P9-CEH-019

THE NEW WESTMINSTER DICTIONARY
OF CHRISTIAN SPIRITUALITY

THE NEW
WESTMINSTER
DICTIONARY
OF
CHRISTIAN
SPIRITUALITY

EDITED BY

PHILIP SHELDRAKE

WESTMINSTER
JOHN KNOX PRESS
LOUISVILLE · KENTUCKY

© SCM Press Ltd 2005

First published in Great Britain in 2005 under the title The New SCM Dictionary of
Christian Spirituality

First American edition
Published by Westminster John Knox Press
Louisville, Kentucky

PRINTED IN GREAT BRITAIN

05 06 07 08 09 10 11 12 13 14 – 10 9 8 7 6 5 4 3 2 1

Library of Congress Cataloging-in-Publication Data is on file at the Library of Congress,
Washington, D.C.

ISBN 0-664-23003-2

CONTENTS

INTRODUCTION

The field of spirituality has changed radically in the twenty years since the late Gordon Wakefield edited the first SCM *Dictionary of Christian Spirituality*. The most significant development in the intervening years has been the growth of spirituality as a major academic discipline with its own methodology. This factor radically reshapes how a dictionary needs to be constructed and so the decision was taken to create a completely new dictionary rather than to update the old one.

At a time when the theme of 'spirituality' is of widespread interest, this new dictionary will be a vital reference work for everyone who wishes to deepen their general understanding of spirituality and knowledge specifically of the Christian spiritual tradition in all its forms. More particularly, the dictionary is intended to offer a fundamental study tool for students and academic teachers across the English-speaking world.

The scope of the dictionary is deliberately limited to *Christian* spirituality. This does not imply exclusivity but underlines the conviction that there is no such thing as 'generic spirituality' because spirituality is always *particular* – that is, grounded in historical-cultural contexts. Equally, despite a contemporary tendency to distinguish 'spirituality' (experience, practices and lifestyles) from 'religion' (interpretation, belief-systems and institutions), spirituality inevitably reflects underlying beliefs about human existence even if these are only implicit. Because the word 'spirituality' is now used so broadly, any attempt to control such an amorphous subject would have been impossible without clear boundaries. Hence we decided to limit the dictionary to a single tradition. Nevertheless, the dictionary tries to do justice to the ways in which Christian spirituality engages with other world faiths.

In today's global Christianity, spirituality is a plural and complex reality. For this reason, no single definition of 'spirituality' was imposed on the contributors. However, if 'spirituality' is not to embrace absolutely anything, we still need to ask what we mean by the word. A dictionary dedicated to 'Christian spirituality' involves a particular horizon of meaning. It refers to the ways in which the particularities of Christian belief about God, the material world and human identity find expression in basic values, lifestyles and spiritual practices. To put matters more classically, Christian spirituality embodies a conscious relationship with God, in Jesus Christ, through the indwelling of the Spirit, in the context of a community of believers. The intimate relationship between spirituality and theology is clearly illustrated by the number of explicitly theological themes among the entries.

In the past, 'spirituality' tended to imply a distinction between spiritual and material levels of human existence, between 'interiority' or a life of prayer and an outer, everyday, public life. Probably the most radical shift in perception about 'Christian spirituality' over the last twenty years has been the ways in which it has increasingly embraced the *whole* of human life – albeit from the perspective of a relationship with God. This has at least three consequences for the dictionary. First, alongside classic themes such as asceticism, contemplation and discernment, the new dictionary includes ground-breaking entries on aspects of material culture such as clothes, food and architecture, as well as entries on subjects such as sexuality, public life, business and sport. Second, it is possible to detect a blurring of boundaries between spirituality and ethics as the former focuses more on lifestyles and the practice of everyday life and the latter focuses more on human qualities rather than simply on the morality of individual actions. This growing encounter between spirituality and ethics is reflected throughout the dictionary. Third, several entries describe the ways in which spirituality is expressed through the arts, literature and film – both historically and in contemporary culture.

The dictionary is ecumenical and international. A serious effort has been made to do justice to a broad spectrum of Christian traditions as well as to acknowledge the global and plural nature of spirituality. The final selection and balance of entries (and of contributors) still involved some difficult choices.

In the light of the above, I am confident about two things. First, even without an imposed definition, readers will find a surprising degree of consensus about the central values and foundations of 'Christian spirituality'. Second, readers may nevertheless be surprised by what is unexpected and challenging. The portrait of Christian spirituality that emerges from the entries clearly shows a balance of interiority and exteriority, the personal and the collective, intense desire for God and fearless engagement with the world of everyday events in its ambiguous mixture of beauty and pain.

It will be useful for readers to know that, in structuring the dictionary, four crucial principles were adopted:

1. There are no individual biographical entries or entries on texts (apart from some biblical ones). This decision was taken because of a greatly increased ecumenical and cultural range of topics and the danger of having to make arbitrary selections. So, it was decided to focus the entries on themes, movements, regions or periods. Information about *specific people or texts* may be pursued by using the comprehensive 'Index of People and Texts' at the end, as well as the bibliographies that follow each entry.

2. A separate section of short essays has been created at the front of the dictionary. These provide a survey of the content, methods and current debates within a still relatively young academic field – topics that merited a longer treatment than was possible in standard A–Z entries. This section clearly illustrates the interdisciplinary nature of contemporary spirituality.

3. The field of spirituality, with its predecessors 'ascetical theology', 'mystical theology' and 'spiritual theology', has generated a wide range of themes and metaphors. Many of these have become 'classic' in their own right and every effort has been made to retain these as entries. However, spirituality continually changes and so there was a need to balance 'classic' entries with more recent topics. Thus, some familiar themes, which are synonyms for or aspects of other topics, are listed but readers are directed elsewhere.

4. The question of geographical boundaries is delicate in a world that is increasingly

conscious of global horizons and multiculturalism. This dictionary cannot pretend to be universal or comprehensive. Any process of selection is contentious and clear choices of emphasis were made. Because it was likely that the dominant readership would be in the English-speaking world, greatest attention has been given to its major regions. In Europe, beyond Britain and Ireland (plus historic links with Scandinavia), entries have been limited to regions with the greatest impact on the broad history of spirituality (e.g. Flemish mysticism or the French School). Spirituality in other continents is represented by survey articles (with titles chosen by the contributors) – because even a mainly 'Northern' readership must nowadays relate its preoccupations to a global context.

This project was first conceived under John Bowden, the last Director of an independent SCM Press, and commissioned by Alex Wright, the first publisher after SCM amalgamated with a larger family of companies. Since then I have worked as Editor with Anna Hardman, Alex Knights and now Barbara Laing and Mary Matthews. Thanks are due to them and to their colleagues at Westminster John Knox Press for steering the dictionary through to publication. I owe a particular debt of gratitude to Hannah Ward and Jennifer Wild not only for their meticulous copy-editing of such a complex text and for creating the Index of People and Texts but also for their thoughtful advice on several technical issues and for good humour and patience in dealing with overdue entries and last minute revisions!

Editing this dictionary over four years with no administrative assistance has been a mammoth task. In this context, I want to offer my warm gratitude to an informal, ecumenical group of advisors in the UK, Ireland, Australia and North America, many of them colleagues in the Society for the Study of Christian Spirituality. Particular thanks are due to Michael Barnes, Douglas Burton-Christie, Mark Burrows, Steven Chase, Sarah Coakley, James Corkery, Lawrence Cunningham, Elizabeth Dreyer, Andrew Hamilton, Arthur Holder, David Lonsdale, Bernard McGinn, Gordon Mursell, Stephanie Paulsell, Sandra Schneiders, Peter Tyler and Claire Wolfteich. Their assistance has influenced the shape of this dictionary in many different ways although I take full responsibility for the final decisions. I could not have completed the task without them. Of course, the greatest thanks are due to the contributors themselves for committing their time and expertise to this project. Finally, I want to thank Susie who, apart from contributing her own entries, has offered wise advice and loving support throughout.

PHILIP SHELDRAKE
UNIVERSITY OF DURHAM, ENGLAND

CONTRIBUTORS

A. M. (Donald) Allchin, *Honorary Professor of Theology at the University of Wales, Bangor, and Anglican priest and writer who has been working in recent years on early Welsh and Celtic spirituality.* **Anglican Spirituality; Caroline Divines; Welsh Spirituality**

Elizabeth Arweck, *Research Fellow at the Institute of Education, University of Warwick, and Co-Editor of the* Journal of Contemporary Religion. **Movements, New Religious**

J. Matthew Ashley, *Associate Professor of Systematic Theology, Department of Theology, University of Notre Dame, Indiana.* **Latin American Spirituality; Liberation Spirituality**

Wilkie Au, *Adjunct Professor in the Department of Theological Studies, Loyola Marymount University, Los Angeles.* **Holistic Spirituality; Pastoral Care and Spirituality**

Michael Barnes SJ, *Director of Studies at the Centre for Christianity and Interreligious Dialogue at Heythrop College, University of London.* **Spirituality and the Dialogue of Religions (*essay*); Yoga; Zen and Christianity**

Alan Bartlett, *Programme Director MA in Theology and Ministry, Tutor in Church History, Spirituality and Anglican Studies, Cranmer Hall, St John's College, University of Durham.* **Incarnation; Redemption**

Stephen Barton, *Reader in New Testament in the Department of Theology, University of Durham and also Assistant Curate of St John's Church, Neville's Cross.* **Synoptic Gospels, Spirituality of**

Tina Beattie, *Lecturer in Christian Studies and Convenor of the MA in Religion and Human Rights in the School of Humanities and Cultural Studies, University of Surrey, Roehampton.* **Mary and Spirituality; Motherhood of God**

Margaret Benefiel, *O'Donnell Chair of Spirituality at the Milltown Institute of Theology and Philosophy in Dublin. Teaches and writes in the area of spirituality, leadership, and organizations.* **Business and Spirituality; Leadership**

Dianne Bergant CSA, *Professor of Old Testament Studies at the Catholic Theological Union, Chicago.* **Song of Songs**

Michael Birkel, *Professor of Religion at Earlham College, Richmond, Indiana.* **Quaker Spirituality**

Michael W. Blastic, OFM CONV., *Associate Professor at The Franciscan Institute, St Bonaventure University, St Bonaventure, NY, and editor of Franciscan Studies.* **Poverty**

Vivian Boland OP, *lecturer in theology at St Mary's College, Strawberry Hill and at Blackfriars Hall, University of Oxford.* **Analogy; Aristotelianism; Scholasticism; Thomist Spirituality**

Mary C. Boys, *Skinner and McAlpin Professor of Practical Theology at Union Theological Seminary, New York.* **Anti-Semitism; Holocaust; Judaism and Christianity**

Ian Bradley, *Reader in Practical Theology and Church History at the University of St Andrews and a minister in the Church of Scotland.* **Scottish Spirituality**

Rosalind Brown, *Vice Principal of the Diocese of Salisbury Ordained Local Ministry Scheme,*

and Academic Staff Member of the Southern Theological Education and Training Scheme.
Hymns and Spirituality

Frank Burch Brown, *Frederick Doyle Kershner Professor of Religion and the Arts at the Christian Theological Seminary, Indianapolis.* **Aesthetics; Architecture and Spirituality; Art and Spirituality; Beauty**

Mark Burrows, *Professor of the History of Christianity at Andover Newton Theology School, Massachussetts.* **Allegory; Poetry and Poetics**

Douglas Burton-Christie, *Professor of Theological Studies at Loyola Marymount University; serves as editor of the journal* Spiritus. **Desert**

Michael Casey ocso, *a monk of Tarrawarra Abbey, Australia, since 1960 and writer of several books and many articles on different aspects of monastic spirituality.* **Apatheia; Cistercian Spirituality; Silence**

Steven Chase, *Associate Professor of Christian Spirituality, Western Theological Seminary, Holland, Michigan.* **Intercession; Mystery; Praise; Recollection; Thanksgiving; Victorine Spirituality**

John Chryssavgis, *theological advisor to the Ecumenical Patriarch on environmental issues, studied in Athens (Greece) and Oxford (England) and has taught theology in Sydney (Australia) and Boston (USA).* **Greek Spirituality; Iconography; Orthodox Spirituality; Philokalia**

Andrew Ciferni o. praem., *a member of Daylesford Abbey in Paoli, Pennsylvania; also the president of the Norbertine Order's Commission on Canonical Life and Spirit of the Order.* **Canonical Communities; Conventual Life; Norbertine Spirituality**

Padraigín Clancy, *a folklorist and historian who lectures and facilitates retreats in Ireland, Britain and the USA on Irish/Celtic heritage and spirituality, frequently contributes to Irish national radio and television and resides on Inis Mór, the Aran Islands.* **Irish Christian Spirituality**

Anne M. Clifford csj, *Associate Professor of Theology, Department of Theology, Duquesne University, Pittsburgh.* **Feminist Spirituality**

Francis X. Clooney sj, *Professor in the Department of Theology, Boston College and Visiting Academic Director for Vaisnava and Hindu Studies at Oxford University.* **Hinduism and Christianity**

Christopher Cocksworth, *Principal of Ridley Hall, an Anglican Theological College in the Cambridge Theological Federation.* **Charismatic Spirituality; Spirit, Holy**

Peter G. Coleman, *Professor in the Department of Psychology, University of Southampton.* **Ageing**

Don H. Compier, *Dean of the Community of Christ Seminary, Independence, Missouri.* **Election (Predestination); Rhetoric**

Walter E. Conn, *Professor in the Department of Theology and Religious Studies, Villanova University, Pennsylvania, and editor of* Horizons, *the journal of the College Theology Society.* **Conversion**

Joann Wolski Conn, *Professor in the Department of Religious Studies, Neumann College, Pennsylvania, and also a spiritual director.* **Growth, Spiritual; Women and Spirituality**

James Corkery sj, *Jesuit priest and theologian, currently Head of the Department of Systematic Theology and History at the Milltown Institute of Theology and Philosophy, Dublin.* **Spirituality and Culture (*essay*)**

David Cornick, *General Secretary of the United Reformed Church (UK) and a Fellow of Robinson College, University of Cambridge.* **Reformed Spirituality; Taizé, Spirituality of**

L. William Countryman, *Sherman E. Johnson Professor of Biblical Studies at The Church Divinity School of the Pacific, Berkeley, California.* **Forgiveness**

Ewert Cousins, *Professor Emeritus, Fordham University, New York and General Editor of the 25-volume series,* World Spirituality: An Encyclopedic History of the Religious Quest. *Also co-developer of the World Commission on Global Consciousness and Spirituality for the Twenty-First Century.* **Global Spirituality**

Michael Crosby OFM CAP., *Coordinator of the Beatitudes Program and Tobacco Program Coordinator, Interfaith Center on Corporate Responsibility (ICCR), New York City.* **Beatitudes; Social Justice**

Paul G. Crowley SJ, *Associate Professor of Theology, Religious Studies Department, Santa Clara University, California.* **Enlightenment Thought**

Lawrence S. Cunningham, *John A. O'Brien Professor of Theology in the Department of Theology, University of Notre Dame, Indiana.* **Catholicity and Spirituality; Roman Catholic Spirituality; Vatican II and Spirituality**

Oliver Davies, *Professor of Christian Doctrine at King's College, University of London.* **Compassion; Holiness**

Tom Deidun *taught New Testament at Heythrop College, University of London from 1980 to 2002, specializing in Pauline studies, and now teaches language and exegetical courses at Birkbeck College FCE, University of London.* **Pauline Spirituality**

Robert Doran SJ, *Director of the Lonergan Research Institute, and Professor of Systematic Theology at Regis College, University of Toronto.* **Affectivity**

Michael Downey, *Professor of Systematic Theology and Spirituality at St John's Seminary, Camarillo, and the Cardinal's Theologian, Archdiocese of Los Angeles.* **Appropriative Method; Charism; Lay People and Spirituality; Trinity and Spirituality**

Elizabeth Dreyer, *Professor of Religious Studies at Fairfield University, Connecticut.* **Humility; Prayer**

Michael S. Driscoll, *Associate Professor in Liturgical Studies, Department of Theology, University of Notre Dame, Indiana.* **Adoration; Baptism; Enthusiasm; Festivals, Religious; Interiority; Penitence**

Rudolph van Dijk, O. carm., *member of the Titus Brandsma Institute, Nijmegen, The Netherlands.* **Devotio Moderna**

Luke Dysinger OSB, *monk of St Andrew's Abbey, Valyermo, California.* **Acedia; Combat, Spiritual; Early Christian Spirituality; Perseverance; Purity of Heart; Tears, Gift of (Penthos); Virginity**

Keith Egan, *The Joyce McMahon Hank Professor in Catholic Theology, St Mary's College, Notre Dame, Indiana.* **Ascent; Carmelite Spirituality; Contemplation; Dark Night**

Charles Elliott, *formerly Dean of Trinity Hall, University of Cambridge, works in UK prisons and elsewhere using a process of organizational change based on the establishment's memories of its best work.* **Memory**

Robert Ellsberg, *Editor-in-Chief of Orbis Books and author of* All Saints *and* The Saints' Guide to Happiness. **Catholic Worker Movement; Martyrdom**

James Empereur SJ, *formerly Professor of Liturgical and Systematic Theology at the Jesuit School of Theology, Berkeley, California, at present parochial vicar and liturgist at the San Fernando Cathedral, San Antonio, Texas.* **Humour; Leisure; Ritual**

Philip Endean SJ, *Tutor in Theology at Campion Hall, University of Oxford, and Editor of* The Way. **Spirituality and Theology (*essay*); Jesus, Society of (Jesuits); Person**

Leif-Gunnar Engedal, *Professor of Practical Theology at the Norwegian Lutheran School of Theology, Oslo.* **Scandinavian Spirituality**

Eduardo Fernandes SJ, *Associate Professor of Pastoral Theology and Ministry, Jesuit School of Theology, Berkeley, California, where he teaches missiology, pastoral theology and ministry.* **Hispanic Spirituality**

Donna Freitas, *Assistant Professor of Religion, St Michael's College, Colchester, Vermont, and author of books on dating and spirituality, and women's pop culture and spirituality.* **Chastity; Mujerista Spirituality; Sport and Spirituality**

Laurence Freeman OSB, *Benedictine monk and Director of The World Community for Christian Meditation, a global contemplative network committed to the teaching of meditation as a way of inner and outer peace.* **Meditation; Presence of God**

Richard Gaillardetz, *Murray-Bacik Professor of Catholic Studies at the University of Toledo, Ohio.* **Communion/*Koinonia*; Ecclesiology and Spirituality**

Michael Paul Gallagher SJ, *Professor of Fundamental Theology at the Gregorian University, Rome.* **Faith; Inculturation**

Ann L. Gilroy, *Director of Undergraduate Studies, School of Theology, University of Auckland, New Zealand.* **Devotions; Devotions, Popular; Devotional Manuals**

George Gispert-Sauch SJ *teaches at Vidyajyoti, the Jesuit theological faculty in Delhi, India.* **Asia, Spiritualities in**

Anthony Gittins CSSP, *Bishop Francis X. Ford Professor of Catholic Missiology at the Catholic Theological Union, Chicago.* **Mission and Spirituality**

Jane Gledhill *has taught English Literature at a number of English universities and is currently contributing courses on Literature and Spirituality for the MA on Christian Spirituality at Sarum College, Salisbury.* **Literature and Spirituality**

Peregrine Graffius OSM, *formerly Prior General of the Servite Order; served as Magnus Cancellarius of the Pontifical Faculty 'Marianum' in Rome, Italy 1971–77.* **Servite Spirituality**

Howard J. Gray SJ, *Rector of the Jesuit community at John Carroll University, University Heights, Ohio, Assistant to the President for University Mission and Identity, and Adjunct Professor of Religious Studies.* **Detachment; Examination of Conscience/Consciousness; Imagination; Indifference; Spiritual Conversation**

Mary Grey, *D. J. James Professor of Pastoral Theology at the University of Wales, Lampeter.* **Creation Spirituality; Ecological Spirituality; Environment**

Colleen M. Griffith, *Faculty Director of Spirituality Studies at the Institute of Religious Education and Pastoral Ministry, Boston College, Chestnut Hill, Massachusetts.* **Education and Spirituality**

George Guiver CR, *Superior of the Community of the Resurrection; also teaches in the Theological College at Mirfield, West Yorkshire.* **Office, Divine**

Sergei Hackel, *Archpriest in the Russian Orthodox Church, Editor of* Sobornost *(incorporating* Eastern Churches Review*) and Editor of religious programmes in the BBC Russian Service. Formerly Reader in Russian Studies, University of Sussex, England.* **Russian Spirituality; Staretz**

Roger Haight SJ, *Professor of Systematic Theology at Weston Jesuit School of Theology, Cambridge, Massachusetts.* **Grace**

Robert Hale OSB cam., *Camaldolese monk at Big Sur Hermitage, California.* **Camaldolese Spirituality; Eremitical Spirituality; Monasticism; Stability**

Andrew Hamilton SJ, *teaches systematic theology and early church history at the United Faculty of Theology in Melbourne, and is also Publisher at Jesuit Publications, Australia.* **Australasian Spirituality; Exile**

Bradley Hanson, *Director of the Grace Institute for Spiritual Formation and Professor Emeritus of Religion at Luther College, Decorah, Iowa.* **Lutheran Spirituality; Pietism**

David Hay, *a zoologist and currently Honorary Senior Research Fellow in the Department of Divinity and Religious Studies at Aberdeen University. Previously Reader in Spiritual Education at the University of Nottingham and before that Director of the Religious Experience Research Unit, Oxford.* **Experience, Religious**

Diana L. Hayes, *Associate Professor of Theology, Georgetown University, Washington, DC.* **African-American Spirituality**

Susie Hayward *is a psychotherapist and humanistic psychologist. She is the consultant for Human Development at the monastery of Ampleforth Abbey, North Yorkshire, England.* **Addiction; Clothing; Food; Psalms**

Thomas J. Heffernan, *The Kenneth Curry Professor, Departments of English and Religious Studies, Program in Medieval Studies, University of Tennessee, Knoxville.* **Biographies, Spiritual; Hagiography**

Noreen Herzfeld, *Professor of Computer Science, St John's University, Collegeville, Minnesota.* **Imago Dei**

Linda Hogan, *Lecturer at the Irish School of Ecumenics, Trinity College Dublin, Ireland.* **Conscience; Virtue**

Arthur G. Holder, *Dean and Vice President for Academic Affairs, and Professor of Christian Spirituality, Graduate Theological Union, Berkeley, California.* **Discipline; Knowledge; Vocation; Wisdom**

Edward Howells, *Lecturer in Christian Spirituality at Heythrop College, University of London.* **Apophatic Spirituality; Darkness; Neoplatonism; Nothingness**

John Inge, *Bishop of Huntingdon, England, and previously Vice-Dean of Ely Cathedral.* **Pilgrimage; Shrines**

Werner Jeanrond, *Professor of Systematic Theology at the University of Lund, Sweden.* **Agape; Charity; Love**

Terrence Kardong OSB, *a monk of Assumption Abbey, Richardton, North Dakota and Editor of the* American Benedictine Review. **Benedictine Spirituality; Labour, Manual;** *Lectio Divina;* **Obedience**

Madge Karecki, *Associate Professor of Missiology and Christian Spirituality in the School of Religion and Theology, University of South Africa (UNISA).* **African Spirituality**

John Kater, *Professor of Ministry Development and Director of the Center for Anglican Learning and Leadership, Church Divinity School of the Pacific, Berkeley, California.* **Reign of God**

Kenneth Kearon, *Secretary-General of the Anglican Communion. Previously, Director of the Irish School of Ecumenics, Trinity College, Dublin, Ireland.* **Ecumenical Spirituality; Peace**

John Keenan, *Professor Emeritus of Religion, Middlebury College, Middlebury, Vermont.* **Buddhism and Christianity**

Heshmat Keroloss *teaches dogmatic theology, patristics, and Orthodox spirituality at St Athanasius Coptic Orthodox Theological College, Melbourne, Australia.* **Coptic Spirituality**

Gillian Kingston, *Local Preacher of the Methodist Church in Ireland, currently Convenor of the Church's Faith and Order Committee and Moderator of the Church Representatives' Meeting of Churches Together in Britain and Ireland. She also sits on the Methodist/Roman Catholic International Commission.* **Methodist Spirituality**

Cheryl A. Kirk-Duggan, *Professor of Theology and Women's Studies and Director of Women's Studies, Shaw University Divinity School, Raleigh, North Carolina.* **Womanist Spirituality**

Elisabeth Koenig, *Professor of Ascetical Theology at General Theological Seminary, New York.* **Cross and Spirituality; Imitation of Christ; Jesus and Spirituality**

Celia Kourie, *Professor of Christian Spirituality in the School of Religion and Theology, University of South Africa (UNISA).* **African Spirituality**

Louise Kretzschmar, *Professor of Theological Ethics in the School of Religion and Theology, University of South Africa (UNISA).* **African Spirituality**

Belden Lane, *Hotfelder Distinguished Professor of Humanities, Department of Theological Studies, St Louis University, Missouri.* **Calvinist Spirituality; Puritan Spirituality**

Dermot Lane, *President of Mater Dei Institute of Education, a College of Dublin City University, Ireland.* **Eschatology**

James F. Lawrence, *Dean, Swedenborgian House of Studies at the Pacific School of Religion, Berkeley, California.* **Swedenborgian Spirituality**

Kenneth Leech, *Community Theologian formerly based at St Botolph's Church, Aldgate, London.* **Drugs**

Bruce Lescher, *Director of Sabbatical Programs, Jesuit School of Theology, Berkeley, California, where he also teaches Christian spirituality.* **Diakonia and Diaconate**

Valerie Lesniak, *Assistant Professor of Spirituality in the School of Theology and Ministry at Seattle University, Washington; previously taught at Heythrop College, University of London for several years.* **Contemporary Spirituality (*essay*); New Age; North American Spirituality**

Ann Loades CBE, *Emerita Professor of Divinity, University of Durham.* **Eucharistic Spirituality; Sacramentality and Spirituality**

Arthur Long, *formerly Principal of the Unitarian College Manchester and Honorary Lecturer, Department of Religions and Theology, University of Manchester, UK.* **Unitarian Spirituality**

David Lonsdale *teaches Christian spirituality in graduate spirituality and pastoral theology programmes at Heythrop College, University of London; also the author of a number of books and articles on Ignatian spirituality.* **Consolation; Desolation; Discernment; Election, Ignatian; Ignatian Spirituality**

Gerard Loughlin, *Senior Lecturer in Theology at the University of Durham.* **Film and Spirituality**

Andrew Louth, *Professor of Patristic and Byzantine Studies at the University of Durham, and priest of the Russian Orthodox Patriarchal Diocese of Sourozh.* **Asceticism; Deification; Fools, Holy**

Harriet A. Luckman, *Associate Professor and Director of the Spirituality Institute, College of Mount St Joseph, Cincinnati, Ohio.* **Celibacy; Dualism; Piety; Sanctification; Singleness**

Anne Luther, *Director of Retreats International, Loyola University, Chicago.* **Retreats**

Thomas Martin OSA, *Associate Professor in the Department of Theology and Religious Studies at Villanova University, Pennsylvania.* **Augustinian Spirituality**

Jane F. Maynard, *Interim Missioner for Adult Formation, The Episcopal Diocese of Olympia, Seattle, Washington.* **Reflection**

Bernard McGinn, *Naomi Shenstone Donnelly Professor of Historical Theology and the History of Christianity, School of Divinity, University of Chicago.* **Mysticism (*essay*); Apocalyptic Spirituality**

John A. McGuckin, *a priest of the Romanian Orthodox Church, Professor of Early Church History at Union Theological Seminary and Professor of Byzantine Christian Studies at Columbia University, New York.* **Byzantine Spirituality; Cappadocian Fathers; Hesychasm; Jesus Prayer; Macarian Spirituality; Theoria**

Mark A. McIntosh, *Associate Professor of Theology, Loyola University, Chicago, and a priest of the Episcopal Church.* **Ascetical Theology; Glory; Mystical Theology**

David McLellan, *Professor of Political Theory, Goldsmiths College, University of London.* **Marxism and Spirituality**

John Melloh SM, *Professional Specialist, Theology, and Director of the John S. Marten Program in Homiletics and Liturgics at the University of Notre Dame, Indiana.* **Preaching and Spirituality**

James Miller, *Assistant Professor and Coordinator of Graduate Studies in the Department of Religious Studies, Queen's University, Kingston, Ontario.* **Daoism and Christianity**

Mary Milligan RSHM, *Professor of Biblical Studies at St John's Seminary, Camarillo, California.* **Religious Life**

Patrick Moore FSC, *a member of the De La Salle Brothers, an international Roman Catholic teaching order and presently Scholar-in-Residence at Sarum College, Salisbury, England.* **Cambridge Platonists; Christian Humanism**

Jeremy Morris, *Dean of Trinity Hall, University of Cambridge.* **Anglo-Catholic Spirituality; Oxford Movement**

Michael P. Morrissey, *Research Consultant at the Institute of Reading Development, Novato, California.* **Afterlife; Hope**

Saskia Murk Jansen, *Fellow of Robinson College, University of Cambridge.* **Beguine Spirituality; Bridal Mysticism (Brautmystic)**

Paul D. Murray, *a married lay Roman Catholic theologian, is a Lecturer in Systematic Theology, Department of Theology and Religion, University of Durham. He serves on the Faith and Culture Committee of the Catholic Bishops' Conference of England and Wales and on the British Roman Catholic–Methodist Committee.* **Freedom; God, Images of**

Gordon Mursell, *Dean of Birmingham Cathedral, England.* **Carthusian Spirituality; English Spirituality; Sabbath; Suffering**

Robert Cummings Neville, *Professor of Philosophy, Religion and Theology at the School of Theology, Boston University, Massachusetts.* **Confucianism and Christianity; Symbol**

Suzanne Noffke OP, *a member and former President of the Sisters of St Dominic of Racine, Wisconsin; also a Catherine of Siena scholar and historian of her congregation, and Scholar in Residence in the Department of History of the University of Wisconsin-Parkside.* **Abandonment; Soul**

Michael S. Northcott, *Reader in Christian Ethics in the School of Divinity, University of Edinburgh.* **Cities and Spirituality**

Joan M. Nuth, *Associate Professor of Theology and Director of the Ignatian Spirituality Institute at John Carroll University, Cleveland, Ohio.* **Emotions; English Mystical Tradition; Women Medieval Mystics**

Rebecca Nye, *Senior Research Associate in Children's Spirituality, University of Cambridge, and Director of Empirical Research for the Centre for the Theology of Childhood, Texas.* **Adolescents and Spirituality; Children and Spirituality**

George O'Har, *Adjunct Assistant Professor in the Department of English, Boston College, Chestnut Hill, Massachusetts. He previously researched technology, science and society at MIT.* **Technology and Spirituality**

Thomas O'Loughlin, *Head of the School of Humanities, University of Wales, Lampeter.* **Celtic Spirituality; Gnosticism; Pelagianism**

Alan G. Paddle, *research scholar at the Union Theological Seminary in New York City.* **Syriac Spirituality**

Garnet Parris, *Director of the Centre of Black Theology, Birmingham University, England, where he researches African Diaspora issues. He is a native of Trinidad and Tobago.* **Black Spirituality; Pentecostal Spirituality**

William B. Parsons, *Chair of the Department of Religious Studies at Rice University, Houston, Texas.* **Nature Mysticism**

Stephanie Paulsell, *Associate Dean for Ministerial Studies and Senior Lecturer on Ministry at Harvard Divinity School.* **Attentiveness; Intellectual Life and Spirituality; Journal, Spiritual**

Steven Payne OCD, *a member of the Washington Province of Discalced Carmelites, President of the Carmelite Institute, Washington, DC, and lecturer in Carmelite Studies at the Washington Theological Union.* **Simplicity**

Martyn Percy, *Principal, Ripon College Cuddesdon, Oxford and Professor of Theological Education, King's College, University of London.* **Fundamentalism; Secularization; Society and Spirituality**

David Perrin OMI, *Associate Professor of Spirituality and Ethics at St Paul University, Ottawa; formerly Dean of the Faculty of Theology 1998–2002.* **Ecstasy; Illuminative Way; Purgative Way; Unitive Way; Visionary Literature**

Marygrace Peters OP, *Prioress of the Dominican Sisters of Houston, Texas and formerly Associate Professor of Church History, Aquinas Institute of Theology, St Louis, Missouri.* **Tradition**

Mark Pryce, *Anglican priest, currently Vicar of Smethwick, Birmingham, England, a multiethnic inner-city parish; also a writer, lecturer and retreat-giver, focusing especially on issues of gender, masculinities and the spirituality of contemporary poetry.* **Friendship; Masculine Spirituality; Relationships**

Ian Randall, *Deputy Principal and Lecturer in Church History and Spirituality, Spurgeon's College, London.* **Baptist Spirituality; Evangelical Spirituality**

Thomas Rausch SJ, *T. Marie Chilton Professor of Catholic Theology at Loyola Marymount University, Los Angeles.* **Community; Discipleship; Priesthood and Spirituality**

Myles Rearden CM, *Vincentian priest and scholar in Ireland.* **Vincentian Spirituality**

Jane C. Redmont, *The Graduate Theological Union, Berkeley, California and formerly Bogard Teaching Fellow at The Church Divinity School of the Pacific.* **Celebration; Joy; Mercy**

Roland Reim, *Director of Ministerial Development at the Southern Theological Education and Training Scheme (STETS), Salisbury.* **Ministry and Spirituality**

William Reiser SJ, *Professor of Theology at the College of the Holy Cross, Worcester, Massachusetts.* **Consumerism**

Lucien Richard OMI, *ordained priest and member of the Oblates of Mary Immaculate; also Professor of Theology at Boston University, Massachusetts.* **Hospitality;** *Kenosis*

Joanne Maguirre Robinson, *Professor in the Department of Religious Studies, University of North Carolina-Charlotte.* **Absorption; Annihilation, Spiritual**

Janet K. Ruffing RSM, *Professor in Spirituality and Spiritual Direction, Graduate School of Religion and Religious Education, Fordham University, New York.* **Affirmative Way; Direction, Spiritual; Kataphatic Spirituality**

Robert J. Russell, *Founder and Director, The Center for Theology and the Natural Sciences and Professor of Theology and Science in Residence, The Graduate Theological Union, Berkeley, California.* **Spirituality and Science (*essay*)**

Don E. Saliers, *Wm R. Cannon Distinguished Professor of Theology and Worship and Director of the Masters of Sacred Music Program, Emory University, Atlanta, Georgia.* **Music and Spirituality; Spirituals**

Sandra M. Schneiders IHM, *Professor of New Testament Studies and Christian Spirituality at the Jesuit School of Theology, Berkeley, California.* **Christian Spirituality: Definition, Methods and Types; Spirituality and Scripture** (*essays*)**; Exegesis, Spiritual; Johannine Spirituality**

Robert Schreiter, *Vatican Council II Professor of Theology at Catholic Theological Union, Chicago, and Professor of Theology and Culture, University of Nijmegen, The Netherlands.* **Non-violence; Reconciliation**

Jan Schumacher, *Associate Professor of Church History at The Norwegian Lutheran School of Theology, Oslo.* **Scandinavian Spirituality**

Frank Senn, *Pastor of Immanuel Lutheran Church, Evanston, Illinois.* **Reformation and Spirituality**

John Shea OSA, *Visiting Associate Professor of Pastoral Care and Counselling at the Institute of Religious Education and Pastoral Ministry, Boston College, Chestnut Hill, Massachusetts.* **Spirituality, Psychology and Psychotherapy** (*essay*)

Philip Sheldrake, *William Leech Professorial Fellow of Applied Theology, University of Durham, England and a former President of the international Society for the Study of Christian Spirituality.* **Spirituality and History; Interpretation** (*essays*)**; Bridgettine Spirituality; Cyberspace; Desire; Gilbertine Spirituality; Grandmontine Spirituality; Journey, Spiritual; Light; Military Orders; Moravian Spirituality; Oratorian Spirituality; Place; Postmodernity; Practice, Spiritual; Rules, Religious; Sacred; Senses, Spiritual; Time; World**

William Short OFM *Professor of Spirituality at the Franciscan School of Theology and Graduate Theological Union, Berkeley, California.* **Franciscan Spirituality; Mendicant Spirituality**

Gemma Simmonds CJ *is doing doctoral studies in systematic theology at St Edmund's College, University of Cambridge, England.* **Apostolic Spirituality; Formation, Spiritual; Vows**

Joan Slobig SP, *former General Councillor of the Sisters of Providence, St Mary-of-the-Woods, Indiana; also a clinical psychologist and Administrator of St Ann Health Care Clinic.* **Providence**

C. Arnold Snyder, *Professor of History, Conrad Grebel University College, University of Waterloo, Canada.* **Anabaptist Spirituality**

William C. Spohn, *Augustine Cardinal Bea Distinguished Professor of Theology in the Department of Religious Studies, Santa Clara University, California.* **Ethics and Spirituality**

Stephen J. Stein, *Chancellor's Professor of Religious Studies, Indiana University, Bloomington, Indiana.* **Shaker Spirituality**

Bryan Stone, *E. Stanley Jones Professor of Evangelism at the School of Theology, Boston University, Massachusetts.* **Evangelization and Spirituality**

Elizabeth Stuart, *Professor in the School of Cultural Studies, King Alfred's College, Winchester.* **Homosexuality and Spirituality**

Jeremy Taylor, *co-founder and Past President of the International Association for the Study of Dreams (IASD); has taught psychology and dream work at the Starr King School for the Ministry in the Graduate Theological Union, Berkeley, California; a Unitarian Universalist minister.* **Dreams and Dreaming**

Carolyn Thompson, *part of the UCC Disabilities Ministries and Disability Project Coordinator, Cambridge, Massachusetts. She was also part of the WCC drafting team for A Church of All and For All – An Interim Statement.* **Disability**

William M. Thompson-Uberuaga, *Professor of Systematic Theology in the Department of*

Theology, Duquesne University, Pittsburgh. **French School of Spirituality; Jansenism; Quietism; Saints, Communion of; Sulpician Spirituality**

Angela Tilby, *Vice-Principal of Westcott House, an Anglican Theological College; teaches spirituality and early church history in the Cambridge Theological Federation.* **Cosmology; Media and Communications**

Joan H. Timmerman, *Professor Emerita, College of St Catherine, author and lecturer now residing in Anaheim, California.* **Body and Spirituality; Eroticism; Sexuality and Spirituality**

Peter Tyler, *Course Director of the MA in Christian Spirituality and Director of the Spirituality Programme, Sarum College, Salisbury.* **Alumbrados; Sufism and Christianity; Triple Way**

Ann Belford Ulanov, *Christiane Brooks Johnson Professor of Psychiatry and Religion at the Union Theological Seminary, New York.* **Prayer, Psychology of**

Benedicta Ward SLG, *member of the Sisters of the Love of God and Reader in the History of Christian Spirituality at the University of Oxford.* **Anglo-Saxon Spirituality**

Susan J. White, *Harold J. and Anna H. Lunger Professor of Spiritual Resources and Disciplines at Brite Divinity School, Texas.* **Spirituality, Liturgy and Worship (*essay*)**

Ulrike Wiethaus, *Professor of the Humanities, Interdisciplinary Appointments, Wake Forest University, North Carolina.* **Medieval Spirituality in the West; Nominalism**

Andrew Wingate, *Director of Interfaith Relations in the Diocese of Leicester.* **Islam and Christianity**

Daryold Corbiere Winkler CSB, *member of the M'Chigeeng First Nation (Anishinaabe) on Manitoulin Island, Canada, and a doctoral candidate in systematic and historical theology at Saint Paul University, Ottawa, Canada.* **Native North American Spirituality**

James Wiseman OSB, *a monk of St Anselm's Abbey, Washington, DC, and Associate Professor of Theology at the Catholic University of America where he was Chair of the Theology Department for five years.* **Flemish Mysticism**

Claire Wolfteich, *Associate Professor of Practical Theology and Spiritual Formation in the School of Theology, Boston University, Massachusetts.* **Spirituality and Social Sciences (*essay*); Public Life and Spirituality; Work**

Richard Woods OP, *Associate Professor of Theology at Dominican University, River Forest, Illinois.* **Dominican Spirituality; Rhineland Mystics**

James Woodward, *Master of the Foundation of Lady Katherine Leveson and Director of the Leveson Centre for the Study of Ageing, Spirituality and Social Policy, Temple Balsall, West Midlands.* **Death and Dying; Healing and Health**

N. T. (Tom) Wright, *Bishop of Durham, England, biblical theologian, writer and broadcaster.* **Lord's Prayer; Resurrection**

Wendy M. Wright, *Professor of Theology and John C. Kenefick Faculty Chair in the Humanities, Creighton University, Omaha, Nebraska.* **Marriage, Family and Spirituality; Sacred Heart; Salesian Spirituality**

Amanda Zilberstein *is pursuing research on the function of the image in Christian spirituality East and West.* **Image and Spirituality**

ABBREVIATIONS

CWS   Classics of World Spirituality, New York: Paulist Press, 1978–

DS   *Dictionnaire de spiritualité ascetique et mystique: doctrine et histoire*, ed. M Viler et al., Paris: Beauchesne, 1932–

PL   *Patrologia Latina*, ed. J. P. Migne, Paris, 1844–55

RB   Rule of Benedict

ST   *Summa Theologiae* of Thomas Aquinas

WS   *World Spirituality: An Encyclopedic History of the Religious Quest*, gen. ed. Ewert Cousins, New York: Crossroad, 1985–

Other abbreviations are occasionally used (with explanation) in some entries.

ESSAYS

Christian Spirituality: Definition, Methods and Types

1. Definition

A. *Spirituality as lived experience*

Spirituality, like experience, is notoriously difficult to define. However, in the last two decades during which spirituality has emerged as a focus of widespread interest in and outside the churches and the academy a certain consensus has built up around the need to distinguish between and to define both the human experience denoted by the word and the academic discipline which studies that experience. Spirituality as lived experience can be defined as conscious involvement in the project of life integration through self-transcendence toward the ultimate value one perceives. This general definition is broad enough to embrace both Christian and non-Christian religious spiritualities as well as secular spiritualities. However, it is also specific enough to give the term some recognizable content.

First, spirituality is not a doctrine or simply a set of practices but an ongoing experience or life project. Second, its ultimate purpose is life integration. Thus, negative patterns such as alcoholism or consumerism (which can become the organizing principle of a person's life) do not constitute a spirituality. Third, the process of self-transcendence rules out a narcissistic self-absorption even in one's own perfection. And fourth, the entire project is oriented toward ultimate value, whether this is the Transcendent, the flourishing of humanity, or some other value.

The ultimate value which generates the horizon of any spirituality relates the one who lives that spirituality to the whole of reality in some particular way. When the horizon of ultimate value is the triune God revealed in Jesus Christ and communicated through his Holy Spirit, and the project of self-transcendence is the living of the paschal mystery within the context of the church community, the spirituality is specifically Christian and involves the person with God, others and all reality according to the understanding of these realities that is characteristic of Christian faith. For example, trinitarian monotheism, incarnation, a morality which is based on the dignity of the person created in the image and likeness of God, sacramentality, are constitutive features of Christian spirituality, not because it is a spirituality but precisely because it is Christian.

The contemporary understanding of Christian spirituality differs significantly from that which preceded it in the modern period. First, the emphasis is on the *holistic* involvement of the person in the spiritual quest which is itself understood holistically.

Thus, the body as well as the spirit, gender and social location as well as human nature, emotion as well as mind and will, relationships with others as well as with God, socio-political commitment as well as prayer and spiritual practices, are involved in the spiritual project. Second, the emphasis on the spiritual life as a *personal* project highlights the uniqueness and initiative of the individual in contrast to an earlier understanding of spirituality as the more or less uniform behavioural application of Church doctrine. Third, the understanding of spirituality as a project of self-*transcendence* emphasizes an openness toward the infinite that does not deny the particularity of the individual seeker but subverts any tendency to reduce spirituality to the purely private or narcissistic quest for one's own self-realization. The contemporary recognition of the necessity of the *community context and the commitment to social transformation* contrast with the overly individualistic understanding of spirituality encountered in many manuals from the eighteenth to the twentieth century.

B. Spirituality as an academic discipline

The contemporary academic discipline of spirituality which studies the lived experience of Christian faith has a long and complex history. In the patristic and early medieval periods, prior to the divorce between spirituality and theology in the thirteenth century, spirituality as living and lived faith was the context and the purpose of all study, both sacred and profane. Theology was articulate spirituality and spirituality was lived theology. Scripture was the source and norm of all knowledge.

When theology relocated from the monastery to the universities in the high Middle Ages this integrated approach to knowledge was shattered. In the schools philosophy became the 'handmaid of theology' which began its long journey into modernity understanding itself increasingly as a 'scientific' rather than a spiritual enterprise. 'Mystical theology' or the wisdom acquired in prayer through meditation on the Scriptures became, virtually exclusively, a monastic enterprise.

As theology entered the modern period it embraced the increasingly rationalistic ideals and agenda of the Enlightenment. By the nineteenth century it had become, in both Catholicism and Protestantism, a highly scholastic discipline, whereas spirituality was now considered a non-academic practice of devotion or piety or even the cultivation of mystical prayer which was suspect in both branches of Western Christianity.

From the eighteenth to the mid-twentieth century the discipline of 'spiritual theology' emerged in Catholic seminaries as a sub-discipline of theology. It derived its principles from systematic and moral theology and was organized according to the scholastic patterns of theology in general. Future clerics studied it in order to be able to guide the faithful, especially 'persons seeking perfection', in the confessional. It was defined as the 'science of perfection' and usually subdivided into 'ascetical theology' which dealt with the active stages of the spiritual life (the purgative and illuminative ways) and 'mystical theology' which dealt with the higher reaches of contemplation (the unitive way). The discipline of spiritual theology was deductive in method, prescriptive in character, and concerned primarily with the practice of personal prayer and asceticism. It was the task of the confessor or spiritual director to mediate the general theory to the particular individual taking account of her or his temperament and individual traits, but it was assumed that the spiritual life was essentially the same for all (although not all attained its full realization). The individual's experience was defined by rather than contributed to the general theory. Manuals of spiritual theology (e.g., those of A. Rodriguez, A. Tanquerey, and A. Saudrau) were textbooks for confessors rather than products of research in spirituality or explorations of actual experience.

In the 1970s and 1980s a new discipline, which gradually came to be called (at least by most of its practitioners) 'spirituality' rather than 'spiritual theology', began to emerge in the academy. The reasons for the new interest are complex, cultural as well as theological, but the interest centred on the experience of the search for meaning, transcendence, personal integration and social transformation which engaged many people in the West in the aftermath of the world wars, the depression, the cold war, the theological and ecclesial upheaval of Vatican II, and the explorations of 'inner space' that the development of the human and personal sciences, especially clinical psychology and psychoanalysis, had unleashed. Although many people found resources for their spiritual quest in the mainline churches, an increasing number of people did not. They turned to eastern mystical religions, to mind-expanding drugs, to 'new religious movements', to occult practices, or to idiosyncratic syntheses of beliefs and practices. Others began to discover riches in the Christian tradition that had been underemphasized or even deliberately obscured for centuries, for example the mystical literature, monastic practices, retreats, personal spiritual direction, and various kinds of group spiritual practice which seemed to offer a more personal and authentic religious experience than did the routines of organized religion.

Some scholars in the traditional theological disciplines, i.e., biblical studies, church history, systematic and moral theology and practical theology, became interested in studying what was occurring in the culture and the churches under the vague term 'spirituality' and its relation to the classical texts and traditions. By the early 1980s these scholars were beginning to realize that they shared an interest which did not have a recognized place in the theological academy. They began to reflect on that interest, raise questions about its subject matter and specific focus, try to articulate their methodology, and to distinguish the field from other disciplines.

The contemporary research discipline of spirituality was born of this growing interest in studying Christian religious experience, both as it had occurred in the past and as it was evolving in the present. In rapid succession new publishing ventures were undertaken to provide critical English language translations of the spiritual classics (e.g. the Paulist Press series, Classics of Western Spirituality) and analytical studies of figures, movements, and schools of spirituality within particular historical periods (e.g. Crossroad's World Spirituality series). The Society for the Study of Christian Spirituality was formed to bring scholars together annually and in 1993 the Society founded a newsletter, *Christian Spirituality Bulletin,* which, in 2001, became a refereed academic journal, *Spiritus.* During this period several seminaries, theological schools and consortia in the United States and Europe began to offer courses in spirituality and graduate programmes at the master's and doctoral level were initiated. The number of students seeking preparation in the field of spirituality, either in its more practical expressions in ministry or as a research discipline, increased notably during this period. By the 1990s, despite ongoing challenges from without and considerable confusion within, spirituality was emerging as a new, interdisciplinary research field distinct from systematic and moral theology on the one hand and from psychological or pastoral counselling on the other, although related to both.

2. Methods

As scholars began to interact in the context of the emerging discipline major questions arose concerning the definition of the discipline, the object of its study, and the methods by which to pursue research in the field. A lively exchange on these subjects in the form of major definitional articles by senior scholars in the field took place in the pages of the *Christian Spirituality Bulletin* (see vols 1.1 and 1.2 [1993]; 2.1 [1994]; 4.1 and 4.2 [1996]; 5.1 [1997]; 6.1 [1998]) and continued in *Spiritus.* In general, three approaches to the study of spirituality began to be recognized: the historical, the theological and the anthropological or hermeneutical.

The historical approach consists basically in the use of contemporary historical methodology for the study of Christian religious experience as it is mediated in texts and other artefacts. It differs from church history and historical theology primarily in its focus on such topics as mysticism, saints, schools of spirituality, movements such as monasticism or the *vita apostolica*, that is, on the lived experience of the faith in various historical contexts rather than on ecclesiastical life or the development of theology. The historical approach is more easily situated in the secular or religious university context where its basic methodology and categories are already established. Historical studies in spirituality are more methodologically defined, more clearly related to the field's predecessors, and provide essential resources for all other research in the field.

The theological approach, more easily situated in the denominational seminary, sees spirituality as one area of theological investigation among others (such as systematic theology, moral theology, or biblical studies). It uses the categories of theology to examine the practice of Christian faith. Thus spirituality is understood as a form of practical theology. This approach is closer to the nineteenth- and early twentieth-century understanding of spiritual theology described above (and its practitioners sometimes prefer that terminology) but it is both more holistic and integrated in its approach and less dogmatic and prescriptive than its predecessor. The theology operative in the theological approach to spirituality is contemporary critical rather than scholastic theology. But the theological approach is necessarily denominational and often more interested in contributing to the formational agenda of the churches than in research.

The anthropological or hermeneutical approach is distinctively new in that it sees Christian spirituality not as a particular subject matter or as an area of Christian theological study but as a regional area within the broader field of spirituality which is neither necessarily religious nor necessarily Christian. It begins with the recognition that the capacity for the spiritual quest belongs to the *humanum* as such and can be, and has been, realized in many ways within the traditions of the great world religions and in primal religions. This approach is more at home in the graduate theological or religious studies context. It is interdisciplinary, cross-cultural, and interreligious in its approach, taking seriously its own Christian focus but oriented primarily toward research into what is actually experienced in the Christian search for God in its concrete and experiential reality and in the constructive work of reinterpreting that experience in and for the contemporary context.

The three approaches are mutually enriching and scholars espousing all three recognize that they share common, as yet unresolved, disciplinary questions. Particularly urgent are questions about the *self-implicating nature of studies in this field* and how this feature can be a resource for research rather than a threat to appropriate critical rigour. The methodological question of *interdisciplinarity*, that is, of how to relate the specifically Christian resources derived from biblical, historical and theological studies to such non-theological disciplines as psychology, sociology, aesthetics and science in order to analyse religious experience in its concrete, holistic particularity is far from resolved. Finally, the scholar of Christian spirituality faces the challenge of how to be fully involved in the broader discussion of the human quest for the ultimate while remaining focused on *Christian* experience. The discipline of Christian spirituality is a bona fide field-encompassing field of study which is not only a valuable resource for Christian practice but is also a serious and challenging field of research whose results are increasingly important in the postmodern world marked by passionate interest in ultimacy and meaning and also by dangerous religious extremism and even fanaticism.

3. Types of Christian spirituality

While it has been correctly maintained that all spirituality which is authentically Christian is related normatively to Scripture and lived within the context of the Church's faith and practice the fact is that the lived experience of Christian faith is enormously varied in practice. It resists all attempts to adequately or comprehensively catalogue it. Any typology depends on the principles of division used and these are usually dictated by the focus of the researcher's interests.

An ancient principle divides spiritualities into active and contemplative depending on the relative dominance of human effort and divine influence in the overall experience. Closely related is the distinction between apophatic (ineffable and imageless) and kataphatic, or more richly imaginative and symbolic, experiences of one's life with God. Also related is the distinction between apostolic spiritualities and more monastic ones. The last also suggests a taxonomy of spiritualities according to the charisms and spiritual traditions of different religious orders (e.g., Benedictine, Carmelite, Dominican) or denominations (e.g., Lutheran or Catholic).

Spiritualities have long been distinguished by state of life or vocation, for example marital/religious or clerical/lay. And within the religious category the basic types (eremitical/communitarian; monastic/mendicant/ministerial; cloistered and non-cloistered) have been studied as types. In recent years the determining influence of gender (masculine/feminine) and/or sexual orientation (hetero-/homosexual) has become a focus of particular attention.

Spiritualities of particular dimensions of human experience, for example work, culture, art, social involvement, peace, ecology and so on, have been elaborated in recent years as individuals and groups have focused their spiritual quest through the lens of these commitments or experiences. Particularly significant today is feminist spirituality, which may be religious or secular, but which involves a serious critique of traditional androcentric and patriarchal Christian spirituality and the effort to elaborate an alternative that will be life-giving for women and other oppressed groups, liberating also for men, and protective of the environment.

This survey of types of spiritualities is suggestive rather than exhaustive of the rich variety within Christian spirituality. The twenty-first century bids fair to be a time of burgeoning interest in and commitment to the quest for the ultimate among people of all religions and none. The discipline of spirituality will be a formidable resource for understanding this phenomenon, critiquing it, and perhaps for helping to guide it.

Kenneth J. Collins (ed.), *Exploring Christian Spirituality: An Ecumenical Reader*, Grand Rapids, MI: Baker Books, 2000; Michael Downey, *Understanding Christian Spirituality*, New York: Paulist Press, 1997; Cheslyn Jones, Geoffrey Wainwright and Edward Yarnold (eds), *The Study of Spirituality*, New York and Oxford: Oxford University Press, 1986; Bernard McGinn, *The Presence of God: A History of Western Christian Mysticism*, 3 vols, New York: Crossroad, 1991, 1994, 1998; Sandra M. Schneiders, 'The study of Christian spirituality: contours and dynamics of a discipline', *Christian Spirituality Bulletin* 6.1 (Spring 1998), 1, 3–12; Philip Sheldrake, *Spirituality and Theology: Christian Living and the Doctrine of God*, Maryknoll, NY: Orbis Books, 1998.

SANDRA M. SCHNEIDERS

Contemporary Spirituality

Any spirituality is embedded in the culture of its time and place. The diversity of voices discernible in contemporary spirituality both in traditional and in non-traditional settings are in dialogue with the vast and rapid changes the world has been undergoing in the past forty years. The accelerated rate of change in society is unprecedented, constraining individuals and communities to seek meaning in the churning seas of new global realities. New technologies like the Internet keep our minds flooded with information and link us through electronic mail in a sheer instant with one another around the globe. World events are broadcast via satellite the moment they are happening, shrinking the distance between regional occurrences and popular consciousness. Extraordinary scientific discoveries in quantum physics, genetics and the evolution of our universe radically challenge our reliance on mechanistic thinking and demand that we conceive of things in holistic ways. In a short span of time, people witnessed the Berlin Wall coming down, the former Soviet Union collapsing, China opening its doors to world trade and South Africa peacefully ending apartheid. Political fortresses crumbled, changing the geopolitical landscape quickly. The world feels smaller as tragic events of human sufferings and environmental disasters are shared globally. Our interconnectedness as a planet is experienced economically, politically and socially every day by the clothes we wear, the food we eat, the means we use to travel and the music that we hear. Paradoxically, as the world's interconnectedness is experienced on local and global levels, tolerance for religious diversity and cultural pluralism is tested by various forms of fundamentalism and stereotyping. Today, as political and religious factional differences erupt, terrorism grows as a major political force on the world stage. In the religious world, Christianity's centre of gravity has shifted from the northern hemisphere to the southern where independent charismatic churches are growing rapidly. The Islamic world is far from being monolithic, as different societies live out Islamic practice in diverse ways. Buddhism itself is made up of over two hundred distinct bodies. We can now talk of the world as having a theodiversity that is akin to the earth's biodiversity.

1. Postmodern world

The view of the world is no longer predominantly western, European-centred, and Christian. It is a world that is multicultural in perspectives, multi-regional in politics, and multi-faith in religious beliefs. We live in what is called a postmodern world. The major beliefs of Enlightenment and modern thought that shaped the predominantly Western world view: 1. the value of unending progress at whatever cost to the planet; 2. the singular power of the rational mind to arrive at universal truths and certainty; and 3. the modern construction of the self-sufficient individual – all are challenged by the contemporary global scene. In contrast, the postmodern consciousness acknowledges 1. the organic and limited nature of the world itself and the interdependency of the human species with all that exist; 2. the ambiguous and multifaceted character of human consciousness and the recognition of the partial, conditioned reality of all truth claims; 3. the awareness that the human person is not self-contained but internally constituted by a whole range of relationships. All of these factors contribute to the various voices being heard in contemporary spirituality. Seven will be described: 1. the appeal to spirituality rather than to religion; 2. the appeal to the contemplative resources of the world traditions; 3. the proliferation of spiritualities – the appeal of the hybrid; 4. the appeal of psychology; 5. the appeal of the sciences; 6. the appeal of cosmology and ecology; 7. the appeal of practices in spirituality.

2. Trends in contemporary spirituality

A. The appeal to spirituality rather than to religion

As the complexity of the pluralistic present-day world permeates human consciousness and ordinary life, individuals find themselves seeking ways to put together the disparate elements of their existence, and to find some meaning in their multifaceted yet fragmented world. The appeal to spirituality has captured the religious imagination of contemporary people as encompassing these spiritual quests more than an appeal to organized religion or to systematic theology. By centring attention on practical lived human experience, spirituality is viewed as a more inclusive, tolerant and flexible canopy under which to pursue the mysteries of the human spirit and the Sacred. Spirituality has become ecumenical and interreligious and not the reserve of any one tradition. Protestant writers like Richard Foster, Rowan Williams, Kenneth Leech, Tilden Edwards and Alan Jones have made spirituality more appealing to Protestant congregations. Catholic writers such as Diarmuid O'Murchu, Barbara Fiand and Joan Chittister contribute to the popularity of spirituality in Catholic communities. Thich Nhat Hanh and the Dalai Lama write prolifically about Buddhism to wide audiences. Abhishiktananda, Bede Griffiths and the transpersonal psychologist Ken Wilber unravel the intricacies of Hinduism for Westerners. The newly translated poetry of the thirteenth-century Sufi Jalalu'ddin Rumi by Coleman Barks and works about Islam by Karen Armstrong introduce people into the mystical traditions of Islam. There is fresh interest in Jewish mysticism found in the cabbala and the writings of the Zohar.

Spirituality is not restricted to religious settings but can be found in a multitude of social locations. For any change in social consciousness, there appears a new spirituality to accompany it. For example, the growing concern for the environment has spawned creation-centred spirituality and ecological spirituality; the woman's movement birthed feminist and womanist spiritualities and the corporate world produced a spirituality of work and the marketplace. The turn to spirituality informs contemporary religious consciousness as the turn to the subject marked Enlightenment thought.

The appeal to spirituality is not only a popular cultural phenomenon but has generated its own academic discipline. Graduate programmes in spirituality can be found at many universities in various countries. Scholarly journals, like *Spiritus,* and academic societies, such as the Society for the Study of Christian Spirituality, are giving coherence to the vast interest in popular spirituality as well as studying classical historical religious expressions. Spirituality's interdisciplinary approach bodes well for its future as a source for integration, applying multiple interpretations from other disciplines like sociology, psychology, history, economics and biology to human religious experiences. Key players in the establishment of spirituality as an academic discipline have been Sandra M. Schneiders, Brad Hanson and Bernard McGinn in the United States and Philip Sheldrake in England.

B. The appeal to the contemplative resources from the world traditions –
the development of the inner self

The breakdown of traditional structures of meaning brought on by the failures of modernity has contributed to a loss of meaning in the postmodern world. In the experience of loss and absence, spiritual seekers have turned inward and outward for alternative visions of authenticity. Significant developments, such as the Western world's exposure to Eastern meditation practices, the enthusiasm for the earth-based and shamanistic wisdom of Native American, Celtic and other aboriginal cultures, and the challenges articulated by feminist and liberation spiritualities to established ways of thinking, coalesced and contributed to the increased interest in the contemplative resources from all the religious traditions. Individuals seek out spiritual directors, engage in silent retreats, read the spiritual classics and the Scriptures, participate in ecumenical and interfaith services and belong to prayer or meditation sitting groups. A spiritual pluralism is an acceptable trait even for those rooted within traditional denominations. Spiritual writers like Thomas Merton (1915–68), Bede Griffiths (1906–93), John Main (1926–82) Anthony de Mello (1931–87), Basil Pennington (1931–) and Henri Nouwen (1932–96) pointed the way, writing about prayer, meditation and their own personal spiritual journeys. Ecumenical communities like Taizé founded in 1940 and Iona in 1938 enjoyed a renaissance of interest, especially among young adults. Writers like William Johnston, *Arise My Love: Mysticism for a New Era* (2000) and Wayne Teasdale, *The Mystic Heart: Discovering a Universal Spirituality in the World's Religions* (1999) attest to an interreligious spirituality using the world's spiritual traditions.

Contemplative resources of other religious traditions are being uncovered and made accessible to wider audiences. Take for example, the one hundred and thirty seven volumes in The Classics of Western Spirituality published by Paulist Press, which covers Jewish, Christian, Islamic and Native American spiritualities in a series that is still ongoing. Contemplative resources are now criss-crossing borders every day in the spiritual lives of individuals. Popular books and articles on prayer and Eastern meditation techniques abound. Classes on yoga and tai chi, workshops on chanting, drumming, walking the labyrinth, ritual practices drawn from indigenous cultures and the monastic practice of *lectio divina* are sponsored not only by church groups and spirituality centres but by individual practitioners of spirituality. The popularity of these gatherings contributes to the dislodging of these practices from particular theologies. Themes such as transformation, solitude, interiority, the search for wisdom, contemplative prayer and spiritual growth draw the attention of people across religious and cultural worlds. The appeal to contemplative practices acts as a counterbalance to the frenetic and superficial contexts of many. A side effect of individuals discovering various spiritual alternatives within their own and other religious traditions has been the possibility of envisioning an authentic spirituality detached from church affiliation.

C. The proliferation of spiritualities – hybrid spiritualities

Both within and outside of religious settings, an array of spiritualities are emerging, growing from special interests and needs. Individuals take responsibility for their own spiritual growth and seek out what assistance they need. Contemporary spiritualities value the process of seeking and appreciate the effects of intentional spiritual practices on one's lifestyle. The metaphor of the spiritual journey captures the perpetual migration from interest to interest, need to need, and practice to practice. Eclecticism accompanies the seeking. Hybrid spiritualities are commonplace. An individual feels free to choose from the rich tapestry of spiritual and psychological options and to belong to multiple communities at the same time for differing degrees of spiritual support. Pragmatism attaches value to the beneficial and visible effects of spiritual disciplines in one's life. It is not uncommon to hear people describe themselves as some form of hybrid, like a Christian Buddhist, or hesitate about claiming a totalizing religious identity, not unlike the dilemma of claiming a pure ethnic identity in today's multicultural world.

D. The appeal of psychology

Thomas Moore's bestseller *Care of the Soul: A Guide for Cultivating Depth and Sacredness in Everyday Life* (1992), M. Scott Peck's *The Road Less Traveled: A New Psychology of Love, Traditional Values and Spiritual Growth* (1978) and Gerald May's *Addiction and Grace: Love and Spirituality in the Healing of Addictions* (1988) have gone through multiple printings and are indicative of an array of other self-help spiritual manuals from which one can choose. These works blend together a variety of sources, among them Jungian psychology, Buddhist principles, psychotherapeutic techniques and classical Christianity. Readers are urged to take responsibility for their feelings and to be accountable for their own happiness. Workshops, retreats, support groups and small prayer/interest circles gather like-minded people together in an otherwise solitary search. Topics of interest range from dreams, journal writing, caring for the soul, friendship, healing, forgiveness, non-violence, creativity, the enneagram, addiction, ecology, psychology, spiritual direction, self-esteem, nature, love, pain, relationships, the body, marriage, ageing, justice and prayer styles. The appeal to psychology in spiritualities has had many positive effects in promoting self-knowledge, increased self-awareness, self-esteem and the integration of affectivity, sexuality and creative energies in a person's life. Negatively, psychology plays a role in the privatization of contemporary spiritualities by promoting deep introspection, personal healing, personal happiness and personal growth to the detriment at times of social and communal relationships and commitments.

E. The appeal of sciences: formation of a new consciousness; complementarity and uncertainty principles

Quantum physics' notion of complementarity: you need more than one version of the truth to make sense of the world; the notion of uncertainty: the way we look at the world changes it, therefore we can never know all aspects of reality – these provide a new vocabulary for contemporary seekers to understand the tentativeness and partialness of everyday life. Other concepts from the sciences such as energy, interconnectedness, participation from within, fields of influence, the properties of light, probability, the quantum vacuum and chaos theory are framing the way people are voicing their spiritual experiences. Spirituality is providing space for a new relationship with science to emerge.

The dualistic and rational legacy of the Cartesian-Kantian world view of mind and body, sacred and profane, and masculine and feminine misses the mark in light of the contemporary religious search for integration and wholeness. Holon/holism in quantum theory, which describes when individual parts of a system are so fully integrated that they behave as a unified whole, has been adopted to express the postmodern awareness. A person's physicality, affectivity, volition and intelligence are experienced as a webbed entity, impossible to separate. The sensual, the bodily, the psychological dimensions of spirituality are now critical factors in any spirituality. All of life is sacred and embodiment is the way of being spiritual in the world. Thus, themes of wholeness, wellness, balance and healing are prevalent in contemporary spiritualities. It becomes impossible also to separate the human person from the netted reality of creation or the social and political interdependencies of the planet. Paradoxically, as holism pervades consciousness, the richness of diversity is enhanced. Spiritualities from Africa, Asia, South America, and from differing subgroups in the cultures, such as indigenous peoples, women, men, gay and lesbian people, are contributing to the dismantling of old constructs and voicing new options for contemporary spirituality.

F. The appeal of cosmology and ecology: the sacredness of the earth

Popular imagination was forever changed when the planet could be viewed from outer space as one Earth. Ecological and environmental movements emerged in order to care for the earth and ensure the planet's survival. New cosmological stories explain the emergence of the universe and are reshaping our understanding of the role the human species plays on the planet. The earth is now seen as a living organism, interdependent, possessing an inherent intelligence. The essence of life is self-organizing, self-maintaining, self-renewing and self-transcending. Creativity, not adaptation, is the basic element of evolution. As we learn more about the story of the earth, our own spiritual story changes. We are more conscious of our own interdependency on the planet and the effects of our lifestyles upon the continuance of the planet for future generations. Eco-justice is intrinsically linked to social justice. Ecotheologian Thomas Berry, *The Great Work: Our Way to the Future* (1999), Rosemary Radford Ruether, *Gaia and God: An Ecofeminist Theology of Earth Healing* (1992), Brian Swimme, *The Hidden Heart of the Cosmos: Humanity and the New Story* (1996), Rupert

Sheldrake and Matthew Fox, *Natural Grace: Dialogues on Science and Spirituality* (1996) contribute to the effort of telling this new story.

The appeal to the sacredness of the earth is found in a flurry of writings on nature, the natural world, geography, landscape, the importance of place, ecology, Celtic culture, creation-centred spirituality and Native American spiritualities. The prevalence of nature in recovering the sense of the Sacred is attested to throughout the history of spirituality. Today, however, open and green spaces, forests, oceans, mountains, meadows, rivers, deserts and the wilderness are not only appreciated as natural cathedrals, sacred places and sanctuaries for humans to commune with the Holy but as living created ecosystems which have their own right to exist as conscious life forms and living subjects.

G. The appeal of practices in spirituality: the recovery of the body

Resurgence in interest in spiritual practices characterizes contemporary spirituality. What classifies as a spiritual practice is also undergoing redefinition. Yoga, tai chi, meditation, chanting, spiritual reading, journaling, fasting, rituals, volunteering, almsgiving, the practice of non-violence, retreats, creative projects, recycling, mindful homemaking, vegetarianism, massage, physical exercise, riding public transport instead of driving a car, backpacking and simplifying one's lifestyle all fall under the heading of spiritual practices. Contemporary embodiments of spiritual practices do not deny the body, materiality or the commonplace realities of existence. Often practices are tied to beneficial results experienced in one's life, such as increased sense of self-esteem, lessening of anxiety, and the sense of contributing to the sustainability of the planet or the easing of another's suffering. Spiritual disciplines so quickly associated with pragmatic results run the risk of becoming yet another product to be tried, consumed and discarded at will. Dorothy Bass, *Practicing Our Faith: A Way of Life for a Searching People* (1998) and Robert Wuthnow, *After Heaven: Spirituality in America since the 1950s* (1998) argue for an approach to spirituality which is rooted in practices. As people gather in small enclaves to do their practice, what we know of as the communal body/community is being reformulated as well.

As the culture of the third millennium continues to develop, one can expect to hear these and other voices transforming the way we live and understand spirituality.

Thomas Berry, *The Great Work: Our Way into the Future,* New York: Bell Tower, 1999; Michael Downey, *Understanding Christian Spirituality,* San Francisco: Harper, 1997; Ursula King (ed.), *Religion and Gender,* Oxford: Blackwell, 1995; Diarmuid O'Murchu, *Reclaiming Spirituality,* Dublin: Gill & Macmillan, 1997; Robert Wuthnow, *After Heaven: Spirituality in America since the 1950s,* Berkeley: University of California Press, 1998.

VALERIE LESNIAK

Interpretation

The study of Christian spirituality involves critical issues of interpretation of traditions and texts. Interpretation is essentially a quest for understanding. This is a complex matter because understanding is associated with 'meaning' rather than purely with gathering factual information.

Because the study of spirituality is self-implicating, it is not only *informative* but also *transformative*. When we approach particular traditions or texts we clearly seek *information*. This includes historical data, textual analysis, an understanding of theological frameworks and a determination of the kind of spiritual practice being represented. However, beyond *information* lies a quest for the 'truth' or wisdom embodied in a tradition or text and how this may be accessed. This confronts us with the questions 'what difference does this make?' and 'what could or should our response be?' This *transformative* dimension of the study of spirituality involves *judgement* (this makes sense, is important and of value) and *appropriation* (we seek to make this wisdom our own).

A rich approach to 'understanding' in Christian spirituality inevitably means that the Enlightenment ideal of a single method, in a free-standing field of study, has to be abandoned. Indeed, in the academic world more broadly the notion of internally consistent but mutually exclusive disciplines separated by hard boundaries is breaking down. The identity of an area of study is no longer found in maintaining sharp distinctions of method. In this context, Christian spirituality is generally agreed to be *interdisciplinary* (albeit with a special relationship to theology).

In the first instance, an interdisciplinary approach expands the disciplines on which the process of interpretation draws. Depending on the nature of the tradition or text under consideration, the classical approach drew on historical, linguistic and literary methods. Because of the religious nature of what is being interpreted, theological tools were also necessary aids to analysis and evaluation (Sheldrake, 1998, 88–93). To these must now be added the methods of modern philosophy, social sciences and psychology along with critical questions addressed by feminist, liberationist and cultural theory.

However, the approach to interpretation nowadays implies more than an expansion of methods. Precisely because spiritual traditions and texts are viewed as sources of *wisdom*, interpretation has shifted beyond methods to hermeneutical theory – the nature of interpretation itself. This asks what 'world of meaning' is presented in a tradition or text and what kind of wisdom is available. Such an approach to interpretation recognizes that what is present in traditions and texts is not reducible to what we know cognitively. Because such wisdom is profoundly challenging and is likely to change us if we pursue it, a contemplative approach must be added to an intellectual one (Schneiders, 1999a, pp. 11–25).

Every act of interpretation is value laden and involves commitments that are far from simple. Because, for many Christians, certain spiritual texts have the status of wisdom documents, there is a particular edge to the scholarly question of interpretation. If our interest is not purely literary or antiquarian, the question of *why* we read such texts and what we read them *for* are central. *How* we proceed to read texts is intimately related to *why* we read them.

In this context, scholars now refer to an 'appropriative method' in relation to interpreting Christian traditions and texts, whether scriptural or spiritual. This means that the purpose of interpretation is not merely accurate knowledge but *application* and the purpose of application is *appropriation*. Understanding is concerned with meanings but also with purpose and values. To be appropriated, texts need to be understood, as it were, from the inside out (Downey, 1997, pp. 126–31; Schneiders, 1999b, *passim*; Williams, 2000, ch. 4).

While spiritual texts are historically conditioned, some cross the boundaries of time or place and retain their importance in new contexts. This is what is implied by the term 'classics' (Tracy, 1991, ch. 3). Such texts disclose something that remains compelling. They continue to challenge readers and bring them into transforming contact with what is enduring in the Christian tradition. The nature of a text's literary genre often influences its popularity and effectiveness (Sheldrake, 1995, pp. 172–3). In general, the strength of classics is that they are capable of moving a reader to a response.

A vital aspect of the power of classics is that they are *committed texts*. Spiritual classics offer a particular interpretation of events, people or teachings. Every spiritual classic has a specific 'take' on the tradition it promotes. In interpreting a spiritual classic, we unavoidably engage with this commitment and the vision of 'truth' embodied in the text.

In a genuine classic there is always a paradoxical tension between particularity and universality. Every classic begins by being embedded in a particular cultural and historical milieu. Yet the 'universality' of the classic refers to its paradoxical capacity to disclose a world of meaning and to evoke transformation in a potentially infinite succession of readers in quite different milieux (Tracy, 1994, p. 115). The category of 'a classic' is not limited to written texts but may be extended to events, persons or even buildings that have some form of revelatory status (Tracy, 1994, p. 118).

We are inevitably aware of different cultural and theological perspectives when we read a text from another time or place. If interpretation is meant to serve contemporary appropriation, we cannot avoid the question of how far to respect a text's conceptual framework, structure or dynamic. Certain responses would be naive. We may ignore the author's intention and the text's structure entirely and simply pick and choose from the text as it suits us. The opposite danger is to assume that only the author's intention is normative. Even assuming that we can accurately reconstruct this, such an approach subordinates our present horizons to the past. Both approaches assume that the 'meaning' of a text is straightforward. A more fruitful, while more complex, approach to interpretation is to engage in a critical *dialogue* with the text. Such a dialogue allows the wisdom of a text to challenge us while at the same time according our own horizons their proper place.

A text's historical context is an important starting point. Spiritual classics were written for clearly identified audiences with specific concerns. The insights of literary criticism also suggest that however familiar words may seem, the experiences and assumptions that lie behind them are different to our own. We are also dealing not with two disconnected moments (our own and that of the author) but with the history of interpretation in between. This history affects our own moment of reading.

While historical knowledge has to some extent a normative role in interpreting texts, there are limits to its value. For example, what we encounter in a text is not direct experience of another time but what the text claims about it. In other words, texts are themselves interpretations of experience, not merely records of it. However, the interpreted nature of texts does not undermine their value. Indeed, subsequent reflections by the author may be more relevant to those who seek to use a text than the original experience alone.

However, the conventional approach to textual interpretation inherited from the nineteenth century, and current until fairly recently, had as its basic principle that the values that a modern reader brings to a classic text are a problem for correct understanding (Sheldrake, 1995, ch. 1). Recent developments in hermeneutics define a broader approach where the possibilities of a text, beyond the author's original conception, are evoked in a creative way by the new religious world in which it finds itself.

The example of music is helpful in understanding this new approach to interpretation. Musicians interpret a text, the score. They may be technically faultless in following the composer's instructions. Performers cannot do simply anything and call it a Beethoven symphony. Yet, a 'good' performance is more than this. It will also be creative because the composer did not merely describe how to produce sounds but sought to shape an experience. Thus, there is no single, definitive interpretation of a text as new aspects are revealed whenever the text confronts new horizons and questions (Lash, 1986, ch. 3).

This image of performance leads us to the core of the interpretative process. Without ignoring the technicalities of a text, or the intention of the author, we reveal new and ever richer meanings every time we read (perform) it. We interrogate the text but our questions are, in turn, reshaped by the text itself. This process is sometimes referred to as the 'hermeneutical circle'. One of the most influential figures in the development of a broader interpretation theory was the German philosopher Hans-Georg Gadamer. He stressed that a text must 'break the spell' of the reader's presuppositions which initially gave the reader an entry point. The text corrects and revises our preliminary understanding (Gadamer, 1979, pp. 324–5).

Gadamer's theory assumes that texts have an 'excess of meaning' beyond the subjective intentions of the author. This is what enables a spiritual classic to come alive in the present. The reader's present situation affects the meaning of the text and the text alters the reader's understanding of the present. Gadamer further concluded that understanding, interpretation and application were a unified process. In Gadamer's view, the weakness of earlier theories of interpretation was that they detached the practical application of a text (for example, in preaching) from technical analysis. In fact we come to a deep understanding of a text only by applying it to the present (Gadamer, 1979, pp. 274–5). In the dialogue between text and reader the aim is to fuse both horizons in an interpretation that is always new. Thus a spiritual classic is not a timeless artefact that demands mere repetition. Understanding the text implies a constant reinterpretation by people who question it from within their own historical circumstances. A concrete example is the Rule of St Benedict. Over the centuries, this produced strikingly different monastic lifestyles while enabling the maintenance of a common core or 'family resemblance'.

Gadamer's theory is complemented by the approach of Paul Ricoeur. Ricoeur emphasizes that once wisdom has been fixed in a written text there follows a radical 'distanciation' of the discourse from its original production. First, the text is distanced from its author who effectively 'loses control'. The text takes on a life of its own as a medium of meaning. Second, the text is distanced from the original audience. A written text inherently becomes available to whoever cares to read it. Third, the text is distanced from its original context (decontextualization) which makes the text able to function in later and different situations (recontextualization). In summary, Ricoeur's emphasis on 'distanciation' enables the text to transcend the limitations of its origins in order to function potentially in any context (Ricoeur, 1976, *passim*).

Contemporary approaches to interpretation suggest the need for what are nowadays referred to as a 'hermeneutics of consent' and a 'hermeneutics of suspicion'. In the first case, we 'consent' to a text in that its origins, the author's intention and the consensus of interpretation over time continue to exert some kind of normative role that prevents us from exploiting the text for our own ends (e.g. Gadamer, 1979, pp. 325–41). However, in the second case, we recognize that the questions provoked by our contemporary situation may be critical of aspects of the text and its assumptions. For example, we are nowadays more aware of the social conditioning of texts and of the need to expose hidden biases against certain ideas or groups of people, particularly biases that continue to influence us (e.g. Schüssler Fiorenza, 1983, *passim*; John, 1988, pp. 143–55).

Two final questions remain. First, can classical texts eventually become unusable? Second, what is a 'community of capable readers' of spiritual texts? Precisely because the presuppositions of a classic are alien to modern people there is a problem. An interesting example is the fourteenth-century English mystical text, *The Cloud of Unknowing*. This has become outstandingly popular in recent times – in fact has been reprinted almost annually since the mid 1960s. Yet what are we to make, for example, of the statement that we are to view the self as a 'foul, stinking lump of sin' (Chapter 40)? The text appears suspicious of the body and of the material world. It also seems to be highly individualistic compared to contemporary sensibilities and clearly assumes that contemplation is open only to a spiritual elite.

So, may people eventually be forced to say that a text is now unusable because it is riddled with assumptions radically out of tune with modern knowledge or values? Even a tentative answer depends on the foundations already described. The first is that 'meaning' does not reside solely in a fixed text but is also established in the conversation between the text and the contemporary reader. The notion of the 'classic text' presupposes that certain documents have shown a capacity to break free from the constraints of their original contexts. This means that they can no longer be seen as tied absolutely to the assumptions of the original author or the original audience. Such texts have already proved capable of being persistently reinterpreted. It may be possible to argue that in a contemporary rereading of the text apparent clashes of culture can be understood differently or interpreted as of secondary importance compared to the fundamental spiritual wisdom of the text (Sheldrake, 1995, pp. 184–92).

In the case of a text that exists to be *performed*, such as Ignatius Loyola's *The Spiritual Exercises*, the imperative of adaptation to the needs of retreatants is built into the text itself and is reinforced in the earliest practical interpretations of it. Thus, according to the text's own logic, 'the Exercises' is not simply the written document but is also what emerges in every use of the text as a medium of spiritual development.

Because the 'meaning' of classic texts is never definitively fixed, it does not seem likely in principle that we will reach the limits of possible interpretations and therefore of 'usefulness'. Obviously there are changes of taste that result in certain texts receding into the background, perhaps to be rediscovered in another age. However, in itself this does not imply the loss of classic status. I may well believe, following David Tracy once again, that texts can be judged according to 'criteria of adequacy', that is, the text meets the basic demands of human living, and 'criteria of appropriateness', that is, the text is faithful to a specifically Christian understanding of existence (Tracy, 1975, pp. 72–9). However, the precise way these criteria are interpreted and applied is also a matter of context. We have to admit that our judgements are not eternally conclusive.

The capacity of texts to reveal new levels of meaning relates closely to the final question of who is capable of interpretation. In practice, 'the community of capable readers' changes over time. For example, in the case of the Ignatian Exercises, interpretation is no longer limited to the perspectives of a male, Roman Catholic clerical religious order, the Jesuits. Lay people, not least women, are not passive recipients of an interpretation established elsewhere but are inherent to the very process of interpretation and the establishment of meaning (Lonsdale 2000, Introduction and ch. 10). Even more radically, given the Reformation origins of the Exercises, the 'community of capable readers' nowadays includes people beyond Roman Catholicism who have benefited from the Exercises and have joined the ranks of those who guide others through the process (Sheldrake, 1990, *passim*).

Much of this essay has been concerned with the *process* of interpreting texts and traditions. However, the final question reminds us that the question of who offers authoritative readings of spiritual classics is at least as important. This final question also illustrates that the history of interpretation involves issues of power (see Ricoeur 1981, pp. 63–100). In the context of Christian spirituality, the reality of power cannot be avoided in how spirituality is defined, who appears in its 'official' history and who is enabled to become an effective interpreter of texts and traditions.

———

M. Downey, *Understanding Christian Spirituality,* New York: Paulist Press, 1997; H.-G. Gadamer, *Truth and Method,* London: Sheed & Ward, 1979; O. John, 'The tradition of the oppressed as the main topic of theological hermeneutics', *Concilium* 200 (1988); N. Lash, *Theology on the Way to Emmaus,* London: SCM Press, 1986; D. Lonsdale, *Eyes to See, Ears to Hear: An Introduction to Ignatian Spirituality,* rev. edn, London: Darton, Longman & Todd/New York: Orbis Books, 2000; P. Ricoeur, *Interpretation Theory: Discourse and the Surplus of Meaning,* Fort Worth: Texas Christian University Press, 1976; P. Ricoeur, 'Hermeneutics and the critique of ideology' in J. B. Thompson (ed.), *Hermeneutics and the Human Sciences,* Cambridge: Cambridge University Press, 1981; S. Schneiders, *The Revelatory Text: Interpreting the New Testament as Sacred Scripture,* Collegeville: The Liturgical Press, 1999a; S. Schneiders, *Written that You May Believe: Encountering Jesus in the Fourth Gospel,* New York, Crossroad, 1999b; E. Schüssler Fiorenza, *In Memory of Her: A Feminist Theological Reconstruction of Christian Origins,* New York: Crossroad, 1983; P. Sheldrake (ed.), *Ignatian Spirituality in Ecumenical Context, The Way Supplement* 68, Summer 1990; P. Sheldrake, *Spirituality and*

History: Questions of Interpretation and Method, rev. edn, London: SPCK/New York: Orbis Books, 1995; P. Sheldrake, *Spirituality and Theology: Christian Living and the Doctrine of God,* London: Darton, Longman & Todd/New York: Orbis Books, 1998; D. Tracy, *Blessed Rage for Order,* New York: Seabury Press, 1975; D. Tracy, *The Analogical Imagination: Christian Theology and the Culture of Pluralism,* New York: Crossroad, 1991; D. Tracy, *On Naming the Present: God, Hermeneutics and Church,* New York: Orbis Books, 1994; R. Williams, *On Christian Theology,* Oxford: Blackwell, 2000.

PHILIP SHELDRAKE

Mysticism

1. The Nature of Mysticism

There is no universally agreed-upon definition of mysticism, any more than there is for religion. In common parlance, the word is often taken to refer to anything that is strange or mysterious. More narrowly, it can be understood to indicate the quest to attain union with God. Here it will refer to those elements in Christian belief and practice that concern the preparation for, the consciousness of, and the effects attendant upon a heightened awareness of God's immediate and transforming presence. Since God cannot be present the way a created thing in the universe is present, many mystics insist that true consciousness of God is best realized through absence, that is, through a process of negation that strips away all experiences, images and concepts to aim toward the mystery that lies beyond both affirmation and negation.

The legitimacy of the term mysticism, which first appeared in the seventeenth century, has been questioned. While the word is modern, the use of 'mystical' as a qualifier for elements in Christian practice and thought is old. The Greek adjective *mystikos* is derived from the verb *myein* meaning to close the mouth or the eyes. Ancient writers used the adjective and terms like 'mystic things' (*ta mystika*) in reference to the mystery cults, but by the second century CE, beginning with Clement of Alexandria, the word began to be adapted by Christians to signify the hidden realities of the Christian life. Its primary employment was in relation to the spiritual meaning of the Bible, but it was also used to point to the inner power of Christian rituals and sacraments; even the vision of God was described as mystical (*theoria mystike*). Around the year 500 the unknown author who used the pseudonym Dionysius (see Acts 17.34) created the term 'mystical theology' to indicate the knowledge (or better super-knowledge) that makes contact with the unknown God. Dionysius was also among the first to use the term 'mystical union' (*henosis mystike*).

A broad and flexible understanding of mysticism need not take the language of union with God as the defining characteristic. While many mystics have used such language, others have avoided it and preferred different modes of expression. A broad understanding also emphasizes that mysticism is essentially a process, a life commitment to attaining God. The significance of the effect of mystical consciousness on the life of the mystic is important because the Christian tradition has always insisted that the only way to validate the claims of mystics is through the impact their inner transformation has upon their lives and the lives of those they influenced. Seeing mysticism as part of a process also emphasizes that mysticism is an element within Christian faith, not some special kind of religion. Finally, a flexible view allows for distinguishing between more or less explicit forms of mysticism. For example, while all Christian mysticism is rooted in the Bible, this does not mean that one can find explicit mysticism in the Bible to match the sense in which Origen of Alexandria in the third century, or Bernard of Clairvaux in the twelfth, wrote as mystical theologians.

2. The development of explicit forms of mysticism

A. Monastic mysticism

The historical evolution of explicit forms of Christian mysticism can be portrayed according to a model of gradually accumulating and interactive layers of tradition. In that sense, mysticism again emerges as one element in the broader Christian dynamic of handing on the faith. Mystics embark upon their pursuit of God within the community of belief and worship on the basis of studying the biblical text, participating in the Church's liturgical and sacramental life, and reading the classics of the mystical tradition.

The first and foundational layer of the Christian mystical tradition began in the third century in the writings of the great exegete and catechist, Origen (d. 254). Although Origen's predecessor Clement of Alexandria had already introduced the use of elements of Greek philosophical mysticism in the service of Christian teaching, especially the notions of contemplation of God and divinization, it was Origen's biblically based programme of the soul's purification from vices through loving devotion to the Word made flesh that set forth the first full exposition of Christian mysticism. According to Origen, the anagogic, or uplifting, interpretation of the Scriptures, especially the Song of Songs, enables the devout believer to attain divinizing union with God. Many of the major themes of subsequent Christian mysticism (e.g. the role of love and knowledge, the relation of action and contemplation, union as a loving union of wills) found their first full presentation in Origen's writings.

The importance of Origen's biblical mysticism stems not only from his own writings, but also from the fact that Origenist mysticism was taken up in the fourth and fifth centuries by monastics to help hand on the wisdom of the desert. The monastic practice of flight from the world in order to undertake a specialized life of prayer and penance, either as a solitary (the eremitical way) or in community (the coenobitical way), became the institutional matrix for most forms of mysticism down to the twelfth century. Monastic mysticism was essentially biblical and liturgical in the sense that the monastics sought God in and through personal appropriation of the spiritual meaning of Scripture cultivated within the liturgical life of the monastic community. Monastic mystics rarely talked about their own experience of God; they rather sought to express the path to mystical transformation through biblical exegesis and treatises of a mystagogical character (i.e., designed to guide readers into the consciousness of God's presence).

Crucial figures in the formation of monastic mysticism were Evagrius of Pontus (d. 399) in the East, and John Cassian (d. 435) in the West. To be sure, Origenism was not the whole story of the first layer in the development of mysticism. The great Fathers of the undivided Church who helped establish the orthodox doctrines of the Trinity and Christology also made significant contributions to the development of the monastic mysticism that was to remain dominant down to the end of the twelfth century. In the East, Gregory of Nyssa (d. 395) showed how divine infinity attracted believers to endless loving pursuit (*epektasis*) of God, both in this life and in the next. In the West, Ambrose of Milan (d. 397) was instrumental in conveying the Greek erotic mysticism of the Song of Songs to Latin readers. Above all, it was Augustine of

Hippo (d. 430) who shaped mysticism in the medieval West. The Bishop of Hippo's accounts of his ascents to brief touching of God in the *Confessions*, and especially his preaching on the mystical dimensions of the Psalms, are classic mystical texts that retain their power even today. His teaching on the immanence of the Trinity in the soul, the necessary mediation of the total Christ, Head and members, in finding God, as well as his analysis of the various kinds of visionary experience, provided doctrinal foundation for many forms of later mysticism. At the end of the ancient world, Gregory the Great (d. 604), the first monastic pope, synthesized mystical teaching under the themes of compunction and contemplation.

Among the most influential of the early mystics was the mysterious Dionysius, probably a Syrian monk of *c*. 500. His writings sketched a programme of ascent to God through the necessary, but insufficient, use of symbols, rites and positive assertions about God designed to lead on to the negative theology that strips all predications from God and prepares for the mystical theology in which the soul, following the example of Moses, finds God in the darkness of unknowing. Dionysius' form of Christian Neoplatonic mysticism was introduced into the West in the ninth century through the translations of John Scotus Eriugena. This Irish scholar developed his own systematic form of Christian Neoplatonism with a strong mystical flavour in his masterwork, the *Periphyseon* (*On the Division of Nature*).

The twelfth century saw both the summation of monastic mysticism, especially in the writings of the Cistercian and Victorine mystics, and the appearance of elements hinting at important shifts in mysticism that were to become evident after the year 1200. The growth of first-person accounts of visionary experiences of Christ fore-shadowed the explosion of visionary mysticism in the later Middle Ages. The greatest mystic of the era, Bernard of Clairvaux (d. 1153), brought the erotic mysticism based on the Song of Songs to new heights. Bernard also stressed the need for personal experience as a criterion to be co-ordinated with that of the biblical witness. The proper balance between what Bernard called 'the book of experience' and the book of the Bible was to remain an issue for centuries. The major Victorine mystics, especially Hugh (d. 1141) and Richard (d. 1173), witness to the desire to systematize traditional teaching on prayer, contemplation and ecstatic experience, showing the importance of mysticism in the Scholastic theology.

B. The new mysticism

At the beginning of the thirteenth century new forms of religious life encouraged innovative ways of describing close encounters with God. The mendicant orders of Franciscans and Dominicans and independent forms of religious life such as that of the Beguines provided impetus for the new mysticism of the late Middle Ages. Although this mysticism built on the riches of the monastic contemplative tradition, it was novel in its break with the monks' stress on flight from the world and in its message that mystical contact with God was accessible to all Christians. The new mysticism was also not limited to the learned Latin tongue, but was most often expressed in the developing vernaculars of Western Europe. The new mysticism invited the participation of women in a powerful way. Many of the late medieval women mystics wrote in the vernacular, making use of language that often seemed excessive in relation to previous mysticism, especially in their appeal to sexual imagery and their claims to have attained complete identity with God.

Of course, generalizations about women mystics are no more true than those about male mystics. What is most impressive is sheer number of important women mystics evident from the thirteenth century on. In Germany we find the Beguine Mechthild of Magdeburg (d. 1282), the Cistercian nuns of Helfta in Saxony, and a number of fourteenth-century Dominican nuns. In Italy, Clare of Assisi (d. 1253), Angela of Foligno (d. 1309), and Catherine of Siena (d. 1380) are the most famous of a host of ecstatic and visionary women. The Dutch-speaking areas provided the Cistercian Beatrice of Nazareth and the Beguine Hadewijch in the thirteenth century, as well as a number of lesser-known women in the centuries that followed. In France another Beguine, Marguerite Porete (d. 1310), was executed for dangerous ideas found in her mystical treatise *The Mirror of Simple Annihilated Souls*. In England the *Showings* of the anchoress Julian of Norwich (d. *c.* 1420) remains one of the most popular of all mystical texts.

The new mysticism was not just the province of women. The period between 1200 and 1500 saw some of the greatest male mystics of the Christian tradition. The writings of Francis of Assisi (d. 1226), like the Bible, are mystical in an implicit more than in an explicit sense, but due to his reception of the stigmata, Francis became an image of the ideal mystic. The works of Bonaventure (d. 1274), the premier mystical theologian of the Franciscan tradition, were instrumental in this process. The Seraphic Doctor brought the systematic impetus of the Victorines to a new level – an organized mystical theology that was given a new orientation through the image of Francis as the perfect *imitatio Christi*.

No less significant was the 'mysticism of the ground' created by the German Dominican, Meister Eckhart (d. 1328). Eckhart preached that 'God's ground is the soul's ground and the soul's ground is God's ground', pointing to the deep inner identity with God that could be reached through the new awareness found in total detachment. Aspects of his daring message were deemed theologically unacceptable by Pope John XXII who condemned twenty-eight extracts from his writing and preaching. Eckhart's followers, particularly Henry Suso and John Tauler, remained true to his memory, though they sought to qualify some of the more daring aspects of the mysticism of the ground. Other fourteenth-century mystics, especially the Dutch John Ruusbroec (d. 1381), worked out a form of mysticism close to that of Eckhart, but more careful of doctrinal limits. The fourteenth century also witnessed significant mystical texts in English produced by Richard Rolle (d. 1349), the Augustinian Walter Hilton (d. 1396), and the anonymous author of *The Cloud of Unknowing* and its related treatises (c. 1380s).

Debates over the differences between true and false mysticism pervaded the four-teenth and fifteenth centuries. At the root of the dispute was the new conception of mystical union that had emerged in the thirteenth century and how this concept was thought to affect the relation between the mystic and the institutional Church. The traditional monastic view of union centred on the loving uniting of the divine and human wills often expressed through an appeal to the erotic intercourse of lovers in the Song of Songs. It insisted on the continuing distinction of the two subjects, taking its motto from the Pauline text, 'The one who adheres to God becomes one spirit' (1 Cor. 6.17). Beginning with some of the thirteenth-century women, such as Hadewijch and Marguerite Porete, and developed in Eckhart's mysticism of the ground, a new concept of union of identity was created according to which God and human, at least in some way, become absolutely one in a bottomless abyss of mutuality and equality. Proponents of this form of union of identity or indistinction also appealed to biblical texts, such as Christ's prayer, 'That they all may be one, even as You, Father, are in me, and I am in You' (John 17.21). But if mystics came to see themselves as identical with God, what did this mean for their relationship to the Church? Were they no longer bound to the ecclesiastical authority and the sacramental life? Were they perhaps even above the moral law? Accusations that some mystics had reached such conclusions and adopted a life of 'freedom of the spirit' (2 Cor. 3.17) were to trouble Western Christianity for centuries.

C. The crisis of mysticism

The sixteenth century created little that was new in the story of Western mysticism, but many of the trends and issues that first emerged about 1200 reached fruition at this time. The fragmentation of Christendom in the Reformation debates also had a profound effect on mysticism. Neither Martin Luther nor John Calvin were mystics in the classic sense, but both Reformation leaders used elements of the mystical tradition in their theologies, so that later Protestant mystics, such as John Arndt (d. 1621), and even the theosophically inspired Jacob Boehme (d. 1624), could claim to be reviving aspects of Reformation theology that had been neglected. The Pietist movement of the seventeenth and eighteenth centuries continued the line of Lutheran Protestant mysticism.

Other churches and groups that had broken with Rome in the sixteenth century also produced their own forms of mysticism. The radical spiritual reformers of the sixteenth century, who went further than Luther and Calvin in their stress on inner religion without institution, absorbed elements of late medieval mysticism, especially the stress on detachment and inner identity with God found in the mysticism of the ground, but they did so within an ethical and individualistic framework that was post-medieval, as can be seen in the writings of Valentin Weigel (d. 1588), who lived as a Lutheran pastor while keeping his true sympathies hidden. In the mainstream Church of England a rich vein of mystical prose and especially poetry emerged in the seventeenth century with such figures as George Herbert (d. 1633) and Thomas Traherne (d. 1674). Coming out of the Calvinist reformed tradition, the seventeenth-century English Puritans also composed mystical poetry and prose treatises.

The major forms of mysticism of the sixteenth and seventeenth centuries were not surprisingly found in Catholic Europe. Female mystics continued to appear in Italy (e.g. Catherine of Genoa, Maria Maddalena de' Pazzi), but it was in sixteenth-century Spain that early modern mysticism reached its first peak. The suspicions of mysticism evident in the late Middle Ages were revived in Spain beginning in the 1520s when the *Alumbrados* (illuminated ones) were accused of many of the same errors as the medieval Free Spirits. But the atmosphere of suspicion and repression did not snuff out the extraordinary mystical fervour that was nurtured by new forms of religious life and the reform of older orders. Ignatius of Loyola (d. 1556), the founder of the Jesuits, was a perfect representative of the mystical ideal of *simul in contemplatione activus* (i.e., being at once active and contemplative). Although some later Jesuits continued to follow the mystical path, the leadership of the order turned against mystical prayer. The greatest Spanish mystics were nurtured by the reform of the Carmelite order. Teresa of Avila (d. 1582), the initiator of the reform, wrote two of the most important mystical classics, an autobiographical *Life* and a treatise called *The Interior Castle*. Her confessor and assistant, John of the Cross (d. 1591), was not only a premier mystical poet, but the author of a four-volume commentary on his poems that forms one great treatise on the negative and positive aspects of the path to mystical union with the Trinity.

The seventeenth century marked a watershed, the era when the ongoing disputes over the nature and legitimacy of mysticism reached a crisis that was partly internal and partly external. Internally, the trajectory stressing the role of inner experience in accounts of mysticism finally seemed to implode as the concentration on the investigation of inner states, especially of rapture and union, became so dominant that it ruptured the connection between the mystical element and the broad context of Christian life. Mystics seemed to some observers, both then and now, to be creating a separate sphere of religion. The emergence of the category of 'mysticism' (first found in France as '*la mystique*') has been seen as a sign of this shift. The internal crisis was exacerbated externally by the Enlightenment criticism of traditional forms of Christian belief and practice, something which helped undercut the world view that had nourished mysticism over the centuries.

During the seventeenth century the major arena of mysticism shifted to France. The Golden Age of French mysticism included such figures as Francis de Sales (d. 1622), Pierre Cardinal Bérulle (d. 1629), and the Ursuline missionary to Canada, Marie de l'Incarnation (d. 1672). Important French mystics were also involved in the Quietist controversy at the end of the century. In 1687 a Spanish priest resident in Rome, Miguel de Molinos, was condemned to perpetual imprisonment for mystical errors characterized as Quietism (i. e., belief in a state of inner passivity so extreme that one could no longer be troubled to perform good works or to avoid evil ones). In the 1690s similar errors were ascribed to Madame Guyon (d. 1717), a prolific mystical author whose writings are reminiscent of some of the more excessive medieval female mystics. Guyon was defended by Archbishop Fénelon (d. 1715), who saw in her a classic mystic who based her life on pure love of God. Fénelon's defence, however, was singled out for condemnation (albeit a mild one) by Pope Innocent XII in 1699.

The effect of these internal and external blows marginalized mysticism in much of Western Europe. This is not to say that mysticism totally died out after 1700. Indeed, in Russia, well removed from the enlightened West, mystical currents continued to flourish and reached new heights in the late eighteenth and in the nineteenth centuries. In Protestant lands mysticism found a place among the Free Church traditions nourished both by the Radical Reformers and (strangely enough) the Catholic Quietists. In Catholicism, for several centuries mysticism tended to be reduced to paranormal experiences of rapture, stigmata and inedia (living without food) found among uneducated women carefully supervised by clerical handlers. Even in the first half of the twentieth century mysticism was generally viewed either psychologically, as an example of aberrant psychic states, or as a suspect phenomenon to be measured by guidelines set down according to a few respected mystics, notably Teresa and John of the Cross.

The significance of mysticism as an integral aspect of Christian life and practice, however, did re-emerge during the course of the twentieth century, both through the writings and witness of modern mystics (e.g., Teilhard de Chardin, Simone Weil, Thomas Merton), and through the investigations of theologians, philosophers and other scholars of religion. Recognition of the power of mysticism to transform not only individual consciousness, but also social and institutional structures, contributed to this renewed appreciation of the necessity of the mystical element in Christianity. The full story of this revival remains to be written, but we can agree with Karl Rahner who said that the Christian of the future will be either a mystic – or will not be a Christian at all.

Hans Urs von Balthasar, *The Glory of the Lord: A Theological Aesthetics,* 7 vols, San Francisco: Ignatius Press, 1982–89; Michel de Certeau, *The Mystic Fable vol. 1, The Sixteenth and Seventeenth Centuries,* Chicago: University of Chicago, 1992; Steven T. Katz (ed.), *Mysticism and Philosophical Analysis,* Oxford: Oxford University Press, 1978; Joseph Maréchal, *Studies in the Psychology of the Mystics,* Albany: Magi Books, 1964 (the original French contained two volumes, only one of which is available in English); Bernard McGinn, *The Presence of God: A History of Western Christian Mysticism,* New York: Crossroad, 1991– (three volumes of the planned five have thus far appeared: *The Foundations of Mysticism* (1991); *The Growth of Mysticism* (1994); and *The Flowering of Mysticism* (1998)); Friedrich von Hügel, *The Mystical Element of Religion as Studied in Catherine of Genoa and her Friends,* 2 vols, London: Clark & Dent, 1961 (first published in 1908).

BERNARD MCGINN

Spirituality and Culture

Different verbs could be used to express the relationship between spirituality and culture. Spirituality could be said to reflect culture, or to challenge, or enhance, or transform, or even undermine it. To some extent, one's understanding of the relationship between spirituality and culture is a variant of one's understanding of the relationship between grace and nature. Grace can be seen primarily as healing nature, or as building on it, or as elevating, perfecting and even transforming it. A complication exists in the fact that grace and nature never show up in a neatly identifiable manner – with grace clearly 'here' and nature clearly 'there'. The same is true of spirituality and culture: as they concretely exist, they are never actually separate; and it is an abstraction, a falsification of reality, to imagine them separated. For this reason, it is difficult to specify, precisely, the nature of their relationship. Nonetheless some attempt will be made to do so here.

1. Spiritualities in cultures and cultures hosting spiritualities

'Spirituality' refers to how we live our lives. 'Culture' does the same; in a nutshell, culture is the way we live together. So are the two identical? No. For in spirituality there is more of an element of conscious choosing, by individuals or groups, to live their lives in a particular – a deeper – way. Spirituality is about life lived at depth. (Sheldrake, 2000, p. 40). The reason it cannot be simply identified with culture is that, not infrequently, spiritualities seek wisdom beyond the cultures in which they exist, so that they at once belong to a culture and at the same time attempt to enrich that culture from elsewhere. However no spirituality is independent of the culture in which it arises and no culture is devoid of implications for spirituality.

'Culture' is how we think and value, how we behave together, how we shape and fashion our material world; in other words, it is ideational, performative and material (see Schreiter, 1997, p. 29). Our beliefs, attitudes and values, our behaviours and rituals, our visible and material creations are all elements of culture and constitute, together, the whole that is more than the sum of the parts and that is always present when human beings live together. Culture is the water we swim in, the air we breathe. We both construct and shape it and we receive and assimilate it; we are in it and it is in us.

'Spirituality' exists in all the dimensions in which culture does: the ideational, the performative, the material. In 'postmodern' cultures, which are characterized by plurality, eclecticism and a refusing of the gap between 'popular' and so-called 'high' culture, there is a plurality of spiritualities and these function, sociologically speaking, more or less as 'subcultures'. This is because, like culture, they are 'the way people live' – in this case, particular people within the overall culture who have chosen to organize their existence according to what they believe and value in relation to the material, human and transcendent world. Spiritualities vary hugely. Yet no spirituality – in its expression and development – escapes reliance on the culture that 'hosts' it.

'Experience is always defined in cultural terms, even when it is religious' (de Certeau, 1966, p. 4). Spiritualities, as articulated, practised and materially expressed, bear the marks of their cultural contexts, even if they also challenge those contexts. There are only spiritualities-in-cultures and cultures-hosting-spiritualities.

2. Relationship: a certain 'mirroring', a certain 'correcting'

It is difficult to characterize the relationship between things that are never separate. However, it is not impossible. There is a certain mirroring element to the spirituality–culture relationship. This is evident in the fact that the plurality of cultures across the world today is reflected in the plurality of spiritualities that are found also across the world. Ideally an essay such as this would do more than acknowledge those many cultures and spiritualities, devoting space to Asian and African spiritualities and even to the spiritualities that are found in smaller, indigenous cultures throughout the world. However, it is so-called 'postmodern' cultures, characteristic today of Europe and the U.S.A. in particular, that must engage us mainly here. These cultures are *mélanges* of many subcultures and are marked by eclecticism, diversity and a certain synthetic character. In them the grand narratives have been set aside and increasing importance is given to local stories. Postmodern cultures celebrate endless local stories and manifest a relativism about world views and ways of living that is reflected in the abundance of spiritual practices and understandings that abound today and that are relativistically assessed ('true for me', 'true for you', etc.). It is not like times past, where 'culture' was a normative notion and spirituality had to do with the devotional and (sometimes) practical aspects of the religion that had the dominant place in that (normatively conceived) culture.

There is, then, today, a tendency towards correspondence between culture(s) and spirituality(ies): because the former are relativistic and eclectic, the latter are relativistically understood and free to combine elements in a pot-pourri that draws from a wide variety of traditions. This correspondence does not mean that all spiritualities will mirror their cultures unthinkingly. For example, it was suggested recently that Europeans' obsession with genetically modified foods was an exaggerated expression of fervour arising from the need to find a 'larger than life' issue (Reid 2001). In other words, it was really an absence of sacredness in the secular culture that led to something being made 'sacred' (Woodward 1994: 'In a secular culture where nothing is sacred, anything can be sacralized'). Here the spirituality–culture relationship is more dialectical than continuous, less a mirroring than a 'holding a mirror up to'. Nonetheless the role of the culture remains decisive in the generation of any 'spiritual' quest, whether the latter runs in tandem with or runs counter to the culture's own thrust. Furthermore, no matter how challenging, how arresting, a particular spirituality will be in a culture, it will still be very difficult for it to rise above the parapet of the culture's panoply of spiritualities. Indeed it is a cultural phenomenon today that people seek out the arcane, the esoteric, the different and unpredictable (see Drane, 2000, p. 157); and so it can be said that it belongs to the culture to go against the culture! In a sense, therefore, the cultural co-opts what challenges it. Again and again postmodern cultural forces canonizing both unabashed eclecticism and political correctness make it very difficult for any particular spirituality to command more than relative attention. This poses a problem with regard to the relationship between Christian spirituality and culture, since Christian spirituality is, on the one hand, respectful of cultural diversity while, on the other hand, committed to following a specific 'way' that is centred on the person of Jesus.

3. Models for relating spirituality and culture

How is the relationship between Christian spirituality and culture to be conceived? There are what might be called 'models' for envisaging this relationship. Some of these models place a priority on 'culture', others on 'Christian spirituality', still others somewhere in between. Models that prioritize culture – call them 'anthropological' models – tend to place their trust in cultural elements themselves as the very lifeblood of an authentic spirituality. Proponents of such models point out that there is no spirituality that is not already inculturated. This means that any meeting between spirituality and culture is in reality an encounter between cultures (see Sievernich, 2003, pp. 50–51). Models that prioritize spirituality tend to place their trust in specific traditions, rituals and practices of the Christian community, particularly as people have personally experienced these. And they tend to view the culture as that into which the spirituality must simply be translated (Bevans, 1992, pp. 30–46, translation model; see also pp. 47–62 for an anthropological model).

The first kind of model tends to have difficulty with the 'authenticity' mentioned above (that is, with the notion of generating an 'authentic' spirituality) because authenticity cannot come from within the culture alone but must, in some way, be guided by a standard or by criteria to which the culture itself can be subjected. The second kind of model tends to have difficulty with the culture, which it conceives, somehow, as apart from the Christian spirituality it espouses and as being to that spirituality much as clothing is to a naked body – necessary so that the body can be seen but not really essential to its existence.

Neither model is satisfactory, the first being too immanent, the second too transcendent. The tendency of the first is to affirm from the outset the human creation that culture is and to forget that cultures, like all human creations, exist under the dialectic of sin and grace and so possess dimensions that are welcoming of the Christian reality and dimensions that are quite opposed to it. The tendency of the second model is to start by looking outside the culture for, as it were, a prior Christian content for the spirituality and to seek, then, simply to translate this into cultural terms – as if a spirituality could be found that were not already inculturated. The first does not take Christian specificity seriously enough; and it fails to recognize that cultures vary hugely in their receptivity for the Christian 'way'. The second does not take the cultural embeddedness of all things human, spirituality included, seriously enough; and it tends to view culture merely as 'clothing' for a kind of naked or alone-standing reality that is just awaiting contemporary dress. In the end, neither model takes culture, in its specificity, seriously enough. These two models might seem, at first glance, to be inductive and deductive respectively. In reality each involves a certain prior commitment, the former to context, the latter to tradition. Neither is radically inductive, although some models for relating spirituality and culture have become such because they begin, literally, from expressions of on-the-ground spiritualities in particular subcultures and try to read, from them, the contours of emerging spiritualities. Can a more satisfactory one be found?

In the search for a more satisfactory model of the relationship between Christian spirituality and culture, it will be necessary to keep in mind that, in postmodern cultures, non-normativity is more or less culturally prescribed. This means that the very suggestion that a particular spirituality might command more attention than others is automatically counter-cultural, for it is swimming against the tide of politically correct, cultural forces that champion the bland equality of all ways and are resistant to all normativity. Yet, the question of whether, for those individuals and groups who wish to live out a specifically Christian spirituality, it is possible to envisage the spirituality–culture relationship in an entirely non-normative manner is one that will not simply disappear. This is because cultures (and subcultures) are not neutral vis-à-vis Christianity. Thus the question remains: can a model for relating spirituality and culture be found that is respectful both of the plurality of spiritualities and of Christian specificity? I attempt to sketch the outlines of such a model below.

4. Towards an adequate model of the spirituality–culture relationship

The insight from the anthropological model that the spirituality–culture relationship always entails an encounter between cultures is valid, including when the spirituality is Christian. For there is no uninculturated spirituality, Christian or otherwise. When relating spirituality and culture, the spiritual and the cultural are found – albeit differently – on both sides of the relationship. Thus the relationship between spirituality and culture may be thought of according to the image of a dialogue between persons. Persons in dialogue are not separated from each other by some kind of clear dividing line. Rather A is in B and B is in A. This is true also in the 'dialogical relationship' between Christian spirituality and culture. This dialogue is analogous to the dialogue that is Christian prayer, on one side of which is the divine seeking the human and on the other side of which is the human opened up to the divine. Christ is central to one side, but he is incarnate in the human world. The human is central to the other side, but is opened for receiving the enfleshed Word. On each side, then, is a divine-human reality, not equal, of course, for Christ is human by self-emptying and the human is divinized by gift (grace). The dialogue is a genuine one because God enables the human, created side to be a real partner. In the dialogue, each side is open to the other: Christ to the human, the human to Christ – in other words, drawing in our analogy, Christian spirituality to culture and culture to Christian spirituality. Thus, in the dialogue, the culture is impinged upon by the challenges that the spirituality embodies and the spirituality willingly self-empties in order to become incarnate afresh – this time in those dimensions of this particular culture that have been prepared and graced to receive it. Revelation occurs here – not as a word spoken and received, but rather as relationship: divine–human encounter. The dimensions of the culture that accord with God's intent for humanity and, as such, can 'make a home for' the Christian way are noted and approached, while the anti-divine dimensions of the culture are noted, and firmly set aside (see Boff, 1979, ch. 9, pp. 141–7). The normative is clearly present. Yet the process is gentle, akin to what occurs in genuine Christian prayer.

This imagined dialogue model of the relationship between Christian spirituality and culture will not be welcomed everywhere. Some will argue that it makes any culture and Christian spirituality equal partners. They will say that the culture(s) in which Christianity flourished (Semitic, Greek) possess a normativity that others do not. Andrew Beards argues that this is true for Joseph Ratzinger and, in an even more radical way, for Bernard Lonergan (see Beards, 2000, pp. 161–210, esp. pp. 176–95). Maybe so; but theirs is a worrying viewpoint that – without wishing to be classicist regarding culture, as in the Christian past – could lead nonetheless to culture's dialogue-partner in the image just outlined being less kenotic and more 'pushy' than Christ ever was, or could be. Also, it could lead to an overlooking of the hidden presence of Christ in all cultures, despite their human imperfections. Here there is no question of denying the normative element in inculturated Christian spiritualities – and there is no other kind – any more than it is a matter of denying the normativity required towards cultures; for all cultures need purifying, some more than others. Here it is a matter rather of recognizing the elements of a graced relationship: the relationship between Christian spirituality and culture, in which God's pattern of self-humbling in Christ – 'stooping' to make his home in those dimensions of the culture that can house Christian faith today – is met by the culture's graced responses to these kenotic overtures. Could it be said that, wishing to become incarnate in cultures, Christian spirituality does not think its cultures-of-origin a thing to be grasped and so, on its side, there is cultural self-emptying and a seeking of incarnation in new cultures? And could it be said that cultures, disarmed by so sensitive an approach, are opened to the gift being offered and thus converted, so that their open-to-the-divine dimensions are widened and their anti-divine dimensions reduced? If so, then the 'dialogical' model of the spirituality-culture relationship can be seen as a double letting go, as a conversation in which kenosis and conversion become the names of the partners in dialogue.

Andrew Beards, 'Christianity, "interculturality," and salvation: some perspectives from Lonergan', *The Thomist* 64.2 (April, 2000), 161–210, esp. Part II, 'Culture, Christianity and cultural normativity', 176–95; Stephen B. Bevans, *Models of Contextual Theology*, rev. and expanded edn, Maryknoll, NY: Orbis Books, 2002; Leonardo Boff, *Liberating Grace*, Maryknoll, NY: Orbis Books, 1979; Kenneth J. Collins (ed.), *Exploring Christian Spirituality: An Ecumenical Reader*, Grand Rapids, MI: Baker Books, 2000; James Corkery, 'Continuing to think about faith and culture', *Studies* 92.365 (Spring 2003), 19–26; Michel de Certeau, 'Culture and spiritual experience', *Concilium* 9.2 (November 1966), 3–16; John Drane, *The McDonaldization of the Church: Spirituality, Creativity, and the Future of the Church*, London: Darton, Longman & Todd, 2000; Philip Endean (ed.) et al, 'Postmodernism: A contribution to spirituality?' *The Way*, July 1996 (entire issue); T. R. Reid, 'In Europe, the ordinary takes a frightening turn: health scares confound continent', *The Washington Post* (Thursday, 1 March 2001), p. A01; Robert J. Schreiter, *The New Catholicity: Theology Between the Global and the Local*, Maryknoll, NY: Orbis Books, 1997; Philip Sheldrake,

'What Is Spirituality?', in Kenneth J. Collins (ed.), *Exploring Christian Spirituality: An Ecumenical Reader*, pp. 21–42; Michael Sievernich, 'Jesuit theologies of mission', *The Way* 42.1 (January 2003), 44–57; Kenneth L. Woodward, 'On the road again: Americans love the search so much that the idea of a destination is lost', *Newsweek* (28 November 1994), 44.

JAMES CORKERY

Spirituality and the Dialogue of Religions

The dialogue between Christianity and other religions was once conceived solely in terms of theological debate. Now, thanks in no small measure to the influence of a number of single-minded individuals, a strong experiential element has been added to the more intellectualist discussion of common themes and ideas. The origins and development of this shift are difficult to trace but at least four layers or strands can be noted, if not precisely distinguished.

First, the dialogue with Eastern forms of meditation has reawakened an interest in neglected or forgotten practices within Christianity itself. J.-M. Déchanet, perhaps the earliest to bring yogic techniques of meditation into Christian prayer, claims that he was influenced by the teaching of William of St Thierry. He represents the belief, rather more strongly felt today, that a proper balance of physical and mental is essential for the spiritual life. Through his contact with a Hindu guru, Swami Satyananda, John Main learned a simple method of praying with a mantra, a word or prayer which would evoke an awareness of the Spirit which dwells in the heart. Later, on becoming a Benedictine monk, Main was led to a similar form of prayer in Cassian and the *Cloud of Unknowing*. His teaching is kept alive today by a wide network of Christian meditation groups.

A second strand is represented by contemplative missionaries. Jules Monchanin and Swami Abhishiktananda (Henri le Saux) founded the Śantivanam ashram out of the conviction that the Christian faith would only ever become rooted in India through the witness of a liturgical and contemplative life in tune with the rhythms of Indian spirituality. Their successor, Bede Griffiths, was responsible for an inculturated Christianity which was one of the more extraordinary results of the post-Vatican II era. A similar motivation can be discerned in the practice of Jesuits like William Johnston, Hugo Enomiya Lassalle and Kakichi Kadowaki in Japan. Their efforts to engage with Zen Buddhism have caught the popular imagination – as did the extraordinary inner journey of Thomas Merton.

A third layer reinforces the inner journeys of these pioneers with a more external or public form of spiritual practice. At Assisi in October 1986 Pope John Paul II met with other faith leaders for a public demonstration that religions could be united through prayer. The event, which caused a great deal of controversy at the time and still raises awkward theological issues, has inspired a number of imaginative imitations in different parts of the world. Inter-faith celebrations, in which people of different faiths listen to each other's prayers and recitations in respectful silence, are now fairly common. The Monastic Inter-faith Dialogue (DIM), mainly in Europe and North America, has developed a rich and impressive tradition of hospitality between faiths. The sight of Tibetan lamas and Shi'a ayatollahs attending compline alongside their brothers and sisters of another tradition is one of the more extraordinary fruits of the dialogue and ensures that the personal encounter grows out of and returns to the daily life of a community of faith.

Fourth, but by no means the least important: if personal and meditative prayer is often led back to its roots in some sort of common liturgy, it also develops shared commitments and common action. In India, where Christians are a tiny minority, dialogue often takes place at the level of experiences of living and working together, whether in Hindu or Christian ashrams. The Zen teacher Thich Nhat Hanh, through his friendships with Merton and the peace activist Dan Berrigan, has brought a whole new dimension to the dialogue with his espousal of 'engaged Buddhism'. The community-based experiments of more active contemplatives like Franco Sotto-cornola in Japan and Aloysius Pieris in Śri Lanka reflects a similar conviction. The latter in particular has been scathing in his criticism of the West's 'spiritual colonial-ism' which picks up the East's methods of meditation but ignores the poverty and injustice by which they are surrounded. For Pieris inter-faith prayer, whether person-al or public, always has an ethical and even political dimension.

These four layers, all too generally sketched here – personal discovery, missionary inculturation, public celebration and concern for the common good – raise a number of questions for Christian spirituality. Does not *common prayer*, whether liturgical, meditative or devotional, imply a single focus, or at any rate some shared understand-ing? What are the limits to inter-faith hospitality or *communicatio in sacris*? Can Eastern meditation techniques be used by Christians? If prayer for the Christian is essentially a response to God's prior Word, how can other forms of address, which name God differently, be incorporated into that prayer? Can 'inter-faith prayer' be anything more than the expression of a lowest common denominator which turns out in the end to be so vapid as to be meaningless?

In recent years Christian spirituality has become more open to other cultural influences. The interest in other religions can be understood as another dimension of the more general shift from a static self-referential approach to the Christian life to a more dynamic or open-ended concept of the spiritual journey in which what is 'other' is to be welcomed as an invitation into a deeper faith rather than marginalized as a threat to be avoided. Such openness is much to be welcomed. It does not follow, how-ever, that a dialogue between persons of faith which takes place at the level of shared prayer and interiority grants some privileged short cut towards inter-religious under-standing. Nor does the identification of commonalities or some sort of 'mystical core' between the religions overcome the need for careful discernment and a more consciously theological or interpretive dialogue. This immediately raises the question whether spirituality is a sufficiently robust term to cope with the complex theological and ethical issues which the encounter of religions raises.

Certainly, when coupled with inter-faith dialogue, the term 'spirituality' can be made to cover phenomena of bewildering complexity and dubious provenance, from yogic retreats and tantric massage to mystic conversations and New Age paraliturgies. It can also become subtly elitist, replacing traditional or supposedly outmoded insti-tutional religion with the pursuit of certain privatized inner states which encourage a culture of spiritual 'self-making'. Some accounts of the relationship between spiritu-ality and inter-faith dialogue tend to speak as if they are coterminous, two sides of one reality, denoting a holistic integration of body, mind and spirit. But what is it that makes for such harmony? And how to distinguish the integrity of faith from a personally appropriated fusion of disparate spiritual experiences?

At issue here is not some cross-religious phenomenology of spiritual experience but, more profoundly, the role which inter-religious relations play in the process of self-understanding. No doubt the experience of dialogue with other religions opens up all sorts of possibilities for personal enrichment, for exploring the 'sacred space' where the prayer, rituals and spiritual wisdom of the world's religions intersect with one another. But it is easy to ignore a more fundamental question: not so much about discernment, which remains always problematic when one ventures across the boundary between one religious tradition and another, but about the boundary itself. Does the experience of crossing the boundary, of entering into a relationship with what is other, have something to teach me about how I am to understand and live my own life of faith?

In order to address that question some account must be taken of the experience of dialogue as an interpersonal encounter. For Christians what differentiates dialogue from any other form of mission or witness is *learning*; the aim is not to proselytize but to understand and in understanding to learn more about what God may be saying to the participants through the encounter. In recent years a typology has established itself: the dialogues of common life, common action, religious experience and theological exchange. First appearing in Vatican documents in the early 1980s, but owing its existence more to the experience of the Church in south Asia and the Far East, this typology offers a useful shorthand for a complex and diffuse phenomenon. While there is no agreement about the relationship of the forms, it makes sense to distinguish between the largely *affective* dialogues of life and action, which provide the interpersonal context, and the more *cognitive* dialogue of theological exchange which concentrates on communicating and explaining the truths of faith.

On this account, religious experience often plays a mediating role. Most of the experiences of dialogue noted earlier begin either with theological or with ethical issues which both join and divide people. They become rooted at a more personal level of faith when the 'edges' of faith are explored in prayer and formalized in ritual and shared religious experience. However, while it is arguable that the meeting of persons of faith at the level of prayer and meditation is the most creative catalyst for the interfaith encounter as a whole, it does not follow that religious experience can be neatly separated from 'common life' and 'common action'. It would be more accurate to speak of the sharing of religious experience as an intensification of what has already been perceived at the interpersonal level. Once sensitized to the complex ethical demands made by the other, perceptions change irrevocably and faith takes on a new responsibility – for itself *and* for the other.

To shift attention in this way to the formative practices of Christian faith through dialogue with the other is not to say that commonalities cannot be identified between Christian spirituality and the spiritual practices of other religious traditions. The first two 'pillars of Islam', the testimony of faith or *Shahadah* and the precept to pray five times day, express 'submission' to the sovereignty of God, while Buddhist meditation is rooted in the practice of *satipatthana*, the 'setting up of mindfulness' of the present moment. Christians will find evocative parallels and connections with their own spirituality in these two themes. But similarities do not imply equivalence. Neither expresses a response to the God revealed in Jesus Christ; nor can they be accommodated in any straightforward fashion with the traditional forms of Christian prayer. Islam expressly denies the divine sonship of Jesus and thus avoids any such filial language to speak of human intimacy with God. Buddhism goes further in refusing to name ultimate reality, let alone speak of a mediator between human and divine. It sometimes seems as if such different traditions of spiritual practice have very little in common. The point, however, is that it is not similarity but the very 'otherness' of these traditions, their refusal to sink differences, which opens up the space of dialogue. Each, in its own way, acknowledges the risk of reducing the Ultimate to some controllable form.

The question, therefore, for any spiritual tradition is not about how different forms of prayer or techniques of meditation can be said to express a common religious experience. Rather it is to ask how *any approach to the Ultimate or any address or response to God is possible in the first place*. To put it in the familiar Christian terms of Paul's struggle with the newness of the gospel revelation, the Spirit of Christ draws him towards God, interceding 'with sighs too deep for words' (Romans 8.26). The Spirit enables the Word of God to be heard and a response of faith to be made. Thus, if the forms or methods of another religious tradition dispose the individual to become sensitive to the movements of the Spirit, to what is always *God's* work, they need not be incompatible with a traditional Christian spirituality founded on Jesus' response to the Father's blessing. More radically, in provoking theological reflection about what 'the other' may be saying, they may deepen Christian life and learning.

Whatever else 'common life' and 'common action' teach the Church, positive experiences of inter-religious relations make the maintenance of borders impossible. At the same time, they raise the most awkward questions about what is, and what is not, of God. It is, of course, true that some basic principles of discernment are needed, but more desirable is a theology which sees in the exchange an image of the welcoming and hospitable God whom Christians experience in Jesus. As far as public or liturgical prayer is concerned, much depends on how hospitality is practised and how the virtues of being by turns host and guest are understood. To return to John Paul II's celebrated meeting at Assisi, a distinction was made there between people of different faiths *coming together to pray* rather than *praying together*. Listening attentively while others pray, supporting them in faith through one's presence, is unproblematic; developing some sort of 'shared formula' is much more difficult.

At the more personal level, the experience of many individuals and groups of inter-religious prayer and meditation has developed a considerable wisdom. None of the practitioners mentioned above is engaged in some sort of uncritical syncretism of religious practice. Rather those ascetical and meditative practices which lead to forms of physical relaxation and peaceful attention (whether Yoga, Zazen, T'ai Chi etc.) are developed as acceptable ways of disposing the individual for the transforming action of God's Spirit. The general yogic method of concentration, which involves the centring of attention on one focus in order to overcome distractions, can act as an effective *introduction* to prayerful contemplation. Indeed, there are forms of Christian meditative and devotional prayer (using simple invocations, an icon, exposition of the Blessed Sacrament) which approximate to versions of this practice. Beyond that, questions about the adaptation and use of particular Eastern techniques for Christian meditation prayer cannot be addressed without reference to the particular traditions in question (see, e.g., two more detailed discussions in this volume: 'Zen and Christianity' and 'Yoga').

Meditative prayer is never a mechanical exercise aimed at achieving some monistic stillness. Properly adapted, techniques may well lead to a contemplation of the horizons of God's unceasing action in the world. Nevertheless, for Christians so engaged, the primary concern must be for the integrity of the Christian faith – a faith which, while it demands a certain passivity in the face of God, never allows the obliteration of the self. Inter-faith prayer, whether understood as no more than listening in silent support of the other, as a shared form of words in which common commitments are made, or as an individual appropriation of the wisdom of meditative practice, will always involve a very personal – and perhaps painful – process of self-abandonment. Such a practice of faith, exercised in responsible relationship with the other, has its active and its passive elements which mirror the example of Christ's relationship with the Father. He both speaks and acts for the sake of the Kingdom of God but obediently undergoes a *kenosis* which submits ultimately to the will of the Father. For Christians the following of Christ has times for speaking and times for listening – times when they may confidently take the initiative and times when they must follow the work of the Spirit who, as the one who witnesses to Christ, goes before the Church.

A Christian spirituality of dialogue does not, therefore, allow for any finished 'state of consciousness', let alone some pan-religious integration of different experiences. As with the dialogues of life, action and even theology, engagement with the other through some sort of shared religious experience demands a willingness to keep moving back and forth from the familiar to the unfamiliar, learning that God is to be found precisely in the crossing, where the borders are riskily transgressed. In imitation of that dialogue which is revealed within the trinitarian relations, Christian spirituality appears as intrinsically dialogical and relational. Christians exist in relationship with the other; that is to say, they are committed always to living 'in between' *this* concrete moment in history and the fullness of meaning which can only be anticipated in hope. Through participating in the never-ending relationship of Father and Son united by the Spirit of love, Christians learn how to relate to others. The analogy of a mutual indwelling, or *perichoresis*, teaches the virtues and practice of hospitality and welcome.

To pray 'in the Spirit' is, according to Paul, to call upon God as 'Abba'; the Spirit's primary role is to form in human beings the same relationship, to make them children after the manner of Jesus' relation with the Father. But this is itself *God's* action, the work of the Spirit, which, like Jesus entering into the mystery of his own death and resurrection, opens up the possibility of resolution, of that tantalizingly close vision of peace and harmony, but does so in an unexpected and sometimes subversive way. The death and resurrection of Jesus challenges the all too human tendency to short-circuit the inevitably difficult and sometimes quite tortuous processes by which human beings make sense of their lives in face of the transcendent. It breaks all conceptual forms and linguistic constructs which risk the domestication of the divine, which would presume to make God instantly accessible.

This is what makes Christian spirituality different from some generalized account of 'spiritual wisdom'. Rather, a Christian spirituality of inter-faith dialogue is concerned with a vision of spiritual wholeness and harmony which is rooted not in the interpretation of more or less discrete or private 'supernatural' experiences but in the conviction that God's Spirit, who led Jesus into the desert and consoled him in times of dereliction, continues to guide God's people even, and perhaps especially, in the challenging and confusing experience of inter-faith encounter.

Michael Barnes, *God East and West*, London: SPCK, 1991; Abhishiktananda (Henri le Saux), *Saccidananda*, Delhi: ISPCK, 1974; Abhishiktananda, *Prayer*, Delhi: ISPCK, 1967; Bede Griffiths, *Return to the Centre*, London: Fount, 1978; Bede Griffiths, *The Marriage of East and West*, London: Fount, 1984; Jules Monchanin and Henri le Saux, *Ermites du Saccidananda*, Paris: Casterman, 1956; Aloysius Pieris, *Love Meets Wisdom*, New York: Orbis Books, 1988; Thich Nhat Hanh and Daniel Berrigan, *The Raft Is not the Shore*, New York: Orbis Books, 2001.

MICHAEL BARNES

Spirituality and History

Christianity is critically preoccupied with 'history' and 'time' for the doctrine of the Incarnation places God at the heart of human history.

> By affirming that all 'meaning', every assertion about the significance of life and reality, must be judged by reference to a brief succession of contingent events in Palestine, Christianity – almost without realising it – closed off the path to 'timeless truth'. (Williams, 1990, p. 1)

Consequently, Christian spirituality embraces an affirmation of 'history' as the context for spiritual transformation. Even Augustine's eschatological theology of history, one of the most influential Christian historical theories, did not render temporal history meaningless even if it distinguished between sacred and secular 'history'. While he rejected a progress model of history, and no age could be closer to God than any other, the thread of sacred history ran through contingent history and each and every moment was therefore equally significant (Markus, 1970, Chapter 1).

Philosophers, historians and anthropologists are also concerned with the importance of a historical consciousness. 'History' and, more broadly, 'time' are important categories in human cultures.

> Few factors in a culture express the essential nature of its world picture as clearly as its way of reckoning time: for this has a determining influence on the way people behave, the way they think, the rhythm of their lives and the relationships between them and things. (Gurevich, 1985, p. 94).

In approaching the relationship of spirituality and history, one fundamental factor is how we view the importance of 'history' itself. Western cultures currently appear to be becoming history-less and memory-less. In the long term this will have a serious impact on our spiritualities. There is a weariness with history and with the notion of being involved in a stream of continuities through time. To base one's life on tradition or to hark back to the past appears to be a distraction. It is common these days for people to believe that 'history' signifies only the past. The past is what has happened rather than something that sustains our present and invites us to reflect on the future and on what we aspire to.

This weariness with history relates to a number of probable factors. Rapid social changes and the decline of traditional communities have broken many people's sense of living connections with the past. 'History' and 'tradition' are also perceived by some people as conservative forces from which we need to break free if we are to live a more mature and rational existence. The power of history-as-myth to sustain entrenched social, religious and political divisions tends to reinforce this negative view. Beyond this, there is a desire for immediacy sustained by consumerism (and reinforced by aspects of information technology) that tends to encourage a memory-less culture without a sense of historical identity. Perhaps the most powerful factor during the course of the twentieth century was the death of 'history-as-destiny' based on faith in the inevitability of progress after a century of industrial growth and imperialistic expansion. Such a belief in 'history' as a progressive force evaporated in the face of the slaughter of the 1914–18 war, mid-century totalitarianism and the horrors of the Holocaust and Hiroshima.

Despite contemporary misgivings, historical consciousness is a fundamental element in the interpretation of spiritual texts and traditions and reminds us of the irreducibly contextual nature and particularity of spiritual values. Serious consideration of the complexities of history has been a major development in the academic study of spirituality over the last thirty years or so. Before that time, spirituality tended to pay little attention to context, whether of historical texts and traditions or of the contemporary interpreter. Studies of classic traditions did not reflect on the contingency of their theological or cultural assumptions. In the case of classical writings, problems of interpretation were not a major issue in a world where Christians had little sense of historical distance from the perspective of ancient authors.

One reason why the study of spirituality in theological circles now pays greater attention to the complexity of historical interpretation lies in an important shift provoked by a change of language associated with the Second Vatican Council in the early 1960s. The use of the phrase 'signs of the times' by Pope John XXIII, and its repetition in the Council documents, was effectively a recognition that history was not incidental to but the context for God's redemptive work. Every historical moment has a dynamic of its own where the presence and power of God may be perceived. Consequently, faith is not opposed to history, and no separation is possible between religious history and world history (Ruggieri, 1987, pp. 92–5).

Spiritualities do not exist on some ideal plane outside the limitations of history. The origins and development of spiritual traditions reflect the specific circumstances of time and place as well as the psychological state of the people involved. They consequently embody values that are socially conditioned. To take one example, the emphasis on radical poverty in the spirituality of the thirteenth-century mendicant movement was not simply a 'naked' scriptural value but a spiritual and social reaction to particular conditions in society and the Church at the time – not least to what were seen as their prevailing sins (Le Goff, 1981, *passim*).

This does not imply that spiritual traditions and texts have no value beyond their original contexts. However, it does mean that to appreciate their riches we must take context seriously. The concept of 'context' was imported from the fields of history and the social sciences. It has become a primary framework for the study of spiritual traditions. All spiritual experience is determined to some degree by culture – that is, a system of meaning or a world view in the sense used by anthropology. Culture 'denotes an historically transmitted pattern of meanings embodied in symbols, a system of inherited conceptions expressed in symbolic forms by means of which men [*sic*] communicate, perpetuate, and develop their knowledge about and attitudes toward life' (Geertz, 1973, p. 89). Spiritual traditions, and the texts that are their 'products', are cultural expressions.

Spirituality is thus never pure in form. 'Context' is not a 'something' that may be added to or subtracted from spiritual experiences or traditions but is the very element within which these find expression (Sheldrake, 1995, pp. 58, 84–6, 167–8; de Certeau, 1966, pp. 3–31). This contradicts an older conception of Christian spirituality as a stream of enduring truth in which the same theories or images are simply repeated in different guises. Even spiritual theologians as sophisticated as Karl Rahner and his brother Hugo appeared at times to place a figure like Ignatius Loyola essentially outside the limitations of history. His spirituality was 'not really an event in the history of ideas that could be inserted, if we were so to choose, in the "Tridentine" or "Baroque" periods . . . It is something of exemplary value in a quite fundamental way, for an age that is only just starting'. In a footnote, Karl Rahner developed this thought further by suggesting that 'Ignatius has something almost of the archaic and archetypal about him . . . He has nothing that really belongs to the Baroque or the Renaissance about him' (Rahner, 1964, pp. 85–7). The writings of the Rahner brothers led the Catholic Reformation historians Outram Evenett and John Bossy to point out the danger of making spiritual experience or teaching 'a region of certainty transcending any historical or psychological conditions' (Evenett, 1968, pp. 55–6 and 126–32).

These comments about culture and context in relation to spirituality would now be widely accepted. However, a comparison of three classic histories of spirituality written during the twentieth century soon reminds us of how substantial the changes have been over the last fifty years.

P. Pourrat's four-volume *La Spiritualité Chrétienne* was published shortly after the First World War. His unified approach to spiritual doctrine led him to suppose that the same theology of prayer, virtue or spiritual growth could be found in all spiritual traditions. Different 'schools' of spirituality or different national 'types' of spirituality differed only in presentation. The cultural dominance of the Graeco-Latin forms was unquestioned. Pourrat effectively ignored the existence of other spiritual 'cultures' (e.g. Celtic in the West or Syriac in the East). He also limited his attention to monasticism and mysticism with virtually no reference to lay or 'popular' spirituality.

Louis Bouyer's three-volume (in the English edition) *A History of Christian Spirituality* was published in the early 1960s around the time of the Second Vatican Council. Bouyer was still preoccupied with the essential unity of spirituality and often lacked an awareness of differences between or even within 'schools' of spirituality. However, in other respects his volumes were a considerable advance on Pourrat. The cultural perspective was broader (e.g. Syriac and Celtic traditions do get a mention), lay spirituality has more substantial treatment and his third volume offered, for its time, a relatively sympathetic treatment of Orthodox, Protestant and Anglican spiritualities. Women were, however, still relatively invisible.

Finally, the three Christian volumes within the Crossroad series, World Spirituality: An Encyclopedic History of the Religious Quest, appeared in the late 1980s. These differ vastly from Pourrat and Bouyer. Most significantly, they are collections of specialist essays by teams of international and ecumenical scholars rather than grand surveys by single authors. The history of spiritual traditions is to be seen as inherently plural, linked to specific social, cultural and theological contexts. We can no longer expect a single person to have the detailed knowledge to write a multi-volume history. While by no means perfect, the volumes offer a much better balance between Eastern and Western Christianity and make other efforts to express the cultural plurality of spirituality beyond a Graeco-Latin hegemony. The spirituality of lay Christians and women's perspectives are better represented and there is an acceptance that earlier condemnations of dissenting spiritualities need to be revised.

While pluralism and context are now accepted as the unquestioned background to the study of historical spiritualities, the way in which contextual studies developed raises questions for people who are concerned with the specifically religious themes of spirituality. For example, the history of spirituality has come to mean the study of how religious attitudes and values are conditioned by surrounding culture and society. This brings historical spirituality close to the study of *mentalités*, or world views, so beloved of French historians in the second half of the twentieth century. This 'social' version of history is informed by anthropology and religious sociology. The limitation of such an approach to spirituality, if it is exclusive, is that it tends to abandon theological sources and the questions raised by theological theory. We need a middle way between the older (exclusively theological) approach to spirituality and the newer stress on changing social contexts (Bynum, 1982, pp. 3–6).

One case study is the recent treatment of early Christian asceticism and monasticism. A contextual approach tends to resituate asceticism in a broader world than monasticism or even patristic Christianity and approaches its history with questions drawn from a wide range of disciplines. This raises many new and interesting questions. The problem is that such an approach *in isolation* often leaves little room for the theological goals that were the active horizons of Christian asceticism (Stewart, 1996, pp. 11–15).

The contextual nature of spiritual traditions means that the process of historical analysis must nowadays address a number of critical questions (Sheldrake 1995, Chapters 3, 4 and 7). First, in any given tradition or text how was holiness conceived? Which categories of people were thought of as holy? What places or things were deemed to be particularly sacred – and, negatively, who or what was excluded from the category 'holy' or 'sacred'? For example, close association with sexual activity (marriage) or with physical reality (manual labour) was for many centuries difficult to connect with ideas of holiness. Second, who creates or controls spirituality? For example, to what degree does the language of spirituality reflect the interests and experience of minority groups (who nevertheless controlled spiritual resources) such as clergy or monastic personnel? Third, what directions were not taken? In other words, to what degree has it been assumed that the choices made were in some absolute way superior to those that were rejected? For example, what were the real motives for the condemnation as heretics of the medieval women's spiritual movement, the Beguines? Was it a genuine concern for the spiritual welfare of lay people or a suspicion of lay people not sufficiently under clerical control? Finally, where are the groups that did not fit? For example, why was it that, within the Western Catholic tradition, the experience of lay Christians and women especially was largely ignored until recently in the formulation of spiritual theory?

All historical studies involve choices and this affects our interpretation of spiritual traditions. First, *time limits* are chosen. In other words, writers decide on the appropriate boundaries within which to date spiritual movements and thus to understand them. For example, our sense of the continuity or discontinuity between the spirituality of the Middle Ages and that of the Protestant Reformation will be affected by an apparently simple matter of how and where authors choose to divide a multi-volume history (Raitt, 1987, Introduction). Second, traditional histories reveal a *geographical bias*. We make assumptions about where 'the centre' and 'the margins' are in the history of spiritual traditions. For example, until recently, the spirituality of Celtic Christianity was usually treated in terms of its absorption into a homogenized Latin tradition around the eleventh and twelfth centuries rather than on its own terms. Third, we choose *certain evidence as significant*. So, for example, if studies concentrate exclusively on mystical texts or monastic rules the impression is given that spirituality is essentially literary, is to be found exclusively in privileged contexts, and may be distinguished from the mere devotional or 'popular' religion.

Finally, despite the complexity of contemporary approaches to history and its relationship to spirituality, a viable sense of historical *narrative* is still important, as Paul Ricoeur reminds us. Narrative, he argues, is vital to our individual and collective identities – and, implicitly, to our spiritual well being: '[T]ime becomes human time to the extent that it is organised after the manner of a narrative; narrative, in turn, is meaningful to the extent that it portrays the features of temporal existence' (Ricoeur, 1984, vol. 1, p. 3). On the one hand, Ricoeur shares a postmodern scepticism for meta-narratives. However, he also refuses to equate this renunciation with the impossibility of seeing history as a form of narrative at all. If we reject the possibility of mediating narratives altogether this is not the liberating experience that it may appear. On the contrary, it is profoundly oppressive because without narrative we risk two things. First, we undermine a key element of human solidarity (we bond together by sharing stories) and, second, we remove a key incentive for changing the status quo as well as an important means of bringing this about. 'We tell stories because in the last analysis human lives need and merit being narrated. The whole history of suffering cries out for vengeance and calls for narrative' (Ricoeur, vol. 1, p. 75).

Narrative is a critical key to our identity for we all need a story to live by in order to make sense of the otherwise unrelated events of life and to find a sense of dignity. It is only by enabling alternative stories to be heard that an elitist 'history', even of spirituality, may be prised open to offer an entry point for the oppressed who have otherwise been excluded from 'official' history. Without narrative, a person's life is just a random sequence of unrelated events, and suffering and loss remain unintelligible. Rather than reject narrative entirely we need to ask 'whose narrative is told?' 'Who belongs within the story?'

L. Bouyer, *A History of Christian Spirituality*, 3 vols, London: Burns & Oates, 1968; C. Walker Bynum, *Jesus as Mother: Studies in the Spirituality of the High Middle Ages*, Berkeley: University of California Press, 1982; M. de Certeau, 'Culture and spiritual experience' in *Spirituality in the Secular City, Concilium* 19, 1966; L. Dupré and D. Saliers (eds), *Christian Spirituality: Post-Reformation and Modern*, WS, New York: Crossroad, 1989; C. Geertz, *The Interpretation of Cultures*, New York: Basic Books, 1973; A. J. Gurevich, *Categories of Medieval Culture*, London and Boston: Routledge & Kegan Paul, 1985; J. Le Goff, 'Francis of Assisi between the renewals and restraints of feudal society' in *Francis of Assisi Today, Concilium* 149, 1981; B. McGinn, J. Meyendorff and J. Leclercq (eds), *Christian Spirituality: Origins to the Twelfth Century*, WS, New York: Crossroad, 1986; P. Pourrat, *La Spiritualité Chrétienne*, 4 vols, Paris, 1918; K. Rahner, *The Dynamic Element of the Church*, London: Burns & Oates, 1964; H. O. Evenett, *The Spirit of the Counter-Reformation*, Cambridge: Cambridge University Press, 1968; J. Raitt (ed.), *Christian Spirituality: High Middle*

Ages and Reformation, WS, New York: Crossroad, 1987; P. Ricoeur, *Time and Narrative*, 3 vols, Chicago: University of Chicago Press, 1984–88; G. Ruggieri, 'Faith and history' in G. Alberigo, J.-P. Jossua and J. A. Komonchak (eds.), *The Reception of Vatican II*, Washington, DC: The Catholic University of America Press, 1987; P. Sheldrake, *Spirituality and History: Questions of Interpretation and Method*, London: SPCK/New York: Orbis Books, 1995; C. Stewart, 'Asceticism and spirituality in Late Antiquity: new vision, impasse or hiatus?', *Christian Spirituality Bulletin* 4.1 (Summer 1996); R. Williams, *The Wound of Knowledge*, London: Darton, Longman & Todd/Boston: Cowley Publications, 1990.

PHILIP SHELDRAKE

Spirituality, Liturgy and Worship

The dialectical relationship between Christian spirituality and Christian common prayer can be traced to the very beginnings of the Church's life. Indeed, already in the New Testament we find participation in worship regarded not only as a sign of the health of our relationship with God but also as a contributor to well-being of that relationship. When St Paul, for example, is encouraging the Corinthian church to move toward holiness of life, he urges them to look to their celebration of the Lord's Supper as both a teacher of righteousness and as the litmus test for any claim that the community is truly the Body of Christ (1 Cor. 11.17–32). This approach sets the pattern for all future conversation between liturgy and spirituality (in all their various forms): the common prayer of the Church provides guidance for Christian devotional life and the yardstick against which it is measured.

The liturgy offers a variety of resources for the spiritual formation of Christian people. First and foremost, Christian public worship serves as a primary 'school of prayer' for those who wish to live intentionally before God, a model for all of the other forms of prayer undertaken. The images and gestures of the liturgy shape the religious imagination out of which prayer emerges; the actions of the liturgy give form and content to meditation, specific liturgical prayers provide a language for private devotional prayer. Over and over again, spiritual guides advise those under their care to absorb the prayer of the liturgical assembly and to allow it to become the formative principle for the entire life of prayer. In a similar way, the actions of the liturgy shape the other disciplines and devotional praxis of the Christian spiritual life. The literature of spirituality often commends regular meditation on the various physical elements of corporate worship: kneeling, offering, grateful receiving, processing, beating the breast in penitence. In this way, certain key patterns of behaviour become habitual for those who allow themselves to be moulded by the liturgy.

Another way in which the liturgy undergirds Christian spirituality is by providing a context within which worshippers can experience the encounter with God. To enter into the spirit of the liturgy is to enter into the arena within which the triune God is actively engaged in restoring and renewing worshippers as they make themselves available to divine power. At the same time, worshipping in faith, hope and love allows participants to make their relationship with God visible through the signs and gestures, words and songs of worship. By giving voice to the praise of God, to the petition for forgiveness, to thanksgiving and to offering, the Christian liturgy gives participants an opportunity to express the subtleties and complexities of the divine–human relationship, and thereby to deepen it. In the liturgy the Christian believer attempts to stand before God 'without an alibi', and with this kind of radical honesty comes the potential for spiritual healing, growth and maturity.

The spiritual life entails not only an individual's relationship with God, but also the relationship between the individual and the world, and Christian common prayer also contributes to this aspect of spirituality by providing a blueprint for human relationships both within and outside the community of faith. As it offers visions of genuine holiness, as it invites acts of reconciliation with God and neighbour, as it offers images of the future of the world and its contents, the liturgy reorders all our dealings with others and casts a new light on the world, relativizing human structures of power, status and authority. The community structured by the Church's liturgy is a community of equality, where gifts are for sharing and not for hoarding or for personal prestige, and where the ministry of reconciliation is the highest calling.

When lived fully and intentionally, the Christian life presents the believer with innumerable temptations, trials and injuries, and if there is any one clear witness in the Christian tradition about the role of the liturgy in the spiritual life it is that by immersion into the words and actions of worship Christians can tap into a deep wellspring of strength in times of spiritual crisis. This happens in innumerable ways. In baptism Christians put on the 'armour of salvation', in the Lord's Supper they partake the spiritual food necessary for the arduous journey of faithfulness, in the absolution of sin they are given a fresh spiritual vitality to resist the lure of evil. Often, it is those who feel the weight of marginalization and oppression, who are cut off from the power-structures of society, who are especially attuned to the spiritual sustenance to be found in Christian worship. The common prayer of the Church is their 'balm in Gilead', the medicine for the 'sin-sick soul', and the liturgical assembly is the infirmary within which that medicine is administered.

Those who understand the Church's liturgy as a primary resource for the devotional life of individuals and communities also wish to argue for its indispensable place in negotiating the major issues of human existence and in the making of meaning. All Christians are called to 'work out their salvation in fear and trembling' in whatever social location they occupy, and questions of human identity and vocation are a part of the spiritual journey of every person. In all of its varied forms, Christian worship addresses these questions both directly and indirectly: in baptism the washing with water speaks of new birth into a particular kind of life in the world; in the Eucharist the sharing of bread and wine speaks of the Christian imperative to share the generosity and hospitality of God which we have been offered, in the exchanging of the peace gestures of reconciliation model the true community of peace and equality. In all of this, Christians are to recognize that their true vocation is to become liturgical persons, and thereby to understand our true identity as children of God and disciples of Jesus Christ.

At the same time the liturgy enables people to find spiritual meaning in their most basic life commitments: mating, parenthood, work. Although it is only in the modern period that people have been free to make independent choices in these matters, the notion that these ordinary social circumstances have spiritual value is as old as the Church itself, and this spiritual value is revealed most powerfully in worship. In the context of the rites of marriage, for example, all of the aspects of human pair-bonding – sex, child-rearing, household economics – are revealed as aspects of the Christian vocation of husband and wife, and as signs of the love of God to the world. In this way, their life together comes to be understood as forming a 'Church in microcosm'. In the eyes of the liturgy, the marriage also becomes a recapitulation of Eden, a fresh opportunity for a godly relationship between men and women.

Because the liturgy makes no sharp distinction between 'sacred' and 'secular', it is a natural starting point for a renewed vision of the place of work in the quest for God. The essential 'materiality' of the various rites is disclosed in the reverence with which they invite us to deal with elements of the created order and the work of human hands – wine, water, bread, oil. While the message of the liturgy is that all of life comes to us as gift, and that we human beings do not create from nothing, it is also true that human work has the potential to become a part of the overall work of God: creative, transformative and redemptive. The Jewish tradition of Sabbath-keeping, transformed into the Christian Sunday 'day of rest', speaks of liberation from compulsive drudgery and rigidly defined roles, from all those things that inhibit a free and exuberant response to the Spirit's promptings.

Spirituality is often studied as something which primarily concerns the personal quest for an encounter with God and for godly living. But the community-forming action of common prayer allows Christians to recognize the communal aspect of their spiritual calling. Christian spiritual guides have always encouraged those under their care to re-imagine what human society might be by regarding it through the lens of liturgy. Washed in one baptism, fed by one eucharistic food, joined in one prayer and praise, the liturgical assembly becomes the sign of the beginnings of the new world which God is always in the process of creating. The liturgy, then, is understood as the stage on which the actors in this new world rehearse their roles and relationships with one another. In the equal sharing of gifts, the liberal offering of service, the free and joyful raising of voices, worship invites the community to model godly human relationships, restored and renewed in the light of the resurrection. In this way, mutual love becomes not just a vague ethical mandate, but the visible expression of new life in Christ.

The community shaped by the Church's liturgy not only comprises those who share the same temporal and spatial geography, but is linked with the whole 'communion of saints', past, present and future. Although the unity to which the Church is called has never been fully realized (and although that failure of unity shows itself most clearly at the font and the holy table), those who understand the liturgy as a primary model for the spiritual life find more that unites the Christian family of churches than divides it. The spirituality that arises out of the common worship of the Church is a spirituality which is keyed to the deep union of those bonded together by a common baptism, those who raise their voices as one in supplication, thanksgiving, rejoicing and intercession before God. With this heavy emphasis on unity, however, the danger of spiritual exclusivism, of an excessive distinction between 'insiders' and 'outsiders', is always present. But because the liturgical community constituted by the liturgy is the ongoing, visible representation of Christ in the world, it is constantly called to relate to that world in the way that Christ related to it: over and over again breaking down boundaries so that all people might become fully human.

This conviction provides the basis for a spirituality of responsible and holy living rooted in the liturgy. Not only does Christian worship provide spiritual resources for resisting temptation to sin, but in various other ways it makes its own moral demands on participants. The spiritual kinship shared among all those in the liturgical assembly requires that each one is responsible not only *to* others but *for* others as well. Worshippers are reminded of this call to mutual care and concern in the sharing of food at the Lord's Supper, in the washing of feet on Maundy Thursday, and in prayers of petition and intercession for one another. But the liturgy also makes demands on behaviour within the wider human community as well. In baptism Christians commit themselves to bearing the image of Christ so that all might know the love of God. In intercessory prayer believers not only ask God to intervene in the situations prayed for, but commit themselves to intervening in those situations. When the peace of Christ is exchanged, believers commit themselves to do whatever possible to reconcile themselves with all those whom they have wronged. Week by week, as worshippers are made aware of their own sinfulness in the words and actions of the liturgy, they also recognize the need to approach others with the same measure of grace and mercy with which they have been approached by God.

In a world of hurry and rootlessness, the task of locating ourselves in time and space is increasingly difficult. In its annual journey through the Christian year, which stands as an antidote to the idea of time as a mere commodity, the liturgical assembly is invited to ponder the spiritual value of time and to consider each moment as full of salvific potential. To punctuate the day with prayer in the Daily Office is to make the ordinary rhythm of day and night transparent to the activity of God. At the same time, the overarching vision of the liturgy seeks to place all human temporal constructs against the backdrop of the eventual end of all time; this eschatological spirituality of time frees believers for deep human encounter 'in the meantime', knowing that the end time is secure. All time is seen, from this perspective, as a vehicle for liberation of humanity and for participation in the compassionate mission of God.

Space too becomes a vehicle for holy encounter when approached from the perspective of the liturgy. In the New Testament the correlation is made between the liturgical environment and the Christian life; we are to be built as a temple of the Holy Spirit. At the same time the physical building in which worship takes place draws believers toward godly insight. The various liturgical furnishings have a pedagogical function in this way of looking at things: the font stands as a reminder of the baptismal vocation, the holy table as a call to meditate on Christ's sacrifice, the pulpit speaks of the centrality of the Word in the Christian life. But in addition to providing lessons in the necessary content of prayer, liturgical space can also focus and intensify prayer. Many Christians whose prayer is hesitant find solace and encouragement by praying in a place where past prayers have been answered and where the daily and weekly prayers of the Christian community are made. More importantly, however, the space in which Christians pray makes the holiness of all space apparent and declares that space, like time, can be a sacrament of the love of God.

Perhaps the greatest challenge to the relationship with God is the experience of human mortality. Sickness, dying and death are not only the occasion for physical pain and existential anxiety, but also have the potential to isolate us from other people, and to reconstruct our self-image. At the very least, human frailty poses critical questions to Christian believers: On what do we rest our hope, firmly and finally? Can we rely on the promise of resurrection? Because the liturgy is rooted in and reflects the whole range of human experience, including the limitations of our bodies, it provides a singular opportunity for godly insight in the face of human mortality. Within the rites of baptism, the Lord's Supper, penance, the forty days of Lent and Christian burial lie a wealth of images and ritual patterns that allow for deeper devotional reflection and more intentional praxis.

Historically, the rituals of healing, including prayer, anointing with oil and the laying on of hands, have been the primary means by which people have been able to find explicitly Christian meaning in the experience of illness. By linking the rites of healing to the healing of Jesus, and to the promise of human wholeness and reconciliation described in the Gospels, the Church evokes powerful images which allow the mystery of human suffering to be understood as a mystery in which God can be known and named. In the same way, the Eucharist presents us with images of our future incorruptible state, and the rites of penitence allow us to express honestly our often ambiguous responses to the experience of sickness and dying.

All of the above describes what might be called a distinctively *liturgical* approach to spirituality, one which lifts up a deep and intrinsic connection between the public worship of the Christian Church and the spiritual formation of its members. This approach is implicit in the writings which emerge from a wide range of spiritual traditions, and not only those which would immediately be considered 'high church': we find it advocated by Quakers and Benedictines, Presbyterians and the Orthodox. All those who wish to explore the liturgy as a resource for spiritual development, as an aid to spiritual insight, and as a model for the spiritual disciplines have a rich treasury of historical resources from which to draw, arising from every century of the Church's life. Used with creativity and care, these can help Christian believers meet the contemporary spiritual challenges of aimlessness, isolation and moral uncertainty.

Paul Bradshaw, *Two Ways of Praying: Introducing Liturgical Spirituality*, London: SPCK, 1995; Alan Jones, *Passion for Pilgrimage*, San Francisco: Harper & Row, 1989; Kevin Irwin, *Liturgy, Prayer, and Spirituality*, New York: Paulist Press, 1984; Philip Pfatteicher, *Liturgical Spirituality*, Valley Forge, Pennsylvania: Trinity Press International, 1988; Don Saliers, *Worship and Spirituality*, Philadelphia: Westminster, 1984; Susan J. White, *The Spirit of Worship: The Liturgical Tradition*, London: Darton, Longman & Todd/New York: Orbis Books, 1999.

SUSAN J. WHITE

Spirituality, Psychology and Psychotherapy

1. Spirituality

Spirituality is defined broadly as *that which gives meaning to life and allows us to participate in the larger whole.* This definition includes Christian spirituality and the spirituality of other religious traditions. For the Christian, that which gives meaning to life is Christ, or the Spirit, or God, and the larger whole we respond to is in Christ, or in the Spirit, or in God. This definition includes those who are not religious, that is, those who do not find meaning or the larger whole in God. This definition also allows for a dialogue with various psychological understandings of the person, some of which have profound understandings of meaning and the larger whole, even if these understandings are not described in spiritual or religious language.

2. Psychology and spirituality

Three influential traditions have contributed to our understanding of how psychology is understood in the culture and of how psychology interfaces with spirituality: 1. the psychoanalytic tradition with its founder, Sigmund Freud (1856–1939); 2. the behaviourist tradition with its founder, J. B. Watson (1878–1958); and 3. the humanistic tradition represented by Carl Rogers (1902–87). A major reason why psychology is seen as antagonistic to religion is that Freud, Watson and Rogers were antagonistic to it. Each of these figures had personal reasons for rejecting religion, and all three were united in wanting to liberate humanity from what they perceived as the authoritarian and irrational control of religion.

A. *Sigmund Freud*

Freud, who experienced prejudice because he was a Jew, sees religion as infantile, neurotic and illusory. Religion is the projection of our 'childish helplessness' and our need for a father's protection onto God. Religious beliefs are illusions, the fulfilment of 'the oldest, strongest and most urgent wishes of mankind'. We believe in God, he says in *The Future of an Illusion*, because we need a provident God who protects us from the terrors of nature, because we need a just God who gives us a moral law that allows us to live in harmony, and because we need a compassionate God who offers us life after death. In addition, Freud sees religion as an agent of the superego, a part of the personality constellated in early childhood. As an early and uncritical internalization of values that come from one's parents and the culture, religion is an immature way of controlling our instincts. Freud wants humanity to grow up. He wants us to move from unconsciousness to consciousness and from fantasy to fact. Only science 'can lead us to a knowledge of reality outside ourselves'.

B. J. B. Watson

Watson believes that all of our behaviour is determined by the external environment. Behaviourism is not concerned with any kind of introspective mentalism, be that in terms of the 'unconscious', or 'consciousness' or 'feeling'. It is concerned only with studying human activity which can be directly and externally observed. For Watson, 'the prediction and control of behaviour' is what the science of psychology is about. Raised by a religious mother who wanted him to study for the ministry, Watson came to reject religion, seeing it as an imposed system of unquestioned concepts which are steeped in childish fear and irrational control. In *Behaviorism*, Watson advocates replacing religion with 'better ways of living and thinking' so that 'the world finally becomes a place fit for human habitation'.

C. Carl Rogers

Rogers stresses the 'actualising tendency of the organism' in its environment. He believes that if we were always loved and accepted 'unconditionally', we would trust our experience and be in touch with our feeling, and therefore be fully actualized and healthy. Unfortunately, we all grow up with some degree of 'incongruence', that is, we deny or distort what we are actually feeling in order to be worthy of the love of significant others. To move from 'incongruence' to 'congruence', that is, to become actualized and healthy by allowing into our self-concept all the organism is actually experiencing, we need the help of another person who is there for us with three 'necessary and sufficient conditions' – empathy, congruence and unconditional positive regard. At one point, Rogers says that he means by unconditional positive regard what the theologian means by 'agape' (God's unconditional love). Although pastoral counsellors and others found an implicit religiousness in Rogerian theory, Rogers himself rejected religion. As a young man, he was studying for the ministry, but he switched to psychology, believing that religious beliefs would limit his freedom.

Although perhaps less influential in the culture, there are a number of psychologists whose thinking is quite open to spirituality and/or religion. Prominent among them are William James (1842–1910), Carl Jung (1875–1961), and Viktor Frankl (1905–97).

D. William James

In *The Varieties of Religious Experience*, James understands religion in terms of spirituality. James uses three experiential criteria – immediate luminousness, philosophical reasonableness, and moral helpfulness – in order to make a 'spiritual judgement' on the truth of religion. Defining religion in personal rather than institutional terms, he sees it as 'the feelings, acts and experiences of individual men in their solitude, so far as they apprehend themselves to stand in relation to whatever they may consider the divine'. Not about God, religion is about our experience of God, and it is about the meaning of that experience for our living. This experience has two aspects: 'feeling', and 'the conceptual'. Feeling is primary in religion; it is 'what actually occurs'. The 'creeds and dogmas' are secondary, dependent on our actual experience of God if they are to have any meaning at all.

Two modes of finding happiness relate to our experience God: there is the healthy-minded person for whom happiness is 'congenital' and there is the 'sick soul' for whom happiness is 'an impossibility'. For the sick soul, the only way to religious happiness is to be 'born again'. There must be a conversion or unification bringing the person to wholeness and peace. The 'ripe fruits' of conversion lie in the 'the saintly character', who experiences 1. a 'feeling of being in a wider life than that of this world's selfish little interests' and 'a conviction, not merely intellectual, but as it were sensible, of the existence of an Ideal Power'; 2. a 'sense of the friendly continuity of the ideal power with our own life'; 3. an 'immense elation and freedom, as the outlines of the confining selfhood melt down'; and 4. a 'shifting of the emotional centre towards loving and harmonious affections'. In the saintly character, the experience of God and living spirituality go together.

E. Carl Jung

Central to Jung's understanding of the person is the notion of 'individuation', the natural process of becoming a whole person, 'a Self'. Although all of life is meant to be this process, the second half of life is the more significant part of individuation because then the conscious part of our personality wants to be transformed by the contents of the unconscious, first by events repressed in our personal unconscious and then by some of the 'archetypes' in our 'collective unconscious'. Consciousness and the unconscious are opposites, and individuation is always a 'reconciliation of opposites'. The archetype that first wants to come to consciousness is the 'shadow', the dark, earthy, socially unacceptable part of the self. Then the contrasexual archetypes, the 'anima', or the feminine side of the man, and the 'animus', or the masculine side of the woman, seek to come to consciousness. Finally, the Self, the overarching archetype of individuation, seeks to become conscious.

As a process of becoming whole, individuation is a quest for the unique meaning and purpose of life. One must separate from collective thinking and then begin to remove one's projections. One must acknowledge the shadow, a part of me that I unconsciously project onto those I despise. One must acknowledge the anima or the animus, a part of me that I unconsciously project onto the opposite sex. And one must acknowledge the Self which means that one also acknowledge the 'image of God' that lies within. For Jung, 'the Self' and 'the image of God' are psychologically indistinguishable, 'two sides of the same coin'. Usually, we project 'the image of God' onto the Bible, or onto the Church, or onto some religious figure, but to realize the Self we must remove the projection. 'Too few people', says Jung in *Psychology and Alchemy*, 'have experienced the divine image as the innermost possession of their souls.' In the process of individuation, psychotherapy, spirituality and religion are of one piece.

F. Viktor Frankl

Known best, perhaps, for *Man's Search for Meaning*, Frankl's analysis of human existence is inherently spiritual. Essential to humanity and to spirituality are three possibilities – freedom, responsibility and the will-to-meaning. Freedom is the ability I have to take a stand in relation to my instincts, my inherited dispositions and the influence of the environment. Responsibility means that only I can determine the concrete meanings and values for my life. Together freedom and responsibility are a will-to-meaning, calling me to find the unique meaning of my life. The essence of the human and the essence of the spiritual are in our search for meaning. Religion, as part of the search for meaning, 'adds immeasurably to human vitality'. It offers 'ultimate meaning' – especially as we face suffering, guilt and death – but this meaning can only be realized in freedom, responsibility and as a will-to-meaning.

As Frankl finds in *Man's Search for Ultimate Meaning*, 'religion is genuine only where it is existential, where man is not somehow driven to it, but commits himself to it by freely choosing to be religious.' We tend to suffer, however, from 'repressed religiousness', partly because we are afraid our experience of God will not be respected by others and partly because the life of religion has 'three stumbling blocks' – authoritarianism, rationalism and anthropomorphism – which distort the meaning of religion and keep our experience of God from becoming conscious. Frankl's psychotherapy is 'logotherapy', a therapy that challenges one to find meaning in life. When we are challenged to find meaning, we may find religious meaning. Logotherapy may lead to religion, and genuine religion is eminently logotherapeutic. In Frankl's psychology, as in the psychology of James and Jung, psychotherapy, spirituality and religion all function together.

3. Psychotherapy and spirituality

Psychotherapy relates to spirituality much as the psychology from which it comes relates to it. Many psychotherapists, including many who are psychoanalytic, behavioural and humanistic, are not interested in addressing either a spiritual or a religious dimension of the person in psychotherapy. Many other psychotherapists, perhaps influenced by the thinking of James, Jung, Frankl and a number of other thinkers, see the spiritual and/or the religious dimension of the person as integral to the work of psychotherapy.

In the past few years, psychotherapists as a whole have taken a new interest in spirituality. Some of the factors contributing to this interest are: 1. an understanding of spirituality defined less by a given spiritual or religious tradition than by the need to find personal meaning in life; 2. an understanding that spirituality is a legitimate dimension of the human and not something 'other than' or 'added on' to our humanity; 3. an understanding that spirituality is existential, personal and concerned with growth while religion is conventional, public and concerned with ritual observance; 4. the emergence of feminist and postmodern thinking which prefers relationship over formal structures and immediacy over timeless realities; and 5. the general acceptance within the culture of a 'holistic' and a 'well-being' perspective on the person, allowing the person to be seen in and as a larger whole. At present, psychotherapists relate to spirituality in three broad categories:

A. Psychotherapists who have little or no interest in spirituality and/or religion

Psychotherapists in this long-standing category find spirituality and religion incompatible with psychology. Many in this category, including many in the psychoanalytic and behaviourist traditions, make a distinction between what we know from psychology as a science and what we know from spirituality or religion as mythology. Psychology is objective, based on research and empirical data, while religion is inherently subjective, based on folklore and tradition. Some in this category are completely dismissive of spirituality and/or religion. Some in this category have a personal interest in spirituality and/or religion, but they see this interest as in a different realm than that of psychology and they feel it is inappropriate or unprofessional to discuss spiritual and/or religious concerns with their clients. Most of those in this category make clear dichotomies in their understandings of the secular and the sacred, the human and the divine, reason and faith, science and religion, 'this world' and 'the next'.

B. Psychotherapists who are interested in the integration of spirituality and/or religion with their understanding of psychotherapy

The distinguishing characteristic of the professionals in this category – many of whom have a newer understanding of spirituality – is that they are interested in finding ways to integrate spirituality and/or religion in their practice of psychotherapy. Psychotherapists in this category come from all the helping professions, including psychologists, psychiatrists, social workers, family therapists and hospice counsellors, and they represent all the different psychotherapeutic approaches, including the psychoanalytic, the analytical (Jungian), the cognitive-behavioural, the existential, the humanistic, the transpersonal, the experiential and the systemic. Many of the psychotherapists in this category have a holistic understanding of the person, and many have their own spiritual and/or religious convictions. The overriding concern of the psychotherapists in this category is to make the resources of spirituality and/or religion available to their clients – especially around values such as hope, trust, forgiveness, serenity, responsibility, surrender, gratitude, prayer, meditation, contemplation, meaning in life and the love of God.

C. Psychotherapists whose interest in spirituality and/or religion defines their understanding of psychotherapy

Those in this category have a foundational understanding of the person as inherently spiritual and/or inherently religious. In this category are pastoral counsellors whose religious affiliations allow them to be sensitive to the spiritual and/or religious concerns of their clients. In this category are (1) analytical (Jungian) psychotherapists for whom 'integration' is a human and spiritual journey; (2) psychotherapists in the Buddhist tradition for whom 'enlightenment' and 'compassion' are essential to human and spiritual realization; (3) transpersonal psychotherapists for whom the development of 'consciousness' is essential both to human and spiritual becoming; (4) psychotherapists for whom 'transcendence', or 'the sacred', or 'wholeness', or 'well-being', or 'ultimate concern', or 'ultimate meaning' is both a human and a spiritual goal; (5) a variety of religious psychotherapists for whom the Bible or a set of religious beliefs provides clear and/or sufficient criteria for psychotherapeutic practice.

Viktor Frankl, *Man's Search for Ultimate Meaning*, Cambridge, Massachusetts: Perseus, 2000; Sigmund Freud, *The Future of an Illusion*, trans. W. D. Robson-Scott, London: Hogarth Press, 1962; William James, *The Varieties of Religious Experience*, Cambridge, Massachusetts: Harvard University Press, 1985; William R. Miller (ed.), *Integrating Spirituality into Treatment: Resources for Practitioners*, Washington, DC: American Psychological Association, 1999; Edward P. Shafranske (ed.), *Religion and the Clinical Practice of Psychology*, Washington, DC: American Psychological Association, 1996; John Swinton, *Spirituality and Mental Health Care: Rediscovering a 'Forgotten' Dimension*, London: Jessica Kingsley, 2001.

JOHN SHEA

Spirituality and Science

The goal of this essay is to suggest fruitful ways to introduce the key discoveries of the natural sciences into the academic study of Christian spirituality. Methodological questions about the developing relations between science, theology and spirituality deserve much more attention than is possible here (see Russell, 2004a; Russell, 2004b). Suffice it to say that I will draw on research material in the burgeoning field of 'theology and science' in order to bring theology, after it has been reconstructed in light of science, into conversation with Christian spirituality. (Note: both introductory and research materials are included in the bibliography.)

1. The pre-scientific, immediate experience of nature as an experience of God the creator

Our most basic spiritual interaction with nature is one in which we experience the world with a minimum of second-order reflection. This is the experience of 'being in the world', of the sheer, surprising and compelling taste and touch of the natural world around us and within us and through it of God the creator. Spiritualities associated with this include the numinous encounter with the Holy in and through nature (a kataphatic spirituality), mystical union with the divine source of nature (an apophatic spirituality), and union with nature-as-community (a relational spirituality).

2. The mathematical laws of nature and the ascent to the transcendent God

For many scientists, the laws of physics are approximations of the underlying, fundamental laws of nature which represent the rationality and intelligibility of nature. This view opens onto several insights for theology and spirituality.

A. The laws of science and the divine Logos

Why is nature intelligible to us? As Albert Einstein remarked so eloquently, 'The eternal mystery of the world is its comprehensibility' (Einstein, 1978). One theological response dates back to Justin Martyr (100–165 CE): the rationality and intelligibility of nature is grounded in the Greek concept of *logos* which the Gospel of John identifies with the incarnate Word (John 1.1–3). The *logos* is also present in our capacity to reason, an aspect of the *imago dei*. Hence our ability to formulate the laws of nature reflects the divine *Logos* within us, as Thomas Torrance and John Polkinghorne suggest (Torrance, 1981; Polkinghorne, 1994, esp. p. 74). Our thirst to discover these laws, and our joy in their discovery, reflects what Paul Tillich called an Augustinian/Franciscan spirituality of 'participation in ultimacy' (Tillich, 1967: 'Experience and Systematic Theology', pp. 40–6).

B. The laws of science and the 'mind of God'

Mark Richardson has identified three distinct genres in the writings on science and spirituality (Richardson, 2002). In the 'rationalist-speculative' genre typified by Paul Davies, the fundamental theories of science provide an ascent from the material world to a Platonic realm of mathematics held within 'the mind of God' (Davies, 1992). Theoretical science is 'thinking God's thoughts after God', leading to what Einstein called a 'cosmic religious feeling'.

C. Scientific instruments and the immanence of God in nature

'Affective-holistic' writings capture the way scientific instruments – the Hubble telescope, electron microscope, gene sequencers – offer a 'window on nature' far beyond the routine experiences of life. We can 'see' and 'hear' nature in ways simply unattainable without science in a seemingly endless growth of scope (think light years) and depth (think subatomic). Richardson's examples here include essays by Pauline Rudd, Joel Primack and Brian Swimme. Such instrument-enhanced experience of the universe can also lead through and beyond nature to the God who is its Creator, as Augustine described eloquently in the *Confessions* – the God who relishes the sheer joy of God's creation and delights in 'behemoth' (Ps. 104.26).

D. Cosmology and creation theology

We now turn to the primary literature in 'theology and science' which Richardson calls 'critical-historical.' This genre relates the theories of science to historical, philosophical and systematic theology. Our first topic is cosmology and creation theology; (for details see Russell et al., 1993).

Cosmology and creation ex nihilo. Big Bang cosmology portrays the universe as expanding in time from its beginning, 't=0', some 13 billion years ago. If t=0 is, in fact, an absolute beginning of all that is, it would offer stunning but indirect evidence of the universe being the creation of God ex nihilo. (The sheer existence of the universe, even if it is eternally old, is our 'primary evidence' for God, as Thomas Aquinas argued.) The discovery that all things have a common origin at t=0 can inspire a spirituality of cosmic unity with even the farthest reaches of the universe. In addition, the fundamental laws and natural constants that characterize our universe are precisely what is needed to make the evolution of life possible (the Anthropic Principle), as described in detail by Barrow and Frank J. Tipler (1986). For some scholars, such 'fine tuning' provides further evidence that the universe is the creation of God and new grounds for a spirituality of cosmic purpose (Murphy and Ellis, 1996).

Big Bang cosmology, however, has undergone important modifications in the past decades, leading to inflationary and quantum cosmology. Will these cosmologies be open to a fruitful interpretation by Christian spirituality? Conversely, might the spiritualities of research cosmologists inspire them to develop new scientific models of the universe?

Quantum mechanics in relation to divine agency and relationality. Does God really act in nature? And can God's action be consistent with, and not a violation of, science? In the growing literature on 'divine action', the goal for many scholars is to make a credible argument for 'non-interventionist objective divine action'. Here 'objective' signifies that God really does act in the world. 'Non-interventionist' means that God acts without suspending or violating the scientific laws of nature; this entails that God's actions are 'hidden' from science. Since the 'laws of nature' are, ultimately, our description of God's regular, faithful action (i.e., general providence), it makes good theological sense that God's additional, special action (i.e., special providence) should be consistent with these laws even while leading to something radically new in nature. (See, for example, Russell et al., 1993; Russell et al., 1995; Russell et al., 1998; Russell et al., 1999; Russell et al., 2001.)

Contemporary physics has broken with the mechanistic view of nature inherited from Newtonian physics and Enlightenment philosophy. Instead of the closed, deterministic world of Newton, physics now offers real hope for an indeterministic view of nature in which the future is genuinely open to non-interventionist divine agency. An indeterministic interpretation of quantum mechanics, for example, makes it possible to think of God as acting together with nature to bring about quantum phenomena both in routine and in novel ways without violating natural processes.

Quantum mechanics also suggests that physical entities at the subatomic level are more complex ontologically than our ordinary world of waves and particles. For compelling theoretical and experimental reasons, and within specific philosophical interpretations, quantum systems are seen as 'non-local' and hence 'non-separable': the individual properties of particles which had once been bound together but are now widely separated display remarkable correlations that defy classical explanation. Such 'non-separability', in turn, suggests a 'wholeness' or 'unity' to nature, and one which is much more ontologically subtle than the mechanistic 'web' or 'interaction' models drawn from ecology. Quantum non-separability also offers a powerful metaphor for the spiritual experience of intrinsic relationality within the divine life and of the unity of creation – humanity, ecology, universe. Conversely, if we look at quantum non-separability through the lens of trinitarian spirituality, what new insights might we discover for further scientific research at the level of fundamental physics?

E. Biological evolution and God's action as continuous creator

Contemporary biology interprets the evolution of life on earth as a consequence of random genetic and environmental variations together with natural selection. Given the ubiquitous role of 'chance' in nature, can evolution be interpreted theologically as due to the ongoing action of God? Atheists like Richard Dawkins say 'no!', but Christians like Arthur Peacocke say 'yes!'. According to 'theistic evolution,' God acts through law *and* chance; indeed God created the universe ex nihilo such that it would be compatible with God's continuous creating activity (*creatio continua*) (Peacocke, 1979).

Now we can take theistic evolution one step further. We know that quantum physics is involved in the production of genetic mutations. If, as suggested above, we interpret quantum physics as open to God's non-interventionist action, then theists can claim (without recourse to 'Intelligent Design') that evolution is indeed the way God creates life, mind and, in humanity at least, creatures capable of moral agency and spiritual experience. This in turn leads to a spirituality of gratitude that recognizes the evolutionary processes out of which we, and all life, arose as the ongoing gift of the immanent Creator.

F. Biological evolution, death as constitutive of life, and natural theodicy

Biological evolution also involves suffering, disease, death and extinction and these 'natural evils' pose a profound challenge to Christian faith: 'natural theodicy'. Biological death is not the consequence of 'the Fall' (Gen. 3); instead it is *constitutive* of life. Sentience in complex organisms entails the experience of joy and of suffering, and in the predator–prey cycle, most animals die an anguishing death as the food for others. Moreover, without the death of organisms and the extinction of species, the evolution of complex life on earth would not have occurred. Does God, by creating life through evolution, allow – even cause – natural evil?

Scholars such as Arthur Peacocke (Peacocke, 1993) and Ian Barbour (Barbour, 1990) have responded to this challenge by turning to a kenotic theology of God's redemptive suffering for humanity by extending it to include the whole sweep of life on earth. As Holmes Rolson puts it, all of nature is 'cruciform' (Rolston, 1987, pp. 144–6, 289–92). The implications for Christian spirituality are enormous. If evolution, and not just humanity, is the scope of Christ's compassion, then our experience of the presence of God in and with the suffering of the poor and oppressed should now include solidarity with all living creatures. But the cross of Christ without his resurrection at Easter would be an unmitigated tragedy. Can we then understand in the hope offered by Christ's resurrection to include all living creatures? We will return to this crucial question below.

G. Christian spirituality in light of humanity's evolutionary origins

What are some of the implications for Christian spirituality of the biological evolution of *Homo sapiens*?

Ethics. In humanity, at least, self-consciousness and rationality are the products of biological evolution because of their adaptive advantage. But what about moral norms? According to Francisco Ayala (Ayala, 1998b), evolution bequeathed us the capacity for morality, but the actual content of moral norms is not determined by biology (*pace* such sociobiological proponents as Ruse, 1995). Instead it may be based on the revelation of God or philosophical argumentation. What about the evolution of the 'soul'? The evolution of the capacity for sin? The evolution of the capacity for spirituality? Key readings here include Murphy (1998).

Genetics. The biochemistry of our genes is shared by all life on earth, leading us to a spirituality of community with nature. Genetic variation, in turn, is a driving factor in evolution and, as we have just seen, a locus of God's continuous creation. Genetic diversity produces both human diversity which we celebrate and human unity as a species that cultural divisions cannot overcome. These aspects of genetics offer the basis for a Christian spirituality of gratitude, unity and human worth. But genetic variation also gives rise to thousands of diseases whose treatment may require genetic engineering, and with it comes a variety of contested ethical issues. How are we to respond spiritually to these diverse and even contradictory aspects of genetics?

Neuroscience and the mind/brain problem. If mental states arise from brain states ('bottom-up causality'), how does the mind influence the brain ('top-down causality' and/or 'supervenience')? (See Russell et al., 1999). How do we understand our experience of Christian spirituality, including discernment and discipleship, if the neurosciences so strongly stress only 'bottom-up causality'?

Artificial intelligence. Is 'embodiment' the crucial distinctive between human rationality and artificial intelligence/robotics? Is there is a connection between our fascination with, even our personalizing of, computers and the *imago dei* as the capacity for relationality, as Noreen Herzfeld suggests (Herzfeld, 2003).

Technology. Once again Barbour provides an excellent typology that parallels attitudes towards nature and towards technology and this can be generalized to include our attitudes towards technology as they reflect our spiritual relation to nature. A spirituality of 'work as prayer' modelled after St Benedict can lead to the stewardship of nature. In light of evolution, though, Philip Hefner views humanity's relation to nature as 'created co-creators'. (See Hefner, 1989; Hefner, 1993.) But technology also tempts us into a 'power over' nature, and as Ian Barbour warns, we must not let 'dominion' (Gen. 1.26) erode into the sin of domination. A classic document is White (1967); for a recent response see Barbour (1993, Chapter 3). Here, the ecofeminist critiques of Merchant (1980) and Ruether (1992) must be considered carefully – that science and technology are in many ways linked to dominance and patriarchal models of God, humanity, and the earth; this in turn lead us to a spirituality of confession and repentance.

H. The cosmological far future and the experience of resurrection faith

The cosmological far future clearly challenges the eschatological future promised by God at Easter. According to science, the earth will be destroyed in the nova of the sun in 5 billion years. Even if humanity migrates to the stars, earth's cornucopia of life will be lost. Beyond this is the inevitable dissolution of our galaxy and the end to the physical conditions required for life, leaving a lifeless universe to expand and cool for ever or recollapse into a fireball (the cosmological 'freeze or fry' scenarios).

In contrast, Christian eschatology, based on the bodily resurrection of Jesus of Nazareth, looks to the coming reign of God and with it God's transformation of the universe – not just the earth – into the new creation. Can we discover ways to respond to these conflicting expectations? What we need is a spirituality whose eschatological horizon is the universe and in which all creatures find hope and eternal life in God's new creation – and which offers a fresh assessment of scientific cosmology. This spirituality might depict humanity's role in nature as 'eschatological companion', to borrow a phrase from Russell (2003). Meanwhile, research in theology and science here is truly a 'frontier field' (Polkinghorne and Michael Welker, 2000; Russell, 2002a).

Francisco J. Ayala, 'The difference of being human: ethical behavior as an evolution-ary byproduct' in Holmes Rolston III (ed.), *Biology, Ethics and the Origins of Life*, Boston: Jones & Bartlett Publishers, 1995, pp. 117–35; Francisco J. Ayala, 'Human nature: one evolutionist's view' in Warren S. Brown, Nancey Murphy and H. Newton Malony (eds), *Whatever Happened to the Soul? Scientific and Theological Portraits of Human Nature*, Minneapolis: Fortress Press, 1998; Ian G. Barbour, *Ethics in an Age of Technology*, Gifford Lectures 1989–91, San Francisco: HarperSanFrancisco, 1993; John D. Barrow and Frank J. Tipler, *The Anthropic Cosmological Principle*, Oxford: Clarendon Press, 1986; Paul C. Davies, *The Mind of God: The Scientific Basis for a Rational World*, New York: Simon & Schuster, 1992; Albert Einstein, 'Physics and Reality' in *Ideas and Opinions*, New York: Dell, 1978, pp. 283–315; Philip Hefner, 'The evolution of the created co-creator' in Ted Peters (ed.), *Cosmos as Creation: Theology and Science in Consonance*, Nashville, TN: Abingdon Press, 1989, pp. 211–34; Philip Hefner, *The Human Factor: Evolution, Culture, and Religion*, Theology and the Sciences Series, Minneapolis: Fortress Press, 1993; Noreen Herzfeld, *In Our Image: Artificial Intelligence and the Human Spirit*, Minneapolis: Fortress Press, 2003; Carolyn Merchant, *The Death of Nature: Women, Ecology, and the Scientific Revolution*, New York: Harper & Row, 1980; Nancey Murphy, 'Human nature: historical, scientific, and religious issues' in Warren S. Brown, Nancey Murphy and H. Newton Malony (eds), *Whatever Happened to the Soul? Scientific and Theological Portraits of Human Nature*, Minneapolis: Fortress Press, 1998; Nancey Murphy and George F. Ellis, *On the Moral Nature of the Universe: Theology, Cosmology, and Ethics*, Theology and the Sciences Series, Minneapolis: Fortress Press, 1996; A. R. Peacocke, *Creation and the World of Science*, The Bampton Lectures, 1979, Oxford: Clarendon Press, 1979; John Polkinghorne and Michael Welker (eds), *The End of the World and the Ends of God: Science and Theology on Eschatology*, Harrisburg: Trinity Press International, 2000; W. Mark Richardson, 'Introduction' in W. Mark Richardson and Robert John Russell (eds), *Science and the Spiritual Quest: New Essays by Leading Scientists*, London and New York: Routledge, 2002, pp. 1–20; Holmes Rolston III, *Science and Religion: A Critical Survey*, New York: Random House, 1987; Rosemary Radford Ruether, *Gaia and God: An Ecofeminist Theology of Earth Healing*, San Francisco: HarperCollins, 1992; Michael Ruse, 'Evolutionary Ethics' in Holmes Rolston III (ed.), *Biology, Ethics and the Origins of Life*, Boston: Jones & Bartlett Publishers, 1995; Robert John Russell, 'Bodily resurrection, eschatology and scientific cosmology: the mutual interaction of Christian theology and science' in Ted Peters, Robert John Russell and Michael Welker (eds), *Resurrection: Theological and Scientific Assessments*, Grand Rapids, MI: Eerdmans, 2002, pp. 3–30; Robert John Russell, 'Five attitudes towards nature and technology from a Christian perspective' *Theology and Science* 1.2 (October 2003), 149–59; Robert John Russell, 'The importance of the natural sciences to Christian spirituality as an academic discipline' in Bruce Lescher and Elizabeth Liebert (eds), a book of essays in honor of Sandra Schneiders, to be published by Paulist Press in 2006; Robert John Russell, 'Science' in *Blackwell Companion to Christian Spirituality*, ed. Arthur Holder, Oxford: Blackwell, 2004; Robert John Russell, Nancey C. Murphy and Chris J. Isham (eds), *Quantum Cosmology and the Laws of Nature: Scientific Perspectives on Divine Action*, Scientific Perspectives on Divine Action Series, Vatican City State: Vatican Observatory Publications/Berkeley, CA: Center for Theology and the Natural Sciences, 1993; Robert John Russell, Nancey C. Murphy and Arthur R. Peacocke (eds), *Chaos and Complexity: Scientific Perspectives on Divine Action*, Scientific Perspectives on Divine Action Series, Vatican City State: Vatican Observatory Publications: Berkeley/CA: Center for Theology and the Natural Sciences, 1995; Robert John Russell, Nancey Murphy et al. (eds), *Neuroscience and the Person: Scientific Perspectives on Divine Action*, Vatican City State: Vatican Observatory Publications/Berkeley, CA: Center for Theology and the Natural Sciences, 1999; Robert John Russell, Philip Clayton et al. (eds), *Quantum Mechanics: Scientific Perspectives on Divine Action*, Vatican City State: Vatican Observatory Publications/ Berkeley, CA: Center for Theology and the Natural Sciences, 2001; Robert John Russell, William R. Stoeger sj and Francisco J. Ayala (eds), *Evolutionary and Molecular Biology: Scientific Perspectives on Divine Action*, Vatican City State: Vatican Observatory Publications/Berkeley, CA: Center for Theology and the Natural Sciences, 1998; Paul Tillich, *Systematic Theology*, 3 vols, Chicago: University of Chicago Press/New York: Harper & Row, 1967; Thomas F. Torrance, *Divine and Contingent Order*, Oxford: Oxford University Press, 1981; Lynn White Jr, 'The historical roots of our ecologic crisis', *Science* 155 (1967), 1203–7.

Further reading

Introductory material
Ian G. Barbour, *Religion and Science: Historical and Contemporary Issues*, San Francisco: HarperSanFrancisco, 1997; Ted Peters, 'Theology and the natural sciences' in *The Modern Theologians: An Introduction to Christian Theology in the Twentieth Century*, 2nd edn, ed. David F. Ford, Cambridge, MA: Blackwell, 1997, pp. 649–68; W. Mark Richardson and Wesley J. Wildman (eds), *Religion and Science: History, Method, Dialogue*, New York: Routledge, 1996 (Appendix A includes an extensive bibliography); Robert John Russell and Kirk Wegter-McNelly, 'Science' in Gareth Jones (ed.), *The Blackwell Companion to Modern Theology*, Oxford: Blackwell, 2004, pp. 512–56; Christopher Southgate, Celia Deane-Drummond et al. (eds), *God, Humanity and the Cosmos: A Textbook in Science and Religion*, Harrisburg: Trinity Press International, 1999.

Research material
Ian G. Barbour, *Religion in an Age of Science*, Gifford Lectures, 1989–90, San Francisco: Harper & Row, 1990; Arthur Peacocke, *Theology for a Scientific Age: Being and Becoming – Natural, Divine and Human*, enlarged edn, Minneapolis: Fortress Press, 1993; John C. Polkinghorne, *The Faith of a Physicist: Reflections of a Bottom-up Thinker*, Princeton, NJ: Princeton University Press, 1994.

ROBERT JOHN RUSSELL

Spirituality and Scripture

1. History

Christian spirituality, that is, the lived experience of Christian faith, originated in the experience of Jesus' resurrection by his first disciples. Convinced that Jesus, who had died by crucifixion, was truly alive in their midst, these first followers began to celebrate and proclaim his new life among them even under threat of persecution and death. From the very beginning the Church drew the categories in which to articulate the salvation they had experienced in Jesus from the Hebrew Scriptures. They presented him as the fulfilment of the Law and the prophets, the antitype of such Old Testament figures as Isaac, Moses, the Isaian Suffering Servant, the paschal lamb, and even as the incarnation of Sophia, the personified Wisdom of God. Thus, Christian spirituality was pervasively biblical from its inception.

Within decades of the resurrection the Church began to commit the kerygma and commentaries upon it to writing, first in the letters of Paul (the epistles and Hebrews) which began to circulate in the 50s and 60s, then, between the late 60s and the turn of the century, in several narrative accounts of the life, death and resurrection of Jesus (the Gospels and Acts), and toward the end of the century in an apocalyptic document (Revelation). The pseudepigraphal 'pastoral' and 'catholic' epistles were early Christian writings which were also included in the canon of the New Testament. A reference to Christian writings as 'Scripture' is found in 2 Peter 3.16 (*c.* 100–125), and in Justin's *Apology* 1.67 (*c.* 150) there is an indication that these writings were being read with the Hebrew Scriptures in the liturgy. The earliest reference to the Hebrew scriptures as the 'Old Testament', according to Eusebius (*Historia Ecclesiastica* 4.26), is that of Melito of Sardis and dates to *c.* 170 while Tertullian seems to have been the first (*c.* 200) to refer to the Christian writings as the 'New Testament'. In short, Scripture not only funded the original expression of Christian spirituality but that spirituality led to the production of a new body of Scripture which, in combination with the Hebrew Scriptures, forms the Christian canon, the body of literature which the Church recognized as the inspired mediation of revelation. This Bible became the norm of Christian faith and life. Christians preached their faith, celebrated it sacramentally, and prayed in biblical language. Christian theology, which focused on Jesus as the Christ and the triune God revealed in him, developed from the beginning by meditation and as commentary upon Scripture. For the first 1200 years of its existence the Church's spirituality and theology were rooted in Scripture and came to expression in biblical images and language.

In the high Middle Ages, as the locus of theology shifted from the monastery to the university, philosophy rather than Scripture became the primary tool for theological reflection. And as theology itself became the primary way of thinking about and explaining the faith the role of Scripture in the lived experience of faith was relativized. Theology, often virtually equated with 'tradition' or official church teaching, began to exercise a certain control over Scripture, especially among the majority of Christians who were dependent on the preaching of the clergy, themselves dependent on or merely repeaters of the established teaching.

At the time of the Reformation (1500s) a major point of contention between Protestants and Catholics was the role of Scripture in the faith and spirituality of believers. For the Reformers, Scripture, understood as the inspired Word of God, was the sole authoritative source of revelation and every Christian was capable of deriving the 'plain sense' of the text by prayerful reading. For Catholics, tradition assumed a practical ascendancy in relation to the Bible whose interpretation was considered beyond the ability of the layperson. Thus, the laity tended to ascribe to the magisterium, that is, to the hierarchy in its teaching role, the authority Protestants ascribed to Scripture. The Protestant branch of Christian spirituality remained deeply biblical, although interpretation of the text was often idiosyncratic or literalistic. Catholic spirituality tended to be sacramental, with the emphasis on ritual rather than Scripture, and doctrinal, with the emphasis on theology and tradition rather than Scripture which had been reduced, for the most part, to a quarry of proof texts.

Vatican Council II confirmed and built upon the liturgical and biblical renewal which had been under way in Europe since the 1940s. In the Dogmatic Constitution on Divine Revelation (*Dei Verbum*) it recognized that Jesus Christ is the sole 'source' of revelation which is mediated by tradition in its fullness (i.e., not merely in magisterial teaching) which comes to normative expression primarily in Scripture; that all members of the Church had a right to rich biblical nourishment in liturgy, sacraments and preaching, which should be offered in the vernacular, and should be encouraged to read and pray with Scripture; that the primary pastoral role and responsibility of the clergy was the ministry of the Word and therefore that all theological education should be scripturally based; that the Church as a whole is the interpreter of Scripture and, in its leadership as well as its membership, is subject to, not master of, the Word of God. All of this underlay the felicitous formulation that 'Scripture is the pure and perennial source of the spiritual life' (*Dei Verbum* 6.21).

This renewed understanding of the role of Scripture in the faith life of Christians not only promoted increased understanding between Protestants and Catholics but also created a ravenous interest in Scripture among Catholics who had been long deprived of this spiritual nourishment. Lay people and religious flocked to biblical lectures and courses, made biblically based retreats, and listened to lectionary readings and homilies on them in their own languages. Meanwhile, Catholic and Protestant biblical scholarship became intimately intertwined and mutually enriching and many scholars devoted considerable time and energy to opening the Bible's riches to the people of God.

2. Interpretation

Because Scripture is a book(s) whose meaning is achieved in reading, the role of Scripture in the spirituality of believers, individually and corporately, depends on interpretation. In different periods of the Church's history the nature of texts in general and of sacred texts in particular as well as the nature and appropriate methods for interpreting Scripture has been differently understood, leading to differences in the role the biblical text played in spirituality.

Christianity arose in and from first-century Judaism and shared its conviction that every word of Scripture was God's word and that the task of interpretation was to find meaning worthy of God in every text. Thus, biblical interpretation could only be properly performed by a believer. The major differences between the Jewish and Christian understandings of Scripture was that, for the Christians, the Bible included a New Testament, and all of Scripture, Old as well as New Testament, was about Jesus Christ. Thus, the primary challenge concerning Scripture for the early Church was how to understand the relationship between the testaments and interpret Scripture accordingly.

The early Church rejected the attempts of some of its members to abandon the Old Testament as worthless or even dangerous (e.g. Marcion, second century) and of others to harmonize the diverse Gospels into a single text (e.g. Tatian, third century). This affirmation of diversity in unity, one Bible but two Testaments and four Gospels, challenged the Church to develop a hermeneutics capable of dealing with such complex richness. For the early Christians Jesus, risen and still present in the community, was the hermeneutical principle for all biblical interpretation. The Old Testament was the background of the New and the New Testament the fulfilment of the Old. This conviction gave rise to two types of Christian exegesis. One, the rabbinical method, sometimes used by Paul, scrutinized every word of the text for meaning useful in the Christian context, whether or not its literary context supported such an interpretation. The other, allegorical or spiritual interpretation, was much more widely used.

Origen (c. 185–254), the greatest scripture scholar of Christian antiquity and the primary hermeneutical theorist of the period, produced a stunning body of biblical interpretation using the allegorical method which he developed following Clement of Alexandria. He developed the theory of a 'more than literal' meaning in the biblical text which, through its most influential proponent, Augustine of Hippo (354–430), virtually controlled biblical interpretation until the late Middle Ages. For the ancients Scripture had a 'literal sense', which they equated with the historical meaning, and a 'spiritual (often called allegorical) sense', which was its real religious and/or theological meaning for the believer. Origen often expanded this basic twofold sense into a threefold model patterned on ancient anthropology (body, soul, spirit) in which there was an historical, a moral and a spiritual meaning. By the Middle Ages this model had become a fourfold one embracing the literal (historical), allegorical (theological), tropological (moral) and anagogical (eschatological) meanings. It is important to note that the term 'allegorical' was used in a variety of ways to mean all 'spiritual' or more-than-literal interpretation, or the theological meaning, or a one-to-one correlation between elements in the text and realities of Christian faith and life. Although pre-critical exegesis was sometimes far-fetched or strained it was much more often theologically sober and based on often quite remarkable critical work.

Although it is difficult to trace the understandings and uses of the various 'senses' of Scripture whose proponents were often not totally consistent in their theory or systematic in their practice, it is significant to note the basic principles that motivated the earliest interpreters. They were convinced that all Scripture was the word of God written for our salvation, that Christ was the meaning (hidden or evident) of Scripture as a whole and of all its parts, and that it was intended to nourish the spirituality of its readers, both the individual and the Church as a whole. Furthermore, they saw the text itself as virtually sacramental, that is, as human language which mediated divine reality. Consequently, the text could and did have a plurality of possible meanings, both those intended by the human author writing under the influence of the Holy Spirit and those unknown to the writer which would be discovered, under the influence of the same Spirit, by readers down through the ages.

In the theological schools of Christian antiquity where study depended upon the practice of a rigorous ascetical life, in the deserts where monasticism was born and where rumination of Scripture was the primary spiritual practice, in the monasteries of the Middle Ages where the practice of *lectio divina* or prayerful meditation on the inspired text was complemented by the Daily Office consisting primarily of the chanting of the psalms, and in the sacramental practice of the local churches, the Bible was the context and content of the spirituality of the Church.

This changed radically as the polemics of the Reformation, the methodological explosion and objectification of the scientific revolution, and the rise of Enlightenment criticism subverted the intimacy of the Bible as word of God with the believer as hearer and doer of the word. Catholics were largely estranged from the Bible as the Roman Church sought to suppress the potential for dissent that 'private interpretation' of the Bible (meaning independent access to biblical revelation) represented. Protestants became embroiled in struggles over the implications of the 'higher criticism' for the faith of ordinary believers. No matter how individuals or authorities in the churches dealt with the issue of Scripture it was no longer possible to live within the faith-saturated climate of the first naivety or immediacy to the meaning of the text which had nourished the spirituality of Christians for centuries. While Protestant biblical fundamentalism struggled with an ever more radical scholarship and Catholic magisterial literalism sought to 'protect' the laity from the inroads of scientific knowledge, Protestant piety in general and Catholic monastic spirituality remained pervasively biblical. But for the mainstream Catholic laity non-biblical devotions became more central to their spirituality than Scripture.

Several important developments in the twentieth century have led to a renewal of the relationship between Scripture and spirituality. As has been mentioned, biblical and liturgical renewal in Catholicism began in Europe decades before Vatican Council II opened in 1962. The gradual entrance of Catholic scholars into the mainstream of modern biblical scholarship was officially recognized in 1943 by Pius XII in his encyclical *Divino Afflante Spiritu*. The liturgical renewal in Europe refocused attention on the great themes and motifs of the Old and New Testaments, and the pervasively biblical character of Christian initiation and life. By the time the Council opened, the way had been prepared for Catholics to reclaim the Bible as the primary source of their spirituality, and the conciliar documents, especially those on divine revelation, the Church and the liturgy, encouraged this development. This led to considerably more contact between Protestants and Catholics, in Bible study groups, in the charismatic renewal, and in the retreat movement which turned preferentially to biblical sources.

Biblical scholarship itself, which had been rigidly historical critical for more than a century and a half and notable for its lack of interest in the theological or spiritual dimensions of the text and the general spiritual aridity of its results, began in the second half of the century to be influenced on the one hand by the increasing demand of believers for spiritually relevant interpretation and on the other hand by the emergence of new methods of biblical interpretation. Many of these new methods, for example literary ones such as redaction, narrative, and reader response criticism, feminist and other forms of liberationist criticism, ethical, post-colonial and other forms of pragmatic interpretation, were frankly concerned with the interaction of interpreter and text and the implications of that interaction for the reader, the Church and society. The collapse of the Enlightenment ideal of 'objectivity' and the turn to the subject made biblical criticism much more sensitive to the spirituality dimensions of the text and the reader.

Developments in methodology led to developments in hermeneutics, or the theory of text interpretation. Most notably modern interpreters rediscovered the pre-critical conviction that texts can have multiple meanings. Modern hermeneutical theory does not attribute this phenomenon to divine agency implanting more-than-literal meanings in the text but to the nature of texts themselves, which are always somewhat indeterminate, semantically autonomous in relation to the intention of the author, and thus always 'completed' by the interpretive activity of the reader. Meaning is no longer understood to reside inertly in the text but to arise in the interaction of the reader with the text. This approach to text and interpretation opened readers to the possibility of new, plural and deeper meanings in the biblical text than could be attained by historical critical exegesis alone, which was focused on the one correct interpretation presumed to be authorially controlled and basically historical.

Finally, late in the century, spirituality emerged in the academy as the focus of a research discipline and the biblical foundations of Christian spirituality began to be studied in earnest not only by biblical scholars but by scholars in the new field of spirituality. The two fields began to influence each other. At the same time, practitioners such as spiritual directors, pastoral counsellors and retreat leaders were becoming increasingly interested in nurturing the biblical foundations of the spirituality of their clients and the work of both biblical scholars and scholars in the field of Christian spirituality was mined as resources.

3. Conclusion

The foundational, intimate and vigorous mutual relationship between Scripture and Christian spirituality which had, in many respects, gone underground in the post-Reformation period re-emerged in the twentieth century as central to the vibrant renewal of spirituality on the one hand and biblical studies on the other. This re-emergence is not a return to pre-critical biblical interpretation or a revival of pietistic spirituality. Rather, it is part of the post-critical reappropriation of many dimensions of human experience that had been banished to the private sphere in the heyday of objectivism and scientism. It has been fostered by the tidal wave of interest in spirituality as a source of existential meaning and a force for personal and social transformation, the rapid proliferation of new, non-objectivistic methods of biblical interpretation, new hermeneutical theories which create a space for the transformative dimensions of reading, and theological developments in which reflection on faith is no longer imprisoned in philosophical scholasticism. There is every reason to believe that what the Council declared in principle will become reality in Christian experience, namely, that Scripture will indeed be the pure and perennial source of the spiritual life of the Church.

———

The Cambridge History of the Bible, 3 vols, Cambridge: Cambridge University Press, 1970, 1969, 1963 respectively; Stephen C. Barton, *The Spirituality of the Gospels*, London: SPCK, 1992; Sandra M. Schneiders, 'Scripture and spirituality' in *Christian Spirituality: Origins to the Twelfth Century*, ed. Bernard McGinn and John Meyendorff, WS, vol. 16, New York: Crossroad, 1985, pp. 1–20; Sandra M. Schneiders, 'Biblical spirituality: life, literature, and learning' in *Doors of Understanding: Conversations in Global Spirituality in Honor of Ewert Cousins*, ed. Steven Chase, Quincy, IL: Franciscan Press, 1997, pp. 51–76; Michael Whelan, *Living Strings: An Introduction to Biblical Spirituality*, Newtown, Australia: E. J. Dwyer, 1994; Amos N. Wilder, *Jesus' Parables and the War of Myths: Essays on Imagination in the Scripture*, ed. James Breech, Philadelphia: Fortress Press, 1982.

SANDRA M. SCHNEIDERS

Spirituality and Social Sciences

Spirituality does not exist in a vacuum. Social, cultural, economic and political con-texts shape how one understands oneself, the world and the divine. Indeed, context moulds the practice of faith. The social sciences are vital tools for understanding the context of individuals' and communities' spiritual lives. By no means should the social sciences be used in a reductionist way to explain away religious experience. Yet they are important tools in describing the relationship between faith and context, and thus they serve as helpful partners to theology.

Social scientific approaches to the study of spirituality incorporate a variety of dis-ciplines, including anthropology, history, psychology, sociology, political science and economics. It will be useful to briefly explore each in turn. While these necessarily brief discussions focus on ways that spirituality scholars and guides make use of the social sciences, it should be noted at the outset that the social scientific theorists have presented sharp challenges to spirituality, describing spirituality or religion as a kind of divinization of society (Durkheim), as the 'opiate' of the masses (Marx), and as psychological 'illusion' (Freud). These challenges must be addressed in a more full discussion of each social science than can be included in this overview essay.

1. Anthropological approach

An anthropological approach to the study of spirituality has gained prominence as scholars and practitioners seek common ground with persons of different religious faiths (and with those outside of any tradition). Illustrated by the work of Sandra Schneiders, the anthropological approach emphasizes the universality of the human search for self-transcendence. Scholars seek to understand and interpret spiritual experience as such. Anthropological definitions of spirituality tend to be quite broad, lacking explicit references to particular theological beliefs. Rather, they point to the common desire across cultures to find meaning in life and to relate one's life to an ulti-mate value (Schneiders, 1986). Hence, such definitions lend themselves to inter-faith dialogue and to initiatives in spirituality that go beyond church walls, extending, for example, into secular spaces such as the workplace and the political forum (note that the *Spirituality and the Secular Quest* volume in the Crossroad 'World Spirituality' series examines a wide variety of 'secular' spiritual practices: see Van Ness, 1996). Anthropological perspectives also serve an important role in the task of inculturation – increasingly important in an era of globalization. That is, religious leaders and theologians must consider how to embed spiritual practice in local cultures, even as Christianity proclaims a truth that transcends culture. How, for example, can worship reflect the language, music, style and food of a culture? Anthropology can be very useful in bringing cultural sensitivity to the study of spirituality and to the practice of spiritual guidance (on the latter point, see the collection of essays in Rakoczy, 1994). The anthropological approach emphasizes the interdisciplinary nature of the study of spirituality, and it incorporates research in a variety of social sciences as it seeks to understand human experience.

2. Historical approach

Historical analysis also serves as an important method in the study of spirituality. Indeed, Christian spirituality may be especially called to attend to historical particularity, for Christianity asserts that God broke into human history at a specific time and place in the revelation of Jesus Christ. The faith is historical, affirming a meeting point of the universal, transcendent and the particular, contingent. The medievalist Bernard McGinn has made the case that spirituality must be analysed through a historical-contextual approach, which can uncover the contours of a community's spiritual practice in relationship to a given time and place. In his multi-volume study on the development of Western Christian mysticism from its origins into the Middle Ages, for example, McGinn situates Christian mystics within their wider social, cultural and philosophical milieux, constantly exploring the interweaving of religious experience and historical context.

As historical study gained currency, questions about method and objectivity came to the fore. Histories of spirituality inevitably offer only a limited, selective picture of the community's experience. Some scholars focus on intellectual history, placing importance on the development of ideas. Others focus on a spiritual elite or on the leaders who became dominant in the tradition, neglecting popular faith. Historians tend to prioritize certain periods of history or locales as they tell the story of Christian spirituality. In noting this partiality and process of selection in the writing of the history of spirituality, Philip Sheldrake asserts that history is not purely 'scientific' or objective. Rather, one must read history with a critical eye, attuned to the ways in which histories of spirituality prioritize certain kinds of religious experience, religious people and communities while omitting others (Sheldrake, 1998).

Because history has overlooked vibrant forms of spirituality, scholars are now giving new attention to less studied subjects – medieval women mystics, lay people, Asians, Latin Americans and Africans. Historians research not only intellectual currents and church leaders, but also popular spirituality. For example, Robert Orsi has done ground-breaking work on popular devotions to the Virgin Mary and to St Jude (Orsi, 1988, 1998). Still, much work needs to be done to uncover and interpret the spiritual practices of a wide range of Christians in the past, and to track how the past relates to the contemporary situation.

3. Sociology and spirituality

While history looks at the past, tracing change over time, sociology explores more the social dynamics of groups in the present. Sociology can be an important tool in the study of spirituality, for the practice of faith occurs in the interplay between the individual and communities of which she is a part. Christian spirituality is not a purely individual affair, isolated from human relationships. Rather, social context, social dynamics and social institutions all affect spirituality. (Although it should be pointed out that so too can spirituality influence society.) Indeed, sociologists bring a keen awareness that social institutions such as the Church and the family play a critical role in transmitting religion and making it plausible (on the key role of 'plausibility structures' for religious socialization, see, for example, Berger, 1969). With secularization and a loss of confidence in institutions and authorities, 'secondary institutions' such as small groups have flourished as social contexts to support the spiritual quest of individuals (see Wuthnow, 1994, 1998; Heelas and Woodhead, 2001).

Social change clearly carries spiritual implications. According to sociologist Peter Berger, for example, pluralism challenges the taken-for-grantedness of religious belief and practice, undermining religious certainty and leading to a more consumerist – but also perhaps more authentic – spirituality. Spirituality then becomes a matter of choosing faith, rather than resting in certain knowledge or blind trust in institutions (Berger, 1979, 1998). In another example of social change, shifting marriage patterns and increasing professional roles for women raise new questions about vocation and call for wise discernment among expanding social and economic choices. Sociologists, economists and historians each play a part in documenting and interpreting such changes, aiding theologians, spiritual guides and other pastoral leaders who must respond to the new situation (see Wolfteich, 2002). Sociologists bring information and analysis that complements but does not replace the task of theology.

Some contemporary writers have seen the task of social analysis as critical to effective and faithful spiritual guidance. Carolyn Gratton called on spiritual guides to actually be social analysts and critics, in order to transform deforming social structures and cultural norms that undermine the Christian spiritual life. For example, Gratton points to the western overemphasis on productivity and perfectionism as factors that hinder persons' ability to pray and to be in relationship with God (Gratton, 1993). Kathleen Fischer invokes the social sciences as tools to uncover destructive cultural norms concerning gender, norms which if not challenged can lead to misguided spiritual direction and discernment. For example, she notes that because of their socialization, women may wrongly attribute passivity with obedience to God. Thus, they lose an ability to claim their freedom and to change their social circumstances (Fischer, 1991).

4. Psychology and spirituality

Such critical perspectives on spiritual direction point to the fact that spirituality is not just about individual religious experience. Rather, social contexts influence individual experience, and vice versa. Of course, spiritual guides must attend to the dynamics of an individual life. Because psychology is the social science that focuses most on the individual per se, it complements other social sciences as a tool for understanding and guiding spirituality. Psychology has strongly influenced contemporary spirituality. Indeed, much popular spirituality sounds quite a bit like self-help literature. Unfortunately, pop psychology too often eclipses theology within spirituality. Yet, attention to human development and psychology has a long, respected history within Christian spirituality. The 'care of souls' in the tradition melded spiritual, pastoral and ethical guidance, although of course this preceded modern psychology (see, for example, Gregory the Great, *The Book of Pastoral Care* and contemporary theologian Thomas Oden's book *Care of Souls in the Classic Tradition*). Scholars in spirituality such as Joann Wolski Conn use developmental psychology to analyse classical spiritual writers and traditions (e.g. Thérèse, Salesian tradition). She also brings a critical perspective on developmental psychology as she analyses women's spirituality. Wolski Conn asserts that relationality is an important component of each life stage, that spiritual and psychological maturity entails both intimacy – traditionally defined as a feminine quality – and autonomy – traditionally defined as a male virtue (Wolski Conn, 1996).

Psychology plays an important part in many retreats and much spiritual direction. With a rise in professionalization, many western spiritual directors are trained today on models similar to those of clinical pastoral education (CPE), with supervision, verbatims, and theological reflection. Spiritual guides often adopt methods used in psychotherapy, such as reflective listening and a carefully delineated relationship with the 'client'. In retreats and popular books, personality measures such as the Myers-Briggs scale and the Enneagram aim to help individuals to discern their spiritual paths, cherish and build upon their own gifts, and deepen understanding of others.

5. Political and economic analysis

Political and economic theory also has informed Christian spirituality, particularly among the base communities of Latin America. Liberation theologians such as Gustavo Gutiérrez, Juan Luis Segundo, and Jon Sobrino insisted that true spirituality works for the political and economic liberation of the poor. Gutiérrez, for example, pointed to the tradition of Christian spirituality to show that spirituality is always concretely linked to historical movements, including the historical process of liberation moving in Latin America. Gutiérrez defined spirituality simply as 'the following of Jesus' (Gutiérrez, 1984, p. 1). In his view, the movement of the poor to assert their human dignity set the stage for an encounter with Christ; certainly it was part of the path of following Jesus. Liberation spirituality emphasized the practice of faith and critiqued traditional notions of spirituality that associated religious practice exclusively with personal piety or church attendance. Belief and private piety was insufficient. Rather, prayer must be united to concrete acts of solidarity and liberative action on behalf of the poor. According to liberation theology, spirituality cannot be apolitical; it either resists or supports the structures of oppression. The social sciences, then, become important tools in theological and spiritual work – they offer tools for analysing oppressive political, economic, and social structures and pointing the way toward a future.

Liberation theology and spirituality has drawn fire for its use of Marxist theory, resulting for example in the Vatican statement *Instruction on Certain Aspects of 'Theology of Liberation'* (1984). The statement affirmed that Christians should exercise a 'preferential option for the poor', but critiqued what the hierarchy saw as a dangerous use of Marxist analysis and a unilateral emphasis on earthly, institutional oppression (rather than the individual bondage to sin). The *Instruction* argued that Marxist theory might appear appealingly 'scientific', but in fact advances a global vision of reality that demands a critical eye from Christians. Thus, debates about liberation theology were at least in part debates about the use of the social sciences in theological reflection and spiritual practice. Gutiérrez and other liberation theologians had established a powerful argument for the relevance of political and economic analysis to

Christian spirituality by casting Christian life in terms of human solidarity, structural critique, and political transformation by and for the sake of the oppressed. Yet their reliance on the social sciences raised important questions at the same time.

6. Debates about the value of the social sciences

While practical theologians, liberation spiritualities and scholars in spirituality have turned to the social sciences, the relevance of the social sciences to Christian spirituality is not uncontroversial. The social sciences carry implicit values and world views, even while claiming objectivity. The practical theologian Don S. Browning has pointed out, for example, the value-laden content of psychological theories used in pastoral care (Browning, 1976). Feminist writers such as the psychologist Carol Gilligan critique male bias in developmental theory (Gilligan, 1982). Still, such scholars would not abandon the use of the social sciences; rather, they caution that social scientific theories cannot be taken as value-free. The Vatican made a similar argument in its statements about liberation theology: the human sciences may have an instrumental value for theologians, but they must be studied critically – and finally, only theological criteria can establish truth. The British theologian John Milbank goes a step farther. He argues that the social sciences offer secular interpretations of the world at variance with the core values of Christianity. Hence, he would reject the use of the social sciences to bolster or guide Christian spirituality. Faith and social science are two alternative, incompatible discourses. Christianity must explain the world on its own terms; it must claim its power as a 'metadiscourse' (Milbank, 1990).

7. Social sciences complement central role of theology

Undeniably, the practice and the study of spirituality demand careful theological reflection. The social sciences cannot and must not replace theological analysis of the spiritual life in context. For while history can shed light on the development of faith, and sociology can illuminate the powerful effects of social groups on religious practice, and psychology can bring to light the dynamics of life stage development, none of these inquiries can establish the truthfulness and fidelity of any particular spiritual path. For that critical task, theology must guide. Every spirituality carries implicit or explicit theological assumptions; these assumptions must be identified, tested and reflected upon in light of the norms and wisdom of the tradition, the Scriptures, reason and experience. For example, a spiritual path or practice usually would define implicitly the highest good toward which human beings should move. A spiritual director would carry certain understandings of human nature (theological anthropology) and our capacity to know God (epistemology). Theology as a mode of reflection enables us to sift out the beliefs embedded in spiritual practice so that they can be seen and evaluated. Most clearly, theology should be a prayerful and humble endeavour to know God. It thus is intimately linked to spirituality; one without the other would make no sense. The social sciences aid the human task of understanding and guiding spirituality in all its complexity. They complement, but do not replace, the important role of theology.

_____

Peter L. Berger, *The Heretical Imperative*. New York: Anchor Press/Doubleday, 1979; Peter Berger, 'Protestantism and the quest for certainty', *The Christian Century* (26 Aug.–2 Sept. 1998), 782–96; Peter L. Berger, *The Sacred Canopy: Elements of a Sociological Theory of Religion*, Garden City, NY: Doubleday, 1969; Don S. Browning, *The Moral Context of Pastoral Care*, Philadelphia: Westminster Press, 1976; Kathleen Fischer, *Women at the Well: Feminist Perspectives on Spiritual Direction*, New York: Paulist Press, 1991; Carol Gilligan, *In a Different Voice: Psychological Theory and Women's Development*, Cambridge, MA: Harvard University Press, 1982; Carolyn Gratton, *The Art of Spiritual Guidance*, New York: Crossroad, 1993; Gustavo Gutiérrez, *A Theology of Liberation: History, Politics, and Salvation*, Maryknoll, NY: Orbis Books, 1973; Gustavo Gutiérrez, *We Drink from Our Own Wells: The Spiritual Journey of a People*, Maryknoll, NY: Orbis Books, 1984; Paul Heelas and Linda Woodhead, 'Homeless minds today?' in Linda Woodhead (ed.), *Peter Berger and the Study of Religion*, London: Routledge, 2001; Bernard McGinn, *The Flowering of Mysticism: Men and Women in the New Mysticism (1200–1350)*, vol. 3 of *The Presence of God: A History of Western Christian Mysticism*, New York: Crossroad, 1998; Bernard McGinn, *The Foundations of Mysticism*, vol. 1 of *The Presence of God: A History of Western Christian Mysticism*, New York: Crossroad, 1991; Bernard McGinn, *The Growth of Mysticism*, vol. 2 of *The Presence of God: A History of Western Christian Mysticism*. New York: Crossroad, 1996; John Milbank, *Theology and Social Theory: Beyond Secular Reason*, Oxford: Blackwell, 1990; Susan Rakoczy (ed.), *Common Journey, Different Paths: Spiritual Direction in Cross-Cultural Perspective*, Maryknoll, NY: Orbis Books, 1994; Sacred Congregation for the Doctrine of the Faith, *Instruction on Certain Aspects of the 'Theology of Liberation'*, Boston, MA: St Paul Editions, 1984; Sandra Schneiders, 'Theology and spirituality: strangers, rivals, or partners?', *Horizons* 13.2 (Fall 1986), 253–74; Philip Sheldrake, *Spirituality and History: Questions of Interpretation and Method*, Maryknoll, NY: Orbis Books, 1998; Peter H. Van Ness (ed.), *Spirituality and the Secular Quest*, New York: Crossroad, 1996; Claire Wolfteich, *Navigating New Terrain: Work and Women's Spiritual Lives*, New York: Paulist Press, 2002; Joann Wolski Conn, *Women's Spirituality: Resources for Christian Development*, New York: Paulist Press, 1996; Robert Wuthnow, *After Heaven: Spirituality in America since the 1950s*, Berkeley: University of California Press, 1998; Robert Wuthnow, *Sharing the Journey: Support Groups and America's New Quest for Community*, New York: Free Press, 1994.

CLAIRE E. WOLFTEICH

Spirituality and Theology

When the term 'spirituality' first came to denote an academic discipline – probably in France during the first half of the twentieth century – it represented a liberation. What it replaced, 'ascetical and mystical theology', seemed to imply an excessively rigid and elitist conception of divine action, and to depend on hopelessly overdrawn distinctions between nature (our effort) and grace (God's gift). Nevertheless, 'spirituality' in the 1950s was still clearly a branch of theology, and really only practised in Catholic faculties. Often classified under the subheading of moral theology, it was a marginal, somewhat esoteric activity. Its concerns were principally with the distinctive identity of consecrated life, and with the forms of prayer cultivated in monastic and quasi-monastic traditions. This understanding of the matter continues to be institutionally influential, particularly in Roman Catholic ecclesiastical faculties.

However, the cultural changes of the second half of the 1900s, catalysed for Catholic traditions of Christianity by the Second Vatican Council, have rendered 'spirituality' no longer exclusively confessional. 'Spirituality' is now concerned with a far richer range of human experience. Clearly the old answers to the questions about what spirituality is, and about its appropriate place in the academy, will no longer suffice. But it is not yet clear what the new answers should be.

1. Theory and experience

Typically, modern students of spirituality have made their own a dictum of the theologian Karl Rahner. Near the beginning of his *Foundations of Christian Faith* – the nearest thing he wrote to a summary statement of his own theology – Rahner says:

> When I love, when I am tormented by questions, when I am sad, when I am faithful, when I feel longing, this human and lived existential reality is a unity . . . that is not *fully* communicated by the idea of this reality that makes it an object to be reflected on academically. (Rahner, pp. 15–16, retranslated)

The spiritual tradition is full of apophatic tropes, full of assertions that what it is trying to talk about is somehow – to use a phrase from Hopkins' 'The Wreck of the *Deutschland*' – 'beyond saying sweet/Past telling of tongue'. How such statements are to be understood varies in context: within spiritual literature in the narrow sense there is a spectrum running between the disciplined negative theology of a figure like Denys the Areopagite (Turner) to the recognition we find at the outset of Ignatius Loyola's *Spiritual Exercises* that people open to the spirits (both good and evil) will often not be able to articulate precisely or accurately what is happening within them. When Rahner speaks of 'unity' in the passage quoted above, he is alluding to his conviction that truth is always more than the merely 'objective', more than what can be measured neutrally. An important element in truth is its transformative effect on one who knows and experiences it.

In a number of ways, the contemporary study of spirituality depends on some kind of disjunction between doctrine and the spiritual. Students of spirituality are frequently interested in how poetry, the visual arts and music articulate human relationships with God. Yet, as Robert Frost famously noted, poetry is what is lost in translation; and attempts to reduce to theological prose the Verdi *Requiem*, or the paradoxes of John Donne's sonnets, or even the rhetorical balance of a text like Teresa of Avila's *Interior Castle*, are laughably heavy-footed. Another standard observation generating an interest in 'spirituality' is a sense of intuitive affinities somehow transcending beliefs. So George Eliot appears as a powerful witness to Christianity even though she herself had ceased to be a mainstream believer by the time she wrote her novels; so too we hope that a focus on experience, deeper than mere beliefs, will enable adherents of different faiths to relate constructively in peace with each other. Moreover, the spiritual occurs in contexts unrecognized by official church theology. Drawing on a tradition going back to William James, figures such as Alister Hardy and David Hay have discerned a widespread openness to the spiritual among those untouched by the Church and sceptical or ignorant of its teachings. 'I am not religious but I am spiritual' has become a standard turn of phrase.

'Spirituality' appears as fresh and exhilarating because it promises a connection with the rich reality of things, of a kind that more theoretical approaches to religion and to Christianity somehow lack. But a question obviously arises. For all their differences, the approaches to 'the spiritual' evoked above are at one in implying that 'the spiritual' transcends mere theory. At first sight, then, there is an incoherence built into the very idea of a special study of 'spirituality': it is offering yet another theory of what is supposed to be beyond theory. Moreover, supposing that this paradox can somehow be resolved, there remains the vexed question of how this special kind of 'spiritual' theory, allegedly more in touch with the experience itself, relates to more prosaic ways of articulating and studying the same subject matter, such as the theological traditions of different religions, or indeed the human sciences.

This problem can obviously be named more briefly and in more familiar terms: the relationship of the nascent discipline of spirituality to (Christian) theology. But it is important not to fall too quickly into that shorthand, in particular not before taking stock of the complex human reality that generates it. Despite the confidence with which people sometimes address the issue, there is a widely acknowledged controversy about what 'spirituality' means, and indeed also considerable vagueness about just what is involved in the term 'theology'. The question nevertheless arises from habits of thought deeply embedded in our culture, reflected in many traditionally established ways in which we evoke the spiritual. At the same time, there is nothing particularly religious about the problem. Ultimately, this issue is simple: lived experience is somehow richer than mere words. Actually being short of money is rather different from the ability to read a bank statement; the experience of watching an exciting football match somehow involves more than an awareness of the rules of football or a knowledge of sports science. More technically, there are branches of study such as 'applied physics' or 'applied economics', paying more explicit attention to how physics and economics function in practice, and raising exactly similar questions about disciplinary identity and boundaries. The issues about spirituality and theology parallel more general questions about how theory of any kind relates to lived reality.

2. Disciplinary imperialisms

Two extreme positions obviously suggest themselves. On the one hand, we could imagine a generic study of 'spirituality' understood independently of Christianity. Within this discipline, Christian spirituality (however defined) would be one sort of spirituality among others, and only this branch of spirituality would require the deployment (more or less critically and exclusively) of Christian theology. On the other hand, we could regard Christian theology as the governing discipline, define 'spirituality' in some problematic way as one area of the Christian life among others, and postulate that spirituality was authentically Christian if and only if it conformed to criteria already supplied by theology.

Both of these positions are manifestly absurd unless they are nuanced. The disjunction between experience and understanding implicit in a study of spirituality as 'pure experience' cannot be absolute, given that our words and theories are in important ways constitutive of our experience. Similarly, an insistence on Christian theology as normative must stop short of the claim that theology already says everything that needs to be said, if only because of the contradiction between such an attitude and an openness to the freedom of God. Its structures have to be open to extension and development in the light of new evidence if knowledge is to grow.

Both extreme positions, nevertheless, influence the contemporary literature. Writers whose primary interests are not theoretical often imply one or the other position, and the opposite one may then be invoked as a corrective. Moreover, both positions can appear in qualified and more defensible forms that provide important elements in any tenable account of the relationship between theology and spirituality. The doctrine of Jesus Christ as truly divine and truly human, for example, will not specify *exhaustively* what does and does not count as authentic Christian spirituality, but it may enable us nevertheless to specify *minimal conditions* which any spirituality must satisfy if it is to be authentically Christian (for example, that it not involve a systematic and principled degradation of the human). Conversely, the abiding appeal to the universality of spiritual experience represents an important, permanent challenge to any spiritual tradition. If it is consistently to speak of a God active in *all* things, a tradition must be open to how its conventional constructions, and its natural tendency to identify divine activity with its own sphere of influence, are permanently prone to subversion. We need an account of theology as normative for spirituality in a way that keeps it open to the unconventional and unpredictable; we need an account of spirituality as universal but not shapeless.

3. Two models

This outline of the issues probably represents the limit of consensus among those explicitly concerned with 'Christian spirituality'. To begin to move further, it may be helpful to return to the tension between theory and reality found in other contexts besides the explicitly religious. The analogies offered so far for the tension between theology and spirituality in fact fall into at least two different kinds. The distinction between pure and applied physics or pure and applied economics is rather different from that between a knowledge of the rules of a game and the experience of watching it or playing it. In the first case, the 'pure' discipline purports somehow to describe reality, and the 'applied' discipline arises because there are certain practical issues that arise which the pure discipline cannot deal with. So, for example, when people refer to canon law as applied ecclesiology, there is implicit here a recognition that the idealistic discourse of ecclesiology cannot handle certain intractable practical issues. But the 'pure' discipline has its own integrity, and its central practitioners can normally conduct their business without attending to the 'applied' one. But such an account of the matter does not match the relationship between, say, the rules of tennis and the Wimbledon final, or between a musical score and a live performance. Here, the theory is self-consciously incomplete. It refers forward to a creative activity for which it specifies a framework, but which it in no sense purports to prescribe.

In terms of these two accounts of the relationship between theory and practice, theology is an interestingly borderline case. Some practitioners do proceed as if 'theology' somehow describes reality: 'God is one and God is three', for example, is understood as a complex metaphysical description of the divine being; the implication is that were our theology only developed enough such talk would become perspicuous. On such a construction of theology, 'spirituality' appears as an 'applied' discipline, appropriate for questions of lived practice where the 'pure' theory somehow appears inadequate. Spirituality is to theology as engineering is to physics – there are close connections between the two, but spirituality is nevertheless autonomous, and can move beyond theology's restrictions. So it is that an author like Sandra Schneiders can claim that 'spirituality is an autonomous discipline which functions in partnership and mutuality with theology'. Specialists who think in this way will be keen to set up faculties and institutes specifically of spirituality. They will of course cultivate cordial relationships with their theological colleagues, but they will also guard their autonomy.

Schneiders has argued her case forcefully, clearly and influentially. Figures such as McGinn, McIntosh and Sheldrake argue in different ways for a closer and more organic connection between theology and spirituality, while sharing Schneiders' rejection of a model of dependence.

One way of articulating such a position is to suppose that Christian theology is, of its very nature, incomplete. Christian dogmas are not descriptions but abstractions. 'God is three and God is one' is not a report, but rather a formula forestalling our idolatrous tendencies to construe the mystery of God in terms of the created realities with which we are more familiar. To understand the formula aright just is to be open to the ongoing and unpredictable action of a self-communicating God in human experience. Dogma is epistemologically dependent on discipleship, on particular patterns of experience of God, and only makes sense when understood in that context – just as a musical score only makes sense as a set of instructions for performance. Such an approach moves towards regarding theology and spirituality as two names for the same activity, with at most differences in emphasis. There are organic links between the study of the rules of football, and the study of the skills of one particular player (let us call him Algernon). True, we may draw on many other resources to explain why Algernon plays as he does – genetics, cultural studies, physics, biology, economics. But the study of the rules of football nevertheless has a special place in our account of Algernon's brilliance, in that we cannot even recognize Algernon's activity as *football* unless these rules are invoked. So, too, we may of course draw on a whole range of academic disciplines to interpret Christian spirituality, but Christian theology remains the definitive frame of reference within which this interdisciplinary activity occurs. The contemporary development of 'spirituality' as an academic discipline appears as an enrichment and reform within the theological enterprise rather than as something fundamentally different. If, administratively, theology and spirituality appear as separate entities, this is merely a pragmatic measure, reflecting dysfunctions in the practice of theology rather than any convictions about the more-than-theological identity of spirituality.

If this analysis of the contemporary discussion is correct, then the differences between contemporary specialists in spirituality regarding spirituality's links with theology turn, not on a disagreement about spirituality, but rather on understandings of what is involved in the theological enterprise more broadly. Specialists in spirituality are united in an insistence that human experience is a genuine source of wisdom and knowledge about God, that this experience requires a form of interpretation drawing eclectically on a whole range of academic methods, and that the proper study of spirituality requires us to go beyond a sense of truth as merely neutral and objective. What remains contentious is whether such a study of spirituality represents a departure from theology, or a summons to theology to conduct itself properly. That question is a matter both of high academic speculation and local academic politics.

Within a Christian perspective, the question of just how spirituality claims its place in the academy is interesting, but comparatively unimportant. What matters is that spirituality be studied as well and as creatively as possible. The question about theology and spirituality appears more momentous than it really is because, in daily academic politics, it touches into far more controversial questions about the status of Christianity in the academy and in secular culture generally. Even in a confessional faculty, an advocacy of 'spirituality' as emancipated from theology may represent a reaction against church authority's efforts to regulate 'theology'. In more secular settings, such an advocacy may be associated with a radically pluralist account of Christianity's relationship to what western scholars, massively and unconsciously influenced by Christianity, call 'other religions'. For its part, a pluralist secular academy may find Christianity's claim to definitive ultimacy problematic, and adopt the term 'spirituality' more or less consciously, more or less coherently, more or less benignly, as a means of marginalizing Christianity. There are questions here about the absoluteness of Christianity, about its canons and procedures in argument, and about its status in the secular world – questions which are indeed important. But they are not, despite the language sometimes used, really questions about Christian spirituality, and they need to be dealt with on their own terms.

Bradley C. Hanson, 'Spirituality as spiritual theology' in Bradley C. Hanson (ed.), *Modern Christian Spirituality: Methodological and Historical Essays*, Atlanta: Scholars Press, 1990, pp. 45–52; Alister Hardy, *The Spiritual Nature of Man*, Oxford: Oxford University Press, 1979; David Hay, *Exploring Inner Space: Is God Still Possible in the Twentieth Century?*, London: Penguin, 1982; William James, *The Varieties of Religious Experience: A Study in Human Nature*, London: Penguin, 1982 [1901]; Bernard

McGinn, 'The letter and the spirit: spirituality as an academic discipline', *Christian Spirituality Bulletin* 1.2 (Fall 1993), 1–10; Mark McIntosh, *Mystical Theology*, Oxford: Blackwell, 1998; Karl Rahner, *Foundations of Christian Faith: An Introduction to the Idea of Christianity*, London: Darton, Longman & Todd, 1978; Sandra M. Schneiders, 'Theology and spirituality: strangers, rivals, or partners?', *Horizons* 13 (1986), 253–74; Sandra M. Schneiders, 'Spirituality in the academy', *Theological Studies* 50 (1989), 676–97; Sandra M. Schneiders, 'Spirituality as an academic discipline: reflections from experience', *Christian Spirituality Bulletin* 1.2 (1993), 10–15; Philip Sheldrake, *Spirituality and Theology: Christian Living and the Doctrine of God*, London: Darton, Longman & Todd, 1998; Denys Turner, *The Darkness of God*, Cambridge: Cambridge University Press, 1998.

PHILIP ENDEAN

ENTRIES A–Z

Abandonment

Abandonment can be understood in a predominantly active sense (abandonment to God) and in a predominantly passive sense (abandonment by God).

1. *Abandonment to God*. In Matt. 6.25–34 (Luke 12.22–31) we are told not to worry about tomorrow, since God knows our needs. Rom. 8.28 and 1 Peter 5.6–8 reinforce that message. Jesus teaches his disciples to pray that God's will be done (Matt. 6.10), and in Gethsemane gives the example: 'Not my will but yours be done' (Luke 22.42).

The theme of abandonment to God saw its earliest theological development mainly in patristic treatments of God's providence. By the Middle Ages increasing emphasis was being placed on the identity of providence with the divine will and pleasure and on renunciation of one's own will so as to conform to God's. The use of the term *abandonment* for this specific attitude became more prominent from the late sixteenth through the early twentieth centuries.

Basic to this evolving understanding was the concept of providence as God's will explicitly directing or at least permitting all that is and all that happens, in the life of the individual as well as in the world as a whole. This notion of abandonment was discussed most often in reference to the more unpleasant aspects of life: poverty, distress, illness, death – but usually coupled with the theme of equanimity in the face of either poverty or wealth, distress or joy, illness or health, life or death. Abandonment to God was characterized as essentially a fruit of perfect love, wherein the human will freely and fully embraced the divine will and pleasure (God's *pleasure* being applied to events which cannot be foreseen). It could, of course, admit of stages of surrender along the way; but only with perfect charity could one live in a *state* of true abandonment. Abandonment was thus more than mere obedience to God's already perceived will, and more than patience or resignation, which still bore elements of fear or coercion. It was for some authors beyond even indifference in the Ignatian

sense (*Spiritual Exercises* 23), since when one has fully embraced God's will in all things, indifference loses its reason for being – though Francis de Sales did call abandonment 'holy indifference' (*Entretiens spirituels* 2).

This concept of abandonment as total loving conformity to God's will and pleasure presumed not mere passive acceptance but an active embrace which also cultivated the other virtues. And though it sometimes seemed to glorify suffering as a good in itself, its most balanced proponents insisted that to desire suffering absolutely was to be less than unconditionally abandoned to God's will.

It remained for the later twentieth century to develop more fully the aspect of human freedom and responsibility in relation to conformity with the divine. The Second Vatican Council of the Roman Catholic Church already revealed this shift when it emphasized the pursuit of fully human solutions to human needs (*Gaudium et Spes* 11). One should not, for example, in the name of abandonment to God's will, neglect one's health and then rejoice in the resultant illness as a sharing in Christ's cross (except repentantly). One should not exhort the poor and oppressed simply to embrace their lot as the will of a provident God who will later make up for it in eternity. God's will and pleasure are, in this interpretation, inextricably bound up with our freedom and responsibility in bringing creation to its fulfilment.

What then remains of the tradition of abandonment to God? The goal of human life for the Christian is still conformity with the divine. And this is not realized without the abandonment of one's circumscribed, self-centred plans and desires for what one shall be in life or in death. In this sense, abandonment to God remains an essential goal of Christian life.

2. *Abandonment by God*. The concept of abandonment by God has direct roots in Scripture. The story of Job and a number of the Psalms wrestled with the mystery of faith confronting seemingly undeserved suffering and desolation. But for Christian spirituality this mystery is most poignantly expressed in Jesus' cry on the cross:

'My God, my God, why have you forsaken me?' (Matt. 27.46). Christians in every age have turned to this cry to discern and interpret the meaning of apparent abandonment by God.

Most especially in the face of a sense of *spiritual* abandonment we find the insistence that what seems to be the absence of God is in fact a particular kind of presence. Catherine of Siena's observation (placed in God's mouth) is typical: 'I come and go, leaving in terms of feeling, not in terms of grace, and I do this to bring them to perfection. When they reach perfection I relieve them of this "lover's game" of going and coming back. I call it a "lover's game" because I go away for love and I come back for love – no, not really I, for I am your unchanging and unchangeable God; what goes and comes back is the feeling my charity creates in the soul' (*Dialogo* 147).

Abandonment by God who is in essence faithful can never be a literal reality but only the desolate person's perception of his or her relationship with God in faith at a given moment. Ultimately, it is only from the vantage point of abandonment to God that one finds meaning in a sense of abandonment by God. And, paradoxically, it is out of the depths of the experience of the sense of abandonment by God that one discovers the full freedom inherent in abandonment to God.

See also **Darkness; Dark Night; Detachment; Providence; Purgative Way; Quietism.**

Jean-Pierre de Caussade, *The Sacrament of the Present Moment*, trans. K. Muggeridge, San Francisco: Harper & Row, 1982; M. Viller, 'Abandon', *DS*, vol. 1, cols 2–25.

SUZANNE NOFFKE

Absence of God

see **Apophatic Spirituality**

Absorption

Christian mystics, who continually struggle with ways to translate their experiences into language, occasionally describe union with God as absorption into God. For such writers, absorption indicates a condition beyond simple contact with the divine that nevertheless stops short of absolute identity. This state of absorption must be reached through withdrawal from the physical world and from active works: individuals on the path to this type of union must reject self-absorption and absorption in material things in order to reach a state of contemplation of God to the exclusion of all else. For some writers, absorption is one of the stages on the way to union without distinction (*see* Annihilation, Spiritual); more often, however, absorption is itself the culmination of a mystical path. It is essential to note that 'absorption' indicates that an ontological distinction remains between creature and creator even when identity seems obscured by the appearance of the union. Absorption might indicate a fusion of wills, but it never goes so far as to indicate an identity of being.

Christian authors borrowed seminal ideas from Plotinus (d. 170) in developing this description of mystical union, as Plotinus also aimed at what can be termed a mystical absorption in the One. For him, the goal of the soul is return to God through purification from the sensible world. This process results in union with, sometimes expressed as absorption into, God. For Christian mystics, the underlying theological assumptions for this type of union include a belief in the dignity of humanity as made in the image of God, which indicates that the soul is part of the divine being. Yet this Neoplatonic idea is coupled with a recognition that human beings, in their willful desires and materiality, can never become God. This is the foundation for the insistence on ontological distinction even within union.

The writers who employ this word are many and diverse. Augustine uses the term in an arresting way when, in his *Confessions*, he describes the universe as a huge sponge that absorbs its creator in all its pores. Absorption as the culmination of the individual mystical encounter can be found in the works of writers such as Evagrius Ponticus (d. 399), Richard of St Victor (d. 1173), Johannes Tauler (d. 1361), and Francis de Sales (d. 1622). Perhaps the most extensive use of this term can be found in the writings of John of the Cross (d. 1591) and Teresa of Avila (d. 1582). In true mystical union, John argues, the soul is utterly absorbed in God. Teresa describes the soul in union with God as a sponge in water: the soul is absorbed in God while God is completely in and through the soul.

Images of absorption are often found alongside other metaphors that express union of wills: for instance, iron in fire, rivers flowing into the sea, liquefaction or melting, and mystical marriage. These metaphors show that the mystical self seems to be wholly, but is not actually, absorbed into the All. Nevertheless, the dramatic image of absorption into God caused several authors who used it to be accused of pantheism.

See also **Mysticism (*essay*); Annihilation, Spiritual; Contemplation; Unitive Way.**

Kieran Kavanaugh, (trans.), *John of the Cross: Selected Writings*, CWS, New York: Paulist Press, 1987; Bernard McGinn, *The Presence of God: A History of Western Christian Mysticism*, New

York: Crossroad, 1994– (3 vols to date, 5 to be published); Bernard McGinn, 'Ocean and desert as symbols of mystical absorption in the Christian tradition', *Journal of Religion* 74.2 (April 1994), 155–81.

JOANNE MAGUIRE ROBINSON

Acedia

Originally one of the eight principal *logismoi* (tempting-thoughts or passions) of early Christian monastic literature, acedia came to be included among the medieval seven deadly sins. Although generally translated as 'sloth', the terms 'apathy' or 'spiritual weariness' are closer to the original meaning. Thomas Aquinas (d. 1274) cited John Damascene's definition of acedia as 'weariness in the face of work' (*ST* 2a2ae 35. 1). Aquinas adapted this to the spiritual life by redefining acedia as *tristitia spiritalis boni*, sadness or listlessness in response to the need to strive for some spiritual good (35. 2. 1). In this sense it represents the sapping or depletion of that spiritual 'good zeal' recommended by St Benedict in his Rule (ch. 72).

A more complete and detailed description of acedia than that of Aquinas is found in chapter 12 of the *Praktikos* by Evagrius of Pontus (d. 399):

The demon of *acedia*, also called the noonday demon (cf. Ps. 90:6), is the most oppressive of all the demons. It attacks the monk at about 10 am and besieges his soul until about 2 pm. First it makes the sun seem to be moving slowly or not at all, so the day appears to be fifty hours long.

Then it compels the monk to keep looking out of his window; it forces him to race out of his cell to watch the sun to see how much longer it will be until 3 pm, and it makes him look all around in case any of the brothers has come [to visit him]. Then it makes him hate the place and his way of life and his manual labor. It makes him think there is no love remaining among the brothers; no one will come to console him.

If anyone has recently offended the monk, the demon adds this too so as to increase his hatred. It makes him desire other places where what the things he needs will be easy to obtain, and where he could practice an easier, more productive trade. After all, the demon adds, pleasing the Lord does not depend on being in a particular place: God is to be worshipped everywhere (cf. John 4:21–4).

It joins to these the memory of the monk's family and his former way of life. It points out

that he still has a long time to live while conjuring before his eyes a vision of how burdensome the ascetic life is. Thus, as they say, [the demon] employs every device it has to make the monk abandon his cell and give up the race.

In this vivid and even humorous depiction Evagrius lays open the whole spectrum of the widely varying manifestations of acedia. Although most often thought of as akin to depression, Evagrius makes it plain that this vice may appear in either a depressed or an agitated form. While often experienced as slothful inactivity and apathy, acedia may also manifest as eagerness or compulsion to do anything, everything, except the spiritual good that is most needful. It may even masquerade under the guise of prudence. These different manifestations all have in common a single goal: namely, to create within the victim an affective or intellectual state that causes him to ignore or abandon his spiritual project.

The cure for acedia therefore lies in cultivating the virtue of perseverance. Evagrius and his disciple John Cassian recommend a variety of spiritual remedies intended to assist the Christian in persevering in his or her spiritual goals. Chief among these are: the practice of psalmody; the deliberate choice not to leave the place where spiritual discipline is practised; meditation on the fact of one's mortality and frailty; and respect for one's body, practically manifested through reasonable attention to one's physical well-being (Evagrius, *Praktikos* 27–9; Cassian *Institutes* 10, *Conferences* 5). Aquinas particularly recommends taking a nap and/or indulging in a warm bath (*ST*, 1a2ae 38. 5).

Perhaps the simplest spiritual remedy for acedia, and the one chosen as the introduction to the whole Greek collection of the *Sayings of the Desert Fathers* is found in the first saying of Abba Antony. While struggling with the demon of acedia Antony cried out to God, 'How can I be saved?' In answer he was given a vision of himself sitting down at his work, intermittently standing for prayer with outstretched arms, then sitting back down to work for an interval. 'Do this', he was told, 'and you will be saved.' Simple, short prayers offered at regular intervals during work throughout the day serve to consecrate, little by little, the whole of ordinary life. No room is left for acedia, since all ordinary activity is thus gradually incorporated into the project of spiritual progress.

See also **Asceticism; Desert; Discipline; Early Christian Spirituality; Eremitical Spirituality; Monasticism.**

B. Ramsey (trans.), *John Cassian: The Institutes and The Conferences*, New York: Paulist Press, 2000; R. E. Sinkewicz (trans.), 'On the eight thoughts', 'The monk', 'Chapters on prayer', *Evagrius of Pontus: The Greek Ascetic Corpus*, Oxford: Oxford University Press, 2004; Thomas Aquinas, *Summa Theologiae*, London: Black-friars edn with notes and appendices, vols 20 and 35, esp. vol. 35, Appendix 1.

LUKE DYSINGER

Addictions and Spiritual Recovery

Addiction is a spiritual disease. Everybody has the ability to connect with the soul and spirit of others. Because addiction is a direct assault against the Self, it is also a direct attack on the spirit or soul of the person suffering from an addiction. A person's spirit sustains life; addiction leads to spiritual death. (Nakken, 1996, p. 54)

Addiction is an insidious disease. It is habitual, demanding and seductive. As its pervasive, intense tendency grows and spreads not unlike a cancer, it destroys the body, mind and soul. Addiction is counter to spirituality. Of all the human conditions addiction is possibly the one that is developing fastest in the world. It could be said that addiction is global and consumerist. As addicts suffer, others grow rich. Those who provide and push substances are economically gratified at the expense of those who, for example in the developing world, harvest the poppy for heroin. Criminality grows on the back of those who become poor through the need to gratify their addiction by any means – stealing being a prime example. Then they, too, become criminals. It is a vicious circle. There is no good in addiction.

Addiction is a multifaceted disorder, deeply complex in its manifestations. Addiction is included as a group of diseases by the World Health Organization in the *International Classification of Diseases* (tenth edition, categories F10–19). This intimates to us that addiction cannot be thought of as something that can be controlled by the individual. Rather the addict is one who is out of control. Will or self-will alone cannot be counted upon to overcome this disease. It is an illness and must be understood as such. Because of the complexity of addiction it is hard to say how a person, or who, becomes an addict. It could be said that the addictive tendency is intrinsic to the human condition and has always been so but has only been termed as such in the past century. The word 'addiction' first appeared in the *Oxford English Dictionary* in 1906 and the

first recorded use of 'addict' as a noun is from 1909 (Farrell Brodie and Redfield, 2002, p. 2).

An attempt to define addiction conclusively will always be limited until such time as the disease is fully understood. Within such limitations we can be sure that no particular personality type is more likely to become an addict than any other, nor can we say why one person is able to contain an addiction and another will die in a gutter. People suffering from addictions have a low sense of self-esteem. They have few of the inner resources that enable self-comfort and inner harmony. The chances are that as children they were brought up within a dysfunctional family and environment where they were treated in abusive ways, overtly or covertly, either physically, emotionally, verbally or sexually – often in combination. The developmental process from child to adult will not only be damaged psychologically but spiritually. There will be a loss of identity, a loss of self, and a sense of non-being. Taking these factors into consideration, it is hardly surprising that the embryo addict will look for a panacea to numb the pain. A depleted sense of well-being, an ever-widening hole of emptiness and yearning for completeness and fulfilment may lead to an addictive craving for destructive and self-abusive practices. 'I am – but only if I have . . .' becomes the cry for help. The substance or practice from which addiction follows can only temporarily assuage the pain and give a sense of well-being which disguises itself as satisfaction or love or fullness. This powerful and destructive cycle can spiral out of control leaving in its wake guilt, shame and self-loathing.

Addictions come in all shapes and sizes and fit into many categories and styles. Some addictions are better known than others and are considered more respectable – even a part of our culture and society particularly in the West. They are well tolerated. Alcohol, smoking and substance abuse fall into this category and are seen as acceptable though destructive. The first two are a development of social activities encouraged through media and advertising and the third is a leisure activity although criminalized. Narcotics also hold a certain kind of cult status. Other addictions are physically harmless to the addict themselves but are societally intolerable. Paedophilia is unquestionably considered the worst and could lead to imprisonment. Kleptomania falls into this category as well.

In the United States it has been estimated that there are more than two hundred classified addictions. They range from eating disorders to sexual disorders; from leisure pursuits such as football to workaholism; from loving too much to spending too much and even to spiritual addiction. Each has its own impulse urge and intensity but all have elements in common. The addict is temporarily filled with an initial sense of gratification and a rise in self-esteem. As the addiction becomes more habitual so the need for gratification becomes more immediate, more desperate. The denial of the condition is paramount to its parasitic life along with its obsessive and self-absorbed preoccupations. The force of the dependency is such that the ensuing loss of identity, status, relationship and self is so powerful that the object of the addiction and its acquisition is more important than life itself.

Addiction is not purely a psychological condition – it is a symptom of something much deeper and more profound, so much so that it can be considered to be a spiritual crisis. It could be said that the power of addiction is so strong and pervasive, so spiritually denying that only a force stronger than the power itself can bring about a recovery. Recovery appears to be effective only when it encompasses a programme such as the Twelve-Step programme, which is based on a process of tight principles. These principles are religious in style and encourage a personal belief system based on spiritual self-discovery and personal enhancement. It is also vital for the addict to believe in the programme and to desire recovery. Without these conditions it is unlikely to succeed.

The Twelve-Step programme of Alcoholics Anonymous and its many similar fellowships was co-founded in 1935 in the United States by 'Dr Bob' Smith and Bill Wilson; their experiences and ideas were published in 1939 in the 'Big Book' considered to be a bible by recovering addicts. This book is strikingly honest, highly anecdotal and rhetorical. Recovery is spoken about in spiritual terms; the guidance is both practical and experiential. In other words the process is a spiritual one – a way of life. The Twelve Steps require an honest admission that the addict is helpless and that only a Power greater than themselves can restore them to sanity. Importantly, a highly confessional approach is taken, repentance is requested and forgiveness asked.

Although the recovery programmes mention God there is a qualification, 'as we understood Him'. This spiritual way of life is not dogmatic. It aspires to no particular religious affiliation; rather it is a search for self, reality and truth. It is highly personal, subjective and flexible. For these reasons programmes are often considered self-absorbed and introspective, simply reversing one addiction for dependency on another, that of the programme. However, many members develop a spirituality that is profound; they change one

way of life for another that enhances their well-being. They stay sober 'one day at a time'. Perhaps for most, if not all, this is their first experience of a trusting community, a place of acceptance, a fellowship of understanding and unconditionality where the addict discovers autonomy, self-control and that they are not god but God is God.

> Encouraging people to develop spiritually does not mean we impose a morality so much as we encourage them to develop their own. If that sounds dangerous, remember that recovering addicts are told to find a God of their own conception. It may be a daffy concept of the divine, but one is better than none given the alternative: drugs and the god of self. (Ringwald, 2002, p. 244)

Janet Farrell Brodie and Marc Redfield (eds), *High Anxieties: Cultural Studies in Addiction*, Berkeley: University of California Press, 2002; Susie Hayward, 'Spiritual Addiction' in *The Way*, 40.4 (October 2000), 314–20; Craig Nakken, *The Addictive Personality*, New York: MJF Books, 1996; Christopher D. Ringwald, *The Soul of Recovery: Uncovering the Spiritual Dimension in the Treatment of Addictions*, Oxford: Oxford University Press, 2002; Martin Weegmann and Robert Cohen (eds), *The Psychodynamics of Addiction*, London and Philadelphia: Whurr Publishers, 2002.

SUSIE HAYWARD

Adolescents and Spirituality

As many Christian biographies attest, the adolescent period can be one of spiritual awakening associated with conversion experiences, urges to seek meaning and truth, and a capacity to exercise autonomy in faith choices, to embrace or reject religious commitment. Empirical study and experience in the new profession of 'youth ministry' suggest yet further layers of complexity.

The parameters of adolescence are challenging (age 11–25?), so few scholars address the whole range. A sequence of patterns may better depict spiritualities of adolescence (see Nelson, 1997: joining, drifting, searching, owning), since a hallmark of adolescence itself is change rather than stability. Significant distinctions reflecting the changing cultural scene (e.g. spirituality of 'baby boomers', generation 'x', generation 'why?') between modern cohorts have also qualified attempts to define adolescent spirituality.

Historically adolescence is ambiguous too, being recognized only lately in Western societies thanks to education, deferment of working life and affluence-enabling teenage leisure culture.

In other places or at other times characteristics of 'adolescent spirituality' described recently in the West may not hold true. In the past, the Church's treatment of adolescents' spiritual lives included taking seriously their desires to test and develop vocation in religious houses, and requiring protection from sexual urges and inexperience in worldly matters. As 'Sunday school' assistants from the 1800s onwards, adolescent spirituality (though perhaps simply equated with religious knowledge) seems to have been regarded as robust enough to exercise a teaching ministry with younger children.

A key feature of contemporary adolescent spirituality is a propensity to split off from institutionalized Christianity, and find its language redundant and spiritually empty. In this age range, church attendance has declined catastrophically in many countries, yet cognitive (interest in matters of belief), emotional (finding God a source of support) and social factors (fellowship) continue to motivate a personal faith and spirituality. The 'homelessness' of adolescent spirituality has been noted in the work and mission of the YMCA where it has been linked with current pluralism of spiritualities and religions. Young people are able to 'travel' more easily than before into new, deliberately 'different' territories of information and practice. Moreover they are attracted to this itinerant style rather than the establishment of a spiritual 'home' or mother tongue. Adult Christians have tended to view these patterns of church rejection and DIY spirituality as a threat to be countered, rather than as gifts of latitude, critical comparison and liminal voice to complement the more conservative spirituality of most established Christian communities. In their own struggle with this, adolescents can be attracted by spiritual situations with extremely clear boundaries – providing an exaggerated sense of 'home' – which might be found in Christian youth groups, sects, passionate adherence to a specific church practice, rule of life or spiritually justified good cause. It is not clear whether confinement to such a home at this stage of life protects or petrifies adolescent spiritual development.

James Fowler's 'Stages of Faith' model offers one way to interpret these tendencies in adolescent spirituality and psychology. Adolescents commonly exhibit features of 'synthetic–conventional' faith (Fowler's stage 3). Faith is fuelled by a need to find a valid way to invest loyalty, a way that supports the relationship of ideas and actions, and the interrelating of individual and group identity. If a way of relating thus is found, it can support strong, idealistic levels of commitment to the new 'family unit' –

e.g. the faith community, admired figures or new idea. A primary spiritual need for adolescent faith is to develop identity through relationship.

Youth spirituality may be best served in terms of loving, Christ-like relating – through accepting and accompanying, rather than dictating the criteria of belief and behaviour on adult terms. A major figure in youth spirituality, Mike Yaconelli (Youth Ministry and Spirituality Project, San Francisco Theological and Princeton Seminaries, USA), suggests contemplative, creative spiritual traditions (e.g. *lectio divina*) that engage with the depth, rather than the restrictive boundaries of religious truth claims, may be valuable both for youth and those working with them. Such approaches may better harness their capacity for relationship and intimacy as a source of meaning, provide enough of a home or structure, but appeal also to the spiritual desire for search, discovery and entering places of mystery. Yaconelli also leads the critique of applying marketplace values, rather than discerning Christian spiritual values, to work with adolescents. Too often, he argues, teenagers are viewed as 'potential customers' in a vast spiritual marketplace where Christian marketing must succeed (or fail) to make them exclusive purchasers of our brand.

See also **Children and Spirituality.**

M. Barnes (ed.), *The Way Supplement 90, The Spirituality of Young People,* (Autumn 1997), especially J. S. Nelson, 'Faith among adolescents: joining, drifting, searching, owning', 60–75; and J. Pridmore, 'The adolescence of Jesus and growing up in Christ', 3–10; M. Eastman, *Theological Approaches to Adolescence: Spirituality, Adolescence and Faith Development,* London: Frontier Youth Trust, 1997; J. Fowler, *Becoming Adult, Becoming Christian: Adult Faith Development and Christian Faith,* Blackburn, Australia: Dove Communications, 1984; K. Hyde, *Religion in Childhood and Adolescence: A Comprehensive Review of Research,* Birmingham: Religious Education Press, 1990; *Youth A Part: Young People and the Church,* London: National Church House Publishing, 1996; Mark Yaconelli, 'Youth ministry: a contemplative approach', *Christian Century* (April 1999), 450–4 and www.youthspecialities.com/articles/Yaconelli

REBECCA NYE

Adoration

Adoration, according to the traditional divisions of prayers into five types, consists of the worship of God alone. Among the Fathers who identify adoration, St Augustine in the *City of God* (10.1) spoke clearly about the absolute worship given to God alone (Latin *latria*) while St Ambrose in his *Commentary on Ps. 98* extends adoration to Christ. Cyril of Jerusalem in his *Mystagogical Catechesis* (5.22) writes, 'Bow down and in adoration and veneration say Amen.' Yet the distinction between adoration and veneration is not clear. Confusion still remained at the Second Council of Nicaea in 787 (*DS* 601), which dealt with the question of the veneration of icons. This Council also made recourse to the term *latria*, restating that it is worship rendered only to God.

Medieval theology classically distinguished between the supreme worship offered to the Trinity (Gr. *latreia*; Lat. *adoratio*) and veneration of the angels and saints (Gr. *douleia*; Lat. *veneratio*). Due to the religious excellence of the saints, service is rendered to them as beings lesser than God. Regarding the veneration of Mary, who has a most privileged place among all the servants of God, the term of *hyperdulia* was coined to indicate her superiority among the saints.

Medieval eucharistic theology with the doctrinal development concerning real presence and transubstantiation underlines the idea of adoration. St Thomas Aquinas in his hymns for the feast of Corpus Christi speaks explicitly of this truth as seen in the hymn *Adoro te devote*. The Council of Trent in the thirteenth session articulated this doctrine as follows:

> There is, therefore, no room for doubt that all the faithful of Christ may, in accordance with a custom always received in the Catholic Church, give to this most holy sacrament in veneration the worship of *latria*, which is due to the true God. Neither is it to be less adored for the reason that it was instituted by Christ the Lord in order to be received. For we believe that in it the same God is present of whom the eternal Father, when introducing him to the world, says: 'And let all the angels of God adore him' (Heb 1:6); whom the Magi, falling down, adored (Mt 2:11); who finally, as the Scriptures testify, was adored by the Apostles in Galilee (Mt 28:17). (chap. IV, cf. *DS* 1643)

During the seventeenth century, the so-called 'French School' developed a spirituality of adoration. Being strongly christocentric, this school conceived of the interior life of perfection as a participation in the mysteries of Christ, where the Eucharist plays a dominant role. According to Jean-Jacques Olier, 'Christianity consists in these three points: . . . to look upon Jesus, to unite oneself to Jesus, and to act in Jesus. The first leads us to respect and to religion; the second to union and to identification with Him;

the third, to an activity no longer solitary, but joined to the virtue of Jesus Christ, which we have drawn upon ourselves by prayer. The first is called adoration; the second, communion; the third, cooperation' (*Introduction to the Christian Life and Virtues* 4.62; see Thompson, p. 229).

Pope Paul VI, who authored the reform of the reform of the liturgy at the Second Vatican Council, also maintained the devotional practice of eucharistic adoration. In his encyclical *Mysterium Fidei* he stated, 'In the course of the day the faithful should not omit visiting the Blessed Sacrament, which in accordance with liturgical law must be reserved in churches with great reverence in a prominent place. Such visits are a sign of gratitude, an expression of love and an acknowledgment of the Lord's presence.' Pope John Paul II in *Dominicae Cenae* restates the rapport between the Eucharist and adoration, making a case for reservation of the holy sacrament as worthy of the cult of *latria*. In the most recent encyclical *Ecclesia de Eucharistia* Pope John Paul II reminds pastors of their responsibility to encourage, also by their personal witness, the practice of eucharistic adoration, and exposition of the blessed sacrament in particular, as well as prayer of adoration before Christ present under the eucharistic species. The Pope asks, 'How can we not feel a renewed need to spend time in spiritual converse, in silent adoration, in heartfelt love before Christ present in the Most Holy Sacrament? How often, dear brothers and sisters, have I experienced this, and drawn from it strength, consolation and support!' (*Ecclesia de Eucharistia*, 48). He recalls that the practice of adoration is supported by the example of many saints. Particularly outstanding in this regard was Alphonsus Liguori, who wrote: 'Of all devotions, that of adoring Jesus in the Blessed Sacrament is the greatest after the sacraments, the one dearest to God and the one most helpful to us' (*ibid.* 49). The theme of eucharistic adoration has marked the spirituality of John Paul II as seen in other documents as well, such as in the Apostolic Letters *Novo Millennio Ineunte* and *Rosarium Virginis Mariae*. Adoration is seen as a complement to worship whereby it prolongs and increases the fruits of our communion in the body and blood of the Lord.

See also **Spirituality, Liturgy and Worship** (*essay*); **Devotions; Eucharistic Spirituality; Prayer.**

John Paul II, *Letter on the Mystery and Worship of the Eucharist*, Dominicae Cenae, *to all the Bishops of the Church*, Boston: St Paul Editions, 1980; *Encyclical Letter*, Ecclesia de Eucharistia, *to the Bishops, Priests and Deacons, Men and Women in the Consecrated Life and all the Lay Faithful on the Eucharist in its Relationship to the Church*, Washington, DC: United States Conference of Catholic Bishops, 2003; Michael O'Carroll (ed.), *Corpus Christi: An Encyclopedia of the Eucharist*, Wilmington: Michael Glazier Press, 1988; Jean-Jacques Olier, *Lettres de M. Olier*, 2 vols, ed. É. Levesque, Paris: J. de Gigord, 1935; Paul VI, *Encyclical Letter*, Mysterium Fidei, *On Eucharistic Doctrine and Worship*, Glen Rock, NJ, Paulist Press, 1966; William Thompson (ed.), *Bérulle and the French School*, New York and Mahwah: Paulist Press, 1989.

MICHAEL S. DRISCOLL

Aesthetics

'Aesthetics' comes from the Greek *aisthetikos*, meaning 'perceptible' or 'concerning perception'. Although Alexander Baumgarten (1714–62) coined the term to refer to a philosophy of 'sensory cognition', and especially of beauty, it was Immanuel Kant (1724–1804) who expanded aesthetics to include a general philosophy of beauty, taste and art. Kant also discussed aesthetics in relation to symbol and imagination. And he supplemented the idea of beauty with that of the sublime – the awe-inspiring in nature, art and thought which later Romantic theorists (more than Kant) associated with the holy in religion. Kant thus established something like the modern meaning of aesthetics.

Since beauty, art and imaginative expression all play a role in religious experience and spiritual practice, we can legitimately speak of theological aesthetics. In the tradition of patristic and medieval theology, from Augustine (354–430) through Thomas Aquinas (*c.* 1225–74) to modern exponents such as Hans Urs von Balthasar (1905–88), God is seen not only as in some sense the supreme artist but also as (invisible) beauty itself, and the source and goal of all earthly beauty. From this point of view, beauty is the attractive radiance – or splendour – of a form which has integrity and good proportion and is pleasing in the very act of being perceived.

By and large, Christian theologians have focused more on 'transcendentals' such as goodness, truth and beauty than on art. Indeed, they have focused more on truth and moral goodness than on beauty itself. When attending to beauty, moreover, theologians prior to the modern era have focused more on intellectual, moral and spiritual beauty than on sensory beauty. In fact, the arts have commonly been assigned a place on the lower rungs of the ladder of spiritual ascent. It is significant that in the twentieth century, in the most comprehensive theological aesthetics ever written, Hans Urs von Balthasar gave relatively little space to the arts and artistry. Similarly, in an earlier era, Jonathan Edwards (1703–58) made much of beauty, theologically, but his idea of 'primary beauty' was essentially moral and non-sensuous.

Several of the many reasons for the relative neglect of the arts in Christian theology can be summed up succinctly. Christians have worried, first, that art may be seductive in its sensuous appeal; second, that art too often falsifies what it represents; third, that art can over-indulge the emotions; and, fourth, that art is often merely entertaining or virtuosic. There is the additional fact that, prior to the modern era, many of the arts were not so widely accessible and not so pervasive in culture.

Regardless of the relative neglect of the arts in formal theology, in practice Christians have made abundant use of various arts. Many forms of art have in fact often been accorded high spiritual standing by those engaged in worship, although different arts have been privileged (or rejected) by different traditions. Some religious groups have favoured an aesthetic of 'less' – such as the austere beauty and formal simplicity of chant and Cistercian architecture. Other groups (especially when well endowed, financially) have favoured an aesthetic of 'more' – such as the ornate and theatrical forms of Baroque religious art and the oratorios of Handel (1685–1759).

Aesthetically, every religious tradition is both selective and creative, and in ways that shape its identity. The Eastern Church, while rejecting instrumental music and sculpture, has gloried in chant and has embraced icons, which it has regarded as central to worship and prayer and as windows on eternity. Again, Western Catholicism has only intermittently welcomed dance or drama in worship. But it has developed the liturgy itself as a kind of drama and has made much use of sculpture (above all, the crucifix). As is well known, moreover, medieval Gothic churches were specifically designed to emulate the order of the divinely created cosmos, to represent religious history past and future, to provide a setting for the holy mystery of Communion, and to create a sense of the heavenly Jerusalem. For their part, Protestants have minimized or prohibited images and have often simplified their architecture, partly to enhance preaching. Yet music, and particularly hymnody, plays an especially crucial part in Protestant worship and spirituality. John Calvin (1509–64), though exhorting musical moderation, regarded music as one of God's greatest gifts, endowed with 'almost incredible power'. Martin Luther (1483–1546) placed music second only to theology and the Word of God as deserving of praise.

John Wesley (1703–91) looked on the hymns of his prolific brother Charles (1707–88) as 'practical divinity' expressed in word and song. African-American singing of spirituals and gospel music has exhibited a freedom of expression that carries particular spiritual significance within that community.

Most of the best-known art has for several centuries been created independently of the Church. Accordingly, one pressing question, from the standpoint of religious aesthetics, has to do with what spiritual value to ascribe to nominally secular arts, or possibly to art in general. Unfortunately, when Kant set the tone for the modern approach to aesthetics, he did so in a way that made it difficult to see any intrinsic and intimate connection between aesthetics and spirituality. Kant was intent on establishing the sphere of pure beauty and aesthetic judgement as independent of any considerations of truth or morality, let alone holiness. In Kant's philosophy, the claims of taste are subjective (though universal), and have to do with formal qualities that happen to please us, rather than with concepts of reality or with moral imperatives.

Kant himself acknowledged that the aesthetic symbol can give rise to thought and that art often has secondary ties to other spheres such as religion and morality. Yet when subsequent theorists – such as Benedetto Croce (1866–1952), R. G. Collingwood (1889–1943), and Susanne Langer (1895–1985) – focused on art as expression, intuition and symbolic form, they were inclined to emphasize the autonomy of art. Although acknowledging that artistic forms use 'non-discursive' symbols to shape perceptions related to life, they argued nonetheless that aesthetic feelings and attitudes are essentially and everywhere quite different from ideas, commitments and religious beliefs. And the New Criticism and related movements in literary theory of the mid twentieth century, while often seeing poetry (broadly speaking) as a special way of knowing, sealed it off from other modes of insight or expression. One might say that never before had art been seen as so special, so unique. But neither had it ever been so in danger of seeming superfluous to larger human interests and to a culturally embodied spirituality.

In the last decades of the twentieth century, aesthetics took a decidedly new turn, rejecting the formalism and purism pervasive in so much modernist theory. Postmodern theory – feminist, neomarxist and deconstructionist – uncovered the designs of politics, race, gender, and class hidden in the very fabric of the 'work of art', whose alleged wholeness and self-contained perfection was now deconstructed. Other thinkers, building in part on philosophers such as John Dewey (1859–1952) or Martin Heidegger (1889–1976), or on the theologian Paul Tillich (1886–1965), began to take a more constructive approach, showing how art is integrally involved in cultural meanings (however unstable and shifting) and how even nominally secular art can be spiritually vital, as a primary expression of what Tillich called 'ultimate concern'. At the same time, theology itself was developing a more positive stance toward the body, senses and creation. Spirituality and embodied imagination were interrelated. Recently, moreover, theorists have emphasized the extraordinary diversity of art and its cultural variability, instead of trying to make all genuine aesthetic experience conform to one pattern.

One effect of all this has been to open up a more spacious and flexible approach to aesthetics – one that can be amenable to a fully fledged theology of art or theological aesthetics. Aesthetics has begun to figure more prominently now in ecotheology, liturgy and a spirituality of nature and place. Aesthetics has also contributed to practical theology by returning in a non-elitist mode to the question of taste (broadly conceived), especially when addressing controversies over such matters as church music and worship style. Finally, there has been a resurgence of interest in the theological and moral aspects of beauty itself, often linked now to concerns for social justice, liberation, and peacemaking.

See also **Spirituality and Culture; Spirituality, Liturgy and Worship (*essays*); Architecture and Spirituality; Art and Spirituality; Beauty; Hymns and Spirituality; Images and Spirituality; Literature and Spirituality; Music and Spirituality.**

Hans Urs von Balthasar, *The Glory of the Lord: A Theological Aesthetics*, 7 vols, various translators, San Francisco: Ignatius Press, 1982–89; Jeremy S. Begbie, *Voicing Creation's Praise: Towards a Theology of the Arts*, Edinburgh: T & T Clark, 1991; Frank Burch Brown, *Good Taste, Bad Taste, and Christian Taste: Aesthetics in Religious Life*, New York: Oxford University Press, 2000; John W. de Gruchy, *Christianity, Art, and Transformation: Theological Aesthetics in the Struggle for Justice*, Cambridge: Cambridge University Press, 2001; Richard Viladesau, *Theological Aesthetics: God in Imagination, Beauty, and Art*, New York: Oxford University Press, 1999; Nicholas Wolterstorff, *Art in Action: Toward a Christian Aesthetic*, Grand Rapids, MI: Eerdmans, 1980.

FRANK BURCH BROWN

Affectivity

Contemporary developments enable greater precision on the role of the affections in the spiritual life than is found in most traditional literature.

Bernard Lonergan distinguishes non-intentional from intentional feelings. Non-intentional feelings include states like anxiety and fatigue, which have causes, and trends like hunger and thirst, which have goals. They are non-intentional inasmuch as they do not arise out of an apprehension of their causes or goals or of any object. They occur, and from their occurrence one diagnoses the cause or goal. Intentional feelings are responses to apprehended objects. The major classes of objects to which they respond are, on the one hand, the satisfying or dissatisfying, and, on the other hand, values. The two classes are not mutually exclusive, for what is satisfying may also be truly worthwhile; but they are also not mutually inclusive, for what is genuinely worthwhile may also be disagreeable. The differential is that value carries us to self-transcendence, and on that basis Lonergan distinguishes vital, social, cultural, personal and religious values in an ascending order.

The link between feelings and values highlights the role of feelings in decisions and discernment. Ignatius of Loyola speaks of three times of decision. In each instance affectivity is a criterion of what method to employ and what course of action to choose. In the first time, one has been so moved by God that one has no doubt what to do. In the second, one is agitated and experiences alternations of consolation and desolation, and must practise what Ignatius calls the discernment of spirits. And in the third, one is tranquil and so is antecedently disposed to employ more rational means, such as weighing the pros and cons of the various alternatives.

These moments are exhaustive of all possibilities. Either there are no further questions about what is to be done (first time) or there are (second and third times). And if there are, either one is moved affectively in diverse and conflicting directions (second time) or one is not (third time).

Ignatius identifies the criterion both of what method to employ and of what course of action to choose with what he calls equanimity or equilibrium. Thus, in the second time, when affective apprehension is only of *possible* values, one should choose what leads to equanimity. In the third time, a test is whether one preserves and deepens the equanimity that enabled one to employ this method in the first place. The first time is so clear precisely because it places one in such a state of equanimity that there is no need for further deliberation. (The practice of discernment is also engaged in independently of such moments of decision. Discernment is a matter of noticing constancy in, or departure from, the state of equilibrium.)

But what precisely is this state of equilibrium? It is a ground of affective self-transcendence. More precisely, such equilibrium is constituted not by homeostasis but by the creative tension or functional interdependence of limitation and transcendence. That tension is *felt* in the sensitive psyche, and these feelings are ciphers, indeed criteria, of genuineness. Concupiscence is the tendency to distort the tension in either direction. Sin is capitulation to that tendency. Grace preserves us in the inner harmony felt in the psyche as the equanimity or equilibrium that enables us to transcend ourselves.

The origination of such equanimity is complex, but besides more or less normal favourable circumstances in a person's life, there is the experience that Ignatius calls consolation without a cause. Karl Rahner interprets this as consolation with a content but without an apprehended object. In this sense, consolation without a cause is in its originating moment non-intentional, at least in that it does not arise from the apprehension or representation of any object. One is in love, and then one discovers who it is whom one loves. Subsequent moments, of course, are intentional, and Ignatius tells us we must watch them very carefully.

One way to monitor this course (or to engage in what today is called an examination of consciousness) is by attention to symbolic responses. A symbol is an image of a real or imaginary object that evokes a feeling or is evoked by a feeling. One's affective state can be mediated to oneself by the symbols to which one responds, including the dreams of the morning, in which the subject anticipates engagement in his or her world.

Lonergan identifies sanctifying grace with the dynamic state of being in love with God, loving with God's love, the basic fulfilment of our conscious longings. In proportion to the consistency of that state, affectivity is of a single piece. Religious and affective development converge in their finality when the goal of each is a dynamic and habitual state of being in love.

See also **Discernment; Emotions; Eroticism; Examination of Conscience/Consciousness; Sexuality.**

Robert M. Doran, *Theological Foundations I: Intentionality and Psyche*, Milwaukee: Marquette University Press, 1995; Robert M. Doran, *Theology and the Dialectics of History*, Toronto: University of Toronto Press, 2001, chs 2, 6–10; Bernard Lonergan, *Method in Theology*, Toronto: University of Toronto Press, 1999, pp.

30–41, 57–69, 101–24; Bernard Lonergan, *A Third Collection*, Mahwah, NJ: Paulist Press, 1985, chs 3 ('Mission and the Spirit'), 7 ('Healing and creating in history') and 11 ('Natural right and historical mindedness', esp. pp. 174–5); Karl Rahner, *The Dynamic Element in the Church*, trans. W. J. O'Hara, Montreal: Palm Publishers, 1964, pp. 84–170.

ROBERT M. DORAN

Affirmative Way

The Affirmative Way is knowledge of God and an experience of God disclosed through the Christian mysteries of creation and incarnation. As knowledge of God and as a way of speaking about God, the Affirmative Way holds that the creation is the result of God's activity and that God is truly manifested in the world. However, it also emphasizes that scriptural images and concepts describing God are always analogical. Everything positive in them must be ascribed to God but in a way that preserves the difference between God who is also more than (eminently so, to a higher degree) and 'beyond' any single attribute or naming of God. The Pseudo-Dionysius in the *Divine Names* suggests that the more God is 'like' light, the more likely humans are to create an idol out of an attribute. Thus in the use of affirmations of God, it is always necessary to assume that God is both similar to the affirmation and also dissimilar to it.

The Affirmative Way is often referred to as kataphatic spirituality or mysticism in its distinct way of apprehending God's self-disclosure to the recipient through the transparency of the cosmos, the natural world, the person of Jesus Christ, symbols, relationships and sacramental worship to God in and through created realities. The experience of God is mediated through the creation and human consciousness.

The Affirmative Way is rooted in the conviction that the cosmos is our home and that according to the teaching of the First Vatican Council (1870) 'God ... may be certainly known by the natural light of human reason, by means of created things, because ever since the creation of the world, his invisible nature has been clearly perceived in the things that have been made (Rom. 1.20); but that it pleased his wisdom and bounty to reveal himself and his eternal decrees in another and a supernatural way; as the Apostle says: "In many and various ways God spoke of old to our fathers by the prophets; but in these last days he has spoken to us by a Son" (Heb. 1.1–2)' (*DS* 3004).

The Affirmative Way celebrates the original blessing and goodness of the created world and responds to it with gratitude, praise and even ecstasy. The beauty of the cosmos and of its incredible variety of creatures leads to appreciation, communion and 'mystical amazement'. The creation itself becomes the primordial sacrament of God's presence to humanity. The distinction between God and the created order is maintained through a theology of panentheism, in which everything is *in God* and thus God's presence may be experienced in and through the creation. In a time of ecological devastation and crisis wrought by humanity's failure to realize its interdependence with the earth, this appreciation leads to justice-making and compassion for the earth itself.

Together with the cosmos itself, Christians believe that Jesus is the incarnation of God, the 'image of the invisible God' (Col. 1.15) and that through Christ, believers experience God (John 14.9 and 1 John 1.1–2). As Edward Schillebeeckx asserted, Christ is the primordial sacrament of encounter with God. Thus, a Christ-mysticism is central to the affirmative way for Christians. If Christ is the image of God, and humanity is made in this same image, then the Christian Affirmative Way constitutes the mystical transformation of the Christian into this Christ transparency.

As a way of approaching God, the Affirmative Way includes meditating on the central symbols of faith, especially as described in the Scriptures, often an affective relationship with Jesus fostered through imaginative contemplation of Christ's life, ministry, death and resurrection through texts and/or material images, and through the progressive assimilation of these mysteries through the Eucharist and its liturgical seasons. It may include, together with the creation itself, all of the material culture of Christianity, including sacraments, sacred places, pilgrimage, service, the use of devotional objects, and popular devotions.

It might well be argued that the Affirmative Way is the predominant spiritual path of Christians in their life of faith. As a mystical path, no less than the often preferred apophatic way, mystical experience in this path may develop through an increasing simplicity of interior processes and a deepening transparency of the Christian mysteries to a real union with God through this more holistic and embodied process.

See also **Spirituality, Liturgy and Worship (*essay*); Art and Spirituality; Beauty; Creation Spirituality; Ignatian Spirituality; Incarnation; Kataphatic Spirituality; Nature Mysticism; Pilgrimage; Ritual; Sacramentality and Spirituality.**

Harvey Egan, *Christian Mysticism: The Future of a Tradition*, New York: Pueblo, 1984; Matthew Fox, *Original Blessing: A Primer in Creation Spirituality*, Santa Fe, NM: Bear & Co. Press, 1983; Dorothee Soelle, *The Silent Cry: Mysticism and Resistance*, Minneapolis, MN: Fortress Press, 2001.

JANET K. RUFFING

African Spirituality

1. *The rich history of African Christianity.* The vast African continent is characterized by diversity with various ethnic and cultural groups existing side by side. The rich spiritual traditions of Africa pre-date recorded history, and yet are of value for the twenty-first century, as evidenced by the bourgeoning interest in African spirituality. There is no one single African spirituality due to the fact that Africa boasts a large variety of diverse religions, inter alia, African Traditional Religions, Hinduism, Buddhism, Judaism, Christianity and Islam. Christians now number over 393 million. The African Initiated Churches (AICs), which have over 6,000 denominations in South Africa alone, the largest of which is the Zion Christian Church, portray evidence of a spirituality that is truly culturally based, and is not held hostage to western norms.

Africa's rich spiritual heritage was not always seen in a positive light by Western dualistic scholarship. Early Christian missionaries often ignored the spiritual heritage of the indigenous peoples of Africa. However, from about the 1960s, a distinctly African theology began to take shape, giving academic form to earlier, more 'popular' African Christian preaching, insights and practices. This process was accelerated with the now famous speech of Pope Paul VI to the bishops of Africa in Kampala, Uganda in 1969, in which he stated that African history is 'a drama of charity, heroism, and sacrifice, which makes the African Church great and holy from its very origins'. Highlighting the contribution of early North African writers, inter alia, Tertullian, Origen, Augustine, and Cyprian, Paul VI urged African Christians to give a genuinely African expression to the Christian faith.

Such appreciation of African culture and its value for Christianity came at a time when many African countries were seeking independence from their colonial rulers. It was just the encouragement that African theologians needed to bring the richness of an African world view into dialogue with Christianity. Notwithstanding the aforementioned multiplicity of spiritual traditions in Africa, it is possible to delineate certain general features that constitute an African spirituality. Five elements will be discussed, with particular reference to the interface between African traditional spirituality and African Christian spirituality.

2. *African traditional spirituality and African Christian spirituality.* Although contemporary estimates with respect to the adherents of African Traditional Religion are approximately only about 10 per cent, the culture and spirituality of Africa remains powerful and pervasive. This is clearly seen as follows.

A. *Awareness of the deity.* In African traditional spirituality, prayer is based on the belief that the visible world is influenced by, and indeed dependent on, the invisible world. The Zulu people speak of the Supreme Deity as *Nkulunkulu* (the Great, Great One) who is called upon to assert his/her presence on all of life. Life–death, good–evil, love–hatred, all of these are bound up in the world. Since the deity ultimately triumphs over evil, his/her power is readily available in coping with the exigencies of life. Africans live with a sense of the presence of the deity who can be called upon at any time for help.

African Christians have a strong awareness of the spiritual dimension of life, including God, angels, evil spirits and Satan. Many of Africa's inhabitants live in close proximity to death, suffering, illness, oppression and uncertainty. For African Christians, God is not just a name, still less *deus absconditus*, but a real and powerful presence. Prayer is an appeal to a living God and salvation is understood in concrete terms.

B. *Creation and a holistic world view.* Within the African world view the presence of the deity is manifested in creation. The whole cosmos is an epiphany of the divine; hence, all of creation is good. Concretely, this means that all of creation is sacred and all the fruits of the earth are worthy offerings to the Lord. It is for this reason that some religious groups in Africa worship in sacred groves or forests while others congregate for worship on mountains or near rivers.

African Christian spirituality is holistic and incarnational. There is no separation between the sacred and the secular, the spiritual and the physical. Rather, all of these are woven into a seamless robe of Christian experience. Thus, African preachers such as Archbishop Tutu move effortlessly from prayer to social justice. Religion, morality, dancing, praying, eating, laughing and communal worship – everything from the mundane to the mystical – are all part of African spirituality.

C. *Family/Community.* African spirituality is essentially communal in nature. At birth a person is incorporated into the life of the family and larger community. This gives a profound sense of belonging and a sense of identity which forms the foundation of personal development. Almost all African languages have a proverb that expresses this: *Umuntu ngumuntu ngabantu* (in Zulu): 'A person becomes a person with others.' Therefore, hospitality is an important value in African life, encompassing members of the extended family. It can, however, exclude enemies or strangers who might be potentially dangerous to family interests. As such Christianity challenges this concept of hospitality so as to extend it to all.

African Christian experience is also strongly communal. Participation and belonging to the wider group is central, and particular attention is paid to facilitating harmony and communal well-being. This is particularly true of church services, weddings, funerals, Easter Celebrations (which receive much more attention than the feast of Christmas) and women's or youth meetings. All believers are one in the body of Christ.

D. *Ancestors.* Since Africans live with a profound sense of the bond between the visible and invisible, and due to the value of the extended family, African spirituality has deep respect for the ancestors. Relationships with those who have made a positive contribution to the family, clan or tribe continue after the death of the person. The living members of the community recognize the gifted heritage of the ancestors and thus accord them special veneration. The ancestors become mediators between the living and God, the protectors of the family and the guardians of morality.

In African Christian spirituality, there are intense debates concerning the role of ancestors. At one extreme, the ancestors are embraced as an essential part of African culture and are sometimes seen to be part of the 'great cloud of witnesses' of Heb. 12.1. At the other extreme, they are rejected as part of a pre-Christian past. Some African Christians venerate the ancestors, the *badimo* (in seSotho), as an essential part of their heritage and identity, but not as mediators between themselves and God, since Christ is now the complete sacrifice and mediator.

Certain African scholars portray Christ as the Proto-Ancestor: he is the Mediator, who is ever-present, giving life and watching over his descendants; he is the Eldest Brother of the anointed ones (*Mulaba-Mukulu*), the model to be imitated; he is also Healer and Chief; above all he is the Liberator who brings his people out of suffering into the promised land.

E. *Public worship.* The notion of religious activities separate from other aspects of life is not to be found in traditional African spirituality.

Unlike Christians who gather for public worship on a Sunday, no one particular day is used for public worship. Rather, public gatherings and rites of passage such as birth, puberty, marriage and death are all times of worship, celebration and community interaction.

African Christian spirituality, especially as reflected in public worship, is filled with music, song and rhythmic movement. Popular songs and choruses have simple lyrics, and repetition invites identification with the deeper, experiential meaning of the words, engendering a religious experience and a sense of belonging. The rituals exert a creative power in the lives of worshippers, and there is a strong sense of the immediacy of God's presence.

In many churches, ample opportunity is provided for extempore and individual responses to God. Less formal liturgies express the orality characteristic of traditional African ritual, allowing for participation by a large number of people in public worship. The Bible is important, and African Christians are proud to be 'the people of the book'. Preaching is central, especially in African evangelical and charismatic churches. Exuberant sermons, often using rhetorical devices, such as repetition of key phrases, images, allegories and stories are common, not only in Sunday services, but also at funerals, weddings and other gatherings.

3. *African spirituality and contemporary challenges.* Given the inroads of secularism, the harmonious view of life and relationships, characteristic of traditional African spirituality, is currently under threat, especially among young people. John Mbiti's famous statement that Africans are 'notoriously religious' may no longer strike such a strong chord. Therefore, perhaps two of the most important issues for African Christian spirituality are *inculturation* and *moral formation*. A rediscovery of the foundational values of African culture can enrich Christianity, and can in turn be deepened by gospel values, leading to societal transformation, on the African continent and elsewhere.

African spirituality offers a holistic way of life, and as such can be of benefit to Western Christianity, infusing the latter with insights and experiences that have largely been forgotten in our postmodern world.

E. Fashole-Luke et al. (eds), *Christianity in Independent Africa*, London: Indiana University Press, 1978; John Mbiti, *African Religions and Philosophy*, London: Heinemann, 1969; Burnet Ntsikana, *The Life in Ntsikana: His Prophecies and His Famous Hymn*, Staten Island: Mission

Press, 1902; Jacob K. Olupona, *African Spirituality: Forms, Meanings and Expressions*, New York: Crossroad, 2000; A. Shorter (ed.), *African Christian Spirituality*, New York: Maryknoll, 1978; Elochukwu E. Uzukwu, *Worship as Body Language: Introduction to Christian Worship: An African Orientation*, Collegeville, MN: The Liturgical Press, 1997.

MADGE KARECKI, CELIA KOURIE,
LOUISE KRETZSCHMAR

African-American Spirituality

Africans came to the United States in diverse ways, some directly from Africa as indentured servants or slaves, others by way of 'seasoning' periods in the Caribbean islands of Santo Domingo, Cuba or Jamaica, and some few, as free Africans. However they came, they carried, on their backs, in their minds and within their souls, the richness and texture of lives lived for generations in towns and villages in West and Central Africa.

This heritage was rooted in a spirituality that saw no separation between sacred and secular worlds; all of life and creation were interconnected and sustained by a God of creation. This spirituality provided the foundation for Africans of many nations and tongues to come together as a new people seasoned by slavery and shaped by resistance to society's denial of their humanity. The world view, traditions, stories, musicality and religious beliefs of their African ancestors were preserved, completely in some cases, partially in others, built upon, meshed with new understandings, experiences and ideas, and passed down from generation to generation. Somehow, they were able to retain and maintain many aspects of their African heritage, which enabled them to withstand the trauma of enslavement.

African-American spirituality is a result of the encounter of a particular people with their God in circumstances not conducive to faith. It is their response to God's action in their lives in ways that revealed to them the meaning of God for themselves as well as providing them with an understanding of themselves as beings created by God. Because that encounter was in many ways unique, forged as it was from the systematic oppression and dehumanization that was the life of African Americans for over four hundred years (roughly 1545–1965), their spirituality is also unique, a combination of the influence of diverse cultures (African, Caribbean, Spanish, French and English) and with a persistent emphasis on freedom. African-American spirituality, therefore, cannot be understood without the knowledge and understanding of who African Americans are, how they came into being, and why they have somehow been able to mature, develop and persist as a people of faith in the face of seemingly insurmountable odds.

The African Traditional Religions (ATR) practised by the many people of the West Coast of Africa though differing in some aspects had much in common. There was an acknowledgement of a Creator God who sustained the world and its creations, lesser gods who served as intermediaries between God and the people, and the ancestors who were those deceased that had led lives worthy of respect and veneration. The world was a sacred world full of the presence of the holy and therefore requiring guidance from spiritual leaders who helped the people to live in harmony with the sacred. Religion was not a separate, private entity but communal, instrumental in constructing family and individual identities and building community. Life could not be lived or sustained apart from that community.

This understanding travelled with the slaves through the Middle Passage and remained with them throughout slavery. Evidence of this can be seen in the Afro-Catholic religions of Santeria, Condomble and Vodoun, which simply syncretized African, usually Yoruban, beliefs with Roman Catholicism. However, aspects also remained in the USA in Protestant Christianity as well as especially in the 'praise houses' of the Carolinas where slaves came together to praise God and 'catch' the spirit while participating in a ring shout. The slaves believed that God was with them, protecting them and preparing them for their eventual freedom.

The spirituality of African Americans expresses a hands-on, down-to-earth belief that God saw them as human, created in God's own image and likeness, and intended them to be a free people. It is a spirituality that is often seen as Old Testament in its emphasis on judgement and justice but New Testament in its recognition of Jesus as Liberator. God is a God of righteousness that rights all wrongs, condemns wrongdoing and punishes those doing wrong, yet that same God is a God of justice and love who has experienced poverty and oppression and promises salvation, both here and in the hereafter, to all who believe.

African-American spirituality is contemplative, holistic, joyful and communitarian. It is a spirituality expressed in contemplative prayer and a deeply conscious prayer life that is not passive but leads to action on behalf of justice. Unlike the Western prayer tradition, there is no separation between the sacred and secular worlds; they are interwoven and lived as one

world in which all of life and the holy are intimately engaged. This spirituality calls forth the
joy of knowing and loving God and acknowledges receiving the grace of God in expressive
and ecstatic song, story, dance and preaching. It
is also communitarian in that it serves to weave
together communities of faith made up of those
connected not merely by kinship or blood ties
but by ties of shared oppression and dehumanization. These communities are revealed not just
in worship services but also in activities that give
life to the community, such as educational and
charitable programmes.

African-American spirituality is also grounded
in a devotion to the Holy Spirit and her ability
to create possibility in the face of denial. The
Holy Spirit sustains and nurtures the African-
American community throughout its struggles,
enabling it to express its joy in ways that reveal
the interconnectedness of God and humanity in
a world graced by God yet stained by sin.
Historically, this belief was revealed in those
songs known as spirituals wherein God, named
as Creator and/or Saviour (for usually there is no
distinction between God and Jesus), was called
upon to act and did act in ways that revealed
God's solidarity with those enslaved or in other
ways oppressed. These songs in later years were
found to contain coded messages that provided
guidance for escaping slaves on their way north,
further evidence of how the sacred and secular
worlds were intimately intertwined in their lives.

The spirituality of African Americans is active
and engaged, encouraging them to participate
in their own liberation regardless of risks.
Historically, this was evidenced in every act of
rebellion against the institution of slavery and its
Jim Crow aftermath as well as against any efforts
to impose forms of Euro-American culture that
negated Black humanity. Men and women such
as Richard Allen, founder of the first independent Black Church (African Methodist Episcopal,
1787), and Elizabeth Clovis Lange, founder of
the first Black Catholic women's religious order
(Oblates of Providence, 1829), refused to accept
the biased efforts to restrict the education and
elevation of their Black brothers and sisters.

This resistance was also seen in the Civil
Rights Movement where the faith-based efforts
of African Americans coalesced in a force that led
to the overturning of laws that had supported
centuries of discrimination and racism. The
Reverend Martin Luther King Jr, following in the
footsteps of God-inspired men and women like
Nat Turner, Denmark Vesey, Harriet Tubman,
Sojourner Truth, and countless others, preached,
especially in his 'Letter from Birmingham Jail',
the centuries-old understanding of African

Americans that God was with them in their
struggle, acting in their history to bring about the
elimination of unjust laws and discriminatory
practices against them and supporting them in
their non-violent efforts to right the wrongs of
centuries.

The Black Church, both Protestant and
Catholic, from its beginnings as an 'invisible
institution' (Raboteau, 1978) during slavery,
helped enable African Americans, slave and free,
to grow in their self-understanding as they grew
in their understanding of God. Forced to imbibe
a Christianity that had lost touch with its liberative origins in Jesus Christ, Black preachers,
teachers and elders were able to look beyond
these distortions and recover a Christian faith
that challenged the racist teachings of slave masters, preachers and teachers who falsely taught
that God had ordained their enslavement and
dehumanized treatment.

Born of constant struggle, the spirituality of
African Americans, in the aftermath of the Civil
Rights and Black Power/Nationalism Movements (1956–68) gave birth to a Black theology
of liberation. Grounded in the Black historical
experience, this theology articulated the faith
belief of persons of African descent in the USA, a
faith that denied their stereotyping as a people
without a past, a culture or a faith. God was not
only with them in their struggle; God was one of
them, poor, oppressed and 'Black'. It brought
together the African traditions of the slaves, the
persistence of their belief forged and articulated
in the sermons, prayers and songs of their slave
religion, and the ongoing struggle to stay alive
and move forward that was and continues to be
their experience after slavery. It is a theology of
hope and realism, that recognizes the hand of
God in human history as well as the participation
of Black men, women and children with Jesus in
bringing about that 'new world' where all will
find justice and peace.

Today, the needs of African Americans have
changed as they have finally begun to achieve a
success and status in American society long
denied them. This presents a challenge to the
Black Church and the Black community. Some
have moved away from the Church, no longer
feeling the need for faith or pursuing other
alleged spiritualities that promise wealth and
prosperity while losing sight of the importance of
family and community, while others, left behind
in urban ghettos, have fallen victim to despair.
God, however, is still present and active helping
African Americans to reclaim their spirituality
and adapt it, responding to these new challenges
by revealing to them new ways to be faithful and
encouraging them to reach out to those most in

need in the often impoverished and increasingly unchurched communities around them. This brings a message not of passivity but of active faith rooted in hope and focused on bringing about change in those communities. The African-American encounter with God is not over and as they grapple with new challenges of secularism, homophobia, sexism and classism, they continue to call upon their God to provide them the strength and direction they need in order not to just survive but to thrive.

See also **Spirituality and Culture** (*essay*); **Black Spirituality; North American Spirituality.**

Black Bishops of the US (RC), *What We Have Seen and Heard: A Pastoral Letter*, St Anthony Messenger Press, 1984; Flora Wilson Bridges, *Resurrection Song: African American Spirituality*, Maryknoll, NY: Orbis Books, 2001; William E. B. DuBois, *The Souls of Black Folk*, New York: Bantam Press, reissue edn, 1989 [1903]; Peter Paris, *The Spirituality of Black People: The Search for a Common Moral Discourse*, Minneapolis, MN: Fortress Press, 1994; Jacob Olupona (ed.), *African Spirituality: Forms, Meanings and Expressions*, New York: Herder & Herder, 2001; Albert Raboteau, *Slave Religion: The 'Invisible Institution' in the Ante-bellum South*, New York: Oxford University Press, 1978; Carlyle Fielding Stewart, *Black Spirituality/Black Consciousness: Soul-Force, Culture and Freedom in the African American Experience*, New York: African World Press, 1999.

DIANA L. HAYES

Afterlife

Belief in some form of afterlife is an essential feature of all religions. Indeed, the ultimate goal of every spiritual journey is victory over death through the passage into another realm of being. The world's religions and philosophies have offered various answers to the problem of death, such as reincarnation in Hinduism and Buddhism, metempsychosis in the ancient Greek mystery cults, and the continuation of a person's 'ka' (life force) and 'ba' (unique personality) beyond death in the mortuary cults of ancient Egypt. Based on its Greek and Jewish roots, Christianity developed its belief in the afterlife in terms of the immortality of the soul and the resurrection of the body.

The great insight of Greek philosophy was that humans are not 'mortals' but embodied souls engaged in a movement toward immortality. This view reached its consummate articulation in Plato's dialogues, where the afterlife is depicted mythically and is grounded in a doctrine of moral retribution – as in the later books of the Old Testament, the just alone reap the heavenly reward.

The biblical notion of resurrection derived from the Jewish apocalyptic hope that emerged around the second century BCE. During the Maccabean period, there arose the possibility of an afterlife (Dan. 12.2; 2 Macc. 7.9–14) in contradistinction to the purely this-worldly eschatology of the prophets. This new hope came to fruition around the time of Jesus when various Jewish groups understood afterlife as some form of resurrection, a hope that was tied to the imminent reign of God's kingdom. The definitive historical realization of this eschatological hope was Jesus' own resurrection. However, the New Testament authors were of a sufficient Greek mentality as to express the meaning of resurrection in the language of the immortal soul. Paul, for example, speaks of the movement of human existence beyond its present structure of death as a transformation into an immortal state effected by the grace of God (1 Cor. 15.42–55). Paul conceived of resurrection as the putting on of a spiritual body over our earthly one. His vision of the resurrected Christ assured him that the transfiguration of reality in history had already begun and would soon be fulfilled by Christ's second coming.

With the disappointment in the imminently expected parousia, Paul's eschatology was revised to incorporate his concern with the manner of life that must be lived in order to insure the believer's imperishability. That manner of life is beautifully described in his famous hymn to love (1 Cor. 13) where, of the three theological virtues, *agape* is accorded the highest rank because, as the very essence of God, it outlasts the conditions of existence in this world. Love alone brings us into the sphere of perfection and promises us an imperishable body as we enter the glory that will soon be revealed to us (Rom. 8).

In the Church's early theological thinking on afterlife, Greek immortality and Jewish resurrection merged and were kept in some equilibrium. However, a pronounced shift occurred in the medieval period when the concrete demands of history outstripped the faraway parousia. The unity of body and soul, present and future, and individual and community, began to derail into a dualism. The Greek influence came to predominate. Consequently, the resurrection of the dead, which for Jesus and his Jewish followers had a distinctively communal character, yielded to an emphasis on the immortality of the individual soul. The accommodation with the Greek concept emerged more strongly in the late medieval dogmas, a trend that reached its peak at the Fifth Lateran Council in 1513 when the Church affirmed the immortality of the soul as a dogma of the faith. The Church eventually came to define afterlife as comprising three realms beyond death – heaven, hell, and purgatory – based on their scriptural antecedents and theological development in the patristic period. Because the afterlife is an empirically unknowable reality, to be affirmed only in faith, hope and love, its depiction is ineluctably symbolic and speculative. The human imagination knows no bounds in envisioning its wonders and horrors, as demonstrated in Dante's *Divine Comedy*.

Contemporary theology has steered away from traditional Christianity's mythological portrayal of heaven, hell and purgatory as actual locations populated by spiritual souls with physical properties. Today theologians attempt to penetrate to the spiritual meaning behind the doctrinal utterances by distinguishing between symbolic discourse and religious message. In this light, heaven, hell and purgatory represent destinies of the soul beyond this world in a trajectory of what one is already experiencing in this life. Eschatological statements then are about humans existing *now* in relation to their possible future that is envisioned analogously. There are certain experiences that teach us that our essential humanity is not intrinsically conditioned by space and time, such as an experience of personal love or intense creativity. All love desires eternity, and God's love not only desires it but effects it, even in the midst of suffering and loss. Such was the disciples' experience at the cross followed by the Easter revelation. In this sense then heaven represents the state of perfection constituted by the beatific vision in eternal fellowship with God. Hell is the opposite of God's blessing, the state of being excluded from fellowship with God by the exclusion of God's grace due to sin. Purgatory represents the intermediary realm between this world and heaven, whereby one dwells in a state of purification antecedent to the state of perfection.

To lose one's life is to save it (Mark 8.35). Christianity's hope is not a survival or reincarnation of some remnant of our earthly existence (Mark 12.25; 1 Cor. 15.50), but rather a spiritual transformation of our being through grace in death. It is not coming to life again through resuscitation or reanimation; it is a passage into eternal being. What awaits us in the afterlife is unknowable, but those who abide in love may find solace in the words of Paul: 'No eye has seen, nor ear heard, nor the human heart conceived, what God has prepared for those who love him' (1 Cor. 2.9).

See also **Death and Dying; Eschatology; Hope;** **Redemption; Resurrection; Salvation; Soul.**

———

Monica Hellwig, *What are they saying about Death and Christian Hope?* New York: Paulist Press, 1978; John Hick, *Death and Eternal Life*, Louisville, KY: Westminster John Knox Press, 1994; Morton Kelsey, *Afterlife: The Other Side of Dying*, New York: Paulist Press, 1979; Hiroshi Obayashi (ed.), *Death and Afterlife: Perspectives of World Religions*, New York: Praeger, 1992.

MICHAEL P. MORRISSEY

Agape

The Greek word *agape* is used in the New Testament in order to refer to the Christian understanding of love: God's love and human love. The First Letter to John (1 John 4.8 and 16) describes God as *agape*. In ordinary Greek, the verb *agapao* meant to receive somebody as a guest, to like somebody. *Agape* was to become the distinctive expression for Christian love over against other expressions of love, such as *eros*, a word never used in the New Testament, or *philia*, which means friendship and is used in the New Testament, though not as widely as the words from the *agape* family that appear in every book of the New Testament.

Since the early Church, *agape* can also refer to the Christian table fellowship that in response to Jesus' example has been understood as a community not only of friends. Rather the original Christian table fellowship was to include the outsiders, the others, e.g. customs officers, women, sinners, the sick, the poor, the unclean and the handicapped. This meaning of *agape* picks up the original secular connotation of the term: to welcome somebody generously. In the name of Jesus Christ the Christian community is called to practise a hospitality that transcends the normal social, ethnic, political and religious boundaries. The love feast held by Christians in connection with the celebration of the Lord's Supper was the theological and the social centre of the emerging Church and has remained a powerful and provocative symbol of Christian charity.

There has been much Christian suspicion against the Greek word *eros*. *Eros* could be identified either as the Greek god of love or as Plato's desire for ascent to and union with the ultimate good, beauty and truth. For Plato, only humans can love, the gods cannot since they already possess perfection. The Christian spirituality of love attempted to distance itself from Greek philosophy by stressing the theological experience of a loving God who in Jesus Christ gathers all human beings in an eschatological community characterized by the praxis of *agape*. Thus, *agape* meant more than desire for union; it always includes action on behalf of the other – God and fellow humans.

The debate on the relationship between *eros* and *agape* has been rekindled many times in Christian spirituality though with a somewhat shifting focus. The early Church Fathers explored the connections between the Platonic philosophy of love and Christian spirituality. This exploration reached its climax with Augustine (354–430): on the basis of God's prior act of love, the human being can desire to ascent to the knowledge of the highest good, God. Augustine distinguished between *amor sui*, self-love based on wrong desire, and *amor dei*, love of God based on right desire. The various mystical movements have enlarged the horizon of a spirituality of love by stressing the ecstatic dimensions of love and have thus been able to retrieve passion and aspects of the erotic into Christian spirituality.

Within the framework of a reconstructed Reformation theology, Anders Nygren (1890–1978) identified *agape* as the fundamental motif of Christian faith that found its highest biblical expression in Paul's thinking. Nygren distinguished sharply between *agape* (God's spontaneous and gratuitous love) and *eros* (the human desire and hubris to reach God). *Agape* and *eros* can never be mediated. Nygren's position has been much criticized, partly for overlooking the elements of *eros* implicit in New Testament spirituality, partly for dichotomizing love of God and human self-love and for thus denying human freedom as a necessary condition for love.

Recent phenomenology and feminist thinking have both stressed the significance of the human self's desire for God in Christian love as well as the need to include the human body in any conception of a spirituality of love. The desire to be transformed by God by the praxis of love offers a new matrix for the understanding of body, self, sexuality, eroticism, passion, subjectivity, friendship, and eschatological community.

See also **Charity; Eroticism; Eucharistic Spirituality; Love.**

William Klassen, 'Love: NT and Early Jewish Literature', in *The Anchor Bible Dictionary*, vol. 4, New York: Doubleday, 1992, pp. 381–96; Jean-Luc Marion, *Le phénomène érotique*, Paris: Grasset, 2003; Anders Nygren, *Agape and Eros: The Christian Idea of Love* [1930–36], Chicago: University of Chicago Press, 1982; Gene Outka, *AGAPE: An Ethical Analysis*, New Haven and London: Yale University Press, 1972.

WERNER G. JEANROND

Ageing

1. *Introduction.* Gerontology – the study of ageing – has come to take increasing note of the spiritual lives of older people (see McFadden, 1996). Spiritual belief and practice are seen as resources in combating the losses and stresses which almost inevitably accompany the ageing process. However, much more empirical research is required, preferably conducted in conjunction with scholars in the field of theology and religious studies, into the functioning of religious and spiritual traditions in later life.

In the following sections a brief and necessarily selective review will be given of what the religious traditions themselves have to say about ageing and spirituality, recent empirical evidence on this subject, and the current state of knowledge on spirituality and adaptation to ageing.

2. *Ageing and spirituality in religious traditions.* Up until the latter part of the twentieth century elderly people in most times and places were a small part of the population. Attention to the needs of the elderly and their position in society, however, belied their numerical unimportance. The historical roots of attitudes to old age within Western society have been the subject of much study, but the conclusions are complex (see Minois, 1989). The Hebrew Scriptures provide some of the most influential images of age. The range of themes in these writings is very broad: historical accounts which are realistic in their depiction of power and frailty and which above all demonstrate the importance of family life for all age groups; calls within the prophetic and psalmist writings for greater sensitivity to the needs of elderly people; and explicit focus on the personal dimension of ageing, especially physical deterioration, within the wisdom writers.

Although the New Testament repeats Jewish prescriptions not to neglect the elderly, the much stronger emphasis within Christianity on ongoing life with God beyond death diminished any special importance attributed to reaching old age per se. Terms such as 'life course' emerged towards the end of the Middle Ages as people began to contemplate life as a journey. Disregard of ageing may also have been encouraged by the medieval characterization of Jesus's age of death as 'the perfect age'. Middle age was depicted as the high point of life in representations of the life course with figures ascending and descending a rising and falling staircase.

In the later twentieth century attempts have been made to recover a more profound spiritual view of the meaning of age. The 'rise and fall' model has been criticized for encouraging fear of the losses of ageing without recognition of its strengths and compensations, and for leading the Christian Church to emphasize a 'sustaining' model of pastoral work with older people rather than one which challenges them to give witness and prophecy. A number of Christian writers have looked for inspiration to secular authorities such as the life-span developmental theorist Erik Erikson who proposed a series of ascending psychosocial challenges throughout life, beginning with the emergence of 'trust' in childhood and culminating with 'integrity' in old age. There is need for more profound consideration of Christianity's own traditions, for example, descriptions of the role of 'elders' within the New Testament, within the writings of the early Fathers of the Church, and within desert and monastic spirituality.

Much recent attention has been given to the unbroken tradition of respect and dignity shown to older people within Eastern religions. It is perhaps significant that the original Buddhist insights on the meaning of life were based on explicit confrontation with the painful realities of the deterioration that comes with age. Hindu thinking about age was similarly transformed. But whereas in Buddhism, old age, disease and death came to be seen as the major enemies to be defeated by means of ascetic renunciation of the world throughout life, Hinduism located the meaning of ageing within the context of a broader familial and social model of the stages of life. Ageing is regarded as a final stage of life for which a special task is appropriate. The suffering and losses are a key to the liberation experience. They waken people to reality. The resultant virtues of confrontation with finitude, the wise use of declining powers and abilities, and the creative response to limits are increasingly appreciated by Western thinkers (see Ram-Prasad, 1995).

3. *Associations between age and spirituality in empirical research.* Both the historical and scientific literatures suggest that issues of meaning and spirituality become more salient as people age. It would appear more important for older people to have answers or at least strategies for dealing with questions about life's meaning. Surveys, in the USA, Britain and other countries of Western Europe indicate that age is associated with religious practice and belief. Many of these differences could also be cohort effects reflecting social changes in attitudes to religion particularly over the past century. Longitudinal evidence, although limited in scope, does support the view that non-organizational religious activities such as prayer and religious reading increase in later life.

The most substantial evidence on age differences in uses of religion comes from Kenneth Pargament's research programme on religion and coping in the USA (Pargament, 1997). Older people were more likely to use spiritually based ways of coping (e.g. looking to religion for different ways to handle the problem), do good deeds, seek support from clergy or church members, and try to avoid their problems through religion (e.g. pray or read the Bible to take their minds off the problem). Older people were less likely to voice their discontent with God or the Church and plead with God as ways of coping with their negative events. Of course these too could be cohort rather than age effects.

General conclusions about the relationship between age, religion and spirituality should not be used to mask diversity. Studies have illustrated how older people can abandon as well as embrace the path of religion. Partly this may reflect disillusionment with religious organizations, particularly in their response to older people in times of difficulty such as bereavement. But religious doubts can surface at any age, and it is important to understand their origins and outcomes.

Much stronger than the association with age is that between gender and religion, at least in Western societies. In both old and new forms of religion women practitioners outnumber men. They also rate their own religious activities as more meaningful to them, and they are more likely to turn to religion as a way of coping with life's difficulties. Explanations for these phenomena include women's greater socialization to expression of emotion, and their greater caregiving role and consequent need for support within this role. Religious organizations need to consider their response to the greater longevity of older women and the increasing numbers living alone in an ageing population. They should also reflect on what more could be done to minister to the spiritual needs of men. There is some evidence to support the theory of a gender cross-over effect with advanced age, with men becoming more receptive to belief, and women more sceptical.

4. *Spirituality and adaptation to ageing.* United States studies demonstrate consistent links between religious practices and reduced onset of physical and mental illness, reduced mortality, and likelihood of recovery from or adjustment to physical and mental illness (see Moberg, 2001). Interpreting findings on older people is particularly problematic, however, because religious practice, and especially attendance at religious services, also reflect better functional health. The

literature on religion and ageing also suffers from an absence of studies on those hostile or indifferent to religion, and assessments of the beneficial or other effects of non-religious and non-spiritual perspectives on life's meaning. It is likely that people continue or adopt religious practices in part at least because of the benefit they perceive they obtain from them. Therefore the only fair comparison is with people who claim benefits from other forms of belief, not only from those who find little benefit in religious practice.

It is also important not to rely solely on US studies, that is, on a society with high levels of religiosity. There is some evidence from less religious societies such as Britain that spiritual belief is not necessarily associated with favourable health outcomes. This may reflect differences in degree of belief. Uncertain levels of belief, for example, are known to be associated with death anxiety. Our recent study on older people's adjustment to spousal loss showed higher levels of depression in those with low to moderate levels of strength of spiritual belief than in those with very strong or no beliefs (Coleman et al., 2002). Surveys on religiosity and self-esteem also suggest a curvilinear relationship between self-esteem and religious coping. Feelings of self-worth tend to be lowest for those with a little religious involvement.

A significant feature of current research on adaptation to ageing is the differentiation between adaptive and maladaptive religious coping and the construction of appropriate measures. Some American gerontologists have even argued that a concept of 'positive spirituality' should be included in normative models of 'successful ageing'. It would seem very important to involve theologians in this work so that the measures employed do justice to the complexity of religious experience, in which negative and positive thought and feeling are often interrelated.

Future research in this field should also give more attention to comparing different religious groups and cultures, rather than proceeding on the assumption that all types of religion function in the same way. Any comparative work, inevitably controversial, has to be preceded by careful description of religious cultures. An illuminating example of such work in the field of ageing studies is Rory Williams' *A Protestant Legacy*, a detailed study on attitudes to death and illness among older Aberdonians (Williams, 1990).

P. G. Coleman, F. McKiernan, M. Mills and P. Speck, 'Spiritual belief and quality of life: the experience of older bereaved spouses', *Quality in Ageing: Policy, Practice and Research* 3 (2002), 20–6; S. H. McFadden, 'Religion and spirituality' in J. E. Birren (ed.), *Encyclopedia of Gerontology*, vol. 2, San Diego: Academic Press, 1996, pp. 387–97; Georges Minios, *History of Old Age: From Antiquity to the Renaissance*, trans. Sarah Hanbury Tenison, Chicago, IL: University of Chicago Press, 1989; D. O. Moberg (ed.), *Aging and Spirituality: Spiritual Dimensions of Aging Theory, Research, Practice, and Policy*, New York: Haworth Press, 2001; K. I. Pargament, *The Psychology of Religion and Coping: Theory, Research, Practice*, New York: Guilford Press, 1997; C. Ram-Prasad, 'A classical Indian philosophical perspective on ageing and the meaning of life', *Ageing and Society*, 15 (1995), 1–36; R. Williams, *A Protestant Legacy: Attitudes to Death and Illness among Older Aberdonians*, Oxford: Clarendon Press, 1990.

PETER G. COLEMAN

Allegory

Allegorical interpretation (*allegoresis*) emerged in the early centuries of Christianity as the dominant spiritual method for the reading of the Bible. The original Greek word, *allegorein*, 'to interpret allegorically', derives from *allos*, 'other', and *agoreuein*, 'to proclaim in the assembly [*agora*]'. To allegorize was to publicize a meaning other than the obvious or literal one, revealing a meaning supposedly hidden *in* the text and *from* the reader. It was also a way of retrieving from obscure narratives a meaning with universal significance, since an allegorical reading offered readers an intelligible meaning from such texts. Such interpreters, according to Philo, were not 'citizens of a petty state' accessible through the literal sense but rather belonged among 'citizens of a greater country, namely, this whole world' (*De somniis* 1.7,39).

The origin of allegorical reading in the ancient world can be traced to the sixth century BCE, among pre-Socratic interpretations of Homeric texts. These texts sought to rescue a philosophically legitimate meaning from the crude and immoral stories about the gods. The approach distinguished what was written, in the text's plain sense, from what was presumed to be its true philosophical meaning. The plain sense of a text, in other words, comes to serve as the occasion for an interpretation which reveals the text's deeper meaning. The apostle Paul borrowed this widely used method in order to interpret 'Scripture' (i.e., the Old Testament). He establishes the rationale for this method with his claim that 'whatever was written in former days was written for our instruction' (Rom. 15.4). Biblical texts had an original historical meaning, but their true spiritual meaning depended upon an interpretation that pointed to Christian fulfilment. Paul utilized allegorical interpretation in reading the Genesis narrative of Sarah and Hagar (Gen. 21.8–21; see Gal. 4.24), interpreting the two women and the mountains of Zion and Sinai as types of the old and new covenants. He applies a similar allegorical approach in order to locate typological texts of Scripture in the letters to the Corinthians (see, for example, 1 Cor. 5.6–8, and 9.8–14, 10.1–5; 2 Cor. 3.12–18).

In the early Church Fathers, varieties of allegorical or spiritual interpretation prevailed in the exposition of Scripture. This was influenced in part by the dominant influence of a Platonic world view, which distinguished the realm of unchanging truth from the vicissitudes of history and experience. These authors self-consciously identified their use of this method with the Pauline precedent. Origen, for example, spoke of 'the hidden splendour of doctrines concealed in the lowly and contemptible literal phrase'. Allegorical reading as a spiritual form of interpretation sought to understand 'the meaning' hidden in the mere words, since 'the treasure of the divine meanings remains enshrined in the frail vessel of the humble letter' (alluding to 2 Cor. 4.7; see De principiis 4.1.7; 4.3.14). He also refers to 'our allegories, which Paul has taught' (In Genesin 3.5), using allegorical reading in order to discover 'a sense worthy of God' when the plain meaning of the narrative suggested 'offensive features, stumbling blocks, and impossibilities' that interpreters could not properly ascribe to God (De principiis 4.2.9). Jerome's phrase, 'according to the allegory, that is, the spiritual understanding', is characteristic of this tendency (see In Amos, PL 25, 1025D); he could still presume to contrast the breadth and depth of allegorical reading with what he called 'the thin lines of history' found in a biblical text (PL 25, 1063D). Augustine offers a subtle deepening of this approach, suggesting that allegorical reading discerns not only the meaning of language but of events: 'Where the apostle calls something 'allegory,' he finds it not in the words but in the fact' (On the Trinity 15.9.1). He follows Jerome's lead in comparing history and allegory, suggesting that these terms designate the difference between 'fact' and 'mystery' (On John's Gospel 50.6).

The allegorical approach to biblical interpretation became the dominant exegetical method in early Christian exegesis, establishing Scripture as the object of a spiritual form of reading. As such it remains the foundation for theological study until the central Middle Ages. This interpretive method was not simply one means of reading biblical texts. It established the

basic spiritual approach used by interpreters. Throughout the broad period leading toward modernity, allegorical, moral and anagogical interpretations establish the texture for the spiritual engagement with Scripture. In fact, Hugh of St Victor describes the literal sense, by which he meant grammar and history, as the wax of the honeycomb; the honey gained through the reader's chewing (ruminatio) of the text represents the spiritual senses of allegory, which was primarily useful for theology, and tropology, which established the basis for preaching. The approach found its classic expression in the formulation: 'The letter teaches events, allegory tells us what we should believe, morality what we should do, and anagogy points to life's goal.' Henri de Lubac has recently described the denouement of this development in the 'mystical tropology' that flowered in twelfth-century Cistercian exegesis. At the hands of monastic interpreters, the hermeneutical task was not only that of ascribing a Christian meaning to an originally Jewish text but rather that of discerning a transformation of meaning based upon the monastic conversion of life (conversatio morum). By this means, one left behind sinful worldly habits and entered into a life shaped by the spiritual virtues of monasticism (see Medieval Exegesis 9). With the rise of the universities as the new context for academic theology, this approach adapts to different sensibilities through an increased emphasis upon the literal sense. Thus, with Thomas Aquinas and the mendicant theologians more broadly, we find an expansion of the literal sense to include figurative readings, together with a steady diminishment of allegorical interpretation (see, for example, ST 1a. 1.10.) This tendency of spiritualizing the literal sense, and the consequent diminishment of the so-called spiritual senses, gains momentum among Renaissance humanists interested in the historical meaning of ancient texts.

Early Protestants, particularly those trained in these circles, continued this tradition. Their theological programme 'back to the sources' (ad fontes) usually meant not simply an emphasis of ancient sources such as the Bible but also a retrieval of the historical meaning of these texts. For Reformed interpreters like Zwingli and Calvin, the spiritual meaning of a given text is to be found within the historical sense. The rise of historical criticism during the nineteenth century moves away from the spiritual readings of a text (i.e., its traditioned meaning), and largely abandons allegory as a proper method of exegesis. Philip Schaff speaks for this departure when he disparages 'the wild allegorical exegesis' that 'turns the Bible into a nose of wax and makes it to teach anything pious or orthodox'. Spiritual reading continues to find legitimacy among Roman Catholic scholars in this period, influenced as they were by an ecclesial reading valuing the traditional readings of the early Fathers and medieval doctors. This found expression in their quest for a *sensus plenior* alongside historical readings. But even this tendency wanes with the reforms in biblical scholarship stimulated by the Second Vatican Council, effecting a renewed emphasis upon the critical study of Scripture in order to establish a scholarly legitimate and ecumenically fruitful approach to scripture studies.

Allegorical reading has been largely discredited in modern biblical scholarship. But it is still true that interpreters standing within the Church's life of prayer and sacrament approach the text not strictly as a historical source. It remains for them a witnessing text belonging to the Church as a confessional community. This offers a certain parallel to allegorical reading, that is, as a proclamation of 'another' meaning in and for 'the [Christian] assembly'. Griffiths (1999) suggests that our culture stands in need of retrieving a lost form of 'religious reading', one based on a spiritual engagement with authoritative texts characterized by 'the basic metaphors . . . of discovery, uncovering, retrieval, opening up' (p. 41). In this sense, the interpreter discerns meaning not in or behind a text but also *before* a text (Schneiders, 1999, pp. 157–79). Such a spirituality of reading approaches Scripture as a historical and witnessing text, and thus as revelatory in a manner not limited by its presumed original meaning. It carries, in other words, both a historical and experiential sense, the latter shaped by later sensibilities including those conveyed by the spiritual and theological insights of the earlier tradition. Such an approach carries distinct echoes to ancient and medieval allegorical reading, since it acknowledges the importance of the dialogue that occurs between what might be called the text's original and the acquired meanings arising from later contexts.

See also **Spirituality and Scripture** (*essay*); **Exegesis, Spiritual; Medieval Spirituality in the West; Early Christian Spirituality;** *Lectio Divina.*

Mark Burrows, '"To taste with the heart": allegory, poetics, and the deep reading of Scripture', *Interpretation* 56 (2002), 168–80; Henri de Lubac, *The Four Senses of Scripture*, vol. 2 of *Medieval Exegesis*, Grand Rapids, MI, and Edinburgh: Eerdmans, 2000; G. R. Evans, *The Language and Logic of the Bible: The Earlier Middle Ages*, Cambridge: Cambridge University Press, 1984; Karlfried Froehlich (ed.), *Biblical Interpretation in the Early Church*, Philadelphia, PA: Fortress Press, 1984; Paul Griffiths, *Religious Reading: The Place of Reading in the Practice of Religion*, New York and Oxford: Oxford University Press, 1999; Sandra Schneiders, *The Revelatory Text: Interpreting the New Testament as Sacred Scripture*, Collegeville, MN: The Liturgical Press, 1999; Beryl Smalley, *The Study of the Bible in the Middle Ages*, Notre Dame, IN: University of Notre Dame Press, 1964; Jon Whitman, *Allegory: The Dynamics of an Ancient and Medieval Technique*, Cambridge, MA: Harvard University Press, 1987.

MARK S. BURROWS

Alcoholics Anonymous

see Addictions and Spiritual Recovery

Alumbrados

The term *alumbrado* (lit: 'enlightened', 'illumined') seems to have originally been one of mockery and abuse used to denote 'excessive piety and to suggest hysteria and hypocrisy and fraudulence' (Hamilton, 1992, p. 28). At the beginning of the sixteenth century it began to be associated in Spain with a loose-knit group who were condemned at various times by the Church and state. The propositions for which they were condemned were first collected together in the Edict of Faith issued by the Inquisitor General, Alonso Manrique (Archbishop of Seville) on 23 September 1525. The edict contained 48 propositions directed against '*alumbrados, dexados e perfectos*' (lit. 'the enlightened, abandoned and perfect'), which comprised a collection of questionable and heretical statements held by and attributed to the group. As well as certain apocalyptic statements they included propositions such as 'prayer must be mental and not vocal'; the denial of the necessity of any sacramental intermediary between God and humans – thus rejecting the efficacy of external works as well as the authority of the Church to interpret Scripture; contempt for the cult of the saints, the worship of images, bulls, indulgences, fasting and abstinence. Although the propositions for which *alumbrados* groups would be condemned over the next hundred years varied, these early condemnations set the pattern for much of what was to come. That is, the *alumbrados* were seen as a sect denying the authority of the Church in a whole host of matters, emphasizing personal salvation, especially through direct prayer, to the detriment of works and often having a special place for women and Jewish *conversos* ('new' Christians with Jewish ancestry). A key phrase used in the condemnation was *dejamiento* (lit.

'abandonment') which was used to describe the type of prayer advocated by the *alumbrados*. It is unclear what exactly was meant by the term. However, it seems to have arisen as a variant of the prayer of *recogimiento* (lit. 'gathering together') popularized and taught by reforming Spanish Franciscans at the beginning of the sixteenth century, most notably described in Francisco de Osuna's *Third Spiritual Alphabet*. The teaching of *recogimiento* placed an emphasis on the importance of withdrawing from activity once or twice a day, usually to a dark room, for quiet contemplation with lowered or closed eyes. The teaching of *dejamiento*, often ascribed to Isabel de la Cruz, suggested that such a withdrawal was unnecessary and the contemplation could continue in all states and places – even allowing evil thoughts and temptations to arise. It is notable that many of the *alumbrados* were associated with Franciscan groups.

It was for the above activities, then, that the first group of *alumbrados* were arrested and tried in Toledo in 1524: Isabel de la Cruz, Pedro Ruiz de Alcaraz, Maria de Cazalla and Gaspar de Bedoya as well as many others. These arrests and trials would continue for the next 15 years. The group was centred on Guadalajara and Escalona and contained a high number of Jewish *conversos* and lay women. Condemned to public penance in the streets of Toledo, Guadalajara, Escalona and Pastrana they were ordered to enter 'perpetual reclusion'. However, in most cases this ended after ten years or so.

The inquisitors seemed somewhat divided after this first trial of *alumbrados* and their ambiguity over the importance and origins of the heresies remained. Later commentators have equally been divided over whether the group was a 'movement' of interior Christianity akin to Erasmianism (Bataillon) or a native, heretical Protestant sect with justification by faith as their basic doctrine (Márquez). Hamilton, following Márquez, suggests their emphasis on the working of the Spirit in the individual, their pessimism about human nature, their interest in St Paul and their quest for greater simplicity in religion ally them to the movement of Catholic reform at the time of the northern European Reformation, known as *evangelism*.

Despite this ambiguity the charge of *alumbradismo* was something that would be used by the Inquisition for the rest of the sixteenth century and into the seventeenth century. After the first trials of Toledo the only other significant groups to be tried were those found over fifty years later in Extremadura and Andalusia. These groups, known as the '*alumbrados* of Llerena' (in the late seventeenth century) and the '*alum-*

brados of Seville' (in the early seventeenth century) had certain similarities with the earlier groups but tended to emphasis a teaching of antinomianism, that is, that they had attained such a state of perfection that they could not sin. They emphasized spectacular acts of ecstasy, raptures and trances and, according to the Inquisition's accounts, indulged in various and diverse sexual acts.

The effects of the movement were far-reaching from the point of view of the study of Spanish spirituality of the sixteenth century – largely negative. St Ignatius of Loyola was accused of *alumbradismo* tendencies several times both in Alcalá and Salamanca where his attachment to groups of women and emphasis on individual study of the Scriptures were considered suspect. It is noteworthy that the final text of the *Spiritual Exercises* omits the meditation on the coming of the Holy Spirit at Pentecost. Likewise, SS Teresa of Avila and John of the Cross were both at different times accused of the heresy. The Fourth Mansion of Teresa of Avila's *Interior Castle* contains a detailed account of the advantages of *recogimiento* prayer over forms more akin to *dejamiento*.

The charge of *alumbradismo* lingered on into the late seventeenth century when it was usually associated with claims of false mysticism, imposture and excess until it was gradually replaced by claims of Quietism and Molinosism.

See also **Mysticism** (*essay*); **Carmelite Spirituality; Ignatian Spirituality; Sufism and Christianity.**

M. Bataillon, *Erasmo y España*, Mexico: Fondo de cultura económica, 1982; A. Hamilton, *Heresy and Mysticism in Sixteenth Century Spain: The Alumbrados*, Cambridge: James Clarke, 1992; H. Kamen, *The Spanish Inquisition*, London: Weidenfeld and Nicolson, 1997; A. Márquez, *Los alumbrados: orígenes y filosofía (1525–1559)*, Madrid: Taurus, 1980; *Francisco de Osuna: The Third Spiritual Alphabet*, CWS, trans. Mary E. Giles, New York: Paulist Press, 1981.

PETER TYLER

Almsgiving

see **Practice, Spiritual**

Anabaptist Spirituality

The sixteenth-century reforming movement called Anabaptism received its name because its adherents opposed infant baptism and practised adult baptism, following confession of faith, as a sign of repentance, rebirth and commitment to live a new life. The first known adult baptism took place in Zurich, Switzerland in January of 1525. Anabaptists soon were found up and down the Rhine, from Switzerland to the Netherlands and to Poland in the east, south to Moravia and Austria and points in between, resolutely opposed by Catholic and Protestant authorities alike.

Anabaptist spirituality is given expression in the booklets, songs, letters, anthologies and collections of Scripture passages they compiled for the edification of church members. Some of this literature was printed; more was circulated in handwritten copies. These sources are supplemented by judicial transcripts still extant in European archives, in which many thousands of arrested and imprisoned Anabaptists give testimony to their faith and practice, often under threat of torture and impending death. Remarkably, in spite of the lack of centralized leadership, Anabaptist testimonies reveal a coherent spiritual path, integrating an inner process of spiritual transformation with a clear understanding of the expected outward 'fruit' of the inward change. This spiritual path was constructed, defended and taught with biblical materials, interpreted and organized in a recognizably Anabaptist way. The surviving Anabaptist traditions (the Swiss Brethren – later also the Amish – the Mennonites and the Hutterites) came to agree on most crucial interpretive issues, with relatively minor differences, and outlined very specific 'rules of discipleship' for their members. These mature Anabaptist traditions have been handed on to succeeding generations down to the present day.

Anabaptism emerged as a Reformation movement, but Protestant principles were developed in a unique manner. Anabaptists insisted that spiritual regeneration and the living of a new and holy life were necessary and visible correlatives to saving faith. Such teaching was denounced by mainline Protestants as 'a new sort of monkery'. In many important ways the Anabaptists uniquely fused late medieval, christocentric, ascetic piety with biblicist Reformation principles.

Early witnesses report that Anabaptist preachers (men and women) called individuals to repentance and conversion. In many cases the call to repentance elicited emotional responses of contrition from hearers, and requests for baptism as a sign of repentance and the intention to live a new life. Anabaptists urged their listeners to 'fear God' and turn away from self-will and the world. The sinner's only hope was to accept the Good News, trusting in the saving power of Christ crucified. The Anabaptists were convinced that God would turn away no sincerely penitent person. The impediments to a spiritual life, they believed, were not 'predestined' by God, but self-chosen. Blocking the efficacious reception of God's grace were self-will, love of the flesh, love of the world, love of ease and comfort, and fear of the consequences of a full commitment of faith – that is, fear of the high cost of being a true follower and disciple of Christ in word and deed.

The Anabaptists spoke not of 'faith alone', but of the 'obedience of faith'. True faith entails a new birth, a spiritual regeneration by God's grace and power; 'believers' are those who have become the spiritual children of God. The beginning of the Anabaptist path to salvation was thus marked not by a forensic understanding of salvation by 'faith alone', but by the entire process of repentance, self-denial, faith, rebirth and obedience. It was this process that was marked by the biblical sign of baptism.

Some of the central themes and attitudes of an earlier mystical tradition were appropriated (and modified) by the Anabaptists, particularly in the way the initial stages of the spiritual path were understood and described. Central among these was the cultivation of an attitude of *Gelassenheit* (yieldedness; abandonment, the quintessential Christlike virtue) and 'the birth of Christ within'. These christocentric emphases were heartily embraced by the Anabaptists. Given the 'birth of Christ within', the mystical and the Anabaptist traditions expected the same virtues of Christ's nature to be reflected in the reborn: humility, patience, complete yieldedness to the will of God, perfect love, obedience.

Setting out on the narrow way of salvation through repentance, self-denial, trust, rebirth and obedience was a commitment that fell to every man and woman personally – no infant could repent, be reborn, or promise to live a new life in obedience to Christ. In their emphasis on spiritual regeneration the Anabaptists shared an important point of departure with contemporary spiritualists, such as Caspar Schwenckfeld and Sebastian Franck. Nevertheless, unlike the spiritualists, the Anabaptists were convinced that the Christian life could not be private, subjective or individual, but rather would necessarily be lived in full view of the world, in the incarnate body of Christ in the world, the Church. Water baptism marked the beginning of the outer life and witness to the new spiritual being in Christ.

Many early Anabaptists spoke of a threefold baptism of Spirit, water and blood. The 'baptism of the Spirit' pointed to the inward process of repentance, yielding and rebirth – the true and efficacious baptism. Nevertheless, persons baptized by the Spirit would testify to their new spiritual birth by water baptism, as commanded (and exemplified) by Christ himself. Water baptism in the Anabaptist understanding was the visible, outward seal and testimony, before the believing community, that a covenant had been made with God in the heart to turn away from self-will and to accept God's will in all things, following after Christ in obedience even unto death. The public commitment and promise of water baptism was a 'testimony of a good conscience before God', a public seal of the spiritual baptism which preceded.

In the second place, the sign of water baptism was a covenant made with the Church that confirmed an individual's intention to join the body of Christ as a full member. And finally, water baptism testified that an individual was now ready to accept the possibility of the baptism of blood – the suffering to be expected by those who publicly follow the crucified Christ. Given the intense persecution suffered by the early Anabaptists because of their adherence to adult baptism, the baptism of blood was a real possibility that had to be faced before the acceptance of water baptism.

Water baptism was central to Anabaptist spirituality, not because of any sacramental function (the water conveyed no grace), but because this public, outlawed sign testified to an individual's experience of spiritual regeneration and linked that inner experience to a visible, continuing life as a member of the body of Christ in the world. The 'Anabaptist' label, although it focused on the secondary act of water baptism, was in the end not an ill-chosen name to describe the movement, especially when 'baptism' was understood to encompass baptism in Spirit, water and blood.

The visible practice of Anabaptist spirituality was to have both individual and collective expressions. Baptized individuals were expected to manifest a Christlike life, measured by the biblical witness of Christ's words and example. In the first place, members of Christ's body were expected to be ready to share their material goods with those in need. Communal sharing was the Anabaptist norm. In the second place, Jesus' words that one's speech is to be 'yes' and 'no' (Matt. 5.33–37) were taken not only as forbidding the swearing of oaths, but even more, as enjoining truthfulness: those who are pure of heart will speak and live truthfully. Finally, the vast majority of Anabaptists (there were some early exceptions) believed and practised 'nonresistance to evil' in their manner of living, avoiding litigation or participation in warfare and violence. As Christ allowed himself to be led to the cross, so also the members of his body were expected do likewise. Being reborn by the power of God was expected to bear the visible spiritual fruit of compassionate, sharing love,

truthfulness and peaceableness, a mirror image of Christ himself.

Individual expressions of a reborn nature were cemented by communal practices in the 'communion of saints', the Church. Anabaptist Church practices attempted to reflect New Testament command and practice. The initial commitment of baptism reflected the command in Matt. 28.19–20 and Mark 16.15–16; it was celebrated in the community and was understood to signify a commitment to live a new Christlike life, as outlined above. Baptism also bound members to fraternal admonition and discipline (the Ban), following the directions given in Matt. 18.15–17. The celebration of the Lord's Supper was limited to baptized members, and was preceded by an examination of relationships and the 'worthiness' of participants (1 Cor. 11.23–29). The celebration of the Supper commemorated Christ's sacrifice, but also recalled and celebrated again the covenant of Christ's living members with Christ the head and with each other. By the middle of the sixteenth century, the celebration of the washing of one another's feet began to be observed in Anabaptist communities, following Christ's practice and command, as a sign of humility and willingness to share all things with the members of Christ's body (John 13.1–15). Anabaptist ecclesial practices were based on direct New Testament commands, but also were communal occasions for commitment and recommitment to the spiritual path of repentance, yieldedness, rebirth and a new life that set out to follow after Christ in obedient discipleship.

Approximately 2,500 Anabaptists were martyred from 1525 to 1600. Surviving testimonies give witness to the spiritual disciplines that sustained these martyrs. These disciplines centred first of all on the words of Scripture, remembered, recalled and internalized to an astounding degree. Anabaptist prisoners (many admitting illiteracy) frustrated clergy and ruling authorities with copious biblical texts; the Bible was their rule of life. Anabaptists also were noted for fervent prayers of the heart, with a particular fondness for the Lord's Prayer, interpreted in typically Anabaptist ways. Finally, Anabaptists composed literally thousands of hymns which they set out to sing 'in a spiritual manner', recalling words and examples from Scripture as well as their own teachings and their history of martyrs and witnesses. Their clandestine worship services were occasions for strengthening their faith collectively through prayer, preaching and song.

Anabaptist spirituality was thus penitential, regenerationist, communal, biblical and christocentric. The Anabaptist witness was to live simply and with integrity in this world, enabled by

God's grace, according to the principles of the kingdom announced by Jesus.

See also **Baptist Spirituality; Reformation and Spirituality.**

Primary sources: Cornelius J. Dyck (trans. and ed.), *Spiritual Life in Anabaptism*, Scottdale, PA: Herald Press, 1995; Daniel Liechty (trans. and ed.), *Early Anabaptist Spirituality: Selected Writings*, New York: Paulist Press, 1994; Robert A. Riall (trans.) and Galen A. Peters (ed.), *The Earliest Hymns of the Ausbund: Some Beautiful Christian Songs Composed and Sung in the Prison at Passau, published in 1564*, Kitchener, ON: Pandora Press, 2003; Thielman J. van Bragt, *The Bloody Theater or Martyrs Mirror of Defenseless Christians*, trans. Joseph Sohm, Scottdale, PA: Herald Press, 1950.

Secondary sources: Timothy George, 'The spirituality of the radical Reformation' in Jill Raitt (ed.), *Christian Spirituality. High Middle Ages and Reformation*, New York: Crossroad, 1987, pp. 334–71; Walter Klaassen, *Anabaptism: Neither Catholic nor Protestant*, 3rd edn, Kitchener, ON: Pandora Press, 2001; C. Arnold Snyder, *Following in the Footsteps of Christ. The Anabaptist Tradition*, Traditions of Christian Spirituality Series, London: Darton, Longman & Todd/New York: Orbis Books, 2004; C. Arnold Snyder, 'Mysticism and the shape of Anabaptist spirituality' in C. Arnold Snyder (ed.), *Commoners and Community: Essays in Honour of Werner O. Packull*, Kitchener, ON: Pandora Press, 2002, pp. 195–215; George H. Williams, 'German mysticism in the polarization of ethical behavior in Luther and the Anabaptists', *Mennonite Quarterly Review* 48 (July 1974), 275–304.

C. ARNOLD SNYDER

Analogy

Struck by the fact that the same term is often used for things that otherwise seem quite different, philosophers applied themselves to understanding the basis for this. Analogy refers to theories about these uses of language, particularly, but not only, in relation to God. Although his account of theological language in *Summa Theologiae* 1.13 has become the classical starting point for reflection on analogy, Thomas Aquinas usually prefers the adverbial term 'analogically' (*analogice*) although he uses the nominal form 'analogy' (*analogia*) also.

The analogical use of language in relation to God contrasts with metaphorical use on the one hand and with univocal and equivocal predication on the other. Most of our language about God is metaphorical. The statements that God is a rock or a fortress are clearly not to be understood literally while at the same time they express something true about the character of God in relation to God's people.

When terms such as 'good' and 'wise' are used of God it seems inadequate to regard them simply as metaphors. The negation of the metaphor – for example, 'God is not a rock' – leaves us untroubled whereas the negation of terms such as these – for example, 'God is not good' – obliges us to think again. Justice is done to the intention of the speaker in these cases only where such terms are understood literally of God.

But how can this be? It seems to involve some kind of blasphemy to think that the attributes of God might be caught and held within human language and within the human modes of thinking to which that language gives expression. At the same time scriptural and philosophical traditions support the possibility of human discourse about God. The alternative seems to be silence or a purely negative understanding of theological language. This is not the position taken by Christian philosophers and theologians for whom the use of such language for God is neither univocal (meaning exactly the same) nor equivocal (meaning something totally different). It is rather 'analogical'.

The understanding of analogy developed from the application of a threefold way of talking about God that had been received from later Greek philosophy but that was also supported by Scripture. This threefold way works as follows. Because God is the cause of all that is, things may legitimately be said of God from our experience of the world, for example that God is powerful. This first step is supported by St Paul's comment in Romans, 'ever since the creation of the world his eternal power and divine nature, invisible though they are, have been understood and seen through the things he has made' (1.20).

The second step is based on the belief that God is the transcendent cause of the world, in other words God is the source of everything while not himself being a part or element within the world. God is then said to be 'more than powerful' or 'super-powerful' to indicate that the quality we feel obliged to attribute to God is attributed in a way that is beyond its use at our creaturely level. This step is supported by, for example, the words of Isaiah, 'as the heavens are higher than the earth, so are my ways higher than your ways and my thoughts than your thoughts' (55.9).

The third step is based on the need to negate what is affirmed of God in order to discount the claim that human thinking and speaking can catch or hold the divine nature. This *via negativa* is an essential aspect of human discourse about God and there may be times when this is the aspect of theological language which needs most emphasis. It is supported by, for example, the paradox implied in Ex. 16.10, 'the glory of the Lord appeared in the cloud'.

Some strands of mystical and spiritual experience within Christianity testify to the *via negativa*, that God is not any of the things we think, imagine, experience or say about God. The theological tradition supports this too while situating the *via negativa* within a full understanding of theological language where positive and negative are complementary. In Pseudo-Dionysius this takes the form of a dialectic involving positive and negative moments. In Thomas Aquinas it takes the form of a carefully worked out account of analogical predication whereby we know what we mean to say about God but do not know how what we mean to say is actually found in God.

The most important criticisms of analogy emerge from the concern that it inevitably involves some kind of univocation, bringing the divine and the creaturely within a shared conceptuality in order to compare them. For proponents of analogical predication it is true that creatures may be said to be like God but in no way may God be said to be like creatures.

See also **Apophatic Spirituality; Aristotelianism; God, Images of; Scholasticism.**

David B. Burrell, *Knowing the Unknowable God: Ibn Sina, Maimonides, Aquinas*, Notre Dame, IN: University of Notre Dame Press, 1986; Ralph McInerny, *Aquinas and Analogy*, Washington, DC: The Catholic University of America Press, 1996; Edward Schillebeeckx, 'The non-conceptual intellectual dimension in our knowledge of God according to Aquinas' in *Concept of Truth and Theological Renewal*, London and Sydney: Sheed & Ward, 1968, pp. 155–206; Janet Martin Soskice, *Metaphor and Religious Language*, Oxford: Clarendon Press, 1985.

VIVIAN BOLAND

Anchorites

see Eremitical Spirituality

Anglican Spirituality

The publication of the anthology of text, *Love's Redeeming Work: The Anglican Quest for Holiness*, in 2001 was a sign of the growing interest in the subject of post-Reformation Anglican spirituality. The volume is the first major collection of material on this subject brought together from the period from the mid sixteenth to the late twentieth century. Putting texts together in this way reveals unexpected facts. To give one example, a perusal of the index reveals that the word 'Eucharist' merits more entries than any other word in the volume. The strongly sacramental character of Anglican spiritual life, increasingly evident since the revival which began in the 1830s, was evidently also characteristic of the earlier periods of post-Reformation Anglican history.

This emphasis on liturgy and sacrament evident throughout the collection brings us at once to the consideration of the one book which, after the Bible, has been central to the spiritual life of the Anglican Churches, *The Book of Common Prayer*. Archbishop Rowan Williams, in his introduction to the first section of the work, points to some of the paradoxical characteristics of that book which have brought this about. There is a quality both Catholic and Protestant, which flows from the pen of Archbishop Cranmer himself, which has had consequences which that writer may neither have foreseen nor altogether desired. Rowan Williams writes:

The Book of Common Prayer remained through most of this period as a touchstone of the Church's identity and integrity. Its evolution is remarkable. Beginning in piecemeal translations and adaptations of liturgical material, it was already, by the time of its second (1552) version, providing a consistent style of reflection and public prayer that consciously set out to mould an entire religious sensibility. Cranmer, architect though not exclusive author of the 1549 and 1552 books, can be credited with the extraordinary achievement of expressing a fairly radical Protestant doctrine of dependence upon grace at all points, in a language not only weighty and authoritative in itself but also evocative of ancient and medieval piety. Protestant theology is made to speak a dialect deeply rooted in Greek and Latin liturgy, and so acquires an added depth and seriousness: *this* it seems to say, is what the true tradition of the Church has been saying all along. (Rowell, Stevenson and Williams (eds), 2001, p. 10)

C. S. Lewis, taking a slightly different view of the intentions of the translators sums it up thus. 'They wanted their book to be praised not for original genius but for catholicity and antiquity and it is in fact the ripe fruit of centuries of worship' (Lewis, 1957, p. 93).

It was not only the tone and quality of the book which were to prove of decisive importance for the future development of Anglicanism. It was its all-inclusive character. In a single medium-sized volume the reader was presented with all the texts essential for maintaining the church's life of prayer and worship and for conducting the individual Christian from baptism in infancy, through confirmation into maturity, to marriage, confession, to the encounter with sickness and the moment of death. If the eucharistic part of the book gives the outlines of the calendar and lectionary for Sundays, the part which provides for morning and evening prayer also provides the rules for the recitation of the psalter and the regular reading of the Bible day by day. At the end of the volume, there come the services for the ordination of bishops, priests and deacons, services in which the laity seldom participated, but which they could here read and examine if they wanted to understand more about the structure of the church's corporate life. Here indeed was an eminently corporate expression of the church's life and worship in which nothing was hidden, all open to inspection.

For the great majority of worshippers, particularly in the first three centuries after the Reformation when most were still illiterate, the character of the book impressed itself through its regular use, week by week, in church, and sometimes even day by day at home. But there were those of a more enquiring and analytical mind who looked at the book as a whole and saw its total pattern and meaning. Such was William Gladstone (1809–90) a young man on holiday in Naples in 1823, one who had grown up in an evangelical milieu and who had probably thought of Christianity principally in individualistic terms. 'It presented to me Christianity under an aspect in which I had not yet known it; its ministry of symbols, its channels of grace, its unending line of teachers, joining from the Head; a sublime construction based throughout upon historic fact, uplifting the idea of the community in which we live, and of the access which it enjoys, through the new living way to the presence of the Most High' (Morley, 1903, p. 87).

Gladstone's particular vision of the Prayer Book is characteristic of the early nineteenth century, the period of romanticism which provided the background for the Oxford Movement. But it points us to aspects of *The Book of Common Prayer* which were to some extent evident from the beginning, and which can still attract newcomers to Anglicanism today. If it could have a Protestant interpretation, it could also have a Catholic interpretation. There is thus no problem in understanding how it was that the Prayer Book itself and the way in which it was used had become the subject of bitter controversy already in the early years of Elizabeth I.

These controversies often touched on detailed matters of rite and ceremony. But they also touched upon deeper and more vital matters, taking us sometimes behind the controversies of the sixteenth century into the heart of the New Testament. H. A. Hodges in discussing how it is that Cranmer's communion rite has through the centuries constantly given rise to theological interpretations more 'realistic' than his own, points us to the words which Cranmer himself puts at the end of the Prayer of Humble Access. There we pray that through the sacrament 'we may evermore dwell in him and he in us' (Hodges, 1956, p. 33). There is at the heart of Cranmer's rite a Johannine sense of the mutual indwelling of God and human beings which has entered deeply into the whole Anglican tradition of faith and worship and has reappeared in a variety of ways at a variety of times.

There is another reason why the controversies about *The Book of Common Prayer*, already in full swing in the 1570s, have come to have such a special place in Anglican tradition. On the side of the Prayer Book they engaged the activity of the most searching and influential theologian that England has produced in the centuries since the Reformation, Richard Hooker. If there is an irenic stream in Anglican theology, from the seventeenth century onwards, much of it can be attributed to him. But greater than his desire to make peace is his longing to reveal to his contemporaries the glory of God, present and at work in the whole of God's creation, the glory of God present and resplendent in the face of Jesus Christ, the eternal Word through whom all things were made.

C. S. Lewis, in words which sum up his understanding of Hooker and reveal how deeply he himself was influenced by him, writes

Every system offers us a model of the universe; Hooker's model has unsurpassed grace and majesty . . . few model universes are more filled – one might say more drenched – with Deity than his. 'All things that are of God (and only sin is not) have God in them and he then in himself likewise; yet their substance and his wholly differeth.' God is unspeakably transcendent, but also unspeakably immanent. 'All kinds of knowledge, all good arts, sciences and disciplines, come from the Father of lights and are so many sparkles resembling the bright fountain from which they arise.' We must not think that we glorify God only in our specially religious actions. 'We move, we sleep, we take the cup at the hand of our friend', and glorify him unconsciously as inanimate objects do, for 'every effect proceeding from the most concealed instincts of nature manifests his power'. We do not always know when we are praying for 'every good and holy desire hath the substance and the force of prayer ... there is natural intercourse between the highest and the lowest powers of man's mind'. We meet on all levels, the divine wisdom shining through 'the beautiful variety of all things in their manifold yet harmonious dissimilitude'. (Lewis, 1957, p. 460)

In his systematic study of the thought of Richard Hooker, Olivier Loyer has a whole section on the nature of prayer. 'Prayer if we grasp it in its true movement is a recapitulation of our humanity which we offer to God ... Man is desire, movement towards his true end which is God; it has the substance and content of prayer even if not its form. It is for each one of us to give it its form by the offering of desire' (Loyer, 1979, pp. 353ff.). The desire for God is at the very heart of human nature. What makes us become fully human is the longing to go always beyond ourselves into God. But this longing can be fulfilled only in the gift of God which goes beyond all that we could ask or think. It is as God comes to us that we find we can come to him. 'This line of thought makes the Eucharistic sacrament the completion of the liturgical celebration, the theology of the incarnation, the crown of the theology of the Word and Prayer' (Loyer, 1979, p. 447). It is a great misfortune that Loyer's work, published in 1979, has still not been made available in English. Like Lewis's work, it brings us to the heart of Anglican spirituality.

See also **Anglo-Catholic Spirituality; Cambridge Platonists; Caroline Divines; English Spirituality; Evangelical Spirituality; Oxford Movement; Puritan Spirituality.**

———
A. M. Allchin, *The Joy of All Creation: An Anglican Meditation on the Place of Mary*, 2nd rev. edn, London: Darton Longman & Todd, 1993; T. S. Eliot, *For Lancelot Andrewes*, London, 1928; H. A. Hodges, *Anglicanism and Orthodoxy*, London, 1956; C. S. Lewis, *Oxford History of English Literature: 16th Century, Excluding Drama*, Oxford: Oxford University Press, 1957; Olivier Loyer, *L'Anglicanisme de Richard Hooker*, 2 vols, Université de Paris-Lille, 1979, vol. 1; H. R. McAdoo, *Anglican Heritage: Theology and Spirituality*, Norwich: Canterbury Press, 1991; H. R. McAdoo and Kenneth Stevenson, *The Mystery of the Eucharist in the Anglican Tradition*, Norwich: Canterbury Press, 1985; John Morley, *The Life of W E Gladstone*, London, 1903, vol. 1; Michael Ramsey, *The Gospel and the Catholic Church*, London, 1936; Geoffrey Rowell, Kenneth Stevenson and Rowan Williams (eds), *Love's Redeeming Work: The Anglican Quest for Holiness*, Oxford: Oxford University Press, 2001; Rowan Williams, *Anglican Identities*, London: Darton, Longman & Todd, 2004,

A. M. ALLCHIN

Anglo-Catholic Spirituality

The spirituality of Anglo-Catholicism represents a distinctive strand within the churches of the Anglican Communion, though it has similarities with Roman Catholicism and Eastern Orthodoxy. Its founding inspiration was the Oxford Movement, but it assumes continuity with earlier elements of the Anglican tradition. It has continued to develop and to exert influence within worldwide Anglicanism into the twentieth century and beyond.

Many of the early protagonists of the Oxford Movement, such as John Henry Newman (1801–90) and Edward Bouverie Pusey (1800–82), were converts to 'High Churchmanship' from Evangelicalism. Sharing with Evangelicals a commitment to church renewal, a passionate earnestness, a suspicion of 'worldly' recreation, and an intense search for personal holiness, they contrasted themselves with the 'High and Dry' school of traditional Anglicanism, which they held to have become compromised and formalistic. On biblical inspiration they were conservative, accusing critical biblical scholars of rationalism.

Yet they did not share the Evangelicals' emphasis on the all-sufficiency of Scripture. Instead, valuing highly the tradition of the early, undivided Church, they saw its authority as co-extensive with Scripture. They re-emphasized the Church's institutional history and form. Anglo-Catholicism was emotionally intense, and yet drawn to aspects of the pre-Reformation Church, including the revival of religious orders, the reintroduction of the language and symbolism of eucharistic sacrifice, the revival of private confession, and, for many clergy, clerical celibacy. Its spirituality was Evangelical in spirit, but High Church in content and form.

Anglo-Catholic spirituality has drawn inspiration from two sources in particular, the early Church, and the seventeenth-century 'Caroline Divines'. Nevertheless, its innovatory character within Anglicanism has been marked by its willingness to draw liturgically and theologically also from Orthodox and Roman Catholic sources, by its renewal of interest in liturgical matters, and by a certain rebellious spirit, suspicious of compromise and called by one scholar 'counter-cultural' (Shelton Reed, 1996, p. xxi).

Five major distinguishing elements can be

identified. Anglo-Catholic spirituality is, first, *ecclesial*, attending closely to the corporate forms, practices and constitution of the Church. Anglo-Catholics' concern to defend the catholicity and apostolicity of the Anglican churches has led them to emphasize the conviction that priority in the formation and shaping of Christian discipleship is to be given to disciplined membership of the Christian community. Correspondingly, the traditions of the Church are highly valued, as well as its unity across time and space, and the communion of the saints.

Second, related to this is the strongly *sacramental* character of Anglo-Catholic spirituality. Whether or not formally affirming the five sacraments 'of the Church' as well as the two 'dominical' sacraments of baptism and Eucharist, in practice most Anglo-Catholics have used sacramental language and symbolism with a scope comparable to that within Roman Catholicism. In particular, regular participation in the Eucharist is strongly urged as a mark of Christian belonging, with daily Eucharist offered in many churches. Until recently, the practice of fasting before Communion was also common. Major festivals of the Christian year and saints' days are marked with Eucharists (or 'Masses') of special solemnity. Behind this sacramentalism lies a conviction of the transparency and the potential sacramentality of the created order: just as Christ's divinity was co-present in and with his humanity, so God's grace is mediated through material means.

Third, in order to maintain this sacramental and ecclesial character, Anglo-Catholic spirituality is strongly *liturgical*. Reviving or innovating processions, festivals, liturgical vestments and a rich variety of liturgical texts, it has re-emphasized public worship as vital to the formation of Christian discipleship. The regularity of liturgical worship symbolizes the sanctification of all time as an arena of Christian conversion. Along with attention to liturgical text and practice has gone commonly a concern to raise and intensify the aesthetic experience of worship, through colour, symbolism and imagery, and music. The Anglo-Catholic revival particularly promoted and was fuelled by what has come to be called the 'English choral revival' of the nineteenth century. Its liturgical practice has tended to value contemplative silence, too, and a sense of mystery.

As well as the corporate experience of faith, the individual's journey within the life of faith is also a matter of paramount concern. The particular framework within which this is placed is holiness, or *sanctification* – the fourth element. The guiding presumption (see, for example, Newman's *Lectures on Justification*, 1838) is that the grace of God, freely given and instantaneously effective in justification, is appropriated by and for the believer through a lifelong attention to the search for personal holiness. Though this has sometimes led to accusations of 'works theology', sanctification is not to be confused with an argument from merit. It is a practice of humility and discipline, which requires careful attention to regular prayer, contrition and spiritual contemplation. Anglo-Catholics value a regular pattern of daily prayer, corporate worship, ordered reading of Scripture, regular spiritual retreats and private confession. The revival of private, or auricular, confession was a particularly contentious aspect of the Anglo-Catholic revival in the nineteenth century, though its practice (now commonly termed 'reconciliation') is generally not controversial today. The contemplative, disciplined character of Anglo-Catholic spirituality is also evident in its strong support for the development of practices of spiritual direction. Collections of letters of spiritual counsel by Keble and Pusey were published posthumously, for example (Keble, 1870; Pusey, 1901).

Despite its commitment to public worship, Anglo-Catholicism has also sought to renew and expand the community of faith. The fifth element of its spirituality, then, is *evangelism*. Anglo-Catholics were pioneers of parish missions, and developed a significant, if always numerically small, commitment to mission and ministry in the slum areas of the great industrial cities of Britain, which has been matched elsewhere, including North America and South Africa. Yet, in line with its theology of sanctification, the Anglo-Catholic ethos of evangelism has generally been gradualist. Instead of conversion as sudden and disruptive, it has been seen as processive and lifelong, the consequence of the sustained practice of devotion within the life of the Church. According to what was sometimes called the 'doctrine of reserve' – a doctrine traced back to primitive practice (Williams, 1838) – Anglo-Catholics have assumed that the depth of Christian faith required spiritual maturity in time. In some cases this has encouraged a revival of techniques of catechesis thought to have been common in the early Church. Latterly, in Europe and North America, the evangelistic commitment of Anglo-Catholicism has often been blunted by internal division.

These five elements represent an 'ideal type', and are not always equally true of Anglo-Catholic churches and believers. Anglo-Catholic spirituality increasingly in the late twentieth century has been somewhat diffuse, and difficult to separate altogether from other currents within worldwide Anglicanism. It has sometimes shaded into theological liberalism, particularly on issues of sexual ethics. Anglo-Catholicism has been sharply divided over the possibility of the ordination of women. But it remains a potent source of theological inspiration within Anglicanism.

See also **Anglican Spirituality; Caroline Divines; Ecclesiology and Spirituality; Evangelical Spirituality; Oxford Movement; Sanctification.**

Primary sources: J. Keble, *Letters of Spiritual Counsel*, London: Parker, 1870; J. H. Newman, *Apologia pro Vita Sua*, London: Longman, 1864; E. B. Pusey, *Spiritual Letters*, London: Longman, 1901; I. Williams, *Tract 80: On Reserve in Communicating Religious Knowledge*, London: Rivington, 1838.

Secondary sources: W. O. Chadwick, *The Spirit of the Oxford Movement: Tractarian Essays*, Cambridge: Cambridge University Press, 1990; W. S. F. Pickering, *Anglo-Catholicism. A Study in Religious Ambiguity*, London: SPCK, 1989; J. Shelton Reed, *Glorious Battle: The Cultural Politics of Victorian Anglo-Catholicism*, London: Tufton Books, 1996; W. N. Yates, *Buildings, Faith and Worship: The Liturgical Arrangement of Anglican Churches 1600–1900*, Oxford: Clarendon Press, 1991.

JEREMY MORRIS

Anglo-Saxon Spirituality

1. *Sources for the seventh century*. There are many sources in both Latin and in Old English to draw upon in building up a picture of the inner life of Anglo-Saxon Christians of the sixth to the eleventh centuries. Evangelization of the sixth-century Germanic settlers in Britain came from different places: there were the existing British Christians, the missionaries sent by Pope Gregory from Rome, contacts with Christian Gaul, as well as missionaries and preachers from Ireland and Iona. In effect, the message they brought came originally from Rome coloured by the different ethos of each group and they intermingled freely, creating a homogeneous Christian nation out of disparate tribes and peoples.

Bede. The chief sources for knowing about them at this early stage are the works of the Venerable Bede (673–735) the greatest scholar of his age and the only Englishman to have been accorded the title of Doctor of the Church. He made it his life's work to offer the new Christians the traditions of Mediterranean Christianity, linking them with the world of the New Testament and the Fathers of the Church, not just as a part of the past but as a new and living people of

God. He did this in three ways: first by his work on the text of the Latin Bible; second, through his commentaries, in the tradition of the Fathers of the Church, on the Bible and his sermons, third, by making a unique record of the conversion of the English in his *Ecclesiastical History of the English People*.

Other sources. In addition to Bede's work, there are saints' lives from this period, showing what the Christian hero was like for a people who were emerging from a military-style paganism. There are, for instance, the lives of St Cuthbert, St Columba, St Wilfred, St Gregory the Great, St Guthlac of Crowland, as well as the many succinct portraits in the *Ecclesiastical History of the English People*, of saints such as Hilda, Aidan and Theodore, all showing the ideals which would inspire others. Another dimension is to be found in their poetry, where the oral sagas of heroic deeds, of exile and homecoming, of desire and fulfilment, loyalty to a lord, love for ones' kin, all found written as well as sung expression in great poetry such as *The Seafarer*, *The Wanderer*, and above all *The Dream of the Rood*. Carvings as well as illuminated manuscripts, the Ruthwell and Bewcastle crosses as well as the Lindisfarne Gospel, add to the picture, with the sense of the enormous value placed on the beauty of the Word of God, the centrality of the Scriptures, as well as the continuation of the intricate symbolic art combined with the written words of the new faith. Excavations and archaeology at Suttton Hoo and Mildenhall fill out the picture given by written documents.

2. *Aidan and Augustine*. The basis of Anglo-Saxon spirituality was formed by Aidan of Iona and by Augustine of Canterbury. Augustine landed at Thanet in 597, coming from Rome through Gaul, bringing the gospel from a Mediterranean church, and so linking the new converts with the earliest days of Christianity. Aidan brought Romano-Irish traditions to the north at the same time. Augustine was a monk, as were his companions and as were Aidan and the Irish missionaries, which gave English Christianity a monastic ethos of devoted study and prayer from the start. Augustine brought with him a silver cross and an icon of Christ, and offered King Aethelbert and his thanes a new and better kingdom. His approach was in line with the policies of Pope Gregory the Great who sent him, in that he was prepared to build on the existing ideals and customs of the English and transfigure rather than destroy and replace them. It was a conversion out of love and not by force, as with Aidan who advocated a gentle approach to the Anglo-Saxons. Augustine began by praying

and fasting in a small church with the queen and her court, establishing a lasting link between Church and state which was dependent on unity of prayer and reality of conduct. Similarly, in the north, Aidan and his successors were advisors and friends of the kings. The Latin liturgy was established and formed a framework for English devotion, giving a new shape to the year with the centrality of Easter, the winter feast of Christmas, and the saints' festivals throughout the cycle of months. Mass and the Daily Office of the monks made a new and lasting pattern to daily life. This also prompted a love of reading and writing among the converts, who found in literacy a new freedom. Along with this love of Latin literacy went a care for those who could not read and write to ensure that their sophisticated understanding of sign and symbol should be absorbed into the new skills of literature by translation. The Anglo-Saxon glory in gold became a love for the beauty of holiness. Awareness of the terrors of both nature and supernature around them as well as of sin within led to a strong emphasis on penance, personal as well as corporate, which coloured devotion and affirmed the centrality of the cross and the last judgement. Love of a lord was transferred to love of the high King of Heaven and love of kin could be the basis for care for membership of the company of the Church. This instinctive need for companionship was transferred also to the saints, who were known as always present and always available in prayers, miracles and visions.

3. *Tenth century.* The first flowering of Anglo-Saxon spirituality was tested by the Viking invasions of the eighth century, but this was followed by another great age of spirituality in the tenth century, the age of King Edgar, and the bishops Dunstan, Oswald and Aethelwold. There are fewer sources available for this era than for the previous golden age but its ethos can be known through saints' lives and documents such as charters. There is also the monastic agreement called the *Concordia Regularis* and the prayer books of Hyde and Newminster, which show the continued influence of monasticism and also the deepening link between Church and state. Manuscripts such as the *Benedictional of St Aethelwold* display the high artistic integrity brought to the service of the gospel.

Conclusion. The chief characteristics of Early English spirituality come from the fact that their own pagan past was not destroyed but was transformed by the light of the gospel. A serious, practical and lasting spirituality was the result, based on the Scriptures and the liturgy of the Church.

See also Celtic Spirituality; English Spirituality; Medieval Spirituality in the West.

Primary sources: Bede, *Ecclesiastical History of the English People*, ed. and trans. J. McClure and R. Collins, World Classics Series, Oxford: Oxford University Press, 1994; Bede, *Two Lives of St Cuthbert*, ed. and trans. B Colgrave, Cambridge: Cambridge University Press, 1940.

Secondary sources: Douglas Dales, *Light to the Isles*, Cambridge: Lutterworth Press, 1997; Gordon Mursell, *English Spirituality from the Earliest Times to 1700*, vol. 1, London: SPCK, 2001; Benedicta Ward, *High King of Heaven: Aspects of Early English Spirituality*, London: Mowbray, 1999; Benedicta Ward, *The Venerable Bede*, London: Cassell, 1981/2000.

BENEDICTA WARD

Annihilation, Spiritual

(Medieval Latin: *adnichilate*; French: *anichilacion*.) The notion of spiritual annihilation as the culmination of the mystical process becomes most prominent toward the end of the thirteenth century, due in large part to the resurgence of ideas regarding the possibility of the absolute oneness of Creator and creature. A tendency toward positing a possible annihilation of the soul is particularly strong among women writers during this time, yet it can be found at other stages of Christian speculative thought.

Ideas about annihilation have their roots in Neoplatonic emanationism and the writings of certain of the Greek Fathers, which describe the procession and return of the soul to its primal reality in God. In annihilation, the soul and God become united without distinction or mediation. This union can only be attained through the complete abnegation of the created will; in other words, the human has to abandon all human powers in order to become 'no-thing' or 'no-self' and thus return to the primal, precreative state. Self-abnegation, perfect humility and a recognition of human wretchedness are keys to this process of annihilation. Such a doctrine goes well beyond the more common description of the mystical loving union of wills in which distinctions are maintained.

The idea of annihilation of the soul was relatively rarely expressed in the Christian tradition as a whole, not least because the prevailing Augustinian tradition denied that the soul and God could share an identity. The theological anthropology that underlies this doctrine of annihilation generally holds that the postlapsarian human condition is one of abject wretchedness in which creatures have become utterly alienated from the Creator through sin and wilfulness. Arguing that the true nature of the soul is one of precreated union with God, however, opens the door for complete union with God even within earthly life, the realization of which is a creature's highest calling.

Several notable authors throughout the tradition have posited some type of annihilation. Some of the Beguine mystics, such as Hadewijch of Antwerp (thirteenth century) and Marguerite Porete (d. 1310), capitalized on the potential of these ideas for the mystical path. Porete went so far as to claim that, in the state of annihilation, a soul can become 'what God is'. These authors influenced Meister Eckhart (d. 1327), who in turn influenced Johannes Tauler (d. 1361) and John Ruysbroeck (d. 1381). Tauler, for instance, insisted, as did the Beguines, that one could fall into the abyss of Godhead, which was a fall into a mutual abyss and union. Angela of Foligno (d. 1309), Ubertino of Casale (d. 1330), Jacopone da Todi (d. 1306) and Catherine of Genoa (d. 1510) also used annihilation in their writings, although not to the extent found in a writer such as Porete.

Spiritual annihilation can also be seen as an ingredient in the so-called 'Quietism' and 'Semi-Quietism' of the seventeenth and eighteenth centuries. Quietist authors shared a negative theological anthropology and believed that passive contemplation and the annihilation of the will could enable even the wretched creature to become united to God. This theme is found most prominently in the writings of Miguel de Molinos (d. 1696), who argued that a human being must annihilate the human powers to follow the 'inward way' of absolute passivity, thus serving God (who then dwells within the soul) as a senseless body, not as a human being with an active will. Other authors in these 'movements' who employed 'annihilation theology' include Madame Guyon (d. 1717) and François Fénelon (d. 1715).

History has shown that those who made these claims were often subject to suspicion by the Church, in large part because of a perceived antinomianism and indifference to external works, such as the sacraments and prayer. A condemnation of the Beguines and Beghards at the Council of Vienne (1311–12), for instance, centred on their claims to the possibility of perfection (sinlessness) in this life and consequent indifference to external works (fasting, praying, external authority). Meister Eckhart and Miguel de Molinos were both accused of similar errors.

Another type of spiritual annihilation (technically referred to as 'annihilationism') is the total annihilation or oblivion of the wicked after death, instead of eternity in hell, as part of God's plan. Some writers, such as Horace Bushnell (d. 1876) and Albrecht Ritschl (d. 1889), argued for annihilation or 'conditional mortality', which meant that divinely granted immortality could be withheld because of sinfulness. This doctrine is generally held today among Adventist groups.

See also **Mysticism** (*essay*); **Absorption; Apophatic Spirituality; Jansenism; Quietism; Unitive Way.**

———

Louis Dupré, 'Jansenism and Quietism' in *Christian Spirituality: Post-Reformation and Modern*, ed. Louis Dupré and Don Saliers, New York: Crossroad, 1991, pp. 121–42; Bernard McGinn, *The Presence of God: A History of Western Christian Mysticism*, New York: Crossroad, 1994– (3 vols to date, 5 to be published); Ellen Babinsky (trans.), *Marguerite Porete: The Mirror of Simple Souls*, CWS, New York: Paulist Press, 1993.

JOANNE MAGUIRE ROBINSON

Anthropology, Christian

see **Person**

Anti-Semitism

Although the term anti-Semitism – coined in 1879 by German journalist Wilhelm Marr to describe Jews as a separate and treacherous 'race' – is of modern origin, hostility toward Jews has a long history. The Graeco-Roman world tended to regard Jews warily because of their refusal to follow its religious beliefs and practices, while according respect to Judaism because of its antiquity and ethics. Christianity, which had emerged from biblical Israel and was an illicit, fledgling religion until the fourth century, sought to legitimize itself against its more established rival, Judaism. This defensive posture flowered in centuries of anti-Jewish teachings. The development of 'race science' in nineteenth-century Europe built upon and exacerbated feelings against Jews as cultural outsiders. Thus, the Nazis found a fertile ground for their anti-Semitic policies. Treating Jews as racial pariahs, they stripped Jews of all privileges of citizenship, confined them in sordid ghettos and labour camps, and finally sought to exterminate them.

While the horrors of the Shoah (Holocaust) awakened many in the world to the injustice of anti-Semitism, this 'longest hatred', as Robert Wistrich has termed it, persists. Anti-Semitic incidents in Europe have increased since the beginning of the third millennium. In the Arab world, criticism of Israel often manifests itself in demonization of Jews. Denial of the Holocaust and recycling of traditional anti-Jewish myths that once circulated widely in the Christian world (e.g. the blood libel) are widespread. Modern technology facilitates the dissemination of hate materials, whether in the multi-part Egyptian television series, *Horseman without a Horse*, based on the anti-Semitic forgery from Czarist Russia, *The Protocols of the Elders of Zion*, shown throughout the Muslim world during Ramadan 2002, or in the use of the Internet as a conduit for the transmission of anti-Semitism by white supremacist or other hate groups.

The role Christianity has played in legitimizing, fostering or even engendering anti-Semitism bears profoundly on Christian spirituality. A distinction is useful in analysing Christian accountability for anti-Semitism. *Anti-Judaism* refers to Christianity's negative theological judgement of Judaism because Jews do not accept Jesus as the Son of God. *Anti-Semitism* denotes hatred of, and hostility toward, Jews; it may be based on little or no theological animus. The distinction is significant for Christians because it focuses on the theological legacy that they must confront: the 'teaching of contempt' (as historian Jules Isaac termed it) that poisoned relations with Jews. The distinctions, however, are not absolute. Without question, Christianity's anti-Jewish teaching and preaching of the Church fostered and exacerbated anti-Semitic attitudes and actions.

Christianity's legacy of anti-Judaism spans many centuries and reflects considerable variations. The polemics in New Testament texts, particularly in the Gospels of Matthew and John, reflect the intensity of intra-Jewish debate; later ages seldom took note of this inner polemic. Moreover, the process by which the church and synagogue parted ways was painful and protracted. The writings of the early Church Fathers continued the debate by presenting Judaism as an obsolete religion, albeit in varying ways. In the late second century, the Bishop of Sardis (in modern Turkey), Melito (d. *c.* 190), preached an eloquent sermon articulating what became the leitmotif of anti-Judaism: in killing Jesus, the Jews had murdered God. This charge of 'deicide' echoed in the Church for nearly two thousand years, formally repudiated only in 1965 by the Second Vatican Council in its decree, *Nostra Aetate*. Augustine of Hippo (354–430), who argued that Jews should for ever be condemned to wander the earth as punishment for rejecting Christ, and John Chrysostom (347–407), who preached vitriolic sermons against the 'Judaizers', intensified the rivalry. Canonical legislation in the early medieval period enforced the boundaries between Christians and Jews.

Over time, the Church allowed or even en-couraged defamation of Jews, although various popes periodically issued statements denouncing violence against Jews and condemning forced baptisms. The Crusades and Inquisitions revealed the cruel underside of Church teaching. While in many times and places Christians and Jews co-existed warily, if often peacefully, church leaders overall treated Jews harshly. Martin Luther's *On the Jews and their Lies* (1543) recommended that synagogues be set afire, rabbis forbidden to teach, and Jewish homes destroyed. Thus was established a pattern of vilification of Jews that served the interests of Nazism.

History offers a sobering lesson about Christianity's complicity in anti-Semitism. Although it took until late in the twentieth century for the Church to repent formally from the sin of anti-Semitism, its commitment to fostering relations with Jews reveals awareness of the imperative to act from an ethic of reconciliation.

See also **Holocaust; Judaism and Christianity.**

Robert Chazan, *Medieval Stereotypes and Modern Antisemitism*, Berkeley: University of California Press, 1997; Edward M. Flannery, *The Anguish of the Jews*, rev. edn, New York and Mahwah, NJ: Paulist Press, 1985; John Gager, *The Origins of Anti-Semitism: Attitudes toward Judaism in Pagan and Late Antiquity*, New York: Oxford University Press, 1985; Gavin Langmuir, *Toward a Definition of Antisemitism*, Berkeley: University of California Press, 1990; Gregory Paul Wegner, *Antisemitism and Schooling in the Third Reich*, New York and London: Routledge, 2002; Robert Wistrich, *Antisemitism: The Longest Hatred*, New York: Pantheon Books, 1991.

MARY C. BOYS

Apatheia

Apatheia describes an advanced state in spirituality characterized by freedom from the dominance of the 'passions' as expressed through carnal desires or thoughts. It is not equivalent to 'apathy', but under grace is the outcome of long and vigorous practice in self-discipline.

1. *Meaning.* The word *apatheia* is Greek for a condition of 'passionlessness'. It emerged as an ethical ideal in the Stoic tradition and was given a Christian sense especially by Clement of Alexandria who saw it as a state of quiet self-possession, marked by wisdom and virtue without the inconsistency resulting from unchecked instinctual desires. The ascetical aspect of the theme was embraced by the Desert Fathers and developed systematically by Evagrius of Pontus (345–400). By long practice the monk hoped to

subdue unruly appetites of attraction or repulsion (concupiscible and irascible appetites) and so enable the passionate sectors of the soul to be at peace. For Evagrius this inner harmony which was 'the health of the soul' (*Praktikos* 56), had a strongly somatic component and was expressed concretely in freedom not only from the acts but also from the 'thoughts' and even dreams of gluttony, fornication, covetousness, anger, sadness, acedia, vain glory and pride. In this tradition *apatheia* is primarily a moral not a psychological state.

2. *Western developments*. John Cassian (360–435) westernized the teaching of Evagrius and through his influence on Gregory the Great (540–604) caused much of it to be absorbed into the mainstream of Latin spirituality. Cassian's preferred synonym for *apatheia* was a phrase based on the Beatitudes and already used in the tradition: 'purity of heart'. This term was understood as meaning singleness or simplicity of heart and denoted a lack of inner division or inconsistency.

Among the twelfth-century Cistercians, under the influence of Augustinian notions of *ordo*, the theme was restated in terms of the ordering of the affections (*ordinatio caritatis*), subordinating the 'lower' movements of passion to the 'higher' movements of reason and spirit.

3. *Function. Apatheia* was never seen as an end in itself. The literature suggests that passionlessness is to be sought because it serves as a doorway to a range of experiences that are closer to the ultimate meaning of the spiritual journey: the tears of compunction, a quiet mind and heart, freedom from sexual disturbance and anger, spiritual gnosis and wisdom, contemplation, unceasing prayer, charity, perseverance. In his first *Conference*, John Cassian makes a distinction between purity of heart (or *apatheia*) as the immediate goal of the monk's striving; and the ultimate goal of finding entrance into God's kingdom. In the final analysis *apatheia* represents an ideal of unbroken union with God prepared for by the progressive elimination of immaturity, multiplicity and materiality. In the strict sense such an ideal presupposes a life of extreme detachment possible only for a few; more loosely, however, it may be understood as an invitation to the conscious channelling of energies until finally they become focused on 'the one thing necessary'.

See also **Purity of Heart.**

Marcia L. Colish, *The Stoic Tradition from Antiquity to the Early Middle Ages* (2 vols),

Leiden: Brill, 1985; Evagrius Ponticus, *The Praktikos Chapters on Prayer*, ed. and trans. John-Eudes Bamberger, Cistercian Studies Series 4, Spencer, MA: Cistercian Publications, 1970; Harriet A. Luckman and Linda Kulzer (eds), *Purity of Heart in Early Ascetic and Monastic Literature: Essays in Honor of Juana Raasch, OSB*, Collegeville, MN: The Liturgical Press, 1999; Juana Raasch *OSB*, 'The monastic concept of purity of heart and its sources', 5 articles in *Studia Monastica* 1966–70; Columba Stewart, *Cassian the Monk*, New York: Oxford University Press, 1998, esp. pp. 40–61.

MICHAEL CASEY

Apocalyptic Spirituality

Every day Christians say the prayer that Jesus taught his disciples without perhaps noticing that one of its major petitions – 'Thy kingdom come' (Matt. 6.10) – expresses the hope that God will soon establish his definitive rule on earth. Many other passages found in almost every strand of the New Testament express the strength of the apocalyptic element among the early Christians who saw Jesus' resurrection from the dead as the beginning of the triumph of the kingdom of God and a sign of his imminent return, or parousia. Early Christianity has been described as an apocalyptic sect of late Second-Temple Judaism, a characterization that is helpful as long as we realize that apocalypticism comes in many varieties, then and now.

Modern scholars have continued to debate the definition and significance of apocalypticism. Here the term will be used to indicate the set of beliefs, often associated with the Revelation of John, that deals with divine control over history and the imminent end of the present age. In this sense apocalypticism is a species of eschatology (belief about the last things) that frequently, though not necessarily, involves millenarianism (expectation of a coming better age on earth) and messianism (hope for a saviour who will initiate the new era). More concretely, Christian apocalypticism is living in the shadow of the second coming.

Apocalypticism arose in Judaism in the third and second centuries BCE, a time of difficulty and persecution for the Jews. As represented by the canonical book of Daniel, apocalypticism is in part a reaction to the crisis of persecution, though there is no simple relationship between crisis situations and apocalyptic beliefs. The learned apocalyptic seers sought to encourage and console the faithful by writing pseudonymous revelatory texts in which God, through heavenly emissaries (usually angels), conveyed a message about the meaning of current trials, announced an imminent final struggle between the forces of good and evil, and promised an ultimate reward to those who remained steadfast in the time of suffering. While the genre 'apocalypse', or mediated revelation, was used to convey both mysteries about the universe, especially the heavenly world (the vertical dimension), and the secrets of history and its approaching end (the horizontal dimension), apocalypticism is mostly used in connection with the latter aspect.

In their efforts to strengthen and encourage believers to hold fast to their faith, apocalyptic authors utilized the symbolism of the cosmic conflict between good and evil found in the ancient myths of the Near East about the primordial struggle between the creator God and the forces of chaos portrayed by the dragon of the abyss. In its power to move and sustain hope, the apocalyptic imagination has always been deeply symbolic. Apocalypticism is fundamentally confrontational – the contrast between good and evil is couched in absolute terms, both in its heavenly and its earthly manifestations. Finally, apocalypticism involves complex interminglings of pessimism and optimism: pessimism about the growing role of evil in the world, yet fundamental optimism about God's breaking into history to reward his faithful.

The significance of apocalyptic expectation of the imminent return of Jesus in the first century of Christianity is undeniable. Some scholars have seen a basic shift in the second century CE as Christians replaced apocalyptic hopes with an institutionalized Church. Apocalyptic texts and themes did begin to receive spiritualized interpretations in the second and third centuries, but fervent forms of apocalypticism did not die out, either then or in later Christian history. New forms of apocalyptic hopes, such as those associated with Joachim of Fiore (d. 1202) and his followers, show the significance of the apocalyptic element in Christianity. Debates about the imminence of the end, the identity of Antichrist, and the possibility of an earthly millennium were widespread among the competing forms of Christianity in the sixteenth and seventeenth centuries. Although the rise of the Enlightenment cast doubts on many aspects of apocalyptic hopes and fears, literal forms of apocalypticism, such as the Dispensationalist Fundamentalism created in the nineteenth century, continue to be strong today.

One of the main reasons for the persistence of the apocalyptic element in Christianity over two millennia has been the way in which its symbolic power answers to key aspects of the human condition, especially temporality and theodicy.

What is the meaning of everyday existence? How are human beings to make sense of their day-to-day striving to attain more permanent value? Apocalypticism builds a bridge between the confusions and trials of quotidian existence and a universal structure of meaning rooted in divine purpose. How can a good God have created a universe in which evil so often seems to have the upper hand? Apocalyptic conviction that the justice of God will triumph in the end helps provide courage to go forward in difficult circumstances.

While the positive aspects of apocalyptic beliefs are undeniable, apocalypticism, especially in its literal forms, has also been the source of many evils. These include not only the foolishness of unfulfilled predictions, but also the way in which apocalyptic exclusivism has often included a thirst for vengeance leading to violence against others in the name of the coming Lord. (Literal apocalypticists often seem to have no trouble hating the sinner more than the sin.) For these reasons many contemporary Christians view apocalypticism as a superseded stage of religion, a neurosis to be overcome. Nevertheless, the significant role that apocalypticism played in the origins of Christianity, as well as its persistence over the centuries, argue that attempts to expunge the apocalyptic element from Christianity not only risk failure, but may even be detrimental to essential aspects of Christian spirituality. Apocalypticism is integral to New Testament teaching about the stance that Christians should take toward Christ's action in history.

Caught between dangerous forms of literal apocalypticism, such as those current among fundamentalists, and the emergence of various forms of secular apocalypticism (e.g. radical ecologies and scientistic attempts to realize human perfectibility), Christians of the third millennium need to pursue the difficult task of creating forms of apocalyptic spirituality that take the symbols of biblical texts about the end seriously but not literally. This task must begin from an honest admission of the ambivalences of the apocalyptic approach to reality and the dangers to which it is prone. To live in the shadow of the second coming is not an easy task.

Practising an authentic apocalyptic spirituality is a delicate balancing act between fidelity to essential values of Christianity and the danger of slipping into their perversions. For example, conviction of God's control over history, even in the midst of crises and tragedies, can degenerate into a sense that believers exercise a similar power by way of their special access to 'the times or periods that the Father has set by his own authority' (Acts 1.7). The need for watchfulness and steadfast endurance proclaimed in the Synoptic Little Apocalypse (e.g. Matt. 24.42; Mark 13.33–37; Luke 21.36), can encourage self-righteousness among those who think they alone are favoured by God. Indignation against evil political and social forces, evident in John's Revelation, has empowered Christian resistance over the centuries, but has also led to violent forms of revolutionary apocalypticism in which humans have elected themselves to be chosen instruments of God's vengeance. The call to moral decision at the heart of the apocalyptic imperative has led to forms of the moralism that find it all too easy to judge others. Finally, avoiding literal apocalypticism by reinterpreting the biblical images of the imminence of the end into symbols of the immanent fate of the soul (*my* end, rather than *the* end) risks privatizing the social and world-historical aspects of the apocalyptic vision.

Among the marks of authentic apocalyptic spirituality are endurance in persecution, resistance to the power of evil, watchfulness for the coming of Christ, and hope in a final triumph of justice that will involve a transcendence over death. Resurrection from the dead is an integral part of the apocalyptic message. If many of these characteristics sound like fundamental Christian values, it may be because apocalypticism is, after all, an essential part of the message of the gospel. Over the centuries, many Christian teachers have been able to avoid the dangers of literal apocalypticism while still being inspired by the core of Christian apocalypticism – conviction of the coming of the risen Lord. To cite just one example, Cyprian of Carthage's treatise *On the Lord's Prayer* makes the following comment about the petition 'Thy kingdom come':

> Dearest brethren, it may be that Christ himself is the kingdom of God, he whom we desire to come each day, he for whose swift return among us we are longing. He is himself the resurrection, because in him we rise again; so too he can be understood as the kingdom because in him we are to reign.

See also **Eschatology; Hope; Lord's Prayer.**

———

Malcolm Bull (ed.), *Apocalypse Theory and the Ends of the World*, Oxford: Blackwell, 1995; Jacques Ellul, *Apocalypse: The Book of Revelation*, New York: Seabury Press, 1977; Frank Kermode, *The Sense of an Ending: Studies in the Theory of Fiction*, Oxford: Oxford University Press, 1966; Christopher Kleinhenz and Fannie J. LeMoine (eds), *Fearful Hope: Approaching the New Millennium*, Madison: University of Wisconsin Press, 1999; Bernard McGinn, John J. Collins and Stephen J. Stein (eds), *The Encyclopedia of Apocalypticism*, 3 vols, New York: Continuum Press, 1998; Bernard McGinn (ed.), *Apocalyptic Spirituality*, CWS, New York: Paulist Press, 1979.

BERNARD MCGINN

Apophatic Spirituality

Apophatic spirituality has three aspects.

1. It is the 'unsaying' (*apophasis*) of language for God, a mode of discourse in which God is approached using a dialectical structure of affirmation and negation, with an emphasis on the negative element or moment. The rationale for the unsaying of language for God is God's objective transcendence of all human language.
2. It is detachment from or the stripping away of attitudes, mental images and ideas which are considered to stand in the way of the active pursuit of relationship with God. This is a path of training (*ascesis*) and the transformation of human desires which focuses on what must be removed in order to 'make room' for God.
3. It is a way of dereliction and suffering, usually understood as patterned on the cross of Christ. Christ's life lends the central images and path for much apophatic spirituality: the passion and the cross in particular give shape to the paradox of 'losing and finding' which characterizes the way of negation.

All three of these aspects are interwoven in the history of Christian apophatic spirituality, as shown in the following examples.

The *apophasis* or unsaying of language has biblical roots, most importantly in the story of Moses meeting God in 'thick darkness' (Ex. 20.21) and in a 'cloud' (Ex. 24.15), and in the christological motifs already mentioned of divine presence in suffering and loss, especially in the passion and the cross. The institution of monasticism was the breeding ground of apophatic practice, placing the practice of detachment at the heart of Christian spirituality and cultivating practices of inner and outer poverty, as well as of silence and solitude. But the influence which did most to make apophatic spirituality a distinct strand within Christianity was its conversation with Neoplatonism, specifically the introduction of the dialectical language of Plato's *Parmenides*. In Neoplatonism, the technique of dialectic was applied to the divine One, for instance by Plotinus (c. 205–70), with the intention of representing the One's simultaneous immanence and transcendence. The Neoplatonic language of simultaneous divine presence and absence, immanence and transcendence, became the language of Christian apophaticism, giving structure to subsequent centuries of reflection on the divine transcendence.

Gregory of Nyssa (c. 335–c. 395). Gregory of Nyssa, the fourth-century Cappadocian Father, was the first Christian writer to develop a full theology of *apophasis*. At the centre was his understanding of God's nature as inexhaustible, so that the human soul is drawn out in an endless pursuit (*epektasis*). Drawing on the Jewish exegete, Philo, Gregory adopted the negative term 'darkness' as his primary metaphor for the divine nature, using the Old Testament image of Moses meeting God in the 'cloud', and he also invoked the New Testament 'no one has ever seen God' (John 1.18). 'This is the seeing that consists in not seeing, because that which is sought transcends all knowledge, being separated on all sides by incomprehensibility as by a kind of darkness' (*Life of Moses* 2.163). It is a 'luminous darkness', in that Moses 'saw' God in the darkness – a 'seeing' by being drawn into God's inexhaustible nature – yet still 'dark' in that the divine nature can never be grasped (*see* Darkness). The use of phrases such as 'seeing in not seeing' and 'luminous darkness' is typical of the deliberately paradoxical, dialectical structure of affirmation and denial which characterizes apophatic spirituality.

Dionysius (fl. c. 500). It was Dionysius, the obscure Syrian monk, who systematized the theology of *apophasis* for the first time in Christianity. He was influential not only in the East but in the West, largely through John Scotus Eriugena (*c.* 810–*c.* 877), leading to the flowering of apophatic spirituality in the high medieval period in the writings, for instance, of Meister Eckhart (*c.* 1260–*c.* 1328; see further below), the *Cloud of Unknowing* (fourteenth century), Nicholas of Cusa (1401–64), and John of the Cross (1542–91; see further below).

Dionysius links his study of how we use affirmations and denials in our language for God to the question of how symbols in general represent God. Symbols from creation, the Bible and the liturgy lead us to God. But those symbols which are 'incongruous' and words which are dissimilar – words such as invisible, infinite, ungraspable – are better than those which are similar, such as Word, Mind and Being, according to Dionysius, because they more adequately express the divine transcendence. Indeed, he

argues, the point is not to express the divine transcendence, because this is inexpressible, but to move our minds beyond both affirmation and denial. 'Here, renouncing all that the mind may conceive, wrapped entirely in the intangible and invisible, he [the seeker] belongs entirely to him who is beyond everything. . . . One is supremely united by a completely unknowing inactivity of all knowledge, and knows beyond the mind by knowing nothing' (*Mystical Theology* 1.3 [1001A]).

Like Gregory of Nyssa, Dionysius uses the image of Moses' ascent of Mount Sinai to meet God in the 'cloud' as a scriptural basis for his theology of 'unknowing' (*agnosia*). But the key move is that beyond the negation of knowing to the 'negation of negation', where the mind shifts 'beyond unknowing' to an inexpressible, hidden union with God. Dionysius gives this a theological basis in his treatment of the Trinity: the Trinity holds together 'the assertion of all things, the denial of all things, [and] that which is beyond all assertion and denial' (*Divine Names* 2.4 [641A]). The linguistic process of affirmation and denial leads to union with God as Trinity.

Meister Eckhart (c. 1260–c. 1328). Meister Eckhart, the German Dominican theologian and noted preacher, roots his apophatic spirituality in the same dialectical flow of the Trinity into creation first elucidated by Dionysius. God as Trinity both remains within and flows out, at once, so that for us to speak of God is to enter into this flow at the same time as remaining outside it. Successful language for God seeks to approximate to the divine relationship with creation which is one of simultaneous unity and difference. The guiding metaphor of this relationship is the 'ground' (*Grunt*), for Eckhart: humans and all creation share the same 'ground' with God, yet they do so dialectically – the 'ground' is both the most intimate reality shared with God within all things and beyond all things as their source.

Eckhart delights in wordplay designed to move his listeners and readers through affirmation to the negation of their understanding of God (this is Eckhart's ascesis), and then to a transforming 'negation of negation', following Dionysius, which takes them beyond the confines of language and into the divine 'ground'. This is especially evident in Eckhart's *German Sermons*, where metaphors are chosen for their ability to collide with and contradict one another, producing an 'explosion' of language as the meanings fall apart, out of which a new understanding is born. The process is often repeated many times over in the course of a single sermon, with the aim of transforming the listener's understanding in such a way that the divine ground 'breaks through' and comes to 'birth' within them.

John of the Cross (1542–91). Linguistic apophasis is an important part of the thought of the sixteenth-century Spanish Carmelite John of the Cross, particularly in his language of light and darkness. But most distinctive of his spirituality is the way that elements of asceticism and suffering patterned on Christ – the second and third aspects outlined above – are combined with the linguistic aspect. The bodily sufferings of Christ were generally emphasized in late medieval piety, and in John this emphasis is internalized, being applied to the loss of mental images and spiritual practices on the path to union with God. There is a severe process of ascesis through the active and passive 'dark nights' of the soul, in which all former spiritual attitudes and ideas are removed. Union with God is found by passing through a state of 'annihilation' which is patterned on Jesus' dereliction on the cross (*Ascent of Mount Carmel* 2.7.9–11). This moment corresponds to Dionysius' negation of negation, as darkness gives way to simultaneous light. Yet for John, the difference is that apophasis is no longer primarily a linguistic method – though it is this as well; it is now a psychological state, corresponding to Christ's suffering on the cross.

Conclusion. Apophasis is an element in much Christian theology and practice, but apophatic spirituality is, more specifically, an understanding of the role of 'unsaying' of language for God, which is given shape in a spiritual path. The figure of Dionysius did most to define this tradition. In modernity and postmodernity, we find echoes of apophatic spirituality, inasmuch as theologians and spiritual practitioners continue to be concerned with the role of dialectical language (for instance, Hegel and Karl Barth, from different perspectives), and with God's transcendence and the role of silence in prayer. In postmodernity, there is a new emphasis on the 'otherness' of God and the sense of God's absence, which parallels the loss of the certainties of modernity (Jacques Derrida, Emmanuel Levinas, et al.). But these remain disparate elements of apophasis, only obliquely related to the earlier tradition; there is yet to be a rebirth of a truly apophatic tradition in Christianity.

See also **Asceticism; Abandonment; Annihilation, Spiritual; Cappadocian Fathers; Carmelite Spirituality; Darkness; Dark Night; Desolation; Neoplatonism; Rhineland Mystics.**

Primary sources: There are many figures who may be regarded as primary sources of apophatic spirituality. Some key texts by the four main authors above can be found in: *Gregory of Nyssa: The Life of Moses*, trans. by Abraham J. Malherbe and Everett Ferguson, CWS, New York: Paulist Press, 1978; *Meister Eckhart: The Essential Sermons, Commentaries, Treatises, and Defense*, trans. Edmund Colledge and Bernard McGinn, CWS, New York: Paulist Press, 1981; *The Collected Works of John of the Cross*, trans. Kieran Kavanaugh and Otilio Rodriguez, Washington, DC: Institute of Carmelite Studies, 1991; *Pseudo-Dionysius: The Complete Works*, trans. Colm Luibheid, CWS, New York: Paulist Press, 1987.

Secondary sources: Deirdre Carabine, *The Unknown God: Negative Theology in the Platonic Tradition: Plato to Eriugena*, Louvain: Peeters/ Grand Rapids, MI: Eerdmans, 1995; Oliver Davies and Denys Turner, *Silence and the Word: Negative Theology and Incarnation*, Cambridge: Cambridge University Press, 2002; Michael Sells, *Mystical Languages of Unsaying*, Chicago, IL: University of Chicago Press, 1994; Denys Turner, *The Darkness of God: Negativity in Christian Mysticism*, Cambridge: Cambridge University Press, 1995.

EDWARD HOWELLS

Apostolic Spirituality

Apostolic spirituality derives its identity from that claimed by Christ (John 20.21) as the one sent by the Father, who in turn sends his followers to proclaim the reign of God (Luke 10.1–9) by preaching the Good News and doing works of healing and liberation from sin (Matt. 10.1; Mark 3.13–15; Luke 9.1). In classical Greek the word *apostollein*, 'to send forth', designates an ambassador or messenger, and comes to refer also to those sent as missionaries (2 Cor. 8.23). The word 'apostle' in the New Testament belongs specifically to the Twelve (Matt. 10.2–4) who are chosen by Jesus (Acts 1.2), witness to the resurrection (Acts 4.33), teach within the community and speak in the name of Jesus (Acts 6.2), in whose name they do works of healing (Acts 5.12). The apostle is a steward of the mysteries of Christ (1 Cor. 4.1), a fellow-worker with God (1 Cor. 3.9) who is called through grace (Gal. 1.15). Personal experience of the living Jesus and witness to the resurrection are required for specific membership of the Twelve (Acts 1.21–22). The term 'apostle' has varied and sometimes ambiguous meanings in the New Testament, which have led to considerable disputes about its exact derivation and meaning (*NJBC* 81, pp. 149–57). The link with the Old Testament is unclear, but some scholars see a link with the Old Testament notion of the prophet, sent to preach God's will to the people, and at times even giving bodily expression (Jer. 20.7–13) to God's self-giving love for humankind (John 3.16), which finds its ultimate expression in the *kenosis* of Jesus (Phil. 2.6–8). All God's people share in that prophetic call of Christ (*Lumen Gentium* 12), whose mission was not only accomplished by his actions but by the very fact of his living human life and sharing human suffering. The description 'apostle' or 'apostolic' comes to be given to all those who receive the Holy Spirit and, through the power of God, bear witness to Christ's presence in the world through their lives, sharing in his work of sanctification (John 20.21–23) confident that his power shines in human weakness (2 Cor. 12.10), and that he is with them to the end (Matt. 28.19–20).

The primitive roots of the consecrated life lay in the choice for a radical following of Christ and dedication to God, which expressed itself in the *fuga mundi*, the repudiation of life as lived in 'the world' for a solitary and penitential life withdrawn from earthly attachments (*NDT* pp. 670–3). From this developed monastic life, supported by rules, which not only gave structure to the pursuit of holiness, lived in common, but came to embody the spiritual teaching of the monastic founder and offered a path to holiness for those who would follow. This spiritual teaching emphasized the virtues required for a life of self-denial, organized around regular worship and concentrated on total dedication to the things of God. From early on in monastic history, however, some of those who remained 'in the world' also sought a greater sanctification of their lives through association with those living under vows by becoming oblates or, with the advent of the mendicant orders, members of 'third orders'. There remained nevertheless a sense of the split between the consecrated or contemplative life of the religious and the secular life of the lay person. Spiritual teaching tended to concentrate on devotions, a rhythm of prayer during the day akin to that of the religious, or a spirituality that turned away from the material world to seek fusion or union with God, rather than on a theology that saw work and life in the world itself as potentially holy.

The emergence of forms of religious life more dedicated to engagement with the world produced a theology and spirituality of the imitation of Christ, which aimed less at the assimilation of the soul into the life of Christ itself and more at becoming 'another Christ' in the world through the exercise of good works. This form of religious life became designated as 'active', in opposition to the 'contemplative' form of monastic life. In the aftermath of the Catholic Reform, founders such as Ignatius Loyola or Louise de Marillac and Vincent de Paul inspired lay people to share in their work and prayer through sodalities or lay associations of 'apostolic' inspiration. At the same time, within Protestant circles, the religious and apostolic nature of life in the world found expression through a way of living centred not on the division between lay and religious Christians, but on ready access to the Bible as a source of inspiration and personal and collective prayer.

The identification of religious congregations by the labels 'active', 'contemplative' or 'mixed' tended to create false divisions based on misleading value judgements that continued to see as more perfect the life more withdrawn from 'the world'. It failed to make clear that all those who seek God are called into a relationship that is essentially contemplative, and all contemplation of God finds its ultimate expression in love of one's neighbour and the proclamation of the reign of God.

The spiritual genius of Ignatius Loyola is best expressed in his *Spiritual Exercises*, whose aim is for 'the Creator to deal directly with the creature, and the creature directly with [the] Creator and Lord' (*Spiritual Exercises* 15). This free and open relationship between Creator and creature enables God to liberate the one making the exercises from inordinate attachments. Like the disciples on the road to Emmaus, a more intimate experience and understanding of Christ as revealed in the Scriptures enables them to make better sense of their own story, and reflection on lived reality enables them to gain a fuller understanding of the Scriptures, which reveal God at work in the events of human history. Through this radical encounter with God in Christ we reach an 'intimate knowledge' of God which enables us to 'find God in all things'. The one who allows God's liberating work to be done becomes free to discern and choose God's will in whatever way that is manifested, putting no premium on any particular choice or way of life (*Spiritual Exercises* 23), desiring to live only in God's love and grace through the exercise of the gifts God has given (*Spiritual Exercises* 234).

While the Ignatian tradition does not hold a monopoly of apostolic spirituality, it is primarily through that insight that we are helped to see all human states and activities as potential calls to holiness and intimacy with God. The Second Vatican Council placed especial emphasis on the universal call to holiness, in which all human activity can come to be seen as a participation in the work of the Creator (*Gaudium et spes* 34) who is continuously at work in the salvation of humankind (*Gaudium et spes* 1). All are called to a union with Christ that expresses itself in apostolic service in keeping with the gifts and vocation of each individual. More recently the enthusiasm for Ignatian spirituality outside the confines of Roman Catholicism has led to a new assimilation of the spiritual traditions of the past in the ecumenical context of today. Within this shift also lies the spirituality of Taizé, which combines the insights of the monastic life and the imperative of apostolic expression with a firm commitment to ecumenism.

The firm emphasis given in Vatican II to the universal call to holiness and the sacred inspiration of all human activity undertaken under God gave rise to renewed reflection on the different states of life within the Church. The disappearance of inappropriate monastic customs in many apostolic religious congregations led to a reappraisal of the varying spiritual traditions from which they sprang. At best, this has reminded religious that contemplation lies at the heart of all consecrated life, and all contemplation has an apostolic purpose in the proclamation of the reign of God, through the witness of life and action. The breakdown of false divisions between clergy, religious and laity has also led to an increased sense of the value of lay life and activity and the legitimate call to holiness that exists within engagement with the world. Whether fostered in numerous groups and movements associated with the traditions of the consecrated life, the charismatic renewal, or through specifically lay movements such as the Christian Life Communities, Julian Groups, Focolare and the like, apostolic spirituality supports and nurtures the pursuit of holiness within the entire spectrum of human relationships and activities among all who follow Christ and share in his office as prophet, priest and king (*Catechism of the Catholic Church* 900–13).

See also **Augustinian Spirituality; Beguine Spirituality; Canonical Communities; Conventual Life;** *Devotio Moderna*; **Dominican Spirituality; Examination of Conscience/ Consciousness; Franciscan Spirituality; Ignatian Spirituality; Imitation of Christ; Jesus, Society of; Lay People and Spirituality; Mendicant Spirituality; Oratorian Spirituality; Religious Life; Rules, Religious; Salesian Spirituality; Taizé, Spirituality of; Vatican II and Spirituality; Vincentian Spirituality.**

Catechism of the Catholic Church, London: Geoffrey Chapman, 1994; *Gaudium et spes*, in *The Documents of Vatican II*, ed. W. Abbott, London: Geoffrey Chapman, 1967; *The Spiritual*

Exercises of St Ignatius, ed. L. Puhl, Chicago, IL: Loyola University Press, 1951. *Lumen Gentium* in *The Documents of Vatican II*, ed. W. Abbott, London: Geoffrey Chapman, 1967; *New Dictionary of Theology* (NDT), ed. J. Komonchak et al., Dublin: Gill & Macmillan, 1990; *New Jerome Biblical Commentary* (NJBC), ed. R. Brown et al., London: Geoffrey Chapman, 1989.

GEMMA SIMMONDS

Appropriative Method

One of the more significant developments in recent studies of Christian spirituality is the awareness of Christian spirituality as a distinct discipline, with identifiable subject matter and precise methods for understanding this subject. While the Second Vatican Council (1962–65) did not make a clear departure from earlier approaches to Christian spirituality, the conciliar teaching on other matters pertinent to Christian life provided orienting principles that have given shape to a contemporary Christian spirituality. Foremost among these are: (1) the formative role of the Word; (2) the Church as the whole people of God; (3) the Liturgy as source and summit of the Christian life; (4) the Church as a sacrament in and to the world.

These conciliar orientations awakened a deeper awareness of the Spirit's presence in a wide range of life experience, not just in the lives of vowed religious, monks and clergy. A recognition of the breadth of the Spirit's presence and action has called for a much wider focus in exploring Christian spirituality and for finding new tools or methods for understanding Christian spirituality, as well as refining others. The subject matter of a specifically Christian spirituality might be understood to be concerned with the Holy Spirit at work in human life, history, the world and the Church: (1) within a culture; (2) in relation to a tradition; (3) in light of contemporary events, hopes, sufferings and promises; (4) in memory of Jesus Christ; (5) in efforts to combine prayer and action; (6) with respect to charism and community; (7) as expressed and authenticated in praxis.

Perhaps no one has contributed more to methodological maturation in the field of Christian spirituality than have Bernard McGinn and Sandra Schneiders in the United States, and Philip Sheldrake in Britain. In several seminal essays, Schneiders identifies four methods for studying Christian spirituality: theological; anthropological; historical; interpretive. The appropriative method is much in line with the interpretive, but is somewhat less cognitive in its operation and its aim. 'Appropriation' and 'appropriative' bespeak an approach to Christian spirituality that aims more precisely at transformation through the personal appropriation of knowledge gained through the study of this subject matter, so that one might be better able to assist in the spiritual transformation of others. The governing concern in the appropriative method, much as in Schneiders' interpretive method, is threefold: (1) to gain from and to contribute to the cumulative knowledge of the Christian spiritual life; (2) to be transformed personally through the appropriation of this knowledge; (3) to aid in the transformation of others through the knowledge appropriated. Underpinning this method is the conviction that all authentic knowledge is ipso facto transformative.

A brief example of how one might employ the appropriative method will have to suffice. First, examine the *Charter of Charity*, one of the foundational documents of Cistercian spirituality, which stipulates the need for periodic visitation of monasteries by abbots of other monasteries in order to insure the integrity of life and the harmony within a particular monastic community. Second, given the current difficulties in the local churches throughout the world, one might come to recognize the need for greater accountability on the part of the diocesan bishop, an accountability that could be assured by establishing a framework for diocesan visitations by bishops of other dioceses. This would entail a deeper recognition of a call to greater accountability and a willingness to accept constructive criticism of oneself. Third, one would then seek to pass on to others a deeper appreciation of accountability and transparency in all areas of life, and how this might be assured in greater measure through establishing frameworks which allow for alternative perspectives to be brought to a particular life situation. All this might be the yield of the appropriative method employed in order to understand a seemingly irrelevant medieval monastic document.

The appropriative method is particularly well suited to serve the subject matter of Christian spirituality, described in various ways as Christian religious experience *as such*, with attention to the experiential dimensions of Christian life in the Spirit. To avoid the excessive focus on the individual in some earlier approaches to Christian life in the Spirit, some contemporary approaches highlight the relational dimension of Christian spirituality, indeed of the whole Christian life. This is aided by a renaissance of interest in the doctrine of the Trinity, often understood to communicate the life of God as personal and relational. Thus, as lived experience or as subject of inquiry, Christian spirituality

may be understood as the quest to be conformed to the person of Christ, brought into communion with God and others through the gift of the Spirit.

Because of the breadth of its subject of concern, approaches to understanding Christian spirituality are, in the main, interdisciplinary, relying on the insights and methods of a range of disciplines. Thus in employing the appropriative method, there is reliance on the gains of disciplines that may seem far afield of the subject of Christian spirituality, such as literary criticism or feminist biblical hermeneutics. In similar vein, the appropriative method relies on the theological, anthropological and the historical, and is best exercised in critical correlation with them. It is in such methodological interdependence that the nature of the discipline of Christian spirituality as a field-encompassing field stands forth. As an emergent discipline Christian spirituality may be said to be methodologically preoccupied. But such is the case with any discipline whose subject matter is still being weaned from under the tutelage of other disciplines with their own subject matter and methods.

Michael Downey, *Understanding Christian Spirituality*, New York and Mahwah, NJ: Paulist Press, 1997, ch. 6, 'Studying spirituality', esp. pp. 129–31; Sandra M. Schneiders, 'A hermeneutical approach to the study of Christian spirituality', *Christian Spirituality Bulletin* 2.1 (Spring 1994), pp. 9–14.

MICHAEL DOWNEY

Architecture and Spirituality

Human beings experience every space – even in nature – as both an opening and an enclosure. The open sky itself is perceived in most premodern settings as also a kind of dome. Architecture comes about when we erect artificial openings and enclosures in order to house and shape our activities – as with domed worship spaces, which traditionally provide a meeting place between heaven and earth. Although such built environments need to be practical and structurally sound, they can also be shaped artistically, and in such a way as to give the 'spirit' – human and divine – a special opening or symbolic habitation. Consecrated buildings, together with their environs (including gardens, cloisters, courtyards and labyrinths), can provide a place and path by which worshippers are reoriented toward a blessed way of life.

Architecture is closely connected to the history and spirituality of a given community. When the early Christians were still a persecuted minority, they gathered for worship in houses or specially modified 'house churches'. The best-known surviving example of such a *domus ecclesiae* is the house church at Dura Europas, Syria, dating from the third century and replete with baptistry and wall paintings. Once Christianity was officially legalized under the Emperor Constantine in the fourth century, churches suddenly became public structures that needed to accommodate large numbers of worshippers.

In reaction against paganism, Christians declined to use the architectural styles of Roman and Greek temples. Those would not have been practical in any case, since pagan temples were designed as dwelling places of gods whose worshippers gathered outside in order to make sacrifices. It was therefore the Roman basilica – a style of building used for law courts and commerce – that Christians adapted most often for their own worship. They took advantage of its oblong shape and terminal apse to construct a processional space: a long nave with side aisles, lighted from above on either side by a clerestory, and entered through an atrium. By the fifth century the church was typically oriented toward the east (as the term 'orient' implies), where there was a bishop's throne and an altar for Communion. The half dome of the apse would typically be adorned with mosaics showing Christ himself amid biblical and ecclesiastical figures. The first St Peter's basilica (as documented in surviving drawings and paintings) and St Mary Major in Rome are prime examples of the style. Alternatively Christians employed some form of domed central or circular plan, which was favoured for martyria. St Vitalis in Ravenna, Italy, exemplifies this pattern. Approaching either kind of the church, one would normally pass through a narthex – where unbaptized neophytes would wait after the homily and during Communion until being readmitted for the final blessing. The baptistry was commonly a separate structure, often octagonal in shape, recalling the 'eighth day' of creation: the day of rebirth and resurrection.

In the medieval West, the basilica was further modified in Romanesque and the Gothic styles. Romanesque (called Norman in England), which flourished in the eleventh through the mid twelfth centuries, was particularly associated with monastic pilgrimage churches. It made use of tunnel and groin vaulting, rounded arches and thick stone walls to create impressive interiors that could rise to great height, though the heavy vaulting was limited in the width that it could span safely. Many naves were modified by the addition of flanking auxiliary chapels and the construction of large transepts, which resulted in

a cross shape. Ambulatories and radial chapels were added to the choir so that pilgrims could visit holy relics without disturbing Mass at the high altar. Prominent examples include Durham Cathedral in England (which anticipates Gothic), St Sernin in Toulouse, France, and the abbey churches of Maria Laach in Germany and Fontenay, France.

No style is more closely associated with Christianity than Gothic, which Abbot Suger (*c.* 1081–1151) inaugurated in the mid twelfth century at the royal abbey church of St Denis, France. As Gothic developed – with pointed arches, ribbed vaulting and flying buttresses that transferred weight to the exterior – the structure no longer needed thick walls and massive pillars. Consequently Gothic churches (which were often cathedrals dedicated to the Virgin) could feature large expanses of stained glass and dizzying height – although, in England, it was length that took precedence.

In its conception, Gothic architecture's orderly design reflected Neoplatonic theologies of divine light and of geometrical beauty in creating a structure that exhibited both rationality and mystery. A Gothic church was envisioned both as the form of the body of Christ and as the bejewelled, heavenly Jerusalem – a foretaste and promise of which is provided by Christ's gracious presence in Communion. Of the vast number of Gothic churches, those in the Isle de France region in and around Paris – such as Notre Dame de Paris, Laon, Rheims and Chartres – are among the most outstanding. On the English side, distinctive contributions include the cathedrals at Salisbury, Wells, Lincoln and York, as well as the later, 'perpendicular' design of King's College Chapel, Cambridge, with its intricate fan vaulting.

Eastern churches, meanwhile, had realized the potential of a centralized structure surmounted by one or more domes. Justinian's great sixth-century Church of Holy Wisdom (Hagia Sophia) in Constantinople had been a primary inspiration, even influencing ambassadors from Russia in 987 who, reportedly, returned to their homeland saying they could not forget such beauty or the sense of divine presence it conveyed. They insisted on being baptized, as Prince Vladimir was soon to be, along with his people. Especially following the iconoclasm of the eighth and early ninth centuries, Byzantine churches abandoned longitudinal plans. They embraced centripetal spaces that would lift one's eyes to the dome and that put the worshipper in more immediate visual contact with icons, with the clergy and with the liturgical action. The narthex at the west led into the central domed space – the nave –

beyond which, at the east end, would lie the screened-off *bema* or sanctuary, the province of clergy alone. It was not the crucified Christ that came to dominate here, visually, but a half-length image of Christ as '*Pantokrator*' – the one who at once rules the world and holds it, containing and transforming all who enter. Such is the style that prevails today in Eastern Orthodoxy, albeit regionally modified.

With the rise of Protestantism in the sixteenth century, there was a new emphasis on the church as the gathered people, and on the preached word. Protestants reduced visual ornamentation and, over time, simplified the structure when possible, often eliminating such things as subsidiary chapels (having no need for relics or multiple altars). Especially when Calvinist, they insisted that the true temple is not the building but the heart in which Christ dwells. In this way a Protestant church building could return to being a house of the assembly (*domus ecclesiae*) rather than a sacred house of God (*domus dei*).

The extreme example of such an ideal is the New England Puritan meeting house, a multi-use square or rectangular space of frame construction, having no steeple and displaying no images, but featuring a massive, elevated pulpit positioned on the central axis, with sounding board directly above. In the nineteenth century, the evangelical movement extended this tradition by calling for worship spaces to function as auditoriums and amphitheatres that would enhance visual and auditory contact between ministers and very large congregations. That tradition survives in the 'megachurches' prominent in suburban America today.

Back in the late seventeenth century, a different approach likewise had proven to be compatible with Protestantism – namely, the simplified forms and uncluttered sight lines of neoclassical architecture (even while reviving some elements once associated with pagan temples). Exemplified by the 'auditory' churches built by Christopher Wren (1632–1723), this influence crossed the Atlantic in the form of white-painted, steepled neoclassical churches that have become iconic of 'classic' American spirituality.

Catholics themselves had at times given considerable prominence to preaching; the Jesuits, among others, designed spaces with that idea in mind. Yet, following the Renaissance and the 'Counter Reformation' of the sixteenth century, Baroque and Rococo architecture was above all an art of splendour, majesty and drama. While retaining the basic form of the basilica, such architecture introduced highly ornamented and curvilinear surfaces that would dazzle the eye. Ceilings were spectacular, employing tricks of perspective to create exhilarating illusions of height and depth and a sense of visual drama.

After the ascendancy of neoclassicism, the nineteenth-century revival of Gothic and Romanesque architecture on both sides of the Atlantic was fed, in part, by a Romantic reaction against the spiritual aridity of the industrial and scientific revolutions. The liturgical movements of the twentieth century (both Catholic and Protestant) encouraged more modest plans, however – plans that would not distance congregations from the clergy or from each other but draw them together around the table. This impetus, ratified and intensified by Vatican II (1962–65), was compatible with the formal simplicity of much modernist architecture – represented remarkably if idiosyncratically by Le Corbusier's pilgrimage chapel at Ronchamp, France (1955). In stressing simplicity and lay participation, Catholics were coming to resemble Protestants, who in turn were becoming more 'Catholic' in their attentiveness to liturgy.

Most recently, while secular architecture has grown more eclectic as part of its 'postmodern' identity, church architecture has been accused of becoming, too often, utilitarian and unimaginative. Yet one discerns signs that Protestants and Catholics alike may be yearning again for at least a provisional (albeit pluralistic and multicultural) sense of 'sacred space'. It seems possible that a new sacramental imagination will result in a sensibility capable of envisioning the house of the church as also – in some sense – the house of God.

See also **Aesthetics; Art; Beauty; Place.**

Karsten Harries, *The Ethical Function of Architecture*, Cambridge, MA: MIT Press, 1997; Richard Kieckhefer, *Theology in Stone: Church Architecture from Byzantium to Berkeley*, New York: Oxford University Press, 2004; Jeanne Halgren Kilde, *When Church Became Theatre: The Transformation of Evangelical Architecture and Worship in Nineteenth-Century America*, New York: Oxford University Press, 2002; Thomas F. Mathews, *Byzantium: From Antiquity to the Renaissance*, New York: Abrams, 1998; Steven J. Schloeder, *Architecture in Communion: Implementing the Second Vatican Council through Liturgy and Architecture*, San Francisco: Ignatius Press, 1998; Otto von Simson, *The Gothic Cathedral*, expanded edn, Princeton, NJ: Princeton University Press, 1988.

FRANK BURCH BROWN

Aristotelianism

Aristotle (384–322 BCE) was Plato's most brilliant student. He spent twenty years in the

Academy before leaving to establish his own school and to develop an alternative approach to philosophy. Aristotle's school, the Lyceum, had a colonnaded walk or '*peripatos*' and from this his followers became known as Peripatetics.

It seems that most of the works of Aristotle are lost but a substantial number of lecture notes, working drafts and accounts of his lectures written by others, survived to be put in order by Andronicus of Rhodes in the first century BCE. Aristotle wrote on virtually every topic of philosophical interest and his importance is second only to that of Plato in the history of Western philosophy. Indeed at certain times and for certain issues he is the more important philosopher of the two. While Samuel Taylor Coleridge declared that every human being is born either an Aristotelian or a Platonist, the late ancient world, in particular Plotinus and the Neoplatonists, sought to reconcile the two philosophies. Theologians in both Muslim and Christian worlds, taunted by the anti-philosophical with what they claimed were the insoluble disagreements of the philosophers, continued the project of trying to reconcile the two great Greek thinkers while putting their work at the service of the respective faiths.

Raphael's painting of *The School of Athens* illustrates the major perceived difference between Plato and Aristotle. Where Plato, idealist and transcendentalist, points to the heavens above as the place where truth is to be sought, Aristotle, empiricist and immanentist, directs the onlooker to the world beneath his or her feet. But this is not to say that Aristotle is blind to spiritual realities. In his account of mind he stands in the mainline Greek tradition for which intellectual knowledge must be immaterial if it is to have those characteristics of universality, immutability and objectivity, which were the agreed criteria for what could count as true knowledge.

Book 12 of Aristotle's *Metaphysics* predicates of the first 'unmoved mover' an activity that is absolutely immaterial and in which the distinction between knowing subject and known object disappears. The only object worthy of the thinking of the first unmoved mover is that very thinking itself so that Aristotle's 'god' may be defined as 'thought thinking itself'. In the case of both Plotinus and Pseudo-Dionysius the Areopagite, scholars have sometimes postulated some contact with Indian thought as an explanation for the mystical element in their understanding of mind. In fact one need look no further than Aristotle as background to those aspects that were thought to reveal contact with some oriental source.

Metaphysics 12 is not the only place where Aristotle speaks about the creative power of mind. In his work *On the Soul* he says that mind has the capacity to produce its own objects – something that is clear from the power of the human mind to abstract universal concepts from the data of sensation (*On the Soul* 3). The most empirical and least romantic of the Greek philosophers, Aristotle reports straightforwardly on what he observes about everything including human knowledge. He sees that human knowledge cannot be explained without appealing to a non-physical, non-material power that alone can explain its transcendence: the fact that the reach and exercise of human knowledge go beyond what sensation can provide or explain, even while it remains always dependent on sensation.

Aristotle believed that the ultimate end or flourishing of human life is to be found in this spiritual realm, the realm of thought. If fulfilment (*eudaimonia*) is found in that activity which is the highest exercise of a nature's highest power, then human fulfilment is found in *theōria*, the mind's enjoyment of truth. A spiritual and religious interpretation of this was helped by the fact that Aristotle described it as a 'divine' activity in us (*Ethics* 10.7). In other parts of his *Ethics*, however, Aristotle offers an alternative, more secular, account of human flourishing in terms of the appropriate enjoyment of the full range of human goods: health, wealth, power, knowledge, friendship, esteem, family life, and so on.

Later Aristotelians, especially Christians, gave Aristotle's *theōria* a strongly religious interpretation, relating it to established traditions concerning contemplation. Thomas Aquinas, for example, was aware of Aristotle's varying response to the question of humanity's ultimate goal and is clear that Aristotle did not realize where human fulfilment is actually to be found. The Latin translation of Aristotle's *eudaimonia* is *beatitudo*, a term like *contemplatio* already laden for Christian thinkers with a rich tradition of biblical and theological significance. For Christian faith the blessedness (*beatitudo*) promised by God is the happiness of seeing God as God really is (1 John 3.2) and becoming like God through sharing in the divine nature, which is love (2 Peter 1.4; 1 John 4.8). If Aristotle provides philosophical resources for articulating a Christian theology of knowledge, love and friendship, a radical transformation of Aristotle's *Ethics* was still necessary to make it useful to Christian theology. Aristotle could never have considered, for example, that the knowledge and love presupposed for friendship might also be possible between human beings and God.

The major issue on which Aristotle disagreed with Plato was the question of forms or ideas. He argued against Plato that good is not a general term corresponding to a single idea. Things are good in relation to the achievement of their specific functions and there is a kind of analogy or proportion between our different uses of the term. But he had problems more generally with Plato's theory. There is ample evidence for on-going debate about it within the academy itself, not only from those passages of the *Metaphysics* where Aristotle rehearses the difficulties, but in the often more telling arguments recorded by Plato himself in his dialogue *Parmenides*. As a way of responding to some of these difficulties later Platonism placed the originally separated ideas within the divine mind so that they became 'the thoughts of God'. This interpretation of Plato was destined to have a long history and became central for medieval Christian thinkers who received it in two significantly different versions, one from Augustine and the other from Pseudo-Dionysius.

Aristotle is often regarded as having given due metaphysical weight to individually existing things in contrast with Platonism's tendency to symbolize and to generalize. If Platonism tends to make individual things occasions or stimuli for the remembrance of higher realities, Aristotle's philosophy encourages the valuing of things in and for themselves. A substantial proportion of his surviving work is concerned with the natural world, with animals, plants, weather and planets, whose constitution and behaviour are carefully observed. Aristotle's amazement at the variety and quirkiness of things is infectious: it is in such wonder, he says, that philosophy is born.

Not surprisingly Aristotle's work was highly regarded by his Christian followers for this evaluation of creation. Albert the Great led the work of integrating Aristotelian philosophy into Christian theology but it was Thomas Aquinas in particular who used the new philosophy not only in his ethical and political thought but also in specifically theological contexts, when considering the sacraments, the incarnation and grace, for example. His Christian faith enables Thomas to go far beyond Aristotle in his appreciation of the physical world, developing an account of the essential unity of body and soul in human beings that has been described as 'the highest encomium of human body' (Bernardo Bazan).

Aquinas is also indebted to Aristotelianism for his understanding and evaluation of creation. This is paradoxical because Aristotle himself had no doctrine of creation, believing that the world always existed and that what required

explanation within it were change and motion rather than its dependence for its being on some transcendent cause. This did not prevent Aquinas and other Christian Aristotelians using Aristotle's language of being and causality to speak about the relationship of dependence in which all things stand towards God. In fact Aristotle's conviction that the world is eternal helped Aquinas to clarify what creation means, since the relationship signified would hold even of an eternal world.

Aristotelianism continued to be important for philosophical and scientific work down to modern times. Aristotle's logic remained fundamental to all understanding of argument and demonstration until the work of Frege in the nineteenth century. Aristotle's ethical theories continue to inform philosophical debate, especially his account of the virtues and in particular what he has to say about prudence or 'practical wisdom'. Aristotle's politics continue to repay study, in particular his understanding of the human being as naturally social and linguistic, and his treatment of friendship without which civil society cannot be what human beings require. Thomas Aquinas, as already noted, did not hesitate to use these ideas in developing his theology of charity as friendship even with God.

See also **Analogy; Body and Spirituality; Choice; Christian Humanism; Contemplation; Cosmology; Deification; Desire; Ethics and Spirituality; Friendship; Intellectual Life and Spirituality; Joy; Neoplatonism; Person; Scholasticism; Soul; Virtue.**

Richard C. Dales, *The Problem of the Rational Soul in the Thirteenth Century*, Leiden: E. J. Brill, 1995; James C. Doig, *Aquinas' Philosophical Commentary on the Ethics: A Historical Perspective*, Dordrecht, Boston, London: Kluwer Academic Publishers, 2001; Joseph Dunne, *Back to the Rough Ground: 'Phronesis' and 'Techne' in Modern Philosophy and in Aristotle*, Notre Dame, IN and London: University of Notre Dame Press, 1993; Husain Kassim, *Aristotle and Aristotelianism in Medieval Muslim, Jewish and Christian Philosophy*, Lanham, MD: Austin and Winfield, 1998; Martha C. Nussbaum and Amélie Oksenberg Rorty, *Essays on Aristotle's De Anima*, Oxford: Clarendon Press, 1992; Philip Merlan, *Monopsychism Mysticism Metaconsciousness. Problems of the Soul in the Neoaristotelian and Neoplatonic Tradition*, The Hague: Martinus Nijhoff, 1963; Ferdinand van Steenberghen, *Aristotle in the West: The Origins of Latin Aristotelianism*, Louvain: E. Nauwelaerts, 1955.

VIVIAN BOLAND

Art and Spirituality

A work of art, as we usually think of it today, is a human artefact produced not only with skill and know-how but also with some degree of creativity or inspiration, and in such a way as to be aesthetically rewarding: beautiful, expressive or imaginative. Art has come to be seen as the form of culture that is perhaps richest in spiritual vitality and imaginative depth – addressing and engaging us wholly (as the poet T. S. Eliot observed). All in all, the arts can probe the human heart, reveal the glories and miseries of social existence, contemplate nature, envision previously unimagined possibilities, offer enjoyment of aesthetic forms in themselves, enrich worship, arouse emotions, move the will, and sometimes provide a quasi-sacramental sense of divine grace and a foretaste of heavenly joy.

The arts have been prized religiously for certain reasons marginal to aesthetics as such. In particular, they have been valued as a powerful aid to memory and an effective means of religious education, especially for the illiterate. The concept of art as a Bible for the poor, articulated most notably by Pope Gregory the Great (c. 540–604), has been applied above all to the visual arts, which are our primary concern here.

Following the iconoclastic controversies of the eighth and ninth centuries, no form of art was more highly esteemed than icons. Yet the Eastern Church, for which icons are indispensable, has never regarded icons as art in the usual sense, since they are to be produced prayerfully, according to strict guidelines, and under spiritual direction. While it is said of icons (as well as other religious images) that the devotion paid to the image is referred to its prototype (Jesus or Mary or the saints), icons are looked on as more than visual aids to prayer. They are windows on eternity, a beautiful threshold to higher, sacred reality, functioning in a virtually sacramental fashion. Mostly non-naturalistic in style, and often arranged on an iconostasis, they call the worshipper to a higher reality that can transfigure the human. Among the most famous icons are the *Trinity* by the Russian monk Andrei Rublev (c. 1360/70–c. 1430), and Our Lady of Vladimir (twelfth-century Russian).

In considering the spiritual significance of icons and other kinds of religious art, it is helpful to observe that theological reflection on art has often lagged behind practice. Early Christian murals, mosaics, catacombs and sarcophagi receive little theological comment in their time. Yet, especially after the fourth century, such art was more extensive than anything one might expect on the basis of certain attacks on images

by Church Fathers – attacks that we now realize were intermittent in any case. In this art Old Testament themes are popular, including Moses striking the rock, Abraham offering Isaac, and the deliverance of Daniel from the lion's den. Christ is shown as a good shepherd, philosopher, healer, wonder-worker, and ruler. Surprisingly, the first depictions of the crucifixion do not appear until the fifth century, and are not widespread until the seventh.

Medieval stained glass reaches an apex in Gothic churches and chapels such as Chartres Cathedral and the Sainte-Chapelle (Paris), although it passes relatively unnoticed by medieval theologians. And manuscript illumination – such as that found in the Lindisfarne Gospels, the Book of Kells, and in the many medieval books of hours used for private devotion – creates a delightfully rich visual symbolism that fits devotional needs but that is inadequately accounted for by the more didactic justifications of art offered periodically by the Church.

It is significant and exceptional when Abbot Suger of St Denis (c. 1081–1151) evidently draws on Neoplatonic theology to interpret the spiritual efficacy of the architectural and liturgical art he has provided for his abbey church – a bejewelled crucifix, chalice, gilded portals, stained-glass windows, and a choir in the new style later known as Gothic. Yet Suger says little about the artistry as such, dwelling instead on the fact that the work is costly, sumptuous and luminous. Again, during the Counter-Reformation, Ignatius of Loyola (1491–1556), in his Spiritual Exercises, stresses the importance of visualizing sacred settings, persons and events – but without mentioning how art might aid in the process. That possibility nevertheless comes to fruition with the Mannerist paintings of El Greco (1541–1614) and with Baroque artists such as Jusepe Ribera (1591–1652) and Peter Paul Rubens (1577–1640).

With or without the explicit support of theologians, visual art has generally blossomed in the context of the liturgy, reaching one of its high points in relation to Communion. Panel paintings often were made into altarpieces placed on and behind the altar. This practice culminated in impressive polyptychs such as Hubert and Jan van Eyck's Ghent Altarpiece (1432) and the Isenheim Altarpiece by Grünewald (c. 1470/80–1528). Alternatively, a reredos was provided, being the sculpted and carved counterpart to the altarpiece. The subjects depicted have included not only saints' lives but also, fittingly, the crucifixion and the last judgement. Church interior walls and domes have likewise invited much visual art, some of the most famous examples being mosaics such as those in Ravenna (fifth and sixth centuries) and frescoes produced by Giotto (1266/7–1337) for the Arena Chapel in Padua and by Michelangelo (1475–1564) for the Sistine Chapel in Rome. The remarkable *Last Supper* by Leonardo da Vinci (1452–1519) appropriately adorns a wall of a monastic refectory in Milan.

Sculpture has found a conspicuous place mainly in Western Catholicism. Particularly striking examples include the Romanesque sculptures at the church of the Madeleine at Vézelay, France, and Gothic figures on the portals, archivolts and tympana at Chartres Cathedral. Tombs, side chapels and shrines have likewise attracted religious sculptures, among the most famous being Michelangelo's Vatican *Pieta* (1500) and his *Moses* (1516) for the tomb of Pope Julius II, as well as Bernini's masterpiece *Saint Teresa in Ecstasy* (1645–52). Many sculptures have been lost, having been a prime target of Protestant iconoclasts and French revolutionaries.

The relation of visual arts to spiritual practice changed markedly with the Reformation. While Martin Luther generally allowed images in church, he discouraged their veneration and thereby circumscribed their spiritual function. John Calvin prohibited images altogether in the sphere of public worship or private devotion, associating them not only with idolatry but also with the veneration of relics. Calvin allowed religious paintings in the home or civic space, however, as long as their use was historical and instructional. During the same period, graphic artists produced large quantities of prints of a religious sort – many of them anti-Catholic. A century later, the most famous of all Protestant artists, Rembrandt (1606–69), created paintings and works of graphic art in which penetrating observation combines with human compassion and a poignant sense of the necessity and availability of divine grace.

As church patronage dwindled even in Catholic circles after the eighteenth century, much of the art having religious significance was produced outside the church. In the nineteenth century depictions of mountains, seascapes and waterfalls often dealt with the sublime – a sense of the infinite and the awe-inspiring – as in the paintings of Caspar David Friedrich (1774–1840) and J. M. W. Turner (1775–1851). Similarly, American landscape art like that of Albert Bierstadt (1830–1902) rendered the 'book of nature' as God's second 'scripture'. Near the end of the century religious themes recurred almost decoratively and nostalgically among the Symbolists and Pre-Raphaelites. Van Gogh

(1853–1900) expressed human suffering and spiritual longing with vibrant intensity, while Paul Gauguin (1843–1903) invoked the exotic and mythic in his paintings from Brittany and Tahiti. In the twentieth century avant-garde artists drew on mystical and esoteric sources, as in the work of Wassily Kandinsky (1866–1944) and Piet Mondrian (1872–1944). A peculiarly mundane yet compellingly unconventional rendering of religious themes marked the work of Stanley Spencer (1891–1959), whereas Francis Bacon (1909–2001) exposed the horrible and the grotesque. Abstract Expressionists such as Barnett Newman (1905–70) and Mark Rothko (1903–70) invested their existential abstractions with a sense of the simultaneously tragic and metaphysical. Photographers such as Ansel Adams (1902–84) looked to nature as a kind of secular spiritual preserve.

As Christianity has expanded geographically, it has shown new faces, artistically: the Virgin of Guadalupe in Hispanic contexts, for instance, and in China a Virgin Mary whose appearance resembles that of the popular Buddhist bodhisattva, Guan-yin. From the mid twentieth century to the present, there has also been a considerable cross-pollination between high arts and popular arts. Film and video have emerged as accessible media of spiritual and moral imagination. Recent examples include *Babette's Feast* (Gabriel Axel, 1988), *Decalogue* (Krzysztof Kieslowski, 1988) and Peter Jackson's popular film version of J. R. R. Tolkien's *Lord of the Rings* (2001–03).

See also **Aesthetics; Architecture; Beauty; Film and Spirituality; Image and Spirituality.**

John Dillenberger, *A Theology of Artistic Sensibilities: The Visual Arts and the Church*, New York: Crossroad, 1986; John Drury, *Painting the Word: Christian Pictures and their Meanings*, New Haven and London: Yale University Press, 1999; William A. Dyrness, *Visual Faith: Art, Theology, and Worship in Dialogue*, Grand Rapids, MI: Baker, 2001; Robin Margaret Jensen, *Understanding Early Christian Art*, London: Routledge, 2000; Roger Lipsey, *An Art of Our Own: The Spiritual in Twentieth Century Art*, Boston: Shambhala, 1989; David Morgan, *Visual Piety: A History and Theory of Popular Religious Images*, Berkeley: University of California Press, 1998.

FRANK BURCH BROWN

Ascent

'Ascent' is a metaphor used widely in world religions. It tells the story of the upward journey of the soul to the divine or to the heaven(s). Christian spirituality and mysticism have used this metaphor constantly. Influenced by Neo-platonism, Christian and otherwise, this metaphor has deeply significant roots in Hebrew and Christian texts. In the Hebrew Scriptures figures taken up by God were Enoch (Gen. 5.24) and Elijah who 'ascended in a whirlwind into heaven' (2 Kings 2.1–12).

The mountain is a ubiquitous image of ascent. Moses and Elijah have been types of those who ascend the mountain to God. 'Moses entered the cloud, and went up the mountain. Moses was on the mountain for forty days and forty nights' (Ex. 24.17–18). Elijah 'got up, and ate and drank; then he went in the strength of that food forty days and forty nights to Horeb, the mount of God. There the Lord was present to Elijah in the "sound of sheer silence"' (1 Kings 19.8, 12). The tradition has seen these events as transformative or deifying. Gregory of Nyssa (d. *c*. 395) retold the Mosaic Sinai event in his *Life of Moses* where he describes that experience as ending in the darkness of apophatic experience.

In the Christian Scriptures a classical figure of ascension was Paul who 'was caught up into Paradise and heard things that are not to be told, that no mortal is permitted to repeat' (2 Cor. 12.4). In the Western tradition of ascent, Augustine led Christians within. To go up would be to go deep within. Moreover, the experience of Monica and Augustine at Ostia became a classic moment in the literature of ascent. Augustine wrote: 'At that moment we extended our reach and in a flash of mental energy attained the eternal wisdom which abides beyond all things (*Confessions* 9.10.25). Augustine's writings, influenced by Platonists, resonate with Plotinus' description of the ascent of the soul to the Good. Yet, Augustine thoroughly grounded his spirituality of ascension in Christ and upon biblical themes. Augustine's impact on the Christian spirituality of introversion and ascension has been incalculable (see especially his *Confessions* and *On the Trinity*.)

Another major influence in the development of the metaphor of ascent was Pseudo-Dionysius (*fl*. 500) whose *Mystical Theology* describes the ascent of the soul/mind into a darkness of un-knowing. Dionysius worked out of a hierarchical structure that was ontologically based. Origen (d. *c*. 253) had introduced to the literature of ascent the stages of purification, illumination and union or perfection. Pseudo-Dionysius cast this division into the well-known form inherited by the tradition.

In his *The Journey of the Soul into God* Bonaventure gathered up the tradition of ascension/ introversion in a powerful exploration of the ecstatic experience of St Francis in which 'Christ is the ladder and the vehicle'. The soul's journey culminates in a passing over into the triune God.

The tradition of ascent has benefited from the genius of many Christian writers: Origen, Gregory of Nyssa, Augustine, Pseudo-Dionysius, Bonaventure, John of the Cross and many others. Writers like these have taken the tradition of ascent and expressed it in new and unique versions, building on the past but injecting new perspectives into the tradition. One must pay close attention to each text of ascent. Otherwise one may universalize aspects of ascent without warrant. In the sixteenth century Bernardino de Laredo OFM, composed *The Ascent of Mount Sion* which influenced Teresa of Avila whose stages of prayer are similar to Laredo's.

John of the Cross expressed the ascent tradition in his commentaries, one of which is entitled *The Ascent of Mount Carmel*. The earliest ascent tradition emphasized the intellect, but, as in Teresa and John of the Cross, ascent, since the Middle Ages, has been perceived as largely culminating in contemplation that is love.

Contemporary Christians should take more account of the theme of ascent in the life of Jesus. Like Moses, Jesus 'went up the mountain' where he taught his disciples (Matt. 5.1–2). Jesus was also known to withdraw to a mountain to pray (Luke 6.12); and in Luke 9.28ff. Jesus was transfigured on the mountain. Jesus rose or was raised from the dead. Descent and ascent are often best described in a dialectical relationship. Thus, in the incarnation, God's descent occurred so that the human person may ascend to God. Moreover, the ascension or exaltation of Jesus has been neglected for too long in the understanding of the Christian ascent to God. The modern metaphor of ascent should take into account the descent of the Holy Spirit who brings about the presence of Christ. Christians would also benefit from retrieving a corporate sense of the ascent as in Vatican II's perception of the spiritual journey 'not as individuals without any bond between them' but as the people of God (*Lumen Gentium* 9).

See also **Apophatic Spirituality; Growth, Spiritual; Illuminative Way; Journey, Spiritual; Neoplatonism; Purgative Way; Purification; Transfiguration; Triple Way; Unitive Way.**

———

Bernard McGinn, *The Presence of God: A History of Western Christian Mysticism*, 3 vols, New York: Crossroad, 1991, 1994, 1998; J. D. Tabor, 'Heaven, Ascent to', *The Anchor Bible Dictionary*, ed. D. N. Freedman, vol. 3, New York and London: Doubleday, 1992, pp. 91–4; Denys

Turner, *The Darkness of God: Negativity in Christian Mysticism*, Cambridge: Cambridge University Press, 1995.

KEITH J. EGAN

Ascetical Theology

Beginning with the works of Giovanni Battista Scaramelli SJ (1687–1752), a distinct discipline, termed 'ascetical theology' to distinguish it from 'mystical theology', was focused on the active human pursuit of Christian perfection. This perhaps questionable early modern formulation (discussed below) should not eclipse the more fundamental and historically ubiquitous role of an ascetical dimension in the Christian spiritual life.

The Greek concept of *askesis*, meaning exercise or training (see 1 Cor. 9.25), seemed a helpful notion to early Christians seeking to interpret the impact of Christ's calling his followers to self-denial and fidelity to himself, especially in terms of sharing in his suffering and death (see, e.g., Mark 10.34ff.). The apostle Paul directly and frequently considers how this adherence to Christ in his death, by means of the rite of baptism (Rom. 6), should liberate one from the constraints of one's 'old' sinful existence and issue in a 'new creation' living freely from the risen life of Christ. In this sense the ascetic dimension of the Christian spiritual life is a manifestation of the continually unfolding power of the death and resurrection of Christ within the lives of believers and of the community – such that one is free to overcome sinful habits and to live with unhindered, even sometimes heroic, charity towards others. For writers such as Athanasius of Alexandria (*c.* 296–373), the ascetic dimension of Christianity was exemplified by the pioneer of desert eremiticism Antony of Egypt (*c.* 251–356); far from any manner of self-preoccupied moral self-improvement, Athanasius understands Antony's asceticism as a striking witness to the world of the power of Christ's victory on the cross over evil, a victory capable of transforming the most basic structures of human bodily, spiritual, moral and communal life. A somewhat different approach to ascetical theology develops from other Alexandrian teachers, chiefly Clement (*c.* 150–*c.* 215) and Origen (*c.* 185–*c.* 254), who adapt for Christian use the common Hellenistic pedagogical sequence of ethics, contemplation of nature, and contemplation of the divine (a path which is later received as the more familiar spiritual stages of purification, illumination and union). While this scheme has its benefits in clarifying the inner dynamic of the spiritual life and its orientation towards everfuller encounter with God, it has sometimes had

at least two disadvantages: it tends to delimit the ascetical as a preliminary stage of moral struggle for beginners, rather than perceiving it in more positive terms as an ongoing dimension of spiritual freedom; and, inextricably connected with this, it has shifted the focus from the new life won by Christ and lived into by the community towards an interior battle to achieve self-denial by individuals. By the later Middle Ages, such significant spiritual teachers as Meister Eckhart (*c.* 1260–1327) were well aware of and warn against the paradox of an asceticism that seeks to perfect the self by too self-preoccupied a self-denial that covertly enthrones the self all the more. For the most part, however, what might be called ascetical theology in the medieval period was an aspect of Christian moral theology, with a particular emphasis on the practical appropriation of grace in the transformation of behaviour. With the early modern fragmentation of theology into discrete disciplines, the proper focus of ascetical theology becomes a subject of debate. One view insisted that ascetical theology covered the ordinary approach of the spiritual life towards perfection, and reserved mystical theology to mean extraordinary states of grace. Another more dominant view draws the line between ascetical and mystical theology according to whether the spiritual state considered is a normal act of Christian virtue aided by grace (ascetical) or a more passively received 'infusion' or experience of divine presence (mystical). More recently, these divisions have come to seem artificial and the study of Christian spirituality has tended to examine an ascetic strand in the spiritual life without demarcating it in terms of phases, level of proficiency, or manner of divine involvement, but locating it instead in all those dimensions of spirituality that attend to freedom from sin, the search for spiritual integrity, and the struggles of love and justice. Particularly noteworthy in this regard would be the ascetical theology implicit in the works of liberation and womanist theologians, calling their communities to repentance and freedom from the sinfully degrading self-images that have been culturally imposed on them.

See also **Mysticism** (*essay*); **Asceticism; Mystical Theology.**

Primary sources: *Athanasius: Life of Antony*, trans. R. Gregg, CWS, New York: Paulist Press, 1980; *John Cassian: Conferences*, trans. B. Ramsey, New York: Newman Press, 2000; *Evagrius: Praktikos*, trans. J. Bamburger, Kalamazoo, MI: Cistercian Publications, 1970.

Secondary Sources: John Chryssavgis, *In the Heart of the Desert: The Spirituality of the Desert*

Fathers and Mothers, Bloomington, IN: World Wisdom, 2003; Olivier Clément, *The Roots of Christian Mysticism*, New York: New City Press, 1995; Rowan Williams, *The Wound of Knowledge: Christian Spirituality from the New Testament to St John of the Cross*, London: Darton, Longman & Todd, 1990.

MARK A. MCINTOSH

Asceticism

From the Greek *askeo*, to train (or literally: to work with raw materials). Virtually all religious traditions require some training, some asceticism, of their committed followers. Despite this fact, the origins of Christian asceticism are to be found in its Jewish roots, and particularly in the influence on early Christianity of the ideal of martyrdom and the associated apocalyptic ideal of living in preparation for the coming holy war that would usher in the coming reign of God: something that formed the inspiration of the community at Qumran. What is perhaps a continuation of this tradition can be found among the 'sons and daughters of the covenant' in early Syrian Christianity.

It is in this apocalyptic context that the earliest Christian uses of *askeo* are to be found (Polycarp, *Philippians* 9.1; *Martyrdom Polycarp* 18.2); indeed, it might plausibly be maintained that the driving inspiration of Christian ethics until as late as the fifth century focused on an *askesis* or training that would ensure steadfastness in the face of the threat of martyrdom. It was not long before Clement of Alexandria, at the end of the second century, began to speak of such preparedness as 'spiritual' or 'gnostic' martyrdom, ranking such lifelong *askesis* higher than the momentary steadfastness required of literal (or 'simple') martyrdom (cf. *Stromateis* 4. 4.15.3–4), a development made all the more easy by the fact that *martyria* primarily means 'bearing witness', actual physical martyrdom being the final test. Clement and others, such as his fellow Alexandrian Origen, lace this fundamentally Christian understanding of *askesis* with notions of classical, primarily Platonic, provenance, which required of the philosopher (in antiquity as much someone committed to a life in search of wisdom, as an adept at argumentation) an ascetic training to free the soul from the body and bodily concerns, thus enabling it to commune unhindered with pure intellectual or spiritual reality: an idea summed up in Socrates' idea of philosophy as *melete thanatou*, preparation for (or training in) death.

The emergence in the fourth century of more structured forms of asceticism that came to be called monasticism, with the monk inheriting the role of the martyr (as intercessor and intimate with the divine), led to more explicit reflection on asceticism. Pre-eminent among the pioneers of ascetic theology was Evagrius, one of the Fathers of the Egyptian desert, a disciple of both the great Macarii (of Egypt and of Alexandria), and before his arrival a pupil of two of the Cappadocian Fathers, Basil the Great and Gregory Nazianzen, and protégé of Melania. From Evagrius' writings we can derive fundamental principles of Christian asceticism of virtually universal influence. Central to Evagrius' asceticism is the notion that the purpose and natural state of the intellect (*nous*) is communion with God in prayer. For such prayer, the intellect needs to be capable of unwavering attention and freed from any kind of distraction. These distractions arise from the lower parts of the soul, the desiring and the aggressive parts (following an analysis of the soul going back at least as far as Plato); Evagrius develops a classification of eight principal tempting or distracting thoughts (*logismoi*) to help in forming a strategy to quell such distractions and attain a state of 'dispassion' (*apatheia*), in which a state of pure prayer becomes a realistic possibility. Such attentive prayer is understood as an expression of love, for in the state of *apatheia* the intellect is free to attend to God, and also to discern and attend to the needs of others. The eight principal 'thoughts' – gluttony, lust, avarice, anger, grief, listlessness, vainglory and pride – are the source of the Western list of seven deadly sins, though, in contrast to the Western list, this classification is primarily diagnostic, intended to be of assistance to a 'spiritual father' (or *geron*, 'elder'), without whose guidance no ascetic endeavour is to be undertaken.

Various other traditions of asceticism emerge from the monastic movement of the fourth century and later. A rather different approach from Evagrius' can be found in groups of homilies, letters, treatises and *erotapokriseis* ('questions-and-answers') that exist in different collections, generally ascribed to Macarius (of Egypt, mostly, though their provenance seems to be Syrian), traditionally called the 'Macarian Homilies'. This tradition sees the heart (*kardia*) as the organ of prayer, and lays stress on true prayer as being the result of the coming of the Holy Spirit and also on the felt experience of his coming. Asceticism in this tradition is seen as making ready for the coming of the Holy Spirit, which also draws on the ancient tradition of Christian martyrdom. A prominent aspect of this ascetic tradition is the notion of combat with the demons, something also found in Evagrius, who classifies the demons in the same way as his *logismoi*: this, too, makes contact with the tradition of Christian martyrdom, as persecutors were regarded as instigated by demons, and the holy war of the eschaton was deemed a struggle with the powers of darkness, the martyrs being the front-line troops. The competitive sense, often found in asceticism throughout the ages, and always felt to be at odds with virtues such as humility, is probably best understood in the context of combat with the demons. Rather different from either of these traditions are those traditions of asceticism that emerged in the context of monks living in community ('coenobitic' monasticism), the pioneers of which were Pachomius and Basil the Great: in these traditions stress is laid on the way in which life in community provides ample opportunity for acts of love and also practice in curbing one's self-will. A notion of immense influence first clearly emerges in the six-century writings ascribed to Dionysius the Areopagite: that of the 'three ways', for Dionysius himself, rather the three aspects of our attaining union with God – purification, illumination and union or perfection. For Dionysius these are intimately bound up with the sacramental nature of the Church.

As the centuries passed, there emerge masters of asceticism who draw on all these traditions; in the East notable examples are Diadochus of Photike (fourth century), Maximus the Confessor, John Climacus, author of the *Ladder of Divine Ascent*, and Isaac of Nineveh, 'the Syrian' (all seventh century), Symeon the New Theologian and his disciple Niketas Stethatos (eleventh century), and more recently Nikodimos of the Holy Mountain (eighteenth century). One ascetic practice that emerges in the Byzantine tradition and comes to assume central significance is practice of the Jesus prayer.

In the West, the history of asceticism and ascetic theology has similar roots and draws on similar sources, especially monastic, as in the Christian East. These monastic sources were partly native to the West (e.g. Martin of Tours, and the circle of ascetics associated with the island of Lérins), but mostly drawn from the East, by translators and interpreters, notably John Cassian, born in Scythia (present-day Romania), who died in Marseilles. The monastic tradition in the West came to be dominated by Benedict and his Rule. In the Middle Ages, various rather different ascetic traditions developed: especially those associated with the mendicant friars, and also lay movements, such as the *Devotio Moderna*. Characteristic of much of this late medieval devotion were methods of meditation and associated practices such as recitation of the rosary.

The word 'asceticism' in modern (and indeed older) use often evokes hair shirts, flagellation, excessive fasting and lengthy vigils. This article has sought to explore the roots of Christian asceticism. Many of these practices do, however, share these roots. If the reality of martyrdom for early Christians taught them that on earth they were no more than strangers or exiles, 'resident aliens' (as *peregrini* might be translated), with no abiding city, but rather in search of a heavenly city, 'whose builder and maker is God' (Heb. 11.10, 13; cf. Eph. 2.19), the various practices of asceticism can be seen as reinforcing this awareness. It is in such a context that external ascetic practices such as fasting, almsgiving, pilgrimage, and even the extreme condition of holy fools, begin to make sense. The dominant form in Christian history of such disjunction from the world has been monasticism, where almost the whole of Christian asceticism has its roots. An acute question today is how the riches of the Christian tradition of asceticism can become a resource for Christians living in the world, especially for married Christians. There is need for the development of an 'asceticism of marriage', understanding the desires and fantasies of the individual as encountering reality in the 'other' of spouse and family, and the 'raw materials' of everyday life as being fashioned into something beautiful, through openness to God's grace and in which that grace is manifest. The understanding of such asceticism could well find inspiration in many of the established traditions of Christian asceticism, especially perhaps those that regard life with others as the fundamental ascetic discipline.

See also **Ascetical Theology; Discipline; Fools, Holy; Martyrdom; Monasticism.**

Gabriel Bunge OSB, *Earthen Vessels. The Practice of Personal Prayer according to the Patristic Tradition*, San Francisco: Ignatius Press, 2002; *Evagrius of Pontus: The Greek Ascetic Corpus*, trans. with intro. and commentary, Robert E. Sinkewicz, Oxford Early Christian Studies, Oxford: Oxford University Press, 2003; *John Climacus: The Ladder of Divine Ascent*, trans. Colm Luibheid and Norman Russell, CWS, Mahwah, NJ: Paulist Press, 1982; Mother Maria Skobtsova, *Essential Writings*, trans. Pichard Pevear and Larissa Volokhonsky, Modern Spiritual Masters Series, Maryknoll, NY: Orbis Books, 2003; Anselme Stolz OSB, *L'Ascèse chrétienne*, Chevetogne: Éditions des Bénédictins d'Amay, 1948; V. Wimbush and R. Valentasis (eds), *Asceticism*, New York: Oxford University Press, 1995.

ANDREW LOUTH

Asia, Spiritualities in

Geographically Asia covers the continent east of the Suez Canal and the Ural range of mountains. But the western part of southern Asia was the home of Semitic races with long contacts with the Greek and Roman empires. To most people today 'Asia' means the civilizations produced by and around China, India, Iran, Japan, Korea and the Indonesian islands. It is to this cultural Asia that this article mostly refers. This dictionary focuses on movements of spirituality found among *Christians*. This short article cannot cover all the religions of Asia, each of which has developed many forms of spirituality. Information about these religions and spiritual paths will be sought in dictionaries or encyclopedias of religions and specialized literature.

West Asia is of course the birthplace of Jesus and of the early stages of the Jesus movement. In the first three centuries the Church spread not only westward and northward, to Europe and the Roman North Africa, but also eastward, into the heart of Semitic Asia, in what is today Lebanon, Syria, Turkey, Armenia, Iraq and Arabia. From this West Asian world the Christian faith infiltrated into central Asia, the heart of China, Mongolia and to East Asia on the one hand, and on the other to Persia (Iran), the Indian subcontinent and the islands beyond. This article does not touch the development of spirituality in the early centuries of Christianity, generally covered in studies on patristics (*see* Early Christian Spirituality).

In the course of the centuries practically all the churches of Europe and America have sent missionaries and established Christian communities all over Asia, each bringing its characteristic form of Christian life and its spiritual traditions. We shall not study here the forms of spirituality practised by Asian oriental Christians derived from their liturgies and patristic traditions, or Western spirituality exported by Iberian and other Catholic missionaries to India, South East Asia, the Philippines or China, or the Anglican, Methodist, Pentecostal or other traditions which took roots in the various Christian communities of Asia. We shall rather pay attention to those spiritual trends that have been influenced or derived from the spiritual religious traditions of Asia.

1. *Yoga and Zen.* The trends of Asian spirituality assimilated and developed by the Christian communities are generally influenced by the Indian traditions of metaphysical advaita and spiritual interiority. The aim is to come into contact with the 'real Self' by 'blocking the fluctuations of consciousness' (*cittavrttinirodha*) of our empirical self, in Patanjali's classical expression, Yogasūtras 1.1.2 (third century?). Thus one develops a higher level of consciousness where the subject is directly aware of the Self, unconditioned by limitations from outside, an experience of the subject *as subject* (*ātmatvena*), as Śankara (eighth century CE?) puts it. Yoga was perhaps the first important spiritual tradition which India offered to Christians. Besides the classical Indian texts one can read the work of Mircea Eliade, *Yoga, Immortality and Freedom*, published in French in 1954 and in English in 1958 (London: Routledge & Kegan Paul).

The Christian reception of the Yoga tradition was well articulated by the Belgian Benedictine monk J.-M. Déchanet who in 1956 published *La voie du silence: L'Experience d'un moine* (Bruges: Desclée de Brower), translated into English as *Christian Yoga* (London: Burns & Oates 1960). Numerous books on Yoga and 'Christian Yoga' have since been published both in Asia and in the West. Déchanet acknowledges that his book is oriented to a practical aim and is a 'complete transposition' of the Indian tradition to the context of the Christian faith. Zen is the Buddhist adaptation of Yoga. Its practice requires the creation of an appropriate physical space, normally in a monastery close to nature, an interior space for the spiritual search, an internal structure consisting of discipline, community and the master, and a goal of awakening in simplicity to the experience of non-duality.

Both Yoga and Zen can be practised for many different purposes. Some seek from it a therapeutic physical exercise. Others want to achieve inner quiet and a psychic equilibrium, useful even for success in professional life. Others find it a help to a higher degree of contemplation; for some it is a means of self-liberation; others go to it in the spirit of the Mahayana to be enabled to help others; while the original *zazen* aims at *satori* (*wu* in Chinese), the actualization of one's true nature and reordering of one's relation to the universe. In Yoga the highest ideal is spoken of as pure existence (*kaivalya*) without objective consciousness (*asamprajñāta*). The claim that the oriental techniques of meditation cannot be imported into a Christian practice does not seem to correspond to the experience of many Asian Christians.

Yoga involves as a preliminary stage the control of breath, the *prāṇāyāma*. It seems that this spiritual tradition was also adopted in the Muslim Sufi spirituality and probably influenced the development of the Jesus Prayer in Oriental Christianity. In his Spiritual Exercises, Ignatius of Loyola teaches among others 'three methods of prayer' of which the first consists in repeating slowly the words of a prayer in unison with the breathing rhythm.

Influenced by the same Yoga tradition, the *nāma-japa* is the recitation in low voice or in chant of the names of God, widely practised in Asia, with or without the help of beads and symbolized by prayer wheels and prayer flags. Christians also frequently use *bhajans*, short invocations sung antiphonally by the leader and the congregation, generally to the accompaniment of the tabla and manual harmonium.

2. *Dialogue and inter-religiosity*. In Asia a great variety of religious traditions have generally co-existed in harmony. Asian religions and ways of life have no hard boundaries to define them. In China, Confucianism, Buddhism and Daoism are blended in a single cultural unity, so that it is impossible to count the members of each religion separately. Similarly in rural parts of India, Sikhism, Hinduism and/or Jainism may be equally owned by the same people, and at the popular level there is a considerable sharing of the spiritual practices of all religions. The same is the case in Indonesia. Christians too live comfortably in various spiritual traditions, even if generally they keep the primary identity of their Christian parents, while not a few Asians of various religions live as non-baptized Christ-bhaktas by making the message and person of Jesus a central point of reference in their lives. The slogan 'To be religious is to be inter-religious' may be new in the West but has been lived in Asia for centuries. The coexistence with other religions even in the situation of minority, as is the case of Christians in most of Asia, is experienced as normal and does not create inner conflict. Rather, it is source of spiritual richness. Today theologians explore the validity and implications of this double belonging and propose new theological vistas to accommodate it.

3. *Ahimsā and ecology*. Another influential feature of Asian spirituality is its stress of *ahimsā* or non-violence in the relation with the external world. *Ahimsā* is the first and most fundamental of the *yamas* or five 'restraints' that the candidate to yoga must begin to practise. Ancient monastic traditions too made it the first of their vows. Mahatma Gandhi developed it into a political theology and praxis. He called it the 'soul force'. It involves a spirituality of action and struggle attuned to human dignity. While he found a confirmation of this principle in the writings of Thoreau and Tolstoy, its roots go deep in the Indian tradition and are shared with much of the rest of Asia. Hinduism and its sister tradition of Jainism, so influential in Gandhiji's native

Gujarat, make *ahimsā* the foundation of the spiritual life. Etymologically, ahimsā is not absence of violence, but is an inner attitude: it derives from a 'desiderative' root and could be translated as the 'non-desire to hurt'. Already in 1958 Pius Régamey OP, published in French a seminal book which articulates the Christian reception of the Gandhian ahimsā. Thomas Merton wrote a significant Preface for the English translation (*Non-violence and the Christian Conscience*, London: Darton, Longman & Todd, 1966). In Asia ahimsā extends not only to human beings but also to the animal world and even to the whole of nature. Sensitivity to nature is an important element of Asian spirituality. Although in some traditions of Asia, for example the Sāmkhya of India, nature (*prakṛti*) is dialectically contrasted with spirit (*puruṣa*), in most cultural contexts nature is perceived very much as the 'home' in which the spirit lives. Koyama calls the 'Asian' a 'cosmological' and even 'botanical' spirituality, in contrast with the 'eschatological spirituality' deriving from Semitic West Asia and developed in Europe. Even the belief in transmigration implies that the animal world is closely related to us. Asia therefore warmly welcomes and contributes much of its own to the ecological movement. It fits with the Asian sensitivity. The respect for the cow in India is only a primordial model of the respect due to all animal life. In the art of Japan and other oriental countries there is a fine blending of nature and the human. Harmony is the best word to describe this. The Korean dances present it visually.

The primeval or tribal world has a different kind of cultural sensitivity, but here too nature is a primordial value to be protected. Indian tribals, Christians included, have strongly protested against the violation of nature involved in the mega industrial undertakings of huge dams with an indiscriminate cutting of trees and destruction of the habitat of people and animals. The forest is the home of the spirits, both benevolent and malevolent, and a respect for the continuity of the environment is essential for the survival of the tribal culture. Not strangely, Indian rural women have embraced the trees to protect them from being cut.

Recently the Federation of Asian Bishops' Conferences (FABC) has insisted on 'harmony' as essential to Asian spirituality. Harmony is the presupposition of ahimsā. The sense of harmony pervades much of the traditional Chinese and Japanese world view.

4. *Ashrams and contemplation*. The home of Yoga and Zen, Asia has a long tradition of contemplative spirituality. Salvation is sought in a new con-

sciousness of oneness with the Absolute Reality. Hinduism and Buddhism have developed sophisticated practices of contemplation to attain liberation. Not surprisingly, the contemplative streak is strong in the spiritual make-up of Asian Christians. A typical evidence of this are the Christian ashrams developed mostly in the twentieth century. An ashram is a kind of retreat centre, different from the institutions known in the West. It has a stable community where contemplation and work, manual and intellectual, blend together. However, it does not impose any spiritual path on its members – each one has to find his or her own, under the guidance of the guru, the central figure of the ashram. The ashram is a place of inter-religious encounter. It keeps the doors open to the occasional visitors who want only a few days or even hours of spiritual experience. The openness of the ashram extends ideally to members of either gender and also to families. The contemplative dimension of Asian spirituality may be the explanation of the abundance of candidates for the Catholic religious life found in most countries of the continent.

5. *Liberation spiritualities*. Asia has generated at least three types of liberation theology with a liberation spirituality. First, the *minjung* theology of Korea. Its focus is the 'people', that is the common men and women in so far as they are marginalized in society without power of their own, victims of systems that impose a way of life not of their choice. The minjung conscientizes people and with the help of popular stories, mask dances and irony awakens a sense of *han*, a feeling of deep anger for the injustice of the situation. If Latin American liberation theology stressed the problem of 'bread', the material poverty of the masses, minjung theology starts from the experience of powerlessness and aims at an adequate sharing of power among all the people.

India has produced dalit theology. The dalits are the originally untouchable castes, believed socially to consist of polluted and polluting people, to be avoided and not allowed to mix with caste society or use the common village resources, e.g. wells. Dalit theology has developed into dalit spirituality, an awareness of the equality of all human beings and leading to a loud vindication of rights. For centuries dalits have sought 'salvation', that is, an escape from their condition, by converting to other religious bodies, Islam, Sikhism, Buddhism, Christianity or new Hindu sects. The starting point of dalit theology is the 'pain-pathos' of the condition of those deprived of social dignity. Its spirituality consists of an internalization of the message of

the cross/resurrection as the source of liberation. Liberation starts within, with a rejection of the myth of pollution, and leads to action for an equal place in society.

Finally the Philippines have developed what they call the theology of struggle that involves an effort of discovering the liberation of the oppressed in the struggle itself, and not just in its future outcome. Perhaps theirs is closer to the Latin American liberation theology, their main concern being the economic situation of the poor. However, the elements of power and of dignity cannot be separated from the poverty factor.

The three forms of Asian liberation spirituality can be related to the three temptations of Jesus.

See also **Spirituality and the Dialogue of Religions (***essay***); Buddhism and Christianity; Confucianism and Christianity; Hinduism and Christianity; Inculturation; Islam and Christianity; Jesus Prayer; Liberation Spirituality; Sufism and Christianity; Yoga; Zen and Christianity.**

Swami Abhishiktananda (Dom Henry Le Saux), *Prayer*, Delhi: ISPCK, 1967, 1972, 1989; Michael Amaladoss, *Making Harmony: Living in a Pluralistic World*, Delhi: ISPCK, 2003; *Asian Christian Perspective on Harmony*, A Document of the Theological Advisory Commission of the Federation of Asian Bishops' Conferences, FABC Papers no. 75, Hong Kong: FABC, 1996 (cf. also no. 76); Virginia Fabella and R. S. Sugirtharajah (eds), *Dictionary of Third World Theologies*, Maryknoll, NY: Orbis Books, 2000 (with appropriate bibliographies); Yves Raguin, *The Depth of God*, Weathampstead: Antony Clarke, 1979; Choan-Seng Song, *The Compassionate God. An Exercise in the Theology of Transposition*, London: SCM Press, 1982.

G. GISPERT-SAUCH

Attentiveness

Attention, writes Pierre Hadot, 'is the philosophical attitude *par excellence*. It is also the attitude of the Christian philosopher' (Hadot, 1995, p. 130). By attention, Hadot means a self-consciousness that is not self-obsession, but an examination of one's motives and intentions in every moment. It denotes both a 'moral conscience' and a 'cosmic consciousness'. In other words, 'the "attentive" person lives constantly in the presence of God and is constantly remembering God, joyfully consenting to the will of universal reason, and he sees all things with the eyes of God himself' (*ibid.*, p. 130).

Hadot has in mind the practices of cultivating

attention developed by the Stoics, inherited by Christian philosophers like Clement of Alexandria and institutionalized in Christian monasticism. But we can look even further back to see that the cultivation of attention is central to a Christian orientation to the world. A generous capacity for attention marks the life of Jesus himself.

The Gospels describe Jesus as a person wholly able to be present to another, without turning the other into something easily received or managed. Jesus makes himself available to sick people, disabled people, broken-hearted people. He attends to those whose sins are known and condemned by their communities. He makes himself present to those on the margins of their communities: women, children, tax collectors, prostitutes. The Gospels describe him receiving each person carefully, in an unrushed, non-judgemental way. The Samaritan woman at the well, the woman caught in adultery, the tax collector Zacchaeus, the children shooed away by his disciples: all receive his careful attention. In the story of Mary and Martha, Jesus commends this way of attention and urges Martha to choose it over distraction, even in the midst of great busyness.

One of the strongest appeals for the cultivation of attention as a Christian practice was made in the twentieth century by the philosopher Simone Weil. In her meditation on what she called 'a Christian conception of studies' (Weil, 1951, p. 58), Weil argued that the development of attention is the 'real object and almost the sole interest of studies' because, without a well-honed capacity for attention, we can neither pray nor be present to those who suffer. 'Warmth of heart', she writes, 'cannot make up for it' (ibid., p. 58).

According to Weil, attention is the very 'substance of prayer' (ibid., p. 59). Students do not, however, cultivate attention through 'contracting their brows, holding their breath, stiffening their muscles' (ibid., p. 60). The kind of attention that bears fruit in prayer must be pursued with desire, pleasure, joy and love. 'Twenty minutes of concentrated, untired attention is infinitely better than three hours of the kind of frowning application that leads us to say with a sense of duty done: "I have worked well!"' (ibid., p. 61).

Not only is attention the indispensable condition for presence to God in prayer, it is also necessary for presence to our suffering neighbour. The cultivation of our attention through study helps us, Weil argues, to empty our soul 'of all its own contents in order to receive into itself the being it is looking at, just as he is, in all his truth' (ibid., p. 65). A well-developed capacity

for attention allows us to be present to what is other than ourselves – God or our neighbour – without trying to turn that other into ourselves.

Study is one practice of Christian spirituality that privileges the cultivation of attention. There are many others. The Rule of St Benedict, for example, urges us to seek Christ in attention to the stranger and the guest through embodied practices like the washing of feet. *The Way of the Pilgrim* teaches a repetitive prayer, the Jesus prayer, that fully engages the body in practices of attention by teaching us to pray the prayer with every breath we exhale. In study and in conversation, in prayer and in the careful tending of the bodies of others, we have the opportunity to nurture an attentiveness that deepens our engagement with God and the world.

Pierre Hadot, *Philosophy as a Way of Life*, ed. Arnold I. Davidson, trans. Michael Chase, Oxford: Blackwell, 1995; *The Rule of St. Benedict*, trans. Timothy Fry, Collegeville, MN: The Liturgical Press, 1982; *The Way of a Pilgrim*, trans. R. M. French, San Francisco: Harper-Collins, 1991; Simone Weil, 'Reflections on the right use of school studies with a view to the love of God', *Waiting for God*, trans. Emma Craufurd, New York: Perennial, 1951.

STEPHANIE PAULSELL

Augustinian Spirituality

St Augustine of Hippo (354–430), monk, bishop and theologian, left a spiritual legacy that may be viewed from two perspectives: his actual teaching and writings, subsequent appropriations of this legacy. In common with all the Fathers of the Church, what today is called spirituality was for him one dimension of a total Christian self-understanding that had not yet begun to divide into distinctive categories such as doctrine, liturgy, the Scriptures and the spiritual life. Augustine's spirituality manifests a thematic rather than a systematic unity, being held together by a series of recurring and interconnected concepts that constitute his distinctive spiritual vision. These are especially prominent in his best-known works: *Confessions*, *Tractates on the Gospel of John*, *Explanation of the Psalms*, *The Trinity*, *The City of God*, and his *Sermons*. In general, later Augustinian thinkers or movements tended to emphasize or systematize some particular aspect of his thought, the results being an approach to or school of spirituality both rooted in and yet distinctive from the actual spiritual vision of Augustine of Hippo. The following can be considered the essential elements or themes of Augustine's spirituality.

1. *Jesus Christ*. Christ as Way and Homeland (*Via* and *Patria*) is one of many christological affirmations employed by Augustine to assert the central place and role of Jesus Christ, Son of God, for humanity. Augustine's spirituality is profoundly christological both in its content and in its method, in no small part a result of the fourth-century struggles associated with the Nicene–Arian crisis. And to affirm the centrality of Christ is likewise to affirm the centrality of the Trinity for Augustine's spirituality. It is Christ who reveals the Father and promises the Spirit; it is the Father who sends the Son; it is the Spirit who enflames the hearts of the members of the Body of Christ. Every dimension of Augustine's spirituality is vitally linked to the identity and work of the Son of God. This finds expression not only in a consistent attention to orthodoxy (True God and True Man, Sole Mediator, etc.) but by the creative employment of key scripturally based titles such as Christ the Word (*Verbum*), Physician (*Medicus*), Teacher (*Magister*) and Poor (*Pauper*). His most original christological affirmation is that of *Christus Totus* – the Whole Christ, a proclamation of the profound union between Christ and his body the Church, a union that will only be totally realized eschatologically.

2. *Grace*. From his earliest writings to his final work Augustine reveals a profound sensitivity to the radically gratuitous nature of God's initiative towards humanity. If creation manifests the first instance of this initiative, God's response to the disobedience of Adam and Eve with their disruption of the human–divine covenant manifests an even more radically gracious initiative: the Word becoming flesh. The name of this initiative is grace and stands at the centre of the human experience of the mystery of God's free love for humanity. This affirmation of grace is profoundly christological yet deeply anthropological, since grace reveals both God's loving initiative in Christ as well as a total and desperate human dependence upon this initiative. 'What do you have that you have not received' (1 Cor. 4.7) is one key text among many that Augustine employs to affirm God's absolute sovereignty in the process of salvation, confirming as well the total human incapacity without this sovereign initiative.

3. *Inner-directed*. 'Our heart is restless' Augustine insists at the outset of his *Confessions* (1.1.1). God alone offers the heart true and lasting satisfaction. Such emphasis on the heart directed towards God highlights the importance of interiority in Augustinian spirituality. It is upon the heart that God has stamped the divine image (Gen. 1.27; see *Tractates on the Gospel of John* 18.10), the awareness of which becomes an unrelenting summons for the Christian to turn within to discover and cherish that divine presence, seal and identity. The heart (*cor*) can be viewed symbolically as representing the unlimited depths within every human being wherein all are called to discover, find and embrace the divine presence. However, the constant call to 'return to yourself' (*On True Religion* 72.102) identified with this heart-emphasis is never meant to be a selfish movement into solitude but serves, rather, as the only sure beginning for discovering one's true and authentic self before God.

4. *Communal*. The emphasis on interiority is matched by a just as insistent emphasis on the shared nature of Christian existence: 'shared was our loss, shared be our finding' – '*communis fuit perditio, sit communis inventio*' (*Sermons* 115.4.4). If Augustine's own human make-up was decidedly social, poignantly portrayed in the *Confessions* as communion in both sin and grace, this was only further intensified by his experience of the African Church of his day, torn by conflict between Catholic and Donatist. This experience only intensified Augustine's awareness of the importance of communal unity: 'the Church is the unity of Christ' (*Sermons* 21D (159B).17; see *Sermons* 47.28). He found in the description of the unity of the first Christian believers in Jerusalem (Acts 4.32) the hallmark for every Christian community: 'one soul and one heart intent upon God' – '*anima una et cor unum in Deum*'. It became the foundational text for his monastic Rule (1.2), but served above all as an indispensable ecclesial ideal.

5. *Love*. 'Love and do what you will' (*Tractates on the Letters of John* 7.8) boldly sums up the centrality of love in the spirituality of Augustine. He explored in depth the relationship between love of God and love of neighbour, one result being his classic *frui/uti* distinction: God alone is to be loved as an end – effectively subordinating all other loves to this end. Both enthralled and terrified with the scriptural affirmations that 'God is love' (1 John 4.6) and Christ's own description of the final judgement in terms of neighbourly love of the poor Christ (Matt. 25.31–46; see *Sermons* 389.5), Augustine consistently placed Jesus' love command as the summation of the whole Christian life.

6. *Truth*. Augustine's insistence upon the pivotal role of love is complemented by a persistent effort to link it to truth: 'truth alone is victorious,

and the victory of truth is love' (*Sermons* 358.1). Grounded in New Testament affirmations of Christ as Truth (e.g., John 14.6) Augustinian love thus becomes a love of truth and the truth of love (see *City of God* 19.19; *Explanation of the Psalms* 99.7; *On the Trinity* 4.proem.). Truth is in essence theocentric: 'where I have found truth, there have I found my God' (*Confessions* 10.24.35). This insistence upon the pursuit of truth gives Augustinian spirituality a deeply intellectual character, where reading, study and dialogue can be seen as spiritual exercises (see *Retractations* 1.27; *On the Trinity* 9.12; *Letters* 157.3; *On True Religion* 17; *Sermons* 4.1).

7. *Monastic*. Upon his conversion, Augustine embraced the ascetical life, foregoing marriage and family, wealth and career. When he returned to his native Africa, now a servant of God (*servus Dei*), the equivalent of a monk, he gathered around himself a community of like-minded ascetics. Living on the remains of his family estate they dedicated themselves to prayer, work and study. His unexpected call to serve the church of Hippo Regius led him to establish a lay monastery there and upon becoming bishop he turned the episcopal residence into a monastery of clerics (see *Sermons* 355–6). The monastic Rule he wrote for the lay monastery, based upon the ideals of the primitive Jerusalem community and his own distinctive emphases (interiority, humility, fraternal correction, forgiveness, grace, etc.), lent its authority to the shaping of Western monasticism.

8. *Progressive*. There is an inherent dynamism and vitality to Augustinian spirituality. His controversies with the Donatists and the Pelagians led him to emphasize the unfinished nature of the Christian life, leading to an ever-increasing emphasis on the notion of progress (*proficere*, *proficiens*). Thus the Christian life is a pilgrimage, demanding ongoing conversion, the taking up of new challenges, requiring an ever-fresh response to God's call: 'If you say you've finished, you're finished!' (see *Sermons* 169.18). Yet this demanding pilgrimage becomes possible because Christ remains both the way and the destination: 'God as Christ is the homeland of our journey, the man Christ is the path there: we journey to him, we journey through him' (*Sermons* 123.3.3).

9. *Scriptural*. Augustine's spirituality is a product of his own encounter with the Word of God which supplies it with both content and vocabulary. Sharing with all patristic authors a profound awareness of the centrality of the biblical

word for faith, worship, prayer and daily living, Augustine's thought is thoroughly scriptural. There are certain biblical texts that occur repeatedly in his writings (e.g. Gen. 1.27; Job 7.1; Isa. 7.9, LXX; John 1.14; Rom. 5.5; 7.24–25a; 11.33–36; 1 Cor. 1.31; 3.6–7; 4.7; Gal. 5.6) and likewise can be said to manifest his distinctive spiritual vision. This profoundly scriptural spirituality is exemplified in the *Confessions*, where scriptural text and Augustinian voice become virtually one.

10. *Legacy*. Both the volume and depth of his writings and the authority of his name gave Augustine a unique and prominent role in the development of Latin Western Christianity. While virtually all the spiritualities and theologies of the West manifest this impact, certain movements and ages reflect a particularly Augustinian character: the canonical movement of the eleventh and twelfth centuries exemplified by the Victorines of Paris and the mendicant Order (Hermits) of Saint Augustine (1244) are two prominent examples. Key Protestant Reformers likewise looked to Augustine as their inspiration as did Jansenius of Ypres. The Augustinian nature of these instances continues to be a source of research and debate. Augustine remains a prominent spiritual voice today, his particular emphasis on self and interiority, grace and freedom, Church and community continuing to attract the attention and comments of contemporary thinkers.

See also **Canonical Communities; Grace; Interiority; Jesus and Spirituality; Love; Mendicant Spirituality; Monasticism; Victorine Spirituality.**

T. J. van Bavel OSA, *Christians in the World: Introduction to the Spirituality of Augustine*, New York: Catholic Book Publishing Co., 1980; Mary T. Clark RSCJ, 'Spirituality' in *Augustine through the Ages: An Encyclopedia*, ed., Allan Fitzgerald, Grand Rapids, MI: Eerdmans, 1999, pp. 813–15; Carol Harrison, *Augustine: Christian Truth and Fractured Humanity*, Oxford: Oxford University Press, 2002; Michele Pellegrino, *Spiritual Journey: Augustine's Reflections on the Christian Life*, Villanova, PA: Augustinian Press, 1996; Adolar Zumkeller, OSA, *Augustine's Ideal of the Religious Life*, trans. Edmund Colledge, New York: Fordham University Press, 1986.

THOMAS F. MARTIN

Australasian Spirituality

In both New Zealand and Australia, indigenous peoples had their own cultures and spiritualities before Christianity arrived with explorers and colonizers. Only relatively recently has the spiritual depth of these indigenous cultures been widely recognized. In Australia, the most striking feature of indigenous spiritualities was the recognition that creative beings were responsible for the features of the land. The stories of the dreaming spoke of the creative activities, the time of creation and of relationships to the land. The world was seen as a closed, self-regulating system in which the parts were alive, conscious and related. In New Zealand, Maori spirituality was pragmatic, centred on honour, and – in myths of arrival by canoe – emphasized the importance of place and its attainment.

The spirituality of the new migrants was shaped by the character of the many churches from which they had originated. The challenges which they faced in establishing and commending their churches in the new lands gave a distinctive cast to their spirituality. In Australia, which began as a convict settlement, the churches never had a privileged place. Those who built church communities worked under great difficulties, venturing long distances into thinly settled land. After the Treaty of Waitangi in 1840, Maori embraced Christianity in great numbers, and also adapted it to their own cultural norms, sometimes forming churches that were very creative in their adoption of Christianity.

The poor resources with which Christians built ensured that there was little space for original reflection on distinctively Australasian Christianity or for original theological thinking. Most Christian writing in the new settlements was designed to make available to Australians the resources of the founding churches, and to strengthen the denominational identity of their adherents. This often encouraged a negative form of self-identification, by which the identity of Protestant Christians was given by being non-Catholic, and vice versa. In missionary contexts, the form of Christian faith and life first brought to the native peoples was generally that of the founding churches. It was modified substantially in being received.

Reflection on what was distinctively Australasian in the encounter of colonists with the new lands and their people was rarely undertaken in explicitly Christian discourse. It fell more generally to poets and historians. In both Australia and New Zealand, there was a tension between emphasizing the unique qualities of the new world and stressing the Western cultural tradition from which both countries drew, between the images of rural life and those of the urbanized reality. The historians and poets have generally provided the myths through which people read what it means to be Australian, and have framed the questions asked about the distinctively local appropriation and living out of Christian faith. The Australian myth of the bronzed bushman was propagated by poets, and later questioned by Henry Lawson and others. In New Zealand, Thomas Bracken proposed the same ideal. The war historian C. E. W. Bean provided the basis for the myth of the Anzacs that reflected the heavy loss of life among young male Australians in the 1918 war. Later, more explicitly spiritual poets like James Baxter and James McCauley reflected on the founding of the two countries, and McCauley picked up a strand of religious speculation about the place which the new world had in God's providence.

The themes of Australian and New Zealand life were also systematized by historians. Of these Manning Clarke has been particularly important in Australia, setting Australian history within the large theological structure of sin and fall, grace and redemption, and emphasizing the distinction between the archetypically Protestant, Catholic and Enlightenment strands of Australian history. More recent historical writing and argument about the dispossession of the indigenous people in Australia has also influenced reflection on Australian identity. It is found in popular works, based on reading and anecdotal evidence, by Donald Horne and others. These popular works have provoked widespread interest and debate about the heart of Australian spirituality.

Contemporary Christian spirituality in New Zealand and Australia is expressed notably in popular writing about prayer and about the shaping of Christian community. It is also expressed in hymnody which picks up the emphasis on social justice, community adopted by the churches.

Explicit treatments of Christian spirituality has generally taken up the themes developed in secular reflection on culture, and has related them to Christian faith. In general, there are five dominant themes expressed in Australian spiritual writing, which have resonances in that of New Zealand.

The first is the nature of life in Australia, and particularly the natural environment of a relatively narrow coastal strip that supports most of the population, with a huge, mainly dry or desert area in the centre of the land. The interrelationship between desert and sea is picked up in biblical reference, and the desert is seen as a natural spiritual home. The heavily populated coastal strip is often presented as an image of exiles camped around the perimeters of an alien continent.

A second theme, closely associated with the environment, is the relationship between indigenous Australians and the white settlers. This has two aspects. Many commentators conclude that aboriginals can communicate the secret of living in Australia, particularly through a message of deep respect for the land and of a non-exploitative attitude to it. Their attitude to the land has been commended particularly by those who wish to develop a spirituality open to environmental concerns. Aboriginal spirituality is also commended for its emphasis on the connection between all beings and particularly between human beings. This has been seen as a corrective to Western individualism.

Also pertinent to reflection on the place of indigenous Australians is the expropriation of land and the mistreatment of the indigenous peoples by the later settlers. It is a commonplace that an Australian spirituality must reckon with the sin at the heart of Australian settlement and the need for healing. Healing can come only through reconciliation between the indigenous Australians and the dominant newer arrivals. The relationship between Maori and Pakeha (New Zealanders of European origin) also forms a central theme of New Zealand spirituality.

The third theme of Australasian spirituality also deals with the local peculiarities of New Zealand and Australian societies. In both, power and government are exercised by populations of largely European descent in a geographic environment that is not European. The Asian context of Australian life and the Pacific context of New Zealand life mean that the spirituality of the later settlers continues to reckon with a strong sense of being out of place.

Fourth, Australia and New Zealand have been celebrated as egalitarian and informal societies. More recently, the relatively flat distribution of wealth and the protected working conditions that underlay this characterization have been destroyed by neo-liberal economic consensus and the forces of globalization. The egalitarian myth, however, influences reflection on Australian spirituality, and supports the strong emphasis on social justice and progressive reform in much of Christian spiritual writing. It also stands in some tension with strongly hierarchical constructions of church life, as well as with the notably individualist trends of contemporary culture. Feminist spirituality, in particular, includes a strong emphasis on justice and equality.

The extent to which these four themes are given prominence in reflection on Australasian spirituality perhaps depends on a larger question that is sharply pointed by the contemporary context. Reflection on spirituality must decide how it is to handle an Australasian reality characterized by declining church attendance and allegiance and a wider population increasingly ignorant of religion and untouched by churches. Confronted by this question, some propose that spirituality must again base itself on the Scriptures and the foundational elements of the tradition. Others insist that Christian spirituality must find common ground with the spiritual yearnings and sustenance found within the culture, and particularly with marginal aspects of that culture. This question is being pressed more urgently in an intellectual environment where foundational and overarching narratives meet with some scepticism.

———

James Belch, *Making Peoples: A History of the New Zealanders, From Polynesian Settlement to the End of the Nineteenth Century,* Honolulu: University of Hawaii's Press, 1996; James Belch, *Paradise Reforged: A History of the New Zealanders, From the 1880s to the Year 2000,* Honolulu: University of Hawai'i Press, 2001; Manning Clark, *A History of Australia,* Carlton: Melbourne University Press, 1962–1987; Donald Horne, *The Lucky Country,* Ringwood: Penguin, 1998; David Tacey, *Re-Enchantment: The New Australian Spirituality:* Pymble: Harper Collins, 2000.

ANDREW HAMILTON

Australian Aboriginal Spirituality

see Australasian Spirituality

Baptism

Baptism from the Greek verb *baptizein* means to 'plunge' or to 'dip'. Many ancient religions knew the practice of ritual ablutions. Muslims and Hindus typically wash themselves as they enter mosques or temples. The Jews also had purification ceremonies in the form of baths (*mikvah*) to re-establish ritual purity. Additionally Jews knew of a baptismal ritual for the proselytizing of Gentiles who sought membership into the Jewish community. The Essene community at Qumran had similar religious practices, whereby after three years of instruction, baptism took place once the candidates confessed their sins and praised God. Unlike other forms of baptism, this rite was repeatable and all members of the community would renew their membership through such purification rituals on an annual basis. Against the Jewish backdrop John the Baptizer practised a purification ritual that was essential to his prophetic call (Mark 1.4–6). For John to plunge a follower under water symbolized conversion. Although Jesus did not need to undergo John's ritual baptism he did so to signify acceptance of his own mission and link it to John's prophesy (Mark 1.9–11; John 1.32–34).

The term baptism in the Christian context is derived from the Church's sacramental practice of washing by a triple immersion in the name of the Trinity (Matt. 28.19). The ritual action of plunging catechumens into water symbolizes the burial into Christ's death (Rom. 6.3–4; Col. 2.12), from which they rise up by resurrection with Christ as 'new creatures' (2 Cor. 5.17; Gal. 6.15). This sacrament is also called 'the washing of regeneration and renewal by the Holy Spirit' (Titus 3.5), for it signifies and brings about the birth of water and the Spirit without which no one 'can enter the kingdom of God' (John 3.5). A third name for this sacrament is 'enlightenment' because those who receive the catechetical instruction are enlightened in their understanding. Having received in baptism the Word, 'the true light that enlightens every person' (John 1.9), those baptized have been 'enlightened' (Heb. 10.32), they become 'children of light' (1 Thess. 5.5), indeed, they become 'light in the Lord' (Eph. 5.8).

A secondary name for this sacrament is 'christening' which refers to the anointing of the catechumen with chrism. The name Christ means 'the anointed one'. As Christ was anointed priest, prophet and king, so too newly born Christians share in the threefold mission of Christ (to teach, govern and sanctify) each person according to his or her God-given gifts and position in the Church, the Body of Christ. A rich theology of Christian vocation and mission can be derived from both the washing in water and the anointing with sacred chrism.

Baptism along with confirmation and the Eucharist comprise the sacraments of Christian initiation and together they lay the foundations of every Christian life. Baptism is the basis of the whole Christian life, the gateway to life in the Spirit and the door that gives access to the other sacraments. Through baptism Christians profess to be freed from sin and reborn as children of God; they become members of Christ and are incorporated into the Church. The gradual process by which one becomes a Christian is called the catechumenate, which consists of four stages. Like all human rites of passage, the Christian rites of initiation follow a general pattern consisting of (1) entrance to the catechumenate after an initial period of inquiry, (2) election during which those to be initiated are instructed and formed in the teaching and life of the community, (3) the rites of initiation (baptism, confirmation and first Communion), rites by which the former catechumens and elect

are now fully incorporated into the life of the Christian community, and (4) the period of mystagogy ('explanation of the mysteries'), a continued process of further incorporation into the community by exploring what the 'mysteries' received signify and what their implications are for ongoing life in the community. Liturgical evidence from the early centuries of Christianity indicates that ritual variations existed from place to place. For example, in Spain the formula was in the name of Christ and not the Trinity, in Milan there was an additional foot-washing as a part of the rite, in the East there were several anointings. Nonetheless the washing ritual, whether by full immersion, by effusion (pouring water) or by aspersion (sprinkling), was the central feature of baptism and the catechumenate was a gradual process whereby Christians were formed in a holistic manner, intellectually, spiritually and ethically.

Since the Second Vatican Council the revised Order of Christian Initiation in the Roman Catholic Church has retrieved many ritual elements of the process that had been lost over time. The liturgical and spiritual experience of parishes around the world of the new rite has been most positive not only for the candidates but also for their sponsors and for parishioners in general. Also for the first time in the history of the Church a rite specifically for infant baptism was devised which clearly takes into consideration the condition of infants who are being initiated into the Church.

Baptism is rich in imagery and symbolism. The fifth-century poem of Pope Sixtus III that is found on the walls of the baptistery of St John Lateran, the cathedral of the city of Rome, captures the multifaceted beauty of this fundamental sacrament of Christian vocation:

> Here a people of godly race are born of heaven;
>   the Spirit gives them life in the fertile waters;
> The Church-Mother, in these waves, bears her children
>   like virginal fruit she has conceived by the Holy Spirit.
> Hope for the kingdom, you who are reborn in this spring
>   for those who are born but once have no share
>   in the life of blessedness.
> Here is to be found the source of life,
>   which washes the whole universe,
>   which gushed from the wound of Christ.
> Sinner, plunge into the sacred fountain to wash away your sin.
> The water receives the old man,
>   and in his place makes the new man to rise.

You wish to become innocent: cleanse yourself
in this bath,
> whatever your burden may be, Adam's sin
> or your own.

There is no difference between those who are
reborn;
> they are one, in a single baptism, a single
> Spirit, a single faith.

Let no one be afraid of the number of the
weight of his sins:
> he who is born of this stream will be made
> holy.

See also **Spirituality, Liturgy and Worship**
(*essay*); **Conversion; Eucharistic Spirituality;**
Ritual; Sacramentality.

Maxwell Johnson, *The Rites of Christian
Initiation: Their Evolution and Interpretation*,
Collegeville, MN: Pueblo, 1999; Maxwell
Johnson (ed.), *Living Water, Sealing Spirit:
Readings on Christian Initiation*, Collegeville,
MN: Pueblo, 1995; Paul Turner, *Halleluja
Highway: A History of the Catechumenate*,
Chicago: Liturgy Training Publications, 2000;
Edward Yarnold, *The Awe-Inspiring Rites of
Initiation: The Origins of the R.C.I.A.*,
Collegeville, MN: The Liturgical Press, 1994.

MICHAEL S. DRISCOLL

Baptist Spirituality

Over the four centuries since the Baptist movement began there has been inevitable development. Baptists today are found all over the world,
with the largest Baptist presence being in North
America, followed by countries in the two-thirds
world such as Nigeria. Although there is diversity, there are certain elements that have characterized and still characterize Baptist spirituality.
The first is personal faith. The classic of Puritan
spirituality, *Pilgrim's Progress*, written in 1678 by
John Bunyan (1628–88), is the story of Christian
and his spiritual journey. He reaches the cross,
where he experiences conversion, and then goes
on through various and varied experiences until
he reaches the heavenly city. Bunyan was part
of a Baptist/Congregational Church and his
emphasis on a personal response to God is
typical of Baptist piety.

Baptist stress on faith and conversion is, however, shared with other Protestant believers.
What was immediately distinctive about Baptists
in seventeenth-century England was their practice of the baptism of believers and their repudiation of infant baptism. John Smyth (c. 1550/
1570–1612), a Church of England priest and
lecturer, became a Separatist, and with a group
that he led moved to Holland in 1607 to escape

religious persecution. There Smyth came to the
firm belief that the only valid baptism was that of
a believer, on profession of personal faith. Dutch
Anabaptist influence may have contributed to
his reaching this conviction. After Smyth had
baptized himself, he baptized other members of
his group, and the first English Baptist Church
was formed, in Holland, in 1609.

Although some Baptists have seen baptism as
primarily a human act of witness, in which the
believer expresses obedience to Christ, others
have understood it as a spiritual experience and a
means of grace. Andrew Fuller (1754–1815), the
leading English Baptist theologian of the eighteenth century, said that immersion in water in
the name of Christ was for the remission of sins.
'Not', he continued 'that there is any virtue in the
element . . . but it contains a sign of the way in
which we must be saved . . . the sign, when rightly used, leads to the thing signified.' In the twentieth century, H. Wheeler Robinson, Principal of
Regent's Park College, Oxford, argued that the
thinking about water baptism that was among
Baptists placed too much emphasis on personal
faith, neglecting 'the spiritual energies which
that act of faith mediates'. The classic modern
exposition of the meaning of baptism for
Baptists, *Baptism in the New Testament*, by
George Beasley-Murray, Principal of Spurgeon's
College and then a professor at Southern Baptist
Theological Seminary, Louisville, Kentucky, also
argued for a close association between the work
of the Spirit and baptism.

For Baptists the Christian life is nourished
primarily by the Bible, prayer and the fellowship
of believers within the life of the church. Early
Baptist meeting houses were usually domestic in
scale. Here the believers met around the Bible on
Sundays and at midweek meetings to listen, discuss and pray. Often midweek meetings allowed
greater participation by the congregation. In the
Baptist context, prayer, whether corporate or
individual, has usually been spontaneous.
Typically, Baptists have not used prayer books.
Historically, the sense of fellowship in Baptist
congregations has been strong. John Smyth,
following the Separatist tradition, saw church
members as bound together in a mutual
covenant. The church members committed
themselves to obey God and carry out the 'duties
of love' to each other.

In the nineteenth century, as Baptist congregations in Britain and America grew larger, there
was much less sense of sharing: the preacher was
seen as the person with the inspired message and
the people were present to receive it. This was the
era of great preachers such as Charles Haddon
Spurgeon (1834–92), the Victorian 'Prince of

Preachers', who attracted so many people to his preaching in London that the Metropolitan Tabernacle, which could accommodate 4,600, was built in 1861 to house his congregation. The sermons of Spurgeon were printed and were distributed and bought around the world. Other famous British pulpiteers of the later nineteenth and early twentieth century were Alexander Maclaren (1826–1910) and John Clifford (1836–1923), and in America Harry Emerson Fosdick (1878–1969), famous for his ministry at Park Avenue Baptist Church, New York.

A further emphasis in Baptist spirituality has been on the freedom of conscience of the individual. Thomas Helwys (1550–c. 1616), a lawyer, who was the leader of the first Baptist congregation meeting on English soil, published in 1612 a remarkable plea for toleration and freedom of worship. His book, *The Mystery of Iniquity*, was the first book in the English language to argue the case for religious liberty. He ended his life in prison. In America, the concept of 'soul freedom' was promulgated by Roger Williams (1603–83), and this expression became a Baptist distinctive, especially in America. The placing of such a high value on freedom does not mean that Baptists espoused rampant individualism. In Baptist life, the meetings of the church members are occasions for seeking 'the mind of Christ' together, and there has also been a tradition of exercising church discipline where members have acted in a way that has been seen as inconsistent with their church membership.

Personal freedom is, therefore, held in tension with the obligation to live a life of obedience to God. Especially from the nineteenth century onwards, many Baptists gave prominence to the Holy Spirit and the life of holiness. A leading American Baptist who conveyed this message was Adoniram Judson Gordon (1836–95), of Clarendon Street Baptist Church, Boston. In Britain the most famous Baptist advocate of the holiness spirituality of the Keswick Convention was F. B. Meyer (1847–1929). 'My remedy for all our ills', said Meyer in 1920, 'is a deeper spirituality.' Although not in this holiness tradition, Wheeler Robinson explored the area of pneumatology in relation to spirituality. His book, *The Christian Experience of the Holy Spirit* (1928), owed a great deal to his own experiences in prayer. In the later twentieth century, Baptists took a greater interest in contemplative spirituality. In America this movement received impetus from E. Glenn Hinson, a Southern Baptist scholar, while in Britain Margaret Jarman, the first woman minister to be President of the Baptist Union, led the Baptist Union Retreat Group, formed in 1988.

The Lord's Supper has rarely been central within Baptist spirituality, but a significant early Baptist confession of faith, the *Second London Confession* (1677), drew from Calvinistic thinking about its spiritual significance. Participants at the Lord's Table, this confession said, 'spiritually receive, and feed upon Christ crucified'. This perspective was taken up by C. H. Spurgeon in a number of his sermons. Spurgeon affirmed: 'At this table Jesus feeds us with His body and His blood. His corporeal presence we have not, but his real spiritual presence we perceive.' Another sermon, 'The object of the Lord's Supper', ended in mystical vein, with an appeal: 'Come and put your finger into the print of the nails, and thrust your hand into his pierced side.' Spurgeon and Meyer were two influential Baptist ministers who insisted on weekly celebration of the Lord's Supper.

A final characteristic of Baptist spirituality has been a strong commitment to mission. Although some high Calvinists, such as John Gill (1697–1771), were not evangelistically disposed, the overwhelming majority of Baptists have been activist and conversionist in their outlook. In 1785 Andrew Fuller published a highly significant book, *The Gospel Worthy of all Acceptation*, in which he argued for a theology which had at its heart the offering of the gospel to all. Fuller had enormous energy and became the driving force behind the Baptist Missionary Society. Another Baptist pastor, and a friend of Fuller's, John Sutcliffe, was behind the issue of a 'Prayer Call' which had as its focus 'the spread of the Gospel to the distant parts of the habitable globe'. Sutcliffe's challenge was taken up not only by Baptists but also by Independents, and in continental Europe as well as Britain.

Baptist commitment to worldwide mission is especially associated with William Carey (1761–1834) in England and with Adoniram Judson (1788–1850) in America. The organized Protestant missionary movement in Britain is usually dated from the publication in 1792 of William Carey's *An Enquiry into the Obligation of Christians, to Use Means for the Conversion of the Heathen*. In 1792 Carey also preached his memorable sermon, 'Expect great things, attempt great things', to the Northamptonshire Baptist Association. It was decided, despite reluctance on the part of some, to form a Baptist Society for mission, and Carey became a pioneer Baptist missionary to India. Adoniram Judson and his wife, Ann, left America in 1812 as London Missionary Society missionaries bound for India. On the voyage Adoniram's studies convinced him that the Baptist position on baptism was correct. After their arrival in India the

Judsons were baptized and later led Baptist missionary work in Burma.

In the twentieth century, three American Baptist leaders have had worldwide influence in shaping approaches to mission. Walter Rauschenbusch (1861–1918) was the primary theologian of the social gospel movement in the early twentieth century. He combined inner piety with a message of social salvation. Martin Luther King Jr (1929–68), followed in this spiritual tradition, with his dream that all people would join hands together. The most famous evangelist of the twentieth century, Billy Graham, exemplified many aspects of Baptists priorities, notably adherence to the Bible, as seen in his often-repeated statement, 'The Bible says', and also the sense of obligation to seek the conversion of others. These features lie at the heart of Baptist spirituality.

See also **Anabaptist Spirituality; Evangelical Spirituality; Puritan Spirituality; Reformation and Spirituality; Reformed Spirituality.**

J. R. Coggins, *John Smyth's Congregation*, Scottdale, PA: Herald Press, 1991; A. R. Cross and P. E. Thompson (eds), *Baptist Sacramentalism*, Carlisle: Paternoster Press, 2003; G. A. Furr and C. W. Freeman (eds), *Ties that Bind: Life Together in the Baptist Vision*, Macon, GA: Smyth and Helwys, 1994; P. J. Morden, *Offering Christ to the World: Andrew Fuller and the Revival of English Particular Baptist Life*, Carlisle: Paternoster Press, 2003; I. M. Randall, *Spirituality and Social Change: The Contribution of F. B. Meyer*, Carlisle: Paternoster Press, 2003.

IAN M. RANDALL

Beatitudes

'Beatitude' originates from the Latin *beatus*, derived from the Hebrew *ashre* and the Greek *makarios*. In selecting the Greek adjective *makarios* to render the Hebrew *ashre*, the Septuagint translators intended to suggest a happiness that flows from justice, or having a right relationship with God. In contrast to *eulogia*, which connotes a cultic blessing that is efficacious in its pronouncement, *makarios* characterized the type of person who is truly fortunate in the standing of the community. *Eulogia* was a 'top-down' form or recognition for right living; *makarios* came to a person from 'below', a communal recognition of valued/honourable behaviour.

Before the Exile beatitudes were used infrequently (i.e., 1 Kings 10.8); in the post-exilic period they became more abundant. Gradually, with Wisdom or sapiential literature, the beatitudes came to reflect the prevailing ethos motifs of the culture. These are articulated primarily in the Psalms, then in the Proverbs, and thirdly in Isaiah, with some in Ecclesiastes and Job.

Those (the third person is dominant) considered beatitudinal by the community trust (Ps. 40.4; Prov. 16.20), fear (Ps. 112.1; 128.1; Prov. 28.14), and obey the Lord (Ps. 1.1; 119.2; Prov. 8.32). They are the ones whom the Lord has chosen (Ps. 65.5) and who have received God's forgiveness (Ps. 32.1–2).

God is never called *makarios* in the New Testament, except for 1 Tim. 1.11; 6.15. Neither is the term applied to non-humans. Twenty-eight of the forty-four beatitudes found in the New Testament are in Matthew and Luke. Thirteen are found in their 'beatitudes' from the Sermons on the Mount and the Plain. Outside the sermons, *makarioi* are found at Matt. 11.6/Luke 7.23; Matt. 13.16/Luke 10.23; Matt. 16.17; Luke 1.27–28; Matt. 26.46/Luke 12.43, 37–38; as well as Luke 1.45; 14.14 and 15.

Most translated *makarios* as a state of being 'blessed', 'happy' or 'fortunate'. However, such images seem overly individualistic and not cognizant of the strongly communitarian nature of the house churches that constituted the Gospels' world. At the heart of household relations during the first century (as well as ours, if we probe deeply enough), was the notion of honour and shame. Given the honour/shame culture that defined household belonging in the first-century world, it seems more appropriate to consider *makarios* as a term of honour for those in the households of Matthew and Luke who exhibited certain situations or stances in the community. Thus 'how honourable' are those/you who . . .

The first eight beatitudes found in Matthew's Gospel constitute the opening of the Sermon on the Mount, the first of Jesus' basic teachings. Thus they can be considered a summary of the entire message of Jesus. The beatitudes honour 'those' who are poor in spirit, who mourn, who are non-violent, who hunger and thirst for righteousness/justice, who are merciful, pure of heart, makers of peace and persecuted for righteousness/justice. In his ninth beatitude Matthew's Jesus honours 'you' who are persecuted. This seems to begin a Matthean triad wherein the one who is blessed receives a name (salt of the earth and light of the world) and, finally, a commission: 'let your light shine before others, so that they may see your good works and give glory to your Father in heaven' (Matt. 5.11–16).

The use of the second person defines the audience of Luke's four beatitudes: 'you' who are poor, hungry and who mourn ('now') as well as those who are hated, excluded, reviled and defamed (Luke 6.20–23). This would follow the Lucan tendency to praise those who were unable to have access to resources as more closely following the poor and rejected Jesus. Immediately following these four beatitudes the Lucan Jesus offers their antithesis by uttering four 'woes' (*ouai*) to those ('you') in his audience who now are rich, full, laugh and are well spoken of (Luke 6.24–26).

Matthew does not have such juxtaposition in his version. However, where Luke contrasts beatitudes and woes, it seems that Matthew considers the opposite of the beatitudes that honour certain behaviours in his house churches those who put stumbling blocks (*skandalizoi*) on the path of others' discipleship (Matt. 11.6; 16.17, 23).

Whether the beatitudes are Matthew's or Luke's, they reveal an ethos, spirituality or code of conduct which not only characterize the unique cultural dynamics of households which constituted their respective communities, they also help define the relationships that determined whether or not one would be considered worthy of belonging to that community. This belonging outlines the honoured way of living promoted by members of that community to be normative of discipleship. They offer a way of life that stands opposed to the cultural norms and universally accepted 'beatitudes' of every generation.

See also Synoptic Gospels.

Hans Dieter Betz, *The Sermon on the Mount, Including the Sermon on the Plain (Matthew 5:3—7:27 and Luke 6:20–49)*, Minneapolis: Fortress Press, 1995; Michael H. Crosby, *Spirituality of the Beatitudes Revisited*, Maryknoll, NY: Orbis Books, 2005; Michael H. Crosby, 'The Beatitudes: General Perspectives', in Francis A. Eigo (ed.), *New Perspectives on the Beatitudes*, Villanova, PN: Villanova University Press, 1995; Jacques Dupont, *Les Béatitudes*, Paris: Gabalda, 1969–73.

MICHAEL H. CROSBY

Beauty

Rarely the primary focus of theology and spirituality, beauty nonetheless plays an important part in both. From Clement of Alexandria (*c.* 150–*c.* 215) and Augustine (354–430), through Bonaventure (*c.* 1217–74) and Thomas Aquinas (*c.* 1225–74), to Hans Urs von Balthasar (1905–88) and Paul Evdokimov (1901–70), theologians of many kinds have held that beauty finds its perfection in God. All created beauty, they have said, reflects and participates to some degree, at least by analogy, in beauty that is divine. The higher forms of beauty, moreover, can attune the soul spiritually and morally.

The main inspiration for such views in antiquity was the philosophy of Plato (*c.* 428–*c.* 348 BC) as reinterpreted through the Neoplatonism of Plotinus (*c.* 205–70) and the Christian mysticism of Dionysius the Pseudo-Areopagite (*c.* 500). Medieval Scholastics also drew on Aristotle (384–322 BC) when they framed the idea that beauty – along with goodness, truth, and unity – is a 'transcendental' property of being, so that, to the extent that something exists, it is also in some measure beautiful.

In all of this, the idea of beauty itself has never been overly precise or fixed. For the ancient Greeks, beauty (*kalon*) had to do not only with aesthetics but also with goodness. It is that which merits recognition and admiration and pleases through proportion and symmetry. Since proportion can be expressed numerically, beauty also has had a distinctly mathematical and rational dimension.

Medieval ideas of beauty (*formositas*) retained much of this intellectual and spiritual tenor while placing renewed emphasis on delight. In the eyes of Scholastic philosophers, culminating in Thomas Aquinas, beauty consists in harmonious proportion, integrity and radiance or 'splendour' of form. At the same time, beauty gives delight in the very act of its being perceived.

For centuries theological discussions of beauty tended to treat only peripherally what we think of as the arts, which due to their intimacy with the senses were often seen as spiritually inferior and as potentially seductive. Even in approaching the Bible, which says little about beauty but which encourages music-making, for instance, theologians long paid particular attention to Wisd. 11.21, which stresses the rational aspect of creativity by declaring that God made all things according to 'measure and number and weight'.

Both the Neoplatonic and Scholastic traditions had another side – one that, far from hurrying past sensible beauty, sought to glory in it appropriately. This could lead to a broadly sacramental approach to such arts as church architecture, stained glass and manuscript illumination. In Byzantine and Eastern Catholic aesthetics the beauty of the church's form, liturgy and icons was held in high spiritual regard from the beginning. The church space was regarded as providing for a glorious meeting between heaven and earth, its beauty serving to transfigure the spirit and senses together.

Western church arts, during the Renaissance and Baroque eras, became more preoccupied with dramatic artistic representation while gradually gazing less intently at beauty's transcendental dimension. By the eighteenth century, when the idea of the 'fine arts' took hold in Europe, beauty was increasingly understood in subjective terms. While Immanuel Kant (1724–1804) could still regard beauty as a symbol of the morally good, beauty was essentially set free from any necessary grounding in reality and was divorced from any inherent connection to morality.

With the rise of Romanticism, artistry was interpreted more in terms of genius and self-expression than in terms of beauty per se. Meanwhile, the religious aspects of beauty, though claimed for the Church by Victorians such as John Henry Newman (1801–90), had been transferred in large part to the idea of the sublime. The latter had to do with those aspects of nature and experience that by their immensity or grandeur inspire awe and wonder. The sublime was likened (and in some cases assimilated) to the idea of the holy, as later interpreted by Rudolf Otto (1869–1937).

The American Calvinist theologian Jonathan Edwards (1703–58) had earlier pointed in a different direction by interpreting primary beauty as a kind of harmonious 'consent to being' in general: a moral disposition of benevolence – like God's own beautiful generosity – toward all that exists. Secondary beauty, Edwards said, appears in natural forms and in the world's harmonious order, mirroring the divine. Two centuries later another Calvinist, Karl Barth (1886–1968), would claim that Mozart's radiantly beautiful music conveys a sense of the goodness of creation and presents audible parables of the kingdom of God. A contemporary of Barth – von Balthasar – helped inspire a resurgence of interest in theological aesthetics overall by his massive effort to show that God's self-revelation takes place in forms that are beautiful, though at times humble and even ugly by worldly standards. In recent years more eclectic and multicultural theologies of beauty have been marked, often, by an explicit concern for justice and liberation.

See also **Aesthetics; Art.**

Hans Urs von Balthasar, *The Glory of the Lord: A Theological Aesthetics*, 7 vols, various translators, San Francisco: Ignatius Press, 1982–89; Edward Farley, *Faith and Beauty: A Theological Aesthetic*, Aldershot: Ashgate, 2001; Alejandro García-Rivera, *The Community of the Beautiful: A Theological Aesthetics*, Collegeville, MN: The Liturgical Press, 1999; John W. de Gruchy, *Christianity, Art, and Transformation: Theological Aesthetics in the Struggle for Justice*, Cambridge: Cambridge University Press, 2002; Richard Harries, *Art and the Beauty of God*, London: Mowbray, 1993; Patrick Sherry, *Spirit and Beauty: An Introduction to Theological Aesthetics*, 2nd edn, London: SCM Press, 2002.

FRANK BURCH BROWN

Beguine Spirituality

The Beguines were religious lay women who chose to live lives of chastity and service to others outside the aegis of an established order. The movement began in the early thirteenth century and has continued, although in a much altered form, to the present day. Alongside the Dominicans and Franciscans, the Beguines were part of the movement that sought to bring God into the marketplace. Previously the religious life had been led behind the walls and closed gates of monasteries, mostly situated outside the towns. The two mendicant orders sought to change this, combining the itinerant lifestyles of the twelfth-century *wanderprediger* with the sanction of the Church in the form of an authorized rule. This way of life was not open to women, so many of those drawn to living lives close to the apostolic ideal turned to the Beguines to realize their ambition. Although they had no authorized rule, the Beguines had received papal sanction for their way of life in 1215. In the early years of the thirteenth century, they were considered by many to be an example of the holiest way of Christian living as they combined lives of poverty, chastity and obedience with service to the sick and the poor and a dedication to working for their living rather than begging as the mendicant orders did.

The thirteenth century was a period of social change and increasing urbanization in Northern Europe. The towns rapidly became the centres of population and of increasing commercial activity, and it is against this background that the great upsurge of popular piety, of religious movements seeking to emulate apostolic poverty, should be seen. The developing urban society was more mixed in terms of its members' origins than society had been previously. It was dominated by the principle of achievement, achievement measured by wealth and ostentation. Like the men who joined the mendicant orders, the women who became Beguines in the early years of the thirteenth century were mostly from aristocratic or wealthy merchant families. By choosing to live lives of poverty emulating the apostolic ideal they hoped to atone in some way for the sins committed in the acquisition of the wealth they saw around them. Beguines followed no authorized rule so the details of their daily lives varied considerably according to when and where they lived. Some women were able to live as Beguines within their families, others lived together in small or large groups, though as the thirteenth century progressed the larger communities became the norm.

The thirteenth century was the great period of the flowering of Beguine spirituality with mystic writers such as Mechtild of Magdeburg, Hadewijch and Marguerite Porete. Another mystic writer often associated with the Beguines is Beatrijs of Nazareth who went to a Beguine school before becoming a nun and later prioress at the Cistercian convent of Nazareth. This remarkable period came to an end with the trial of Marguerite Porete for heresy and her execution in 1310 and the associated Council of the Church at Vienne in 1312 during which the entire movement was condemned as potentially heretical. Thereafter, although the movement continued, as the lovely Beguinages in Belgium and elsewhere from later periods testify, it did so in a much attenuated form.

Mechtild of Magdeburg was born in the vicinity of Magdeburg in 1207, probably of wealthy and possibly aristocratic parents. In 1230 she moved to Magdeburg where she spent the next forty years as a Beguine. In 1270 she joined a convent in Helfta and died there twelve years later in 1282. Her book *Flowing Light of the Godhead* is a collection of texts written at different times of her life. Books I–V were written between 1250 and 1259, Book VI between 1260 and 1270, Book VII between 1271 and 1282 in Helfta. Using the imagery of bridal mysticism she speaks of the relationship between her soul and God as between a bride and her bridegroom, moving from the erotic passion and longing of the new bride to the warm intimacy of an established marriage at which point the soul is described as *husvrouwe*, that is, 'lady of the house' or 'chatelaine' (not 'housewife' as some have mistranslated it!).

We have no comparable dates for the Flemish Beguine Hadewijch. From the scant information in her texts it is thought that she must have been writing before 1245. Tradition, based on a much later note in one of the manuscripts of her work, suggests that she may have been a Beguine in Antwerp. However, no evidence has yet been found to locate her definitively in Antwerp or any other Belgian city. Her work is found in just five closely related manuscripts and comprises forty-five poems in stanzas, thirty-one letters, fourteen visions, a list of 'perfect ones', and a collection of some twenty-nine other poems of which sixteen are definitely attributed to her. Developing a variant of bridal mysticism, namely courtly mysticism, to an extraordinary pitch Hadewijch speaks of her relationship with God

as that between a courtly lover and his highborn mistress. Her work shows such a remarkable level of education as well as familiarity with the conventions of the courtly love lyric that it has been argued that she too must have been from an aristocratic family. Another possible explanation could be that she, like at least one other early Beguine we know of, had been a court musician before becoming a Beguine.

A contemporary of both Hadewijch and Mechtild was Beatrijs of Nazareth. Beatrijs was born in 1200, of a wealthy and highly respected burger family. Before entering one of her father's foundations as a nun, Beatrijs was educated by the Beguines where her *Vita* describes her as receiving an excellent education. In 1237 she was elected prioress in her father's foundation of Nazareth where she remained until her death in 1268. The only work we have by Beatrijs is a short prose text, *The Seven Manners of Loving*, written in Middle Dutch and a, substantially altered, Latin translation. It is interesting to note that although her *Vita*, written in Latin by her confessor, makes much of her ascetic practices, there is no reference to asceticism in her own text.

We know little of the life of Marguerite Porete, although we know more about her death. She was burned at the stake as a lapsed heretic in Paris on 1 June 1310. Her book *The Mirror of Simple Souls* had previously been condemned and publicly burned at Valenciennes and it is thought that she may have been a Beguine in that town. From the account of her trial and condemnation it appears that one of the reasons for her condemnation and eventual execution was that she had written in her native tongue, rather than in Latin, of matters deemed too complicated for lay men and women to understand. The other Beguines mentioned above wrote in their native languages too, they are important witnesses for the development of vernacular theology, but this practice ceased almost completely after the Council at Vienne in 1312.

The spirituality that grew out of the Beguine movement was one that required the business of everyday life to be practised. Because their spirituality was one of active service, those elements of mystic grace which prevented such service, or diverted attention from it, such as visions, ecstasies and trances, were dismissed as juvenile. Similarly any inclination toward excessive asceticism was rejected as making the Beguine less able to serve others. Paradoxically, these women who lived working lives of service to others spoke of themselves and of their relationship to God in the most refined terms of courtly love. This paradox is indeed one of the defining elements of their spirituality: that one is closest to union with

God's divinity when living with his humanity a life of service, despised and rejected by others. Using the feminine noun *minne*, 'love', to speak of God enabled them to explore the ambiguities inherent in a relationship in which the love wherewith we love God is the love wherewith he first loved us, the love indeed that is God, love that is suffering service. Loving God without measure, burning with longing for his presence, striving to satisfy God while certain of never being able fully to do so, love is at once both pain and delight. Suffering is not just the means to union, it is the *locus* of union itself. These themes also reveal the debt owed by these women to the inspiration of the Cistercians and the Victorines of the previous century.

See also **Bridal Mysticism; Cistercian Spirituality; Medieval Spirituality in the West.**

Primary sources: Beatrijs of Nazareth, *The Seven Manners of Loving*, in *Medieval Netherlands Religious Literature*, trans. Edmund Colledge, London: Heinemann, 1965; *Hadewijch: The Complete Works*, trans. Mother Columba Hart, CWS, London: SPCK, 1980; Mechtild of Magdeburg, *Flowing Light of the Godhead*, trans. C. M. Galvani, ed. S. Clark, New York: Garland, 1991; *Marguerite Porete: The Mirror of Simple Souls*, trans. Ellen I. Babinsky, New York: Paulist Press, 1993.

Secondary sources: Herbert Grundmann, *Religious Movements in the Middle Ages: The Historical Links between Heresy, the Mendicant Orders, and the Women's Religious Movement in the Twelfth and Thirteenth Century, with the Historical Foundations of German Mysticism*, trans. Steven Rowan, Notre Dame, IN: University of Notre Dame Press, 1995; Bernard McGinn, *The Flowering of Mysticism: Men and Women in the New Mysticism – 1200–1350*, vol. 3 of *The Presence of God: A History of Western Christian Mysticism*, New York: Crossroads, 1998; Saskia Murk-Jansen, *Brides in the Desert: The Spirituality of the Beguines*, London: Darton, Longman & Todd, 1998.

SASKIA MURK JANSEN

Benedictine Spirituality

This entry will be based solely on the Rule of Benedict (RB), the sixth-century Italian text that has guided much of Western monasticism. Another possible source would be *Dialogue II* of Pope Gregory I, which recounts the life of the saint, but that text tells us more about the spirituality of Gregory than it does about Benedict. One could also attempt to distil a spirituality from the history of Benedictinism,

but that history is so long and varied as to make the task unmanageable.

The Rule of Benedict itself is a fairly heterogeneous document drawn from many earlier monastic sources. This has contributed to its remarkable staying power, but it does not make the task of finding its spiritual node (if indeed one exists) any easier. Nevertheless, the present author will venture the following passage as quintessentially Benedictine:

> Thus the first step of humility is to utterly flee forgetfulness by keeping 'the fear of God always before one's eyes' (Ps 36:2). We must constantly recall the commandments of God, continually mulling over how hell burns the sinners who despise God, and eternal life is prepared for those who fear God. We should guard ourselves at all times from sins and vices, that is, of thoughts, tongue, hands, feet or self-will, but also desires of the flesh. Let each one take into account that he is constantly observed by God from heaven and our deeds everywhere lie open to the divine gaze and are reported by the angels at every hour. (RB 7.10–13)

Since it is so harsh in tone, to choose this passage as the key to Benedict's spirituality is perhaps to risk bringing the saint or oneself into bad repute. The modern sensibility is generally repelled by the image of a stern, judgemental God gazing down from heaven at the foibles of humanity. As for Benedict he seems to have a universal reputation as a balanced, and even gentle, spirit, which is not conveyed by this passage.

Yet simply on the basis of quantitative word study, this text is very representative of Benedict. For the same constellation of unfashionable ideas: fear of God, divine retribution, flight from sin, God as judge, angels as reporters, appears no less than four times in the Rule (RB 4.44–9; 7.10–13; 7.26–30 and 19.1–7). Most of these passages are copied directly from another sixth-century Rule, the Rule of the Master, but their ultimate source seems to be St Basil the Great (fourth century), whom Benedict calls 'our holy father' (RB 73.5).

In presenting the reader with such a stern picture of God, Benedict is only echoing the spirit of his age. Anyone who has gazed on the frescoes and mosaics of Christ in the apses of medieval churches, and especially at Cefalu and Monreale (Sicily), realizes that those people thought of Christ in very formidable and exalted terms. What is more, for Benedict Christ is virtually synonymous with God, since his abundant use of the word *Dominus* includes both. So for

Benedict, there is no companionable levelling of God with humanity.

To say that the monk must 'fear' this redoubtable God does not call for abject terror, but it does demand reverential awe. One would expect to find that atmosphere in the Benedictine liturgy: 'When we wish to propose something to powerful people, we do not presume to do so without humility and reverence. How much more should we petition the Lord God of the universe with great humility and devotion' (RB 20.1–2).

Another expected locus of God's presence is in the abbot, whom Benedict says 'is believed to hold the place of Christ in the monastery' (RB 2.2). Although Benedict somewhat tones down the almost divine status of the abbot in the Rule of the Master, he still presents him as a figure of tremendous spiritual authority. Consequently, the virtues of obedience, silence and humility (RB 5–7) toward the abbot predominate in the Rule. None of this is unusual for the sixth century, which was a period when leaders of all types demanded absolute submission from their subjects. It does not seem particularly attractive to our own age.

But there is another dimension to Benedict's spirituality, an aspect that is mostly absent from the Rule of the Master and which is probably more compelling to our own time. In brief, Benedict also locates his formidable God/Christ in the weakest and most marginal persons, and so he demands that they, too, be treated with reverential awe.

A prime example of this is found in RB 36, a chapter on the care of the sick. The discussion begins with reference to Matt. 25.36 and 40 where Christ praises the just in the last judgement because 'I was sick and you visited me. What you did to one of these little ones, you did to me.' Benedict's use of this almost shocking passage shows that he means to ground compassionate care of the sick monks on a solid theological base: Christ himself is served in these weak and marginal members. Later he shows that such a spirituality is hard to keep in focus, but it can be done if the caregiver is 'God-fearing'. Thus the qualification for this job is not technical but spiritual.

The same adjective is used in RB 53.21 to describe the guest-master. Indeed, Matt. 25.35 is again quoted at the beginning of this famous chapter to argue for hospitality: 'I was a stranger and you took me in.' To understand the context of this discussion, it should be remembered that travel in the sixth century was a harzardous business. Those who showed up at the door of the monastery usually had nowhere else to go, so to turn them away would have been tantamount to murder. What is more, many of them were poor pilgrims, dependent on whatever the monks provided for them. Consequently, to see Christ in these people was an act of faith that was based on the fear of God.

Of course, hospitality was also extended to the affluent benefactors of the monastery, but Benedict wryly comments that 'the very fear of the rich wins them respect' (RB 53.15). Thus he neatly distinguishes between worldly respect and fear of the Lord. But it would not be right to put too much stress on the word 'fear' in all of this. In fact, the monks considered the stranger a veritable gift of God, much in the spirit of Abraham, who said to the three angels: 'Sirs, if I have deserved this favour, do not go past your servant without a visit' (Gen. 18.3; see RB 53.14).

This same attitude toward the weak and poor is seen again in RB 66.3, concerning the work of the gatekeeper. For this role, Benedict prefers a wise old monk who will stay at his post. But his primary qualification is again that he is 'God-fearing', so that when 'someone arrives or a poor person cries out, he will respond 'thanks be to God!'' No doubt the temptation for someone unconvinced by the radical spiritual vision of Jesus and Benedict would be to treat the rich at the gate with deference and the poor carelessly.

Of course, the gospel ideal is that there should be no weak or marginal persons in society, but rather a basic equality in Christ. Benedict wants his monastery to be such a world, as he shows near the end of the Rule in RB 72. In that short chapter, he rings the changes on mutual love among the members, and he shows that this respect is based on the presence of Christ in each one. After running through a series of biblically inspired verses on communal love, he concludes with the timeless aphorism: 'Let them prefer absolutely nothing to Christ' (RB 72.11).

Thus the Rule of Benedict, after its initial introduction of an exalted God/Christ, to whom we owe the greatest reverence and awe, ends by insisting that this same God is found not only in the powerful persons in our lives, but especially in the lowly and the powerless. To them is owed that special religious devotion called 'fear of the Lord'.

See also **Christ-centred Spirituality; Hospitality; Labour, Manual; Monasticism;** *Lectio Divina*; **Poverty; Stability.**

A. Borias, 'Christ in the Rule of St. Benedict', *Monastic Studies* 10 (1974), 97–128; T. Kardong, *Benedict's Rule: A Translation and Commentary*, Collegeville, MN: The Liturgical Press, 1996; T. Kardong, 'Benedictine Spirituality' in *New

Dictionary of Christian Spirituality, Collegeville, MN: The Liturgical Press, 1993, pp. 84–91; A. de Vogüé, *La Règle de Saint Benoît* IV–VI, Paris: Cerf, 1972.

                                        TERRENCE G. KARDONG

Bible and spirituality

see Spirituality and Scripture (*essay*)

Biographies, Spiritual

Spiritual biographies are life studies written by or about men and women who are driven to discover God as the ground of their being. The genre in the Christian tradition begins with the Gospels and includes diverse narratives, letters, diaries, prison journals, memoirs, full biographies and autobiography. These narratives depict subjects of every shade of human imagination from an incarnate God, to simple men and women transformed beyond their own recognition through their confrontation with divinity.

The entirety of Christian spiritual biography has as its central concern the imperative of a personal discovery of God in the depths of one's being, a discovery that alone brings peace and surcease. St Augustine opens his *Confessions* (398) with an observation that humans praise God instinctually, 'The thought of you stirs him so deeply that he cannot be content unless he praises you, because you made us for yourself and our hearts find no peace until they rest in you' (1.1). A millennium and a half later St Edith Stein concurs, writing in her autobiography *Life in a Jewish Family* (1934–42), 'Those who seek the truth seek God, whether they realize it or not.' Augustine and Stein believed such praise flows from an innate desire to seek the soul's profoundest truth.

While all biography employs chronology and anecdote, spiritual biography employs anecdote as a means of constructing a chronology of a life seen through a causal teleology. Matthew begins his Gospel with the acknowledgement that Jesus is the Messiah and part of the evidence for this is evident in his royal genealogy. All four Gospels demonstrate the truth that Jesus is the prophesized Messiah and his concrete deeds the proof of that. Hildegard of Bingen in her *Life* puts it succinctly stating that 'outer realities teach us about inner ones'. These narratives often use familiar situations to reveal the dynamic truth in the deep recesses of the soul in dialogue with divinity. They seldom employ anecdote to chronicle the historic context of an event, crucial though it may be.

The soul's immateriality ensures that the ultimate quest is non-material. Consequently the narrative continually circles back to confront the discovery of such spiritual truth apart from its physical existence. Writing in *If We Are Really Christians Then What is God?* Kierkegaard has harsh words for those who confuse this search, 'The most terrible blasphemy is the one in which "Christianity" is guilty, which is, to transform the God of the Spirit into a ridiculous piece of nonsense.' The history of the search, the resultant biography, is an illustration of one's search for meaning given the reality of a God whose existence calls the individual into being and without which there would be no individual. Frequently such narratives illustrate the bitter struggle for such truth, depicting the heights and depths of emotional existence. Writing from Bedford jail in his *Grace Abounding to the Chief of Sinners* (1666) – a work indebted to Augustine and Thomas à Kempis – John Bunyan commented on a recent experience he had of God 'that I have been in my spirit so filled with darkness, that I could not so much conceive what that God and that comfort was with which I have been refreshed'.

For Augustine and most of the notable spiritual biographies in the Christian tradition such primal truths are only accessible through a dialogue with God and depend on God's making them accessible to us. In the prison memoir *Passion of Perpetua and Felicity* (203), the young slave Felicity represents this indwelling in her acknowledgement that although she was going to suffer as a martyr, '. . . then there will be another inside me, who will suffer for me, because I am going to suffer for him'. This dialogue with the Lord, this chronicle of the depths of the human soul, is not mere metaphor – as Teresa of Avila states in the Fifth Dwelling of *The Interior Castle* – providing verisimilitude to aid understanding. Such a dialogic reality is apprehended only by faith.

Yet the paradox of faith as presented in many of these biographies is that God, while recognized in the smallest of things – for Julian of Norwich a humble hazelnut – is found outside of things. In his *Letters and Papers from Prison* (1943) Dietrich Bonhoeffer remarks, 'the spirit always seems to want some visible token of this union of love and remembrance and then material things become the vehicles of spiritual realities'. In *The Imitation of Christ*, Thomas à Kempis (1380–1471) noted, 'the more a man departs from earthly solace the more he draws near to God'. Indeed such biographies view with skepticism mediators to facilitate their quest. In his *Journal* (1694) George Fox is scathing in his contempt for those who sought to guide him, concluding, 'I saw all the world could do me no good.' Fox's suspicion, shared by Thomas Brown in *Religio Medici* (1635–42), stated that he borrowed 'not the rules of my religion from Rome or Geneva but the dictates of my own reason'.

The account of the spiritual life invariably reduces the narrative to this exclusive dialogue between subject and God. While other characters may be part of the narrative they are peripheral to the goal of discovery, of enlightenment. Such exclusion reaches an apogee in the spiritual biographies by and about monks and the cloistered life. In the preface to the Japanese edition of *The Seven Storey Mountain* (1949), Thomas Merton remarks, 'My monastery is not a home . . . rather [it is] a place in which I disappear from the world as an object of interest in order to be everywhere in it by hiddenness and compassion. To exist everywhere I have to be No-one.' Exclusion from the world leads us paradoxically back to the world and to a deeper discovery of self and God. Edith Stein (1934) puts it masterfully, 'I even believe that the deeper one is drawn into God, the more one must "go out of oneself." That is, one must go to the world to carry the divine life into it.'

Spiritual biography therefore is a narrative that seeks to capture that mysterious journey out of the self towards God only to discover paradoxically that the journey has sometimes unwittingly led to an unveiling of the true self, the ground of whose being is God.

See also **Devotional Manuals; Hagiography; Journal, Spiritual.**

Saint Augustine, *Confessions*, ed. and trans. R. S. Pine-Coffin, London: Penguin, 1961; Dietrich Bonhoeffer, *Letters and Papers from Prison*, ed. Eberhard Bethge, London: SCM Press, 1971; John Bunyan (ed.), John Stachniewski, *Grace Abounding with Other Spiritual Autobiographies*, Oxford: Oxford University Press, 1998; Patricia Cox, *Biography in Late Antiquity: A Quest for the Holy Man*, Berkeley: University of California Press, 1983; Thomas Merton, *The Seven Storey Mountain*, San Diego: Harcourt Brace Jovanovich, 1990; Edith Stein, *Life in a Jewish Family: Her Unfinished Autobiographical Account*, Washington, DC: ICS Publications, 1986; St. Teresa of Avila, *The Interior Castle*, trans. Mirabai Starr, New York: Riverhead Books, 2002.

THOMAS J. HEFFERNAN

Black Spiritualities

Black spirituality should be seen as a term which encompasses the totality of beliefs, power, values and behaviours that moulds the understanding, capacity and consciousness of Black people in relation to divine realities. Within this framework, spirituality enables people to interpret, adapt and formulate their understandings of God within a specific context.

Black spirituality is something of a misnomer as the word 'Black' has been politicized and is now an umbrella term that embraces Black Africans in the Sub-Saharan region and Africans in the diaspora, namely, African Caribbeans and African Americans of both North and South Americas, and, finally, African peoples in Europe. This geographical span ensures that one should properly speak of 'Black spiritualities'. In addition, the fact that many Black people belong to the various churches of the West means that many of the spiritualities within Western traditions are part of the hybridity of Black spiritual life. Black spirituality should not be seen as confined to the Christian faith community as it also includes the religions of ancient Africa, Black adaptations of Hebraic, Jewish, Christian and Islamic beliefs and rituals. Additionally, it can also include, traditional African religions and numerous derivatives found in the Black Diaspora: Umbanda and Candomble (Brazil), Shango (Trinidad), Santeria (Cuba, Puerto Rico) and Verdun (Haiti).

However, Black spirituality within Europe, the Americas and the Caribbean does owe something to inherited traditions of African spirituality. African spirituality has some characteristics that distinguish it from other racial groups. It sees the supernatural as a mere extension of the natural order and regards all of life as permeated with forces or powers in some relationship to humanity. One enters into communion with this other reality in a prescribed way to receive its benefits and avoid penalties. This spirituality embraces a Supreme being, ancestors, spirits resident in or associated with certain natural phenomena, and living humans who possess gifts of healing or of making mischief. These are all united in one comprehensive, invisible system that has its own laws that sustain the visible world and ordinary life for the good of all.

Spirituality is expressed and exercised through prayers, rituals, symbols, dance and other art forms or representations. The prayers of African religion address all aspects of personal and community life. This includes all the major events that affect us from the cradle to the grave, the environment in which humanity exists, and expressions of joy and praise, blessing, the arrival of rain for planting and individual and community health. The spirituality that emanates from these prayers is an all-embracing spirituality: the physical world is embraced in the spiritual, the physical is lifted up into the spiritual. Prayer is the medium in which God and the spiritual realm is approached in a manner which demands that worshippers seek to be pure before God, as God is seen as pure and clean. Prayers are offered which affect all areas of life, for example, purification of a new home, new fields, new working season and tools (for planting, hunting and fishing), the start of new fires, and the first-fruits of the harvest before the new crop is eaten.

Humility is a great spiritual element in prayer, as the worshipper seeks a good relationship with the spiritual realm. Therefore, people call on God as Father, Creator and Giver of all, and think of themselves as God's children. The elements of love, honour, respect, adoration and admiration towards God, and at times to forefathers of the family, are all part of a relationship of humility. Joy, thanksgiving and praise come out strongly in African prayers, as the soul gives itself back to God through praise and joy. These elements are often accompanied by singing, dancing, clapping and communal celebration since most of the religious exercises are done on a community basis. They express the feeling that people's prayers have been answered whether to God or in the spiritual realm. In general, African people approach life in a celebratory attitude, despite the adversities and frustrations of life. Celebration through dance and music characterizes their life. Similarly, when speaking of the music of Black slaves in the United States, we are reminded that this music was characterized by 'a strong emphasis on call and response, polyrhythms, syncopation, ornamentation, slides from one note to another, and repetition. The words expressed Biblical themes and the music was influenced by Western hymnody and secular music, but the style of the "Negro Spiritual" was African' (MacRobert, 1988, p. 31). It is this form of spirituality that enabled Black peoples in the diaspora to build a spirit of resistance to the many problems they faced in the West and to demonstrate an alternative spirituality to that which prevailed around them. The thrust of this spirituality was crystal clear in the period of slavery in the West, where the worship of slaveholders and slaves could not have the same meaning, as essentially they did not have the same opportunities in life. The rationale for this is a simple one, if spirituality and worship is inseparably connected to life, then the worship and spirituality of slaves and slaveholders had to be different as their economic and social realities were vastly different. Similarly, the process of racism calls for an alternative spirituality.

In the spirituality of Black Christians, the Bible plays a significant role and the expectation of seeing God in the routine of everyday events is paramount. This is also accompanied by a sense of celebration often expressed in movement and dance in Black/Black-led Churches, as well as thanksgiving to a God who is 'a rock', 'a shepherd', and the one who 'puts people in power' and can also 'pull them down'.

In the United States, and the United Kingdom, as well as South Africa, Black theology seeks to provide a theological underpinning for Black spirituality. This theology seeks to understand God in the context of the Black experience and rejects the universal claims of European and white North American theology and challenges the hegemony that this theology has created. The sources of Black theology are Black experience, Black history, Black culture, revelation and Scripture and tradition. This theology seeks to enable Black people to interpret, adapt and formulate their understandings of God within a specific context. Additionally, there has been a challenge within Black theology to address the issues of sexism present in the Black Churches and to give a proper place to the experience and spirituality of Black women, areas that have been long neglected in the theological realm of the Black community. This approach is understood as womanist theology. Both these theological approaches have been instrumental in developing Black spiritualities among the African diaspora and in the case of womanist theology, this has served as a corrective to our understanding of the spirituality of Black women and ensures that records of their spiritualities are preserved. These spiritualities and theologies contribute to the fuller understanding of Black spiritualities in the African diasporan communities in the West and to the understanding of those churches commonly referred to as belonging to the Traditional African Religion network in the West and on the continent of Africa.

See also **African-American Spirituality; Liberation Spirituality; Womanist Spirituality.**

R. Beckford, *Jesus is Dread: Black Theology and Black Culture*, London: Darton, Longman & Todd, 1998; M. Hersokivitis, *The Myth of the Negro Past*, Boston: Beacon Press, 1941, 1958, 1990; C. Lincoln (ed.), *The Black Experience in Religion*, New York: Anchor Books, 1974; I. MacRobert, *The Black Roots and White Racism of Early Pentecostalism in the USA*, New York: Palgrave Macmillan, 1988; C. Fielding Stewart, *Soul Survivor: An African American Spirituality*, Louisville, KY: Westminster John Knox Press, 1997.

GARNET PARRIS

Body and Spirituality

1. *Two conceptions of the body.* Two conceptions of the body figure in the intellectual history of the West. The Greek conception is a more or less extreme dualism. In Platonic thought the body is the prison of the soul; Aristotelian dualism construes a human being as consisting of parts, so that we are said to 'have' a body, while the soul is the substantial form of the body. The biblical conception, on the other hand, views a human being in substantial unity, using terms such as flesh, soul and breath of life to designate the whole. In the New Testament St Paul develops a theology of the body as *soma* rather than *sarx*. *Soma* is the earthly as well as the heavenly body, the unity of the whole person. It is subject to sin and death here on earth, but is destined to be exalted and transformed by the Spirit/*Pneuma*. When *sarx* alone is used (flesh) it can mean the mortality of the body, the locus of human sin, the person as earthly minded. Christian philosophy and theology have not yet found a unified position that is continuous with both the biblical view and the Neoplatonic view in which the first theologies were written. The anthropology of St Thomas Aquinas used the Aristotelian categories of form and matter to express the relationship of body and soul. The body expresses the soul, and only through bodily expression does the soul achieve its concrete reality. The soul cannot fulfil itself without making use of matter. The body is the medium of all communication. Moreover, the soul fulfils itself in proportion as human beings live 'with bodily men in a bodily world'.

The current Christian theology of the body is in accord with more positive principles. The body is the prime symbol; all experience and expression of mental and spiritual states is through the body. All religious ritual uses the bodily senses and positions to enable receptivity to the divine presence and to respond to it.

2. *Ambiguity about the body in the tradition.* There is, however, ambiguity about the body in the Christian tradition. Historically sensuality is subordinated to reason, and repressed in the name of perfection. God is made flesh, becomes embodied as a sexual person like us. In this event our bodies too are blessed and reaffirmed in their holiness. Yet this incarnation was interpreted in the early Christian centuries as having happened asexually. Suspicious of sexuality, the early Christian Church decreed that God became human but not through a genital act. For many today, this interpretation drains the concept of the incarnation of its power.

3. *Current recovery of the integral unity of body–mind.* The second half of the twentieth century saw a recovery of the value of bodiliness. Sensuality is that aspect of human consciousness which is bound up with the body, and presents material things to the mind in concrete acts of knowledge and will. Sensuality is necessary and good. It is not to be extinguished in Stoic or Manichaean fashion but increasingly integrated into the whole person. Consonance between the inner and the outer self is the meaning of integrity. The fact that this task is never completed to perfection during our life is part of the human situation. This first and more original sense of the word sensuality is not the same as its derogatory sense, which in many Western countries was its usual and common meaning. Sensuality in the concrete is always affected by the world and its history, and is shaped too by the wrong decisions made in our own lifetime. That we are sensual beings not only faces us with a task (that of a growing integration), but is also an occasion of limitations (wrong choices) which must be overcome by the grace of God.

Self-understanding includes a *sense of embodiment* – what having a body, being a body-ed self means. Sometimes the experience is one of integration – body and self are one. Athletes experience this when they are able to perform complicated physical tasks with both ease and skill. This is part of the high that comes in sports, for player and spectator alike (e.g. the runner in *Chariots of Fire* saying, 'When I run I feel God's pleasure'). Something similar often occurs in lovemaking when the barrier of separateness is momentarily transcended and lovers experience a communion that goes beyond the joining of bodies. But at other times – in illness or after abusive eating or drinking, self and body seem disconnected, linked only in an uneasy truce. That was the agony of St Paul, 'My body follows a different law that battles against the law which my reason dictates . . . What a wretched man I am!' (Rom. 7.23–24). Some images of our bodies are fleeting – for example, we can't move well, then we feel strong and agile again. Other images are internalized and become part of the characteristic way we see our self – our body is clumsy or sickly or fat-and-ugly. These images of our embodiment become a significant part of our sexuality.

Self-esteem correlates to our images of the physical body. Are we physically strong or weak? Able or handicapped? Beautiful or scarred? Too tall or too short? These assets and limitations may be illusory from a spiritual perspective; yet a person's acceptance of or resistance to them is critical to entering spiritual adulthood. How we feel about ourselves, whether we respect ourselves, determines the quality of our life, our capacity to succeed in business, relationships, healing and intuitive skills. Self-understanding and acceptance, the bond we form with ourselves, is in many ways the most crucial spiritual challenge we face. No one is born with healthy self-esteem. We must earn this quality in the process of living, as we face our challenges one at a time. The challenge to each of us is: Given your particular body, environment and beliefs, will you make choices that enhance your spirit or decisions that drain your power into the external things around you? Our spiritual task regarding bodiliness is to undo the bonds of fear and shame that tend to control us. If a person suffers from low self-esteem, she cannot act on her best impulses because her fear of failure is too intense. Spirituality, however, measures our success not by what we have achieved but by how much we have learned. By its very nature it directs us into new cycles of learning that are sometimes uncomfortable. Spiritual maturity is finding our own voice, the capacity to stand one's ground as a reflection of a genuine inner belief. Self-knowledge and self acceptance are also expressed in our occupations, which are part of our lives, and therefore are part of our spirituality.

Another aspect of our embodiment is *gender* – what being a woman or a man means. This awareness comes in part from our sex, that is, from the fact that our reproductive system is female or male. But our sense of our self as a man or a woman involves much more than a check of reproductive organs. Gender goes beyond biology to social expectations. Each culture forms its own roles and rules of gender. Our society's expectations about what is masculine and feminine play an important role in our growing sense of what being a woman or a man means. Our awareness that we are a woman or a man is central to our sexuality. Initially we come to this sense through the messages we receive from others, especially from our parents. As we participate in school and church and neighbourhood we learn broader expectations of femininity or masculinity. In our community and in the media, we find role models who show us what being a woman means. We discover both the benefits and the burdens of our gender. For both men and women, maturity urges us to question cultural definitions and social norms of gender that distort our common humanity.

A third aspect of embodiment is our awareness concerning the *movement of our affections*, the feelings that we have toward persons of the same and of the opposite sex. Each must come to terms with her own affections. Most of us, both women and men, find that our own feelings do not fit neatly into the culture's narrowest definitions of acceptable heterosexuality. We are drawn, to different degrees and with different intensity, toward both men and women. Some of us find that our strongest emotional orientation is toward persons of the same sex. This level of self-awareness – the ways we are moved emotionally by women and by men, the sense we have of our self as primarily gay lesbian, bisexual or heterosexual – is part of our sexuality.

Several movements of the past century have contributed to the recovery of the value of bodiliness to spirituality.

Feminist spirituality looked to the transcendent character of the female body, studying life stages, and working out a spirituality of generativity, shown especially in motherhood. Eco-feminism has drawn a homology between the human body and the earth, going so far as to suggest that the disvaluing of the human body is a causal factor in the environmental crises that are becoming more apparent each decade.

Forms of spiritual practice, ancient and new, such as fasting and asceticism, singing and dancing, yoga and meditation, running and sports, study and good works, even the taking on of a pilgrimage, affirm the effectiveness of manipulating the body and breath to bring about healing, clarity and expanded consciousness.

Scientific research continues to affirm the connection of body, mind and spirit: Dr Candace Pert, Teilhard de Chardin, SJ, and Dr James Prescott. As neurobiologist Dr Pert has proven, neuropeptides – the chemicals triggered by emotions – are thoughts converted into matter. Our emotions reside physically in our bodies and interact with our cells and tissues. In fact, Dr Pert can no longer separate the mind from the body, she says, because the same kinds of cells that manufacture and receive emotional chemistry in the brain are present throughout the body. As Dr Pert said on Bill Moyers' TV documentary, *Healing and the Mind*, 'Clearly there's another form of energy that we have not yet understood . . . Your mind is in every cell of your body.'

New Age spirituality is not dualistic, but finds spiritual power in nature and in things. It tends to use the language of energy rather than that of personal relationships and transcendent spirits. Energy is a neutral word that evokes no religious associations nor deeply held fears about one's relationship to God. Spiritual crises are described as energy disorders. Experiences that carry emotional energy in our energy systems include past and present relationships, both personal and professional; profound or traumatic experiences and memories; and belief patterns and attitudes, including all spiritual and super-stitious beliefs. The emotions from these experi-ences become encoded in our biological systems and contribute to the formation of our cell tis-sue, which then generates a quality of energy that reflects these emotions. When someone praises you, you feel a positive energy – a surge of personal power within your body. Positive and negative experiences register a memory in cell tissue as well as in the energy field.

Our relationship to power is at the core of our health. Of course, money doesn't guarantee health, but poverty, powerlessness and illness are undeniably linked. When you have trouble mak-ing money or you suddenly lose money, your biological system may weaken. Carolyn Myss, a popular spokesperson for the close relationship between spirituality and illness maintains in her book *Anatomy of the Spirit* that

> unused sexual juice may manifest as hot flashes. Unused creative energy or creative conflicts may also be expressed as hot flashes. In women most problems with bleeding and irregular periods frequently come from hav-ing too much emotional stress combined with the belief that one has no power over one's life choices, that one's choices are controlled by others. Bleeding abnormalities are often exacerbated when a woman internalizes con-fusing signals from her family or society about her own sexual pleasure and sexual needs. For instance, a woman may desire sexual pleasure but feel guilty about it or be unable to ask directly for it. She may not even be conscious of this inner conflict. (Myss, 1966, p. 143)

Self-pleasuring by genital self-stimulation is a pervasive human experience, reported by sex-ologists to be enjoyed by 95 per cent of men and 50–90 per cent of women. In recent years, from being categorized as a moral evil, self-pleasuring has been proposed as an aid for understanding one's body and for learning how to express love in a bodily way. Moreover, self-intimacy can be seen as a practice promoting integration of body, mind and spirit and, hence, spiritual growth. At the very least, it has come to be seen as a remedial practice for unlearning the shame and guilt that has characterized the experience of sexual arousal for many. Persons who were abused as children or women who were abused in violent relationship can relearn, through gentle self-stimulating touch, the goodness of their own bodies and the delight of sexual pleasure and heal some of the wounds they carry. Our spiritual task will always be to make our sexual lives free instead of compulsive, generous instead of selfish; fruitful rather than manipulative.

See also **Affectivity; Asceticism; Eroticism; Person; Sexuality.**

Peter Brown, *The Body and Society*, New York: Columbia University Press, 1988; Carol P. Christ and Judith Plaskow (eds), *Womanspirit Rising. A Feminist Reader in Religion*, New York: HarperCollins, 1992; Bill Moyers, *Healing and the Mind*, New York: Main Street Books, 1995; Carolyn Myss, *Anatomy of the Spirit*, New York: Three Rivers Press, 1996; James W. Prescott, 'Body pleasure and the origins of violence', *The Futurist* 9.2 (April 1975), 64–74; Joan Timmer-man, *The Mardi Gras Syndrome: Rethinking Christian Sexuality*, New York: Crossroad, 1984.

JOAN H. TIMMERMAN.

Bridal Mysticism (Brautmystic)

Narrowly defined, these terms refer only to mys-ticism using the metaphor of the soul as the bride of Christ to speak of mystic union with God. The notion of a consecrated virgin as a 'spouse of Christ' is a very early Christian concept and is still part of Christian thought today. Similarly, the exploitation of the language of the Song of Songs to illustrate the relationship between the soul and God has a long and distinguished history in Christian thought. The love poem in which the bride speaks of her longing as she awaits the return of her bridegroom was origin-ally included in the Jewish canon because the language was used in the Bible to describe the relationship between God and the tribe of Israel. It was therefore accepted into the Christian canon and Origen was the first to use the metaphor to speak of the individual soul rather than either Israel or the Church collectively. The imagery was popularized by the great Cistercian abbot Bernard of Clairvaux, in a series of ser-mons on the Song of Songs. It is a remarkable testament to the charismatic power of Bernard that he was able to speak to an audience of grown men of the love between the soul and God in unambiguously erotic language while keeping their attention focused on the spiritual import of what he had to say : 'Take heed that you bring chaste ears to this discourse of love; and when you think of these two lovers, remember always that not a man and a woman are to be thought of, but the Word of God and a soul' *(Sermon 61.2)*.

The imagery passed into more common use and can be found in the work of mystics such as Richard of St Victor, the Beguines and Ruys-broeck. The Beguine Mechtild of Magdeburg, for example, speaks of her relationship with God in this way in her *Flowing Light of the Godhead*: 'You (the soul) are like a new bride whose only love has left her sleeping from whom she cannot bear to part for even one hour . . . I (God) await you in the orchard of love and pick for you the flower of sweet reunion and make ready there your bed.' The soul replies, 'Ah my beloved I am hoarse in the throat of my chastity but the sweetness of your kindness has cleared my throat so that now I can sing' (*Flowing Light of the Godhead*, Book 2.25).

Numerous mystics, male as well as female, speak of their visionary marriage to God. There are several occurrences of mystics receiving stigmata in the form of a ring round their ring finger following their visionary marriage, for example Catherine of Ricci in 1542. Male mystics also speak of their mystical marriage to personifications of the virtues – such as that of Francis of Assisi to 'Lady Poverty'. The use of the erotic imagery of bridal mysticism leads naturally to visions of being pregnant, sometimes with the Holy Ghost, sometimes with the Word himself, and hence to at times very detailed descriptions of '*imitatio Mariae*' in which the nun or mystic shadows to a greater or lesser degree the experience of Mary during the nine months of her pregnancy. Imagery derived from the Song of Songs continued to be used throughout the Middle Ages and beyond by mystics and others including Teresa of Avila and John of the Cross. For example, in his *Spiritual Canticle* John of the Cross writes:

There he taught me a science most delectable;
And I gave myself to him indeed reserving nothing;
There I promised him to be his bride.
(*Spiritual Canticle* 407)

Echoes of the metaphor can also be found in the writings of Luther and the Anabaptists.

Another definition of the term *brautmystic* is much broader: the use of sensual language and images to describe the soul's relationship with God. Sensual language of course includes the erotic language of the Song of Songs mentioned above, but it is notable how the image of the soul as nurseling, suckling and obtaining nourishment at the breast of God, can at times merge almost indistinguishably with it. For example, in the following passage from Teresa of Avila: 'But when this most wealthy Spouse desires to enrich and comfort the Bride still more, He draws her so closely to Him that she is like one who swoons from excess of pleasure and joy and seems suspended in those Divine arms and drawn near to that sacred side and to those Divine breasts. Sustained by the Divine milk with which her Spouse continually nourishes her and growing

in grace so that she may be enabled to receive His comforts she can do nothing but rejoice' (*Conceptions of the Love of God* 4.384–5).

Another metaphor that is frequently included under *brautmystic* using this broader definition is that of courtly mysticism – the soul as the lover of a highborn mistress. This metaphor was drawn, not from the Hebrew Scriptures, but from the popular courtly love lyric in which the lover speaks of his love, his fear that it may be unrequited and his determination to prove himself worthy of the object of his love. Although both the bride and the courtly lover long for the return of their beloved and unashamedly demand the joyous fulfilment of their needs, the bride waits secure in the knowledge that she is loved and that the bridegroom will return. An important element of the relationship between the soul as bride and God as bridegroom is the mutuality of their love. The lover on the other hand often doubts the return of his beloved and declarations of love alternate with anger before reaching resolution in renewed, if resigned, professions of undying love. The bride occupies herself with charitable works and prayer while waiting for her bridegroom's return. The lover may be engaged in similar acts of service but does so as a way of earning his beloved's affection, not as the fruit of a fulfilled marriage.

The details of the relationship between the soul and God are clearly different in these different metaphors, but all the metaphors are fluid in terms of gender. Bernard of Clairvaux speaks of himself and his monks as brides, while numerous Beguines speak of themselves as men in love with a highborn woman – God. Christ is spoken of as a mother feeding her children from his breasts, and for Bernard and other Cistercians the image of the bride with breasts flowing with milk calls to mind an abbot preaching to his monks and giving them spiritual guidance. Similarly, all the metaphors have in common the unusual characteristic that they employ strong language that is unambiguously drawn from bodily functions often condemned by the Church to speak of the highest spiritual good – namely a sense of being one with God – experiencing God in the integration of the erotic and the holy.

See also **Beguine Spirituality; Carmelite Spirituality.**

Primary sources: *Bernard of Clairvaux on the Song of Songs i–iv*, Kalamazoo: Cistercian Publications, 1971–80; John of the Cross, *The Spiritual Canticle*, trans. and ed. E. Allison Peers, Garden City New York: Doubleday Image Books, 1961; Mechtild of Magdeburg, *Flowing*

Light of the Godhead, trans. C. M. Galvani, ed. S. Clark, New York: Garland, 1991; Teresa of Avila, *The Complete Works of St Teresa of Jesus,* trans. and ed. E. Allison Peers, London: Sheed & Ward, 1973.

Secondary sources: Bernard McGinn, *The Growth of Mysticism: Gregory the Great through the Twelfth Century,* New York: Crossroad, 1994; Barbara Newman, *From Virile Woman to WomanChrist: Studies in Medieval Religion and Literature,* Philadelphia: University of Pennsylvania Press, 1995; Nelson Pike, *Mystic Union: An Essay in the Phenomenology of Mysticism,* Ithaca: Cornell University Press, 1992.

SASKIA MURK JANSEN

Bridgettine Spirituality

St Bridget of Sweden (more accurately Birgitta *c.* 1302/3–73) was a visionary and founder of the Bridgettine Order. The daughter of a wealthy family, Bridget married at thirteen and had eight children, one of whom, St Catherine, became first abbess of the Order. After the death of her husband in 1341, Bridget had a series of visions and spiritual experiences derived from close meditative reading of the Scriptures. She became the most influential spiritual and theological figure in medieval Scandinavia. Her *Revelations* and the devotions inspired by them were immensely popular not least because they offered details of Jesus' earthly life. They also had a wide influence in the later Middle Ages – including on Margery Kempe, the English fourteenth-century mystic. Bridget was one of several important medieval mystics (famously, Julian of Norwich) to speak of Christ as Mother. Overall, the *Revelations* were outstanding examples of the affective, christocentric spirituality of her age. However, the text is problematic because it was not composed by her but written down in Latin by her spiritual directors who certainly interpreted the visions and may have altered the content.

Bridget's visionary experiences did not lead to a withdrawal into pure interiority. On the contrary, the visions were directed very much to the Church and to the world and called for conversion. Her visionary experience appears to have impelled Bridget towards a public role in the Church and on the political stage and given her an authority to speak. She was vocal in attempting to persuade the popes to return from Avignon to Rome and also challenged corruption and spiritual decay in the Church at large. In 1349 Bridget went to Rome where she lived for the remainder of her life and worked for reform in the Church and for the development of her Order of the Most Holy Saviour, or Bridgettines.

The original house of the Bridgettine Order was begun in 1346 at Vadstena, a royal castle donated by King Magnus of Sweden. Construction was halted in 1348 because confirmation of Bridget's Rule (based on her visions) was initially refused as it did not conform to the regulations of the Fourth Lateran Council of 1215 that all new foundations must adopt an ancient rule. In the end, against Bridget's wishes, the nuns of the Order had to adopt the Rule of St Augustine with Bridget's Rule merely a supplement. However, by 1378 Pope Urban VI allowed the two Rules to be given equal weight. The original structure of the Order was for double monasteries of women and men, segregated but with a common church. Theoretically there were to be sixty nuns and twenty-five monks (thirteen priests, four deacons and eight lay brothers) in each house. Bridget's Rule was bold in asserting the dominance of the nuns. This was based on Bridget's understanding of the relationship of Mary and her Son and particularly her vision of the Virgin as head and queen of the apostles in heaven. Thus the abbess, representing the figure of Mary, governed the internal life of the whole monastery. Under her, a Confessor General (prior of the monks) acted as the spiritual guide for both women and men. The strongly christocentric spirituality of the Order is underlined by the nuns wearing white linen bands on top of their heads in the form of a cross on which five pieces of red cloth are sown to mark Christ's wounds.

The Bridgettine Rule prescribed a strict life of contemplation and study and many of the members, both women and men, became scholars. One of the most famous monasteries of any kind in England during the later Middle Ages was the Bridgettine Syon Abbey on the outskirts of London, founded in 1415 by King Henry V in thanksgiving for victory at Agincourt. Syon was noted for its scholarly and humanist associations. It produced the largest single group of spiritual works in print immediately before the Reformation – Richard Whitford being its most prolific author. Another monk, Richard Reynolds, was part of the circle of Sir Thomas More and the English Humanists and a confidant of Queen Catherine of Aragon and was one of the first group of people to be executed in 1535 for refusing to acknowledge King Henry VIII as head of the English Church.

Because of the Order's demography the Reformation seriously depleted its numbers. The French Revolution at the end of the eighteenth century led to further decline. The monks died out finally in the nineteenth century (a small community has recently been refounded in the United States). Four female monasteries of the original Order that survived the French Revolution still exist, one of them in England. There is also a less enclosed Bridgettine congregation of sisters, founded in the early twentieth century by a former Swedish Lutheran Elizabeth Hasseblad, that has convents in Europe, Central America and India. No branch of the Bridgettine family currently has double houses.

See also **Mysticism** (*essay*); **Augustinian Spirituality; Canonical Communities; Jesus and Spirituality; Rules, Religious; Visionary Literature; Women Medieval Mystics.**

Marguerite Tjader Harris (ed.), *Birgitta of Sweden: Life and Selected Revelations*, CWS, New York: Paulist Press, 1990; Roger Ellis, *Syon Abbey: The Spirit of the English Bridgettines*, Salzburg: Analecta Cartusiana, 1984; Bridget Morris, *St Birgitta of Sweden*, Woodbridge: Boydell & Brewer, 1999; Patricia Ranft, *Women and the Religious Life in Premodern Europe.* New York: St Martin's Press, 1996.

PHILIP SHELDRAKE

Buddhism and Christianity

In a world of ever more porous cultural and religious boundaries, whether welcomed and sought or resisted and feared, Christians find themselves unavoidably engaged with other faith traditions. The old culture-bound strategy of exclusion and refutation no longer reinforces the confidence and increases the numbers of Christian practitioners, but hastens instead the marginalization of the traditional Churches.

Indeed, with a solid push from the World Council of Churches and the Second Vatican Council in the latter half of the twentieth century, both Protestants and Catholics for the last several decades have been exploring other religious traditions while witnessing to the Christian gospel in the context of a plurality of traditions. Buddhism is one of the major world faith traditions with which many Christians have found rich and rewarding points of encounter and even resources for personal transformation. Central to the encounter of Christian spirituality with Buddhism has been the impact of Zen (Chan) meditative practice. In particular, the Sambô Kyôdan lineage of Japanese Zen has had a significant influence on Christian meditation teachers. This is treated in this dictionary by a separate entry on the meeting between Zen and Christian spirituality.

The present entry deals more broadly with the wider impact of Buddhist teaching and practice on Christian spirituality. Perhaps the most notable impact on Christian spirituality and theology is visible in the widespread reconfiguration of Christian mission that reflects a pervasive change in attitude among missionaries of mainline denominations. While fundamentalist and more evangelical missionaries for the most part set their aim on conversions to the gospel and away from other paths, Christian thinkers and preachers from many mainline Protestant and Catholic traditions – having studied the cultures in which they live and work – have come to adopt a more nuanced approach. They appreciate the riches and beauty they find in Buddhism (and in other traditions) while at the same time witnessing to the truth of the gospel, preaching doctrine, and welcoming inter-faith dialogue. The shift is from conversion to witness, from cultural isolation to dialogue and discussion.

All over the Buddhist world, church-sponsored centres for such dialogue and interaction can be found: in Taiwan the Taipei Ricci Center; in Japan the Institute of Christian Culture/Oriental Religions in Tokyo, the Nanzan Institute for Religion and Culture in Nagoya, and the NCC Center for the Study of Japanese Religions in Kyoto; in the Philippines the Gowing Memorial Research Center; in Hong Kong the Christian Study Centre on Chinese Religion and Culture; in Korea the Seton Inter-religious Research and Spirituality Center and the Institute of Religion at Sogang University; and in Thailand the FABC Office of Ecumenical and Interreligious Affairs and the interfaith endeavours of Payap University in Chiang Mai. Now for over thirty years, these and other centres have sponsored dialogues on a host of subjects – and have published numerous scholarly journals and insightful books on the interaction between Christian faith and Buddhist doctrine and philosophy. Their work has provided a significant impetus for theological interpretation of the nature of mission and indeed the nature of the Christian Church itself, and has engaged some of the finest minds in the Christian traditions.

Another point of rich contact between Christian spirituality and Buddhism is the dialogue between Buddhist monks and those Christian traditions that embrace monasticism. Throughout the entirety of its history Buddhism has been a monastic tradition. The Roman Catholic, Orthodox and Anglican traditions, where monasticism remains vibrant, have launched monastic exchange programmes with Buddhist religious communities. Christian monks spend months living and practising within Buddhist monasteries, and Buddhist monks in Christian monasteries. They learn one another's life rule, liturgical practice and prayer methods, which are then passed on through articles and books to other Christian practitioners. Prominent among the participants and supporters of this inter-change have been Christian monks and nuns – Thomas Merton, Thomas Keating, Elaine MacInnes and Wayne Teasdale – and their Buddhist counterparts – Thich Nhat Hanh, the Dalai Lama, Norman Fischer, Eshin Nishimura and Ven. Yifa.

There are also numerous contact points between Buddhists and Christians in areas of social engagement, both in Asian countries and in the West. Not infrequently, inter-faith dia-logue runs into dead ends where the partners may either embrace a respectful silence as the best option or else soldier on until new insights illumine as-yet unthought approaches. A third option is for Christians and Buddhists to engage in shared social action – in peace activities, social welfare programmes, political efforts to bring about justice. Of particular note is the broad and shared effort to address the persecution of Tibetan Buddhists in Tibet, a political cause that attracts support from a broad array of religious practitioners. Also notable are the social and economic 'liberation' efforts of Christians and Buddhists in Southeast Asia, such as A. T. Ariyaratne in Sri Lanka, Sulak Sivaraksa and Phra Prayudh Payutto in Thailand, Frank Tedesco in Korea, and also in Korea the Christian Minjung (peoples') theological move-ment, represented by such activists as Ahn Byung, a New Testament scholar, and the poet Kim Chi-ha.

On a more theological and philosophical level, the efforts of scholars and theologians have transformed modern Western understandings of Buddhism and its potential impact on Christian faith. While previous generations constructed caricatures of the religions against which they competed, such misconstruals are less likely to occur today because of many well-researched studies of the basic history and doctrine of the traditions. Thinkers in the West have at their dis-posal hundreds of books on Buddhism in Euro-pean languages. In addition, the languages of Buddhism – Sanskrit, Tibetan, Chinese, Japanese – are now widely taught in colleges and universi-ties in Europe and the United States. Thus today any attempt at caricature is immediately recog-nized as uninformed and theologically narrow, no matter how weighty its institutional pedigree.

Scholarly and inter-faith groups abound, providing dialogue venues for academics and practitioners of Buddhism and Christianity. The European Network of Buddhist–Christian Studies and its American counterpart, the Society for Buddhist–Christian Studies, both sponsor conferences and publications. Here in the culturally Christian West, the membership of

these organizations is largely Christian, by con-trast to Japan, for example, where Buddhist–Christian meetings are heavily Buddhist.

The specific philosophies that inform Bud-dhism have impacted Christian thinking in different ways. The modern Japanese Kyoto School philosophers developed their unique way of thinking by bringing Buddhist philosophy into intentional dialogue with and critique of Western philosophy. They wrote very difficult books that were rather inaccessible to westerners until the last fifteen or twenty years, when – building on previous efforts at interpretation and translation – the Nanzan Institute for Religion and Culture undertook to translate and publish the major works of Kitarô Nishida, Hajime Tanabe and Keiji Nishitani, as well as in-depth studies on the development and import of their thinking.

More classical works of Mahâyâna Buddhist philosophy have also had a profound impact on Western Christian thinkers of the last gener-ation. The Mâdhyamika philosophy of founding Mahâyâna master Nâgârjuna (c. 150 CE) presents a critical approach to both religious affirmation and negation, offering a means whereby one can abide in the dependently arisen awareness of the emptiness of all things. The Yogâcâra philosophy of Asanga and Vasubandhu introduced Bud-dhists to a critical understanding not only of the patterns of meaning but also of the conscious-ness that engenders meaning, whether deluded and awakened. These are the two foundational philosophies of Mahâyâna Buddhism, permeat-ing all later Buddhist traditions in China, Korea and Japan. They draw also on the slightly earlier *Perfection of Wisdom Scriptures*, which were appropriated and culturally embodied in the Chan (Zen) traditions as well. These traditions in Buddhist thought offer philosophical models for comparative interplay with Christian texts. They may also serve as startlingly elegant philosoph-ical frameworks for thinking anew the 'Good News', for doing theology within ever-surprising contexts.

See also **Spirituality and the Dialogue of Religions** (*essay*); **Zen and Christianity.**

Ruben L. F. Habito, *Living Zen, Loving God*, Boston: Wisdom, 2004; James W. Heisig, *Philosophers of Nothingness: An Essay on the Kyoto School*, Honolulu: University of Hawaii Press, 2001; John P. Keenan, *The Meaning of Christ: A Mahâyâna Theology*, Maryknoll, NY: Orbis Books, 1989; Robert H. King, *Thomas Merton and Thich Nhat Hanh: Engaged Spirituality in an Age of Globalization*, New York and London: Continuum, 2001; Paul F. Knitter,

Introducing Theologies of Religion, Maryknoll, NY: Orbis Books, 2002; Donald W. Mitchell and James Wiseman, *The Gethsemane Encounter: A Dialogue on the Spiritual Life by Buddhist and Christian Monastics,* New York and London: Continuum, 1999; Terry Muck, 'Living in God's Grace' in Harold Kasimow, John P. Keenan and Linda Klepinger Keenan (eds), *Beside Still Waters: Jews, Christians, and the Way of the Buddha,* Boston: Wisdom, 2003; Nagao Gadjin, *The Foundational Standpoint of Mâdhyamika Philosophy,* Albany: State University of New York Press, 1989; Thich Nhat Hanh, *Going Home: Jesus and Buddha as Brothers,* New York: Riverhead Books, 1999; Joseph Stephen O'Leary, *Christian Truth and Religious Pluralism,* Edinburgh: Edinburgh University Press, 1996; Maurice Wiles, *Christian Theology and Inter-Religious Dialogue,* London: SCM Press/ Philadelphia: Trinity Press, 1992.

JOHN P. KEENAN

Business and Spirituality

The past fifteen years have witnessed an explosion of books, articles, workshops and conferences on the topic of spirituality and business. Over three hundred books have appeared, conferences have been organized in fifteen countries, and the Academy of Management, the professional organization for business and management scholars, has established a new interest group in 'Management, Spirituality, and Religion'.

International in scope, the spirituality in the business movement bridges cultures, continents and religions, appearing in such diverse places as Australia, China, Canada, England, France, Germany, India, Ireland, New Zealand, the Netherlands, the Philippines, Scotland, Singapore, Switzerland, the United States and Wales.

Only time will tell if this movement is a mutant offspring or the evolved child of the historical coupling of faith and work. Early forebears of the spirituality in business movement include John Calvin, who wrote about 'secular' work as a divine calling, the papal encyclical *Rerum Novarum* (1891), and nineteenth-century American businessmen John Wanamaker and Samuel Jones, who sought to operate their businesses by biblical principles. More recently, the not-so-distant US ancestor of the spirituality in business movement was the 'Ministry of the Laity' movement, which started after World War 2 and emphasized business and other 'secular' work as divine vocations.

Popular writers and speakers in the current movement of spirituality in business are primarily business leaders and consultants who have discovered a spiritual path and want to introduce others to the benefits of integrating spirituality into the workplace. Seeking to motivate, inspire and instruct, they fall into two groups: first, those who define spirituality broadly, seeking to include adherents of all religions as well as those who claim no religious affiliation; and, second, those who focus solely on Christian faith. Both groups argue that spirituality in business improves morale, increases employee fulfilment, builds stronger teams and increases profits. Religious leaders, including Christian pastors and theologians, have been slow to take interest in the topic, thus most of the conversation has occurred without the benefit of dialogue with those trained as leaders in religious traditions.

Scholars, wary of the sweeping claims made in the popular literature, seek to investigate those claims, with most of the scholarly work thus far being done by management scholars. The driving question behind most of these academic studies has been, 'How does spirituality affect organizational performance?' Quantitative researchers focus on defining and measuring spirituality in business as a precursor to creating instruments that can measure the influence of spirituality on a company's bottom line. Qualitative researchers seek to describe how spirituality gets manifested throughout an organization and then generate hypotheses about the impact a spiritual organization has on organizational performance. While many researchers who focus on spirituality and organizational performance insist on the necessity of solely using this empirical approach if spirituality is to be accepted in the academy, another group of scholars decries this narrow focus, fearing being co-opted by the management academy. They claim that different research methods are needed in this new field of spirituality in business, methods that go beyond the positivist, empiricist approach traditionally used by social scientific researchers. Scholars from the field of spirituality have just begun to explore what they can contribute to this conversation.

Since by its very nature spirituality connects with all of life, it is not surprising that spirituality is now engaging the realm of business. The tension and the opportunity lie in maintaining the integrity of each as they engage with one another.

See also **Leadership.**

Margaret Benefiel (in press), 'Pathfinders and trailblazers: exploring the territory of spirituality in organizations', *Managerial Finance*; R. Giacolone and C. Jurkiewicz (eds), *Handbook of Workplace Spirituality and Organizational Performance,* Armonk, NY: Sharpe, 2003; K. Lund

Dean, C. Forniciari and J. McGee, 'Research in spirituality, religion, and work: walking the line between relevance and legitimacy', *Journal of Organizational Change Management* 16.4 (2003), 378–95; M. McLoughlin, *2003 International Faith and Work Directory*, Cumming, GA: Aslan, 2003; D. W. Miller, 'The faith at work movement', *Theology Today* 60 (2003), 301–10.

MARGARET BENEFIEL

Byzantine Spirituality

The empire of Christian Byzantium, in its heyday, stretched from the Balkans to the Russias and from Africa to the Adriatic, with its heartland always in Greece and Asia Minor, and its capital at the 'Queen of all Cities' – Constantinople (now Istanbul). It endured from the fourth to the fifteenth centuries, always seeing itself as the direct continuation of the ancient Roman imperium. One of its liveliest channels of interest was the spiritual life, as can be witnessed by the great body of literature it produced in the process of defining, defending and clarifying its spiritual and mystical identity. The poet Yeats was not far off the mark when he reflected on the way ordinary life had been so closely merged with the religious imperative in the East Roman Empire, saying: 'I think that in early Byzantium, as maybe never before or since in recorded history, religious, aesthetic and practical life were one.' The credal structures, hagiographies, liturgical forms and monastic prayer disciplines that soon became constitutive of worldwide Christianity all originated in the Byzantine world, a fertile melting pot of religious passion and mystical speculation for most if its long life. It is difficult to sum up the 'Byzantine tradition' as a single factor because, at least from the fourth to the eighth centuries (before the expanse of Islam began to cut off the Christian communities of Syria and Africa from the international Oecumene) the Byzantine world was a truly international mix of Egyptian (Coptic), Nubian, Ethiopic, Syrian and Greek elements. One of the chief characteristics of the Byzantine tradition is precisely this rich cultural fusion of important base elements, which in many instances were spread among the Great Churches (Rome, Constantinople, Alexandria, Antioch, Jerusalem, Kiev, for example) by a lively monastic and pilgrim traffic. But certain common characteristics of Byzantine spirituality can be briefly noted here.

One of the chief defining markers of the Byzantine spirituality was its ascetical tone. From the earliest appearance of monks and hermits in Egypt, Syria and Palestine, they were eagerly welcomed by Byzantine patrons, and in the great cities of the empire there was always an avid readership for hagiographic tales of the 'desert fathers'. Most of Byzantine anthropological theory followed ascetical principles. The soul or the spiritual intellect was regarded as the Hegemonikon (ruling identity) of a human being, a divinely graced potentiality for transcendent communion, but one that was always challenged by material distractions (the passions of body and psyche) that could easily put into disarray the fundamental anthropological rationale, which was the ascent of the soul to the goal of divine communion (a process frequently summated by the East Christians as the path to deification). Constant purification of the heart through prayer and acts of renunciation was seen as essential to the mainstream of all Byzantine types of spiritual life.

In addition to this, the Byzantine Church focused profoundly on liturgical life. Here, from ancient times, the great church services were called 'The Mysteries', and were approached with great ceremony and awe, as powerful channels of the divine presence. The border between the great liturgical ceremonials and the ritual patterns of daily life were not so strictly demarcated, and innumerable smaller rites served to protect farm animals, and vineyards, houses and people, in a web of blessing services, healings and intercessions, extant in the service books, that demonstrate a deep sense of the Byzantine desire to consecrate the earthly environment. The ritual of the blessing of the waters, celebrated on the feast of the Theophany (the Baptism of Jesus on 6 January) typically demonstrates this deeply 'ecological' sense of the Byzantine desire to render the environment sacred, and luminous.

Icons also, at least from the sixth century onwards, came to have a similarly potent place in the spiritual lives of the East Romans. Unlike the more functional Western Church, religious art was never explained in Byzantium (or perhaps explained away) as having a primarily didactic function (teaching the unlettered or suchlike). In the Byzantine Church the icon was seen as a mystery on its own terms, a channel of divine grace and power. Innumerable stories tell of miraculous healings or apparitions associated with icons. The cult of the Holy Virgin, the local saints, and the defending angels, closely allied with their local churches and the associated icons, provided a web of kinship bonding whereby a typical Byzantine Christian understood his or her place in the cosmos. The intercession of Christ and the saints was always understood quite locally and concretely. The character of this can be seen abundantly in the innumerable hagiographies (lives and legends of the local saints) that Byzantium seemed to produce incessantly.

The religious poetry of Byzantium remains one of the world's undiscovered wonders. Master poets and musicians such as Romanos the Melodist in the sixth century, John of Damascus in the eighth, or Symeon the New Theologian in the eleventh, produced rhapsodic works of immense beauty, retelling the biblical narratives in an extended commentary-midrash on the holy text and, in the process, unravelling and reweaving the simple biblical tales into rich and detailed tapestries of meaning. This poetic chant was typically sung throughout church services lasting several hours, and the communication of the gospel truths through the medium of these strangely harmonized Byzantine chants gave even the new hymnic genres a mystical and hypnotic character. It is one that is still readily observable in the great ceremonies of the Orthodox Church's Passion Week, or the other major festivals (such as Christmas or Pascha) when these hymns provide the organizing structure of the services.

Byzantine spiritual writing is quintessentially and predominantly monastic. In studying this long literary history one can see several schools of thought coming to an ever closer alignment after the fifth century. The Syro-Byzantine writers particularly stressed the need of the believer to keep an open and perceptive 'heart' before the face of God in prayer. God, so they taught, looked only at the heart, and if it were not alive to the divine presence, and generously responsive to God, working out its discipleship in 'heartfelt' generosity, then the life of the spirit would be rendered pointless. Greek and Egyptian Byzantine writers, on the other hand, spoke often of the need for the intellect to rise from material obsessions and creaturely defilement, through a purification of the soul, until the Nous (spiritual intellect) was capable of receiving revealed intimations of the divine presence in a luminous and wise state of perception. The twin tracks of the deepening focus of the heart, and the purified and luminous vision, eventually merged in Byzantium to produce a distinctive 'Hesychast' school of theology that itself came to be characteristically descriptive of 'Byzantine spirituality' in all its forms. The Hesychast tradition can still be witnessed in the monasteries of the Eastern Orthodox world, and is preserved in a central collection of ascetical and mystical texts called the Philokalia.

After the collapse of Byzantium as an independent Christian power in the fifteenth century, its spiritual traditions remained alive in the variegated families of the Orthodox and Oriental

Churches, despite their collective oppression by often hostile external forces. Today the Byzantine Christian tradition is becoming more known to the West through the processes of the large ethnic diasporas that occurred in the twentieth century. An especially fertile meeting ground has been provided in modern America, where the Orthodox communities are significant in both numbers and vitality, and can once more enjoy the privilege of the investigation and re-appropriation of their ancient traditions in freedom and security.

See also **Early Christian Spirituality; Hesychasm; Orthodox Spirituality.**

J. M. Hussey, *The Orthodox Church in the Byzantine Empire*, Oxford: Clarendon Press, 1990; V. Lossky, *The Mystical Theology of the Eastern Church*. Cambridge: Clarke & Co. [1957] 1973; J. A. McGuckin, *Standing in God's Holy Fire: The Byzantine Tradition*, Traditions of Christian Spirituality, ed. P. Sheldrake, London: Darton, Longman & Todd/New York: Orbis Books, 2001; L. Ouspensky, *Theology of the Icon*, vols 1–2, New York: SVS Press, 1992; T. Spidlik, *The Spirituality of the Christian East*, Kalamazoo, MI: Cistercian Publications, 1986.

JOHN ANTHONY MCGUCKIN

Calvinist Spirituality

A focus on the adoration of God's glory and the centrality of union with Christ form the core of the Calvinist conception of the spiritual life. In his *Institutes of the Christian Religion*, Calvin gave 'the highest degree of importance' to 'that joining together of Head and members, that indwelling of Christ in our hearts – in short, that mystical union' by which 'we put on Christ and are engrafted into his body' (*Institutes* 3.12.10) Flowing from this core are accompanying themes that characterize Calvinist piety in its varied expressions.

Balancing the love of God and the fear of God as essential in Calvinist spirituality. Calvin stressed the interweaving of desire and awe as a central dynamic of the Christian life. In his first catechism he defined 'true piety' as that 'which loves God as Father as much as it fears and reverences Him as Lord' (*Catechism*, p. 2). His God was a father 'inclined to allure us to himself by gentle and loving means', one who created the world as a theatre of God's glory, using beauty to attract God's children in every possible way ('Sermon on Deuteronomy' 28.46–50, *Calvini Opera* 28.441). Knowing God, for Calvin, was thus inescapably a matter of enjoying God. Yet he also knew that the human desire for the divine could easily be twisted to other ends. Hence, those 'who have been endowed with this piety dare not fashion out of their own rashness any God for themselves' (*Catechism*, p. 2). The danger of idolatry requires the continual testing and refining of desire in the presence of a majestic Lord, jealous of all other lovers. A restless longing for beauty necessarily tempers itself through the touchstone of Scripture and the exercise of self-forgetfulness. 'We are not our own,' Calvin emphasized (*Institutes* 3.7.1). We are the dearly loved children of a radiant God of matchless glory. As a result, the knowledge of God and the knowledge of ourselves are inseparably knit together.

In the subsequent history of Calvinist spirituality, one finds a tension between those who shared Calvin's own tendency toward personal anxiety, ever seeking assurance of their salvation, and those who could rest in the words of the Heidelberg Catechism, 'My only comfort is that I belong – body and soul, in life and in death – not to myself but to my faithful Saviour Jesus Christ' (Heidelberg Catechism 1562, question 1). Apprehensiveness and confident joy are thus intertwined realities in the devotional life of Reformed Christians.

Being engrafted into Christ by word and sacrament. Given the importance that the Calvinist tradition attributes to mystical union with Christ as the central project of the Christian life, preaching becomes basic to that process in offering what amounts to the 'real presence' of Christ in the preached Word. Calvin insisted that 'God is nigh to us, face to face' in the mystery of preaching ('Commentary on Haggai' 1.12, *Calvini Opera* 44.94). Calvinist piety is thus inescapably biblical. Similarly, the role of baptism is crucial in incorporating the faithful into the covenant bond of Christ's body, as is the mystery of the Eucharist in feeding the faithful on the life-giving flesh (*caro vivifica*) of Christ's body. Calvin spoke of a 'true and substantial partaking of the body and blood of the Lord' in the sacrament of the Lord's Supper (*Institutes* 4.17.19). One of the Genevan Reformer's distinctive contributions to the understanding of Scripture and Eucharist alike was the importance he gave to the presence and witness of the Holy Spirit in assuring one's reception of Christ and his gifts. His short treatise on 'The Life of the Christian', found in chapters 6–10 of the third book of the *Institutes*, underscores the idea that growth in the Christian life is a gradual process of being engrafted into Christ by the work of the Spirit, never a matter of instant perfection.

The corporate, covenantal reality of Calvinist spirituality. Like Cyprian, Calvin insisted that one cannot have God as one's Father without also having the Church as one's Mother. The Church precedes the individual, receiving separate believers into her common life. It is she who 'gives us birth and nourishes us at her breast' (*Institutes* 4.1.1, 4). The Reformed tradition emphasizes this corporate nature of the Christian life in its focus on God's covenant as a communal affair, joining together the people of God in a relationship initiated by God alone. Similarly, Calvinist piety stresses the centrality of corporate worship, understanding private devotion to draw its strength and correction from the life of the community. In the Reformed tradition, an individualistic search for interior meaning has never been as important as the ethical and social implications of the lordship of Christ. Its emphasis on personal conversion and sanctification focuses on Christ and one's neighbour more than on the attainment of individual perfection. Given the importance that Calvinists also attribute to the structuring of church life, they have at times manifested a penchant for disciplined order and rationality.

The active, 'worldly' dimension of Calvinist piety. Gratitude and grace provide the impulse to Christian action in Calvin's thinking, with the third use of the law giving concrete shape to the exercise of love. For Calvin, the law functioned not only in the ordering of civil society and in driving sinners to recognize their need of God's grace, but also as a guide in living out the Christian life. Hence sanctification assumed for Calvinism the importance that justification had been given in the Lutheran tradition. The goal of Reformed Christian discipleship is to bring all human experience (secular and sacred) under the lordship of Christ. To this end, the Calvinist doctrine of vocation called laity and clergy alike to incorporate every sphere of their lives into Christ's service, seeing the Christian life as more a matter of engagement than withdrawal. The analysis and redemption of social structures thus became an accompanying dimension of Calvinist spirituality. Calvin himself urged legislation to secure balcony rails for the protection of small children in the houses of Geneva. His efforts to introduce a silk-weaving industry to provide jobs for the poor were, for him, a natural expression of the 'practice of piety'. From Abraham Kuyper to H. Richard Niebuhr, the Calvinist spirit has been recognized as actively engaged in the transformation of culture. Reformed Christians possess an innate suspicion of otherworldliness.

Given this reality, Max Weber observed the impact of the 'worldly asceticism' of Calvinist spirituality on economic changes in the early modern period. Reformed sermons on frugality, simplicity and the practice of charity, however, contributed as much to the criticism of capitalism as to its rise. A Calvinist attentiveness to the operation of Divine Providence in the workings of nature and the unfolding of history has always made Reformed Christians sensitive to the beauty and wonder of creation as well as to political and social developments in cultural life.

These themes have all been expressed in the Calvinist tradition through devotional manuals like Lewis Bayly's *The Practice of Piety* and Richard Baxter's *The Saints Everlasting Rest*, the spiritual diaries of Elizabeth Rowe and Cotton Mather, the sermons of George Whitefield and Alexander Whyte, the hymns of Isaac Watts and Gerhard Tersteegen, the meditative poetry of Edward Taylor and Anne Bradstreet, and the literary creativity of John Milton and John Bunyan. The theological integrity and social activism of Reformed piety are seen in the works of John Williamson Nevin, P. T. Forsyth, Thomas F. Torrance, Reinhold Niebuhr, Karl Barth, George MacLeod of Iona, and Allen Boesak in South Africa. Calvinist spirituality exerts significant influence in various Reformed, Presbyterian, Congregationalist and even Anglican and Baptist Church bodies. Historically, its social and spiritual ideals have profoundly influenced the cultural (and even political) life of the Netherlands, the United Kingdom (especially Scotland), the United States, South Africa and Korea.

Calvinism long laboured under the stereotype of a dark and brooding theology, fixed on a sovereign God's condemnation of sinful humanity. Despite emphasis on the 'horrible decree' of predestination in the Calvinism that developed after Calvin, the doctrine of election never formed the heartbeat of Reformed piety. Communion with Christ, as emphasized here, was a much more dominant motif.

As a subset of Reformed piety emerging out of the sixteenth-century Swiss Reformation, Calvinist spirituality should also be distinguished from its Zwinglian predecessor. The latter was narrowly bibliocentric in its reform of worship and piety, producing a devotion that remained largely inward and rational, more individualistic in its practice of the spiritual life. Ulrich Zwingli's understanding of the believer's subjective 'remembrance' of Christ in the Eucharist has deeply influenced the history of Reformed spirituality, but John Calvin's more churchly piety stands closer to the mainstream of the Reformation (and Catholic) traditions.

See also **Election (Predestination); Puritan Spirituality; Reformation and Spirituality; Reformed Tradition.**

William Bouwsma, 'The Spirituality of John Calvin' in J. Raitt (ed.), *Christian Spirituality: High Middle Ages and Reformation*, New York: Crossroad, 1989, pp. 318–33; John Calvin, *Institutes of the Christian Religion*, trans. Ford Lewis Battles, 2 vols, Philadelphia: Westminster Press, 1960; John Calvin, *Catechism (1537)*, trans. Ford Lewis Battles, Pittsburgh: Pittsburgh Theological Seminary, 1972; Howard G. Hageman, 'Reformed Spirituality' in F. Senn (ed.), *Protestant Spiritual Traditions*, New York: Paulist Press, 1986, pp. 55–79; Elsie Anne McKee, *John Calvin: Writings on Pastoral Piety*, New York: Paulist Press, 2001; Howard L. Rice, *Reformed Spirituality*, Louisville: Westminster John Knox Press, 1991; Ronald S. Wallace, *Calvin's Doctrine of the Christian Life*, Edinburgh: Oliver & Boyd, 1959.

BELDEN C. LANE

Camaldolese Spirituality

Camaldolese spirituality is a particular expression of Benedictine spirituality, but also very much rooted in the pre-Benedictine eremitical heritage of Egypt and Palestine. The Camaldolese family of monks and nuns thus follows the Rule of St Benedict, and provides monasteries for communal life, but also includes hermitages (and ashrams), and is even open to monastic mission. This 'threefold good' of community, solitude and mission even unto martyrdom, which the Camaldolese feel is firmly rooted in Scripture and in the life of Jesus, was spelled out in explicit monastic terms by the contemporary disciple of St Romuald, St Bruno-Boniface, himself martyred in mission (d. 1009). The very charismatic St Romuald (c. 950–1027) is looked to by the Camaldolese family as the father of the Camaldolese reform movement, but neither he nor St Benedict is considered 'founder' of the Camaldolese in the way that in later centuries the Franciscans, for instance, would consider St Francis, or the Dominicans St Dominic. Rather, the Camaldolese see themselves as living within the larger context of the ancient monastic heritage of East and West, and firmly rooted in the Scriptures. The Camaldolese see their scriptural roots in the desert experience of Elijah and John the Baptist and especially of Jesus, as well as in the communal experience of the first apostles and disciples, called into koinonia by Jesus, and also in the apostolic mission even unto death (the biblical roots of the 'threefold good').

Romuald, a nobleman of Ravenna, was so grieved that his father had killed another in a duel that he entered the Abbey of St Apollinare in Classe to do penance. The Byzantine influence over the whole area was expressed in the abbey church in its magnificent mosaics, with their paradise and paschal themes, which shaped Romuald in Eastern spirit, as well as in the Benedictine, from his first formation. After three years in the Abbey, Romuald felt a strong attraction to solitude, and was permitted to retire to the west of Venice under the guidance of an old hermit Marinus. From there Romuald accompanied the Doge of Venice, who had undergone a powerful conversion experience and wished to retire into solitude, and an abbot to the famous Abbey of St Michael of Cuxa in Catalonia, a flourishing community of the Cluniac reform. Here all three were permitted to live in solitude, where Romuald, over a period of perhaps ten years, deepened his study of Scripture and of the monastic heritage, in its full 'threefold good' range, from the coenobitic to eremitic and even to monastic mission. Here he was ordained priest, and returned to Italy in 988. He was by then renowned for sanctity and his charismatic gifts, and Emperor Otto III appointed him abbot of St Apollinare in 998. But the community did not accept his reforming spirit, so he retired into solitude again. He would emerge periodically to establish a little community of hermits or monks, or renew a community, or defend the poor, and toward the end of his life, around 1023, he established in the Tuscan mountains the hermitage of Camaldoli. Scholars debate the etymology of 'Camaldoli', but it is possibly a conflation of *campus Romualdi*, 'field of Romuald'. About two miles below the hermitage was founded, especially for the young and infirm monks, a monastery which with the hermitage has constituted one monastic family since. That hermitage-monastery then founded or renewed many other houses, and became early on the head of the Camaldolese Congregation, officially recognized as one of the earliest congregations by Pope Paschal II in 1113.

We have no writings from St Romuald, just a *Short Rule* recorded by his contemporary disciple St Bruno Boniface, but it sums up much of the substance of desert spirituality:

Sit in your cell as in paradise; put the whole world behind you and forget it; like a skilled angler on the lookout for a catch, keep a careful eye on your thoughts. The path you must follow is in the psalms – don't leave it . . . take every chance you can find to sing the psalms in your heart and to understand them with your head; if your mind wanders as you read, don't give up but hurry back and try again. Above all realize that you are in God's presence; hold your heart there in wonder as if before your sovereign. Empty yourself completely; sit waiting, content with God's gift, like a little chick tasting and eating nothing but what its mother brings.

St Peter Damian (1007–72), monk, bishop, cardinal, Doctor of the Church, wrote the *Life of Romuald* and was decisive in bringing his own austere monastery of Fonte Avellana (still flourishing today) and the monasteries founded from it into the ambit of the Romualdian reform. Like Romuald he was born in Ravenna, but of a poor, struggling family. With the help of his elder brother he received a fine theological education in Faenza and Parma, and in 1035 he entered Fonte Avellana. A prophetic voice against abuses of the Church, he was a key figure in the eleventh-century Church reform. He was an eloquent poet, one of his most famous hymns being in honour of St Gregory the Great, 'Anglorum iam apostolus'. He wrote extensively, and his delightful treatise *Dominus Vobiscum* offers a solid theological basis for solitary prayer, insisting that the whole Church is present in each Christian:

Indeed, the Church of Christ is united in all her parts by such a bond of love that her several members form a single body and in each one the whole Church is mystically present, so that the whole Church universal may rightly be called the one bride of Christ, and on the other hand every single soul can, because of the mystical effects of the sacrament, be regarded as the whole Church . . . For indeed, although the holy Church is diversified in the multiplicity of her members, yet she is fused into unity by the fire of the Holy Spirit. (chs. 5, 6)

Other notable figures of the Camaldolese family include Guido of Arezzo (d. 1050), 'the father of modern music', who laid the groundwork for modern notation. Gratian (d. *c.* 1179), 'the father of canon law', gathered together some four thousand patristic, conciliar and papal decrees regarding key areas of church discipline, thus indicating its deeper traditions (Dante placed Gratian, along with Romuald and Peter Damian, in paradise). Lorenzo Monaco (d. *c.* 1424), perhaps the most important Florentine artist of the first half of the fifteenth century, had a significant influence on Fra Angelico and the art of the later Renaissance. Ambrose Traversari (d. 1439), general of the order, humanist and pioneering ecumenist, translated many of the

Eastern Fathers into Latin; Pope Eugene IV described him as 'the light of the Church'. Fra Mauro (d. 1459) was the careful cartographer whose maps of a round world significantly aided Columbus and other explorers.

All this creativity took place in Camaldolese monastic communities that were rigorously committed to the regular observance of liturgy, personal prayer, silence and hospitality.

Recent Camaldolese notables include the Oxford educated Fr Bede Griffiths, whose life, ashram in India and many writings have significantly contributed to inter-religious dialogue, especially with Hinduism. And Fr Cyprian Vagaggini, *peritus* at Vatican II, played a major part in the shaping of the new Roman Catholic liturgy and liturgical spirituality and theology today. The arts, especially music and painting, continue to flourish within Camaldolese houses.

In the sixteenth century a strictly eremitical congregation was established, Monte Corona, and in the seventeenth a strictly coenobitical. This latter was reunited in the last century with the Congregation of Camaldoli, which has always retained the full range of forms of monastic life, including eremitical to coenobitical. Today there are two men's congregations, Camaldoli and Monte Corona, which share a common liturgical calendar, as well as many independent communities of Camaldolese nuns. This Camaldolese family is present now especially in Italy, the United States, Poland, France, Brazil, Columbia, India and Tanzania. Its ecumenical oblate family is numerous and expanding.

The monastic life predates Christian division, and so the Camaldolese have been very committed to the ecumenical dialogue, at least since the time of Ambrose Traversari. More recently the Camaldolese, particularly in America, have been committed to dialogue with the Anglican Communion. Thus the Fellowship of St Gregory and St Augustine (cf. www.anglican-roman catholic.com), the Friendship Covenant with the (Anglican) Order of the Holy Cross, and so on. The Camaldolese monastery in Rome, St Gregory the Great, is one of the most ancient of 'living' monasteries, and it is from here that Pope Gregory sent St Augustine and his company of monks to England; thus the ecumenical significance of this monastic seat, that Archbishops of Canterbury with Popes have visited in recent decades and from which have published ecumenical joint statements. The Italian monastic communities are also very involved in the dialogue with Orthodoxy, with the Italian Evangelical Churches, and with the Italian Jewish community. And the Camaldolese ashrams in India, continuing the rich heritage of Dom Bede Griffiths, are particularly involved in the Christian–Hindu dialogue. The American Camaldolese houses are also very involved in the dialogue with Hinduism, as well as Buddhism and Taoism (thus the Camaldolese Institute for East–West Dialogue). The Vatican has very much encouraged this particular commitment of the Camaldolese to ecumenical and inter-religious dialogue.

See also **Benedictine Spirituality; Eremitical Spirituality; Monasticism.**

Peter-Damian Belisle (ed.), *The Privilege of Love: Camaldolese Benedictine Spirituality*, Collegeville, MN: Liturgical Press, 2002; Robert Hale, *Love on the Mountain: The Chronicle Journal of a Camaldolese Monk*, California: Source Books, 1999; Thomas Matus, *The Mystery of Romuald and the Five Brothers*, California: Source Books, 1994; St Peter Damian, *Selected Writings on the Spiritual Life*, London: Faber and Faber, 1959; Lino Vigilucci, *Camaldoli: A Journey into Its History and Spirituality*, California: Source Books, 1988.

ROBERT HALE

Cambridge Platonists

The Cambridge Platonists were a group of seventeenth-century scholars who saw a great harmony between the light of natural reason and the divine revelation which came through Scripture. In an age of religious dissension and controversy they believed in freedom of conscience and the ability of a person to recognize the truths of God because they were previously implanted in the human heart and mind. They were opposed to the use of enthusiasm in religion and substituted a more balanced approach enlightened by reason. The Platonic and Neoplatonic traditions of inward learning characterized their theological thought. The modern reader, however, often finds difficulty with their arguments because their seventeenth-century prose is discursive rather than analytical, and filled with allusions to classical Greek and Latin texts. Their message, however, was not reserved for a university elite but was open to anyone with an open mind illuminated by reason and Scripture.

The Cambridge Platonists believed that God made human beings in his image, and so righteousness, fairness and benevolence are deeply imprinted in the soul of all creatures. External law is only effective because it is built on the internal law written into the human heart. For the Cambridge Platonists there was no opposition between the rational and the spiritual.

However, the rational is more like an intuitive faculty which had long been cultivated in the Platonic and Neoplatonic traditions.

The senior member of the group was Benjamin Whichcote who entered Emmanuel College, Cambridge in 1628 and eventually became a Fellow and a most effective tutor. He later became Provost of King's College. Although Emmanuel was initially a Puritan foundation, the Cambridge Platonists abandoned its Calvinist theology although they retained its moral earnestness. Two of Whichcote's students at Emmanuel were Nathaniel Culverwell and John Smith. Culverwell became a Fellow of the College, and since he died young his principal work *An Elegant and Learned Discourse of the Light of Nature* was published posthumously in 1652 during the Commonwealth. John Smith, son of a small farmer, was eventually a Fellow of Queen's College and as Dean there he spread the ideals of the Platonists in his religious instruction in the university. Other members of the group included Ralph Cadworth and Henry More. Cadworth moved from Emmanuel to become Master of Christ's College and propagated his ideas there, as did More who expressed himself through poetry as well as in his philosophical and theological writings. As a group, the Cambridge Platonists were inheritors of the Renaissance revival in Platonism, but they were equally influenced by the later interpretations of Plotinus. As one of their contemporaries observed, the purpose of these Fellows of Cambridge colleges was to bring the Church back to her old muse, Platonic philosophy. In their attempt to harmonize reason with revelation they turned to early Church theologians such as Clement of Alexandria and Origen. Their favourite passage of Scripture was Prov. 20.27, 'The spirit of man is the candle of the Lord.' The candle is fragile but it contains the same light as comes from divine illumination.

See also **Anglican Spirituality; English Spirituality.**

Anna Baldwin and Sarah Hutton (eds), *Platonism and the English Imagination*, Cambridge: Cambridge University Press, 1994; Gerald R. Cragg (ed.), *The Cambridge Platonists*, New York: Oxford University Press, 1968; C. A. Patrides, *The Cambridge Platonists*, Cambridge: Cambridge University Press, 1980.

PATRICK MOORE

Canonical Communities

1. *History*. Until the advent of the mendicants in the thirteenth century consecrated life in the Western Church took two basic forms: the lay monastic movement of the desert and the movement of clerics and/or virgins and widows sharing a common life and ministry in a cathedral or other urban churches. Eusebius of Vercelli (d. 371), Paulinus of Nola (d. 431) and, above all, Augustine of Hippo (d. 430) bear witness to this latter movement. Such clerics and/or religious women living together, serving the local church and ministering to and at its common prayer were enrolled on a list (Gk. *kanon* and Lat. *canon*) of that church. Augustine's Rule for his *monasterium clericorum*, which was later to exercise tremendous influence on canonical life in the Gregorian Reform of the eleventh and twelfth centuries, seems not to have had much influence after his own death and the disappearance of the Church in North Africa. Nonetheless the common life of clergy and pious women was a frequent reality throughout the Western Church. These groups were called chapters or canonries and their non-cathedral urban churches called collegiate churches.

Charlemagne called upon Chrodegang of Metz (d. 766) to draw up a rule for the canons of his realm. Chrodegang borrowed heavily from the Rule of Benedict and insisted on the *capsa communis* or renunciation of private ownership. This stipulation was almost entirely eliminated in the Rule of Aachen (816). Private ownership inevitably led to the breakdown of the common life. The renewal of the Church led by Gregory VII, especially in its focus on the reform of the clergy, created a favourable environment for the renewal of the canonical life for both canons and canonesses. The period between the Synod of Rome in 1059 and the advent of the friars at the beginning of the thirteenth century saw the halcyon days of the canonical movement.

This period witnessed reform-minded clergy of cathedral and collegiate churches and many houses of canonesses returning to full common life and shared ownership. This was especially true in Mediterranean areas such as Italy (at the Lateran Basilica in Rome, Fano, Florence and Lucca), southern France (Avignon, Arles), Spain (Pamplona, Osma, Toledo) but also occurred in Austria (Salzburg), England (Carlisle) and Ireland (Down Clogher and Dublin). Reform communities were marked by a preference for non-urban or eremitical sites and by adherence to the monastic institutions of Augustine and more specifically to the rediscovered Rule of Augustine. Observance of this Rule gave rise to the distinction between secular canons (cathedral or collegiate clergy not bound by a rule) and canons regular who professed a common life according to the Rule of Augustine. Canons regular adhering to the stricter Augustinian *Ordo*

Monasterii were dubbed the *ordo novus* while those observing the more moderate *Regula Tertia* were called the *ordo antiquus*. Eventually all came to follow the more moderate form of Augustine's Rule.

Having had no intention of abandoning the pastoral care or preaching for which they were ordained, twelfth-century canons regular frequently established their canonries along routes where they might care for pilgrims or in conjunction with guest houses/hospitals where they could minister to the poor, the sick and the dying. In Eastern Europe communities of canons regular made pioneer settlements in unchristianized areas and often became cathedral churches or canonries responsible for the pastoral care of a clearly circumscribed area. Other activities of these houses were often sacred study, spiritual writing and the copying of manuscripts.

In the integration of pastoral care with contemplative monastic conventual observances the canons and canonesses regular broke new ground and came into conflict with those who were discomfited by the rise of a form of religious life that did not fit easily into twelfth-century categories. The challenge of a new religious life form gave rise to, and is witnessed to in, contemporary dialogues between monks and canons regular. In retrospect we can see that the canonical *propositum* set the stage for the mendicants.

The reform of the common life of the clergy was but one aspect of a return to the *vita apostolica* fostered by the Gregorian Reform. As such it integrated the equally strong drive and proposal towards a more evangelical life of the laity. Gathered around a core group of ordained clergy was a much larger number of lay brothers and professed sisters or canonesses who played a critical role in the canonries' works of hospitality and care for the sick. This occurred both in the reform and/or resettlement of older canonries and in the foundation of many new reformed canonries. Almost all new foundations were double monasteries and some, e.g. Saint-Victor, Saint Genevieve and Windesheim, gave birth eventually to independent communities of canonesses.

New foundations of this latter type were more numerous in northern Europe, for example Arrouaise (1090), Saint-Victor (1108), and Prémontré (1121) – all in northern France – and Marbach (1093) in Germany, Rolduc and the Canons Regular of the Holy Cross or Crosiers (1210) in the Low Lands. But similar foundations were also made in Mediterranean lands, for example Saint-Ruf near Avignon (1090) and Coimbra in Portugal (1131).

Unlike Cluny that imposed its *ordo vivendi* on its many and widespread dependent daughters, most reform houses of canons and canonesses were strictly local and autonomous even though other reform houses might borrow from their customaries. The Premonstratensians, on the other hand, adopted many of the governmental structures of the Cistercians, for example a system of regular visitations, an annual general chapter and constitutions binding all houses. Between 1050 and 1131 many houses of Canons Regular of Saint Augustine were founded in the Low Lands, Switzerland and Austria. One of these abbeys, Windesheim, numbered among its members Jan Ruysbroeck, Geert Grote and Thomas à Kempis, spiritual leaders of the fourteenth-century *Devotio Moderna*.

By the end of the twelfth century there were hundreds of houses of canons and canonesses regular from Scandinavia to Palestine and from Spain to the missionary frontiers of Eastern Europe. In almost all cases the women's communities, usually against their will, had been cut off from their original double monasteries and resettled in another location. But the profession of stability for life in one monastery for both men and women and the strict enclosure of women made canonical life and ministry less than fully responsive to the growth of cities in the late twelfth and early thirteenth centuries and there was a subsequent decline in their numbers. The newly founded mendicant orders were better able to respond to the need for popular preaching and urban pastoral care but the canons regular had prepared for their advent by integrating for the first time pastoral care with a contemplative common life and prayer. The sixteenth century saw a rebirth of some communities of canonesses (Lateran, Windesheim, Congregation of Notre Dame) who were at that time able to minister outside a strictly cloistered environment.

The Reformation, the secularization of monasteries by Joseph II of Austria, and the French Revolution saw the closing of hundreds of European houses of canons and canonesses. In the nineteenth century some communities were refounded and flourished. Missionary activity was taken up by some of these canonries and communities of canons and canonesses regular have been established in North and South America, India and Africa. The communist suppression of church life in Eastern Europe after World War 2 saw the closing of many abbeys and convents. Many of these are presently in a process of refounding with varying degrees of success. In 1959 the autonomous canonical congregations of Nicholas and Bernard (the Grand Saint-Bernard) and St Maurice of Agaune in

Switzerland, the congregation of the Lateran and the Austrian canons regular formed a papally approved Federation of Canons Regular of Saint Augustine. Communities of canonesses remain, for the most part, independent, exceptions being those of the Lateran, Windesheim, the Congregation of Notre Dame (the Roman Union, the Jupille Union and the German Union), and the Canonesses of the Holy Sepulchre.

Pastoral care in parishes, retreat work, liturgical apostolate, hospitals and schools have been and remain important apostolates of canons and canonesses regular in the twentieth and twenty-first centuries.

2. *Spirituality*. The constants in the spirituality of canonical communities since the Gregorian Reform are:

1. The pursuit of the *vita apostolica* (cf. Acts) of the primitive Jerusalem community as embodied in Augustine's *monasterium clericorum* at Hippo. The contemplative communion of heart and mind intent on God is given expression and a daily renewed impetus through the conventual observances lived in tension with the demands of the community's ministries.
2. Profession of stability to a local church rather than to a monastic community and the particular shape this gives to the ongoing *conversatio morum* of the members. This self-donation to a local church demands integration of pastoral care and a contemplative conventual life. Each of these two essential dimensions of canonical life informs the other.
3. The high priority accorded the solemn public celebration of the liturgy *in medio populi* that marks a post-Vatican II shift from a commitment to a *splendor cultus* intended to stir up the faith of the laity who observed it to a dedication to celebration of the church's public worship in a manner that invites and encourages the full participation of all present.

See also **Augustinian Spirituality; Bridgettine Spirituality; Conventual Life; Gilbertine Spirituality; Norbertine Spirituality.**

Caroline Walker Bynum, 'Docere verbo et exemplo: an aspect of twelfth-century spirituality', *Harvard Theological Studies* 31, Missoula, MT: Scholars Press, 1979; Caroline Walker Bynum, *Jesus as Mother: Studies in the Spirituality of the High Middle Ages*, Berkeley and London: University of California Press, 1982; *Canonicorum Regularium Sodalitates*, Canonia Vorau (Austria), 1954; Dominique-Marie Dauzet, en collaboration (eds), *La voie canoniale dans l'église aujour-*

d'hui, Bruxelles and Namur: Vie Consacrée, 1994; George Lawless, *Augustine of Hippo and His Rule*, Oxford: Clarendon Press, 1987.

ANDREW CIFERNI

Cappadocian Fathers

The Cappadocian Fathers is a collective title for a close-knit group of important fourth-century Greek theologians and ascetics who lived in eastern Asia Minor (modern Turkey near the Syrian borders). They have traditionally been regarded as the 'Three' (Basil of Caesarea, Gregory of Nyssa his brother, and Gregory of Nazianzus their friend who is more commonly known in Eastern Orthodox literature as Gregory the Theologian). We ought to add in another theologian to their midst, Amphilochius of Iconium, Gregory Nazianzen's cousin, and also a fifth Cappadocian 'Mother' – Macrina, the elder sister of Basil and Gregory Nyssa, who was both Gregory's earliest teacher and played an instrumental role in Basil's conversion to asceticism. Macrina was a leading force in the female ascetic movement in Cappadocia, probably under the influence of Bishop Eustathius of Sebaste, a radical monastic leader and pro-Nicene apologist of the fourth-century Church. Basil, who was first a deacon serving with Eustathius, later fell out with him over significant theological and personal matters and (probably as a result) he curiously makes no reference to his sister Macrina in all his writings. It is much otherwise with Gregory of Nyssa, whose *Life of Macrina* is an important treatise on the immortality of the soul and on the freedom from fear which the ascetic life can afford to the soul of the believer. All the Cappadocian men (all of them from a wealthy background) achieved high rank in the churches and used their episcopal preaching to advocate the Nicene Christology of the Homoousion (the Son of God as co-equal and co-essential with the Father) and the divinity of the Holy Spirit. Gregory Nazianzen was the one who pressed most insistently for a clear expression of the Homoousion of the Son and Spirit, thus being the chief architect for the classical doctrine of Trinity. The two Gregories lived to see their theology vindicated at the Ecumenical Council of Constantinople in 381, where Gregory Nazianzen briefly presided. Apart from their monumental standing in the history of doctrine, the writings of the three major Cappadocians were important in establishing some foundational trends of Christian spirituality.

Basil of Caesarea (330–79). Basil is often known as the 'father of Eastern monasticism'. From his early association with Eustathius of Sebaste and Gregory of Nazianzus (since both early influences were already ascetics before him), Basil came slowly to realize that his future did not lie in the rhetorical and legal career he had first mapped out for himself. His dynamic and charismatic personality soon attracted to himself many monastic disciples in the Cappadocian region, and soon he succeeded (controversially) to the office of the metropolitan archbishop of Cappadocia's greatest city, Caesarea. From this power base Basil founded numerous philanthropic works, staffing them with monastics, and thus giving a paradigm of a church administered by an ascetic bishop, using monks to service an array of hospitals and schools as part of the official ecclesial 'mission'. His vision of ascetical 'activism' was summed up in his gathering together of a set of basic instructions for monks. Basil was not so much the inventor of these (some scholars, even from antiquity, have attributed the original materials to Eustathius) but was more a collator and organizer of genius. To this extent the *Great Asceticon* (there also exists a variant edition of a *Smaller Asceticon*) achieved ever-increasing popularity among monastics of subsequent generations and became a foundational text for monastic life, both in the Eastern and Western Churches. The *Asceticon* combines a list of biblical paradigms and inspirational material, with an overarching vision of monasticism as *opus Dei*, a labour for the glory of God, whereby the monk can dedicate his energies as an ascetical offering. Basil's ascetical rules were crucial in establishing the sevenfold pattern of monastic prayer offices, beginning with the midnight vigil and proceeding through regular 'hours' to mark out the whole monastic day as one of prayer. Most of Basil's literary works represent his sharply 'practical' character, preferring to take the common man's angle, though his sermons reveal him to be a brilliant expositor. One of his chief works, *The Hexaemeron Homilies*, which he delivered to a group of local workers on the nature of God's creation, demonstrates him at his best. The moral significance is never far away from Basil's explicit goals in writing, and his ascetical theology manifests a highly practical, organized and ethical tone.

Gregory Nazianzen (c. 329–90). Gregory, Basil's close friend from youth, was one of the most learned academics of his century and one of the greatest of all Christian poets and theologians. He too was highly significant as a theorist on Christian monasticism, but has largely been overlooked because of the attention Basil has received. Gregory followed a slightly different approach to ascetical theory to Basil. He believed that 'ascetical labour' did not necessarily demand a person should engage in manual works, and he was not a strong advocate of the Egyptian style of monastic life. For him the essence of ascetical 'withdrawal' was to provide a relative seclusion so that the mind and soul could reflect in a deep and sustained way on the nature of life and the movings of the Holy Spirit. For Gregory, reading and intellectual culture were fundamental preparatory steps in preparing the soul for the visitation of God. He described the spiritual life in favoured terms of luminous vision (frequently citing his favourite verse of Plato: 'God is to the soul what the cosmic sun is to this world'). His young disciple, Evagrius of Pontus, would take his ideas to a new pitch in the next generation. Gregory describes the spiritual life as a slow and sure progress into the sanctuary of the Cosmic Temple, a progressive moving through life away from material obsessions to spiritual refinement. It is an upward ascent of the soul to light which will be fulfilled in the Next Age when the soul enters the presence of the Holy One in the heavenly sanctuary, and will there receive angelic transformation. More than the other two, Gregory Nazianzen was heavily influenced by Origen's mystical theology, although he is careful to correct his earlier mentor's theory on the pre-existence of souls, which was already beginning to attract hostile attention in his time. Using the example of his own career, he advocated an ascetical lifestyle that did not need to be coenobitic or eremitical to be authentically monastic. His was a voice that carried for later Byzantium (where he was the single most widely read author after the Bible), and his notions of an ascetic lifestyle that made allowances for personal charism, and the concept of 'city-monasticism', both had a lasting impact. For a brief time he occupied the world's centre stage, assuming the leadership of the Nicene party at Constantinople when Theodosius took the capital and exiled the Arian majority there. Gregory presided over the Second Oecumenical Council (Constantinople 381) as a passionate advocate for the co-equal divinity of the Holy Spirit, a theology he felt was absolutely necessary for, and could be demonstrated existentially in, the spiritual progress of the Christian to God, a progress he called 'deification' or the advancement into the divine presence of the mere creature. Deification (the West would prefer the synonym 'grace') mysteriously enfolded and transfigured mortality into immortal glory and noetic enlightenment. Gregory was rejected by the conciliar fathers for refusing to compromise on policy matters, and so retired to his estates in Cappadocia where he wrote a remarkable (and sombre) series of final poems, reflecting on the 'fragility of human life'. They demonstrate, with an unblinking eye, the state of corruptible mortality before the eternal radiance of God, and ask (at times in a manner reminiscent of the ancient psalmists) why it is that God so often delivers suffering as the lot of those who wish to follow him most closely. They are, perhaps, among the most intriguing, and are certainly the most 'personal', of all patristic writing from the early period.

Gregory of Nyssa (d. c. 395). Gregory of Nyssa was the younger brother of Basil and Macrina, and was educated by his ascetical sister (who was the first in the family to transform their country estate into a monastic settlement). As a young man he was trained in rhetoric by Gregory of Nazianzus, who also guided him away from the pursuit of a secular career in law by reminding him that the Church needed his services. When Basil became Archbishop of Caesarea he used his family as pawns in Church politics, and Gregory was blown along for most of the time his dominant brother was alive, with the storms that usually attended him; being compelled by Basil to take up the insignificant village of Nyssa as its bishop. After Basil's death Gregory emerged into the limelight. At first he continued his brother's apologetic against Arianism (Basil's old enemies had attacked his reputation posthumously). This foray into doctrinal apologetic marked his rapid development as a brilliant theologian and spiritual teacher. At the end of his life he was cited by the emperor as one of the 'arbiters of orthodoxy in the Eastern Church'. In these latter years Gregory revealed more and more of his character as a leading spiritual master. Today, in the Western Church, he is perhaps the most well known of the three major Cappadocians as a mystical teacher. Gregory is the most overtly Platonist of the three and uses ideas from Stoicism and Middle Platonism that resonated with the emerging Hellenistic mysticism of his day (Plotinianism) to describe the passage of the soul through life as an ascent and a constant 'stretching out' (*epektasis*) of mortal being to God. In the 390s he wrote the *Commentary on the Song of Songs*, dedicated to his friend the deaconess Olympias. Possibly he wrote the *Life of Moses* at this time, though some have argued for an earlier dating. Both works develop the idea of perfection as *epektasis*. The creaturely soul reaches out in an endless arc comprised of cycles of repentance and longing. As the creature advances in the love and embrace of God, it experiences the unapproachable deity authentic-

ally. Even though God is unlimited and incomprehensible, the creature's endless reaching out in love (which always takes that creature a little further into the Inexhaustible One) is itself a strangely paradoxical experience of Limited Being participating directly in Unlimited Being (*Metousia Theou*). Gregory radically transformed the Neoplatonic concepts of participation in, and return to, God. His work set out to eliminate pantheistic elements in the notions and to elaborate the Christian distinction between creature and Creator, yet in a way that articulated a profound sense of Christian *Theosis* as the goal and telos of the redemptive task of the Word bringing the world to (new) life. He vehemently opposed the Platonic (and Origenian) idea of pre-existence of souls – and argued instead that the creation of humanity was designed as that part of the creation of Intelligences through which the material universe was destined to participate in God noetically. In his trinitarian thought Gregory elaborated a theology that tried to exclude subordinationism within the inner life of God, and in Christology he presented a more worked-out version of anti-Apollinarian thought than most theologians before him (thereby insisting on the full humanness of Jesus). Gregory retained the Origenian view of *apocatastasis*: all souls even those in Hell will one day return to their source in God, for the process of conversion is irresistible since it is the pattern and meaning of the entire cosmos. His influence was especially marked on the later Byzantine spiritual writers: Pseudo-Dionysius, Maximus the Confessor, John Damascene and Gregory Palamas. In the medieval West he had numerous admirers too. John Scotus Eriugena, who also translated the works of Pseudo-Dionysius, was responsible for passing on Gregory's thought to twelfth-century Western anthropological and mystical writers. Accordingly, the concept of the three spiritual steps which Gregory regularly advocated (following the Syrian tradition of Pseudo-Macarius), namely purification, noetic enlightenment and unitive ascent, came to be highly descriptive of later Western mystical writing. Gregory differed from his namesake of Nazianzus in that he returned to the notion he found first in Philo, and so he uses the motif of the theophany on Sinai to describe the highest intimations of the human experience of the divine in terms of obscure darkness (*gnophos*) rather than the Nazianzen's radiant illumination (*photismos*). The Christian image of mystical apprehension as an enveloping darkness of unknowing owes much to his work.

See also **Early Christian Spirituality; Deification; Orthodox Spirituality.**

D. F. Balás, *Metousia Theou: Man's Participation in God's Perfections According to St. Gregory of Nyssa*, Rome: IBC Libreria Herder, 1966; V. E. F. Harrison, *Grace and Human Freedom According to St. Gregory of Nyssa*, New York: Edwin Mellen Press, 1992; J. A. McGuckin, *St. Gregory of Nazianzus: An Intellectual Biography*, New York: St Vladimir's Seminary Press, 2001; A. Meredith, *Gregory of Nyssa* (writings with commentary), London: Routledge, 1999; H. Musurillo (ed.), *From Glory to Glory: Texts from Gregory of Nyssa's Mystical Writings*, New York: Scribner's, 1961; B. Otis, 'Cappadocian Thought as a Coherent System', *Dumbarton Oaks Papers* 12 (1958), 95–124; P. Rousseau, *Basil of Caesarea*, Berkeley: University of California Press, 1998.

JOHN ANTHONY MCGUCKIN

Carmelite Spirituality

About 1200 CE a group of hermits settled on Mount Carmel in a ravine at the Wadi Ain-es-Sah about four kilometers south of Haifa. These lay hermits sought, between 1206 and 1214, ecclesial recognition from Albert, Patriarch of Jerusalem whose letter to them, a 'formula of life', is the foundational document of Carmelite spirituality.

This brief formula described a simple semi-eremitic way of life in which the first Carmelites lived in separated cells, observing solitude and silence. They were to remain in or near their cells, 'meditating day and night on the law of the Lord'. When possible, they met early in the day for the celebration of Eucharist in an oratory which was situated in the midst of the surrounding cells of the hermits. A modern commentator has called the place described in this formula 'a mystical space' oriented to contemplation. Albert's formula of life made no mention of pastoral ministry.

The incursions of Muslim armies into the Latin Kingdom of Jerusalem made life for the Carmelite hermits problematic. By 1238 some of the Carmelites were emigrating to the West where they made eremitic foundations in Cyprus, Sicily, England and France. The Carmelite hermits arrived in the West when mendicants, the Dominicans and the Franciscans, were flourishing and rapidly increasing. The Carmelite hermits soon determined that their formula of life required revision if they were to prosper in the evangelical climate after the pastoral initiatives of the Fourth Lateran Council. A general chapter in 1247 sought the needed revisions from Pope Innocent IV who appointed two prelates (former Dominicans) to oversee the revision of the formula of life which became an official rule (*regula*) on 1 October 1247. Slight changes in the rule introduced coenobitic elements into Carmelite life, for example a common refectory, less silence and the recitation of the Divine Office in common. Crucial to this revision was the permission to make foundations not only in out-of-the-way places but elsewhere as well. With dispatch, foundations were made in cities, some with universities – London, Pisa, Cologne, Cambridge, Paris, Oxford, Bologna etc. The Carmelites thus aligned themselves with the friars, and they eventually became a student order which meant that they educated their members for pastoral ministry, some of whom, like John Baconthorpe and Thomas Netter, became prominent theologians at medieval universities.

The Second Council of Lyons in 1274 affirmed the Dominicans and Franciscans but put the future of the Carmelites and the Augustinian friars on hold. This decision was reversed in 1298. From then on the Carmelites never looked back on their identity as a mendicant order; nor have any of the Order's reforms called this identity into question. Once the Carmelites became mendicants the basic paradox of their life became solitude within a ministerial community just as the original paradox had been solitude within community.

The first extant Carmelite constitutions (1281) advised younger members of the Order of its heritage. From the time of the prophets Elijah and Elisha, the constitutions said, Carmelites had lived near the fountain of Elijah on Mount Carmel as 'true lovers of solitude in order to pursue the contemplation of heavenly things'. Here was expressed the kernel of the original Carmelite charism: solitude for the sake of contemplation.

The Dominicans and Franciscans had charismatic founders, but the Carmelites were without a celebrated founder. The medieval Carmelites soon looked to Elijah for inspiration and as their 'founder'. They also associated themselves with Mary to whom their oratory on Mount Carmel had been dedicated. They called themselves 'Brothers of Our Lady of Mount Carmel'. Thus Carmelite spirituality has been marked by the call to prophetic contemplation and to a Marian affiliation. In the fourteenth century a Carmelite literary tradition further developed the Elijan and Marian character of the order. Before 1391, the Carmelite Felip Ribot compiled documents supposedly from the tradition but which were, in fact, a sampling of legends edited and given expression by Ribot himself. One of these documents, *The Institution of the First Monks*, made explicit the contemplative, mystical character of the Carmelite vocation. This book, which was influenced by John Cassian's writings, became a staple of Carmelite spiritual reading into the seventeenth century. The mystical writings of Teresa of Avila and John of the Cross have resonated with the mysticism of the *Institution*.

The Carmelites, unlike the Dominicans and the Franciscans, did not have what would later be called a second order of Carmelite women or a third order for the laity until 1452 when the papal bull *Cum Nulla* permitted the formal acceptance into the order of women and lay affiliates. This entry of women into the Carmelite family, which has been highly significant for Carmelite spirituality, occurred under the leadership of the prior general and reformer Blessed John Soreth (d. 1471).

During the later Middle Ages the Carmelites, like other religious orders, grappled with the need for reform and a number of Carmelite reform movements arose in an attempt to restore the original contemplative charism of the Order. However, not until the reforming activities of Teresa of Avila (d. 1582) and her collaborator John of the Cross (d. 1591) did an effective, enduring and thoroughgoing reform occur. The Teresian reform resulted in 1593, after the death of John of the Cross, in the creation of a separate order known as the Discalced Carmelites.

Inspired by the 'holy fathers' of the thirteenth century who had lived on Mount Carmel, Teresa impressed upon her followers that Carmelites 'are called to prayer and contemplation'. She wanted her daughters to be detached from what kept them from God, to be humble and to practise the prayer of recollection. This prayer of recollection stressed attention to the presence of Christ. Before she died Teresa established seventeen cloistered Carmels for women which were small enough for contemplative solitude but large enough to support the community. Teresa had a gift for warm, engaging prose which she wrote for the instruction of her daughters. Her masterpiece *The Interior Castle*, along with her other writings, are classics in the Western contemplative tradition as are the poetry and commentaries of John of the Cross. John's analysis of the dark night experiences have been given much attention; he is, however, every bit as much a lucid teacher of the journey to the transforming union with God in love. Together Teresa and John introduced Carmel to the mysticism of the Song of Songs tradition, the final stages of which are spiritual betrothal and spiritual marriage where one encounters the loving union with the triune God. For their teachings on the spiritual life Teresa and John, as well as Thérèse of Lisieux, have been declared Doctors of the Church

The Carmelites of the Ancient Observance, those who did not become Discalced Carmelites, underwent in seventeenth-century France a contemplative reform. The leading light of this Touraine Reform was the blind lay brother John of St Samson (d.1636).

Thérèse of Lisieux (d. 1897), with her simplicity and her recovery of love as the heart of the spiritual life, has been extraordinarily influential on countless people throughout the world. John of the Cross's writings were particularly influential on the young woman from Lisieux whose *Story of a Soul*, which speaks passionately of God's love in her life, has been translated into numerous languages. Elizabeth of the Trinity (d. 1906), who, like Thérèse, died in her twenties, articulated a spirituality that emphasized a profound relationship with the triune God. Two Carmelites, Edith Stein and Titus Brandsma, both martyred by the Nazis in 1942, have awakened a renewed interest in Carmel's spirituality and prayer.

Since the Second Vatican Council, the study of Carmel's classic texts has awakened a keen interest among Carmelites and others in retrieving the original charism of the Rule of St Albert as well as in recovering the wisdom of Carmel's saints and Doctors of the Church. Carmelite spirituality, with its call to solitude, prayer, contemplation and union with God in love, is a resource for all who search for a deeper meaning in human existence and for all who desire to participate in the life of a more contemplative Church. This contemplative spirituality serves as the primary focus of cloistered Carmelite nuns but also as the necessary partner in the pastoral ministry of Carmelite friars as well as in the ministries of Carmelite sisters and lay Carmelites. The Carmelite charism, in fact, like the charisms of all religious communities, is a gift for every baptized Christian who discovers an affinity with Carmel's contemplative tradition.

See also **Eremitical Spirituality; Mendicant Spirituality**.

Keith J. Egan, 'Carmelite Spirituality', in *The New Dictionary of Catholic Spirituality*, ed. Michael Downey, Collegeville, MN: The Liturgical Press, 1993, pp. 117–25; Kieran Kavanaugh and Otilio Rodriguez (eds), *The Collected Works of St John of the Cross*, rev. edn, Washington, DC: Institute of Carmelite Studies, 1991; Kieran Kavanaugh and Otilio Rodriguez (eds), *The Collected Works of St Teresa of Avila*, Washington, DC: Institute of Carmelite Studies, 1976, 1980, 1985; John Clarke (trans.), *Story of a*

Soul: The Autobiography of Saint Thérèse of Lisieux, 3rd edn, Washington, DC: Institute of Carmelite Studies, 1996; Kees Waaijman, *The Mystical Space of Carmel: A Commentary on the Carmelite Rule,* trans. John Vriend, Leuven: Peeters, 1999; John Welch, *The Carmelite Way: An Ancient Path for Today's Pilgrim*, New York: Paulist Press, 1996.

KEITH J. EGAN

Caroline Divines

The term Caroline Divines would seem at first sight to refer to a group of theologians writing in the reigns of Charles I and Charles II. But it is generally accepted that the words have a wider meaning. *The Oxford Dictionary of the Christian Church* says simply, 'Anglican divines of the seventeenth century especially when considered exponents of High Church principles'. Here we shall take it as including the two writers who were founders of this school, Lancelot Andrewes (1555–1626) and his contemporary Richard Hooker (1554–1600). We shall note that the group includes not only theologian bishops, for example John Cosin, Jeremy Taylor, John Bramhall and John Pearson, but also a remarkable group of theologian poets, John Donne, George Herbert, Henry Vaughan and Thomas Traherne, whose works are widely studied across the English-speaking world, most often in departments of English literature.

As suggested elsewhere, a large part of Hooker's theology is linked with the defence and explication of the Church's tradition of worship as contained in *The Book of Common Prayer*. Even a slight acquaintance with the sermons and devotions of Lancelot Andrewes will convince us that he too is a teacher for whom prayer and worship, theology and proclamation are intimately bound together. Andrewes' preaching is doxological and kerygmatic, expressing a theology of prayer and praise. It is significant that the Russian Orthodox scholar Nicholas Lossky gives his study of Andrewes' sermons the subtitle *The Origins of the Mystical Theology of the Church of England* (Lossky, 1991).

Central for the whole theological movement which develops from the work of Hooker and Andrewes is the significance given to the human body and to the material world of which it is a part, in our approach to God and in God's approach to us. 'As Andrewes clearly shows in one of his Christmas sermons, adoration, and therefore prayer, thanksgiving and praise, directly concern the body, because on the one hand it is a creature of God no less that the soul and on the other hand, and above all, because Christ now has a body himself, something that has

restored to material life all its holiness'(Lossky, 1991, p. 302).

Such an understanding of things can lead to a perception of the bodily world as full of the energies of God's glory, something which we find in many ways in the writers of this period both in poetry and prose.

In the first part of Jeremy Taylor's *Holy Living*, one of the most influential devotional books of the time, there is a whole section on the reality of God's presence in the world, and of our consequent calling to recognize and rejoice in it. So Taylor writes, 'God is wholly in every place, included in no place, not bound with cords (except those of love), not divided into parts, not changeable into several shapes, filling heaven and earth with his present power and his never absent nature: so St Augustine expresses this article. So that we may imagine God to be as the air and the sea and we all included in his circle wrapped up in the lap of his infinite nature, as infants in the wombs of their pregnant mothers' (Taylor, 1989, p. 35). Taylor goes on to encourage the Christian actively to realize this sense of God's presence throughout his life, day by day: 'Let everything you see represent to your spirit, the presence, the excellency, the power of God, and let your conversation with the creatures lead you unto the creator, for so shall your actions be done more frequently with an actual eye to God's presence by your often seeing him in the glass of creation. In the face of the sun you may see God's beauty; in the fire you may feel his heat warming you. It is the dew of heaven that makes your fields give their bread, and the breasts of God are the bottles that minister drink to your necessities' (Taylor, 1989, p. 39).

These passages give us a sense of joy and confidence in God which Taylor deepens further on: 'If we walk with God in all his ways as he walks with us in all ours, we shall find perpetual reasons to enable us to keep that rule of God, "Rejoice in the Lord always and again I say rejoice."' Taylor then quotes a saying attributed to St Antony of Egypt: 'There is one way of overcoming our ghostly enemies, spiritual mirth and a perpetual bearing of God in our mind' (Taylor, 1989, p. 41).

We note here that Taylor is not afraid to use maternal images in speaking of God. We are held in God's presence 'Like infants held in the wombs of their pregnant mothers'. We are refreshed when thirsty from 'the breasts of God, the bottles that minister drink to your necessities'. Lancelot Andrewes, in a sermon which discusses the various meanings of the Hebrew word for blessing, moves in the same direction, 'the word *barak* is applied to knee and signifies, as it were, the mother's tenderness to the babe sitting on her knee . . . when the babes are upon their mother's knee, they kiss them, they wish them well, they cherish them; so doth God, setting us on his knee, so that *blanda est in Deo matrum affectio*' (Andrewes, 1657, p. 90).

We also find in the writers of this school an unexpected tendency to ponder the place of Mary in the scheme of redemption, above all her intimate and necessary role in the mystery of the incarnation. The Anglican theologians of this period accepted certain clear limitations in this development of Marian thinking. They do not for instance allow for any direct invocation of Mary or the saints, since we have direct access to God through Jesus Christ himself, the one mediator between God and human beings. They prefer to think of Mary as the representative of God's people Israel, sometimes as the representative of all humankind before God. They usually avoid the thought of her as representing God's mercy towards our sinful humanity. But if from time to time they distinguish their position from that of Rome, they also distinguish themselves from the silence about Mary which was characteristic of most of the Protestant world of their day. Quite a number of writers of this school seem willing and indeed anxious to enter into these questions, from Andrewes himself until Thomas Ken at the beginning of the eighteenth century.

So for instance in a sermon on Hannah's song of thanksgiving for the birth of her child Andrewes contrasts it with Mary's Magnificat: 'Hannah prayed alone, but as for Mary's prayer it was accompanied by the desire and prayer of all creatures as both prophets and apostles do show . . . The Virgin's key of prayer accompanied with the prayer of all God's people in all ages opened the doors of heaven so as they "dropped down righteousness"' (Andrewes, 1657, pp. 567–78). Thus Mary's yes to God is placed at the heart of the longing and desire of all God's people of all ages. In a Christmas sermon, preached before the court at Westminster, Andrewes speaks with emphasis of the role of Mary in the whole mystery of the incarnation:

This we are to hold, to conceive is more than to receive. It is so to receive as to yield somewhat of our own. A vessel is not said to conceive the liquor that is put in it? Why? Because it yieldeth nothing from itself. The Blessed Virgin is and therefore is because she did. She did both give and take. Give of her own substance whereof his body was formed; and take or receive power from the Holy Ghost, whereby was supplied the office and efficacy of the masculine seed. This is *concipiet*. (Andrewes, 1841–54, vol. 1, p. 139)

Of all the Caroline Divines who wrote about Mary it seems to be Mark Frank (1613–64) who in his sermons has contributed most on this subject. A student at Cambridge, he became a Fellow of Pembroke College before the Civil War. During the Commonwealth he seems to have lived a life of active retirement: on the restoration of the monarchy he became Master of the college where he had earlier been a Fellow.

He too sees Mary's calling in the light of the history of Israel. We note his understanding of the blessings promised to Israel in Deuteronomy 28 as fulfilled in her:

Blessed of God, Blessed of Man; Blessed in the city and blessed in the field. Cities and countries call her blessed; blessed in the fruit of her body her blessed child Jesus. Blessed in the fruit of her ground, her cattle her kine and her sheep, in the inferior faculties of her soul and body. All fructify to Christ. Blessed her basket and her store, her womb and her breasts; the womb that bear him and the paps that gave him suck . . . the earth filled with the blessings which she brought forth into the world, when she brought forth the Son of God.

Here we see a vision of Mary's place within creation, the good earth open to God's grace and mercy which showers down upon it, the land of promise, the heart of creation as it turns towards God (Frank, 1851–53, vol. 2, pp. 47–8).

In commenting on the Gospels Frank sees the stable at Bethlehem as the house of prayer for all people: 'Hither they come to worship, hither they come to pay their offerings and their vows; here is the shrine and altar, the glorious Virgin's lap where the saviour of the world is laid to be adored and worshipped' (Frank, 1851–53, p. 49). For him our closest identification with Mary comes at the Eucharist, where we find ourselves at one with the Lord's mother. The Lord comes to none more fully 'than in the blessed sacrament to which we are now agoing. There he is strangely with us, highly favours us, exceeding blesses us, there we are all made blessed Marys and become mothers, sisters and brothers of our Lord, where we hear his work and conceive it in us, while we believe him who is the Word and receive him into us too.' (Frank, 1851–53, pp. 50–1).

· In these two lines of thought, the thought of the bodily nature of God's creation and our part in it, the thought of Mary's role within the whole scheme of redemption, we see characteristic features of the thought and devotion of the writers known as the Caroline Divines. Some of these lines are taken up again in the nineteenth century and twentieth century, and analysed in new ways.

See also **Anglican Spirituality; Cambridge Platonists.**

G. W. O. Addleshaw, *The High Church Tradition: A Study of the Liturgical Thought of the Seventeenth Century*, London, 1941; Lancelot Andrews, *Apospasmatia sacra*, London 1657; Lancelot Andrewes, *Works*, ed. J. P. Wilson and John Bliss, 11 vols, Library of Anglo-Catholic Theology, Oxford, 1841–54; Mark Frank, *Sermons*, 2 vols, Library of Anglo-Catholic Theology, Oxford, 1851–53; Nicholas Lossky, *Lancelot Andrewes, the Preacher: 1555–1626. The Origins of the Mystical Theology of the Church of England*, Oxford: Oxford University Press, 1991; Olivier Loyer, *L'Anglicanisme de Richard Hooker*, 2 vols, Paris: Université de Paris-Lille, 1979; H. R. McAdoo, *The Eucharistic Theology of Jeremy Taylor Today*, Norwich: Canterbury Press, 1988; Kenneth Stevenson, *Covenant of Grace Renewed: A Vision of the Eucharist in the Seventeenth Century*, London: SPCK, 1994; *Jeremy Taylor: Selected Works*, ed. Thomas K. Carroll, CWS, New York: Paulist Press, 1990; Jeremy Taylor, *Holy Living*, ed. P. G. Stanwood, Oxford: Oxford University Press, 1989, vol. 1, p. 35.

A. M. ALLCHIN

Cartesianism

see **Enlightenment Thought**

Carthusian Spirituality

The Carthusian Order takes its name from La Grande Chartreuse, the remote and mountainous spot in the diocese of Grenoble where St Bruno, formerly master of the cathedral school at Cologne, founded a small monastery in 1086. The name is significant: like their contemporaries the Cistercians, the early Carthusians made no particular claims to originality, and simply called their foundation after its place name rather than after its founder. They saw themselves as existing within the broad tradition of Western monastic life; and, like the Cistercians, they sought what they believed to be the primitive simplicity of the first apostles and the earliest monks. Thus all the early charterhouses (or Carthusian monasteries) had just twelve monks (the number of the apostles), together with sixteen lay brothers (*conversi*) living a less solitary form of the life close by and attending to many of the monastery's physical and practical needs.

The early Carthusians sought to withdraw from the secular world in order to live a carefully crafted synthesis of the solitary and the monastic life, for which St Bruno and the fifth prior, Guigo I (prior 1106–36) were primarily responsible. But this was not so much a flight *from* the world as a flight *for* it. One of the other early priors of the Grande Chartreuse began a charter dated 1156 with the words, 'We unworthy and useless poor men of Christ (*nos indigni et inutiles pauperes Christi*), who dwell in the desert of the Chartreuse for love of the name of Jesus . . .' The eleventh and twelfth centuries saw an eruption of interest in love both human and divine – the lyrics of the troubadours and the writings of St Bernard of Clairvaux are two of the most famous examples of this interest – together with a number of experiments in monastic and solitary life which reflect a turning-away from military and mercantile values in the search for a deeper and purer form of Christianity. The early Carthusians believed that the highest form of Christian love – both of God and of neighbour – might be practised only by those who had decisively abandoned the values of the world. In the Customs (*Consuetudines*) of the Order, Prior Guigo I took the familiar contrast between the biblical figures of Mary and Martha to set out the purpose of Carthusian life: '[Mary] follows in the footsteps of Christ and, by being at leisure, sees that he is God; she purifies her spirit and directs her prayer into her heart, listening within herself for what the Lord may say to her; and thus, to the limited extent to which she can, through a glass darkly, she tastes and sees how good the Lord is; and in this way she prays as much for Martha as for all those who work like her' (*Consuetudines Cartusiae* 20.2).

All the principal features of Carthusian spirituality derive from this fundamental vision. The reference to 'leisure' should not be misunderstood: the life of each Carthusian monk or nun (communities of women followed slightly later) was seen as rooted in a 'working leisure' (*otium negotiosum*), work and prayer each fulfilling the other. The primary 'work' of the Carthusian was from the beginning the copying of appropriate manuscripts, a form of 'silent preaching' (*praedicatio muta*) which conformed entirely to the severe asceticism of the monastery. And even this work was to be permeated by prayer.

In order to carry out their vocation, the Carthusians showed from the very beginning a primary concern to define and maintain their boundaries. St Bruno wanted a clearly demarcated space (or *desertum*) where his careful fusion of the monastic and solitary ways of life could be practised without distraction. From the beginning, the prior of the Chartreuse was forbidden to leave the *desertum*, and in practice the general of the Order almost never has. Carthusians refused to possess anything, or to receive any income, beyond their boundaries. The structure of the Order, with a fixed number of choir monks and lay *conversi*, was designed to make each house as self-sufficient as possible; and the *conversi* were understood to have a distinctive and valid vocation of their own: they were not simply there to enable the choir monks to fulfil theirs. As Guigo I put it, the monk is to travel, but not to Jerusalem or even to the nearest town: rather to humility and patience. It was the inward journey that counted, even though this journey was accomplished in community. The monk was to seek to be obedient to this inner yet corporate calling.

From the outset, a rigorous poverty was enjoined on members of the Order. Carthusians were glad to serve the poor of the world who came to their houses in search of sustenance. But their primary concern was with souls, and (again from the start) they were more preoccupied with attending to spiritual than to physical poverty. The poverty of the monks themselves, freely embraced, was a prophetic sign to the world: an active and uncompromising imitation of Christ. St Hugh of Lincoln (*c.* 1140–1200), the most famous English Carthusian and the only one to become a bishop, continued to practise the rigorous asceticism of Carthusian life after leaving the charterhouse at Witham in Somerset to become Bishop of Lincoln; but he also defended the poor and even, when necessary, defied the king (who memorably exclaimed to him, 'What heavy demands you make on us!'). Hugh's biographer also commends his care of lepers and his 'maternal tenderness' to his fellow monks (Adam of Eynsham 1, p. 85; 2, p. 13).

The same was true of solitude, which from the start was integral to Carthusian spirituality, even though it was a corporate one (each monk or nun lives in an individual 'cell' or small house opening off a cloister: they meet together only for specified activities such as the daily Mass, the long night office and the weekly walk). It was the solitude of John the Baptist, through which he acquired the grace and virtue to recognize and baptize Jesus and to endure martyrdom for the sake of Christ; and the Baptist remains the primary patron saint of the Order. True solitude, within a carefully regulated common life, made possible an accurate self-knowledge, a recognition of one's own sinfulness, which in turn allowed one to expose oneself entirely to the love and grace of Christ. And it was this shared solitude (*solitudo pluralis*) which was conceived of as a flight for the world, a prophetic sign to it, rather than an escape from it.

Carthusian liturgy was, from the outset, markedly austere, pruned of anything that might be considered unnecessary, and structured in such a way as to provide a proper balance between prayer and work in the daily life of the monk. Thus the antiphonary is restricted almost entirely to scriptural sources, and the repertoire of chants strictly limited so as to minimize the need to keep learning new ones. Mass was celebrated much less frequently than at (say) Cîteaux, let alone Cluny. But prayer, in the form both of the Daily Office and of personal devotion, was enjoined throughout the daily life of the monk or nun. Carthusians were also expected to give time to a careful and focused spiritual reading, with the soul biting and chewing on the grape of God's word (as Prior Guigo II, who died in 1188, put it in his *Scala Claustralium*, or 'Ladder of Monks'), as well as to the practice of meditation both on the words of the Bible and on the experiences of each day.

The early Carthusians, 'aflame with divine love' (*divino amore ferventes*) as St Bruno put it, sought to respond to the love of God by separating themselves from all that might constrain or compromise it, and by seeking to make their own the simplicity and single-mindedness of the apostles and the early practitioners of the spirituality of the desert. In their long night office, recited together in the monastery church while the world sleeps, Carthusians exemplify a vocation that is no easy or cosy escape from the needs of the world. As a modern Carthusian writer puts it, 'We do not keep vigil for ourselves alone, but for the whole Church, the light of our faith steadfast against the darkness. We have to be the vigilant heart of the Church.'

See also **Eremitical Spirituality; Monasticism.**

Adam of Eynsham, *The Great Life (Magna Vita) of St Hugh of Lincoln*, ed. D. L. Douie and D. H. Farmer, 2 vols, Oxford Medieval Texts, 2nd edn, Oxford: Clarendon Press, 1989; Anon (a Carthusian), *The Way of Silent Love* (1993), *The Wound of Love: A Carthusian Miscellany* (1994), *The Call of Silent Love* (1995), *Interior Prayer* (1996), all London: Darton, Longman & Todd; David Hugh Farmer, *Saint Hugh of Lincoln*, London: Darton, Longman & Todd, 1985, repr. Lincoln: Honywood, 1992; Dennis D. Martin (ed.), *Carthusian Spirituality: The Writings of Hugh of Balma and Guigo de Ponte*, CWS, New York: Paulist Press, 1997; Gordon Mursell, *The Theology of the Carthusian Life in the Writings of St Bruno and Guigo I*, Analecta Cartusiana 127, Salzburg: Institut für Anglistik und Amerikanistik, 1988.

GORDON MURSELL

Cataphatic

see Kataphatic

Catholicity and Spirituality

For purposes of this entry the term 'catholicity' is not understood as a denominational tag (e.g. Catholic as opposed to Protestant or Orthodox) but as a theological term which, among other things, is canonized in the historic creeds. The word 'catholic' does not occur in the New Testament but appears very early in the writings of the Apostolic Fathers. As an adjective the word, from its Greek roots, means something like 'of the whole' or 'universal'. It was first used in the early second century to distinguish the entire body of the Church as opposed to this or that particular church community. By the fourth century it took on a more precise signification, namely, the teaching and practice of the apostolic or 'great' Church as opposed to a heretical or schismatic community. Hence, 'catholic' began to be a synonym for 'orthodox' – the right believing and right worshipping Church as distinguished from those Church bodies broken off or out of unity with the holders of the apostolic faith. After the great schism of 1054 the East has preferred the term 'Orthodox' to describe themselves, and the West, by contrast, became more familiarly known as the Catholic Church.

Towards the close of the nineteenth century the term 'Catholic' took on a pejorative meaning for some, mainly, German, historians (e.g. von Harnack) to describe a deformation of evangelical faith with the late third-century rise of elaborated liturgies, the cult of Mary and the saints, monasticism, the structures of the episcopal hierarchy (and especially Roman claims about the Bishop of Rome), and so on.

Catholicity, understood as that tradition of Christian belief and practice which makes a central claim of apostolic succession and continuity, has, despite various ways of disagreement about who may claim to be truly Catholic, certain common characteristics. Attempts to adjudicate those disagreements about what and who is Catholic tend to look back to tradition, especially as enshrined in credal affirmations, church councils, and long-standing liturgical practice to make normative claims.

Catholic spirituality, in the first place, privileges the liturgical and sacramental life of the Christian community. Through entrance by the sacramental signs of initiation that cluster around baptism, the Christian has the right and obligation to enter into and participate in the eucharistic liturgy which re-enacts, re-presents and re-members the paschal mystery of Christ's passion, death and resurrection. The eucharistic liturgy is, as the Second Vatican Council asserted, the 'apex' of the Church's life.

The liturgical emphasis of Catholicism also gives a special place to other sacramental signs ranging from reconciliation after sin to ordering the priesthood (the ordination of bishops and priests) or sanctifying the married state or healing the sick and dying through anointing. The emphasis on sacramental signs has also encouraged, through a long period of historical evolution, the development of other visible ways of mediating the trinitarian revelation to humanity through material gestures (ceremonies), visual representations (icons), sacralizing space (shrines, pilgrimage sites etc.), and so on. These somewhat epiphenomenal signs of catholicity must be seen as the working out of a certain logic which puts faith in the capacity of signs to mediate grace. Catholic spirituality, in its various forms, has been traditionally iconic and, further, because of its liturgical bent, sympathetic to sacred space(s).

The Catholic tradition also sees the Church, not only as an earthly reality, but as a communion of those who see the face of God in eternity, having passed through a purification in death. That capacious kind of ecclesiology allows place for a whole range of practices characteristic of the tradition: veneration of Mary, the angels, and the saints; prayers for the dead; intercessory prayer, and so on. The complex iconographical decoration of many traditional churches – with its mosaics, stained glass, icon screens, and so on – are visual attempts to enhance this large understanding of the Church.

The temptation of a Church tradition preoccupied with the liturgical life is to ignore the world outside the sanctuary; to radicalize the distinction between sacred and profane. Hence, the Catholic spiritual tradition has encouraged movements, intentional communities, and small groups to form as 'little churches' to provide for the needs of the world through a whole complex of outreach – missionary, charitable, educational etc. Such movements have a nexus to some of the other characteristic forms found in the Catholic tradition: the emergence of the monastic charism and other forms of the regular (i.e., life under a rule (*regula*)). Such groups have always been seen as ways of being Christian and, in some instances, have exerted a powerful influence on the shape of piety and spiritual practice. Out of such movements and their founders/foundresses have come 'schools' of spirituality which derive from the particular insights of a person or a community of persons who have attempted to see a new way of living out the gospel. Such 'schools' tend to privilege a certain canon of biblical texts, develop a pedagogy of prayer, and thirst for intense spiritual experience. Such 'schools' enter into the living tradition as a resource for spiritual development and intensification. Thus, Orthodox Hesychasm or forms of unceasing prayer, Catholic Franciscan identification with the poverty of Christ or the affective piety of the French School, all enter into the larger Catholic tradition to provide people with diverse ways of being Christian within the large stream of the Catholic tradition broadly understood.

The distinction between the Catholic tradition and the tradition(s) deriving from the Protestant Reformation is not an impermeable one. Some Reformation Churches (e.g. Lutheran) still reflect many 'catholic' characteristics while others (the Free Church bodies) show fewer. Even within the Catholic tradition there are variations and nuances as one sees, for example, in the 'wings' of the Anglicans which stretch from Evangelical orientations to those of the High Church. Such variations inevitably find their sense from the canon of formal liturgical and sacramental practice and a hierarchical order that holds custody over such practices.

See also **Sacramentality and Spirituality.**

Lawrence S. Cunningham, *The Catholic Experience,* New York: Crossroad, 1985; Avery Dulles, *The Catholicity of the Church,* Oxford: Clarendon Press, 1983; Jean-Marie Tillard, *L'église locale: ecclesiologie de la communion et catholicité,* Paris: Cerf, 1995.

LAWRENCE S. CUNNINGHAM

Catholic Worker Movement

'The Catholic Worker' – both the movement and the newspaper of the same name – was launched on 1 May 1933 in New York City. It was the product of two remarkable figures, Dorothy Day (1897–1980) and Peter Maurin (1877–1949) who had met some months before. Day was a journalist, a recent convert to Catholicism after years of immersion in the radical social movements of the day. Following her conversion she had searched for a way to reconcile her Catholic faith with her commitment to the poor and social justice. She found her answer after meeting Maurin, a French immigrant and itinerant philosopher. He inspired her to launch a newspaper that would proclaim the social implications of the gospel. Thus, *The Catholic Worker* was born.

Maurin and Day were not content simply to denounce social conditions. They sought to inspire a 'personalist revolution', showing how the world could be different if people took responsibility for their neighbours instead of trusting in the beneficence of the state or institutional charities. First in New York and then across the country Catholic Worker 'houses of hospitality' were established to serve the poor and carry out the 'works of mercy' – feeding the hungry, clothing the naked, sheltering the homeless. The Catholic Workers embraced voluntary poverty and combined their service with direct action against the forces of war and injustice.

From its early days in the heart of the Depression, *The Catholic Worker* documented labour struggles and the plight of the poor. But increasingly the movement became known for its pacifist stance. Throughout World War 2 and then into the Cold War and the Vietnam era, Day and her associates were at the centre of a small but growing Catholic peace witness. Day herself was arrested on numerous occasions for acts of civil disobedience, notably her refusal to comply with compulsory civil defence drills. She also advocated resistance to the military draft and refused to pay federal income taxes as a way of protesting war. Though for most of her career Day's radical positions left her isolated from the mainstream, by the time of her death in 1980 she was widely recognized as the conscience of the American Catholic Church. In 1999 the Vatican authorized the introduction of her cause for canonization; she was officially proclaimed 'Servant of God'.

The spirituality of the Catholic Worker was rooted in the twin commandments of the gospel: to love God and to love one's neighbour as oneself. A key text for Day was the parable of the last judgement in Matthew 25 in which heaven hinges on service to Christ in the disguise of the poor. Day's personal spirituality was rooted in the Eucharist, daily prayer and reading of Scripture. A Benedictine oblate since 1955, she revered the monastic values of work, community, hospitality and peace. She also drew on the spirit of St Francis in her espousal of voluntary poverty. Her favorite saint, however, was St Thérèse of Lisieux with her 'little way'. In this spirit, Day always emphasized that it is not the large projects and accomplishments that are critical for our salvation, but the doing of small things with love and faith. Each day at the Catholic Worker, she believed, brought a repetition of the miracle of the loaves and fishes.

Since its origins the Catholic Worker has remained a lay movement, with no official authorization from Church officials. Today there are more than a hundred and fifty Catholic Worker communities across North America, mostly in poor urban centres, though there are also a number of affiliated farming communities. Most of them are marked by a similar spirit of functional anarchy, and by the same combination of service to the poor and activism on behalf of peace. But they also share an atmosphere of precariousness and vulnerability that comes with life among the very poor.

For many decades the Catholic Worker movement has served as a powerful leaven within the Church, anticipating such principles as the 'preferential option for the poor', and recovering the all-but-forgotten memory of gospel nonviolence. Although many Catholic Worker principles are now accepted by the mainstream Church, the Worker continues to serve as a prophetic witness, and for many of those who pass through its houses, it remains a school of holiness and Christian action.

———

Dorothy Day, *Loaves and Fishes,* Maryknoll, NY: Orbis Books, 1997; Robert Ellsberg (ed.), *Dorothy Day: Selected Writings,* Maryknoll, NY: Orbis Books, 1992; Brigid O'Shea Merriman, *Searching for Christ: The Spirituality of Dorothy Day,* South Bend: University of Notre Dame Press, 1994; Mel Piehl, *Breaking Bread: The Catholic Worker and the Origins of Catholic Radicalism in America,* Philadelphia: Temple University Press, 1982; Rosalie Riegle, *Dorothy Day: Portraits by Those Who Knew Her,* Maryknoll: Orbis Books, 2003; Rosalie Riegle (ed.), *Voices from the Catholic Worker,* Philadelphia: Temple University Press, 1993.

ROBERT ELLSBERG

Celebration

Celebration is by nature a communal and public reality. It holds a privileged place in the Christian life and the life of the Church, drawing communities and persons through 'the deep anthropological demands of the heart' (Elizondo and Matovina, pp. 21–2). Though it may be spontaneous, Christian celebration is more often, like sabbath time, set aside in time and space, marking the transitions of human life, the seasons and feasts of the Christian year, the sacred mysteries of faith, and the meeting of all these. Celebrations are moments of grace. In the joy and intensity of these moments, human beings, even when they prepare and lead the celebration, know themselves to be guests at the table.

Like its biblical antecedents, Christian celebration offers praise to God, sings of deliverance, welcomes the estranged (Luke 15.11–32), celebrates forgiveness and reconciliation, repentance and return. Its focus is on passages and seasons, but also on struggle, endurance, survival, life itself, and Christ in all of these.

Its concentrated form, summit and core, is in worship or liturgy. Celebration is thus an ecclesial reality par excellence. 'If the Church did not celebrate the liturgy, it would cease to be the Church' (Corbon, p. 79).

For the more liturgical churches, celebration means especially the Eucharist or Divine Liturgy. Christian liturgical celebration, however, takes many forms within the Church universal: services of worship and praise, communities anchored in word and song, communions praying with image and sacrament. In many Christian communities processions, pilgrimages and devotions are major forms of celebration of the mysteries of God's presence. The assembly gathers inside church buildings, but also on streets, at shrines and in homes. Especially in the larger public gatherings, the assembly expands, welcoming people from beyond the Christian community (Elizondo and Matovina, pp. 21, 82).

Liturgical celebration is a local reality. In it is manifest and present the Church universal, but always in a particular time and place and culture (Corbon, pp. 80–1). The celebrating church is a particular church, just as persons and cultures are particular (Lumbala, p. 5).

In the post-colonial era especially, a deeper awareness of the organic and intimate relationship between culture and religion has enriched the entire Church. Celebrations of the gospel have always existed in diverse cultural incarnations, but shifts in power dynamics within the Church as well as developments in scholarship, travel and communication have contributed to the appreciation of this variety within the Body of Christ. Contemporary Church reform (e.g. in the Roman Catholic Church, the Second Vatican Council's Constitution on the Sacred Liturgy, *Sacrosanctum Concilium*) has both reflected and encouraged these developments.

Liturgical celebrations, rooted in and vehicles of tradition, are marked by both fidelity and freedom. Like human cultures, they evolve (Elizondo and Matovina, pp. 21, 37–41). The sacred mysteries they celebrate are fundamental: liturgical celebration flows from and points to its source, the self-communication of the Triune God (Corbon, pp. 11, 17–18).

Human beings are members of creation; they are embodied, not souls encased in foreign flesh. For Christians, God is incarnate; salvation comes to body and spirit, inside human, earthly, and cosmic history; resurrection is bodily. Celebration, then, is always bodily, sensory and sensual, incorporating and hallowing the things of earth. It is memory of Jesus' earthly ministry, presence of the risen Christ, and hope for the time when God will be all in all.

Human persons are not only part of creation; they are fundamentally social (Lumbala, p. 6). Although celebrations may be led by clergy and other pastoral agents, it is the community as a whole which celebrates. The primary agent of celebration is the whole body of Christ.

Authentic celebration is revelatory of God and reveals persons to themselves. It is formative of communities and individuals. It welcomes and evangelizes. Suspending ordinary time, it also sends participants out 'to proclaim what it has celebrated' (Fleming and Tufano, p. 11), to make the earth a place of celebration, to live out 'the drama of divinization in which the mystery of the lived liturgy is brought to completion in each Christian' (Corbon, p. 152).

See also **Spirituality, Liturgy and Worship** (*essay*); **Eucharistic Spirituality; Food; Incarnation; Joy; Music and Spirituality; Praise; Ritual; Sabbath; Thanksgiving.**

Jean Corbon, *The Wellspring of Worship*, trans. Matthew J. O'Connell, foreword by Edward J. Kilmartin, New York: Paulist Press, 1988 (original edition: *Liturgie de Source*, Paris: Les Editions du Cerf, 1980); Virgil Elizondo and Timothy M. Matovina, *San Fernando Cathedral: Soul of the City*, Maryknoll, NY: Orbis Books, 1998; Austin Fleming with Victoria M. Tufano, *Preparing for Liturgy: A Theology and Spirituality*, rev. edn, Chicago, IL: Liturgy Training Publications, 1997; Thomas A. Kane, *The Dancing Church Around the World*, Two-disc DVD, Cambridge MA: Tomaso Production/Crawfordsville, IN: Wabash Center for Teaching and Learning in Theology and Religion, 2004; François Kabasele Lumbala, *Celebrating Jesus Christ in Africa: Liturgy and Inculturation*, Maryknoll, NY: Orbis Books, 1998.

JANE CAROL REDMONT

Celibacy

The notion and practice of celibacy dates from such Latin writers as Seneca and Cicero, and the word itself was coined to refer to the unmarried state of both men and women. Groups such as the Essenes and Philo of Alexandria's *Therapeutai* adopted celibacy for spiritual purposes, believing living in such a state would allow them a freer, purer spiritual life. Early Christian groups such as the Syrian 'Sons and Daughters of the Covenant' and various Christian Gnostic groups adopted celibacy as the preferred state of the truly spiritual person. They believed living in imitation of the unmarried Jesus would bring them closer to the Son of God, purer vessels of the Holy Spirit, and more worthy sons and daughters of God. Celibacy was also practised in early Christian apocalyptic groups who believed the end of the world was imminent.

Celibacy was by no means a universally accepted lifestyle in the early Christian communities. Documents reveal the ongoing struggles within these communities concerning the practice which in the early Jewish/Christian world was seen as contrary to the commandment of God to go forth and multiply. Those who chose a lifelong celibate lifestyle were often considered extreme with many of those documents considered marginal and non-canonical, such as the *Acts of Paul and Thecla*. Paul himself complains that while the other apostles could have their wives, he and Barnabas were forbidden by them to marry. Yet Paul has long been cited as the New Testament source for the value and superiority of the celibate lifestyle. Paul advocated celibacy primarily because he viewed family life as a distraction and a source of troubles, and, together with the first Christians, he believed the end of the world was imminent. Paul explains his views of marriage and celibacy in 1 Cor. 7.25 where he admits that while he has no command from the Lord, his own opinion is that the life free of the responsibilities of marriage was to be preferred. However, in this same letter (9.3–7), Paul complains about his unmarried status by asking, 'Do we not have the right to be accompanied by a wife as the other apostles and brothers of the Lord and Cephas?' With the rise of the early ascetic and later monastic movements, the lifelong practice of celibacy eventually found its way into the centre of ecclesiastical life and teaching, and was considered the superior choice of those who sincerely wanted to follow a devout Christian lifestyle.

The first institutional steps to advocate the practice of mandatory clerical celibacy came at the Council of Elvira in *c.* 306. Through the instigation of a Spanish bishop, the council formulated the rule that bishops, priests and deacons are to refrain from sexual relations with their wives (canon 33). It was also decided that deaconesses who married after their consecration were to be dismissed. The rule, however, met with much heated debate and resistance from the majority of the bishops, and it was a rule that appears to have been considered optional for the next 800 years in the West concerning all ordained clergy, and 300 years in the East for bishops and men who were ordained to the priesthood before marriage. So debated was the topic that at the Synod of Gangra in *c.* 358, the ascetical spiritual teaching of Eustathius of Sebaste, that celibacy was a superior state of life and only unmarried priests were worthy of the priesthood, was declared anathema by the 17 bishops who presided. The superiority of celibacy for the spiritual life, however, gained ecclesiastical ground with such monk bishops as Basil of Caesarea (d. 379) in the East and Ambrose of Milan in the West. It was not, however, until Lateran II in 1139 that mandatory clerical celibacy was adopted in the West for all ordained clergy, though it can be argued the rule was often ignored even by popes. The Orthodox, on the other hand, rejected the practice of mandatory celibacy for all priests, particularly at the Synod of Constantinople in 691.

Martin Luther rejected the teaching that celibacy was superior to the married state as unbiblical (1521, Augsburg Confession 23, Apology 23). The Lutheran reform stressed celibacy was a gift worthy of praise; however, it rejected the notion of celibacy as a means to gain merit in the eyes of God. The Council of Trent responded to the Reformers in 1563 by condemning all who taught that virginity and celibacy was no better or holier than marriage (Denzinger-Hünermann, *Enchiridion symbolorum* 1810). While the question of celibacy was a dividing point among Roman Catholics and the Protestant Reformers, small groups within the Protestant reform – such as the Shakers – practised lifelong celibacy and virginity as a spiritual calling.

The practice of mandatory clerical celibacy in the Roman Catholic Church has come under much heated discussion following the sex abuse scandals which came to widespread public attention in Boston, Massachusetts early in 2002, and continue to come to light throughout the United States and other parts of the Catholic world. Mandatory celibacy has also come into renewed debate as the Catholic Church faces a crisis in the number of priests available for the celebration of the Eucharist. While celibacy retains its value as a unique spiritual gift, the renewed respect given to marriage at Vatican II has begged the question of the merit and validity of mandatory celibacy for the clerical state.

Outside the clerical culture, celibacy and virginity were often adopted by women as a way in which to free themselves from undesired marriages and the dangers of childbirth. Prior to the feminist movements of the late 1960s, the vows of celibacy – especially life in a religious order – provided them with the freedom to pursue education and careers usually undertaken only by men. Historically, in the early Church, groups of male and female celibates considered themselves living the angelic life which was considered above the human life as the angels have no bodies and are purely spiritual beings. By living as the angels, and as the virginal Christ, these early Christian celibates believed they could intercede

for the rest of humankind by standing in the threshold between heaven and earth. In medieval piety the state of perpetual celibacy and virginity was seen as allowing the monk or nun to be espoused to the Bridegroom, Christ, and permitted them an intimacy with God that was not allowed the married. Mandatory clerical celibacy came to be seen as the spiritual marriage between the celibate male priest and the female Bride of Christ – the Church – and gave rise to the notion of the priest being 'married' to the Church to whom he owed complete fidelity and service.

The practice of celibacy whether lifelong or temporary has long been a respected and valued spiritual practice not only among Christians, but also among most of the major world religions. Celibacy, whether temporary or permanent, has long been recognized as providing those who have the gift with deep spiritual insight, clarity of vision and the leisure to study and meditate on religious and spiritual truths. Celibacy as a rare gift will always exist within religious traditions providing an insight and vision of value to the wider body of humanity.

See also **Chastity; Body and Spirituality; Practices, Spiritual; Priesthood and Spirituality; Religious Life; Sexuality; Virginity.**

Elizabeth Abbott, *A History of Celibacy,* Cambridge, MA: De Capo Press, 2001; Suzanna Elm, *Virgins of God, The Making of Asceticism in Late Antiquity,* Oxford: Oxford University Press, 1996; Eugene C. Kennedy, *The Unhealed Wound: The Church and Human Sexuality,* New York: St Martin's Press, 2001; Sandra M. Schneiders, *Selling All: Commitment, Consecrated Celibacy, and Community in Catholic Religious Life,* New York: Paulist Press, 2001; A. W. Richard Sipe, *Celibacy in Crisis: A Secret World Revisited,* Brunner-Routledge, 2003; H.-J. Vogels, *Celibacy: Gift or Law? A Critical Investigation,* Tunbridge Wells: Search Press, 1992; Vincent L. Wimbush (ed.), *Ascetic Behavior in Greco-Roman Antiquity,* Minneapolis, MN: Fortress Press, 1991.

HARRIET A. LUCKMAN

Celtic Spirituality

This is one of the more controversial topics in contemporary spirituality, especially in the English-speaking world; whose proponents claim that it is a lost, but recoverable, Christian or pagan wisdom ideally suited to contemporary situations, but whose existence its opponents deny on either conceptual or historical grounds, or both. A starting point is to observe what its devotees claim for it. The basic image is that there is a 'Celtic' region or fringe in north-west

Europe (Wales, Ireland and Scotland are seen as the territory of this people) where a different people, 'the Celts', lived and where their descendants still live, who are characterized by a different attitude to the world, nature, art and spiritual realities, which has enabled them to adopt/ adapt Christianity in a very different way to that which has become dominant in the Western world. This 'Celtic Christianity' is seen as similar to other 'native spiritualities' in attitude, sensitivity and forms (so, particularly for North Americans, the 'Celtic' is the place where Christianity can interface with the religions of the First Nations), and it is marked off from other Christianities that are less in touch with basic human sentiments. Thus it is defined by its difference from 'Roman Christianity' and 'Western Christianity', and has links with the various forms of Eastern Christianity whence it is often represented as derived from a 'Celtic Church'. It is characterized by a more sensitive liturgy which has a role for sacred space and place (so it values pilgrimages and holy wells), it values people in its liturgy over regulated forms, it gives adequate expression to the insights of wise women (hence a renewed interest in saints and their cults), and it is not 'sin-soaked' as it rejected the dour Augustine for the more upbeat message of the Celt, Pelagius. For some people, Celtic Christianity also was able to accommodate the wisdom of the Celtic pagan past and preserve its 'earthy' knowledge of seasons, the power in nature, and an ability to interact with spiritual powers in the universe which have been ignored to the detriment of human beings and the environment – and there is often an overlap between 'Celtic spirituality' (sometimes used in contradistinction from 'Celtic Christianity') and New Age writings.

Given that its proponents make such a claim about its antiquity and its links with particular cultures and the past, it is somewhat ironic that all its headline claims about the past are rejected by historians whether in Celtic studies (see Meek) or theology (see O'Loughlin). There never was a people who referred to themselves as 'the Celts': there were Irish, Welsh and Bretons who did not recognize any special affinity between them or any common characteristic that distinguished them collectively from other groups. The term 'Celtic' was coined by philology to express common characteristics of a language-family, but major expressions of those languages (i.e., the languages behind modern Welsh and modern Irish) were not mutually intelligible in the historical period. It is used by analogy by literary historians and archaeologists to refer to literature and art, which does not fall

within the mainstream of Western culture when that is defined by relationship to the Graeco-Roman past. However, it is singularly inappropriate when referring to Christianity in those lands in north-west Europe. Christianity arrived there through its westward spread within the Roman Empire, established itself there using the Western Latin liturgy and that Christianity expressed itself as part of Western Christendom looking explicitly to Rome as its patriarchal centre until the Reformation. There never was a 'Celtic' rite, much less a 'Celtic' Church; every theologian writing in those lands saw themselves belonging to a single religious body – hence their ability to integrate with locals in monasteries and schools when on the continent. In regard to the claims that the Christianity in those lands made 'space' for the pre-Christian past there are further difficulties. Our knowledge of that past comes either from classical authors who presented the religion of Gaul (it is an assumption that this is similar to that of the insular lands several centuries later) to their Graeco-Roman audience in terms of the 'natural religion' as imagined by the Stoics so that the descriptions are as valuable for the history of Stoicism as of Gaul, or from later Christian authors who interpret the past in terms of Old Testament confrontations with non-Israelite priests (e.g. 1 Kings 18) and theories of Christianity as the perfection of a religious quest (e.g. Acts 17), which tells us more about their theology than their society. For instance, the 'druids' (itself a linguistic nonsense: the Old Irish word for wizard is *drui* and the plural is *druid*) are supposed to come from Gaul, Wales and Ireland, yet the basic references to them are only from Ireland in relatively late Christian sources where what is said of them is derived wholly from Dan. 1—4!

How then can the distinctive Christian world that is found in early medieval texts from those lands be accounted for? First, while the medieval West certainly had an image of its religious unity (expressed in maps, law and language) it had no experience of the actual uniformity in such matters as liturgy or the desire for uniformity in doctrinal expressions that characterize recent centuries. For example, only with print did liturgical uniformity over a wide area become possible, while only with the Reformation did the desire for such uniformity become a force in ecclesiastical politics. The earlier the period one looks at in the West the more one finds that local connections produce distinctive patterns in spirituality relating to local patterns of settlement, legal background and language use. So, for example, a saint's life from Ireland will draw on the great hagiographical models (Athanasius, *c.*

296–373, and Sulpicius Severus, *c.* 360–*c.* 420) for its form, but express sanctity in a society that was non-urban, without a legacy of Roman administration, with its own traditions of law and social interaction, and in Latin which was learned as a second, specific-use language. Second, later myths of historical continuity that late medieval standard forms of theology or the religious life 'go back to the beginning' are confounded by finding Christian expressions from the period before those standard forms emerged. For instance, the later standard form of Western monasticism, that is Benedictinism and its offshoots such as the Cistercians, emerged with Benedict of Aniane (*c.* 750–821) but the monastic texts from Ireland come from before that time when there was a much more varied monastic landscape across the West, where John Cassian (*c.* 360–435) was the leading theorist – an influence which explains the similarities of that monasticism with that of the East. Equally, the interest in the universe as sacramental reflects a common theme of pre-university theology, but when it is found in an insular text is taken as being somehow distinctive of works written in that area. Third, the various areas of the Latin world produced distinctive elements that later either became part of the mainstream or disappeared with the gradual spread of greater uniformity in practice or teaching: thus early medieval Spain produced the theology of the Eucharist as the sacred object, while early medieval Ireland produced a new system of penance standing behind the later development of auricular confession and indulgences.

The historical task is not that of finding a 'Celtic spirituality', but being sensitive to the variations found throughout the medieval world and then comparing them with other local theologies from the period; this process then leaves open the theological task of seeing whether or not these various phenomena pose questions as to the nature of later uniformities or contemporary assumptions.

The current interest in 'the Celtic past' whether or not it is well founded historically has produced some interesting effects in Christian communities. First, it has often highlighted the historical nature of Christian belief and practice emphasizing the extent to which culture and spirituality interact. Second, under the category of 'Celtic' many groups have sought to experiment with liturgy, for example a sacred year or the practice of pilgrimage, where those practices are not part of their recent church-memory. Third, it has been used in several ecumenical endeavours to construct a common remembered past that bypasses memories of division stem-

ming from the Reformation and its aftermath through the intellectual device that that which is now proposed is 'older' than the period of division. Whether or not this current interest will be long-standing – it arose at a time when there is a widespread fascination with the 'Celtic' as an 'alternative' culture – only time will tell, but for many who have come in contact with it, it has revealed a more basic perception that Christianity has a genius for pluriformity and for adapting itself to local life-situations without losing its catholicity and world (*oikoumene*)-wide vision.

See also **Asceticism; Desert; Eremitical Spirituality; Hagiography; Irish Christian Spirituality; Monasticism; Pelagianism; Scottish Spirituality; Welsh Spirituality.**

Donald E. Meek, *The Quest for Celtic Christianity*, Edinburgh: Handsel Press, 2000; Thomas O'Loughlin, *Celtic Theology: Humanity, World and God in Early Irish Writings*, London: Continuum, 2000; Thomas O'Loughlin, 'Medieval church history: beyond apologetics, after development: the awkward memories', *The Way* 38 (1998) 65–76; Thomas O'Loughlin, *Journeys on the Edges: The Celtic Tradition*, London: Darton, Longman & Todd/New York: Orbis Books, 2000; Thomas O'Loughlin, '"Celtic spirituality", ecumenism, and the contemporary religious landscape', *Irish Theological Quarterly* 67 (2002) 153–68; Thomas O'Loughlin, '"A Celtic theology": some awkward questions and observations' in J. F. Nagy (ed.), *Identifying the 'Celtic'*, Celtic Studies Association of North America Yearbook 2, Dublin: Four Courts Press, 2002, pp. 49–65.

THOMAS O'LOUGHLIN

Centring Prayer

see Meditation

Charism

Charism is to be understood in terms of God's gift and giving. One may be endowed with certain natural gifts and talents, which may be nurtured or neglected. These may be used for personal gain or put to the service of some wider purpose. Charism, on the other hand, is a gift that may or may not be rooted in natural endowment, and is always given and received for the good of a body of persons and its common life, purpose and sense of destiny.

In the history of Christian spirituality many religious orders and congregations have emerged as a result of a charism given to a particular person or group in order to respond to the needs of the Church and society at a particular time and place. Katharine Drexel, the Philadelphia heiress to a generous financial estate, used that gift as well as her natural abilities to establish the Religious Congregation of the Sisters of the Blessed Sacrament. Her effort to establish this sisterhood for the purpose of serving the needs of 'Indians and Colored People' in the United States cannot be properly understood solely as a communal enterprise aimed at addressing the racial inequality so prevalent in her own time and place. It was rather more a response to a gift given by God present and active in her own heart and in the hearts of the first of her companions who were moved to attend to the poor and marginalized members of the Body of Christ in the Church and world of the early to mid twentieth century. The charisms of many religious congregations and orders of men and of women have been and are still discerned in response to shifting modes of perceiving and being, as well as in light of changing needs in society and Church.

Far too often in the history of Christian spirituality, the term 'charism' has been rather narrowly associated with religious congregations and orders. In addition, it has often been associated with a sense of personal call as well as the gift or gifts needed to persevere in that call, which more often than not entailed a call to religious life or priesthood. In urging vowed religious to return to the charism of their founders, the Second Vatican Council prompted fuller exploration not only of the specific charisms that prompted the foundation of religious institutes, but also required more serious and careful reflection on the very nature and function of charism, with particular attention to its biblical mooring.

Turning to the corpus of St Paul, all who make up the body are gifted, no matter how insignificant the gift may seem. Just as the members are many, so are the gifts of the Holy Spirit which inspire, enliven, enlighten and heal the Body with God's own breath, balm and brightness. In the midst of such an abundance of gift and gifting, there is a need for discernment of distinct charisms, which differ according to the needs of the body in a particular time and place.

In light of an emerging ecclesial reality among the earliest Christian churches at Ephesus Paul emphasizes Christ's headship, as he does with the Colossians. In the Church at Philippi, however, his emphasis is on Jesus Christ as exemplar in his self-giving. Whatever there may be in the way of coherence and consistency in the Pauline vision of a new community, it emerges from an effort to articulate a vision in response to quite diverse situations.

In this schema, charism is ineluctably related to vision. Vision is first and foremost. 'Without a vision, the people perish' (Prov. 16.9). Charisms are to be discerned in light of a vision and are to be put to its service. It is precisely the ability to articulate a vision in a persuasive and compelling way that lies at the heart of the charism of leadership. Whatever sense of call to which one may lay claim, and whatever charisms may be discerned for fidelity to it, the call and the charism do not exist as purely personal, individual entities, but are always to be understood in relation to the wider body, whose good the charism is given to serve.

––––––

'Charism' in Karl Rahner and Herbert Vorgrimler (eds), *Dictionary of Theology*, New York: Crossroad, 1981, pp. 64–5; Wilfred Harrington, 'Charism' in Joseph Komonchak, Mary Collins, Dermot Lane (eds), *The New Dictionary of Theology*, Wilmington, DE: Michael Glazier, 1987, pp. 180–3; J. Koenig, *Charismata: God's Gifts for God's People*, Philadelphia, PA: Westminster Press, 1978; Edward Malatesta, 'Charism' in Michael Downey (ed.), *The New Dictionary of Catholic Spirituality*, Collegeville, MN: The Liturgical Press/Glazier, 1993, pp. 140–3.

MICHAEL DOWNEY

Charismatic Spirituality

The heart of charismatic spirituality is the conviction and experience of the present, empowering activity of the Holy Spirit in and through the life of the believer and the church community, including the manifestation of the Spirit's gifts (*charismata*) and ministries familiar in at least some of the New Testament churches (e.g. Rom. 12.6–8; 1 Cor. 12.28–31; Eph. 4.11–12).

Although we will concentrate upon charismatic spirituality as evidenced in the contemporary charismatic movement, it is important to recognize that charismatic forms of spirituality have occurred and reoccurred at various times in the history of the Church. Indeed, the ancient and catholic antecedents of today's charismatic spirituality are increasingly charted by contemporary charismatics as they seek to demonstrate the authenticity of both their religious experiences and their vision for the health of the Church. Charismatics, with proper justification, point not only to the charismatic life of many New Testament churches but also to the continuing acceptance of various *charismata* in the patristic period, as well as to the expectation of the demonstrable presence of the Spirit in Christian initiation in the early centuries of the Church, referring to various writers, and by no means only the notoriously charismatic Tertullian and the Montanists.

Again on sound historical grounds, charismatics draw attention to charismatic activity among the Desert Fathers and Mothers, the Celtic monks and saints and the leaders or founders of religious orders or movements of renewal in the Western Church, including Hildegard of Bingen (twelfth century), Francis of Assisi (thirteenth century), Thomas Münster, Ignatius Loyola (sixteenth century), George Fox (seventeenth century), George Whitefield, John Wesley and Jonathan Edwards (eighteenth century). The post-patristic life of the Eastern tradition has been less noticed by charismatic apologists but there is much from the Eastern Church that resonates with the experience of charismatics, for example in the writings of Symeon the New Theologian (tenth to eleventh centuries), the various writings of the Philokalia and the ministry of Seraphim of Sarov (nineteenth century).

The origins of the contemporary charismatic movement can be traced to the middle of the twentieth century when phenomena associated with the Pentecostal churches began to break out in other historic ecclesial communities. Momentous experiences of being filled with the Holy Spirit, speaking in tongues, new-found joy, freedom and vitality in worship, prophetic words and pictures, evidence of miraculous healings through expectant prayer and the laying on of hands, increased recognition of the presence of evil began to occur in Anglican, Baptist, Lutheran, Mennonite, Methodist, Presbyterian and Roman Catholic circles.

Originally described as the neo-Pentecostal movement, this mid twentieth-century outbreak of charismatic spirituality was related to but distinct from the Pentecostal movement, the beginning of which is usually dated to the Azusa Street revival of 1906–13. It was similar to its Pentecostal elder in some of the fundamental features of its spirituality – the *felt* presence and power of the Holy Spirit leading to exuberant forms of worship, expectations of the discernible activity of God in worship and ministry and a heightened eschatological consciousness. However, it was different – and remains different – from classical Pentecostalism. Sociologically charismatics tended to be more 'affluent and white' and significantly less 'poor and coloured'. Ecclesially, they sought to remain in and to influence the historic Churches, while becoming increasingly ecumenical, at least to charismatics in other traditions. Pragmatically, they were less committed to evangelism and to worldwide mission than their Pentecostal peers. Theologically, they were generally not convinced by some of the theological positions of Pentecostalism, particularly in terms of the relation between a post-baptismal or post-conversion experience of the Spirit and Christian initiation itself.

Although the charismatic movement remains strong in many of the historic denominations it is more prevalent beyond them. This is due to a number of factors. Some twentieth-century charismatics disagreed with the strategy to 'stay and renew', preferring to 'leave and begin again'. Many found that they were unwelcome or that the culture and structure of their Church were insufficiently malleable for the new life of the Spirit. House churches, new Churches and new affiliations of Churches resulted in the West. However, the most significant growth in worldwide charismatic life beyond the historic Churches has taken place among independent and indigenous Churches in Asia, Africa and South America. Despite their charismatic practice, most of these Churches – in whatever part of the world – are not affiliated to Pentecostalism itself and many do not even describe themselves as charismatic. This has led some analysts to describe them as neo-charismatic, or as a 'third wave' of the Spirit's renewal of the Church. At the beginning of the twenty-first century the total numbers of Pentecostal, charismatic and neo-charismatic Christians in the world was estimated to be 523 million, representing 27.7 per cent of global Christianity, and it has been predicted to be the fastest growing form of church life in the early decades of the century.

As we said earlier, the heart of charismatic spirituality is the conviction and experience of the present, empowering activity of the Holy Spirit in and through the life of the believer and the church community. Some charismatics would describe this experience as 'baptism in the Spirit' and, like Pentecostals, define it as a necessary stage in Christian initiation (usually accompanied by a gift confirming the Spirit's presence) and one distinct from conversion and water baptism. However, most charismatics, while affirming the importance of empowering experiences of the Spirit, are more relaxed about both the description and the definition of the experience. Often it will be called 'being filled with' or 'released by' the Spirit. Generally, its exact relation to profession of faith in Christ and water baptism will be left unclear and a variety of interpretations, appropriate to different ecclesial traditions, recognized and allowed. Nevertheless, a 'personal Pentecost', an 'individual epiclesis', remains at the centre of charismatic spirituality. An implicitly trinitarian event (in which the Spirit of God renews a person's devotion to Christ and empowers a person's witness to Christ and work for the reign of God), the 'baptism', 'filling' or 'release' of the Spirit equips believers with gifts to minister within the body of the Church and empowers them with capacities to serve the world for the sake of the coming kingdom of God.

Charismatic spirituality offers a number of gifts to the Church as a whole to 'promote the body's growth in building itself up in love' (Eph. 4.16). It has learnt about the *sovereignty* of God. Through the present, dynamic activity of God, the graces and powers of the people of God have been released from their clericalization in the systems of the Church. Likewise, the reductionism of rationalism has been challenged by manifestations of the miraculous. Charismatic spirituality has discovered *catholicity*. Charismatics have found out what it means to be part of the body of Christ in a particular community. The exercise of gifts and ministries by all members of the body offers a profound example of ecclesial life to other Christians. Furthermore, although many charismatics are broadly evangelical, charismatic renewal at its best has led to a remarkable dismantling of walls between Christians and an openness to signs of the Spirit's work in 'the other'. Charismatic spirituality has also proved to be *apostolic*. Again, at its best, it has been fired by a vision for the life of God's kingdom to be seen on God's earth. The heartbeat of charismatic spirituality is eschatology. It longs to see the demonstration of God's rule over sin, sickness, suffering and death. It sends people out from the church to confront evil, tell others of Christ and to heal the sickness of individuals and communities. The lungs of charismatic spirituality are worship – worship of the sovereign God who acts today, worship as members of the body of Christ, each with a gift to contribute to the 'common good' (1 Cor. 12.7), and worship that anticipates the coming of the new heavens and the new earth where souls and bodies, people and communities, humanity and the whole of creation are fully renewed by the Spirit of God.

Nevertheless, despite the considerable strengths of contemporary charismatic spirituality, a number of weaknesses are evident in at least some of its expressions. In theology, the relationship between the activity of the Holy Spirit and the function of the human spirit is often confused, repeatedly, for example, with regard to the relationship between human faith and divine healing – the latter often being made entirely dependent on the former. In eschatology, the tension between the presence and the coming of the kingdom is sometimes threatened, and there has been a tendency to downplay the reality of the cross and to overplay the power of the resurrection in Christian life. In worship, the place of Christ's priesthood is often eclipsed by his kingship. In ecclesiology, the visible structures of communion are often undervalued and the wisdom of the Church's history ignored. In ministry and mission, charismatics have been prone to judge methods by their immediate success rather than by their theological value, and they have been easily seduced by the latest fashion in spiritual life and church practice.

The challenge to charismatic spirituality is to allow its fundamental openness to the Spirit to reveal its weaknesses and to lead it into all truth, so that its challenge to the whole Church to remain dependent on the perpetual presence and power of the Spirit can be fully heard.

See also **Charism; Emotions; Ecstasy; Evangelical Spirituality; Holiness; Pentecostal Spirituality; Pietism; Postmodernity; Presence of God; Quaker Spirituality; Shaker Spirituality; Spirit, Holy; Tears, Gift of (Penthos); Trinity and Spirituality; Visionary Literature.**

Stanley M. Burgess and Eduard M. Van Der Maas, *The New International Dictionary of Pentecostal and Charismatic Movements*, rev. edn, Grand Rapids, MI: Zondervan, 2000; Heribert Mühlen, *A Charismatic Theology: Initiation into the Spirit*, London: Burns & Oates, 1978; Léon Joseph Cardinal Suenens, *A New Pentecost?*, London: Darton, Longman & Todd, 1975; Jean-Jacques Surrmond, *Word and Spirit at Play: Towards a Charismatic Theology*, London: SCM Press, 1994; Vinson Synan, *The Century of the Holy Spirit: 100 Years of Pentecostal and Charismatic Renewal*, Nashville, TN: Thomas Nelson, 2001; Max Turner, *The Holy Spirit and Spiritual Gifts: Then and Now*, Carlisle: Paternoster Press, 1996.

CHRISTOPHER COCKSWORTH

Charity

In the context of Christian spirituality, charity (from the Latin *caritas*) is often used synonymously with Christian love, or it can refer to the concrete attitudes and actions towards God and the neighbour that are expected of every Christian. In a secularized context charity often refers to different kinds of benevolent and philanthropic actions on behalf of individual human beings, groups or peoples who require help and assistance. Charitable institutions and associations may aim at alleviating acute emergencies (e.g. war, natural catastrophes, illness, epidemics) or at transforming unjust structures and situations.

Charity understood as one of the three theological virtues – the others are hope and faith – is discussed by Paul (1 Cor. 13, 1 Thess. 1.3 and 4.8; Gal. 5.5–6; Col. 1.4–5) who considers it the greatest of these virtues. Later theology has distinguished these three God-given virtues from natural virtues. Charity has an eschatological character: it originates in the triune God who is love (1 John 4.16) and it gives expression to God's coming reign, to its creative and redemptive nature as well as to the corresponding human praxis which is inspired by the Holy Spirit.

Christian charity often refers to the overall purpose and concern of individual or corporate services by Christian churches and movements. In response to Jesus' teaching that every person is our neighbour (Luke 10.25–37) and that whatever we do to a person in need we do to the Son of Man himself (Matt. 25.31–46), Christian spiritualities have developed many ways of addressing the needs of men, women and children individually or socially. Religious orders, lay movements, local, regional and universal groups of Christians have identified pressing needs in Church and society and developed ad hoc or institutional strategies of dealing with them. Individual Christians have reacted to such needs either spontaneously or by devoting their entire life to works of love, compassion, justice and solidarity. At times, Christians have co-operated with state bodies, with international institutions (e.g. International Red Cross, the United Nations, UNICEF), and more recently also with help organizations of other religions. Since the emergence of the modern and secular welfare state, traditional concerns of Christian charity have been taken over by state agencies (especially in northern Europe) or been affirmed and actively supported by the state (according to the principle of subsidiarity). Moreover, non-governmental organizations and non-religious associations promoting aspects of charity have grown in recent decades – with or without the active support of Christian churches or movements. Thus, today Christians have no monopoly of caring for the people whose needs they may have been first to identify and address: the sick, the handicapped, the dying, prisoners, orphans, widows, refugees, asylum-seekers, outcasts, exploited women and children, victims of tyranny, torture, epidemics, famine, and underdevelopment etc.

In response to their divine vocation, Christians must remain sensitive to detect new and emerging needs, including the systemic needs of an exploited universe and the dilemma of deciding which need is most deserving at a given time and place. This is not easy as a result of the increasing level of mass media information on particular needs and the implicit emphasis on immediacy in these media. Christians must also be aware of the danger of reducing other human beings to mere objects of charity. People in need must never be deprived of their human integrity. Christian charity must therefore keep in mind that all of its actions are to affirm and enable other persons to be themselves as fully as possible and strive to avoid creating or sustaining unnecessary forms of dependence. Human freedom, emancipation and justice are goals, and must not become victims of Christian charity. Christian charity must help build just structures and institutions and not replace them by mere acts of charity. Hence, Christian charity requires an ongoing process of theological examination and self-critique.

See also **Love.**

Stanley Hauerwas, *Community of Character: Towards a Constructive Christian Social Ethics*, Notre Dame and London: University of Notre Dame Press, 1981; Werner G. Jeanrond, *Call and Response: The Challenge of Christian Life,* Dublin: Gill & Macmillan, 1995; Søren Kierkegaard, *Works of Love* [1847], Princeton: Princeton University Press, 1995; Hans Küng, *Global Responsibility: In Search of a New World Ethic,* London: SCM Press, 1991; Stephen G. Post et al. (eds), *Altruism and Altruistic Love: Science, Philosophy, and Religion in Dialogue,* Oxford: Oxford University Press, 2002.

WERNER G. JEANROND

Chastity

Chastity implies remaining faithful to a vow that may or may not require sexual abstinence. Culturally, a vow of chastity is most often associated with a celibate lifestyle, typically of lifelong virginity, as in the case of Catholic priests, monks and nuns. Historically and outside of the religious life, concern for the preservation of chastity, understood as virginity, most often arose with regard to unmarried women. Hence the creation of the famous medieval device: the chastity belt, which was designed to protect a woman's sexual purity. Further, in *A History of Celibacy*, Elizabeth Abbott quickly informs her reader that, while historically the meaning of chastity is not exhausted by celibacy, throughout her book she will go along with the cultural association and use the terms chastity and celibacy interchangeably.

Within the area of Christian spirituality, chastity has often been associated with a state of virginity as well. Chastity as abstinence, not only from sexual activity, but even the thought of sexual activity, was prized in monastic culture. This was especially the case within the writings of the medieval mystics. For example, in Hildegard of Bingen's *Scivias*, upholding a vow of chastity, interpreted as lifelong virginity, was considered the pinnacle of human devotion to God. Yet Hildegard also warns that it is not a vow to take lightly. One who pledges virginity and then fails to uphold this vow falls so far from God's grace, they are left with no hope of approaching near the pinnacle of the virgin lifestyle again.

Despite Abbott's reduction of chastity and celibacy to interchangeable terms, and both the societal and monastic tendency to associate one with the other, chastity and celibacy are not one and the same. At the core of chastity is a vow regarding sexual activity, but not exclusively toward the end of refraining from sexual activity altogether. A vow of chastity sets the boundaries surrounding when sexual activity is morally permissible and when it is not. Thus, it is possible for two people to engage in chaste sexual activity, if this activity occurs within the boundaries of a chaste marriage. In St Augustine's treatise *The Good of Marriage*, he refers to chastity as the 'crown of marriage'. Yet for Augustine, chaste sexual activity fulfils its promise as the 'crown of marriage' in a very narrowly defined set of circumstances: a marriage is chaste only when sexual activity between married persons occurs for the sole purpose of procreation.

In another, more contemporary treatment of chastity, Annemarie Kidder urges, in *Women, Celibacy and the Church*, that it is crucial to differentiate between the two terms. Unlike Abbott, Kidder argues that celibacy is only one means of expressing the vow and therefore it is a mistake to reduce chastity to celibacy. She explains that chastity understood as total sexual abstinence is generally expected across traditions from Christians who choose to remain single for life, who identify as gay or lesbian, or who have not yet entered into a marital commitment. Kidder also reiterates that sexual activity within marriage is chaste by way of the fidelity expressed between a man and a woman within the marital bond. Yet, Kidder also argues that an understanding of chastity, interpreted as total sexual abstinence for the single person, should be abandoned. She believes that this interpretation again engenders a mistaken reduction of chastity to celibacy and promotes an unhealthy spiritual attitude toward sexuality.

Finally, there is an interesting cultural divide regarding the issue of chastity emerging among young adults, beginning with Generations X, Y, and now among the Millenials. There is a growing tendency among younger generations to delay marriage decades beyond their parents and grandparents. On one end of the divide are those who, distanced from their religious upbringing, identify as 'spiritual, but not religious', or speaking as gay/lesbian persons for whom 'chaste marriage' is not a possibility (as it is illegal), disregard the Christian teaching to refrain from sexual activity until marriage. Preservation of chastity understood as sexual abstinence outside of marriage is either discarded as an outdated moral expectation, or reinterpreted to better fit the cultural shift in dating practices.

On the other end of the divide, led by the Evangelical Christian youth movement are teenagers and twenty-something's who are committed to preserving a celibate or chaste lifestyle until marriage. This movement was popularized by a pioneer book by Joshua Harris, entitled *I Kissed Dating Goodbye*, which urges total sexual abstinence among non-married persons, including abstention from male–female friendships to protect oneself from lustful thoughts, as the only legitimate path for committed Christians. This book has inspired countless similar texts on purity, chastity and abstinence directed at the growing contingent of Evangelical Christian youths in the United States. In addition, concern for the preservation of sexual purity among Evangelical young adults has led to the development of new, ritual expressions of chastity. In a ring ceremony (primarily) young women of twelve to fifteen years pledge themselves as 'brides of Christ' by placing a 'promise ring' on their left hand to signify the vow of chastity they will keep until they marry.

Emerging generations seem caught between interpreting chastity in its strictest sense, understanding even the thought of sex prior to marriage as a violation, and stretching the boundaries of 'chaste activity' to accommodate contemporary lifestyles and culture, in ways that far exceed the views of St Augustine that have long defined the traditional, Christian understanding behind the meaning of chastity.

See also **Celibacy; Body and Spirituality; Practices, Spiritual; Priesthood and Spirituality; Religious Life; Sexuality; Virginity.**

———

Lisa Sowle Cahill, *Sex, Gender, and Christian Ethics*, New Studies in Christian Ethics 5, Cambridge: Cambridge University Press, 1996; Elizabeth Clark (ed.), *St. Augustine on Marriage and Sexuality,* Washington, DC: The Catholic University of America Press, 1996; John

Grabowski, *Sex and Virtue: An Introduction to Sexual Ethics*, Catholic Moral Thought Series, Washington, DC: Catholic University of America Press, 2003; Joshua Harris, *I Kissed Dating Goodbye: A New Attitude toward Relationships and Romance*, Sisters, OR: Multnomah, 1997; Annemarie S. Kidder, *Women, Celibacy, and the Church: Towards a Theology of the Single Life*, New York: Herder & Herder, 2003; Albert Plé, *Chastity and the Affective Life*, trans. Marie-Claude Thompson, New York: Herder & Herder, 1966.

DONNA FREITAS

Children and Spirituality

1. *Historical overview*. Historically the spirituality of childhood has received scant attention. Children's religious and general education, discipline and moral formation overshadowed Christian interest in their spirituality. From the writings of theologians, Christian educators and parents in the past it appears the child's spiritual life was equated with such issues, or deemed to be contingent upon sufficient development in these domains. Spirituality was configured as something for which children would be passively prepared by others, rather than actively engaged with in their own right, or capable of their own spiritual experience or knowing. Contemporary study suggests this pessimistic expectation of children's spirituality points to weakness in adult perception rather than basis in childhood reality.

A key problem for historical study in this area is a lack of evidence in children's own voices. The situation is worse even than the documentation of women's authentic spiritual voices – beset by being unheard, silenced, spoken for by others or having to speak in the accepted 'accents' of others. Those few children whom history has documented were regarded as 'exceptional', rather than normal, and adults often interpreted evidence of their spiritual vitality as a channel of divine communication, rather than integral to the child's being themselves.

2. *Historical relation to Christian theology*. The undervaluing of childhood spirituality in Christian thought and practice is perplexing in the light of Jesus' rich and provocative treatment of children in the Gospels (J. Berryman). Subsequent Christian theology has given uneven attention to childhood (infant baptism, original sin, abortion), focusing on issues which have potentially negative repercussions for the spiritual state of the *adult*. Children have often been negative examples for 'mature' adult spirituality (e.g. St Paul, 1 Cor. 13.11, Augustine's *Confessions*), or a site for exploring adult spiritual responsibilities

(as domestic church leaders, evangelists or educators). However, F. Schleiermacher, H. Bushnell and K. Rahner (see Bunge) engaged with childhood in ways that draw positively on its autonomous spiritual richness, developing more rigorously the position identified in poetic writings of Thomas Traherne, and the poetry of Wordsworth and other romantics, that is, that childhood is a natural sanctuary for spiritual qualities for which adults must constantly struggle: openness, perceptual far-sightedness and an everyday sensitivity to experiences of sacred transcendence and immanence.

3. *Modern trends*. The twentieth century witnessed a multi-disciplinary awakening in the study of childhood generally. However, cognitive developmental psychology of children's religion served further to focus on religious life in intellectual, linguistic terms (naturally limited for a child), and deterred the study of any more affective spiritual capacity or its role in early Christian life. Nevertheless empirically informed writers (such as P. Ranwez, A. Rizzuto and A. Vergote) were instrumental in their recognition of the wider parameters required to perceive childhood spirituality, the need for more naturalistic observation of children's religious response and to attend to the emotional significance, rather than surface content, of their religious understanding.

This need to reach an understanding of children's spirituality on children's terms should not be confused with other efforts to adopt more 'child-friendly' approaches to church. The latter are rarely motivated by considerations of the child's capacity for meaningful spiritual experience, but rather are concessions to the Christian politics of inclusion, or concessions to the perceived impoverished psychology of the child as needing entertainment, distraction, physical activity and additional explanation and clarity. Indeed, hallmarks identified by current scholarship (see below) suggesting children's spiritual potential is best evoked in intimate, safe sacred spaces, and attended by penetrating freely chosen creative thought and play, silence or stillness, moods of deep joy, wonder and fascination with mystery, may be *least* well served in much of modern 'child-friendly' church practices.

A growing consensus of scholars demonstrates a marked shift away from evidence of intellectual religious understanding and its language as prerequisites for childhood spirituality, picking up themes echoing across modern literature on Christian spirituality. Spirituality in childhood offers, sine qua non, the need to grapple with themes of knowing rather than knowledge about, connative rather than dennotative insight, and a spirituality based on first-hand 'being' rather than accumulated evidence of good works, appropriate religious behaviours or theological sophistication.

4. *Contemporary research findings.* Since the mid 1980s a new research field in children's spirituality has developed, attracting cross-disciplinary attention (e.g. *International Journal of Children's Spirituality*). Indeed Christian-focused contributions are outnumbered by others motivated by secular, psychological, multi-faith or educational concerns for the spiritual realities of childhood. Many document the integral nature of spirituality in childhood experience (R. Coles, C. Erricker, D. Heller, B. Kimes Myers, R. Nye, E. Robinson), delegating faith nurture to a secondary role, or even citing religious teaching as tending to stifle spiritual life. Common to this research initiative has been the value placed on analysis of children in their own words and other expressions, revealing an embarrassingly rich landscape of spiritual experience (e.g. among 7-year-olds surveyed 80 per cent reported an experience of the presence of God – K. Tamminen, Finland), spiritual meaning-making and engagement with spiritual questioning at every age, among children of all faiths and none. Though many children employ 'God-talk' in their expression, few children identify the Church, its representatives, its concerns or its function as connected to their spirituality. The challenge to present Christian religious language and practice as empowered to meet and deepen children's spiritual capacities and needs remains widely underestimated by most Christian communities' approaches to faith nurture.

Empirical research has recognized the mystical predisposition of children's psychology among some of the key characteristics of their spirituality. For example, the formative experience from infancy onwards of dependence and relationship, of self and other distinctions and fusion, and the emotional extremes arsing in this are natural forms of the kind of spirituality described by R. Otto (*The Idea of the Holy*). Also the precedence of emotional sensitivity and the language of the non-verbal domain in younger children (rather than intellectual and verbal reasoning) supports more acute perceptions of qualities of the sacred presented through time, space, pattern or symbol, and an ability to enter into these unselfconsciously, even to a point of being overwhelmed and easily accepting the ineffability of the sacred. Older children (approx 4–10) can experience narrative (religious or secular) as having a powerful capacity to hold

(and develop) the emerging 'logic' of spiritual feelings and thoughts, going deeper by dwelling in the story world rather than by attempts to analyse or extract meanings from them. Christian spiritual traditions like Ignatian Spiritual Exercises and *lectio divina* place value on similar skills.

5. *Educational implications.* Key developments in Christian approaches to children's spiritual nurture share twin guiding principles – a generous, radical regard for the child's spiritual potential implied in the Gospels *and* the need for close observation of children at their most natural (e.g. at play) and their responses to the sacred. The work of J. Berryman (USA) and S. Cavalletti (Italy) exemplifies this, espousing in so doing the primary need for spiritual nurture to adopt not merely a spiritual message but also suitable spiritual media to withstand contemporary children's often more exacting thresholds for authenticity in encounters with religious language. These 'media' include the attention to the spiritual quality (mutual respect and openness to discovery) of both teacher–child and peer relationships, and the role played by the physical and emotional environment in shaping (or mis-shaping) spiritual life.

Thus there is a dramatic shift away from seeing children as objects of religious education to whom spiritual life is introduced once understanding is established, towards the more radical notion that children may be an important subject of spiritual life. As a consequence of our closer reflection on the meaning of childhood and observation of them at play, at rest, in terms of their relationships of dependence and trust, and their instinctive thirst for meaning, freedom and love, analyses of children's spirituality offer opportunities for natural laws of spiritual being to be inferred, as well as shedding fresh light on a Christian view of personhood. The educational implications are not only to the way children are nurtured by Christians in ways that support both the child's spiritual present and adult future, but also set a challenge for adult life to relate with awareness to their own childhood as an 'abiding reality' (Rahner) for their total spiritual identity.

───────

E. Bernstein and J. Brooks-Leonard (eds), *Children in the Assembly of the Church*, Liturgy Training Publications, 1993; J. Berryman, *Godly Play: An Imaginative Approach to Religious Education*, Minneapolis: Augsburg Fortress Press, 1995; M. Bunge (ed.), *The Child in Christian Thought*, Grand Rapids, MI: Eerdmans, 2001; S. Cavalletti, *The Religious Potential of the Child,* New York: Paulist Press,

1983; D. Hay, with R. Nye, *The Spirit of the Child*, HarperCollins, 1998; K. Rahner, 'Ideas for a theology of childhood' in *Theological Investigations* 8, *Further Theology of the Spiritual Life* 2, trans. David Bourke, New York: Herder & Herder, 1971; *International Journal of Children's Spirituality*, Carfax Publishing, 1996–.

Cross-cultural perspectives, especially from the developing world, have been absent from most of the scenes described here. However see www.viva.org/tellme/resources/articles/gods_heart/theology.html for a collection of resources and projects that are seeking to remedy this.

REBECCA NYE

Choice

see Discernment

Christ-Centred Spirituality

see Jesus and Spirituality

Christian Humanism

Christian humanism is an ideal which grew out of the Italian Renaissance in the late fourteenth century and spread throughout Europe in the two succeeding centuries. The revival of interest in the classical world of Greece and Rome gave rise to the educational ideal of *studia humanitatis* wherein the human person is the proper study of a Christian illuminated by achievements of the ancients. The use of classical studies began with Petrarch who saw Augustine not so much as a theologian but as a soul searching for God and who did so through the affective as well as intellectual dimension of life. Petrarch and his followers created a shift in emphasis away from the monastery to the court, away from the theologian to the poet and away from the medieval schoolman to the artist. In Christian humanism the human person is viewed as a co-creator who participates with God's creation in an active manner.

Petrarch made a leap of the imagination back over the 'Middle Ages' to return to the ideals of the classical world. This new use of history was to have a great influence on the later Reformers who attempted to do the same by appealing to the early Church. The rediscovery of Greek and Roman texts required new linguistic skills of the humanists, and this was another element inherited by the Reformers. Where the medieval schoolmen had been interested primarily in the philosophical thought of the ancient world, the Christian humanists were concerned with oratory, poetry, history and political thought. Cicero, as a rhetorician, had a special influence and the quality of written and spoken eloquence was characteristic of the Renaissance.

The movement of Greek manuscripts and scholars to the West after the fall of Constantinople in 1453 brought a renewed interest in Neoplatonic thought. This gave the humanists a new tool with which they could educate in the new learning not only the young, but adults such as merchants and lawyers. The latter organized academies and combined philosophical discussion with works of charity within the community.

Florence became the centre of Christian humanism when the leading merchant family, the Medicis, commissioned Marsilio Ficino (1433–99) to translate all of Plato's work into Latin. His translations and letters spread this new learning throughout the courts of Europe. He revived the ancient concept of the philosopher as 'the doctor of the soul' and offered counsel and guidance not only to those of the Medici circle but, through his eloquent letters, to men and women throughout the courts of Europe. For Ficino there was no conflict between humanism and Christianity. Indeed for him the former would serve as the vehicle for the regeneration of religion. Although artists were originally seen as only craftsmen, the philosophical and religious thought of the Christian humanists at the court of the Medicis was shared with young artists such as Michelangelo and Botticelli.

The humanists' idea that we share in the creative activity of God incorporated the artist, the sculptor and the poet into the movement of Renaissance Christian humanism. Humanists did not see themselves as imitating the achievements of the classical world so much as continuing them. They reached back over the middle centuries to 'converse' with their predecessors, much as Petrarch wrote to Cicero after discovering the latter's letters.

Ficino saw the two traditions of Hebrew revelation and the philosophical thought Plato inherited from his predecessors as coming together in Christ, the divine Logos. Thus, rather than there being a conflict between Christianity and humanism, they were allies.

The new learning of classical Greece and Rome had a great influence on John Collet, the early sixteenth-century Dean of St Paul's Cathedral in London. After studying in Florence and elsewhere on the continent, Colet founded St Paul's School with lay masters rather than clergy as teachers according to the new principles of Christian humanism wherein religion could be best taught by studying texts from the Greeks and Romans. This curriculum was to characterize secondary education in the 'public' (that is, independent) and grammar schools in England for the next three hundred years. The ancient languages were seen primarily as a literary study which best revealed the ethical truths of Christianity. Two of Colet's friends, Thomas More and John Fisher, brought the most eminent Christian humanist Desiderius Erasmus to England to be the first teacher of Greek in Cambridge. In the same year as Thomas More wrote *Utopia*, Erasmus produced an edition of the Greek New Testament. He was a translator, commentator, satirist and embodied the humanists' qualities of courtesy and deep Christian faith.

Perhaps the most eloquent statement of Christian Renaissance humanism was Baldassare Castiglione's sixteenth-century *The Book of the Courtier*. Castiglione embodied all the attributes of a Renaissance humanist. He was a soldier, writer, Latin and Greek scholar and friend of the painter Raphael. He observed that the ancients held art and artists in high esteem and this became a characteristic of Renaissance thought. It was, interestingly enough, two women who presided over the conversations recorded in his book. The final speech is given by Pietro Bembo, later a cardinal who speaks of the soul's journey to God as the fulfilment of the life of the Christian humanist.

The period of the Renaissance embodied the ideal of Christian humanism. Although it was not in opposition to the clerical or monastic worlds, it spoke of a new world of the court and urban life. Most of its participants were lay and the spirituality experienced in conversation and in the academies expressed itself in works of charity which assisted those in the community in greatest need. Perhaps the most significant element of Christian humanism was the aesthetic in which the creative capacities of the human being reflect those of the divine creator.

In succeeding centuries this ideal can be seen in the work of some writers, usually those concerned with the imaginative life. Thus in the last century personalities as distinct as Dorothy L. Sayers and T. S. Eliot were described as Christian humanists.

See also **Aesthetics; Art; Literature and Spirituality; Poetry and Poetics.**

Marsilio Ficino, *Letters*, 7 vols, London: Shepheard-Walwin, 2003; Marsilio Ficino, *Platonic Theology*, 4 vols, London: Harvard University Press, 2004; James Hankins, *Plato in the Italian Renaissance*, New York: E. J. Brill, 1999; Anthony Levi, *Renaissance and Reformation: The Intellectual Genesis*, New Haven: Yale University Press, 2004; Michael Shepherd, *Friend to Mankind*, London: Shepheard-Walwin, 1999.

PATRICK MOORE

Christian Life

see Discipleship

Cistercian Spirituality

The twelfth-century Cistercian version of Benedictine monasticism was a product both of the reformist movement associated with the papacy of Gregory VII (1073–85) and the cultural renaissance then occurring in Western Europe. The group of monasteries following the reform expanded rapidly due to effective economic management, extensive networking and, most of all, because of its self-projection through the accomplished literary expression of its spirituality under the influence of St Bernard of Clairvaux (1090–1153).

1. *Foundation values.* The monastery that came to be called Cîteaux, from which the name Cistercian derives, is situated 20 km south of Dijon, the capital of Burgundy. It was founded from Molesme, itself a reformed abbey, in 1098. The founders of the New Monastery were a group of about twenty monks under the leadership of Robert (1028–1111), Alberic (1050–1108) and Stephen (1059–1134) some of whom returned to Molesme with Robert in 1099. Together these three men revamped traditional monasticism with a view to ridding it of the accretions of earlier periods and making it suitable for their own time.

After some initial years of hardship, the New Monastery began to grow, making its first foundation in 1113, the same year that Bernard and a group of thirty companions entered the novitiate. Thereafter through natural increase, aggregation and incorporation the Cistercian enterprise expanded rapidly. By 1153 it numbered 352 abbeys. From 1125 the nuns' monastery of Tart was associated with Cîteaux and from 1147, provision was made for much closer links between the monasteries of nuns and those of the monks. The number of nuns continued to grow until the 1220s when restrictive measures were taken.

The primary constitutional texts that document the reform comprise the *Exordium Parvum* (an extended narrative preamble with archival material), the *Charter of Charity* (which defines relationships between monasteries and makes provision for visitation and general chapters) and the *Institutes* (a cumulative body of statutory law). Although the redactional history of these texts is complex and disputed, there is sufficient clarity to be able to establish the animating principles of the Cistercian movement.

Like most contemporary reform initiatives,

the Cistercians aimed primarily at a return to the integral observance of the Rule of St Benedict. In practice this involved a move away from population centres into newly settled areas and a simpler and more austere lifestyle with the emphasis on personal and communal poverty, symbolized by manual work. To achieve a high level of solitude, a greater distance was established between the monastery and 'the world': geographically, architecturally and by monastic discipline. Lay brothers (*conversi*) were introduced as the mainstay of the monastery's economy and, to some extent, to serve as the monastic interface with the outside. The total effect of the reforms was to focus attention on the internal life of the monastery, with its daily round of liturgy and monastic observances and, inevitably, on intracommunity relationships. This led to a growing emphasis on the contemplative character of Cistercian life. As early as 1132 in a bull of Innocent II the purpose of the exemptions being granted was stated thus. 'That you may more freely attend to the divine services and, with the power of your mind purified, you may more sincerely give yourselves to contemplation.' The three recognized priorities at that stage were liturgy, asceticism and contemplation. To these must be added a growing awareness of the importance of fraternal relations: the monastery was to be seen not only as a 'school of the Lord's service' but also as a *schola caritatis*, a school of love.

2. *The flowering of Cistercian spirituality*. The ideals of authentic observance, poverty, contemplation and community that were espoused by the early Cistercians did not differ substantively from those present in many other contemporary monastic movements. However, the intensely focused lifestyle and the high educational standards of many entrants led to the development of a comprehensive spiritual vision suitable for the times, first given expression by the abbatial ministry of teaching and later published in literary form. Cistercian spirituality has been called 'the school of self-knowledge' because, beyond the pragmatism of the Benedictine programme, it continued to emphasize interiority after the manner of Evagrius and John Cassian, but broadened this teaching by incorporating the theological and anthropological perspectives of Origen, Augustine and Gregory the Great and gave it relevance by incorporating the contemporary interest in the theme of love.

Following are the major authors of this first period of Cistercian history. Although each wrote with a distinctive style, the content and vocabulary of their teaching are similar. The most characteristic Cistercian genre was the free-wheeling sermon; but treatises, letters, commentaries, anecdotal literature, hagiography and many other kinds of writing are also in evidence. It is due to these later authors that the founding ideals found such ample expression and a wide following in the twelfth and thirteenth centuries: St Bernard of Clairvaux (1090–1153); William of Saint-Thierry (1075–1148); Blessed Guerric of Igny (1080–1157); St Aelred of Rievaulx (1109–67); Isaac of Stella (d. 1167); Gilbert of Swineshead (d. 1172); John of Forde (d. 1214); Beatrice of Nazareth (1200–68). To this list, however, scores of other writers from most European countries could be added. Not all the available material has been published and, apart from a few famous authors, not very much of the vast collection has been the subject of scholarly scrutiny.

3. *Later development*. The founding of the College of St Bernard in Paris in 1245 began a process by which the masculine branch of the order (at least) began to move away from its lifestyle-generated spirituality towards a more intellectual approach, somewhat open to Scholasticism. The period from the late thirteenth to the fifteenth century was, in addition, marked by newer options for religious life, changes in the cultural ambience, war, plague, litigation and a general decline in the life of the Church. As a result, numbers decreased and perhaps there was some diminishment in fervour. Cistercians (especially in the Germanic countries) continued to write during this period but for the most part their writings are little known and did not have a great influence on subsequent history.

The effects of the Reformation on Cistercian monasticism were severe and the controversies of subsequent centuries were not sympathetic to Cistercianism. In many European countries monasteries were suppressed or directed towards active apostolates and, as a result, monastic populations were dispersed, disheartened or lacking in focus.

A new reform was initiated by Armand-Jean de Rancé, Abbot of La Trappe in France (1626–1700) under the banner of 'Strict Observance'. De Rancé supplemented the administrative measures of his radical reform by extensive teaching, hoping to guide his monks back to the fervour of primitive Cîteaux and beyond. His severity suited the age; his books were widely read and he attracted many candidates.

4. *Modern period*. As with other monastic orders, the nineteenth century was one of geographical expansion for the Cistercians with foundations

in Algeria, Australia, China, North America, Palestine, South Africa and elsewhere. Within the Order polarization between 'strict observance' and 'common observance' led to legal separation in 1892. The Order of Cîteaux continued to be divided into more or less regional congregations, which offered the possibility of adaptation and pluriformity. The Strict Observance (or Trappists) insisted on a more uniform observance and a high level of austerity.

Both Orders continued to expand geographically in the twentieth century, especially in Africa, Asia and Latin America. Both Orders have made provision for the active involvement of Cistercian nuns in their own government and for general chapters involving both abbots and abbesses. All experienced numerical decline in years following Vatican II. The desire for greater contact between the Orders was evinced at the time of the ninth centenary of the foundation of Cîteaux and a synaxis involving all branches of the Cistercian family was held. This gathering included independent congregations of nuns not juridically part of either Order but sharing its spirituality: Bernardines and the Congregation of St Bernard of Las Huelgas. It remains to be seen what will be the long-term effects of this initiative. Many monasteries all over the world currently have programmes for the associates or lay Cistercians.

During the twentieth century many Cistercians, especially from the Strict Observance, have written books and articles on aspects of spirituality. The most famous of these was certainly Thomas Merton (1915–68). After a disturbed upbringing in France and England, Merton became a Catholic while studying at Columbia University. In 1941 he became a Trappist at Gethsemani abbey and was soon put to work on various projects that used his literary and linguistic skills. In 1947 he published his best-selling autobiography *The Seven Storey Mountain*, followed in 1953 by his monastic journal *The Sign of Jonas*. A stream of publications followed, even after he retired to a hermitage on the property in 1965. These, together with his collected letters and journals, not only evidence Merton's growing expertise in monastic questions and in spirituality, but also chronicled his expanding interest in social questions such as race relations and the peace movement, Latin America, indigenous cultures, environmental questions, calligraphy, photography, experimental poetry, Zen Buddhism and inter-religious dialogue. After completing *Contemplative Prayer*, he set off on a monastic pilgrimage to Asia (described in *The Asian Journal*). He died as a result of accidental electrocution during an inter-monastic congress at Bangkok. His books and studies of his works continue to be published 35 years afterwards.

See also **Benedictine Spirituality; Camaldolese Spirituality; Monasticism.**

————

Cistercian Publications located at Western Michigan University Kalamazoo, Michigan, has published approximately 250 volumes of texts and studies on Cistercian matters. See www.cistpub.wmich.edu; *Cistercian Studies Quarterly* published in the USA, is one of several international journals dedicated to publishing articles on Cistercian spirituality; *Exordium: A program of Reflection and Study on the Values of the Cistercian Reform* is available at www.ocso.org.

Bernard de Clairvaux: histoire, mentalité, spiritualité, Sources Chrétiennes 380, Paris: Cerf, 1992; *Spiritualité Cistercienne*, Bibliothèque de spiritualité 15; Paris: Beauchesne, 1998. This volume contains all the Cistercian articles previously published in the *Dictionnaire de Spiritualité*. For political reasons the general entry on Cistercian spirituality by Edmond Mikkers was located within the article 'Robert de Molesme' (pp. 432–546); Constance Hoffman Berman, *The Cistercian Evolution: The Invention of a Religious Order in Twelfth-Century Europe*, Philadelphia: University of Pennsylvania Press, 2000; Laurence S. Cunningham, *Thomas Merton and the Monastic Vision*, Grand Rapids, MI: Eerdmans, 1999; A. J. Krailsheimer, *Armand-Jean de Rancé: Abbot of La Trappe*, Oxford: Clarendon Press, 1974 ; Jean Leclercq, *Saint Bernard and the Cistercian Spirit*, Cistercian Studies Series 16, Kalamazoo, MI: Cistercian Publications, 1976 ; Louis Lekai, *The Cistercians: Ideals and Realities*, Kent, OH: Kent State University Press, 1977; André Louf, *The Cistercian Way*, Cistercian Studies Series 96, Kalamazoo, MI: Cistercian Publications, 1983; Pauline Matarasso, *The Cistercian World: Monastic Writings of the Twelfth Century*, Harmondsworth: Penguin, 1993; Martha G. Newman, *The Boundaries of Charity: Cistercian Culture and Ecclesiastical Reform, 1098–1180*, Stanford: Stanford University Press, 1996; Chrysogonus Waddell, *Narrative and Legislative Texts from Early Cîteaux*, Studia et Documenta IX, Cîteaux: Commentarii Cistercienses, 1999.

MICHAEL CASEY

Cities and Spirituality

More than 50 per cent of humanity now lives in big cities, cities of a size thousands of times larger than the small city of Jerusalem at the time of Christ. Modern post-colonial cities from Sao

Paulo to San Francisco, from London to Lagos and from Singapore to Sydney are multicultural and multilingual gatherings of peoples from many nations brought together by the twin forces of territorial colonization and economic globalization. The birth of the Church in Jerusalem was a multicultural event at which people from more than thirty nations, gathered in Jerusalem, heard the Disciples moved by the Holy Spirit at Pentecost address them in many tongues. From Jerusalem Christian worship and spirituality spread along the trade routes to cities and peoples throughout the Roman Empire beginning with the extraordinary missionary journeys and travails of St Paul and St Barnabas and their associates.

The association of early Christianity with such major imperial cities as Rome, Thessalonica, Ephesus and Corinth placed Christian spirituality in direct contest with the pagan and mystery cults of these places, and with the Roman imperial cult. The city therefore was a place of persecution as well as witness for the first Christian centuries. But after the conversion of the Emperor Constantine Christianity became the public cult of imperial Rome with dramatic consequences for Christian spirituality. Some clergy and lay people sought an escape from the corrupting influence of Rome on the Church and turned to the desert as the way to recover a holy life. The spirituality of the Desert Fathers gave rise to the monastic movement in which the desert itself became a city as solitary monks and holy men gathered together into communities of prayer and counsel, and these communities were often gathered together on the edge, the boundary between the city and the wilderness, a kind of mediating place between the noise and bustle of the city and the quiet contemplative spaces of the desert.

Through the Middle Ages monastic spirituality exercised an enormous influence over the shape and development of Christian cities as communities of monastics gathered in cities, and the monasteries gave spiritual shape to the medieval cities of Europe. Many cathedrals were homes to religious communities and the shape and pattern of daily prayer and the liturgical year reflected the monastic rule. Medieval cities were thus shaped by Christian spirituality both spatially and temporally.

The modern industrial and global city is shaped more by economic exigencies than spiritual community, and urban churches struggle with a deep spiritual alienation from Christian worship. Production, consumption and entertainment run on a 24-hour seven-day-a-week clock and the urban masses are in thrall to the fetishism of commodities which displaces the spiritual quest with the false gods of fashion and technology.

Christian spirituality in the postmodern city takes on a range of forms in response to the new urban reality. Some churches seek to reconnect with mass urban culture through a new aesthetic of worship which embraces modern urban styles from hip hop music through multi-media presentations and art installations. This reconnection often engages also with older more traditional symbolic forms such as the labyrinth, icons, plainsong chants and dramatic performances of biblical stories. The most popular form of Christian spirituality in the world-class cities of the last hundred years has been Pentecostalism, which spread from a church in Azusa Street, Los Angeles to become a truly global urban mass movement infecting churches of every kind from Roman Catholic to African Independent. The emphasis on the work of the Holy Spirit in the life of the individual, and its expression in energetic and participative public worship, embraces key features of global urban culture including both individual autonomy and mass participation in popular culture.

Pentecostalism has particular appeal as the spirituality of the poor and marginalized in the postmodern city. Many black-led churches in Britain have adopted this spiritual style as black immigrants found their 'mother' church of the Empire rejected them on arrival in Britain. Industrial workers in the nineteenth century experienced a similar alienation from Christianity in the city and the resultant chasm between working-class culture and urban Christianity produced a whole raft of initiatives through the twentieth century to try to bridge the gap. The worker-priest movement and industrial mission involved attempts in mid century to refound Christian spirituality in the factory setting and the artisan housing estate. Clergy and lay workers in urban priority areas speak of a sense of spiritual reality which is sharper than it is in the suburban church. They indicate by this that people whose lives are shaped by living on the edge – both economically and geographically – are closer to the heart of God, less protected by material goods, more vulnerable, more dependent on one another, and hence more open to spiritual reality, demonic and divine. The poor as the liberation theologian Gustavo Gutiérrez indicates 'drink from their own wells' of spirituality and community.

Ignatian spirituality is another growing spiritual form in the city. Living in the postmodern city shapes modern sense perception in a distinctive way, providing endless forms of electronic entertainment and auditory and visual distraction while at the same time cutting city-dwellers off from the naturally based rhythm of the seasons and of the natural world. Ignatian spirituality as it has been adapted for lay people and retreatants in recent decades re-engages the senses and the emotions in the quest for holiness and contemplation. It provides to the postmodern seeker a new imaginary in which it becomes possible to follow the way of the desert in the global city.

Raymond Bakke, *The Urban Christian,* Bromley: MARC, 1987; Derwas J. Chitty, *The Desert a City: An Introduction to the Study of Egyptian and Palestinian Monasticism under the Christian Empire,* Crestwood, NY: St Vladimir's Seminary Press, 1999; Gustavo Gutiérrez, *We Drink From Our Own Wells: The Spiritual Journey of a People,* Maryknoll, NY: Orbis Books, 1990; Michael Northcott, 'Worship in the city' in Michael Northcott (ed.), *Urban Theology: A Reader,* London: Cassell, 1998, pp. 221–6; John and Angela Pearce, *Inner City Spirituality,* Nottingham: Grove Booklets, 1987.

MICHAEL S. NORTHCOTT

Clothing

We are born naked. Almost immediately we are clothed and named. Our identity and gender is further established by the choice of the colour we are given to wear: for example, pink for a girl, blue for a boy. We become a fully fledged member of the family into which we are born and part of its history. Clothes pay a vital part in our lives; they are, you could say, a second skin and foundational to our spirituality and identity. Our first skin, naked and bare, would probably survive without clothes in a temperate climate and a heated home. Nakedness is vulnerable. Perhaps the mystery that clothes afford our nakedness will provide not only protection but also invisibility. Clothes have as many 'skins' as we have personae. Our personae – our many different faces – that make us who we are, require just as many different sorts of clothes to wear. Underclothes, leisure clothes, sports clothes, summer clothes, winter clothes and business clothes all shape our identity and hold our personal thumbprint.

Clothes and identity. 'When we encounter a stranger as initially mysterious and inaccessible, we refer to clothing styles and physical appearance, in the absence of any other means, as a reliable sign of identity. Clothing is frequently seen as symbolic of the individual's status and moral-

ity, whether actual or contrived' (Finkelstein, 1991, p. 128).

Clothes are about bodies and dressed bodies are inseparable from the self. The social world is clothed rather than unclothed. Nakedness is private, personal and often hidden even from the eyes of the person to whom the body belongs. Clothes are basic to our needs and, indeed, are a fact of social life. The whole process of clothing ourselves is learnt and practised from our earliest childhood; it is ritualistic in nature and individualistic in its approach. Wearing the correct and appropriate clothes makes us feel at ease within the society to which we belong, while inappropriate dress can leave us uncomfortable and vulnerable. There can be a tension between who we are and how we display ourselves – an indicator perhaps of being in the right or wrong place, the right or wrong society or the place where I desire to belong. Furthermore it is through the expression of the clothes we wear that we are identified, approved of and often judged, and by which our identity is firmly stamped.

The relationship that we establish with our way or code of dress, signals to others the culture of which we are a part or to which we aspire – its class or style and even our moral or political persuasion (e.g. controversies over Muslim women wearing the 'headscarf' and Punjabi women wearing 'trousers'). However, because clothes 'do not speak', misinterpretation, criticism and judgement can follow in the bid to discover the wearer's authenticity and genuineness. Categorization of the 'outsider' by their 'strange' dress or adornment (e.g. the 'punk') can threaten and be threatening and create an alienation that marginalizes. In fact 'appearance can be deceptive' and the *real* person behind the impression of their clothing may not be easily found.

Clothes and gender. Clothes are a construct of society, its philosophy towards the body and the morality on which it imposes its constraints and rules. Nowhere can this be better seen than in the effects that gender has on clothing. Masculinity and femininity are immediately determined and obviously seen in the sexed-clothed body. Classically the female stereotype accentuates the waist and bosom to display her body shape, its *décolletage* and female form; while the male stereotype displays his form by sporting broad-shouldered jackets and tightly crotched jeans. It is only since the early 1960s in Western society that trousers have been an accepted form of female clothing. Clothes silently speak of gender and the identity that the individual needs to portray. These conventional boundaries are transgressed by some people who find their personhood through cross-dressing.

In association with gender, yet separate from it, clothes play an important part in conveying our sexual being. Our sexuality and sexed-self is played out either consciously or unconsciously in the specific ways we select our clothing to attract another. In this respect clothing and correct body language must be in harmony for the desired effect to be achieved. In contemporary culture clothing and its healthy sexual expression is played out in an ever-changing confrontation between sexual display and modesty. Conversely clothes can play an unhealthy part in forms of sexual deviation and fetishism.

Clothes and Christian virtue.

Seek by every means to check the luxury of dress which is excessive and hateful to God . . . These garments, betraying a nakedness of soul, display in themselves signs of arrogance and pride and wantonness and vanity . . . [these clothes can lead] to lust, unholy intercourse, indifference to reading and prayer and the ruin of souls. (Letter from St Boniface to Cuthbert, Archbishop of Canterbury, 747)

Christianity, on the whole, has not favoured clothes and clothing, dress and dressing. The Christian world has tended to regard delight and pleasure in personal appearance, through any form of adornment, as vain and even sinful. Asceticism, even to wearing clothing that might harm and chastise the body (e.g. a hair shirt), was held as virtuous until recent times. On the one hand, the naked body was deemed as shameful and, on the other hand, the clothed body, particularly the female clothed body, was seen as a distraction to modesty, humility and chastity – at least a possible vehicle towards waywardness and at worst towards prostitution.

Christianity derives from a humble foundation. The message of the gospel narratives is radical and compels towards an option for the poor and the marginalized. Jesus was humble; he was born and 'wrapped in swaddling cloths' (Luke 2.7, KJB); after he was crucified his tunic 'seamless, woven in one piece from the top' (John 19.23, NRSV) was divided into four pieces. Clothes are, within the scriptural narratives, predominantly used symbolically to show dependency on God alone (e.g. Matt. 6.25, 29; 10.10) or as a contrast of radical opposites as in the demonstration of wealth versus poverty (e.g. Luke 16.19; James 2.2–4). Clothes are not treated pejoratively for their own sake but solely for the sake of excessiveness and surfeit. Dress should reveal a humble state of mind: 'And all of you must clothe yourselves with humility in your

dealings with one another'(1 Peter 5.5). Furthermore dress is equated with simplicity. For example, adornment and preoccupation with the body might distract from devotion to the poor: 'women should dress themselves modestly and decently in suitable clothing, not with their hair braided, or with gold, pearls, or expensive clothes, but with good works. As is proper for women who profess reverence for God' (1 Tim. 2.9–10).

Clothes and ritual. Ecclesiastical clothing, such as vestments, does not have the intention of adorning the celebrant but are specifically worn as a spiritual act in the commemoration of the Last Supper. Interestingly the early Church advised priests to wear their ordinary clothes to identify with the people they served, but gradually distinct types of clerical clothing began to be worn. These have prevailed over centuries with little change but many adaptations. Liturgical finery with its symbolism in colours and applied decoration has, as with fashion, been dependent on the taste of the period and its culture to portray either greater or lesser wealth – or a more ornate or simple style of liturgical practice.

The clothing of the monk is an occasion of profound importance and spiritual significance. The former life of the candidate and the packing away of his secular clothes are movingly given over to a new birth, an acceptance by the community and the taking of a new name – a new personal and spiritual identity. The whole role of the habit of religious, both male and female, brings about a corporate and distinguishable identification marker, which symbolize both simplicity and modesty but are specific to the ethos of the order, its rule and its way of life. After the Reformation, both the symbolism of simplicity and of separation from the material world extends more broadly into the lives and clothing of Christian groups such as the Puritans, the early Quakers and the Amish.

Clothing and its consequences. In Western contemporary society, the fashion industry has become an over-influential and exploitative force – a negative identity marker. Dingy sweatshops and appalling working conditions have provided poverty-stricken countries with cheap labour to satisfy the demands of an ever-growing consumerist society. There is an increasing obsession with the *new* in all aspects of life. Possessions are not valued highly and become easily disposable. Boredom and possible addiction follow. To numbers of people, logos and designer labels give the impression of wealth and celebrity, while in reality they result in loss of true identity. To be ethical in matters of clothing is difficult. To discover the sordid source of the clothing we wear is even more difficult. There is no easy solution.

Nevertheless, from medieval weaving, intricate embroidery and lace-making to the haute couture and catwalks of New York, Paris and London, the manufacture and design of beautiful and sometimes experimental clothes and textiles are an important part of material culture and creative artistry. Clothing is, at best, an art form. Not only does it provide information about patterns of life and living but clothing also plays an important role in anthropology and sociology and the understanding of human identity. Clothing has been a major industry and provider of skilled work for millions of people both before and after the Industrial Revolutions for which it was largely responsible.

Clothes are integral to our identity and our identity is integral to our spirituality. Clothes must not be reduced to a mere extravagance or to some sort of unnecessary frivolity. To be religious and to be spiritual does not necessitate disinterest in appearance, or denegation of the human form, or even a false humility. As Christians, if we are to take seriously the theology of the body and embodiment, then we will make sure that we pay attention to our clothes and to the way we dress. As both consumers and Christians we will take care to choose and buy clothes that are manufactured ethically and be aware of the politics that surround their industry.

See also **Body and Spirituality; Consumerism; Sexuality.**

Christopher Breward, *The Culture of Fashion*, Manchester and New York: Manchester University Press, 1995; Joanne Entwistle, *The Fashioned Body: Fashion Dress and Modern Social Theory*, Cambridge: Polity Press, 2000; J Finkelstein, *The Fashioned Self*, Cambridge: Polity Press, 1991; David R. Holeton, 'Vestments' in Paul Bradshaw (ed.), *The New SCM Dictionary of Liturgy and Worship*, London: SCM Press, 2002; Françoise Piponnier and Perrine Mane, *Dress in the Middle Ages*, New Haven: Yale University Press, 1997; Aileen Ribeiro, *Dress and Morality*, Oxford: Berg, 2003; Naomi Tarrant, *The Development of Costume*, London: Routledge, 1994.

SUSIE HAYWARD

Combat, Spiritual

The use of military metaphor to depict the inward struggle against sin and vice long predates Christianity; but its frequent use in the New Testament epistles, especially by St Paul

(Rom. 7.23; 2 Cor. 10.3–6; 1 Tim. 1.18), made the theme of spiritual warfare a Christian commonplace. It has been employed by spiritual writers in every epoch of Christian history as a means of portraying the arduous, heroic nature of the quest to avoid sin and attain holiness.

Three caveats should be observed in regard to this theme. First, it is essential to clearly define both the opposing 'enemy' and the 'battleground' on which spiritual combat is waged. St Paul explicitly states that our fight (*agon*) is not against human beings or temporal governments: our battle is joined against 'spiritual wickedness in heavenly places' (Eph. 6.12). The demonic powers that tempt to sin constitute the enemy; the battleground is the heart or 'innermost self' of the Christian. Any other use of the notion of spiritual warfare by Christians, as for example in attempting to rationalize the use of physical violence in the cause of religion, is a perversion of this concept. Second, there is a regrettable tendency in some modern authors to describe extraordinary and bizarre manifestations as 'spiritual warfare'. Above all this term describes the ordinary, daily, and often quite banal, experience of struggle against sin. The notion of 'spiritual combat' is not chiefly concerned with phenomena that require the attention of an exorcist. Third, the language of spiritual warfare inevitably suggests at least a hint of Pelagianism; so it is important always to begin with the Christian's absolute dependence on the grace of God. Even though the battleground is the individual Christian heart, the Christian who avoids sin and grows in holiness is not the true victor: that title and dignity belong to Christ alone, as the Book of Revelation makes clear (5.12–13; chs 20—21). The Christian never fights alone, and victory is always the gift of God.

During the first three Christian centuries a vivid and public symbol of spiritual warfare was found in the martyrs' struggle. Although instigated and conducted by civil authorities who tried to compel apostasy, martyrdom was regarded within the Church as the external manifestation of an invisible and deeper spiritual combat. In *The Martyrdom of Saints Perpetua and Felicity* the young matron and catechumen Perpetua vividly depicts this conviction by recounting a dream in which she envisions her imminent death and that of her companions in the arena as a gladiatorial combat against the devil. The civil authorities were not thus the real enemy: they were the dupes and agents of the true unseen adversary.

In the developing Christian ascetical tradition, Perpetua's understanding of spiritual combat was applied to the interior 'arena' of the heart.

The most eloquent exponent of this tradition is the desert hermit Evagrius Ponticus (d. 399). In his *Praktikos*, Evagrius explains that victory in the daily battle for virtue begins with faith in and wholehearted reliance on Jesus Christ, who alone is able to communicate in prayer the deeper meaning of the daily struggle. With the help of Christ the Christian ascetic learns to recognize the tactics of the demonic enemy. Ever attentive to his own unique constellation of weaknesses and strengths, the ascetic, or *praktikos*, learns the identity, the order and the frequency of the most common demonic assaults: gluttony, lust, avarice, dejection, wrath, acedia, vainglory and pride. He also learns how to appropriately employ in each of these assaults fitting spiritual remedies, such as fasting, keeping vigil, psalmody, prayer and charitable deeds. Particularly important for Evagrius is the memorization and use of suitable biblical verses in verbal 'contradiction' (*antirrhesis*) of the offending tempting thought (*logismos*).

Along with other Desert Fathers Evagrius emphasizes the critical importance of directing the powerful but dangerous energy of anger (*thumos*) solely against the demonic sources of temptation, and never against an offending brother or sister. Tricking the Christian into wrongly identifying another human being (rather than the demon) as the enemy is a common demonic ruse. Evagrius' disciple John Cassian particularly emphasized that treasured friendships can easily become unintended casualties of spiritual warfare whenever the perilous weapon of anger is deployed (*Conference* 16).

The goal of spiritual warfare and of all Christian asceticism is the attainment of both charity and that state of inner freedom from compulsion called *apatheia* or 'purity of heart' that is the necessary precondition for spiritual vision, contemplation. Texts on the art of spiritual warfare have taken the form of handbooks on Christian asceticism. Among the most influential of these are: the ascetical treatises of Evagrius Ponticus (partly preserved in the Orthodox *Philokalia*), the *Institutes* and *Conferences* of Cassian *The Spiritual Ladder* of John Climacus; the *Spiritual Exercises* of Ignatius Loyola and the *Spiritual Combat* attributed to Scupoli.

See also **Asceticism.**

C. Luibheid (trans.), *John Climacus: The Ladder of Divine Ascent,* New York: Paulist Press, 1982; B. Ramsey (trans.), *John Cassian: The Institutes and The Conferences*, New York: Paulist Press, 1997; Scupoli, *The Spiritual Combat*, numerous editions, various publishers; R. E. Sinkewicz

(trans.), 'On the Eight Thoughts', 'The Monk', 'Chapters on Prayer', *Evagrius of Pontus: The Greek Ascetic Corpus,* Oxford: Oxford University Press, 2004.

LUKE DYSINGER

Commitment

see **Discipleship**

Common Life, Brothers and Sisters of

see **Devotio Moderna**

Communion/*Koinonia*

In the last fifty years biblical studies, ecumenical studies, ecclesiology, theological anthropology, trinitarian theology and Christian spirituality have all benefited from renewed reflection on an ancient Christian concept, communion/ *koinonia.*

1. *Biblical background.* There is no corresponding Hebrew term for the Greek word *koinonia* and it only rarely appears in early Greek translations of the Old Testament. The Greek concept does not appear to have been used by Jesus himself and first makes its appearance in the New Testament in Paul's first letter to the Corinthians. The term was translated into Latin as *communio* and is frequently translated into English as 'communion', 'fellowship', 'participation in' or 'sharing in'. If one includes all related forms of the noun *koinonia,* it appears in the New Testament 36 times, most frequently in the Pauline corpus. Etymologically, its meaning is grounded in the Greek root *koinon,* meaning 'common'.

Koinonia has a rich semantic field of meaning in Paul's writing. In 1 Cor. 1.9 Paul expresses gratitude for the Corinthians having been called by God into 'fellowship' (*koinonia*) with Christ. A parallel usage is found in Paul's benediction to the Corinthians at the conclusion of the second epistle: 'The grace of the Lord Jesus Christ and the love of God and the fellowship (*koinonia*) of the holy Spirit be with all of you' (2 Cor. 13.13 NAB). Although 1 Cor. 1.9 refers to fellowship with Christ, Phil. 2.1 refers to a *koinonia* in the Spirit. Both passages, however, articulate an enduring relationship with God effected in baptism. Also, 2 Cor. 13.13 may bear a more ecclesial sense in which *koinonia* is a gift *from* the Spirit, suggesting that it is the Spirit who brings about a shared relationship among believers. That Paul's understanding would seem to incorporate both a vertical element of *koinonia* (e.g. fellowship with

Christ or the Spirit) and a horizontal one (e.g. fellowship among believers) is evident in 1 Cor. 10.16–17. 'The cup of blessing that we bless, is it not a participation in the blood of Christ? The bread that we break, is it not a participation in the body of Christ? Because the loaf of bread is one, we, though many, are one body, for we all partake of the one loaf' (New American Bible). This passage appears in the context of Paul's treatment of the vexing Corinthian dilemma regarding the suitability of eating food sacrificed to idols. Paul wants to stress that the *koinonia* in Christ manifested in the Eucharist also creates unity among believers. This unity of believers must be considered when such questions are addressed. According to Paul, communion/*koinonia* is first effected in baptism and then further manifested in the Eucharist. This sacramental *koinonia*, in turn, places ethical expectations on members of the Christian community; the freedom proper to believers as followers of Jesus is conditioned by the obligations imposed upon them by their shared *koinonia*.

The dual dimensions of Paul's usage of *koinonia* – fellowship with God in Christ and the Spirit and fellowship with other believers – is articulated even more explicitly in the Johannine literature:

> for the life was made visible; we have seen it and testify to it and proclaim to you the eternal life that was with the Father and was made visible to us – what we have seen and heard we proclaim now to you, so that you too may have fellowship with us; for our fellowship is with the Father and with his Son, Jesus Christ. (1 John 1.2–3)

This passage highlights the simultaneity of the shared life among believers and their shared life with God, that is to say, 'with the Father and with his Son'. The author's intention apparently was to forestall any idea that fellowship with God provided a freedom to do as one wishes in the sphere of human relationships. The author of 1 John insists that true fellowship with God bears within it an ethical and even ontological imperative; one cannot separate fellowship with God from fellowship with fellow believers. The communal dimension of the Christian experience of *koinonia* is further reflected in Acts 2.42 in which the *koinonia* among the disciples is evident in their sharing all things in common.

When one considers both the Pauline and Johannine references above, what is striking is the connection between the spiritual life of the Christian and an incipient trinitarian theology. These passages relate the believer to a *koinonia*

'in Christ' (1 Cor. 1.9), 'of the holy Spirit' (2 Cor. 13.13) and 'with the Father' (1 John 1.3). Yet nowhere is the term *koinonia* used to describe the relationships *among* the trinitarian persons, a strictly post-biblical development. Likewise, while the biblical usage of the term *koinonia* includes an ecclesial dimension, only in the post-biblical period will *koinonia* actually be equated with the Church or used to describe the communion that exists among various local churches.

2. *Contemporary developments.* Modern theology and spirituality have taken a renewed interest in the concept of *koinonia*, often treated under its most common Latin translation, *communio*. It has been particularly influential in ecclesiology and ecumenism. In ecclesiology, the early Christian use of *koinonia* as a way of describing the bond of unity among the various local churches within the whole body of Christ is seen as a helpful corrective to a universalist ecclesiology that subsumes local churches into the universal Church (e.g. the ecclesiology of baroque Catholicism) and a congregationalism that reduces the universal Church to a confederation of autonomous local churches (the church polity of many evangelical Bible churches). It has also been influential in the development of eucharistic ecclesiologies that would see the Eucharist as the most profound sacramental expression of what it is to be church. In ecumenism, *koinonia* often refers to the spiritual unity that already exists, albeit imperfectly, among various Christian churches but which still demands a more visible expression.

Another fruitful line of development explores the conviction of early Christian writers that *koinonia*/communion describes not only the believer's relationship with the triune God but also the perichoretic relationship of the trinitarian persons. God is not a self-contained divine monad; God's action in the economy of salvation reveals a God who does not just *enter into* relationships of one kind or another, but rather, a God who is, in the divine being, perfect relationship. In trinitarian reflection, divine persons are understood, not as autonomous individual entities, but as differentiated relations. God's reality is most adequately affirmed, not as perfect self-sufficiency, but as perfect relatedness. God is *koinonia* in God's very being. From this perspective Jesus Christ is, for humankind, the prime analogate for an understanding of divine personhood, and as the incarnation of the second person of the Trinity, he is also the key to understanding the nature, demands and possibilities of authentic human personhood. The implications of these assertions are immense.

Much of Western philosophy, ancient and modern, has been based on a 'substance ontology', that is, an ontology that analyses being as encountered in individual substances. However, if the source of all being, God, is not an individual anything but perfect relationality, and if, according to the doctrine of *creatio ex nihilo*, all that is proceeds from the creative act of God, then a substance ontology must give way to a 'relational ontology'. 'Personhood', an inherently relational category, supplants 'substance' as the starting point for modern metaphysics. This line of development places the concept of *koinonia*/communion, grounded in the triune being of God and manifested in the life and teaching of Jesus, at the forefront of contemporary theology and spirituality. If authentic existence is now understood not in terms of self-sufficiency, but in being-for-others, then spirituality can no longer be conceived as the exploration of one's private relationship with God. Humans are made for communion. One's spirituality is realized in one's relationship to God, other persons and the cosmos itself. As the biblical witness consistently affirmed, being with God and being with others are intimately related. Consequently we find much contemporary writing that attends to a spirituality of communion in which communion with God is encountered in one's experience of communion with the other.

This spirituality has appealed to Christian feminists concerned with the damaging effects of patriarchy on the flourishing of women and the welfare of humankind. Some feminist thinkers have claimed that the roots of patriarchy lie in a substance ontology's tendency to engender relations of competitiveness and a view of power as domination. In contrast, the call to communion encourages a vision of human flourishing that is grounded not in competition and domination but in mutuality and co-operation. Likewise, spiritualities of communion have found a sympathetic hearing among those with deep ecological concerns who see in the notion of communion an openness to cosmic relatedness that would challenge the dominant anthropocentric view of creation.

See also Ecclesiology and Spirituality.

_____

Thomas F. Best and Günther Gassmann (eds), *On the Way to Fuller Koinonia*, Faith and Order Paper 166, Geneva: WCC Publications, 1994; Michael Downey, *Altogether Gift: A Trinitarian Spirituality,* Maryknoll, NY: Orbis Books, 2000; Catherine Mowry LaCugna, *God for Us: The Trinity and Christian Life,* New York: HarperCollins, 1991; J.-M. R. Tillard, *Church of Churches: The Ecclesiology of Communion,* Wilmington: Glazier, 1992; John D. Zizioulas, *Being as Communion,* Crestwood, NY: St Vladimir's Seminary Press, 1985.

RICHARD GAILLARDETZ

Community

Every human community is constituted by persons united by bonds of communion and mutual love. Just as Christians confess God as a Trinity of persons in communion, so too the kingdom of God preached by Jesus envisions the reconciliation and communion of all people in the Spirit. Thus community is intrinsic to the meaning of Church.

The Church (*ekklesia*, 'those called out') is the community of the disciples of Jesus, 'a people made one with the unity of the Father, the Son, and the Holy Spirit' (*Lumen Gentium* 4; Cyprian, *On the Lord's Prayer* 23). The roots of ecclesial community lie in God's covenant people Israel, and in the renewed Israel gathered by Jesus in his movement, with 'the Twelve' (Mark 3.13–19) representing the twelve tribes at its centre. The author of Acts describes the apostolic church of Jerusalem as a community devoted 'to the teaching of the apostles and to the communal life (*koinonia*), to the breaking of the bread and to the prayers'. This idealized vision of early Christian life involved prayer and worship, shared goods and mutual assistance (see Acts 2.42–47). Other New Testament expressions of the communal nature of the Church include Paul's letters in which he describes the Church as the one body of Christ, united by baptism and Eucharist and equipped with a diversity of gifts and ministries manifesting the inner life of the Spirit (1 Cor. 10—12); the Petrine tradition reflected in 1 Peter which sees the Church as a holy people of God; and the Johannine epistles which understand the Church as a community guided by the Spirit. The communal nature of Christian life has been manifested in a diversity of ways in the history of the Church.

1. *Monastic communities.* After Constantine's Edict of 313 and the establishment of the Church, bishops became public officials as well as church leaders. As the communitarian dimension of the Church began to be overshadowed by its structural and institutional elements, many lay men and women withdrew to the deserts of Egypt, Syria and Palestine to live an ascetical life as hermits or 'monks' (*monos*, 'alone'). Athanasius' *Life of Antony* (356) idealized their way of life and drew many to join their colonies, called *lavras*. Pachomius (*c.* 292–346), a monk

who had served in the Roman army, is considered the first to begin organizing these colonies into communities. The monks lived together in common houses or buildings grouped around a church. Each monk had a cell, but they would come together for meals and a common order of prayer, manual labour, and later study, all under the direction of a leader or superior (*abba*, 'father'), to whom the monks pledged obedience, in addition to the poverty and chastity they already observed. Pachomius left writings that would later be published as a text of Rules for these 'coenobitic' (*koinos bios*, 'common life') communities. But it was the Rules of Basil of Caesarea (*c.* 330–79) that was to give lasting guidance to the monastic movement in the East, tempering its often unruly individualism and securing it in the Church. Monasticism also flourished in the West, building on an earlier ascetical movement. Monastic communities developed in North Africa, France and Ireland and were spread by Irish monks to Britain, Gaul, Germany and Switzerland. From these communities would develop a rich flowering of religious congregations and 'orders' that would offer a specifically communal expression of the Christian life.

Benedict of Nursia (*c.* 480–547) is considered the father of Western monasticism. His Rule is both moderate and practical; it describes a community life revolving around the *opus Dei* (work of God), gathering eight times each day to pray the monastic office, *lectio divina*, a meditative reading of Scripture and other spiritual works, and *labora*, the manual labour by which the monks supported themselves. Benedictine monasticism spread throughout Europe, largely as a result of the reform of Cluny (910). And other communities or orders have followed Benedict's Rule down to the present day, including the Camaldolese hermits founded by Romuald of Ravenna (*c.* 950–1027), the Carthusians of St Bruno (1032–1101) and the Cistercians founded by Robert of Molesme and companions in 1098.

2. *Apostolic communities.* New communities emerged in the Europe of the twelfth and thirteenth centuries, influenced by an evangelical movement known as the *vita apostolica* or 'apostolic life'. Like the monastic movement, the *vita apostolica* was essentially a lay movement that stressed evangelization and radical poverty, as did the communities that it inspired. The Humiliati, the Waldensians and the Poor Catholics were mixed communities of men and women. The Beguines were women who lived together and practised a type of voluntary poverty; they have been described as the first identifiable women's movement in Christian history. Francis of Assisi's (1182–1226) community of 'lesser brothers' began as a lay movement but later underwent a clericalization because of its preaching mission. Similarly, Clare of Assisi's (*c.* 1193–1253) sisters had hoped to live an apostolic life like their Franciscan brothers, but were required by the Church to become a cloistered religious community. The Dominicans, an order of priests and brothers founded by Dominic de Guzman (1172–1221), were religious from the beginning.

The medieval confraternities provided another type of community for lay people. These voluntary associations, dedicated to a more intense devotional life and works of charity, gathered men and sometimes women together by class and trade. Confraternity members gathered for occasional banquets or communal meals; they participated in special Masses and processions and accompanied their dying members in their final hours, praying for them and escorting them to their place of burial. Thus they fostered a spirit of fraternity and mutual support. They also took on various ministries directed towards the poor, providing help for the most vulnerable members of society. By the fifteenth century there were fraternities throughout Italy, France, Spain and Germany.

3. *Post-Reformation communities.* The Reformation's rejection of monasticism meant that community life virtually disappeared in those parts of Europe that became Protestant. But the Reformation's radical 'left wing' proved the exception; from it came new communities in the Anabaptist tradition, among them the Swiss Brethren, Moravians, Hutterites and Mennonites. These Christians understood their communities as alternative societies based on a radical gospel discipleship. Some, refusing to bear arms, were later known as peace Churches. Others, like the Hutterites, practised a community of goods. While many of these communities did not survive the sixteenth century, they witnessed to a radical discipleship that was not to reappear in Catholicism until the twentieth century. Their tradition lives on in the Quakers, Moravian Brethren and Mennonites.

The sixteenth century also saw the founding of new religious communities, nourished in part by the spirit of reform awakened in the Catholic Church. Teresa of Avila initiated a reform of the Carmelites in Spain. Another reform movement within the Franciscans led to a new order, the Capuchins (1526). Others included apostolic clerical communities, prominent among them the Theatines (1524), Barnabites (1533) and

Jesuits (1540). Numerous apostolic communities of men and women were founded in succeeding centuries. In France alone, more than four hundred congregations of apostolic women religious were established between 1800 and 1880.

4. *The contemporary Church*. The twentieth century saw the foundation of numerous new communities, both religious and lay. A liturgical renewal within the Reformed Churches of Switzerland led to a rediscovery of the monastic life by a community of Protestant women at Grandchamp near Neuchâtel (1936). Other examples of Protestant communities in the monastic tradition include Pomeyrol and the Marienschwestern of Darmstadt. Taizé, a monastic community founded by Roger Schutz in France (1944), began within the Protestant tradition but is now ecumenical, with both Catholic and Protestant members. The Little Sisters and Little Brothers of Jesus, inspired by Charles de Foucauld (1858–1916), seek to live among the poor, as do the Missionaries of Charity, founded by Mother Teresa (1910–97)

The twentieth century also saw the establishment of a number of lay communities. The Catholic Worker movement, founded by Dorothy Day and Peter Maurin (1933), marked the emergence of a radical Catholicism in the United States. There are now more than 185 Catholic Worker communities worldwide, many of them serving the poor and homeless in the inner cities of the United States. Iona, an ecumenical community established on the site of a former Benedictine monastery in Scotland (1938) by George MacLeod, has served as a creative force for the renewal of the Church in Scotland. Jean Vanier's L'Arche communities, in which mentally handicapped people live together with other men and women 'assistants', now number over 120 communities in 30 different countries. The Focolare Movement, founded by Chiara Lubich (1943), brings together Christians, people of other faiths, as well as those with no religious convictions in a movement seeking greater solidarity and communion among peoples. Today over 2 million people are involved on a regular basis. At its heart are small communities of lay people, both single and married, who work outside the community but share a life together.

One of the most significant developments in the late twentieth century has been the development of small faith communities. There are numerous expressions of this impulse that brings Christians together weekly in small groups for reflection on Scripture, shared prayer, community and ministry, often directed towards the poor. In the years after the Second Vatican Council, the *comunidades de base* or basic Christian communities of Latin America played a key role in the renewal and re-evangelization of the Latin American Church. It is estimated that there are between 180,000 and 200,000 such communities in Latin America. Other communities have multiplied around the world, giving Christians the opportunity to share their faith in small groups. They include communities growing out of renewal movements such as the charismatic renewal and the RENEW programme, the Jesuit sponsored Christian Life Community, base communities or house churches in third world countries, and faith-sharing communities established in parishes throughout the world.

Thus the Christian tradition has fostered diverse expressions of community life beyond that of the local parish or church throughout its history. In religious orders and congregations, men and women have committed themselves by vows to a shared life of prayer, worship, and ministry. Other communities have brought together men and women to serve the disadvantaged and witness to justice. Many seek to live a simple life in solidarity with the poor. The contemporary Church has also seen an explosion of small faith-sharing communities in countries throughout the world. In an increasingly divided world, they foreshadow the reconciliation and communion of peoples in the fullness of the kingdom.

See also Ecclesiology and Spirituality; Lay People and Spirituality; Liberation Spirituality; Religious Life.

Marcello de Carvalho Azevedo, *Basic Ecclesial Communities in Brazil: The Challenge of a New Way of Being Church*, Washington, DC: Georgetown University Press, 1987; Marie-Dominique Chenu, *Nature, Man and Society in the Twelfth Century*, Chicago and London: University of Chicago Press, 1968; Maureen Flynn, *Sacred Charity: Confraternities and Social Welfare in Spain, 1400–1700*, Ithaca, NY: Cornell University Press, 1989; C. H. Lawrence, *Medieval Monasticism: Forms of Religious Life in Western Europe in the Middle Ages*, London: Longman, 1984; Bernard J. Lee, *The Catholic Experience of Small Christian Communities*, New York: Paulist Press, 2000; Thomas P. Rausch, *Radical Christian Communities*, Collegeville, MN: The Liturgical Press, 1990.

THOMAS P. RAUSCH

Compassion

'Compassion' is a term widely used in our society. It is suggestive of an active concern for our neighbour, including a willingness to help, even perhaps to put oneself at risk for the sake of another. Martha Nussbaum has identified three elements to compassion: a response of emotion, cognition and will. When we are compassionate, we perceive another's suffering, are moved by it and seek to come to their aid. Compassion needs to be distinguished from 'empathy' therefore, which is merely a cognitive state (after all, those who wish to inflict suffering need to understand what suffering is), from pity (we may pity someone but choose not to help them) and from mercy (which implies a power relation – we may feel compassion for those to whom we cannot show mercy, for sound practical reasons, as when a judge feels obliged to impose a strict sentence on a young offender from a poor background as a deterrent to others). 'Compassion' is also suggestive of a certain physicality of feeling, since 'passions' are experienced in the body. This is captured by the Latin *misericordia*, but is notably absent from the terms that have in general been used to convey the key Hebrew and Greek words which stand at the centre of the thematics of God's 'compassion' in the Old and New Testament. The Hebrew *rachemim* is cognate with *rechem*, meaning womb, and is at times used in the intensely physical context of a mother's care and concern for the children of her own body. It derives from the social world of sibling relations and is a familial term in parallel with *chesed*, meaning 'loving-kindness'. Similarly the original meaning of *splanghna*, a word of great importance in New Testament writings, is 'viscera' or 'entrails'.

Rachemim (or the verb *racham* 'to show compassion') is used throughout the Old Testament but consistently with regard to God's self-declaration in Exodus. Here reference to the compassionate acts of God, who liberated his people from slavery in Egypt, is combined with divine theophany of the Name (see Ex. 3; 6.1–13; 33.12–23). God promises to allow his goodness to pass before Moses and to proclaim before him the Name, adding: 'and I will be gracious to whom I will be gracious, and will show compassion on whom I will show compassion' (33.19). The link between *rachemim* and the Name (Yahweh) appears also in rabbinic sources, as we find in the Exodus Rabbah: 'and when I show compassion for my world I am called Yahweh'. Compassion thereafter becomes a quality of those who follow the Lord, as can be seen in texts such as Ps. 112.4: 'They rise in the darkness as a light for the upright; they are gracious, compassionate and righteous.' The deuteronomic texts are full of imperatives concerning the showing of compassion to 'widows and orphans' and 'strangers'. For a prophet such as Zechariah, the failure of God's people to 'show kindness and compassion to one another' is the reason for God's wrath (Zech. 7.8–14), and it is Zechariah too who points to the eschatological compassion of God (Zech. 10.6).

There are a number of Greek equivalents for the term *racham* in the Septuagint, especially *eleeo* and *oiktiro*. Both lack the visceral character of the Hebrew word and are equally to be translated into English as 'mercy' or 'pity'. *Splanghna* and the verb *splanghnizomai* on the other hand do carry the visceral or organic feel of the Hebrew terms. These words are in general distinctive to the New Testament (they do occur in another early text, the *Testimony of the Twelve Patriarchs*, but may be a later Christian interpolation). They seem to acknowledge the corporeal character of the Hebrew equivalents. In the New Testament *splanghna* and *splanghnizomai* are generally reserved for Jesus alone, especially in his role as healer, although they are also attributed to figures who represent divine forgiveness and mercy in three parables of Jesus, including the parable of the wicked servant, the Good Samaritan and the Prodigal Son. The Song of Zechariah seems to refer to Jesus himself as the 'compassion' of God: 'By the tender mercy (*splanghna*) of our God, the dawn from on high will break upon us' (Luke 1.78). The terminology of *splanghna* is used also in the Pauline epistles to refer to the 'compassionate heart' which is the foundation of the Church and of its shared life in Christ. Towards the beginning of the letter to the Philippians, Paul states: 'For God is my witness, how I long for all of you in the compassion of Christ Jesus' (Phil. 1.8). For the author of the first letter of John, the failure to act upon compassionate feeling means that God's love does not abide in us (1 John 3.17).

The centrality of 'compassion' in both Old and New Testaments marks Christianity out as a religion for which the ethics of compassion plays a key role. Although 'compassion' is absent from the traditional virtues of Christian tradition, historical Christianity has implicitly upheld the values of a creative 'suffering with' as a key element within the *imitatio Christi*. The relatively modern popularity of words built around the compound con-passio ('suffering with') as we find in English and some romance languages (cf. also German: *Mitleid*) owes much to Judaeo-Christian tradition therefore, which has frequently been at odds with the more negative attitude to compassion which has been apparent among philosophers, from Plato and the Stoics, to Kant and Nietzsche.

We cannot conclude a discussion of compassion without noting the extent to which globalization and the power of the mass media have established compassion and 'the politics of compassion' as a powerful motivational force in today's world. Some of the best-known spiritual figures of recent times, such as Mother Teresa, are specifically associated with compassionate living. One of the effects of this may well be to increase the awareness of Christ as 'the compassion of God' within the Christian Church.

See also Charity; Cross and Spirituality; Love; Social Justice; Reconciliation.

Oliver Davies, A *Theology of Compassion*, London: SCM Press, 2001; Edward Farley, *Divine Empathy: A Theology of God*, Minneapolis, MN: Fortress Press, 1996; Gerard W. Hughes, *God of Compassion*, London: Darton, Longman & Todd, 1998; Martha Nussbaum, 'Compassion: the basic social emotion', *Social Philosophy and Policy* 13.1 (Winter 1996), 27–58; Jon Sobrino, *Compassion: The Shaping Principle of the Human and of the Christian*, Regina: Campion College, University of Regina, 1992.

OLIVER DAVIES

Confucianism and Christianity

Confucianism began when Confucius (551–479 BCE) gathered around him a group of disciples with whom he studied and edited ancient texts, practised rituals attributed to the ancients, and commented on public affairs. The age was a time of weak central government in China, with small states competing for hegemony and warlords the only source of social stability, of which there was little. Confucius' collected sayings, *The Analects*, complain about the loss of two things necessary for high civilization, the virtue of humaneness and the effective practice of ritual propriety. The Chinese word for humaneness, *ren*, is also often translated as love, benevolence and humanheartedness. Confucius and his followers understood humaneness to be, paradoxically, ready at hand at all times if only we notice and also the virtue of the sage that requires a lifetime to perfect. The core of humaneness is learned through perfected family relations, parents loving children and children loving parents. The Confucian Mencius (371–289 BCE) emphasized humaneness. Ritual propriety is expertise in social patterns that are preconditions for civilized and humane interactions. As developed by the Confucian Xunzi (c. 310–211 BCE), rituals are learned patterns of social interactions that include gestures and modes of eye contact, language, conventions of greeting, precedence and respect, and religious family and court rituals. The Confucian complaint was that in the time of

social anarchy the well-practised rituals that made possible things such as decent family life, economically productive village life, and the high culture of imperial civilization simply did not exist. Confucius claimed to be reviving the preferable rituals of the ancients, although scholars believe he was rather inventive himself.

During the magnificent Dang (Tang) Dynasty (618–907 CE) Confucianism shared influence at the imperial court with Daoism and Buddhism, and also to a lesser extent with the other religions whose practice in China was encouraged, including Nestorian Christianity, Judaism, Islam and Manichaeism. Christianity was introduced to the imperial court by the monk A-lo-pen in 635 CE, and its flourishing was described in a monument, now in Sian, erected in a Christian monastery in 781. By the end of the Dang Dynasty religious tolerance was greatly diminished and Christianity virtually disappeared. During the Song Dynasty (960–1279) Confucianism radically reorganized itself by engaging both the metaphysics and the meditation practices of Buddhism and Daoism, creating what is known as neo-Confucianism. In addition to its political interests, neo-Confucianism emphasized the cultivation of inward sageliness in continuity with the great ontological principles of nature, including Nothingness, the Great Ultimate, Dao, Yin and Yang, Principle (the source of harmony), and Material Force. Confucianism continued to develop until the Marxist revolution of the mid twentieth century when most of its intellectual leaders had to flee to Taiwan, Hong Kong or the United States. These expatriates and their students intensely engaged the Western traditions, including Christianity and Western philosophy, and are known as New Confucians because they develop Confucianism for a global conversation and religious reality. Tu Weiming, now a professor at Harvard, is one of the leading New Confucians to present Confucianism as a religion that engages Christianity.

The first well-documented engagement of Christian spirituality with that of Confucianism was begun by Matteo Ricci, a Jesuit who came to China in 1582, learned classical and vernacular Chinese, translated the Confucian classics into Latin, and taught Western science to the Chinese. He argued that 'original Confucianism' (not the neo-Confucianism of his contemporaries) was very close to Christianity and entered into debates both as a Confucian and as a Christian. Although he made many converts to Christianity, he did not insist that they abandon their rites of ancestor worship, which he regarded as not true worship but only a showing of deep respect. Eventually, fellow Christians in Europe criticized him for compromising Christianity too much to give it spiritual vitality in China and his position on ancestor rites was repudiated. Roman Catholic Christianity in China then kept a European rather than indigenized Chinese form far longer than it would have if his creative engagement had been supported.

Contemporary Confucian and Christian spiritualities can be compared on many topics, of which three will be mentioned here. Since Ricci's time filial piety, which includes rites to honour ancestors, has been controversial. The heart of filial piety is to take into oneself the virtues of the parents so that they fulfil their obligation to make their children virtuous people. Becoming virtuous is an obligation children owe parents and its accomplishment sets parents free. Confucians imagine virtue always to be passed down through the generations, not acquired *de novo* by individuals in their own time. Hence the importance of honouring ancestors, the source of this generation's virtue. Of course Confucians, like others, sometimes have wretched parents with little virtue to pass on. So the ritual source of virtue needs to connect up with more remote ancestors. Confucius, living in a time of failed families, said that virtue derives from the legendary sage emperors of the mythic past. Christians have been more forthright than Confucians in noting that families are often dysfunctional, and have transferred many of the supportive roles Confucians seek in family relations to life in religious communities. Nevertheless, Christians are much like Confucians in saying that virtue derives from the past, from Jesus in the Christian case. 'Taking on the mind of Christ' (1 Cor. 2) is structurally similar to the Confucian taking on the virtue of the ancestors, and the piety and spiritual practices to accomplish this are interestingly similar.

The second comparative topic in spirituality is devotion to Heaven or God. Confucians believe that the inmost perceptive and responsive centre of human nature derives from Heaven, or Principle, yet in most people this *imago dei*, in Christian terms, is obscured or insufficiently developed. The spiritual project of becoming a sage, the most important task of Confucian spirituality, requires returning to this Heavenly Principle, learning to see it in oneself and all things, and conforming life to the harmony dictated by Heavenly Principle. Tu Weiming goes so far as to say that this can require a Kierkegaardian-like commitment of faith to the project of sagehood, recovering the divine principle. This bears obvious analogies to Christian commitment to God.

The Christian case, however, often represents God as a person, or takes the person of Jesus to be the symbol of God, devotion to whom amounts to devotion to God, and this is not the case with Confucianism. Like Confucianism (and most religions), Christianity has conceptions of God ranging from the highly anthropomorphic to the highly abstract, transcendent or supra-personal. Christianity fixed the centre of gravity for its rhetoric, however, in the personalistic language of the Bible. Confucianism, by contrast, fixed the centre of gravity of its rhetoric in an anti-anthropomorphic phase of its development, rejecting the personal God Shang-di (whom Ricci likened to the Christian God) for an impersonal Heaven or, more abstractly, Principle. Christian spirituality has rather great continuity of its popular forms in which God is very personal, Jesus a personal friend, and angels guard the soul, with its more elite theological and mystical forms in which God is the Creator, the One, the Act of Esse, the Ground of Being, or even the Abyss of Nothingness. Confucian spirituality, by contrast, is limited by its impersonal rhetoric to elite reflective forms and coexists in East Asia with Buddhism, Daoism and shamanism for popular forms of religious life.

The third comparative topic is humaneness or love. In both traditions these are extremely complicated and far-reaching terms, not given to easy definition. In both they are human virtues, derived from a divine or ontologically prior source, and used to characterize the most important cosmological as well as personal and social processes. The interesting comparative difference, however, concerns what might inhibit or distort humaneness or love. In the Confucian case, the inhibition lies in selfishness, and the remedy is education undertaken as a personal quest for sageliness. In the Christian case the inhibition lies in sin, which though involving selfishness manifests a deeper contradiction. The remedy in Christian spirituality is handing over the soul to the mind of Christ to be remade. Furthermore, Christ is thought to be able to remake souls because of who he was historically and is ontologically. Sin is a bondage from which release is required, whereas selfishness is a developmental problem. Despite many parallels, and a vast plurality of positions within both Christianity and Confucianism (Orthodox Christianity, for example, emphasizes sin as a developmental problem inhibiting *theosis,* a position quite close to Confucianism), the spiritual flavour of the two traditions regarding the task of manifesting love is very different. The flavour of Confucian spirituality is increased harmonization. The flavour of Christian spirituality, by contrast, is radical remaking.

A final comparative comment is that, whereas both Confucianism and Christianity have had moments and movements of very individualistic spirituality, both more fundamentally understand spirituality to require the renovation of the community. Because Confucians understand people to be defined in part by ritual, they are essentially communal; Christians identify the spirituality of loving God with loving neighbours. For the Confucian sage as well as the Christian saint, personal virtue is social holiness.

John H. Berthrong, *Transformations of the Confucian Way,* Boulder, CO and Oxford, UK: Westview Press, 1998; Herbert Fingarette, *Confucius: The Secular as Sacred,* New York: Harper & Row, 1972; Ian Gillman and Hans-Joichim Klimkeit, *Christians in Asia before 1500,* Ann Arbor: University of Michigan Press, 1999; Robert Cummings Neville, with a Foreword by Tu Weiming, *Boston Confucianism: Portable Tradition in the Late-Modern World,* Albany: State University of New York Press, 2000; Tu Weiming, *Humanity and Self-Cultivation: Essays in Confucian Thought,* Berkeley: Asian Humanities Press, 1979; reissued Boston: Cheng and Tsui, 1999; John D. Young, *Confucianism and Christianity: The First Encounter,* Hong Kong: Hong Kong University Press, 1983.

ROBERT CUMMINGS NEVILLE

Conformity

see **Prayer**

Conscience

Conscience is a complex entity which refers to the inward workings of the mind and heart. Although vague and ambiguous it has been used within the Christian tradition from the beginning to suggest moral self-governance. Conscience is intensely personal. It embodies the person's deeply held moral convictions, and refers to the inner sense of right and wrong as the basis of the individual's decisions. Within the tradition since Jerome conscience has signified two related aspects of the ethical life. As the habitual conscience it signals the person's innate disposition towards the good, what is known as 'the spark of conscience'. However it also refers to particular moral judgements, a process called the actual conscience. In each of its aspects conscience highlights the importance of freedom in morality because conscience is the process by which the individual comes to a personal evaluation of the right and good in each situation. Moreover this personal, self-conscious ethical activity, which is called conscience, is part of the

very dignity and uniqueness of being human. Thus although its workings may be impaired, it is never extinguished in the person.

Although the language of conscience has a broad resonance in Western culture, the Christian tradition gives a particular orientation to the meaning of conscience. As the source of free and responsible decision-making, conscience is regarded as the primary authority in ethics, and always to be obeyed. However it is not seen in isolation from the other authoritative sources of Christian morality, which include the teaching of Jesus; the collective wisdom of the tradition preserved in the Church's norms and principles; and the guidance of the magisterium. Conscience therefore takes its place as one of a number of sources of moral discernment. It is shaped by the collective experience of the church community and formed in dialogue with the tradition's central beliefs. It is to this dialectic of the personal and the communitarian that the term 'informed conscience' refers. This integration of collective moral wisdom with personal insight is precisely the goal of an informed conscience.

Conscience is not merely a synonym for subjectivism, although in some of their aspects they may appear to be indistinguishable. For the Christian, conscience is the place where human beings work towards discerning the objective good in each situation. Conscience is thereby best understood as the person's consciousness of the obligations due to the other and to God, as well as his or her apprehension of natural law. Thus conscience is not only an expression of personal judgement, it also aspires to be a reflection and embodiment of divine and natural law. Yet it is only through personal discernment that one can come to ascertain the demands of natural law. Conscience is thus situated within the context of the objective moral order, under the guidance of a personal and loving God. It expresses the irreducible quality of the person's moral discernment, but always in light of its formation within the objective moral order.

As the moral faculty that belongs to the person by nature, conscience forms the basis of our capacity to judge our own and others' actions. However, given the complexities of ethical decision-making, the exercise of this function can be difficult. Indeed not only can decisions of conscience be ambiguous, they can also be erroneous. Thus the question arises as to whether the conscience should always be obeyed, even if it is in error. In fact the earliest Christian discussions of conscience in the Pauline letters already gave attention to this difficulty. In his response to the community at Corinth regarding the acceptability of eating meat that had been offered to idols,

Paul taught that whatever the cause of the conscience's error, its force is binding. However, patristic theologians were reluctant to adopt this radical position of the binding force of an erroneous conscience, and even the recognized medieval authority Peter Lombard, following Augustine, held that in instances of conflict between conscience and Church teaching, the conscience should always give way. Nonetheless in a major refutation of the existing teaching Aquinas contested this and in so doing bequeathed to the tradition one of the most significant and enduring ethical principles: that of the primacy of (even an erroneous) conscience.

Thus the conscience is at the centre of moral perception and decision-making. As an integrating force, the discernment of conscience draws on many aspects of the person's life, including its rational, emotional, intuitive, imaginative and spiritual ones. And although often neglected in ethics, spiritual discernment plays a crucial role in the moral life, in particular through the workings of conscience. Decisions of conscience are enhanced by prayerful reflection and stillness and form an important part of the interior life of the person. Moreover as the 'most secret core and sanctuary' of the person (which is how Vatican II described it) conscience signifies a place wherein the spiritual and the ethical are mutually engaged.

See also **Conversion; Ethics and Spirituality; Discernment; Person.**

S. Callahan, *In Good Conscience: Reason and Emotion in Decision Making*, New York: Harper-Collins, 1991; W. Conn, *Christian Conversion, A Developmental Interpretation of Autonomy and Surrender*, Mahwah, NJ, Paulist Press, 1986; E. D'Arcy, *Conscience and Its Right to Freedom*, London: Sheed & Ward, 1961; P. Delhaye, *The Christian Conscience*, New York: Desclée Company, 1968; J. Mahoney, *The Making of Moral Theology: A Study of the Roman Catholic Tradition*, Oxford: Clarendon Press, 1987.

LINDA HOGAN

Consolation

From the Middle Ages onwards 'consolation' has had both non-religious and religious meanings and has been used regularly in both contexts (*Oxford English Dictionary*). In this article, however, the focus is the meaning of 'consolation' in Christian religious settings. '(Spiritual) consolation' is the equivalent of the earlier terms, '[ghostly] comfort' or 'solace'. In Christian literature from the Middle Ages to the present, two senses and uses of 'consolation' may be identified; one is general while the other (and

later), more technical and specific usage is associated particularly with Ignatian spirituality. As a general term in both religious and non-religious writings, 'consolation' includes: (1) 'the action of consoling, cheering or comforting'; (2) 'the state of being consoled; alleviation of sorrow or mental distress'; (3) 'an act or instance of consolation'; (4) an agent or cause, such as 'a person or thing that affords consolation; a consoling fact or circumstance' (*Oxford English Dictionary*). What gives Christian spiritual consolation its specific character is the fact that such an action of comforting or encouraging or a state of being consoled is rooted in religious faith or belief, in an appreciation of an aspect of the saving mystery of God set forth in Christ. The Christian tradition also holds such spiritual consolation to be the effect of the action of the Spirit of God in the human soul. The hymn *Veni, Sancte Spiritus* illustrates the range of phenomena encompassed by the term 'consolation'. The Spirit is addressed as 'best comforter', 'enlightener of hearts and minds' and 'the soul's sweet guest'. In the hymn, metaphors of consolation given by the Spirit also include: rest in time of hard work, a cooling breeze in the heat of summer, comfort in anguish, healing, thawing frozen hearts and bringing order into disordered lives. In Christian literature experiences of consolation range from mild mental and spiritual satisfaction or restfulness to intense joy and delight in the mystery of God, to extraordinary visions, locutions and ecstasies. It would be a mistake to conclude, however, that in its Christian sense 'consolation' includes only pleasant, enjoyable states of mind and heart. Consolations may also be painful, as for example when men or women become profoundly aware of the depth of their own involvement in sin and evil. While that may be a painful experience, it is genuine consolation when it is grounded in faith and hope and leads to repentance and reconciliation. Christian spiritual traditions consistently recognize the ambiguity of all religious experience and hence the need to distinguish between true and false consolation.

The second, more specific and technical use of 'consolation' occurs in the language and practice, from the mid sixteenth century to the present day, of Ignatian spirituality. In this context 'consolation' certainly carries the range of meanings mentioned above, but the word and the experiences to which it refers are also put to particular use in discernment of spirits, where 'consolation' is correlated with its opposite 'desolation'. In discernment, the ability to distinguish between true consolation, which is the work of the Spirit of God, and false consolation, an instance of evil masquerading as good or of a lesser good seeming to be the greater, is clearly crucial. Criteria for distinguishing between them, however, lie not so much in the kinds of experiences that they are as in the direction in which they are moving a person or group and the choices or actions in which they issue or are likely to issue. Consolation is genuine if it draws in the direction of (greater) effective love of God and of others and the world in God, irrespective of whether the experience itself is pleasant or painful. The basic principle in this approach to discernment is to move with and build on true consolation and to act against false consolation. Thus, critical theological reflection on consolation and desolation is a powerful tool for dealing with the ambiguity of religious experience and distinguishing between good (or better) and evil (or less good) choices and actions.

See also Desolation; Discernment; Ignatian Spirituality.

Michael Buckley, 'Discernment of spirits' in The New Dictionary of Catholic Spirituality, ed. Michael Downey, Collegeville, MN: The Liturgical Press, 1993; Maureen Conroy, The Discerning Heart: Discovering a Personal God, Chicago, IL: Loyola University Press, 1993; David Lonsdale, Dance to the Music of the Spirit: the Art of Discernment, London: Darton, Longman & Todd, 1993 (published in the USA as Listening to the Music of the Spirit, Ave Maria Press, 1993), ch. 4; Virginia Varley, 'Fostering the process of discerning together' in Discerning Together, The Way Supplement 85 (Spring 1996), 84–97.

DAVID LONSDALE

Consumerism

While consumerism can refer to watching out for the interests of consumers or to the idea that the consumption of material goods is economically and politically beneficial to societies, from the perspective of Christian spirituality consumerism points to personal and social disorder. The gospel wisdom about not storing up treasures on earth (Matt. 6.19) and Jesus' warning that 'one's life does not consist in the abundance of possessions' (Luke 12.15, NRSV) underscore the disorder in an individual's life caused by excessive attachment to material goods. The ethical teaching that the goods of creation are intended for the use of all and that the right to private property needs to be situated within an understanding of the common good highlights the disorder in society that has resulted because the world's resources have been distributed so unevenly (see, for example, the Vatican II document Pastoral Constitution on the Church in the Modern World 69 and Paul VI, On the Development of Peoples 23).

The consumption of material goods is essential to human well-being; all of us are consumers. But with consumerism the realm of human needs expands, steadily incorporating what is superfluous. In order to address consumerism, therefore, one has to locate the human person in her or his relatedness to other human beings. One also has to take into account the human being's relatedness to the earth itself, not to mention the responsibility we bear as creation's stewards, since 'The earth is the LORD's and all that is in it' (Ps. 24.1). Forgetfulness of the environment paves the way to depletion of natural resources and ecological disaster – a driving concern of many contemporary religious writers ('ecological theology'). The reasons why human beings are drawn to over-consume range from being quite simple (the desire for possessions as signs of status, as ways of mediating the ontological insecurity which comes from being finite, as expressions of free choice) to being quite complex (how cultures 'construct' their definition of what it means to be human; the connection between consumption, capitalism and the globalization of economies).

The right use of goods is by no means an exclusively Christian concern and consumerism as a symptom of spiritual disorientation is not just a modern phenomenon. For centuries the practice of poverty undertaken by religious has enabled individuals to overcome their attachments to material things by cultivating interior freedom and concentrating on only the most basic needs, an extension of the idea that one finds life by losing it (Mark 8.35). The vow of poverty consequently subverts consumerism and the cultural forces that diminish human dignity by evaluating persons in terms of their ability to purchase. The practice of religious poverty is deeply counter-cultural.

Perhaps the strongest defence against consumerism for the Church at large, however, is what John Paul II has referred to as an 'authentic globalized culture of solidarity' (Ecclesia in America 55). Solidarity as an expression of religious belief is grounded upon a 'preferential option for the poor', that is, an insertion of mind, heart, and imagination in the biblical portrayal of God as so attentive to the cry of the poor as to be practically deaf to any other concern. This prayerful insertion yields a perspective that evaluates social and economic policies in terms of their effects upon the most vulnerable members of the human community. The preferential option shapes one's politics and it certainly refashions one's behaviour as a consumer. One finds the strength to resist the pressures and allurements of consumerism as one develops strong ideological and affective ties with the people whom capitalism and globalization are content to consign to the bottom of the world's economies.

Consumerism cannot be combated solely on the basis of individuals choosing to consume less, however. In so far as the survival of the prevailing economic and social systems depends upon increased consumption of goods and further exhausting the earth's resources (thereby mortgaging humanity's future), the solution to consumerism has to involve globalized solidarity – a concerted effort on the part of all human beings to alter the way nations go about their business (Lodziak, 2002, p. 159). Consumerism can certainly be viewed as a sign of spiritual malaise, but salvation in this case cannot be achieved solely by practices like almsgiving, asceticism and serving the poor. The justice that God desires (see Isa. 58.6) probably means that economic and social systems must be substantially reconfigured.

See also Clothing; Food.

Conrad Lodziak, *The Myth of Consumerism*, London/Sterling, VA: Pluto Press, 2002; Lizabeth Cohen, *A Consumers' Republic: The Politics of Mass Consumption in Postwar America*, New York: Alfred A. Knopf, 2003; Alan Durning, *How Much Is Enough? The Consumer Society and the Future of the Earth*, London/New York: W. W. Norton, 1992; John Francis Kavanaugh, *Following Christ in a Consumer Society: The Spirituality of Cultural Resistance*, Maryknoll, NY: Orbis Books, 1981; John Paul II, *On Social Concern (Sollicitudo Rei Socialis)*, Washington: United States Catholic Conference, 1988; Vincent J. Miller, *Consuming Religion: Christian Faith and Practice in a Consumer Culture*, New York: Continuum, 2003.

WILLIAM REISER

Contemplation

The word contemplation has been used with a wide variety of meanings. It can stand for simple or even philosophical reflection. The concern in this entry is with the religious meanings of contemplation and, in particular, its Christian religious meaning. Religiously contemplation sometimes refers to meditation. But the chief concern here is with contemplation as an intensification of a transforming awareness of divine presence. Contemplation transforms one's spiritual resources and effects a deeper practice of virtue. The Christian tradition has also seen a life of virtue as a prerequisite for contemplation

as well as a foretaste of heaven. The issue at stake in the study of contemplation is both the possibility and the nature of transformative encounters with the divine. Christians perceive contemplation as a divine gift or grace.

The term contemplation originated with the Latin *templum* which represented the designated place in the heavens where the soothsayer discerned for a client the design of the gods. Hence *templum* or temple became the dwelling place of gods; at the temple one was in the presence of the gods. In Greek the word for contemplation is *theoría* – for Christians a beholding or vision of God that brings one into union with God.

Contemplation as articulated in the Christian tradition has significant roots in ancient Greek philosophy especially in Plato and Aristotle. Philo and later Plotinus had significant impact on Christian thinking about contemplation. In Christianity Greek thinking about contemplation was combined with a biblical tradition of encounters with God in which key figures of the Hebrew Scriptures had paradigmatic contemplative experiences of God, for example Moses and Elijah on Sinai/Horeb (Deut. 34.10; 1 Kings 19.13–14) and in the Christian Scriptures the experience of Jesus at the Transfiguration (Luke 9.28–36) as well as Paul's experience of being taken up into the third heaven (2 Cor. 12.2). Christians also turned to John's Gospel where the union between Christ and the believer is portrayed as a transformative experience.

The history of how contemplation has been understood in the Christian tradition is rich and varied. Many key Christian thinkers have contributed to that tradition. There is space here for only some of the more prominent voices in that tradition. Gregory of Nyssa's (d. 394) *Life of Moses* described the journey to the contemplative encounter with God by way of the experience of Moses. Gregory's apophatic understanding of contemplation, that is, contemplation that culminates in a divine encounter with darkness and unknowing, has had a deep and long-lasting effect on what has been called negative or apophatic theology, whereas Origen (d. *c.* 254), to whom Gregory was much indebted, espoused a contemplation of light. John Cassian (d. 430), a writer much read in the monastic tradition and throughout the Middle Ages, spoke of purity of heart as the way to contemplation, and he also wrote of purity of heart as contemplation itself, a contemplation that is 'fiery' and 'wordless'.

Augustine of Hippo, who died the same year as John Cassian, turned Western Christians to the journey within, and his report of his contemplative experience of God shared with his mother at Ostia has made an indelible mark on the spiritual consciousness of the West. About the year 500 CE, Pseudo-Dionysius composed a brief work, *Mystical Theology*, which described the climax of the journey into God as the experience of utter darkness and silence. This treatise has had a large and decisive impact on the Christian mystical tradition.

Pope Gregory the Great (d. 604), an author who greatly influenced the medieval tradition of contemplation, insisted that contemplation be rooted in meditation on the Word of God. Christian reflection on contemplation has been at its best when this intimate connection between contemplation and the Word has been operative. Gregory also saw contemplation as the human person's spiritual destiny, a conviction repeated often in the tradition.

Origen had used the Song of Songs to articulate the deeper experiences of God. Bernard of Clairvaux (d. 1153), like others before him, followed Origen's lead. However, Bernard's vivid and powerful language in his *Sermons on the Song of Songs* was immensely influential on the Western tradition. After Bernard and throughout the rest of the Middle Ages visionary literature became prominent especially among many medieval women visionaries. The importance of these visionaries needs to be balanced with a sense that visions and other psychological phenomena are not integral to the contemplative experience of the divine. Moreover, there has been a healthy scepticism about psychological phenomena sometimes associated with contemplation. This scepticism was strongly endorsed by John of the Cross. The later Middle Ages stressed detailed steps in meditation, a trend that may, then and in early modern times, have made contemplation seem a remote possibility in the life of the Christian.

Medieval monasticism was perceived as a contemplative life because it purported to be a life within which contemplation of heavenly things was facilitated. Thomas Aquinas (d. 1274) defended the new style of life espoused in the thirteenth century by the mendicant orders, especially his own Dominican Order, which he saw as a sharing with others the 'fruits of contemplation'. For Thomas the contemplative encounter with God constituted the ultimate and crowning experience of the human person. Though Thomas said that the highest knowledge of God is reached in mystical contemplation, this knowing of God goes beyond any concepts of God. Knowing has always been associated with contemplation, but more often than not Christian contemplation is associated with a loving encounter with God. This contemplative experience brings into a creative unity knowing and loving. Thomas spoke as did those before him of the delight that contemplation brings to the one who receives this gift.

At the time of the Reformation, Protestant religious figures set aside the language of mysticism and contemplation. In modern times there has been a trend to retrieve the contemplative tradition among Protestant writers. Ignatius of Loyola (d. 1556) used a fluid contemplative vocabulary. Sometimes contemplation meant for him a prayerful meditation especially about Christ. Ignatius himself had mystical experiences which deeply influenced his teaching on prayer. One of his associates, Jerome Nadal, spoke of Ignatius as a 'contemplative in action', which neatly addressed the supposed disconnection between action and contemplation which became a false dichotomy in many Christian conversations. Contemplation of the divine, in fact, integrates all facets of life.

Teresa of Avila (d. 1582) and John of the Cross (d. 1591) gave to the tradition an enduring understanding of contemplation which they articulated in the imagery of bridal mysticism. For them the spiritual life culminates in spiritual betrothal and finally in spiritual marriage. These two Spanish Carmelites also emphasized the gifted, passive nature of contemplation; they saw contemplation as God's work within the human person. For them and the authentic Christian contemplative tradition, contemplation is the encounter with the Christ that culminates in the experience of the triune God. Teresa popularized her version of the stages of the contemplative experience. John of the Cross described the finely tuned signs of the passage from discursive meditation to the gift of what came to be known as infused contemplation. For John of the Cross contemplation began with what he called the dark night of the senses and grew to become simple loving attention to the presence of God. Teresa taught that authentic contemplative experience is verified by a down-to-earth love of neighbour. After John of the Cross's time, various writers made room for what they called acquired contemplation about which there has been ongoing controversy.

Mysticism in Western Christianity became suspect from the late seventeenth century until the middle of the twentieth century. Consequently contemplation was portrayed as an esoteric and elitist event. Thomas Merton (d. 1968), Karl Rahner (d. 1984) and others have democratized contemplation removing its elitist character as did Vatican II's doctrine of the universal call to holiness. Rahner has situated contemplation within ecclesial and sacramental dimensions. Current contemplative prayer forms like centring prayer and Christian meditation have also brought contemplation within the reach of ordinary Christians. These forms of prayer dispose the human person to allow God to do what only God can do. The challenge remains for Christians to know that, while contemplation is not elitist, it demands solitude in some form, the practice of virtue and meditation, especially reflection on the life of Christ. Further challenges are the embracing of inter-faith dialogues concerning contemplative practices that have the potential of healing religious divisions. For Christians themselves there is the challenge of becoming more contemplative churches as a basis for ecumenical harmony and for action on behalf of justice and peace, that is, to become contemplatives in action.

See also Mysticism (essay); Apophatic Spirituality; Illuminative Way; Kataphatic Spirituality; Meditation; Mystical Theology; Prayer; Purgative Way; Senses, Spiritual; Triple Ways; Unitive Way.

Cuthbert Butler, *Western Mysticism: The Teaching of Saints Augustine, Gregory and Bernard on Contemplation and the Contemplative Life*, New York: Dutton, 1923; 'Contemplation', in *DS* 2.2. 1643–2193; Bernard McGinn, *The Presence of God: A History of Western Christian Mysticism*, 3 vols so far, New York: Crossroad, 1991, 1994, 1998; William Shannon, 'Contemplation, contemplative prayer' in *The New Dictionary of Catholic Theology*, Collegeville, MN: The Liturgical Press, 1993, pp. 209–14.

KEITH J. EGAN

Conventual Life

In religious life as in all human life the ritual surface structures of a community express and shape the deep psychospiritual structures of that group. Until modern times, except for the eremitical life in its purest form, consecrated life has almost always been a life in common. The sharing of financial resources, residence, meals, prayer, ministry and governance was and is seen to reflect and form the members' commitment to a communion of life rooted in and directed back to the communion of life shared by Father, Son and Holy Spirit. This life is believed to be an embodiment of the ideal life of the apostolic community of Jerusalem (cf. Acts 4.31–35) and a model of life for all the Church. The conventual life is the name we give to the concrete shape of the spaces, timetable (*horarium*) and rituals which shape and express the evangelical communion of those who have committed their lives to one another in service to the Church.

The specific shape of conventual life has changed and will continue to change through various cultures and periods of history. In analogy with Christology, ecclesiology and sacramentality, we can say that there is a spectrum of expressions of conventual life from 'high' to 'low'. Members of the pre-mendicant communities professing stability for life to one monastic community (monks and nuns) or to a local church (canons and canonesses) have led and continue to lead a more elaborated conventual life. In these communities the entire life is seen in a certain sense to be a ritualized life of worship. Church, chapter room and refectory traditionally arranged around a central cloister garden are the 'stations' to and from which the community members process. Mendicants, clerks regular, missionary and apostolic communities of men and women usually follow a less regulated conventual life more in keeping with their many forms of ministry outside their place of common residence.

The concrete forms of conventual life are meant to deepen in the members of a community their awareness of and commitment to the values of the group. Thus 'high' forms of conventual life will almost always include a repertoire of gestures in which the members and their religious superiors express their reverence and respect for one another. This may range from the ritual washing of feet to bows of respect and signs indicating the granting and accepting of pardon for offences. Meals are begun and ended with prayer and often are taken in silence while one of the members reads to those eating. The *horarium* is intended to assure a balance among the elements of individual prayer such as *lectio divina*, the celebration of the Eucharist and the Liturgy of the Hours, manual labour, other works of the house, sacred study, ministry, recreation and rest. The times allotted to these activities flows from their importance relative to the charism of the founder, the tradition of the community and its particular circumstances.

The community's calendar, based principally on the church's liturgical calendar, gives to the common life its particular texture of seasons, fasts and feasts. Calendar habitually indicated changes of religious habit appropriate to seasons and special feasts. Calendar indicated similar changes in diet. Calendar also marks the remembrance of nodal events in the life of the community and recalls to memory the lives and deaths of deceased members and benefactors.

In the Roman Catholic Church, since the Second Vatican Council (1962–65) almost all communities of consecrated life have adapted or even abandoned the forms of conventual life handed down to them over the centuries. The Council's retrieval of a sense of local church, the subsequent diminishment of demands for worldwide uniformity throughout religious communities and a renewed study of the charism of religious institutes created possibilities for the inculturation of religious life that could not but have a significant impact on the forms of conventual life that both express and shape the charism of communities of consecrated life.

See also **Apostolic Spirituality; Canonical Communities; Mendicant Spirituality; Monasticism; Religious Life; Rules, Religious.**

ANDREW CIFERNI

Conversion

Most simply, conversion is a kind of change, usually understood positively as a change for the better (change viewed negatively, or in terms of what one leaves behind, is sometimes called deconversion). In religious contexts, conversion often means a new allegiance to an organized group of believers, either a change from one group to another, or from no previous group. Occasionally whole communities adhere to a new religious group, but usually conversion is understood in terms of individuals. Conversion also means transformation, a profound experience of personal, interior change. The depth of a particular conversion is sometimes emphasized by saying that someone has become a new, a different person. But even the most thoroughgoing conversion is not alchemic transmutation. Conversion as transformation makes sense only if personal identity remains while much of even great importance about a person changes. A transformational conversion experience may accompany a new group allegiance, may occur within a group as intensification of faith, or may involve no group.

The life of John Henry Newman (1801–90) exemplifies these different meanings of conversion. At the age of fifteen Newman, raised as a conventional Anglican, experienced a profound conversion that intensified his faith and changed his life. This occurred privately and within the Anglican Church, though Newman did become more evangelical than his parents. A decade later at Oxford, as Newman was drifting toward Liberalism, a cognitive conversion brought him to an Anglo-Catholic position. Two more decades later (1845), Newman, now a High Churchman and prominent Oxford Tractarian, after many years of agonizing deliberation, changed allegiance from the Anglican Church to the Roman Catholic Church, the conversion for which he is famous. Some viewed this as a conversion in the most positive sense; others, of course, saw it negatively as a change for the worse, a deconversion (J. H. Newman, *Apologia pro Vita Sua*, 1864).

The Christian understanding of conversion as a moral-religious reality finds its roots in the Hebrew Scriptures: the history of Israel is the story of a people repeatedly being called to conversion, called to turn back to its covenant with the God it has adulterously abandoned. David is the model of how this call works in the individual sinner's life (2 Sam. 11—12). The story of Job, who comes to recognize the mystery of God, underscores the fundamental truth that even the just person is called to conversion.

John the Baptist continues the prophets' call to conversion in the New Testament. And after John's arrest, Jesus takes up the call and makes it central to his preaching: 'The time has come . . . the reign of God is at hand. Be converted and believe in the good news' (Mark 1.15).

The key biblical words for conversion are *naham* and *shub* in Hebrew, and *metanoia* and *epistrophe* in Greek. If conversion means a radical turning, or a redirecting of one's life, the first word in each pair, emphasizing repentance, specifies a turning *from* (sin), while the second indicates a turning *toward* (God). Emphasis on conversion as repentance for sin has probably kept Christians from thinking of Jesus as having experienced conversion, even though he did present himself to John for baptism. It has been the extraordinary experience of Paul on the road to Damascus, rather, that has dominated Christian thinking about conversion in the New Testament (especially accounts in Acts). Many contemporary theologians, however, realizing the full *religious* depth of conversion beyond the moral, recognize in Jesus' response to crises in his life and ministry a transformation of faith, a rethinking of his relationship to the Father that defines the very essence of religious conversion.

Though rooted in the prophetic call of the Hebrew Scriptures, and absolutely fundamental to New Testament teaching, conversion was by no means exclusive to Judaism and Christianity. Indeed, the early Christian meaning of this fundamental reality was elaborated in a cultural context of mutual influence where it shared the term *epistrophe* with Middle- and Neo-Platonism as well as with Stoicism and Gnosticism. Judaism and Christianity might have been alone among ancient Mediterranean religions in demanding conversion, as A. D. Nock (*Conversion*, 1933) claims, but philosophic conversion as the object of education, a moral-intellectual 'turning of the soul', was already established with Plato (*Republic* 7.518D).

The philosophic search for truth becomes the Christian yearning for God in Augustine, whose *Confessions* recount his intellectual, moral and religious conversions. Indeed, the *Confessions*' eloquent articulation of the profound *experience* of interior transformation has given Augustine a pre-eminent place in Christian spirituality. Though medieval spiritual writers like Meister Eckhart continued to focus on the experience of Christian life, the dominant Scholastic mode of theology effectively lost the experience of conversion in the metaphysical analysis of faith, grace and justification. Luther best marks the return of conversion as experienced to a central place in reflection on Christian life. However else they differ, Luther and Ignatius of Loyola share the reality of conversion in their personal experience as well as in their analyses of the spiritual life. Despite the enormous influence of Ignatius' *Spiritual Exercises* on individual lives, however, it would be some four centuries before formal Roman Catholic theology was ready to recognize in the experience of conversion the significance which had become a primary characteristic of Protestant theology.

Philip Spener and Pietism in Germany, John Wesley and the founding of Methodism in England, and Jonathan Edwards and the Great Awakening in New England are only three of the many persons and events that would have to be mentioned in any complete survey of conversion in Protestantism. More than anything else, perhaps, these were responsible for the popular religious revivalism that carried into and through the nineteenth century. Even high Anglican divines like Pusey, who held to baptismal regeneration, did not dispute in most cases the need of 'a solid and entire conversion'.

It was in the revivalist context at the beginning of the twentieth century, when psychology was still in its infancy as a science, that William James' classic *Varieties of Religious Experience* (1902) established a presumption in favour of adolescence as the common time for conversion. Despite C. G. Jung's later emphasis on the religious possibilities of the mid-life crisis, most psychological studies of conversion have followed James in seeing it as an essentially adolescent phenomenon.

Only in recent decades has developmental psychology – notably the psychosocial life-cycle approach of Erik Erikson – reoriented the psychological study of conversion by relativizing the identity crisis associated with adolescent conversion as just one of several critical turning points in the larger personal context of the lifecycle. From this perspective, conversions of adolescence and youth (even those expressed in reli-

gious language) appear to have a distinctly moral emphasis. At the same time, the older adult's crisis of integrity vs. despair not only echoes Jung, but correlates closely with contemporary theological analyses of specifically religious conversion as the total reorientation of one's life through unconditional surrender to God in Jesus Christ by the power of the Spirit – a surrender of one's claim to absolute autonomy. If the gospel makes it clear that this interior transformation must be realized in justice and love of neighbour, contemporary theologians have clarified that these must take social structural as well as interpersonal shape.

Rooted in biblical and historical sources, nourished by theological sensitivity to personal and social experience, and supported by psychological approaches attuned to personal development and the possibilities of self-transcendence, the contemporary discipline of Christian spirituality is in the process of effecting a critical retrieval of conversion as the foundation of authentic Christian life.

See also **Desire; Growth, Spiritual; Person.**

W. Conn, *Christian Conversion*, New York: Paulist Press, 1986; E. H. Erikson, *Childhood and Society*, 2nd edn, New York: Norton, 1963; C. G. Jung, *Modern Man in Search of a Soul*, New York: Harcourt, Brace & World, 1933; J.-M. Le Blond, *Les conversions de saint Augustin*, Paris: Aubier, 1950; E. Liebert, *Changing Life Patterns*, 2nd edn, St Louis: Chalice 2000; B. Lonergan, *Method in Theology*, New York: Herder & Herder, 1972; L. R. Rambo, *Understanding Religious Conversion*, New Haven: Yale University Press, 1993.

WALTER E. CONN

Coptic Spirituality

The Coptic Orthodox Church of Egypt was founded by St Mark the Apostle around the middle of the first century AD , and is one of the four primary Sees in the world, besides the churches of Jerusalem, Antioch and Rome, joined later on by the See of Constantinople (Malaty, 1987, p. 7). The Coptic Church has a profound and rich spirituality that is rooted in the eschatological spirit of the early Church of the first century, the ascetic experience of the monastic life of the fourth century, the religion of ancient Egypt, the patristic tradition of the great Fathers of the Church, as well as a glorious history of remarkable events.

1. *From eschatology to asceticism.* Out of genuine response of Jesus' call, 'The time is fulfilled and the kingdom of God is at hand. Repent and

believe in the gospel' (Mark 1.15), and believing Jesus' promise, 'Behold, I am coming quickly' (Rev. 22.7, 12, 20), early Christians lived with an eschatological zeal, 'looking for and hastening the coming of the day of God' (2 Peter 2.12). They fervently integrated this belief in their worship and prayed 'Amen, Even so, come, Lord Jesus' (Rev. 22.20; on this, see Zizioulas, 1985).

Thus the ideal of virginity was adopted with great enthusiasm and asceticism became a main feature of the spirituality of the early Christian communities. St Paul's exhortation (in 1 Cor. 7, especially verses 32–35) has been a source of inspiration for many (see Clark, 1986). This was manifested in the Coptic Church in particular. It reached its maximum expression in the monastic movement of the fourth century, and it is still lived out in the contemporary Coptic Orthodox Church. This is shown not only in the numerous monasteries and convents which are spread all over Egypt, but also in the hundreds of celibate young men and women who dedicate their life to service in the Church. Modern Copts have great love for monasteries. Parish churches always conducted trips to the monasteries and many people of all ages joyfully join such trips, this is beside the small groups and individual spiritual retreats in which people spend some time at the monasteries' retreat houses.

2. From asceticism to monasticism Monasticism is 'Egypt's greatest gift to the world' (Baynes and Moss, 1948). This statement is based on the great influence of the *Vita Antonii* through which St Athanasius, the twentieth Patriarch of the Coptic Church and champion of Orthodoxy against Arianism, wrote aiming to introduce monasticism to the enthusiastic Christian ascetics who were eager to know about the life of the great Egyptian monk. Athanasius composed it *c.* AD 357 shortly after the death of the great hermit in AD 356, and addressed it to the monks who asked him for an account of how Antony came to practise asceticism (Quasten, *Patrology* 3.39). The *Vita* was the most important document of early monasticism which became a source of inspiration for the Christian ascetic movement as a whole (Kannengiesser, 1995, p. 479). The *Vita* 'introduced the church to a new phenomenon and stimulated universal imitation and emulation. Even in the story of the conversion of Augustine the *Vita Antonii* plays a part, and innumerable Greek lives of the saints were planned on the pattern which it had established' (von Campenhausen, 1998, p. 82). St Athanasius was 'the first authority in the Christian church who recognized the importance of monasticism for the Christian way of life' (Kannengiesser, 1995, p. 479).

As St Athanasius presented the ascetic ideal to all, educated and uneducated alike, he believed that it had to be established on Christ and the Orthodox teaching of the Church. 'In this sense Athanasius strove to combine monasticism with Nicene Orthodoxy and blended them in the depth of popular feeling and the consciousness of the church' (von Campenhausen, 1998, p. 83). The strong relation between dogma and virtue or right doctrine and righteous life has been always an essential characteristic of Coptic Spirituality (Rousseau, 1985). St Athanasius saw in asceticism, along with martyrdom, a strong proof of the truth of the Christian faith. In his treatise *On the Incarnation,* he invites those who have any doubt about Christianity to 'come up and see the demonstration of virtue in the virgins of Christ and the youth who live a pure life in chastity, and the belief in immortality in such a great company of martyrs' (Athanasius, 1971, p. 255).

In the *Vita Antonii* we read that St Antony 'persuaded many to choose the monastic way of life and in his way monasteries came into being in the mountains, and the desert filled with monks . . . They registered themselves for citizenship in heaven' (*Life of Antony* 14). The great influence of Coptic monasticism has to do also with the unique experience of the Desert Fathers whose profound sayings were recorded in the well-known *Apophthegmata Patrum* which became a source of spiritual guidance and education for many generations and many churches until this day.

St John Cassian was among Western figures who came to Egypt and lived among the spiritual Fathers of the Desert and recorded their spiritual wisdom in his *Institutions* and *Conferences.* St Basil the Great who came also to Egypt and was influenced by the Pachomian *koinonia,* or the communal life shared by monks who live together in one monastery. In Basil's travels to the monastic centres in Egypt and other countries in 356 he rejoiced at meeting monks 'at whose continence *(encrates)* in living he marveled' (*Letter* 223). Upon his return to Cappadocia, Basil adopted the ascetic life himself and founded monastic life in the coenobitic (or communal) form in a number of monasteries following and developing the Pachomian monastic style. This was one of Basil's greatest achievements (Beatrice, 1987, p. 221) in which he reconciled the two main forms of monasticism, the solitary and the communal (Gregory Nazianzen, 1953, p. 80; Lowther Clarke, 1913, p. 46).

Monasticism provided Orthodox spirituality with fundamental values that have been applied by all Christians, such as renunciation of the world, mortification of the body and purification of passions, and spiritual discipleship to a spiritual father. All these were taken in a spiritual way that fits the ordinary Christian person who lives in the society.

3. *Saints and martyrs.* An essential feature of Coptic spirituality is the veneration of saints and martyrs. The icons of the saints in Coptic churches, the joyful celebrations of saints' feast days, the reading of saints' lives in every liturgy (recorded in a book called the Synaxarium) and the placing of martyrs' relics in churches: all these are common practices that express the honourable place of the saints, the crown of whom is the mother of God, St Mary. Saints are perceived not as extraordinary exceptions but as living examples of faithful obedience to the gospel's call for perfection in submission to God's will and word.

4. *Glorious historical events in Egypt.* Copts take pride at the flight of the holy family to Egypt which happened as a response to a divine commandment (Matt. 2.13–15) and in fulfilment of Old Testament prophesies (Hos. 11.1; Isa. 19.1, 19, 21). This is for Copts a great blessing to their country which developed in them a genuine sense of the sacredness of space and place. Copts know the various stations of the holy family's trip in Egypt. Monasteries and churches were built on many of those stations, and Copts love to visit them and receive their blessings.

5. *Persecution and martyrdom.* Copts were exposed to severe persecutions throughout their history. This allowed them to experience God's power and protection which preserved the Church and the Christian faith till this day in spite of all challenges. It also enhanced in them their eschatological spirit and ascetical zeal. They understood their life on earth as a continuous preparation for eternal life. Even when persecution ceased they had interest in pursuing a spiritual martyrdom, according to St Paul's exhortation of dying daily (Rom. 8.35–37; Ps. 44.42), and according to Clement of Alexandria and Origen's idea of the martyrdom of the conscience (*Orthodox Spirituality*, 1987, pp. 7f., 91f.).

6. *Prayer and fasting.* Coptic spirituality has been faithful to the gospel's teaching on prayer and fasting as two necessary aspects of spiritual life and as two powerful weapons in spiritual warfare against demons (Matt. 17.21).

A remarkable event took place in the history of the Coptic Church as a result of prayer and fasting. During the Fatimid era the Coptic Patriarch Abraam Ibn-Zaraa, the sixty-second Patriarch, who was enthroned in the year AD 975, was exposed to a terrible challenge. Being provoked by a Jewish minister who hated Christians, the Fatimid Caliph Al-Muizz told the Patriarch that if Christians have a verse in their Bible that says 'If you have faith as a mustard seed, you will say to this mountain move from here to there and it will move' (Matt. 17.20; Mark 11.23), then he had to do it to show that their faith was true through moving the Muqatam Mountain, otherwise all Copts would be subject to the sword. The Patriarch asked for a three-day respite, during which a special prayer and fasting were commanded to people. And at the end of the three days all gathered at the mountain and Copts started praying 'Lord have mercy', and the mountain started to move up. The Caliph was terrified and cried for safety and he spared the lives of the Copts and became a good friend to the Patriarch (Malaty, 1987, pp. 104–5).

A monk of the Eastern Church, *Orthodox Spirituality: An Outline of the Orthodox Ascetical and Mystical Traditions,* Crestwood, NY: SVS Press, 1987, pp. 7f., 91f.; Athanasius, *On the Incarnation* 48 in Robert W. Thompson (ed. and trans.), *Athanasius: Contra gentes and De incarnatione,* Oxford: Clarendon Press, 1971; Norman Baynes and H. St L. B. Moss, *Byantium,* Oxford: Clarendon Press, 1948, p. xxxi; Pier Franco Beatrice, *Introduction to the Fathers of the Church,* Holy, Vicenza: Edizioni Instituto San Gaetano, 1987; Hans von Campenhausen, *The Fathers of the Church,* Peabody, MA: Hendrickson, 1998; Elizabeth A. Clark, *Ascetic Piety and Women's Faith: Essays on Late Ancient Christianity,* Lewiston: The Edwin Mellen Press, 1986; W. K. Lowther Clarke, *St. Basil the Great: A Study in Monasticism,* Cambridge: Cambridge University Press, 1913; Gregory Nazianzan, *Oration* 43.62 on St Basil, trans. Leo P. McCawley et al., *The Fathers of the Church: A New Translation* 22, New York: The Fathers in the Church Inc., 1953; Charles Kannengiesser, 'Athanasius of Alexandria and the ascetic movement of his time' in Vincent L. Wimbush and Richard Valantasis (eds), *Asceticism,* New York/ Oxford: Oxford University Press, 1995; Heshmat Keroloss, 'Virginity in the Early Church: The Meanings and Motives of Sexual Renunciation in the First Four Centuries', unpublished Ph.D Dissertation at Fordham University, New York, 1996; Tadros Malaty, *Introduction to the Coptic Orthodox Church,* Ottawa, Ontario: St Mary Coptic Orthodox Church, 1987; Philip Rousseau, *Pachomius: The Making of a Community in Fourth Century Egypt,* Berkeley: University of California Press, 1985; Tim Vivian (ed. and trans.), 'Life of Antony by St Athanasius of Alexandria', Coptic Church Preview 15.1, 2 (Spring and Summer 1994); John Zizioulas, 'The early Christian community' in Bernard McGinn et al. (eds), Christian Spirituality: Origins to the Twelfth Century, New York: Crossroad, 1985.

HESHMAT KEROLOSS

Cosmology

Beliefs about the nature of the universe inevitably have an impact on Christian spirituality. Christianity inherited a positive view of the created order from Judaism, and a more ambivalent view from Greek philosophy. Highly influential in early Christianity was the cosmology proposed by the Stoic philosophy which had a wide influence in the Graeco-Roman world. Stoic thought is also reflected in Hellenistic Jewish writing, in Paul and in the early Christian apologists. The Stoics saw the universe as a rationally ordered whole. It was an organism, not alien to humankind. The Emperor Marcus Aurelius described the universe as the 'dear city of God'. Animated by divine reason, the 'logos', the world would ultimately collapse in fire, though it would then be reborn.

A more pessimistic approach to nature is reflected in the various Gnostic teachings, which involved both psychological and metaphysical speculation. Gnostics, borrowing some aspects of Platonism, presumed a hierarchy of being in which only the truly spiritual could reach salvation. Matter was despised, the body was to be treated with indifference. These attitudes were not confined to Gnostics but became incorporated into the Christian ascetic tradition. In general, though, the Jewish and classical heritage ensured that the human person was seen as a kind of microcosm of the universe as a whole.

Ptolemy, a second-century Greek astronomer, synthesized the speculations of earlier philosophers to produce a theory of planetary motion which became the official cosmology of the medieval Church. Ptolemy's universe was earth centred, though the earth was seen as a dark, sluggish place, round which the planets revolved encased in an ascending series of crystal spheres which transmitted various influences to the earth. Beyond the planets were the fixed stars which did not move. Ptolemy's universe was a static hierarchy, an organic whole radiating from God to earth. The darkness of the night sky was caused merely by the shadow of the earth. To the medieval mind the universe, though huge, was finite, and full of divine radiance. Though awe-inspiring it was still 'home'. The Ptolemaic universe provided physical and spiritual answers to the questions of existence and its influence lasted for over a thousand years.

The Ptolemaic map of the universe was replaced as the telescope began to reveal that the movements of the heavenly bodies suggested a sun-centred universe. The laws of motion and gravity, discovered by Isaac Newton, provided a successful mechanical model to explain how the solar system worked. Nature became distanced from humanity as it became the object of human interrogation and exploitation. The universe was no longer seen as an interconnected organism, but more as machine. In consequence Christian spirituality was driven inward, confined to private feelings and moral choices. The machine model of the universe has lasted for three hundred years and has been hugely successful. It has contributed to a major change in the context of Christian spirituality, to a sense of alienation from nature and the body. God, in Newtonian physics, is outside the universe and is unable to interact with it. It is no accident that Newton was a Unitarian, denying the Trinity and the incarnation.

The twentieth century saw revolutions in cosmology as Newtonian certainty about the machine-like regularity and predictability of nature gave way to Einstein's General and Special Theories of Relativity. Einstein's further discovery of quantum mechanics undermined the notion that every event in the universe could, in theory, be predicted. The impact of recent science suggests a return to a model of an interconnected, interactive universe in which humanity is deeply embedded. Much contemporary spirituality both within and without the Christian tradition is 'holistic' in response to this contemporary cosmology.

See also Spirituality and Science (essay); Creation Spirituality.

For further reading, see the bibliography in Spirituality and Science (essay).

ANGELA TILBY

Counsels, Evangelical

see Vows

Creation Spirituality

In its deepest meaning 'creation spirituality' focuses on the practice of awe and mystery that are at the heart of creation. Its emphasis is on all living things as created and blessed by God. As such they reveal the wisdom of God immanent in the world. In its contemporary form it is frequently associated with the US theologian Matthew Fox, although in reality it is much older, being in fact an abiding dimension of both

Jewish and Christian faiths, even if at times obscured by a more pessimistic attitude to the natural world.

In its current manifestation 'creation spirituality' belongs within a wider spectrum of evolutionary thinking about and a changed relationship with the earth. The need to place the human story within the cosmic story is an urgent plea. Brian Swimme and Thomas Berry provide inspiration here, as well as insights from quantum physics of the interconnectedness and interpenetration of all dimensions of existence. A creation-centred perspective views the entirety of life as sacred, thus rejecting any dualistic split between the sacred and profane. In a cosmic perspective human beings lose their place of privilege, yet still retain a unique responsibility within the vast scheme of things – a point stressed by ecofeminist theologian Sallie McFague.

In Matthew Fox's work 'creation spirituality' challenges the centrality of the fall and original sin in the Western tradition – without denying the reality of sin – making *original blessing* the central focus. His contribution has been to offer a practice of 'creation spirituality' in a fourfold path, a practice that has become well known internationally. These steps are not linear but 'spirally interwoven'. The *via positiva* is the practice of awe, wonder, gratitude and delight in creation; the *via negativa* is the practice of letting the dark be the dark. Instead of conquering pain by asceticism or will power, letting pain be pain means allowing ourselves to experience it as well as giving up the will to control everything; the *via creativa* invites humanity to reconnect with its own creative power, to give birth to new ideas and imagination and to new expressions of God. The final movement, the *via transformativa,* calls us to bring the insights of compassion, wisdom and justice on the three other paths with a view to changing self and society. An integral part of the practice of this form of 'creation spirituality' is the stress on both prophecy and mysticism, the prophet being the 'mystic in action'. There is also a call to recover a cosmology respectful of the earth by paying attention to other cultures remaining more faithful to the earth, for example indigenous Indians of North America and Aboriginals in Australia. The principal argument is that 'creation spirituality' – as defined by Fox – is the underlying authenticity of Christian faith that has been suppressed by the Western fall tradition, with its overemphasis on guilt: with the loss of 'the cosmic story' has come the loss of eros and mysticism, the scapegoating of women and earth alike, culture's loss of childhood innocence and a dysfunctional Church.

While there is much here that is positive, 'creation spirituality' needs to be put in a wider framework – and some of Fox's claims modified. It is undeniable that there has been an over-emphasis on fall and guilt, a turning away from the earth so that humanity lost consciousness of the wider cosmic picture, but the recovery and 'turn to the earth' called for by many theologians means holding both creation and redemption together as interwoven journeys. It means acknowledging original blessing together with all creation's need for healing and redemption in this 'broken web' (Catherine Keller's image). Replacing one set of dualisms for another is unhelpful: for example, resisting darkness as 'sin' by embracing it as wholly positive in the *via negativa*, risks ignoring the whole intricate, ambiguous web of suffering and evil in which many poor communities are trapped. This 'darkness' – if that is the appropriate metaphor – is far from positive and a spirituality of resistance might be more appropriate here. Letting pain be pain is in many cases unhelpful – even cruel – advice. Feminist theology has been active in disclosing the mechanism by which guilt and sin of disordered sexuality is projected onto women, a mechanism that eludes any facile categorizing. Third, labelling ancient sources as 'creation-positive' (Celtic spirituality, Benedictines, Hildegard of Bingen, for example) and others as guilty of 'redemption dualism' (Augustine, Luther) ignores the enormous complexity of these authors' wrestling with good and evil, and the persistence of dualisms within their thought that was impossible to escape, given the categories of their time.

A more fruitful understanding of creation spirituality recognizes the uniqueness of a starting point where the earth is exploited as never before in its history. Our 'ecological footprint' is immeasurably heavier than that of our ancestors. So, 'conversion to the earth' and the search for resources for her healing take place in explicit recognition of the interwovenness of the need for redemption of earth, her creatures and human beings alike. Thus recovery of 'creation-friendly' sources such as the creation stories (Gen. 1 and 2) focus on creation as blessing and the goodness and promise of creation, *if and only if her limits and needs are respected*. Third, whereas resources such as Jewish messianic peace and the flourishing of earth and people alike (Isa. chs 11, 35 and 61) or the Orthodox Church's spirituality of praise for creation are a precious heritage, they are reclaimed in a totally different context, a context of urgency where life on earth itself is threatened. Fourth, there are ways in which 'creation spirituality', far from romanticizing the past, focuses on developing areas of the tradition which may be considered blind spots, for example, the lack of honour given to women and children as God's good creation or the ethics of vegetarianism at a time when animals are being hunted to extinction. It can also grapple with the complexity of the natural world which demands far more than ecstasy and wonder at sunrises, for example, but as much the terror-stricken cry of Job at God's revelation of the mystery, cruelty and ambiguity of creation and the sovereign reign of God in and through it all.

'Creation spirituality' does recall humanity to responsible action and contemplative praise at a time of ecological crisis. (The reclaiming of the Jubilee traditions of the book of Leviticus at the time of the global debt crisis is an example.) It does promise a corrective to the path of 'flight from the earth' (either through despair of the material world or as an attempt to escape from responsible stewardship) and embraces all living things in the rhythm of praise for the Creator, whose presence among them it celebrates. But, although it provides many valuable points of contact with all faiths and the secular world, its deepest insight is that ultimately, the sacredness of the earth/Gaia/the Universe is as originating in and sustained by God, in whom creation finds its ultimate home.

See also **Spirituality and Science (*essay*); Cosmology; Ecological Spirituality; Ethics and Spirituality; Feminist Spirituality; Liberation Spirituality; Orthodox Spirituality; Sacred; World.**

Matthew Fox, *Original Blessing: A Primer in Creation Spirituality*, Santa Fe: Bear & Co., 1983; D. Hessel and R. Rasmussen (eds), *Earth Habitat: Eco-injustice and the Church's Response*, Minneapolis: Fortress Press, 2001; Sallie McFague, *Models of God: An Ecological Theology*, Philadelphia: Fortress Press, 1993; Vincent Rossi, 'Liturgizing the world: religion and science and the environmental crisis in light of the sacrificial ethic of sacred cosmology', *Ecotheology* 3 (July 1997), 61–84; B. Swimme and T. Berry, *The Universe Story*, New York: HarperCollins, 1992.

MARY C. GREY

Cross and Spirituality

The fact of Jesus' execution on a cross has shaped the Christian understanding of spirituality from the earliest creeds and scriptural testimonies to present-day struggles for social and political liberation. As the identifying symbol of the Christian movement, the cross has challenged followers of Jesus to find their own ways to express sacrificial love. Again and again, inter-preters of the tradition have represented the cross as the very gateway to discipleship. Scripture and theology, worship, military and political action, prayer and poetry, iconography and architecture, music and dance, all have focused on the cross as the emblem of specifically Christian spirituality. That an instrument of torture should become the sign of God's overweening love has provoked and perplexed not only those within but also those outside the Church.

Within twenty years of Jesus' death, Paul declared the crucifixion of Jesus 'a stumbling block to Jews and folly to Gentiles' (1 Cor. 1.23) But he exclaims that he never boasts 'of anything except the cross of our Lord Jesus Christ' (Gal. 6.14), and goes on to argue that Christian spiritual maturity comes exclusively through baptism into Christ's death on the cross. 'Do you not know that all of us who have been baptized into Christ Jesus were baptized into his death?' (Rom. 6.3) Baptism initiates a spiritual process, an ongoing event, through which one is constantly shaped and reshaped according to the model that is Christ crucified himself. This means that the astonishing dynamism of resurrection reality must always be held in tension with the suffering of the cross: 'I want to know Christ and the power of his resurrection and the sharing of his sufferings by becoming like him in his death,' Paul says (Phil. 3.10). The difference between the *teleioi* (the 'maturing', 'perfecting' ones) and those Paul labels 'babes in Christ', or 'people of the flesh', or those dominated by 'jealousy and strife', is that the mature have been trained to recognize God's power in the crucified Christ, and their spiritual maturity consists precisely in this: they rely totally on God's life-in-the-midst of death, rather than on themselves. They are endlessly alert and ready to encounter Christ's power through the sharing of his sufferings. Paul never loses sight of how physical this process is. We 'are always carrying in the body the death of Jesus, so that the life of Jesus may also be made visible in our bodies', where 'the life of Jesus' designates not the earthly, pre-crucified ministry, but the resurrection-life of Jesus (2 Cor. 4.10). Thus the cross signifies that Christians are called to participate spiritually and intentionally in both Jesus' death and in his resurrection.

Each of the four Gospels interprets the meaning of the cross differently, eliciting a distinct spiritual response. Matthew values Jesus' obedience to God, his steadfastness in his mission and his solidarity with the pain and hope of his people. Jesus' death on the cross continues his life and work and anticipates the future kingdom of God. Moreover, Matthew testifies that Jesus predicted both his death and the kingdom during the Last Supper in promising his disciples that he would 'never again drink of this fruit of the vine until that day when I drink it new with you in my Father's kingdom' (26.29). The community that lives after him is asked to live spiritually in relation to Jesus and in the light of God's kingdom by loving one another as Jesus loved them.

The spiritual theme for Mark is discipleship even to the cross. He understands Jesus' ministry to involve an inevitable sequence of events whose climax is Golgotha. Through the cross, Jesus is made known as the Son of God who wins salvation for the new community of faith – a community called to follow him in faithful discipleship. Thus Jesus' call to follow him is equivalent to an invitation to take the way of the cross. 'If any want to become my followers, let them deny themselves and take up their cross and follow me' (8.34–38).

Luke brings two distinctive emphases. On the one hand, he inserts a psychological and spiritual theme when Jesus says, 'If any want to become my followers, let them deny themselves and take up their cross *daily* and follow me' (9.23, my emphasis). On the other hand, Luke's identification of Jesus' passion as that of the Suffering Servant in Isaiah emphasizes the salvation-historical necessity of the cross, the universality of his mission, and highlights Jesus' exaltation and vindication as the salvific event (24.46–47). Spiritually, this suggests that believers should mirror that universality through gracious acceptance of others, Gentiles, Jews and criminals in particular. Moreover, they should also embody the righteousness, humiliation and lowliness of the Servant.

John 'spiritualizes' the cross more than the synoptic authors do, stressing the intimate connection between Jesus' crucifixion and his exaltation. The life of the Son of God is best understood as a journey: he comes from his pre-existent state in heaven, dwells among women and men, then returns to heaven. In essence, John overcomes the scandal of the cross by interpreting it in terms of Jesus' exaltation (12.32–36). Of spiritual significance for believers are the moments on the cross when Jesus confers a familial relationship on the beloved disciple and Mary, then gives up his spirit (19.26, 30). Orthodox Christian faith sees the establishment of the Church and Christian tradition in these acts. Christian spirituality is thus understood to be informed by Jesus' spirit.

An avid reader of Paul, Augustine elaborates on Paul's teaching regarding the cross. Through the cross, Christians learn to obey the demand for righteousness. For Augustine, the sign of the cross, inscribed on the forehead of catechumens and the baptized, replaces circumcision and impels them to be conformed to the mysteries that the cross represents, namely, the incarnation and passion of the Lord. Christian people should avoid behaviour that contradicts a life conformed to the cross. For example, they should not go to theatres where lewd acts are performed.

In his sermons, Augustine develops the meaning of the cross in terms of other images: a mousetrap, a fishhook and a lion trap. The mortal flesh of Christ is like bait which fools the devil, who loves to kill sinners. But Christ the innocent one's death was undeserved. Thus the devil is compelled to hand over the debtors. Augustine uses these images to strengthen faith in God. Though it took the devil's appetite for killing, the compassion of Christ is now fully disclosed: Christians know they are beloved and thus are empowered to love others.

Similarly, the lampstand images the cross. Augustine uses Matthew 5.15 ('Nobody lights a lamp and puts it under a tub, but on a lampstand, so that it may shine on all who are in the house') to encourage Christians not to take credit for any virtue or good deeds they have done, because God's grace is always the source. The house is the world, the lampstand is the cross of Christ, the lamp shining from the lampstand is Christ hanging on the cross. That it was the Son of God who loved his enemies even as he hung on a cross should not be taken to mean that others are incapable of doing what Christ did. Augustine points out that Stephen, who was not God incarnate, was able to forgive his enemies even while he was being stoned. Always, the cross means that the capacity for such love comes from the grace of God. Augustine believes that the Eucharist empowers Christians to renounce their own claims to compassion irrespective of God's grace. Inducting them into the sacrifice of the cross, the Eucharist is a source of progressive spiritual renewal in which old meanings are dismantled and new ones brought in.

Numerous interpreters of the biblical and patristic material have explicated the meaning of the cross for spiritual experience, growth and maturity. Bonaventure linked increase in compassion with a meditation process that culminated in receiving the imprint of Christ crucified on one's heart. Julian of Norwich identified her own near-death experience with Jesus' dying on the cross and believed that she thereby was made whole and more capable of loving herself and others. Ignatius of Loyola trained retreatants in the use of his Spiritual Exercises to 'imagine Christ our Lord suspended on the cross' so that they might engage in a colloquy with him on the subject of their own sins, thus preparing themselves for later stages of the Exercises and, ultimately, the discernment of their own ministry. Teresa of Avila spontaneously felt that the crucified Jesus was etched deeply into her heart as she prayed through her own pain of abandonment, both by God and other people. And her associate in the Carmelite reform, John, not only appended the cross to his own name, but developed a spiritual theology describing the believer's passage through dark nights of sense and of spirit that somehow mirror Jesus' suffering and culminate in spiritual maturity. Bonhoeffer saw the cross as the most explicit symbol of suffering that was not natural, but undertaken for Jesus Christ's sake.

Some contemporary liberation theologians, feminists and womanists find themselves repelled by the cross because they believe that it has perpetuated the suffering of oppressed groups, especially women, people of colour and inhabitants of the third world. They point out that an ascetic and moralizing focus on the cross, or a 'spiritual' one, can render meaningless the importance of the cross in history, specifically in personal stories of people struggling against tyranny. Others point out that the symbol of the cross continues to raise stress levels in Jewish–Christian relations. And psychologists warn against masochistic identification with Jesus in his suffering. Nevertheless, the cross endures as the primal Christian image that draws lovers of God into experiences of solidarity and commitment, mystery and glory, transforming sorrow and profoundest joy.

See also **Abandonment; Jesus and Spirituality; Imitation of Christ; Suffering.**

Dietrich Bonhoeffer, *Meditations on the Cross,* Louisville, KY: Westminster John Knox Press, 1996; Charles B. Cousar, *A Theology of the Cross: The Death of Jesus in the Pauline Letters,* Minneapolis: Fortress Press, 1990; Elizabeth Dreyer, *The Cross in Christian Tradition: From Paul to Bonaventure,* New York: Paulist Press, 2000; Douglas John Hall, *The Cross in Our Context: Jesus and the Suffering World,* Minneapolis: Fortress Press, 2003; J. B. Green, 'Death of Jesu,' in *Dictionary of Jesus and the Gospels,* ed. Joel B. Green et al., Downers Grove, IL: Intervarsity Press, 1992, pp. 146–63; Luke Timothy Johnson, 'Cross, crucifixion' in *The Oxford Companion to Christian Thought,* Oxford: Oxford University Press, 2000.

ELISABETH KOENIG

Crusades

see **Military Orders**

Cyberspace and Spirituality

The development of information technology (IT) is a major challenge to spirituality in the twenty-first century. From the first invention of tools, people's relationship with God has been conditioned by technological development. The machine technologies of the Industrial Revolution had an immense impact on people's sense of identity and on the self-understanding of society. The workplace gradually separated from living, machinery substituted for human labour and communication across vast distances was greatly extended. At every stage, religious people have faced a choice: condemn such developments or engage with the changes.

IT is more challenging than machine technology because it concerns communication and knowledge. Its purpose is to increase understanding as well as to produce complex links with people worldwide. Inevitably, its messages imply values and social actions. IT offers immediacy as a key value by means of an unprecedented concentration of economic and interpretative power. Its interactive process is not only shaped by people but unavoidably shapes people as well.

IT is a kind of 'embodiment' of human creativity, meaning, value and consciousness. Exploration of the Internet offers relatively unrestrained access to all the knowledge currently available. However, a striking aspect is that IT creates a new kind of social 'space', 'cyberspace', for dwelling, communication and connection. So 'cyberspace' suggests more than 'information technology' or 'Internet' because it highlights the fact that the critical questions are more about *people* than technology. Cyberspace makes a qualitative rather than purely quantitative change to the way we exist: it affects our relationships with each other; it affects how we think of ourselves; it affects what we perceive as 'real'.

The potential of this 'space' for communicating is not in doubt. For example, in terms of human community, people who are housebound may belong to a wider community than their physically circumscribed world. As a space for knowing, the Internet democratizes education by means of distance learning, by placing more material in the public domain and by offering access to texts, artwork or music that are otherwise difficult to obtain.

However, there are questions. First, is virtual space really a place of human *encounter* rather than a protected existence? A recently coined word 'technomonasticism' implies a new kind of community. Yet, alongside the 'technomonastics' there are also 'lurkers' whose anonymous presences browse the Net without identifying themselves or interacting. A high proportion of 'hits' on any web page is of this kind. One response to this perception is to say that this confirms the age-old wisdom that real community demands active commitment and contribution by all members. However, there is another way of looking at things. In 'physical' space, people who are silent are not necessarily uncommitted. They may actually make a significant contribution to community – indeed monastic communities build silence into their lifestyle yet tell of an intimacy between members.

Second, a common reason to access the Internet is electronic mail. E-mail has substantially increased contacts with family and friends. Communication is relatively immediate, effortless and cheap. An increasing number of people think of themselves as part of a 'virtual family' – an immense network in comparison to connections in three-dimensional space. But how real is Internet intimacy? An extreme example is the growth of sexual encounters on the Internet. Can we talk about 'virtual adultery' or 'virtual abuse'? Or, because this is not an encounter 'in the flesh', is it not a 'real' relationship?

Third, what is the impact of 'cyber-travel' on the human spirit? In the past, journeys away from familiar places and meetings with strange people with different customs disturbed our assumptions and world views. Does travel through virtual space possess the same power to challenge? A potential weakness is that technology can promote variety without disturbance. It may simply create an *illusion* of life-changing encounters or the illusion that we can eliminate effortlessly what separates us. However, travel in virtual space is as protectively packaged as air-conditioned tourism. We 'visit' people who are thousands of miles away but it is a journey without real movement. We are not aggravated by strange diets, heat or health hazards. The immediacy of encounters on the Net is selective. We can always click 'Exit' whenever we wish.

Another ambiguity about 'virtual community' is that a major attraction of cyberspace is its potential for individual empowerment. On one level this is a major improvement. People can work, play or learn in their own place and at their own pace. From one perspective, the new culture of information is radically focused around the individual. I can even programme the environment so that *my* preferences inform my Internet activity. Add to this the growing possibility of 'virtual worlds' (from virtual 'tours' of historic buildings to the total immersion of MUDs or multi-user domains) and the dividing line between imagination and reality is blurred. I can regularly take on whatever persona I want

beyond the limits of my physical gendered self. Without care and reflection, such possibilities immerse people in false models of the world so that they are distracted from effective action in real environments.

To be fair, there is a positive side. Cyberspace enables the creation of communities of interest that are otherwise unavailable. In terms of building faith communities, new options open up. On a simple level, electronic mail has given new birth to the ancient art of 'spiritual guidance by letter'. 'Retreats in everyday life' are now offered by means of web sites.

This enhanced capacity for exchange and the multitude of sources also raise questions for serious reflection by traditional faith communities. How does the passing on of tradition fit into this new digital culture that places a bewildering array of resources at people's finger tips? 'Traditions' now exist in a fast-moving, fluid, plural and egalitarian world where boundaries are crossed at will and there are few constraints about the material, ideas and views to which we have access. At the end of the Middle Ages Church people worried about the effect of printing and how it enabled material to be spread beyond the control of Church authority. However, the printed word, like the older manuscript tradition, has texts that are relatively fixed. Now it is the very notion of fixedness that is challenged by cyber-texts. All this challenges understandings of a 'religious tradition' as simple, universal and timeless. A sense of independent choice is always now available.

One of the most awesome possibilities implied by cyberspace is the transcendence of physical limits. Cyberspace is a kind of 'metaphysical gateway' which transports us beyond the equations of physics into an 'other' realm. 'Space' and 'place' take on wholly new meanings and co-ordinates. Some commentators talk of a kind of new physical/spiritual dualism. Physical interaction occurs in many subtle ways. Cyber-community may actually offer more limited interaction. When the Jewish and Christian traditions use the language of 'face to face' to describe union with God, this image is not purely incidental. It reveals something vital about interpersonal encounter. The Christian vision of human nature places a high degree of importance on embodiment. The doctrine of incarnation suggests that God becomes *flesh*. Human embodiment is a kind of 'sacrament' of God's presence. Human destiny is described in terms of *bodily* resurrection. If we bypass fleshliness this creates a privileged, disembodied world that lifts the initiates into a new dualism where 'perfection', as with Gnosticism, is found on some kind of elevated *mental* plane. At the extreme end of speculation, there are claims that cyberspace will become a form of 'life beyond life' if, as some suggest, individual memory can be downloaded and permanently digitalized. If technically possible, it would shift the heart of human existence from bodiliness to patterns of data. However, other commentators speak of *virtual embodiment* and suggest that what is happening in cyberspace is simply the collapse of conventional boundaries between the physical and non-physical.

The more advanced frontiers of speculation are already talking of cyberspace as a kind of 'beyond'. The language used is quasi-mystical. However, the ambiguity of cyberspace in relation to classic approaches to mystical transcendence is beginning to be addressed by some scholars of religion (e.g. Carlson, 2003; Ward, 2000). The apparent ability of the human subject to master the world through technologies seems to overcome the limits of space and time and therefore to 'flatten out' the mystery of transcendence. One way of interpreting the culture of cyberspace is as a form of absolute immanence or 'total presence'. Such a culture offers simultaneity in which 'time' is merely simulated and 'place' is ubiquitous and therefore finally displaced, omni-directional and without any real centre. Yet, it is open to question whether, as some suggest, this signals yet again the death of God. It may be argued, for example, that the apparently all-encompassing vision offered by cyberspace merely cloaks another version of ultimate unknowing. As in classic apophatic mystical texts, the human subject endlessly desires and seeks, but never fully captures, the ultimate 'causality' of its world. Thus in the technological universe, we remain ever on the move, passing from image to image with an endless pattern of connections but also displacements. Desire creates ever new images yet never quite achieves 'the whole', totality.

Cyberspace offers exciting possibilities and even more extraordinary speculations. However, this underlines the need for discernment in the use of new technologies. Discernment has always been a central spiritual value in the Christian spiritual tradition. Now, once again, we have to be capable of discriminating in the potential of cyberspace between what is dehumanizing and what is enhancing, what fragments and what binds us together, what is intellectually and spiritually bankrupt and what will develop human well-being.

See also **Spirituality and Science (*essay*); Body and Spirituality; Images and Spirituality; Media and Communications; Person; Technology and Spirituality.**

James Bailey, *After Thought: The Computer Challenge to Human Intelligence*, New York: Basic Books, 1996; Tom Beaudoin, *Virtual Faith: The Irreverent Spiritual Quest of Generation X*, San Francisco: Jossey-Bass, 1998; Derek Burke et al., *Cybernauts Awake! Ethical and Spiritual Implications of Computers, Information Technology and the Internet*, London: Church House Publishing, 1999; Thomas Carlson, 'Locating the mystical subject' in Michael Kessler and Christian Sheppard (eds), *Mystics: Presence and Aporia*, Chicago: The University of Chicago Press, 2003; Gordon Graham, *The Internet: A Philosophical Inquiry*, London and New York: Routledge, 1999; Michael Heim, *The Metaphysics of Virtual Reality*, Oxford and New York: Oxford University Press, 1993; David Porter (ed.), *Internet Culture*, London and New York: Routledge, 1997; Graham Ward, *Cities of God*, London and New York: Routledge, 2000; Margaret Wertheim, *The Pearly Gates of Cyberspace: A History of Space from Dante to the Internet*, London: Virago Press, 2000.

PHILIP SHELDRAKE

Daoism and Christianity

The comparative study and practice of Daoist and Christian spirituality is ancient but little studied. Early contacts between Christianity and Daoism date back to 635 or when a Monophysite Christian mission to China was established, remarkably, in the precincts of a Daoist abbey near Chang'an (present-day Xi'an), the then capital of the Tang dynasty (608–916 CE). At that time, Daoism, the indigenous organized religion of China, enjoyed a high degree of imperial patronage. The first Tang emperor, who was not himself of noble birth, had claimed to be descended from Laozi, the reputed author of the Scripture of the Way and its Power (*Daode jing c.* fourth century BCE), one of the most prized Daoist scriptures. Laozi was held to be a personification of the Dao – the impersonal cosmic power that gives life and creativity to the myriad creatures – who had appeared not only in China but also in India, as the Buddha, and in the West, as Mani. During the Tang dynasty, Chang'an was perhaps the most cosmopolitan city in the world and was the site of theological controversy and syncretism among Daoists, Confucians, Buddhists, Zoroastrians and Christians.

The literary output of this heady religious melting pot includes the recently retranslated 'Jesus Sutras', which fuse Christian, Daoist and Buddhist terminology into a unique Chinese Christian creation. A stone stele dated to 781 written by the Chinese Christian monk Jingjing records that a virgin gave birth to the holy one in the Roman Empire, that Persians followed the light to give him gifts and subsequently spread the doctrine of light to dispel darkness throughout the world. No mention is made of the crucifixion, presumably because it would be impossible to imagine that a divine being might undergo such inhuman cruelty.

Daoist and Christian spirituality must first of all be understood as a spirituality of salvation into which one must be initiated. The mystery of salvation (the Way) is in both cases revealed through a human who is subsequently understood to be a divine being, and is recorded in written documents transmitted through a priestly lineage. In Daoism, the goal is to recover one's original nature through initiation into the arts of longevity and immortality. Two main forms of Daoism exist in the present. In the Way of the Celestial Masters, the adept hopes to attain a transcendent state (immortality) by petitioning the celestial spirits who are in charge of the bureaucracy of the heavens. In the Way of Complete Perfection, adepts nurture an immortal embryo within the body through meditative practices involving the manipulation of Qi (vital energy) that is stored and processed in the internal organs and which flows through twenty-four conduits or meridians.

Both major forms of spiritual practice may be compared to elements of Christianity. The spirituality of the Way of the Celestial Masters may be termed a liturgical spirituality whose power depends on the authority of the priests to petition the spirits in accordance with sacred liturgies that are not generally accessible to the public. As in pre-Vatican II Catholicism, the power of the (male) priests is based chiefly in their mastery of the classical language in which the sacred documents are written. The priests offer liturgies on behalf of the laity in the hope of winning salvation in the afterlife. Today the main duties of these priests is in performing rituals of exorcism and healing, and funerals.

The spirituality of the Way of Complete Perfection is a monastic spirituality in which Daoists seek their own salvation under the guidance of a master. Open to both men and women, such Daoists dedicate themselves to attaining a transcendent unity with the Dao by means of a spiritual training that involves the whole body. As in classical Christian theology, Daoism proposes that this transcendence must involve the whole body viewed, in Daoism, as a complex of physical and spiritual energy in constant interaction with its environment. Daoism thus emphasizes a 'bio-spirituality' in which the major organs of the body figure prominently. The Way of Highest

Clarity, for instance, developed a repertoire of meditation techniques that involved visualizing the deities who inhabit the stars of the Northern Dipper (Ursa major) descending into the corresponding organs of the body to effect a bio-spiritual transfiguration. The aim is to produce a body of refined spirit energy that is not constrained by the ordinary limits of time and space.

The hagiographies of such people, termed 'immortals', 'transcendents' or 'perfected', are a staple of Daoist sacred literature. Such figures are gifted with a wide range of paranormal powers such as multi-location and shape-shifting. Some simulate their own deaths and leave behind an earthly corpse. Others, like Jesus, ascend into the heavens in broad daylight and attain the highest rank of celestial immortality. Such perfected ones preside over a richly textured celestial world of immortals, spirits, ghosts and demons.

By the time of the Jesuit missions of the sixteenth to eighteenth centuries and the Protestant missions of the nineteenth and twentieth centuries, Daoism no longer occupied such a privileged position in Chinese society. Having become more fused with popular religion and local religious movements, it was regarded by Western Christians as a form of magic or popular superstition, a negative value judgement that persists to this day. Any spiritual value that the tradition contained was thought to be located in the 'mystical' texts of ancient proto-Daoist wisdom tradition, the *Daode Jing* and the *Zhuangzi*. Such texts were interpreted as espousing a form of personal, mystical apprehension of the impersonal Dao, a form of mysticism compatible with perennial philosophy and New Age personal spirituality.

It is increasingly common to associate Daoism with a range of non-religious healing practices such as Taiji quan (T'ai-ch'i-chü'an) and Qigong (Ch'i-kung) that have grown out of the longevity and martial arts practices associated with Daoist religious training. Increasingly it is common for Christians to be engaged in these practices and to have to assess whether or not they are in conflict with Christian spiritual practices. Moreover, hybrid forms of Christian discipleship are emerging that are focused on combining Christian theology with Chinese healing practices. This practical syncretism, coupled with the reassessment of Daoist values and practices by Chinese Christians means that the twenty-first century may witness as fruitful an encounter between Daoists and Christians as occurred in seventh-century China.

See also **Spirituality and the Dialogue of Religions** (*essay*).

Hans Küng and Julia Ching, *Christianity and Chinese Religions,* New York: Doubleday, 1989; James Miller, *Daoism: A Short Introduction,* Oxford: OneWorld Publications, 2003; Martin Palmer in association with Eva Wong, Thalling Halbertsma, Zhao Xiaomin, Li Rongrong and James Palmer, *The Jesus Sutras: Rediscovering the Lost Scrolls of Taoist Christianity,* New York: Ballantine Wellspring, 2001.

JAMES MILLER

Dark Night

Common to religions of the world are the metaphors of light and darkness. Christianity from early on turned to these metaphors, for example in the Gospel of John. Gregory of Nyssa (d. *c.* 395), taking his cue from Exodus 20.21, described the experience of Moses as an encounter with God in darkness. Pseudo-Dionysius (*fl. c.* 500) saw union with God as taking place in the darkness of unknowing. These two authors have given permanent direction to apophatic mysticism, that is, the experience of God in utter darkness. However, the classic expression of the dark night as purification or liberation from what keeps one from union with God in love has been by the Spanish Carmelite John of the Cross (d. 1591). For John the dark night experience purifies the human heart so that it may live in love of God and consequently in love of all creation. John composed a poem, 'Dark Night' and two unfinished commentaries on this poem: *The Ascent of Mount Carmel* and *The Dark Night.* These commentaries were meant as spiritual guidance especially for the Carmelite nuns and friars of his time but as well for the clergy and laity for whom he served as a spiritual guide.

Some time after his nine-month imprisonment at Toledo in 1577–78, John composed his poem, 'Noche oscura' ('Dark Night'), recognized as one of the great poetic compositions of Spanish literature. The poem, much influenced by the language and imagery of the Song of Songs, was composed from the perspective of one who has already experienced union with God in love. The commentaries on the 'Dark Night' tell of the struggle and pain but also of the growth and joy encountered in this contemplative journey that prepares one for intimate union with God. The suffering comes not from God's always loving presence but from human weakness and resistance, conscious and unconscious, to the poverty of spirit and emptiness required so that one may welcome and embrace God's love which fills this emptiness.

The first book of the *Dark Night* commentary describes the passive purification or liberation of the senses which is an initiation into a dark and purifying contemplation. This purification brings about a freedom of spirit 'as one liberated from a cramped prison cell', great delight and enrichment with the fruits of the Holy Spirit.

The second book of the *Dark Night* speaks of the passive purification of the spirit. Passive in both books means that this liberation is God's work, a work that the human person cannot achieve on her own. Contemplation for John is 'nothing else than a secret and peaceful and loving inflow of God' (*Dark Night* 1.10.6). The dark nights, especially the dark night of the spirit, prepare one for living with loving attention to God for whose love the human person was created.

The two commentaries, *Ascent* (2.13) and *Dark Night* (1.9), contain John's classical signs for passing from discursive meditation to contemplation. Meditation becomes problematic because one is called to allow God's love to do its work unimpeded by human thought. John of the Cross chided the spiritual guides of his time for hindering their directees from making this passage into purifying contemplation. Modern spiritual literature often extrapolates John of the Cross's imagery of the dark night to illustrate corporate experiences of oppressive suffering that are not amenable to human efforts.

The human person, or the soul, to use John's expression, 'departs in the dark night from herself and from all creatures, fired with love's urgent longings, and advances by the secret ladder of contemplation to perfect union with God, who is her Beloved salvation' (*Dark Night* 2.21.10).

This intimate union with God in which one becomes like God through participation renders the human person capable of loving all things as they were meant to be loved. The dark nights, however dark they may be, are a secure path to God and are always about life, light and love.

See also **Apophatic Spirituality; Darkness; Carmelite Spirituality.**

Kevin Culligan and Regis Jordan (eds), *Carmel and Contemplation: Transforming Human Consciousness,* Carmelite Studies 8, Washington, DC: Institute of Carmelite Studies, 2000; Keith J. Egan, 'Darkness, Dark Night' in Michael Downey (ed.), *The New Dictionary of Catholic Spirituality,* Collegeville, MN: The Liturgical Press, 1993; Constance FitzGerald, 'Impasse and dark night' in Tilden Edwards (ed.), *Living with Apocalypse: Spiritual Resources for Social Compassion,* San Francisco: Harper & Row, 1984, pp. 93–116; Kieran Kavanaugh and Otilio

Rodriguez (trans.), *The Collected Works of Saint John of the Cross,* rev. edn, Washington, DC: Institute of Carmelite Studies, 1991.

KEITH J. EGAN

Darkness

Darkness is most commonly used as a metaphor for deprivation in Christian spirituality, as also in the Bible and generally in human experience. Darkness is the deprivation of sight, with which one is usually equipped. In the Bible, darkness is a metaphor for lacking understanding or good judgement (Job 12.25; Eph. 4.18), for places where God is absent (Ps. 74.20; John 1.5), for painful experiences of the absence of God (Job 23.17), and for the time of judgement in the last days (Ezek. 32.8; Mark 13.24). In contrast, God is light: 'God is light and in him there is no darkness at all' (1 John 1.5). It is strange, then, to find God also being referred to as dark, and darkness being valued as a place of positive communication with God. In the story of Moses, Moses speaks to God by drawing near to the 'thick darkness where God was' (Ex. 20.21), and he speaks to God in the midst of a 'cloud' on Mount Sinai (Ex. 24.16). The darkness of night is also elsewhere the place where God speaks: to Jacob in his vision, to the boy Samuel, to Jesus who prays at night. Darkness is not simply a name for deprivation but is part of a larger word-play of light and darkness, which is designed to say paradoxical or difficult things about God and spiritual progress. This is more clear where the statements are deliberately paradoxical, as in the statement, 'Even the darkness is not dark to thee, the night is as bright as day' (Ps. 139.12).

The darkness of God is the darkness of an excess of light, a metaphor for God's transcendence of everything that we are or can conceive. The Jewish philosopher and exegete Philo (*c.* 20 BCE–*c.* 50 CE) was the first to make darkness a primary metaphor for God, in contrast to the Platonists who preferred light as the metaphor for the divine One. He took the story of Moses as his source, using the image of God as darkness to stress the absolute divine transcendence of created being. Yet darkness is not only divine transcendence, for Philo, but the hidden communication of God: it is a darkness suffused with unseeable, incomprehensible light. Gregory of Nyssa (*c.* 335–*c.* 395), the Christian Cappadocian Father, pursued this image, saying that Moses' first theophany of God as light in the burning bush was inferior to his second, where he saw God as darkness, because as we progress spiritually, we become more aware of how much remains uncontemplated in God. We move from light to darkness. Yet, again, this is a paradoxical,

'luminous darkness', because Moses 'grew in knowledge' even while seeing that 'what is divine is beyond all knowledge and comprehension' (*Life of Moses* 2.162–3).

It was this understanding of darkness as, at once, the transcendent incomprehensibility of God and God's most intimate communication with humanity that became a key part of the tradition in Christianity known as apophatic or negative theology. In Dionysius (*fl. c.* 500), the obscure Syrian monk whose work was formative of the apophatic tradition, darkness and light are the focal images of a wide-ranging analysis of the interplay of positive and negative symbols in spiritual progress. He draws on the sense from Genesis of darkness as prior to the light of creation, contrasting our present created light with the uncreated God in darkness. But having denied that God is light, he points out that we must also then deny that God is darkness: 'darkness and light, error and truth – it [the supreme Cause of all] is none of these. It is beyond assertion and denial' (*Mystical Theology* 5 [1048A–B]). Darkness helps us to see beyond our false conceptions of God to the one who is beyond language, transforming our understanding by means of a dialectical process. Paradoxical phrases like 'luminous darkness' are designed to expand our understanding beyond the familiar meanings of light and darkness, to catch a glimpse of God as God really is, beyond all description.

In the late Middle Ages and in the modern period, darkness, in common with other metaphors for the spiritual life, became more internalized, describing subjective states of the soul rather than the objective relationship of God with creatures. The transition is most clear in John of the Cross (1542–91), whose 'dark night of the soul' has become a common term for spiritual suffering. However, John of the Cross retains the dialectical language of Dionysius and his goal is to show how subjective feelings of darkness may be filled with the objective divine light. He says that we feel our darkness most acutely when we are being illuminated by God's light, because of our spiritual poverty, and the greatest darkness of all is experienced when looking directly at God (*Dark Night* 2.5.2). Darkness, correctly discerned, is the communication of God and the mark of spiritual progress.

Darkness has remained a key metaphor among spiritual writers in recent times, for instance in Thérèse of Lisieux, T. S. Eliot, and R. S. Thomas. More than marking subjective feelings, its dialectical use is able to show the paradoxical presence of God even in what is experienced as deprivation.

See also **Apophatic Spirituality; Dark Night; God, Images of; Light; Mystical Theology.**

Primary sources: There are many figures who may be regarded as primary sources of the language of darkness. Some key texts by the three main authors above can be found in:
Gregory of Nyssa: the Life of Moses, trans. Abraham J. Malherbe and Everett Ferguson, CWS, New York: Paulist Press, 1978; Pseudo-Dionysius: The Complete Works, trans. Colm Luibheid, CWS, New York: Paulist Press, 1987; The Collected Works of John of the Cross, trans. Kieran Kavanaugh and Otilio Rodriguez, Washington, DC: Institute of Carmelite Studies, 1991.
Secondary sources: 'Nuit (Ténèbre)' in DS, vol. XI, pp. 519–25; Andrew Louth, The Origins of the Christian Mystical Tradition from Plato to Denys, Oxford: Clarendon Press, 1980; Denys Turner, The Darkness of God: Negativity in Christian Mysticism, Cambridge: Cambridge University Press, 1995.

EDWARD HOWELLS

Death and Dying

In Western society, death is often thought of as simply the end and this view is encouraged by a prevailing reductionist scientism. This materialist view affirms that human beings are no more than complicated psychophysical organisms. There are interesting paradoxes involved with secular views of death. On the one hand death is seen as the ultimate terror to be avoided or postponed. On the other hand life can be regarded as so broken, disabled or fading as not to be worthwhile or of any social value – hence it may be neglected or even extinguished by voluntary or involuntary euthanasia.

For Christian theology, in its understanding of the doctrine of Christian hope, there is an insistence that death must be taken seriously as the ending of individual existence. Resurrection, therefore, is seen as a new creation by which God transcends all that we can think or imagine. In this perspective the resurrection of Jesus Christ is seen as the foundation for future hope. Belief in life after death has always been at the heart of Christianity. Death happens to us all but for the Christian it is not an ultimate disintegration. Beyond death the Christian is offered the endowment of a new body of a kind foreign to this present age (1 Cor. 15.35–54) and this renders death an essential preparation for resurrection in Christ (1 Cor. 15.49). So what matters most for the Christian is not death but a person's union with and in Christ (2 Cor. 5.17).

In this context death and dying are the ends of a process which begins in everyone at conception – even our bodily form is shaped in part by the death of some of its proliferations before birth. Ageing is part of dying and leads to death, whether by accident or disease. Hence the Christian Church has never sought to disguise the absence of this normal process but rather, in the light of its belief in the resurrection, to look forward to the vital nature of the life beyond.

The Christian Church has had a particular concern for the care of the vulnerable, sick and dying. It is part of the Christian vocation to encourage prayer and assure the dying person that prayer is being made for them. Many dying people need to be reminded of a trust which they have ceased to exercise, or for which they have seen no need before. Christians can and have played their part in collaborating in shared care with others for the dying. At the heart of this shared Christian care is love.

Death is the temporal limit of all finite existence. Its meaning depends upon the perspective from which it is viewed, that is, biological, psychological, sociological or theological-spiritual. In Christian theology death is interpreted in relation to God the Creator, Judge and Redeemer of life. The death and resurrection of Christ are central in this interpretation. Modern theology emphasizes the multidimensionality of death, including the possibility of its being the natural conclusion of life. Theologians have argued that death belongs to the limitation of human life as created by God. It follows that under the condition of sin death confronts us as guilty creatures unable to justify our lives and that through faith in Christ we are 'liberated from natural death', that is, set free to live and die in the confidence that God, who is gracious and faithful, is Lord not only of life but also of death.

Christian spirituality should take note of these significant denials of death in modern culture. The widespread denial of death is a recurrent theme in modern literature as well as in many scientific studies. Both denial and acceptance of death in modern culture are rooted in the conviction that death is the ultimate reality. Modern fear of death focuses as much on the processes of dying as on death itself. Having learned to value independence and activity, and to abhor dependence and passivity, many persons above all fear the helplessness of dying. This fear of complete dependence is intensified by the possibility of being kept alive artificially by modern medical technology, when all valued life capacities are irretrievably lost.

In conclusion we should note the following: the value of the diversity of biblical understanding of death; the profound relationality of human existence and the ultimate Christian confidence that in the face of death we are all held by the grace of God. Another significant aspect of this theology is the awareness of the incompleteness of the work of redemption and of the continuing groaning of creation. Faith in God refuses to justify the horrors of history or the tragedies of personal experience. The resurrection of Christ from the dead is the basis and paradigm of hope in God's final victory over evil.

In the light of all this we might see death and the thought of death as a spiritual opportunity to reorientate our priorities away from the worldly towards the religious, away from the material towards ultimate questions of truth and love. Mortal illness might serve to orientate us away from excessive concerns with status. The thought of death might be able to usher us towards a profounder sense of our priorities. The prospect of our own death may draw us towards a way of life that we value in our hearts.

See also **Health and Healing; Resurrection.**

John Bowker, *The Meanings of Death*, Cambridge: Cambridge University Press, 1993; Nicholas Peter Harvey, *Death's Gift*, London: Epworth Press, 1985; Peter Houghton, *On Death, Dying and not Dying*, London: Jessica Kingsley Press, 2001; Gillian Rose, *Love's Work*, London: Chatto & Windus, 1995; Rachel Stanworth, *Recognising Spiritual Needs in People Who Are Dying*, Oxford: Oxford University Press, 2004; Averil Stedeford, *Facing Death*, London: Sobell Publications, 1994; James Woodward, *Befriending Death*, London: SPCK, 2005; James Woodward (ed.), *Embracing the Chaos: Theological Responses to AIDS*, London: SPCK, 1990.

JAMES WOODWARD

Decision-Making

see Discernment

Deification

Deification (or divinization, in Greek: *theosis*): the doctrine that the destiny of human kind, or indeed of the cosmos as a whole, is to share in the divine life, and actually to become God, though by grace rather than by nature. The doctrine, that has become particularly characteristic of Eastern Orthodox theology, developed out of a host of suggestions in the Bible that human engagement with God involves a profound intimacy. These include the affirmation that Israel's God is 'near to it' (Deut. 4.7), that Israel's relationship to God is that of a 'son' (e.g. Ex. 4.22), that Israel is God's, 'called by name' (Isa. 43.1). Such sugges-

tions are multiplied in the New Testament: the notion of sonship becomes central (cf. Matt. 6.9–13; Rom. 8.14–17; Gal. 4.4–7), the notion of transformation into the Lord's glory appears (cf. 2 Cor. 3.18; 1 Cor. 13.12–13), and there are explicit assertions that 'we shall be like him' (1 John 3.2), and 'become partakers of the divine nature' (2 Peter 1.4).

In early patristic thought, these hints are drawn together by the centrality of the doctrine of human creation in the 'image [*eikon*] and likeness [*homoiosis*] of God' (Gen. 1.26), and combined with the Platonic ideal of assimilation to God, *homoiosis theoi* (*Theaetetus* 176B), as well as the general philosophical conviction that genuine knowledge, being knowledge by participation, entails assimilation of the knower to the known. All of this is given sharper focus through reflection on the purpose and significance of God's assumption of humanity in the incarnation, and the insight that the human response to God's becoming human is humankind's becoming God, expressed in lapidary form in Athanasius' assertion that '[the Word] became human that we might become God' (*On the Incarnation* 54). Such a doctrine is already explicit in such early theologians as Irenaeus and Clement, and is developed by later theologians such as Athanasius and Gregory of Nazianzus (who coined the term *theosis*), Cyril of Alexandria and especially Maximus the Confessor. It also became an important theme in Byzantine ascetic theology. In the fourteenth-century Hesychast controversy, the doctrine became controversial, the notion of deification being held to blur the distinction between the creature and the uncreated God; to defend the by then traditional teaching Gregory Palamas invoked the distinction, already found in an inchoate form in the Cappadocians and Maximus, between God's essence, which is unknowable and imparticipable, and his energies, which are uncreated and therefore fully divine, but knowable, participation in which entails deification.

In the West, the theme of deification became less important (though it is still significant for Augustine), being overshadowed by an understanding of the human relationship to God based on the distinction between nature and grace. However, among many of the so-called 'mystics', the doctrine of deification remained central, though it attracted the same kind of suspicion from theologians as did the Byzantine Hesychasts. Twentieth-century ecumenical dialogue has led to renewed interest in the doctrine of deification, and it has been suggested that the doctrine is much more significant in the West than has often been thought: even, for instance, in Martin

Luther. In this context, it is perhaps useful to distinguish between the doctrine of deification, as it developed in Greek patristic theology, and the theme or metaphor of deification, which, given the biblical evidence cited above, is hardly likely to be completely neglected in any biblically informed theology. The patristic doctrine of deification goes beyond being merely a theme, and incorporates the following points. First, and most important, human destiny is seen in terms of deification; the arc of creation to deification, in which creation finds its fulfilment, is the principal arc of human destiny, transcending the lesser arc, that has come to dominate Western theology, of fall to redemption. Second, deification involves a fundamental change in human nature (in this context the word 'ontological' is often used); it is not a matter of an altered estimate of the human condition, as redemption has sometimes been considered in the West, or even altered patterns of moral behaviour: it involves a breaking of, and reconstruction of, the heart, as the ontological centre of human beings. Consequently, third, deification, though quite beyond human achievement, is not to be accomplished without the most strenuous human effort: it demands a serious asceticism, as the human is shaped to the presence and activity of the divine.

See also Byzantine Spirituality; Cappadocian Fathers; Early Christian Spirituality; Hesychasm; Orthodox Spirituality.

Jules Gross, *The Divinization of the Christian according to the Greek Fathers*, trans. Paul. A. Onica, Anaheim, CA: A & C Press, 2002 (originally published in French in 1938); M. Lot-Borodine, *La deification de l'homme selon la doctrine des Pères grecs*, Bibliothèque Œcuménique 9, Paris: Éditions du Cerf, 1970 (originally published as articles in 1932, 1939 and 1950); Friedrich Normann, *Telihabe – ein Schlüsselwort der Vätertheologie*, Münsterische Beiträge zur Theologie 42, Münster: Aschendorff, 1978; Norman Russell, *The Doctrine of Deification in the Greek Patristic Tradition*, Oxford Early Christian Studies, Oxford: Oxford University Press, 2004.

ANDREW LOUTH

Depression

see Desolation

Desert

It would be difficult to overestimate the significance of the desert in the Christian imagination. But the role it occupies within Christian spirituality is complex. It is first of all an actual geographical locale, within which crucial experiences of encounter with God occur. But it is also a mythic place, a place of dreams and fears that has come to occupy a central place within the religious imaginations of Christians. These two aspects of the desert are not unrelated to one another. If one considers the foundational desert encounters in Jewish and Christian experience (e.g. Moses and the burning bush, Jesus and the forty days in the wilderness, the early Christian monastics in the deserts of Egypt and Judaea), one recognizes that the desert is both actual place and rich, ambiguous metaphor. That is, an actual encounter in a desert landscape stands at the heart of the experience, but the religious imagination makes the desert into something that can continue to feed the soul long after the desert itself is but a distant memory.

The story of Antony of Egypt offers a good example of this process. Athanasius' *Life of Antony* describes Antony's experience of long years living in the Egyptian desert, first in the region near the Nile river valley, and then far beyond that in the more remote 'great desert' toward the Red Sea. This is a real desert, arid, hot, with little water and food. It is also a place of great beauty. Antony actually lived in this landscape and traces of this desert can be discerned in his story. However, the desert is already mythologized in Athanasius' telling of the story: it is home to the demons, a difficult and treacherous domain in which the monk is tested, purified, made whole. It is also, in Athanasius' telling, a paradisal reality, a place to which the monk is drawn in order to discover and create a new Eden. The monk's struggle in the desert is a battle against principalities and powers, a journey into the very depths of the soul, the means by which the soul can come to know God.

While actual deserts have continued to play a role in shaping persons and communities in the Christian spiritual tradition, it is the myth of the desert that has had the more wide-ranging and enduring influence on the Christian imagination. Already in the early monastic tradition, there is evidence that the desert myth had begun shaping Christian experience. In a process that one scholar has described as the 'desertification' of early monastic experience, the story of Antony's solitary struggle in the desert proved so imaginatively compelling and dramatically alluring that it came to stand as the emblematic monastic story, thus obscuring and rendering less compelling other and different experiments in ascetic living (e.g. those more communal in character or those located in towns and villages rather than in deserts). As an imaginative space that described the immense range and depth of the spiritual journey, the desert had an undeniable power that often enabled it to dwarf other, less compelling images of the spiritual life.

One sees evidence of this power within the subsequent history of Christian spirituality, art and practice. The spiritual ideal of the desert, especially the notion of the desert as a place of testing and purification, became associated in the Christian imagination with the *via purgativa* and more broadly with the apophatic spirituality of the *via negativa*. It is in this sense that figures as diverse in sensibility and geographical locale as the early Cistercian monks, Julian of Norwich, John of the Cross, Seraphim of Sarov and Abbé Huvelin can be considered exemplars of 'desert spirituality'. One also sees the enduring power of the desert ideal in the myriad visual depictions of St Antony's story in the history of Western art, by artists such as Sassetta, Grünewald and Bosch, for whom Antony's story proved a necessary lens through which to examine the challenges and possibilities of their own times. Finally, one must reckon with the ongoing presence of the desert as an inspiration to countless generations of Christian ascetics who continue to understand their lives as continuation of the ancient desert ideal.

Does the desert as an actual geographical place still have a role to play in shaping the Christian imagination? The witness of the Trappist monks of Tibhirrine, killed in 1996, in part for their refusal to leave their Muslim friends who were embroiled in the Algerian civil war, provides us with a more recent image of Christians who have chosen to enter the desert to follow Christ. As harrowing and compelling as the stories of Jesus and Antony, the story of these monks hidden away in the desert of Algeria reminds us yet again of the power of the desert to draw forth from persons of faith their deepest and most generous response to God.

See also Asceticism; Early Christian Spirituality; Eremitical Spirituality; Monasticism; Place.

Isabel Colegate, *A Pelican in the Wilderness: Hermits, Solitaries and Recluses*, Washington, DC: Counterpoint, 2002; Belden C. Lane, *The Solace of Fierce Landscapes: Exploring Desert and Mountain Spirituality*, New York: Oxford University Press, 1998; Andrew Louth, *The Wilderness of God*, Nashville, TN: Abingdon, 1991; Bernard McGinn, 'Ocean and desert as symbols of mystical absorption in the Christian tradition', *Journal of Religion* 74.2 (1994), 155–81; Benedicta Ward, 'The desert myth: reflections on the desert ideal in early Cistercian monasticism' in M. Basil Pennington (ed.), *One Yet Two: Monastic Tradition East and West*, Kalamazoo, MI: Cistercian Publications, 1976.

DOUGLAS BURTON-CHRISTIE

Desire

Desire is the heart of all spirituality. It is an energy that powers spirituality but, conversely, spirituality is concerned with how people focus desire. Christian spirituality embodies the sense that humanity has a longing that can only be satisfied in God. Consequently, its greatest teachers focused on how desire should be channelled.

As Walter Conn suggests, the most fundamental human desire is for transcendence. How can we transcend ourselves in relationships with the world, other people and God? (Conn, 1998, p. 5). Many people find it difficult to think of desire as a key to spirituality. Part of the problem is the effect of various ascetical trends inherited from the early Christian centuries which set the tone for so much that came afterwards. These presented the ideal human as free from need and desire – especially apparently inescapable dependencies on food and sex.

Western spirituality has also been powerfully influenced in recent centuries by the Enlightenment, associated with a strong emphasis on individuality and on rationality. Where love has been allowed a role, it was spiritual, disinterested, universal love *(agape)* rather than engaged, passionate, particular love *(eros)*. Only *agape* was generally associated with God even though *eros* played an important role in the theology of significant spiritual figures such as the fourteenth-century Dominican, Meister Eckhart.

Yet, desire has a particular association with eros-love. It is best understood as our most honest experience of ourselves, in all our complexity and depth, as we relate to people and things around us. Desire is not the same as instincts but actually involves a reflective element. Desire is associated with our capacity to love truly. This proves itself in focused attention and a quality of dedication that is deeper than duty or will power. It is perhaps what St Augustine means by 'intention' and the author of the English mystical text, *The Cloud of Unknowing*, by 'naked intent'.

Desire is powerful. The fourteenth-century Italian mystic Catherine of Siena recognized the positive power of desire when she wrote that it is one of the few ways of touching God because 'you have nothing infinite except your soul's love and desire' (*Dialogue*, p. 270). Meister Eckhart suggested that the reason why we are not able to see God is the faintness of our desire.

Scripture and desire. Many Christians have not instinctively related to the biblical idea of a God passionately engaged with creation and whose very existence is a continuous movement out of self. A more familiar influence is the image of a passionless, detached God whose perfection (based on the philosophy of Aristotle) is to be self-contained and at rest. Yet both the Hebrew and Christian Scriptures are full of the themes of desire, yearning and longing. The writers of the Psalms were never afraid to express deep and powerful emotions of this kind in relation to God:

> As a deer yearns for running streams, so I yearn for you, my God.
> I thirst for God, the living God; when shall I go to see the face of God?
>
> (Ps. 42.1–2)

God, too, is a God who desires us and yearns for us. The consoling prophecy of Second Isaiah to the defeated and exiled people of Israel portrays God's desire as so great that the people's image or name is carved into the palm of God's hand:

> Zion was saying, 'Yahweh has abandoned me, the Lord has forgotten me.'
> Can a woman forget her baby at the breast, feel no pity for the child she has borne?
> Even if these were to forget,
> I shall not forget you.
> Look, I have engraved you on the palms of my hands . . .
>
> (Isa. 49.14–16)

In the New Testament Mark 10 highlights the different qualities of human desire. The rich man desires to be good and to love God (verses 17–22) but also wants material security. The text does not present a crude contrast between love of God and love of other things. Rather, that man's deepest desire for God was still not free to find full expression. The sons of Zebedee (verses 35–40) desire to be with Jesus but also seek the status that they believe the kingdom of God will bring. To desire fully to 'be with' Jesus is to risk sharing in who Jesus really is and thus in a process of stripping away more superficial desires. The blind beggar, Bartimaeus (verses 46–52), contrasts strongly with the spiritual blindness of both the rich man and the disciples. His deep, intensely focused desire is not merely for healing but to follow Jesus. In this case, singleness of desire brings both healing and discipleship.

Teachers of desire. Many of the greatest spiritual teachers use desire as a central metaphor of the human search for God and God's search for humanity. One only has to consider Augustine, Gregory of Nyssa, medieval monks using the Song of Songs, Beguines such as Hadewijch, Bonaventure, Eckhart, Catherine of Siena, Julian

of Norwich, the author of *The Cloud of Unknowing*, the great Carmelites Teresa of Avila and John of the Cross, Ignatius Loyola, the Anglicans George Herbert and Thomas Traherne and the Wesley brothers. All of them, in different ways, taught that spirituality centres on desire.

A key teacher of a spirituality of desire is Ignatius Loyola (1491–1556), the sixteenth-century Basque noble and founder of the Jesuits. Both his life and his teachings speak of desire in relation to prayer and discernment in everyday life. From the moment his military career ended as the result of wounds at the battle of Pamplona 1521, Ignatius began a journey of desire. During his painful convalescence he struggled to discover his heart's desire. A period as a hermit at Manresa, university studies, the creation of the famous Spiritual Exercises, and his founding of the Jesuits, was a gradual process of learning how to focus his desire on choosing well. In his Spiritual Exercises, Ignatius invites the one making the retreat 'to ask God our Lord for what I want and desire' at the beginning of every period of prayer. Running through Ignatius' spirituality of desire is the quest for spiritual freedom from misplaced or superficial desires that imprison us (what he called 'disordered attachments') and an ever greater ability to centre authentic desire on God. Authentic desires arise from the essential self rather than from immediate reactions to situations and experiences. Such desires reach into the heart of identity. At this level 'Who am I?' and 'What do I want?' coincide. 'To ask God our Lord for what I want and desire' is an invitation to acknowledge an immediate sense of need but only as a starting point for a gradual unfolding of what we are most deeply concerned about.

A spirituality of desire. Is God a God of desire? The seventeenth-century Anglican mystic Thomas Traherne had no doubts about it. Traherne is one of the most striking spiritual writers on the subject of desire – ours and God's. '[God's] wants put a lustre upon his enjoyments and make them infinite' (*Centuries of Meditation*, 1.44). It is because God is a God of desire that engaging with desire is the heart of prayer. Desire, or its equivalents, plays a major role in the approach to prayer from the Desert Fathers and Mothers to the great Western mystics. As Abba Joseph said to Abba Lot, with his fingers 'like ten lamps of fire', 'If you will, you can become all flame' (Ward, 1975, p. 103). Throughout Julian of Norwich's *Showings*, 'longing' or 'yearning' are key experiences not only in our forgiveness by God and conversion from sin but also in our developing relationship to God. For the author of *The Cloud of*

Unknowing, 'Now you have to stand in desire all your life long' (ch. 2).

Delight, play and pleasure are not concepts that many people instinctively associate with spirituality. We may admit that the word *desire* has some kind of spiritual dimension but its passionate, even sexual, connotations seem to lack the sober quality needed for serious seekers. From Buddhist ascetics to Christian contemplatives a culture of detachment has predominated. This way of passionlessness affects the spiritual self-understanding of the majority of people who lead sexually active lives. Yet, of all the aspects of the practice of everyday life, sexuality is arguably the most powerful in terms of spirituality.

Desire implies incompleteness because it speaks of what we are not, or do not have. Desire is, therefore, a condition of openness to future possibility. While desire is grounded in the present it also points beyond. As Augustine affirmed to God, 'Our hearts are restless until they find their rest in You.' Clearly, such ideas have a great deal to do with our experience of choice and change. Desire comes into its own as the condition for discerning what our choices are and how to choose authentically. Being people of desire also means that the spiritual journey is essentially a story of continual transition. In this way, desire becomes a powerful metaphor for spiritual transformation.

See also **Affectivity; Agape; Body and Spirituality; Bridal Mysticism; Conversion; Detachment; Discernment; Election, Ignatian; Emotions; Eroticism; Ignatian Spirituality; Love; Sexuality.**

Anon., *The Cloud of Unknowing,* CWS, New York: Paulist Press, 1981; Augustine, *Confessions,* there are a variety of modern editions available; Catherine of Siena, *The Dialogue,* CWS, New York: Paulist Press, 1980; Walter Conn, *The Desiring Self,* New York: Paulist Press, 1998; Meister Eckhart, *Teacher and Preacher,* CWS, New York: Paulist Press, 1986; Julian of Norwich, *Showings,* CWS, New York: Paulist Press, 1978; Philip Sheldrake, *Befriending our Desires,* 2nd edn, Ottawa: Novalis/London: Darton, Longman & Todd, 2001; Thomas Traherne, *Centuries,* London: Mowbray, 1975; Benedicta Ward (ed.), *The Sayings of the Desert Fathers,* Kalamazoo, MI: Cistercian Publications, 1984.

PHILIP SHELDRAKE

Desolation

This entry will focus on 'desolation' as a term referring to a painful spiritual, mental and affective state characterized by, for instance, dreary sorrow, wretchedness or, negatively, a lack or deprivation of comfort or joy. The term has particular use and importance in the context of discernment of spirits in Ignatian spirituality where it refers to any experience that is contrary to consolation. Ignatius Loyola gave as examples of desolation, 'darkness and disturbance of the soul, attraction towards what is low and of the earth, anxiety arising from various agitations and temptations. All this' he added, 'tends to a lack of confidence in which the soul is without hope and without love; one finds oneself thoroughly lazy, lukewarm, sad and as though cut off from one's Creator and Lord' (*Spiritual Exercises* 317). A tendency to cynicism or self-absorption, moral and spiritual lethargy, an aversion to opening oneself in love towards God and others or a focus on gratification of immediate personal needs may also be included among symptoms of spiritual desolation. Although in the Christian spiritual tradition discussion normally focuses on experiences of desolation in individuals, 'group desolation' is also a recognizable phenomenon with a potentially destructive impact on a group or community.

In the traditional language of Ignatian spirituality, genuine consolation is attributed to the action of 'good spirit(s)' or influences and desolation to 'bad' or 'evil spirit(s)' or influences. Just as consolation is a sign of a person being in right relationship with God and with others in God, so spiritual desolation, for those who are seeking to live such a relationship, is as an indicator either of something wrong in relationship with God, others and the world, or of influences within a person or group which are potentially destructive of such right relationship. Hence, in discernment of spirits, reflecting on consolation and desolation helps towards distinguishing between those elements in experience which lead to human flourishing through an ordering of life in love of God and others and the world in God (consolation) and those which draw a person in a contrary direction and are destructive of human good (desolation).

It is clear that there are both similarities and differences between desolation in the sense described here and depression. On the one hand, they belong to two different kinds of discourse: one has to do with ethical and spiritual experience and behaviour within a theological framework of understanding, the other with clinical and psychological diagnosis and treatment, a difference which suggests two distinct conditions. Nevertheless, they may in certain cases have not only similar causes (e.g. trauma, loss, grief, personal neglect, oppressive living conditions) but also similar symptoms (as described above). Moreover, they sometimes exist together in the same person at the same time, and experience suggests that clinical depression may also be a cause of spiritual desolation. Any wise discernment process will be careful to distinguish between these two conditions and to deal with each by appropriate means.

Contemporary Ignatian spirituality makes use of the strategies for understanding and dealing with desolation suggested by Ignatius Loyola and they have proved wise and effective over time (cf. *Spiritual Exercises* 314–36). Underlying these strategies is the presupposition that desolation, painful and potentially destructive though it is, can also, if rightly handled, make for good. The following are some examples of such strategies. Honest consideration of one's recent conduct, to see if the cause of present desolation lies there, militates against laziness, rationalization or self-deception. Critical reflection on the experience and speaking of it to a wise friend help a person to understand the subtle workings of desolation and make for objectivity as well as support and encouragement. Calling to mind previous experiences of consolation may be an aid towards recognizing that present experience, though painful, is likely to be temporary. Being careful not to make any important decisions in desolation forestalls any destructive outworking of the experience. Finally, opening to God in prayer and faith not only acts against the thrust of desolation towards self-absorption and self gratification but also reflects a trust in God as the ultimate source of all grace and true consolation. These suggestions enshrine the basic principle that good discernment means moving with and building upon consolation and acting against desolation.

See also **Consolation; Discernment; Ignatian Spirituality.**

For further reading, consult the bibliography to the entry on **Discernment.**

DAVID LONSDALE

Detachment

Detachment is an act of spiritual freedom. It is also the virtue of habitually choosing out of freedom not compulsion, fear, or routine. Therefore, it is a virtue that allows a person to review competing goods and choose that which most fulfils one's life ideals or values. In the Hebrew Scripture the great model of detachment is Abraham who left his homeland and offered to sacrifice his own son and became, through his fidelity to the Lord, the father of a great people. For Christians, Jesus walks in that same path of fidelity to the call of the Lord. The hymn from Philippians (2.1–11) provides the classic Christian meditation on this fundamental paradigm of detachment.

Within the Christian ascetical tradition detachment is a prerequisite for discipleship, to leave behind what does not allow a man or woman to follow the call of Christ. Within Christian tradition there have been a number of terms that spelled out applications of this Christlike detachment: abnegation, forgetfulness of self, humility, mortification, renouncement, renunciation, self-denial, self-sacrifice and, more recently, apostolic availability, mobility and spiritual freedom. What all these terms have in common is an agreement that at the heart of the Christian experience is the acceptance of the absolute character of God's will. Therefore, detachment and discernment are intimately linked so that a person is detached in order to find how God calls and then to what specific action God calls.

Within the Christian tradition detachment transcends any one way of life – contemplative or active, religious, clerical or lay – and is an element in all ways of Christian life. A developed prayer life demands a detachment, openness to God's guidance and response. An active ministry presumes a listening heart, the willingness to look at all the ways God calls one to action for the kingdom.

The asceticism that is part of detachment is not the end of detachment. Detachment is fully compatible with a love of creation, with a warmly human response to other people, and with a deep reverence for learning art, science and technology. Detachment guides the affective determination to find God in all things because it both takes seriously the dignity of every creature and the creature's relationship to the only absolute, God. The end of detachment, then, is love but a love attuned to God's priorities. Such is the spirituality of detachment that shapes the Ignatian and Teresian traditions. It is also the spirituality that moulds the Vatican II call to the Church to be a servant to the world in the promotion of peace and social justice, in ecumenism, as an extension of friendship to other faiths. Operating in this social context, detachment is not only a personal virtue but an institutional one as well, a corporate freedom that seeks through communal discernment the ways any group, precisely as a group, can determine the authentic call of God and then have the courage to follow that call. Institutional detachment, like individual detachment, confronts vested interests and selfish securities. It summons churches and nations to live beyond themselves for a world more just, more peaceful and more humane.

See also **Abandonment; Asceticism; Discipline; Discernment; Examination of Conscience/ Consciousness.**

R. Oechslin, G. Bardy, H. Martin, 'Depouillement' in *DS* cols 455–502; Leif E. Vaage and Vincent L. Wimbush (eds), *Asceticism and the New Testament,* New York and London: Routledge, 1999.

HOWARD GRAY

Devotio Moderna

The *devotio moderna* (*c.* 1375–1600) is a movement of interior reform that has its roots in the Dutch and German-speaking worlds of the late Middle Ages and early modernity. To say this is already to specify *devotio moderna* to some extent as regards content, period and location. It appears as spiritually akin to the reform movements taking place at the time, especially in religious orders throughout Europe.

Its discernible origins as a movement are to be found in the life and work of Master Geert Grote (1340–84) from Deventer. After being prey as a young cleric to the decadence of Church life in the fourteenth century, to the extent even of his having applied for lucrative benefices, he was converted around 1374. He made over his family home as a house where devout, poor women could live in freedom, and moved into the Charterhouse at Monnikhuizen (Arnhem), got to know its rich literary culture thoroughly, and then returned back into the world after three years. By being ordained deacon, he obtained a licence to preach in the diocese of Utrecht. He travelled tirelessly around this district as a reform preacher in order to denounce lapses in celibacy among the clergy, lapses in poverty among religious, lapses in morality among the laity, and sectarianism and heresy at every level of the Church. At this time of the Western Schism (1378–1417), which split the Church into two allegiances (Rome and Avignon), he put before his audience both orally and in writing the ideal of a discipleship of Christ expressed principally through a personal sense of responsibility for the whole of the body of Christ as represented by its head, and in a sense of spiritual bonding with Christ. He pointed young people towards religious houses open to reform; through his letters he encouraged those who had become unsettled; and more generally he fostered individual and communal prayer through a vernacular Book of Hours (*horarium*), developed by him out of the official ecclesiastical breviary – a work disseminated very broadly. With his friend, the school director in Zwolle, Johannes Cele (1350–1417), he initiated the late medieval school reform in the Netherlands, which had as its main goals the gospel as the basis of a style of education sensitive to children, and the formation of Christian conscience or community spirit.

Grote's concern for reform was very fruitful. First, with his friend, the priest Florens Radewijns (1350–1400) he laid the foundations for the Brethren of the Common Life: clerics and lay people who lived together in semi-religious community, following the model of the primitive Jerusalem community (Acts 2.44–47; 4.32–35), without a religious rule or profession. Thus the house which Radewijns had as curate at Deventer became the *Heer-Florenshuis,* the spiritual centre of a devout movement of brothers that underwent further development during the time when Radewijns was rector. In the same year as his early death, Geert Grote also founded a house for the Brothers in nearby Zwolle. After his death, the independent group of women living in Grote's parental home developed, under the protection of Johannes Brinckerninck (1359–1419) into a parallel group of Sisters.

Second, the collections of books owned by Grote and the first Brothers such as Radewijns, Brinckerninck, Gerard Zerbolt (1376–98) and Johannes van den Gronde (d. 1392) stimulated the development of a literary culture that had a decisive influence on the movement's further development. They began busily to buy, read, copy, exchange and collect books. The central rationale was the conviction that a good Christian book contains the whole patrimony of the Church, and that every interior reform should begin with a return to these primordial sources. For this purpose, the Brothers gathered around them young men especially, who, through their activity as copyists, would be constantly enriched by the fruits of the Church's life as it had been lived over the centuries. A distinctive feature for this regime of piety became the *rapiarium,* a personal collection of texts culled from what people read. Almost every member had one of these.

Third, along with this literary culture and the educational reform, there developed a system of hostels. Hostels grew up alongside many of the Brothers' houses: specially designated lodgings under the leadership of a Procurator, which provided for the boys who went to school spiritual guidance and help with school work, as well as board and lodging. However, it was only rarely that the Brothers of the Common Life undertook school administration or teaching. They preferred to exert their educational influence through sitting on appointments committees, through enterprises of continuing education such as conferences (*collationes*), and through personal counselling.

From this first form of *devotio moderna*, the Brothers and Sisters of Common Life, two further forms soon arose. Both the Heer-Florenshuis and the Meester-Geertshuis founded from Deventer independent monasteries in the tradition of the Canons Regular under the rule of St Augustine, in Windesheim (1387) and in Dipenveen (1400). There were three reasons why this new development took place: (1) the Brotherhood was not fully a religious order, and could provide only an unstable foundation for a juridically assured future; (2) the Brothers and Sisters had taken from their founder the additional goal of reforming the consecrated life of their time along the lines of the 'new interiority'; (3) some of the Brothers and Sisters preferred, out of a sense of personal calling, a more regulated form of consecrated life. Out of the Windesheim monastery, its two daughter monasteries in Niewlicht (Hoorn) and Marienborn (Arnhem), and the new model foundation at Eemstein, there grew the Windesheim Congregation (1395), that at the beginning of the sixteenth century extended to 102 monasteries for men and women, to say nothing of the numerous convents of canonesses that were not part of the Congregation, but lived according to the Windesheim rules, and – with the exception of ten to fourteen convents that came together in the Venlo Chapter (1455) – did not form any federation.

The *devotio moderna* originated in the area around Deventer, with Zwolle as a second centre. However, even in the fourteenth century, there was also a focus around Amersfoort, Utrecht and Delft, with Willem Clinckaert as the leading figure. Here there soon arose a preference for the Rule of the Franciscan Third Order, leading to a third form of life according to the *devotio moderna*. In 1399, some houses of Brothers and Sisters took this semi-religious Rule as the inspiration for a form of tertiary life, closer to that of religious orders. At the same time, they founded in Amersfoort the Chapter of Utrecht, which by the beginning of the sixteenth century had grown to 166 houses, mostly of female tertiaries. This Chapter was also the source of a further, smaller federation of monasteries of Augustinian canons, when in 1418 some of its houses went over to the Augustinian Rule and founded the Chapter of Sion. This latter chapter would come in the sixteenth century to include 14 houses, both male and female.

Following the example of the federations just mentioned, the houses of the Brothers and Sisters themselves also came together. Thus the houses in the Northern and Southern Netherlands formed the Colloquium of Zwolle (some time after 1430), and the north German houses of Brothers the Colloquium of Münster. Meanwhile, the houses of Brothers in southern Germany resembled traditional foundations, and formed the General Chapter of Marienthal (1471) as canons regular.

As it spread, the *devotio moderna* gradually institutionalized, as can be seen also in the other two forms of life. The Utrecht Chapter was followed by federations of female tertiaries in the Southern Netherlands and in the Rhineland, with the foundations of the Chapter of Cologne (1427) and the Chapter of Zepperen (1443). But the strongest influence of the movement of interior reform came through the Windesheim Congregation, which extended northwards as far as Bordesholm (Denmark), eastwards as far as Jasenica (Poland), southwards as far as Zurich, and westwards to the Atlantic and to the North Sea.

The spirituality of the *devotio moderna* is very much under the influence of the Brabantine mysticism of Jan van Ruusbroec (1293–1381) and his disciples, and also of the Rhineland mysticism as practised above all by Johannes Tauler (c. 1300–61) and Heinrich Suso (c. 1295–1366). In the movement's collecting, copying and reading, preference was shown also to authors from other schools of spirituality, such as the Carthusian, Ludolf of Saxony (1295/1300–78) and the Franciscan, Bonaventure (c. 1217–74). Because it arose in lay circles and among those who were only semi-cloistered, and because of its vigorous literary culture, the *devotio moderna* gave rise to a rich literature, in which the vernacular languages, as well as the more usual Latin, had a major place. Because it was situated on the threshold between the world and the cloister, the *devotio moderna* played a decisive role in the establishment of mysticism as a social reality, a process that took place between the late medieval period and modernity. Especially after the second half of the fifteenth century, it developed along more ascetical lines, under the influence of reform efforts from the centre of the Church. But its basic characteristics are indisputably of a mystical character.

The human person is created in the image of God and called to likeness with God. Through original sin, it fell away from its original similarity to God. Irresistibly, the divine questing love (*Minne*) seeks to unite itself with the soul that is its own, and which has this love as a final goal (*telos*). The immediate aim (*skopos*) of this love is a permanent collaboration with the desire for God to be found in the person's soul. The desire associated with the divine *Minne* arouses the self to conversion (*Bekehrung*) and transformation (*mystischer kêr*). Once the person submits, purity of heart is their only task. This enables the person to hand themselves over into the risky adventure that is the divine questing love (*Minne*). Its active role is restricted to the practice of the virtues. The natural space for this is the 'common life', which in the earthly forms it takes represents the common life of the three divine Persons in the one divine essence. Through this transformation, the person becomes a *ghemeyne mensch* (a person of both action and contemplation), and their essence a *Minne* that embraces God, the neighbour, and the self in one single, undifferentiated movement of love.

It is particularly the early literature of the *devotio moderna* movement that brings out this mystical tendency, for example the two best-sellers written by Gerard Zerbolt van Zutphen before his early death: *The Reformation of the Soul's Powers* and *The Spiritual Ascensions*. Besides these manuals for the spiritual way, we should also mention the modest output of the Windesheim Canon, Gerlach Peters (d. 1411), with his sensitivity for the difference between spirits, and the numerous works of Hendrik Mande (*c.* 1360–1431), an oblate (*Donat=donné*, an associate without being vowed) of Windesheim, who enjoyed the reputation of being a 'Ruusbroec of the North'. Among the Windesheim canonesses, we should mention the Utrecht hermit, Sister Bertken Jacobs (1426/7–1514), with her delicately sensitive writings, and the prioress of the Galilee convent in Ghent, Alijt Bake (1415–55), who wrote, among other works, a spiritual autobiography describing her development. There was a significant flowering of literature later in the movement as well, with the anonymous treatise *De Evangelische Peerle, Van den Tempel onser sielen* (*The Gospel Pearl: On the Temple Which Is Our Soul*) and with the work of Maria van Hout (1470–1547).

Nevertheless, the climax of the *devotio moderna* came before the middle of the fifteenth century. In 1441, Thomas à Kempis (1379/80–1471) completed his *Imitation of Christ* in four books after twenty-one years of compilation and editing. It is to be noted – a point decisive for the understanding of his spirituality – that what is now book III came after what is now book IV. This work, indisputably a classic of world literature, has been repeatedly translated and edited all over the world up to our own day. *The Imitation of Christ* is not only the climax of late medieval affective spirituality, but also an inheritance that can be held in common from the time of what was still an undivided Church, because it

has been used in numerous different church communities and faith groups. *The Imitation of Christ* can, more than any other book, serve as a powerful instrument of true ecumenism between the Churches and the different religions.

———

K. M. Becker, 'From the Treasure-House of Scripture: An Analysis of Scriptural Sources in "De imitatione Christi"', *Instrumenta patristica et mediaeualia; Research on the Inheritance of Early and Medieval Christianity* 44 (Turnhout, 2002) 233–55, Bibliography; H. Blommestijn, C. Caspers and R. Hofman (eds), *Spirituality Renewed: Studies on Significant Representatives of the Modern Devotion*, Studies in Spirituality Supplements 10, Louvain/Paris/Dudley, MA: Peeters, 2003; G. Épiney-Burgard, *Gérard Grote (1340–1384) et les débuts de la Dévotion moderne*, Veröffentlichungen des Instituts für europäische Geschichte Mainz 54, Wiesbaden, 1970; G. H. Gerrits, *Inter timorem et spem: A Study of the Theological Thought of Gerard Zerbolt of Zutphen (1367–1398)*, Studies in Medieval and Reformation Thought 37, Leiden, 1986; R. R. Post, *The Modern Devotion. Confrontation with Reformation and Humanism.* Studies in Medieval and Reformation Thought 3, Leiden, 1968; G. Rehm, *Die Schwestern vom gemeinsamen Leben im nordwestlichen Deutschland. Untersuchungen zur Geschichte der Devotio moderna und des weiblichen Religiosentums*, Berliner Historische Studien 11, Ordensstudien V, Berlin, 1985; J. van Engen, *Devotio Moderna. Basic Writings*, CWS, New York, 1988.

RUDOLPH VAN DIJK
(TRANS. PHILIP ENDEAN)

Devotional Manuals

Devotional manuals are handbooks containing collections of prayers, instruction, general guidance for the spiritual life and exhortation for moral living. They are for personal use or to expand and enrich the basic structure of liturgy or formal prayer. Devotional manuals may be loosely divided into three categories: (a) those concerned with spiritual direction and the spiritual life; (b) collections of prayers, and (c) sermons, tracts, exhortatory texts and counsels for a moral life.

(a) Manuals that deal with the spiritual life were often compiled and reworked from the writings of the 'the masters' of the spiritual life, for example, Augustine of Hippo, Dionysius the Pseudo-Areopagite, Bernard of Clairvaux, Anselm, Bonaventure and Hildegarde of Bingen. Some are more original. The Beguine, Margaret Porete's (d. 1310), *Miroir des simples ames*, circulated widely in Europe as the work of an 'unknown French mystic'. Walter Hilton's (1340–1396) *The Ladder of Perfection*, although intended for the spiritual direction of an anchoress, became an individual's handbook for the contemplative life. Ignatius Loyola's (1491–1556) *The Spiritual Exercises* outlines a process of discernment for the spiritual life and remains a valued resource for spiritual directors; Teresa of Avila (1515–1582) used an experiential narrative form in *The Way of Perfection* and *The Interior Castle* to describe for her nuns the stages of growth in contemplative prayer. Along with the work of John of the Cross, Teresa's writing has been seminal in the development of spiritual direction in contemplative prayer. Francis de Sales' (1567–1622) *Treatise on the Love of God* and *Introduction to the Devout Life* were written particularly for the laity and illustrate the eclectic use of sources on the contemplative tradition reworked with the religious thought of his time. John Wesley drew on eighteenth-century manuals, including Robert Nelson's *The Practice of True Devotion* and Nathaniel Spinckes' *A Complete Manual of Private Devotions* in shaping the Wesleyan (Methodist) spirituality.

(b) Among collections of prayers, the Psalter (psalms, canticles and prayers drawn from the Bible) has been the most influential. Used initially by monastics and clerics for daily prayer, it was used increasingly by laity after the twelfth century, increasingly so after the advent of the printing press. *The Book of Common Prayer* of the Anglican Communion first introduced in 1549 has been an influential devotional and liturgical manual containing guidelines for the liturgy of the Sacraments as well as prayers and devotional practices. It has been revised at different periods and adapted by various local synods of the Communion. The Catholic *Missal* provided a similar collection of liturgical practice, scriptural readings and devotional prayer. Catholic compilations of prayers for daily life, especially prayers before and after the reception of Communion, the daily examination of conscience, and explanations of popular devotions, were found under such titles as '*A Treasury of Divine Grace*' and '*The Garden of the Soul*'. These collections, popular among the laity before Vatican Council II when the liturgy was in Latin, waned in popularity with the introduction of the vernacular for the liturgy. Hymnals can also be included as manuals in this category as they are used for liturgical worship as well as for personal and group prayer.

(c) Thomas à Kempis' (*c*. 1380–1471) *Imitation of Christ*, a pastiche of Scripture and pious interpretation which has been an influential devotional text in Catholicism and in Reformed

Christianity, represents a devotional manual which provides counsel for the moral life. Handbooks of this kind which encouraged a particular way of devotional life were produced in the Pietist Movement. Philipp Jakob Spener's (1635–1705) exhortatory text, *Pia desideria: or Heartfelt Desires for a God-Pleasing Improvement of the True Protestant Church* and Johann Friedrich Stark of the Halle School, *Daily Handbook for Days of Joy and Sorrow* (1728) are examples of handbooks providing encouragement for the daily life of virtue and discipleship of Christ. The basis for moral exhortation was an interpretation of Scripture and an appeal to the emotional response of devotees. The eighteenth-century popular series of woodcuts, *Le Miroir du Coeur: Images Morales,* provide advice graphically by illustrating the moral person's advance through life to a happy death and eternal life in heaven through the practice of virtue and contrasting these images with the sinful person's journey to hell after following the devil into sin. Collections of tracts and sermons were also available as aids for preaching and teaching in most Christian traditions.

See also **Beguine Spirituality; Spiritual Direction; Discernment; English Mystical Tradition; Ignatian Spirituality; Mary and Spirituality; Office, Divine; Virtue**.

Caroline Walker Bynum, 'Women mystics and eucharistic devotion' in *Fragmentation and Redemption,* New York: Zone Books, 1992, pp. 119–50; Margaret R. Miles, *The Image and Practice of Holiness: A Critique of the Classic Manuals of Devotion,* London: SCM Press, 1988.

ANN L. GILROY

Devotions

Devotions, the heartfelt reverence towards God, Jesus Christ, Mary or the other saints, denote practices and prayers which focus on human life touching the sacred. Devotions and their associated practices have been important in Christianity and lie along the spectrum between private personal prayer and public liturgy. Devotions can be local and contextual, such as the veneration of Our Lady of Guadalupe by South Americans, or of more universal significance, such as devotion to the Rosary in the Catholic Church. The objects of devotion provide inspiration, fervour and moral support for believers. Devotees believe that through venerating the holy they will be favoured in the circumstances of their lives and drawn into a closer relationship with God. For example, the devotion around early Christian martyrs and their burial sites, which venerated the martyrs' sacrifice of their lives for Christ, prefigured belief in the communion of saints and the later widespread practice in the European Church of interring the bodies of significant people in church buildings and of displaying their relics for public veneration.

The objects of devotion are usually a person and the extensions of the person, namely the things associated with the person. Aspects of the life of Jesus, particularly his birth and death, have been a fertile field for the devotional imagination. The now popular practice of using a nativity scene as a devotional aid for the Christmas season traces its origins to Francis of Assisi (1182–1226). The crucifix is not only an aid for meditation and prayer but the cross is a universal Christian symbol. Paintings, icons and sculptures portraying the passion of Jesus provide an affective aid for devotional life. Prayers, such as the Stations of the Cross, and hymns, such as the Wesleyan corpus, provide a framework for reflection on the salvific nature of Jesus' passion and death.

Devotions are also associated with the sacramental life of the Church. For example the veneration of the eucharistic host and the practice of Benediction have developed alongside the eucharistic liturgy. The practices of regular examination of conscience, confession and penitential practices developed with the sacrament of penance.

Mary and the saints are also frequently the object of devotion because of their relationship to God and the belief that they can intercede with God to influence human affairs. Mary as Mother of Christ has been venerated in the Christian Church under many titles, images, prayers and songs. Other saints are also honoured because their relationship with God is believed to enable them to bestow particular graces and blessings on devotees.

Some places associated with a person or sacred events also have devotional significance particularly as places of pilgrimage. The Holy Land is significant as the land of Jesus' life and death. Bethlehem, Nazareth and Jerusalem draw pilgrims who pray at such holy sites as the Nativity, the Via Dolorosa and the Church of the Holy Sepulchre. Marian shrines, associated either with an appearance of Mary or an image with reputed miraculous powers, also attract devotion. Lourdes, in France, is associated with appearances of the Virgin Mary to the peasant girl, Bernadette Soubirous, in 1858, and for the spring water reputed to have miraculous healing qualities. Pilgrims, particularly the sick, flock to the site of the apparitions to pray for healing and to bathe in the waters. The shrine of St James the Apostle at Compostella and the home town of

Francis and Clare in Assisi are other places of devotional pilgrimage. The birth or death places of saints around the Christian world have likewise become the focus for devotion. These can be as local as, for example, the home of Blessed Mary MacKillop in Sydney, Australia, or more widely known, as is the former leper colony on Molokai Island, Hawaii, the site of Blessed Damien's ministry.

The practices associated with devotions are varied and include the recitation of prayers, fasting, pilgrimage, processions, prayer meetings, hymn-singing, novenas, vigils and the decoration of shrines.

See also **Adoration; Devotions, Popular; Devotional Manuals; Examination of Conscience/Consciousness; Eucharist; Fasting; Mary and Spirituality; Piety; Saints, Communion of; Vatican II and Spirituality.**

Louis Dupré & Don E. Saliers (eds), *Christian Spirituality: Post Reformation and Modern*, London: SCM Press, 1989; Cheslyn Jones, Geoffrey Wainwright and Edward Yarnold (eds), *The Study of Spirituality*, London: SPCK, 1994.

ANN GILROY

Devotions, Popular

Popular devotions describe the veneration given to particular aspects of God, Mary or the saints. Popular devotions, so named because they attract the religious imagination of adherents, usually develop alongside the more formal liturgies of the Christian liturgical calendar. Their popularity is often limited to a specific locality or context and is fostered by perceived graces, favours, miraculous healings and moral benefits for devotees.

Many popular devotions arose in the medieval period of Christianity when the sense of the holy and belief in the manifestation in miracles was more widespread than in contemporary times. For example, the fourteenth-century devotion to the childhood of Jesus found prominence in a particular statue of the Infant Jesus brought from Spain to Prague in the Czech Republic. The church housing the statue was demolished in war and the forgotten statue was rediscovered, repaired and placed in a place of honour by a priest in the seventeenth century who was reported to have heard the child Jesus say, 'The more you honour me the more I will bless you.' Devotion to the Infant of Prague was fostered by reports of miracles attributed to praying before the image. The church containing the Infant of Prague became a place of pilgrimage and copies of the statue circulated as the devotion grew.

The passion and cross of Jesus have been the object of popular devotion. Since St Helen discovered the 'true cross', splinters of the cross have proliferated through the Christian world. Despite the suspicious authenticity of these fragments, devotion developed around the cross and its healing power. Likewise the relics of the saints, displayed at shrines, became sites of pilgrimage and prayer and places where grateful devotees bestowed riches. Many bejewelled, embroidered and gilded statues and caskets witness to the devotion of the faithful in European and South America churches. Other items, such as olive wood from the garden of Gethsemane, fragments of Jesus' swaddling cloths and the shroud of Turin, have become objects for popular devotion and valued for their symbolic holiness more than their authenticity.

The eucharistic devotions of the Middle Ages focused on the presence of Christ in the Communion host and developed the devotional practices of processions, blessings, vigils of adoration, prayers and hymns. Eucharistic devotion continued into the twentieth century in forms of Benediction and Eucharistic Adoration. The devotions commonly took place in the parish church and the devout gathered regularly to pray with the priest.

Popular devotions to Mary remain important for Catholic and Eastern Christians. Mary's role of motherhood has particular significance in the religious imagination, obvious in art, poetry and music through the centuries. Notable Marian shrines and places of pilgrimage include Lourdes in France, Fatima in Portugal, Walsingham in Norfolk, England, Knock in Ireland and Medjugorje in Bosnia-Herzegovina. Mary is also honoured by the proliferation of titles that describe her place in the popular imagination. She is called Our Lady of Guadalupe, Our Lady of Perpetual Succour, Mary Help of Christians, Mother of God, Immaculate Conception, Star of the Sea, Mystic Rose, and Mother of the Oppressed. She is venerated through prayer, song, art, and practices such as the decoration of her shrines, the wearing of a scapular or miraculous medal and participation in charitable works. The most popular Marian devotion is the recitation of the Rosary on a circlet of beads arranged in decades. The 'Hail Mary' is recited mantra-like on each bead as devotees meditate on mysteries of the life of Christ decade by decade.

Popular devotion has also extended to include the honouring of saints and holy people. Some like Francis of Assisi, Mother Teresa and Oscar Romero have a more universal Christian significance because of the witness of their inclusive love, their care of the poor and the quality of their discipleship. Others' significance is fostered through their religious orders: Benedict, Dominic, Ignatius Loyola, Louise de Marillac, Vincent de Paul, Elizabeth Seton, Catherine McAuley and Mary Ward. Again devotion to some saints has a national or cultural significance, as Rose of Lima for Peru, Brigid and Patrick for Ireland, George for England, David for Wales, Mary MacKillop for Australia. Further, special powers of patronage are attributed to some saints. St Cecilia is the patron of musicians, St Joseph of carpenters and St Luke of doctors. Despite research into St Christopher revealing the a-historicity of this person and his being dropped from the Catholic Calendar, devotion to him has continued. Many keep a St Christopher medal in their vehicles as a plea to Christopher, the Christ-child bearer, to keep them safe while travelling.

Some popular devotions grew up in response to particular circumstances and waned when the circumstances changed. An example is the devotion to the Sacred Heart of Jesus which grew out of the reported visions of the Heart of Jesus and his promises of salvation to Margaret Mary Alacoque in the seventeenth century. Promoted initially by the Visitandine Sisters and Jesuits as an antidote to Jansenism and secularity in France, the devotion gained new life with the nineteenth-century missionary movement. At a time when the sense of humanity's sinfulness, their distance from God and impending doom was felt acutely, the devotion promoted a sense of hope and reliance on the mercy of the loving heart of Jesus. It encouraged repentance for sins, the dedication of families to the Sacred Heart and fervent reception of Communion especially on the first Friday of each month in honour of Christ's death. Since the Vatican Council II's (1962–65) updating of theology and liturgy which has promoted a sense of hope in universal salvation, this devotion has largely lost popular appeal although the feast of the Sacred Heart remains in the liturgical calendar.

A contemporary popular devotion is demonstrated by the honouring of the Holy Spirit in the charismatic movement. Adherents use the Bible, particularly the books that reveal the activity of the Spirit among early Christians, as a source of meditation, prayer and preaching. Their devotional practices include personal prayer, small group instruction and hymn-singing. Within the group meeting their prayer emphasizes glossolalia, extempore praying, prophesying, exorcisms and healings.

The World Wide Web provides a plethora of resources for devotions. Websites give information on traditional devotions as well as such resources as a daily prayer, Scripture reading, sermons and tracts, music and questions for personal reflection and moral guidance.

See also **Charismatic Spirituality; Devotions; Devotional Manuals; Examination of Conscience/Consciousness; Eucharistic Spirituality; Fasting; Hope; Jansenism; Lay People and Spirituality; Mary and Spirituality; Meditation; Perfection; Piety; Sacramentality and Spirituality; Secularization; Spirit, Holy; Vatican II and Spirituality.**

Carolyn Walker Bynum, *Holy Feast Holy Fast*, Berkeley: University of California Press, 1987; Carolyn Walker Bynum, *Fragmentation and Redemption: Essays on Gender and the Human Body in Medieval Religion*, New York: Zone Books, 1992; Eamon Duffy, *The Stripping of the Altars: Traditional Religion in England 1400–1580*, New Haven and London: Yale University Press, 1992; Louis Gougaud, *Devotional and Ascetic Practices in the Middle Ages*, trans. G. C. Bateman, London: Burns, Oates & Washbourne, 1927.

ANN GILROY

Diakonia and Diaconate

The Greek word *diakonia* means 'service', and in the New Testament it also came to identify a ministerial role within the Christian community. It is the root of the English words 'deacon' and 'diaconate'.

The linkage between 'service' and 'ministry' flows from the witness of Jesus, as in Mark 10.45: 'For the Son of Man came not to be served but to serve (*diakonein*), and to give his life as a ransom for many.' Jesus, the minister par excellence, renders service.

New Testament. In the New Testament, *diakonos* (servant, or minister) and its cognates *diakoneo* (to serve or minister) and *diakonia* (service, ministry) occur one hundred times. These words usually refer to simple acts of service, as when Peter's mother-in-law waits on Jesus and the disciples (Mark 1.31) or when Martha is distracted from listening to Jesus by her serving (Luke 10.40). In later New Testament writings, however, *diakonos* designates an office or role within the Christian community. In Phil. 1.1 Paul speaks of elders (*episkopoi*) and deacons. In Rom. 16.1, he calls Phoebe a *diakonos*. And 1 Tim. 3.8–13 lists the qualities expected of deacons, qualities similar to those of the *episkopoi*. It is not clear from these texts, however, what duties these *diakonoi* fulfilled.

One long-standing tradition within Christianity ascribes the beginning of the diaconate to the seven disciples chosen to assist with distribution of food to the widows in Acts 6. Irenaeus of Lyons (born *c.* 150), one hundred years after the writing of Acts, first made this claim. However, Acts never designates these disciples as deacons, and they are described as doing much more than distributing food; Stephen, for example, preaches just like the apostles in Acts 6—7.

100–200 CE. Christian texts up to the third century (for example, the letters of Clement of Rome and Ignatius of Antioch, the *Didache* [*c.* 90], and *The Shepherd of Hermas* [*c.* 140]) mention deacons, often in the context of the tripartite structure of bishop (*episkopos*), priest (*presbyteros*), and deacon (*diakonos*). This early stage of development, however, was marked by a diversity of ministerial functions based upon the local customs of a given community. Some communities were headed by *episkopoi*, others by *presbyteroi*. The *diakonoi* were clearly to be exemplary persons who embodied Christian qualities. They assisted the leaders, but their precise role is unclear. They probably had responsibility for the care of the poor. These various ministries were understood more organically than hierarchically; that is, they were all integral to caring for the Body of Christ.

200–400 CE. During this period deacons reached the height of their influence in the Western Church. In Rome, for example, Pope Fabian (235–250) divided the city into seven administrative districts (echoing the seven disciples in Acts 6) and placed each district under the direction of a deacon. Deacons functioned as chief administrators for bishops, having control of personnel and finances. They were the normal liaison between bishops and the faithful. The *Didascalia Apostolorum* (*c.* 250) states that deacons are 'the bishop's ear, mouth, heart, and soul'. Deacons managed the Church's charitable outreach: visiting the sick, providing for the poor, assisting the dying. Deacons stood in as proxies for absent bishops at the Council of Arles (314). Liturgically, they also played visible roles; they assisted with the baptism of catechumens; at the Eucharist they read the Gospel and distributed Communion. The Council of Elvira (306), in Canon 77, suggests that deacons could be leaders of rural churches.

The decline of the diaconate. The fourth century, however, brought changes to the ministerial structure of Christianity and ushered in a decline in the diaconate. The conversion of the Emperor Constantine in 313 led to the recognition of Christianity as the official religion of the Roman

Empire. To cope with the influx of large numbers of converts, the Church adapted the administrative structures of the Roman Empire. Bishops, especially in urban areas, became administrators over geographic regions rather than pastors of local parishes. Increasingly, presbyters presided at the Eucharist and assumed a more prominent role in ministry. The councils of Arles and Ancira, both held in 314, instruct deacons to no longer preside at Eucharist. The tripartite ministry of deacon-presbyter-bishop came to be understood in hierarchic terms: the higher offices contained the lower. Gradually, by the year 800, the diaconate came to be seen as a stage in the process of becoming a priest rather than a vocation in itself. In the Roman Catholic Church, this view continued into the twentieth century.

Deaconesses. Deaconesses existed in both East and West in the early centuries of Christianity. In Romans 16.1 Paul designates Phoebe as a deacon. Deaconesses served the bishops in capacities that were not possible for male deacons. They ministered to women by assisting with baptisms, instructing the newly baptized, acting as messengers between bishops and women, taking Communion to the sick, and having oversight of widows and orphans. In the East, the law codes of Justinian (*c.* 550) indicate that the Church of St Sophia in Constantinople was allotted forty deaconesses while small churches were allotted six. Deaconesses also served in the West and are occasionally referenced in church documents, but they were not widely accepted. The Synod of Nimes (394) forbade the ordination of deaconesses, and later councils repeated this stricture. Even in the East the office of deaconess went into decline after the sixth century.

The Orthodox tradition. Among the Orthodox Churches, deacons ceased having a primary role focused upon charity and instead came to play an important role in the celebration of the Eucharist. St John Chrysostom (d. 407), saw the diaconate as primarily a liturgical institution. The Council of Trullo (692) stated that there was no identity between the liturgical diaconate and the service of charity found in Acts 6. Orthodox deacons were ordained to be liturgical assistants to priests and bishops. They had an especially prominent role in leading litanies and were often chosen for their ability to sing.

Churches of the Reformation. As a general rule, the Churches of the Reformation broke with the concept of the diaconate as a step to the priesthood. The Church of England and the Anglican Communion that grew from it are a notable exception in retaining the traditional diaconate as part of the threefold division of the clergy. Other Churches of the Reformation sought to restore the diaconate as a service to the poor and an integral part of the Church's social mission. Martin Luther based his view of the diaconate upon Acts 6. He saw the role of deacons as distributing alms to the poor. Hence within Lutheranism there has been a reluctance to see deacons as part of the clergy; rather, they are ministers of service and social outreach.

The Reformed Churches trace their roots to John Calvin. In his *Institutes of the Christian Religion* he argues for two types of deacon: those who administer the affairs of the poor (for example, oversee the distribution of donations), and those who personally care for the poor and sick. In general, Churches tracing their roots to Calvin do designate men and women as deacons. They are usually not considered clergy. They are involved in parish work, social and medical outreach, teaching and missionary activity. In many Reformed Churches, the diaconate is communal: deacons are elected to a board for their local church and serve a designated term. Such boards assist in managing the temporal affairs of the church, and in pastoral and charitable outreach.

The renewal of the diaconate. The nineteenth and twentieth centuries witnessed a renewal of the diaconate, often in response to social conditions brought on by industrialization and urbanization. In 1833, a Lutheran lay man, Johannes Wichern, began the 'inner mission' movement of the diaconate. His 'brothers' went on mission within Germany, working in jails, slums and areas where clergy were not likely to go. In 1962, there were still over 4500 Brüdern in Germany. Also in the 1830s, Theodore Fliedner, a Lutheran pastor, gathered an association of women in Kaiserworth, Germany, to care for the sick and destitute. Thousands of women joined this endeavour, and the movement flowered into deaconess hospitals in many countries. Some within the Anglican Church followed this development with interest, and in 1889 the General Convention of the Episcopal Church passed a canon setting apart deaconesses who, at that stage, were carefully distinguished from the all-male clerical diaconate. Several training schools were then begun. These women were ordained and carried out charitable works.

In 1964, the Roman Catholic bishops gathered at Vatican Council II called for the renewal of the diaconate in *Lumen Gentium*, the dogmatic constitution on the Church. In less than forty years since then, nearly thirty thousand deacons have been ordained worldwide, about half of them in the United States. The renewal of the diaconate in Roman Catholicism has led to interest in other denominations as well. In 1982, the World Council of Churches published a document entitled *Baptism, Eucharist, and Ministry*. This document stated that 'churches not having the threefold ministry [of bishop, priest, and deacon] . . . need to ask themselves whether the threefold pattern as developed does not have a powerful claim to be accepted by them'.

Conclusion. Linguistically 'service', *diakonia*, and 'community', *koinonia*, share *koinos* (that which is common) at their root. From the very beginning Christians understood ministry as service for the upbuilding of the community. They embodied this vision in the office of deacon and deaconess. Today various denominations enflesh this vision in different ways. But whether deacons and deaconesses are ordained, whether they serve a bishop or a local congregation, whether they function liturgically or in social service, individually or in groups, they continue their witness of Jesus who came not to be served but to serve.

James Monroe Barnett, *The Diaconate: A Full and Equal Order*, Valley Forge, PA: Trinity Press International, 1995; Richard T. Nolan (ed.), *The Diaconate Now*, Washington, DC: Corpus Books, 1968; Jeannine E. Olson, *One Ministry Many Roles: Deacons and Deaconesses through the Centuries*, St Louis, MO: Concordia Publishing House, 1992; Kenan Osborne OFM, *The Diaconate in the Christian Church: Its History and Theology*, Chicago: National Association of Diaconate Directors, 1996.

BRUCE LESCHER

Direction, Spiritual

Spiritual direction is an ancient ascetical practice in which one person serves as a guide, conversation partner, and co-discerner with another who seeks to explore, reflect on, and grow in his/her spiritual life. Not limited to Christianity, spiritual direction participates in the archetypal relationship named in various religious traditions as: guru/disciple; shaman/initiate; murshid/ mureed; rebbe/hasid; elder (abba, imma)/ neophyte; roshi/student; anamcara (soul-friend)/ seeker and director/directee. Each of these relationships implies an existential inequality between the guide and the seeker in terms of spiritual development, human experience and/or maturity. These relationships imply the seeker's need for spiritual initiation, formation and guidance at the beginning of a particular spiritual path and lifestyle.

Christianity developed from the relationship of a community of disciples with their itinerant rabbi-teacher Jesus who practised both individual and communal 'spiritual direction' together with his preaching and healing ministries. The Christian practice of spiritual direction occurs within this faith context in which Jesus promises the indwelling gift of the Holy Spirit to his followers. In Christian spiritual direction, both director and directee engage in a conversational process in order to listen to, interpret and discern the 'leadings' of the Holy Spirit, the true director, in all arenas of the life of the directee. In order to do so, the director asks facilitating questions and offers responses that help directees articulate their unique faith experiences, grasp their implications, and make choices in the light of this mysterious faith reality. Scripture, the mysteries of Christian faith and Christian spiritual traditions provide a primary interpretive horizon for this reflective interpretation. The growing practice of group spiritual direction is grounded in the same assumptions.

An ongoing process of discernment is the core of this process as both conversational partners seek to discover the origin, meaning, direction and purpose of religious experience. Hence, spiritual direction is not limited to initial stages of spiritual formation, but may remain an important although not absolutely necessary spiritual practice for the mature Christian and even mystic throughout the life-cycle. Although contemplative prayer, meditation, and ritual worship constitute important and privileged occasions of religious experience, they are not the exclusive focus of spiritual direction. Of equal importance are spontaneous experiences of God in daily life, the directee's organic growth in the virtuous life (an ethics of character) the loving quality of relationships, and activities of care, creativity and compassion within work and ministerial life.

Historically, spiritual direction has alternated between charismatic and institutional forms although a charismatic element has been significantly present. For instance, the early fourth-century Christians, primarily laity, who created Egyptian eremetical and coenobitic monastic life initiated an entirely charismatic form of spiritual direction based on the elder/neophyte relationship. Elders who had learned the way of their own hearts to God in solitude and had successfully undergone the temptations and challenges of life in the desert were sought out by others through spiritual affinity – a mutual attraction and agreement to enter into this sacred relationship. Gradually, an originally oral wisdom tradition emerged within these communities captured in the stories and sayings of the desert abbas and ammas. The central practice of these extraordinary interviews was 'the manifestation of the heart' of the person seeking guidance. This is the disclosure of interior movements, stirrings, affections, temptations, desires and preoccupations before they become sinful behaviours or patterns of resistance to grace in contemplative practice. This trusting self-disclosure of both positive and negative interior movements provides the data for discernment that leads to increasing self-understanding, moral and spiritual growth. The desert elder, through teaching stories and aphoristic 'words', compassionately supported directees in confronting their human weaknesses and struggles and frequently evoked a change in consciousness that released them from a compulsive preoccupation with a theme or negative emotion. Eventually, newcomers to the desert were required to choose an elder and consult him or her frequently, often living with the elder or building one's hut in the same compound as the elder. Experienced desert-dwellers sought one another out in mutual support and self-disclosure on an as-needed basis. Hence, the relationship was entirely charismatic. The elder was recognized as such not by virtue of age but by virtue of their charismatic gift of discernment and spiritual guidance.

As Benedictine monasticism became the dominant form of religious life from the sixth century on, the central charismatic core of the spiritual elder was incorporated into the institutional role of the abbot/abbess and the novice director. Community life itself and its liturgical prayer life provided the primary *schola* – a form of guidance together with the Rule itself. The *seniores*, the experienced members, often served the professed community with individual guidance as members sought them out.

Although the clergy confessor gradually took over the functions of spiritual direction within the confessor role from the time of the Fourth Lateran Council (1215), a charismatic tradition of spiritual direction persisted through the medieval period. Lay mystics, often women, but sometimes men as well, were recognized for their holiness of life because of the visibility of their mystical experiences or the wisdom of their counsel and sought out by others. Julian of Norwich, Richard Rolle, Catherine of Siena, Hadewijch of Antwerp, and Gertrude the Great are among this group. Within religious communities, women continued to offer spiritual guidance although they were often officially unrecognized in this role and experienced conflict with the increasing clerical monopoly of spiritual direction.

The merging of the function of spiritual direction with the role of the confessor in the sacrament of penance intensified in the Catholic response to the Reformers at the Council of Trent (1545–63). Increased attention was given to the priest 'director of conscience' who was charged with assessing the authenticity and orthodoxy of penitents who reported mystical experiences as well as hearing confession of sin and imposing penances. This development threatened the long-standing charismatic approach to spiritual direction, and represented the most complete institutionalization of this ministry. Even under these circumstances, there were some gifted priest confessors/spiritual directors such as Francis de Sales, John of the Cross, Augustine Baker and a large number of Jesuit directors beginning with Ignatius himself and later ones such as Père Grou. Too frequently, the confessor/penitent model of spiritual direction became authoritarian and sin-focused, resulting for many in mediocre or oppressive spiritual direction. Because the terminology of director and directee are associated with this particular model of spiritual direction, the renewal of the former charismatic, non-institutional model of spiritual direction occurred more slowly in the Reformed and Evangelical Christian traditions than among Roman Catholics after Vatican II.

The contemporary practice of spiritual direction, when it retains this vocabulary, requires a radical redefinition of these terms. The ministry of spiritual direction is no longer dependent on ordination for its authentication. There are wide agreements across Christian traditions that spiritual direction is a charism given for the good of the community and recognized by those seeking spiritual direction who call others into this ministry. Once again, the Holy Spirit is the true 'director'. The director does not impose his or her theology, opinions or spiritual path upon the one seeking direction, but rather tries to discover and support the 'spiritual direction' the Holy Spirit is already initiating in the directee's life. The sacrament of reconciliation has become distinct from spiritual direction in North America, Europe and Australia except at times within the seminary context itself. In many other parts of the world, spiritual direction remains tied to the confessor role and has not yet become widely available to lay Christians in significant numbers.

Since the 1970s, the relationship between spiritual direction and various forms of psychotherapy continues to develop. Because psychology and clinical therapeutic experience has furthered the understanding of human personality and the psychology of meditation, spiritual directors require a basic understanding of the complementary and overlapping roles of therapy and spiritual direction. Because spiritual direction is also a helping relationship, directors need to understand the dynamics of transference and counter-transference as they affect spiritual direction. Directors also need to recognize when to refer directees to appropriate forms of counselling or therapy and learn to work in tandem with other professionals. In the beginning of this vigorous dialogue, spiritual direction became more psychologically oriented than previously. With more recent studies disclosing the importance of spirituality to physical and psychological health, some forms of therapy and counselling have become more concerned with spirituality. Both spiritual directors and therapists need to recognize their specific competencies and work carefully within their own disciplines.

Although spiritual direction is widely acknowledged to be a charism, a gradual professionalization of spiritual direction is welcomed by some and resisted by others. There are more than three hundred 'training' programmes in spiritual direction, a handful existing within institutions of higher learning, responding to the need for mentoring persons discerning a call to this ministry. A collegial organization, Spiritual Direction International, with its own journal *Presence,* is an international network of spiritual directors that has recently become inter-religious as well as interdenominational. The necessity of professional ethics, including the maintenance of appropriate boundaries in the relationship, is also widely recognized.

Among current trends, increasingly, spiritual directors are companioning directees who engage in some form of dual practice, such as insight meditation or zazen as an important spiritual exercise, yet retain Christianity as their primary faith horizon. Still others are attempting to offer spiritual direction across religious traditions altogether.

See also **Mysticism; Spirituality, Psychology and Psychotherapy** (*essays*)**; Asceticism; Attentiveness; Buddhism and Christianity; Charism; Contemplation; Conversation, Spiritual; Conversion; Discernment; Eremitical Spirituality; Experience, Religious; Intercession; Interiority; Meditation; Monastic Spirituality; Prayer; Retreats; Spirit, Holy; Zen and Christianity.**

Peter Ball, *Anglican Spiritual Direction*, Cambridge, MA: Cowley Publications, 1998; William Barry and William Connolly, *The Practice of Spiritual Direction*, San Francisco: Harper Collins, 1982; Tilden Edwards, *Spiritual Director/Spiritual Companion: Guide to Tending*

the Soul, Mahwah, NJ: Paulist Press, 2001; Kathryn Dyckman, Mary Garvin and Elizabeth Liebert, *The Spiritual Exercises Reclaimed: Uncovering Liberating Possibilities for Women*, Mahwah, NJ: Paulist Press, 2001; Frank Houdek, *Guided by the Spirit: A Jesuit Perspective on Spiritual Direction*, Chicago: Loyola University Press, 1996; Gerald May, *Care of Mind/Care of Spirit*, San Francisco: Harper, 1982, 1992; Janet Ruffing, *Spiritual Direction: Beyond the Beginnings*, Mahwah, NJ: Paulist Press, 2000.

JANET K. RUFFING

Disability

The daily news frequently includes stories about disability: an auto accident leaves a man paralysed from the waist down, a woman in her prime is diagnosed with Parkinson's disease, new parents are told their baby has cerebral palsy, a young adult leaves college because of mental illness, soldiers return from battle minus legs, arms, hands and sanity, a responsive two-year-old quits talking and withdraws into the shell of autism. Not so common are the stories about how these people move on with their lives.

Helen Keller said, 'Life is a great adventure, or nothing at all', but these encounters with disability are not adventures planned with great anticipation. How does one find hope and meaning in life after sustaining a serious injury or receiving a devastating medical diagnosis? Where does one find the faith and strength to negotiate this new terrain of disability? How do individuals with significant impairments or chronic illness live with dignity and purpose when much of society views them as pitiful victims whose lives are not worth living, and thinks they would be better off dead?

Conservative estimates indicate there are over 500 million people with disabilities worldwide, at least one-twelfth of the population. As people age they are more likely to become disabled, and disability is more prevalent in regions of the world that experience great poverty. Some disabilities are readily apparent; others are less obvious. Family members, friends, caregivers and co-workers are greatly affected by an individual's disability. The extent to which an individual is 'handicapped' by a particular impairment will be greatly influenced by the physical, cultural and religious environment in which the person lives.

Christian Scripture and tradition have left their mark on how people perceive disability. Many have taken spiritual comfort in knowing that since Christ suffered on the cross he can understand their afflictions. The concepts of self-sacrifice and perseverance have encouraged many to nobly ignore their own distress while pressing on to some greater goal or service. Anticipation of an afterlife without pain has sustained people through the hardships of their earthly existence. A spirit of charity inspired the building of hospitals, asylums and special schools.

Sometimes the dualistic mind/body split that values the intellect as being a truer reflection of God's image worked to the advantage of intelligent individuals with physical disabilities; it did not matter so much that the body was impaired if the mind was rational. But this concept is not helpful or comforting to people with mental retardation or mental illness. And individuals with physical incapacities have been made to feel that they personify the weaker, more corrupt estate ascribed to the body in this dualistic concept. With the still common belief that disease and disability are in some way punishment for sin, it is no wonder that such conditions remain cloaked in shame. Religious prohibitions against the participation of people with dysfunctional body parts have ostracized many disabled people. Attempts to bring wayward bodies into line through practices of austere deprivation and punishment have also caused great harm.

Christian spirituality should be salvific; it proclaims transformation and resurrection. Disability is one of those life events – like earthquakes, acts of violence, and profound changes in human relationships – that turns life upside down. Nothing is the same as it used to be, and the future is still unknown. Being on the border of this new and unfamiliar land of disability is not a comfortable spiritual position. Trust and hope are needed, but the tendency is to grab frantically for explanations and solutions – anything to make order out of the chaos. The real challenge is to stay awhile with the unsettled feelings and the realization that one is not in total control. Lament, anger, grief and acknowledging one's vulnerability and fear are all appropriate spiritual responses. Then with quiet waiting and listening a person may hear God's voice more clearly. In the mystery of this sacred in-between space new possibilities can take root, and that which seemed dead can find new life.

Christian spirituality is incarnational – the body matters. Christians believe in a deity who came to earth in a human form to show people God's ways. In his earthly life Jesus went about feeding, touching, healing human bodies and minds. People perceive, respond and participate in the world through their bodies; the mind or soul cannot really be separated from the body. All parts of the body are important and each has a purpose. There is integrity to this creation. To ignore or mistreat any part of the body is to do damage to the whole. This is a particularly important message for people with disabilities who are often made to feel inadequate because parts of their bodies or minds work in unique and different ways, or made to believe that some parts of themselves are unworthy and should be kept hidden. Nourishing the body with healthy food, getting adequate rest, experiencing soothing touch, can make a body feel valued. Spiritual practices that physically involve the body in movement such as yoga or dance can bring renewed connection and awareness of the self. Praying with bodily motions, making or listening to music, painting or working with clay, can bring enjoyment and express an embodied spirituality and a relationship to God that is not solely dependent on an intellectual mastery of words.

Rarely does disability get discussed without the subject of healing coming into the conversation, but what is meant by Christian healing? Western society's approach to disability has been dominated for decades by a medical model that focuses on curing a specific impairment or ailment through some treatment regime or surgery. The emphasis is on correcting the deficit in the individual. But for the person with the disability this can become an unending process in the hands of professionals; the more she becomes the object of their procedures, the more she loses her own integrity and sense of self. If healing is to be more about restoring wholeness than fixing an individual, then spiritual practices that foster connection, that encourage remembering and offer reconciliation are needed. When Jesus healed people he also restored them to a valued place in their communities.

Those parts of both individual and socio/political bodies and life experiences that have become estranged need to be reclaimed. Becoming whole is a process of integration, not segregation. This spirituality of Christian healing and forgiveness is an ongoing process of recovery. The challenge is to reconcile the disparate parts, for people to remember their stories and who they are, to welcome even the least significant or least capable, and know that it is all holy and acceptable before God.

Besides working for cures and prevention in the attempt to manage disability, people try to sort it into categories, rank it by severity or prevalence, and predict its outcome. This tends to channel thinking into rigid patterns that classify people as healthy or sick, strong or helpless, obstinate or compliant, acceptable or unacceptable. People look for either/or explanations, but disability does not fit neatly into these boxes. Stereotypes leave no room for the ambiguity and fluctuation that characterize this life, and they deny people the choice of being uniquely themselves. Disability is full of unpredictability and paradox. It has a cruciform shape that calls one to stand in the centre, in the mystery, and to hold the tension between the extremes. This position of uncertainty requires mindfulness, balance and imagination to resist the easy black or white answers that some suggest. Wrestling with God and oneself to discover meaning and purpose in a life with disability requires persistence and patience. It also helps to have a sense of humour.

In this struggle people with disabilities will often find themselves on the margins where they have only a meagre share of what is important to those in the middle of the circle. Sometimes it can feel as though one is clinging to the bare edges of life. Discrimination is an experience common to disabled people worldwide, and it is very wearing. It requires constant vigilance to be always on guard, pushing back against some bureaucratic regulation, metaphor or pejorative statement that threatens to undermine one's sense of personhood. Without resilience and a strong faith plus some real material supports, the experience of being disabled and marginalized can be so demoralizing and exhausting that some people just give up.

But being on the margins may also provide a sense of purpose. It is a position that can stimulate critical thinking and political analysis. The person on the boundary between the accepted way and a different world can sometimes see what is out of view to others. From this perspective she may be able to hear the voices or see the faces of those who have been missing from the picture. Or it may be that the disabled person living on the border is more inclined to think outside the box. He uses his ingenuity to design something new precisely because the old system, the status quo, literally does not work for him. Being a prophetic voice is lonely work that requires a special kind of confidence. The pioneer needs a spirituality that reminds him that he is a beloved child of God.

Christian spirituality is about relationship and communion, *koinonia*. Everyone needs community. This can be especially true for people with disabilities, who – unlike other minority groups – do not all speak the same language, have the same skin colour or share a common heritage. It is the Church's mandate to be a place of welcome to all people without discrimination. Through God's grace in baptism Christians are united with Christ and each other. Here is a place of true belonging. It is in this community of mutual interdependence that members can guide and correct one another in love and call forth each other's gifts. Here is a place for joy and celebration. In Africa the Ubuntu philosophy says, 'a person is a person through other persons', or 'each individual's humanity is ideally expressed through his or her relationship with others . . .'. All people have gifts and experience to share, including people with physical, mental and sensory impairments. God's invitation is for everyone to participate.

See also **Baptism; Body and Spirituality; Communion/*Koinonia*; Community; Dualism; Healing and Health; Hope; Incarnation; Memory; Perseverance; Reconciliation; Suffering.**

A Church of All and For All: An Interim (Theological) Statement, document PLEN 1.1, Geneva, Switzerland: Central Committee of the World Council of Churches, 2003 (Drafted by the Ecumenical Disability Advocates Network, Justice, Peace and Creation Team); Nancy Eiesland, *The Disabled God: Toward a Liberatory Theology of Disability*, Nashville: Abingdon Press, 1994; William C. Gaventa and David L. Coulter (eds), *Spirituality and Intellectual Disability: International Perspectives on the Effect of Culture and Religion on Healing Body, Mind, and Soul*, New York: Haworth Press, 2002; Roy McCloughry and Wayne Morris, *Making a World of Difference: Christian Reflections on Disability*, SPCK: London, 2002; Augustine Shutte, *Philosophy for Africa*, Rondebosch, South Africa: UCT Press, 1993; South African Governmental White Paper on Welfare as cited in paper by Dirk J. Louw, 'Ubuntu: an African assessment of the religious other', <www.bu.edu/wcp/Papers/Afri/AfriLouw.htm>; John Swinton, *Spirituality and Mental Health Care: Rediscovering a 'Forgotten' Dimension*, London and Philadelphia: Jessica Kingsley, 2001; Brett Webb-Mitchell, *God Plays Piano, Too: The Spiritual Lives of Disabled Children*, New York: Crossroad, 1993.

CAROLYN R. THOMPSON

Discernment

Discernment of spirits is a form of critical reflection on human and specifically religious experience, either of individuals or of a group or community. Its purpose is to ensure that, within a context of a living relationship with God, religious experience, subjected to critical reflection, may be a basis for right choice and action. The need for discernment, as a process of *critical* reflection, is rooted in fundamental ambiguities inherent in human moral and religious experience as such.

Human beings, faced with moral choices, find themselves subject, individually and corporately, to contradictory inner and external influences, some of which incline them to good, others to evil. Moreover, it is often difficult to distinguish, in practice, between good and evil pressures or 'stirrings' in a person, a group or community, an institution, a nation state or globally. That is because what is in reality an influence or force for evil not infrequently appears under the guise of good, and is attractive precisely for that reason. The need for discernment, therefore, is clear in a view of the world as a field in which, on the one hand, there are undoubtedly forces at work for good, and yet, at the same time, other, contradictory influences work in an opposite direction to forestall, undermine, divert, corrupt, pervert or otherwise destroy the good and its effects. Truly identifying and disentangling these two opposed sets of factors is a notoriously complex and subtle process.

Human beings who engage with God typically want God to guide their lives. Religious experience, however, is no less ambiguous than any other area of human experience. The glow of a bright idea is no indication of a divine origin and divine inspiration is claimed for the most inhuman acts. The inherent ambiguity of both moral and religious experience lays bare the need to distinguish, individually and corporately, those impulses, moods, desires or other affective stirrings which lead to fullness of life in the love of God and those which appear to be 'of God' and yet are in reality destructive, the opposite of what they seem.

The Hebrew Scriptures, especially through the stories they recount, show an awareness of the need for discernment, though they do not offer systematic discussion of the topic. The need is apparent, for example, in Moses' exhortation to the people to 'choose life' (Deut. 13.15–20); in the accounts of the disputes between true and false prophets (Deut. 18.21ff.); and in the stories and metaphors used to give an account of Wisdom (e.g. Prov. 6, 7; Wisd. 8, 9), who makes possible the ordering of personal and corporate life in accordance with God's will and desire. The New Testament concern for discernment emerges from this experience of Israel. The early Church was occupied with the need to test the influences that affected the Christian community, especially the destruction created by the apparently good (e.g. 2 Cor. 11.13–15). Paul, consequently, developed criteria for discriminating between the works of 'the flesh' and those of 'the Spirit' (of God), (e.g. Gal. 5.16–26; 1 Cor. 3.3). The Gospels portray Jesus constantly as called upon to distinguish between good and evil 'spirits', between 'light' and 'darkness' in the environment and culture which he inhabited.

The First Letter of John exhorts the recipients to 'test the spirits to see if they are of God' (1 John 4.1). For the New Testament writers, to live by the Spirit is to have a proper Christian order in the corporate life of the community and in a person's own life, an order which involves particular ethical qualities and reflects in some way the life, death and resurrection of Jesus. Examination of key New Testament texts reveals an understanding of discernment as (1) a charismatic gift given by the Spirit for the good of the community, and (2) a Christian ability to reflect upon a range of spiritual experiences in order to determine which lead towards God in a path of Christian discipleship and which lead away from God.

Down the centuries the Christian Church developed its teaching on discernment on the basis of biblical data and further experience. Key figures in this development are: Origen (184–254); John Cassian (c. 360–435); John Climacus (sixth century), and subsequently, in the West, Denis the Carthusian (c. 1450); Ignatius Loyola (c. 1492–1556); John Cardinal Bona (mid seventeenth century); Giovanni Battista Scaramelli (mid eighteenth century). In the East the collection of texts known as the *Philokalia* (published 1782) draws together texts from previous centuries.

At the present time, especially in the Anglophone Christian world outside the monastic tradition, reflection on theory and practice of discernment derives mainly from the guidelines set out by Ignatius Loyola in, notably, the *Spiritual Exercises*, his *Spiritual Journal*, the *Constitutions of the Society of Jesus* and a few important letters.

From these and other sources it is possible to identify key features of Christian discernment. First, it emerges as a process of critical reflection which seeks to draw both affectivity (feeling, desires, impulses, moods) and understanding, reason, judgement and choice into a creative partnership. Thus it seeks to go beyond, on the one hand, a rationalism or a crude dogmatism which would devalue affective experience and, on the other hand, the domination of an individual or community by subjectivity, sentimentality, unreflective piety or uncritical enthusiasm. Second, if the Christian 'task' is to order personal and corporate life in the love of God and in love of others and the world in God, according to the pattern of the life, death and resurrection of Jesus in the power of the Spirit, then Christian discernment is an instrument to that end. It is an attempt to help persons and communities to tune in to what the Spirit of Christ is doing and desires to do in the world. Third, Christian discernment is based on an assumption that the mystery of God approaches human beings through experience. Its aim is to discriminate between those affective stirrings which lead to greater love of God and of others in God, after the pattern of Jesus' life and death, and those which lead in the opposite direction and are thus potentially destructive of human beings and communities.

Crucial to this discrimination is a distinction such as Ignatius Loyola made between two kinds of affective 'movements of the spirit', consolation and desolation. In the *Spiritual Exercises* Ignatius distinguished, at least implicitly, between true and apparent consolation, on the one hand, and desolation on the other. He also set out clear guidance, tested by experience, for identifying true consolation, apparent consolation and true desolation and for dealing with each (*Spiritual Exercises* 313–36). Whereas the mark of true consolation is its capacity to deepen love of God and of others in God, apparent consolation and desolation move a person in the opposite direction. The difficulty lies in distinguishing between the two movements because of the inherent ambiguity of moral and religious experience, mentioned above, by which evil appears as good and the good is liable to be undermined or corrupted in subtle and hidden ways. The aim of discernment, therefore, is to understand the truth behind the appearances: to distinguish true consolation from apparent consolation and from desolation and to make choices grounded in the movements of true consolation.

In recent times the notion and practice of discernment have been developed in the Christian community in a number of ways. The Second Vatican Council recommended to Roman Catholics the discernment of the 'signs of the times': movements of the Spirit of God in the contemporary world. Liberation communities and theologians use discernment to distinguish between what does or does not accord with God's will in situations of institutionalized injustice and oppression, in order to make choices for liberating praxis. Feminist theologians have developed criteria by which to distinguish, in specifically women's experience, between what is of God and what is not, taking into account the fact that conventional notions of what is 'good' in and for women are embedded in patriarchal value systems and are at best untrustworthy and at worst destructive. Finally, it may be argued that the contemporary world has features which make the call to discernment more urgent than ever. There is widespread and profound suspicion of authority and the choices it makes or imposes. While some religious pluralists claim that all truth and value are relative, religious fundamen-

talists insist that they have exclusive access to absolute truth and to God and act upon that claim. The name of God is invoked to justify acts of extreme brutality and inhumanity. In such circumstances it is as incumbent as it ever was on all religious groups to identify, scrutinize and reappraise critically the processes by which they 'test the spirits', make choices and justify the choices that they make.

See also **Consolation; Desolation; Conversion.**

Michael Buckley, 'Discernment of spirits' in Michael Downey (ed.), *The New Dictionary of Catholic Spirituality*, Collegeville, MN: The Liturgical Press, 1993; Maureen Conroy, *The Discerning Heart: Discovering a Personal God*, Chicago: Loyola University Press, 1993; Philip Endean and Jackie Hawkins (eds), *Discerning Together*, *The Way Supplement* 85 (Spring 1996); 'Discernment' in Kathleen Fischer, *Women at the Well: Feminist Perspectives on Spiritual Direction*, London: SPCK, 1989; David Lonsdale, *Dance to the Music of the Spirit: The Art of Discernment*, London: Darton, Longman & Todd, 1993 (published in the USA as *Listening to the Music of the Spirit*, Notre Dame, IN: Ave Maria Press, 1993).

DAVID LONSDALE

Discipleship

The evangelists uses two different words to express the concept of discipleship, so central to the ministry of Jesus, the noun *mathetes*, 'one who learns', and the verb *akolouthein*, 'to follow after'. The English 'disciple' comes from the Latin *discipulus*, 'pupil'. *Mathetes* occurs more than 250 times, mostly in the Gospels and Acts. *Akolouthein* appears 56 times in the Synoptics and 14 in John; though sometimes used of the crowds, when used of individuals (Mark 1.18; Luke 5.11; John 1.43), it shows the special relation of the disciples to Jesus. The evangelists also speak of a new kind of family, based not on traditional bonds of clan, kinship or patriarchy, but on one's acceptance of the kingdom of God (Mark 3.33–35). At times, the theme of the new family merges with that of the disciples (Luke 14.26; John 19.26–27). But it is the language of discipleship that is most evident.

The relation of master/disciple occurs rarely in the Old Testament and the word *mathetes* does not appear in the Septuagint. While the New Testament uses *mathetes* for the disciples of John the Baptist and occasionally for the disciples of the Pharisees, its usage in reference to the disciples of Jesus is unique. First, unlike the case of discipleship in Rabbinic Judaism, where the disciple chose the master, Jesus chose and called his disciples (Mark 1.17; 2.14). While he called all to repentance, to act with mercy and love, to forgive, and to welcome the kingdom, only some received a personal invitation to be in his company and to follow him as disciples.

Second, there was an inclusive character to Jesus' call to discipleship; his invitations were not restricted to the ritually pure, the religiously observant, or even to men. Among those who followed him were 'tax collectors and sinners' (Mark 2.15) as well as a group of women (Luke 8.2).

Third, being a disciple of Jesus demands a religious conversion that goes beyond the requirements of the law, a radical break with one's past. The disciples 'left everything' (Luke 5.11), giving up parents, family, children (Luke 14.26), jobs (Mark 2.24), and possessions (Mark 10.21). They shared Jesus' itinerant life and poverty (Matt. 8.20). For some it meant celibacy for the sake of the kingdom of heaven (Matt. 19.11–12). The omission of 'fathers' from the new family of disciples in Mark 10.30 and the inclusion of women suggests that the break with one's past meant a break with one's culture as well.

Finally, being a disciple of Jesus meant sharing in his ministry. Unlike the disciples of the Pharisees who were concerned only with learning the teachings of their masters, the disciples of Jesus were sent out to heal the sick, cast out unclean spirits, and proclaim that the kingdom of God was at hand (Mark 6.7–13; Luke 10.2–12). Like Jesus, they must be willing to take the last place and serve others (Mark 9.35), even to sacrifice their lives (Mark 8.35; John 15.12–13).

In the post-Easter communities, discipleship was understood as including the following of Jesus in his passage from death to life. Paul sees the Christian life, from its beginnings in baptism to its ultimate victory over sin and death as a participation in Christ's paschal mystery (Rom. 6.3–5; Phil. 3.8–11). The central part of Mark's Gospel is an instruction on discipleship as the Christian 'way' (Mark 8.27—10.52) that includes the taking up one's cross and coming after Jesus (Mark 8.34–35).

In subsequent Christian history discipleship became practically synonymous with Christian life. The Acts of the Apostles frequently refers to the early Christians simply as 'the disciples'. Martyrdom in the early centuries, the monastic life, the *vita apostolica* or 'apostolic life' in the late Middle Ages, Thomas à Kempis' classic fifteenth-century *Imitation of Christ*, the communities of the radical Reformation, the *Spiritual Exercises* of Ignatius of Loyola, Dietrich Bonhoeffer's *The Cost of Discipleship*, the stress on the social/political character of Christian discipleship in Johann Baptist Metz or Latin American liberation theology – all represent different efforts to express and live out a life of Christian discipleship.

Against the tendency to identify discipleship with the pursuit of perfection in the 'consecrated life', Vatican II emphasized that all Christians are called to holiness (*LG* 5). For many today, sensitivity to social disparity has made simplicity of life and solidarity with the poor important aspects of Christian discipleship. Thus discipleship means a following of Jesus that ought to shape all dimensions of a Christian's life, personal, social, sexual, economic and political. At the heart of Christian discipleship is always the *imitatio Christi*.

See also **Apostolic Spirituality; Discipline.**

Bruce Chilton and J. I. H. McDonald, *Jesus and the Ethics of the Kingdom*, Grand Rapids, MI: Eerdmans, 1987; Martin Hengel, *The Charismatic Leader and His Followers*, Edinburgh: T & T Clark, 1996; John P. Meier, 'The disciples' in *A Marginal Jew, Vol. 3: Companions and Competitors*, New York: Doubleday, 2001, pp. 40–124.

THOMAS P. RAUSCH

Discipline

A discipline is a practice or system of practices undertaken by an individual or a community as part of a programme of training or instruction. In the Christian context, it is thus closely related, both etymologically and functionally, to the concept of discipleship. Historically, the term 'discipline' has been used in three distinct ways in discourse about Christian spirituality:

1. *Ecclesiastical rules and sanctions*. In this sense, 'church discipline' refers to a Christian community's regulation of the behaviour or belief of its members, especially through exclusionary practices such as excommunication, banning from fellowship, or shunning. The New Testament basis for such practices can be found in passages such as Matt. 18.15–20 and 1 Cor. 5.1–5. In the early Church, discipline was exercised principally through the practice of public penance known as *exomologesis* ('confession'), with carefully modulated grades of exclusion from and readmission to the worshipping community. In the Middle Ages, discipline took the form of auricular confession to a priest with absolution followed by stipulated acts of satisfaction; this continues to be the prevailing approach to discipline in Roman Catholic and Eastern Orthodox churches today. In various ways, the Churches of the Reformation sought to restore a more systematic and rigorous public enforcement of communal norms concerning morality,

church attendance and devotional practice, but these efforts are less prevalent among Protestants today, except in some evangelical and fundamentalist circles.

2. *Ascetical exercises of mortification.* The Latin word *disciplina* has often been taken as equivalent to the Greek *ascesis* ('exercise') and thus used to refer to stringent acts of mortification and self-denial. In particular, the term has long been associated with the practice of flagellation. The Rule of Benedict and other early monastic rules prescribed beating or whipping as a means of chastisement for disobedient or negligent monks. By the eleventh century, largely through the influence of Peter Damian, flagellation (self-inflicted or administered by a religious superior) with a whip of cords that came to be known as 'the discipline' was a common ascetic exercise in religious communities, and it has sometimes made its way into popular devotional practice among the laity.

3. *Spiritual practices more generally.* In contemporary discourse about Christian spirituality, reference is now more often to a wide range of 'spiritual disciplines' conceived both more broadly and more positively, as practices of devotion and training in discipleship. Perhaps the best-known categorization is that set forth by Richard Foster in *Celebration of Discipline*: the 'inward disciplines' of meditation, prayer, fasting and study; the 'outward disciplines' of simplicity, solitude, submission and service; and finally the 'corporate disciplines' of confession, worship, guidance and celebration. Advocates of these spiritual disciplines note that all of them appear throughout Scripture, including accounts of Jesus' ministry. Because they are embodied activities that involve the whole person in doing what Jesus did and commanded, these disciplines form Christian character and virtues more effectively than mere verbal admonition that appeals to the intellect or the affections but fails to engage the body and the will. There is of course a danger of turning these disciplines into a sombre and legalistic list of duties, or a way of claiming hypocritical superiority over others. But properly understood and practised, the spiritual disciplines are God-given means of grace, effective in the formation and training of Christian disciples.

See also **Asceticism; Discipleship; Formation, Spiritual; Penitence; Practice, Spiritual; Purgative Way.**

Tilden Edwards, *Living in the Presence: Spiritual Exercises to Open Your Life to the Awareness of God,* San Francisco: HarperSanFrancisco, 1995;

Richard J. Foster, *Celebration of Discipline: The Path to Spiritual Growth,* third edn, San Francisco: HarperSanFrancisco, 1998; S. L. Greenslade, *Shepherding the Flock: Problems of Pastoral Discipline in the Early Church and in the Younger Churches Today,* London: SCM Press, 1967; Howard Thurman, *Disciplines of the Spirit,* reprint edn, Richmond, IN: Friends United Press, 1977; Dallas Willard, *The Spirit of the Disciplines: Understanding How God Changes Lives,* reprint edn, San Francisco: HarperSanFrancisco, 1991; Vincent L. Wimbush and Richard Valantasis, *Asceticism,* New York: Oxford University Press, 1995.

ARTHUR G. HOLDER

Discretion

see **Discernment**

Divinization

see **Deification**

Dominican Spirituality

Many years before the official foundation of the Order of Preachers (Dominicans) in 1216, two aspects of the medieval movement known as the *vita apostolica* characterized the spirituality and mission of St Dominic and became twin pillars of later Dominican spirituality: evangelical preaching and the contemplative, scholastic and liturgical life of the Canons Regular of St Augustine.

The preaching ministry arose when in 1203 Dominic, then an Augustinian canon, accompanied Bishop Diego of Osma on a diplomatic mission for the King of Castille. En route to Denmark, Dominic and Diego encountered the mission of the Cistercian abbots who had been ordered by Pope Innocent III to preach against the dualistic heretics of southern France. Assuming direction of the faltering mission, Diego laid the foundations for an order of evangelical preachers by insisting on simplicity of life, gospel poverty and humility. After Diego's death in 1207 and the withdrawal of the Cistercians, Dominic remained in France to continue the mission, eventually gathering around himself a band of similarly dedicated preachers.

The original character of the Order and its spirituality was thus shaped by the personality and background of St Dominic, the demands of the apostolic task he had inherited, and the social-cultural circumstances of the early thirteenth century during which the Order took form. But it would be mistaken to assume that there is a single Dominican spirituality distinct from other forms of Christian spirituality or that it possesses an official spiritual doctrine. Diverse and inclusive, Dominican spirituality is nevertheless characterized individually and collectively by several recognizable attributes.

1. *Diversity in membership.* Women played an important role in the preaching mission of Diego and Dominic from the beginning. The establishment in 1206 of the convent of nuns at Prouille as a refuge for women converted from the Albigensian heresy was the first 'Dominican' foundation. After receiving approval of the Order from Pope Honorius III in 1216, Dominic soon founded other monasteries for nuns, and the 'Sisters Preachers' were fully incorporated into the Order in 1267. Lay associates of the Order existed informally from the beginning and by 1286 were recognized as integral members. Thus although not familial in the manner of monastic orders such as the Benedictines, the Dominican 'Family' is comprised of a variety of brothers and sisters – the clerical friars and co-operator brothers; the contemplative nuns; and the religious sisters, diocesan clergy, and vowed lay persons of both sexes. Each group is distinctive, having its own government, constitutions and procedures. Egalitarian and democratic from the beginning, Dominicans elect their leaders for limited terms and determine policy by vote in local, regional and international assemblies (chapters).

2. *Contemplation and action.* In the papal letter of Honorius III to Dominic and the first friars in 1216, the Pope described the purpose of Order as '. . . a life of poverty and regular observance and . . . preaching the Word of God and proclaiming the name of our Lord Jesus Christ throughout the world'. According to the prologue of the earliest Constitutions, the Order 'is known from the beginning to have been instituted especially for preaching and the salvation of souls'.

When Dominic decided to establish an order of preaching friars and sisters, he modelled it on what he knew from experience. The Rule he chose, which was approved by the first members of the Order, is that of St Augustine. The character of the Order of Friars Preachers and therefore its spirituality are thus rooted in its origins as an order of Canons Regular, priests living in common and following a monastic rule. And although canons were not monks, a liturgically focused life of contemplation was specifically their calling. Contemplation has remained a central part of Dominican spirituality ever since. Canons were also actively involved in various ministries. Action, therefore, has always been the other pole of Dominican life and spirituality.

In the early 1220s Bishop Jacques de Vitry described the Dominicans at Bologna simply as a house of canons following the Rule of St Augustine (*Histories of the East and of the West*). 'They have fused an order of preachers to an order of canons. This felicitous mixture of good elements attracts, stimulates, and fires up a great many people to follow them; each day this holy and distinguished congregation of Christ's students both grows in number and expands in charity.'

William Hinnebusch concludes that the spirituality of the Friars, and by extension all Dominicans, is characteristically

theocentric, Christological, sacerdotal . . . monastic, contemplative, and apostolic. It is, in truth, the spirituality of Christ the Preacher and of the Apostles. The primary intention is to elevate the friar to the heights of contemplation, but going beyond this, Dominican contemplation itself is intended to fructify in the apostolate for souls, especially through preaching, teaching, and writing. Contemplation is the generic element, the one the Friars Preachers share with other contemplative Orders, the salvation of souls through preaching is the specific note distinguishing Dominicans from all other Orders. (Hinnebusch, 1965, p. 2)

3. *A functional spirituality.* Benedict Ashley similarly identifies four fundamental characteristics of Dominican spirituality. First, the mission of the Order of Preachers is *evangelization* – spreading the gospel of Christ by preaching. Since such evangelical preaching is primarily the responsibility of the whole community, Dominican life and spirituality are fundamentally *communal*. *Worship and prayer* are primary expressions of that communal identity. *Spiritual discipline* is an important aspect of Dominican spirituality, especially the observance of evangelical poverty and study, notably of Scripture (Ashley, 1990, pp. 20–2). Dominic's replacement of manual labour by study was of significant consequence for the Church as a whole, according to Hinnebusch, for with this innovation, 'for the first time in a thousand years of monastic history, a religious Order incorporated into its rule sections dealing with the academic life' (Hinnebusch, 1965, p. 105).

The traditional emblems of the Order reflect these elements clearly. The 'motto' of the Order found on seals, stationery, documents and inscriptions contains the Latin words *Laudare, Benedicere, Praedicare*: 'to Praise, to Bless, to Preach'. These words indicate the primary mission and therefore the spirituality of the Order as a whole: prayer and worship; evangelical ministry, expressed in sacramental administration, missionary work, teaching, healing and parochial care; and preaching in its many forms, including writing and the expressive arts.

The single word *Veritas*, 'Truth', often inscribed over the Dominican seal, summarizes the goal and ideal of the Order. By this is meant the whole range of divine, physical and human Reality. Thomas Aquinas would write three volumes on the meaning of truth (*De Veritate*), but for him, as for all Dominicans, the chief instance and perfect exemplar was Eternal Truth, expressed substantially and historically in Jesus Christ: 'In other men we find many participated truths, insofar as the First Truth gleams back into their minds through many likenesses; but Christ is Truth itself' (*Commentary on the Gospel of John*, Chap. 1, Lect. 8, No. 188.) The quest for Truth in all its forms – theological, philosophical, scientific, historical and artistic has always been the star that guided the Dominican spirit.

A third epithet has traditionally illustrated the spirituality of the Dominican Order: *Contemplata aliis tradere*, 'to hand on to others what we have learned in contemplation'. Also drawn from the teachings of St Thomas Aquinas (*ST* 2a2ae.188.6), this phrase is meant not to distinguish the mystical, contemplative dimension of Dominican spirituality from its active expression, but to unite them. Nor are they related as a means to an end: they form a single, unified goal.

4. *A Tradition without a method*. Unlike that of many religious orders and congregations, Dominican spirituality characteristically lacks a preferred method, or a technique, or a favoured set of exercises. Rather, a great variety of approaches can be found in the history of the Order, from the synoptic intellectualism of Albert the Great and Thomas Aquinas to the mystical lyricism of Henry Süs (Suso) and the artistic genius of Fra Angelico. The prophetic apocalypticism of Vincent Ferrer and Jerome Savonarola are matched by the mystical activism of Catherine of Siena and the Franciscan-like humility and compassion of Martin de Porres.

In general terms, however, the characteristic elements found in Dominican spirituality wherever it flourishes will include the following: (1) the constitutive priorities of preaching, community life, prayer, and study; (2) poverty of spirit; (3) the primacy of Truth; (4) contemplation expressed in active ministry. To these may be added the quest for ever closer union with God through conformity to Christ under the influence of the gifts of the Holy Spirit, a recurrent theme in the writings of the spiritual masters of the Order and one which characterizes the lives of its greatest saints. Preachers, theologians, philosophers, missionaries, spiritual directors, reformers, healers, scientists, historians, painters, sculptors, musicians and poets – all have successfully embodied the spirit of the Order, each contributing to and drawing from its spirituality in a distinctive but recognizably Dominican way.

See also **Canonical Communities; Mendicant Spirituality.**

Benedict Ashley, *The Dominicans*, Collegeville, MN: The Liturgical Press, 1990; Ambroise Gardeil, *The Gifts of the Holy Ghost in Dominican Saints*, Milwaukee: Bruce, 1937; William Hinnebusch, *Dominican Spirituality: Principles and Practices*, Washington, DC: The Thomist Press, 1965; Edward Schillebeeckx, 'Dominican spirituality, or the counter-thread in the old religious story as the golden thread in the Dominican family-story', *Dominican Topics in South Africa*, March, May and August, 1975; Anselm Townsend (ed. and trans.), *Dominican Spirituality*, Milwaukee: Bruce, 1934, translation of *La vie spirituelle* 4 (Aug. 1921); Simon Tugwell, *The Way of the Preacher*. London: Darton, Longman & Todd, 1979; Richard Woods, *Mysticism and Prophecy: The Dominican Tradition*, London: Darton, Longman & Todd/New York: Orbis Books, 1998.

RICHARD WOODS

Doxology

see **Praise**

Dreams and Dreaming

The scientific evidence is overwhelming and unambiguous: all human beings dream, whether they recall these nightly adventures upon awakening or not. The phenomenon of involuntary 'rapid eye motion', (also called 'REM'), in sleep and its association with dreaming is readily observable and demonstrable in all people (and in all complex, warm-blooded animals as well).

The scriptures and sacred narratives of all the world's many religious traditions also speak with a single voice on this question: human beings are in closer and more direct communion and communication with the divine in our dreams than any other state of consciousness.

Curiously, at the same time, the actual practice of paying close attention to, and analysing, dreams with an eye to discovering their deeper spiritual significance is generally disparaged and/or forbidden in the practices of all the more prominent religions (although it still remains a regular element in the customs and procedures of many less widely accepted, occult, nativist, and 'fringe' Churches and religious communities).

Perhaps the most important reason for this curious state of affairs is that all dreams (even the nasty ones we tend to call 'nightmares'), come ultimately in the service of physical, emotional and spiritual health and wholeness. Dreams shape and deliver their healing messages in a universal language of symbol and metaphor. The Swiss psychiatrist and historian of world religion, Carl Jung, called these repeating symbols and metaphors 'archetypes of the collective unconscious'. It is this ubiquitous healing and wholeness-promoting quality of dreaming that is primarily responsible for the unambiguously privileged position that dream wisdom holds in the sacred narratives of the world.

The subsequent disparagement of dreams as a source of spiritual insight and guidance also stems directly from this privileged position dreams hold in world religious traditions: if actual work with dreams were not disparaged and forbidden, it would then always be possible (and over time, ultimately inevitable), that anyone could lay claim to the special authority of dream revelation, since the experience of dreaming is universal, and comes alike to all, regardless of class, caste, privilege, education or special religious training. Indeed, if these dreamers also happened to be more or less scruffy and malcontent, then ironically their dream-inspired messages would be even more likely to carry weight and authority, because of the repeated association of scruffiness and malcontentedness with the 'authentic voice of prophecy' in virtually all religious traditions. In such a situation, it would be nearly impossible for any merely human authority, in any specific local gathering, to stand effectively against whatever heretical notions any community members might derive from their private and personal dreams, precisely because the transpersonal 'scriptural authority' of dreaming as a means of direct communion with the divine is so clear and unambiguous.

Many 'reform movements' within the major world religions have tried repeatedly to return to their respective scriptural practices of remembering and sharing dreams (at least at the beginnings of their reform efforts), in an effort to 'restore' the 'ancient covenant', and return to a 'purer' and 'more direct' relationship with the divine, which they often feel has been betrayed, or at least made more distant and less effective, by the practices of the professional priestly class. Again and again, at the idealistic beginnings of such reform movements in Judaism, Christianity, Islam, Hinduism, Buddhism and many others besides, the reformers begin by re-establishing the communal dream-sharing and interpretation practices recounted and celebrated in their own sacred narratives, only to discover that the subsequent divisions and differences of opinion fracture and fragment the 'solidarity' of the reform movement to such an extent that these practices are once again abandoned and 'outlawed'.

The price that is paid for this disparagement of dreams and dreaming is inevitably an increased sense of distance from direct revelation and personal experience of 'God's will', and an increased rigidity in protecting the newly revised dogma from any further 'heretical' revision. This repeating pattern is in itself an example of a repeating 'archetypal drama'.

In the late twentieth and early twenty-first centuries, particularly in the Western hemisphere, there has been a revived interest in remembering dreams and searching for their deeper psychological meanings and creative inspirations, largely inspired by the clinical insights of Jung, Freud and others. This 'lay' dream work movement has also created renewed interest in the more spiritual levels of dream experience, and has led many individuals to add dream-sharing and dream exploration to their personal spiritual practice, regardless of the specific religious traditions from which they come.

Jeremy Taylor, *Dream Work*, Mahwah, NJ: Paulist Press, 1983.

JEREMY TAYLOR

Drugs

The use of psychoactive drugs for spiritual purposes is very ancient. One-tenth of the Rig Veda refers to a drug called *soma*, often identified with the mushroom *amanita muscaria*, though some believe that it was cannabis. Cannabis is certainly mentioned within a religious context in many ancient texts. In the ancient Greek *Materia medica*, it is clear that plant wisdom is linked with priestly learning and folk traditions. The amanita mushroom has been seen as the basis of many cults, and J. M. Allegro associated it with the beginnings of Christianity – a view which attracted no scholarly support. The ritual and sacramental use of drugs other than alcohol is more common outside the Jewish and Christian traditions, although the Native American Church has used peyote for a long time.

The value of certain drugs in raising the level of consciousness and enhancing religious experience was discussed by William James in 1902. James ascribed 'metaphysical significance' to his experiences under nitrous oxide. Later Aldous

Huxley discussed the same issues in relation to mescaline, and in the early 1960s Leary and his colleagues at Harvard experimented with psilocybin, making religious claims for that drug.

It was the increased use, in the late 1960s, of LSD-25 (lysergic acid diethylamide) which led to widespread debate in the West about the role of these substances in spiritual development. The word 'psychedelic' (mind-expanding), first used by Humphrey Osmond in 1957, became popular in these years. The main effects claimed for LSD were the intensifying of experience, the illumination (or altered perception) of reality, and the temporary dissolution of the boundaries of the ego. Richard Alpert wrote of its ability to allow people 'to break out of certain limited perceptual vantage points and understand alternative possibilities of reality'. It was therefore argued (e.g. by Leary, Alpert and Watts) that this and related drugs were of great value in aiding spiritual growth. Parallels were made with mystical experiences (as in the research of Pahnke).

One of the most important and influential writers in this area, the late Alan Watts, argued that LSD helped people to discover the central human experience, known in Zen as *satori* and in Hinduism as *moksha*, an experience which changes all others, and brings about a cosmic consciousness. There was, he argued, no essential difference between the experiences with or without the aid of chemicals, and he suggested that LSD should be taken in a retreat house under the guidance of a spiritual director.

Others claimed that most psychedelic experiences were low-grade alterations of consciousness which in fact diminished consciousness, integrity and personality. Allan Y. Cohen argued that the opening up of the deeper regions of consciousness through drugs could, and did, lead many to move beyond the drug experience into more authentic spiritual paths. He referred to 'the journey beyond trips' and called such journeyers 'meta-hippies'.

The word 'entheogen' was introduced by C. A. P. Ruck in 1979, as an alternative to 'psychedelic', to describe plants and chemicals which awaken or generate mystical experiences. (A few years earlier the pharmacologist C. R. B. Joyce had coined the word 'theopharmacology' to describe the growing interest in chemicals and religion.)

However, since the 1960s there has been a marked tendency to devalue regular drug use. Many spiritual writers have warned against reliance on chemicals as a route to God. Some claim that the main value of these agents was to enable some people within a materialistic culture

to experience a breakthrough to neglected or suppressed areas of consciousness. But continued reliance on them was more likely to lead to spiritual decline. Hence the interest shifted away from drugs towards non-chemical approaches to spirituality. However, the possible contribution of certain drugs as aids to spiritual perception should not be ruled out.

The comparison, often associated with Marx, of religion itself to an intoxicant or an opiate, in fact goes back to the eighteenth century. As psychopharmacology has developed, the study of what Huxley termed 'the chemical conditions of transcendence' has become more sophisticated. The connection between the use of chemicals and religion (including its pathological forms) has come to be seen as more complex than earlier mechanistic and deterministic writers held. The use of drugs in a religious context raises issues such as the relation between chemical changes and personality, between body and spirit, questions which are central to all incarnational religion.

Allan Y. Cohen, 'The journey beyond trips: alternatives to drugs' in David E. Smith and George R. Guy (eds), *It's So Good Don't Even Try It Once: Heroin Perspectives*, Englewood Cliffs, NJ: Prentice Hall, 1972, pp. 186–96; Harvey D. Egan, 'Christian mysticism and psychedelic drug experience' in *Studies in Formative Spirituality: Spiritual Formation and Mysticism* vol. 5.1 (February 1984), 33–41; Robert Forte (ed.), *Entheogens and the Future of Religion*, San Francisco: Council on Spiritual Practices, 1997; Mike Jay (ed.), *Artificial Paradises*, London: Penguin, 1999; Kenneth Leech, *Drugs and Pastoral Care*, London: Darton, Longman & Todd, 1998; Kenneth Leech, *Youthquake: Spirituality and the Growth of a Counter-Culture*, London: Sphere, 1976; Nicholas Saunders, Anya Saunders and Michelle Paul, *In Search of the Ultimate High: Spiritual Experience through Psychoactives*, London: Rider/Random House, 2000; Huston Smith, *Cleansing the Doors of Perception: The Religious Significance of Entheogenic Plants and Chemicals*, New York: Jeremy P. Tarcher/Putnam, 2000.

KENNETH LEECH

Dualism

Dualism approaches the question of God, creation, the human person and the struggle with evil as two realities which fundamentally oppose one another. This opposition is often viewed as irreconcilable opposites engaged in warlike struggle with one another where one must triumph over the other. Such warring opposites most often are seen as 'good and evil', 'light and darkness' or 'spirit and matter'. In religious thought, dualism begins on the level of the divine that consequently manifests itself in cosmology and the human person.

Dualistic outlooks have been apparent in nearly all religious traditions and vary in level of opposition and antagonism. In radical dualism, the two opposite principles are equal in power and eternal, and often are portrayed as being at war with one another. Zoroastrianism and Manichaeism taught the eternal battle between the kingdom of light and the kingdom of darkness, and such cosmic warfare is also evident in much of the apocalyptic literature of Judaism such as in the War Scroll of Qumran and works known as the Old Testament Pseudepigrapha. Early Christianity included dualistic tendencies in the New Testament book of Revelation (the Apocalypse) and in what are now considered non-canonical works such as the *Apocalypse of Peter*, and the *Didache*. God, the world and the human struggle are defined in terms of irreconcilable differences between two incompatible realities reduced to simple concepts of right or wrong, good or evil, God or Satan, the body or the spirit.

Radical dualism not only separated the two as warring opposites, but attributed absolute corruption to the human body and material creation. Radical dualism was in large part rejected by the early Christian communities, though it continued to find a home in certain Gnostic and early ascetical groups. Far more prevalent and enduring in Christian spirituality has been moderate dualism which sees the primacy of good and the spiritual over the struggle with evil and the limitations of matter. Many surviving writings of such early Christian writers such as Origen and some of the ascetical movements continued to view the body as separate and inherently inferior to the soul. Origen himself traced the existence of material creation and the human body as a consequence of the fall of the soul. Radical dualism viewed the human body and the material world as entirely corrupt and the enemy of the soul and spirit. Moderate dualism was found in some Stoic schools and moderate early Christian ascetical groups saw the body and creation as a meritorious training ground for strengthening the spirit which would eventually discard both the material world and the body in order to achieve perfect freedom and eternal life.

While radical dualism was quickly rejected by Christianity, moderate dualism on the other hand, influenced the writings of such early theologians and spiritual writers as Basil of Caesarea, Gregory of Nyssa, Athanasius of Alexandria, Ambrose and Augustine. A dualism of body and spirit is evident in much of the surviving early Christian literature, especially when discussing human sexuality. Most surviving texts of this period consider God and the human person originally and ideally asexual, with Augustine in particular teaching that sexual relations were a consequence of the fall and original sin was passed on via sexual intercourse.

Throughout its history, regardless of denomination, Christian spirituality has continued to embrace moderate dualism, particularly in matters of the human body and soul. There has been and continues to be a lack of positive constructive understanding of the unity of body and soul, material and spiritual, and a healthy understanding and regard for human sexuality and emotion. While asceticism need not be considered essentially dualistic in theory, nevertheless in practice and theology it can easily be seen that a dualism of body and spirit has often influenced ascetical theologies and lifestyles. Contemporary efforts in the field of spirituality, especially feminist spirituality, and psychology have made attempts to achieve a more holistic, creation-centred spirituality and so have made efforts to correct the centuries long imbalance between body and soul in traditional Christian spirituality.

See also **Asceticism; Early Christian Spirituality; Body and Spirituality.**

U. Bianchi, *Selected Essays on Gnosticism, Dualism, and Myetriosophy*, Leiden: Brill, 1997; John J. Collins, *Apocalypticism in the Dead Sea Scrolls*, London and New York: Routledge, 1997; John W. Cooper, *Body, Soul, and Life Everlasting: Biblical Anthropology and the Monism–Dualism Debate*, Grand Rapids, MI: Eerdmans, 1989; Bart D. Ehrman, *Jesus: Apocalyptic Prophet of the New Millennium*, Oxford and New York: Oxford University Press, 1999; Gillian McCulloch, David A. S. Fergusson, *The Deconstruction of Dualism in Theology: With Special Reference to Ecofeminist Theology and New Age Spirituality*, Carlisle: Paternoster Press, 2003; Elaine Pagels, *The Origin of Satan*, London: Vintage, 1996.

HARRIET A. LUCKMAN

Early Christian Spirituality

The period covered by this article extends from the end of the first century to the pontificate of Gregory the Great (604).

1. *The persecuted Church.* Early Christian spiritual writings, texts that mention or are concerned with prayer, the vision of God and spiritual progress, are strongly coloured by the threat of

persecution and the possibility of martyrdom. Even though official persecution of Christians by imperial authorities was often sporadic and sometimes half-hearted, there existed within the Christian community throughout the whole of the period prior to Constantine's peace of the Church (313) an awareness that Christianity was universally viewed with suspicion and hostility by 'the world'. *Martyria,* 'bearing witness' to Christ, was not only the task of celebrated heroes: ordinary Christians could give witness to the inner meaning of their faith at all times by publicly adhering to strict moral codes already foreshadowed in the concluding moral exhortations of St Paul's epistles, and regularly reiterated by the Apostolic Fathers (*Didache,* Barnabas, Hermas) and apologists (Justin). Early Church leaders such as Clement of Rome (*c.* 96) and Ignatius of Antioch (*c.* 107) encouraged the faithful to see a parallel between the external 'arena' of public martyrdom and their interior, daily struggle against sin. Spirituality was thus inextricably intertwined with adherence to a demanding ethical code: prayer and a sense of God's nearness were both means and fruits of living a life that proclaimed Christian moral identity to an unbelieving world.

This interrelationship between martyrdom, morality and spirituality is vividly attested in the prison diary of the young matron Perpetua (203), a text that provides an unparalleled window into the spiritual life of a devout lay woman. Her steadfast adherence to Christianity in the face of threat attests to her moral heroism (*Mart. Perpet.* 1.1–2), while her status as a martyr-in-training enables her to make bold requests of God in prayer (1.3). She is granted a mystical vision of ascent to heaven on a ladder of virtues, where Christ the Good Shepherd invites her to partake of a kind of eucharistic banquet (1.3). In subsequent visions she discovers the martyr's powers of intercession, is able to obtain release from suffering for her deceased pagan brother, (2.3) and perceives her imminent death as a successful gladiatorial struggle against Satan. (3.2–3).

The martyrs' spiritual prerogatives of bold prayer, effective intercession and contemplative vision were progressively understood as available to all Christians who undertake the *ascesis* ('training') of rejecting sin and serving Christ. In the writings of Irenaeus of Lyons (200), Clement of Alexandria (215), and Origen (254), Middle- and Neo-platonic notions of ethical purification (*katharsis*), contemplative vision (*theōria*) and mystical exegesis (*allegoria*) were applied to the Christian Scriptures and to spiritual theology, yielding methods of biblical interpretation and models of spiritual progress. In his *Letter to Donatus* Cyprian (258) urged all Christians to ascend to God by an alternating rhythm of Scripture reading (*lectio*) and personal prayer (*oratio*). This early witness to the practice of *lectio divina* was amplified by Clement and Origen, who described the supreme heights to which the Scriptures can carry the devout Christian. The Bible may be read at different levels: first at the historical or literal level, based on grammar and history; superior to it is the ethical or moral sense; and highest of all are the spiritual, allegorical or *epoptic* senses, conveying theological mysteries. Roughly parallel to this exegetical method is a model of spiritual progress based on traditional Greek pedagogy: the Christian initiate first undergoes purification from sin (ethics); then learns the rudiments of doctrine reflected in creation and nature (physics); and finally perceives deeper mysteries transcending words and concepts (enoptics/epoptics/theology). Origen associated this highest level with the Song of Songs, and for many centuries commentaries on this biblical book served as the customary means of describing the highest levels of Christian prayer and contemplation. This Alexandrian vocabulary of mystical exegesis and spiritual progress was adapted and refined by the monk Evagrius Ponticus (399) whose psychological insight enhanced his methodical description of virtue, temptation and prayer. These provided the basis and standard vocabulary for the developing mystical theology of the Christian East, and, through the *Institutes* and *Conferences* of Evagrius' disciple John Cassian (420), the Latin-speaking West.

2. *The state Church.* Constantine's edict of toleration (313) and the eventual establishment of Christianity as the sole licit religion of the Roman Empire meant a drastic reversal in popular Christian self-understanding. The faith that had been forbidden now became the key to political success, and the once-persecuted religion now set eagerly about the project of persecuting pagans and heretics. To many of the faithful it seemed that the vast influx of dubious catechumens diluted the spiritual fervour of an earlier, more perilous era. The phenomenal success of monasticism during this period reflected, at least in part, a popular desire to preserve the spirituality of the church of the martyrs. Monks and nuns presented new models of spiritual heroism: their spiritual practices and often remote geographical sites symbolized rejection of 'worldly' culture; they became the intercessors and seers of the new age; and many of them, especially the hermits, offered spiritual guidance to those who sought it.

Monks and nuns preserved and augmented the pattern of regular prayer every few hours that Tertullian (225) and Cyprian (258) had urged on all Christians. In the monasteries methods of liturgical and private prayer were formalized that alternated kataphatic (image-filled) psalmody with intervals of silent, apophatic (imageless, wordless) self-offering. Monastic life found its greatest hero and model in Antony (356), whose biography by Athanasius (373) became an almost instant bestseller. The developing institution of monasticism found its organizing principles in the *Ascetikon* of Basil of Caesarea (379), the *Institutes* of Cassian, and later in the West in the Rule of Benedict of Nursia (*c.* 540)

Throughout the latter half of the fourth century the liturgy came to be regarded, like meditation on the Scriptures, as a privileged means of contemplative exercise and mystical ascent. The mystagogical and catechetical homilies of Cyril of Jerusalem (387) and Ambrose of Milan (397) present the liturgy as both a means of Christian catechesis and a spiritual exercise through which the soul perceives God and is mysteriously transformed. The trinitarian and christological controversies of the same century contributed to this increasingly mystical understanding of the liturgy. St Athanasius' (373) objection to the Arians' use of the word *homoiousios* ('of like substance') to describe Christ's relationship to the Father was rooted in his doctrine of *theosis,* divinization. We are saved through a mystical transformation: 'He became human so that we might be made God' (*de. Incarn.* 54.3); and unless Christ is fully divine – of the same substance (*homoousios*) – as the Father, Christ cannot divinize. The liturgical celebrations where the transforming sacraments of baptism, the Eucharist and ordination are celebrated came to be regarded as unique occasions of *theosis*. In the daily monastic and cathedral celebrations of the Liturgy of the Hours, psalmody acquired an increasingly privileged place; and like the sacraments, chanted psalms were believed to have power to heal and restore the soul. The liturgy was a foretaste of the bliss of heaven, an awakening of an ever-deepening desire for God, a 'straining forward' (*epektasis*) that, according to Gregory of Nyssa (395), will grow even stronger in the world to come. This esteem for liturgical prayer attained its zenith in the magnificent if esoteric writings of Dionysius the Aereopagite (*c.* 520), who celebrates both the apophatic divine darkness (*The Mystical Theology*) and the radiantly kataphatic, complex creation (*The Celestial and Ecclesiastical Hierarchies*). For Dionysius all grace is mediated through visible and invisible ranks of angels, sacraments and ecclesiastical offices. To contemplate a sacrament or a psalm is to be drawn into the divine rhythm of eternal outpouring, indwelling and reunion. Dionysius' breathtaking vision would directly influence the mystical theology, ecclesiology and sacramental theology of the Christian West through translations into Latin; while his influence in the East would be felt chiefly through his commentators, including Maximus Confessor (662).

3. *The Church in a collapsing empire.* Constantine had envisioned Christianity providing moral and spiritual support for a distended empire that was widely and accurately perceived as collapsing. Christian spirituality naturally came to mirror the anxieties of a culture sliding towards dissolution. In Christian spiritual literature and art there is a clearly discernible shift from an early, popular image of Christ the 'divine physician' and Good Shepherd (often modelled on Orpheus and Apollo) to a later and much sterner visage of Christ the lawgiver and judge, guarantor of morality and good order. This autocratic, impassive, even imperial Christ is the direct precursor of the later Pantokrator of Eastern apses, the inflexible presider over the horrific last judgements of Western cathedral tympana. In an earlier era of apparent stability it had been possible to stress Christ's power to heal every human failing: indeed, some theologians, including Origen, Evagrius, and Gregory of Nyssa, dared hope that on the last day all would be saved in the *apokatastasis*, or 'restoration' of all beings to union with God. According to this doctrine all punishment, whether in this life or the next, is remedial and therapeutic. Jerome (420), Augustine (430), and later the Emperor Justinian I (565) found this teaching repugnant; and each contributed in his own way to a series of anti-Origenist councils that repeatedly condemned the *apokatastasis* as blasphemous. Throughout the fifth and sixth centuries it became progressively more difficult to imagine divine punishment as anything but retributive and well deserved. Augustine plumbed the psychological depths of human guilt and concluded that the majority of the human race is condemned to eternal torment in the world to come, and that the utterly undeserved gift of salvation is inexorably and obscurely bestowed only upon an invisible minority.

Augustine's meditations on original sin and predestination proved congenial to a Western mindset increasingly influenced by Germanic legal notions of just retribution and painful expiation for crimes. The 'crime' of sin sullied the honour of God which could only be restored by the suffering of the criminal. Subtly but steadily prayer, spiritual practices and the sacraments came to be regarded less as opportunities for the vision of heaven and *theosis* than as occasions for expiation and reparation. Nevertheless, even as Christian spirituality shifted into a more sombre mode, models of hope and images of the divine compassion regularly emerged. Benedict's practical, compassionate condensation and mitigation of the rigorous 'Rule of the Master' provided a prudent, gentle model of community life that proved its worth throughout the next fifteen hundred years. Biblical exegesis, especially in the West, remained a fruitful means of transmitting experiences of prayer and spiritual progress through allegorical commentaries. And Gregory the Great, the 'first medieval pope', offered living examples of holiness and contemplation in his homilies and *Dialogues*, as well as practical advice for bishops and pastors in his *Pastoral Rule*.

See also **Asceticism; Cappadocian Fathers; Monastic Spirituality; Orthodox Spirituality.**

Louis Bouyer (ed.), *A History of Christian Spirituality*, 3 vols, New York: Seabury, 1977; Andrew Louth, *The Origins of the Christian Mystical Tradition from Plato to Denys*, Oxford: Oxford University Press, 1981; Bernard McGinn, *Christian Spirituality: Origins to the Twelfth Century*, WS, No. 16, New York: Crossroad, 1987; Bernard McGinn, *The Foundations of Mysticism*, London: SCM Press, 1992; Johannes Quasten, *Patrology*, 4 vols, Westminster, MD: Christian Classics, Inc., 1988; Simon Tugwell, *Ways of Imperfection*, Springfield, IL: Templegate, 1985.

LUKE DYSINGER

Eastern Christian Spirituality

see **Orthodox Spirituality**

Ecclesiology and Spirituality

Christians profess faith in the triune God whose very being is disclosed as life-giving relationship. This God brings into existence humans who find their fulfilment in vulnerable companionship and common labour. From the very beginning of human history, in the Judaeo-Christian telling of it, humans were made for communion with God and one another.

1. *Biblical foundations for the relationship between Church and spirituality*. The biblical antecedent to the creation of the Christian Church, the calling forth of Israel as a covenantal community, manifests God's determination to engage not isolated individuals but 'a people'. For the people of Israel, covenantal living meant a communal living in fidelity to Torah. The spirituality of the Old Testament is a spirituality shaped by the demands of faithful covenant living, and the consequences of infidelity to that covenant.

Baptism, Church and Christian living. Early Christian reflection on the meaning and shape of Christian community occurs in the emerging theology of baptism. Early Christians understood themselves to be forged, through faith and baptism, as a new people of God. According to what was likely an ancient baptismal catechesis found in 1 Peter, baptism inserted one into a 'chosen race, a royal priesthood, a holy nation, a people of his own' (1 Peter 2.9 NAB) where the priestly life of the community lay not in any ritual action but in everyday holy living. St Paul also assumed a thoroughly ecclesial understanding of baptism. Baptism initiated the believer into the 'one body' (1 Cor. 12.13), the Church. Individual believers did not *make* a church; initiation into the Church through faith and baptism *made* the believer. By faith and baptism believers were drawn simultaneously into both communion (*koinonia*) with God and communion with the members of the Christian community (cf. 1 Cor. 10.16–17; 2 Cor. 13.13). This new form of Christian living was given shape by the cross and resurrection of Christ (Rom. 6.3–11), the 'paschal mystery', which served as the very grammar of the Christian life. During the Reformation, Martin Luther would develop this theme in his *The Holy and Blessed Sacrament of Baptism*. The Christian life, Luther held, was to be a daily living out of the death to sin and resurrection to new life effected by faith and baptism.

The new ecclesial relationship established in baptism unfolds along three axes. Vertically, if you will, believers are baptized into communion with God in Christ by the power of the Spirit. Baptism initiates believers into the life of worship. St Thomas Aquinas wrote that the sacramental 'character' imparted by baptism was nothing other than a participation in Christ's priesthood, empowering the believer to participate fully in the worship of the Church (*ST* 3.63.3). This relation is inseparable from the horizontal dimension of Christian living in which faith and baptism establish a communion of believers grounded in communion in Christ. These two dimensions must be conjoined with a third dimension, the movement outward toward the world in mission.

This mission is no extrinsic task imposed upon the Church from without, it is the very *raison d'être* of the Church. Indeed the Church's mission derives from its trinitarian origins. Salvation history reveals a God who sends forth the Word and Spirit in mission as the very expression and fulfilment of God's love for the world. God's Word, spoken into human history from the beginning of creation and made effective by the power of the Spirit, in the fullness of time, became incarnate as Jesus of Nazareth. The origins of the Church, in turn, are inextricably linked to Jesus' gathering a community of followers whom, after his death and resurrection, were empowered by his Spirit to continue his mission to serve, proclaim and realize the coming reign of God.

Eucharist, Church and Christian living. Early Christian understandings of the Eucharist reinforced the relationship between baptism, Church and spirituality. Paul saw the Eucharist as a deepening of the experience of twofold communion with God in Christ and communion within the community of believers (1 Cor. 10.16–17). At the same time, the Eucharist was a ritual re-enactment of the paschal mystery (1 Cor. 11.23–26). To celebrate the Eucharist was not just to be spiritually nourished by the bread of life, it was to be transformed. In this spirit St Augustine could, centuries later, exhort believers to recognize the transformative power of the Eucharist: 'Be what you see, and receive what you are' (*Sermon* 272).

Many Christian traditions have preserved an ecclesiology and spirituality nourished by the celebration of the Christian liturgy. Eastern Christianity celebrates the divine liturgy as a sacramental foretaste of the heavenly banquet in which all the saints live in perpetual praise of God. Eastern liturgical spirituality sees the celebration of the liturgy not as an escape from the world but an opportunity to see the world with transformed vision.

The Church as a community of disciples. The word 'disciples' appears in the New Testament over two hundred times and it indicates the dominance of an understanding of the Church as a school of discipleship in which Christians are formed through the proclamation of the Scriptures and the engagement of such distinctive ecclesial practices as the communal 'breaking of the bread' and the giving of alms. As a community of disciples the Church is not its own lord; to be a member of the Church is to be in the company of disciples who, by definition, are dependent upon their master, Christ. It means also being in a community that is *in via,* 'on the way'. The journey of Christian discipleship leads one to follow and emulate 'the master'.

The Second Vatican Council employed a similar image, that of the 'pilgrim' (Dogmatic Constitution on the Church, *Lumen Gentium* 7), to describe the Church. The Church is con-

ceived, not just as a Church of pilgrims, but as a 'pilgrim Church', a community which 'will reach its perfection only in the glory of heaven (48)'. The twin images of discipleship and pilgrimage highlight the way in which the Christian life is marked by confident assurance that we are not traveling through this life in vain but are being 'led' by the Spirit of God, and the humble recognition that as pilgrims and disciples we have not yet arrived. The Church is always both holy and yet a Church *semper reformanda,* ever in need of reform and renewal.

The Church and the reign of God. When we look to the Gospels, it is striking how seldom Jesus makes reference to any 'church' that would come after him. By contrast, Jesus' preaching is filled with references to the kingdom or reign of God. Jesus did not present the reign of God as a future time of divine judgement. His preaching of the coming reign of God could only be understood in the context of his own ministry to the sick, the possessed, the poor, the outcast and the oppressed. These deeds were themselves recognized signs from the Hebrew Scriptures of the end times. Yet for Jesus, God's reign was not just a future expectation but a divine reality present in his own person and work. If the Church is to remain faithful to Christ's own mission it can never exist merely for its own sake but only as an instrument in service of Christ's mission to proclaim and realize, by grace, the coming reign of God.

2. *Contemporary perspectives.* Contemporary Christianity is more sensitive to the diversity of theological understandings of the Church found in various Christian communities today. Pentecost becomes the powerful symbol of the Church animated by the Holy Spirit who unites believers within the body of Christ, not by imposing a stifling uniformity in the spiritual life, but by allowing believers to discover a spiritual unity 'each in their own language' (Acts 2.8).

This diversity is seen by many as good and wholly appropriate in the light of a contemporary stress on the diverse inculturations of the gospel in the lives of particular Churches. The mutually constitutive relationship between ecclesiology and spirituality is nowhere more evident than in the way diverse ecclesiologies conceive the relationship between Church and world. Ecclesiologies that are heir to an Augustinian pessimism are more inclined to see the spiritual life as a call to gospel fidelity and prophetic witness with little expectation of genuine social transformation. Such ecclesiologies can, but need not be, sectarian in focus, viewing the Church as an 'oasis of grace' in a hostile and fallen world. Ecclesiologies that are heir to a more Thomistic anthropology or an Enlightenment optimism are inclined to define the spiritual life in terms of a more or less critical, yet dialogical, engagement with the world.

Finally we might note that past Catholic–Protestant polemics about the relationship between charism and institution in the life of the Church have largely given way to a recognition of the complementarity of charism and church office. There is a growing recognition in ecumenical dialogue that office without charism becomes arid and legalistic; charism without office becomes chaotic and sectarian. The contemporary challenge is to overcome this historical opposition in favour of understanding of the inseparability of institutional and spiritual dimensions of Christian ecclesial life.

See also **Charism; Ministry and Spirituality; Communion/***Koinonia***; Ecumenical Spirituality.**

Michael L. Budde and Robert W. Brimlow (eds), *The Church as Counterculture*, Albany: State University of New York Press, 2000; Paul D. Hanson, *The People Called: The Growth of Community in the Bible*, Louisville and London: Westminster John Knox Press, 2001; H. Richard Niebuhr, *Christ and Culture*, New York: Harper & Row, 1951; Letty Russell, *Church in the Round: Feminist Interpretation of the Church*, Louisville: Westminster John Knox Press, 1993; Juan Luis Segundo, *The Community Called Church*, Maryknoll, NY: Orbis Books, 1973; J.-M.-R. Tillard, *Flesh of the Church, Flesh of Christ*, Collegeville, MN: The Liturgical Press, 2001.

RICHARD GAILLARDETZ

Ecological Spirituality

Ecological spirituality is both ancient and new. As a spirituality of living gently with the earth, living as if the earth mattered, it has been implicit in many forms of Christian spirituality, especially that of religious orders like the Franciscan and the Benedictine as well as in churches that emphasize a sacramental tradition. But as an explicit form of spirituality it has only recently emerged as a response to the crisis of the environment and the threat to the very survival of the planet. After Lynn White Jr's article (1967), suggesting that theology must take some responsibility for the ecological crisis, various attempts were made to encourage ecological awareness in theology and to prioritize ethical thinking in this area, but it would be some time before the real urgency of the situation would energize influential movements in spirituality. In fact it was from those countries suffering most from the earth's exploitation that the impetus would first come. The Earth Summit at Rio de Janeiro in 1992 marked a turning point. Its 'Letter to the Churches' called for repentance for past neglect and for re-conversion to the earth. Three years later, Leonardo Boff's book *Ecology and Liberation: a New Paradigm* signalled that 'the earth' had been the forgotten dimension of liberation theology and was herself in need of liberation. 'Nature' had now become *the new poor* of liberation theology. Since the early nineties, there has been a growing involvement of the Churches in conversion to the earth: in fact, the movement 'Justice, Peace and Integrity of Creation' was launched in Basel in 1989. The more recent *Kairos* movement in Europe, calling on the Churches to repent, includes a substantial element of conversion to the earth.

Many forms of ecological spirituality have begun to emerge. Inevitably, one of the early tendencies, still popular in some circles, was what could be called a 'hermeneutics of retrieval' – namely, the reclaiming of specific persons and movements deemed to be 'creation-friendly', such as Francis of Assisi and Hildegarde of Bingen. But this in itself failed to shift the prevailing view that the earth's sole purpose in existing is to serve the needs of human beings. An approach was needed offering a lens through which earth and her creatures were seen as having intrinsic value as God's good creation; in other words, a shift from anthropocentrism to an organic perspective of the valuing of all life forms in the web of life. This would provide an authentic basis for ecological spirituality.

A first step was to consider human beings as the stewards of creation – and this remains a popular approach with many church communities. Attitudes of domination or dominion over creation could now give way to the call to take responsibility for the earth and the just management of her resources. Responsible stewardship forms an important part of ecological spirituality, and will continue to play a significant role in decision-making; yet it still does not go the whole way in recognizing the inherent value of every life form *in itself* as part of creation. So the appearance of creation spirituality – in its many forms, and often associated with Matthew Fox – is welcomed as placing a priority on the reverencing and valuing of all living things as part of God's good creation.

Two more radical movements, both influencing Christian spirituality, are *deep ecology* and *ecofeminism*. Deep ecology – often associated with the Norwegian Arne Naess, values all ecosystems within the web of life. Interdependent and interconnecting relations with all dimensions of earth/air/water/plants – as well as other levels of imagination and emotion – form part of the constitutive relations of humanity. Like the Gaia hypothesis (James Lovelock) deep ecology argues against any radical discontinuity between humans and all other organisms – a principle that challenges traditional Christian thinking. It is prophetic in the rigorous demands it makes for a lifestyle promoting the flourishing of all organisms, but its counsels of perfection may not actually be achievable goals for many who cope with the conflicting demands of life – for example, veganism or living without a car are not options for all.

Ecofeminism, a global activist movement as well as a spirituality, links the oppression of women with that of the earth. It grounds a philosophy showing the interconnections of the system of 'mastery' or logic of patriarchal domination over women, earth, animals and the interactions between gender, race and economic poverty. In particular, the environmental exploitation and degradation are linked with the feminization of poverty. Its spirituality highlights the sacredness of the earth and challenges the boundaries erected by Christianity between 'spirit' as superior and beyond nature, and the physical/bodily/sexual/*earthy* realities of nature, traditionally considered as inferior. Some of its forms reclaim the ancient goddess spiritualities of many cultures, seeking in its rituals to honour the earth's seasons and rhythms and draw strength in the connections between these and human experiences. Reclaiming the goddess – seen as the divine as immanent – has brought the figure of the divine as female to the fore and in many circles encouraged the honouring of female sexuality, despised in much of traditional Christian theology. From the early seventies, that is, twenty years earlier than most liberation theologians, Christian feminist theologians made these connections between women, nature and oppression, calling for the reshaping of our relationship with nature as integral both to the reshaping of the human person in just relation and to the achieving of social justice.

Although ecospiritualities take diverse forms, they also share many dimensions. Christian ecospirituality has a *mystical* dimension, fostering awe, wonder and reverence in creation and God's presence within it. Part of this is also learning *from* nature (see Ps. 104 or Job 12.7–9, for example), and rediscovering those dimensions of Jewish and Christian Scriptures that encourage this. Both Scripture, poetry and art sustain this mystical dimension: poets have been faithful to the earth at times when theologians have transferred their attention to beyond it. At the same time it is *prophetic* in its denunciation of

lifestyles of excess and exploitation, and visionary in its call to simplicity in the light of the messianic dream of the 'peaceable kingdom' where human beings, animals and all creation live in harmony (see Isa. 11). Both mystical and prophetic dimensions seek liturgical expression. Praise and thanksgiving are constant elements in worship, but particularly powerful is the recovery of prophetic lament, where sorrow and grief for what has been destroyed and lost are given liturgical space. The sacramental tradition that reverences the natural world as gift and as radiating the presence of God (a constant valued tradition in the liturgy of the Orthodox Church), now takes on new significance when the continued existence of this world is threatened. At the same time the prophetic aspect inspires a new ethics, calling for lifestyles of living more respectfully with the earth and organizing active protest about such issues as compassionate methods in farming, the manipulation of nature through GM crops, and the need to halt desertification in many parts of the world.

Such spirituality seeks to ground major themes in theology. Redemption and salvation include the well-being and flourishing of all earth's ecosystems. The cross of Christ is planted anew in places of suffering where the earth's very survival is in question. Eschatology, the hope of eternal life and heaven, are in some way dependent on the earth's inclusion in resurrection and the risen life. But if there is one fruit of eco-spirituality to be emphasized it is that of 'joy'. Living in right relation with the earth and all creation is a joyful experience, a foretaste of the fullness of the new creation and the coming of the peaceable kingdom.

See also **Creation Spirituality; Environment; Feminist Spirituality; Ethics and Spirituality; Liberation Spirituality; Orthodox Spirituality.**

Leonardo Boff, *Ecology and Liberation: A New Paradigm*, Maryknoll, NY: Orbis Books, 1995; Yvone Gebara, *Longing for Running Water: Ecofeminism and Liberation*, Minneapolis: Fortress Press, 1999; Mar Paulos Gregorios, *The Human Presence: Ecological Spirituality and the Age of the Spirit*, New York: Amity House, 1987; Alvin Pitcher, *Listen to the Crying of the Earth: Cultivating Creation Communities*, Cleveland, OH: Pilgrim Press, 1993; Anne Primavesi, *Sacred Gaia: Holistic Theology and Earth System Science*, London: Routledge, 2000; Rosemary Radford Ruether, *Gaia and God: an Ecofeminist Theology of Earth Healing*, San Francisco: HarperCollins, 1992; Lynn White Jr, 'The historical roots of the ecological crisis', *Science* 155 (1967), 1203–77.

MARY C. GREY

Ecstasy

In general the word ecstasy, based on the Greek noun *ekstasis*, means 'a state of being beyond reason and self-control'. It refers to a certain uncontrolled state of being 'beyond one's own self'. This state of overwhelming emotion exhibits itself as a trance-like state accompanied by rapturous delight. But various authors from Greek and biblical times, through to our own days, have understood this phenomenon in various ways and attributed its origin to differing causes.

In the Old Testament 'ecstasy' referred exclusively to 'prophetic ecstasy'. In prophetic literature this is not to be confused with 'divine inspiration', which is more commonly reflected in expressions like 'the hand of Yahweh came upon me' (Ezek. 3.22). However, in the books of Daniel (chs 8 and 10) and Job (4.12–16), as well as Ezekiel (1.28—2.2 and 3.22–24) there is clear indication that the authors of these texts underwent ecstatic experiences that signalled a profound experience attributed to their God Yahweh. The ecstatic experience of the Old Testament writer clearly attributed the experience to the eruption of the *truth of Yahweh* in their life. This truth, as oracle or message, was passed on to the people of Israel in order to correct shortcomings and to guide them into the promised land.

In the New Testament Paul of Tarsus is a good example of one who experienced ecstasy as a result of his personal relationship with the Christian God. Paul narrates, in a general way, these ecstatic experiences in 2 Corinthians 12.1–4 which he says 'cannot be put in human language'. The use of the word to describe the events of 2 Corinthians 12.1–4 is consistent with the understanding of ecstasy in the Greek tradition. Furthermore, in 2 Corinthians 12—14 Paul talks about 'spiritual gifts' and their role in building up the Christian community. In particular he mentions 'the gift of tongues'. This gift was often expressed in an 'ecstatic state', that is, the individual was moved beyond his or her own self-control and began speaking in a strange language. This phenomenon required an interpreter for any message to be brought to the Christian community. Through the ecstasy of the 'gift of tongues' the charismatic wisdom of the Holy Spirit was evident in the nascent churches of Jerusalem so that the people of God would enter ever more deeply into the life of the resurrected Christ.

As the Christian churches became established and more widespread, theologians and writers were hesitant to recognize any concept of divine inspiration that 'annihilated the self' or involved intense 'irrational experiences'. Thus in the Patristic period, generally speaking, there was a divergent appreciation of the ecstatic phenomenon. Notwithstanding the explicit narratives in the biblical literature, there existed a strong opposition to any acceptance of the ecstatic phenomenon in the Christian journey. Gregory of Nyssa (d. 394) was the major exception to this trend. Without hesitation he was able to describe the characteristics of ecstasy and describe them in relationship to the spiritual development of the soul as a prelude to the beatific vision. In a certain way he christianized the language and theology of the ecstatic experience. Others would follow suit and develop their perspectives along this line.

By the twelfth century it had become accepted that ecstatic experiences were a pinnacle in what had become known as the contemplative life (in opposition to the active life). Ecstatic experiences were seen as a reflection of a high degree of Christian holiness. By this time God is well established as the protagonist of this 'invasion of the soul' that elevates the person beyond the norms of human living in order to experience a certain intimacy with God. This 'stupor' and 'trance-like' state associated with 'infused contemplation' brought about a certain modification of consciousness in order to know the transcendent God. No longer is the object of one's contemplation an 'object', but indeed has been transformed into a 'subject' through this personal encounter. Through this encounter the Holy Spirit gives the individual a new way to know God by the encounter of absolute Love with human understanding. In this way love and intelligibility become one.

Bonaventure (d. 1274) is a good example of this approach to ecstasy. He taught that, in the ecstatic trance, 'the soul' experienced the immediate presence of God and thus came to know God directly. This 'union of love' had as its result the development of a certain wisdom in the individual. This is to say that Bonaventure taught that ecstasy was a transformative experience; not being a permanent state of mind, the ecstatic experience, in its short-lived span, shaped the human faculties more closely to those of the divine will. Furthermore, he taught that ecstasy was possible as the way for all Christians, should God so choose, and not only for those who 'trained' in such matters such as clerics or religious sisters and brothers.

Progressively ecstatic experiences became closely associated with mysticism, especially 'advanced stages of mysticism'. With this understanding the appreciation of ecstasy as an 'out of self' experience was easily acknowledged and accepted. Theologians disagreed, however, on various components of the ecstatic experience. With the rise of speculative theology associated with the scholastic theologians such as Aquinas (d. 1274) and Albert the Great (d. 1280) many different answers were given for various questions associated with ecstatic experiences. For example, are ecstatic experiences accompanied by visions? Are they more closely associated with the will (the seat of love) or the intellect (the seat of knowledge)? And has the individual any degree of self-awareness or not during the ecstatic experience?

By the sixteenth century Teresa of Avila (d. 1582) spoke of ecstasy as a form of mystical union of the soul with God; it is an 'elevation' of the soul to God. Teresa gives great importance to ecstatic phenomena and writes about this mystical union during the ecstatic state as a 'union of love'. This loving grace of God is so intense that the suspension of the normal human faculties is necessary, that is, the disproportionate nature of our humanity to that of God's divine nature necessitates a cessation of normal human consciousness in order to be elevated to union with the 'consciousness of God'. Thus, we are reminded once again of the similarity of this description with that of the Greek use of the word. For the Christian, however, the transient 'out of self state' is not a journey into 'nothingness', but it results in an intimacy with the Christian divine Other and a concomitant transformation of self into divine Love.

John of the Cross (d. 1591), a contemporary of Teresa of Avila, did not give the importance to ecstatic experiences that Teresa was wont to do. He carefully constructed a synthesis of the spiritual journey that gave a place for ecstatic experiences, but he did not see these as the pinnacle of spiritual development. Rather John saw these as preparatory, a transformative stage, on the way to the more intimate grace given by God in the 'spiritual marriage'. John talks about 'raptures' in *The Dark Night* 2.1–2, but warns that the pilgrim should not seek to become attached to these phenomena; they are not, in themselves, expressions of holiness but are a stage in the journey toward the fullness of divine love. True ecstasy in John, however, is identified by the 'departure of the human soul from the body' to be united with the 'divine Soul of God', as he recounts in the *Spiritual Canticle B*, st. 13.2–5.

In summary, therefore, ecstasy refers to a phenomenon with widespread interpretations and understandings. It has been appreciated in different ways throughout the history of Christianity. Inasmuch as it manifests itself in the body through, for example, a trance-like stance, immobility, tears, or in some cases levitation and stigmatization, it also manifests itself interiorly with a suspension of normal cognitive behaviour. Understood within the Christian tradition, ecstasy comes solely as a result of God's initiative: God 'touches the soul' in order to reveal the intimacy of God's love. God is free to bestow this gift of love on whoever is chosen as a kind of transient 'beatific vision'. When it is authentic ecstasy results in the transformation of the individual which is exhibited in expressions of charity, humility, self-sacrifice and, in general, to a radical commitment to the Christian way of life. Ecstasy, with its strong biblical foundations, has withstood the test of time as an authentic Christian experience that witnesses to the diverse ways that God journeys with humanity and calls us to the fullness of life.

See also **Mysticism (*essay*); Illuminative Way; Unitive Way.**

Martin Buber, collected by P. Mendes-Flohr (ed.), *Ecstatic Confessions,* San Francisco: Harper & Row, 1985; Thomas Katsaros, *The Western Mystical Tradition: An Intellectual History of Western Civilization,* New Haven, CT: College and University Press, 1969; Joan M. Lewis, *Ecstatic Religion: A Study of Shamanism and Spirit Possession,* 2nd edn, London: Routledge, 1989; Teresa of Avila, *Interior Castle,* Sixth Mansions, ch. 5; Marcel Viller (ed.), *DS,* vol. 4(2), cols 2045–189.

DAVID PERRIN

Ecumenical Spirituality

While it is common to date the emergence of the Ecumenical Movement to the Edinburgh Missionary Conference in 1910, it is possible to trace its roots back much further, even back as far as the Reformation itself. A major influence was the establishment in the late eighteenth and nineteenth centuries within the Protestant churches of Bible and Missionary Societies, Sunday School Societies, bodies such as the World Evangelical Alliance (1846), and, from the middle of the nineteenth century, student movements such as the Young Men's Christian Association (1844), the Young Women's Christian Association (1854), and a little later the World Student Christian Federation (1895), and the Student Christian Movement. Organizations such as these, which transcended the Protestant denominations, were hugely influential in introducing generations to the faith, worship and spirituality of their fellow Christians in other traditions, and gave their members early experiences of what would later be called ecumenism.

For the formal beginning we should look to the series of huge missionary conferences which took place in Europe and North America in the latter part of the nineteenth century and which culminated in the Edinburgh Missionary Conference of 1910, where 'the theme of Christian unity is running through the whole conference like a subterranean stream' (Morrison). Thus the missionary imperative of the church became an important strand in the ecumenical movement. Themes on 'Faith and Order' and 'Life and Work' led to the inauguration of the World Council of Churches in 1948, the first genuinely international ecumenical instrument involving most of the major world confessional families, except the Roman Catholic Church, which had to await the dramatic changes of the Second Vatican Council (1962–65) for its formal commitment to the rapidly developing Ecumenical Movement.

Common Bible study was a key feature of the movement, and Christians together rediscovered the centrality of Jesus' prayer to God 'that they may be one . . . that the world may know that you have sent me' (John 17.21), thus linking the impetus to unity with that towards mission. Further shared biblical study uncovered the importance of reconciliation as a key gospel value (2 Cor. 5.18–20). Christians can only become 'ambassadors of reconciliation' if they themselves demonstrate that reconciliation in their own lives and ecclesial organizations.

Weaving like a thread through this twentieth-century history is the Week of Prayer for Christian Unity, proposed in 1908, and now a universal focus for ecumenical prayer and activity. The simple act of joining together in prayer with others with whom one does not routinely pray, using models and forms of prayer which are unfamiliar and unusual, opens up new riches of spirituality to be found in other denominations.

Ecumenism, of course, flourishes outside the formal Ecumenical Movement, and three strands can be identified: (1) theological convergence across denominations, (2) the uncovering of shared liturgical roots, and (3) liberation movements.

1. At the beginning of the twentieth century, denominational studies provided the key to understanding the Christian faith. Mainly European in origin, these denominations were exported largely intact through nineteenth-century Christian missionary expansion into every part of the world. The lines of association and relationship for newly established missionary parishes and congregations stretched back to Europe or North America, rather than locally to fellow Christians in other congregations. Different organizational models were expressed in different liturgical practices, which in turn reflected different theologies and patterns of belief. Such differences, so long familiar in Europe and North America that they had ceased to cause offence or even be noticed, jarred not only with the missionaries themselves (as reflected in the Edinburgh Conference already mentioned), but also in the minds of younger theologians and church leaders, many of whom had begun their spiritual journeys in the world-wide and non-denominational student movements of the late nineteenth and twentieth centuries. These radical young churchpeople sought theological insight from the great theologians of their day, irrespective of their denominational allegiance.

2. Alongside this, research into the origins of spiritual, liturgical and worship practices uncovered shared patterns at the heart of all liturgy and a new depth of spiritual experience to be uncovered in neighbouring Christian traditions. Today, shared theological sources and common liturgical reforms are the norm between the various world confessional bodies. Institutional co-operation at local, national and international levels flows naturally from such.

For increasing numbers today, common theological roots and similar liturgical expressions means that their spirituality, while still rooted in one denomination or another, is essentially ecumenical, and so the key features of an ecumenical spirituality are becoming more apparent. Such a spirituality is rooted in engagement with other believers, the sharing of insights with fellow travellers on the journey of faith, and common action on matters of common concern. The spirituality of the Orthodox tradition, with its emphasis on the dynamic relationship within the Holy Trinity, has been very influential in modelling this new ecumenical spirituality in terms of dialogue one with another at every level of faith and practice.

3. Denominational division has been further undermined by a series of discourses developing around black, feminist and other liberationist spiritualities. Ecumenical spirituality seeks to integrate these insights within more traditional expressions of faith, such that current twenty-first-century patterns of belief and practice are largely unrecognizable from their nineteenth- and twentieth-century denominational antecedents.

This does not mean that the current picture is all ecumenical. The demise of denominational divisions has been replaced by new divisions which transect the older ones. Divisions between liberal and conservative, and catholic and evangelical, have introduced new fault lines within the Christian family. Each has found new allegiances across denominational lines, and in that way may be said to be ecumenical in a sense.

However, the commitment to dialogue, which is at the heart of an ecumenical spirituality, has found strong opposition in those who are often termed fundamentalist, one of whose defining features is the refusal to dialogue at all, fearing that dialogue with its negative overtones of compromise and negotiation poses dangers for religious truth itself. It is for those committed to dialogue as a way to deeper truth and religious insight to demonstrate the value of an ecumenical spirituality as an essential feature of modern Christian faith and practice.

Tosh Arai and Wesley Ariarajah (eds), *Spirituality in Interfaith Dialogue*, Geneva: WCC, 1989; Don E. Saliers, 'Christian spirituality in an ecumenical age' in L. Dupré and D. E. Saliers (eds), *Christian Spirituality: Post Reformation and Modern*, London: SCM Press, 1990.

KENNETH KEARON

Education and Spirituality

Education and spirituality are neither strangers nor mere acquaintances. They are distinct, though related human activities that have much in common. Both aim for fuller knowledge of the truth for the sake of living it, however that truth is perceived. Both are committed to specific practices that help persons to orient their lives in meaningful ways. Each enterprise draws upon traditions from the past, placing value on the centuries-old achievements of earlier generations. And each is committed to fostering more expansive and inclusive ways of thinking and acting in relation to self, world and others.

Spiritual principles can be found in all forms of humanizing education. Whenever education engages the depths of persons, encouraging them to seek purposeful ways of being, it tends toward the spiritual, broadly construed. When educators look upon the co-participants in a learning process with respect and reverence, viewing them as subjects and agents rather than passive receptacles for knowledge, they advance a spiritual understanding of the person. And in so far as the learning communities that are integral to the practice of education are places of honest dialogue, in which diversity is welcomed and creative tensions are regarded as fruitful, the communal dimension of spirituality is apparent.

Education at its best can and does call forth a person's spiritual vitality. Practices of attentiveness, critical reflection and discernment with regard to creation, society and culture are recognizable features of good education. Such practices help to constitute more contemplative, deliberative and socially conscious selves. When educators incorporate these practices intentionally into pedagogical processes, they advance the spiritual dimension of life.

Historical figures from the Christian tradition have highlighted aspects of educational activity that are spiritual. Augustine, for example, influenced heavily by Plato, claimed that truth was lodged deeply within persons. Education became the opportunity for inward reflection on that truth. In *De magistro*, Augustine described the role of the educator as one of evoking what the students already knew from 'the Teacher within'. Thomas Aquinas, by contrast, relying on Aristotle as his philosophical mentor, remained convinced that the first source of knowledge was the data of the senses, and that persons could be aided enormously by another, a teacher, in coming to new understanding. While he saw value in a discovery method, he preferred a didactic form of instruction. In addition, Thomas was convinced that knowledge of the truth was to serve a doing of the good.

In the seventeenth century, John Amos Comenius, the founder of modern educational theory, asserted that all persons, being created in the image and likeness of God, had a God-given capacity for learning. Comenius favoured an education that was grounded in experience, an observation of things rather than ideas, according to one's inherent interests and abilities. Exerting formative influence on educational giants that followed him, figures like John Dewey, Jean Piaget and Maria Montessori, Comenius thought about education in spiritual terms as the pursuit of wisdom.

In the twentieth century, Alfred Whitehead boldly proclaimed that the essence of true education is religious. He viewed it as an activity that served to guide human beings toward their highest achievement. According to Whitehead, education at its best inculcated 'duty and reverence'. A sense of duty or responsibility enabled participants in the teaching–learning dynamic to realize how knowledge could change a course of events. And reverence, ever a spiritual value, became the stance of those who caught sight of the possibilities inherent in the present moment, the now that held within it the reality of the past and the promise of a future.

In his classic text, *Education at the Crossroads*, the twentieth-century philosopher Jacques Maritain wrote that the nature of education belonged to the sphere of ethics and practical wisdom. He too saw the educational task to be one of engaging the 'inner vitality' of persons, guiding them toward their fullest and truest achievements. A 'complete and integral' idea of the person was the prerequisite for this task, the aim of which was to shape a human being of sound judgement and moral virtues who assumed responsibility for the civilization in which he or she was involved. From this perspective, education could not escape spirituality.

In the twenty-first century, the religious education theorist Thomas Groome has highlighted many ways in which educators can and do nurture spiritual growth. These include teaching others to notice their lives in the world, to reflect critically on their assumptions and experiences, to put their praxis in dialogue with the wisdom of long-standing traditions, to appropriate those traditions for themselves, and to make decisions regarding their future praxis in light of this appropriation. Parker Palmer, who likens education to a spiritual journey, invites all those involved in the enterprise to see its potential to lead persons beyond half-truths and narrow concepts to 'whole sight', a more authentic and inclusive knowing.

When education has a spiritual vision, it can usher in these rounder and fuller ways of knowing. In fact it can bring people to spiritual wisdom for life. Devoid of such vision, education quickly becomes utilitarian, subject to a narrow pragmatism in which specific training becomes the immediate goal. While there is always a place for specialized training, the aim of education is forever wider. Keeping education and spirituality aligned assures that education remains a humanizing activity that helps to order and sustain life. Recognition of the intrinsic links between the two enterprises is ultimately to the great benefit of each.

See also **Knowledge; Moravian Spirituality; Wisdom.**

D. E. Cooper, *Authenticity and Learning*, London: Routledge & Kegan Paul, 1983; John Dewey, *Democracy and Education*, New York: Macmillan, 1916; Thomas H. Groome, *Educating for Life*, New York: Crossroad, 2000; Jacques Maritain, *Education at the Crossroads*, New Haven, CT: Yale University Press, 1943; Parker Palmer, *To Know as We Are Known: Education as a Spiritual Journey*, San Francisco: Harper & Row, 1983; Alfred Whitehead, *The Aims of Education and Other Essays*, New York: Free Press, 1929.

COLLEEN M. GRIFFITH

Election (Predestination)

Christian doctrines of election attempt to express key spiritual insights and experiences in theological language. Election (God's choice of us) affirms that God has always loved us first, unconditionally and freely. This immense and wholly gracious gift of the divine affection comprises the basis of our relationship with God, always shaping the possibility of our spiritual response. The doctrine of predestination represents one way to emphasize these realities by stressing that election of specific individuals has been God's plan from the very beginning. Unfortunately, the history of Christian theology suggests that this manner of speaking about divine love can spark controversies that may detract attention from the strength of the originating spiritual impulse.

The various positions on election and predestination emerge from diverse interpretations of biblical material. Theologians invariably refer to two principal themes of the Hebrew Bible, namely the choice of Israel as Yahweh's own and God's immense power. In the New Testament the Gospels depict Jesus' proclamation of God's unmerited compassion. In light of his conversion experience, Paul would build on this tradition to develop his highly influential doctrine of salvation by grace alone (see especially Galatians and Romans). He draws out the implication already present in the Hebrew Bible, namely that God's choice of 'Jacob' entails the divine rejection of 'Esau' (Mal. 1.2–3, quoted in Rom. 9.13). Perhaps wishing to stress that gracious election forms part of the very character of God, Ephesians 1.4 declares that God 'chose us in Christ before the foundation of the world'.

St Augustine of Hippo (354–430) shared Paul's sense of being a redeemed sinner. His interpretation of the apostle's doctrine of election is a leading theme in many of his voluminous works. He also defended Christianity at a time when Graeco-Roman philosophy and religion was still very influential. The consequent stress on God's sole, absolute power conditions Augustine's embrace of double predestination. This theological variant affirms that God has from eternity chosen both who would be saved and who would be damned. St Thomas Aquinas (1224–74) would give these ideas systematic expression in Question 23 of the First Part of his magisterial *Summa Theologica*. He anticipates later developments in the Reformed tradition by placing the doctrine of predestination under the heading of providence in his extended treatment of the doctrine of God.

The Protestant Reformation featured the rediscovery of Pauline and Augustinian doctrines of election. In general terms the Lutheran, Anglican and Reformed theologians all affirmed predestination, and sometimes even double predestination. Against the advice of his peers, John Calvin (1509–64) chose to devote considerable space to the issue. Like Augustine and Aquinas before him he was careful to commend respect for God's mystery. Like them he also believed that attention to the doctrine brought spiritual benefits such as consolation (recall that he is writing on behalf of persecuted Protestants, especially in his native France) and humility. His rhetorical prose went to unprecedented lengths to describe and defend God's choice to damn the reprobate. He ensured that the doctrine of double predestination would be specially associated with his theology. And he spurred controversies that would recur for centuries.

Under the pressures of warfare, theological conflict and the emergence of modernity, Reformed theologians and confessions after Calvin sought greater degrees of theological certainty. Whereas Calvin placed predestination under the doctrine of salvation, his successors reverted to Aquinas' precedent, giving double predestination even a more central place than it had occupied in Calvin's thought. The Dutch theologian Jacobus Arminius (1560–1609) protested, hoping to preserve some place for human free will by insisting that God had predestined Jesus Christ to be the means of salvation for all who subsequently believed in him. The Synod of Dort (1618–19) established subsequent Reformed orthodoxy by definitively rejecting this position. Nonetheless, the 'Calvinist' and 'Arminian' positions continued to divide the Evangelical movement from the eighteenth century onward. The reverberations have helped shape denominational configurations to this day.

Leading Reformed theologians of the twentieth century creatively reinterpreted the traditional teaching concerning election and predestination. The Dutch theologian G. C. Berkouwer (1903–96) reinvigorated the orthodox position by recalling its spiritual roots. He saw these doctrines as the foundation of a devotional life characterized by gratitude and praise. The famous Swiss theologian Karl Barth (1886–1968) went much further, chastising both Calvin and the subsequent Reformed tradition for departing from the core of the gospel and from the spiritual tone predominant in Augustine and Aquinas. For Barth, God can only be known in Jesus Christ. In Jesus all of humanity is elected, and God's wrath borne by Jesus as our representative will be decisively overcome in the inevitable final triumph of grace. Election continues to be a focus for creative contemporary theology and spirituality. Donna Bowman, for instance, sees affinities between Barth's theology and process philosophy's depiction of God's good primordial aim for all creatures.

See also Spirituality and Scripture; Spiritu-

ality and Theology (*essays*); Pauline Spirituality; Augustinian Spirituality; Thomist Spirituality; Reformation and Spirituality; Calvinist Spirituality; Reformed Spirituality; Evangelical Spirituality.

Carl Bangs, *Arminius: A Study in the Dutch Reformation*, Nashville, TN: Abingdon, 1971; Karl Barth, *Church Dogmatics II.2: The Doctrine of God*, Edinburgh: T & T Clark, 1957; G. C. Berkouwer, *Divine Election*, Grand Rapids, MI: Eerdmans, 1960; Donna Bowman, *The Divine Decision: A Process Doctrine of Election*, Louisville, KY: Westminster John Knox Press, 2002; John Calvin, *Institutes of the Christian Religion*, Philadelphia: Westminster, 1960, 3.21–4, pp. 920–87; Thomas Aquinas, *Summa Theologica*, Allen, TX: Christian Classics, 1981, pp. 125–33.

DON H. COMPIER

Election, Ignatian

This is a term used in Ignatian spirituality, the tradition of Christian discipleship inherited from Ignatius Loyola (1492–1556). Ignatius believed that each human being is created for a purpose, which is, 'to praise, reverence and serve God our Lord and by so doing to save his or her soul' (*Spiritual Exercises* 22). He likewise held that, since human well-being and good order are rooted in consistency between that ultimate purpose and the choices which men and women make in particular circumstances, then if human beings are to flourish, those choices need to be consciously related to that purpose. Ignatius also recognized that all human decisions are liable to be influenced by many different and mutually contradictory influences, since hearts and wills may be besieged by a variety of internal and external factors, including disordered patterns of thinking, feeling and acting. His book, *The Spiritual Exercises*, has a practical aim: 'the overcoming of self and the ordering of life on the basis of a decision made in freedom from any ill-ordered attachment' (21), a decision, that is to say, which accords with the ultimate purpose of human living. It is to the process of making such choices that the term 'Ignatian election' refers (Latin *electio*: 'choice' or 'decision'). The Spiritual Exercises offer a comprehensive method for making good choices which consciously embody a Christian commitment or a desire for such a commitment.

This method is a major element in the dynamic of the Exercises. The aids Ignatius provides are intended to enable those who make the Exercises to come to a decision, either about the shape and direction of their life as a whole or about the conduct of some aspect of it. Key elements of the process are listed here. First of all, there is a presupposition that good Christian choices are made in a setting of assiduous prayer. In the thirty-day form of the Exercises, four or five hours a day are spent in prayer. After the first part ('week') of the Exercises, immersion through gospel contemplation in the mystery of the incarnation and the story of the birth, early life and ministry of Jesus shapes decision-making in that the central issue for the person who undertakes this prayer is how the pattern of Jesus' life can best be embodied in his or her particular human life. Second, the 'Rules for discernment' (313–36) provide guidance on how reactions to the material presented for prayer may be 'to some extent' understood and handled as a basis for making good choices by a method of discernment of spirits. Third, Ignatius intersperses periods of contemplating the life of Jesus with other exercises, of his own composition, intended to provide further guidance in Christian decision-making (135–74). These exercises have various effects: for example, they offer those who make the Exercises a way of clarifying for themselves what they really desire, and they provide insight into subtle paths by which people are commonly deflected from making good choices or, having made them, from carrying them out. They also identify values which operate, or should operate, in the making of good Christian choices and help towards the concrete embodiment of those values in personal and corporate life. Fourth, Ignatius further clarifies the process of choosing by guidance on different circumstances and ways in which good choices may be made (175–89).

This takes place typically in the second week of the Exercises. The choice made is then further reflected upon, challenged, clarified and confirmed (or identified for further consideration) in the exercises of the later weeks, where the focus of prayer is first the passion and death and then the resurrection of Jesus.

In the last forty years, much effective work has been done on ways in which the elements of this paradigmatic decision-making process may, with suitable adaptation, shape public and private, individual and communal choices, both in day-to-day Christian living and at major turning points.

See also Discernment; Ignatian Spirituality.

Philip Endean and Joseph A. Munitiz (eds), *St Ignatius of Loyola: Personal Writings*, London: Penguin, 1996; Michael Ivens, *Understanding the Spiritual Exercises*, Leominster, UK: Gracewing, 1998; David Lonsdale, *Eyes to See, Ears to Hear: An Introduction to Ignatian Spirituality*, 2nd, rev. edn, London: Darton, Longman & Todd/ Maryknoll: Orbis Books, 2001.

DAVID LONSDALE

Emotions

Emotions are strong feelings experienced in response to stimuli. They can be categorized in various ways. Scholastic philosophy divided them into those which manifest the concupiscible appetite (directed toward pleasure or pain) such as love and hatred, desire and aversion, joy and sorrow, and those which manifest the irascible appetite (directed toward success or failure) such as hope and depression, courage and fear, and anger. The American psychiatrist Willard Gaylin uses a different categorization: emotions concerned with individual or group survival, such as anger, anxiety, guilt, shame, pride; emotions that exhibit caution, such as irritation, boredom, envy, and feeling exploited; and emotions that signal success such as pleasure and feeling touched or moved.

Through the centuries of Christianity, emotions have been considered differently with respect to their relationship to spiritual development. Much early spirituality, influenced by ancient Platonic and Stoic philosophy, strove after *apatheia*, the indifference to and freedom from emotion in one's spiritual practices. It was believed that turning away from all creatures and eliminating the emotions elicited by them would make one more open to experiencing the presence of God in contemplation. Writers like Clement of Alexandria, Evagrius and Origen thus tended to treat the emotions with suspicion. However, when directed toward God or against evil, these same emotions were often considered virtues. For example, even in the highly apophatic Dionysian mystical tradition, the yearning for God is considered essential to the attainment of contemplative union with God, and such union is expected to result in the experience of joy.

When translated to the West, chiefly by Cassian, this striving after *apatheia* was modified to mean control of the emotions rather than their elimination, with the goal of attaining a simplicity or single-mindedness with which to encounter God. With Benedictine monasticism came the practice of *lectio divina*, the strongly affective reading of Scripture, which positively engaged the emotions as a way to contemplation. This emotion-filled expression of devotion came to a peak in the twelfth-century Cistercians and the thirteenth-century spirituality of Francis and women visionaries. These two tendencies – the Greek *apophatic*, which attempts to leave feeling behind, and the Latin *kataphatic*, which cultivates the affective life as a way to God – are two streams which influenced the development of Christian mysticism and continue to exist today as alternative methods of contemplation.

The ancient tradition of the discernment of spirits used emotions as indicators of whether one was accepting or rejecting the will of God. This practice was fine-tuned by Ignatius of Loyola (1491–1556) whose two sets of Rules for the Discernment of Spirits in the *Spiritual Exercises* focus primarily on experiences of consolation and desolation as ways of discovering whether one's motivations, experiences and choices have their source in God or in the forces of evil.

In an effort to counter rationalistic notions of religion, two post-Enlightenment theologians placed strong emphasis upon the role of emotion as an integral element of the human religious impulse. Friedrich Schleiermacher (1768–1834) defined religion as the feeling of absolute dependence upon the divine, and listed a series of emotions indicative of an innate religiosity in the human: desire, reverence, humility, gratitude, compassion, sorrow and zeal. Similarly, Rudolph Otto (1869–1937) described the fundamental religious experience as having two emotion-laden components. In relation to the *mysterium tremendum et fascinans*, one simultaneously experiences both fear and fascination, the emotional tension of being both repelled by and attracted to the Holy.

Contemporary spirituality benefits from modern psychology's understanding of the role of the emotions in human growth and development. The American Jesuit William Barry uses the psychology of human relationship, including the role the emotions play in its development, as an apt analogy for one's relationship with God. Consistent with the Ignatian tradition, Barry insists that emotional honesty before God is the way to foster that relationship. One must be willing to share one's emotional depths and be aware of and receptive to the feelings evoked through one's encounter with God. Similarly, the American psychiatrist Gerald May has written a series of books which focus on the human emotional life as an integral element of a healthy spirituality. He is particularly helpful in his discussion of how our morally neutral emotions can either be put to the service of God or can degenerate into self-serving addiction. In either case, the role of the emotions in one's spiritual development is crucial.

An important part of spiritual direction therefore consists in helping a person to notice emotional reactions, or the lack thereof, to what is experienced in prayer, and to place them trustingly into one's relationship with God. This is not usually difficult with positive emotions such as love, gratitude or joy. But the negative emotions, like fear, guilt and especially anger, are often suppressed or denied, setting up an impassable roadblock to spiritual growth. If one's relationship with God is to grow, one must be willing to be transparent before God in the complicated mystery that is the human emotional life.

See also **Spirituality and Psychology (*essay*); Addiction; Affectivity; Affirmative Way; Apatheia; Apophatic Spirituality; Ascetical Theology; Asceticism; Consolation; Darkness; Desire; Desolation; Detachment; Direction, Spiritual; Discernment; Eroticism; Holistic Spirituality; Joy; Kataphatic Spirituality; Lectio Divina; Tears, Gift of (Penthos).**

William Barry, *God and You: Prayer as a Personal Relationship*, New York: Paulist Press, 1987; Willard Gaylin, *Feelings: Our Vital Signs*, New York: Harper & Row, 1979; Gerald May, *Addiction and Grace: Love and Spirituality in the Healing of Addictions*, New York: HarperCollins, 1988; Gerald May, *Will and Spirit: A Contemplative Psychology*, HarperSanFrancisco, 1982; Gerard Sitwell, *Spiritual Writers of the Middle Ages*, New York: Hawthorn, 1961, pp. 11–21; Roberto Mangabeira Unger, *Passion: An Essay on Personality*, New York: The Free Press (Macmillan), 1984.

JOAN M. NUTH

English Mystical Tradition

The term refers to five mystical writers who flourished in late medieval England, although the uniqueness of each precludes considering their writings as a cohesive tradition in the usual sense of the word. Their commonality resides in the fact that all were rooted in the broader traditions of English spirituality, all wrote in English, and all were products of the fourteenth century.

The Yorkshireman Richard Rolle (*c*. 1300–49) studied briefly at Oxford but left without a degree to pursue the eremitic life. Dependent upon the largesse of patrons, Rolle lived in various locations, ending his days at Hampole near a Cistercian nunnery where he probably served as spiritual guide. The most prolific of the English mystics, Rolle wrote in both Latin and English in a variety of genres: lyric poetry, commentaries and meditations on Scripture, and treatises on the spiritual life. The lyrics reveal Rolle's poetic tendency, something equally evident in his highly alliterative and melodious Latin prose.

Rolle authored two commentaries on the book of Psalms, one in Latin and one in English, and two meditations on the passion of Christ in the tradition of affective piety. Rolle's most original contributions to mystical literature are found in his spiritual treatises, notably *The Fire of Love* and *The Mending of Life*. His description of the spiritual life is dependent upon the 'three ways' of spiritual progress and upon the writings of Bernard of Clairvaux and Richard of St Victor. Yet Rolle describes growth in the spiritual life in a unique fashion, founded upon his own religious experience. After a period of purgation, one experiences the 'opening of the heavenly door' (Rev. 4.1) which creates an intense longing for God. This leads into mystical union with God, typified by experiences of heat, sweetness and song, which Rolle probably meant as metaphors descriptive of the spiritual senses.

We know nothing of the author of *The Cloud of Unknowing* (fl. 1380s), although there is growing consensus that he may have been a Carthusian. Besides *The Cloud*, he authored several other works, all of which reveal a skilled theologian and wise spiritual director. While the subject matter of *The Cloud* is difficult, and its practice even more so, the book is written in such a clear, direct style with the use of concrete images, that it makes the exercise of apophatic contemplation seem attainable for those moved to leave discursive meditation behind. *The Cloud* author followed the apophatic mysticism of pseudo-Dionysius, the late fifth-century Syrian monk, interpreted in light of the 'ordering of charity' created by the twelfth-century Cistercians and Victorines. Thus, for *The Cloud* author, love replaces reason as the power of the soul open to union with God, something Dionysius does not do. While this gives *The Cloud* a warmer, more devotional ambience, it also opens the door to voluntaristic and anti-intellectual interpretations. The essence of *The Cloud*'s teaching on contemplation is simple in the extreme. Moved by the call to contemplation, one focuses one's desire upon God alone, leaving behind all images and sensual feeling. To achieve this, the author suggests placing all creatures beneath oneself in 'a cloud of forgetting', concentrating instead upon the 'cloud of unknowing' which exists between the self and God, smiting upon it with the 'naked intent' of the will through which alone union with God is possible.

The most certain fact about Walter Hilton is that he died an Augustinian canon at the priory of Thurgarton in March 1395/6. He probably studied both law and theology at Cambridge, earning the title 'Master' which appears on several manuscripts of his works. He lived as a solitary for a time, but eventually found the 'mixed life' of the Augustinian canons better suited to his temperament. Several letters reveal him to be a wise spiritual director, advocating styles of spirituality appropriate to lay people interested in pursuing a vibrant spiritual life. Hilton's masterpiece is *The Scale of Perfection*, regarded by some as the most complete, succinct and balanced treatment of the interior life produced in the Middle Ages. His teaching applies to all the baptized, not merely to those called to the eremitical or vowed life. Obviously indebted to Augustinian theology, *The Scale* focuses on the notion that the human soul was created in the image of God and subsequently defaced by sin, but through Christ the grace necessary for its reformation has become available. Hilton describes this reform in four stages, based upon an interpretation of Romans 8.30. One first experiences a call from a life of self-absorption into the desire for God. 'Reform in faith' takes place when one begins to reject sin and advance in the exercise of Christian virtue, a process aided by penance and meditation upon the life of Christ. The third stage is the beginning of the 'reform in feeling' of Christ's image in the soul attained by those who dedicate themselves to contemplation. This is typified by such an intense desire for God that even the inclination toward sin begins to disappear and one lives only for the love of God. The fourth stage is the fullness of 'reform in feeling' enjoyed only by the blessed in heaven.

Unlike the mystics described thus far, the anchoress Julian of Norwich (c. 1342–c. 1416) was a visionary, a fact that places her in continuity with the women visionaries who flourished on the Continent during the thirteenth and fourteenth centuries. In 1343, in the midst of a debilitating illness, she received sixteen 'showings' of the love of God for humanity, combined with a vision of the Crucified. She recorded this experience sometime afterwards (Short Text), but about twenty years later completed an extended version (Long Text) which can properly be considered a theological tract. In it Julian plumbs the depths of her experiences to reveal their theological significance, covering all the main areas of Christian doctrine: incarnation and redemption, ecclesiology, the one and triune God, theological anthropology, creation and eschatology, integrating them into a cohesive whole. In the Short Text the foundational symbol is the suffering Christ. This is expanded in the Long Text into the Parable of the Lord and the Servant, an elaborate conflation of many scriptural images, encompassing the whole story of salvation from humanity's creation into the as yet unfulfilled future. Julian's most original theological ideas include the fact that God looks upon humans only with love even in their sin, and the fact that 'all will be well', a promise that hints at universal salvation. She is also unique in her treatment of the motherhood of Christ, which she transformed from an occasional metaphor for Christ's redemptive activity into a way of understanding the essence of God. Julian's discussion of the spiritual life is related to her theology of the economic trinity; we are beneficiaries of God's gracious works toward us, works of nature (creation), mercy (redemption) and grace (final salvation).

The lay woman Margery Kempe (c. 1373– c. 1440) lived out her call to holiness neither in anchorhold nor monastery but in the world. We know more about her than we do about the others, since her *Book,* discovered in 1934 at the home of William Butler-Bowden, is an autobiography, the first of that genre in the English language. Like Julian, Margery was a visionary, and her *Book* contains many allusions to the tradition of Continental women visionaries. The daughter of a prominent citizen of King's Lynn, Margery married at age twenty a local burgess, John Kempe. After the birth of her first child, she was afflicted by a mental illness from which she was healed by a vision of Christ. Shortly thereafter she experienced a conversion, adopting strict habits of prayer and fasting which drew the hostility of her neighbours, but she found solace in frequent visions of Christ and Mary. Always anxious about her spiritual progress, Margery constantly sought out preachers and spiritual guides for reassurance. After about twenty years of marriage during which she bore fourteen children, Margery persuaded her husband to agree to her long-cherished wish for celibacy, which gave her more freedom to pursue her religious life in earnest. She travelled on pilgrimage to the Holy Land, where the gift of tears which she had first experienced at her conversion changed significantly. She began howling and wailing uncontrollably at any mention of Christ's passion. Upon her return to England, her unusual behaviour caused so much attention that she was arrested and questioned for heresy on several occasions, although she was never convicted. Compared unfavourably with Julian, Margery has been accused of hypocrisy, self-aggrandizement and hysteria. However, scholarship today is generally more favourable toward her, appreciating her unique vocation. Margery's *Book* provides us with a rare glimpse into the inner life of a medieval lay woman who fought against tremendous odds for the opportunity to practise her spirituality. Margery's account of the spiritual life is unparalleled for its candour, simplicity and attention to detail, rooted in that tender devotion to the humanity of Christ that was the heart and soul of all late medieval spirituality.

See also **Mysticism (*essay*); Affectivity; Augustinian Spirituality; Carthusian Spirituality; Contemplation; English Spirituality; Eremitical Spirituality; Illuminative Way; Imago Dei; Kataphatic Spirituality; *Lectio Divina*; Medieval Spirituality in the West; Motherhood of God; Mystical Theology; Purgative Way; Tears, Gift of (Penthos); Triple Way; Unitive Way; Victorine Spirituality; Women Medieval Mystics.**

The Cloud of Unknowing, trans. and ed. James Walsh, New York: Paulist Press, 1981; Walter Hilton, *The Scale of Perfection,* trans. and ed. John P. H. Clark and Rosemary Dorward, CWS, New York: Paulist Press, 1991; Julian of Norwich, *Showings,* trans. and ed. Edmund Colledge and James Walsh, CWS, New York: Paulist Press, 1978; Margery Kempe, *The Book of Margery Kempe,* trans. and ed. B. A. Windeatt, Harmondsworth: Penguin, 1985; Joan M. Nuth, *God's Lovers in an Age of Anxiety: The Medieval English Mystics,* London: Darton, Longman & Todd/Maryknoll, NY: Orbis Books, 2001; Nicholas Watson, *Richard Rolle and the Invention of Authority,* Cambridge: Cambridge University Press, 1991.

JOAN M. NUTH

English Spirituality

1. *Introduction.* It is not easy to define the characteristics of Englishness. In the early twentieth century, the Conservative politician and Prime Minister Stanley Baldwin (1867–1947) suggested that English people 'grumble, and . . . always have grumbled, but . . . never worry . . . It is in staying power that [the English person] is supreme' (*On England,* pp. 3–4). He went on to argue that English people possessed a number of distinctive characteristics, among them 'a profound sympathy for the under-dog', the capacity to laugh in the face of adversity, and 'a diversified individuality' and corresponding resistance to uniformity (*ibid.,* pp. 4–5). These characteristics are evident throughout the English spiritual tradition: the combination of Celtic, Roman, Scandinavian, Anglo-Saxon, Norman and (more recently) Asian and Afro-Caribbean blood, together with the combined impact of insularity, landscape and climate, appear to have issued in an emphasis on independence, a preference for empiricism

over metaphysical speculation, and perhaps for words, literature and drama more than for music and the visual arts.

2. *Anglo-Saxon spirituality*. The latter preference may be the result of a relatively cold and dark climate, or (more likely, perhaps) of the Protestant Reformation in the sixteenth century. Prior to that defining event, the English spiritual tradition was for the most part Catholic and orthodox, though sometimes reflecting a tension between its insular (that is, Irish, Scottish and Welsh) and continental Roman inheritances. The two achieved a synthesis in the writings of the Northumbrian monk Bede the Venerable (673–735), the first great figure in English spirituality. Bede wrote about Celtic saints like Aidan and Cuthbert in such a way as to make them not only exemplars of a humane and Catholic culture, but also figures of awesome holiness and power. Bede's achievement was to integrate history, biblical exegesis and patristic theology in a way that encouraged Christians to enlarge their imaginative world view, and to live more consciously in the company of the saints and with an active expectation of the world to come.

3. *Medieval spirituality*. The Norman Conquest of the mid-eleventh century inevitably drew England into a more European ambience; and the achievement of St Anselm (1033–1109), a Norman monk who became Archbishop of Canterbury in 1093, was to show how spiritual life could become a lived response to Christ's atoning work on the cross, by means of which God's honour (disfigured by human sin) is restored, and the place of human beings with it. The emphasis on the passion and the humanity of Christ, and on the terrible consequences of human sin and evil, is characteristic of the medieval period: lay spirituality and vernacular art alike reflect the importance of penance, as well as the practice of pilgrimage, a concept that is central to the writings of such diverse figures as Geoffrey Chaucer (1340–1400) and Margery Kempe (c. 1373–c.1438).

Kempe's extraordinary and autobiographical *Book* is characteristic of much late medieval women's piety in its emphasis on a deeply personal, even intimate relationship with Christ, though it is exceptional in the way that relationship is firmly set in the context of a married lay woman in an increasingly urban and mercantile society: Margery bargains and argues with God as much as she does with archbishops and others. The group of writers often known as the Middle English mystics all reflect the centrality of the Christian's relationship with Christ, but in different ways. Richard Rolle (c. 1300–49) spent much of his life as a hermit in Yorkshire before dying of the plague that was to cast such a shadow over late medieval England: he draws extensively on his own personal experience in developing a spirituality that is at once passionate and mystical, and rooted in the solitary life. The anonymous author of the fourteenth-century *Cloud of Unknowing* draws on the apophatic tradition associated with the fifth-century Syriac writer known as Pseudo-Dionysius to emphasize the beauty and mystery of God, but develops that tradition in a new way by stressing that love and desire, not knowledge, are primary in our search for God. 'For not what you are, nor what you have been, does God behold with his merciful eyes, but what you want to be' (*Cloud* 75). The influence of St Augustine, evident here, is even stronger in the work of the Yorkshireman Walter Hilton (c. 1343–96), whose *Ladder* [or *Scale*] *of Perfection* is a remarkable guide to the spiritual life, much of which is of enduring value to all Christians.

Arguably the greatest of the Middle English mystics was Julian of Norwich (c. 1342–c. 1417), who became a solitary anchoress in one of England's most prosperous towns, but at a time of both personal and national upheaval – her own serious illness is the crucible of her spirituality, but the terrible consequences of both the Black Death and the Peasants' Revolt (1381) were the background against which she wrote. Her *Shewings* (or *Revelations of the Divine Love*) exists in both a short and longer version, the latter the consequence of twenty years' reflection by the author in which her original experience of God during illness were set in the larger context of a trinitarian theology of love. Both versions represent a profound fusion of personal experience and deeply pondered theological reflection, in which the suffering of humanity is embraced and transformed by the maternal love of Christ, in whose sufferings we find both the reflection and the redemption of our own.

4. *The Reformation period*. Many of the deepest themes of medieval English spirituality endure beyond the Protestant Reformation; but there can be no denying the impact of a movement which in England was largely imposed from above, the consequence of centralized Tudor power and politics. Yet without the growing confidence and literacy of lay Christians, and the early death of the Catholic Queen Mary Tudor in 1558, its course would have been very different. A national church and Prayer Book replaced the international perspectives of Catholicism; church buildings changed in character from

being the scene of holy rites and things to being meeting-places for the godly; and no longer could inherited belief, priesthood or dogma go unquestioned. In the writings of the Catholic Thomas More (1478–1535) and the Protestant William Tyndale (1494–1536) a longing for holiness and integrity was inseparable from the most violent attacks on one another – a reminder that the search for truth mattered far more than the desire for tolerance or reconciliation.

5. *The Anglican spiritual tradition.* The development of the Anglican spiritual tradition was indelibly marked by its two greatest literary monuments – the *Book of Common Prayer* of 1549 (revised in 1662) and the Authorized (or King James) Version of the Bible of 1611. Their names alone reflect something of the emerging temper of Anglicanism: a common prayer book really did seek to address and embrace the concerns of lay Christians living in the world, and to offer them a way to holiness that refused to separate the ethical from the spiritual, the street from the sanctuary, while the dedication of the new Bible, which describes James I as 'a most tender and loving nursing father', is a sharp reminder that this is an English Bible for an English church. The great figures of the early Anglican tradition – Richard Hooker (c. 1553–1600), its first outstanding theologian; Lancelot Andrewes (1556–1626), the epitome of scholarly holiness; John Donne (1572–1631), George Herbert (1593–1633) and Jeremy Taylor (1613–67), who perhaps supremely exemplify the integrity of a distinctively Anglican spirituality in a troubled and turbulent age – developed what came to be known as 'practicall divinitie': a Christian way of life in which worship, preaching, study, family prayer and moral uprightness were integrated into a seamless whole. In the nineteenth century the leaders of the Oxford Movement (notably John Keble (1792–1866) and Edward Pusey (1800–82)) sought to renew this tradition in the face of growing scepticism by developing an Anglican spirituality in which patristic theology, the beauty of sacramental worship and a passion for social justice were integrated in a remarkable synthesis.

6. *Reformed spirituality.* The Protestant tradition of John Calvin took a different route: the term 'Puritan', applied to many in Reformed Christianity, was originally an insult, directed at those who sought to recover the purity of scriptural religion. Like all who have sought a return to a supposed original and pristine Christian life, the Puritans were in fact profoundly influenced not only by Calvin but by patristic and medieval forebears such as Augustine of Hippo and the Franciscan William of Ockham. The sober doctrine of double predestination, whereby God was believed to have predestined some to eternal salvation and many more to damnation, is often taken as the single controlling feature of Puritan spirituality. In fact it embraced much more: a new emphasis on the Holy Spirit, seen as the free and untrammelled presence and power of God at work within the life of the Christian, preparing us for the transforming process of regeneration. And this led to a recovery of the New Testament virtue of *parrhesia*, boldness, which is the fruit of our assurance of salvation. Richard Baxter (1615–91) and John Bunyan (1628–88) developed a deeply personal Reformed spirituality rooted in these principles, yet interpreted in such a way as to make them both accessible and attractive. The hymns of Isaac Watts (1674–1748), the fiction of Daniel Defoe (1660–1731), and the radical principles of the Levellers and the Quakers enlarged still further both the perspectives and the appeal of Puritan spirituality.

Later English Protestant spirituality was dominated by two different movements. The Methodists, and supremely the lives and work of the brothers John and Charles Wesley (1703–91 and 1707–88), brought a new prophetic energy to English Christianity, yet one drawing upon a striking range of biblical, patristic and continental as well as English sources. Their passionate longing to show how God in Christ could and did change lives, and society too, was in the end too much for the then Church of England to contain: yet Anglicanism did manage to embrace, if not to control, the Evangelical movement, whose principal figures (John Newton (1725–1807), Hannah More (1745–1833), Charles Simeon (1759–1836) and John Stott (b. 1921)) remained within the established Church. This movement too drew upon ancient sources, and in its willingness to challenge secularism by affirming a full-blooded and unapologetically scriptural holiness it renewed the life and vitality of English Christianity.

7. *Roman Catholic spirituality.* The Roman Catholic tradition within English spirituality did not die out at the Reformation, though for some time exiles like the Benedictine Augustine Baker (1575–1641) and small communities of recusants largely kept it alive. Much Catholic piety in the sixteenth and seventeenth centuries was of a firmly traditional kind, intended to help Catholics survive spiritually in an age of terrible persecution; later figures, above all the former Anglican John Henry Newman (1801–90), succeeded in developing a Catholic spirituality

which managed to be both scholarly and passionate, uncompromising in its demands and (like the Tractarians and Evangelicals) firmly *contra mundum* in nature, and imbued with a burning longing for the renewal of both church and society.

8. *Conclusion.* Twentieth-century English spirituality became more diffuse and eclectic as old certainties lost their grip, and monstrous evils like the Holocaust (as well as the sheer pace and scope of social change) subverted the dominance of mainstream Christianity and opened the way to patterns of spirituality that embraced peacemaking, feminism and the protection of the environment, as well as to the recovery of earlier customs such as the practice of pilgrimage to holy places such as the medieval shrine of Our Lady of Walsingham. Yet these challenges in turn elicited from the older traditions a willingness to engage with and respond to, not simply withdraw from, the values of contemporary society; and the start of the third Christian millennium witnessed an energy and adventurousness in the spiritual life of English Christianity which appeared to presage more than simply its early demise.

See also **Anglican Spirituality; Anglo-Saxon Spirituality; English Mystical Tradition; Medieval Spirituality in the West.**

Eamon Duffy, *The Stripping of the Altars: Traditional Religion in England 1400–1580*; New Haven and London: Yale UP, 1992; Gordon Mursell, *English Spirituality: From Earliest Times to 1700*, London: SPCK and Louisville, KT: Westminster John Knox Press, 2001; Gordon Mursell, *English Spirituality: From 1700 to the Present Day*; London: SPCK and Louisville, KT: Westminster John Knox Press, 2001; Geoffrey Rowell (ed.), *The English Religious Tradition and the Genius of Anglicanism*, Wantage: Ikon, 1992; Geoffrey Rowell et al. (eds), *Love's Redeeming Work: The Anglican Quest for Holiness*, Oxford: Oxford University Press, 2001; Martin Thornton, *English Spirituality: An Outline of Ascetical Theology According to the English Pastoral Tradition*, London: SPCK, 1963, repr. Cambridge, MA: Cowley Publications, 1986; Gordon S. Wakefield, *Methodist Spirituality*; Peterborough: Epworth Press, 1999.

GORDON MURSELL

Enlightenment Thought

The 'Enlightenment' describes an array of intellectual, scientific, political and religious developments. It is generally thought to begin somewhere in the mid seventeenth century and to extend through the period of the French Revolution (1789) and its aftermath. The oft-quoted founding tract of the Enlightenment is Immanuel Kant's *What is Enlightenment?* and its battle cry, '*Sapere aude!*' (loosely translated, 'dare to think for yourself').

In general, Enlightenment thought reflected several reactions against the last vestiges of late medieval thought: a confidence in individual autonomy, the use of critical reason, the supremacy of nature over law, a qualified optimism about the future course of humanity in the face of evil, a belief in progress, and a spirit of toleration (Livingston, pp. 5–11). It was accompanied by faith in clarity of scientific methods, suspicion of religious dogmatism and traditions, and the emergence of secular forms of community and government. In the realm of theology, it gave rise to theories of natural religion and to religious rationalism, quasi-scientific theologies, critical approaches to sacred texts (theories of hermeneutics), and an emphasis on a philosophic (not religiously derived) ethics.

With intellectual roots in France, Germany and England, and following upon the Thirty Years War (1648 marks the Treaty of Westphalia), Enlightenment thought often evinced deep hostility to the intolerance exhibited by religion in Europe, but not necessarily to religion itself. Indeed, there was a new-found fascination with philosophies of God, with non-Christian religions such as Confucianism, and with spiritual practices such as Quietism. Philosophical debates over the existence and nature of God were a hallmark of the period. What all of these positions had in common was a loss of 'the key to the symbolic language of medieval Christendom' (Gay, p. 352).

The Enlightenment crossed confessional boundaries. Kant, David Hume and Gottfried Wilhelm Leibniz were Protestants. Yet the major source of Enlightenment thought was Catholic France, where the luminaries were Voltaire, Denis Diderot and Jean-Jacques Rousseau. They and other *philosophes* and *encyclopédistes* often took adversarial positions toward Christian orthodoxy and the religious authority of the Church. There and in other parts of Europe and America, 'freethinking' became institutionalized in such groups as the Freemasons and Rosicrucians, but also in groups like the Quakers.

Yet not all Enlightenment thinkers were hostile to traditional forms of religion. Some tried to establish it on scientific grounds. In Isaac Newton's *Optiks*, for example, God is the provident governor of a universe who 'forms matter and associates it according to mechanical laws that are rationally determinable' (Buckley, p. 143). Theories of divine providence are seen as concomitants of natural theologies that find the evidence and attributes of God in the order of creation, thus bypassing revelation and the traditional warrants for religious faith. Newton was followed by a series of Anglican theologians such as Bishop Samuel Clarke who endeavoured to establish natural theologies of God on the basis of Newtonian physics (universal mechanics). Deism, where 'God' is construed as a provident but disengaged governor of a mechanical universe, became a philosophic alternative to theological faith. In the United States, Jefferson and Franklin, among others, were deists in the mainstream of Enlightenment thought. But it was a relatively short step from some of these theologies to the conclusion that nature was free-standing, apart from any God whatsoever. Baron Paul Henri D'Holbach's arguments for atheism in his *Système de la Nature* can be understood as the inexorable result of these scientific and philosophical developments.

If Christian spirituality is understood as a way of orienting one's life toward the God of Jesus Christ, then Enlightenment thought itself gave rise to a broad palette of possibilities, most of them somewhat distant from traditional forms of Christian religion, both Catholic and Protestant. While Kant himself never abjured religion or his Christian faith, the content of faith grew less substantial or significant among many Enlightenment thinkers, especially as Nicene orthodoxy gave way to Unitarianism or even atheism. But among several deist thinkers there is to be found a tendency toward awe before what some saw as the designs of an all-provident God inscribed in 'Nature'. Where supernatural revelation had ceased to claim authority, now supplanted by Nature, there still remained a general religious pietism, especially among Protestants, coupled with the admonition toward good works. Kant's ethical imperative and moral warrant for the existence of God constitutes the most theoretical exposition of this blend of natural religion with religious piety. In this kind of religiosity, Jesus was viewed as a moral exemplar but not as the Son of God consubstantial with the Father. In the words of Thomas Paine, he 'was a virtuous and amiable man', and according to Jefferson, he presented moral precepts that 'would be the most perfect and sublime that have ever been taught by man' (Buckley, p. 40).

But the Enlightenment, a movement fixed on the rejection of traditional forms of religion, paradoxically generated significant reactions and movements within the worlds of both Catholic and Protestant religion on the level of popular piety and religious practice. Enlightenment accents upon theism, providence and ethical religion were evident in Protestant preaching and also in efforts, especially in France and Germany, to strip Catholic churches of the trappings of medieval religion. Catholicism, particularly in France and Germany, witnessed a proliferation of new spiritual practices and devotions.

In France, the groundwork for religious responses to Enlightenment thought had already been laid in the late sixteenth and early seventeenth centuries by members of what is now known as the 'French School' and such spiritual masters as Pierre de Bérulle, John Eudes, and Louis de Montfort. This movement emphasized a spirituality marked by a sense of personal abasement before the divine majesty, childlike adherence to the precepts of Jesus, and extreme self-denial (even 'slavery' to Christ in Montfort). The goal of this spirituality was to be a witness to the simple life of Jesus and Mary, lived in a devout religious or apostolic life. This pattern of religiosity was said to have been established by Mary's *fiat* to the will of God (Muto, *Bérulle and the French School*, p. xvi).

This strand of French spirituality fed naturally into the mid seventeenth-century (early Enlightenment period) rise of Jansenism (named after Cornelius Jansen), an austere form of Augustinianism that maintained positions on the free will similar to Calvin's. One of Jansen's major adherents and critical interlocutors was the philosopher-mathematician Blaise Pascal (1623–62), who in his *Provincial Letters* vigorously defended Jansenist teachings against what was said to be the semi-Pelagianism and moral laxity of the Jesuits. Later, François de Salignac Fénelon and Jean-Pierre de Caussade emphasized indifference to the will of God (Quietism), eliciting vigorous responses from J.-B. Bossuet, who opposed this view, and the Jesuits, especially Miguel de Molinos, who tended to support some of its implications for the freedom of will.

These various strands of Catholic thought and piety, which were promoted by spiritual directors and assiduously followed by devoted directees, were an undercurrent of spirituality in eighteenth-century Catholic France. But it must not be forgotten that spirituality in an ordinary sense thrived in the sacramental and devotional lives of people not at all involved in these debates or engaged in spiritual direction. In the wake of the anti-clericalism, defilements of the churches and persecutions of the French Revolution, an intense devotionalism developed within popular French Catholicism. This was typified by renewed devotion to the Eucharist as well as attachment to the human person of Jesus, as exemplified in the Sacred Heart devotion. Retreat movements, lay organizations and sodalities proliferated. After the suppression of the Society of Jesus in 1773, older religious orders were reformed and new orders founded, not only in France, but throughout Western Europe. Many of these groups, of either men or women, were dedicated to the works of mercy such as care for the sick, but also to care of souls, or spiritual direction.

There were correlative effects on Protestant spirituality. In Germany, Pietism, an anti-intellectual movement especially popular among the poor, arose in opposition to rationalist forms of religion, but it also had its Catholic versions, especially in Germany. In England, John Wesley's Methodist movement viewed with suspicion Anglican accommodations to deism. Both Pietism and Methodism stressed heartfelt prayer, communal fellowship, religious enthusiasm and a return to simple living. After the Great Awakening in America, many of these post-Enlightenment spiritual movements came to dominate Protestantism and Free Church traditions there.

The 'spirituality' of the Enlightenment is therefore a multifaceted reality, reflecting the many strands of thought and social development that made up the Enlightenment period itself. It is represented in both the implications of Enlightenment thought, and in the debates that sometimes raged within the churches themselves during this period. Perhaps above all, it was a matter of how the great majority of people practised their Christian religion in a world that was fast rejecting the foundations on which that religion had always stood. In this sense, the Enlightenment is arguably a more radical moment in religious history, and in the history of spirituality, than is the period of the Reformation and early modernity.

Michael J. Buckley, *At the Origins of Modern Atheism*, New Haven: Yale University Press, 1987; Ernst Cassirer, *The Philosophy of the Enlightenment*, Boston: Beacon Press, 1960; Peter Gay, *The Enlightenment: An Interpretation: The Rise of Modern Paganism*, New York: Norton, 1966; James C. Livingston, *Modern Christian Thought, Vol. 1: The Enlightenment and the Nineteenth Century*, 2nd edn, Upper Saddle River, NJ: Prentice Hall, 1997; Frank Manuel, *The Eighteenth Century Confronts the Gods*, Cambridge: Harvard University Press, 1959; William Thompson (ed.), *Bérulle and the French School*, New York: Paulist Press, 1989.

PAUL CROWLEY

Enthusiasm

Enthusiasm, derived from the late classical Greek *enthousiasmos* (from *enthousiazein*, 'to be God-possessed'), means to be inspired or possessed by a god or a divine superhuman power. It is associated with a psychic excitement whereby one can transcend the purely rational order. Enthusiasm historically has been regarded with suspicion. In the seventeenth and eighteenth centuries, both Deists and Calvinists sharply contrasted enthusiasm with revelation and inspiration. Due to religious conflict during the English Civil War, Quakers, Ranters and Oliverians, as well as other splinter groups, were persecuted, much as the Huguenots were pursued in France as false French prophets (*camisards*). Jonathan Edwards, for example, alleged that enthusiasts are those who falsely pretend to be inspired by the Holy Spirit as the prophets were. In Henry More's brief discourse entitled *Enthusiasmus Triumphatus* written in 1662, enthusiasm is defined in the most pejorative light as a distemper. He compares enthusiasm to false inspiration, indicating that enthusiasm is nothing more than a misconception of being inspired. True inspiration is to be moved in an extraordinary manner by the power or Spirit of God to act, speak or think what is holy, just and true. But enthusiasm is a false persuasion of inspiration (sect. 2). In the 1740s the charge of enthusiasm was the ultimate reproach levelled against the revivalism of the Great Awakening. The period that followed, called the Revival, brought about radical religious expression, involving religious behaviour not previously understood or appreciated.

The subject of religious enthusiasm has been of interest in a more positive way since about 1950, when Ronald Knox wrote his lengthy history of enthusiasm. He traces the development of the phenomenon beginning with the Pauline community at Corinth, through the Montanists and Donatists of the early Church up to 1820, focusing upon certain Protestant groups. Enthusiasm in his perspective is a kind of religious eccentricity associated with people gesticulating wildly and screaming in a religious frenzy. Characteristic of religious enthusiasm are the following attributes: excessive piety, schism, appeal to charismatic authority, ultrasupernaturalism, global pessimism, anti-intellectualism and millenarianism. His definition, however, has difficulty in freeing itself from fanaticism and other pejorative interpretations. In an attempt to explain the phenomenon, Knox decides that the theological foundation of enthusiasm is based upon a theology of grace different from the traditional Scholastic view. Rather than grace building upon nature, where inspiration would be fundamentally a natural human capacity, grace in the case of enthusiasm supplements that which is lacking in nature, making the enthusiast privy to superhuman powers. Therefore new faculties are given to persons so that they can perceive deeper into the nature of things. He detects this idea especially in revivalism and religious groups moved by ecstasy. Using the term in a rather precise and technical sense, the notion indicates that one relies solely upon direct divine inspiration, ignoring the existing channels of faith. Within Knox's assessment, enthusiasm is suspect due to its high emotionalism.

At the root of all enthusiasm is a belief in divine illumination, reminiscent of the Gnostic movements throughout history. Gnosticism, believed to have its roots in Persian thought and religion, is based upon a dualism whereby anything material is automatically evil, while the purely spiritual is inherently good. Gnosticism makes recourse to divine illumination a type of purely spiritual knowledge. This interior illumination is of an inspirational kind, but as Knox attempts to demonstrate, it has led to many religious aberrations within the history of Christianity.

In religious terms, enthusiasm took new forms in the amorphous evangelical Christian movements, and especially in the fundamentalist churches. First termed 'Pentecostalism', one notes that largely uneducated segments of the population were attracted to this kind of religious experience. Beginning in 1966, some Roman Catholics were involved in this movement. A growing fear of uncontrolled emotionalism and over-zealous frenzy compelled the United States Conference of Bishops to oversee this problem, especially as it could influence the charismatic renewal in the United States. Similar oversight was exercised elsewhere. Consequently charismatic piety in the Roman Catholic context tended to avoid the extremes that plagued many of the spiritual movements throughout the history of the Church.

See also **Conversion; Charismatic Spirituality; Evangelical Spirituality; Gnosticism; Illuminative Way; Joy; Pentecostal Spirituality; Spirit, Holy.**

Daniel C. Fouke, *The Enthusiastical Concerns of Dr Henry More: Religious Meaning and the Psychology of Delusion*, Leiden and New York: E. J. Brill, 1997; Clement Hawes, *Mania and Literary Style: The Rhetoric of Enthusiasm from the Ranters to Christopher Smart*, Cambridge and New York: Cambridge University Press, 1996; James Hitchcock, *The New Enthusiasts and What They Are Doing in the Catholic Church*, Chicago: Thomas More Press, 1982; Ronald A. Knox, *Enthusiasm: A Chapter in the History of Religion* [1950], Notre Dame, IN: University of Notre Dame Press, 1994; David Lovejoy, *Religious Enthusiasm in the New World: Heresy to Revolution*, Cambridge, MA: Harvard University Press, 1985; Henry More, *Enthusiasmus Triumphatus* [1662], Augustan Reprint Society, Publication no. 118, Los Angeles: William Andrews Clark Memorial Library, University of California, 1966.

MICHAEL S. DRISCOLL

Environment

The environment is the word used to refer to nature and to the interaction of the human with the non-human world. Its meanings include an enormous range of life-forms, from forests and plant world to insects and the entire bird and animal world, from agriculture to climate, from pollution of soil, water and air, to linked issues of poverty and justice. The environment as such only became an explicit subject for Christian spirituality comparatively recently because of the emerging consciousness of the ecological crisis. In 1962 Rachel Carson's *The Silent Spring* shocked concerned people as to the damage inflicted on the earth through pesticides, but it was the article of Lynn White Jr in 1967 that specifically implicated theologians in negative attitudes and practices towards the earth. The text cited as potentially damaging is Gen. 1.28 and there have been many efforts to show that 'dominion' does not necessarily mean exploitation. There is general agreement that damage wreaked upon the earth by human beings is relative to political and economic context, and that the immense environmental crisis we now suffer is both a product of industrializing, capitalist expansion and the system of globalization that maximizes profit whatever the environmental cost.

Religious thinking reacted in different ways. It is widely recognized that capitalist expansion often relied on religious legitimization. The most influential prevailing attitude is that all created things (that is, all life forms) exist solely for the use and benefit of human beings. This anthropocentrism continues to influence attitudes to the environment, justifying a range of policies from fish-farming, experiments on animals, the slaughter of healthy animals in a foot-and-mouth crisis (to preserve the international meat market), to the colossal destruction of the forests across the world. Yet an increasing sense of responsibility towards the environment prompted many churches to develop attitudes of stewardship. Others realized that even responsible stewardship still considers the earth and its resources to exist for the benefit of humanity. So more radical attitudes – influenced by secular movements like 'deep ecology' – see the need to value all forms of life within the great web of life. For Christian theology this means that all the great beliefs of Christianity – God/ Christ/creation/redemption/eschatology/sin/ grace – must be re-thought to include the flourishing of the environment along with humanity. The very word environment came to be seen as inadequate, when viewed under the lens of God's loving care for the whole of creation: it seems to imply more of a backcloth for human activity.

The impact on spirituality has been dynamic and is still evolving. In its most simple expression it means a recognition that Christian spiritual growth takes place in a much more rooted way, linked with place, the quality of relationship with soil and trees, water and the plant world; but more importantly, with the *quality* of interaction between the human and the non-human forms of being. Pastoral care now includes this dimension. Along with this has come a retrieval of Christian traditions on nature/the environment, from the integrated attitudes of Jewish spirituality of 'shalom', to Jesus' own situatedness in the ecology of Israel, and supposed environmentally friendly figures in Christian tradition such as Hildegard of Bingen and St Francis. The link between women and the environment has been made. In poor countries where environmental degradation is acute, the suffering of women is severe, since the provision of water, firewood and fodder for animals is mostly their responsibility. This has become the starting point for ecofeminist spirituality. A third approach comes from liberation spirituality: just as 'the poor' are the focus of liberation theology, so the environment/nature is now to be regarded as 'the new poor' and should be at the centre of responsible action. Serious attention is now given by the World Council of Churches to such issues as climate change.

Although awareness has been raised, the position is still grave. It remains to be seen if Christian spirituality can eradicate the inherited anthropocentric dualisms at its heart that still privilege the human at the expense of other living organic systems. As long as 'the environment' is considered to be the expendable backdrop of human endeavour, and not as sacred in itself, the potential richness of mutual interrelatedness is still an undiscovered spiritual resource.

See also **Creation Spirituality; Ecological Spirituality; Ethics and Spirituality; Feminist Spirituality; Liberation Spirituality; Orthodox Spirituality.**

Leonardo Boff, *Ecology and Liberation – a New Paradigm,* Maryknoll: Orbis Books, 1995; Rachel Carson, *The Silent Spring,* Boston, MA: Houghton Mifflin, 1962; Sean McDonagh, *The Greening of the Church,* London: Geoffrey Chapman, 1994; Rosemary Radford Ruether, *Gaia and God: An Ecofeminist Theology of Earth Healing,* San Francisco: HarperSanFrancisco, 1992; Paul Santmire, *Nature Reborn: The Ecological and Cosmic Promise of Christian Theology,* Minneapolis: Fortress Augsburg, 2000; Lynn White Jr, 'The historical roots of the ecological crisis', *Science* 155 (1967), 1203–77.

MARY C. GREY

Eremitical Spirituality

The word 'eremitical' derives from the Greek *eremia,* which means desert. The desert experience is decisive for the Jewish Scriptures, beginning with Israel's journey to freedom, covenant and the promised land through the harsh Sinai desert. It was on that journey that Moses had the powerful encounter with God in the burning bush, and on the summit of Sinai. The prophets later promise to an unfaithful Israel that God will call her back into the desert: 'I will allure her; I will lead her into the desert and speak to her heart' (Hos. 2.14). And the prophet Elijah returns to the desert, and encounters God now in a new way, at the mouth of the cave of Mt Horeb, in 'a sound of sheer silence' (1 Kings 19.12). The desert was seen as the setting of a place of paradise rejoicing: 'the desert shall rejoice and blossom'.

For the Gospels this prophetic word was fulfilled in Christ, who went to John the Baptist, 'a voice crying out in the desert' (Mark 1.3), to be baptized in the Spirit and affirmed by the Father. Jesus then directly was 'led by the Spirit' out into the desert for forty days, to wrestle with Satan and the fundamental human temptations; then 'angels came and waited on him' (Matt. 4.1ff.). Paul's withdrawal after his conversion 'at once into Arabia' (Gal. 1.17) was perhaps a desert experience. And he would teach that Israel's desert experiences were a type of the Christian journey of faith (1 Cor. 10.11). And the mysterious woman of the Book of Revelation would flee the serpent into the desert 'where she had a place prepared by God' (Rev. 12.6, 14).

The patristic literature drew from all these threads to interpret the Christian life in terms of a journey through the desert, as with Origen and Gregory of Nyssa's *Life of Moses.* And in the third century and thereafter men and women abandoned the cities, also in protest for the easy accommodation of Christianity with the empire, for the desert solitude of Egypt, Syria, Palestine, Arabia and Europe, to live out a spiritual form of the early martyrdom they regarded as the Christian ideal. This vast spiritual experience generated a significant literature, such as Athanasius' *Life of Antony,* Jerome's *Life of Paul,* the *Sayings of the Desert Fathers,* Cassian's *Conferences,* the writings of Evagrius, John Climacus, and so on.

This literature significantly influenced Western and Eastern spirituality thereafter. The Celtic tradition, for instance, honoured the eremitical life in France, Ireland, Scotland and Wales. St Benedict's Rule, which became normative in the West, was written especially for monks living in community, but recognized the possibility of monks going into solitude after a first cenobitic experience; and thus throughout Europe the eremitical life continued to flourish also during the 'Benedictine centuries'. Even urban parish churches would sometimes have an anchorhold attached (thus Julian of Norwich). In the Eastern Church the eremitical was especially esteemed (despite the perplexities of Basil) in centres such as Mt Athos and Mt Sinai, nourishing the decisive hesychast current.

This Eastern heritage influenced also the eremitical renewal in the Western Church in the tenth and eleventh centuries, in saints and traditions such as Romuald and the Camaldolese (see Camaldolese Spirituality), and Bruno and the Carthusians (see Carthusian Spirituality). The hermitages of these reforms were really communities of hermits gathered around a common church, as in the earlier lavra model of Palestine and Egypt. These currents generated a literature also about the 'inner desert' that every Christian is called to enter, to encounter the living God in deeper intimacy. In the pivotal thirteenth century St Francis spent a significant time in solitude and wrote a *Rule for Hermitages.* The first flowering of the Carmelites was in a Holy Land eremitical form, and the giant reformers Teresa and John of the Cross would invoke this spirituality as decisive for their own. The 'English School' of spirituality, including Richard Rolle, the author of the *Cloud of Unknowing,* and Julian of Norwich, would be shaped by the eremitical spirit, and they would impact English Catholicism, both Roman and Anglican.

Even the Ignatian current can be seen to be rooted in the decisive Manresa cave experience of St Ignatius of Loyola, and thus also his profound reverence for the Carthusians and his directives facilitating the transfer of Jesuits to that eremitical Order. And so the many apostolic congregations that have been influenced by the Ignatians continue to harbour, with the Jesuits, an eremitical 'heart of the matter' in their spirituality.

In more recent centuries interest in the eremitical has been renewed East and West through the writings and lives of figures such as Seraphim of Sarov, Charles de Foucauld, Catherine de Hueck Doherty, and especially Thomas Merton. Writers such as Henri Nouwen and Anglicans A. M. Allchin and Sr Benedicta Ward have explored the significance of the eremitical experience for all Christians, also as a protest against too easy an accommodation of established Christianity to secular and consumer collectivistic culture.

Many lay people, and some clergy, Catholic and Orthodox and Anglican, continue to live individual eremitical lives throughout Europe and North America. Moreover, the Camaldolese and Carthusian congregations continue to provide the eremitical form of life for vowed religious. Some Benedictine and Cistercian abbeys have individual hermitages on their grounds for their own religious, and there are some small Franciscan and Carmelite hermitages in Europe and America. And of course very many single people 'in the world' live a virtual eremitical life in their apartments and homes.

The East–West dialogue has made us aware that Christians have no monopoly on the eremitical experience (as they have no monopoly on monasticism, marriage, friendship and other basic forms of human spiritual living). Thus we are becoming more aware of the eremitical traditions in Hinduism, Taoism, Buddhism, etc.

One of the most emphatic champions of Christian solitude, Thomas Merton, sought to nourish his spirituality with virtually all of the above currents. He affirmed, in his many writings, that our collectivistic, mass age is in particular need of the solitary individual, the solitary dimension in everyone, so that we might move beyond the collective false self to an inner true self, which can only be discovered in solitude and silence, there to encounter the living God, and thus there to be united with all of humanity and all of creation at the deepest level.

See also **Benedictine Spirituality; Camaldolese Spirituality; Carmelite Spirituality; Carthusian Spirituality; Desert; English Mystical Tradition; Early Christian Spirituality; Franciscan Spirituality; Grandmontine Spirituality; Monasticism; Orthodox Spirituality.**

Athanasius, *The Life of Antony and the Letter to Marcellinus,* CWS, New York: Paulist Press, 1980; John Cassian, *The Conferences,* annotated by Boniface Ramsey OP, CWS, New York: Paulist Press, 1997; Derwas Chitty, *The Desert a City*, New York: St Vladimir's Seminary Press, 1966; Thomas Merton, *The Wisdom of the Desert: Sayings from the Desert Fathers*, New York: New Directions, 1960; Benedicta Ward (ed.), *Lives of the Desert Fathers*, London: Mowbray, 1981.

ROBERT HALE

Eroticism

The word erotic suggests to many people a perverse preoccupation with sex, associated with pornography. But it is unfair to limit Eros to genital activity.

In early Greek mythology Eros was the vital force active in every area of life. It was considered revolutionary because it was capable of overthrowing the established order of things. In the Hebrew Scriptures' Song of Songs it is an aspect of the divine which occasionally manifests in us. 'For love is strong as death, Passion relentless as hell. The flash of it is a flash of fire, A flame of Yahweh's own self' (8.6). The history of Christian mysticism is replete with figures, such as Catherine of Siena, John of the Cross, Teresa of Avila, Julian of Norwich and others, who use erotic language and images in their descriptions of religious experience. Contemporary Christians report the experience of sexual arousal at prayer and of spiritual growth through sexual practice.

Eros is our passionate drive for life and growth. It is experienced as the desire for union with the Other. It is the traditional name given to the body's desire and delight. Arousal and affection, passion and response, intimacy and appreciation – all are part of Eros. In erotic experience we first feel the connections between presence and pleasure, our separateness and the otherness in the universe. Eros moves in all our longings to make contact, to be touched and to touch. The more common, less feared word for eroticism is romance. The erotic excitement of romance can lead to the broader commitments of mutual love. Sexual satisfaction can mean growth in bodily self-acceptance, in the capacity for sensuousness, in the capacity for play, in the healthy diffusion of the erotic throughout the body (rather than the genitalization of the erotic).

The sensual is another name for the many ways that we are bodily moved, excited, and refreshed. This is the broader meaning of Eros. When we are in love, we notice nature and music in a new way. By contrast, when we are lonely, we are without these delights. But those who are frightened by the surprising stirrings of the body may avoid all sensual arousals fearing that they may lead to a loss of control. Hostility toward the body and fear of emotions are often linked. One who is confused abut masculinity or femininity, or does not understand her own love map (see entry on Sexuality and Spirituality) may find that reaching out to other people in genuine friendship is difficult. If we are afraid of the ways in which our affections are stirred, soon the experiences of joy and beauty become as alien to us as the unwanted sexual stimulation.

Many things have been eroticized – fire, food, power, pain, submission. The eroticization of certain foods as conducive to arousal is an ancient practice. Among these aphrodisiacs are listed oysters, garlic, truffles, chocolate, figs, honey, caviar, pine nuts and strawberries, not to mention the alcoholic and, therefore, inhibition-reducing beverages, such as champagne.

The modern reconstruction of the spirituality of Eros came from feminist spirituality, where writers looked for and found the transcendent within the ultimate symbol of the immanent, the female body. According to such writers, holiness and wholeness do not mean a flight from the sexual. It demands a befriending of the frightening and fascinating force called Eros. It requires that we become more profoundly and freely erotic. Sexual eroticism is a form of physical and emotional liberation as well as of spiritual liberation. The erotic is opposed to the compulsive, unfree lust of the person who has not integrated its power into her life. It can be called spiritual because erotic pleasure is, by nature 'in the moment', an encounter in which we drop most of our physical boundaries in order to enjoy the full measure of human contact. Explored without shame, erotic energy can elevate the human body and spirit into sensations of ecstasy, at times producing altered states of consciousness.

Sexual eroticism normally produces orgasm, and the release of this energy is essential to physical, mental and psychological health. Orgasm is one way – certainly one of the more pleasurable ways – of releasing the 'energy debris' we collect through ordinary human contact. Exercise and creativity are other well-known avenues of release. When a person has no release, however, this energy backs up in the system and, without conscious management, can produce reactions that run the gamut from depression to violence.

The influence of feminist thought in the twentieth century has raised a number of issues which have not yet been resolved. The attempts to distinguish eroticism from pornography have generally failed, on the fronts of both law and art. It has been argued that the right of persons to enjoy erotic language and images has been taken hostage by those who continue to make a commodity of female sexuality and offer it for commercial profit. The eroticization of violence against women, which is characteristic of some pornographic films, has led many to reject explicit sexual art, calling it a preparation for rape.

The last twenty-five years have produced widespread acceptance and availability of commercial pornography. Sold as 'adult entertainment by consenting adults for consenting adults in the privacy of their own home' it has become a sizeable international industry which claims the right of free speech and makes an enormous profit for its purveyors. It has been estimated that 70 per cent of hotel profits come from in-room pay TV, movies which are watched for an average length of seven minutes. Because there is still a social stigma, the ability to watch such material privately has increased its acceptance. The invention of the VCR and the technology of the Internet explain the explosion of wider availability. The computer is now in more than 100 million households. Community standards change as teen rock stars make music videos influenced by explicit sexual imagery, and adult videos show extreme shots of women being raped and murdered, humiliated and degraded. The only material absolutely illegal is child porn. The rest must be judged by a jury. Anti-porn initiatives are making strange bed-fellows of feminists, church groups and governments. The aim is generally not to eliminate all sexually explicit material but rather to apply some standards, distinguishing healthy eroticism from its spurious counterpart.

Another effort, a positive one as contrasted with the fight against pornography, is to encourage a public erotic language. Popular culture, even in traditions such as courtship and wedding rituals, has developed no public language of Eros, leaving the field to clinical language or the vulgarities of slang. Eros, which effects desire and connection, needs better conditions for its spiritual rebirth. The symbols of dualism and separation remain strong in the popular cultures of Europe and North and South America. Symbols of integration and connection will follow the redefinition of eroticism as the force of divine passion.

See also **Body and Spirituality; Desire; Sexuality and Spirituality.**

Bonnie Bullough and Vern Bullough, *Women and Prostitution: A Social History*, New Concepts in Human Sexuality, New York: Prometheus Books, 1987; Riane Eisler, *Sacred Pleasure: Sex, Myth, and the Politics of the Body – New Paths to Power and Love*, San Francisco: Harper-SanFrancisco, 1999; Lynn Hunt (ed.), *Eroticism and the Body Politic*, Baltimore, MD: Johns Hopkins University Press, 1991; *The Complete Kama Sutra*, trans. Alain Danielou, Rochester, VT: Park Street Press, 1994; Audre Lorde, *Sister Outsider: Essays and Speeches*, Santa Cruz, CA: Crossing Press, 1984; John C. Pierrakos, *Eros, Love and Sexuality: The Forces that Unify Man and Woman*, Mendicino, CA: Liferhythm Press, 1997.

JOAN H. TIMMERMAN

Eschatology

Eschatology literally means the study of or discourse about (*logos*) the last things (*eschata*). In this context 'the last things' refers to death, judgement, heaven and hell in relation to the individual (individual eschatology) and also the second coming, general judgement, resurrection and the end of the world for humanity (social eschatology). Within this perspective eschatology, following the creeds, usually appears at the end of the rest of Christian theology, and then more often as an appendix. And yet, contrary to this perceived view, it should be noted that theologies of death, judgement, heaven and hell have been fairly prominent in the history of Christianity, especially in liturgy, art and spiritual practices.

The term 'eschatology' came into prominence only in the late eighteenth and early nineteenth century with the critical study of the life of 'the Jesus of history'. In the first decade of the twentieth century Albert Schweitzer emphasized the presence of what he called consistent or 'thoroughgoing' eschatology within the teaching of Jesus. For Schweitzer, eschatology was the driving force in the life of Jesus and by this he meant that Jesus understood himself to be announcing the end of the world through the proclamation of the reign of God, even though this collapsed with the death of Jesus on the cross. In the 1930s C. H. Dodd put forward a theory of 'realized eschatology' in the life of Jesus suggesting that the reign of God had already come into being, especially according to the Gospel of John. In the 1950s R. H. Fuller proposed the presence of 'an inaugurated eschatology' in the life. In the mid 1980s the US Jesus Seminar argued for a non-eschatological Jesus – a view that has been persuasively discredited by E. P. Sanders and J. P. Meier.

Most theologies of the New Testament suggest that within early Christianity there was a strong sense that the future had already arrived in the death and resurrection of Jesus and that the 'end of ages' had occurred in the Christ-event (1 Cor. 10.11; Heb. 6.5). Within the Pauline tradition one can detect at least two different layers of eschatology. In the early Paul there is an emphasis on the resurrection of Christ and the expected early return of Christ in the parousia (1 Thess.). In the later Paul the focus shifts to a theology of personal death and resurrection in this life brought about through faith and the sacraments of Baptism and Eucharist (Rom. 6.3–6; Col. 2.11–12). In John's Gospel there is the presence of a realized eschatology that sees eternal life as a possession in this life for those who believe in Jesus (John 3.36; 5.24, 40; 6.40, 47, 54, 68; 10.10).

In brief, the early Church believed that in the life of Jesus, especially through his saving death and resurrection, a prototype of the future had been revealed. The paschal mystery of the life, death and resurrection of Jesus was understood as a microcosm of what will happen to the macrocosm of humanity and creation. The end of the world has appeared in embryo in the life and destiny of Jesus as the Christ.

In the light of these biblical perspectives there has been a renaissance within eschatology in the systematic theology of the latter half of the twentieth century. Eschatology has now become more prominent in the rest of Christian theology. For example, Jürgen Moltmann and Karl Rahner suggest that eschatology is not just one area of theology but rather something that should permeate the whole of theology. Further, other theologians argue that the study of eschatology should become more christocentric and that the primary emphasis should be on the arrival of the eschaton in the life, death and resurrection of Jesus; it is the advent of the eschaton 'in Christ' that should inform the particular theologies of the eschata of death, judgement, heaven and hell, and not the other way around as had been the case in classical eschatology. Within this emphasis on the eschaton 'in Christ' there will be recognition of elements of continuity and discontinuity between historical existence and the gift of eternal life. Karl Rahner makes a strong case for the construction of particular principles of interpretation specific to the peculiar character of eschatology if we are to make sense of eschatological statements.

One of the benefits of these twentieth-century developments within eschatology is that it becomes clear from a theological point of view what eschatology *is not*: not a futurology, not a prediction about the end of the world, not secret information about what goes on in the next life. Instead eschatology is ultimately about 'hope seeking understanding', which is addressed to the transformation of humanity and creation as God's promise, revealed in the death and resurrection of Jesus. The object of Christian hope is not simply the cross, nor is it the resurrection, but rather Christ crucified and risen. In the light of the death and resurrection of Jesus as the Christ, the Christian is one who dares to hope for the triumph of good over evil, of justice over injustice and love over hatred in this life and eternity.

Towards the end of the twentieth century and the beginning of the twenty-first century eschatology has been seriously called into question by the advent of postmodernity. Postmodernity is more a mood than a movement, more a reaction against the Enlightenment than a system of thought. In particular, postmodernity is deeply anti-modern, sceptical about all of the grand narratives of life, rejects the notion of an objective world, celebrates difference, and delights in multiplicity. Within this 'philosophy' of postmodernity the human is reduced to the level of a social construction, which enables linguistic and cultural exchanges to take place.

Clearly this outlook of postmodernity leaves very little room for an eschatological narrative. However there is a view among some who claim that postmodernity is an interim development, paving the way and making space for a new kind of religious discourse, including that of eschatology: for example, postmodern talk about a passion for the impossible, the possibility of representing the unrepresentable, of saying something about the unsayable, highlighting the messianic structure of human experience, and ultimately focusing on the apophatic character of all human discourse. These aspirations within postmodernity, it is suggested, have some affinity with eschatology, which it must be remembered also seeks to attend to the messianic character of experience, to imagine the unimaginable, to express the inexpressible in ways that explicitly acknowledge an apophatic element within its statements. However, there is a fundamental difference between eschatology and postmodernity in terms of their respective points of departure. Christian eschatology arises out of a particular interpretation of human experience and locates this interpretation within the historical narrative of the biblical data, arriving at a point of epistemological humility as to the content of its statements. In contrast, postmodernity begins with a deep suspicion towards all systems of thought, which in effect precludes any particular point of arrival. There is no doubt this is a debate which has only begun and it remains to be seen whether some versions of postmodernity and eschatology can fruitfully dialogue with each other in the future.

To conclude, it should be noted that there are certain qualities belonging to eschatology that could contribute to the construction of a distinctively Christian and eschatological spirituality. Briefly these distinctive qualities may be summarized as follows. First of all the shape of an eschatological Christian spirituality would be cruciform; the cross of Christ is at the centre of eschatology and as such is one of the hallmarks of an authentic Christian spirituality. Second, the colour of an eschatological spirituality would be one of a 'bright darkness'. Christian spirituality cannot avoid or escape the darkness of human suffering and death itself; instead Christian spirituality must dwell within the darkness of life and death to see the light and glory of resurrection. Third, the rhythm of an eschatological spirituality would be a paschal process of dying and rising, of passing over and returning, of decentring the self to re-centre the self on Christ crucified and risen. An authentic Christian spirituality, therefore, would include a moment of *kenosis* (self-emptying), which leads to the fullness of life, modelled on the memory of the self-emptying love of Christ on the cross. Finally, an eschatological spirituality would have a dual point of reference, affirming the goodness of the whole of God's creation while recognizing its need for transformation 'in Christ'. A true Christian spirituality, therefore, will have 'a this worldly' and 'an otherworldly' dimension to it, bringing together into a creative unity elements of the mystical imagination and political praxis.

See also **Creation Spirituality; Cross and Spirituality; Hope; Place; Postmodernity; Sacred; Time; World.**

Richard Bauckham and Trevor Hart, *Hope Against Hope: Christian Eschatology in Contemporary Context*, London: Darton, Longman & Todd, 1999; David Ferguson and Marcel Sarot (eds), *The Future as God's Gift: Explorations in Christian Eschatology*, Edinburgh: T & T Clark, 2000; Mary C. Grey, *The Outrageous Pursuit of Hope: Prophetic Dreams for the Twenty-first Century*, London: Darton, Longman & Todd, 2000; Dermot A. Lane, *Keeping Hope Alive: Stirrings in Christian Theology*, Dublin: Veritas/New York: Paulist Press, 1996; Jürgen Moltmann, *The Coming of God: Christian Eschatology*, trans. Margaret Kohl, London: SCM Press, 1996; Peter C. Phan, *Responses to 101 Questions on Death and Eternal Life*, New York: Paulist Press, 1997; Karl Rahner, *Foundations of the Christian Faith: An Introduction to the Idea of Christianity*, trans. William V. Dych, London: Darton, Longman & Todd, 1978.

DERMOT A. LANE

Ethics and Spirituality

Following the foundational biblical witness, most Christian traditions see spirituality and the moral life as integrally connected but not reducible one to another. The Great Commandment's unity of love of God and love of neighbour locates the moral life in a transcendental horizon as a response to God's graciousness in and through specific human interactions (Karl Rahner). The Spirit of God heals moral disorder and internally shapes the virtues and moral character of Christians to conform to the character of Jesus Christ. Prophetic texts and the symbol of the kingdom of God rule out any divorce of piety from moral commitment and faithful action. Ethics brings to lived spirituality the normative considerations that are central to moral experience and the religious tradition. Ethics offers to spiritualities language to make their practices publicly intelligible. The study of spirituality examines practices of piety that provide a transformative and developmental wisdom that is generally absent from ethics.

The relation between the academic study of spirituality and that of ethics depends upon the relation between lived spirituality and morality. Lived spirituality, which is called 'piety' in some traditions, is the affective, practical and transformative dimension of religion; it emphasizes the experience of what is believed. Morality is taken here to be the experience of moral values and development, while ethics or moral philosophy is the formal, critical investigation of the claims, dynamics and grounds of the moral life. The academic study of spirituality stands to lived spirituality as ethics stands to morality. The study of spirituality brings critical resources from theology, psychology and social sciences to bear on the spiritual experience and practices of individuals and groups. In Christian theologies the systematic configuration of spirituality and ethics will be determined by the meaning and relative ordering given to grace and nature, sin and salvation, creation and incarnation.

Although spirituality and ethics have been historically related by reduction or subordination, these approaches are usually considered inadequate. Ethics is collapsed into spirituality by antinomian pietism and certain forms of contemporary experience of the sacred that ignore the moral claims that the sacred makes, particularly the obligation to remedy social injustice and oppression. Some movements ask spiritual experiences to do the work of reflective morality by assuming a direct intuition of God's purposes. Spirituality is collapsed into ethics by the Enlightenment contention that morality is completely autonomous and that spiritual experience can be reduced without remainder to moral values, thereby ignoring the transcendent source and destiny of the moral life.

Subordinating spirituality to ethics or vice versa presents a more persistent challenge to communities of faith. Both are compromised when one is used instrumentally to foster the other. When religious experience and spiritual practices are means for advancing moral purposes, as in some varieties of liberal religion and liberation movements, the transcendence of God is violated by making the absolute serve the relative. Likewise, Luther's warning against 'works' righteousness' targets the Pelagianism that makes moral commitment the instrument of spiritual development, thereby denying the gratuity of God's love in Christ.

Spiritual practices. Every serious spirituality is structured by specific practices, and these practices provide the bridge between the spiritual life and moral development and action. Alasdair MacIntyre proposes that every culture inculcates specific virtues in its adherents through practices that are historically defined, contain internal standards of performance, expand human capacities, and are intrinsically worthwhile. Rightly pursued practices instil virtues, the habits of affection and action that define character. The New Testament communities commended certain practices as constitutive of the life of discipleship: for instance, forgiveness, obedience to God, self-sacrificial love, eucharistic worship, generosity to the poor and mutual forbearance. Rightly intended as expressions of love of God and neighbour, these practices are the psychological vehicles through which the Spirit of God reshapes the Christian's character. Although the immature may approach them as techniques for personal growth or salvation, over time the action of grace can reorient that intention so that the practices are performed from love. A spiritual routine that originally began as a technique can change into a genuine practice done for its own sake as response to God's goodness and beauty. The internal dynamic of practices as intrinsically worthwhile activities guided by the Spirit should counteract tendencies to perfectionism.

Since the gospel is always in dialogue with cultures, there can be no generic Christian spirituality, but necessarily a wide variety of them. Founders of Christian spiritualities articulate the gospel message for a specific time and culture through a distinctive set of practices. Host Christian communities can either welcome these charismatic innovations, as medieval Christianity did in the case of Francis of Assisi, and the Catholic Reformation in the case of Teresa of Avila, or they may fail to accommodate the new spirituality as in the case of the Church of England and John Wesley. The latter may occur particularly when the emergent spirituality levels a moral critique at the host denomination.

Ethics of character. Given spiritualities are congenial to particular types of ethics. The existentialist approaches of Karl Barth and Dietrich Bonhoeffer combined moral intuitionism with the deontology of divine commands. The spirituality of the 'social gospel' movement as expressed by Friedrich Rauschenbusch was more teleological, as are contemporary liberation spiritualities like that of Gustavo Gutiérrez and the feminism of Elisabeth Schüssler Fiorenza. Although obedience to God's will (deontology) and faithful action to transform society (teleology) are components of Christian discipleship, the New Testament places primary emphasis on the radical transformation of believers' hearts and minds in the Body of Christ. Since practices are the core of spirituality, the ethics of character and virtue offers a more adequate ethical partner for the study of spirituality than do deontology or teleology. Moral philosophies such as Kantianism, utilitarianism and social contract theory will be less apt instruments for understanding the impact of spiritualities on moral experience because they formulate universal, impartial moral principles by discounting emotions and the preferences derived from specific ways of life and religious traditions. The ethics of virtue and character attends to moral psychology that distinguishes different regions of moral experience where grace heals and transforms through the discipline of regular spiritual practices:

1. *Perception.* The ability to notice what is morally promising or threatening in particular situations is equally significant in religious experience. Spiritual practices of contemplation, simplicity of life, and service of others can locate experience against a transcendent horizon of God's concern. In this way individual values and persons can be appreciated more for their own worth than for their value to the perceiver.

2. *Emotions.* The deep affections of the heart filter experience and dispose the agent to act in corresponding ways. Meditation on biblical psalms, narratives, and prophecies can tutor the emotions over time to 'take on the mind of Christ'. Right actions not informed by virtuous dispositions, pre-eminently that of love, are worthless, as Paul insists in 1 Corinthians 13. For Thomas Aquinas, the gifts of the spirit are dispositions that bridge the spiritual and moral dimensions of the Christian life. Jonathan Edwards and Ignatius Loyola both made

'ordered affections' the criteria for the practice of discernment.

3. *Identity.* Moral character gradually becomes consistent and integral by commitment to persons, causes and communities. The practice of communal worship, including praise, thanksgiving and preaching of the gospel, locates individual experience in the framework of the people of God extended over time and space. The practice of forgiveness makes it possible for love of neighbour to persist in all seasons, while the practice of solidarity with the poor expressed in service and generosity leads believers to identify with the larger community of humankind and learn God's compassion and justice.

Finally, authentically Christian spiritual practices inculcate the normative pattern of Christian transformation that makes the fundamental moral claim on disciples. The entire life of Jesus Christ from the interactions of the public ministry to the cross and resurrection presents that normative pattern. The biblical narratives offer a 'concrete universal', a paradigm for the Christian way of life. Although that norm is a different sort of criterion than general ethical principles, it is the criterion by which spiritualities are to be judged. Spiritual practices engage the imagination to interpret a way of life that is both faithful to the example of Christ and creatively expresses his attitudes and commitments in different cultural contexts. At the same time, authentic spiritualities do not violate ethical norms and moral virtues, but express a distinctive way of living shaped by the example of Christ. Lived spiritualities that are not anchored in a normative theological and ethical tradition run the dangers of quietism, excess and illusion, as John of the Cross and others have insisted. Consequently, the Christian moral life depends upon the spiritual wisdom and willingness that are inculcated by grace through lived spiritualities.

See also **Spirituality and Scripture** (*essay*); **Affectivity; Discipline; Emotions; Practice, Spiritual; Virtue.**

Dietrich Bonhoeffer, *The Cost of Discipleship*, New York: Simon & Schuster, 1995; James M. Gustafson, *Can Ethics Be Christian?* Chicago: University of Chicago Press, 1975; Gene Outka and John Reeder (eds), *Religion and Morality: A Collection of Essays,* Garden City, NJ: Doubleday, 1973; Karl Rahner, *The Love of Jesus and the Love of Neighbor,* New York: Crossroad, 1983.

WILLIAM C. SPOHN

Eucharistic Spirituality

The twenty-first century finds Christians the inheritors of a complex tradition about the Eucharist ('thanksgiving'). Being a 'companion', that is, eating with someone, is fundamental to human community and to conviviality (life together), irrespective of any specific religious belief. Precisely because it is so central, however, it is unsurprising that human communities find that the offering of hospitality in a shared meal may be charged with significance, depending on the occasion. And those who know what starvation is like or who live in insecurity may be readier both to give thanks for what they enjoy together, and to be more generously charitable and hospitable, not least to strangers, than those whose affluence and experience of stability may disguise from them the extent to which they depend on others, giving thanks for what they receive and are able to share. Participation in eucharistic ceremony is deemed by most, but by no means all Christian communities, to be integral to how human beings become themselves most fully in relation to God.

The emergence of the Christian Eucharist, however, is by no means entirely clear to us, though careful exegesis of New Testament and other closely related texts gives us some clues (Hurtado, 1999). For instance, the injunction to 'Greet one another with a kiss of charity' (1 Peter 5.16) is one indication of how the early experience of worship enabled a gathering of people to overcome major differences in social status in their lives. Joy and fervour seem to have been characteristic of these communities, with Christ revered and experienced as divine, as the one who provides and presides over the meal which believers share with one another and with him. Participation in such a community meant not participating in a range of social events at which other 'gods' were invoked and enjoyed. To that extent, early Christian worshippers were like Jews in renouncing the worship of all other divinities, while profoundly differing from Jews in the reverence given to Christ as divine. After the destruction of Jerusalem in AD 70, moreover, Judaism as it developed had largely to live without sacrifices. Whereas someone in the Temple had offered a substitute for himself, 'as if he were the substitute, substitutes had as it were to be found for the substituted (Fishbane, 1998). The 'breath' of the devout reading of paragraphs in the Torah dealing with the incense offering in the Temple now took the place of the offering of that incense, for example; and acts of ethics and piety structured into the life of communities as ever found ready prompting in the Scriptures which became Christian Scripture too. The humility towards and dependence on God of Psalm 51.17 ('The sacrifices of God are a broken spirit: a broken and a contrite heart, O God, thou wilt not despise') are the words of one 'as if' he had offered sacrifice. Romans 12 exemplifies the point.

Mutual interdependence sustained new Christian communities as it sustained the communities from which they were derived, and eating together was central to identifying specifically Christian groups in contradistinction from other devout believers. That said, very little in the new Christian Scriptures as they were developed over the centuries and accepted as authorized reading (and much remained outside that authorized list) tells us in detail about just how a thanksgiving meal was celebrated. Given the diversity of the record of Christ's eating with his disciples and acquaintances during his earthly life, reflection on the significance of his last meal with those closest to him, meals with Christ risen and glorified, and then post-Pentecost, post-baptism experience (e.g. Acts 2.41–47), a thanksgiving meal could take many forms. It was certainly to be distinguished from the rites of the religions from which Christians wished to be dissociated.

Quite what Christ himself intended by the words recorded of him at his last meal remains somewhat contentious, as is the significance of his death. Two points seem clear, however. One is that the Eucharist had its origin in an occasion of hospitality betrayed (Ps. 41.9; John 13) and of blundering, misplaced expressions of loyalty by those who had not learned that their lives depended on divine fidelity to them rather than on their own resources (Luke 22.34 and parallels). The other point is that Jesus' death was believed to have a 'once-for-all' character in respect of putting human beings into a different relationship with God. If, so to speak, Christ were thought to have reversed the substitution of an animal for a human being by offering himself in place of an animal, at once priest and offering in joyous dedicatory sacrifice, then while Christians might believe themselves to be joined by Christ into his joyous dedication to God, certainly they could not be supposed to be putting themselves right with God (Atwood, 2004, Herbert, 1991, Wesley, 1995). It does not require an understanding of Christ's death as 'sacrifice', however, or the Eucharist as a 'commemorative representation' of his 'sacrificial' death (John Paul II) to make the outrageous claim that in his being betrayed, suffering utter humiliation and a brutal end, human beings are to recognize a supreme manifestation of divine charity, into which they are caught up by participation in the Eucharist. The Eucharist itself, however, depends upon Christ's relationship to God beyond his death, in resurrection and ascension and the transformation of his humanity, and his continued intercessory presence to humanity. It is by participation in the Eucharist that believers are nourished, cleansed, healed and sanctified, and, in anticipation at least, transformed into a new humanity.

As Henri de Lubac has made clear, in the first millennium at least in the West, the Latin phrase *corpus Christi* (body of Christ) meant either the historical body of Christ or the Church, and *corpus Christi mysticum* (the mystical body of Christ) meant the 'eucharistic body', Christ's personal presence in the celebration of the Eucharist, as it became a ceremonial occasion during the first centuries of the Church's life. A twelfth-century monastic text, familiar in many musical settings, captures the significance of 'the mystical body of Christ' in a way which remains profoundly important. It reads: '*O sacrum convivium, in quo Christus sumitur, memoria passionis eius celebratur, mens impletur gratiae, et pignus futurae gloriae nobis datur*'; 'O sacred banquet in which Christ is received, the memory of his passion is renewed, the soul is filled with grace, and the pledge of future glory is given us.' The text centres on the centrality of Christ, risen, ascended and present; the transformative plenitude of grace; and orientation towards a fulfilment of life to which Christ summons his 'body' (Wainwright, 1978). Taking this seriously requires a major shift in the understanding of the trajectory of one's life (Pannenberg, 1983, Grenz, 1991).

That text, however, marked the threshold of a period of intense controversy about the Eucharist which had disastrous consequences for Western Christianity, for relationships with the Orthodox family of churches, and for relationships between Christians today, when some hold that participation in the Eucharist is a means by which communion between Christians will be established, and others deny that the grounds for such intercommunion yet exist. Inherited differences in understanding have thus become major obstacles to precisely the growth in charity and gratitude which lie at the heart of the Eucharist. Controversy centred on just how believers were united to the 'real presence' of Christ in the Eucharist. Were they related to the risen and ascended Christ by faith, and in reconciliation with the Church? In that case, the basic 'elements' of the meal remained what they were. If, however, Christ made himself available to believers in and through the 'elements', then they could be supposed to be transformed in some way, while apparently remaining exactly what they were. To the extent that this latter conviction was given priority, then devotion and piety centred on the bread and wine, on 'words of institution' and so on, rather than on the presence of the Spirit of Christ in the whole ceremony and on the participation of those present. The words *corpus Christi* or *corpus verum* (true body) now came to be used of the Eucharist, and *corpus Christi mysticum* of the Church. However problematic the shift, as we view it in hindsight, the establishment of the Feast of Corpus Christi, inspired by the visions of Juliana, Abbess in Liège, resulted in some of Thomas Aquinas' richest liturgical texts, including hymns.

The second millennium therefore saw controversy about the meaning of this most central ceremony, and that controversy was expressed not merely in verbal argument, but in architecture, music, painting, vestments, movement, decorative arts of all kinds, the degree to which the laity participate, devotional poetry, and intense focus on Christ's body as the source of the Eucharist (Finaldi, 2000, MacGregor, 2000). Recovered in the twentieth century has been a refocusing on the personal presence of Christ and the Spirit sustaining freedom for communion in the Eucharist, and a renewed focus on the social and indeed political implications of eucharistic fellowship. However provisional ultimately such expressions of the Eucharist may be in respect of the divine gift of ultimate fulfilment, we cannot become 'body' of Christ if, for instance, starvation, deep-seated poverty, the displacement and decimation of populations in war, racism, the resort to violence and the provocation of hatred remain characteristic of the dealings human beings have with one another (Codina, 1993, de Gruchy, 1991). Liturgical revisions of eucharistic ceremonies generously allow, as they must, for the variability of meaning and insight inherited by Christian communities, and the attempt to find sufficient agreement in the necessary diversity so that Eucharist becomes 'companionship' and 'conviviality' and does not signify the division and exclusion which so contradict its core meanings. Isak Dinesen/Karen Blixen's superb short story, 'Babette's Feast', makes the point perfectly.

See also **Food; Ecclesiology and Spirituality; Sacramentality and Spirituality.**

———

David Brown and David Fuller, *Signs of Grace. Sacraments in Poetry and Prose*, London and New York: Continuum, 2003; David Brown and Ann Loades (eds), *Christ: The Sacramental Word. Incarnation, Sacrament and Poetry*, London: SPCK, 1996; Larry Hurtado, *At the Origins of Christian Worship: The Context and Character of Earliest Christian Devotion*, Carlisle: Paternoster, 1999; David N. Power, *The Eucharistic Mystery.*

Revitalizing the Tradition, New York: Crossroad, 1992; Susan A. Ross, *Extravagant Affections: A Feminist Sacramental Theology*, New York: Continuum, 1998; Geoffrey Rowell and Christine Hall (eds), *The Gestures of God: Explorations in Sacramentality*, London and New York: Continuum, 2004 (essays from an ecumenical colloquium held in 2003).

Additional reading: Craig D. Atwood, *Community of the Cross: Moravian Piety in Colonial Bethlehem*, University Park, PA: Pennsylvania State University Press, 2004; Charles Caspers, Gerard Lukken and Gerard Rouwhorst (eds), *Bread of Heaven: Customs and Practices Surrounding Holy Communion: Essays in the History of Liturgy and Culture*, Kampen: Kok Pharos Publishing House, 1995; Victor Codina, 'Sacraments' in Ignacio Ellacuría and Jon Sobrino (eds), *Mysterium Liberationis: Fundamental Concepts of Liberation Theology*, Maryknoll, NY: Orbis Books/North Blackburn, Victoria: Collinsdove, 1993, pp. 654–76; William R. Crockett, 'Holy Communion' in Stephen Sykes, John Booty and Jonathan Knight (eds), *The Study of Anglicanism* (rev. edn), London: SPCK/Minneapolis: Fortress Press, 1998; John W. De Gruchy, *Liberating Reformed Theology: A South African Contribution to an Ecumenical Debate*, Grand Rapids, MI: Eerdmans, 1991; Isak Dinesen/Karen Blixen, 'Babette's Feast' in *Anecdotes of Destiny*, Harmondsworth: Penguin, 1958, pp. 23–68 (see also the recent film); Doctrine Commission of the Church of England, 'Retelling the story' in *The Mystery of Salvation: The Story of God's Gift*, London: Church House Publishing, 1995, pp. 102–19; Faith and Order Committee Report to the Methodist Conference 2003, *His Presence Makes the Feast: Holy Communion in the Methodist Church*, Peterborough: Methodist Publishing House, 2003; Gabriele Finaldi et al., *The Image of Christ*, London: National Gallery Company, 2000, distributed by Yale University Press (see especially pp. 169–207 on 'The saving body' and 'The abiding presence'); Peter E. Fink (ed.), *The New Dictionary of Sacramental Worship*, Dublin: Gill & Macmillan, 1990; Michael Fishbane, 'Substitutes for sacrifice in Judaism' in *The Exegetical Imagination: On Jewish Thought and Theology*, Cambridge, MA and London: Harvard University Press, 1998, pp. 123–35; Edward Foley, *From Age to Age: How Christians Celebrated the Eucharist*, Chicago, IL: Liturgy Training Publications, 1991; Stanley J. Grenz, 'Sacramental spirituality, ecumenism, and mission to the world: foundational motifs of Pannenberg's ecclesiology', *Mid-Stream* 30 (1991), 20–34; Adrian Hastings, Alistair Mason and Hugh Pyper (eds), *The Oxford Companion to Christian Thought*, Oxford: Oxford University Press, 2000 (articles on 'Blood', 'Body', 'Eucharist', 'Sacrament', 'Spirituality', 'Symbolism'); George Herbert, 'Sacrifice' in the collection of his work, *The Complete English Poems*, London: Penguin, 1991, pp. 23–31; John Paul II, *Ecclesia de Eucharistia: Encyclical Letter on the Eucharist and the Church*, London: Catholic Truth Society, 2003; Denise Levertov, 'Mass for the Day of St Thomas Didymus' in *Selected Poems*, Newcastle upon Tyne: Bloodaxe Books, 1986, pp. 175–81; Neil MacGregor, *Seeing Salvation: Images of Christ in Art*, London: BBC Worldwide, 2000; Herbert McCabe, 'Transubstantiation and the real presence' in *God Matters*, London: Cassell, 1987, pp. 116–29; David Martin, *Christian Language in the Secular City*, Aldershot: Ashgate, 2002; Wolfhart Pannenberg, 'Eucharistic Piety – a new experience of Christian community' in *Christian Spirituality and Sacramental Community*, London: Darton, Longman & Todd, 1983, pp. 31–49; Margaret Spufford, *Celebration: A Story of Suffering and Joy* (1989), London: Mowbray, 1996; Thomas Aquinas, *Devoutly I Adore Thee: The Prayers and Hymns of St Thomas Aquinas*, trans. and ed. Robert Anderson and Johann Moser, Manchester, NH: Sophia Institute Press, 1993; Evelyn Underhill, *Eucharistic Prayers from the Ancient Liturgies*, London: Longmans, Green, 1939; Evelyn Underhill, *The School of Charity: Meditations on the Christian Creed* [1934] and *The Mystery of Sacrifice: A Meditation on the Liturgy* [1938], London: Longmans, Green, 1956; Geoffrey Wainwright, *Eucharist and Eschatology* [1971], London: Epworth Press, 1978; Charles Wesley Society, *Proceedings of the Charles Wesley Society*, vol. 2, *Hymns of the Lord's Supper: 250 Years*, Madison, NJ: Charles Wesley Society, 1994–96; John and Charles Wesley, *Hymns on the Lord's Supper*, introd. Geoffrey Wainwright, facsimile of the 1745 first edition, Madison, NJ: Charles Wesley Society, 1995.

ANN LOADES

Evangelical Spirituality

Evangelicalism is a pan-denominational movement within Protestantism which took shape in the eighteenth century and was particularly associated with revival in Britain led by John Wesley (1703–91) and George Whitefield (1714–70), and the Great Awakening in North America, where Jonathan Edwards (1703–58) was the leading thinker. David Bebbington, in his book *Evangelicalism in Modern Britain*, has spoken of conversionism, crucicentrism, biblicism and activism as the four hallmarks of evangelicalism. He argues that the decade beginning in 1734 'witnessed in the English-speaking world a more important development than any other, before or after, in the history of Protestant Christianity: the emergence of the movement that became Evangelicalism'.

Although evangelical spirituality (more often known as piety) took different forms, with the Wesleyan stream, for example, emphasizing the possibility of Christian perfection, there have been certain distinctives which have characterized the movement as a whole. Evangelical spirituality is biblically orientated. It is through hearing the message of God's grace in Scripture that a person is converted and experiences assurance of salvation. There is a strong focus on individual Bible reading and serious Bible study as a means of spiritual growth. This attention to the written word was well expressed by John Wesley, who said 'Let me be *homo unius libri*' (a man of one book). One of the most influential evangelical Anglicans of the nineteenth century, Charles Simeon (1759–1836), Vicar of Holy Trinity Church, Cambridge, wrote: 'Religion is the regulation of our lives by God's holy word.'

Often this dedication to Scripture has meant a discipline of daily devotion which involves both reading and prayer. In the midst of a very busy life, William Wilberforce (1759–1833), known for his anti-slavery campaigning in Britain, spent two hours each day before breakfast, praying and studying the Bible. He once wrote: 'I have been keeping too late hours, and hence I have had but a hurried half an hour in the morning to myself. Surely it is the experience of all good men that without a due measure of private devotions the soul grows lean.' Thus reading of scripture was not primarily to acquire knowledge but to deepen a relationship with Christ. As an international evangelical leader of the twentieth century, John Stott, put it, 'to be a Christian is to live . . . through, on, in, under, with, for and like Jesus Christ.'

Personal Bible reading and prayer have been seen as belonging together in the evangelical tradition. But by comparison with the place of prayer in other Christian traditions there were few guides to prayer in the early period of evangelicalism. Simeon's new edition of *Evangelical Meditations* (1802) was popular, as were two other evangelical Anglican contributions, Edward Bickersteth's *A Treatise on Prayer* (1826) and Hannah More's *Spirit of Prayer*. Henry Thornton, an associate of Wilberforce's, wrote a popular book of family prayers. Especially among Free Church evangelicals, however, there has been a fear of using the prayers of others since each person should approach God directly, using their own words.

Corporate spirituality within historic evangelicalism has made the preaching of the Bible central. Martyn Lloyd-Jones (1899–1981), minister of Westminster Chapel, London, and one of the greatest evangelical preachers of the twentieth century, spoke of preaching as 'theology on fire'. Within the life of evangelical congregations, meetings for corporate prayer have been common. John Newton (1725–1807), a former slave trader who became an Anglican clergyman, said: 'I look upon prayer meetings as the most profitable exercise in which Christians can engage. They have a direct tendency to kill a worldly and trifling spirit, to draw down a divine blessing on all our concerns and to deal with differences and kindle the flame of divine love among the brethren.' Newton is also an example of another feature of corporate evangelical spirituality: hymn-singing. The place of hymn-singing was established by Charles Wesley, and Newton, through writing hymns such as 'Amazing Grace', reinforced this aspect.

Expressions of evangelical devotion have in fact been less uniformly individualistic than is often thought. It is true that evangelical commitment begins with conversion, which is almost always regarded as intensely personal, but evangelical piety shares with other approaches to spiritual experience an awareness that individual spirituality is worked out in wider contexts. Thus, as well as public worship, there has been the use of small groups, for example Methodist class meetings. In the later twentieth century evangelical churches of most denominations and in many different countries adopted house groups, at which prayer, Bible study and sharing of experiences take place, as a pattern of mid-week church life.

A further feature of evangelical spirituality has been an emphasis on holiness. Often the primary concern has been for personal holiness, although John Wesley also taught the importance of 'social holiness'. There have been different views about how such holiness is to be achieved. Andrew Fuller (1754–1815), an influential English Baptist within the Calvinistic strand of evangelicalism, typically held that holiness was fostered by the Bible. He wrote: 'The more we read the Holy Scriptures, the more we shall imbibe their spirit and be formed by them as a model.' In the nineteenth century, however, the Calvinist tendency to see holiness as arising from effort was challenged. The new holiness movement, as it was called, found lasting expression in the Keswick Convention, dating from 1875, which had a considerable influence across the world. Here the stress was on the achievement of the holy life through 'full surrender' and 'holiness by faith'.

The Keswick approach to spirituality helped to shape the prevailing pattern of piety within English-speaking evangelicalism for a good part of the twentieth century. Keswick's roots were in the holiness revivalism of the nineteenth century, with its Wesleyan affinities. The British holiness movement owed much to American holiness teachers such as Charles Finney (1792–1875), Phoebe Palmer (1807–74) and Robert and Hannah Pearsall Smith. Keswick's founding fathers, however, such as the Anglican Evan Hopkins (1837–1919), constructed what they saw as temperate holiness doctrine, consonant with the Calvinistic sympathies of much British evangelicalism. Keswick was also interdenominational, its motto being 'All One in Christ Jesus'. Anglicans predominated, with Bishop Handley Moule (1842–1920) being the movement's best-known ecclesiastical figure, but a Baptist, F. B. Meyer (1847–1929), was Keswick's most renowned international speaker. The best known hymn-writer of the Keswick movement was Frances Ridley Havergal (1836–1879), probably the greatest evangelical hymn-writer of the nineteenth century.

Keswick was criticized by some for teaching sinless perfection and for the elitism of some of its early terminology, such as 'the higher Christian life'. A significant evangelical critique of Keswick spirituality was a book written by J. C. Ryle (1816–1900), Bishop of Liverpool, simply entitled *Holiness*. In a famous outburst by one Anglican, Keswick was described as 'damnable heresy'. But Keswick spirituality always taught, according to its leading proponents, that sin could be countered yet never eradicated. This did not, however, satisfy some of those in the Wesleyan holiness Arminian tradition, who held out the possibility that a Christian could be free from sin in this life.

Despite such differences, the outworking of holiness among evangelicals was fairly standard. Seeing the cross of Christ as at the heart of the experience of salvation, evangelicals went on to view the Christian life as one in which disciples of Christ were called to give up their own way and follow the crucified Saviour. There have been many activities which evangelicals have seen as incompatible with holiness. In earlier evangelicalism, the theatre was taboo. In other periods dances and the cinema were regarded as 'worldly'. There was also great concern not to be like the world in the use of Sunday. The Victorian Sabbath was not entirely a creation of evangelicalism, but evangelical spirituality was a strong influence. Commitment to total abstinence also became a feature of many later nineteenth-century evangelicals.

A final feature of evangelical spirituality has been active engagement in evangelism, aimed at bringing people to an experience of conversion. For this to take place, the spiritual life of the Christian has to be properly nourished. Henry Venn (1796–1873), the first General Secretary of the Church of England's Church Missionary Society, said: 'A feeble, nominal Christianity is the greatest obstacle to the conversion of the world.' The sense of duty to evangelize has at times been stimulated by the eschatological views held by evangelicals. Many earlier evangelicals were postmillennial, believing that the gospel would spread throughout the world. Often this led to active social concern. In the later nineteenth century evangelicals tended towards a premillennial view. This generated a feeling of living in the last times. The American evangelist Dwight L. Moody (1837–99) spoke of the world as a wrecked vessel. The call was to save as many people as possible.

New movements influenced evangelical spirituality in the twentieth century. In England the Anglican Evangelical Group Movement, centred on the Cromer Convention, introduced elements of high church devotion, such as the use of retreats, to evangelicals of the 1920s and 1930s. In the same period Pentecostalism became an increasingly important force within world-wide evangelical life, to be followed by the charismatic movement from the 1960s. Both these movements emphasized the Holy Spirit coming with power, bringing gifts such as speaking in tongues, prophecy and healing. Under the guidance of leaders such as John Stott and Billy Graham, evangelicals have become more world-affirming, recovering an older evangelical tradition of social involvement. In evangelical Anglican churches more frequent celebration of the Eucharist is evident.

In recent years there has been an attempt on the part of evangelicals to analyse their spiritual tradition, for instance David Gillett's *Trust and Obey*. For one leading evangelical theologian, Alister McGrath, evangelicalism is 'the slumbering giant in the world of spirituality'.

See also **Anglican Spirituality; Charismatic Spirituality; Conversion; Cross and Spirituality; Holiness; Jesus and Spirituality; Methodist Spirituality; Moravian Spirituality; Pietism; Piety.**

D. W. Bebbington, *Holiness in Nineteenth-Century England*, Carlisle: Paternoster Press, 2000; D. K. Gillett, *Trust and Obey*, London: Darton, Longman & Todd, 1993; J. M. Gordon, *Evangelical Spirituality*, London: SPCK, 1991; B. Hindmarsh, *John Newton and the English Evangelical Tradition*, Oxford: Oxford University Press, 1996; C. Price and I. M. Randall, *Transforming Keswick*, Carlisle: Paternoster Press, 2000; I. M. Randall, *Evangelical Experiences: A Study in the Spirituality of English Evangelicalism, 1918–1939*, Carlisle: Paternoster Press, 1999.

IAN M. RANDALL

Evangelization and Spirituality

Evangelization means literally 'an offer of good news' or 'a welcome message'. That the term should historically be so closely associated with the art of communication, however, may be a liability in modern Western culture, given our predilection for thinking of communication as information delivery, especially in the form of sentences or bits of data. Evangelization may then be reduced to proclamation, and the gospel to a set of propositions. Characterizing evangelization in terms of 'a message' or 'news' may likewise disguise the fact that throughout history, as Scripture testifies, God calls and forms a people who, through its worship and obedience, is itself God's message and offer to the world – a living 'letter', as Paul puts it (2 Cor. 3.3). From the earliest apostolic communities whose visible reconciliation of Jew and Gentile modelled a new social possibility, to the martyr communities of the first centuries that refused to worship the emperor or fight his wars, to the more recent base communities of Latin America in which the poor are both valued and find voice, the Christian witness to the gospel is inseparable from the form of life in which that gospel is embodied. We need not denigrate proclamation, therefore, to insist that at the heart of evangelization is the Spirit's formation of a people (what the early Christians called *ecclesia*) into a distinctive set of habits, practices, disciplines and loyalties that together constitute a visible and recognizable pattern before a watching world (Yoder, 2001). Given that 'the medium is the message', as has frequently been noted, Christian spirituality is no merely private or interior piety but a way of walking, seeing, listening and being present in the world that itself constitutes both a public offer and that to which the offer points. To evangelize is not merely to invite persons to believe the truth of the Christian story in some detached, abstract way, but to invite persons to make the Christian story their own by having their lives patterned after that story and into the very life of Christ. But this invitation requires a community of evangelists whose lives have themselves been saturated by the Christian story such that its beginning is their beginning, its journey their journey, its end their end. In worship, in disciplines such as prayer, meditation or protest, and in practices such as confession, fraternal admonition and eucharistic celebration, we are made faithful 'rememberers' of that story and thus capable of faithfully narrating it and offering it to others. Indeed, our gift to the world as Christians is precisely our difference from the world manifest in a new 'timefulness' made possible by such practices and disciplines. As Alexander Schmemann says, if it were only a soul that needed saving, we would need no 'calendar' (Schmemann, 1997, p. 52). Thus, one of the ways we evangelize the world is by keeping time for it – by remembering the Sabbath, and by 'feasting' properly, with joy and thanksgiving for the gift of life.

Spirituality is thus internally related to evangelization. Moreover, just as evangelization requires distinctive practices of spiritual formation both as the source and aim of its offer, so also this process of 'making' new Christians stands in contrast to other processes of formation and, frequently, as a form of resistance to them. That the Church has something to offer the world is embodied in its visible difference from the world: its refusal of war, violence and revenge in favour of love of enemies, forgiveness and peacemaking; its rejection of an economics of scarcity and competition in favour of material sharing with one's neighbour and extravagance toward the poor; its reversal of deeply ingrained patterns of exclusion and domination in favour of egalitarian embrace. A faith deeply formed by Christian worship, practices and spiritual disciplines is the necessary but also sufficient condition for evangelizing the world.

But then perhaps we can also conclude not only that spirituality and evangelization are internally related, but that this relationship is a two-way relationship. If we can imagine Christian formation as something like a craft apprenticeship which includes the ongoing process of observation, imitation, internalization and innovation (Budde and Bromlow, p. 60) this apprenticeship includes one further dimension – namely, the cultivation of a willingness, confidence and patience to apprentice others. Evangelization is the Church's practice of living the Christian story openly, imaginatively, and in such a way that it can be taken seriously and then accepted or rejected responsibly. Fidelity to the gospel requires that what we have been given as a gift in turn be offered to the world. What we have been given is salvation in Christ in the form of a new peoplehood, the body of Christ. It is this that we extend to the world. But in order for this gift to become a serious option *for* the world, it must be visibly embodied *in* the world.

See also **Conversion; Discipleship; Ecclesiology and Spirituality; Mission and Spirituality; Formation, Spiritual.**

William Abraham, *The Logic of Evangelism*, Grand Rapids, MI: Eerdmans, 1989; Mortimer Arias, *Announcing the Reign of God: Evangelization and the Subversive Memory of Jesus*, Philadelphia: Fortress Press, 1984; Michael L. Budde and Robert W. Brimlow, *Christianity Incorporated: How Big Business Is Buying the Church*, Grand Rapids, MI: Brazos Press, 2002; Darell L. Guder, *The Continuing Conversion of the Church*, Grand Rapids, MI: Eerdmans, 2000; Walter Klaiber, *Call and Response: Biblical Foundations of a Theology of Evangelism*, Nashville, TN: Abingdon Press, 1997; Alexander Schmemann, *For the Life of the World: Sacraments and Orthodoxy*, Crestwood, NY: St Vladimir's Seminary Press, 1997; John Howard Yoder, *Body Politics: Five Practices of the Christian Community Before the Watching World*, Scottdale, PA: Herald Press, 2001.

BRYAN STONE

Examination of Conscience/ Consciousness

The examination of conscience or of consciousness is a personal reflection, which focuses on how God moves and rests within one's life. The term *examination of conscience* has a troubled history because it had long been associated almost exclusively with the mechanical effort to eradicate personal sins and faults. Interpreted in this light, the examination of conscience appeared to be introspective faultfinding. Moreover, as a practice, it was relegated to something one did at the beginning of a dedicated spiritual life but could soon outgrow and, more or less, discard.

However, a renaissance in Ignatian spirituality refocused interest in the insistence Ignatius Loyola made on the role of the examination of conscience in the lives of busy and distracted apostolic workers. The revisiting of the phrase and a renewed appreciation for the power of the practice led to a new term, *examination of consciousness*.

The examination of consciousness engages one's personal integrity, that harmony between what one says and what one does or the integration between values and performance, and the grace to appreciate the accompanying presence of God's Spirit in the life of the sincerely religious person. This emphasis on personal integrity is close to what Ignatius Loyola called 'purity of intention'. It is self-awareness before God.

As a particular practice the examination of consciousness is usually described as having five stages of encounter between the man or woman who seeks and God who responds. The first stage is a request for light, particularly from the Holy Spirit, to see one's present life as God sees that life. It comes from a consciousness that asks to know as it is known, in love and regard by the God who created and nurtured and saved it. The second stage is an act of gratitude and thanksgiving for all the ways that God has donated life and love in an ordinary day. The third stage of the examination is a synoptic survey of where the day reveals personal fears and lapses, sins and struggles, in the honest effort to live a life of companionship with God. The fourth stage moves into contrition, a heartfelt acceptance that where one presently is represents the place where God most loves one. In other words, it is the highly personal acceptance of redemption here and now. The fifth and final stage moves into the future, in the company of God whose great gift is hope.

These five stages represent a developmental model of practical prayer, from light to gratitude to insight to forgiveness to new hope within the life a person has been called to lead in and with God. The five stages of the examination of consciousness are helpful methods or approaches towards settling down and guiding one's mind and heart in the midst of the demands and deadlines that characterize contemporary life. Finally, the examination of consciousness is a movement from reflection about one's service to rededication to that service.

The value of the examination of consciousness lies in the way individuals can adapt the five stages to their particular needs and demands. Some days a person may feel a need for light and that will constitute his or her examination of consciousness. Other days one can discover quickly that some great gift has been given and will spend the fifteen-minute period in thanksgiving. Through adaptation to one's needs and available time, the examination of consciousness provides an orientation and a practical methodology for finding God within one's daily life.

See also **Conscience; Discernment; Ignatian Spirituality; Reflection; Relationships; Retreats; Spirit, Holy; Thanksgiving.**

George Aschenbrenner, 'Consciousness examen', *Review for Religious* 31 (1972), 14–21; Avery Dulles, 'Finding God's will', *Woodstock Letters* 94.2 (Spring 1965), 139–52; Donald St Louis, 'The Ignatian examen', in Philip Sheldrake (ed.), *The Way of St Ignatius*, London: SPCK/St Louis: Institute of Jesuit Sources, 1991, pp. 154–64.

HOWARD GRAY

Exegesis, Spiritual

In the patristic and medieval periods spiritual or allegorical exegesis, which sought the revealed meaning of the biblical text, was contrasted to literal or historical exegesis which was concerned with the words themselves. The ancients recognized the importance of ascertaining the literal sense but considered it imperative to get beyond it to the real meaning. This twofold understanding of the 'senses' of Scripture, which can be traced back to Origen (second century), developed into a threefold and eventually fourfold understanding in which the spiritual sense was subdivided into the allegorical or theological, tropological or moral, and anagogical or eschatological meanings. The goal of exegesis was to attain to the spiritual meaning under one or more of these headings.

Spiritual exegesis responded to several concerns. It allowed the interpreter, by allegorical interpretation, to find a meaning worthy of God in texts which seemed banal or even scandalous. It facilitated, by the use of typology, the christological interpretation of the Old Testament and thus the unity of the Christian Bible. But most importantly, it got beyond a fixation on either the words in themselves or the purely historical reference to the life-giving meaning of the text for the contemporary reader.

With the rise of historical criticism in the modern period spiritual exegesis fell into disrepute among scholars. The text was believed to have only one sense or meaning, namely, that intended by the author, which was presumed to be historical. Allegorical interpretation, which was the very soul of spiritual exegesis, appeared fantastic to the higher critics. This was a major misunderstanding of the ancient notion of allegory which was not merely a one-to-one comparison of the text to some extra-textual reality to which it did not refer. Allegory denoted any kind of more-than-literal language such as metaphor, symbolic discourse or parable. Allegorical interpretation was not only a quest for the meaning of the text 'intended by God' but also attention to the text as literature. The spiritual sense was accessed by careful and critical attention to the letter but went beyond it. Without doubt, it sometimes went beyond not only the literal but also beyond any legitimate sense. This, however, was much rarer than modern exegetes believed to be the case.

Today, biblical scholars are rediscovering the genius if not the actual methods of spiritual exegesis. It belongs to the area of hermeneutics rather than exegesis, that is, to interpretation which is based on critical exegesis but not arrested at the analytical level. As late twentieth-century biblical scholars moved beyond exclusively historical critical approaches they focused first on the biblical writers as authors with theological and other agendas pursued by various rhetorical strategies. This led to a focus on the text itself as literature. And this led inevitably to a focus on the reader whose interaction with the text gives rise to meaning. Readers do not simply work on texts but the text works on the reader, for good or for ill. The pragmatics of reading came into focus and this is the sphere of spiritual interpretation.

Ideology criticism (e.g. feminist) and ethical as well as spiritual interpretation have in common their starting point in the experience of the reader and their purpose which is social and/or personal transformation. The term 'spiritual exegesis' is probably best left in its pre-critical context where it has a specific reference. Its contemporary successor is biblical spirituality as a process of transformative (rather than purely informative) engagement with the text. It differs from patristic or medieval allegorical interpretation and from monastic *lectio divina* in that it makes full use of modern exegetical methods. But it shares the ancient concern with the biblical text as sacred scripture which mediates God's word to and in the Church.

See also **Spirituality and Scripture** (*essay*); *Lectio Divina.*

Raymond E. Brown and Sandra M. Schneiders, 'Hermeneutics' in Raymond E. Brown, Joseph A. Fitzmyer and Roland E. Murphy (eds), *The New Jerome Biblical Commentary*, Englewood Cliffs, NJ: Prentice-Hall, 1990, pp. 1146–65; R. P. C. Hanson, 'Biblical exegesis in the early Church' in *The Cambridge History of the Bible*, vol. 1, Cambridge: Cambridge University Press, 1970, pp. 412–53; David C. Steinmetz, 'The superiority of pre-critical exegesis', *Theology Today* 37 (1980), 27–38; Susan K. Wood, *Spiritual Exegesis and the Church in the Theology of Henri de Lubac*, Edinburgh: T & T Clark/Grand Rapids, MI: Eerdmans, 1998.

SANDRA M. SCHNEIDERS

Exile

The image of exile is a particular form of the journey image. It is distinctive, because it implies both that the travellers are out of the place they recognize as their own, and that, unlike the travelling of pilgrims or tourists, their journey is not chosen but responds to some personal or national catastrophe.

In the older Testament the two dominant narratives are journeys – the Exodus from Egypt into the promised land, and the exile of the Jews into Babylon, followed by their return to Jerusalem. The two journeys coincide in culminating in the possession of the promised land, the first by entry and the second by return. The exile also forms the context within which many of the biblical books were written.

The exile into Babylon is described in many ways. In the simplest view, it embodies God's judgement on the people of Israel for their infidelity. But it also comes to have a larger significance: it can be accepted because in it God's larger purposes are seen to be fulfilled. In the experience of exile is revealed something of God's nature and relationship to the people of Israel. Because the people understand that God is with them in exile, they are entitled to hope that the same God will act freely to restore them. The exile can at once be represented as a revelation of God's continuing mercy and grace within the experience of exile, and as a temporary painful experience in which we wait for God to intervene to bring us home.

The themes of disobedience, exile and hope for a land in which to live happily, associate the exile with other biblical stories, most notably with the story of creation and fall. It was naturally taken up into early Christian reflection on the death and resurrection of Jesus Christ who died outside the city. The exilic condition also was seen to fit Christian experience of being at home neither in Judaism nor in the empire. As resident aliens, they conceived their hope as eschatological.

The theme of exile was enriched and spiritualized in the orphic myths which Plato adapted. The myth of the *Phaedrus* was particularly significant. It depicted the destiny of the soul as being to rise to contemplation of spiritual reality. Some souls fell to earth because they were entangled in the material world. There they were to remain for ten thousand years, and subsequently either to contemplate the good or to fall further into animal life. This journey of ascent, fall and renewed ascent could readily be juxtaposed with the biblical stories of the creation of human beings and their exile from paradise. As Philo had done previously, Origen combines biblical and Platonist imagery. Augustine brings together masterfully the themes of the journeying soul and the exile to Babylon in his exposition of the Psalms. He sees Jerusalem as the home of those whose vision is fixed on eternity, while

Babylon is the home of those who are locked into this world. We spend our lives as sojourners dwelling in a strange land, our hearts properly fixed on the eternal.

Augustine's fusion of the soul's journey with the imagery of the exile to Babylon caught the imagination of his readers, and dominated later use of the theme of exile. It was, however, made more complex by being incorporated into the practices of monasticism and pilgrimage. Pilgrimage allowed pilgrims to leave their homes and journey to the place where Jesus lived and died, and to remember their exile in the place where he was at home. The desert spirituality, too, had to handle the reality of the monks' lives in which the spiritual image of exile was associated with their move away from settled places. The desert, a hard place, embodied the exile of the monk from paradise, but also became his home. This paradoxical interpretation of exile was carried over into the treatment of death, the final exile and the final homecoming.

These images became commonplace in late medieval spirituality. When reflecting on sin, for example, Ignatius Loyola could unselfconsciously use the imagery of the Christian Platonist tradition when speaking of the human condition. He described the soul in the body, as though it were in prison, and the whole person as in exile among wild beasts.

More modern developments in the spirituality of exile are coloured by the Romantic image of the alienated spirit, and by the Marxist location of this image in a historical, social and economic context. The figure of the outsider, alienated from society and culture by economic or psychological factors, is a commonplace in European literature. It is reflected in spiritualities that emphasize liberation from oppression based on class, gender, race or culture. Such spiritualities offer a practical path to liberation.

More recently, many Christian groups have been led by their passionate interest in the experience of refugees and asylum-seekers to appreciate more vividly the reality of exile. Jewish thinkers had earlier returned to the exilic texts when grappling with the theological significance of the Holocaust and the establishment of the State of Israel. When the experience of exile in such concrete and terrible forms presses strongly on the imagination, the use of the metaphor of exile purely for the human spiritual condition becomes problematic. To use the metaphor legitimately, it may be important to have entered the reality of those seeking asylum, and to have been in solidarity with exiles.

See also **Desert; Monastic Spirituality; Pilgrimage; Place; Social Justice.**

R. Klein, *Israel in Exile: A Theological Interpretation,* Philadelphia: Fortress Press, 1979; R. J. O'Connell, *Soundings in St Augustine's Imagination,* New York: Fordham University Press, 1994; E. Wiesel, *Evil and Exile,* Notre Dame, IN: University of Notre Dame Press, 1990.

ANDREW HAMILTON

Experience, Religious

In the beginning, as the French sociologist Émile Durkheim remarked, all is religious. But the Judaeo-Christian tradition has always recognized that there are special occasions when we become directly and vividly aware of the presence of God. The story in the Book of Exodus of Yahweh calling to Moses from the midst of a burning bush on Mount Horeb is a particularly dramatic instance, as is the vision of Yahweh in the temple, described in the Book of Isaiah. The disciples' experience of the transfiguration of Jesus on Mount Tabor and the conversion of St Paul on the road to Damascus are well known examples from the New Testament. Probably the most famous post-biblical description of hearing a call from God is St Augustine's conversion in a garden in Milan during the fourth century, as recorded in his *Confessions.* Subsequent Christian history is filled with similar stories, and modern survey data show that such occurrences, or something very like them, are still reported extremely commonly (if not always as spectacularly) even in highly secularized countries like the United Kingdom.

These accounts are examples of what would nowadays be called 'religious experience'. Something needs to be said about the use of this terminology. To set apart a particular dimension of human experience as 'religious' in contrast with other kinds of experience that are *not* religious, implies that there has been some withdrawal from the sense of a cosmos filled with the presence of God. It indicates a degree of secularization of consciousness, or disenchantment of the world, to use Max Weber's expression. Accordingly, it turns out that the term 'religious experience' has quite a brief history. Thus, the first printed reference noted in the Oxford English Dictionary is to a Quaker devotional work, *A Diary of the Religious Experience of Mary Waring,* published in 1809. Nevertheless its cultural antecedents lie a good deal further back, in doctrinal developments within the Puritan and Pietist branches of Protestant Christianity during the seventeenth century. In both communities there developed an emphasis on the need for a conscious experience of conversion which, in the case of the Puritans in particular, because of their adherence to the doctrine of predestination, was a means of obtaining reassurance that they were members of the elect. In England one of the initiators of this view was William Perkins (1558–1602). Perkins asserted, 'Herein stands the power and pith of true religion, when a man by observation and experience in himself, knows the love of God in Christ towards him.' It has been the watchword of Evangelical Christianity ever since.

At the end of the eighteenth century the emphasis on personal experience (though not necessarily only the experience of conversion), was elaborated theologically by the German Pietist, Friedrich Schleiermacher (1768–1834). He reacted against his sceptical colleagues' dismissal of religion on the basis of abstract philosophical arguments. His central axiom was that religion is not in the first place a matter of intellectual debate, nor of natural science, nor of adherence to dogmatic belief, but is the 'sense and taste for the infinite'. It is founded on the feeling of absolute dependence. He expanded this theme in *On Religion: Speeches to its Cultured Despisers* (1799) and later used it as the basis for a systematic theology in *The Christian Faith* (1821).

Many have been suspicious of Schleiermacher's insistence on the importance of religious experience. His most prominent critic during the twentieth century was Karl Barth (1886–1968) who alleged that he had reduced religion to pure subjectivity, thus leading to the focus of modern liberal theology on human potential at the expense of God's reality. Others have disputed this, asserting that Barth misunderstood the perceptual connotation of the word 'feeling' for Schleiermacher. That is to say, Schleiermacher was not implying that God is nothing but a creation of the human imagination, but that what is taking place is an encounter with divine transcendence. Major students of religion who have been influenced by Schleiermacher's views include Ernst Troeltsch (1865–1923), Rudolf Otto (1869–1937), and Joachim Wach (1898–1955).

Interest in religious experience took a scientific turn towards the end of the nineteenth century, particularly in North America. This was perhaps because Puritan influences, initiated by the arrival of the Pilgrim Fathers in New England in 1620, were still at this late stage dominant in the culture. Consequently when psychology was beginning to emerge as a separate discipline, a small group of scholars in the North Eastern United States began psychological investigations of religious experience, including G. Stanley

Hall, James Leuba, Edwin Starbuck and, most influentially, William James. James's Gifford Lectures at the University of Edinburgh during 1901 and 1902 are still considered to be the classic psychological study of religious experience. Published as *The Varieties of Religious Experience* and intended as a pragmatic defence of religion, the lectures proposed that 'the "more" with which in religious experience we feel ourselves connected is on its *hither* side the subconscious continuation of our conscious life'.

Although he was speaking from a context of New England Protestantism, James's eclectic use of illustrations from many different cultures implied that religious experience is a human universal to be found in some form everywhere. This is of course implicit in Schleiermacher's account of the religious consciousness, and it is a theme that was taken up influentially in the German philosopher/theologian Rudolf Otto's book *Das Heilige*, published in 1917. Otto argued that the sense of the Holy or *numinous* (a term he coined) is *sui generis,* that is to say, it cannot be explained away in other terms. His book offers a moving phenomenology of such experience as an encounter with the transcendent sacred, or as he called it, the *mysterium tremendum.*

The idea that religious experience is a human universal has led to the so-called 'common core' theory of religion. According to this view, however much the religions of the world may differ from each other culturally, they share, almost as their defining characteristic, that they are interpretations of a primary and irreducible encounter with the sacred. One resulting development during the past thirty years has been a growing interest in what it is in our biological nature that makes religious experience possible. In his Gifford lectures at Aberdeen University during the 1960s, the Oxford zoologist Alister Hardy suggested that it is based on an awareness that has evolved in the human species through the process of natural selection because it has survival value. While his hypothesis is naturalistic, Hardy explicitly contradicts those reductionist interpretations of religious experience that see it as symptomatic of false consciousness or pathology.

Hardy also believed that religious experience is much more commonplace than could be suspected from an examination of the secular assumptions of Western society. Subsequent research has confirmed that it is indeed widespread. For example a national survey conducted in Britain to coincide with Millennium 2000 suggested that about three-quarters of the adult population would probably claim to have had such experience. Similar figures are reported for Australia. Very recently there have also been attempts to identify the anatomical site of religious experience in the brain. The neurophysiologists V. S. Ramachandran at the University of San Diego and Eugene d'Aquili and Andrew Newberg at the University of Pennsylvania have each offered differing suggestions for the location of such experience.

The common core thesis has produced much debate. Several students of comparative religion have suggested that a detailed phenomenological analysis of the experiential dimension of different religious cultures refutes the common core idea. They assert that the differences are too wide to be plausibly explained on this basis. There have also been critical reflections on the ontological status of religious experience. Can it, for example, be used as evidence for the existence of God?

Ranged on one side are reductionists who draw upon Enlightenment critiques of religion that dismiss it as a widespread cultural error. Thus Freud interpreted religious experience as possibly symptomatic of a temporary psychosis, while other critics, including Marx, saw it as due to false attribution. A recent version of the latter view is that of the philosopher Wayne Proudfoot in his book *Religious Experience*. Proudfoot bases his critique on the fact that all human experience is already interpreted by the culture to which a person belongs. Hence so-called religious experience is given that attribution because of the religious culture out of which the person speaks and has no absolute validity.

It must be said that if what is described as religious experience is natural to the species, then its very universality makes the ascription 'religious' somewhat debatable. If it is implicitly part of the biological make-up of all human beings, this must include everyone, including those who reject religious belief. One response has been to replace the term 'religious experience' with the more general category of 'spiritual experience', defined as a sense of profound relationship with whatever the individual perceives as ultimate reality. The mystical writing of Richard Jefferies are a secular example of this perspective, as are the views of some recent Marxist writers. The Christian experience of the presence of God would then be a subset within such an overall understanding of spirituality. The case of atheistic religions (e.g. Theravada Buddhism) reminds us that this is an extremely complex issue, lately made more difficult by postmodern discussions of the role of language in the construction of experience.

Against this relativist view, other contemporary philosophers continue to maintain that religious experience is a matter of direct encounter with and recognition of God. Though given varying discursive structure by the cultural apparatus available to the experient, nevertheless it has its own ontological validity. A representative of this stance is William Alston in his book *Perceiving God*.

See also **Mysticism; Spirituality and Psychology; Spirituality and Science; Spirituality and Social Sciences (essays); Conversion; Enlightenment Thought; Feelings; Meditation; Presence of God.**

William P. Alston, *Perceiving God: the Epistemology of Religious Experience*, Ithaca, NY and London: Cornell University Press, 1991; Alister Hardy, *The Divine Flame: An Essay towards a Natural History of Religion*, London: Collins, 1966; David Hay, *Exploring Inner Space: Scientists and Religious Experience*, Oxford: Mowbray, 1987; William James, *The Varieties of Religious Experience*, London: Penguin Books, 1982 [1902]; Rudolf Otto, *The Idea of the Holy*, Oxford University Press, 1923; Wayne Proudfoot, *Religious Experience*, Berkeley, Los Angeles and London: University of California Press, 1985.

DAVID HAY

Faith

Even in ordinary language faith between people implies a special kind of knowing. It involves a decision to trust rather than a logic that verifies. It is more relational than measurable and hence 'a discernment within a commitment' (Avery Dulles). Religious faith is similar because it is 'the knowledge born from religious love' (Bernard Lonergan) and 'only love is believable' (von Balthasar). In the Christian tradition this means recognizing the self-revelation of God in Jesus Christ, but to respond to that gift involves various spiritual conditions. As in human friendship, if we try to stay neutral and outside, we block the growth of intimacy. Faith becomes difficult to reach if the disposition of a person remains closed or shallow. It needs a 'readiness for surprise' (Margaret MacCurtain), because it involves 'God perceived by the heart' (Pascal). As the young John Henry Newman wrote to his unbelieving brother, rejection of faith can stem 'from a fault of the heart, not of the intellect'. He put it more simply later in life: 'We believe because we love.' He was unconsciously echoing Aquinas: 'Where love exists, there is an eye'.

Therefore faith, in practice, cannot be separated from how we live. The courage to live unselfishly is both the gateway into faith and its essential fruit. To stress that faith is more a form of love-truth than of reason-truth does not mean that it is simply a matter of feeling or that it cannot ground itself intelligently (the anti-intellectual tendency called fideism). But faith is more than a matter of the mind and to do justice to it requires a larger spiritual horizon than is common in debates about the existence of God. People tend to identify faith with beliefs or doctrines: these come later as interpretations of the basic recognition 'I believe *in* you' (which is different from 'I believe *that* God exists'). Interestingly in John's Gospel faith never appears as a noun, but the verb to believe occurs more than a hundred times; in this way Christian faith is a dynamism born from recognizing God in Jesus, a choice in action more than a knowledge possessed. Therefore faith has to do with our transformation by the creative artistry of God, who in Christ enters the adventure of our meaning-making and our history-shaping.

Friedrich von Hügel offers an attractive synthesis of the roots of his faith: 'I believe because I am told, because it is true, because it answers to my deepest interior experiences and needs.' He proposes that there are at least three major dimensions to faith – institutional, reflective and mystical. In other words faith is born from hearing the Word in a community. It also grows through questions and the quest for understanding. At a more personal level it fulfils the longings of the heart to relax into the surprise of being loved by God. In recent times much attention has been given to various stages of faith, as explored for instance by James Fowler. A child lives from images, stories and basic trust. A young person's faith needs a sense of friendship with Christ. A more adult stage reaches a capacity for faithful and steady commitment. Midlife can bring more fog and doubt, and yet out of the collapse of old certainties a new compassion can be born, as well as the capacity for deep silence before mystery. Old age is invited to enjoy a grace of serenity and a freedom to surrender one's life gently into the hands of God. To avoid undue clarity we need to recall that faith involves a movement of desire towards Someone whom we never understand. In this sense the object of faith is not merely factual. It is *semper maior*, always greater than our poor images and ideas.

Reflection on faith can focus either on the 'content' of revelation or on the 'act' of the person in accepting God's word. Traditional theology of faith tells us that it has various characteristics: a gift because God chooses to reveal love; a free response involving a life option; a reasonable conviction or assent of the mind but needing a spirit of trust; something certain because it depends on God's promise, but also dark because in this life we do not see; an anticipation or foretaste of the goal of our hearts, attainable only in eternity. All these aspects have implications for spirituality that cannot be explored here. Any spirituality of faith needs to see it as a lifelong adventure with many tones, as the friendship with Christ blossoms into mature discipleship. It is more a drama of companionship and vision than a theory, more an event than a philosophy. It is a lived adventure with alternations of light and dark: in the typically provocative expression of G. K. Chesterton, faith means being able to survive one's moods.

See also **Conversion; God; Images of Love; Knowledge.**

Avery Dulles, *The Assurance of Things Hoped For: A Theology of Christian Faith*, New York: Oxford University Press, 1994; Gerhard Ebeling, *The Nature of Faith*, London: Collins, 1961; Michael Paul Gallagher, *Dive Deeper: The Human Poetry of Faith*, London: Darton, Longman & Todd, 2001; Walter Kasper, *Transcending All Understanding: The Meaning of Christian Faith Today*, San Francisco: Ignatius Press, 1989; Tony Kelly, *An Expanding Theology: Faith in a World of Connections*, Newton: E. J. Dwyer, 1993.

MICHAEL PAUL GALLAGHER

Faithfulness

see **Perseverance**

Family

see **Marriage, Family and Spirituality**

Fasting

see **Food**

Feasting

see **Food**

Feelings

see **Emotions**

Feminist Spirituality

At a minimum, 'spirituality' refers to the 'inner dimensions' of lived experience in respect to what is ultimate. As reflection on lived experience, spirituality is always concerned with particularity, in this essay with Christianity and feminism. Feminist spirituality is both related to and distinct from women's spirituality. Women's spirituality is concerned with the spiritual practices and experiences of women across various historical time periods or religious and cultural groups, while feminist spirituality not only attends to women's experience, it also raises critical awareness of what prevents women from full human flourishing. Feminist spirituality describes approaches to relationship with God, others, the self and the world that critique the oppressive effects of patriarchy, and advocate changes in support of the full human dignity of women and also of men and other creatures diminished by patriarchal systems.

The roots of all Christian understandings of spirituality are traceable to the New Testament and to the presence of the Spirit in the world, which although invisible is ultimate reality. Christian feminist spirituality embraces Paul's insight: 'God's love has been poured into our hearts through the Holy Spirit that has been given to us' (Rom. 5.5). It acknowledges that over the centuries, in spite of the negative effects of ecclesial patriarchy on women, countless women have experienced the Holy Spirit in their lives and have found sources of inspiration and sustenance in the teachings of Jesus Christ and the liturgies and practices of their churches. While affirming this, feminist spirituality, in company with other Christian liberation movements, denounces domination in all unjust systems, while discerning the freeing truth of the gospel.

Because analysis of feminism has relevance for understanding Christian feminist spirituality, this essay will begin with a brief sketch of its historical origins and then will proceed to major facets of contemporary feminist spirituality, many of which illustrate the close relationship of feminist spirituality to feminist theology and ethics.

1. *Historical origins of feminism.* Although the term 'feminism' is widely accredited to Hubertine Auclert, who coined it in 1882, the roots of feminism can be traced to the 1830s and advocacy for the abolition of slavery in England and the United States of America. In this 'first wave of feminism', women raised their voices in condemnation of slavery and proclaimed 'liberty for captives' in Christian churches and other public forums. Many of these women were condemned on biblical grounds (1 Cor. 14.34–35; 1 Tim. 2.11–13), prompting consciousness of the connections between the oppression of slaves and of women and challenge to male interpretations of sacred Scripture (Elizabeth Cady Stanton (ed.), *The Woman's Bible,* 1895–1898). From these beginnings, feminism developed by bringing secular Enlightenment egalitarian thinking and Christian biblical theology to bear on the

androcentric social arrangements that privileged males over females. Nineteenth-century feminism in the West resulted in women attaining important rights such as voting, ownership of property, and education, but the Christian churches' broad support for the 'cult of true womanhood' blocked most development in Christian feminism until the 1960s.

Women's participation in the Civil Rights Movement for support of equality for African Americans in the United States during the 1960s prompted heightened consciousness of the inequality of women and men. Feminism also emerged with renewed vigour in Western European countries, gradually becoming a global reality due to United Nations events devoted to the status of women (e.g. 'UN Decade of Women', 1975–85). The 'second wave of feminism' revived not only women's struggle for political and economic equality but also led to the development of feminist studies as an academic discipline, impacting virtually every field of study. Analysis of gender oppression of women as a cultural construct paved the way for feminist scholars to recognize the wide-ranging effects of patriarchy on every facet of life. These developments and the efforts of women such as Sandra Schneiders, Anne Carr and Joann Wolski Conn resulted in Christian 'feminist spirituality' developing into an academic discipline.

2. *Major characteristics of feminist spirituality.* Since the 1970s many types of feminism and feminist spirituality have emerged. Some give pride of place to women as agents in their own liberative process against the injustice of sexism ('woman-centred feminists'), while others emphasize that both women and men are capable of recognizing and overcoming this evil ('inclusivist feminists'). The judgement of many woman-centred feminists is that Christianity is irredeemably patriarchal and, therefore, inimical to women's spiritual well being. Among the more noteworthy spokespersons of this position is Mary Daly, an American and former Roman Catholic, whose *Beyond God the Father* (1968, 1973) received wide attention. Other feminists have contributed to the body of literature highly critical of Christianity, including the American Protestant Carol Christ who addressed why women need the Goddess in an article by that title (1992), and the British former Anglican Daphne Hampson, author of several notable post-Christian works, including *After Christianity* (1996).

The condemnations of Christianity by women-centred feminists have prompted some Christians to denounce feminism. Inclusivist Christian feminists have rejected both stances. Acknowledging the sin of sexism's effects on Christianity, they engage in reform through *retrieval* of women's contributions to ecclesial life and spirituality by searching for a 'usable past' and by calling for *critique* of patriarchy and *reconstruction* of Christian theology, spirituality and practice.

Retrieval. The past three decades have seen an unprecedented number of monographs devoted to women in the Bible, including Mary and the female disciples of Jesus, and to translations of major works by women of earlier periods honoured for their piety, mysticism and response to the needs of their time. Books retrieving the stories of women's agency in the unfolding story of redemption correct many past misconceptions and provide rich resources for feminist spirituality.

Critique and reconstruction. In addition to retrieval of women's spiritual heritage, critique of patriarchy with accompanying reconstruction plays a major role in Christian feminist spirituality. Among the more pointed critiques of patriarchy are the forms of hierarchical dualism, incorporated from Platonic thought into Christianity. For Plato what was associated with the 'spiritual' was good because it was immortal, while the 'physical' was bad, drawing us earthward. In company with this perspective are the dualistic conceptions of (1) male over female; (2) soul/spirit/mind over the body/emotions; (3) culture over nature. Christian feminism is critical of this ideology because male–female dualism is at the basis of the others, extending superiority to all that is conceived as 'masculine' and inferiority to all that is perceived as 'feminine'.

Platonic gender-based hierarchical dualism incorporated into the Christian tradition has affected all dimensions of Christianity, including the doctrine of God. Critique of the masculinization of God abounds among Christian feminist theologians, whose attention to spiritual and ethical questions exceed the boundaries of theology. Rosemary Radford Ruether, a Roman Catholic, for example, has argued that equating a particular image for God drawn from one gender with who God is, is idolatry. To correct the exclusively male genderization of God and its debilitating effect on women, Ruether calls for the use of images drawn from women's experience to enable bonds of intimacy of women with God (*Sexism and God-Talk*, 1983). Among other fruitful proposals are those of Protestant scholar Sallie McFague who draws attention to biblical motherhood metaphors for God and God's immanence in creation (*Models of God*, 1987)

and Roman Catholic scholar Elizabeth Johnson whose attention to how God symbols function leads her to develop a theology of God centred on in the biblical figure *Hokmah/Sophia*, divine Woman-Wisdom (*She Who Is*, 1992).

Women's sense of self is enriched by a God who is not only 'he' but also 'she'. This insight supports ownership by women of the biblical confession that woman is a full human being made in the 'image of God' (Gen. 1.26–27), thereby countering women's secondary status in church and society associated with women as 'daughters of Eve' (Helen Schengel-Straumann, 'The feminine face of God', *Concilium* 1995/2; Mary Catherine Hilkert, 'Cry Beloved Image', in Ann O'Hara Gruff (ed.), *In the Embrace of God*, 1996).

Christian feminist reflection does not neglect the Trinity. Putting the apparent maleness of the divine three in the background, emphasis is placed on interrelationship and mutuality, values central to feminist ethical discourse, as the core of divine reality and the basis of the world as it ought to be (e.g. Patricia Wilson-Kastner, *Faith, Feminism and the Christ*, 1983).

Psyche-soma dualism has been addressed by many Christian feminists, including, Elisabeth Moltmann-Wendell who speaks of Christianity as 'disembodied' and calls for the rediscovery of the centrality of the body (*I Am My Body*, 1994). Attention to the centrality of the body may rightly begin with an incarnational spirituality that depicts Mary, not as a passive channel through which the divine saviour passed to enter creation (Docetism), but as a woman whose purposeful 'yes' to God resulted in her role as God-bearer (*Theotokos*), giving Jesus Christ flesh in and through her body. But it attends not only to motherhood but also to all aspects of women's experience as embodied selves, including the profound interconnectedness of body-mind-spirit experienced in the bodily seasons of women's lives and expressed in embodied prayer in communal rituals.

The dualism of culture over nature has been critiqued extensively by 'ecofeminism', a term first used by Françoise d'Eaubonne in 1974 to name the commitment of feminists to the ecological health of the planet. Ecofeminism rejects the association of women with nature as a faulty construct, condemning it for objectifying and commodifying women and non-human nature to the advantage of men who occupy the top levels of the social and economic hierarchies. Ecofeminism advocates a fundamental re-envisioning of the dominant anthropocentric conception of reality, emphasizing that humans are not above nature, but are participants in it.

Christian ecofeminist spirituality gives attention to biblically rooted female images and metaphors for God and human kinship solidarity with all creatures. In ecofeminist spirituality, Earth is commonly regarded as a sacred gift and sacrament because all creatures have their origins in God and are revelatory of the divine. Christian ecofeminist spirituality brings together the Christian doctrinal heritage of creation and redemption in prophetic protest of the disregard and damage of creation in a commitment to an eco-justice of right relations with all creatures.

See also **Body and Spirituality; Dualism; Mujerista Spirituality; Liberation Spirituality; Women and Spirituality; Women Medieval Mystics; Womanist Spirituality.**

Anne Carr, 'On feminist spirituality' in Joann Wolski Conn (ed.), *Women's Spirituality: Resources for Christian Development*, New York: Paulist Press, 1986; Elizabeth A. Johnson, *Truly Our Sister: A Theology of Mary in the Communion of Saints*, New York and London: Continuum, 2003; Ursula King, *Women and Spirituality: Voices of Protest and Promise*, London: Macmillan, 1989; *Madelia Lectures in Spirituality*, New York: Paulist Press, 1985–2003; Shawn Madigan (ed.), *Mystics, Visionaries and Prophets: A Historical Anthology of Women's Spiritual Writings*, Minneapolis, MN: Fortress Press, 1998; Mary T. Malone, *Women and Christianity, Vol. III: From the Reformation to the 21st Century*, Maryknoll, NY: Orbis Books, 2003; Rosemary Radford Ruether (ed.), *Women Healing Earth: Third World Women on Ecology, Feminism and Religion*, Maryknoll, NY: Orbis Books, 1996.

ANNE M. CLIFFORD

Festivals, Religious

All religions celebrate special dates as festival days. For Christians Sundays are the major days of the Christian liturgical year, the weekly celebrations of Christ's resurrection. The Scriptures are careful to note that it was the morning of the first day that the empty tomb was discovered. In the early Church, Sunday was called the 'eighth day' as well as the 'first day'. In the Jewish tradition, Saturday or Sabbath was the 'seventh day' corresponding to the first creation account of Genesis. The Christians therefore used the number eight due to its symbolic value. Trying to avoid the idea that the week closed with the Sabbath, and attempting to demonstrate how the New Testament superseded the Old Testament, Sunday designated both the first day (*feria I*) of a new creation and the eighth day (*dies octava*) of the week, a day that stood outside of the calendar, a day that prefigured eternity in time. God created the world in six days and rested on the seventh, but it was on a Sunday that God continued the work of redeeming fallen creation. Sunday came to mean the New Creation. The Fathers of the Church thoroughly imbued with the symbolism of numbers wrote about the number eight, seeing in it a symbol of Sunday, of the resurrection and of the world's renewal through Christ.

Many of the Christian feasts and sacraments were also associated with the eighth-day association. Circumcision, for example, was effected on the eighth day after birth. There were eight people in Noah's ark. Every strophe of Psalm 118 has eight verses. John Damascene talks of eight biblical stories as eight types (*tupoi*) of baptism. For Christians these were veiled references to the day of resurrection and the redemption in the new covenant.

By the second century, the feast of Easter had developed as an annual commemoration. Drawing upon the language of Jewish Passover, Christians reread the event of Christ's death and resurrection as a passing over from sin and death to atonement and life and as a prefiguring of the final Passover, which is the parousia. Both the Jewish and Christian Paschs were feasts of redemption and hope. As Sunday was the weekly celebration of the Lord's death and resurrection, Easter became its annual celebration and to it was attached the awesome rites of initiation of catechumens through the sacraments of baptism, chrismation and Eucharist. Gradually there developed a period of preparation associated with the symbolism of the number forty. As Noah prepared for a new creation in the ark for forty days and nights, as Moses prepared to enter the promised land by wandering in the desert for forty years, and as Christ prepared for his public ministry by fasting and praying for forty days, catechumens prepared themselves in an intense way through prayer and fasting during Lent, the forty days leading to Easter. After Easter, the Church celebrated the Easter joy with the newly baptized for fifty days. The fiftieth day is called Pentecost which celebrates the descent of the Holy Spirit upon the Church and this feast corresponds to the Jewish feast of the fiftieth day after Passover called Shavu'ot. The date of Easter is a moveable feast determined by a complicated computation based upon the lunar calendar and the method of calculation has been disputed throughout Christian history. The question of whether the annual commemoration of the paschal mystery should be celebrated on the fourteenth day of Nisan according to the Jewish computation of Passover (the first day of the full moon in the first month of spring, even if this day does not fall on a Sunday) or if it should be celebrated on the first Sunday after the fourteenth of Nisan, was resolved at the Council of Nicaea (325 CE) in favour of the latter.

Christmas emerged as the feast of the nativity of Christ and was celebrated on 25 December. The date may have arisen in the identification of the Jewish feast of the 14 Nisan with 25 March (a date associated with Christ's death) according to the chronology offered in the Gospel of John. Counting backwards nine months from the date of Christ's resurrection (birth into new life) determined the method for computing the date of Jesus' birth. By the fourth century in Rome the feast was associated with the pagan feast of Invincible Sun (*Sol invictus*) associated with the winter solstice. The pagan feast celebrating the birth of the sun was easily Christianized to signify the birth of the Son of God and the rich imagery of light growing out of the darkness lent itself to the Christian commemoration of Christ's birth. As the Easter season was a cycle of life, Christmastide celebrated the cycle of light. Associated with the theme of light was the feast of Epiphany, which came to commemorate the Magi following the star. But the fuller meaning of epiphany is the 'manifestation' (*epiphania*) of God among us. Linked to this feast was also the baptism of Christ and the wedding feast of Cana, two further events when God became manifest. As Lent was the penitential preparation for Easter, Advent emerged as the period of joyful preparation for Christmas/Epiphany. Just as Easter was the major feast of initiation, epiphany with all of its associations with light and the baptism of Christ became a major secondary feast of initiation with the effect that advent was regarded as a mini-Lent.

While Sunday framed the weekly celebration and Easter and Christmas framed the annual festivals, the Christians arranged other feast days in relationship to the Christ, particularly the days commemorating the saints. A rich theology interprets the saints as those who configured their lives to Christ. In the case of the martyrs, the feast commemorates the day of death with the idea that on these days the martyrs were reborn into new life sharing in the resurrection of Christ. Some of the Christian feast days are paired feasts, placed in parallel to christological feasts. For example, the feast of the Annunciation celebrating the conception of Christ is placed on 25 March (the spring equinox), nine months before the nativity of Christ. The birth of John the Baptist celebrated nine months after his conception corresponding to the autumnal equinox is six months apart from the birth of Christ.

As Christ's nativity corresponded to the winter solstice when the days were getting imperceptibly longer, John the Baptist's nativity corresponds to the summer solstice when the days are gradually growing shorter. This feast in particular typifies John's words that 'Christ must increase while I decrease'.

The particular meaning of the Christian feasts and seasons flows from the idea that the year was a complete unit of time. In celebrating the annual feasts, however, Christians did not understand this as beginning anew each time. Rather, the annual festivals admit to an ongoing transformation of Christian life in time and history.

See also **Spirituality, Liturgy and Worship** (*essay*)**; Celebration; Food; Time.**

Adolf Adam, *The Liturgical Year: Its History and Its Meaning after the Reform of the Liturgy*, Collegeville, MN: Pueblo, 1981; John Paul II, *Apostolic Letter* Dies Domini: *Guide to Keeping Sunday Holy*, Chicago, IL: Liturgy Training Publications, 1998; Maxwell Johnson (ed.), *Between Memory and Hope: Readings on the Liturgical Year*, Collegeville, MN: Pueblo, 2000; Thomas Talley, *The Origins of the Liturgical Year*, Collegeville, MN: Pueblo, 1986.

MICHAEL S. DRISCOLL

Film and Spirituality

Vachel Lindsay (1879–1931) was one of the first writers to analyse narrative cinema as art and as a medium for religious ideas and spiritual sentiments. For Lindsay – writing in 1915 – the silent 'photoplay' offered a universal language of 'hieroglyphic' images which viewers could discuss while watching the film, the auditorium filled with the low hum of the 'conversing audience'. Film, for Lindsay, was sculpture and painting in motion, produced by artists whom the Church should embrace as once it had embraced the great painters and sculptors of the past. 'The kinescope in the hands of artists is a higher form of picture-writing. In the hands of prophet-wizards it will be a higher form of vision-seeing.' But while the film industry saw a market in religious stories from the first – passion plays were being filmed in France and America from as early as 1897 and 1898 respectively – the churches were less convinced by arguments such as Lindsay's.

However, while the ability of film to tell religious stories with power and sometimes subtlety is not in question, its ability to be a spiritual medium is more doubtful. In part this is because the dominant forms of cinema are irreducibly commercial, concerned with entertaining mass audiences. There is still a market for biblical dramas, as Mel Gibson's *The Passion of the Christ* (2004) has shown, and many mainstream directors (e.g. David Fincher, Alfred Hitchcock, Martin Scorsese) have explored religious themes, such as guilt and redemption, in thoughtful and surprising ways, while others – such as the Wachowski brothers in their *Matrix* trilogy (1999/2003) about the Internet – have dressed up their fantasies with religious ideas, winning popular acclaim and commercial success. Religion and pseudo-spirituality still sells. But whether film can attain to the power of religious parable, to the austerity of the great icons, and itself become the occasion of hierophany, is another matter.

Paul Schrader provides a clear and accessible analysis of how it is that certain film directors – Yasujiro Ozu, Robert Bresson, Carl Dreyer – have achieved a 'transcendental style' which evokes a sense of the transcendent, of a spiritual reality beyond what is seen. Schrader claims that the style is universal, apparent in both East and West, in Ozu's Japanese Zen sensibility and Bresson's French Catholicism. The style consists in both the way a story is told – with an apparently artless cold detachment from what is yet carefully observed – and in the narrative arc of its telling, which moves from the mundane, through a moment of disparity or crisis, to a final stasis or quietude, in which the transcendent is revealed: whether as the unity of nature, the ground of being, or as the salvific grace of God.

Schrader defines a form of film which 'induces' a sense of the transcendent, suggesting a spiritual cinematic machine which seems to deny the working of a freely bestowed grace; but perhaps the transcendental style is the form that grace takes in the cinema, since in Catholic thought the supernatural is but the natural restored to its originary beatitude, as when we share our food, or extend a hand in forgiveness. Certain forms of life reveal their createdness (for those given to see). Thus, irrespective of the director's intentions, one can identify aspects of the transcendental style in the work of avowed atheists, such as Pier Paolo Pasolini's *The Gospel According to St Matthew* (1964) or Alain Cavalier's *Thérèse* (1986), a study of St Thérèse (Martin) of Lisieux. Indeed, Nicholas Philibert's small-scale documentary about a French single-room country school, *Être et avoir* (2002), can be read as a spiritual film, since it finds the disparities involved in human socialization and their comforting in the everyday work of a dedicated school teacher exceptional only in the compassion of his daily labour.

The great Russian 'prophet-wizard' Andrei Tarkovsky (1932–86) worked for most of his career under the scrutiny of the atheistic Soviet state, and so could not have made explicitly religious films. He had to show religion as something past, a matter of defeated relics in the modern world. But it is unlikely that he would have made 'religious films', even if he could have done so. Tarkovsky's carefully crafted vocabulary of natural motifs – rain, fire, water, wind and snow – and meditative camera movements (slow zooms and lengthy panning and dolly shots) enables a form of transcendent 'vision-seeing', which is as much about the loss of spirituality as its necessity. *Andrei Rublev* (1966) is about the great fifteenth-century icon painter of the same name, and Tarkovsky's films are in many ways icons rather than metaphors. They consist in images which don't stand in for something else, but are simply themselves, yet within which we can see what cannot be shown (the 'prototype'); *there* but beyond the image. This is to achieve a truly spiritual cinema – a *via positiva* which is at the same time a *via negativa*, a way into the light which resides in the dark; a glimpse of the invisible in the visible, in the depths of the seen.

See also **Aesthetics; Image and Spirituality.**

Mary Lea Bandy and Antonio Monda (eds), *The Hidden God: Film and Faith*, New York: The Museum of Modern Art, 2003; Robert K. Johnston, *Reel Spirituality: Theology and Film in Dialogue*, Grand Rapids, MI: Baker Academic, 2000; Vachel Lindsay, *The Art of the Moving Picture*, New York: The Modern Library [1915] 2000; Gerard Loughlin, *Alien Sex: The Body and Desire in Cinema and Theology*, Oxford: Blackwell, 2004; Stephen Mulhall, *On Film*, London: Routledge, 2002; Paul Schrader, *Transcendental Style in Film: Ozu, Bresson, Dreyer*, New York: Da Capo Press, 1972.

GERARD LOUGHLIN

Flemish Mysticism

Mystical texts written in one or another dialect of Middle Netherlandish first appeared toward the beginning of the thirteenth century, but even at that period some mystics of the Low Countries (such as Mary of Oignies and Margaret of Ypres) are known to us only through *vitae* composed by others. Although these lives are generally considered reliable sources for the teaching of such persons, we are on still firmer ground when dealing with texts composed by mystics themselves. The latter will therefore be the focus of this article.

Two of the most important Flemish mystical writers were Beatrice of Nazareth and Hadewijch of Antwerp. Both flourished in the first half of the thirteenth century and both were influenced by the works of Augustine, Bernard, William of St Thierry, and the Victorines, but the fact that Beatrice belonged to an organized religious community and Hadewijch did not led to far more biographical data being preserved about the former. Beatrice (1200–68) was a Cistercian nun who ended her days as prioress of the monastery of Nazareth in Brabant. Her spiritual journal, now lost, was the basis of the *Life* composed by the chaplain of the community after her death. Beatrice's single treatise, *The Seven Manners of Loving*, was for many centuries available only in a Latin adaptation included as part of the *Life*, but the original vernacular text was discovered in a collection of sermons near the beginning of the twentieth century. It exemplifies many of the themes that would reappear in the works of other Flemish mystics, especially, first, a fervent desire to be united with God and so come to enjoy the peaceful resting in God that results when the mystic's will is merged with the divine will; second, the claim that one can return to one's true being, which has been timelessly in the triune God from all eternity; and, third, the insistence that the divine love that draws us back to that primal unity cannot be mastered or fully grasped, for it draws the soul 'into the incomprehensibility and vastness and inaccessible sublimity and deep abyss of the Godhead, which is totally present in all things and remains incomprehensibly beyond all things'.

These themes are not only found but even more strongly emphasized in the works of Hadewijch, a beguine from Antwerp who has left us a rich variety of writings: 31 letters, 45 poems in stanzas, 16 poems in couplets, and 14 visions. (Another 13 poems in couplets are found in some manuscripts of her work but these are by an otherwise unknown author commonly called Hadewijch II, whose general tone is more abstract than that of the Antwerp beguine.) Of the *Letters*, some are personal missives of spiritual direction, while others could more properly be considered short treatises on the spiritual life. The call to return to one's true being in the divine Exemplar is prominent, as when she writes in *Letter* 6: 'If you wish to attain your being in which God created you, you must in noblemindedness fear no difficulty . . . but valiantly lay hold on the best part – I mean, the great totality of God – as your own good.'

Like Beatrice (and like Flemish mystics of later generations), Hadewijch insists that one can lay hold on this 'great totality of God' only through love (*minne*). No term appears so prominently in her poetry, as in the remarkable concluding lines of her fifteenth poem in couplets: 'O Love, were I but love,/And could I but love you, Love, with love!/O Love, for love's sake, grant that I,/Having become love, may know Love wholly as Love!' Nevertheless, and again like Beatrice, she does not disdain the role of the reason or intellect in the journey back to God. Following the teaching of William of St Thierry, she writes in *Letter* 18 that the soul's power of vision has two eyes, love and reason. The latter 'cannot see God except in what he is not', whereas 'love rests not except in what he is'. Neither is sufficient by itself, but the two are of great mutual help one to the other.

Hadewijch does, however, go farther than Beatrice in the way she expresses the culmination of the soul's union with God. Although Beatrice writes of being made 'one spirit with Christ' (even as does St Paul in 1 Cor. 6.17), there remains a definite sense of distinction between the soul and its Lord. Hadewijch is bolder on this point. When one is fully in the blissful state of resting in God, 'one becomes God, mighty and just' (*Letter* 17), even as she speaks in *Vision* 7 of being so taken up into Christ that 'it was to me as if we were one without difference' (*sonder differencie*). This is the kind of language that has at times led mystical writers to be accused of pantheism or autotheism, but from the context it is clear that Hadewijch is trying to give voice to an *experience* of deep union that is not radically different from the experience of oneness often felt by two human lovers.

Jan van Ruusbroec (1293–1381), the most influential of all the Flemish mystics, definitely knew the works of Hadewijch, for he quotes from them in several of his treatises, though without naming the author. After spending the first twenty-four years of his priestly life as a chaplain at the largest church in Brussels, at the age of fifty he and two like-minded confrères retired to the secluded area of Groenendaal southwest of the city, where they eventually founded a priory following the rule of the canons regular of St Augustine. Ruusbroec had already composed his major work, *The Spiritual Espousals*, while living in Brussels and continued his literary activity at Groenendaal by expanding on various themes treated in the *Espousals*. Like Hadewijch, he uses the terminology of being united with God 'without difference' and speaks of our being able 'to be God with God, without intermediary or any element of otherness that could constitute an obstacle or impediment' (*Espousals*, book 3). Such phrases elicited the criticism of the Parisian Chancellor Jean Gerson in the following generation, but if they are read in context it is clear that they are expressions of mystical consciousness and not claims of strict ontological identity. It is a matter not of fusion but of a communion of love, a point that

Ruusbroec makes explicitly in the final lines of his later treatise, *A Mirror of Eternal Blessedness*.

One further point should be made about his teaching. For all of his eloquent and inspiring language about contemplatively resting in God, Ruusbroec had no tolerance for the quietistic tendencies of his day, known as the movement of the Free Spirit. The Christian ideal was to be rooted in a blissful awareness of oneness with God and *at the same time* to 'go out to creatures in virtue and righteousness through a love that is common to all' (*Espousals*, book 2). In the conclusion of *The Sparkling Stone* Ruusbroec called this ideal 'the common life', attained when one 'is equally ready for contemplation or for action and is perfect in both'.

During the Groenendaal years Ruusbroec received visitors from many parts of northern Europe, among them Gerard Groote (1340–84), the founder of the *Devotio Moderna*. Groote himself translated some of the mystic's works into Latin, while Groote's own disciple Gerlach Peters (d. 1411) composed a *Soliloquium* marked by an affective christocentric mysticism and a Ruusbroeckian insistence that spiritual progress consists in the realization of our likeness to God, who has impressed his image in the depth of our being. Ruusbroec's influence is still more pronounced in the writings of Hendrik Herp (d. 1478), whose *Mirror of Perfection* led to his being called 'The Herald of Ruusbroec'. The Spanish Franciscan Bernardine of Laredo drew heavily on the Latin translation of the *Mirror* in his own *Ascent of Mount Zion*, which in turn influenced Teresa of Avila and other Spaniards of her day.

The final blossoming of medieval Flemish mysticism may be found in *The Evangelical Pearl*, written by an anonymous Brabantine woman who flourished in the first half of the sixteenth century. The work was published in Utrecht in 1535 and in an expanded version three years later in Antwerp. Its author draws not only on Ruusbroec but also on the Rhineland mystics Meister Eckhart and Johannes Tauler, but inasmuch as Ruusbroec and his own disciple Jan van Leeuwen were highly critical of some aspects of Eckhart's teaching, the *Pearl* has what Louis Cognet has called 'a certain composite and inorganic character'. Even so, the fact that it was soon translated into Latin, French and German helped carry the influence of Flemish mysticism into the early modern period and beyond.

See also **Mysticism (*essay*); Apophatic Spirituality; Beguine Spirituality; Bridal Mysticism; Cistercian Spirituality; Contemplation; *Devotio Moderna*; Quietism; Rhineland Mysticism; Unitive Way; Victorine Spirituality; Women Medieval Mystics.**

Primary sources: *The Life of Beatrice of Nazareth, 1200–1268*, trans. and annotated by Roger de Ganck, Kalamazoo, MI: Cistercian Publications, 1991; *Hadewijch: The Complete Works*, trans. Mother Columba Hart OSB, CWS, London: SPCK; New York: Paulist Press, 1980; *John Ruusbroec: The Spiritual Espousals and Other Works*, trans. James A. Wiseman OSB, CWS, London: SPCK; New York: Paulist Press, 1985.

Secondary sources: Louis Cognet, *Introduction aux mystiques rhéno-flamands*, Paris: Desclée, 1968; Albert Deblaere, 'Mysticism. II: Schools of mysticism. B: The Netherlands' in *Sacramentum Mundi: An Encyclopedia of Theology*, London: Burns & Oates; New York: Herder & Herder, 1969, vol. 4, pp. 143–6; Bernard McGinn, *The Flowering of Mysticism: Men and Women in the New Mysticism, 1200–1350*, vol. 3 of *The Presence of God: A History of Western Christian Mysticism*, New York: Crossroad, 1998. (This volume has material on Beatrice and Hadewijch; the forthcoming fourth volume will have a section on Ruusbroec.)

JAMES A. WISEMAN

Food

In contemporary western cultures, food has almost never been simply a matter of survival. Food narrates the collective imagination of those who participate in its rituals of gathering, preparation, eating and drinking, and garbage disposal. It involves a set of images, dreams, tastes, choices and values. Food, particularly as advertised, speaks about the community's links with its own past, its (often not so hidden) sublimation of sexuality and gender definition, and the ideals of diet, bodiliness, and health in a society. (Stephen Happel, in *The Way* 37.1 (1997), p. 3)

Without food we would unquestionably die. At the first flicker of the spark of life the cellular construction that will become a human embryo must feed to survive. Of equal importance is the relationship that is formed *in vitro* between infant and mother at its most vulnerable beginnings. Thus the relevance of food and its significance to spirituality are established at this early stage of life and it is the major source for the physical and emotional survival of the child. Nurture and relationship are important ingredients to the recipe of life.

But food is not simply a matter of nurture and relationship. That is just the beginning. It is far more. Food is a highly political and ethical issue.

It is about values and morality, ritual and celebration, health and ill health, feast and fast, the rich and the poor, the world divided into North and South. Creatively, food and its preparation can be an art form, an indulgence and a fetish, even an addiction. Food well used and resourced sustains – food badly resourced destroys health and local communities.

Food and society. Brillat-Savarin wrote in the early nineteenth century, 'Tell me what you eat: I will tell you what you are.' This quotation has now commonly become the cliché, 'You are what you eat.' It can be said that in the northern hemisphere only the wealthy have the opportunity to eat in ways that value health and body. To eat respectfully, organically, ethically and 'greenly' requires leisure, money and plenty of time. Perhaps organic food speaks to us of the innocence and purity of a lost spirituality. But it comes at a high price. Local and organic foods are expensive. The global food industry has squeezed farmers and small producers out of the market place. The rise in numbers of supermarkets, hypermarkets and fast-food outlets has caused us to become a consumerist society that favours speedy consumption, huge choice and poor quality over careful preparation, seasonally selected and healthy foods. This society has been conditioned to favour cheap and snack food that is easily obtainable and often processed in ways that counter health. People are often ignorant of the political tactics that are used to promote poor standards of eating that pressurize and steal from the developing world where over 840 million people are chronically undernourished. They wonder why the rich world's poor members have become obese, that families no longer eat together and there is a massive increase in eating disorders. There is no morality in this type of food production or its outcome. It is counter to a healthy spirituality of embodiment because it disembodies principles and the valuation of the sacredness of the body and its life.

Food and scripture.
God comes to feed us, to fill us, to love us. 'God pervades the world in the same way as honey in the comb,' says Tertullian. Abundant beyond our wildest hopes, this bread is everywhere before us, sweet like honey in our mouths, given to sustain us. (Douglas Burton-Christie, *Weavings*, July–August 1999, 45)

The Bible abounds with images, metaphors and allegories of food. Food is central to the description of our relationship with God. The constant hunger, yearning and desire to find relationship with God and its need for fulfilment can be found in and through the symbolism of the Bible. From the Genesis account of 'the fall', in the narrative of the Garden of Eden, to the total and unadulterated sensuousness of the Garden of Paradise in the Song of Songs, the mutual desire between God's love for us and ours for God makes it abundantly clear how the language of desire becomes the language of food.

The New Testament gospel narratives teach and instruct us through the actions of God made visible in Jesus Christ how to live our lives through the law of love. One of the principal ways of loving is in the sharing of our selves. This sharing requires selflessness, compassion and constant vigilance towards our neighbour. These attributes and spiritual practices are intrinsic to hospitality. Hospitality is fundamental to Christian virtue and nowhere is it better exemplified than in the teachings of the gospel.

Jesus was radical. He took pleasure in the friendship of and being with outsiders, sinners, ordinary people and the marginalized. He spent time with those who were in need of forgiveness, protection and love. There are a number of stories relating to Jesus' table fellowship that describe how the sharing of food proved to be healing and transformative experiences. This put Jesus in a constant state of ritual impurity: for example the call of Levi, the tax collector and the feast in his house (Luke 5.27–32); the woman who was a sinner at the Pharisee's house (Luke 7.31–34), 'This man welcomes sinners and eats with them' (Luke 15.1–2); the story of Zacchaeus (Luke 19.7). Jesus' message was one of joy that the eschatological banquet was at hand. In these meals he shared the anticipation of that banquet.

In the feeding of the five thousand in all four Gospels (Matt. 14.13–21; Mark 6.30–44; Luke 9.10–17; John 6.1–15), the spiritual symbolism of food is richly represented. The twelve disciples with twelve baskets represent Israel gathered by Jesus and fed by God, sustainer, nourisher and provider. These sequences include strong references to the Eucharist (the food is blessed, broken and given). In Matthew a second feeding (Matt. 15.32–39) explicitly takes place on the non-Jewish side of the Lake of Galilee. Finally at the Last Supper (Luke 22.14–20) Jesus sits and eats with his disciples. This last meal holds the key symbolic reference, in the institution of the Eucharist, for succeeding generations of Christians – Jesus' life, death and resurrection is repeatedly commemorated in the breaking of bread. Jesus' mission was inclusive to the end. Everyone is welcome at the table, even those whose loyalty was suspect to the point of betrayal and death.

Feasting and fasting. To feast is to celebrate. The Christian calendar has always celebrated feast days in commemoration of events in the life of Christ, the saints or the seasons of the year. Food is essential to the celebration of these events. The choice of food is particular to each cultural environment. Special foods are often local and seasonal: for example, in Britain, turkey or goose is eaten at Christmas; in the United States turkey is the chosen meat of Thanksgiving; Easter is celebrated with eggs, the sign of new life in the resurrection, and in Mediterranean Europe a lamb or goat is often roasted whole. The special preparation of the food and the table is highly significant; it is often lavish and extravagant. The care and particularity with which the preparation of these significant occasions is performed is ritualistic and even sacramental. All our senses are employed, touch, smell, taste, hearing and sight. The liturgies of life's significant events are marked through and with food – in baptisms, birthdays, weddings and funerals. Social ties are formed in the intimacy of the partaking, sharing, ingesting of the same foods. This should be a profound expression of love, communion and fellowship – a transformative experience. A feast is not only associated with celebration. It is also importantly related to and consistent with memory, ritual, thanksgiving and cultural identity. The praying of grace, which often precedes a festive meal, bestows a spiritual blessing and recollection on all who have participated in the gathering of the food and on those who will share in the eating.

To fast is to detoxify. Fasting within the Christian calendar holds equal significance with its cycles of feast days and is usually anticipatory of them (e.g. the seasons of Advent and Lent), but not exclusively so. Fasting is a specifically religious and spiritual act and is common to all religions. It is not to be associated with dieting. The intention of fasting is to purify the body by abstaining from eating and drinking in excess in order to control our 'appetites' and 'desires'. It is part of the ascetical and mystical tradition of the Christian Church. It calls for a simplicity of lifestyle and a reverence towards the body and is often seen as a form of penance. It is a way of resonating with poverty and starvation. 'Corporate fasting forges religious identity in associating with the sufferings of Christ and prepares us for the common and joyful celebrations that follow the fast period' (Louth, 2000). The outcomes from fasting, in the correct sense, may well be an intensification of prayer and a heightened awareness of the immanence and presence of God.

Feasting and fasting in proper balance speak to us about moderation in all aspects of living.

The monastic tradition has much to say on this subject, for example, St Benedict's Rule (39.1–11; 41.1–9) and also St Ignatius of Loyola in 'The Rules for Eating' in the Third Week of the Spiritual Exercises (210–17). Unfortunately, there is a paradox, when feasting and fasting become indulgent, feasting can turn to gluttony and then to obesity whilst fasting can turn to self-intended deprivation, and to starvation – today's anorexia and bulimia. These new, complex and sophisticated diseases of abundance are encouraged by the industry of dieting. A further paradox is that the 'luxury' of such diseases does not exist in the starving world. The politics of food and global consumerism do not address this imbalance. If we take seriously the spirituality of the body and its sustenance through food we should eat according to good, healthy and ethical standards.

See also **Addiction; Asceticism; Consumerism.**

Enzo Bianchi, *Words of Spirituality: Towards a Lexicon of the Inner Life*, London: SPCK, 2002, ch. 2, 'Asceticism', pp. 3–5; ch. 33, 'Fasting', pp. 83–5; David F. Ford, *Self and Salvation: Being Transformed*, Cambridge: Cambridge University Press, 1999, ch. 11, 'Feasting', sections 11.1–11.6.3; John Holden, Lydia Howland, Daniel Stedman Jones (eds), *Foodstuff: Living in an Age of Feast and Famine*, London: Demos Collection 18.18, 2002; Leon R. Kass, *The Hungry Soul: Eating and the Perfecting of our Nature*, Chicago: The University of Chicago Press, 1999; Carolyn Korsmeyer, *Making Sense of Taste: Food and Philosophy*, Ithaca: Cornell University Press, 1999; Andrew Louth, 'Fasting' in Adrian Hastings (ed.), *The Oxford Companion to Christian Thought*, Oxford: Oxford University Press, 2000; Roy Strong, *Feast: A History of Grand Eating*, London: Jonathan Cape, 2002.

SUSIE HAYWARD

Fools, Holy

(Greek: *salos*, Slavonic: *iurodivij*) If monasticism is fundamentally a rejection of the compromised standards of normal civilized society, an act of renunciation, *apotage*, or estrangement, *xeniteia*, then the phenomenon of holy folly may perhaps be seen as, in essence, a psychological version of such estrangement, a rejection of the compromised rationality of normal human society by adoption of the patterns of mad or deranged behaviour. Such madness may also be seen as a form of humility, and as a way of imitating the folly of God in the incarnation and the cross (cf. 1 Cor. 1.21–25; 3.18–19; 4.10). The practice of holy folly certainly developed in a monastic context. The earliest example is found in Palladius'

Lausiac History (34), which tells of an unnamed nun who 'feigned madness and demon possession' and was regarded with contempt by her sisters, who called her a *sale*; her way of life is presented as an example of humility, and justified by reference to 1 Cor. 3.18. Her disguise is broken after her piety is disclosed in a vision to a monk, Piteroum, who visits her monastery and reveals her as a spiritual mother. Unable to bear the acclaim, she vanishes from the monastery. A later and very influential example of a *salos* is Symeon of Emesa, known from Evagrius' *Church History* (4.34) and a *Life* written by Leontius of Neapolis. Symeon lives a double life: in private a devout and ascetic monk, but in public given to scandalous behaviour, indulging in gluttony, frolicking with prostitutes and even appearing naked in the women's section of the baths. Leontius' *Life of Symeon* formed a template for later *lives* of Byzantine *saloi*, among whom perhaps the most famous was Andrew the Fool. The 'original' Andrew the Fool seems to have belonged to the fifth century, and thus antedates Symeon, but his *Life* was composed in the tenth century, and Andrew is presented as a 'Scythian', probably a Slav. The *Life of Andrew the Fool* became very popular in Orthodox Russia, and the moment when Andrew saw the protecting veil of the Mother of God over the beleaguered city of Constantinople came to be celebrated on the feast of the *Pokrov* (Protection or Veil) of the Mother of God on 1 October. Holy fools were regarded as sacred figures, with prophetic powers of foresight and the equally prophetic freedom to denounce wrongdoing. Notable Russian *iurodivie* include the fifteenth-century Michael of Kloptso and the sixteenth-century Basil the Blessed, contemporary of Ivan the Terrible, whom he denounced with impunity (it is to him that the cathedral in Moscow's Red Square is dedicated). A holy fool plays a central role in Mussorgsky's opera *Boris Godunov* (especially the original version); there is also something of the Byzantine *salos* in the fool in Shakespeare's *King Lear*. The tradition of holy folly is often regarded as peculiar to the Orthodox tradition, but there is plenty of evidence for such ways of sanctity in the West, though they are not singled out by specific terminology. In the Orthodox tradition holy folly is always presented as feigned. In the West, however, we find examples of a genuine descent into madness, as a redemptive way of exchange, especially in the Jesuit priest who exorcized the nuns of Loudun in the seventeenth century, Jean-Joseph Surin.

See also **Asceticism; Holiness; Orthodox Spirituality.**

Derek Krueger, *Symeon the Holy Fool. Leontius's Life and the Late Antique City*, Transformation of the Classical Heritage 25, Berkeley: University of California Press, 1996; Lennart Rydén (ed.), *The Life of Andrew the Fool*, 2 vols, Acta Universitatis Upsaliensis: Studia Byzantina Upsaliensia 4:1, Uppsala, 1995; Lennart Rydén, 'The Holy Fool' in *The Byzantine Saint* ed. Sergei Hackel, Crestwood, NY: St Vladimir's Seminary Press, 2001, pp. 106–13; John Saward, *Perfect Fools: Folly for Christ's Sake in Catholic and Orthodox Spirituality*, Oxford: Oxford University Press, 1980; Kallistos Ware, 'The Fool in Christ as prophet and apostle' in *The Inner Kingdom: volume 1 of the Collected Works*, Crestwood, NY: St Vladimir's Seminary Press, 2000, pp. 153–80 (originally published in *Sobornost* 6.2 (1984), pp. 6–28).

ANDREW LOUTH

Forgiveness

Forgiveness is an original and basic element of Christian spirituality. Forgiveness, in the Scriptures of Israel, is primarily something that God does for the people of Israel (and sometimes, as in Jonah, for others). Forgiveness among human beings may be held up as a model, as in the story of Joseph; but it is not treated as an obligation. In the Gospels, however, our forgiveness of one another is deeply and directly linked with God's forgiveness of us, as, for example, in the Lord's Prayer: Forgive us our sins, as we forgive those who sin against us. At times, God's forgiveness of us appears to be a free gift with no prior conditions; at other times, it appears to be conditional on our forgiveness of others. Perhaps this ambiguity is best summed up in the parable of the two servants, where the initial gift of forgiveness is free, but the first servant's failure to extend forgiveness to the second results in revocation of his own forgiveness (Matt. 18.23–35).

God's forgiveness of us is indeed an act of gracious generosity. But the spiritual challenge is to appropriate it in a way that treats it as the beginning, not the end, of a process. Hence the importance of repentance and amendment of life. To appropriate God's forgiveness of us means that we grow, change and are transformed. We are not mere consumers of God's forgiveness, but participants in God's work of reconciling the world. Without cultivating a life that manifests and incorporates forgiveness, we cannot truly accept God's forgiveness even for ourselves, for it is not given in a way that privileges one person over others. God forgives all alike.

The experience of being forgiven teaches us the power of forgiveness to create new possibilities and so gives us power to pronounce God's forgiveness even of the sins of others (John 20.19–23). This power is not simply the property of the ordained, for the Gospel of John shows no interest in ordination as such. It is rather an expression of life lived in the newness that forgiveness makes possible. Forgiveness is an extension of the grace of creation, adapting God's creative power to changing human needs. Through it, God intervenes in human history and culture to help us create a new human reality in which hope triumphs over fear and suspicion. Forgiveness opens the gate to the life of the Age to Come by creating the possibility of a human society that can survive and be meaningful in an Age when 'They shall not hurt nor destroy in all my holy mountain' (Isa. 11.9 AV).

Christian piety has committed at least two major errors in speaking about forgiveness. One is the attempt to enhance and magnify the grace of forgiveness by elaborating on the depravity of humanity, which it portrays as being utterly without any goodness until the gift of divine forgiveness transforms it. This is a betrayal of the doctrine of creation. Nothing in Scripture indicates that the fall absolutely erased all value in the original creation. Sin does deserve to be taken very seriously. A world that has lived through the horrors of modern times should never doubt that. But the teaching of forgiveness is not enhanced by exaggerating human sinfulness.

The other grave error has been the tendency to treat forgiveness purely as duty and, worse yet, to impose it on the weak. If forgiveness is treated simply as duty, we tend to fabricate the appearance of it by pretending that the offence was less severe than we know it was or by blaming ourselves rather than the perpetrator or by feigning a generosity we do not truly embrace. Jesus requires that true forgiveness be 'from your heart' (Matt. 18.35). We cannot rise, by will alone, to this height nor can we demand it of others. We reach it by the complex process of living into God's gifts to us. Forgiveness never implies any falsification regarding the gravity of the wrong done.

Recent decades have seen a fresh recognition of the importance of forgiveness in the public as well as the individual or private sphere – for example, in the South African Truth and Reconciliation Commission, which seems to have been at least partially successful in freeing communities to begin living anew. At the same time, there have been criticisms that forgiveness was sometimes urged as a way to avoid the more difficult demands of doing justice. It is important that the weak not be forced into a position of having to remain quiet and forgive their oppressors without the oppressors being pressed in a comparable way to cease their harmful behaviour and to serve justice.

See also **Lord's Prayer; Penitence; Reconciliation.**

L. William Countryman, *Forgiven and Forgiving*, Harrisburg, PA: Morehouse Publishing, 1998; Raymond G. Helmick and Rodney L. Petersen (eds), *Forgiveness and Reconciliation: Religion, Public Policy, and Conflict Transformation*, Philadelphia: Templeton Foundation Press, 2001; Desmond Mpilo Tutu, *No Future without Forgiveness*, New York: Doubleday, 1999.

L. WILLIAM COUNTRYMAN

Formation, Spiritual

The content of training or formation programmes for men and women preparing for ministry in the Christian Churches tends to reflect the role that ministers are expected to play within their respective traditions. Historically emphasis was placed on academic training in Scripture, theology and philosophy, so that the minister could stand as a religious expert within the community. Alongside this was training for particular skills such as preaching or liturgical presidency, or specialization in such matters as canon law or moral theology and ethics. Often the nurturing of the trainee minister's personal life of holiness consisted of formal instruction in and practice of public prayer, largely within a liturgical framework. While the development of a private prayer life was implicit in many formation programmes, the growth of psychology as a science has led to an understanding that it is not incompatible with philosophy, or religious belief and practice and that they can be mutually supportive. The integration of psychological insights with those of the spiritual traditions has led to an understanding that spiritual formation needs to cover the personal psychosexual and social development of the individual in order to lead towards true spiritual maturity and autonomy. Psychology and theology offer valuable hermeneutic tools for interpreting and understanding human behaviour and, as part of spiritual formation, can lead to greater self-awareness, opening to the possibility of interior change and moral development. More recent times have also come to see spiritual formation as a necessary part of all growth in relationship with God and not only a pedagogical means to a practical end in terms of church ministry.

The spiritual formation of the individual has its external and internal sources. Traditionally it has been believed that the living of a way of life centred on God liturgically and in common pursuit of the Gospels is itself formative. Some of the ancient rules of life for religious refer to the living out of that rule as a 'school of the Lord's service' (*RSB* Prologue), a 'pathway to God' (*CSJ* 3), or as being 'on the way to God' (*RSA* 2). But within these and other all-inclusive programmes of formation lies an understanding of the need for specific development of a personal life of prayer and human integration, in which each individual identity grows and matures in relationship with God. If the minister is to lead others in a life of holiness, then that minister must first and foremost submit to the challenge of such a life.

The area of theology that covered spiritual formation was traditionally known as mystical or ascetical theology, and was in some ways considered a protected area, aimed at a religious elite. The revival of catechetical methods of the primitive Church such as the Rite of Christian Initiation of Adults sees the *mystagogia* as an essential part of initiation into mature, autonomous Christian practice for any person whose faith has at its heart the contemplation of God. In no way can psychology be seen as a substitute or replacement for spiritual formation. But the genius of the great masters of the spiritual life such as SS Benedict, Ignatius, Catherine of Siena and Teresa of Avila, as well as Julian of Norwich, Hildegard of Bingen, Meister Eckhart, Jakob Boehme and other mystics, has been their insight into the working of the inner human psyche and the way it relates to external experience through the grace of God. Present-day spiritual formation lays emphasis on the need to understand our inner selves: our personal history, our sexual identity and our patterns of relationship, if we are to develop a life at once authentic, life-giving and leading to spiritual growth.

Spiritual formation is not something that is part of a person's initial training, which, once undergone, can be considered achieved and assumed, like an examination grade. Certain historical phases, such as catechumenate, novitiate or ministerial training, or a long retreat, will be bound by time. But it must remain continuous, since the Christian remains in a position of discipleship for the whole of life. The secular concept of lifelong learning echoes this understanding. There must be periods of renewal, and some religious orders, such as the Society of Jesus, build this into their system of training with the 'third probation' or tertianship, described by Ignatius as a 'school of the heart' (*CSJ* 516). Sabbatical programmes have a similar aim. But religious belief cannot be divorced from the context of life experience. Through the power of desire and symbolic imagination, the thoughtful human being is always exercised by the gap between ordinary human capacity and what she or he may feel drawn to achieve. Spiritual formation becomes a strategy, within the religious impulse, for addressing this moral gap and achieving the radical transformation of the self. While the interior journey, in a secular sense, has self-awareness as its goal, the spiritual journey leads to self-awareness in relationship to God, and under the transformative power of grace. It is the regular practice of the spiritual life in prayer and the virtues, as well as education in the insights of the human sciences, that constitute spiritual formation as the solid grounding for the following of Christ.

See also **Conversion; Journey, Spiritual; Religious Life; Vows.**

Primary sources: *Constitutions of the Society of Jesus (CSJ)*, St Louis: Institute of Jesuit Sources, 1970; *The Rule of St. Augustine (RSA)*, London: Darton, Longman & Todd, 1996; *The Rule of St. Benedict (RSB)*, London: Sheed & Ward, 1970.

Secondary sources: J. English, *Choosing Life*, New York: Paulist Press, 1978; F. Ferder and J. Heagle, *Your Sexual Self*, Notre Dame, IN: Ave Maria Press, 1992; D. and M. Linn and S. Fabricant, *Healing the Eight Stages of Life*, New York: Paulist Press, 1988; G. May, *Addiction and Grace*, San Francisco: Harper, 1988; T. Moore, *Care of the Soul*, London: Piatkus, 1992; S. Tugwell, *Prayer*, vols 1 and 2, Dublin: Veritas, 1974.

GEMMA SIMMONDS

Franciscan Spirituality

Beginning with its founders, Francis of Assisi (1181/2–1226) and Clare of Assisi (1194/5–1253), Franciscan spirituality proposes the words and deeds of Jesus in the gospel as its basic guide; emphasizing the humility of God revealed in the incarnation, the love manifested by Christ's passion, and the goodness of all creation.

'To observe the Holy Gospel of Our Lord Jesus Christ'. If we were to use one adjective to describe the spirituality of Francis, it would be 'evangelical'. The gospel (*evangelium*) contains all that Francis received from God as the 'revelation' of how he should live. In the *Testament* he wrote shortly before his death he makes clear that 'the Most High Himself revealed to me that I should live according to the pattern of the holy Gospel'. He outlined this way of life in the Rule of the Order of Lesser Brothers (*fratres minores, friars minor*). This brotherhood, founded in 1209/10

with the arrival of Francis' first followers, received final approval of its innovative way of life with papal confirmation of the Rule in 1223.

Incarnation. Francis expressed, in words and gestures, his admiration for the humility of God revealed in the 'Word made flesh'. His desire to visualize the events of the birth of Jesus led him to create an early form of the Christmas crèche or nativity scene in 1223. As the first journey of the 'Word made flesh' was made possible by the faithful consent of the 'most blessed virgin Mary', when the Word descended to make its home in her, Francis compares the eucharistic ministry of the priesthood to the role of Mary, who first gave to us the 'body and blood' of the Lord, as he writes in his *Admonitions*: 'Each day He humbles Himself as when He came from the royal throne into the Virgin's womb.'

Creation. Francis, named 'Patron Saint of Ecology' in 1979 by Pope John Paul II, may be best known internationally as a friend of animals and poet of creation. His 'Canticle of the Creatures' (or 'Canticle of Brother Sun') exalts the goodness of the Creator through the cosmic elements of earth, air, fire and water, each called 'Sister' or 'Brother'. 'Praised be You, my Lord, with all your creatures, especially Sir Brother Sun . . . Sister Moon and the stars.' Even death itself became 'Sister Death' in this, one of the earliest of Italian poems, composed by a nearly blind Francis shortly before his death.

Passion and love. Francis is keenly aware that the Son who is 'given to us' does not draw back from suffering in fulfilling the Father's will to share divine life with humanity. The story of the suffering and death of Christ on the cross moves Francis deeply, as he wrote in his *Testament*: 'By Your holy cross you have redeemed the world.' According to his companion, Brother Leo, two years before his death, during an extended retreat on Mount La Verna in Tuscany, Francis showed marks on his body later hailed as *stigmata*, resembling the wounds of Christ's passion. Exposed for the veneration of the faithful before his funeral, the body of Francis itself became an eloquent sign of his compassion with the suffering of Jesus.

Poverty. The suffering and death of Jesus, followed by his being raised up to glory, are the conclusion of the journey of the incarnation. This journey of 'letting go' of everything for the sake of more abundant life for others, makes Francis' dedication to poverty more understandable. The vocabulary that Francis uses reveals his under-

standing of its basis in the life of Jesus, as he writes in the Rule: 'For our sakes, our Lord made Himself poor in this world.' Following the example of their poor Lord, Francis and his brothers make a vow 'to live without anything of their own'. All things instead must be returned, through almsgiving and thanksgiving, to their true owner, the creator of all.

Clare and the Mirror. Clare joined Francis (in 1212), dedicating herself to life 'according to the Holy Gospel'. This she described in the 'form of life', or Rule of St Clare, that she composed for the Order of Poor Sisters (later called Poor Clares). In her *Letters to Agnes of Prague*, Clare emphasizes the bond between contemplation and poverty. Christ is the Mirror into which Clare and her sisters gaze and, in doing so, marvel at the 'poverty of Him Who was placed in a manger . . . O astonishing poverty!' 'That Mirror, suspended on the wood of the Cross' becomes for Clare the one in whom she may 'contemplate the ineffable charity that led Him to suffer on the wood of the Cross'. Clare writes in her *Testament* that the sisters 'whom the Lord has called to our way of life' are to be 'a mirror and example to those living in the world'.

Example and mirror. One outstanding way in which Clare served as an 'example and mirror' was in her care for those who suffered from a variety of diseases. Clare herself suffered from poor health for many years, and wrote tenderly of care for the sick in her Rule: 'everyone is bound to serve and provide for their sisters who are ill'; and they should perform these services 'as they would wish to be served if they were suffering from some illness'. Among the many examples her sisters recalled in the hearings for Clare's process of canonization, one after another they testify to their own healing in her presence, as each 'had received the sign of the cross . . . and been touched with her hand'.

Communities of brothers and sisters. After the death of their founders, the followers of Francis and Clare continued to spread their characteristic spirituality through communities they founded. The Lesser Brothers was organized for men; the Poor Ladies for women; while the Brothers and Sisters of Penance (or Third Order) welcomed married and single men and women, living in their own homes or in small communities, some of which later became religious communities (Third Order Regular). Franciscan spirituality penetrated the wider society largely through the expansion of these 'Three Orders of St Francis'.

Medieval development. Bonaventure of Bagno-regio (1221–74), a master of theology at Paris, brought the insights of Francis into dialogue with the wider Latin and Greek theological tradition. In *The Soul's Journey into God* he outlines a journey of six steps toward God (from creation, through the human person, to the mystery of the Trinity), culminating in a seventh moment of ecstatic rest in the crucified Christ. Angela of Foligno (1248–1309) takes the affective dimension of Franciscan spirituality to new levels. In *The Book of Blessed Angela*, written by her confessor, Brother 'A', this lay penitent, mother and widow recounts her spiritual journey in the vivid language of spousal love.

In the era of reform. Franciscan spirituality contributed significantly to the great mystical movement in sixteenth-century Spain. Through his *Third Spiritual Alphabet*, Francisco de Osuna (1492–1542) served as a guide for those (including Teresa of Avila) practising the kind of quiet prayer known as 'recollection'. In *The Ascent of Mount Sion*, the Franciscan lay brother and apothecary Bernardino de Laredo (1482–1540) described a path of contemplative prayer leading to a union with God based on love, in a movement from recollection, to quiet, to union. In his classic *Treatise on Prayer and Meditation*, the Franciscan reformer Peter of Alcantara (1499–1562) teaches a simple method for prayer, emphasizing the role of feelings over intellectual speculation.

Modern revival. After serious decline in the wake of the Enlightenment and revolutions, a recovery of Franciscan spirituality began, provoked in part by the 1894 publication of a controversial account of Francis *Vie de Saint François* published by the French Reformed scholar Paul Sabatier. In the course of the twentieth century the story of Francis and Clare was retold through biographies by authors as diverse as G. K. Chesterton, Nikos Kazantzakis, Julien Greene and Leonardo Boff. French composer Olivier Messiaen's opera *Saint François d'Assisi* exalts Francis' love of creation and his compassion for the suffering Christ. Films have also popularized aspects of Franciscan spirituality, as in Roberto Rossellini's *The Flowers of St. Francis* (1950), Franco Zeffirelli's *Brother Sun, Sister Moon* (1973), and Liliana Cavani's *Francesco* (1989).

The twentieth century also saw the increasing popularity within the Roman Catholic Church of the Franciscan Third Order for the laity (now called the Secular Franciscan Order), as a means of spreading the message of Franciscan spirituality. Franciscan spirituality also inspires communities in several other Christian Church communities, as witnessed by The Society of St Francis in the Anglican Communion, Franciscan communities among Lutherans, and interdenominational, ecumenical Franciscan communities.

See also **Eremitical Spirituality; Mendicant Spirituality; Poverty.**

———

Primary sources: Regis Armstrong, J. A. Wayne Hellmann, William Short (eds), *Francis of Assisi: Early Documents*, 4 vols, Hyde Park, NY: New City Press, 1999–2001; Regis Armstrong (ed.), *Clare of Assisi: Early Documents*, St Bonaventure, NY: The Franciscan Institute, 1993; Ewert Cousins (ed.), *Bonaventure: The Soul's Journey into God; The Tree of Life; The Life of St. Francis*, New York: Paulist Press, 1978; Paul Lachance (ed.), *Angela of Foligno: Complete Works*, New York: Paulist Press, 1993; Mary E. Giles (ed.), *Francisco de Osuna: The Third Spiritual Alphabet*, New York: Paulist Press, 1981; E. Allison Peers (ed.), *Bernadino de Laredo, The Ascent of Mount Sion; being the third book of the treatise of that name*, New York: Harper, 1952; Pedro de Alcantara, *A Golden Treatise of Mentall Praier*, Ilkley, UK: Scolar Press, 1977, repr. of Brussels, 1632 edn.

Secondary sources: Marco Bartoli, *Clare of Assisi*, trans. Frances Teresa osc, London: Darton, Longman & Todd; Quincy, IL: Franciscan Press, 1993; Margaret Carney, *The First Franciscan Woman: Clare of Assisi and Her Form of Life*, Quincy, IL: Franciscan Press, 1993; Jacques Dalarun, *The Misadventure of Francis of Assisi*, trans. Edward Hagman ofm cap., St Bonaventure, NY: The Franciscan Institute, 2002; I. Arnaldo Fortini, *Francis of Assisi*, trans. Helen Moak, New York: Crossroad, 1981; Agostino Gemelli, *The Franciscan Message to the World*, trans. Henry Louis Hughes, London: Burns, Oates & Washbourne, 1934; Raoul Manselli, *Saint Francis of Assisi*, trans. Paul Duggan, Chicago, IL: Franciscan Herald Press, 1988; Bernard McGinn, *The Flowering of Mysticism: Men and Women in the New Mysticism (1200–1350), The Presence of God: A History of Western Christian Mysticism*, vol. 3, New York: Crossroad, 1998; E. Allison Peers, *Studies of the Spanish Mystics*, 2nd edn, rev., 3 vols, London: SPCK; New York: Macmillan, 1951–60; Ingrid Peterson, *Clare of Assisi: A Biographical Study*, Quincy, IL: Franciscan Press, 1993; W. Short, *Poverty and Joy: The Franciscan Tradition*, Traditions of Christian Spirituality, London: Darton, Longman & Todd/New York: Orbis, 1999.

WILLIAM SHORT

Freedom

Freedom – whether in the sense of religious and cultural nonconformity, moral autonomy, social emancipation, political independence, sexual licence, individualistic self-definition or the ability to purchase and consume in accordance with our super-stimulated desires – is a word with significant yet varied resonance for modern and postmodern sensibilities. Given that Christianity has not infrequently been perceived as being complicit in maintaining the very constraints from which freedom is sought, it is salient to ask what the Christian tradition has to do with this varied aspiration for freedom.

Something of the tension here is manifest in the commonly expressed preference for 'spirituality' over 'religion', with the former referencing a disparate range of practices, therapies and world views promising personal self-development and the latter rules and institutions fostering impersonal conformity. Potentially more fruitful lines of exploration are suggested by the conviction at the heart of Christian tradition that the life of the Trinity is one of perfect, generative freedom in relation – communion – from which we originate, in which we exist and into which we are being drawn as our own fulfilment. Within this perspective, while 'freedom' bespeaks a desire for liberation from that which frustrates and diminishes, such desire may itself need liberating from our capacity for confusion and delusion. As such, the Christian tradition can be heard throughout as the still unfolding story of God's freeing of us for freedom within which Christian spirituality represents the disciplined learning of the ways of God's freedom in relation in the hope that they will come to be run 'in a sweetness of love beyond words' (Rule of St Benedict).

While freedom itself is a scarce word in Scripture, it is notable that the central redemptive event of the Hebrew Scriptures is the liberation from slavery in Egypt, followed by the forty years of desert wanderings through which the Israelites were slowly formed into a people capable of discerning and manifesting God's good order of life and flourishing. Here freedom is not simply from something but towards something. It is not simply event but programme. More than that, it is vocation, calling and destiny.

Likewise, Paul is quite clear that the freedom for which 'Christ has set us free' (Gal. 5.1, 13) is not only freedom *from* external law, sin and death (Rom. 6.15–23) but freedom *for* the law of love and life in the Spirit (Gal. 5.13–14, 16–26; 2 Cor. 3.17; Rom. 7.6; 8.1–17). Far from being an unconstrained autonomy it represents a move from slavery to sin to slavery of Christ (1 Cor. 7.22; Rom. 6.18, 22).

But nor is the life of service of and gradual conformity to Christ conceived as a frustrating heteronomous imposition. In God we are believed to 'live, move and have our being' (Acts 17.28). Hence, human freedom is regarded as finding its true fulfilment not its contradiction in God's will. As Karl Rahner eloquently expressed it, 'Freedom and dependence on God increase in direct rather than indirect proportion.' Or as Thomas Merton, 'It is only the saints who are truly free.' As this also suggests and as Augustine of Hippo maintained so sharply, given the fractured, confused state of our desiring such freedom requires to be continually received anew and grown into further. While it can powerfully inspire resistance to anything that diminishes human life, it becomes nonsensical if asserted as the right to strict self-determination.

With this, while the long march to freedom is perceived within Christianity as a pilgrimage with an ultimately eschatological orientation, its fundamentally relational character resists its confusion with any merely interior or dispositional quality. Even growth in interior freedom – in detachment from distorted desires and for the joyful, liberating embrace of God's good will – necessarily manifests itself in growth in decisions and practices supportive of mutual wellbeing and, likewise, in the desire for structures and social economies generative of the same. Such growth, whether for individuals or communities, presupposes growth in the discipline of discernment, itself intrinsically relational in character given the need both for attentive listening (obedience) and the perspective of others if we are to hear in concert rather than soliloquy.

In the school of Christian freedom, if it is the Spirit working in us who is the teacher, it is in the life, death and resurrection of Jesus that we find the embodied form of freedom truly performed. Here we find one possessed of a staggering ability, born of the Spirit, to imagine, risk, transcend, challenge, suffer and die trusting in the infinitely generative freedom of his relationship with Abba God. If herein lies the gift to the Church, the correlative calling is to be sign and sacrament of the ways of God's freedom and flourishing in relation for the good of the world – it is the calling of the communion of saints.

See also **Discernment; Obedience; Saints, Communion of; Trinitarian Spirituality; Vocation.**

John J. English sj, *Spiritual Freedom: From an Experience of the Ignatian Exercises to the Art of Spiritual Guidance*, 2nd edn, Chicago, IL: Loyola University Press, 1995; Thomas Merton, *Seeds of Contemplation*, Wheathampstead, Herts:

Anthony Clarke, 1972, pp. 149–57; Karl Rahner, 'Theology of freedom', *Theological Investigations VI*, London: Darton, Longman & Todd, 1969, pp. 178–96.

PAUL D. MURRAY

French School of Spirituality

'French School' is a neologism denoting the spiritual programme of Pierre de Bérulle (1575–1629), founder of the French Oratory, and a group of like-minded reformers. Because the spiritual traditions of France cannot be limited to the circles centred around Bérulle, and transcend ethnic/political categories to some extent, some scholars now use 'the bérullian current'. Understood widely, so as to honour the considerable originality of Bérulle's collaborators, this newer term may be the preferable one. 'School' seems less problematic, if one maintains the classical sense of a 'place' of formation.

Bérulle's period, which includes Vincent de Paul, Francis de Sales, Louise de Marillac, Jeanne de Chantal, and other notables, has been called a 'second golden age' of reform later but parallel to the first 'golden age' of reform in Spain under Ignatius Loyola, Teresa of Avila and John of the Cross. The christocentrism of Loyola and Teresa influenced the School, which also shared sensibilities with the Protestant Reformers (priesthood of the laity, universal call to holiness, clerical education and reform), and was likely more influenced by them than it could understand in the anti-ecumenical atmosphere of the times.

Bérulle is the central founder and theologian. Born into the aristocracy and named an honorary chaplain at court (possibly to placate the anti-Huguenot League with which he was associated), he was able to exercise a leading influence. Named a cardinal in 1627, he was at the end in disfavour at court because of his opposition to some of Richelieu's anti-Roman policies. The Oratory concentrated upon the reform of the secular priesthood, the 'order of Jesus', by combining priestly authority and education with holiness. In time it developed into a system of schools somewhat in competition and even conflict with the Jesuits. Both Descartes and Malebranche had been influenced by Oratorian schooling, for example. Bérulle's prominence also brought him into conflict with the Huguenot theologians, forcing him to study the Scriptures and especially the councils and Fathers made available to him in new 'critical' editions. This accounts for the patristic (Augustinian, Dionysian-Greek) tone in his theological spirituality. In many ways, the French School is simply a creative retrieval of the Johannine, Pauline and conciliar-patristic trinitarian Christology. He was also beneficiary to the mystical literature entering France, and disseminated mainly in the circle of Mme Acarie. Educated in the traditional Scholastic theology, it is nonetheless patent that he was seeking a renewal of theology along the lines of the Fathers, who did not separate their theology from their pastoral practice and mysticism.

The 'vows controversy' (1615–23) illustrates how contentious this spiritual-theological reform could be. Miscommunication and ecclesial rivalry forced Bérulle to indicate that the vows of servitude he was asking the nuns to make were but extensions of the baptismal vows. He had established two 'choirs of servitude' (today perhaps 'service'; see Phil. 2.7), the first a Marian, and the second centred around Jesus' own servitude. The motivation was to be formed, like Mary, through a novitiate of participation in Jesus' servitude; in time this could mature into a greater participation in the depths of Jesus' own slavery. One goes to Jesus 'through Mary', in the sense of being formed in the school of Mary. Authors also refer to Bérulle's 'reversal of the hierarchies [of the universe]', inasmuch as Jesus rather than the angels (as in Dionysius the Areopagite to some extent) is the centre. The God-Man is the sun around whom the universe revolves, the 'Copernican revolution', as Bérulle notably described it (*Discourse on the State and Grandeurs of Jesus*, discourse 2).

Bérulle christifies Neoplatonism's '*exitus*' and '*reditus*' pattern. God's going out to us takes place through the incarnate Word, and as we participate in the God-Man through the deifying work of the Spirit, we return back to the inner life of the Trinity. Trinity, Christology, Eucharist (expressive of his ecclesiology) form an interconnected 'chain of love' (*Grandeurs*, discourse 6). The God-Man is at the centre; as we participate in his states and mysteries, which always remain present in their salvific effects through the Spirit, we are simultaneously led into the mysterious depths of the Trinity as well as 'outwards' into the eucharistic heart of the Church and its mission of holiness. A modern sensitivity is his stress upon a 'double' form of participation in Christ, namely, while all are called, at the same time we receive unique forms of such participation. (Karl Rahner suggested that Bérulle is perhaps the only thinker to have offered a theological study of this theme of our participation in Christ.)

Bérulle explored the full range of Jesus' states, from womb and infancy (a special interest, surfacing later in Thérèse of Lisieux) on through to resurrection and Pentecost, along with attention to the states of his mother, Magdalene and others. This school is very Marian; from it later came Louis Grignion de Montfort. One also senses differences between the way in which Bérulle explores our participation in Jesus' mysteries and how Loyola or Teresa of Avila do so. All contemplate both the humanity and the divinity of Jesus, but Bérulle tends to place the accent upon how the divine Son shines through the human states, like a Greek icon. In other words, Bérulle tends to be Johannine. Loyola and Teresa manifest less of this icon-like tone. When Bérulle contemplates the intra-uterine state of Jesus, the only theme explored in his *Life of Jesus*, or the special form of love experienced by Magdalene, whom he names 'an apostle of the apostles' in his *Elevation on Mary Magdalene*, the human dimension is more prominent. He particularly returns to the themes of adoration and servitude. The God-Man reveals both how God deserves to be adored and yet how self-emptying this God is.

Madeleine de St-Joseph (1578–1637), the First French prioress of the discalced Carmelite nuns in France, was both soul guide and disciple to Bérulle (himself a co-founder of these discalced Carmelites). Madeleine is rather prominent among the many women exercising significant roles in the French School. In her letters, she joins Teresa of Avila's thought with Bérulle's, emphasizing love along with adoration (the latter is only a 'pretence' without love). She critiques the tendency of trying to bypass the humanity of Jesus, as if it were a hindrance in the 'higher' stages of the spiritual journey. She counsels that there are many different spiritual paths, and so the director needs to be humble and submissive to the Spirit's promptings. But always one will be 'adhering' to Jesus, if not in explicit words, certainly 'by state' (that is, in the depths of our being).

Charles de Condren (1588–1641), successor to Bérulle as the Oratory's superior, left us very little by way of writings, but so far as we can tell he was particularly devoted to meditating upon the theme of sacrifice. In a way, his greatest 'writing' was his spiritual disciple Jean-Jacques Olier (1608–57), who went on to found the Society of St Sulpice. M. Olier develops the personal, more psychological side of our participation in Christ, complementing Bérulle's more 'objectivist' approach.

Saint Jean Eudes (1601–80), a disciple of Olier's who founded his own Congregation of Jesus and Mary ('Eudists') and cofounded the Congregation of Good Shepherd sisters, focused upon the hearts of Jesus and Mary, and was along with Margaret Mary Alacoque one of the seminal disseminators of the sacred heart devotion, a devotion which might well be something of a corrective to the rigorism of Jansenism. The *Catechism of the Catholic Church* (no. 521) features him in its section on the mysteries of Jesus.

Baron Gaston de Renty (1611–49), an aristocrat who was under Condren's spiritual guidance, is representative of the considerable lay involvement, male and female, in the projects of the French School. A member of the influential Company of the Blessed Sacrament, Renty was especially attracted to contemplating Jesus' infancy. This was the port of entry to all the other mysteries and the only one we should choose. Jesus the infant child was completely dependent upon God through his total dependency upon his parents. Through our own participation in this infancy, we become properly disposed to the kind of dependency upon God which enables us to accept God's will and thus to obediently participate in the other states of Jesus and his saints as is appropriate. John Wesley found Renty's pastoral spirituality significant and included an abridged version of his life in the *Christian Library*.

The focus upon Jesus' humanity and our participation in its states is emblematic of a new humanism. But the traditional and somewhat restorationist dimension is strong. It is the human as transfigured by divinity which is celebrated. An Augustinian stress on sin, moreover, is an issue of some contention. The School's later religious foundations and its mystics and even canonized saints (de Montfort, John Baptist de la Salle, Chaminade etc.) are a testimony to the School's rich mine of insights. Bérulle particularly is a notable example of how to go about linking theology with spirituality, as writers like Karl Rahner and Hans Urs von Balthasar have noted.

See also **Adoration; Annihilation, Spiritual; Augustinian Spirituality; Christian Humanism; Ignatian Spirituality; Incarnation; Jansenism; Jesus and Spirituality; Neoplatonism; Oratorian Spirituality; Quietism; Reformation and Spirituality; Sacred Heart; Salesian Spirituality; Sulpician Spirituality; Trinity and Spirituality; Vincentian Spirituality.**

Henri Bremond, *A Literary History of Religious Sentiment in France*, vol. 3, *The Triumph of Mysticism*, trans. K. L. Montgomery, London: SPCK, 1936; Michel de Certeau, *The Mystic Fable*, trans. Michael B. Smith, *Religion and Postmodernism*, vol. 1, Chicago: University of Chicago Press, 1992; Louis Cognet, *Post-Reformation Spirituality*, trans. P. Hepburne Scott, *Twentieth Century Encyclopedia of*

Catholicism, 41, New York: Hawthorn, 1959; Raymond Deville, *The French School of Spirituality: An Introduction and Reader*, trans. Agnes C. Cunningham, Pittsburgh: Duquesne University Press, 1994; Louis K. Dupré, *Passage to Modernity: An Essay in the Hermeneutics of Nature and Culture*, New Haven: Yale University Press, 1993; William M. Thompson (ed.), *Bérulle and the French School: Selected Writings*, CWS, New York: Paulist Press, 1989.

WILLIAM THOMPSON-UBERUAGA

Friendship

Biblical literature contains compelling stories of friendship, such as those of Jonathan and David (1 Sam. 18—2 Sam. 1), and Ruth and Naomi (book of Ruth). Jesus' relationships with Mary, Martha and Lazarus (John 11) and with John the beloved disciple (John 13.23, 19.25) have inspired reflection on the spiritual qualities of friendship through many centuries. Wisdom literature esteems the values of loyalty and honesty to be found in true friendship (e.g. Prov. 17.17; 27.6; Ecclus. 6.15; 9.10), and psalms lament the pain of abandonment by false friends (e.g. Ps. 41; 88), a theme powerfully emphasized in the betrayal and loneliness of the suffering Jesus (Mark 14.50, 66–72). The joy of companionship is also celebrated (e.g. Ps. 133; Mark 14.40ff.).

The whole economy of grace set out in the biblical scheme of God's creation and redemption of the human race has been characterized as one of friendship: the restoration of friendship with God through Christ and the working of the Holy Spirit through faith and the sacraments (e.g. *Catechism of the Catholic Church* 1468). From this perspective, the friendship Jesus extends to his disciples (John 15) is one of ultimate self-giving love which restores the primal covenantal friendship of humanity and God. Jesus addresses his disciples and hearers as 'friends' (Luke 12.10, 14), and is condemned by some for his living out of God's generous love and forgiveness as 'friend of tax collectors and sinners' (Matt. 11.19; Luke 7.6). Jesus' death establishes a communion with God and a fellowship among believers which is characterized by friendship (e.g. Rom. 7.4; 1 Cor. 14.26, 39; Gal. 4.12ff.; 5.11).

In the eleventh and twelfth centuries the personal relationships of Jesus in Scripture and the classical philosophies of friendship expounded by Plato, Aristotle and Cicero were fused to form a spirituality of friendship, most notably Aelred of Rievaulx's *Spiritual Friendship*, based on Cicero's *De amicitia*. Aelred commends friendship within religious community as both rooted in and a reflection of divine love: it is in our friendships that we experience God's love in a personal way. Anselm's prayers look to Jesus as 'good friend' and to the saints, particularly St John, as 'compassionate friends of God'. Towards the close of his *Proslogion* Anselm expresses the delight of heaven as that of complete friendship with God, self and others (ch. 25). Anselm's letters, and the examples of St Bernard, St Francis of Assisi and St Clare, show the importance of friendship as a source of strength and support in spiritual life. Post-Reformation writers such as Jeremy Taylor extended spiritual friendship to include marriage. However, Francis de Sales and Vincent de Paul advised against particular friendships in religious life as potentially divisive.

Friendship has been the description for a spiritual intimacy with God which is particular and immediate yet includes other human beings. Those influenced by the mystical piety centred on fourteenth-century Rhineland and Switzerland, such as Eckhart, which stressed inner transformation above outward forms of religious adherence, were known as Gottesfreunde – 'God's friends'. The mid-seventeenth-century Quaker movement assumed the title 'Friends' or 'Society of Friends' in reference to the direct experience of the Holy Spirit in the lives of individuals and the non-hierarchical fellowship of believers which characterizes their relationships with God and one another. Many hymns in the Reformed tradition have placed a devotional emphasis on Jesus as friend in expressing God's intimate knowledge and concern for individuals, and modern hymns emphasize Jesus' friendship as a matter of divine solidarity with the human condition in the incarnation.

Friendship features strongly in contemporary spiritualities. Gay and Lesbian theologians such as Elizabeth Stuart and Michael Vasey commend friendship with God and one another as a model for discipleship and ecclesial community to displace hierarchy and the perceived dominance of heterosexual marriage in the Church. James Nelson has argued that a healthy masculine spirituality will foster friendship as a way of overcoming isolation in men and encountering the living reality of God through mutuality and intimacy. Sallie McFague suggests friendship as a metaphor with which to describe the divine–human relationship: a model which conveys qualities of mutuality, companionship and a shared concern for the well-being of the earth. Contemporary spiritual writers such as Kenneth Leech, and Kathleen Fischer writing from the perspective of feminist spirituality, have explored the possibilities of spiritual direction and guidance in ways which are more akin to friendship and companionship in their emphasis on mutuality and co-exploration. Similarly, relational approaches to the sacrament of penance talk of restoring the sinner to God's friendship, and the restoration of harmonious human relationships through social justice and solidarity can also be understood as one of friendship across barriers of class, race and nation (cf. *Catechism of the Catholic Church* 374, 396).

See also **Feminist Spirituality; Homosexuality and Spirituality; Love; Masculine Spirituality; Quaker Spirituality; Sexuality; Social Justice.**

Aelred of Rievaulx, *Spiritual Friendship*, Cistercian Fathers Series, 5, Kalamazoo: Cistercian Publications, 1974; St Anselm, *Proslogion, Prayers and Meditations*, trans. Benedicta Ward, London: Penguin, 1973; Sallie McFague, *Models of God*, London: SCM Press, 1987; Elizabeth Stuart, *Just Good Friends: Towards a Gay and Lesbian Theology of Relationships*, London: Mowbray, 1995; Theodore Zeldin, *An Intimate History of Humanity*, London: Sinclair-Stevenson, 1994.

MARK PRYCE

Fuga Mundi

see **Monasticism; World.**

Fundamentalism

As a term, 'fundamentalism' is arguably so broad and pejorative as to be almost useless. Nevertheless, in connection with religion, the word still carries weight as a signifier of attitude, temperament, doctrine and ideology. But the use of the term is diverse and fissiparous. It can be linked to religious extremism within nationalist movements in almost any world faith. Equally, fundamentalism can be manifest in a variety of political movements ('religio-political activism'). Jerry Falwell's 'Moral Majority' in the USA campaigns for a particularly conservative social outlook. Billy Graham has been a key confidant to Republican Presidents such as Nixon and Reagan. In Central America, the Guatemalan government of Rios Montt (1981) drew heavily on ultra-conservative Protestant outlooks to reform the nation.

There is a great deal of literature on the subject from a variety of perspectives. There are trenchant defences of the term from scholars such as James Packer (*Fundamentalism and the Word of God*, 1958). Thorough histories of the term have also been undertaken (see Harriet Harris, *Fundamentalism and Evangelicals*, 1998). There is also an enormous range of analyses from the social sciences (see Lionel Kaplan, *Studies in*

Religious Fundamentalism, 1987, and Martyn Percy, *Fundamentalism, Church and Society*, 2002). Scholars such as James Barr, Scott Appleby, Martin Marty, Mark Noll, Nancy Ammerman are continuous contributors to debates about its origin, direction and ethos. Their critiques are broadly socio-theological, but extensive psychological and anthropological treatments are also available in abundance. Of special note is the five-volume series that undertakes a substantial global study of fundamentalism, edited by Martin Marty and Scott Appleby (published between 1991 and 1996 by Chicago University Press), which arose out of a major study called The Fundamentalism Project.

History. In terms of Christianity, fundamentalism is a recent movement, opposed to 'the mixed offerings of modernity'. It takes its name from *The Fundamentals*, a series of pamphlets issued in the USA between 1909 and 1916, which sought to argue for and reassert conservative views on doctrine. A world conference on fundamentals was subsequently convened in Philadelphia in 1919, in reaction to liberally inclined theology. In part, this precipitated the formation of the Southern Baptist Convention. But fundamentalism has also spawned countless seminaries, ministries and new denominations.

The spiritual roots of Christian fundamentalism lie in revivalism, holiness movements, nonconformity and an assortment of sectarian responses to the world. In terms of more recent history, 'fundamentalism' has matured into a more comprehensive (postmodern) response that fights on various fronts, often in a sophisticated way (e.g. TV, radio, political lobbying). Similarly, Islamic fundamentalism fights against secularism, Western imperialism/colonialization, social and economic injustice, nominal Islam, 'impure' Islam, Zionism/Israel and the Power of Non-Muslim world. According to Jeff Haynes (*Religion, Fundamentalism and Ethnicity*, 1995), there are now two types of fundamentalism. The first is concerned with the strict ordering of religion and society according to revealed texts. The second, where the boundaries and status of Scriptures are less clear (in religions such as Hinduism and Buddhism), fundamentalism tends to be concerned with cultural or national purity.

So the history of fundamentalism is more about the use of a relatively modern term than it is concerned with tracing one particular movement. From the beginning, fundamentalism has been difficult to define; it is a spongy, imprecise word that covers a considerable variety of individuals, bodies and movements.

Character. The sheer breadth of fundamentalism makes it a difficult movement to characterize. Indeed, because it is not one movement, but rather a term that describes diverse forms of behaviour, belief and practice that are widespread, extreme caution should be observed in using the word at all. Nevertheless, The Fundamentalism Project argues that there are nine characteristics that typify fundamentalism. Five of these are ideological in outlook: a reaction to the perceived marginalization of religion; selectivity of religious essentials and issues; moral dualism; a commitment to an inerrant Scripture and a tendency towards absolutism; millennialism and 'messianic' interests. The remaining four characteristics are organizational: an 'elect' membership (i.e., an elite, whose identity is clear); sharp delineation of boundaries (e.g. 'saved' and 'unsaved', 'church' and 'world'); authoritarian and charismatic leadership (i.e., anointed leader, guru, etc.); and behavioural requirements (e.g. abstinence). The vast majority of the expressions of fundamentalism from within the 'Abrahamic' faiths (i.e., Christian, Jewish and Muslim) exhibit these characteristics. Many expressions of fundamentalism that fall outside this category (e.g. Sikh, Hindu, Buddhist) also share most if not all of these characteristics. In a slightly different vein, Martin Marty sees fundamentalism almost entirely as a matter of 'fighting'. He also notes how the 'mindset' is reliant on control and authority, echoing the work of James Barr, among others.

We can summarize these characteristics in the following way. First, fundamentalism is a movement that engages in 'backward-looking legitimation': the answer to present crisis, whatever it may be, is deemed to have been revealed in the past. Second, fundamentalism is always dialectical: it must exist in opposition to something. (Take liberalism away and fundamentalism has no raison d'etre.) Third, fundamentalism is a tendency – a habit of the heart or mind – more than it is necessarily a specific creed. Fourth, fundamentalism is trans-denominational, trans-religious as well as being sectarian: it is a widely disseminated and pervasive outlook. Fifth, fundamentalism is 'cultural-linguistic': believers are offered a 'sacred canopy' under which to shelter from the threats of modernity, pluralism and other movements or issues that are held to be deleterious and detrimental towards the purity of the faith. Fundamentalism offers to its adherents a near-complete 'world' that can be developed to take on other world views.

Fundamentalism, the Bible and spirituality. A common misconception about fundamentalism is that it is simplistic. On the contrary, the structure of fundamentalistic thinking is, far from being simple and clear, highly complex, differentiated, accommodating and fluid. Exegesis (i.e., reading meaning 'out of' a text), eisegesis (i.e., reading meaning 'in to' a text), interpretation and exposition abound. The Bible can function almost totemically in some communities, while in others it provides illumination, inspiration and canonicity – but is rarely read or regarded as wholly inerrant. There is, in short, no *precise* agreement on the nature of the Bible and what it determines of itself for fundamentalists. Some have 'high' views of inspiration, but have abandoned inerrancy. Others qualify inerrancy, insisting that the doctrine only applies to original autographs, excludes grammatical errors or misspellings, and is exempted from lack of precision in certain matters, or apparent contradictions.

This leads scholars to identify at least five different versions of the doctrine of inerrancy: propositional (absolute); pietistic (i.e., a kind of spiritual biblicism); nuanced (some portions of Scripture weigh more than others); critical (identifies non-essential errors); and functional (limited inerrancy, or particular infallibility). Each of these versions will produce a distinct kind of spiritual harvest. The freedom to interpret some parts of the Bible analogically instead of historically will open up particular vistas of meaning for the reader.

Even in the most tightly defined fundamentalistic communities, there is considerable divergence on what constitutes an inerrant Bible. And bearing in mind that for such communities, authority flows *from* the inerrancy of Scripture (which is to say that ecclesial and ministerial authority is regarded as being *under* the Word), the patterns of authority and teaching in such communities will vary widely. Where there are similarities between them, they may be morphological rather than doctrinal (in other words a matter of style, not substance).

The role of women in faiths and society is an arena where fundamentalistic views can be tested and studied comparatively. In Protestant Christian fundamentalism, the majority of churches and movements will not regard women holding spiritual authority or office to be either appropriate or biblical. But there will be some notable exceptions to this. For example, a small number of 'house churches' will recognize women as having an apostolic ministry of oversight and leadership, although this is still a rare feature in the house-church movement. In Christianity, Judaism and Islam, a more fundamentalistic outlook tends to assign an apparently 'traditional' role to women – as wife, mother and home-maker. In certain religious traditions, women will be barred from certain ritual activities such as public prayer, or will be required to carry out worship in a segregated arena. But at the same time, there are some scholars who take the view that women can be spiritually empowered by what is apparently manifest oppression. Ironic-ally, the spirituality of women in fundamentalist communities can have a powerful leavening effect upon the overall polity of a movement, and several studies have shown that women can feel liberated and empowered by particular expressions of fundamentalism.

Invariably, the roles assigned to women are traced back to (apparent) scriptural norms, but this can lead to some peculiar anomalies. For example, in college and university Christian Unions (IVF in the USA and UCCF in the UK), women are often not allowed to hold authority at particular levels, and some will forbid women addressing main meetings. This tradition is observed in spite of the fact that Christian Unions are not Churches, and the scriptural injunctions pertaining to women holding authority only seem to be applicable in ecclesial contexts. Suffice to say, debate on the issue within any Christian Union would normally be seen as divi-sive. But Christian Unions are by no means unique in holding to a literalist or fundamental-istic interpretation on the role of women. Within mainstream Christian denominations, some will assert that Jesus' choice of male apostles has always implied that women should not hold authority in churches. Some will go further, and argue that the maleness of Christ reveals an absolute truth about appropriate priestly representation.

Thus, a review of the authority of the Bible in different denominations would reveal a similarly significant range of diversity. Some treat the sacred text as a 'rule book' (instructions to be followed, carefully), others as a guidebook (a few rules, many recommendations, warnings, sug-gestions, etc.), and most interchanging between the two. (But is it not the case that the parabolic tradition of Jesus gives the Church precisely this permission to act so fluidly?) Ecclesial com-munities and fundamentalistic movements are unavoidably hermeneutical rather than (vapid-ly) receptive. They are *within* the (ultimate) par-able of Jesus Christ – experiencing God's story of incarnation, redemption and resurrection as it continues to unfold within them and around them: the Word made flesh. This makes them responsive and reflexive in character; their only difference lies in the degrees to which differences and diversity are tolerated.

Conclusion. In talking about fundamentalism, it is important to remember that although (allegedly) inerrant texts frequently play a major part in defining the movement and constituting its identity, other 'agents' may operate just as effectively as fundaments. A pope or guru, a type of experience, or even a moral code, can all func-tion just as programmatically. Fundamentalism remains a broad umbrella term for a cluster of movements that are habitually restless within the world. Fundamentalism seeks clarity in the midst of ambiguity. It strives to locate and cele-brate certainty in the midst of doubt. It antici-pates and expects faith to triumph over secular reason.

At the same time, it cannot be said that funda-mentalism absolutely and necessarily resists modernity. Fundamentalists are remarkably adept at accommodating the world in order to achieve their higher religious, political and social purposes. Thus, while some may decry the influence of the media or the Internet, it is pre-cisely in such arenas that fundamentalists are also to be found at their most active. Fundamen-talism, in other words, does not simply resist modernity; it also engages with it – radically – in order to achieve the restoration of a 'purer' form of faith that will provide a credible alternative to secularity. Fundamentalism therefore continues to be a diverse but pervasive spiritual force with-in most societies at the beginning of the twenty-first century.

J. Barr, *Fundamentalism*, London: SCM Press, 1977; H. Harris, *Fundamentalism and Evangel-icals*, Oxford: Oxford University Press, 1998; J. Haynes, *Religion, Fundamentalism and Ethnicity*, London: Longman, 1995; L. Kaplan, *Studies in Religious Fundamentalism*, Amhurst: University of Massachussetts Press, 1987; J. Packer, *Fundamentalism and the Word of God*, London: Inter-Varsity Press, 1958; M. Percy, *Fundamen-talism, Church and Society*, London: SPCK, 2002.

MARTYN PERCY

Gilbertine Spirituality

The Gilbertine Order, founded by St Gilbert of Sempringham (1083–1189), was the only uniquely English religious order created during the Middle Ages. Gilbert studied in England and France, was ordained *c.* 1123 and became the Rector of Sempringham of which his father was lord of the manor. The story of the foundation of the Order is told in the *Vita* or *Life of Gilbert* composed in 1201 by an unknown canon of the Order and expanded in 1205 as part of the movement for Gilbert's canonization.

On the death of his father, Gilbert built a convent (1131) in the village for seven women who sought to live a monastic life. These women appear to have begun as anchoresses attached to the parish church – a manifestation of the new eremitical strand of spirituality that emerged in the Western Church during the twelfth century. The new community of nuns was placed under the Rule of St Benedict with some Cistercian features, and the eremitical origins were reflected in the emphasis on strict enclosure. The maintenance of this enclosure was the motivation behind the gradual introduction first of lay sisters then of lay brothers (influenced by contacts with the Cistercians at Rievaulx, North Yorkshire) to do the manual labour and to deal with outside business. Indeed, all of the eventual categories of membership were subordinated to the priority of the contemplative nuns.

In the context of his times, Gilbert can be credited with opening up new opportunities for women's spirituality in England. This not only applied to the nuns but even more to Gilbert's recruitment of village girls in simple vows to assist the contemplatives. This creation of lay sisters made religious life available to a class of women who had previously been overlooked. It appears that they assisted at the nuns' liturgy where possible and provision was made for them to receive some teaching from one of the nuns.

A second foundation was made at Haverholme in 1139 and other foundations followed. In the Charter for Haverholme granted by the Bishop of Lincoln there is a reference to the contemplative nuns following 'the life of the monks of the Order of Citeaux as far as the strength of their sex allows'. In 1147 Gilbert visited Bernard of Clairvaux and sought to have his community formally incorporated into the Cistercian Order. This project failed although the *Vita* refers to Bernard helping Gilbert to draw up the *Institutes of the Gilbertine Order* that was to cover all the categories of the Order, male as well as female. On his return to England, Gilbert became Master of the Order and introduced canons regular under the Augustinian Rule to serve the Gilbertine communities as priest-chaplains. Some communities became double (or parallel) monasteries with a prioress in charge of the nuns and a prior to head the canons. There were also communities of canons alone. At least one Gilbertine house, St Katherine in Lincoln, was associated with running a hospital. W. Dugdale's *Monasticon Anglicanum* notes the presence there of twenty lay sisters alongside sixteen brothers although a surviving charter only refers to men.

Eventually, due to some sexual incidents and discontent among the lay brothers (who lost status once another male category, the canons, was introduced), the organization of the Gilbertines was significantly revised. This particularly involved a more rigorous segregation of the different categories of members in daily life and worship. The relatively easy and innovative co-operation of the early years was effectively lost.

At its height, the Gilbertine Order had approximately 700 canons and 1,500 nuns. At St Gilbert's death there were nine double monasteries and four of men, while at the dissolution of the monasteries under Henry VIII the Order totalled twenty-five monasteries. Because of the purely English nature of the Gilbertines (apart from abortive foundations in Scotland and Rome), the Reformation marked the end of the Order.

It is difficult to establish the spiritual ethos of the Order at this distance in time and with such a dearth of writings. How Cistercian was the spirituality? How much help did Gilbert have in drawing up the *Institutes*? How distinctive was the Order in reality? Some sermons survive but no writings by the women. We have to rely mainly on the *Institutes* and the *Vita of Gilbert*. These emphasize classic biblical themes and present the Order in very Augustinian terms as a community of diverse people living together in harmony: women and men, young and old, monastics and clerics, literate and illiterate. The anonymous canon who wrote the *Vita*, paraphrasing Isaiah 11 and alluding to Ps. 148.12, focused particularly on how the four categories of membership present a marvellous unity prefiguring the harmony of paradise.

See also **Augustinian Spirituality; Canonical Communities; Cistercian Spirituality; English Spirituality; Eremitical Spirituality; Rules, Religious.**

Janet Burton, *Monastic and Religious Orders in Britain 1000–1300*, Cambridge: Cambridge University Press, 1994; Sharon Elkins, *Holy Women of Twelfth-Century England*, Chapel Hill: University of North Carolina Press, 1988; Sharon Elkins, 'All ages, every condition and both sexes: the emergence of a Gilbertine identity' in John A. Nichols and Lillian Thomas Shank (eds), *Distant Echoes: Medieval Religious Women*, vol. 1, Kalamazoo: Cistercian Publications, 1984; Brian Golding, *Gilbert of Sempringham and the Gilbertine Order c1130–c1300*, Oxford: Clarendon Press, 1995; Sally Thompson, *Women Religious: The Founding of English Nunneries after the Norman Conquest*, Oxford: Clarendon Press, 1991.

PHILIP SHELDRAKE

Global Spirituality

The term 'global spirituality' reflects one of the major religious phenomena of our time. Over the last hundred years there has emerged an increasing interest in world religions, not primarily in terms of their history and doctrines, but in terms of their spiritual wisdom that can enrich and guide seekers on their individual spiritual journey and at the same time lead to the emergence of a global spiritual community. This is a matter of great challenge and opportunity, for as Philip Sheldrake observes, 'The self-identity of Christian spirituality is in process of a massive transition as it comes to terms with existence in a global, multi-cultural, multi-faith world.'

In his book *The Way of All the Earth*, John Dunne writes: 'Is a religion coming to birth in our time? It could be. What seems to be occurring is a phenomenon we might call "passing over," passing over from one culture to another, from one way of life to another, from one religion to another.' According to Dunne, passing over leads to a return: 'It is followed by an equal and opposite process we might call "coming back," coming back with a new insight to one's own culture, one's own way of life, one's own religion.' Dunne sees this process as characteristic: 'Passing over and coming back, it seems, is the spiritual adventure of our time.'

The meaning of the two terms in our topic, 'global' and 'spirituality', can be seen through the perspective of a 25-volume publishing project entitled *World Spirituality: An Encyclopedic History of the Religious Quest*. In terms of scope this project covers the vast history of spirituality from prehistoric times into the traditions of Asia, Europe, Africa, Australia and North and South America. Although it focuses also on the present and the future, it encompasses the whole of human history. In describing the nature of spirituality, it proposes the following definition:

> The series focuses on that inner dimension of the person called by certain traditions 'the spirit.' This spiritual core is the deepest center of the person. It is here that the person is open to the transcendent dimension; it is here that the person experiences ultimate reality. The series explores the discovery of this core, the dynamics of its development, and its journey to the ultimate goal. It deals with prayer, spiritual direction, the various maps of the spiritual journey, and the methods of advancement in the spiritual ascent.

The meaning of global spirituality can also be seen through the lens of the Parliament of the World's Religions, which held its first meeting in Chicago in 1893. It was at this gathering that Swami Vivekananda electrified a large audience and effectively launched the inter-religious movement. Throughout the next century the movement increased around the world and eventually gained such momentum that many thought the inter-religious movement had become global and there was no need for a Parliament in Chicago. However, it was decided to hold a hundredth anniversary meeting of the Parliament, which took place in Chicago in 1993, with some eight thousand attending. It was at this event that a suggestion was made to hold meetings about every five years. As a result, the next meeting was in Cape Town in 1999 with almost eight thousand attending and most recently in Barcelona with almost nine thousand. The inter-religious movement has now become global, with meetings held increasingly throughout the world, supported by numerous publications.

By looking at the plan of the most recent Parliament in Barcelona, we can get a picture of its scope and content. The Barcelona Parliament took place over one week and consisted of a plenary session each evening along with a total of more than seven hundred sessions throughout the week, covering the wide range of global spirituality. For example, one session involved a Hindu, Sundarararjan, a Confucian, Tu Weiming, and a Christian, Ramon Panikkar, on the topic 'World Spirituality: Into the Future'. Another session was on 'Praying Together' with Marcus Braybrook, President of the World Congress of Faiths, Iman Dr Abdul Jalil and Fr Albert Nambiaparambil.

In order to understand the present and future unfolding of spirituality, it is valuable to situate it in its historical context. The history of spirituality can be expressed in three periods.

1. **The Pre-Axial Period.** The first stage of human consciousness is what existed among indigenous people before the emergence of Axial consciousness.
2. **The Axial Period.** (So named because it was the axis around which history turned.) After a long development of agriculture, river trade, and communication through the use of the alphabet and written texts, a new kind of consciousness emerged: Axial consciousness, which appeared in Asia and Europe between 800 and 200 BCE. Axial consciousness itself, as well as those other developments, provided the basis for the civilizations of the world, along with the emergence of the great world religions: Hinduism, Buddhism, Taoism, Confucianism, Judaism, and later Christianity and Islam.

3. **The Second Axial Period**. This began its emergence about 1900. It is the period in which we now find ourselves, and it continues into the future.

My understanding of these periods is derived from Teilhard's general theory of the evolution of consciousness, with the shift from divergence to convergence taking place in our era.

This global consciousness, made more complex through the meeting of cultures and religions, is only one characteristic of the Second Axial Period. The consciousness of this period is global in another sense, namely, in rediscovering its roots in the earth. At the very moment when the various cultures and religions are meeting each other and creating a new global community, our life on the planet is being threatened. The very tools that we have used to bring about this convergence, industrialization and technology, are undercutting the biological support system that sustains life on our planet. The future of consciousness, even life on Earth, is shrouded in a cloud of uncertainty by the pollution of our environment, the depletion of natural resources, the unjust distribution of wealth and the stockpiling of nuclear weapons. Unless the human community reverses these destructive forces, we may not survive far into the future. The human race as a whole – all the diverse cultures and religions – must face these problems squarely.

In the Second Axial Period we must rediscover the dimensions of consciousness of the spirituality of the primal peoples of the Pre-Axial Period. As we saw, this consciousness was collective and cosmic, rooted in the earth and the life cycles. We must rapidly appropriate that form of consciousness or perish. I am not suggesting, however, a romantic attempt to live in the past, but that the evolution of consciousness proceeds by way of recapitulation. Having developed self-reflective, analytic, critical consciousness in the First Axial Period, we must now, while retaining these values, reappropriate and integrate into that consciousness the collective and cosmic dimensions of the pre-Axial consciousness. We must recapture the unity of tribal consciousness by seeing humanity as a single tribe, and we must see this single tribe related organically to the total cosmos. This means that the consciousness of the twenty-first century will be global from two perspectives: from a horizontal perspective, cultures and religions must meet each other on the surface of the globe, entering into creative encounters that will produce a complexified collective consciousness; and from a vertical perspective, they must plunge their roots deep into the earth in order to provide a stable and secure base for future development.

This new global consciousness must be organically ecological, supported by structures that will ensure justice and peace. The voices of the oppressed – the poor, women, and racial and ethnic minorities – must be heard and heeded. These groups, along with the earth itself, can be looked upon as the prophets and teachers of the Second Axial Period. This emerging twofold global consciousness is not just a creative possibility to enhance the twenty-first century; it is an absolute necessity if we are to survive.

What does this mean for religions in the twenty-first century? It means that they have a double task: to enter creatively into the dialogue of religions and to channel their energies into solving the common human problems that threaten our future on the earth. It means that they must strip away negative and limiting attitudes toward other religions. They must avoid both a narrow fundamentalism and a bland universalism. They must be true to their spiritual heritage, for this is the source of their power and their gift to the world. They must make every effort to ground themselves in their own traditions and at the same time to open themselves to other traditions. In concert with the other religions they should commit themselves to creating the new, more complex, global consciousness we have been exploring.

But to meet, even creatively, on the spiritual level is not enough. They must channel their spiritual resources toward the solution of global problems. For the most part, this calls for a transformation of the religions. Having been formed in the First Axial Period, the religions bear the mark of Axial consciousness in turning toward the spiritual ascent and away from the material. The religions must rediscover the material dimension of existence and its spiritual significance. In this they can learn from the secular that justice and peace are human values that must be cherished and pragmatically cultivated. But they must not adopt an exclusively secular attitude, for their unique contribution is to tap their reservoirs of spiritual energy and channel this into developing secular enterprises that are genuinely human. I believe that it is in this larger context that the emerging spiritual communities of the world must face together the challenges of the Second Axial Period.

In conclusion, the roots of global spirituality go back to the dawn of human history. From the very beginning, in spite of differences, it has had a common core which emerged in diverse ways throughout the unfolding of history. In our era, with increasing communication and with the convergence of cultures, we are beginning to awaken to the fact that we have been on a single spiritual journey from the very outset.

Series: 'Classics of Western Spirituality', 106 volumes (Christian, Jewish, Muslim), Mahwah, NJ: Paulist Press, 1978–; *World Spirituality: An Encyclopedic History of the Religious Quest*, ed. Ewert Cousins. 25 vols, New York: Crossroad, 1985–.

John Dunne, *The Way of All the Earth: Experiments in Truth and Religion*, Notre Dame: University of Notre Dame Press, 1978; Raimundo Pannikar, *The Trinity and the Religious Experience of Man*, New York: Orbis Books, 1973.

EWERT H. COUSINS

Glory

In the Old Testament the glory (*kabod*) of God includes resonances of weight, worth and richness. It is the particular expression of God's holiness and personal character (see Ex. 33.12ff.) and is also envisioned as the hoped-for realization of God's plan of salvation (Isa. 58; 60). In the New Testament, glory (*doxa*) includes both this sense of radiance and manifest goodness and also the common Greek meaning of opinion or reputation. For Paul this radiant and salvific holiness is focused within the world in the figure of Christ (2 Cor. 4.3–6). In other (deutero-) Pauline literature the Holy Spirit is particularly noticed as the sign, within the community, of the coming consummation of Christ's glory to which the world is called (Eph. 1.13–14; Heb. 6.4–5). This theme is developed greatly in the Johannine literature. John portrays the world as caught between a tendency to seek its glory from itself and Jesus' receiving of glory from the Father (John 5). This is a crucial theme in John for it points towards the new adoption or birth of believers in Christ, who come to receive their identity and glory no longer from their biological or cultural status but from their acceptance as God's children in the beloved child Jesus (cf. John 3). Thus, glory has a dual role in Christian spirituality for John: it marks the newly emerging identity of those who believe, and it does so precisely because it is a sharing in 'the glory as of a father's only son' (John 1.14), made known within the transformed community by the hidden presence of the Holy Spirit (John 14.26). Glory is thus the shining into historical visibility of the Father's joy (the Holy Spirit) in the Word.

This theme of the Spirit as the glory of divine delight, poured out transformingly within the world, appears in Augustine (*The Trinity*): the

Bishop of Hippo (354–430) suggests that just as the Father delights eternally in the Son, glorifying him (which is the eternal procession of the Spirit), so the same divine delight of the Spirit is manifest as glory within all creation because it exists as the expression in time of the Word in whom the Father delights. 'That inexpressible embrace, so to say, of the Father and the image [the eternal Word] is not without enjoyment, without charity, without happiness [the Holy Spirit]' who as eternal joy of the divine Persons is also found 'pervading all creatures according to their capacity with its [the Spirit's] vast generosity and fruitfulness' (*Trinity* 6.2.11). Important developments in this Augustinian theme of the divine glory in creation occur with the rise of the Franciscan tradition, especially in the work of Bonaventure (*c.* 1217–74). It reappears most intriguingly in the thought of the Anglican theologian and poet Thomas Traherne (*c.* 1636–74) and the American Puritan divine Jonathan Edwards (1703–58). For both writers, the whole divine economy of creation and salvation radiates the divine glory continually, but only through participation in Christ is humanity enabled to offer creation back through praise to its divine maker, thus realizing the creation's calling to reflect the glory of God.

For a massive survey of the theme of glory in Christian metaphysics, theology and spirituality, see the seven vols of Hans Urs von Balthasar, *The Glory of the Lord: A Theological Aesthetics*, Edinburgh: T & T Clark; San Francisco: Ignatius Press, 1982–9.

Primary sources: Augustine, *The Trinity*, trans. Edmund Hill, New York: New City Press, 1991; Bonaventure, *Collations on the Six Days*, trans. José de Vinck, Paterson, NJ: St Anthony Guild Press, 1970; Jonathan Edwards, *A Jonathan Edwards Reader*, ed. John E. Smith et al., New Haven: Yale University Press, 1995; Thomas Traherne, *Centuries*, ed. H. M. Margouliouth, Oxford: Oxford University Press, 1958.

Secondary sources: Stephen R. Holmes, *God of Grace and God of Glory: An Account of the Theology of Jonathan Edwards*, Edinburgh: T & T Clark, 2000; Denise Inge, 'Introduction', *Thomas Traherne: Poetry and Prose*, London: SPCK, 2002.

MARK A. MCINTOSH

Gnosticism

'Gnosticism' is one of the more poorly defined terms, whether as an abstract name for a spectrum of ideas or as a collective name for a group of devotees ('the Gnostics'), in Christian history; and much of the contemporary debate as to its origins, content and extent is a function of the term's indiscriminate use in both scholarly and popular religious literature. 'Gnosis' ('the knowledge') of Jesus is linked to salvation in several places in early Christian writings (e.g. John 17.3) while there are also warnings of a 'false gnosis', in opposition to Christian faith, in other places (e.g. 1 Cor. 8.1; 1 Tim. 6.20). And, from a later period (Irenaeus (c. 130–c. 200), Tertullian (c. 160–c. 225) and Hippolytus (c. 170–c. 236)) we have condemnations of what was seen as a perversion of Christianity and called 'Gnosticism'. Until the mid twentieth century scholarship saw these early reactions – and until that time these reactions were the sources of all our information – as pointing to a distinct trend or flavour of belief, and so a group affected by that trend, among early Christians. So for some scholars, following the early Fathers, there was the heresy of Gnosticism and a group 'the Gnostics': the movement was then represented as the falsehood that arose from the extreme submergence of Christianity within a Hellenistic religious culture. Other scholars argued that Gnosticism was a diffuse religious movement within the Hellenistic world that combined philosophical ideas with elements derived from the various mystery cults and which was syncretistic in nature: hence it could adopt Christian ideas and names, appearing to overlap with Christianity. Thus the Manichees are seen to fall within the category of the Gnostics: they are not really Christian heretics, but the followers of a materialist dualism which adopts much Christian vocabulary; which offered its initiates the secret knowledge which allowed them to be delivered from the power of Darkness.

This situation changed radically with the discovery of a cache of texts (52 different treatises) in Egypt at the site of the early monastery of Chenoboskion, now Nag Hammadi, on the Nile in 1945. These texts ranged from items that are unexceptionally Christian (albeit unknown to the tradition) to texts that are unambiguously pieces of philosophical speculation, but many treatises fall between these poles presenting Christianity in an esoteric language within a cosmos of many divine/angelic powers. Other texts adopted certain Jewish or Christian notions into a radically different religious cosmos to that of either Jews or Christians, while preserving a veneer of Christian language and symbolism. From the moment of the announcement of the discovery of these texts they were being claimed as 'the library of the Gnostics' – now able to speak for themselves and not just through their enemies – and presented as if they formed a coherent corpus of texts and religious ideas. However, as an earlier generation of scholars assumed links between those criticized by Paul and those later attacked as 'the Gnostics', so more recently many scholars have assumed links between 'the Gnostics' and the target audience (or audiences) of the texts found in Egypt. Actual historical linkages are very difficult to establish, and apart from the fact that these texts were gathered together in specific codices and buried by those monks (and we can only speculate as to the significance of that action: burning would be a far more efficient means of indicating condemnation) we have no evidence that they represent any connected body of thought much less any specific group.

However, if we step back from the search for the Gnostics as a group or Gnosticism as a specific system, it is clear that there were many people in the early centuries of Christianity who sought answers to the human predicament, explanations of the purpose of life, the relationship of good to evil, and liberation from this level of existence through a knowledge of what would save them from this existence within a religious world that has (1) many points of contact with Christianity and its sources (e.g. references to Christ and the angels named in Judaeo-Christian tradition), but which also (2) has many overlaps with other traditions of ancient religious belief (e.g. acceptance of a religious astrology or cosmic determinism), and which (3) was not passed on as part of the inheritance of Christian thought (e.g. material relating to the Great Seth) or has been formally rejected (e.g. that Jesus only appeared to suffer and die on the cross). So rather than describe a group's beliefs, it is more profitable to attempt to isolate some characteristic tendencies in those texts, which lie within that net of criteria. First, many Nag Hammadi texts, in agreement with the claims of early Christian opponents of the Gnostics, see the possession of the secret knowledge about the divinity or the universe as, in itself, conveying salvation. Linked with this is the interest in special select societies of initiates who have privileged access to this knowledge. While initiation was a central concern of early Christianity, mainstream Christianity was missionary rather than sectarian in its impulse. Second, that knowledge is the secret code that unravels the mysteries of the universe (as a material reality) and the locus of humanity's predicament. Linked with this sense of knowing what is really happening in the cosmos is a belief that the responsibility for evil, whether physical (e.g. illness) or moral (e.g. fornication), lies in the cosmos, and the individual is at the mercy of these forces. Third, there is often an anti-world dimension in these beliefs so that the creation is a prison from which to escape rather than as the milieu intended by God and entered and redeemed/sanctified by the Christ. This can be developed in terms of humans not really belonging within their bodies but as sparks of divine fire trapped until they can discover and know their true realm. Fourth, a tendency to merge the divine with the created universe, or the spiritual and material orders, as if they formed an ontological continuity, and in particular to blur the Creator/creation divide (this is, from the standpoint of historic Christian orthodoxy, the fundamental human error). Thus there are other divine beings – one of which, for example, the demiurge could be the creator of the material universe where humans are trapped – between a supreme being and human beings, and these intermediate beings (sometimes with angelic names or sometimes bearing names derived from Greek religious thought) might be hostile to humanity or humanity's destiny.

These ideas, so similar in appearance to orthodox Christianity and its expression, circulated for centuries popping up here and there, sometimes provoking vigorous reaction and at other times just being re-absorbed within the mainstream. For example, it is often shown that the Manichees are an organized group in late antiquity which exhibit many of the characteristics of Gnosticism (cf. Rudolph, *Gnosis*, pp. 326–42), then similarities with the Bogomils (tenth century) are noted, and then that group is linked to medieval groups such as the Cathars (cf. S. Runciman, *The Medieval Manichee: A Study of the Christian Dualist Heresy*, Cambridge 1960). Clearly, many later religious movements both East and West adopted ideas that can be labelled 'Gnostic', but tracing exact lines of influence is often impossible. The mixture of 'secret knowledge' offering to decode the human situation, along with an exotic, esoteric cosmology seems to possess a perennial fascination. Indeed, the attraction shows little sign of abating today. The religious interest in the work of Carl Jung (1875–1961), and his interest in religious symbolism, is frequently related to an explicit interest in 'gnostic' ideas. Many New Age groups structure their beliefs in ways that resemble the ideas found in some Nag Hammadi texts; and this interest can be seen in the religious welcome those texts often receive as the 'secret library of wisdom', which was 'banished' by Christians jealous of its wonders! While from more explicitly Christian circles have come many books in recent years on the 'secret life' of Jesus or which present Jesus as the revealer of a wisdom subse-

quently lost or hidden which rely heavily on both texts and tendencies which fall within the range of 'Gnosticism'.

See also **Augustinian Spirituality; Cappadocian Fathers; Cosmology; Coptic Spirituality; Knowledge; Neoplatonism; New Age.**

G. Filoramo, *A History of Gnosticism*, Oxford: Oxford University Press, 1990; G. Filoramo, 'Gnosis – Gnosticism' in Angelo Di Berardino (ed.), *Encyclopedia of the Early Church*, Cambridge: James Clarke & Co., 1992, vol. 1, pp. 352–4; A. H. B. Logan, *Gnostic Truth and Christian Heresy*, Edinburgh: T & T Clark, 1996; James M. Robinson, 'The discovery of the Nag Hammadi codices', *Biblical Archaeologist* 42 (1979), 206–24; James M. Robinson (ed.), *The Nag Hammadi Library in English*, 3rd edn, Leiden: E. J. Brill, 1988; Kurt Rudolph, *Gnosis*, Edinburgh: T & T Clark, 1983; Richard Smith, 'Afterword: the modern relevance of Gnosticism' in Robinson (ed.), *Nag Hammadi Library*, pp. 532–49.

THOMAS O'LOUGHLIN

God, Images of

Christianity lives between the recognition, shared with the other Abrahamic traditions and beyond, of the profound unknowability of God the infinite, inexhaustible source of all that is and its defining belief in Jesus of Nazareth as *the* expressed image (Col. 1.15) and uttered Word of God (John 1.1–18), God's own body language as it were. With this, it lives between the conviction that as created through the Word in the Spirit all things are able to disclose something of God, albeit only ever partially, and the recognition that on account of sin such disclosure is always in a distorted, disfigured form that disguises and confuses as it discloses.

In this perspective the absolutizing of any image of God is necessarily idolatrous. This extends beyond the prohibition of the worship of 'graven images' (Ex. 20.4) to the need also to recognize the intrinsically limited character even of all genuinely revelatory events. Notably prefacing the second narrative of the revelation of the Decalogue (Ex. 34), for example, is a clear cautionary statement that though 'you shall see my back . . . my face shall not be seen' (Ex. 33.17–23). Within specifically Christian tradition particularly important to recognize here is that this proviso significantly applies even to the humanity of Jesus, regarded in Christian faith precisely as the incarnate, embodied 'form and face of the knowledge of the Father' (Basil of Caesarea, *Letters* 38.8). Given the significance of this for any discussion of the use of images in Christian spirituality and its counter-intuitive character it is worth teasing out a little.

The life, death and resurrection of Jesus as witnessed to in the New Testament writings are understood within Christianity as the fullest possible revelation of God in this order – God's speaking God's Word in human form – in such a fashion as is taken to mean that there can be no other genuine knowledge of God that contradicts what is known of God in Jesus. All of this is compatible, however, with properly recognizing that even the transfigured humanity of the incarnate Word prior to the resurrection and ascension was a limited creaturely reality that could not possibly exhaustively disclose the infinite fullness of God (see Aquinas, *ST* 3a.25.2). Indeed, as much is suggested by the depiction of the risen Jesus' command to Mary Magdalene not to seek to hold on to him (John 20.17). Consequently, the Christian conviction that the interpreted memory of Jesus constitutes the unparalleled criterion for assessing all claims for experience and knowledge of God can be reconciled with a positive acknowledgement of there also being, to borrow Karl Barth's phrase, 'other lights' from which Christianity can itself learn.

Further, given the trinitarian structure of Christian faith, such 'other lights' need not be viewed as alternative sources of revelation competing with the one revelation of God in Christ and the Spirit. The point is that it is authentic to the Christian tradition to recognize that while the Word, the eternal self-expression of God, and the Holy Spirit, the energy of God, might not be fundamentally other than Christianity knows, they are nevertheless always necessarily greater than Christianity yet knows them to be. It is, in this perspective, the Church that belongs to and exists within the Trinity rather than vice versa. Far, then, from promoting any premature exclusive closure, it is the central convictions of Christian faith that should serve to keep it open to the possibility of fresh learning.

In turn, if Christian tradition exists between the necessary use and the necessary unsettling of all images, understandings and concepts of God, an interesting parallel has emerged in some recent epistemology and philosophy of language. Here also there is dual recognition both of the essential role of image, word and concept in constructively shaping rather than just subsequently expressing human experience and of the inevitable partiality and final inadequacy of all of our images, words and concepts even to the task of articulating the complexity and richness of finite reality.

Whether approached, then, within the frame of dogmatic or philosophical theological understanding, Christian tradition is characterized by a concern for an appropriately disciplined regard for images of God. In terms of the actual practice of Christian life and spirituality images of God feature in a variety of ways from the visual or symbolic to the conceptual and from the public and tangible to the personal and imaginative. In each case the same key principles associated with the fundamental theology of revelation apply.

From early on Christians have produced artistic images depicting biblical scenes, the person of Christ and the saints – those regarded as manifesting conformity to the image of Christ and so variously showing what it means for humans truly to be formed in the 'image' and 'likeness' of God (Gen. 1.26). Although the conventions pertaining to such images between East and West may differ, the intent throughout is the same. While at one level they convey knowledge and understanding without resort to words, frequently earning them such descriptions as 'the gospels of the unlettered', their purpose is less to do with the transmission of information and much more to do with the formation of persons. Their purpose, that is, is to draw people through curiosity and attraction into prayerful attendance upon the transforming mystery of God in Christ and the Spirit as disclosed through the visual witness they represent, themselves the fruits of such prior graced attention and transforming encounter on behalf of the artist. As such, while holy images/icons and, likewise, the saints as living icons are themselves appropriately reverenced (*dulia*) in Christian practice, it is the mystery of God disclosed through them that is alone properly worshipped and adored (*latria*). Idolatrous over-regard for images and iconoclastic renunciation of the same each flow from a common failure to observe this principle.

If tangible, artistic holy images are regarded within Christian tradition as flowing from the inspired imaginations and talents of believers, they in turn help to shape the imaginative landscapes of other believers and so feed further processes of creative envisioning. This realm of inner imagining and its relationship with mental prayer, self-knowledge and personal development has long constituted a strong focus of attention in Christian spirituality with it receiving perhaps its most influential treatment in the *Spiritual Exercises* of Ignatius of Loyola and the traditions of spiritual direction that have flown from that work.

Here the point is not strenuously and self-consciously to produce vivid mental pictures for oneself that are themselves taken as meditative experiences. Rather, the point is to seek to move from predominantly cerebral, conceptual or cognitive modes of awareness into more affective modes of awareness by attending to what the less self-consciously stimulated products of the imagination – typically in response to the praying of a piece of Scripture – suggest about the state of the believer's desires, hopes, frustrations and sense of self in relation to others before God. As such, the point of attending to the imagining process in prayer is not as a good in itself but as a means of enabling the believer to experience afresh the gracious, personal call of God to growth and greater freedom in the ways of love. Given, however, the conflicted state of human desiring, the fracturing of the self and the consequently confused state of spiritual imagining, which can disclose and reinforce personal inner demons as well as the ways of grace, the disciplines of spiritual discernment and direction are required if such growth is to take place. The insights and approaches of modern psychotherapeutic modes of analysis are now typically drawn upon to greater and lesser degrees in this process of re-imaging oneself and being re-membered before God.

Moving from the more visual to the more conceptual – while recognizing that for language-using humans it is artificial to distinguish image and concept entirely – a good deal of contemporary theology has addressed itself to the need to revise 'standard' images of God, whether as exclusively male, or as unconnected with and unconcerned for finite this-worldly reality, or as concerned only for humanity rather than the entirety of creation, or whatever. As in the practice of personal spiritual growth and spiritual discernment, so here the intention is to move from inadequate, distorted, even damaging images of God to images more generative of the well-being in relation properly associated with the God of Jesus Christ. Even this important and appropriately liberative intention, however, requires discipline and humility if it is not to descend to the level of creating God in the image we would have God to be. It is, for Christian tradition, the surprising, even scandalous traditions associated with Jesus of Nazareth that form the lens through which such creative discerning is properly done and which open to the possibility of fresh learning and fresh vision while always recognizing that the Word is spoken from a silence, the depths of which can never be plumbed other than by the Spirit who searches out the hidden things of God.

See also **Creation Spirituality; Direction, Spiritual; Discernment; Ecological Spirituality; Ignatian Spirituality; Meditation; Motherhood of God; Trinitarian Spirituality.**

Gerard W. Hughes, *God of Surprises*, London: Darton, Longman & Todd, 1985; Michael Ivens, *Understanding the Spiritual Exercises: Text and Commentary; A Handbook for Retreat Directors*, Leominster: Gracewing, 1998; Sallie McFague, *Models of God: Theology for an Ecological, Nuclear Age*, Minneapolis, MN: Augsburg Fortress 1987.

PAUL D. MURRAY

Grace

The range of meaning of the concept of grace is broad. One should distinguish three spheres of reference. First, the idea has its deepest roots in the character of God as experienced in the Jewish and Christian traditions: God is good, benevolent, friendly, loving, faithfully caring, the gracious giver of gifts. Second, the way God's character towards human beings shows itself in history is understood differently in various theological syntheses along the way of Christian theological history. Grace thus has many distinct technical nuances all of which have a bearing on spirituality. Third, 'grace' or 'graces' commonly refers to the concrete gifts or charisms that God bestows on human beings, ranging from talents accompanying the creation of each individual to extraordinary powers credited to God's Spirit, including specific favours often requested in prayer.

The relevance of the concept and construal of grace to spirituality can be illustrated by the questions to which the theologies of grace respond. Three questions are particularly pertinent. First, what is the nature of God according to Christian revelation? Second, what is the nature of human existence or the human person when conceived as standing before God? This particular question explains why the theology of grace is often called Christian anthropology. Third, how should Christians conceptualize the ongoing dialogical relationship between God and human beings as this unfolds across human history? Both in terms of individual persons and in the larger scheme of the history of the human race, how do Christians understand the continual or intermittent dialogue or interchange between God as grace and human beings in prayer and action? These questions also find responses in other theological topics, such as creation, providence, Christology, redemption and Church. But in the Western Church since Augustine the theology of grace picks up these formal and structural questions in a most direct way. Their elementary or primal character means that all spirituality either unconsciously embodies responses to these questions or explicitly incorporates these themes into its logic.

Four examples of landmark figures in the theology of grace will illustrate how specific interpretations of the functioning of grace have a bearing on spirituality. The first is Augustine who conceived of grace as the working of God as Spirit within the human subject drawing it beyond a person inherently curved in on himself or herself in sin (original sin). Augustine thus understood grace as the antidote to sin and the power by which one longed for and sought ultimate truth, goodness and salvation. He also affirmed that God's grace or Spirit co-operated with human freedom in acts of charity thus laying the groundwork for a view of Christian life that transformed worldly and sinful values into the kingdom of God.

Aquinas applied Aristotelian categories to understand the dynamism of grace. A thing's nature is the structure governing its kind of activity and orienting it to its appropriate ultimate goal. He understood grace as a gift of God that, as an inherent modification of human nature, raised it up and allowed supernatural activities such as faith, hope and love that were oriented to a supernatural life in communion with God. This compact integration of human nature and grace dictated a spirituality of activity, a goal-oriented life of the virtues that in turn sanctified life in this world and served as the theological foundation of medieval Christendom.

Martin Luther formulated a theology of grace as the groundwork of spirituality around a conception of the redemptive work of Christ. He combined a strong conception of human bondage in sin with an equally strong conception of grace that completely freed the Christian who held fast to Christ by faith. This resulted in a tensive spirituality of a consciousness of sin, and gratitude to God, and freedom from all effort at trying to win salvation for oneself: once convinced of the power of sin and the overwhelmingly stronger power of grace, one could not only accept a loving God but also oneself as one actually was.

Karl Rahner's contribution to the theology of grace can be understood against various forms of division or separation between the orders of redemption and creation, grace and nature, the Church and the world. Grace is God's personal gift of love or presence of God's self to every human being, from the beginning, and as the very purpose of creation itself. Therefore the life of all human beings and human history itself unfolds within the embrace of God's personal self-presence, and this is experienced, however anonymously, in every inner appeal to self-transcendence. With this conception Rahner lays the ground work for a spirituality of everyday life in which, with every decision and human response, one continues a dialogue with God that strengthens or weakens one's relation to the ultimate principle of life who, as the absolute future of humankind, awaits each one.

These classic theologies of grace do not negate each other, but draw from the scriptural witness themes that respond to different historical exigencies and provide foundations for different but complementary traditions of the Christian life.

See also **Augustinian Spirituality; Aristotelianism; Charism; Creation Spirituality; Ecclesiology and Spirituality; God, Images of; Holiness; Incarnation; Lutheran Spirituality; Person; Redemption; Virtue; World.**

Augustine, 'On Grace and Free Will' in *Basic Writings of Saint Augustine*, ed. Whitney J. Oates, New York: Random House, 1948, pp. 733–74; Leonardo Boff, *Liberating Grace*. Maryknoll, NY: Orbis Books, 1979; Stephen Duffy, *The Dynamics of Grace*, Collegeville, MN: Liturgical Press, 1993; Roger Haight, *The Experience and Language of Grace*, New York: Paulist Press, 1979; Martin Luther, 'The Freedom of a Christian' in *Luther's Works*, vol. 31, ed. H. J. Grimm, Philadelphia: Muhlenberg Press, 1957, pp. 327–77; Peter C. Phan, *Grace and the Human Condition*, Wilmington, DE: M. Glazier, 1988; Karl Rahner, 'Nature and grace' in *Theological Investigations*, 4, Baltimore: Helicon Press, 1966, pp. 165–88; Juan Luis Segundo, *Grace and the Human Condition*, Maryknoll, NY: Orbis Books, 1973; Thomas Aquinas, *Summa Theologiae*, vol. 30, Blackfriars edn, New York: McGraw-Hill, 1972.

ROGER HAIGHT

Grandmontine Spirituality

The Order of Grandmont, now extinct, had a number of unique features in the history of Western monastic spirituality. The founder, St Stephen of Muret (c. 1054–1124/25), began living as a hermit at Ambazac near Limoges in France c. 1076. The early history of Grandmont is obscure. However, in ways that parallel other new communities of the time, its origins lay in the resurgence of eremitical spirituality sweeping the Western Church and in a small group of hermits gathered informally around Stephen. The discipline was severe, the poverty strict but the rule of silence relatively lenient. The first monastery was built at Grandmont only after his death. The Rule was formally drawn up in the time of Stephen of Liciac, the fourth prior (1139–63), and was based partly on the Rule of St Benedict and on the homilies of St Stephen of

Muret, passed on by oral tradition. St Stephen would call his community neither monks nor hermits nor canons regular and the Order was claimed at various times both for the Benedictine and Augustinian traditions.

The Order modelled itself on the life of John the Baptist and claimed that its only rule was the gospel of Jesus Christ – particularly the emphasis on material poverty. The reputation of the Grandmontines was both for extreme simplicity of life and for generosity to the poor – hence the nickname 'Bonshommes'. Interestingly, alongside the emphasis on solitude was also a stress on hospitality, particularly to the laity. St Stephen of Muret was quoted in the Rule as speaking of the privilege it was for monks to talk to the poor. In order to maintain a simple life and liturgy in simple surroundings, the communities were intended to be small. Originally each house contained only about four choir monks and nine lay brothers.

The Grandmontines had two unique features. First their way of life combined cenobitic monasticism with the solitude of hermits and the poverty of the mendicant orders. Although in its developed form the Order became institutionalized, its spirit remained that of the desert hermitage. Both solitude and poverty were seen as aids to the fundamental purpose of contemplation. Interestingly, while the Rule emphasized perpetual seclusion and detachment from anything that would disturb the isolation of the cloister, its regulations also allowed brothers to leave the enclosure to beg for food and alms if necessary. Recent studies of Grandmontine sites and buildings (e.g. Gilchrist, 1995) note the preference for woodlands and uplands as markers of the quest for liminality. The spirituality of the Order was manifested in simple buildings with a remarkably uniform style (e.g. plain aisleless churches). There was also a symbolism of light marked by a single window in the nave at the west end (creating a dark atmosphere perhaps characteristic of the hermit cave) and a triplet in the apse. The effect was that all light was either morning light from the east or evening light from the west.

The second unique feature of the Order was that the choir monks and lay brothers had equal status with a single choir, single chapter meeting, common refectory and common dormitory. In practice, the lay brothers exercised a great deal of authority. Under the Prior of Grandmont, the other houses were dependent cells jointly led by a choir monk *corrector* or spiritual director and lay brother *curiosis* or procurator. Unfortunately from the 1180s disputes arose between the choir monks who wanted to maintain a strict hermit

life and the brothers who sought some respite. By 1317, as a result of internal crises, the papacy imposed a more traditional monastic hierarchy on the Order. Grandmont became an abbey, the daughter houses were made priories under the authority of a choir monk as prior and the lay brothers were deprived of authority. The Order's uniquely democratic and eremitical character disappeared.

During the Middle Ages there were, as far as we know, only three Grandmontine monasteries in England, Alberbury in Shropshire, Craswell in Herefordshire and Grosmont in North Yorkshire. Only the latter survived to the dissolution of the monasteries at the Reformation.

There was a revival of some aspects of the original spirit with the short-lived foundation in 1643 of houses of Strict Observance under Dom Charles Frémon. However, in general the Order remained relatively small as did its individual houses. It may well have been this fact rather than a disastrous decline in observance that led to the Order's eventual demise. During the last half of the eighteenth century a commission of the French crown drew up criteria for the suppression of small religious houses and according to these criteria decided that individual Grandmontine houses had insufficient numbers to survive. Grandmont itself was finally closed in 1772.

See also **Augustinian Spirituality; Benedictine Spirituality; Desert; Eremitical Spirituality; Light; Mendicant Spirituality; Monasticism; Poverty; Rules, Religious.**

Roberta Gilchrist, *Action and Contemplation: The Other Monasteries*, London/New York: Leicester University Press, 1995; C. A. Hutchinson, *The Hermit Monks of Grandmont*, Cistercian Studies 118, Kalamazoo, MI: Cistercian Publications, 1989; C. H. Lawrence, *Medieval Monasticism: Forms of Religious Life in Western Europe in the Middle Ages*, London and New York: Longmans, 1992; Henrietta Leyser, *Hermits and the New Monasticism: A Study of Religious Communities in Western Europe 1000–1150*, London: Macmillan 1984.

PHILIP SHELDRAKE

Greek Spirituality

1. *Early period*. Though Greece is an ancient country, it is a relatively new nation-state in Europe, enjoying independence from the Ottoman Empire only since the 1820s and autocephaly (or self-government) as a Church only since 1850. As such, the Church of Greece comprises one of some fifteen independent Orthodox Churches throughout the world. While everything Byzantine was for the most part

spurned by the newly established Church of Greece, often uncritically espousing a European classicism or Renaissance in its ecclesiastical, cultural and academic development, it is also noted for exceptional spiritual sages who lived in cities and monasteries. Such personalities deeply shaped the spiritual culture of the Greek Church and *diaspora* both positively and negatively.

In the early centuries, Byzantium left a profound impact on Greek soil. Monastic institutions were founded on Mount Athos (where monasticism was formally established from the tenth century, although informal monastic settlement commenced at least a century earlier), while in northern Greece, Thessalonika was widely known as 'little Byzantium' or 'second Mount Athos'. Central and lower mainland Greece boasted renowned medieval centres of cultural and artistic expression: in Athens (with the spectacular iconography at Daphni (sixth century) and Osios Loukas (tenth century)), as well as on the daring rocks of Meteora (from the fourteenth century). Mistras in the Peloponnese (thirteenth century) and the sacred island of Patmos (twelfth century) were further examples of a creative and thriving spiritual life. During this early period, Greece also produced a number of remarkable saints, such as Nikon 'of Metanoeite' (d. 998), who preached repentance throughout Greece.

2. *An 'occupation' geographically as well as spiritually.* During the Ottoman occupation of Greece (1453–1821), a number of New or Neo-Martyrs influenced the theology and spirituality of the general population. Male and female saints constituted brilliant examples of a spiritual maturity that not only provided spiritual sustenance and guidance during a bleak and sometimes oppressive period; they could also reach out and relate to issues of social concern and justice. Such saints included Philothea of Athens (d. 1589), Kosmas the Aitolos (1714–79) and Nikiphoros of Chios (1750–1821), all of these steeped in and staunch supporters of the spiritual tradition of the Byzantine East. Nikiphoros of Chios, who died in the year of Greece's political liberation and national independence, was asked by Makarios (Notaras) of Corinth (1731–1805) to compose a *New Leimonarion* (or, *New Spiritual Meadow*) – a tribute to the blooming spiritual growth during the same time.

In the period following the Greek independence and autocephaly, a number of intellectuals became more closely familiar with the Western history leading to the Enlightenment than with the patristic notion of illumination. Among these, Adamantios Koraes (1748–1833) espoused a return to classical Greek roots of civilization rather than traditional Byzantine roots of spirituality. This attitude also infiltrated church circles, where clergymen such as Neophytos Vamvas (1770–1855) and Theokletos Pharmakidis (1784–1860) were more interested in philosophical and natural theology, in imitation of their French and German counterparts in theological thought and church life.

Among the more exceptional critics of these arbitrary spiritual developments were Konstantinos Oikonomos (1780–1857), Christophoros Panagiotopoulos (or Papoulakos, 1770–1861) and the military general Makrygiannis (1797–1864). These remained important and influential symbols of an Orthodox spiritual conscience. Another breath of fresh air amid the theological aridity and the lay pietism of this period was Alexandros Papadiamantis (1851–1911), who proved to be an equivalent in Greece to what Fyodor Dostoevsky was for Russia.

3. *Recent developments.* In more recent years, this attachment to Western sources and styles of spirituality has unfortunately persevered in Greek history and life. This is particularly evident with the establishment of religious movements such as Zoe – founded by Fr Eusebios Matthopoulos (1849–1929) and continued by Fr Seraphim Papakostas (1892–1954) – which provided a refuge of spirituality during an inactive period of institutional church life in Greece.

Nevertheless, a number of well-known and deeply respected spiritual guides have also proved to be contemporary witnesses to, and the living continuation of, the spirit of *The Philokalia* (cf. relevant article). These include canonized saints such as Nektarios of Aegina (1846–1920), undoubtedly the most popular of Greek saints. Another example is Savvas the New (1862–1948), the spiritual protégé of Nektarios. Women saints, too, are not unknown during the same period; Methodia of Kimolos (1865–1908) is a case in point. Moreover, perhaps the greatest influence in the artistic and aesthetic revival of Greek spirituality was Photis Kontoglou (1896–1965), who was a prolific author as well as a phenomenal iconographer, arguing for a return to the traditional roots of Orthodox painting and living.

They also include such twentieth-century personalities as Nicholas Planas (a celibate living in the centre of Athens), Dimitrios Gagastathis (1902–75, a married priest living in central Greece), as well as Porphyrios (1906–91, a monk living on the outskirts of Athens). There were also those who lived on the monastic republic of Mount Athos, such as Joseph (1898–1959, at

New Skete), Ephraim (1912–98, at Katounakia) and Paisios (1924–94, near Karyes).

See also **Byzantine Spirituality; Iconography; Hesychasm; Orthodox Spirituality.**

Constantine Cavarnos, *Modern Orthodox Saints Series*, 14 vols, Belmont MA: Institute for Byzantine and Modern Greek Studies, 1971–2000; John Meyendorff, *The Orthodox Church: Its Past and Its Role in the World Today*, New York: St Vladimir's Seminary Press, 1981; Nomikos Michael Vaporis, *Witnesses for Christ: Orthodox Christian Neomartyrs of the Ottoman Period (1453–1860)*, New York: St Vladimir's Seminary Press, 2000; Andrew Walker and Costa Carras (eds), *Living Orthodoxy in the Modern World: Orthodox Christianity and Society*, London: SPCK and New York: St Vladimir's Seminary Press, 1996; Kallistos Ware, *The Orthodox Church*, London/New York: Penguin, 1963, rev. 1990; Timothy Ware, *Eustratios Argenti: A Study of the Greek Church under Turkish Rule*, Oxford: Clarendon Press, 1964.

JOHN CHRYSSAVGIS

Growth, Spiritual

Approaches to this topic are usually framed by Augustine's controversy with Pelagius regarding grace and human effort, questions revived in the sixteenth century. Is spiritual growth entirely the work of the Holy Spirit? Does human action play any part? How is spiritual life related to human nature, to human psychology, to human freedom? Recent questions include: How is spiritual growth related to social structures and to world religions?

Two emphases predominate. In the Reformation tradition, rooted in Paul and Augustine, sin corrupted human nature yet grace abounds initiating and causing any spiritual growth. Here the emphasis would be on the utter inadequacy of all human effort. In the tradition associated with Roman Catholic and Anglican emphasis, rooted in pre-Augustinian theology of graced transformation as deification and supported by Thomas Aquinas, there is a conviction that grace builds on nature. Here the emphasis honours the experience of early monks of Gaul (e.g. Cassian), whose anthropology, essentially eastern Christian in inspiration, was more open to natural possibility than Augustine's. In their theological reflection on experience, Augustine and the monks of Gaul moved in opposite directions.

In the biblical vision, spiritual growth is a matter of fidelity to the covenant, to loving God with one's whole heart, soul, might (Deut. 6.4 NRSV). Maturity is living from 'God's love . . . poured into our hearts through the Holy Spirit . . . given

to us' (Rom. 5.4 NRSV), inclusive love of God and neighbour born of the struggle to discern where and how God is present in the community, in the distribution of the Spirit's gifts, in suffering, in religious and political dissension, even in one's own sinfulness. Growth is primarily a matter of relationship, yet need for adult freedom is also evident in the language of a call to conversion and to fidelity in spiritual darkness.

Spiritual growth in Christian antiquity continued to be understood as union with God, especially in contemplative prayer, and love of neighbour. Insertion into Antiochene, Alexandrian, Byzantine and Roman institutions resulted in evaluating these relationships in terms of ideals of charity, purity of heart and unceasing prayer, as well as war against sexual desire and subjection of passion to reason. Virginity as a means of spiritual growth not only prompted renunciation of sexuality but also legitimated rejection of social conventions regarding family.

Medieval spirituality envisioned spiritual growth as movement into wholehearted conformity to Christ's love and care for all, a care imaged as motherly more often by men, such as Cistercian abbots, than by women, such as Julian of Norwich. New forms of 'apostolic life' promoted spiritual growth outside monastic settings.

Both Protestant and Catholic reformers understood spiritual growth as surrender to God's free love in Christ and as fidelity to one's interior call. Catholics, such as Teresa of Avila and Ignatius of Loyola, relate their experience of spiritual growth as involving both active choice and receptive surrender. Religious upheaval and reform tended to reinforce the need for fidelity to conscience in the midst of uncertainty. Thus, this era developed themes of growth through discernment and explicit self-knowledge. Modern spirituality urged growth through response to new perspectives on faith and doubt, on mission, science, social structures and world religions. Radically new human possibilities and re-examination of religious authority reinforced the demands that spiritual growth include both trust in God's guidance and evaluation of personal decisions.

Contemporary perspectives on spiritual growth reflect awareness of the universal call to holiness, Protestant rediscovery of value in monastic practices such as *lectio divina* and centring prayer, Catholic recovery of the centrality of Scripture and vernacular liturgy, widespread interest in spiritual direction, along with the inseparability of contemplation and action for justice. Ecumenical discussion promotes awareness of both the virtues and temptations of

Catholic and Protestant emphases regarding spiritual growth. Catholic sacramental imagination is primed to appreciate ongoing revelation of God's transforming presence in human experience, yet is led to underestimate the power of sin, especially as it is embedded in social structures of racism, sexism and the corporate greed of economic globalization. Protestant dialectical imagination honours the profound transcendence of God and the power of the cross, yet tends to underestimate the presence of the Word of God in ordinary human experience. Recent questions include: How is spiritual growth related to psychological growth? How is Christian spiritual growth appropriately nurtured by spiritual wisdom from other world religions? If Christian spiritual growth is understood as life in Christ lived with self-appropriation, thus capable of mature self-donation to God and others, then it is compatible, even inseparable from, psychological growth. This is true on condition that psychological development means one grows beyond autonomy into relationships that value vulnerability and mutual self-donation. Christians have recent examples of persons whose authentic Christian growth drew them into prayerful study of Buddhism and Hinduism. Both Thomas Merton and Bede Griffiths found their experience of union with the divine appropriately described in these wisdom traditions.

See also **Spirituality, Psychology and Psychotherapy** (*essay*); **Conversion; Dark Night; Deification; Discernment; Grace; Holiness; Journey, Spiritual; Spirit, Holy; Triple Way.**

Joann Wolski Conn, *Spirituality and Personal Maturity*, Lanham, MD: University Press of America, 1994; Elizabeth Liebert, *Changing Life Patterns: Adult Development in Spiritual Direction*, 2nd edn, St Louis, MO: Chalice Press, 2001; Gordon Mursell (ed.), *The Story of Christian Spirituality: Two Thousand Years from East to West*, Minneapolis: Fortress Press, 2001; Columba Stewart, *Cassian the Monk*, New York: Oxford University Press, 1998; Rowan Williams, *The Wound of Knowledge: Christian Spirituality from the New Testament to St John of the Cross*, 2nd edn, London: Darton, Longman & Todd, 1979; Boston, MA: Cowley, 1990.

JOANN WOLSKI CONN

Hagiography

The word, a compound Greek noun, means to write about the holy. Although there is no attestation of the word in antiquity, the word *agios* applied to a person is used first by Aristophanes in *Aves* 522 and is first given a focused religious

orientation in Paul (1 Cor. 6.1–2), '*kai ouci epii tvn agiwn*', rendered by Jerome as '*et non apud sanctos*'. While the Romans reserved the word *sanctus* for categories of people, poets and prophets (see Strabo, Trag. 2) and Seneca used it to identify certain moral qualities (*Octavia* 408), it never took on the ontological status it had in Christianity. For Paul the *agiwn/sanctos* designated those who explicitly follow and model themselves after the teachings of Christ. Christian virtue, and by extension its practitioner, derived not from the practice of community-sanctioned ideas of virtue (*mos maiorum*), but rather from a wilful disposition to perform actions as if the performance was a ritual re-enactment of how Christ would have acted.

From the earliest period of Christian texts certain individuals are represented as having participated in God's presence in a deliberately imitative manner, and were *sanctii* because of such imitation. Such behaviour gave rise to a christological theology observable as early as Clement of Alexandria's remark that knowledge of God, particularly of the Logos, the second Person of the Trinity, makes us like God, 'For if one knows himself, he will know God; and knowing God, he will be made like God' (*Teacher* 3.1.1). Ritually mimetic behaviour coupled with something like Clement's stoic epistemology even informed those narratives that described the moment of death. Luke presents Stephen, the proto-martyr, as he was being stoned for being a blasphemer, uttering a paraphrase of Jesus' remarks on the cross (Acts 7.59–60). Early biography is encomium and celebrated the heroism of its subject, whether that was David's arrival in Saul's court, his defeat of Goliath, Homer's praise for Hector, or his genealogy and narrative of the deeds of Odysseus. While all are in part studies in biography, neither the anonymous authors of 1 Samuel or Homer are biographers since their principal aim is not to record a life. The genre of biography does not officially appear until Damascius' *Life of Isidore of Alexandria* (d. *c.* 533 BC), the first to actually use the word to refer to his work. From the late fifth century works of biography, like that of Xenophon's *Cyropaedia* and Isocrates' *Encomium on Evagoras* (*c.* 365 BC), portray certain acts as emblematic of virtue worth imitating. From the period of the late Roman Republic, there was an explosion of interest in recording what Pliny called the *exitus illustrium virorum*, exemplified by C. Nepos' *De viris illustribus*, Plutarch's *Parallel Lives*, Suetonius' *De viris illustribus* and Philostratus' *Life of Apollonius of Tyana*. Taken along with the Christian Gospels, all of these works had an influence on the emerging genre of hagiography.

Since the sacred is universal, hagiographers would lessen the particular if it endangered representations of the divine. Christian hagiography is an idealizing genre; it often flattens events and personalities, rendering them with an iconographic two-dimensionality. It is no less a branch of historic writing, however, and much of our historical knowledge comes from the saints' lives. The earliest hagiographies, the stories of the martyrs, are based on the brief Roman transcripts of martyrs' trials, the *cognitio extra ordinem*. These transcripts are terse records of the dialogue between accused and accuser. They seldom contain narrative events beyond the issue being disputed, the question whether is one a Christian and held the *nomen Christianum* in greater regard than that of the emperor. This juridical frame of the *cognitio* further limits detailed narrative representation. The *Acts of the Scillitan Martyrs* (*c.* 180), the *Martyrdom of St Marinus* and the *Acts of Maximilian* illustrate this early stage in Christian hagiography.

Hagiography was the most popular narrative during the Middle Ages with almost nine thousand *Vitae* extant in the *Bibliotheca hagiographica Latina*. Although conservative in certain formal criteria, the genre was dynamic and adopted new models of sanctity commensurate with the age. For example, as the genre matured and the Church went from a persecuted *collegia illicita* to the official religion of the empire (*c.* 313), the exercise of Christian virtue – no longer exemplified by heroic resistance to the death against the hated Roman jurists – was represented in dramatic contests against Satan, *a bellum Satanicum*. The new model of sanctity, no longer a martyr, shunned the world, was a seer, a thaumaturge, who achieved grace through the practice of extreme asceticism. Athanasius' *Life of St Antony* (*c.* 357) and St Jerome's biographies of the great ascetic Paul, Hilarion and Malchus, and Sulpicius Severus' *Life of St Martin* introduce this new model of the holy. The struggle against the temptations of the flesh and the devil, against good and evil, were, to paraphrase the great Spanish hagiographer Prudentius, a psychomachia.

Although there are earlier lives of bishops (e.g. Cyprian), Sulpicius' *Life of St Martin* inaugurated the *vita episcopii*. The bishop as holy shepherd and pastor emerged concurrently with that of the ascetic seer dwelling in the desert fastness. Of particular interest are those instances when the hagiographer is an intimate with the subject. Possidius' *Life of St Augustine* based on four decades of friendship left the most complete list of Augustine's library and Paulinus who was with Ambrose at his death got much of his infor-

mation for his *Life of Ambrose* from Ambrose's sister Marcellina. Motifs from one life are sometimes used to show the influence of the sacral over time. Thus Gervase of Canterbury's *Life of St Thomas* shows the influence of Sulpicius' *Life of St Martin* while Eddius Stephanus' prologue to his *Life of St Wilfrid* is lifted verbatim from the *Life of St Cuthbert*, itself a florilegium of quotations from Evagrius' translation of the *Life of St Antony*. Both Northumbrian lives are nevertheless indispensable for our knowledge of the politics of the seventh-century English Church. *Vitae* were written of the holy abbots, abbesses and founders of religious orders; notable Lives in this category include that of the Lives of SS Benedict, Columba, Hild, Francis and Clare.

While the genre continues to be practised there is less emphasis on the supernatural and more on the idea of self-sacrifice and the social gospel. Some notable lives of modern saints are those of SS Térèse of Lisieux (d. 1897), Francis Cabrini (d. 1917), Maxmillian Kolbe and Edith Stein (d. 1942).

See also **Biographies, Spiritual; Holiness.**

Peter Brown, *The Cult of the Saints: Its Rise and Function in Latin Christianity*, Chicago: University of Chicago Press, 1981; H. Delehaye, *Legends of the Saints: An Introduction To Hagiography*, trans. Donald Attwater, New York: Fordham University Press, 1974; David Hugh Farmer (ed.), *The Oxford Dictionary of Saints*, Oxford: Oxford University Press, 2003; Thomas Head (ed.), *Medieval Hagiography: An Anthology*, New York: Routledge, 2001; Thomas John Heffernan, *Sacred Biography: Saints and their Biographers in the Middle Ages*, Oxford: Oxford University Press, 1988; Herbert Musurillo (ed.), *The Acts of the Christian Martyrs*, Oxford: Clarendon Press, 1972; Thomas Noble and Thomas Head (eds), *Soldiers of Christ: Saints' Lives from Late Antiquity and the Early Middle Ages*, University Park: Pennsylvania State, 1995; André Vauchez, *Sainthood in the Later Middle Ages*, trans. Jean Birrell, Cambridge: Cambridge University Press, 1997.

THOMAS J. HEFFERNAN

Happiness

see Joy

Healing and Health

It is the purpose of this entry to offer a broad understanding of the meanings of health, healing and wholeness. The topics of discussion will include models of health; systems of care; principles of health and healing; our theological resources; and, finally, some challenges for our Christian spirituality. It is not the purpose of this entry to discuss in what way God may intervene in the natural world in order to heal (see Parsons, 1986; Pattison, 1989).

There are two dominant and co-existing models of health that shape both society's and the Church's thought and practice. The first, described as the medical model of health, has the following key features. The condition of illness is generally to be understood as non-voluntary and linked with organic disease. Those who define and exercise power as experts over illness are doctors. Sickness, therefore, is defined as what falls below a socially defined standard of acceptability with regard to bodily and mental well-being. A number of values and boundaries are exercised by society, Church and medical profession (Jones, 1994).

In contrast, the social model of health has grown over the past two decades and the following are its main features. A person is viewed as a whole, with a particular emphasis on the connection between the individual and their environment. The causes of illness, and therefore their treatment, are complex and are shaped by this social, economic and political context. Above all there is an acceptance of the spiritual dimension of health and healing, though not narrowly defined or contained by the Christian tradition (Evans, 1999).

In human terms, for our Christian understanding of health and healing we need to ask first what our experience of healthcare systems is. For most of us our primary point of reference in the maintenance of health and the need for treatment and healing is the doctor and other health-related professionals. We need to safeguard against the reductionism and depersonalization which might arise in the working of these models, professionals or systems. In this context we need to acknowledge that the operation of healthcare systems is often driven by economics and by the relevant science as a consequence of which spiritual care or concern for the whole person is marginalized. Further, there has been an acknowledgement that, despite significant effort, there is a failure of healthcare reforms to provide holistic care for all. Moreover, the further patients move in the healthcare system, especially into hospital treatment, the further they are likely to be removed from a sense of the wholeness of human life in its social or communal settings. Without this, it is necessary for the spiritual dimension to be brought into play. What we can expect of any given system is an important starting point. Our needs and demands must relate to limited resources

and so necessarily to the ability to meet all our expectations for health (Calman, 1998).

Christian spirituality has a particular role to play in shaping and reshaping our views and in challenging our experiences. In Christian terms a person is understood as a unity both within themselves and in relation to their environment. Illness can occur when this unity breaks down or fragments. In this Christian perspective the notion of 'health' includes the spiritual. Our basic human orientation is towards health and not towards sickness. Moreover, health is not merely an individual matter but depends on our setting alongside others. Indeed, its primary goal is others' health and not solely one's own as if we existed in isolation. These values and beliefs take shape in the following way. We are an integrated whole, body, mind and spirit, created to live in community. Health and wholeness are twin concepts signifying the totality of our life in a state of well-being. Sickness and sin interrelate as a reflection of brokenness, though not always in a causal way (Evans, 1999; Aldridge, 2000).

It follows therefore that healing includes a variety of resources, activities and attitudes that move us towards the assertion of wholeness. This may itself include suffering and is always more than mere curing. It is communal as well as individual. Christ's healing ministry is a paradigm for healing and, for the Christian, the resources of prayer, faith and medicine always belong together. 'Miraculous' healing is not contrary to nature, but can be a fuller revelation of the deeper nature of God's world. Healers are persons who move a person towards wholeness – the person being the central healer assisted by others. It follows therefore, that the Church is the corporate expression of the calling to healing (Parsons, 1986). The Church has a concern, therefore, for health and healing and can play a part in the promotion of wholeness (Evans, 1999).

Finally, there are a number of questions that might be addressed in working through these meanings, beliefs and practices in relation to Christian spirituality.

- What are the parts of our lives that are in need of healing?
- What are the dimensions of the society or community around us that need healing?
- In what ways is your faith community a healing church?

See also **Death and Dying.**

David Aldridge, *Spirituality, Healing and Medicine: Return to the Silence*, London: Jessica

Kingsley Publishers, 2000; Alan Beattie, Marjorie Gott, Linda Jones, Moira Sidell (eds), *Health and Well-Being: A Reader*, London: Macmillan and The Open University Press, 1993; Kenneth C. Calman, *The Potential for Health*, Oxford: Oxford University Press, 1998; Abigail Ryan Evans, *The Healing Church: Practical Programmes for Health Ministries*, Ohio: United Church Press, 1999; Linda J. Jones, *The Social Context of Health and Health Work*, London: Macmillan, 1994; Stephen Parsons, *The Challenge of Christian Healing*, London: SPCK, 1986; Stephen Pattison, *Alive and Kicking: Towards a Practical Theology of Illness and Healing*, London: SCM Press, 1989.

JAMES WOODWARD

Heart

see Methodist Spirituality; Moravian Spirituality; Piety; Purity of Heart; Sacred Heart

Hermits and Anchorites

see Eremitical Spirituality

Hesychasm

Hesychasm derives from the Greek word for quietness (*hesychia*). In the Byzantine period, from the sixth century through to the eleventh, 'hesychast' was simply a synonym for a monk or ascetic, who was expected to spend a significant time in quiet withdrawal. In medieval Byzantine times it gained the special sense of that time of retreat monastics might engage in if they moved to a more private lifestyle or to greater solitude in which to seek undistracted prayer. Before the fourteenth-century reappropriation of the word, for new specific resonances in Byzantine religious thought, therefore, the word was clearly a generic one that connoted monastic 'contemplation'. When St Symeon the New Theologian was put under house arrest in his monastery by the Synod of Constantinople in the eleventh century, for example, he described his imprisonment (somewhat ironically) to his disciples as his period of 'longed-for *hesychia*'. The term *hesychia* also began to develop as a precisely technical 'spiritual word' in the works of the Christian monastic writers from the late fourth century onwards. Here it signified that state of quietness achieved by the soul that allowed it to be both free from the loud demands of the mental imagination (noetic activity) and from bodily and psychological desires (*pathemata*). Once quietness of soul had been achieved, according to monastic theorists of prayer, the soul was readied to receive the grace of special communion with God. John of Damascus, in the eighth century, put it succinctly: '*Hesychia* gives birth to

prayer, and prayer is the mother of the vision of the glory of God.'

This concept of hesychasm is rooted in ancient Greek-Christian anthropological doctrines that regard the soul as composite. The *hegemonikon* (the dominant part of a person's psychic life) is *nous*: the spiritual aspect of the psychological life. The presidency of the *nous*, however, is subject to disruption by *epithymia* – desires and needs both bodily and emotive. The direction of the inner life is a fraught thing because, in monastic belief, the demons also war within the bodily and psychic life, trying to counteract the asceticism of the monk and disrupt the spiritual influences of Christ's grace. Stillness of soul was achieved by fasting, prayer and retiring recollection. The ascetic task of quietening outward desires was pursued in the cause of achieving that stillness where the voice of God could be heard. It is useful to note this long history of the term 'hesychasm' because the word is now more commonly used to signify the so-called 'Hesychastic Tradition' of thirteenth-century Byzantium and after. The splitting off of this medieval movement (which to be sure has aspects and emphases all its own) from the earlier use of hesychastic ideas within the ancient monastic literature is a mistake of much modern writing, and makes the medieval Hesychast school appear to be more distinctive than it really is.

By the Byzantine middle ages, the Syrian tradition of the concentration of the soul (a long and ancient monastic school that advocated the heart of the disciple should be assiduously trained to focus on the inner presence of the Spirit of God) had been fused in the common Byzantine monastic literature with the Graeco-Egyptian desert tradition (that advocated the mind of the disciple should be trained through stillness for theoretical vision). The juxtaposition of both trends produced a newly fertile intellectual environment among the monks of Mount Athos and the Sinai region that created a school of thinkers now known as the 'Hesychast Tradition'. They were monastic reformers who emphasized the importance of the Jesus prayer (the frequent repetition of the phrase 'Lord Jesus Christ, Son of God, have mercy on me') as an inner spiritual concentrant. Leaders of the movement such as Gregory of Sinai (1258–1346), and Gregory Palamas (1296–1359) brought about a renaissance in Eastern monastic life, and formed new schools of prayer which used the central motifs of the stilling of the heart through the Jesus prayer, with a specific aim to acquire the awareness of the presence of the Spirit of God indwelling the soul, an experience they frequently evoked as a luminous epiphany, comparable to the vision of Jesus transfigured on Thabor. Some of the major apologetic elements in the medieval Hesychast controversy related to the possibility of seeing the (Uncreated) divine light of God directly with (created) human eyes. The Hesychasts stood for the possibility of this paradoxical claim, as a manifestation of the deifying grace of God incarnate. The Hesychastic synthesis and combination of the themes of luminous vision, quietness of heart and the awareness of the presence of the Spirit within the heart, all conspired to stimulate and produce the Philokalic tradition from the eighteenth century onwards. *The Philokalia* was a major collation of ancient writings favourable to Hesychastic theory produced at this period by Nicodemus the Hagiorite. This new collation assisted in the wide dissemination of the works in print form, and led to a hesychastic renaissance from the eighteenth to the twentieth centuries among Eastern Orthodox monastics. It is this Philokalic school which still today dominates Eastern Christian spiritual tradition.

See also **Byzantine Spirituality; Early Christian Spirituality; Orthodox Spirituality; Silence; Soul; Syriac Spirituality.**

I. Hausherr, *The Spirituality of the Christian East*, Kalamazoo: Cistercian Publications, 1980; C. Jones, G. Wainwright and E. Yarnold (eds), *The Study of Spirituality*, Oxford and New York: Oxford University Press, 1986; B. McGinn and J. Meyendorff (eds), *Christian Spirituality*, vol. 1, *Origins to the Twelfth Century*, New York: Crossroad, 1993; J. A. McGuckin, *Standing in God's Holy Fire: The Byzantine Tradition*, London: Darton, Longman & Todd/New York: Orbis Books, 2001; J. Meyendorff, *Byzantine Theology*, New York: St Vladimir's Seminary Press, 1975.

JOHN ANTHONY MCGUCKIN

Hinduism and Christianity

To trace the reception of Hindu insights and practices into Christian spirituality tells us more about Christian spirituality and Christian perceptions of India than about Hindu traditions in themselves. What matters to insiders may be overlooked by outsiders, while secondary aspects may intrigue newcomers more than the basics of a tradition. Like Christians, by their attitudes and practices Hindus have long aimed at the cultivation and maturation of spiritual perspectives toward the world, life and death, social and religious obligations; Hindu spiritualities too are deeply interconnected with a wide range of social and ritual values and obligations, doctrinal and apologetic developments, and have been influenced by influential personalities and historical turning points. Accordingly, there can be no single 'Hindu spirituality', but only 'Hindu spiritualities' subject to multiple interpretations. In turn, these spiritualities need to be interpreted in the context of the wider range of Indian spirituality, including its Jaina and Buddhist, Muslim, Sikh and other strands. Nor can one even imagine a modern encounter of the 'purely Christian' and the 'purely Hindu'; Nestorian and then Orthodox Christian Churches have had long-term interactions with Indian religious traditions, while the Christian influence on Hindu belief and practice has been significant during Western colonial rule and the neo-Hindu 'reformation' of the nineteenth century.

The history of interaction has been a long one. Over three millennia, the vast civilizations and religions of 'West' and 'East' have touched one another for shorter or longer periods of time, to varying degrees of intensity, and in circumstances more or less conducive to constructive exchange. Merchants and soldiers visited India at least as early as Alexander the Great's fourth-century invasion of north-west India, and we have records of some interaction among Indian religious figures and Christians in the first centuries CE. Scholars have speculated about possible Indian influences on Pythagoras (sixth century BCE), while Plotinus (third century CE) is said to have travelled east in order to investigate Indian wisdom. Some contacts were quite indirect, as when the story of a Buddhist saint, an ascetic and wise figure who renounced the world, became the basis for the legend of St Josaphat. During the Middle Ages India retained the image of a fabulous land of natural and preternatural wonders, exaggerated virtues and vices, intense asceticism, otherworldly detachment and a most intense search for liberation. Intensely fantasized, India was denied the status of a real country, and was to a large extent constructed to serve as Europe's 'polar other', a land of paradigmatic spirituality or, for some, exotic and esoteric spiritualism. Some of these early attitudes toward India have endured even until today in the popular imagination.

With the fifteenth and sixteenth century colonialist entry into India, interaction and then more reliable learning began to increase greatly. Early missionaries often saw the religions of India as quintessential paganism and condemned Hindu image worship as mere idolatry. Untutored in the languages and customs of India, they promoted the view that Christians have nothing to learn from India; even if they had been disposed toward mutual spiritual learning, however, the required warrants for such exchange had not yet been developed. By way of exception, figures such as the Jesuit Roberto de Nobili (seventeenth century) and the Lutheran Bartholomaeus Ziegenbalg (eighteenth century) learned languages, studied the culture deeply and were greatly impressed by the ardour of Hindu devotion and the rigour of Indian religious systems. By their own lights they sought to systematize the best of Indian thought, strip away superstition and uncover the intact natural bases underlying Hinduism and even a lost monotheism thought to have been overlaid by millennia of error. Eighteenth-century Orientalist scholars, British, French and later German, made available key Hindu texts in translation and provided resources for new speculation on the unity of religions according to new categories such as 'religion' and 'spirituality'. The scholarly discovery of Hindu theology in Vedanta, Saiva, Vaisnava, Tantric and other theological traditions made clear that Hindus too, no less than their counterparts in the West, were seeking to balance spiritual and intellectual concerns in philosophically and theologically tenable ways.

Nineteenth-century missionaries and scholars, along with soldiers, travellers and colonial administrators, had still more opportunities to study Hindu spiritual paths and incorporate insights and practices into Christian living. As Europe became more religiously and culturally complex, Christians began studying texts like the *Bhagavad Gita* and *Yoga Sutras* and thinking comparatively about topics hitherto studied only according to biblical and European insights. Even grand theorists such as Hegel had to find a place for India's thinking and spiritual practice in their global systems. The Theosophical Society, New England transcendentalism and (due to the writings of John Woodroffe, 'Arthur Avalon') a growing appreciation of goddesses were all in debt to Hinduism. In the late nineteenth and twentieth centuries we find more deliberate efforts to adopt yoga as a form of spiritual practice in the West, and a growing respect for Hindu non-dualism as a higher wisdom and viable basis for the moral life. Figures such as Ramakrishna Paramahamsa, Swami Vivekananda, Mohandas Gandhi, Sri Aurobindo, Ramana Maharshi and J. Krishnamurti stood forth as exemplars of admirable spiritualities not heavily indebted to Christian influence.

In India itself, the twentieth century saw Christians actively seeking to develop truly Indian Christian spiritualities by removing Western accretions and delving deeply into Hindu sources; for many in Christian ashrams and seminaries and convents etc., this meant introducing Hindu attitudes and symbols into Christian worship and prayer. Figures such as Brahmobandhab Upadhyay, Henri Le Saux (Swami Abhishiktananda), Ignatius Hirudayam, Bede Griffiths, Vandana Mataji, Sarah Grant, Raimon Panikkar and Anthony de Mello, all popularized Hindu spiritual practices and values, for Indians but then, too, readers in the West. Since much of the creative spiritual and theological reflection of Indian Christians in the past fifty years has occurred in the context of the Hindu–Christian encounter, their experience provides a wealth of spiritual insight for Christians globally. Today, too, still easier travel and the arrival of numerous Hindu teachers in the West have guaranteed that large numbers of Christians seeking to meditate and develop inner spiritual values could draw (consciously or not) on Hindu traditions. Myths about 'East' and 'West' have been evaporating and more substantial learning made possible. As the number of Indians living in the West grows, Hindu spirituality can now be studied in a richer, less exoticized context where spiritual insights and practices have been reconnected to ordinary Hindu life, temple worship and belief.

Thematically, the following are some key areas in which Christians have found in Hindu traditions elements to enrich Christian spirituality: the intuition of an ultimate reality underlying and pervading phenomenal multiplicity; alternative understandings of divine inconceivability and differently refined uses of apophatic language; the discovery of more effective disciplines toward appropriating the inner self; yoga as helpful physical practice and a way of life with great psychological and spiritual benefits; spiritual direction as practical guidance along the mystical path founded in a teacher–disciple relationship; an appreciation of the sacrality of nature and a more inclusive respect for all living beings and the environment; non-violence as a viable alternative to warfare and as deeper personal wisdom; vegetarianism as salutary for health but also as an expression of the solidarity of all living beings; the celebration of pluralism and the embrace of diverse conceptions of the divine; an appreciation of goddesses and feminine aspects of the divine; new insights, reflected through Hindu experience, into Jesus Christ, the Spirit and God's creative power; rereadings of the Bible and Christian mysticism in light of Hindu Scriptures which, in turn, have sometimes found a place in prayer and liturgical worship. Some resources, such as rebirth or radical non-dualism, remain challenges marginal to Christian spirituality.

Of course Christians have also found in Hinduism a foil by which to perceive more clearly distinctive Christian (and Western) values, such as egalitarian society, work for justice and the transformation of social structures, the positive evaluation of historical change as progress, and the centrality of love of neighbour as a norm for spiritual maturity. Some theologians and church leaders insist that the uniqueness of Christian spirituality makes it fundamentally incompatible with Hindu spiritualities and immune to their influence, and disparage the value of spiritual exercises such as yoga. Yet even Christian uniqueness is now asserted only in the context of conceding that Hindu (and other) spiritualities offer plausible and attractive paths by which people apparently succeed in achieving mature spiritual lives. On the whole, it seems reasonable to conclude that over the centuries the influence of Hinduism on Christian spirituality has been increasingly significant and largely beneficial and that, in all likelihood, Hindu wisdom will become even more integral to the Christian spiritualities of the future.

See also **Spirituality and the Dialogue of Religions** (*essay*).

Francis X. Clooney, *Hindu Wisdom for All God's Children*, Maryknoll, NY: Orbis Books, 1998; J. M. Dechanet, *Christian Yoga*, New York: Harper & Brothers Publishers, 1960; Jean Filliozat, *Les Relations Extérieures de L'Inde*, Pondichery: Institut Français d'Indologie, 1956; Richard Garbe, *India and Christendom: The Historical Connections between their Religions*, Open Court Pub. Co., 1959; Wilhelm Halbfass, *India and Europe: An Essay in Understanding*, Albany: State University of New York Press, 1988; Krishna Sivaraman (ed.), *Hindu Spirituality I: Vedas through Vedanta*, New York: Crossroad, 1989; K. A. Sundararajan and Bithika Mukerji (eds), *Hindu Spirituality II: Postclassical and Modern*, New York: Crossroad, 1997; Judson B. Trapnell, *Bede Griffiths: A Life in Dialogue*, Albany: State University of New York Press, 2001.

FRANCIS X. CLOONEY

Hispanic Spirituality

'Hispanic spirituality', also sometimes called Latino spirituality because of its Latin American and not just Iberian roots, stems from the writings of Hispanic or Latinos or Latinas, who since the mid 1970s have been concerned about articulating the faith experience of the fastest-growing sector of the US population. This spirituality reflects not only centuries of lived Christianity in Latin America but also a new synthesis or *mestizaje* gradually taking shape on US

soil (see Fernández' introductory work (2000) in the bibliography). Both terms, Hispanic or Latino or Latina (in the case of women), will be used interchangeably in this entry.

While some feel that a more systematic treatise of this form of spirituality has yet to be written, not a surprising observation given the relatively recent articulation of it in print, there are writers from this community who are providing the substance for such a larger work. Their names and contributions appear below together with some general characteristics. Given the incredible diversity found among this population, for example, the fact that the term 'Hispanic' can be ascribed both to someone who has lived in the United States for only a few years or to someone whose family has been living there since the seventeenth century, generalizations have to be made cautiously. Nonetheless, if Hispanic spirituality is in fact a distinct Christian spirituality amid the general US milieu, it must possess some unique features. In general, it can be described under the following headings.

1. *Diverse*. As mentioned above, the peoples called Hispanic or Latino not only have inhabited what is now the United States over different periods of time but also trace their origins to Spain or any of several Latin American countries. This means that the spiritualities which they brought with them or continue to bring with them will be diverse, to say nothing of what happens once they encounter US mainstream. Factors not to be overlooked in this understanding of diversity are the various cultural and religious strands which came together at the time of the Iberian conquests of the Americas in the sixteenth century. Not only did the mixture of the Indigenous and the European, and in some cases the African, produce a new type, the 'mestizo' or 'mulatto' (in the case of African influence because of the slaves brought to the shores of the New World), but the European already reflected a cultural amalgamation of Iberian, Basque, Phoenician, Greek, Roman, Visigothic, North African, Moorish and Jewish cultures (Deck, 1993, p. 47; for an introduction to African-influenced forms, see Julio Sánchez Cárdenas, 1997). Virgilio Elizondo, a pioneer of US Hispanic theology, has written most extensively about this *mestizaje*, especially as it relates to Jesus' own marginal cultural status as a Galilean.

2. *Popular and communal*. Partly because of its socio-historical emergence in a people not unfamiliar with diversity, conquest and resistance, Hispanic spirituality is not that of some elite group. In the words of Allan Figueroa Deck, 'It does not have its gurus, nor does it move in

rarefied circles. This spirituality is bound up with the Hispanic Catholic civilization' (Deck, 1993, p. 46). Several Latino Protestants, such as Justo L. González, have noted the need to take into account these Catholic cultural roots. As in any serious treatment of culture, symbol, ritual and myth assume key roles. Deck notes the difficulty that modern cultures have in understanding the evangelization of the New World. He designates the central issue as being the nature of conversion. 'Modern European and North American cultures have tended to conceive of conversion as Protestants do. For many of us, conversion means a personal decision to believe and follow Christ in the Church. Conversion, in this view, is fundamentally a personal matter' (Deck, 1993, p. 48). Contrasting the pre-Tridentine approach used by the sixteenth-century mendicant friars, Deck sees this conversion as a collective, communal, event, time and circumstances not permitting otherwise. In other words, by trying to focus their energies not on individual conversions but on the conversion of communal symbols, rituals and customs, the missionaries sought to win over the hearts of indigenous peoples to Christ. Evidence of what Deck labels as 'cultural conversion' is found amply today in the persistence of a popular religiosity which can only be understood by exploring its symbols, rituals and cultural myths. Unlike mainstream American Catholicism or mainstream Protestantism which has 'opted to take the route of the cognitive, literate, rational exposition of the faith', Hispanic Catholicism (and Hispanic spirituality by derivation), being rooted in orality and myth, has 'opted for the heart. It seeks to fill the heart first and then, hopefully, the head' (Deck, 1993, p. 49).

This emphasis on the heart as articulated in community is clearly evident in the various recent successful movements such as Charismatic, Cursillo, Marriage Encounter, Renewal and several youth movements which often invite others to experience their Christian faith more vibrantly through an experience of an intense weekend of hearing faith testimonies or sharing their own struggles to follow Christ in the world. They are often very good about providing a supportive community after this intense experience. The importance of these movements is their appeal to the emotive and communal aspects of the culture, especially in a situation where the majority of Hispanics are recent immigrants who often feel isolated in their new country. In a way, they find that they can no longer take for granted the type of popular religiosity they experienced in their native countries.

It is interesting to note, incidentally, that this very persistence of Hispanic popular religiosity in now providing a vehicle for exploring pre-Christian indigenous or African spiritualities. The Latino Catholic writers most associated with the study of popular religiosity or popular religion, as some choose to call it, along with its incorporation into the liturgy are Orlando Espín, Rosa María Icaza and Arturo Pérez-Rodríguez. These writers demonstrate that faith is kept alive at home through practices in daily life and particularly during the principal seasons of the liturgical year, such as Advent and Lent. From a Protestant perspective, Elizabeth Conde-Frazier has penned a significant piece demonstrating similarities and differences in Hispanic Protestant and Catholic practice. As a large number of US Hispanics are now becoming Pentecostal, Samuel Solivan's book, *The Spirit, Pathos, and Liberation*, outlines the unique contribution which this group is making today to world Christianity.

3. *Festive.* Despite a history of suffering and oppression, Latino spirituality is characterized by a life-giving inner strength. The saying *Si no me río, lloro* ('If I don't laugh, I'll cry') reveals a general sunny disposition needed to combat life's difficulties. The large number of family and communal celebrations provides a type of oasis in a life beset with an infinite number of problems which so often plague a population much poorer than the general one. Likewise, art and music play a key role in this affirmation of life. Latinos writing about theological aesthetics as it relates to spirituality now include Alejandro García-Rivera and Roberto Goizueta. For example, Goizueta notes that the aesthetic paradigm has played an important role in the history of Latin American philosophy, in many ways an alternative to the Cartesian epistemological paradigm. For the ancient Aztecs, indigenous inhabitants of Mesoamerica, truth was expressed not in logic but in *flor y canto* ('flower and song'). Is it any wonder, then, that flower and song remain powerful symbols used in worship even to this day? Celebrations are seen as communal events, such as patronal feasts, and many include prayer or meals, dance, processions and poetry. Rites of passage, sacraments or ordinances such as baptism (or *presentación*, i.e., a 'presentation to the community' in the case of some Protestants), first communion, coming of age, marriage, and those surrounding death and remembrance almost always include a common meal.

4. *Relational.* In general, it can be said that compared to US dominant culture, Latinas and

Latinos value belonging over personal achievements. More in tune with traditional societies where the individual derives her or his importance from the group rather than from individual accomplishments, relations take on a singular quality. Family and friends must be consulted when important decisions are made or their welfare should have a priority in the individual's life. For example, Hispanics are less likely to put their elderly in nursing homes or to put up a child for adoption. Whether aged or young, these persons are the responsibility of the community. Similarly, hospitality and care for one's own during times of sickness or imprisonment reveal gospel values. This love and support is not seen as something which ends at death but continues long after, as the importance given to funerals and yearly memorials will attest.

Women, particularly in the role of mother and grandmother, are often the ones who serve as reconcilers, domestic prayer leaders, storytellers, community leaders and care providers. They often lead many popular piety rituals such as praying the rosary, seasonal customs such as the advent practice of *posada* (a novena which re-enacts Mary and Joseph's search for lodging) or blessing their children, especially when they are departing for a journey. Elizabeth Conde-Frazier describes bridal and baby showers where folk wisdom, prayers and biblical teaching were imparted, especially by older women.

Ana María Díaz-Stevens, however, notes that because the sphere of religion has been generally neglected by scholars of the Latino community, not enough attention has been paid to the Latinas who through their religious work have emerged as leaders, especially at the grassroots level (cited in Fernández, 2000, p. 63). There is also the danger in the Hispanic community that women are expected to carry the bulk of the burden of caring for family and community.

In Hispanic Roman Catholic practice, God is found either in the arms of the Virgin Mary or, as in the case of Mexican piety, as Guadalupe, the defender of oppressed peoples. Other Latin American countries honour Mary under other titles and her feast days are cause for great communal celebrations. A similar phenomenon occurs with the saints who are seen as friends and powerful intercessors. Again similar to other traditional societies which engage intermediaries, Hispanic Catholics honour Mary and the saints because they are related to Christ. If I care about you, I will also care about your mother and your friends and family.

As in any honest relationship, persons have the confidence to ask for favours. Thus, intercessory prayers to Mary and the saints for one's loved ones, especially if they be in need of physical or spiritual healing, are common, just as one would not hesitate to ask one's mother or relatives for prayers. Miraculous healings are seen as possible if God wills them.

This relational characteristic of Latino spirituality is particularly seen in the area of social justice. As in the case of the grassroots women leaders mentioned above, the quest for justice cannot be separated from spirituality. As the biblical understanding of justice stresses, justice is about fulfilling one's obligations in a covenant relationship. Ada María Isasi-Díaz and María Pilar Aquino are the two Latinas who have most clearly articulated the relationship of justice to spirituality, especially as it relates to the role of women in the Hispanic community.

5. *Transcendent.* Deck writes that Hispanic spirituality 'unabashedly affirms a transcendent God. Our language is full of references to our dependence on this God who is both near and far' (Deck, 1993, p. 51). There is a basic and constant awareness of the presence of God, a God who becomes human. Devotions around the human Jesus often catch the eye of the outsider: the Christ child, the suffering Christ found in the passion, and those concerning his mother and followers. Yet, these images are only part of the story. For Catholic Hispanics, the Sacred Heart of Jesus, the symbol of the love and mercy of the risen Christ, speaks volumes. And for Hispanics in general, the humanity, and yet transcendence, of Christ, remains essential to their devotion. In reference to the suffering Christ, Orlando Espín writes: 'This dying Jesus, however, is so special because he is not just another human who suffers unfairly at the hands of evil humans. He is the divine Christ, and that makes his innocent suffering all the more dramatic . . . His passion and death express his solidarity with all men and women throughout history who have also innocently suffered at the hands of evildoers' (cited in Fernandez, 2000, p. 52).

See also **Spirituality and Culture (*essay*); Devotions, Popular; Latin American Spirituality; Liberation Spirituality; Mujerista Spirituality.**

María Pilar Aquino, *Our Cry for Life: Feminist Theology from Latin America*, Maryknoll, NY: Orbis Books, 1993; María Pilar Aquino, Daisy L. Machado and Jeanette Rodríguez (eds), *A Reader in Latina Feminist Theology: Religion and Justice*, Austin, TX: University of Texas Press, 2002; Elizabeth Conde-Frazier, 'Hispanic Protestant spirituality' in José David Rodríguez and Loida I. Martell-Otero (eds), *Teología en Conjunto: A Collaborative Protestant Theology*, Louisville, KY:

Westminster John Knox Press, 1997, pp. 125–45; Allan Figueroa Deck, 'Raza cósmica: Rediscovering the Hispanic soul', *Critic* (Spring, 1993), pp. 46–53; Anita de Luna, *Faith Formation and Popular Religion: A Tejana Approach*, Lanham, MD: Rowman & Littlefield, 2002; Virgil P. Elizondo, *Galilean Journey: The Mexican American Promise*, Maryknoll, NY: Orbis Books, 1983; Orlando Espín, *The Faith of the People: Theological Reflections on Popular Catholicism*, Maryknoll, NY: Orbis Books, 1997; Eduardo C. Fernández, *La Cosecha: Harvesting Contemporary United States Hispanic Theology (1972–1998)*, Collegeville, MN: The Liturgical Press, 2000; Alejandro García-Rivera, *The Community of the Beautiful: A Theological Aesthetics*, Collegeville, MN: Michael Glazier/The Liturgical Press, 1999; Roberto S. Goizueta, *Caminemos con Jesús: Toward a Hispanic/Latino Theology of Accompaniment*, Maryknoll, NY: Orbis Books, 1995; Justo L. González, *Mañana: Christian Theology from a Hispanic Perspective*, Nashville: Abingdon Press, 1990; Daniel Groody, *Border of Death, Valley of Life: An Immigrant Journey of Heart and Spirit*, Linham, MD: Rowman & Littlefield, 2002; Rosa María Icaza, 'Spirituality-Mística-Liturgy' in Soledad Galerón, Rosa María Icaza and Rosendo Urrabazo (eds), *Prophetic Vision: Pastoral Reflections on the National Plan for Hispanic Ministry*, Kansas City: Sheed & Ward, 1992, pp. 239–47; Ada María Isasi-Díaz, *En la lucha, In the Struggle: A Hispanic Women's Liberation Theology*, Minneapolis: Fortress Press, 1993; Arturo J. Pérez, *Popular Catholicism*, Washington, DC: Pastoral Press, 1988; Arturo J. Pérez, 'Spirituality' in Allan Figueroa Deck, Yolanda Tarango and Timothy M. Matovina (eds), *Perspectivas: Hispanic Ministry*, Kansas City: Sheed and Ward, 1995, pp. 98–104; Julio Sánchez Cárdenas, 'Santería or Orisha Religion: An Old Religion in a New World' in Gary H. Gossen in collaboration with Miguel León-Portilla (eds), *South and Meso-American Native Spirituality: From the Cult of the Feathered Serpent to the Theology of Liberation*, New York: Crossroad Herder, 1997, pp. 474–95; Samual Soliván, *The Spirit, Pathos, and Liberation*, Sheffield, England: Sheffield Academic Press, 1998.

EDUARDO C. FERNÁNDEZ

Holiness

Holiness in the Old Testament (from the root *qdš*) is unusual in that it does not originate in the secular language of daily life but has exclusively theological meaning. Three kinds of usage can be discerned. In the first place 'holiness' denotes separateness which is associated with purity. This is a theme which finds expression at the material level and which becomes bound up with priestly traditions of ritual and purity (cf. the Holiness Code of Lev. 17—26). Another theme, which functions at the moral level and is associated with prophetic tradition, is that of social relations and the requirements of justice in the right ordering of society. Israel is also set apart by the righteousness visible in her social life. A third is that of the glorious majesty of God (cf. Isa. 6.1–8), which calls forth the praise of the angels ('Holy, Holy, Holy'), repeated in the trisagion of the liturgy.

According to Lev. 19.2, the holiness of God is replicated in the holiness of Israel ('You shall be holy, for I the Lord your God am holy').

The New Testament assumes the holiness of God and is concerned with showing the equal holiness of Jesus who sanctifies others, making them *hagios*. This is developed in the letter to the Hebrews in association with redemptive suffering. The Spirit too sanctifies (upon which Basil the Great will base his argument for the divinity of the Holy Spirit). By baptism and 'renewal' and 'rebirth' through the Spirit, the Christian is made part of the Church, which is called 'a chosen race, a royal priesthood, a holy nation' (1 Peter 2.9). Holiness is defined as 'purity' (1 Tim. 1.5), 'wisdom' and 'innocence' (Matt. 10.16) and a holy life is one consecrated into the holiness of Christ, lived out in mutual love, fidelity to God and hope for the kingdom.

The interconnection between meanings attached to the 'holiness' of God and images of the 'holy life' on earth point to the richness and variety surrounding Christian practices and understandings of holiness. Where the transcendence of God is stressed, as it was by many of the Greek Fathers, the holy life might reflect patterns of withdrawal from the world and elevation of the mind above earthbound images. The spirituality of early eremeticism was one of poverty and purification at the physical level, and of abstraction and raising the mind to God in prayer, at an internal or mental level. The spirituality of the mendicant orders of the thirteenth century strongly reinforced the principle of personal poverty as the mark of holiness, and it was a Dominican (Meister Eckhart) and a Franciscan (St Bonaventure) who composed some of the finest representations of the purifying ascent of the mind to God from this period. On the other hand, where the emphasis lies upon the immanence of God, and specifically upon the Incarnation, the active life, with its commitment to meeting the needs of others, may come increasingly to the fore. The Middle Ages, with its numerous manuals of prayer and piety, shows the evident tension between a life devoted to prayer and a life devoted to action in the world, as well as their complementarity.

The concept of holiness, or 'godliness', emerged with a new intensity during the Protestant Reformation. The Pietists rejected what they perceived to be a formalized Protestant scholasticism in favour of a vital spiritual life of worship and service based upon a radical and straightforward christocentrism. This more small-scale and charismatic spirit flowered in classic texts such as Johann Arndt's *True Christianity* (1605) and Philip Jacob Spener's *Pia Desideria* (1675). The Puritan movement, the spirit of which found enduring expression in John Bunyon's *Pilgrim's Progress* (1678), tended to understand holiness in terms of radical and public conversion.

For many Christians today the concept of holiness combines elements which derive from a commitment both to personal piety and to an active concern for others. Many medieval mystical treatises, including such works as the *Cloud of Unknowing* or the *Revelations* of Julian of Norwich, enjoy a greater popularity today than they did in their own time. They appear to serve as an important counterbalance to the materialism and utilitarianism of our age. At the same time, globalization has led us to develop a keener social conscience than our ancestors had, and we expect holiness of life to include a visible engagement with social issues and the alleviation of suffering. Practices of holiness today are also more likely to include objects and ideas associated with other cultures. The widespread use of icons, which are traditionally associated with the Orthodox world, is an example of this, as is the use of the Jesus prayer. For some Christians, the meditative techniques of Eastern religions offer a valuable resource. If 'spirituality' is a word that is extensively used outside a specifically Christian frame of reference, the idea of 'holiness' remains more closely linked with Christian traditions and with traditional understandings of the nature of God. For all the variety of Christian practice and belief, we can still discern much of the threefold unity of Hebrew holiness in the life of the Church. Christians are a people set apart by and for God in cult and rite, called to practical acts of altruism in social relations, worshipping and honouring with awe the God of glory.

See also **Conversion; Deification; Fools, Holy; Journey, Spiritual; Saints, Communion of; Sanctification; Virtue.**

Stephen Barton (ed.), *Holiness Past and Present*, Edinburgh: T & T Clark, 2003; Margaret M.

Miles, *The Image and Practice of Holiness: A Critique of the Classic Manuals of Devotion*, London: SCM Press, 1988; Donald Nicholl, *Holiness*, London: Darton, Longman & Todd, 1981; Rudolf Otto, *The Idea of the Holy*, Oxford: Oxford University Press, 1923; Philip Sheldrake, *Spirituality and History*, London: SPCK, 1991; John Webster, *Holiness*, London: SCM Press, 2003.

OLIVER DAVIES

Holistic Spirituality

The term 'holistic' has in recent years been applied to such diverse fields as medicine, human development and spirituality. In all these applications, the common meaning reflects a concern for wholeness, a desire for integration and an attempt to understand the connections among the various aspects that constitute a given reality. In the New Testament, the word 'holistic' (from the Greek *holus*) means total or entire, as in the story of the widow's mite in which Jesus commends the woman for putting her *holon ton biov* (everything she had to support her life) into the basket (Luke 21.4). Holistic discernment, for example, invites people to put their whole self into the process, like Luke's widow. Recognizing God as Mystery, a holistic approach to discernment argues for the need to be open to the many and diverse ways that our lives can be influenced by the Holy One in our midst. It is inclusive and takes seriously the knowledge-bearing capacity not only of the mind, but also of the body, emotions, senses, imagination, feelings, intuition and dreams. Like holistic medicine which links physical and mental health, a holistic spirituality respects the psychosomatic or body-spirit unity of the person. Holistic prayer, for example, recognizes that bodily calm can engender internal stillness, and external concentration can focus the spirit's awareness.

As with holistic human development, which views growth as the lifelong effort to integrate the diverse aspects that constitute the self, holistic spirituality sees the struggle for personal wholeness as an integral part of the journey to holiness. This belief is reflected, for example, in Josef Goldbrunner's *Holiness Is Wholeness* (New York: Pantheon, 1955). To regard the spiritual life holistically is to assert the truth of two central beliefs: first, the pursuit of holiness is in no way inimical to healthy human growth; and, second, those who strive to be religious are not exempt from the human condition, but must, like everyone else, work out their growth into wholeness in the context of human struggle. A spiritual life not built on solid human development born of struggle is liable to be superficial and escapist.

Thus, authentic spiritual development requires a commitment to ongoing human growth. Holistic spirituality is developmental in that it views growth as occurring gradually throughout the different seasons of one's life and allows for trial-and-error learning.

Defining the spiritual life as coextensive with life itself, holistic spirituality finds every human concern relevant. God's Spirit can be encountered in all aspects of life and not merely in such explicitly religious activities as prayer and worship. Understanding spirituality holistically involves linking it with every aspect of human development – psychological and spiritual, interpersonal and political. All aspects of a person's life must be subjected to the transforming influence of the Spirit. Antithetical to a dualistic mentality that sees things as irreconcilable opposites, holistic spirituality stresses a complementary attitude that is integrative and inclusive. When, for example, the spiritual is seen as opposed to the material, the development of one's inner life or the spiritual soul is almost exclusively emphasized; affectivity, sexuality and whatever belongs to the life of the body are seen as irrelevant to holiness and spiritual development. Holistic spirituality opposes any such dualism that has plagued spirituality in the Western Christian tradition over the centuries. Platonic devaluation of the world of the senses, Cartesian dichotomization of matter and spirit, and Manichean beliefs that see material things as tainted with sin and the realm of the divine as non-material have separated realities that holistic spirituality insists should be united. Specifically, holistic spirituality opposes pitting the sacred against the secular, 'this world' against the 'next world', the individual against the social, and the spiritual against the material. According to holistic spirituality, the world is a divine milieu and every particle of the created universe is potentially revelatory of God, every bush a burning bush to the eyes of faith (Ex. 3.1–6). By enabling people to forge a more vital link between their faith and their daily lives, a holistic approach to the spiritual life helps them to grow in wholeness by healing the dichotomy between the human and the holy – a division that has forced so many to be schizophrenic in living out their religious beliefs.

See also Spirituality, Psychology and Psychotherapy (essay); Affectivity; Body and Spirituality; Creation Spirituality; Desire; Dualism; Journey, Spiritual.

Wilkie Au, By Way of the Heart: Toward a Holistic Christian Spirituality, Mahwah, NJ: Paulist Press, 1989; Wilkie Au and Noreen Cannon, Urgings of the Heart: A Spirituality of Integration, Mahwah, NJ: Paulist Press, 1995; Wilkie Au, The Enduring Heart: Spirituality for the Long Haul, Mahwah, NJ, Paulist Press, 2000; John Carmody, Holistic Spirituality, Mahwah, NJ: Paulist Press, 1983.

WILKIE AU

Holocaust

The Holocaust defies explanation, but demands examination. As the state-sanctioned, systematic persecution and murder of some 6 million Jews – two-thirds of European Jewry – the Holocaust poses searing questions about how 'civilized' and 'enlightened' moderns could have sought to obliterate an entire people. The Nazi genocide claimed millions of other victims as well, whether those they deemed racially inferior (e.g. Roma [Gypsies], Poles, the disabled) or politically undesirable (e.g. homosexuals, Jehovah's Witnesses, Communists).

The Holocaust indicts Christianity. Its anti-Jewish teachings, which over the centuries varied in intent, virulence and effect, were a necessary if insufficient cause of the Holocaust. Christian teaching and preaching had provided fertile ground on which the genocidal policies of the Third Reich, supported by the myth of the German Volk and theories of race 'science', took root.

Christianity, in both its institutional manifestations and local practice, interacted with the Third Reich in various ways. In some cases, it endorsed National Socialism, most notably in the anti-Semitic German Christian Movement, founded in 1932 in the hopes of forming a national Reich Church. Its members envisioned Jesus as the Aryan exemplar of the 'new' Germany and suppressed the Old Testament. The German Evangelical Church, composed of the Lutheran, Reformed and United Churches and constituting the largest Protestant Church in Germany, denounced this movement. Yet its own alliance of 'throne and altar', an outgrowth of the Lutheran doctrine of the two kingdoms, meant that many of its members were intensely nationalistic. For the most part, the churches were excessively cautious in challenging the state, both out of nationalist fervour and a desire to maintain independence from Nazi control. The Vatican's 1933 'Concordat between the Holy See and the German Reich' illustrates this caution most markedly. Yet even the Confessing Church's Barmen Declaration of 1934, notable for its assertion of God's dominion (Reich) over the state's claims, revealed little concern for the fate of Jews who had not converted to Christianity. This caution, combined with the longstanding 'teaching of contempt' – the denigration of Judaism in preaching and teaching – exposed the Church's proclivity for self-preservation over prophecy. Nevertheless, some Christian leaders both in Germany and abroad condemned Nazi policies and actions, although their condemnations were unsystematic and sporadic. Some Christians joined the ranks of resisters and rescuers. These 'righteous Gentiles' showed exceptional courage and even cunning. Yet research reveals that Christian convictions motivated relatively few of them.

The failures of the Churches during the Holocaust have engendered widespread reflection and reassessment in recent years. The Vatican concluded its statement 'We Remember: Reflections on the Shoah' (1998) with the imperative that the 'spoiled seeds of anti-Judaism and antisemitism must never again be allowed to take root in any human heart'. The Leuenberg Church Fellowship (an alliance of Reformation Churches in Europe) declared in its document 'Church and Israel' (2001) that the Holocaust requires 'permanent theological self-examination and renewal'.

The Holocaust provokes profound questions at the heart of Christian spirituality. Perhaps most radical is the 'God question', to which wide-ranging responses may be discerned. One pole of the continuum may be seen in the position associated with some ultra Orthodox Jews that because the people Israel had sinned, Auschwitz was the retribution of a just God. Countervailing positions include the argument that the Holocaust proves that God is dead because a just God would have prevented Auschwitz, and the daring position associated with Rabbi David Blumenthal that God is an 'abusing' God. Other views speak of God in 'hiding' or in 'eclipse'. For many, divine omnipotence can no longer be asserted: the Almighty does not reign from heaven above but suffers with the people. Among Christian scholars, Jürgen Moltmann has developed a theology of 'divine vulnerability', arguing that God suffers with the martyred and murdered – in the camps and with Jesus on the cross.

In light of the Holocaust, glib assertions about divine providence or pronouncements about redemption as if it were complete reflect 'cheap grace', in the memorable phrase of Dietrich Bonhoeffer. Christian theologies of the past may have fostered passivity in the face of an all-powerful God. After the Shoah (a term meaning 'whirlwind of destruction' that many prefer to the term holocaust, since that latter, biblical term for sacrifice is not an appropriate designation for such an obscene event), humans must reawaken to their obligations as covenant partners and assume proper responsibility for the care of the world. They must use the power their creator has given them, even as they recognize (as the Nazis did not) that their power is given by a God who desires the flourishing of all creation.

No healthy Christian spirituality can avoid wrestling with the Holocaust. It compels one to confront radical evil, rethink the divine–human relationship, and reassess Christianity's relationship with Judaism. To admit the Holocaust into one's spirituality is to confess to the Church's sinfulness and to assume a posture of repentance.

See also Anti-Semitism; Cross and Spirituality; Judaism and Christianity; Redemption.

Victoria Barnett, For the Soul of the People: Protestant Protest against Hitler, New York and Oxford: Oxford University Press, 1992; Doris Berger, Twisted Cross: The German Christian Movement in the Third Reich, Chapel Hill and London: University of North Carolina Press, 1996; Dan Cohn-Sherbok (ed.), Holocaust Theology: A Reader, New York: New York University Press, 2002; Donald J. Dietrich, God and Humanity in Auschwitz: Jewish–Christian Relations and Sanctioned Murder, New Brunswick, NJ: Transaction Publishers, 1995; Michael A. Signer (ed.), Humanity at the Limit: The Impact of the Holocaust Experience on Jews and Christians, Bloomington and Indianapolis: Indiana University Press, 2000.

MARY BOYS

Holy Spirit

see Spirit, Holy

Homosexuality

The Stonewall Riots of June 1969 have come to mark the symbolic beginning of the gay liberation movement. For four days the sexually marginalized patrons of this New York bar kept at bay the police who had come to execute a routine raid. Stonewall has come to symbolize the transformation of homosexual people into gay and lesbian people. People whose sexual desire had been labelled by the medical establishment as pathological and an expression of a pathological self now used that labelling to band together and subvert it. They claimed their own subjectivity, moral agency and rights to self-determination and self-definition. They began to claim a minority voice and a place in culture and represented themselves as a stable oppressed minority group.

A gay and lesbian Christian spirituality began to emerge as members who belonged to this minority group began to reflect theologically and spiritually upon their status and experience. Broadly speaking, four different types of spiritual reflection on homosexuality have emerged from gay and lesbian people themselves – liberal, liberationist, lesbian feminist and queer.

Gay liberal theology like all liberal theological reflection centres the self as the point of contact between God and humanity. The genius of gay liberal theology was to take advantage of the invention of the sexual self in medical and social scientific discourse but to reverse the pathological construction of the homosexual self and claim that for the gay person their homosexuality was their point of contact with the divine. The former Jesuit John J. McNeill is the most prolific exponent of a gay liberal spirituality. McNeill draws a distinction between mature and immature faith. Immature faith is one which confuses the will of God with that of external authorities and confuses God's voice with that of our own 'sadistic superego' that paralyses us with neurotic guilt. A mature 'healthy' faith is one built directly on our own experience, a faith that can lead us to reach out in love to each other. This faith must be grounded in prayer, in the 'direct and immediate' contact with God that no Church can touch or override. For the Church is prone to preach and incarnate 'pathological' religion, a belief system that fears and punishes freedom of thought. Healthy religion on the other hand enables people to achieve *teleios* (Matt. 5.48), not moral perfection but self-realization. Gay and lesbian people have therefore to engage in a process of self-centring as they move towards spiritual maturity and from that internal space which is the space of God they have the obligation to scrutinize and judge all belief systems, rejecting those which stand in the way of the gay self reaching spiritual maturity. For McNeill such maturity is achieved through three stages: the achievement of self-love as a gay person, learning to love another and becoming actively involved in the gay Christian community in order to teach the wider Church that it is possible to be gay and Christian. McNeill's genius was to direct lesbian and gay readers to a sacred space outside the realm of ecclesial authority, a space where it is possible for the lesbian and gay person to hear the voice of God speaking directly to them. This space is their heart/conscience. In going into this space and trusting their experiences, lesbian and gay Christians ironically demonstrate themselves to have a faith much more mature and healthy than many of their fellow Christians. In McNeill's theology, a despised and beleaguered group of people become the bearers of the gospel to their fellow Christians. But any theology centred on the self will fall too easily into the trap of identifying God with the self and absorbing the Other into oneself, and in any case the existence of the sexual self is not an incontestable truth.

Liberationist gay spirituality tends to take a social constructionist approach to sexual identity. Rather than ground spirituality in the gay self, gay liberationists ground it in their experience of oppression. In the writings of theologians such as J. Michael Clark, Richard Clever and Gary Comstock, gay Christians are understood to be an exodus community moving out of oppression into freedom. Salvation is understood to be a communal, historical event and God is to be experienced as the imminent presence propelling this community out of homophobic structures and constructions. Spirituality becomes active involvement in this process. Robert Goss constructs a 'queer' Christology around Jesus' proclamation of the reign of God which involved the political transformation of society. Jesus acted out his message by standing with the oppressed and the outcast of his society and by forming a discipleship of equals in which men and women were equal. The key event that led to Jesus' death was what Goss labels the Stop the Temple action which was Jesus' most transgressive demonstration of the 'egalitarian, unbrokered reign of God'. Goss argues that at Easter Jesus became the queer Christ. This is not any comment upon Jesus' sexuality; rather, for Goss the resurrection is God's 'coming out' on the side of Jesus, confirming his *basileia* message. Jesus' resurrection is therefore the hope for queer people, for it is through it that God turns Jesus into a parable about God and so we know that God is on the side of the oppressed. At Easter God 'raised Jesus to the level of a discursive symbol and praxis, and Jesus became the Christ, the liberative praxis of God's compassion in the world'. So that for all time and space Jesus stands in solidarity with the oppressed who then have a duty to follow him in acting out God's kingdom around them. One of the dangers of gay liberationist spirituality is that it fosters a sense of identity grounded solely in victimhood and does not encourage critical self-examination or contemplation.

Lesbian feminist spirituality seeks to engage in spiritual reflection from the particular perspective of lesbian women. The vast majority of lesbian feminist spirituality is constructed around Audre Lorde's notion of the erotic. Lorde identified the erotic with a deep body knowledge and a drive towards joy, satisfaction and self-fulfilment which may be encountered in sexual relations but may also be experienced in any creative activity. The erotic is our 'yes' within ourselves, our deepest cravings, but we have been taught to fear these and to repress them, to rely upon external authorities rather than our deep internal knowledge, our 'erotic guides'. Carter Heyward, the most influential lesbian theologian, further defined the erotic as power in relation and identified that power with God. Jesus serves as an example of how to 'god', that is, how to live out right relationship by building friendships (including sexual friendships) upon foundations of mutuality. Since God is our power in relation, God is encountered primarily in the act of right relating. The problem with this approach is that it can shrink God to fit our own experience so that our spirituality becomes very narrowly focused on our own lives and we fail to lift our eyes to wider horizons.

Queer spirituality has a completely different starting point to lesbian and gay spirituality. Whereas all lesbian and gay theology assumes a gay subject stable enough to engage in spiritual reflection upon, queer spirituality does not. It follows queer theorists such as Michel Foucault and Judith Butler in taking the view that sexuality and gender are not stable, essential forms of identity that somehow tell the truth about the person but are rather always matters of performance. Sexual orientation and gender cannot then be said to be of ultimate concern nor can they be the point of contact between God and humanity. Queer theologians such as Kathy Rudy, Eugene Rogers and Elizabeth Stuart have all argued that the only form of stable identity is that given by God in baptism. Christian people have an ecclesial identity within which they are under a divine mandate to subvert dominant cultural constructions of maleness and femaleness and related constructions of sexual orientation. Queer theologians argue that queer theory picks up an ancient Christian tradition exemplified in the writings of early Church theologians such as Gregory of Nyssa. Gregory, in his reflections on the resurrection, constructs a body which is fluid. Unlike some early theologians Gregory does not associate change with decay but with movement towards the next life. Reading Gen. 1.27 with Gal. 3.28 Gregory argued that the original human creature was not sexed and it was to this angelic prelapsarian state that human beings would return in the resurrection. This state can to some extent be anticipated in the ascetic life. Gregory then looks to a life beyond gender which can be anticipated in this life, a life beyond gender and beyond sexual orientation which is available to us in Christian worship. This is the vision espoused by queer spirituality which is a very different vision to lesbian and gay spirituality and grounded much more deeply in the Christian tradition.

See also Body and Spirituality; Conscience; Desire; Discernment; Ecclesiology and Spirituality; Eroticism; Feminist Spirituality; Friendship; God, Images of; Liberation Spirituality; Sexuality.

———

Donald L. Boisvert, *Out on Holy Ground: Meditations on Gay Men's Spirituality*, Cleveland, OH: The Pilgrim Press, 2000; J. Michael Clark, *A Place to Start: Toward an Unapologetic Gay Liberation Theology*, Dallas, TX: Monument Press, 1989; Robert Goss, *Jesus Acted Up: A Gay and Lesbian Manifesto*, San Francisco: HarperSanFrancisco, 1993; Carter Heyward, *Touching Our Strength: The Erotic as Power and the Love of God*, San Francisco: Harper & Row, 1989; John J. McNeill, *Taking a Chance on God: Liberating Theology for Gays, Lesbians, and their Lovers, Families and Friends*, Boston: Beacon Press, 1988; Elizabeth Stuart, *Gay and Lesbian Theologies: Repetitions with Critical Difference*, Aldershot: Ashgate, 2002.

ELIZABETH STUART

Hope

Hope is the universal human experience that orients us to the future. Hope is directed not just toward the things of this world, but more importantly toward the world beyond. The fact that humans hope beyond death is reason for believing that we have an eternal destiny. Hope draws us out of the present towards a future whose perspective transforms the present. However, hope is neither wish-fulfilment nor the construction of an imaginary future. It is not centred on dreams of individual happiness or the perfection of society. Rather, hope is an attunement to the divine order of creation. It is the fundamental orientation of the soul toward transcendent reality that makes the soul receptive to the divine indwelling. As the ultimate source of genuine hope, divine grace eliminates from this fundamental attitude anxiety over the future as well as the anticipation of personal rewards. God's grace already given to a person in creation is the basis for trusting in the future consummation of the human–divine relationship.

From a Christian perspective, hope is one of the three theological virtues, eminently related to both faith and love, in the sense of Heb. 11.1: 'Faith is the conviction of things hoped for and the evidence of things not seen.' To face the mystery of reality means to live in light of this faith. The things hoped for are awaited with confidence, and love provides the assurance that the object of our hope is not sought in vain.

Christian hope rests in the belief that love is stronger than death and will ultimately triumph over death. The divine love that has been poured into our hearts from the Holy Spirit (Rom. 5.5) infuses the soul with the hope of eternal union with God. The God of love, then, is the ground of this very hope, the ultimate goal of which is made known wherever love is expressed.

Christian hope is essentially eschatological. The definitive historical realization of this eschatological hope for Christians is Christ's resurrection. For St Paul Christ's resurrection vindicates his life and teaching and is the basis of our faith that God is reconciling the world to himself. Paul's statement in 1 Cor. 15.19, 'If for this life only we have hoped in Christ, we are of all people most to be pitied,' expresses the belief that hope in this life is not enough. In fact, it is worse than nothing, unless this hope is embedded in the assurance that derives from the vision of the Resurrected – the beginning of the transfiguration of this world. For Paul, hope penetrates all creation as it struggles toward salvation (Rom. 8.18–25). Moreover, salvation is not a matter of knowledge. It is not something seen, but instead rests on hope. If salvation were seen, hope would not be necessary (Rom. 8.24). As the ordering virtue that attunes the soul to transcendence, hope seeks its ultimate fulfilment in a transfigured humanity.

According to the Scholastic tradition, faith and hope are formed by love. From this tradition, what Christians have hoped for is entrance into the beatific vision at death, to await the resurrection of all the dead at the end of the world. Unfortunately, when the eschatological things hoped for but not seen are deformed into an expectation of future events that will occur in history, or worse, when human projects of self-salvation seek to realize the expectations historically, then human existence as a tension between the transcendent and the immanent is destroyed, leading to the destruction of the Mystery. Joachim of Fiore's tripartite division of history in the thirteenth century was a medieval vision of hope that led to the modern, secularized ideologies of immanent progress in history that delivered this very spiritual ruin. Joachim's project additionally distorted reality by yielding an apocalyptic theology and spirituality that awaited the new millennium in the divine dispensation for history.

Human history indeed is the locus for the realization of Christian hope. However much hope seeks a more abundant life – one that encompasses a more just and peaceful world – it is irreducible to an intramundane fulfilment. Though the hope of heaven must not divert attention from earthly injustice and suffering, the Christian vision is not a political utopia. To live in hope is to reject any utopianism that would identify the reign of God with any immanent realm of freedom. Trust in the God of love is the only basis for the human expectation of a destiny beyond the grave. We must constantly turn ourselves to that steadfast love to see how it has been and will be acted out in human history.

See also **Afterlife; Death and Dying; Eschatology; Redemption; Resurrection; Salvation; Soul.**

A. J. Conyers, *God, Hope, and History*, Macon, GA: Mercer Press, 1992; A. J. Conyers, *The Eclipse of Heaven: Rediscovering the Hope of a World Beyond History*, Downers Grove, IL: InterVarsity Press, 1992; John Macquarrie, *Christian Hope*, New York: Seabury Press, 1978; John Polkinghorne, *The God of Hope and the End of the World*, New Haven, CT: Yale University Press, 2002.

MICHAEL P. MORRISSEY

Hospitality

Questions about the nature of hospitality have a renewed urgency in light of actual social and political issues. The massive entry of strangers into our living spaces often leads to the polarization of the stranger. The issue of modern society is not how to eliminate the stranger, but how to live with the stranger. Hospitality provides the possibility of a critical stance toward present forms of existence and order in society. It can lead us to an acceptable model of humanhood and call us to social action on behalf of a new Earth. It is an important theme for our own time, which seems over-preoccupied with individual autonomy, individual prosperity, and, marked by a deep ambiguity, fear and distrust of the stranger. Hospitality is also central to the Christian vision and to Christian discipleship.

Hospitality has to do with manifold realities that are complex and touch deep human elements. In antiquity, there is a pervasive consciousness of the singular value of hospitality toward the stranger. Such hospitality was perceived as an important sign of civilization. In ancient Greece, hospitality is acknowledged and celebrated, and the lack of it decried.

Yet, hospitality is founded upon ambivalence evident in the etymology of the word. In Greek, words of the *xen* stem mean 'foreign' or 'strange', but also 'guest'. For example, the verb *xenizo* means 'to surprise', 'to be strange', but also 'to entertain'. In Latin, the word that signifies 'host' is *hospes*, and the word for 'enemy' is *hostis*, from which our word 'hostile' derives. Etymologically, the word for stranger may have a negative meaning, leading to xenophobia, or a positive meaning, when the stranger is given hospitality, *philoxenia*, the love of the host.

Emphasis on hospitality to the stranger has its foundation in both Scriptures. There are many texts in the Hebrew Bible that make clear that hospitality to the stranger is God's wish. In Israel, the commandment to be hospitable is grounded in the remembering of the Israelite's own situation when in Egypt (Deut. 10.19). Numerous texts in the Law concretize this commandment through specific stipulations. Here, in these texts, the stranger is inserted in the class of poor, the widows and the orphans (cf. Jer. 7.1–7; Zech. 7.10; Job 31.32; Lev. 25.35, 39–40). Gen. 18 describes the mysterious depth of hospitality to the stranger. Abraham's hospitality to the three strangers is hospitality to God. Abraham hurries to find food; he kneels before his hosts, washes their feet, gives them bread and milk. These are the eternal gestures, the sacraments of hospitality. The vagrant, the wanderer, far from being despised, oppressed, murdered, becomes the occasion of an encounter with God.

The difference between the Jewish Scriptures and the Christian Scriptures on hospitality to the stranger is Jesus, his person and his message: 'I was a stranger and you received me.' Hospitality is present in much of Jesus' life and ministry. Jesus is born in a stable since there is no other place for him; Jesus is taken out of Israel into Egypt because of Herod. In his ministry, Jesus is a wanderer without home (Matt. 8.20). Jesus has to accept hospitality from various individuals, such as Lazarus and his sisters. Jesus depends on hospitality (Mark 1.29 ff.; 2.15ff.; Luke 9.58). In the Gospel of John, Jesus appears as the stranger in our midst. Christ comes into a hostile world as a stranger (Mark 12.1ff.; John 8.14, 25ff.). Even his disciples do not really know him (John 21.12) and constantly misunderstand him (John 3.4).

Hospitality is the way that should characterize our meeting with strangers. The practice of hospitality was viewed as the concrete expression of love (Rom. 1.9–13; Heb. 13.1–2; 1 Peter 4.8–10). Christians affirm that they 'are no longer strangers but fellow citizens with the saints and members of the household of God' (Eph. 2.19). The fundamental vision of the Christian faith, that of the kingdom of God, has to do with hospitality to the stranger. Hospitality to the stranger has a bearing on eternal destiny, for it has, as Matt. 25 affirms, a bearing on one's relationship to Christ.

Hospitality was a fundamental condition of the mission and expansion of the early Church. The practice of hospitality is presented in the New Testament as the common virtue of Church. Like love, hospitality forges social bonds; it brings forth a sense of unity. There are many hints in the Pauline letters that ordinary Christians travelling to another city could already expect to find accommodations with 'brothers and sisters'. Hospitality is a virtue especially required of bishops. The Christians are invited to accept strangers on trust and in faith. The Church in the Diaspora is to be as a home, *oikos*, for the *paroikoi*, the stranger. Such a practice is evident in the first letter of Peter (1 Peter 4.8–10). For Christianity, hospitality, as expressed in the meals taken by Jesus with those who were at the margin of society, expresses its reality; here is the revelation, sacrament, Word of God. This Christian reality is not simply a thing or object, but the way Christianity exists. Such a reality provides us with an image that brings intelligibility to all occasions of personal and common life. It affects the Christian communities' preaching, worship, ways of caring, ethical concerns and spirituality.

See also **Benedictine Spirituality; Food; Eucharistic Spirituality.**

John H. Eliot, *Home for the Homeless*, Philadelphia: Fortress Press, 1981; John Koenig, *New Testament Hospitality*, Philadelphia: Fortress Press, 1975; Willi Malarcher, 'Hospitality' in *The New Dictionary of Sacramental Worship* ed. Peter E. Fink, Collegeville, MN: The Liturgical Press, 1990, pp. 558–62; Thomas W. Ogletree, *Hospitality to the Stranger. Dimensions of Moral Understanding*, Philadelphia: Fortress Press, 1985; Parker J. Palmer, *The Company of Strangers: Christianity and Renewals of America's Public Life*, New York: Crossroad, 1981; Lucien Richard, *Living the Hospitality of God*, New York: Paulist Press, 2000.

LUCIEN J. RICHARD

Hours, Prayer of the

see Office, Divine

Humility

The meaning and importance of the virtue of humility varies from one setting and time to another. In the ancient Graeco-Roman world, humility was disdained, equated with low social status, lack of freedom and inability to influence the public arena. In Israelite culture, the poor ones of Yahweh (*anawim*) depended on God's special care for the lowly. In modern India, Hindu pacifist Mahatma Gandhi describes humility as the spirit and goal of non-violence, the willingness to approach God with a humble and contrite heart and witness to unobtrusive humility. In the Christian tradition, humility has been a constant, though evolving value.

The term humility is from the Latin term for earth or soil (*humus*), and is an antidote to pride. This virtue played a prominent role in the writings of the fourth-century Desert Fathers and Mothers. In the sixth century, Benedict of Nursia spoke of humility more formally in chapter 7 of his Rule. Imagining the spiritual life as a ladder, he taught that to climb is to descend, but to descend in humility is to ascend to God. In medieval spirituality, humility continued to be central to the spiritual life, second only to charity. In the twelfth century, Bernard of Clairvaux expounds the dangers of pride in *The Steps of Humility and Pride*, and two hundred years later Catherine of Siena writes in her *Dialogue* that the humble soul knows that all she is, and every gift she has comes from God. In the seventh mansions of *The Interior Castle*, Teresa of Avila comments that the foundation of the entire edifice is humility. Martin Luther saw humility as the foundation and fruit of faith. Life's tribulations create awareness of sin and a humbled heart, leading believers to seek God alone.

In contemporary Western cultures, often described as narcissistic and prone to self-delusion, humility has been marginalized. Erroneous understandings and uses of humility are rightly viewed as inimical to healthy psychological development and a barrier to self-realization – especially for women who experience as oppressive the admonition to be humble (1 Tim. 2.9–15; Titus 2). However, genuine humility is not to be confused with humiliation. It does not involve rejection, hatred of oneself or lack of self-esteem and assertiveness. It does not demand that one become a doormat. Rather, humility is linked with truth about oneself and the world. To be humble is to accept one's creatureliness, gifts and sinfulness. Both reason and psychological knowledge can be assets in discovering one's true self, but humility is ultimately the fruit of openness to God's generous love and mystery. To be humble is to be free of pretence, to have oneself in perspective in order to resist exaggeration of either one's gifts or one's faults.

In the Christian life, the model for humble living is Jesus Christ, who refused to cling to divine status (Phil. 2.5–9); possessed a deep reverence for and patience with others; reflected an interior silence and self-possession; and was willing to forgive. Jesus is the antithesis of arrogance and self-preoccupation. He cared about the poor; washed the feet of his disciples (John 13.3);

and forgave those who crucified him. Christianity is constructed on the paradox that life emerges out of death; the humble shall be exalted (Matt. 23.11–12; Luke 1.52); the last shall be first (Luke 13.29–30); to lose one's life is to find it.

Spiritual disciplines can prepare one to receive the gift of humility but one cannot command it, only pray to remain open to it. All baptized Christians can benefit from traditional teaching on humility, provided it is viewed in a broader lay context, distinguished from the monastic emphasis on vows of poverty, chastity and obedience. To practise humility is to assume a counter-cultural stance against a status quo that encourages arrogance and self-aggrandizement at the expense of others (Rom. 12.16). In a world rife with conflict, humbleness points the way to forgiveness and reconciliation.

The fruits of humility include trust in God's saving love; freedom from self to serve others; internal peace extended to all; just action that gives each person his or her due; gratitude for life that comes from and returns to God. Not to boast, not to put oneself first, to be forgetful of self – these dispositions lead one to the truth that all glory and thanks belong to God. Humble persons see themselves, their family and their nation as unexceptional when viewed in the light of God's greatness and the world's magnificence. By living in the truth about oneself and one's world, one cultivates a humility that knows the gifts and miseries of others, responds in compassion and does great things because one's surety is in God. 'Take my yoke upon you, and learn from me; for I am gentle and lowly in heart, and you will find rest for your souls' (Matt. 11.29).

See also Asceticism; Compassion; Detachment; Freedom; Love; Non-violence; Patience; Poverty; Relationships; Simplicity; Social Justice; Virtue.

The Rule of St. Benedict – In English, ed. Timothy Fry, The Vintage Spiritual Classics Series, New York: Vintage Books, 1998; Bernard of Clairvaux, *The Steps of Humility and Pride*, Treatises II, Cistercian Fathers Series 13, Kalamazoo, MI: Cistercian Publications, 1980; R. Bondi, 'Humility: a meditation on an ancient virtue for modern Christians', *Quarterly Review* 3 (Winter 1983), 27–41; M. Casey, *A Guide to Living in the Truth: Saint Benedict's Teaching on Humility*, Liguori, MO: Triumph Books, 2001; D. von Hildebrand, *Humility: Wellspring of Virtue*, Manchester, NH: Sophia Institute Press, 1997 [1948]; G. Maloney, *On the Road to Perfection: Christian Humility in Modern Society*, Hyde Park, NY: New City Press, 1995.

ELIZABETH A. DREYER

Humour

Humour is probably as old as the human race itself, as old as the first meaningful gestures and the beginnings of language. Humour has been a significant theme in theological writings in the course of Western history whether in Erasmus' *In Praise of Folly* in the sixteenth century or the more recent Harvey Cox's *The Feast of Fools*. Humour is valuable in the spiritual life as such. It is a companion to leisure in resisting the workaholism of modern society. It is part of what some spiritual writers call 'wasting time with God'. Humour has a way of breaking the obsession with being in constant motion that often springs from a need to justify one's existence. Humour can temporarily restore a certain playfulness, which is often absent in adult life. Humour seems indispensable to being an effective pastoral minister today. In particular, humour's significance is recognized in the areas of spiritual guidance, biblical preaching and pastoral care with various marginalized groups.

Spiritual guidance. In spiritual guidance as such the use of humour requires sensible discernment. Humour initiated by the director can easily interfere with the process of transparency on the part of the client. On the other hand, humour in response to the client's own attempts to describe humorous situations can assist in the process of self-discovery. Appropriately placed, the laughter of the therapist or director can be as healing as well-focused listening. There is a quality to humour which opens up the human spirit. Through humour the client can recognize the basic incongruities in the issues presented in spiritual direction. Humour may be the least threatening way that the directees have to see the flaws in their character. It is usually easier to work with a director who has a sense of humour. The client will be more comfortable with such directors because often they communicate a sense of flexibility. Laughter can be a creative experience in spiritual direction. The caution is that it must not contaminate the professional relationship.

Biblical preaching. If spiritual guidance is a setting where humour and spirituality meet and assist each other, preaching is the place where the same happens in the public arena. Douglas Adams, in his work on biblical humour, shows how the Bible is inherently funny. By bringing biblical characters to life he not only lifts up elements of humour in the biblical texts that are not often recognized as such, he also shows how humour can be an effective hermeneutical tool for the interpretation of biblical passages.

Through the use of biblical humour the effective homilist can bring to life the parables and miracles of Jesus, the Pauline letters and the Hebrew Scriptures. Often locating biblical humour is done through different forms of storytelling. The effects for the worshippers can be significant: more engagement with the preaching, another access to the scriptural passages, and a more lasting effect of the biblical material on their spiritual lives. Laughter produced by humour in preaching can be a public emotional safety value. Humour is one of the ways that the preacher can break through the armed defences of the worshippers to help them become more spiritually alive. Humour counteracts an unhealthy self-absorption. Humour can remove the blindness that prevents people from seeing the needs of others. Humour also plays an important role in politics where humans tend to be intolerant and take themselves too seriously. Humour is an effective tool for relativizing prejudices and absolute worldviews.

Pastoral care with marginalized groups. Culture, church and synagogue have marginalized certain groups at different times in history. Ethnic groups, women, gays and lesbians and the elderly are notable examples of people who are pushed to the edges of society. Humour can be a way in which these people are momentarily freed from the forces oppressing them. This is possible because humour is an imaginative act and it is the imagination that gives one a sense of liberation. The imagination is the power whereby one can entertain alternatives and live by a self-image that relativizes the one instilled through oppression. Humour is one of the instruments whereby people can acknowledge the fears that paralyse them, the inhibitions that prevent their spirit from expanding but also the hopes that can lift the darkness of depression. Sometimes humour is the only available antidote to the oppression coming from one's place in history, gender, economic status or sexual orientation. For these reasons humour can be a tool in pastoral care for those working with marginalized groups. Whether one is working in spiritual guidance, is present at liturgical celebrations or is a member of a marginalized group, humour can help one re-engage in life.

———

Douglas Adams, *Humor in the American Pulpit from George Whitefield through Henry Ward Beecher*, 4th edn, Richmond, CA: Sharing, 1992; Douglas Adams, *The Prostitute in the Family Tree: Discovering Humor and Irony in the Bible*, Richmond, CA: The Sharing Company, 1997; Jacki Kwan, *Almost Home: Embracing the*

Magical Connection Between Positive Humor and Spirituality, Cameo Publications, 2002; Pam Vredevelt, *Espresso for a Woman's Spirit: Encouraging Stories of Hope and Humor*, Multnomah, 2000.

JAMES EMPEREUR

Hymns and Spirituality

What is a hymn? A hymn is a text that is sung to God by worshippers. It combines words and music, and in worship each person present sings it personally as well as corporately. A hymn takes on new life every time it is sung as the context is always different. It is a theological text and therefore must be doctrinally faithful, but it is also poetry, written to strict constraints of rhyme and metre. Good hymns are understood easily, simple but not simplistic, beautiful and reverent yet thought-provoking and challenging. The music can set the mood, interpret or nuance the words, and embed the hymn in people's memory. The combination of text and tune is significant; texts can be sung to different tunes but some become inseparable, for example 'All people that on earth do dwell' and 'Old Hundredth'.

Hymns are divided into verses, or stanzas, normally of four, six or eight lines, with a total of 24–32 lines being common. Metre varies between hymns but once set it must be continued throughout a hymn since the tune is repeated while the text develops. Texts have a clear beginning and end, the intermediate development of the theme allows the singers to engage before God with theological truths and their own experiences. Good hymns lift people's hearts before God, giving them usable words to express praise or petition, joy or lament, certainties or questions, assurance or ambivalence. Hymns can vivify Scripture, recall the past as a basis for present or future hope, challenge to action or move to commitment. Choosing appropriate hymns for worship is a significant part of pastoral ministry since they must express the congregation's beliefs, experiences and desires with integrity, while liturgical sensitivity is required to understand how hymns work in worship.

In recent years worship songs have grown in popularity. They do not observe the strict structure of hymns and are often much shorter, expressing one basic idea or theme rather than developing a line of thought. Structurally, they share much with choruses from Sunday schools and missions, adapting and bringing that style of singing into regular congregational worship. The metre is frequently irregular and the music written in conjunction with the text, whereas hymn texts and tunes may be paired long after writing.

The overhead projector and PowerPoint, along with the Christian Copyright Licence scheme, have facilitated the rapid legal (and illegal) dissemination of new hymns and worship songs. No longer is it necessary to use hymn books, but where churches abandon them people can no longer ponder hymn texts more slowly, use them in personal prayer or discover hymns not sung in a particular church. Both avoiding all new hymns and abandoning the historical body of hymnody limit singers' formation in the full riches of the Christian tradition. Hymns learned in childhood can be formative, may be all some people know, and are requested frequently at weddings or funerals.

While many people use hymns in private prayer, hymns belong in corporate worship. For many people hymns are the primary means of active participation in the liturgy and become part of tradition, which may make it difficult to introduce change. Frequent singing of a hymn can shape a person's or congregation's beliefs or world view and most denominations publish hymn books that reflect their doctrinal understanding. While retaining their own emphases, most denominations use texts from other Churches and, as texts from earlier generations and overseas are translated, congregations now have a greater breadth of hymnody than ever before. Ecumenical Hymn Societies have been formed in the United Kingdom and in the United States and Canada, to further the study and appreciation of hymnody.

Hymnody in the Christian spiritual tradition. Hymnody is not unique to Christianity and has evolved over the centuries. Some early hymn texts are embedded in the New Testament (Phil. 2.5–11; 1 Tim. 3.16). Hymns from the first centuries are strongly doctrinal rather than narrative (for example, the fifth-century hymn 'Of the Father's heart begotten') and were used to spread orthodox doctrine: Augustine records hymns being sung to counter the Arian heresy, and there are accounts of rival choirs singing at each other over city walls. Ephraim the Syrian (d. 373) was a prolific early hymn-writer; other writers include Clement of Alexandria (d. 220), Ambrose of Milan (d. 397), Prudentius of Spain (d. 410) and Venatius Fortunatus (d. 600).

In the medieval period, Latin chant was dominant in worship with vernacular carols (dancing tunes) sung by the populace outside church. Hymns were primarily for private devotion (for example, Bernard of Clairvaux's 'Jesus the very thought of thee', and 'O sacred head sore wounded') and, in line with the devotion of the period, became much more affective in tone. At the Reformation the Calvinist tradition limited itself to psalms but the Lutheran tradition encouraged the use of popular tunes with new texts in congregational worship – the Passion Chorale was originally a German drinking song. The initially Calvinist Church of England published two volumes of metrical psalms, the Old Version (Sternhold and Hopkins) in 1560 and the New Version (Tate and Brady) in 1696, and only slowly broadened out into metrical paraphrases of other Scripture. Anglican clergy like George Herbert (1593–1633) and Thomas Ken (1637–1711) continued the tradition of writing poetry, which later became hymnody, for their personal devotion, but Isaac Watts (1674–1748), the 'Father of English hymnody' and a member of the Congregational Church, wanted to bring the gospel into the church's song alongside the psalms. He wrote words that congregations could use to express their own praise and adoration to God, blending scriptural ideas and images with personal response, and enabling people to engage emotionally in worship. In an age when visual images were removed from churches, he painted verbal pictures ('When I survey the wondrous cross'). Others followed his lead including Charles Wesley (1757–1834) who is said to have written 7,000 hymns. With his brother John (1703–1791) who translated Moravian hymns, he used hymns in evangelism as well as worship, often addressing hymns to the singer and giving people words with which to respond to God. Methodism was said to be born in song.

Congregational hymn-singing took root in most non-Anglican churches by the eighteenth century. Hymns expressed people's devotion and embedded Christian truths and values in their lives, and denominational hymn books were published for public and private use. In the Church of England, evangelicals introduced hymns in the early nineteenth century, provoking controversy until a court case in 1820 resulted in tacit approval of hymns. John Keble (1792–1866) and John Mason Neale (1818–66) were influential with others in translating texts from the early Church and writing hymns suitable for catholic worship, thus encouraging Tractarians to sing hymns. *Hymns Ancient and Modern* (1861) was not an official Church of England hymn book and hymn-singing in services was not legalized until 1872, although Anglican churches elsewhere were not so restricted. All denominations began to use the German Reformation hymns translated by Catherine Winkworth (1827–88) and the mission hymns generated by overseas missionary work. The spirituals sustained slaves who identified with the biblical heroes and articulated their hope that God would act again to bring deliverance, while gospel hymns, which coupled sentimental words with memorable tunes, emerged from American revival meetings. In the Roman Catholic Church, the Second Vatican Council (1962–65) opened the doors to hymns as a more integral part of eucharistic and other worship.

Hymns continue to be influential as an expression of piety and belief both within and outside the regular worship of the Church. *Songs of Praise* continues to attract a faithful following on British television, allowing people who do not attend church to share in congregational hymn-singing in their homes. Traditions reappear in new forms: the Iona Community continues the appropriation of popular folk tunes as hymn tunes, frequently coupled with texts that address contemporary social issues, and the Taizé community in France has reinvigorated the meditative use of chant. Since the 1960s there has been a hymn explosion. Hymns are a great ecumenical tool of the Church and today few hymn books are published without texts and tunes from all over the world and all branches and generations of the Church.

See also **Spirituality, Liturgy and Worship** (*essay*); **Music and Spirituality; Spirituals.**

Ian Bradley, *Abide with Me: The World of Victorian Hymns*, London: SPCK, 1997; Rosalind Brown, *How Hymns Shape Our Lives*, Cambridge: Grove, 2001; Arthur C. Jones, *Wade in the Water: The Wisdom of the Spirituals*, Maryknoll: Orbis Books, 1993; J. R. Watson, *The English Hymn: A Critical and Historical Survey*, Oxford: Oxford University Press, 1997; Brian Wren, *What Language Shall I Borrow? God-talk in Worship, A Male Response to Feminist Theology*, London: SCM Press/New York: Crossroad, 1989; Brian Wren, *Praying Twice: The Music and Words of Congregational Song*, Louisville, KY: Westminster John Knox Press, 2000.

ROSALIND BROWN

Iconography

History of the icon. 'Iconography' (from the Greek, meaning the writing or painting of images) is a central part of theology, worship and spirituality in the Christian, but particularly in the Eastern Orthodox, Church. Anyone entering an Orthodox church will first observe the role and significance of icons in the entrance to the church, in the central part and dome of the church, as well as separating the main section from the altar area. All images are normally painted in roughly the same distinctive style, the fruit not of artistic creativity alone but of long and deliberate spiritual reflection of the world in relation to God. Manuals of iconography in the second millennium offer precise instructions as to the distinctive shape, features and colours of Christ and the saints.

Throughout the eighth (from 726) and the first half of the ninth (to 843) centuries, the emperors of Byzantium led a movement, known as iconoclasm, to remove icons from Christian churches. In response, John of Damascus (d. 749), Germanos of Constantinople (d. 773), Theodore the Studite (d. 826) and Leontius of Byzantium led a movement of the *iconophiles* (lit., friends of icons) or, pejoratively, as *iconodules* (lit., slaves of icons), articulating at the same time a convincing theological argument against contentions of idolatry. In response to the iconoclastic citation of the Old Testament commandment not to worship graven images, they replied that, in the New Testament, God's eternal Word had assumed flesh and that the refusal to paint icons implied the denial of God's human nature. John of Damascus, the eighth-century champion of icons, states: '[We] do not adore creation; [we] worship the One who assumed creation. ... God has saved [us] through matter. ... Because of the incarnation, [we] salute all creation.' The Seventh Ecumenical Council (787) formally endorsed the use of icons in homes and in churches, recognizing the legitimacy of their veneration or honour – although not their adoration or worship. It declared that the use of icons was a 'guarantee that the divine incarnation of the Word is real and not illusory'.

Spirituality of the icon. Thus, Christian art became as essential a part of Eastern Christian spiritual life and thought as theology and the sacraments. More than merely incidental, ornamental or even instructional, icons are theology and spirituality in colour. They constitute a channel of divine grace and sanctification. They are a liturgical art, a way of prayer, an article of faith, a fact of immediate experience of a mystery beyond experience. The world of the icon offers new insights and new perceptions into reality, revealing the eternal dimension in the world of sense and experience. Icons signify a sacred covenant, a symbolical connection between ourselves and our world, since both humanity and nature are created. Moreover, icons indicate a desire for intimate communion and mutual enhancement between our world and the beyond. This may be a reason for the absence of three-dimensional art in the Eastern Christian Church.

While there is no official condemnation of statues in the early iconographical sources, art is normally two-dimensional, in expectation of the divine third dimension.

The icon restores and reconciles, reminding of another way and of another world. It offers a corrective to a self-centred or world-centred culture that gives value only to the here and now. The icon aspires to the inner vision of all, the world as created and as intended by God. The icon articulates with theological conviction our faith in the heavenly kingdom. The icon does away with any objective distance between this world and the next, between the material and the spiritual, between body and soul, time and eternity, creation and divinity. The icon reminds us that there is no double vision, no double order in creation. The icon speaks in this world the language of the age to come.

The transfiguration and the nativity of Christ. Very often, it is said, the first image attempted by an Orthodox iconographer is that of the transfiguration of Christ on Mount Tabor. This is precisely because the iconographer struggles to hold together this world and the next, to transfigure this world in light of the next. Disconnecting this world from heaven leads to the desacralization of both.

This is why the icon of divine incarnation – either of the birth or of the face of Jesus Christ – is also at the heart of iconography. In the icon of Jesus Christ, God assumes a human face, a beauty that is exceeding (Ps. 44.2). Moreover, in Orthodox icons, the faces – whether of Jesus Christ or of the saints – are always frontal. The conviction is that – as the Orthodox Liturgy of St John Chrysostom says – 'Christ is in our midst.' In iconography, profile signifies sin; it implies a rupture in communication or communion. Faces are frontal, all eyes, eternally receptive and susceptive of divine grace. 'I see' means that 'I am seen', which in turn implies that I am in communion. This is the powerful experience of the invisible and the immortal, a passing over to another way of seeing, a 'Passover' or 'Pascha'.

The icon converts the beholder from a restricted, limited point of view to a fuller, spiritual vision. In this respect, the light of the icon is the light of reconciliation, of restoration and of resurrection. It is not the light of this world; it 'knows no evening', to quote another Orthodox hymn. This is why icons depicting events that occurred in the daytime are no brighter than icons depicting events that occurred at nighttime. The icon of Gethsemane, for example, is no darker than the icon of Pentecost. The icon of the resurrection is no brighter than the icon of the crucifixion. The icon presupposes and proposes another light in which to see things, a 'different way of life', as the Orthodox Easter liturgy states. The icon provides another means of communication, beyond the conceptual, beyond the written, beyond the spoken word. It is the language of silence, of mystery and of the age to come.

Humanity and creation as icons. Thus, iconography depicts God in the divine Word as an icon. It also depicts all of humanity as an icon. The last book of the Christian Scriptures is the Revelation of John the Divine. And revelation implies a manifestation of faces, a vocation to become icons, to discern in all people 'the image of God' (Gen. 1.26). In iconography, then, the human person exists on two levels and worlds simultaneously. The human person is considered a meeting point for all of creation, a bridge between this world and heaven. In the words of the fifth-century ascetic, Nilus of Ancyra: 'You are a world within a world . . . Look within yourself, and there you will discover the entire world.' And in the seventh century, Maximus the Confessor described the human person as a 'mediator'. Theodore the Studite underlined the human implications of the icon: 'The fact that the human person is created in the image and likeness of God means that the making of icons is in some way a divine work.'

Finally, it is not just humanity that is likened to an icon. The entire world is an icon, a window or a point of entry to a new reality. Everything in this world is a sign, a seed. 'Nothing is a vacuum in the face of God,' wrote Irenaeus of Lyons in the second century; 'everything is a sign of God'. Everything and everyone contain this dimension of transparency. And so in icons, rivers too assume human form; the sun and the moon and the stars and the waters: all assume human faces; all acquire a personal dimension; just like people; just like God! Nothing whatsoever is regarded as neutral or as lacking sacredness.

Thus, in the ninth century, Leontius of Byzantium proclaimed: 'Through heaven and earth and sea, through wood and stone, through relics and church buildings and the cross, through angels and people, through all creation visible and invisible, [we] offer veneration and honour to the Creator and Master and Maker of all things, and to God alone. For, the creation does not venerate the Maker directly and by itself, but it is through [us] that the heavens declare the glory of God, through [us] the moon worships God, through [us] the stars glorify God, through [us] the waters and showers of rain, the dew and all creation, venerate God and give glory to God.'

Non-iconic prayer. In conclusion, it is important to mention that the use of iconography reflects the importance also of the absence of icons in theology and spirituality. In the Eastern Orthodox Church, there are two ways of praying: the iconic as well as the non-iconic, sometimes referred to as the negative or 'apophatic' way. On the one hand, there is the positive (also known as the 'kataphatic') or actual representation of the divine through the painting of images and the creation of concepts, whereby human beings make full use of art and imagination to depict and describe the immanence of the divine presence. However, the emphasis in the Christian East has always and primarily been on the transcendence of the divine mystery, beyond human capacity to define or comprehend. This alternative, or rather complementary, way of spirituality is contained in the way of silence characteristic of *The Philokalia.*

See also **Aesthetics; Art; Image and Spirituality; Kataphatic Spirituality; Orthodox Spirituality; Sacramentality and Spirituality.**

David Comler, *The Icon Handbook*, Springfield IL: Templegate Publications, 1995; Paul Evdokimov, *Art of the Icon: A Theology of Beauty*, Redondo Beach, CA: Oakwood Publications, 1990; Ambrosius Giakalis, *Images of the Divine: The Theology of Icons at the Seventh Ecumenical Council*, Leiden: E. J. Brill, 1994; André Grabar, *Byzantium: Byzantine Art in the Middle Ages*, London: Methuen, 1960; Konstantinos Kalokyres, *The Essence of Orthodox Iconography*, Brookline, MA: Holy Cross Orthodox Press, 1985; Gennadios Limouris (ed.), *Icons: Windows on Eternity. Theology and Spirituality in Colour*, Geneva: World Council of Churches, 1990; Cyril Mango, *Art of the Byzantine Empire (312–1453): Sources and Documents*, Englewood Cliffs, NJ: Prentice-Hall, 1972; Leonid Ouspensky, *Theology of the Icon*, New York: St Vladimir's Seminary Press, 1992; Leonid Ouspensky and Vladimir Lossky, *The Meaning of Icons*, New York: St Vladimir's Seminary Press, 1982; Philip Sherrard, *The Sacred in Art and Life*, Ipswich, UK: Golgonoza Press, 1990; Evgenii Trubetskoi, *Icons: Theology in Color*, New York: St Vladimir's Seminary Press, 1973.

JOHN CHRYSSAVGIS

Ignatian Spirituality

Ignatian spirituality is the pattern of Christian discipleship which has its origin and inspiration in the life and legacy of Ignatius Loyola (*c.* 1491–1556). He was born into a Basque aristocratic family (Inigo Lopez were his baptismal names) and educated initially for a career as a soldier, courtier and possibly cleric-diplomat. The story of his 'conversion' is well known. In a battle against French forces at Pamplona (1521) his leg was broken by a cannonball. During his convalescence at Loyola (1521–22), he spent weeks reading and ruminating on the only books available, *The Golden Legends*, a collection of lives of the saints by Jacopo de Voragine, and the *Life of Christ* by Ludolph of Saxony.

Ignatius' own experience is a major clue to his way of understanding and living Christian discipleship. His life after Pamplona presents several phases in which emerge different images of the man which, while distinct, are nonetheless part of an unending search 'to know God's will and have the grace to carry it out'. As a result of his reading at Loyola, the courtier, soldier and trainee diplomat became a pilgrim, intent on a life of austerity in Jerusalem, and incipient evangelizer. It was during his pilgrimage that he spent almost a year living in a cave in Manresa (1522–23), near the monastery of Montserrat. There he adopted a regime of long hours of prayer and (what he later judged to be excessive) austerity. His experience at Manresa later contributed much to his book of *Spiritual Exercises* and his understanding of the vagaries of the human spirit. Since, in order to have a recognized pastoral role in the Church, he had to be qualified, when his Jerusalem project collapsed, he became, in his early thirties, a student, at first among schoolboys and later among teenage undergraduates in Paris (1528–35). Their studies completed, he and his companions set off for Rome as wandering evangelists, preaching in churches, in public squares and on street corners. On arrival in Rome (1537), Ignatius' life changed yet again. He and his companions, after much prayer and heart-searching, formed themselves into the Society of Jesus (Jesuits), with Ignatius as their elected Superior General (1540). As a result, he spent the remaining sixteen years of his life in Rome, fostering the growth of the new religious order, sending its members to all parts of the known world, establishing (mainly) educational institutions and writing the Jesuit Constitutions. Thus, the pattern of Christian discipleship which had evolved in Ignatius' own life also shaped the life of a missionary community of priests and lay brothers.

A considerable corpus of writings by Ignatius is extant. This includes the *Spiritual Exercises*, the *Constitutions of the Society of Jesus*, a *Spiritual Journal*, some dictated Reminiscences (aka the *Autobiography*) and hundreds of letters.

The *Spiritual Exercises* is Ignatius' best-known work. It is a collection of notes intended for those who, having themselves been guided through the Exercises, are accompanying others. The notes include, among a range of helps for Christian living, material for prayer and consideration, guidance for dealing with likely reactions to that material, and aids towards making good Christian choices. The chief aim of the Spiritual Exercises is to enable Christians to order their lives in freedom before God. As means to that end, the book offers a pattern of prayer, meditation, contemplation and reflection, arranged so as to lead people into an increasingly profound experience and understanding of the mystery of God manifest in Jesus, to reflect on their lives in the light of that, and from there to move to making discerning Christian choices.

Certain influences gave Ignatius' approach to Christian discipleship its particular flavour. A love of romances in his youth offered him stories and courtly ideals of self-forgetful service in the company of a worthy king and for the sake of a beloved and admired noble woman. The *Life of Christ* attracted him irrevocably to the persons of Jesus and Mary and drew him into a profound understanding of the incarnation. The lives of the saints awakened in him a desire to distinguish himself as a 'knight companion' in the service of Jesus, 'the Eternal King'. Reflection on his own experience of making and sustaining radical choices about his own future initiated and then deepened his understanding and practice of discernment of spirits. And his time at the University of Paris, his slow journeys through Spain, Northern Europe and Italy and his later position in Rome made him keenly aware of the crisis facing Christianity in the middle decades of the sixteenth century.

From all of this, some fundamental features of Ignatian spirituality emerge. A few assumptions are basic. First, the mystery of God is to be encountered, not only in the Scriptures and the Church, but also in personal and human history and the non-human world (*Spiritual Exercises* 230–7). Second, the life and death of Jesus offer the fundamental pattern for Christian living. The task of Christians, then, is to determine how the life, death and resurrection of Jesus are to shape their own personal and corporate life. Third, God sent the Son into the world to reconcile, heal and redeem. The Christian Church is thus an instrument of redemption, healing and reconciliation established by God to continue the work of the Son in the power of the Spirit. Fourth, just as the journey of the Son into the world was a journey from the heart of love, so Christian discipleship is fundamentally a path of love – love of God and of others and the world in

God – in response to the God who first loved us (cf. *Spiritual Exercises* 91–117, 230–1).

Hence Ignatian spirituality involves, in the first place, a day-by-day engagement with the mystery of God, as shown forth in human history and experience, in Jesus Christ, in the Scriptures and in the life and worship of the Christian community. It also means ensuring, as far as possible, that it is this engagement with the mystery of God that gives shape to personal and corporate life, through an integration of contemplation and action. Ignatius' way, therefore, is a path of reflective discipleship in that reflection on encounters with God in prayer and in life form the basis on which personal and communal choices are made. And a mark of Ignatian Christian discipleship is service grounded in love. In practice this service takes many forms: from daily, unspectacular devotion to family, friends and colleagues, to teaching the young, to supplying clean water in India or Africa, to caring for refugees, to encouraging and participating in Latin American *comunidades de base*, to creating and maintaining vast institutions for the welfare or education of whole populations. All of these forms of service, and an endless variety of others, integrated with a life of prayer, are ways of embodying, personally or corporately, the basic elements of Ignatian spirituality.

The pattern of service, mission and dialogue with contemporary culture, rooted in 'familiarity with God', which was established by Ignatius for the Society of Jesus from the start, has been the hallmark of its work over three and a half centuries. Between the death of Ignatius and the middle of the twentieth century, Ignatian forms of Christian discipleship were fostered across the world largely through Jesuit institutions. The Spiritual Exercises, too, continued to be given. Between the 1560s and the 1960s, however, the usual way of giving the Exercises was through preaching, whether to small groups or large congregations. Hence, an important aspect of Ignatius' legacy, namely the one-to-one conversation and process of personal discernment, which had been Ignatius' own practice, had largely disappeared. The recovery of this method in recent decades represents a reversal of a 300-year-old trend.

The last forty years have also seen a remarkable spread of interest in and practice of Ignatian spirituality across a broad range of Christian churches and traditions. One particularly important development has been enabling lay people, both men and women, first to make and then to give the Spiritual Exercises. Ignatius' bequest, therefore, now has a powerful impact on the formation of Christians in discipleship throughout the world. Current issues in Ignatian spirituality include: contemplation and social engagement; relationships between personal experience and ecclesial authority; problems involved in interpreting and adapting the Spiritual Exercises; continuity and openness to change in current practice and ministry; encounters between Ignatian spirituality and a broad range of very different ecclesiologies; Ignatian spirituality in a context of widespread unbelief, postmodernity and religious and cultural pluralism. And while many Christian women have found their discipleship genuinely enriched and deepened by the Spiritual Exercises, current developments also suggest that critical attention to the whole Ignatian legacy from a contemporary women's perspective will render it a more creative instrument in the formation of both women and men in Christian discipleship.

See also **Consolation; Spiritual Conversation; Desolation; Detachment; Direction, Spiritual; Discernment; Election (Ignatian); Examination of Conscience/Consciousness; Imagination; Indifference; Jesus, Society of; Retreats; Senses, Spiritual.**

Katherine Dykeman, Mary Garvin, Elizabeth Liebert, *The Spiritual Exercises Reclaimed: Uncovering Liberating Possibilities for Women*, Mahwah, NJ: Paulist Press, 2001; Philip Endean, Joseph A. Munitiz, *St. Ignatius of Loyola: Personal Writings*, London: Penguin, 1996; Michael Ivens, *Understanding the Spiritual Exercises*, Leominster, UK: Gracewing, 1998; David Lonsdale, *Eyes to See, Ears to Hear: An Introduction to Ignatian Spirituality*, 2nd, rev. edn, London: Darton, Longman & Todd/Maryknoll, NY: Orbis Books, 2001; John W. O'Malley, *The First Jesuits*, Cambridge, MA: Harvard University Press, 1996.

DAVID LONSDALE

Illuminati

see *Alumbrados*

Illuminative Way

The Illuminative Way refers to the second of a threefold spiritual itinerary that includes the following: Purgative Way, Illuminative Way and Unitive Way. These three 'ways' compromise the 'classical spiritual itinerary'; fairly well defined as such from the thirteenth century on. (See the entry 'Purgative Way' for a brief history of the concept of the 'classical spiritual itinerary'.) John of the Cross carefully analyses the threefold way in his commentaries *The Dark Night of the Soul* (*DN*), *The Ascent of Mount Carmel* (*A*), *The*

Spiritual Canticle (SC) and *The Living Flame of Love (F)*. Since John of the Cross is recognized as the Western mystic that described, systematized and analysed most thoroughly the Purgative, Illuminative and Unitive Ways, his work will be used in a summary way as the basis for the presentation below as well as the other entries concerning the classical spiritual itinerary.

After a period of transition (between the Purgative and the Illuminative Way) one can recognize the entry into what spiritual authors have termed the Illuminative Way, also known as the state of Proficients. The entry into the Illuminative Way is characterized by a significant shift from discursive meditation and active self-discipline to a more contemplative form of prayer and self-possession. The paradox here is that far from becoming 'self-absorbed' and 'self-preoccupied' in this more contemplative stance toward life, the pilgrim, more than ever, sees himself or herself as living from a well of life deep within that expresses itself in an active love towards others, the world and God. The embodiment of spontaneous self-giving love is the hallmark of the Illuminative Way.

The pilgrim is 'illuminated' by the loving grace of God in his or her life in the quiet prayer of loving contemplation. This is in contrast to the 'busy' discursive mental activity that characterized the prayer of the Purgative Way. In the Illuminative Way peace-filled moments of quiet illumine the truth ever more profoundly about one's life in relationship to the truth about God, others and the world. John of the Cross indicates three signs that indicate one is leaving behind his or her central preoccupation with the Purgative Way in order to move more fully into the modality of the Illuminative Way:

> The first is the realization that one cannot make discursive meditation or receive satisfaction from it as before . . .
> The second sign is an awareness of a disinclination to fix the imagination or sense faculties on other particular objects [such as statues or icons] . . .
> The third and surest sign is that a person likes to remain alone in loving awareness of God, without particular considerations, in interior peace and quiet and repose. (*A* 2.13.2–4)

The Illuminative Way is not some blissful state of ecstatic preoccupation of 'nothingness' but rather it is a contemplation that has a certain noetic quality which accompanies it: one is 'illumined' or learns more profoundly about the truth of life in all its aspects. The falsehoods of the self are even more finely stripped away to reveal a truer and more authentic notion of self in relationship to the loving presence of God in the world. The individual becomes more attuned to a realm of reality hitherto he or she was unaware of. One's gaze on the world has shifted and thus one's relationship to it likewise. In the Illuminative Way one's affections are continuously reshaped to be in right relationship to things and others according to the gospel of Jesus Christ. This is in contrast to the havoc that disordered affectivity can wreak on human relationships. John of the Cross describes it this way:

> When this house of the senses was stilled (that is, mortified), its passions quenched, and its appetites calmed and put to sleep through this happy night of the purgation of the sense, the soul went out in order to begin its journey along the road of the spirit, which is that of Proficients and which by another terminology is referred to as the illuminative way or the way of infused contemplation. (*DN* 1.14.1)

The state of the Illuminative Way, in contrast to that of the Purgative Way, may last many years in order to conform the individual more completely to the illuminated 'heart and mind of God'. In fact, in its initial phase the Illuminative Way may not be experienced as 'illuminating' at all. Because the individual is discovering new ways to be in relationship to the world and to others the initial part of this 'illuminative journey' is fraught with confusion and uncertainty, as one might expect when charting a new course into the unknown.

It is in the initial onset of the Illuminative Way that the pilgrim may experience trances and raptures, or often lapses of memory. As the 'light of God's love' shines ever more brilliantly into the soul a certain disorientation takes place that can be experienced in these forms. These phenomena are often popularly associated with the highest levels of mysticism and personal holiness. However, John of the Cross counsels that these should not be paid attention to in any particular way, but should be simply acknowledged without seeking to prolong them or see them as signs of 'holiness'. In as much as the pilgrim seeks to be detached from material possessions in the Purgative Way, the pilgrim here actively seeks to be detached from these phenomena that occur in one's spirit (John calls them 'visions of the soul', *A* 2.23.2) due to the conversion or transition that is taking place in one's entire being. In other words the pilgrim is counselled to continue to go about his or her business mindful that 'no one thing' is the definitive expression of God's loving activity in one's life. The goal of the three ways must always be kept in mind: to understand reality and the world in terms of God's perspective, and thus to be in loving relationship to the world in the same way as God.

The Illuminative Way can be described, therefore, as a slow and gradual process of the 'accommodation of the senses to the spirit' (*DN* 2.2.1); all parts of the body are being brought into harmonious accord with God's loving plan for the world. The pilgrim, in the Illuminative Way, has become radically aware that only God's loving grace can achieve the fullness of life which is desired. As the pilgrim continues to experience this purification there eventually comes what is commonly known as the 'dark night of the soul'.

The 'dark night of the soul' refers to the most intense experience of the purification process cited to this point. Due to the 'divine light' that assails the pilgrim John indicates that she or he 'feels so unclean and wretched that it seems God is against him and he is against God' (*DN* 2.5.5). So intense is this experience that the individual appears completely lost: 'Clearly beholding its impurity by means of this pure light, although in darkness, the soul understands distinctly that it is worthy neither of God nor of any creature. And what most grieves it is that it thinks it will never be worthy, and there are no more blessings for it' (*DN* 2.5.5).

This experience indicates the culminating point of the Illuminative Way. What is happening here is a constitutive and fundamental reorientation of the personality structure. In 'the dark night' no longer can we sustain, in any way, comfortable illusions about who we are before others or before God: radically naked we stand before God and before ourselves in this phase of the journey. John calls this a 'dark night' since the 'natural light' of our own cognitive abilities and faculties that 'makes sense out of things' no longer functions in any familiar way, but the 'light of God' has not yet been revealed in its fullness. Thus the metaphors of 'darkness' and 'dark night' are used by John of the Cross. The 'dark night of the soul' is not a passing psychological state that the pilgrim 'will get over'; it is a theological category that describes the state of existence that opens up the radical awareness of the individual's absolute and utter dependence on God and thus is revelatory of the very nature of God.

What needs to be stressed here, once again, is that the God of 'loving and sweet' presence experienced in the Purgative Way is one and the same as that experienced here in the 'darkness' of the Illuminative Way. As the pilgrim has grown in his or her journey, so too does the intensity of the loving presence of God in his or her life. This awareness, of course, is of no consolation during this 'most terrible' of experiences called 'the dark night'.

What does stand out, however, is that in the public forum the individual experiencing the 'dark night of the soul' will scarcely be seen to be doing so at all. What will be seen abundantly are generous acts of charity, spontaneous acts of forgiveness and reconciliation, and extreme moral integrity. The person will be experienced as joy-filled and exude intense happiness as well as depth of character. There is an acute awareness of the profound love of God that is embodied in the day-to-day life of the pilgrim in this culminating phase of the Illuminative Way prior to entry into the last of the threefold journey, the Unitive Way.

See also **Journey, Spiritual; Purgative Way; Triple Way; Unitive Way.**

E. W. Trueman Dicken, *The Crucible of Love: A Study of the Mysticism of St Teresa of Jesus and St John of the Cross*, New York: Sheed & Ward, 1963; K. Kavanaugh and O. Rodriguez, *The Collected Works of St John of the Cross*, Washington: Institute of Carmelite Studies, 1991; Steven Payne, *John of the Cross and the Cognitive Value of Mysticism*, Norwell: Kluwer Academic Publications, 1990; David B. Perrin, *For Love of the World: The Old and the New Self of John of the Cross*, Bethesda: International Scholars Press, 1997.

DAVID PERRIN

Image and Spirituality

Images in Christian spirituality and religious practice take many shapes and perform many functions. They can be two-dimensional representations such as paintings or icons, or three-dimensional objects such as sculptures or reliefs. Images may take the appearance of architecture – churches and cathedrals – be enacted in religious processions, medieval mystery plays and sermons, take the form of visions and dreams, or be invoked in words and music.

Similarly, images have performed a multiplicity of functions in the Christian tradition – sacramental, devotional, liturgical and so on. Images are credited with healing and miracle-working powers, they bring comfort to the distressed and bereaved, act as symbols of national consciousness, and are used to intercede for the dead or ensure a smooth passage to the next life. Images function in a powerful and immediate way that can prompt strong emotions and responses.

From the Renaissance onwards understanding

of the Christian image has often been dominated by considerations relating to the individual creative personality of the artist. The creation of an art-critical language has had an intellectualizing effect such that the beholder's instinctive and primordial responses to images have been factored out of our conscious experience of the image in what David Freedberg calls the repressive overlay of education. The experience of Christian images in earlier epochs cannot be retrieved other than through the distorted lenses of contemporary cultural attitudes.

The defining attributes of an image are composite and the identity or intent of the person making it is just one part of the mix. In the Orthodox tradition the iconographer is seen as the instrument of other forces – the Church Fathers, the saints (or the image prototype), the Holy Spirit – which are the true authors of the image. Yet there are three other factors, in addition to intent, that exercise a primary influence at the point of contact between image and beholder – locus, iconography and response – and while in any situation or time one of these factors may take precedence over the others, there must be some combination of all four. *Locus* is the place and the context in which the image is viewed; iconography essentially relates to the subject matter and style of the image, and response refers both to the reaction of a specific group of beholders and to the viewing tradition that changes over time. Indeed response is not a passive event but an action predicated by some intention on the part of the beholder and characterized by interaction or dialogue between viewer and that which is viewed. There are, of course, other considerations beyond the four factors, such theology and cultural context, but these tend to be filtered through those already named, thus for example, the artist's intent will be informed directly and indirectly by cultural, psychological and theological factors.

The earliest surviving Christian images are predominantly funerary images from third-century Rome – sculptures and wall paintings found respectively on the sarcophagi and walls of the catacombs. There are a number of difficulties associated with interpreting these images arising from this specificity of time, place and purpose. For a long time historians assumed the combination of the catacombs' location in Rome together with Rome's political dominance meant that all Christian art originated from and was influenced by Rome. This shows how discussion of the role and meaning of the earliest known Christian images is fraught with misplaced assumptions of later eras. Difficulties arise primarily because we have almost no information about the intent of the artists or the response of the beholders to these images. Indeed, the principal reason we know they are Christian images is due to their locus at recognized Christian burial sites.

A major unanswered question is why these images seem to have appeared suddenly in the mid- to late third century. It was once thought that the earliest Christians adhered faithfully to the Mosaic prohibition (Ex. 20.4–5) of the making of graven images and that the only Christians to engage with images were the Gnostics and others drawing on a pagan past. Another view is that the images were made for purely educational purposes, primarily for the benefit of women, the illiterate and the underclass that could not be expected to understand the Christian message otherwise. This view is drawn from Pope Gregory the Great who wrote in the sixth century that what writing presents to readers, a picture presents to the unlearned.

Modern understanding of early and medieval Christian images has until recently been interpreted against the benchmark of theological and other texts. Thus statements such as Gregory's have been accorded influence to the exclusion of other factors, such as letting the images speak for themselves. In the later twentieth century historians began to treat early Christian images as texts to be read and interpreted in their own right and it was recognized that they did not always speak in one voice with the written sources. Some historians (such as C. Arnold Snyder and Margaret Miles) saw images as the most accurate sources for retrieving the voices of the dispossessed – women, poor, illiterate, once again making an implicit assumption that images were preeminently for the unlettered.

The iconography of the catacombs is a mixture of Christian and pagan imagery. In a still predominantly pagan society it is reasonable to assume that artists who worked on the images were often pagan. Some images, such as the Good Shepherd, the fisher of men, the praying person (orant), had pagan origins but were assimilated into Christian iconography. Today the image of the Good Shepherd seems an incontrovertibly Christian image, yet the shepherd carrying a sheep was a popular image in classical art with an antecedent in Hermes the guide to the underworld. The image was associated with hopes for a blessed afterlife and, therefore, particularly suited to a funereal environment. The catacombs also contain recognizably Christian motifs in the form of Bible narratives, such as Abraham sacrificing Isaac, the baptism of Jesus and so on. But the fact that Christians were prepared to use pagan images shows that, in the absence of an explicit Christian locus or iconography such as the catacombs, it may not always be possible to identify particular images as Christian.

By contrast with early Christian art, in the Middle Ages the image functioned in a cultural environment that was overwhelmingly Christian and in which Christian iconographic motifs were well established. There is no ambiguity about the Christian identity of medieval images since image-makers, image-beholders, iconography and locus were all explicitly Christian. The medieval church or cathedral building was a focus for Christian life and worship and was meant to function as an integrated whole drawing the beholder towards the kingdom of God. Images, whether a pilgrim's badge or a stained-glass window, were signs pointing to the divine. Bernard McGinn points to an Augustinian aesthetic in medieval art and images. The Church is a community of the faithful who make up the mystical body of Christ and this universal Church has a locus where the liturgy, prayer and the fabric of the building itself combine to express and meet the divine.

In the later Middle Ages a movement was to emerge that gives us a first real glimpse of images at work in Christian devotional practices. Anne Derbes observes a transition in Christian iconography tracing its roots back perhaps to St Anselm's meditations. In the twelfth and thirteenth centuries the iconography of crucifixes changed from the images of a kingly Christ who transcends all suffering (*Christus triumphus*) to the emotionally charged images of a very human saviour weighed down with pain and suffering (*Christus patiens*). This development paralleled the extraordinary growth of the mendicant movement in Europe and the emergence of a Franciscan aesthetic. St Francis emphasized the importance of earthly life and the need to imitate Christ in order to prepare for the next life. Images became more naturalistic and represent a strongly incarnational spirituality. Like Francis' poem glorying Brother Sun and Sister Moon, images celebrated the beauty of creation and the suffering incarnate God. Images were used less as signs pointing to the kingdom and more as a way to imaginatively and emotionally 're-member' events leading to the passion and resurrection.

Christian images today in some respects have more in common with the early Christian art of the catacombs than that of the Middle Ages or Renaissance Europe. Christians no longer live, for the most part, in a cultural and social environment that is exclusively Christian but in a cultural melting pot. People have access to a wide range of images, both from other Christian traditions, such as Orthodox icons or Celtic spirituality, as well as from non-Christian spiritual traditions. Christian images are used by non-Christians and feature in non-religious contexts and settings. Professional artists that are not necessarily practising Christians have created many of the images present in our churches and cathedrals. American video artist Bill Viola, for example, is not unique among modern artists in drawing extensively on Christian iconography in his work to explore universal spiritual themes, while professing an Eastern Sufi-inspired spirituality. One of the most powerful Christian images of recent years is arguably Anthony Gormley's 20m-high *Angel of the North*, located on a hilltop at Gateshead in northern England. Like images of third-century Rome, modern Christian images are no longer necessarily characterized by an identifiably Christian intent, locus, iconography or response.

The power and immediacy of images has been reflected in various iconoclastic movements that have occurred over the centuries – in Eastern Christendom in the eighth century, in Reformation Northern Europe, and more recently during the French and Russian Revolutions. Iconoclasm has been manifested as an intellectual movement of the rational against the irrational and as a mob desire for destruction. Erasmus, a precursor of the Protestant Reformation, summarized the power of images and the root cause of the fear they have sometimes inspired, writing that 'painting is much more eloquent than speech, and often penetrates more deeply into one's heart'.

See also **Art; Aesthetics; Iconography; Franciscan Spirituality; Orthodox Spirituality.**

Rosemary Cumlin, *Beyond Belief: Modern Art and the Religious Imagination*, Melbourne: National Gallery of Victoria, 1998; Anne Derbes, *Picturing the Passion in Late Medieval Italy: Narrative Painting, Franciscan Ideologies, and the Levant*, Cambridge: Cambridge University Press, 1996; David Freedberg, *The Power of Images: Studies in the History and Theory of Response*, Chicago and London: University of Chicago Press, 1989; Robin Margaret Jensen, *Understanding Early Christian Art*, London and New York: Routledge, 2000; Leonid Ouspensky, *Theology of the Icon*, trans. Anthony Gythiel, Crestwood, New York: St Vladimir's Seminary Press, 1992; V. C. Raguin, K. Brush and P. Draper (eds), *Artistic Integration in Gothic Buildings*, Toronto, Buffalo, London: University of Toronto Press, 1995.

AMANDA ZILBERSTEIN

Imagination

The term *imagination* enjoys a rich history ranging from a merely decorative rhetorical art to an epistemologically secure way of knowing. In its relationship to religious experience and practice imagination has been seen as something of a handmaiden to revelation, systematic theology and pastoral adaptation, or, more often than not, as a subversive power working against the sound asceticism and rigorous discipline necessary for progress in virtue and grace. Fortunately, in more recent times, there has been a firm effort to reclaim the seriousness of imagination both in itself – as a way of knowing, of gaining insight, of developing gifts, of creating new technological and scientific breakthroughs – and in the life of the Spirit. It is this second development that this entry will feature.

The relationship between imagination and spirituality abides in the human heart, as the place of affective knowledge. Spirituality and imagination are ways to come to knowledge by a willingness to enter the world of another. Through analogy, image, symbol and myth, spirituality and imagination reveal new worlds. Spirituality invites men and women into the world of mystery, the abode of God. The unveiling of mystery is always through some medium, either an image (God as Father or Mother) or a symbol (the holy Mount or the cross), or an analogy (the parables of Jesus, 'The Kingdom of God is like . . .'), or a story (the Gospels themselves). Therefore the descriptions of both imagination and spirituality complement one another. They represent ways to enter into the mystery within and beyond human life.

Second, imagination and spirituality reverence the power to create, to make something new. The divine figure of Genesis standing before creation and exclaiming that his handiwork, his divine effort, is 'very good', dramatizes as well the creative exhilaration of every artist, scientist, technologist, writer and performer who makes life out of seemingly formless material. In other words, the act of creation, of making and renewing, from life to forgiveness to the call to mission to the summons to enter death – the cycle that founds spirituality – springs from the imaginative power to make not once but again and again. Consequently, imagination and spirituality both rejoice in life and love as the expression of power.

Third, imagination and spirituality are inherently generative, donating and even sacrificial. The Lord of Genesis gives man and woman the Garden as their own; the God of the patriarchs gives protection and destiny; the God of Exodus gives the Land; the God of Jesus gives his only Son. The Christian revelation of God-in-Christ founds its significance on the washing of the feet, the memorial of the Supper, and the death on the cross. Ignatius of Loyola characterized the risen Jesus, the Consoler, as the one who gives peace and joy and hope to his scattered followers. The artist, the scientist, the performer and the teacher – all who build their lives on imagination have to set their artistic children free. In some way every creative person has to die to sole ownership and let the accomplishment become a gift.

The theological reflection that sees an affinity between spirituality and imagination also expresses some important caveats. Spirituality must be linked to ethical decision-making, to conduct and to the works of mercy. Spirituality demands a fidelity, to the Absolute Mystery of God, which cannot be shared with any other reality. Spirituality builds on belief, conduct and worship in ways that imagination cannot. But insofar as both invite the human heart to know and to celebrate its transcendence, spirituality and imagination represent the search for God.

See also **Spirituality and Culture; Spirituality, Liturgy, and Worship (*essays*); Art; Beauty; Experience, Religious; Image and Spirituality; *Imago Dei*; Ignatian Spirituality; Literature and Spirituality; Senses, Spiritual.**

Paul Avis, *God and Imagination, Metaphor, Symbol, and Myth in Religion and Theology*, London and New York: Routledge, 1999; Northrup Frye, *The Great Code: The Bible as Literature*, London: Routledge & Paul Kegan, 1982; Andrew Greeley, *Religion as Poetry*, New Brunswick and London: Transaction, 1995; Andrew Greeley, *The Catholic Imagination*, Berkeley: University of California Press, 2000.

HOWARD GRAY

Imago Dei

Gen. 1.27 states, 'So God created humankind in his image, in the image of God he created them, male and female he created them.' What constitutes this image of God in humankind is not clearly spelled out in Scripture. That humans are created in God's image is stated explicitly in only three passages – Gen. 1.26–28;5.3; and 9.6 – all of which are attributable to the Priestly writer. The expressions 'in our image' and 'according to our likeness' are used in reference only to the creation of human beings, in conjunction with humans as both male and female and as having dominion over the rest of creation. In Gen. 5.3 both likeness and image are used to draw a parallel between God's creation of humankind and human procreation in the birth of Seth. Gen. 9.6 cites the image of God as a source of value for human life. New Testament references to the *imago dei* are equally few. In 1 Cor. 11.7, Paul writes, 'For a man ought not to have his head veiled, since he is the image and reflection of God.' In other passages, such as Col. 1.15 and 2 Cor. 4.4, Paul refers to Christ as the image of God. In 2 Cor. 3.18 Paul writes, 'And all of us, with unveiled faces, seeing the glory of the Lord as though reflected in a mirror, are being transformed into the same image from one degree of glory to another.' Here the image is not something humans possess, but something in which we grow. This dynamic understanding is particularly emphasized in the Orthodox tradition, where writers traditionally distinguish between the image and the likeness of God (see Lossky, 1985).

Considering the scant number of scriptural references, the concept of the *imago dei* has commanded an unusual amount of attention from theologians. It is a convenient locus for questions fundamental to Christian anthropology such as what it means to be human or what our relationship as humans is to God. Interpretations of the *imago dei* have varied, yet most can be categorized in one of three ways. Substantive interpretations view the image as an individually held property that is a part of our nature, most often associated with reason. Functional interpretations see the image of God in action, specifically our exercise of dominion over the earth. Relational interpretations find the image within the relationships we establish and maintain.

Until the twentieth century, most interpretations of the *imago dei* considered it to be a property possessed by both humans and God, one which distinguishes humans from other animals. The property or set of properties making up the image has varied over time, reflecting the concerns and preoccupations of each age, but has included our physical form (Gunkel), the ability to stand upright (Koehler), our rationality or intellect (Aquinas), our personality (Procksch), or our capacity for self-transcendence (Niebuhr). The quality most commonly cited is reason. Early Christian writers who discuss the *imago dei* in terms of the rational mind include Clement of Alexandria (*Stromateis* 5.14), Origen (*Against Celsus* 4.85), Gregory of Nazianzus (*Orations* 38.11), Gregory of Nyssa (*On the Making of Man* 5), and Augustine (*On the Trinity* 12–14). They are followed in this interpretation in both the Scholastic tradition (Aquinas) and the Reformation tradition (Luther, Calvin). Though dominant historically, substantive interpretations have fallen out of favour among twentieth-century theologians. While we find reason as a part of the *imago dei* in the work of theologians such as Reinhold Niebuhr and Paul Tillich, the strongest proponents of this view today are found primarily among Evangelical writers.

In a 1915 article, 'Zum Terminus "Bild Gottes"', Johannes Hehn suggested that the image of God be understood as a royal title or designation rather than an attribute of human nature. Old Testament scholars Gerhard von Rad and Wilhelm Caspari extended Hehn's work into a functional approach to the *imago dei* that locates the image, not in a quality we possess, but in what we are called to do. In his commentary on Genesis, Gerhard von Rad notes that the noun *selem* is translated as 'duplicate', 'idol', or 'painting' in its occurrences in other Old Testament texts (see 1 Sam. 6.5; Num. 33.52; 2 Kings 11.18; Ezek. 23.14 for other uses of *selem*). He thus suggests that the *imago dei* be understood as our call to be 'God's representative, summoned to maintain and enforce God's claim to dominion over the earth' (von Rad, *Genesis*, p. 58; see also Millard & Bordreuil, 1982, 135–41). This interpretation has been in the ascendancy among biblical scholars throughout the twentieth century (see Jonsson, 1988, p. 219).

A third interpretation is relational. According to Karl Barth, the image of God 'does not consist in anything that man is or does' but is identified with the fact that the human being is a 'counterpart to God' (Barth, 1958, pp. 184–5). Barth interprets the plural in 'Let us make man' as referring to God as a Trinity that contains both an 'I' that can issue a call and a 'Thou' capable of response. We image such a God by being in relationship, first to God and, secondarily, with one another. Although many have differed sharply with Barth on the details of what constitutes authentic relationship, a relational model of the *imago dei* has become the dominant approach among systematic theologians in the mid to late twentieth century. Similar views are found in Brunner, Berkouwer, Bonhoeffer, Pannenberg and Küng. While Brunner initially divides the image of God into two aspects, a formal aspect retained at the fall and a material aspect which is lost, he abandons this distinction in *Man in Revolt*, stressing in its place the image as the whole person, responsible for responding to God and to one another in love. Berkouwer suggests that the analogy between humans and God is neither an analogy of being nor of relationship, but that we image God in our love for others. Pannenberg locates the centre of humanity in the tension between our self-consciousness as individuals and our exocentricity or openness to others. Each of these approaches are essentially relational, though they qualify the relationship in various ways.

See also **Deification; Image and Spirituality; Iconography; Person.**

Karl Barth, *Church Dogmatics*, ed. G. W. Bromiley and T. F. Torrance, trans. J. W. Edwards, O. Bussey, Harold Knight, Edinburgh: T & T Clark, 1958; G. C. Berkower, *Man: The Image of God: Studies in Dogmatics*, Grand Rapids, MI: Eerdmans, 1962; Dietrich Bonhoeffer, *Creation and Fall*, London: SCM Press, 1959; David Cairnes, *The Image of God in Man*, Fontana Library of Theology and Philosophy, London: SCM Press, 1953; reprint, London: Collins, 1973; Gunnlaugur A. Jonsson, *The Image of God: Genesis 1:26–28 in a Century of Old Testament Research*, Coniectanea Biblica Old Testament Series 26, ed. Tryggve Mettinger and Magnus Ottosson, Lund: Almqvist and Wiksell, 1988; Hans Küng, *On Being a Christian*, trans. E. Quinn, Garden City, NJ: Doubleday, 1976; Vladimir Lossky, *In the Image and Likeness of God*, Crestwood, NY: St Vladimir's Seminary Press, 1985; A. R. Millard and P. Bordreuil, 'A statue from Syria with Assyrian and Aramaic inscriptions', *Biblical Archeologist* 45 (1982), 135–41; Wolfhart Pannenberg, *Anthropology in Theological Perspective*, Philadelphia: Westminster, 1984; Gerhard von Rad, *Genesis: A Commentary*, trans. J. H. Marks, London: SCM Press, 1961; Claus Westermann, *Genesis 1–11: A Commentary*, trans. John Scullion, Minneapolis: Augsburg, 1984.

NOREEN HERZFELD

Imitation of Christ

Perhaps the most prevalent metaphor or pattern for the Christian life, the phrase has evoked multiple interpretations, from the literal and simplistic, to the questioning and complexly nuanced. Whether God's grace or human works should be stressed has been a concern, also the relative importance of the individual and the community.

There is continuity between imitation of Christ and the Old Testament notion of imitating God, or following in the way of God: 'What does the Lord require of you but to do justice, and to love kindness, and to walk humbly with your God?' (Micah 6.8). Early theologians regarded Jesus, the saving Son of God, as uniquely capable of imitating and obeying his Father. As a result, the problem for Christians has been to discover in what respects their own lives can be said to trace God's path by following Jesus

Christ. Some, like Stephen, Ignatius of Antioch, Origen and Cyprian, believed this only could be accomplished through martyrdom.

Paul also linked 'being like' Christ with dying as Christ had died, whether literally or metaphorically, and baptism initiated Christians into this process (Rom. 6.5; Phil. 3.10–11). For Paul and the early Church Fathers, not only baptism, but the Spirit-filled Eucharist, united Christians to the cosmic drama of Christ's death and resurrection and anticipated the future coming of Christ in the parousia. Thus, imitation of Christ was both sacramental and ecclesial and was predicated on full participation in the cosmic drama of the gospel narrative expressed communally and liturgically through the Eucharist. Indeed, the very transmission of the Gospels seems to have been motivated by the endeavour to imitate Christ.

From Clement of Alexandria (*c.* 150–*c.* 215) onwards, many Christians have regarded the literal imitation of Christ to be an elementary spiritual stage which one ought to outgrow in favour of a more mature spirituality. Nevertheless, in the medieval period, a real shift to such literal and individualistic interpretations took place. Most renowned among the medieval imitators was Thomas à Kempis (*c.* 1380–1471), whose *Imitation of Christ* defined the phrase in terms of a meditation on the inner life of Jesus, accessed primarily through medieval devotional tradition and à Kempis's own contemplative experience. Francis of Assisi (1181/2–1226), known as the 'Second Christ', intentionally imitated Jesus both in dress and in suffering, to the extent that stigmata appeared on his body. Important also was Bernard of Clairvaux (1090–1153), who practised devotion to Jesus' sacred humanity, but believed in a progressive passage from a carnal to a spiritual imitation of Christ in which one's faith became strong: 'When finally I believed in Christ, that is to say, when I imitated His humility, I came to know Truth.' For Bernard and for many others, one strove to imitate Jesus Christ through humility, gentleness, love and obedience.

Women also have devoted themselves to the imitation of Christ. The example of Hadewijch of Brabant (a Beguine and gifted visionary and poet of the thirteenth century) raises the question of the relationship between the contemplative and the active life. In passionate contemplation she yearned above all 'to be one with God in fruition', until she learned that this was a sign of 'non-full-grownness', and that Jesus preferred her to become 'pure man like myself'. In her case this meant abandoning the quest for mystical union in favour of a daily round of care for lepers. In like vein, the reformer Teresa of Avila (1515–82), whose contemplative life and ministry were initiated by a profound identification with an image of the wounded Jesus, strove constantly to unite in her person the roles of Mary and Martha. Julian of Norwich (1342–c. 1423) believed knowledge of God's love could come from experiencing in her body the same pains as Jesus did in his passion and death, but her interpretation of her near-death experience and its accompanying sixteen visions are now recognized as far from individualistic: their implications are at once political and universal. In some cases, the impulse toward literal interpretation of the imitation of Christ may perhaps have been naive. However, the actual texts of these great mystics testify to a quality of Christian maturity and integration only rarely attained in any age.

Luther (1483–1546) was critical of the ideal of the imitation of Christ because he could not reconcile it with his doctrine of justification by faith, for him, the essential gospel message of grace. He made a distinction between *imitation*, which was a human work, and *conformity*, a process of conformation to Christ through the work of the Holy Spirit. In the twentieth century, Dietrich Bonhoeffer (1906–45) was probably the most fully developed inheritor not only of Luther, but of the ancient and medieval traditions. In the context of Nazi Germany, he asserted that the sole path to Christian freedom was the imitation of Jesus through the injunctions implicit in the Sermon on the Mount. The Holy Spirit would lead one, not to the 'cheap grace' of the bourgeois Church, but to the 'costly grace' required to risk care for those in need (in Bonhoeffer's case, the Jews), even if that meant death on a cross, the ultimate symbol of being for others.

See also **Contemplation; Discipleship; Deification; Discipline; Early Christian Spirituality; Cross and Spirituality;** *Imago Dei*; **Spiritual Formation; Jesus and Spirituality; Love; Martyrdom; Medieval Spirituality in the West; Obedience; Peace; Poverty; Suffering.**

Dietrich Bonhoeffer, *Ethics*; Giles Constable, 'The ideal of the imitation of Christ' in his *Three Studies in Medieval Religious and Social Thought*, Cambridge: Cambridge University Press, 1995; Edouard Cothenet, *Imitating Christ*, St Meinrad, IN: Avvey Press, 1974 (this is a translation of articles from *DS)*; Geffrey B. Kelly and F. Burton Nelson, *The Cost of Moral Leadership: The Spirituality of Dietrich Bonhoeffer*, Grand Rapids, MI: Eerdmans, 2003; Margaret R. Miles, 'An image of the image: imitation of Christ' in her *Practicing Christianity: Critical Perspectives for an Embodied Spirituality*, New York: Crossroad, 1988; E. J. Tinsley, *The Imitation of God in Christ: An Essay on the Biblical Basis of Christian Spirituality*, London: SCM Press, 1960.

ELISABETH KOENIG

Incarnation

The doctrine of the incarnation (as classically expressed, the conviction that the eternal 'Son of God' became the human being Jesus of Nazareth) is the bedrock of Christian faith, on which all other doctrines rest and which is therefore the core of most Christian spirituality. It is also, however, a source for a number of specific themes in the Christian spiritual life.

Its origins lie in the experience and faith of the first generations of Christians witnessed to in the developing New Testament in various places: the vindication of Jesus at the resurrection; reflection on the life story of Jesus (prophet, teacher, miracle-worker, granter of forgiveness) especially in the compilation of the synoptic Gospels; the extrapolation of messianic language, including the use of 'wisdom' typology (Matt. 11.28–30, Col. 1.15–16); Paul's conception of a 'cosmic Christ' alongside his paralleling of Adam and Christ as the Second Adam (Rom. 5.12–21; Phil. 2.5–11); the exaltation of Jesus over angels in Hebrews; the synoptic birth narratives; the self-description of the Johannine Jesus. The evolving conception takes its clearest and most influential form in the prologue to John's Gospel (1.1–14). There, the 'Word' is described both as 'being' God ('the Word was with God and the Word was God') and as 'becoming flesh' ('the Word became flesh and dwelt among us'). Exegesis and interpretation of this are not without their complications, but the majority view is that this 'hymn' communicates the conviction that the man Jesus of Nazareth is the embodiment of an eternal element of God himself. Thus faith in Jesus the Christ as 'Son of God', the union of divine and human in the specific person of Jesus of Nazareth, may be said to represent the pinnacle of New Testament theology.

Its precise formulation was achieved in four centuries of controversy culminating in the trinitarian convictions of the Niceno-Constantinopolitan Creed, that Christ is 'God from God', 'of one being with the Father' ('*homoousios*'), and the christological boundaries of the Chalcedonian definition. The essence of the latter is the defence of the 'two Natures' of Christ, 'truly God and truly human', united in one Person, but without providing a final resolution of how this paradox was to be understood, not least in the consciousness and experience of a real human being, though this is in part to introduce modern categories to the debate.

These formularies retained their almost universal authority until the later Enlightenment and modern periods when the emerging discipline of biblical criticism questioned the historical nature and doctrinal uniformity of the New Testament; historical criticism questioned the assumption that the post-New Testament trajectory was inevitable and correct; and philosophical scepticism questioned both the categories with which the patristic theologians had worked and also the intelligibility of their conclusions. More recent criticisms have pushed these questions further to the point of wishing to deny or at least severely rethink the truth claims of the doctrine of the incarnation (Goulder, Hick, Theissen, the 'Jesus Seminar'). New questions have also been raised by feminist (Heyward, Schüssler Fiorenza), black (Beckford, Cone, Douglas) and developing world (Sobrino) theologians about the validity of the traditional claims made for the salvific significance of the man Jesus of Nazareth.

Some modern theologians have responded either by attempting to defend the traditional 'from above' Christology, for example by expanding the kenotic interpretation of the Incarnation (Gore). Others have responded (crudely, Christology 'from below') by redefining the Incarnation as an expression of the faith that in Jesus, God is discerned as being uniquely present to humankind (Robinson); or that in Jesus, faith in God and human virtue reaches a high point worthy of later celebration and imitation (Schleiermacher, differently Cupitt). It must be noted that other biblical theologians are mounting a sustained defence of the doctrine of the incarnation 'from above', while taking seriously critical readings of the New Testament and tradition (R. E. Brown, Dunn, N. T. Wright), thereby providing an account of Jesus the Christ which gives more value and reality to his real and specific humanity while retaining the doctrinal essence of classic orthodoxy.

These different modes of understanding the incarnation have had varying expressions in the Christian spiritual life.

The first expression is in worship of Jesus Christ. It is rightly noted that the New Testament has examples of worship being directed to Jesus (Matt. 28.19–20; John 20.28; 2 Thess. 1.12; Rev. 1.17) and that this became an important factor in the patristic defence of his divine status (Athanasius). Worship of the Person Jesus Christ has remained a constant feature of Christian worship thereafter, whether in medieval office liturgy, Wesleyan hymnody or modern charismatic choruses.

The second is an appreciation of the salvific significance of Jesus, which may be seen in some patristic writers to give profound value to humankind. So Irenaeus writes that 'the glory of God is a human being fully alive', referring both to Jesus of Nazareth and to the redeemed human life (*Adversus Haereses 4.20.7*). This is linked to patristic understandings of the mode of salvation – by taking humanity into himself, Christ saves all that he 'assumes' (Athanasius) – and of the final destination of human beings, union with God, 'deification' (Gregory Nazianzen).

The third is in a sacramental form. Just as God became incarnate in Christ, so he is 'incarnated' in the Eucharist. So there evolved in the patristic period strongly 'realist' language of the presence of Christ's body and blood in the bread and the wine (Cyril of Alexandria), language which was to be given a particular philosophical rigour in the medieval Western Church in the theology of transubstantiation (Aquinas). Consequently a rich and extensive eucharistic sacramental spirituality has evolved wherein the believer meets Christ in a profound, tangible as well as spiritual, way in the Eucharist (Thomas à Kempis, George Herbert).

A fourth form is in the direct imitation of Christ as providing the perfect model for a human life. This has been understood in a variety of ways but common themes are self-denial (Antony), self-sacrificial service (Mother Teresa), sheer self-sacrifice for others (Maximilian Kolbe) and humility. Arguably the most Christlike of the saints, Francis, strove to copy Christ in all aspects of his life, not least in his poverty, love for the disadvantaged, respect for creation, and humility. It could be argued that Christians have been less alert to the possibility of imitating Christ in his more celebratory aspects of human living: his humour, his robustness, his sheer attractiveness.

A more recent development of these forms argues explicitly that by so valuing humankind and creation by becoming part of it, God is demonstrating his commitment to the value and welfare of his whole creation, not least in its material aspect – remember Fr Dolling's claim that Christ was as concerned for the drains of Poplar as for the souls of those who lived there. In the modern period this variant takes the affirmation of humankind in the incarnation as a basis for social and political action for human welfare, partly in direct imitation of Christ (Luke 4) and partly in a wider extrapolation of this understanding of the character of God in Christ (liberation theology).

A sixth variant, which is evident in the exemplarist theology of Abelard and also in changing patterns of Western art in the thirteenth century, is an appreciation of the suffering which Christ underwent and of the importance for this in showing us the extent of God's love for humankind. Luther was to take this much further in his depiction of the 'God-forsakeness' of Christ, and this understanding has come to be particularly valued by post-Holocaust theologians, trying to retain faith in God in the face of human tragedy (Moltmann). Arguably this interpretation has been assisted by some other aspects of modern Christology which have been more effective in expressing and valuing in a realistic way Jesus' humanity than were the patristic, medieval or Reformation exegetes. Nonetheless the theological and devotional effectiveness of these key modern spiritualities are dependent on an underlying conviction in the truthfulness of the doctrine of the incarnation, that in Jesus Christ, God is specifically and specially present.

In recent generations Julian of Norwich has been highlighted as someone who holds together commitment to the salvific significance of Jesus Christ, of the significance of his incarnation as an affirmation of humankind and as the ultimate demonstration of the love of God. 'This lovely human nature was made for Christ so that man [*sic*] could be created in glory and beauty and saved for joy and bliss' (*Revelations of Divine Love* 62).

See also **Body and Spirituality; Cappadocian Fathers; Cross and Spirituality; Eucharistic Spirituality; God, Images of; Imitation of Christ; Jesus and Spirituality; Liberation Spirituality; Person; Redemption; Resurrection; Sacramentality and Spirituality; Sacred; World.**

R. Beckford, *Jesus is Dread*, London: Darton, Longman & Todd, 1998; M. Bockmuehl (ed.), *The Cambridge Companion to Jesus*, Cambridge: Cambridge University Press, 2001; J. D. G. Dunn, *Jesus Remembered*, Christianity in the Making 1, Grand Rapids, MI: Eerdmans, 2003; J. D. G. Dunn, *Christology in the Making*, London: SCM Press, 1989; Elisabeth Schüssler Fiorenza, *Jesus: Miriam's Child, Sophia's Prophet*, New York: Continuum, 1994/London: SCM Press, 1995; J. Sobrino, *Christology at the Crossroads*, London: SCM Press, 1978; J. Sobrino, *Jesus the Liberator: A Historical-Theological Reading of Jesus of Nazareth*, Maryknoll, NY: Orbis Books, 1993; J. Sobrino, *Christ the Liberator*, Maryknoll, NY: Orbis Books, 2001; N. T. Wright, *Jesus and the Victory of God*, London: SPCK, 1996 (and other vols in this proposed 5-vol. series).

ALAN BARTLETT

Inculturation

A spirituality of inculturation implies a series of conversions, whereby we open humanly to new horizons and recognize the call of God in these new places. Inculturation is a recent word for an old reality. From the very beginning Christianity embraced the adventure of making faith real by reaching out to other peoples. In fact the first outreach from Jewish to Greek cultures caused a major crisis in the primitive Church, as one can see from Acts 15. Two chapters later one has another struggle of interpretations. At first St Paul is disgusted with the display of idols in Athens but then, when he has an opportunity to have contact with the leaders of that culture, his attitude moves from disdain to generosity, and he comments favourably on the altar to the unknown god as an expression of their genuine religious desire. Such a change of disposition is crucial for anyone involved in inculturation. There is a place for negative and prophetic judgement but never at the outset, before entering into relationship with the culture and trying to understand it on its own terms.

The term 'culture' has at least three main fields of meaning. There is the older 'high' sense of creative culture, that is, the realms of thought or artistic production. Then there is the newer anthropological sense of 'ordinary' culture, the set of assumptions underlying the meanings and values of a way of life. Again one may mention the more postmodern approach to culture as a zone of conflict and power struggle: dominant cultures can become oppressive and dangerous. In reflecting on inculturation all three have their relevance but in particular the second or anthropological dimension.

To be involved in inculturation will entail a series of conversions or expansions of horizon as one comes to realize the demands of this slow process of earthing the gospel in new soil. Indeed by echoing the gradually accumulating insights of the Churches on this issue, one may identify some ten stages and new attitudes needed along this road.

1. A first conversion stems from a recognition of the *plurality of cultures* (as against the hidden temptation to think of 'our' culture as the norm).

2. Taking the culturally limited incarnation of Jesus as paradigm, we realize that faith is not tied to any one culture but will grow differently in particular cultural settings, *adapting its language* (in a broad sense) to meet local needs.

3. Next comes the hope for a two-way traffic of *mutual enrichment* between two cultural

horizons and therefore a spirituality of real dialogue is called for.

4. Instead of being directed by experts from outside, real inculturation will mean a *transformation from within* a given culture and involving the entire community. Hence the external agent has to learn humility and patience in order to foster agency and creativity in others.

5. Inculturation aims at giving birth to new cultural expressions, deeply transformed by its meeting with the gospel. The incarnation paradigm of embracing human realities needs also the *redemption model of purification* and conversion.

6. In this light, *skills of discernment* will be needed to sift what is humanizing from what is dehumanizing, because all cultures, being human constructs, are inevitably ambiguous. Discernment focuses on fruits and will ask 'Where are these choices or tendencies leading us long-term?'

7. Key *criteria for a genuine inculturation* include compatibility with the gospel and unity with the universal Church.

8. The *zones for inculturation* include not only the more obvious ones of liturgy or catechesis but ultimately theological thought forms, artistic expressions and the whole lifestyle of a Christian community.

9. The process of *inculturation never finishes* because cultures are in continual evolution and change.

10. Inculturation is not simply a matter for 'mission' territories. The 'new evangelization' also implies a difficult *inculturation of faith in Western cultures* that have largely lost their Christian roots and symbolic memories.

In order to live these various dimensions, a spirituality of adventure, patience and service is needed, rooted in trust that the Spirit is indeed artistically at work in all cultures. Linked with these many challenges of inculturation is the huge change in the demography of the Church. As Johann Baptist Metz has put it, the Catholic Church, for instance, does not 'have' a third-world Church; it is now mainly a third-world Church with its origins in Western Europe.

See also **Spirituality and Culture** (*essay*).

———

Gerald Arbuckle, *Earthing the Gospel: An Inculturation Handbook for Pastoral Workers*, London: Geoffrey Chapman, 1990; Michael Paul Gallagher, *Clashing Symbols: An Introduction to Faith and Culture*, rev. edn, London: Darton, Longman & Todd, 2003; Elizabeth Johnson, 'Between the times: religious life and the post-modern experience of God', *Review for Religious* 53 (1994), 6–28; Franx Xaver Scheuerer, *Interculturality: A Challenge for the Mission of the Church*, Bangalore: Asian Trading Corporation, 2001; Robert J. Schreiter, *The New Catholicity: Theology between the Global and the Local*, Maryknoll, NY: Orbis Books, 1997; Aylward Shorter, *Toward a Theology of Inculturation*, London: Geoffrey Chapman, 1988.

MICHAEL PAUL GALLAGHER

Indifference

One of the great texts of spirituality is the Principle and Foundation, an introductory consideration at the threshold of the Spiritual Exercises of St Ignatius Loyola. In the five paragraphs of the Principle and Foundation Ignatius has laid out a set of principles foundational to the spiritual life: that a human being is free to respond to the loving act of creation, that a network of relationships constitutes creative reality, that the human person is called to use creatures in so far and only in so far as these help a person to praise, to reverence and to serve God, and then that there are two complementary directives called the principle of indifference and the principle of the *magis*. The principle of indifference does not mean affective distancing from or a dismissal of creative reality. Rather indifference is a psycho-religious balance before one commits himself or herself to the use of any creature. The *magis* principle states that once a person has this balance before created reality, then that person should choose only what more leads to the end for which he or she has been created, to stand in the company of the Lord. The proper understanding of spiritual indifference is that it is preparatory to a choice to live a life that wants what God wants. It is a principle of generous and intelligent openness towards the whole context of the life of the Spirit.

In utilizing this principle, Ignatius stood on the shoulders of giants, the great figures of biblical and Christian history who saw that the rational yet ardent service of God could be united in a single act of discerning readiness, that is, both a review of options and a desire to embrace only that option which furthered the presence of God and the work of God in the world. Throughout the Exercises this dynamic of reason and affective readiness to choose generously for the sake of the kingdom acts as a kind of hermeneutic in reading the life and ministry of Christ and in leading the one making the Exercises towards a life of service in the likeness of Christ.

Indifference is a pivotal Ignatian strategy for choice but always in conjunction with the principle of the *magis*. Clearly, then, indifference also presumes a discernment about how and where one is attracted, a solid reading of moods and environment, and a developing sense of ownership about one's personal spiritual history so that one becomes more and more aware of the influences on her or his choice: fear, ambition, anger, insecurity and habit. What gradually emerges is that there are two forces in one's spiritual life, one leads to life and love, while the other leads to death and enmity.

The culture in which one makes decisions about life is also a subtle influence on one's freedom. Therefore, indifference is also important for reading the signs of one's times. Indifference can demand the courage to be counter-cultural, especially when there is pressure to conform, to fit in and to comply, to be friends with the world of ambition and competition.

Finally, indifference operates in group decision-making as well as in individual decision-making. Communal reflection and choices in contemporary Christian life will become more and more important. Conjoined to the shared responsibility to act is a prior responsibility to act spiritually, to act with this combination of indifference and a readiness for the *magis*.

See also **Spirituality, Psychology and Psychotherapy; Absorption; Affectivity; Business and Spirituality; Consumerism; Desire; Discernment; Emotions; Ignatian Spirituality; Practice, Spiritual; Vocation.**

Michael Ivens, *Understanding the Spiritual Exercises*, Trowbridge: Cromwell Press, 1998.

HOWARD GRAY

Intellectual Life and Spirituality

The intersection of the intellectual life and spirituality has a long history in many religious and philosophical traditions. As the work of Pierre Hadot has shown, philosophy in the ancient world was a way of life focused less on propositions to which one might or might not give one's assent and more on spiritual exercises intended, as Hadot puts it, 'to form rather than inform' (Hadot, 1995, p. 20). Many of these spiritual exercises are intellectual practices: reading, listening, thinking, writing, research, dialogue, physics. Stoics, Epicureans, Platonists and others committed their lives to these practices with the goal of transforming their vision of the world, freeing themselves from the tyranny of their passions, and changing their lives.

The development of Christian spirituality is no less tied to the practices of intellectual life. As Bernard McGinn has shown, the Christian mystical tradition has a 'distinctively exegetical character' (McGinn, 1992, p. 3), reflecting its origins in the interpretation of the Bible in worshipping communities as well as the influence of Jewish and Greek exegetical practices. Intellectual practices such as reading, writing and studying languages have a long history as spiritual practices in Christianity, practices intended to make one vulnerable to an experience of God.

Perhaps no text in the history and literature of Christian spirituality so fully grapples with the place of intellectual work in Christian spiritual life than the *Confessions* of St Augustine. Susceptible from his youth to the pleasures of intellectual work, the adult Augustine looks back with shame on his childhood tears over the fate of Dido in the *Aeneid* because he was not moved in the same way by the story of Christ's passion. The Augustine of the *Confessions* tries to pray his way into a new relationship to intellectual work, one focused less on ambition and more on praise: 'For see, Lord, my King and my God, I would wish everything useful which I learned as a boy to be used in your service – speaking, reading, writing, arithmetic, all' (*Confessions* 1.15, p. 33).

The same seductive power that reading exerts over Augustine as a child also contributes to his conversion to Christianity as an adult, a conversion rooted in intense reading experiences. Reading Cicero's *Hortensius*, he is converted to the love of wisdom. Reading the Platonists, he encounters the Word, although not yet the Word made flesh. In comparison with these philosophical works, he finds the Christian Scriptures inelegant, 'unworthy of comparison with the grand style of Cicero' (*Confessions* 3.5, p. 57). But when his mentor, Bishop Ambrose of Milan, introduces him to the allegorical method of reading, the depth and complexity of Scripture unfurls before him in a way he had never experienced. He comes to see Scripture as a cathedral in which 'the vault is high and veiled in mysteries' (*Confessions* 3.5) but whose doorway is low and requires the reader to stoop down in humility in order to enter. He learns to see in the humble style of Scripture a reflection of God's own humility in the incarnation.

The practice of reading is at the centre of the decisive moment of his conversion. Wanting to become a Christian, but struggling with fear and confusion over what such a commitment will mean for him, a child's voice penetrates his anguished internal dialogue. '*Tolle, lege,*' the voice says. 'Take and read.' Remembering how the monk Antony has received God's call through the reading of Scripture, he opens the letters of Paul and reads 'in silence the passage upon which my eyes first fell: *Not in rioting and drunkenness, not in chambering and wantonness, not in strife and envying: but put ye on the Lord*

Jesus Christ, and make not provision for the flesh in concupiscence' (*Confessions* 8.12, p. 183). And although his restless questions about God never cease, from that moment he embraces the Christian faith with both mind and body.

The rest of the *Confessions* is a view into the passionate reading of Scripture that would absorb him for the rest of his life. Such meditation on Scripture that leads one to God eventually comes to be known under the name *lectio divina* and is systematized by its later practitioners. The twelfth-century Carthusian Guigo II, for example, describes the unfolding of *lectio divina* in this way: *lectio*, or reading, is the bottom rung of a ladder of monks, stretching from earth to heaven. *Lectio* leads to *meditatio*, in which the reader brings all the resources of his or her intellect to bear on the text in meditation. *Meditatio* quite naturally leads to *oratio*, prayer. And prayer leaves us vulnerable to an experience of *contemplatio*, a contemplative experience of God's presence which cannot be scheduled or demanded but for which we may prepare through the practice of *lectio divina*. More than one hundred years later, another Carthusian, Marguerite d'Oingt, will add the rung of *scriptio* – writing – to Guigo's ladder, turning it into more of a wheel, a circular path in which one responds to God through writing, which then provides a new text for *lectio*.

Closer to our own day, the philosopher Simone Weil, who was deeply attracted to Christianity, described intellectual work as the pearl of great price, worthy of all our sacrifices to pursue, because it cultivates our capacity for attention without which we cannot pray, nor be present to our suffering neighbour. For her, the fruit of intellectual work lies not in how much we know, but in our ability to be truly present to what is other than ourselves.

A rich intellectual life is the inheritance of every Christian, not just the 'intellectuals'. As we have learned from base communities studying Scripture in places of material deprivation, even those considered 'illiterate' can read deeply, can interpret, can teach. From the child wondering about the stories of Scripture she is hearing for the first time to the scholar pondering the multiple meanings of Hebrew words, the intellectual life of Christian faith belongs to all of us.

See also **Education and Spirituality.**

Augustine of Hippo, *The Confessions of St Augustine*, trans. Rex Warner, New York: Mentor, 1963; Mary Frohlich, 'Spiritual discipline, discipline of spirituality: revisiting questions of definition and method', *Spiritus: A Journal of Christian Spirituality* 1.1 (2001), 78; Guigo II, *The Ladder of Monks*, trans. Edmund Colledge OSA and James Walsh SJ, Kalamazoo, MI: Cistercian Publications, 1981; Pierre Hadot, *Philosophy as a Way of Life*, ed. Arnold I. Davidson, trans. Michael Chase, Oxford: Blackwell, 1995; Marguerite d'Oingt, *Les Oeuvres de Marguerite d'Oingt*, ed. Antonin Duraffour, Pierre Gardette and Paulette Durdilly, Publications de l'institute de linguistique romane de Lyon 21, Paris: Societe d'edition 'Les belles lettres', 1965; in English: *The Writings of Margaret of Oingt: Medieval Prioress and Mystic*, trans. Renate Blumenfeld-Kosinski, Newburyport, MA: Focus Information Group, 1990; Bernard McGinn, *The Foundations of Mysticism: Origins to the Fifth Century*, New York: Crossroad, 1992; Stephanie Paulsell, 'Spiritual formation and intellectual work in theological education', *Theology Today* 55.2 (July 1998), 229–34; Stephanie Paulsell, 'Writing and mystical experience in Marguerite d'Oingt and Virginia Woolf', *Comparative Literature* 44.3 (Summer 1992), 249–67; Simone Weil, 'On the right use of school studies with a view to the love of God' in *Waiting on God*, trans. Emma Craufurd, New York: HarperCollins, 1951.

STEPHANIE PAULSELL

Intercession

Intercession is prayer for, with or on behalf of another community, event, person or group. It can be as simple and spontaneous as the soft utterance of a single name or as complex, ritualized and familiar as ancient prayers from *The Book of Common Prayer* or other set prayers. Inextricably linked to other forms of prayer as well, intercessory prayer is simultaneously a prayer of thanksgiving in that it recognizes in faith that God answers prayer. It is a close relative of petition (asking on behalf of oneself), while at the same time is likewise a prayer of confession of God's wisdom, power and goodness. It is praise in that it remembers God's interceding acts of the past and God's promise to intercede in the future. Intercession, perhaps more than any other form of 'verbal' prayer, also has its efficacious silent side. The name or face remembered of a person in distress, a thought for another in need, prayer for the health and well-being of people known and unknown, all these moments permeate intercession with a grace-filled silence.

As modelled in the life, work and prayer of Jesus Christ, intercession draws us out of ourselves, transforming self-absorption into attention to others and isolation into community. This attention, as George Buttrick notes, requires that 'intercession be specific, it is pondered: it requires us to bear on our heart the burden of those for whom we pray . . . genuine love sees faces, not a mass' (Buttrick, 1993). Intercession is from the Latin *intercedere*, to 'go between', 'to intervene on behalf of another', or in relationships simply to 'exist between'. In intercessory prayer we stand on behalf of another, 'between' another and God, calling God's attention to another and, no doubt, calling another's attention to God. In many forms of Christian spirituality, Mary is a model of this balance 'existing between' humanity and God.

Margaret Guenther notes that intercession is 'a small experience of watching at the foot of the cross; we grow in awareness of the suffering of others' (Guenther, 1998, ch. 3). Simone Weil, one of our most astute writers on intercessory prayer, says simply that prayer *is* 'attention to others'. In her essay, 'Reflections on the right use of school studies,' she writes that 'the key to a Christian conception of studies is the realization that prayer consists of attention'. Such attention is, for Weil, that ability to 'exist between' on behalf of others, to ask of another, 'What are you going through?' Their answer becomes our prayer of intercession.

Intercession has a long history in the Hebrew Bible. Abraham, for instance, pleads for Sodom (Gen. 18.22–23) and Moses frequently mediates and 'stands between God' on behalf of the Hebrew people. In the New Testament, Jesus models intercessory prayer by, for example, praying for Peter, for his disciples' sanctification and for forgiveness of others. Paul tells us that it is 'Christ Jesus, who died, yes, who was raised, who is at the right hand of God, who indeed intercedes for us' (Rom. 8.34). The writer of Hebrews reminds us that it is Jesus, the eternal priest who 'always lives to make intercession' (Heb. 7.25). Struggling to enunciate the difference Jesus makes, Richard Foster notes: 'The new dimension is this: Jesus is entering his eternal work as Intercessor before the throne of God, and, as a result, we are enabled to pray for others with an entirely new authority. What I am trying to say is that in our ministry of intercession . . . we pray by faith alone – Jesus Christ our eternal Intercessor is responsible for our prayer life' (*Prayer*, ch. 17). Nonetheless, in praying for others we soon realize that the results are not always what we hoped; often the results seem non-existent.

To that perennial question of why our prayers at times seemingly go unanswered, Christian spiritual teachers recommend persistence in a twofold meditation: first, meditation on human suffering and misery; and second, meditation on divine mercy. The first is conversation with God concerning humanity's misfortune through recollection of fear, sorrow and humility, and, second, conversation with God centred on divine blessings through recollection of joy, wonder and love (cf. Chase, 2003, ch. 6). The wisdom of the Christian spiritual tradition has always noted that prayer is unanswered only from our limited perspective. Meditation on sorrows and blessings in the context of intercessory prayer is an excellent example of this. Answers are not always clear, yet in intercessory prayer we 'meet in a space between'; what we find there is Christ on our behalf; what we find there is the answer of relationship and love.

During the medieval period the Church prayed not only through Christ but also in the name of angels, Mary and the saints who were seen to 'exist between' those in need and a caring God. Reformation leaders such as Luther and Calvin insisted that intercessory prayer be addressed only to God in the name of Christ through the Holy Spirit. At its core, intercessory prayer is a response to the God who promises to attend to us in our weakness and our poverty. It is conversation with God that clarifies for us that we desire for others far more than we are able to give them ourselves.

The Anglican William Law, in fact, considers intercession to be an exercise of universal love and that intercession amends and reforms the hearts of those who use it. 'For a frequent intercession with God,' Law teaches, 'earnestly beseeching him to forgive the sins of all humankind, to bless them with his providence, enlighten them with his spirit, and bring them to everlasting happiness, is the divinest exercise that the heart of man can be engaged. For there is nothing that makes us love a man so much as praying for him' (Law, 1978, ch. 31).

See also **Charity; Compassion; Love; Mercy; Prayer; Reconciliation; Suffering.**

———

George A. Buttrick, 'Prayer' in Richard Foster and James Bryan Smith (eds), *Devotional Classics: Selected Readings for Individuals and Groups*, San Francisco: HarperSanFrancisco, 1993, pp. 100–5; Steven Chase, *Contemplation and Compassion: The Victorine Spiritual Tradition*, Maryknoll: NY: Orbis Books, 2003; Margaret Guenther, *The Practice of Prayer*, Cambridge, MA: Cowley Publications, 1998; William Law, *A Serious Call to a Devout and Holy Life*, ed. Paul G. Stanwood, New York: Paulist Press, 1978; Simone Weil, 'Reflections on the right use of school studies with a view to the love of God' in George A. Panichas (ed.), *The Simone Weil Reader*, New York: David McKay Company Inc., 1977, pp. 44–52.

STEVEN CHASE

Interiority

Interiority or the interior life is a helpful concept in the study of spirituality in both Christian and non-Christian contexts. Many spiritual writers in both the East and West, especially in the religions of India, use the concept. Although many of the non-Christian religions speak of the interior life, the context is radically different. With Buddhists, for example, interiority means to retreat from the world into a state of nirvana. For Christians the interior life is more a state of prayer than a state of being.

The Scriptures are replete with ideas about the interior life. In the Old Testament with its accent on holistic anthropology, the human person is considered in its totality. The Graeco-Hellenistic dualism, splitting body and soul, is not apparent. The human body is animated by some kind of spiritual principle, of which three Hebrew words (*nephes, ruah, leb*) give indications of the nuanced understanding of the ancient Hebrews as well as the variations in meaning.

The principle of vitality (Heb. *nephes*; Gk. *psyche*; Lat. *anima*) is often translated as soul but one must remember that the Greek dualistic concept of body/soul was foreign to the Semitic mind. The soul, rather than being added to the body, denotes the entire human person. It is necessary to conceive of this as the force of animation closely associated with every living creature, but especially with humans. The term came to be identified with the living individual or the inner feelings associated with a person, such as joy, rest, contentment, love, sadness, pain, bitterness and anxiety. The wide variety of feelings affects the *nephes* in its relationship with God. For example the *nephes* wants God (Isa. 26.9), thirsts for God (Ps. 42.2–3; 63.2), raises itself toward God (Ps. 25.1; 86.4), and rests in God (Ps. 62.2; 63.9). As the principle of vitality, the *nephes* is the spiritual power of a person and the resonator of one's experience with God.

Breath or wind (Heb. *ruah*; Gk. *pneuma*; Lat. *spiritus*) indicates the spirit and is important in the spiritual history of Israel meaning both the spirit of God and of the human person. Literally it means breath, wind or blowing, and it too is a force that provides vital energy from God to all living creatures. Death results when God recalls this breath (Gen. 6.3; Ps. 104.29; Job 34.14). Health and vitality are strictly dependent upon the presence and the dynamism of God's *ruah*. This breath exists in people without belonging to them, as though it was an independent agent. Attached to this concept is the notion of interiority in both the intellectual and affective dimensions. One speaks of the human *ruah* as a stable spiritual disposition and the biblical expression 'a new spirit' (Ezek. 11.19; 18.31) indicates a renewal of the spiritual being in humans. The highest spiritual activities are associated and individuated in the human person, joining again to the *nephes* in its personal and interior aspects.

There is a tendency to oppose the spirit from the flesh, but even the Hebrew notion of flesh (*basar*), due to the psychosomatic unity of the human person, regards the flesh as a spiritual entity. Often the term flesh indicates the human person in its fragility and its finitude. To the Semitic mind the flesh experiences many feelings, such as trembling before God (Ps. 119.120) and longing for God like a dry land (Ps. 63.2). For the people of the Old Testament, the body is far from being a prison for the soul.

The richest term for indicating interiority is the heart (Heb. *leb*; Gk. *kardia*; Lat. *cor*). Being the seat of the emotions, the heart was destined to become the symbol of that which is the core of one's being, the most intimate part of the person that enters into dialogue with God. Much more than simply the affective centre in the person, the heart for the Semitic mind was the interior of the person. Apart from feelings, the heart is also the intellectual principle. God gives a heart with which to think (Ecclus. 17.6). A 'hardened heart' can mean a closed mind as well as someone embittered and calloused. The heart is the source of one's consciousness, intelligent and free personality, the place of decision-making, where the Law is written and where the mysterious actions of God take place.

The Semitic ideas mentioned above are the backdrop for the New Testament understanding of interiority. Against the Jewish dietary laws, Jesus insists that it is not something that enters the body from outside which makes a person good, but that which comes from within (Matt. 23.27–28). Criticizing the Pharisees, Christ demands that they look at the interior of the cup and dish, and not simply the exterior (Luke 11.39). The treasure, representing that which is contained within the human heart, and the good earth, which receives the Word, are images that capture the idea of the interior life.

In the writings of St Paul further development is noted concerning the notion of interiority. Often confused with Hellenistic dualism, St Paul avoids any opposition between body and soul. Although Paul distinguishes between those who are under the power of the flesh (*sarkikoi*) and those under the influence of the spirit (*pneumatikoi*), he holds for a psychosomatic unity of the human person, maintaining the delicate balance of the constitutive parts of the person (*sarx* and *soma, psyche, nous* and *suneidesis*). Paul uses the expression three times 'the interior person' (*ho eso anthropos*, Rom. 7), which is not of biblical origin. In describing the fact of interior alienation of a sinner, there is a connection between the interior person and the transforming power of the Spirit (Eph. 3.16). The interior person is always in a state of becoming, whereby one becomes interiorized to the degree that one is rooted in the love of God (*agape*) and knows the love of Christ that surpasses all human understanding. The interior person is someone filled with the Spirit of regeneration (Titus 3.5) and who moves toward the fullness of God (Eph. 3.19). The dialectic opposing the old Adam against the new Adam is related to the idea of baptism as a progressive change or metamorphosis, where the believer is identified with Christ as an icon of God.

In the Christian tradition, St Teresa of Avila (d. 1582) is certainly one writer who explicitly mentions the interior life. In her work *The Interior Castle*, the principal source of her mature thought on the spiritual life, she accentuates the life of prayer. The interior castle represents the soul in which the Trinity dwells and where one enters into greatest intimacy with God through prayer. When one has passed through the various mansions of the castle, one enters into the most interior chamber where one is most centred with oneself. In her *Way of Perfection*, written about a decade earlier, Teresa instructs her nuns on the spiritual life and how to pray. Using the Our Father as an instrument, the prayer becomes a means of getting in touch with one's interiority and centring oneself in God.

In a similar vein, St John of the Cross (d. 1591), in his *Dark Night of the Soul*, speaks eloquently of the interior life. In his mystical order, the goal of the Christian is to find God who dwells within the soul and to exclude anything that is exterior to the soul. The illumination about which St John speaks is found in the darkness of one's interiority, which he calls the soul. The task of the mystic is toward passivity, allowing God's light to illumine the darkness of the soul.

St Francis de Sales (d. 1622) identifies interiority with the quiet where prayer originates. In his *Treatise on the Love of God*, he instructs the Philothea to actively concentrate on prayer. In opposition to mystical passivity, the spiritual person is active in seeking an intimate rapport with God in the interiority of the heart.

See also **Mysticism** (*essay*); **Contemplation; Public Life and Spirituality.**

Francis de Sales, *Introduction à la vie devote*, Paris: Les Belles Lettres, 1961; Kathleen Healy, *Entering the Cave of the Heart*, New York and Mahwah, NJ: Paulist Press, 1986; Kieran Kavanaugh and Otilio Rodriguez, trans. *The Collected Works of Saint John of the Cross*, Washington, DC: ICS Publications, 1991; Xavier Léon-Dufour, *Dictionary of Biblical Theology*, New York: Seabury Press, 1973; Dorothea Olkowski and James Morley (eds), *Merleau-Ponty, Interiority and Exteriority, Psychic Life and the World*, Albany, NY: State University of New York Press, 1999; Teresa of Avila, *The Interior Castle*, trans. Mirabai Starr, New York: Riverhead Books, 2003.

MICHAEL S. DRISCOLL

Irish Spirituality

At the threshold of the third millennium CE, we encounter Irish Christian Spirituality as we would an intricate design from the Book of Kells; at first glance it appears chaotic and unstructured but a closer look reveals a myriad of discernible elements – magnificently interwoven – in constant movement. These elements have been influenced by the physical, social, historical and cultural story of Ireland. Some have their origin in pre-Christian Celtic and Celto-Megalithic belief and ritual such as the continued faith practice of pilgrimage at holy well and mountain top or the customary making of a cross in honour of the national female patron, St Brigit, at the threshold of spring. Others such as the practice of Christian meditation based on John Main or Tony de Mello are more recent acquisitions to Irish Christian spirituality. Yet other elements such as the formerly widespread devotional practices of the nineteenth-century Catholic Church in Ireland have been in steady decline since the Second Vatican Council.

Indeed, nowadays, some commentators speak about Ireland as a post-Christian society and, given the dwindling attendance at the main Christian Churches on the island plus the growth of the 'Celtic Tiger' economy and its concomitant consumerism, a new secularism is being realized. Furthermore, the ever-changing demographics in Western Europe, in particular the recent influx of migrant workers and refugees from Eastern Europe and Africa, is leading to a new multiculturalism in Irish society which in its turn affects the existing spirituality. One could say that Irish Christian spirituality at the threshold of the third millennium stands itself at a threshold – the threshold between death and resurrection. While old institutional practices die and the seeds of change and renewal are present and germinating in the Christian tradition on the island, nonetheless, a new spiritual vacuum is emerging at the heart of Irish life. How it may be filled and what role Christianity may play remains to be seen. For now we can only record what is; remember what has been and pause for reflection on the way to the future.

The introduction of Christianity into Ireland in the fourth and fifth centuries CE, saw the transition of Irish society from an oral-based Gaelic culture to a literary one. The subsequent growth of the monastic movement in Ireland and the flourishing of learning yielded a large corpus of material, unrivalled in Europe, in Old Irish and Medieval or Hiberno-Latin.

Our material reveals a spirituality in which there exists a strong sense of divine immanence. God is not merely experienced as transcendent but also as immediate, being mediated through creation in all its forms. As the sixth-century Irish missionary to continental Europe, Columbanus, reputedly tells us, 'If you want to understand the Creator know created things' (F. Ní Chuill in Clancy, 1999, p. 183). God is popularly referred to in the literature as *Rí na nDúl* or *Rí na Bhfeart* (King of the Creatures or King of the Heavens), epithets which remain to the present day in the Gaelic language.

It is no surprise, therefore, that there is a strong emphasis in the early Christian period on the Trinity and the holism which it confers. This echoes the pre-Christian emphasis on divine immanence and the triplication of Celtic deities. An early creed attributed to St Patrick is strongly trinitarian as the following extract, translated from the original, indicates:

Our God, God of all men,
God of heaven and earth, sea and rivers,
God of sun and moon and all the stars,
God of high mountains and of lowly valleys,
God over heaven, and in heaven, and under heaven . . .

He inspires all things,
He quickens all things,
He is over all things,
He supports all things . . .

He has a Son
Coeternal with Himself, like to Himself;
Not junior is Son to Father,
Nor Father to the Son.

And the Holy Spirit
Breather in them;
Not separate are Father
And Son and Holy Spirit.
(trans. Carney, 1967).

A comprehensive collection of marginal quatrains and poems from this early monastic period also reveals an intimate awareness of divinity in nature. In this example, bird song – the totem of pre-Christian Gaelic spirituality – invites the poet to prayer:

Learned in Music sings the lark,
I leave my cell to listen;
His open beak spills music hark!
Where Heaven's bright cloudlets glisten.

And so I'll sing my morning psalm
That God bright heaven may give me
And keep me in eternal calm
And from all sin relieve me.
(trans. Flower, 1994)

Hospitality, a perennial characteristic of the Irish, and already of key significance under the Gaelic or Brehon law, emerges also as a central tenet of Christian spirituality in the early period. An early poem highlights the perception that every stranger is Christ:

Chonaic mé coigríoch inné,
Chuir mé bia in áit ithidh dó, deoch in áit óil,
Ceol in áit éisteachta,
Agus in ainm naofa na tríonóide
Bheannaigh sé mé fhéin is mo theach,
Mo ní is mo dhuine,
'S dúirt an fhuiseog, 's í ag seinm;
Gur minic minic minic, a thagann Críost
I riocht an choigríochaigh.

I saw a stranger yesterday,
I put food for him in the eating place
Drink in the drinking place,
Music in the listening place,
And in the holy name of the trinity,
He blessed me my family and people,
And the lark said as she sang:
Often often often Christ comes in the form of a stranger. (trans. Seán Ó Duinn, unpublished)

The all-pervading presence of the divine and the closeness of the otherworld also allows for easy and direct access to the Godhead on the part of the individual and this is strongly indicated in the large corpus of early prayers found uniquely in the Celtic languages. Among these we find the *luireach* (breastplate), a genre of prayer which characteristically calls on the protection of the entire otherworld including the Trinity, angels, communion of saints and ancestors, to assist body, mind and spirit with every action of the night and day. These early prayers are echoed through the millennia in the Irish language folk prayers collected in the twentieth century by an t-Ath Diarmuid Ó Laoghaire sj and are still found and recited among the elderly in Irish-speaking districts.

Pilgrimage both maritime and overland is a common practice in the early period, the remnants of which remain with us today in pilgrimages such as those to Croagh Patrick, Mount Brandon, Lough Derg, Liscannor, Faughart, Glendalough, Ballyvourney and Glen Colmcille to name but a few. This practice is not only inspired by the biblical call to 'the way' but is also influenced by the *imram* (sea voyage) and *eachtra* (land adventure) which were part of Gaelic heroic literature and tradition. In particular there is a strong identification with the journey of Christ who is recognized as the new hero – and the greatest of all. There is a special empathy with his passion and the concept of suffering with him is a central element in Gaelic spirituality.

The early period is characterized then by an extraordinary number of Irish men and women who not only go on short-term pilgrimage but who chose a form of permanent exile or 'pilgrimage for Christ's sake' (*peregrinatio pro Christo*), giving their lives entirely to God by separating themselves from family and kin and pursuing asceticism. By seeking out a *dísert* (desert/wilderness) of mountain, woodland or rocky island, men and women such as Éanna, Brigit, Colmcille (Columba), Íde, Cillian, Caomhán Columbanus, Darerca and Samthann, among others, were responsible for spreading the wisdom of the gospel throughout Ireland, Britain and Europe. Echoing the suffering of Christ their spirituality was strongly penitential and included rigorous fasting and prayer. This penitential tradition eventually led to the *Céili Dé* (culdee) movement of the eighth and ninth centuries and was to influence European Christianity by stressing the importance of private confession, penitence and the need for *anamchairdeas* (soul friendship or spiritual direction).

Responsibility to the dead was also a key element in the spirituality of the early period. A legacy of the pre-Christian era, Gaelic culture held that the soul's journey did not end in this life but continued in the next world, and to the present day when someone dies it is said in the Gaelic language, 'Tá sé imithe ar shlí na fírinne' ('He is gone on the path of truth'). The Rule attributed to St Colmcille, for example, tells us we should intercede for the dead 'with fervour, as if every one of the faithful who died were a special friend of yours'. Equally the ancestors were understood to be assisting the living and were deemed to be especially close at threshold times in the calendar. This belief is evident, particularly, in the folk custom surrounding the Celtic Quarter Day Festivals; St Brigit's Day (*Féile Bríde*), May Day (*Bealtaine*), Lughnasa and Hallowe'en (*Samhain*), elements of which were Christianized and remain with us to the present day.

The celebrated poems of Blathmac show us that by the eighth century there is a 'mature devotion' to Our Lady and a compassion for her suffering son:

Come to me, loving Mary
That I may keen with your very dear one.
Alas that your Son should go to the cross,
He was a great didadem,
A beautiful hero . . .

It would have been fitting for God's elements,
The beautiful sea,
The blue heavens, the present earth,
That they should change their aspect when keening their hero . . . (trans. Carney, 1967)

Jesus is depicted with his mother throughout the early period and referred to as Mac Muire (the son of Mary), Muire being the unique title given to Mary in the Gaelic language. Mary is portrayed as primordial mother, an image more akin to Orthodox representations of her than to the traditional Roman Catholic one. The status afforded Mary in the early spirituality is reminiscent of the status afforded the Irish mythological goddess where we find 'the notion of a great goddess who was mother of the Gods is a central element' (Mac Cana, 1970, p. 86). The concept of Mary as primordial mother is conveyed in the traditional saying still found among Gaelic language speakers in Ireland, 'Tá Dia láidir agus tá máthair mhaith aige' ('God is good and he has a great mother').

The Viking invasions and settlements of the ninth to eleventh centuries and the Norman invasion of the twelfth century signalled the decline of the old native monastic system and opened the way for the introduction of a newly reformed parochial and diocesan structure. The reforms instituted by SS Cellach and Malachy in the twelfth century were accompanied by the arrival of continental orders, bringing new spiritualities, among them the Franciscans, Dominicans, Augustinians and Cistercians. The old themes also remained: 'Again and again we find old attitudes surviving: pilgrimage, asceticism, fasting, alms giving, hospitality, devotions – both native and foreign – to Christ in his passion, to Mary and to the saints and in relation to the after-life. All of these and more were part and parcel of the furniture of Irish Christianity' (Ó Ríordáin, 1998, p. 56).

By the sixteenth century England had colonized and consolidated her rule in Ireland and the Anglican Church in Ireland became the established religion. It was followed within a century by the arrival of other Christian denominations including Presbyterian and Quaker. The Catholic Church which still commanded the loyalty of almost all the people was outlawed and subjected to a penal code. Thus the seeds of ethnic division based on religious difference were sown on the island; in general the Gaelic Irish tended to be Catholic and the new settlers Protestant. The persecution of the Catholic Church for more than a hundred years led to a consolidation of traditional folk practices among the faithful, such as holy well devotion, eucharistic celebration at mass rocks, familial and communal recitation of the rosary and other folk prayers. Emphasis on the passion of Christ continued to pervade the spirituality and was further intensified by the suffering experienced by the people.

Catholic emancipation in 1829 witnessed an institutional renewal in that Church. If the earlier Church had been rooted in the Gaelic culture the collapse of that order and decline of the language meant that this later Church would now look firmly beyond the Alps to Rome in what is referred to as Ultramontanism. Presided over by Archbishop Paul Cullen who was 'firmly imbued with the Roman outlook' the period, sometimes described as the Cullenization of Ireland, concerned itself with the building of an organized and disciplined church with a hierarchy firmly aligned to Rome. Structures were renewed, clergy trained, churches built, and religious orders such as the Redemptorists, Jesuits, Vincentians, Carmelites and Dominicans were invited to expand and participate in the work of reform and popular renewal.

The absence of the Gaelic language meant that devotional literature and practices from Britain and Europe found a new niche in nineteenth-century Irish spirituality. Ultramontanism combined itself, then, with the puritanical cultural Victorianism of the age and a new Catholic piety less tolerant than before emerged. The whole resulted in a devotional revolution which 'moulded the people into a thoroughly sacramental and mass-going church; Sodalities, jubilees, benediction, stations of the cross, novenas, scapulars, missals, prayer books, medals, holy pictures all became part of the Irish Catholic spiritual diet' (Ó Ríordáin, 1998, p. 110). Vocations increased, missionary and teaching orders such as the Mercy and Presentation Sisters, the Christian Brothers, St Patrick's Missionary Society and the Medical Missionaries of Mary were founded and expanded.

Having experienced persecution for so long it is unsurprising that the new-founded Catholicism consolidated itself around the emerging independent Irish state over which it maintained a close influence until the latter part of the twentieth century. Following the Second Vatican Council Catholic religious observances relaxed considerably, and in more recent decades Catholics have enjoyed a looser and, one could say, a more balanced relationship with the institution – an institution which in itself has suffered its own troubles. A new spirit of ecumenism also encouraged by Vatican II gradually combined itself with an economically successful independent Ireland, and the need for conciliation, inclusion and religious toleration on the whole island was recognized. In the early twenty-first century the new tolerance is reflected in the birth of 'The peace process' on the island. Irish national television, for example, now facilitates all the major religions. The Catholic angelus bell sounds daily on the national airwaves but it is now termed 'a pause for prayer' and the images conveyed are multi-denominational.

Since the 1980s a decline in attendance and in vocations has been experienced in the main Christian Churches on the island. Roman Catholic, Church of Ireland, Presbyterian, Methodist and Quaker suffer the same fate. Among the under-forties in particular there are a majority that could be termed à la carte Christians. These are those who tend to appear solely in church to mark the rites of passage – baptism, marriage and funerals – or to mark the central turning points in the liturgical calendar such as Christmas and Easter.

The decline in Christian observance has been accompanied by the emergence of a new spiritual vacuum at the heart of modern Irish life. The void is perhaps partially being filled by the addictions of consumerism, drug abuse and alcoholism, all of which experience higher rates than ever before as do the rates of suicide among the young and depression and loneliness among the elderly. The frenetic pace of modern life means quality time for self and 'the other' has diminished greatly. Familial dysfunction and marital breakdown is widespread and 'Ireland of the welcomes' struggles to survive as it encounters the flood tide of immigration. The gap between rich and poor grows wider and although Ireland is 'awash' with money there are constantly raised Christian and humanitarian voices who remind us that we are creating a less caring society.

Yet while there is a tangible sense of being in a spiritual wilderness the seeds of renewal and change can also be felt. For those who still participate in the Christian life, some of the themes of the early period survive and enjoy a revitalisation under the popular banner of 'Celtic Christianity' or 'Celtic spirituality'. This essentially represents a return to some of the spiritual riches of the early Christian period in Ireland, a new embracing of the native tradition. Being pre-Reformation, 'the Celtic' also provides a safe point of contact between all the Christian churches on the island.

Women both lay and religious within the various Christian denominations are also re-examining their role and re-empowering themselves vis-à-vis male-dominated institutions. Feminist theology is alive and well. In the Catholic Church in particular some women choose to remain and work within present church structures while others have withdrawn to create their own worship and liturgical celebrations.

The monastic life once again is also proving an attractive option. Offering an alternative in an otherwise hectic world, religious orders such as the Benedictines and Cistercians, in stark contrast with others of their contemporaries, enjoy a rise in pilgrim numbers and in vocations.

For the majority who do not participate in the Christian churches, however, the spiritual hunger is perhaps best evidenced in the quest for healthier ways of living, including the pursuit of alternative medicine, yoga, meditation, aboriginal cultures, Eastern mysticism, care for the environment, other major religions and the creative arts. Many of these themes also find their way into the Christian life and in the twenty first century theological institutes tend to offer a cocktail of courses on everything from Enneagram studies to Christian meditation, sacred dance, Scripture classes, psychosynthesis and so on.

Encountering Irish Christian spirituality at the threshold of the third millennium is, as suggested at the outset, akin to encountering an intricate design from the Book of Kells – a certain chaos is apparent, but nonetheless an order emerges from within it. Currently a spiritual vacuum exists but the richly coloured threads of past and present intertwine and grow themselves into a new creation – the shape of which is not yet known but which doubtlessly will possess its own glorious radiance.

For the present we sit as our ancestors did five thousand years ago in the dark Megalithic mound of Brú na Bóinne (New Grange) awaiting the light of the sun or as the Celtic hero Fionn sat awaiting the Salmon of Knowledge or as the 'Cry of the Irish' awaited the salvation brought by Patrick. We are to use the Gaelic word for contemplation 'ag rinnfheitheamh' (at the point of waiting) . . . Solas na bhFlaitheas Dúinn . . . May the Light of Heaven be ours!

See also **Celtic Spirituality; English Spirituality; Scottish Spirituality; Welsh Spirituality.**

James Carney, *Medieval Irish Lyrics with the Irish Bardic Poet*, Dublin: Dolmen Press, 1967; Padraigín Clancy (ed.), *Celtic Threads; Exploring the Wisdom of Our Heritage*, Dublin: Veritas, 1999; Kevin Danaher, *The Year in Ireland: Irish Calendar and Customs*, Cork: Mercier Press, 1972; Robin Flower, *The Irish Tradition*, Dublin: The Lilliput Press, 1994; Proinsias Mac Cana, *Celtic Mythology*, London: Hamlyn, 1970; Michael Maher (ed.), *Irish Spirituality*, Dublin: Veritas, 1981; Robert O' Driscoll (ed.), *The Celtic Consciousness*, New York: George Braziller, 1985; Seán Ó Duinn, *Where Three Streams Meet: Celtic Spirituality*, Dublin: Columba Press, 2000; Peter O' Dwyer, *Towards a History of Irish Spirituality*, Dublin: Columba Press, 1995; Diarmuid Ó Laoghaire, *Ár bPaidreacha Dúchais*, Dublin: Foilseachain Abhair Spioradalta, 1982; John J. Ó Ríordáin, *Irish Catholic Spirituality: Celtic and Roman*, Dublin: Columba Press, 1998; Seán Ó Súilleabháin, *Irish Folk Custom and Belief*, Dublin: Cultural Relations Committee, 1977.

.PADRAIGÍN CLANCY

Islam and Christianity

If Christians can allow themselves to go beyond negative stereotypes of Islam, generated by the media and much popular Christian teaching, and accentuated since the attack on the twin towers on 9.11.2001, there are wide challenges open to them from Muslim spirituality. They need also to go beyond a theological exclusivism, which denies that Muslims worship the same God. If such thinking is in their minds, learning from the other becomes ruled out a priori. Disciplines of prayer, which encourage worship of the demonic or illusory, become themselves dangerous or fanatical. For learning to take place, the Muslim affirmation that the God of Abraham and Moses is also the God of Jesus and Muhammad needs to be accepted as authentic, even if we differ radically on the person of Jesus. Christians need to accept that the oneness of God is something they hold as a central concept with Muslims, even though they experience that God in three ways; and that all Christian prayer is addressed to that one God, whether affirmed as Father, Jesus or Spirit. Prayer is not a tritheist activity. Nor does all authentic prayer have to end 'through Jesus Christ our Lord'. Such would rule out the Lord's Prayer and the daily Jewish prayers of Jesus. Inclusively, we can use such phrases as 'in thy name, O Lord', 'for thy name's sake' or 'in thy merciful Name', in a Muslim–

Christian context. What is implicit for Christians does not always have to be made explicit.

What can Christians then learn from Muslim tradition and practice, and in particular, the five pillars of Islamic faith?

Chris Hewer has summed up the essence of Islam in just one sentence: 'Islam means to live a fully human and balanced life in perfect harmony with God, all other human beings and the whole of creation.' This is an ideal often far from being lived out in practice. But the Christian who moves close to faithful local Muslims can catch glimpses of this vision. This is seen visibly in lives focused upon prayer, symbolized by the *adhan*, the call to prayer, the same throughout the world, with its public witness, 'Come ye unto prayer', with the early morning assertion that 'prayer is better than sleep'. This universal sound demonstrates a willingness to be counter-cultural, within a secular world, and is a challenge to Christians.

Even more challenging is the practice of *salat*, the five-times-a-day prayer, whether in mosque, house or elsewhere. Coming together is preferable, and expected on Friday. The identity of a religious community is affirmed, and their obeisance before God. Such is shown in bodily postures and in the requirement that all sit in rows, without gaps, where social distinctions are broken down. All are equally nothing, before the God who is Lord of all the worlds and master of the day of judgement. To him is owed praise and worship, from him is required guidance and grace. This is emphasized, above all, in the repeated act of prostration, as the forehead touches the ground itself, the proudest part of the human form touches the dust (*sajdah*). This is the sacrament of submission to the almightiness of God. The Christian may think of the prayer of the publican, 'God, be merciful to me a sinner' (Luke 18.13), and he went away justified.

Equally powerful is how formal prayer ends, with the gesture of looking over the shoulder, to right and left, as neighbour and angels are greeted, and blessed. Here there is indicated that great sense of community, with both seen and unseen. Christians have reintroduced the Peace in the Eucharist, with a similar meaning. But the sense of community is often lessened, by lack of proximity to other worshippers.

Much too is to be learnt by fulfilment of the obligation to pray, whether a mosque is available or not. Whether on a journey, in factory or fields, whether with an imam present or not, the same gestures are offered. The saying of Muhammad is that 'the whole earth has been rendered for me a Mosque, pure and clean'. The Christian may be challenged to recall in the encounter between Jesus and the Samaritan woman, Jesus affirms that true worship is neither on Mount Gerezim nor in Jerusalem, but in Spirit and truth (John 4.24).

The Christian may reflect on the obligation to pray 'in season and out', and whether that is being fulfilled, and how prayer and worship are not just about how one is feeling. They may be reminded of the word 'Office', which means 'duty' applied to the monastic times of prayer, and the old matins and evensong. Islam specifies that prayer must be preceded by *niyyah*, 'right intention', and that is enough. In the words of the mystic Rumi, 'Intention is the root of the matter . . . words are the branch.'

This concentration is helped by the practice of *wudu*, ritual washing, as required before all formal prayer. This is primarily to emphasize purity, and if no water is available, clean sand or earth is permissible. Cleanliness of the body becomes linked with cleanliness of the mind, thought and motive. The meaning can remind Christians of the opening eucharistic prayer: 'Almighty God, to whom all hearts are open, all desires known, and from whom no secrets are hid, cleanse the thoughts of our hearts, by the inspiration of your Holy Spirit, that we may perfectly love you, and worthily magnify your holy Name.'

According to some Muslim interpretations a woman's prayer is preferable in her house rather than the mosque, resulting in her not taking part in congregational prayers. However, local customs and traditions perhaps play the major role in such decisions. This is difficult for Christians to understand, and not acceptable to some Muslim women also. But faithful prayer at home can enable the practice to be introduced to children, and the home to have a strongly spiritual dimension, something Christians in the West at least have largely lost.

Key also is *dua*, spontaneous devotional prayer. Kenneth Cragg, former Bishop in Egypt, is the pioneer and most influential of twentieth-century Christians in responding to the theology and spirituality of Islam. He divides *dua* into prayer of 'praise, penitence and petition'. It is offered spontaneously and freely, in the mosque, after formal prayers, and on other occasions. It centres upon 'calling upon the name of God', and includes devotional exercises related to the ninety-nine beautiful names of God. Invoking these names takes the devotee to the heart of Muslim piety, fulfilling the Qu'ranic call to 'desire the face of God'. Allah cannot be imagined or pictured; but these characteristics can be recited as human language allows. The Christian can respond with warmth to most of the names, even if sometimes the interpretation may somewhat differ. The heart is found in these two, *Al-Rahim* and *Al-Rahman*, meaning respectively 'mercy in action' and 'divine mercy in essence' – 'the merciful one' and 'the Lord of mercy'. Christians see God's essence also worked out in doing, above all through the person of Jesus: 'He that hath seen me, hath seen the Father.' One Christian response to the ninety-nine names has been to compose ninety-nine beautiful names for Jesus, and to recite them with devotion.

The practice of fasting, as required in Ramadan, is often understood by Christians only in a limited and sometimes negative way. It is seen as life-denying and oppressive, another example of a religion of law and not grace. This is to fail completely to catch the essence of this remarkable annual period, when a large proportion of Muslims willingly change priorities. Fasting should go along with a renewed commitment to prayer, spirituality and the reading of Scripture. The rhythm of life slows, to demonstrate its aim is to honour God, not to be successful in a worldly way, or attend endless meetings. The symbolism of *Iftar*, the breaking of the fast, displays a sacramental feel to the Christian fortunate enough to attend, as does the evening celebration meal. All this reaches its peak in the last ten days of the month, as the Scriptures are read right through, and some spend several nights in the confinement of a mosque. Congregational numbers become very high, as Eid al-Fitr, the festival at the end of Ramadan, grows near. Christians also have a long fasting tradition, centred on the penitential seasons of Lent and Advent, and on Fridays. Observing Ramadan can encourage Christians to take their own discipline more seriously. Some Christians have shared in particular days within Ramadan, in solidarity and prayer with Muslims, and have broken the fast with them, in a powerful sign of common commitment to peace and harmony.

Hajj, the pilgrimage to Makkah (formerly Mecca), is easily understandable by Christians. Pilgrimage has long been part of their spirituality, focusing particularly on Jerusalem and the Holy Land. There has been a revival of other pilgrimages in recent years, to places like Iona, Taizé, Assisi and other places associated with saints. Muslim obligation is stronger, for those who have means. Powerfully evident is the unity of purpose, as all Muslim travellers focus on one end.

Zakat, the giving of a fixed percentage of capital, to the poor, is economic, but also spiritual. God is creator and sustainer of all, the benificent one, and we owe all to God. There is a special duty to the poor, the special concern of Allah.

Here there are obvious parallels with the Christian understanding, rediscovered by liberation theology, that God has a bias towards the poor. In each Eucharist, the Christian gives their offering, and the prayer is said, 'All things come from you, and of your own do we give you.' Though other offerings are for all the poor, *Zakat* is for poor Muslims primarily. In Christian tradition likewise, there is an obligation to care for those in need 'who are of the household of faith'; but charities such as Christian Aid and CAFOD care for the poor, of whatever faith. This is increasingly the case with Muslim Aid and Islamic Relief.

Mention should be made of Sufism or *tasawwuf* – the mystical dimension of Islam. Emphasis on personal spiritual experience, illumination and union with God has been an inspiration to Christians who find themselves on a journey of the Spirit, which takes them beyond themselves. Repentance, cleansing of conscience, renunciation of the world, poverty, suffering, absolute trust in God, and acceptance of whatever happens in one's life are the basic characteristics of *tasawwuf*. The writings of Sufis contain metaphors, deeply evocative for Christian mystics, and this has enabled them to share in prayer. The most accessible of Sufi writers is perhaps Imam Al-Ghazzali (1058–1111). Deeply versed in philosophy and theology, his experiences with Sufis in his native Persia transformed his understanding. He remained a strict adherent to Islamic law and practice, but saw the heart of faith in absolute trust in God, and ultimate detachment from material things. One of his famous sayings is, 'Those who are learned about, for example, the laws of divorce, can tell you nothing about the simpler aspects of spiritual life, such as the meaning of sincerity towards God or trust in Him.' Christians may see in his writings a likeness to parts of the Sermon on the Mount.

Islamic spirituality cannot be divorced from the Qu'ran, and there is a long tradition of Christian attempts to grapple with the Qu'ran. This is not always easy, because of the nature of the text and the requirement that the true Qur'an has to be the Arabic text. This is not the case with the New Testament, where the translation is the text. Jesus is the Word of God, and the Gospels and epistles the witness to Jesus. There is also a long tradition of learning from the Hadith, the saying of the prophet, and traditional stories from the life of the prophet. These are often quoted in Muslim-Christian dialogue.

Finally, mention should be made of the first pillar of Islam, the *shahadah*. This is the very short credal statement, of belief in the absolute oneness of God, and in Muhammad as his messenger. At one level, Christians cannot accept this, because of the radically different place they have for Jesus. At another level, they can learn much from the repeated remembrance (*dhikr)* of God, and his absolute otherness, which can be compared with the Jesus prayer, or the Hail Mary. Christians can often domesticate God, and limit him to Jesus or the Holy Spirit. Christians can learn from the simplicity of this statement of belief, repeated every time prayer begins. Even the simplest Christian creeds seem complicated, and it is not surprising that many of those who embrace Islam remark on the attraction of a simple, though clearly not simplistic faith.

See also **Spirituality and the Dialogue of Religions (***essay***); Sufism and Christianity.**

Stuart Brown, *The Nearest in Affection*, Geneva: World Council of Churches, 1994; Kenneth Cragg, *The Call of the Minaret*, New York: Oxford University Press, 1956, new edns, Oxford, 1986, 2000; Kenneth Cragg, *Alive to God*, London, New York, Toronto: Oxford University Press, 1970; revised as *Common Prayer*, Oxford: Oneworld, 1999 (also 41 further books by Cragg); Chris Hewer, *The Essence of Islam*, Hampshire: Many Rooms, 2002; Michael Ipgrave (ed.), *Scriptures in Dialogue*, London: Church House Publishing, 2004; Constance Padwick, *Muslim Devotions*, London: SPCK, 1961, 1969; John Renard, *Seven Doors to Islam*, Berkeley: University of California Press, 1996.

ANDREW WINGATE

Jansenism

The special bowstrung-tight tension between attunement to divine transcendence and moral earnestness seems the core of Jansenist spirituality. Honouring the transcendent pole expresses itself in a profound awareness of human 'nothingness' ('apart from God' is the not always expressed condition) and sinfulness. Nothing creaturely is worthy of God; one can only hope that grace will overlook the unworthiness. On the other hand, rather than succumb to quietistic passivity, the Jansenist responds with earnest asceticism. If one is unworthy, perhaps the tension thus experienced can be relieved through seeking maximal purity of moral effort. But of course, the tension is never quite relieved, for the holy One transcends all creaturely efforts. This spiritual practice, which is not without its 'nobility', all too easily 'damages' one or both poles of the tension. On the one hand, the divine Partner becomes a competitor with the human partner; as the one increases, the other must decrease. This would hardly seem consistent

with the Christian view of a compassionate God. On the other hand, the otiose view of God actually hinders human responsiveness; it cramps human creativity and replaces it with fear and subtle forms of human pride. (This description is offered as a model; wide variations exist in practice.)

Just as extreme quietistic passivity seems a constant tendency in Christian spirituality, so too does moral rigorism of the 'Jansenist' type. Donatism and Pelagianism, for example, would be earlier, analogous examples. It is helpful to speculate on why what technically goes under the name of 'Jansenism' emerged in the seventeenth century, although this exercise is rather speculative, given our lack of precise sociological data. It may well represent a reaction to the growing humanism of the times. Its moral rigorism fascinatingly expresses this humanism, inasmuch as the intensified exercise of human acts places a certain premium on the human dimension in spirituality. On the other hand, the heightened sense of human unworthiness and God's holy otherness serves effectively as a purifying critique and near-rejection of the same humanism. Some have speculated that people of the upper middle class effectively rendered impotent by the absolute French monarchy might well be likely carriers of such a spirituality. They would possess the sense of their human dignity on the one hand and yet their impotency on the other. But this seems at best a partial factor, for Quietists and others also come from this class, and naturally it is the writings of this class that have received attention for the most part. History's 'little people' did not yet have their advocates, as in today's history 'from below'.

'Jansenism' derives from the Flemish theologian Cornelius Jansen (1585–1638), whose posthumously published study of Augustine's anti-Pelagianism (the 1640 *Augustinus)* played a role in the reformist movement centred on the convent of Port-Royal near Paris. A few figures are central. Jean Durvergier de Hauranne (known as the Abbé de St-Cyran, 1581–1643) was a confessor and spiritual director for the nuns at Port-Royal, and his retrieval of Augustine's theology of grace exercised a certain influence. Antoine Arnauld (1612–94) defended St-Cyran after the latter's imprisonment and death, and it was in the midst of this polemic that in 1653 Pope Innocent X condemned five propositions teaching an extreme form of anti-Pelagianism (thought to be Calvinist) 'derived' from Jansen's *Augustinus*. Blaise Pascal's sister was a Port-Royal nun, and of course his satirical attacks against the moral libertinism of the Jesuits, along with his sympathies for the more

Augustinian current, are well known. The later condemnation expressed in the papal bull *Unigenitus* (1713) was directed at statements in Pasquier Quesnel's work *Réflexions morales* (1698). This condemnation indicates that Jansenism had lingering effects beyond the seventeenth century.

Part of the seventeenth-century French reformist movement, as we have noted, Jansenist tendencies seem more neo-patristic and even restorationist in some respects. It was symptomatic of the labyrinthine transition the Church was undergoing at the time; hence its unresolved tensions. Its theology of grace (there were several varieties) was a dimension, but perhaps the deepest theological dimension, of this more ample biblical, patristic, ecclesial and political reform effort. Arnauld's *On Frequent Communion* (1643) was pivotal in shaping the movement, illustrating the sacramental aspect of the reform. ('Delaying absolution' to ensure an authentic confession of 'perfect contrition' before communion was the Jansenist moral strategy in approaching Eucharist.) The spirituality of the French School and Jansenism both share a stress upon interior authenticity, but the difference between them surfaces when one recalls that M. Olier very decisively condemned Arnauld's strictures against frequent communion, bringing down upon him a revolt from his more Jansenist parishioners at St-Sulpice. Olier's eucharistic liberalism was eventually vindicated when Pope Pius X in 1905 authoritatively fostered the same. Some think this 1905 declaration marks at least the official end of Jansenism.

See also **Asceticism; Augustinian Spirituality; Calvinist Spirituality; Discipline; French School of Spirituality; Interiority; Practice, Spiritual; Quietism; Sulpician Spirituality.**

Louis K. Dupré and Don F. Saliers (eds), *Christian Spirituality: Post-Reformation and Modern*, New York: Crossroad, 1989; Louis Cognet, *Post-Reformation Spirituality*, trans. P. Hepburne Scott, Twentieth Century Encyclopedia of Catholicism 41, New York: Hawthorn, 1959; Michel Dupuy, 'Jansénisme' in *DS*, vol. 8, cols. 102–48; Leszek Kolakowski, *God Owes Us Nothing: A Brief Remark on Pascal's Religion and on the Spirit of Jansenism*, Chicago: University of Chicago Press, 1995; Ephraim Radner, 'Jansenism' in *The Dictionary of Historical Theology*, ed. Trevor A. Hart, Grand Rapids, MI: Eerdmans, 2000, pp. 277–9; Alexander Sedgwick, *The Travails of Conscience: The Arnauld Family and the Ancien Régime*, Cambridge, MA: Harvard University Press, 1998.

WILLIAM THOMPSON-UBERUAGA

Jesus and Spirituality

Jesus of Nazareth provides Christians with both pattern and power for their life in the Spirit. Moreover, Christian spirituality normally is understood as an invitation to share in Jesus' relationship with his Father, which is experienced and expressed existentially by means of the loving dynamism of the Spirit. Theologians and biblical scholars debate such issues as the meaning of divine sonship, of Jesus' own spiritual development and self-understanding, of the place of prayer in his life, of his experience of the Spirit, of his suffering and death, and of the resurrection.

Although most experts today would deny access either to the consciousness of Jesus or to the actual course of his spiritual development, at least one gospel writer, Luke, deems it important to trace an itinerary of maturation and change. Additionally, Luke discerns, in the events of Jesus' life, a pattern for the spiritual growth of all Christians who are caught up in the course of salvation history. Evidence for this consists in the striking parallels between the career of Jesus in Luke's Gospel and the happenings to the earliest church communities in the Acts of the Apostles. Thus everyone's spiritual understanding could be enhanced through meditation on the significance of Jesus' dedication to God by his parents as an infant (Luke 2.22–24); on his personal accent to their choice as a 12-year-old boy (Luke 2.40–52); on his empowerment by the Holy Spirit (Luke 3.21–22); on his acceptance of rejection, suffering and death as integral dimensions of his calling and his negotiation of these crises through prayer (Luke 9.19, 22, 44, 51; 18.31–33); and his resurrection, ascension and exaltation (Luke 24; Acts).

Prayer. It is commonly assumed that the gospel writers develop Jesus' prayer sayings and behaviour for the benefit of the early church communities; nevertheless, it seems clear that Jesus himself considered prayer as essential for relationship with God. Jesus values the Temple as a house of prayer (Mark 11.17); he encourages the disciples to be bold in their prayer: 'Whatever you ask in prayer, believe that you receive it, and you will!' (Matt. 7.7–11; Luke 11.9–13); he teaches them the 'Lord's Prayer' (Matt. 6.9–13; Luke 11.2–4); denounces the abuse of prayer (Matt. 6.5–8; cf. Mark 12.40; Luke 20.47); and, in the parable of the friend at midnight, challenges them to 'unashamed prayer' (Luke 18.1–5). Noteworthy also is the fact that, during times of stress, crisis, and decision, Jesus preferred to be alone to pray, either in the desert, or on a mountain, sometimes going off very early in the morning, sometimes spending the night in solitary prayer to his Father (Mark 6.46; 14.32–42; Luke 6.12).

Sonship. As Jeremias discovered, the entire gospel tradition asserts that in *all* his prayers, except the cry of dereliction from the cross, Jesus addressed God as 'Father'. In Jesus' Aramaic, this would be 'Abba', a word very out-of-the-ordinary for Judaism and denoting a connection with God as intimate as that found typically in families. Moreover, Paul makes it clear in Rom. 8.15 and Gal. 4.6 that the Christian's experience of adoption as son or daughter of God depends on and reproduces Jesus' own experience. Paul's assessment is based on the experience of Jesus himself: although Jesus believed his relationship with the Father was somehow unique and distinctive, he at the same time offers with his gift of the Lord's Prayer the conviction that the disciples could pray in the same way he did, their relationship with the Father a consequence of his status as God's son.

Holy Spirit. Most New Testament scholars consider it probable that Jesus not only thought of himself as God's son, but also believed himself to be empowered by the Spirit. Twentieth-century research uncovered that Jesus' consciousness of God's Spirit working through him always had eschatological meaning: in him the last events that would usher in the future kingdom were being inaugurated. Additionally, Jesus' sayings testify that the still-future spiritual realm has become present to believers in his person. Thus, the Spirit manifested as power for Jesus, *authoritative* and *effective* power, specifically, the power to heal persons and make them whole, and while also proclaiming good news to the poor. Furthermore, there is clear continuity between Jesus' actions in the Spirit and that of the earliest church communities. Resurrection appearances and outpourings of the Spirit, taken always as signs of the last times, not only provided the basis for the communal and worship experiences of the earliest Christians, but also empowered them for healing and mission.

Rejection, suffering, death on the cross. 'Who do you say that I am?' Jesus asks the disciples (Luke 9.20). When Peter answers, 'The Messiah of God', Jesus 'commands them not to tell anyone, saying, "The Son of Man must undergo great suffering, and be rejected by the elders, chief priests, and scribes, and be killed, and on the third day be raised"' (Luke 9.21–22). That Jesus must suffer is linked to the eschatology of first-century Christianity. The first moments of the last times, inaugurated in his person, combine an 'already' and a 'not yet' (cf. Paul in 1 Cor. 4, 15; Phil. 3). The New Age breaks in with Jesus, but the Old Age endures until the parousia, his second coming. Even though Jesus is Spirit-empowered, he remains subject to the evil of the present age. The New Testament offers several meanings for Jesus' suffering unto death: two temptation sequences in Luke, one in the wilderness and the other on the cross (4.1–13; 23.35, 36–37, 39), represent Jesus as reversing the sin of Adam and Eve and of Israel through his obedience to the Father. Paul, Hebrews and 1 Peter describe Jesus' suffering as the arena in which obedience to God is perfected as a developing process. Generally speaking for Christians through the centuries, experiences of suffering, rejection, persecution and the threat of death denote the possibility of the loss of those things which one holds dear, to which one is inordinately attached, or through which one grasps one's very identity. Suffering is redemptive when it shatters idols and allows God to draw one to himself alone.

Resurrection. Although difficult to conceptualize and subject to a variety of interpretations from the literal through the metaphoric, the resurrection of Jesus is the sine qua non of Christian spirituality. The New Testament testifies that many people believed Jesus had appeared to them after his death, and that this experience, whatever its status, confirmed both Jesus' proclamation of the nearness of God's spiritual realm and the early Christians' own sense of calling to participate in the events that would bring it in. Furthermore, ongoing Christian spiritual traditions have witnessed to the living, risen Jesus Christ, particularly through lives of holiness.

For example, in the view of many ancient and medieval Christians, Mary Magdalene, the prototypical contemplative, epitomizes the transformative process effected in believers by the resurrection. She, who had desired to hold Jesus when she saw him in the garden on Easter morning, is rebuked: 'Do not hold on to me, because I have not yet ascended to the Father' (John 20.17). Mystics from Hadewijch of Brabant and Julian of Norwich to Teresa of Avila and John of the Cross have believed on the model of Mary Magdalene or the Bride in the Song of Songs, that the crucifying absence of the risen Christ works an ever-deeper union with him.

In his seventh-century *Chapters on Knowledge*, Maximus the Confessor created a theological foundation for the belief in holiness as testimony to the resurrection. Maximus asserts that the resurrection guarantees that Jesus Christ as incarnate Word is not only living and available to believers, but also transforms them and brings about their deification. Maximus correlates the stages of believers' spiritual lives with the form in which Christ is able to come to them, and the highest and most perfect form is as risen Lord. The resurrected Christ so powerfully attracts and arouses love in believers that they are drawn out of themselves.

No one testifies more powerfully than Ignatius of Loyola, the founder of the Jesuits, that such ecstasy is for the sake of generous and consciously chosen service to God. In the Fourth Week of his Spiritual Exercises, Ignatius encourages retreatants to enter into the mystery of the resurrection by asking for the grace to be glad and to rejoice intensely because of the great glory and joy of Christ our Lord. When conjoined with the 'Contemplation to Obtain Love' from the same Week, this imaginative entry into the resurrection is intended to bring about the very qualities of joy, intense delight, mirth and heart-ease after sorrow that must have been Jesus' own resurrection experience. For Ignatius, these empowering moments energized Christians for active service to the Church and to the poor.

This theme has become the cry of liberation theologians throughout the third world – many of them Jesuit-trained. In Latin America, Gustavo Gutiérrez and Jon Sobrino, among others, assert that life lived in resurrection fullness only manifests where people repeat the following of Jesus in the spirit of Jesus on this earth. And that means for the *campesino* that Christians will act in such ways that the sufferings of the poor and outcast will not be for naught, and ultimately will be turned into joy.

See also Abandonment; Contemplation; Cross and Spirituality; Deification; Detachment; Discipleship; Early Christian Spirituality; Formation, Spiritual; Holiness; Ignatian Spirituality; Imitation of Christ; Incarnation; Jesus, Society of; Obedience; Medieval Spirituality in the West; Redemption; Resurrection; Suffering; Unitive Way.

———

James D. G. Dunn, *Jesus and the Spirit*, Philadelphia: Westminster Press, 1975; James D. G. Dunn, *Jesus Remembered*, Grand Rapids, MI: Eerdmans, 2003; Ignacio Ellacuria and Jon Sobrino, *Mysterium Liberationis: Fundamental Concepts in Liberation Theology*, Maryknoll, NY: Orbis Books, 1993; Larry W. Hurtado, *Lord Jesus Christ: Devotion to Jesus in Earliest Christianity*, Grand Rapids, MI: Eerdmans, 2003; John Koenig, *Rediscovering New Testament Prayer: Boldness and Blessing in the Name of Jesus*, Harrisburg, PA: Morehouse, 1998; Mark

McIntosh, 'The Eastering of Jesus: resurrection and the witness of Christian spirituality', *The Downside Review* 112 (January 1994), 44–61; C. H. Talbert, *Literary Patterns, Theological Themes and the Genre of Luke-Acts*, Missoula: Scholars Press, 1974; N. T. Wright, *The Resurrection of the Son of God*, London: SPCK/Minneapolis: Fortress Press, 2003.

ELISABETH KOENIG

Jesus Prayer

The Jesus prayer is an ancient monastic spiritual practice that grew from an ascetical device designed to help concentration to become a central devotional aspect of one of the major schools of medieval (and modern) Byzantine spirituality, that is, the Hesychast movement (*see* Hesychasm). The Jesus prayer itself amounts to the short invocation: 'Lord Jesus Christ, Son of [the Living] God, have mercy on me [a sinner].' The Russian Church generally prefers the longer variant to the shorter Greek standard. In the ancient desert communities, the repetition of such short prayers as this, often allied with numerous prostrations, was a standard way of concentrating the monk's attention during long labours or church vigils. For the early ascetics, particularly in Egypt in the fourth century, the inner appropriation of the word of God was seen to be a primary duty of the monk. To this end short biblical verses would be repeated regularly, and many times over, during the course of any given day. Prolonged reflection on, and repetition of, the phrases was felt to be a way of making the word bear fruit. It was in this generic context that increasing attention came to be paid to the Jesus prayer as a pure biblical summation of the essential gospel. The phrase derives generically from the parable of the Tax Collector and the Publican – where two went in to pray, and one proudly told God how much he had achieved, while the other did not dare look up but merely made a prayer for mercy. Jesus' judgement was that: 'It was this man who went home at peace with God.' The monastic teachers also gave high status to this form of prayer, since the acclamation of Jesus as Lord was, in and of itself, taken to be a sign of high spiritual initiation (cf. 1 Cor. 12.3). The power of the Name, working within the inmost heart of the disciple, was expected to bring about a powerful purification and assistance, simply by its enunciation, so sacred was its character. In this the early Church followed closely in the steps of the ancient scriptural understanding of the power of the divine name, and the awesome holiness evoked by its enunciation. The Jesus prayer soon came to be associated with that Syro-Greek spiritual tradition (one which came to be dominant in Byzantium) known as the 'prayer of the heart'. Using the constantly repeated words of the Jesus prayer, a Byzantine monk would seek for 'Hesychia', that spiritual stillness that would concentrate a person's heart on the divine presence and open up, for the eyes of the soul, the possibility of the vision of divine glory. The close association of these three themes, of the Jesus prayer, the warming of the heart, and the vision of divine light, became constitutive of 'Hesychast' spirituality from the Byzantine medieval period to the present in the Eastern Orthodox world. The Jesus prayer is now practised in most Orthodox countries, and has been spread to the West by such spiritual literature as *The Way of a Pilgrim* and other translations of Russian devotional writing as well as the Greek *Philokalia*. Many practitioners of the Jesus prayer will use a woollen rosary, a woven rope with knots within it (sometimes thirty-three, and sometimes a hundred or up to three hundred), counting off the knots with each recitation of the prayer. Spiritual teachers who advocated the use of the prayer generally called for the recitation to be slow and so sustained that the words 'entered into the heart' with the rhythm of the breathing. In this case it is often presumed that the vocalization was hardly breathed out, and that an inbreath carried the first half of the prayer, while an outbreath marked the second half, with the breathing being slowed from the normal (at all costs avoiding a rapid pace of prayer) and some attempt made to 'pull the mind down into the heart', or to 'keep the mind captive in the heart', meaning a constant search for affective concentration. When the heart had absorbed the rhythm of the prayer after many vocalizations, and the heart was concentrated on the divine presence, the prayer led on into mystical awareness. When the mind 'broke free' by distraction or the 'arising of thoughts', the teachers advocated becoming conscious of the words once again, and beginning the process over until the mind could once again be brought captive into wordless contemplation. Some spiritual teachers of the Middle Ages even called for the adoption of a posture of crouching over a low stool with the head tucked into the chest, to assist the effort of drawing the mind into the heart by a corresponding physical posture. Such a position is highly uncomfortable, and some commentators have suggested it was meant to be adopted only in the early stages of the hours spent in the Jesus prayer. Some modern Orthodox monasteries, developing on the Hesychast tradition (such as the Stavropegal Community of St John in Essex or the Romanian Metropolia in Nuremberg),

have even adopted the public recitation of the Jesus prayer as their central 'office' of daily communal prayer.

See also **Hesychasm; Prayer; Orthodox Spirituality.**

R. French (trans.), *The Way of a Pilgrim*, New York: Seabury Press, 1972; I. Hasher, *The Name of Jesus*, Kalamazoo: Cistercian Publications, 1978; J. A. McGuckin, 'The prayer of the heart in patristic and early Byzantine tradition', in P. Allen, W. Mayer and L. Cross (eds), *Prayer and Spirituality in the Early Church* 2, Brisbane: Centre for Early Christian Studies, Australian Catholic University, 1999, pp. 69–108.

JOHN ANTHONY MCGUCKIN

Jesus, Society of (Jesuits)

The Society of Jesus (unofficially known as the Jesuits) is a Roman Catholic religious order founded in 1540 by Ignatius Loyola (1491–1556) and nine others, including Francis Xavier (1506–52). According to its papal Bull of foundation, the Society's aim is 'the progress of souls in Christian life and faith and the propagation of the faith'; among the means named were 'spiritual exercises and deeds of charity' and 'the spiritual consolation of Christ's faithful in the hearing of confessions'.

The Jesuits' distinctiveness consisted less in a commitment to ministry as such than in their refusal to define their commitment in terms of a specific place. The sharpest expression of this refusal was their abandonment of office in choir in the interest of maximizing their availability for service. Even within Ignatius' lifetime, however, they recognized the need for that ministry to be institutionalized. In particular, they founded schools, which came to exert great cultural influence, especially before the politically motivated suppression of the Jesuits in 1773. Restored in 1814, the Society expanded considerably until the 1960s, developing ministries of various kinds in most countries of the world. In the early years of the twenty-first century, it counts some 20,000 members. Recent trends in recruitment are leading to a sharp numerical decline in first-world countries, and significant expansion in Africa, Asia and Latin America.

If spirituality is understood primarily in terms of schools centred on religious orders, discussion of the Society of Jesus overlaps almost completely with discussion of Ignatian spirituality (*see* Ignatian Spirituality). Tellingly, Ignacio Iparraguirre's classic history of the practice of the Spiritual Exercises (written in Spanish) presents the codification of the Exercises in the so-called Official Directory (1599) as one and the same process as the definitive consolidation of the Society of Jesus's spiritual identity. In an alternative, more inclusive account of spirituality, the spirituality fostered by the Ignatian Exercises is older, more fundamental and broader than Jesuit spirituality. This latter arguably only begins to exist as an identifiable subculture under the leadership of the first two non-Spanish General Superiors, Everard Mercurian (in office 1573–80) and Claudio Acquaviva (in office 1580–1615).

Ignatius' movement was initially nurtured in a small circle of about ten, but expanded with bewildering speed once it had been officially ratified. When Ignatius died in 1556, it had approximately 1,000 members; by 1580, its membership was around 5,000 and by 1615 around 13,000. Important centres in Spain and Portugal grew rapidly, in little direct contact with Rome, prone to nationalist influence, and with only tenuous spiritual cohesion. A questionnaire administered in the 1560s and 1570s suggests that only a small proportion of Jesuits had made the Exercises in their full form. Not without conflict, the Society of Jesus gradually developed a distinctive culture centred on the rhetoric of the Exercises. The dominant Jesuit narratives written by Iparraguirre and de Guibert present this process as one of organic development, and it is certainly undeniable that only through such means could Ignatian spirituality have survived historically. But the consolidation arguably involved losses as well as gains: the marginalization of more unitive, 'contemplative' elements in the Ignatian and Jesuit traditions; the giving of the Exercises through sermons rather than one-to-one interview; the loss of any sense that the Jesuit vocation was only one possible outcome of a good Ignatian discernment.

Given the Jesuits' tradition of scholarship, their need to nourish their own subculture, and their long-standing systematic maintenance of archives, their own writing on Jesuit spirituality is relatively plentiful. But on several counts the conventional Jesuit accounts are incomplete and potentially misleading. Scholarly attention has been directed first at the circle round Ignatius, for obvious reasons, and second, at Jesuit involvement through figures such as Louis Lallemant (1587–1635) and Jean Joseph Surin (1600–65) in controversies in seventeenth-century France regarding Jansenism and Quietism – this latter perhaps in reaction to the wideranging and critical work of the former Jesuit Henri Bremond. The tacit, and unwarranted, implication is that not much else is of any great significance. Inevitably, too, because written sources are relatively easy to manage, conventional writing concentrates on what Jesuit superiors and charismatic figures wrote about the spiritual life. An account of Jesuit spirituality, however, needs to consider also how such material functioned in the lives of Jesuits at large, and requires the development of alternative approaches to research.

Jesuit writing on the spirituality of Jesuits also inevitably highlights what is, or is perceived to be, specifically Jesuit, and marginalizes other factors which may be nevertheless of great significance for the student of spirituality. Religious writing on the two most studied Jesuit spiritual figures of more recent centuries, Gerard M. Hopkins (1844–89) and Pierre Teilhard de Chardin (1881–1955), almost inevitably starts from the fact that both were Jesuits, and in so doing already begins to sideline other important realities: the far more determinative spiritual significance of Hopkins's exceptional talent as a poet and Teilhard's as a scientist; the limitations of Ignatian and Jesuit formation as they received it; the serious possibility in both cases that Jesuit commitment may have damaged as much as nurtured their genius. More generally, there is a tendency to present as specifically Jesuit what is of far wider relevance. Thus, 'finding God in all things' and 'contemplation in action' often appear as hallmarks of Jesuit identity (as indeed they arguably are if spirituality is understood as the preserve of those in consecrated life) rather than as possibilities and demands given with Christianity as such.

Changes in the understanding of spirituality have thus rendered the classic accounts of Jesuit spirituality problematic. At the same time, the scholarship that would enable us to establish an alternative account has hardly begun. But we can at least highlight three major Jesuit contributions to Christian spirituality.

First, the focus on ministry characteristic of Jesuit consecrated life has inevitably led Jesuits to particularly intense reflection on the relationship between prayer and work, contemplation and action. The issues here are perennial. They reflect in part what is simply a human need for a balance between work and rest, a need that may obviously be met in a variety of ways. They also reflect the conceptual tension in Christianity arising from the belief that the God who calls human beings to union at once transcends the world and dwells within it, and is hence to be sought through both engagement and withdrawal. The most significant Jesuit account of prayer and action was probably that of Jerónimo Nadal (1507–80) whose works, edited in the twentieth century, were influentially retrieved by a group of Jesuits around Hugo Rahner (1900–

68). There are, however, as yet unresolved questions regarding the precise interpretation of Nadal's doctrine, the real extent of its historical influence, and the purported originality and distinctiveness of his insights. There are also some more problematic traces in Jesuit tradition of a commitment to ministry marginalizing and repressing contemplative impulses.

Second, the Jesuit commitment to service 'at the frontiers', both literally and figuratively at a remove from the official Church's structures, generates a particularly sharp tension in Jesuit spirituality, between charismatic independence of authority and ecclesial allegiance – a tension which has not always been well managed. The Spiritual Exercises are predicated on the belief that God can work directly within the creature – a potentially subversive claim that coexists with the authoritarian rhetoric of readiness to believe that white is black should authority so define it that we find in the so-called 'Rules for Thinking with the Church'. Similarly, Jesuit teaching on government at once stresses a need for obedience and encourages initiative. The contradictions here emerge from a missionary commitment to the quest for God beyond ecclesial convention, from a sense of being sent by Christ beyond the current range of the Church he founded. However much such a commitment to mission merely reflects the gospel, it implies a potentially subversive dissatisfaction with the status quo. Missionary openness needs to be balanced by a rhetoric of reassuring conservatism if it is to maintain its identity as Christian – a point that applies both in terms of ecclesial relations and also within the self's own sense of identity. The Jesuit charism generates both creative and visionary figures like Pedro Arrupe (1907–91), superior general in the immediate aftermath of Vatican II, and much more conformist and authoritarian figures. The conflict here – dramatized for instance in the film The Mission, when the Jesuits in eighteenth-century Paraguay are caught in a dilemma between obedience to authority and their commitment to the people in their care – is probably central to Jesuit identity. A person can retain a sense of missionary commitment in the long term only if they maintain and foster a living relationship with the reality that sends them.

Third, the Jesuits were instrumental in promoting various movements in popular spirituality. At their inception, they were closely allied to lay confraternities, and later founded Sodalities of the Blessed Virgin Mary (which, following Vatican II, transformed themselves into Christian Life Communities). Until liturgical reforms in the twentieth century established the practice

as normative, they were noted for advocating that believers should receive the Eucharist frequently. They were influential in the fostering of devotion to the Sacred Heart of Jesus, notably through the spiritual direction given by Claude de la Colombière (1641–82) to the visionary, Margaret Mary Alacoque. We probably do better merely to note these achievements as facts, rather than speculate on any connections between these devotions promoted by Jesuits in the course of their ministry and the spirituality characterizing Jesuits' personal lives.

See also **Apostolic Spirituality; Ignatian Spirituality; Religious Life; Rules, Religious.**

William A. Barry and Robert G. Doherty, Contemplatives in Action: The Jesuit Way, New York: Paulist Press, 2002; Paul Begheyn, 'Bibliography on the history of the Jesuits: publications in English 1990–1993', Studies in the Spirituality of Jesuits 28.1, 1996; Thomas H. Clancy, An Introduction to Jesuit Life: The Constitutions and History Through 435 Years, St Louis: Institute of Jesuit Sources, 1976; Joseph de Guibert, The Jesuits: Their Spiritual Doctrine and Practice – A Historical Study, St Louis: Institute of Jesuit Sources, 1964 [1942]; John W. O'Malley, The First Jesuits, Cambridge, MA: Harvard University Press, 1993; John W. Padberg (Gen. ed.), The Constitutions of the Society of Jesus and Their Complementary Norms, St Louis: Institute of Jesuit Sources, 1996.

PHILIP ENDEAN

Johannine Spirituality

Introduction. In the first conclusion of John's Gospel, chs 20, 30—31 (ch. 21 is considered by many scholars to be an appendix composed and added by another hand after the completion of the body of the Gospel by the evangelist), the evangelist (who is an anonymous writer traditionally called 'John') makes explicit the connection between the spirituality presented in the text and the spirituality of subsequent readers of the text. The former witnesses to the lived experience of Jesus by his contemporary disciples as it was appropriated in the lived experience of Christian faith by a highly distinctive community of first- and second-generation Christians living somewhere outside Palestine, probably in Asia Minor or Alexandria. The latter is the substantially identical but modally different spirituality which the evangelist proposes to those in the community who were not contemporaries of Jesus or later disciples. John says, 'Jesus did many other signs in the presence of his disciples . . . But these are written that you may believe that Jesus is the Christ, the Son of God, and that by believing you may *have life* in his [Jesus'] name' (translations of the Fourth Gospel are my own unless otherwise noted – in this case, emphasis is added).

This is a capsule expression of Johannine spirituality. The pre-Easter Jesus offered participation in his own divine life to those who responded, by believing in him, to the 'signs' he did in their presence, including both his words and his works ('sign' is a technical Johannine term for Jesus' symbolic actions, including those which are called 'miracles' in the synoptic Gospels). He continues to offer divine life to those who respond, by believing in him, to the Gospel which functions for them as the signs did for the first disciples. Jesus' witness, in both cases, is symbolic but in the first it is historical and in the second, textual.

The substance of Johannine spirituality. The spirituality, or lived experience of faith, of the Fourth Gospel is centred in Jesus who is presented as the Word or Wisdom of God made flesh, the fully adequate expression of God. As incarnate Word the historical Jesus is 'Son' in relation to God who is 'Father'. These terms do not designate divine gender. They are a parental metaphor to present Jesus as one with God ('I and the Father are one', 10.30), sharing God's very life, and sent by God into the world that all who believe in him may have the fullness of divine life (cf. 10.10).

The *life* which Jesus has from God (cf. 5.26) and into which he inaugurates his disciples is a real participation in the life of God which John calls 'eternal life' (*zwhv*) in distinction from human life (*yuchv*) which is subject to death. Those who believe in Jesus are born anew in the Spirit (cf. 35.5) and become in reality children of God (cf. 1.12–13) as Jesus is Son of God.

The life of God which Jesus shares with his disciples is *love*. The first epistle of John says simply, 'God is love'. (N.B. The three Johannine epistles were not written by the evangelist but come from the same community milieu that produced the Gospel and, with some different emphases due to the community situation, share its theology and spirituality.) And God so loved the world, John says, that God sent the only Son (cf. 3.16) who manifested God's saving love by laying down his life for his friends and giving them, as his only commandment, the charge to love one another as he had loved them (cf. 15.12–15).

The love-life of God enters the world as *light* which enlightens every human being (cf. 1.4, 9). A striking feature of Johannine spirituality is that salvation is presented not in terms of expiatory or substitutionary sacrifice but in terms of revelation. In John, the death of Jesus on the cross is not a kenosis but a glorification, the absolute manifestation of the very being of God as love. The symbol of light, especially in the story of the man born blind whom Jesus enlightened by opening his eyes (cf. ch. 9), is a way of talking about divine revelation or the human encounter with the Truth who is Jesus.

The dynamics of Johannine spirituality. Revelation, in John, is not a one-way communication to humans of hidden divine truths. It is a two-way engagement of Jesus and his followers in which they respond by believing in the witness to his own identity as Son of God which Jesus offers through his symbolic words and works. This dynamic of discipleship is carried by a vocabulary of 'language'. Jesus is the Word of God, God's self-expression in the world. Jesus speaks, witnessing to himself, to his union with God, to God's saving will for all people. This is not information but a sharing of his inner being and life, and an invitation to his hearers to respond with a total gift of themselves to him. This mutual self-revelation is the progressive creation of a shared life, a world of 'we' which reflects the union of Jesus and God. By sharing in Jesus' divine life the person ceases to be 'from below', purely natural, and is born 'from above' into the very life of God. Consequently, in John Jesus is preeminently 'teacher' or 'rabbi' and his followers are 'disciples', not because he is informing them intellectually, but because he, the Truth, is the light in which they see God.

The person who encounters Jesus in John's Gospel is called to respond by believing. The evangelist developed a special vocabulary to talk about this response. The term 'faith' is never used in John. The relationship is always a verb, *pisteuvw*, something one does rather than something one has. Furthermore, the evangelist created a grammatical construction of the verb that is peculiar to this Gospel, 'to believe *into* Jesus' rather than simply 'to believe in'. The preposition (*eis*) with the accusative case suggests a progressive entrance into and growth in the relationship. Jesus says, 'If you remain [or continue] in my word you are truly my disciples' (8.31). Believing, in other words, is not notional or intellectual but relational.

Encounter with Jesus in John precipitates a crisis, a point at which one must choose either to become his disciple or to 'go away' and 'die in one's sins' (cf. 8.24). Those who choose to remain with him declare, even when they do not understand, 'Lord, to whom shall we go? You have the words of eternal life' (6.68). Those who go away, like the people who were fed by Jesus in the desert but resisted his teaching on the Bread of Life, declare his word 'a hard teaching' which they cannot accept (cf. 6.60).

Those who come to Jesus, believe in him, remain with him, follow him and gradually become his disciples are born of the Spirit and become children of God, friends rather than servants of Jesus, and friends of one another in the community which is Jesus' bodily presence in the world after the resurrection (cf. 2.19–22). On Easter night the risen Jesus stood among his disciples, breathed into them his Spirit, and sent them as the Father had sent him to take away the sins of the world (cf. 20.19–23). But the sending of the disciples in John is quite different from the commissioning in the synoptics. Jesus had said, in his last discourse to the disciples the night before he died, that they would remain as his presence in the world, doing even greater works than he had done (cf. 14.12). But Jesus prays to his Father that his disciples 'may be one' even as he and God are one 'so that the world may believe' (17.21). The mission of the Johannine community is not to go into the whole world and preach the gospel to every creature but to be a community whose love witnesses to divine life, to be in the world what Jesus had been for them. Jesus is 'no longer in the world, but they are in the world' (17.11) making Jesus present, offering divine life, to their contemporaries down through history.

Characteristics of Johannine spirituality. Johannine spirituality has several distinctive features which are particularly attractive to modern believers. First, it is a *mystical spirituality* in which presence, mutual indwelling, and union rather than dogma or morality predominate. Union with Jesus is the source of intimate knowledge of God and the strength to live as the body of Jesus in the world, to love unto the laying down of one's life. Second, it is an intensely *personal spirituality*. Each disciple is a branch in the one Vine (cf. 15.1–7), one personally called by name by the Good Shepherd (cf. 10.3–6). No one takes Jesus' place in the life of the disciples or brokers their relationship with him. Third, the community of Jesus' disciples is presented as *egalitarian*. The Spirit is given equally to all. Women play prominent roles in John's Gospel and the beloved disciple, the ideal for all disciples, is neither one of the Twelve nor subordinate to Peter. Fourth, the only criterion of holiness in John is *love* of Jesus and his friends. Peter, who denied Jesus three times, is not rehabilitated and commissioned to care for Jesus' (not Peter's) flock, until he has thrice responded to Jesus' question, 'Do you love me?' (cf. 21.15–17). Fifth, the source of life in John is the

Spirit rather than the observance of rules or the practice of rituals. And finally, there is little emphasis in John on this life as a prelude to or testing ground for the next life. Those who believe in Jesus share now in eternal life and *they will never die* even as they pass through physical death (cf. 11.25–26). Christian spirituality is a living of this divine life of love which is expressed in the service unto death modelled by Jesus in washing his disciples' feet (cf. 13.1–20) before his glorification on the cross. Jesus alone is the way, the truth and the life of his disciples (cf. 14.6).

See also **Spirituality and Scripture** (*essay*); **Pauline Spirituality; Synoptic Gospels.**

———

Raymond E. Brown, *The Gospel According to John*, 2 vols, Anchor Bible 29, 29A, Garden City, NY: Doubleday, 1966, 1970; Raymond E. Brown, *A Retreat with John the Evangelist: That You May Have Life*, Cincinnati: St Anthony Messenger, 1998; Demetrius R. Dumm, *A Mystical Portrait of Jesus: New Perspectives on John's Gospel*, Collegeville, MN: The Liturgical Press, 2001; Barnabas Lindars, *The Gospel of John*, New Century Bible, London: Oliphants, 1972; Gail R. O'Day, *Revelation in the Fourth Gospel: Narrative Mode and Theological Claim*, Philadelphia: Fortress Press, 1986; Sandra M. Schneiders, *Written that You May Believe: Encountering Jesus in the Fourth Gospel*, New York: Crossroad, 1999.

SANDRA M. SCHNEIDERS

Journal, Spiritual

Such a wide range of writing has gone under the name 'spiritual journal' that it is difficult to pin down just what this genre represents. The Quaker founder George Fox's famous *Journal* gives a chapter-by-chapter narrative account of his past life, from his childhood through his life of ministry. Dag Hammarskjöld left a manuscript of what he called his 'diary' – later published as *Markings* – that is a collection of meditations on a range of topics, like Pascal's *Pensées*, or Marcus Aurelius' *Meditations*. Some of these meditations are grouped according to the year they were written, while others have specific dates attached to them. Many women's spiritual texts, such as Mechthild of Magdeburg's *Flowing Light of the Godhead* or Catherine of Siena's *Dialogue*, have been described as spiritual journals. But often the designation 'spiritual journal' seems born from a conviction about the spontaneity of women's writing that obscures the literary skill with which women writers constructed their texts. More contemporary notions of a 'spiritual journal' point to a written record of life as it is lived. Thomas Merton's *Sign of Jonas* is one example of this sort of spiritual journal.

Each entry is dated, and the reader has a sense of watching Merton's life unfold day by day.

It is this kind of immediacy, this sort of closeness to daily life, that the term 'spiritual journal' has tried to capture, however imperfectly. And it is the dailiness of the discipline of journal writing that makes the keeping of a journal such a popular spiritual practice. There is something inherently spiritual about keeping a daily account of one's life. The practice of narrating our days hallows them and cultivates our capacity for attention to the present moment.

While the practice of writing a spiritual journal has a long history in Christianity, reading and rereading one's own spiritual journals and the journals of others does as well. Dag Hammarskjöld, like Marcus Aurelius, often writes directly to himself in his Markings: 'do not then anesthetize yourself', he exhorts himself. 'Do what you can.' 'Forward!' This is clearly a journal intended to be read and reread, a journal that is intended not only to record but also to shape a life.

It is precisely this desire to shape our lives – to live with more attention, more love, gratitude for each moment – that keeps us reading and writing spiritual journals. For spiritual journals place our deepest questions and fiercest hopes in the context of everyday life. Reading such journals reminds us to attend more deeply to the significance of each moment as it is lived. And writing a spiritual journal deepens our experience by requiring us to find language to describe it.

See also **Biographies, Spiritual; Devotional Manuals; Lectio Divina; Practice, Spiritual.**

Catherine of Siena: The Dialogue, trans. Suzanne Noffke, CWS, Mahwah, NY: Paulist Press, 1980; John L. Nickalls (ed.), The Journal of George Fox, London: Religion Society of Friends 1975; Dag Hammarskjöld, Markings, New York: Knopf, 1964; Mechthild of Magdeburg: The Flowing Light of the Godhead, trans. Frank Tobin, CWS, Mahwah, NY: Paulist Press, 1998; Thomas Merton, The Sign of Jonas, New York: Harvest, 2002.

STEPHANIE PAULSELL

Journey, Spiritual

The understanding of the spiritual life as a journey with different stages or levels is a widespread theme in Christian spirituality and has been expressed in different times and places as, for example, theosis (or deification), ascent (up mountains or ladders), conversatio (in Western monasticism), the triplex via (or threefold path) or, more recently, in terms adapted from modern psychological theories of growth and development. In broader, less structured terms, the theme of the Christian life as pilgrimage has also been a rich one in spiritual literature from Augustine's City of God to John Bunyan's Pilgrim's Progress to the anonymous nineteenth-century Russian work on the spirituality of the Jesus Prayer, The Way of a Pilgrim.

In the Christian Scriptures, Jesus speaks of himself as 'the way' for all disciples (John 14.6), and in the book of Acts Christianity is described as 'the way' and Christians as 'people of the way' (Acts 9.2; 18.25) – the way of Jesus which all disciples follow after. This following of Jesus Christ, or discipleship, is fundamental to the life of Christians and involves conversion – a turning away from falsehood and a turning towards God. The Christian understanding of the spiritual journey is thus a lifelong process of commitment to this process of turning – in other words, a movement of ongoing transformation. The metaphor of 'journey' attempts to express the radically dynamic rather than static nature of Christian experience and practice. 'Perfection' or 'union' are two concepts that have sometimes been used to express the 'where to?' of the journey, but ultimately the end in view is fullness of life in God.

Beginning with Irenaeus in the second century, who contrasted a developmental understanding of the Christian life with the more static, achieved state of illumination in Gnosticism, patristic theology gradually developed a theory of stages of the spiritual life. The Alexandrian theologian Origen (c. 185–255) explained the contemplative life in Neoplatonic terms as three ascending stages associated with beginners (praxis), proficients (theōria) and the perfect (theologia). The journey was a recovery of the likeness of God in the soul in a movement upwards towards greater light. In the following century, the Cappadocian theologian Gregory of Nyssa (c. 335–95), especially in his Life of Moses, also represented the contemplative journey in terms of stages and ascent but in this case towards darkness rather than light. He used as his framework of reference the story of Moses' experiences in the book of Exodus. Here the metaphor is the ascent of Mount Sinai as Moses enters into ever deeper clouds of darkness in his encounter with God.

Because of Gregory of Nyssa's 'apophatic' understanding of the climax of the contemplative ascent as deep darkness in which God is experienced but never finally known, there is a certain open-ended quality to the journey. There is a greater sense of final 'arrival' in Origen where human perfection is represented by a more Platonic, static union with the Godhead. In contrast, Gregory's portrayal of the spiritual journey is a never-ending progress *towards* perfection in which we strive ever more to be perfect but never conclusively arrive.

Origen's and Gregory's exposition of the spiritual journey (allied with the writings of the sixth-century pseudonymous Dionysius) had a considerable influence in both the East and the West. During the Middle Ages in the West, the conception of the spiritual journey developed strongly in the direction of the 'three ways' (purgative, illuminative and unitive) which are dealt with both in terms of the threefold theory and also individually in other entries in this dictionary. Subsequent spiritual literature is also full of images and metaphors of the spiritual journey – often associated with 'ascent' whether of mountains (for example, the sixteenth-century *Ascent of Mount Carmel* of John of the Cross) or of ladders (for example, the fourteenth-century Walter Hilton's *Ladder* – or *Scale*, from *scala – of Perfection*).

The most dominant Western monastic rule, the sixth-century Rule of St Benedict, described the spiritual journey in terms of the twelve degrees of humility (ch. 7), 'a ladder of our ascending actions'. This is developed further in other monastic works such as the twelfth-century Cistercian, Bernard of Clairvaux's commentary on ch. 7 of the Rule, *Steps of Humility and Pride*. Another influential medieval monastic description of the spiritual journey as an ascent was the twelfth-century Guigo the Carthusian's *Ladder of Monks* but this referred to the ancient monastic contemplative practice of *lectio divina* now structured more systematically as four stages (*see* Lectio).

As already noted, the sixteenth-century Carmelite John of the Cross, in his *Ascent of Mount Carmel*, adopts the metaphor of climbing a mountain, in this case away from a faith and life of prayer based on sense experience through various 'nights' of sensory deprivation, spiritual darkness and purification to the 'summit' of transforming union – a spiritual marriage between God and the soul. Teresa of Avila, John's older contemporary and collaborator in the Carmelite reform movement, vividly describes the spiritual journey in *The Interior Castle* in terms of a progression through the different rooms or mansions of the 'castle' of the soul, clustered in groups corresponding to the threefold way, until the pilgrimage culminates in rooms 5–7 in which takes place a similar transforming union leading to spiritual marriage.

Beyond these and other classic itineraries of the spiritual journey, contemporary developments in spirituality during the last forty years have been significantly influenced by the human sciences, especially psychological theories of various schools. In the context of the spiritual journey this particularly refers to various theories of human development such as those of Erik Erickson and Lawrence Kohlberg supplemented by the work specifically in faith development by James Fowler (*see* Conversion).

Margaret Miles has suggested that the classic metaphor of 'ascent' retains a certain value in that it emphasizes a role for personal work and responsibility as opposed to mere passivity, a dynamic rather than a static vision of the Christian life, and a continuous journey rather than a succession of quite disconnected experiences. However, not only does 'ascent' also suggest a separation of the world of the senses from the spiritual realm, but there are more general questions about the notion of successive stages. First, what is represented by the distinct stages (repentance, enlargement of vision and loving union with God) are present in different proportions at all points of the spiritual journey. Second, in a fundamental way, union with God is not so much a stage above and beyond other stages (achieved essentially through contemplative practice) but, in the sense of the prior actuality of God's grace, is a prerequisite of all spiritual growth. Here Augustine's distinction between operative or prevenient grace (God's initial act) and co-operative grace (what God does 'with' us) is helpful. Third, the notion of distinct stages can support a hierarchy of spiritual and moral values and therefore of lifestyles in which the contemplative way is seen as distinct from and superior to the way of action.

Karl Rahner also questioned the very concept of distinct stages as based on an outdated Neoplatonic anthropology in which the summit of existence is total detachment from human passions. He also rejected an approach which seems, theologically, to involve an objective, continuous and inevitable increase of *grace* or, ethically, the limitation of higher moral acts to one stage rather than another.

While the classic approaches to the spiritual journey in Christian spirituality may continue to offer valuable wisdom for our own times, a contemporary hermeneutic suggests that their sometimes individualistic resonances must nowadays be corrected by a renewed emphasis on the collective understanding of discipleship in the New Testament. The Second Vatican Council described the Christian community as a whole as a pilgrim people 'led by the Holy Spirit in their journey to the kingdom of their Father'

(*Gaudium et Spes* 1). This recovery of a more collective understanding of the spiritual journey also provided a pointer towards the notion of solidarity with others in liberation spirituality as it emerged in Latin America in the 1960s. Here, this led to the use of the Old Testament image of the Exodus where the emphasis is on a desert journey in which God leads the oppressed peoples from a state of slavery to the possession of a land of their own through God's promise and guidance as in Gustavo Gutiérrez' *We Drink from Our Own Wells: The Spiritual Journey of a People.*

See also **Conversion; Deification; Discipleship; Pilgrimage; Triple Way.**

Lawrence S. Cunningham and Keith J. Egan, *Christian Spirituality: Themes from the Tradition*, New York: Paulist Press, 1996; Gustavo Gutiérrez, *We Drink from Our Own Wells: The Spiritual Journey of a People*. Maryknoll: Orbis Books, 1984; Andrew Louth, *The Origins of the Christian Mystical Yradition: From Plato to Denys*, Oxford: Clarendon Press, 1981; Margaret R. Miles, *Practicing Christianity: Critical Perspectives for an Embodied Spirituality*, New York: Crossroad, 1988; Karl Rahner, 'Reflection on the problem of the gradual ascent to perfection' in *Theological Investigations*, London: Burns & Oates, 1967.

PHILIP SHELDRAKE

Joy

'Alleluia', the great cry of joy, is the song of creation, praising the wonders God has made. The Psalms and the book of Isaiah do not speak only of our human rejoicing: trees, mountains, heaven and earth, creation itself sings (Ps. 66.1; 96.12; Isa. 49.13; 55.12). But joy, in the biblical traditions of both testaments, is also a sign of and response to God's action in history: redemption, liberation, healing.

Most of all, for Christians, the alleluia song is the song of resurrection and the sign of the coming of the Holy Spirit. The believers gathered at Pentecost, reports the book of Acts, were so infused with joy that observers suspected them of being drunk on new wine (Acts 2.12).

Christians who sing the resurrection song have known also the betrayal, suffering, cries and awful silence of the cross. Joy, like all realities in the Christian life, exists only in relation to the paschal mystery. As Christians move more deeply into a discovery of the depths of joy, they encounter joy's paradoxes. Christian hope is not the same as optimism; so too joy is no self-satisfied contentment; it is, rather, akin to the peace 'that passes all understanding' (Phil. 4.7).

In both biblical and later Christian sources, untrammelled joy, associated with gratitude, childlike delight, simplicity and purity of heart, also lives despite and in the midst of difficulty, pain, sorrow, opposition and persecution, even death.

Joy is one of the signs of holiness of life, not merely a feeling but a way of being in the world. It is one of the fruits of the Spirit described by St Paul as 'love, joy, peace, patience, kindness, generosity, faithfulness, gentleness, and self-control' (Gal. 5.22). It goes hand in hand with humility and poverty of spirit, the acknowledgement of God's power and of human limitations.

Material poverty and joy are also linked in Christian tradition. Contemporary theologians and spiritual writers have criticized the romanticizing of poverty, noting its social and structural causes (Gutiérrez, 1984, pp. 20 ff.) and distinguishing between voluntary poverty and the destitution that corrodes and destroys. Yet in both contexts the gift of joy occurs. For the privileged, the joy that coexists with simple living is a sign of contradiction to the culture of consumerism. Among the impoverished, joy is both triumph amid misery and companion to the hope for change.

Individual saints are commemorated especially for their joy. Centred on the contemplation of Christ and rejecting the way of the world in the forms of wealth and military armour, Francis of Assisi did not turn from the world itself. Even as death approached, he composed the *Canticle of Brother Sun*, praising creation and the goodness of the creator. Seraphim of Sarov, the Russian *starets*, was also known for his radiant demeanour and joyful communion with God and God's creatures. He addressed guests and conversation partners as 'my Joy', an expression he used also for Mary, Mother of God, to whom he was deeply devoted. He taught that the Spirit brings both rejoicing in God's presence and a foretaste of joy in the world to come. Thérèse of Lisieux discovered and taught 'the little way': ordinary work, ordinary life are enough, provided we walk their path with love and joy.

For the mystics, joy is the very union with God, that knowledge which is also an indwelling. Marguerite Porete speaks of the soul 'swim[ming] in the sea of joy, that is in the sea of delights, flowing and running out of the Divinity. And so she feels no joy, for she is joy itself. She swims and flows in joy, without feeling any joy, for she dwells in Joy and Joy dwells in her . . .' (Porete, 1993, p. 109).

The joy of mystical union is ineffable. Yet – another paradox – it longs to express itself. Faced with the limits and weight of ordinary language, mystics in every era have turned to poetry, dance and music: psalms chanted and sung, the Easter polyphony of the Orthodox Church, the cantatas of Bach and Masses of Mozart, the street processions of New Orleans jazz funerals, the exuberant blend of musical idioms in Pentecostalism worldwide.

Joy is the stance of the Christian who sees with new eyes. It accompanies both conversion – a heart transformed – and liberation – a transformed world. The classic canticle of joy is the Magnificat of Mary, singing of the wonders God has done for one lowly woman and offering thanks for relations of power turned upside down, the beginning of the Messianic era (Luke 1.46–55).

As difficult as the prayer of woe may be, it is often harder to exult than to lament. The Anglican writer Janet Morley, evoking Christ's words to Mary of Magdala before the empty tomb (John 20.11–18), prays that 'we need not cling to our familiar grief, but may be freed to proclaim resurrection' (Morley, 1992, p. 14).

See also **Mysticism** (*essay*); **Abandonment; Beatitudes; Celebration; Charismatic Spirituality; Consolation; Desolation; Ecstasy; Fools, Holy; Franciscan Spirituality; Freedom; Humour; Liberation Spirituality; Peace; Presence of God; Purity of Heart; Resurrection; Silence; Spirit, Holy.**

Gustavo Gutiérrez, *We Drink from Our Own Wells: The Spiritual Journey of a People*, trans. Matthew J. O'Connell, Maryknoll, NY: Orbis Books/Melbourne: Dove Communications, 1984; Damian Kirkpatrick ssf, Philip Doherty ofm Conv. and Sheelagh O'Flynn fmdm on behalf of The Franciscan Association of Great Britain, *Joy in All Things: A Franciscan Companion*, Norwich: Canterbury Press, 2002; Janet Morley, *All Desires Known*, expanded edn, Harrisburg, PA: Morehouse, 1992; *Marguerite Porete: The Mirror of Simple Souls*, trans. Ellen L. Babinsky, CWS, Mahwah, NJ: Paulist Press, 1993; Valentine Zander, *Saint Seraphim of Sarov*, Crestwood, NY: St Vladimir's Seminary Press, 1995.

JANE CAROL REDMONT

Judaism and Christianity

As siblings born out of biblical Israel, Judaism and Christianity began as rivals, developed into enemies and struggle now to reconcile as partners waiting and working for the world's full redemption. They are like no other two religions, historian Amos Funkenstein argues, because 'such strong mutual bonds of aversion and fascination, attraction and repulsion' link them. The tragedy is that for nearly two millennia, the bonds of aversion and repulsion were far greater than those of fascination and attraction.

The sibling rivalry grew out of a disagreement over which was the 'true Israel': the Torah of Moses or the Way of Jesus Christ? From its beginnings, what came to be called Christianity had to legitimize itself vis-à-vis other Jewish movements. Its eventual parting from Judaism was gradual, and no single issue can be identified as *the* cause of separation. Neither can a particular time be determined as the moment of division. Although in some places clearer boundaries between the two traditions were apparent by mid second century, in other areas the split was not definitive for several centuries – as John Chrysostom realized when he raged in his sermons 'Against the Judaizers' in late fourth-century Antioch, where Christians continued to be attracted to Jewish festivals and to the practice of Jewish customs.

As an illicit cult in the Roman Empire, and an insecure minority over against an established tradition, the Christian movement caricatured Jewish leadership (e.g. Matt. 23) and exculpated Roman authorities for their role in the crucifixion of Jesus (e.g. the passion narrative in John's Gospel). Early Christian writers accused Jews of reading the letter but not the spirit of the Scriptures (e.g. Justin Martyr's *Dialogue with Trypho the Jew*), oversimplified debates about Jewish practices, charged the Jews with 'deicide' (Melito of Sardis's *Homily on the Passover*), and asserted that God had ended the covenant with sinful Israel (*Letter of Barnabas*). In short, early Christianity presented itself as having superseded Judaism.

After Christianity became the official religion of the Roman Empire under Emperor Theodosius I (379–95), legislation enshrined supersessionism. Some twenty regional councils issued rulings between 465 and 694 that enforced boundaries between Christians and Jews, such as forbidding mixed marriages or participation in Jewish meals. Other legislation restricted the public character of Jewish life (e.g. prohibiting Jews from holding public office and forbidding the building of new synagogues).

By the High Middle Ages Christian society in Europe had so divorced itself from its origins in Judaism that Jews were regarded as an 'other' threatening the stability of the social order. Accused of ritual murder and blood libel, Jews were segregated in ghettos, their sacred texts burned, expelled from many countries, and even massacred. Jews were no longer regarded merely as religious competitors but as enemies of the Church and a menace to society. Nevertheless, the theological antagonism continued, as illustrated by the Council of Florence's 'Decree for the Copts' (1442): 'Therefore, she [the Holy Roman Church] denounces as foreign to the faith of Christ all those who after that time observe circumcision, the Sabbath and other laws, and she asserts that they can in no way be sharers of eternal salvation, unless they sometime turn away from their errors.' No one who remained outside the Catholic Church, the Council of Florence ruled, could partake of eternal life – 'not only pagans, but also Jews, heretics or schismatics . . . will go to the "eternal fire prepared for the devil and his angels" (Matt. 25.41), unless before the end of their life they are received into it'.

Neither the Reformation nor the Enlightenment broke decisively from such views. Martin Luther's tract of 1543, 'On the Jews and their Lies', spoke of 'this damned, rejected race of Jews'. The Enlightenment brought emancipation for Jews; yet they again became scapegoats for societal tensions in the ensuing economic crises and political upheaval. Modernity also led to the disestablishment of the Churches, thus challenging ecclesiastical power. When National Socialism arose in Germany in the 1930s, the status of the Church was further threatened. Moreover, the dominant Christian culture associated negative developments such as secularism and Marxism with Judaism, thereby exacerbating the long-standing hostility to Judaism. With Church authorities generally reluctant to challenge the Nazi authorities, and a legacy of teachings that disparaged Judaism and vilified Jews, Christianity lacked the soul to defy the Third Reich. As the Catholic bishops of Germany admitted in 1995, the Church community as a whole turned 'their back too often on the fate of this persecuted Jewish people . . . looked too fixedly at the threat to their own institutions and . . . remained silent about the crimes committed against the Jews and Judaism'.

'Aversion' and 'repulsion' in the Christian–Jewish relationship seemed to have reached their apotheosis during the period of the Third Reich. It is premature to assert that 'fascination and attraction' have now achieved ascendancy. Nonetheless, dramatic changes in the relation of Judaism and Christianity are apparent – changes unimaginable in the previous epochs.

Because the charge that Jews were 'Christ-killers' has lingered for so long in formal teaching and popular piety with such tragic effect, reassessment of Christianity's teaching about the death of Jesus is fundamental to reappraising its relation to Judaism. The formulation of the Second Vatican Council in Nostra Aetate, promulgated in 1965, represented the first statement from an official Church body that 'what happened in his passion cannot be charged against all the Jews, without distinction, then alive, nor against the Jews of today'. Thus, 'Jews should not be presented as rejected or accursed by God, as if this followed from the Holy Scriptures.' Since that initial statement, many Christian traditions have issued similar declarations. In addition, numerous pastoral and academic resources now provide more adequate ways of interpreting the passion of Christ.

The Churches have begun to assume responsibility for what their anti-Jewish teachings have cost the Jewish community. In a declaration of 1994, the Evangelical Lutheran Church in America acknowledged 'with pain' Luther's 'anti-Jewish diatribes and violent recommendations', and deplored the 'appropriation of Luther's words by modern anti-Semites'. They called anti-Semitism a 'contradiction and an affront to the Gospel, a violation of our hope and calling', and grieved 'the complicity of our tradition within this history of hatred'.

The onus of responsibility lies within the Christian community, yet many Jews have collaborated with Christians in study sessions, conferences and dialogue groups. While mistrust of Christians understandably lingers in most Jewish circles, a statement published in 2000, 'Dabru Emet', recognized a 'dramatic and unprecedented shift in Jewish and Christian relations'. The changes in the Churches 'merit thoughtful Jewish responses' so that Jews might learn about 'efforts of Christians to honor Judaism'. Although written by only four Jewish scholars, numerous rabbis and scholars signed 'Dabru Emet', and it has circulated widely.

The question of Christian mission to the Jews remains unresolved, a point of contention between Christian denominations and within them. In Evangelical Christianity, a mission to the Jews is fundamental, as is evident in the imperative from the 1991 Lausanne Committee on World Evangelism that the 'whole church' should 'take the whole Gospel to the Jewish people everywhere'. Other traditions reject proselytizing, recommending instead 'dialogue' and 'witness'. An ecumenical group of scholars in the United States published a statement in 2002, 'A sacred obligation', in which they affirmed the enduring quality of God's covenant with the Jews and concluded that Christians, therefore, should not target Jews for conversion.

The relation between Judaism and Christianity involves many vital theological issues, including understandings of such central issues as redemption, salvation and the doctrine of God. It also entails examining components of the other's tradition that have no precise analogy in one's own (e.g. the role of the Land of Israel in Judaism). Situating Christian origins in the context of Second-Temple Judaism has provided a far more nuanced and complicated account of the early Church. Collaboration among Jewish and Christian biblical scholars has afforded rich interpretations of texts and the varying traditions of commentary.

The revitalized relationship with Judaism has enhanced Christian spirituality as well. Studies on the 'Jewishness' of Jesus have opened new perspectives on his mission and ministry, and explorations of the Jewish roots of Christian liturgy have contributed to a deeper understanding of the Church's prayer life. Comparative studies of mystical literature reveal profound commonalities in longing for intimacy with the divine. Contemporary Christian thinkers are deeply indebted to the insights of Jewish thinkers, most notably Martin Buber and Abraham Joshua Heschel.

In many circles of Jews and Christians, what was once a largely disputatious relationship is now characterized more by dialogue, scholarly exchange and collaboration. While distrust has not disappeared, 'strong mutual bonds' of respect are developing, to the enhancement of each tradition – and a blessing to a world so riven with conflict.

See also **Spirituality and the Dialogue of Religions** (*essay*); **Anti-Semitism; Holocaust.**

Mary C. Boys, *Has God Only One Blessing? Judaism as a Source of Christian Self-Understanding*, A Stimulus Book, New York and Mahwah, NJ: Paulist Press, 2000; Jacob R. Marcus, *The Jew in the Medieval World: A Source Book, 315–1791*, rev. edn, Cincinnati: Hebrew Union College Press, 2000; Peter Ochs, Tikva Frymer-Kensky, David Novak, David Fox Sandmel and Michael A. Signer (eds), *Christianity in Jewish Terms*, Boulder: Westview Press, 2000; Clark A. Williamson, *Way of Blessing, Way of Life*, St Louis: Chalice Press, 1999; Robert Wilken, *Judaism and the Early Christian Mind*, New Haven: Yale University Press, 1971; Stephen G. Wilson, *Related Strangers: Jews and Christians 70–170 C.E.*, Minneapolis: Fortress Press, 1995.

Statements are available at http://www.jcrelations.net.

MARY BOYS

Kataphatic Spirituality

Kataphatic spirituality is synonymous with the affirmative way. Based on the theological premise that a relationship exists between the creation and God's self, kataphatic spirituality emphasizes the similarity between God and the creation that emanates from God's self more than its dissimilarity. Although creation is not identical with God, creation exists within God's being, and thus human persons may mystically experience the presence of God in and through creation and incarnation. This view which seeks to resolve the problem of God's transcendence with God's self-revealing and even erotic movement toward God's creatures is theologically named panentheism. Panentheism recognizes all things and persons exist in God. Thus the transformed and purified consciousness of the kataphatic mystic discovers God in all things and all things in God although God is recognized to be always more than any single manifestation or mediation of God's presence to the mystic. This view preserves God's transcendence in this way and bows before God who is ultimately pure Mystery.

Kataphatic spirituality is often, of necessity, contrasted with its opposite, apophatic spirituality. The word 'kataphatic' in Greek means with images while 'apophatic' means without form or images. The relationship between these two spiritual paths has often been asserted to be one of progression. The progression theory assumes most people begin their spiritual itinerary aided by the beauty of nature, reflection upon the Gospels and the symbols of faith in the creed, the development of a personal affective relationship with Christ through meditation and contemplative prayer, and participation in the sacraments and the liturgical life of the Christian community. Eventually, persons will abandon this mediated path to God in their personal prayer for the self-emptying, knowing of unknowing, and dark contemplation of God more typical of apophatic mysticism. This progression is obviously true for some although this apophatic spirituality retains the kataphatic elements of nature, Scripture and sacramental life as the supportive matrix of their apophatic style of contemplative prayer.

Since the Reformation, Roman Catholic mystical theology has manifested a distinct preference for apophatic mysticism and nearly made it definitive of mysticism itself. This bias has resulted in a consequent lack of appreciation for kataphatic spiritualilty and has had the effect of obscuring the full potential of the flowering of a primarily kataphatic mysticism as a lifetime pattern for many people.

Bernard McGinn and Harvey Egan have both proposed a more complex relationship between these two spiritual paths and between the apophatic and kataphatic elements that belong to both paths in significant ways. McGinn's careful study of historical texts suggests two distinctly different experiences of God. He first defines the experience of the presence of God as the core of the mystical element of Christianity that 'includes that part of its belief and practices that concerns the preparation for, the consciousness of, and the reaction to what can be described as the immediate or direct presence of God' (McGinn, 1991, p. xvii). Kataphatic mystics tend to speak of experiences of 'presence'. Yet 'because of the incommensurability between the finite and the Infinite Subject, Christian mystics . . . have never been able to convey their message solely through the positive language of presence'. The language of both presence and absence is required. 'Among the most positive, or cataphatic, mystics, it is primarily a successive experience, as in the coming and going of the Divine Lover . . .' 'Among the negative or apophatic mystics, presence and absence are more paradoxically and dialectically simultaneous' (ibid., p. xviii).

McGinn points to the possibility that there is a distinct difference between these two experiences. The kataphatic love mystic's process of transformation consists of successive experiences of presence with intervening periods of the felt 'absence' of God. The mystic discovers he or she is subject to this alternation of presence and absence without being able to control it. Yet the felt experience of 'absence' may not also be simultaneously an experience of presence. It is possible that God allures the mystic in this lover's game through the surprise and unpredictability of when and where and through which mediation, God's presence will subsequently reveal itself rather than through an absence of mediations altogether. In this process, the mystery of God may expand beyond a christocentric love mysticism or service mysticism to the Trinity itself or to God as utter Mystery. The suffering and pain that impinge on every human life and which kataphatically teach the person on this path to embrace, endure and transmute them through the paschal mystery of Christ may be as important to the transformative process as the obscurity of the mystical experience and the passive purifications in the apophatic mode. A person on this kataphatic path may well experience periods of loss of connection to God's presence when a particular mediation no longer 'works'. This may well be an apophatic phase or brief interval, in which the person can only wait in quiet and openness for a new mediation to emerge if the kataphatic path is to continue as primary. Some of the Beguine mystics, despite their love mysticism, also describe experiences of 'the abyss of God' and

adopt other highly paradoxical phrases that suggest that some may experience a more typically apophatic form of contemplation for some period of time within a predominately kataphatic spirituality.

Egan suggests that a kataphatic process such as the Spiritual Exercises of St Ignatius leads to a 'progressive simplification and eventual transparency of the Christian mysteries'. He suggests that the mystery being contemplated becomes itself something of a sacrament 'of the healing, transforming presence of God'. 'Transparency, not forgetting and unknowing, underpins Ignatius' radical kataphatic mysticism' (Egan, 1984, p. 53). This progressive transparency of a God-sourced, God-infused world carries over to all of life so that eventually the Ignatian mystic becomes capable of 'finding God in all things'.

At the present time, there is fresh interest and attraction to kataphatic spirituality. Influenced by creation-centred spirituality, feminism and the new story of the universe and our earth within it, kataphatic spirituality embraces an unabashedly incarnational and embodied sacramental approach to spirituality. A sacramental rather than an instrumental attitude toward the cosmos and the dazzling beauty of the created world leads to wonder, amazement, appreciation and response to protect and care for the earth itself. The cosmos is once again experienced as a primary revelation of God. The discovery that humans together with all beings on the planet enjoy communion and community with God and with one another expands the sense of rootedness and belonging to both God and the creation as well as intensifies a desire to alleviate eco and human injustice and the suffering it produces. All activities and relationships may become to the one 'who has eyes to see openings to the Divine' and invitations to personal transformation as well as to activities of care, compassion, social justice and creativity.

See also **Mysticism; Spirituality, Liturgy and Worship** (essays); **Affirmative Way; Art; Beauty; Creation Spirituality; Ignatian Spirituality; Incarnation; Nature Mysticism; Ritual; Sacramentality and Spirituality.**

Harvey Egan, Christian Mysticism: The Future of a Tradition, New York: Pueblo, 1984; Bernard McGinn, The Foundations of Mysticism, vol. 1 of The Presence of God: A History of Western Christian Mysticism, New York: Crossroad, 1991; Janet Ruffing, 'The world transfigured: kataphatic religious experience', Studies in Spirituality 5 (1995), 232–59.

JANET K. RUFFING

Kenosis

Kenosis is a Greek word that means emptying. In Christianity, it refers to the self-emptying of Christ as expressed in Paul's letter to the Philippians 2.5–11. This text offers a vision of the Christian faith and a testimonial to the earliest development of Christology. The exegesis of this text has a long history; the text continues today to be one of the most disputed passages in the history of New Testament exegesis. The 'kenotic Christology' of Philippians has been and remains one of the most fruitful in the tradition. Much has been written on the 'hymnic' structure of the text, of its 'pre-Pauline' existence, and its reference to an ancient myth or figure. Many exegetes see the text as having its proper context in the two-Adams typology. In contemporary exegesis, 'incarnational' versus 'anthropological' interpretations have emerged alongside a long-standing debate over the 'ethical' interpretation of the text.

Most contributions to kenotic Christology have come out of the Protestant tradition, influenced by Luther's theology of the cross. Earlier exponents of kenotic Christology – such as Gottfried Thomasius, P. T. Forsyth and H. R. Mackintosh – see in kenosis the means of retrieving the full implications of the reality of Jesus' humanity in its ontological and psychological dimensions. Kenosis is important in the writings of Søren Kierkegaard and Karl Barth.

In Dietrich Bonhoeffer, we find a new form of kenosis that sees the very essence of Christian existence as one of self-emptying. With the 'Death of God' theology and specifically with T. Altizer, we have a radical interpretation of kenosis: the self-emptying of God in Jesus Christ is really his death. The incarnation has to be understood as actually effecting the death of God. According to Altizer, 'Theology is now called to a radically kenotic Christology.'

Contemporary authors have affirmed that a kenotic Christology must be grounded in the mysteries of the Trinity, creation and redemption. For Jürgen Moltmann, the conceptual framework is the doctrine of the Trinity. The self-limitation of Christ on the cross is an expression of the self-limitation within the Godhead. Moltmann sees kenosis as the necessary basis of liberation theology. Hans Urs von Balthasar interprets kenosis from the context of the doctrine of the Trinity, as well. Kenotic self-emptying is God's trinitarian nature and characterizes all of God's works, especially that of creation and redemption. Hans Küng sees Hegel's theological thought as kenotic. Kenosis is not only christological in nature, but it is also the pattern of the threefold movement of all reality. For Karl Rahner, incarnation is a kenosis in which God poses the other as his own reality.

Kenosis is also an important concept for theologians and scientists exploring the meaning of creation. Kenosis, as referring to God's self-limitation, allows creation its own otherness. Creation is the God-given space for freedom. Kenosis offers a new response to the issues of evil and suffering. Kenotic themes are prominent in the writings of process theologians. Kenosis plays an important role in the Buddhist–Christian dialogue. Masac Abe considers Phil. 2.5–11 as the most touching passage in Christian Scriptures. He reinterprets Buddhist emptiness in dialogue with the kenosis of Phil. 2. For him, the kenosis of Christ reveals the genesis of the Godhead.

Kenotic Christology not only must be rooted in the broad framework of God's mystery as he is in himself and as he is for us, but it must also shed light on what the nature of God must be. A kenotic Christology must have real implications for a Christian view of life; as a theological model, it should function as a transformation model. The self-emptying of God in the person of Jesus Christ is the model for human generosity and compassion.

See also **Compassion; God, Images of; Incarnation; Jesus and Spirituality; Love.**

H. Urs von Balthasar, *Mysterium Paschale: The Mystery of Easter*, Grand Rapids, MI: Eerdmans, 1993; John B. Cobb and Christopher Ives (eds), *The Emptying God: A Buddhist–Jewish–Christian Conversation*, Maryknoll, NY: Orbis Books, 1990; Paul Henry, 'Kénose', in *Dictionaire de la Bible*, Supplément 5 (1957), 7–161; Ralph P. Martin, *Carmen Christi: Philippians 2.5–11 in Recent Interpretation and in Setting of Early Christian Worship*, rev. edn, Grand Rapids, MI: Eerdmans, 1983; Ralph P. Martin and Brian Dodd (eds), *Where Christology Began: Essays on Philippians 2*, Louisville, KY: Westminster John Knox Press, 1998; Donald W. Mitchell, *Spirituality and Emptiness: The Dynamics of Spiritual Life in Buddhism and Christianity*, Mahwah, NJ: Paulist Press, 1991; Jürgen Moltmann, *The Crucified God: The Cross of Christ as the Foundation and Criticism of Christian Theology*, San Francisco: Harper & Row, 1974; John Polkinhorne (ed.), *The Work of Love: Creation as Kenosis*, Grand Rapids, MI: Eerdmans, 2001; Lucien Richard, *Christ: The Self-Emptying of God*, Mahwah, NJ: Paulist Press, 1997.

LUCIEN J. RICHARD

Kingdom of God

see **Reign of God**

Knowledge

According to Bernard of Clairvaux, spiritual knowledge can be defined as 'a clear and certain grasp of something unseen'. Knowledge is distinguished from opinion because it does not admit doubt, and from faith in that knowledge fully understands what faith holds only as a mystery (*On Consideration* 3.6). All human knowing is a complex activity, in which Bernard Lonergan (1992) has identified a threefold structure of experiencing, understanding and judging.

A human being can have knowledge of God, the self, other persons and the rest of the created order. Christian spiritual writers have often focused on the first two of these aspects of knowledge, following the example of Augustine who professed a desire to know nothing but God and the soul (*Soliloquies* 1.2.7). But there have always been exceptions such as Julian of Norwich's frequent recollection of her 'even-Christians' and Thomas Traherne's delight in the peculiar wonders of nature. Contemporary spirituality is being challenged to pay even closer attention to these other two aspects. For example, African theologians informed by the concept of *ubuntu* (in which selfhood is discovered through relatedness to others) stress the corporate nature of all human knowing, and recent scientific developments in physics, biology and cosmology open up new realms of knowledge for contemplation and reflection.

The role that knowledge plays in the Christian life has been a matter of debate from the biblical period until now. Depending on the definition employed, knowledge has been seen both positively (as the ultimate goal of the spiritual quest) and negatively (as a potential distraction or temptation, or at least as in need of supplementation by the affective virtue of love).

Positively, both Scripture and the Greek philosophical tradition understood knowledge as a form of intimate participation in which the knower becomes like unto the known. (This self-implicating and relational way of knowing has recently been recovered by feminist and postmodern epistemologies, but with different metaphysical assumptions and stress on the contextualized character of all knowing.) A matter of the heart as well as the head, such knowledge is transformative and life-giving when that which is known is the living God. Thus Isaiah envisions the reign of the ideal Davidic king as a time when 'the earth will be full of the knowledge of the Lord as the waters cover the sea' (11.9). In John's

Gospel, eternal life means 'that they may know you, the only true God, and Jesus Christ whom you have sent' (17.3). Knowledge in this sense is equivalent to wisdom, and virtually synonymous with salvation.

Negatively, knowledge has often been defined more narrowly and ascribed value only within strict limits. Augustine located knowledge within the realm of action and distinguished it from the wisdom proper to contemplation, because 'wisdom is concerned with the intellectual cognizance of eternal things and knowledge with the rational cognizance of temporal things' (*On the Trinity* 12.25). Thomas à Kempis asked whether knowledge was of any use at all apart from the fear of God (*Imitation of Christ* 1.2). The apostle Paul counted knowledge as a spiritual gift but did not think it among the highest gifts, warning that 'knowledge puffs up, but love builds up' (1 Cor. 8.1).

The various schools of Christian spirituality have attempted to explicate the proper relationship between love and knowledge. In the East, the speculative Christian gnosticism of Evagrius and the affective materialism of Pseudo-Macarius were effectively synthesized by later writers such as Maximus the Confessor, Symeon the New Theologian and Gregory Palamas. In the West, Dominicans have stressed the primacy of the intellect and identified the vision of God as the goal of the spiritual journey, with love as the fruit of knowledge. Holding to the primacy of the will, Franciscans have tended to see knowledge as necessary but insufficient, so that knowledge is but an intimation of the ecstasy of love in which God is more 'tasted' than 'seen'.

Ultimately, Christians must confess that their knowledge this side of heaven is always incomplete and imprecise. 'Now I know only in part; then I will know fully, even as I have been fully known' (1 Cor. 13.12). All earthly knowledge – especially knowledge of God – is subject to the dialectic movements of affirmation and negation. It is for this reason that Christian spiritual teachers so often resort to the language of paradox in order to speak of that 'learned ignorance' in which the self-revelation of God is received as gift and invitation to communion.

See also **Affirmative Way; Apophatic Spirituality; Contemplation; Interiority; Kataphatic Spirituality; Love; Mystery; Revelation; Unitive Way.**

Bernard J. F. Lonergan, *Insight: A Study of Human Understanding*, ed. Frederick E. Crowe and Robert M. Doran, Toronto: University of Toronto Press, 1992 [1957]; Mary McClintock Fulkerson, *Changing the Subject: Women's*

Discourses and Feminist Theology, Minneapolis: Fortress Press, 1994, esp. ch. 1: 'Constructing a feminist liberation epistemology'; J. I. Packer, *Knowing God*, Downers Grove, IL: InterVarsity Press, 1973, 1993; Parker J. Palmer, *To Know as We Are Known: Education as a Spiritual Journey*, San Francisco: HarperCollins, 1993; Kevin J. Vanhoozer, 'Theology and the condition of postmodernity: a report on knowledge of God' in Kevin J. Vanhoozer (ed.), *The Cambridge Companion to Postmodern Theology*, Cambridge: Cambridge University Press, 2003.

ARTHUR G. HOLDER

Labour, Manual

Christianity has a rather undeveloped work ethic, and even less has been said about the value and meaning of manual labour. Although work is one of the most important human activities, the Bible has surprisingly little to say about the topic. People in the Hebrew Bible are rarely shown working, and in the New Testament only Paul makes work a necessary aspect of spiritual progress (1 Thess. 4.11; 2 Thess. 3.10).

When the gospel moved out of Palestine into Graeco-Roman culture, it suffered the prejudices of that culture against physical work. For complex reasons, the Mediterranean world relegated hard physical work to slaves. It was considered beneath the dignity of a free person. Therefore, when the Egyptian monks did field work (fourth century), they were either being counter-cultural or simply continuing their own peasant background.

They were also solving the practical problem of feeding themselves without begging, which was the tradition of the monks of the Far East. But even those monks who longed to 'pray always', recognized that a healthy, balanced life requires physical activity as well as mental and spiritual effort (*Sayings of the Desert Fathers*, Antony 1). Monks in Syria did not honour that principle and sometimes wound up begging or disparaging the work of ordinary people.

The difficult balance between the physical and the spiritual continues to be the point of monastic controversy and struggle throughout the ages. Whereas the Rule of the Master (RM) forbids the monks to do field work because it will make it impossible for them to fast (RM 86), St Benedict tells his community that 'they are truly monks when they live by the labour of their hands' (Rule of Benedict (RB) 48). It was assumed that one could easily meditate while doing simple manual labour.

This may sound like a solid argument for a holistic spirituality of manual labour, but it should not be overly relied upon. Benedict does not emphasize work nearly as much as is sometimes claimed. He says nothing about work as therapy or work as an ascetical means of purification. Nor does he discuss the intrinsic value of work as co-creation with God. He simply wants the monks to 'do what needs to be done' (RB 48.6).

Nevertheless, when the Cistercian monks wished to reform Benedictine monasticism in the twelfth century, one of their principal themes was a return to the manual labour demanded by the Rule of Benedict. They claimed, rightly, that the dominant Cluniac interpretation of the Rule had so emphasized the public liturgy that little time was left for work. Indeed, the Cluniac monks spent about eight hours a day in church and about three hours in housework. That does not mean that the Cluniac life was easy, for the exact performance of the liturgy is by no means so.

For their part, the Cistercians shortened the public liturgy so as to have more time in the fields. Along with this, they refused to accept the donation of churches and estates from which to collect rents. They really wanted to be 'blue-collar monks', and for a while they were. The medieval miniature paintings of the white monks clearing the wastelands of Europe with hoe and mattock are not false. Yet we should not retroject our modern romantic notions of outdoor work on the medieval monks. Their own views were much more theological and pragmatic.

But it must be added that this experiment did not work. The Cistercians found they could not pray the entire Divine Office and still find enough time in the fields to make a living. The economy of Europe was becoming monetary at this time, which had the effect of downgrading the value of manual labour. And so the White Monks had to introduce a whole class of 'family brothers', who worked long hours in the fields but spent little time in church.

This example shows that the manual labour of monks, and of everyone else, depends on the customs and values of the surrounding society. Moreover, in our own time, technological change has eliminated much physical work, at least in the industrialized countries. This means that what hard work remains is done by the poor and the uneducated, leaving the prestige of manual labour at the same low level it was in Roman times.

In this situation, a voice like that of Wendell Berry can make us aware that something important has been lost. As long as we live in an embodied condition in the physical world, we need to acknowledge that fact by working with our bodies. The degradation of the earth by remote, abstract forces can be countered by direct, hands-on knowledge of the world, the kind that can only be gained through honest physical work. To do so is a spiritual as well as a physical exercise.

See also **Benedictine Spirituality; Body and Spirituality; Cistercian Spirituality;** *Lectio Divina*; **Syriac Spirituality; Work.**

G. Constable, *The Reformation of the Twelfth Century*, Cambridge: Cambridge University Press, 1998; J. Leclercq et al., 'Lavoro', *Dictionario degli Istituti di Perfezione* 5.515–48 (1973).

TERRENCE KARDONG

Ladder

see Ascent

Latin American Spirituality

Culturally and religiously speaking, Latin America stretches from the desert south-west of the United States to Tierra del Fuego, some 13,000 kilometres to the south, making it more than twice as large as Europe. There are at least six distinct zones: the southern cone, made up of Argentina and Chile; Brazil, including the immense tropical forests of the Amazon river watershed; the northern Andes (including Bolivia, Peru, Ecuador, Columbia); Mesoamerica, stretching from Costa Rica north into Mexico; northern Mexico and the border region with the United States; and, finally, the Caribbean, including both the islands themselves and the Caribbean coastal regions of South and Central America. Latin America counts thousands of distinct language and culture groups among the indigenous peoples, overlaid historically by highly complex civilizations in Mesoamerica and the central Andes and then by the cultures brought by Spain and Portugal with the sixteenth-century conquest (to a lesser extent, too, by France and Britain), and those that came subsequently from Africa with the slave trade.

As a consequence of this complexity, few generalizations that would rise above the level of the trivial can do justice to, say, the Peyote Hunt of the Huichol Indians in the Sierra Madre Mountains of Mexico and the activism of base Christian communities in the slums of Santiago – both of which equally deserve to be treated under the category of spirituality. If there is a general feature it is the one identified by Virgil Elizondo in speaking of the culture and spirituality of Mexicans and Mexican-Americans:

mestizaje. The history of spirituality in Latin America is a history of the encounter and mixing of different cultures. This means too that spirituality in Latin America is particularly tied to negotiating the challenges to meaning, and to life itself, that come from invasion and subjugation, as well as from living as a *mestizo*, as someone both in and in between cultures. This has resulted in great creativity and diversity in Latin American spiritualities.

History. The mixing of cultures in Latin America began in Neolithic times with successive waves of hunter-gatherers passing through from the north. Agriculture and the first Neolithic village settlements began in the third millennium (a little later in Mesoamerica). As with similar cultures around the world, their spiritualities centred on the multifold epiphanies of the sacred in the natural world and the need for human beings to integrate themselves into the interplay of sacred forces that impinged on their reality and determined their fate. Urban civilizations began developing in Mesoamerica in the first millennium before Christ. These civilizations (the Olmec, Toltec, Maya and Aztec peoples, among others, and later, the Incas in the Central Andes) developed highly sophisticated religions, with a professional priestly class, complex mythologies and elaborate rituals predicated on a complex understanding of the interrelationship between space and time. Their spiritualities had a strong sense of the fragility of a world hospitable to humans and the need for humans to participate in its continuation and regeneration. They were also thoroughly embodied. This can be seen both in the centrality of sacred places, manifested in both the great ceremonial sites and in domestic shrines, and in the stress on the human body itself as a locus for sacred powers. While much of the spirituality focused on the need to attend to the regeneration and stabilization of a social and natural environment always under threat, and thus was tightly integrated into social and political structures, there were intriguing beginnings of a more 'Ecclesiastes-like' spirituality of scepticism and a search for transcendent truth beyond this world: in the schools of higher learning, or '*calmecas*' of the Aztecs, for instance.

The Spanish conquest of the sixteenth century brought with it a vibrant, expansionary – in many ways militaristic – spirituality of a nation forging its identity out of the re-conquest of the Iberian Peninsula. The significant presence of religious orders in the Americas, particularly the Franciscans and the Jesuits, meant that many of the riches of European Christian spirituality were brought to Latin America; but the exigencies of evangelization and the milieu of Counter-Reformation Spain and Portugal had a greater impact. The spiritualities they inculcated emphasized all of the sacraments, the cult of the saints, especially Mary, and certain sacramentals (holy water, penitential rituals, pilgrimages). This was probably in part because these practices were contested by Protestants, and in part because they provided points of contact with indigenous spiritualities, with their concern for past generations and their embodiedness. Religious confraternities, or *cofradías*, a prominent feature of Spanish and Portuguese popular religion, were introduced as ways of organizing the indigenous peoples. For the latter, they became a way of continuing clan- and kin-based religious associations, and, thereby, some of the spiritual practices of their ancestors. As a rule, then, spiritualities in Latin America did not experience the disembodiment, interiorization or privatization characteristic of much of European spirituality after the Reformation. Spirituality was based and expressed in the local community, and very much tied to struggles for cultural identity.

Perhaps the most dramatic instance of this is the devotion to the Virgin of Guadalupe in Mexico and US south-west. The tradition of her apparition to a Nahuatl-speaking Indian, not long after the conquest, goes back to the sixteenth century, although its precise historicity is contested. What is not contested is that veneration of 'la morenita', identified both with Mary and with the Aztec mother-goddess, Tonantzin, defines a whole cluster of spiritual practices, including pilgrimages, fiestas, the creation and keeping of domestic altars, and so on, that has enabled the indigenous peoples and Spanish-Indian *mestizos* of Mexico, and later the Mexican-American *mestizos* of the US south-west, to survive and assert their dignity as a people, under extremely hostile conditions. The spirituality deploys and integrates into corresponding elements from Spanish Catholicism the embodiedness of ancient Mesoamerican spiritualities, the focus on the sacredness of the body, especially the heart, and the prominent place of food and fiestas, among others. Her cult, which has many analogues, such as the Virgen de la Caridad of Cuba, has expanded beyond the boundaries of Mexican and Mexican-American communities, and even outside the boundaries of Christianity. It provides an example of the creativity and robustness of Latin American spiritualities' response to adverse conditions of conquest and cultural subalternation.

Three other developments have shaped Latin American spirituality. The first is the slave trade. Over the course of four centuries, millions of Africans were brought to Latin America, particularly to the Caribbean region and Brazil, the latter of which received over three and a half million slaves. They were in many ways able to maintain their own religious traditions, albeit covertly, and as they gained greater freedoms in the nineteenth century, these traditions re-emerged, although now melded with Catholic practices. The second is the wave of Protestant missionary activity in the nineteenth century, coming especially from the United States. In the twentieth century, Pentecostalism arrived, again from the United States, with its distinctive spirituality. In the past decades it has experienced dramatic growth, quickly developing its own indigenous Churches. Finally, the reorientation of the Latin American Roman Catholic Church effected at the meeting of Latin American Bishops at Medellín in 1968 catalysed the development of liberation theology and its distinctive spirituality of action for justice.

Modern trends. This brief and very simplified historical sketch can indicate the complexity of the spiritual landscape in Latin America today. In the past the virtual hegemony of Roman Catholicism in the region provided a framework for approaching its religion and spirituality, but this has changed dramatically over the past fifty years. Although Roman Catholicism still predominates, various Protestant denominations, and above all Pentecostalism and related Holiness movements, have made major inroads in Latin America. The flourishing of syncretic religions, such as Santería in Brazil and the Caribbean, and the more public assertion of indigenous spiritualities in places like Chiapas, southern Mexico, add further complexity. Finally, the globalization of religions and spiritualities that is so evident in the United States is also increasingly manifest in Latin America. Thus, for example, in Mexico and Brazil, Buddhism is on the rise among the upper classes; while, ironically, the Japanese who brought it abandon it in order to assimilate more quickly.

Three features may still be asserted of spirituality in Latin America. First, it is intensely communal. Even the more privatized patterns of Protestant spiritualities that emphasize one's personal relationship to Christ take on communal features in Latin America, mainly because the flourishing of the individual cannot be conceived in a Latin American context in a purely 'spiritualist' way; neither can it be disconnected from the flourishing of the individual's local community. Second, it is embodied: Latin

American spiritualities live in and through all five senses. This can be seen in processions and fiestas, from the celebration of 'Las Posadas' in San Antonio, Texas, to Carnival in Rio de Janeiro. Third, in Latin America, as in North America, individual spiritualities tend more and more to be a bricollage of beliefs and practices drawn from the great diversity of spiritual traditions now present there. This is as evident in Santería in the Caribbean as it is in Brazilian women who are members of a base Christian community, with its liberationist spirituality, but also attend Pentecostal prayer meetings. What is interesting is that whereas in North America this construction of individual spiritualities is emblematic of the middle and upper classes, in Latin America it is just as marked among the poor.

See also Liberation Spirituality.

D. A. Brading, Mexican Phoenix: Our Lady of Guadalupe: Image and Tradition Across Five Centuries, Cambridge: Cambridge University Press, 2001; David Carrasco, Religions of Mesoamerica: Cosmovison and Ceremonial Centers, San Francisco: Harper & Row, 1990; Guillermo Cook (ed.), Crosscurrents in Indigenous Spirituality: Interface of Maya, Catholic and Protestant Worldviews, New York: E. J. Brill, 1997; Gary Gossen with Miguel Léon-Portilla (ed.), South and Meso-American Native Spirituality: From the Cult of the Feathered Serpent to the Theology of Liberation, WS, vol. 4, New York: Crossroad, 1993; Christian Smith and Joshua Prokopy (eds), Latin American Religion in Motion, New York: Routledge, 1999; Lawrence Sullivan, Icanchu's Drum: South American Religions: A Search for Orientation, New York: Macmillan, 1988.

MATTHEW ASHLEY

Lay People and Spirituality

Addressing the subject of spirituality and lay people, or a lay spirituality, entails the recognition of the central, foundational role of baptism in the Christian spiritual life. Lay spirituality is none other than life in Christ through the presence and power of the Spirit to the glory of the Father. The spirituality of lay people is rooted in the gift of the Spirit given in baptism by which they become members of a people (laos), a holy people, a royal priesthood, sharing in the mission of Word and Spirit, becoming a sacrament of communion and justice in the world. This spirituality is shaped by the formative role of the Word of God in Scripture, by ongoing participation in the sacramental life of the Church, and by taking up the daily commitment to discipleship as part of Christ's body, the Church. Common understandings of the term 'lay' as unlettered or non-professional can muddle the fundamental dignity of all the baptized, ordained and non-ordained, who together make up a holy people, the people of God (laos theou).

In baptism one is initiated into a way of life rooted in the covenant. This covenant is rooted in the love of God given in Christ and the on-going gift of the Spirit, the life of God pouring itself forth. Christian life in the Spirit is shaped by an awareness of responsibility more than obligation, a responsibility springing from membership in God's holy people. The mature and responsible Christian is committed to being and building the body of Christ in the Church and in the world, so that both will be transformed by love.

All too often in Christian history, the 'common' spirituality of the baptized has been understood as less essential than particular priestly, religious or monastic spiritualities. The former has often been thought to derive from the latter, as seen in efforts to apply the wisdom of the Rule of Benedict to life 'in the world', or in the efforts of members of third orders to adhere to a mitigated rule of life based upon that of the Franciscans, the Dominicans or the Carmelites. This tendency to work within a model of derivation is not found only among Roman Catholics. In any case, in speaking of a lay spirituality, we move in precisely the opposite direction. Specific spiritualities such as Franciscan, Ignatian or Benedictine are only properly understood when they are seen as specifications or distinctive manifestations of the baptismal spirituality to which all are called by virtue of their membership in God's people. In that sense, they are derivative of and dependent upon a baptismal spirituality. Said another way, all authentic Christian spirituality is cultivated, nurtured and sustained by Word, sacrament and belonging to a community of discipleship. All the baptized, whatever their situation in life, are called to the fullness of life in Christ by the presence and power of the Holy Spirit as this is discerned in and through membership in God's people, the Church.

Baptism: participation in the mission of Word and Spirit. By baptism, one bears the name Christian. Whatever one's way or walk in life, whatever the calling, or particular vocation, it is in service of the common call given as a gift in baptism. And the one, common call is to participate in the mission of the Word and the Spirit and, by so doing, to share in the very life of God.

Who is God? God's name above and beyond

all naming is love. God is love (1 John 4.8). What is love? Love is the life that pours itself forth – as gift. The gift of God's life, which is love, is constantly, everywhere and always pouring forth as gift.

Word is God's love made visible, tangible and audible. Word is God's love seen, touched and heard. Every Christian calling is to continue to render love visible, tangible and audible, so that God is seen and touched and heard amid a broken world. The one call of all who live in Christ through the gift of the Sprit is to cultivate, to nurture, to sustain all manifestations of love – through preaching, teaching, catechesis and sacramental celebration, but also in art, literature, works of mercy, family life, tending the sick and promoting a society more just and a Church more in keeping with the reign of God – God's hope, desire, intention for the world now and to come, a world in which truth, holiness, justice, love and peace will hold sway.

The *Spirit* is God's love creating, animating and bonding. The Spirit is God's very life toward us, for us, with us and within us. Christian life in the Spirit, or the Christian spiritual life, entails participation in all creative, animating, bonding and unifying expressions of divine love, becoming a sign of reconciliation of peace amid a world so deeply divided. By the gift of the Spirit, God dwells within the human heart endowing the Christian with firm faith to walk in the light of Christ, abundant hope to move forward in the face of every obstacle, and love's flourishing so that all the living might share in the divine life – even now.

The Spirit has been given in baptism, and sealed and strengthened in confirmation. The fruits of the Spirit are the gift to every one of the baptized: love, joy, peace, patience, kindness, generosity, faithfulness, gentleness, self-control. Against these there is no law (Gal. 5.22–26). The various disciplines of the spiritual life, such as abstinence, fasting, methods of prayer, making retreat, are properly understood not as ends but as means of growing to fuller maturation in the Spirit, being conformed to the person of Christ, brought into deeper communion with God and others.

Because the spiritual life has often been understood as the prerogative of monks and nuns, clergy and religious, lay persons are still often at a loss for understanding spiritual growth and development as part of the responsibility entailed in their baptismal promises. Many are at sea, left wondering: how is the spiritual life to be cultivated amid the cacophony and clutter, the break-neck speed at which many, if not most, Christians move through life? How are the fruits of the Spirit, the seeds of which are given in baptism, nurtured? How are Christians, often deeply divided themselves, to live together in these dark days in the communion of the Spirit, participating more fully in the mission of Word and Spirit, becoming a sign of reconciliation and peace? Answering these questions provides occasion for each one, in light of the specific gifts given, to give shape to a particular spirituality. But any spirituality which is first and finally baptismal, that is, lay, will be (1) informed by the Word of God in Scripture; (2) strengthened by ongoing participation in the liturgical life of the Church, and (3) given particular shape through a sense of responsibility springing from membership in God's holy people.

Informed by the Word. Because of the renewal of Church life and practice prompted by the Second Vatican Council, Catholics have grown in an appreciation of the importance of sacred Scripture. However, many still tend to think of the Word of God in Scripture as secondary to the sacraments. Nonetheless, the Catholic tradition has consistently affirmed the crucial importance of both Word and sacrament, expressed in the words of Augustine:

> Brothers and Sisters, here is a question for you: which to you seems the greater, the Word of God or the Body of Christ? If you want to give the right answer you will reply that God's word is not less than Christ's Body. Therefore, just as we take care when we receive the Body of Christ so that no part of it falls to the ground so, likewise, should we insure that the word of God which is given to us is not lost to our souls because we are speaking or thinking about something different. One who listens negligently to God's word is just as guilty as one who, through carelessness, allows Christ's Body to fall to the ground.

Central to any lay spirituality is the discipline of slow, careful pondering of God's Word in the pages of the Bible, Sunday by Sunday, year by year, day by day. If there is one, prime disposition, a single attitude to be cultivated as a spiritual discipline central to a lay spirituality it is active receptivity, learning how to receive the gift of the Spirit in and through the Word of God in Scripture.

Strengthened in worship. In the waters of baptism, by the anointing in the Spirit in confirmation, and through the ongoing celebration of the Eucharist, the Christian is brought into a way of life rooted in worship and service. Living for the glory of God the Father, through Christ, in the Spirit, which is the very heart of the Christian life, is a life of worship and of service, whatever one's particular service in the Church or to the larger human family might be. For the lay person, the question is this: is worship really at the centre of my life, and do I see service as a source of spirituality? Or, do I think of spirituality as something associated with the 'interior life', or with a particular devotion, or a prayer technique? Do I see worship and service as ways of being and building the body of Christ? And do I recognize that everything I say and do are ways of becoming a living doxology, a living act of praise to the Father, through Christ, in the communion of the Spirit. Living a life rooted in worship and service entails living what is said and done in liturgy, and understanding oneself as first and finally a member of God's people.

In relation to God's people. By baptism, one is incorporated into the people of God, the body of Christ. All, not just some, are called to live the fullness of the Christian life, through witness, worship and service.

Witness includes, but is not limited to teaching, catechizing, proclaiming the word, prophetic utterance, faithfulness in illness, challenging structures and systems that depersonalize and dehumanize, constant prayer, hoping when there seems to be no reason to hope.

Worship involves full, conscious and active participation in the sacramental worship of the Church, but also include any and all activities through which God is praised and glorified.

Service is expressed in manifold ways, but is expressed most concretely by attending to the material needs of those in our families, neighbourhoods, workplaces and communities, as well as the wider human family.

A lay spirituality is none other than life in Christ through the gift of the Spirit. Every spiritual discipline and all spiritual growth and development is to be understood and evaluated in light of the common Christian call to share in the mission of Christ and the Spirit, being and building the body of Christ as a sacrament of truth, holiness, justice, love and peace in and to the world.

See also **Baptism; Ecclesiology and Spirituality; Ministry and Spirituality; Mission and Spirituality.**

John Paul II, 'Apostolic exhortation on the laity' (*Christifideles Laici*), *Origins* 18.35, pp. 261–83; National Conference of Catholic Bishops, *Called and Gifted for the Third Millennium*, Washington, DC: United States Catholic Conference, 1995; Susan K. Wood (ed.), *Ordering the Baptismal Priesthood: Theologies of Lay and Ordained Ministry*, Collegeville, MN: The Liturgical Press, 2003.

MICHAEL DOWNEY

Leadership

From the beginning spirituality and leadership have lived in dynamic tension with one another. Sometimes abiding in harmony, sometimes clashing in dissonance, spirituality and leadership have coexisted as both foes and friends.

Early Christians drew on biblical stories and exhortations to build a foundation for their understanding of leadership. From Moses, Deborah, Isaiah and the kings of Israel to Jesus, the disciples, Paul, Phoebe and the deacons and elders of the New Testament, biblical rolemodels and teachings inspired and instructed leaders. The Bible's exemplary prophets, kings and disciples provided illustrations of spiritually grounded leaders and hence visions of leadership to which to aspire, at the same time that stories of such characters as Saul, Eli and Judas warned leaders of how far they could fall if they abandoned their spiritual core.

As the Church grew into an institution, especially after 330 CE when Constantine declared Christianity the state religion, questions about the relationship among power, authority, leadership and spirituality assumed centre stage. Arguments revolved around the source and style of authority. For some, leaders gained their authority through Jesus Christ by appointment of the Church hierarchy. Once appointed, leaders had the right to command and control those beneath them, with little accountability. In this view leaders who claimed authority based on Holy Spirit's inspiration and guidance were usually seen as threats to legitimate authority. For others, leaders gained their authority first from Jesus Christ and secondarily through multiple sources such as Scripture, personal holiness and the gifts of the Holy Spirit. Leaders were to be servants, serving the people as Jesus had served the disciples. In this view, leaders who claimed authority based on the inspiration of the Spirit were taken seriously and assisted in their discernment of the Spirit's guidance. Once such a leader failed to exhibit personal holiness or reliance on Scripture, or failed to exercise servant leadership, the leader could be rebuked and held accountable.

In actual practice, most held some combination of various elements of these two views of leadership, tending more toward one or the other. While the institutional Church tended toward the former, monasticism kept the latter view alive for centuries. The writings of such monastic leaders as St Benedict, St Bonaventure and St Teresa are full of exhortations to the abbot or abbess to be steeped in Scripture, holy, filled with the Holy Spirit, and a servant to the brothers or sisters. Bonaventure's writing, for example, typifies this literature by focusing on six characteristics that leaders of monastic communities should exhibit: devotion to God; zeal for righteousness (both in oneself and others); compassion; patience; a life that serves as a role-model to the community; and discernment.

Martin Luther, John Calvin, Richard Baxter, George Fox and other Reformation leaders revisited questions of spirituality, authority and leadership, often leaning toward the latter view in the early days of their movements and eventually incorporating elements of the former view as their denominations became established. Born out of a revolt against authority, Reformation churches discovered that spiritual leadership's integral relationship with authority could not be ignored.

With the advent of the twentieth century, a confluence of factors returned the latter view of leadership to the fore. The Church (both Catholic and Protestant) began to take seriously such cultural developments as the rise of modern science, historical consciousness and the turn to the subject, thus causing scholars to question the authoritarian view of leadership held by the institutional Church. Vatican II thrust this thinking from a small group of scholars out into the Catholic Church as a whole. Meanwhile, Protestant churches were being influenced by the anti-authoritarian movements of the 1960s and the literature on servant leadership. Liberation theology in Latin America, Africa and Asia, political theology in Europe, and feminist and womanist theology all presented more collaborative, socially aware understandings of leadership which influenced the Church widely.

At the same time, the twentieth century saw the rise of secular leadership theory. Apparently at odds with religious understandings of leadership, since secular theories focused on leader effectiveness and organizational performance, while religious understandings stressed the importance of virtuous leadership for its own sake, secular theories unexpectedly met religious understandings in the last decade of the twentieth century. A growing chorus of secular voices had been arguing that spirituality was necessary in organizations for ethical behaviour, for job satisfaction and employee commitment, and for productivity and competitive advantage. Increasingly, this point was being demonstrated empirically. Along with the spirituality in organ-

izations theme in the chorus ran the spiritual leadership variation on the theme. Numerous popular and scholarly speakers and writers argued that spiritual leadership should form the backbone of the spiritual organization.

A number of contemporary degree programmes, writers and trainers in spiritual leadership now seek to integrate elements of the two strands. Some continue to emphasize religious leadership models, integrating aspects of secular leadership theory which serve their purposes. Others draw on the religious literature and then broaden it, seeking to base their understanding of spiritual leadership on the wisdom of religious traditions while creating a more inclusive model for the twenty-first century. They then integrate insights of secular leadership theory which they find compatible with spiritual leadership. Still others attempt to create a model of spiritual leadership which is entirely separate from religion, believing that such a model is more accessible to a wide audience and more easily integrated with secular leadership theory.

A subset of both the academic literature on leadership and the academic literature on spirituality in organizations, the academic literature on spiritual leadership is still in its infancy. Its current development, driven by management scholars, focuses on building a testable theory of spiritual leadership using social scientific constructs. Scholars in the academic field of spirituality have yet to enter the dialogue.

See also **Business and Spirituality.**

M. Downey (ed.), *That They Might Live: Power, Empowerment and Leadership in the Church*, New York: Crossroad, 1991; L. W. Fry, 'Toward a theory of spiritual leadership', *Leadership Quarterly* 14 (2003), 693–727; R. Giacolone and C. Jurkiewicz (eds), *Handbook of Workplace Spirituality and Organizational Performance*, Armonk, NY: Sharpe, 2003; C. Gratton, 'Selected bibliography on the topic of spiritual formation and leadership', *Studies in Formative Spirituality* 3 (1982), 165–72; E. Townes, 'A womanist perspective on spirituality in leadership', *Theological Education* 37.1 (2000), 73–96.

MARGARET BENEFIEL

Lectio Divina

An ancient Christian term referring to the prayerful reading of the Bible. *Lectio divina* is sometimes translated 'spiritual reading', but that seems too pallid and subject to excessively broad interpretation. The literal translation 'reading from God' can remind us that Scripture is God's word in writing. If *lectio divina* is not tightly restricted to the Bible itself, at least it should only be applied to Christian literature that is solidly based on Scripture.

An interesting text on the subject of *lectio divina* is the Rule of St Benedict (RB), ch. 48. Here the great Italian legislator arranges that his monks will have at least three hours daily where they are 'free (*vacare*) for *lectio divina*'. Along with manual labour and the Divine Office, *lectio divina* forms one of the three basic activities of Benedict's community. Hence the famous motto 'work and pray' is not accurate, unless *lectio divina* is implied in 'pray'.

The term *vacare* is very revealing, for it is a clear indication that *lectio divina* was not just another form of work for the monks. And yet, it was not easy for most of them, and so monitors were to check to see that those who were bored (*acediosus*, RB 48.18) did not disturb others. Perhaps it was thought of as a form of holy leisure, where they were to spend meaningful, but not productive, time with the word of God.

If *lectio divina* was not thought of as work, neither was it simply a matter of studying the Bible during these hours. True, Benedict usually manages to reserve for *lectio divina* those hours when the mind would be freshest, but desire for God, not intellectual sharpness, is the primary requisite for fruitful *lectio divina*. Of course, the more one knows about the text of Scripture, the better one can pray it. Most ancient monastic libraries included commentaries on Scripture by the church Fathers, and surely the monks included them in their *lectio divina*.

But the Bible was the main focus of monastic *lectio divina*. In RB 48.15, each monk is to accept a book from the 'library' (*bibliotheca*) for Lenten reading; this may well refer to the various fascicles into which ancient Bibles were bound. At any rate, Benedict calls Scripture 'a completely reliable guidepost' (*rectissima norma*, 73.3), so it would be the centre of any reading programme that he would institute.

We can gain some further insight into the nature of ancient monastic *lectio divina* from the way people read in those days. In short, they did so out loud, even to themselves. And so even though Benedict allows the monks to substitute reading for siesta, he has to warn them to avoid disturbing the sleepers (RB 48.5). Although such a method of reading could be socially difficult, it did affect the reader quite differently than does our modern practice of silent perusal. When ancient people read, they involved most of their faculties: tongue, ears and eyes.

As anyone knows who has tried it, such a practice is ideal for memorization, and it seems this was a major part of *lectio divina* for the early monks. Pachomius demands that new recruits be able to memorize large parts of the Bible (Rule, 139–40), no doubt to enable them to participate in the Divine Office, which was mostly done by heart. Benedict likewise tells the brothers to spend the time after Vigils memorizing psalms and lessons they will need (RB 8.3).

But the Scripture memorized in *lectio divina* was more for private prayer than for the Office. Indeed, the term *meditare*, which is used in this connection (RB 48.23), should probably not be translated 'meditate' but 'ruminate'. Once a biblical passage had been gotten by heart, it could be 'chewed over' or meditated at any time. Such meditation is far from an abstract exercise, for it has Scripture as its basis and it involves the repetition of the very word of God. In fact, this form of prayer predominated in the Church until the Bible was separated from mental prayer in the late Middle Ages.

Although Benedict never says so, it is very likely that he concurs with the other early monastic legislators that this practice of ruminating the word of God should continue during periods of work. Since most monastic work was simple and repetitive, it would be possible to combine it with this form of prayer. And thus *lectio divina* could function as the wellspring of a life of continual prayer.

See also **Spirituality and Scripture; Exegesis, Spiritual; Leisure; Labour, Manual; Meditation; Memory; Senses, Spiritual.**

Michael Casey, *Sacred Reading*, Ligouri, MO: Triumph Books, 1996; Terrence Kardong, 'The vocabulary of monastic *Lectio* in RB 48', *Cistercian Studies* 16 (1981), 171–81; Ambrose Wathen, 'Monastic *Lectio*: some clues from terminology', *Monastic Studies* 12 (1976), 207–15.

TERRENCE KARDONG

Leisure

History. Leisure or the free time that we experience whether planned or unplanned was not a specific topic of writers except in passing until modern times. Negative attitudes toward the body in the Middle Ages as well as the Calvinistic spirituality of the Reformation prevented any view of leisure as a good in itself. It has become more the focus of writers in modern times for several reasons. Modernity and its industrial and technological developments have given the ordinary person more free time. Over the past century modern society has produced in people such leisure-time activities as sports, shopping, technological games and increasingly organized vacations and travel. To the extent that these activities often amount to more work for people than play, the value of them and, thus, the meaning of leisure, have come into question. The religious strictures against leisure with their implied 'leisure is the workshop of the devil' kind of mentality have continued to lessen. And now, leisure itself has become the object of philosophical and theological reflection. Hugo Rahner in his *Man at Play* addressed leisure theologically and Joseph Pieper spoke of leisure in more psychological terms. For the latter it is a kind of ritual.

Approaches to leisure as a spiritual value. Leisure can be seen as a time for creativity. This may be the creativity of the artist, the scientist or the ritualist. All require the leisure that gives the necessary psychological space for the imagination to be activated, to follow its own rhythm and to be free of distraction. The media continually find ways to fill up leisure time. This can have a salutary effect as when it brings people together around sporting events, news that broadens people's cultural horizons, and that kind of religious and cultural programming which enhances personhood even when the television viewer is seeking entertainment or distraction.

Leisure is usually defined in opposition to work. But leisure as a spiritual value does not mean that one does nothing or wanders aimless from one thing to another in search of nothing in particular. Leisure becomes spiritually fulfilling when it provides the opportunity to read good literature, pursue a hobby such as birdwatching, practise the piano, go to a play, or spend time playing games with one's children. Leisure is not a way to escape the world but to enter more profoundly into present reality. Whatever one does in leisure time is to help one find a home here, to experience dwelling in this world as happy.

Leisure time provides the opportunity to grow more fully as human beings. This is especially important for people for whom their work may not be a fulfilling experience. But in order for this to be so one must experience leisure as full of meaning. People are not finding meaning and significance for themselves in the trivial ways their culture suggests for leisure time: sports, technological games, overly organized vacations or more work disguised as play. In order for that to happen one must make a connection with reality by means of the imagination. And so there is a need to act in ways in leisure time that exercise one's imaginative powers. One should move from leisure time to one's work time with a feeling of refreshment not dullness. When Joseph Pieper spoke about being in tune with the world, he meant that our restful and/or playful time is one where people are imaginatively connected with life not where they are anaesthetized by the trivial and dull.

As modern technology makes it possible for people to have more hours of leisure in a week, it is more important that individuals become more intentional regarding this free time. This does not mean turning leisure time into another kind of work time, but to let oneself get lost in this free time as one gets lost in a good conversation, an intriguing play or in sensuous expressions of love. It is moving from chronological time to chairotic (grace-filled) time, which can be called liminal time.

This liminal quality is what makes leisure time become sacred time. Much can be learned from those cultures for whom leisure time has been less separated from daily living and for whom leisure is a much more wholesome experience. A paradigm of leisure time is the Hispanic celebration of fiesta. Fiesta is a family-oriented celebration that brings together the many scattered and fragmented parts of what is supposed to be close-knit relationships. Others can learn from the Hispanic fiesta how leisure can be sacred time. Fiesta is sacred because it is more than empty time. It can be the time of healing. Whether the participants are suffering from alienation, hopelessness or oppression or whether from fragmentation due to drugs, crime or children caught up in gangs, the imaginative power of the fiesta provides alternative self-images to those who are powerless, alienated or marginalized. Fiesta is healing because it is an affirmation of life. It is a concrete expression of why life is worth living. It is also a counter-cultural experience because it challenges all those cultural ideologies that are destructive of the spiritual quality of leisure such as workaholism, ambition and consumerism. Fiesta is a temporary reprieve from that. It cannot be reduced to play. It is a celebration of life. Leisure can be no less than that.

See also **Celebration; Sport and Spirituality; Work.**

Jonathan Gershung, *Changing Times: Work and Leisure in Postindustrial Society*, Oxford: Oxford University Press, 2001; Timothy Jones, *Awake my Soul: Practical Spirituality for Busy People*, New York: Galilee, 2000; Troy Messenger, *Holy Leisure: Recreation and Religion in God's Square Mile*, Minneapolis: University of Minnesota Press, 1999; Joseph Pieper, *In Tune with the World*, New York: Harcourt & Brace, 1965; Adolfo Quezada, *Sabbath Moments: Finding Rest for the Soul in the Midst of Daily Living*, Totowa, NJ: Resurrection Press, 2003; Hugo Rahner, *Man at Play*, New York: Herder, 1967.

JAMES EMPEREUR

Liberation Spirituality

Liberation theology can refer generally to a large family of theologies, present on every continent except Antarctica, that focus on the superation of unjust social, political and economic structures as an integral part of Christian faith. The perspective from which these structures are identified and addressed, however, can be variously situated in terms of economic class, race and ethnicity (e.g. black theology), gender (feminist theology), and more recently, even biological species (ecological or environmental theology). Here we consider only Latin American liberation theology, which arose in the 1960s and 1970s in Central and South America.

As with many twentieth-century spiritualities, liberation spirituality stresses the need to resist and overcome (1) the restriction of spirituality to some relatively small group of Christian elites, (2) spirituality's privatization, and (3) its excessive interiorization. For liberation spirituality this is most manifest in the essentially communal and ecclesial framework of liberation spirituality, and in its focus on following Jesus, particularly the Jesus who came to proclaim and effect an 'integral liberation' (as Gustavo Gutiérrez first named it) of all human beings, but especially the poor and marginalized, from everything that prevents them from having life, and having it to the full. A brief consideration of these two aspects provides a framework for considering two principal authors of liberation theology and spirituality: Gustavo Gutiérrez and Jon Sobrino. I then close with a few remarks on new trends in liberation spirituality.

1. *The communal dimension.* Liberation spirituality has always had a strong communal dimension, a dimension that is usually expressed ecclesially. This is due in part to its birthplace. Latin American spirituality in general has a strong communal dimension, and it has almost always been intimately tied to struggles for identity, or even survival, within a history of conquests, war and grinding poverty and oppression for the region's poor majorities. This communal dimension may also be explained in part by the fact that some of its principal architects were trained in Europe during a time when the historical, social and ecclesial dimensions of spirituality were being stressed, by figures such as M.-D. Chenu, for instance.

As a social movement, liberation theology and spirituality have important roots in new pastoral strategies implemented in the mid twentieth century by the Roman Catholic Church to reach the laity and involve them in the Church's life.

Popes Pius X and Pius XI both emphasized this need. The resulting 'Catholic Action' movement, with ancillary movements such as the Young Christian Students, emphasized communal reading of Scripture and prayer, and concrete action for incarnating a life of faith. Not only did many later advocates of liberation spirituality participate in these communities, but they provided a precedent for the base Christian communities, which were promoted particularly after the meeting of Roman Catholic bishops of Latin America at Medellín in 1968. These communities have been both the root of liberation spirituality's vitality and a laboratory for its ongoing creation. Finally, the communal-ecclesial dimension has also given liberation spirituality a distinctive connection to the institutional Church. Indeed, some of the most important figures in the development of liberation spirituality have been bishops: inter alia, Cardinal Paulo Evaristo Arns, Pedro Casadáliga, Oscar Romero and Samuel Ruiz. The pastoral letters and homilies of prelates such as these are an important source for the study of liberation spirituality.

The communal dimension of liberation spirituality is strongly evident in Gustavo Gutiérrez's work. The subtitle of his primary work on liberation spirituality, *We Drink from Our Own Wells*, is 'the spiritual journey of a people'. Gutiérrez takes up the spiritual motif of 'journey', rerooting it in its biblical locus of the Exodus. He thinks of it not primarily as the journey of the individual soul to God, but of a people toward a new way of life: one of profound and integral communion (friendship) with each other and with God. Remarkable in this regard is Gutiérrez's appropriation of John of the Cross, rereading John's itinerary of the spiritual life (including the forms of the dark night) to describe the struggle of Christian communities to live a more human life, a struggle that is at the same time physical and spiritual.

2. *A spirituality of discipleship.* It may be that the Franciscan and Jesuit allegiances of important proponents of liberation spirituality, such as Leonardo Boff, Juan Luis Segundo and Jon Sobrino, have contributed to the heavy emphasis in liberation spirituality on the spiritual practices of engaging the New Testament accounts of Jesus as historical accounts, and imitating the Jesus found thereby. Ewert Cousins, speaking of Francis of Assisi, has called this a 'mysticism of the historical event', which finds in historical events of the past not just the instantiation of universal forms and archetypes to be eventually transcended and left behind in the spiritual itin-

erary, but perduring loci for a spirituality that is fulfilled precisely in embracing and transforming one's own historical times more radically (which is to say, evangelically). These writers have taken up and reconfigured the distinctive forms of the *vita mixta* of contemplation and action found in the Franciscan and Ignatian traditions. Thus, they advocate a form of 'contemplation in action', insisting, however, that not just any action can serve as the context and basis of such a spirituality, but only the action of struggling for life and justice for the poor. Ignacio Ellacuría, for instance, called this 'contemplation' and Leonardo Boff speaks of 'contemplatives in liberation'. This 'praxis' or 'active life' of solidarity with the poor and struggling for justice on their behalf provides a context for the 'theoria' both of contemplation and also of speculative theological production.

When liberation theologians emphasize 'the historical Jesus', therefore, it is more accurate to relate this emphasis not primarily to one or other of the 'quests' for the historical Jesus, but rather to the tradition of *lectio divina*, and the meditative reading of the New Testament laid out, for instance, in the Second Week of Ignatius of Loyola's Spiritual Exercises. It is, accordingly, an approach to Jesus that stresses not so much factual knowledge as it does an affective knowledge that leads to love and imitation of Jesus in one's own historical circumstances. Jesuit theologians Juan Luis Segundo and Jon Sobrino have written extensively on this. Sobrino sees the spiritual life as a process of making real, and really effective (which means transformative), in one's life and historical circumstances, the basic structure of Jesus' life. He understands this structure in terms of the basic christological loci: incarnation, cross, resurrection and second coming. A spiritual life that recapitulates the structure of incarnation, for instance, is one that enters wholly, honestly and tenaciously into historical reality, especially where it is threatened by sin and death. As the classic mystical tradition asserts the possibility of moments, however fleeting, in which we can experience the final *telos* of union with God, for Sobrino we can live in some ways and fleetingly, as persons 'already risen', risen into the fullness of life for all that is the *telos* of history, however much this 'experience' often comes in mystery and a 'dark current of hope' that is the correlate in his spirituality to Gutiérrez's talk of the 'dark night of injustice'.

3. *Recent trends.* Changing circumstances in Latin America in the 1980s and 1990s, not surprisingly, had an impact on liberation theology

and spirituality. There has been a broadening of the vision of poverty and injustice so as to grapple with the oppression of indigenous peoples, of women and even of nature. A good example of this trend is the work of Francisco Boff and Ivone Gebara. Boff has recently written passionately on the need to incorporate ecological concern within liberation theology and spirituality, looking particularly at the devastation being visited on the Amazon River Basin. This has been a natural evolution for him, drawing once again on the legacy of Francis of Assisi. Gebara is a good example of someone who has not only taken up this ecological vision, but also the plight of the indigenous (again in Brazil), all within the broader framework of feminist concerns. Like many feminists, her spirituality tends to be more daring in its appeal to sources outside the Bible and mainline Christian traditions, although the spiritualities of Francis of Assisi and Teilhard de Chardin figure prominently.

A second striking development is the growing emphasis on martyrdom. This is not surprising given the fate of countless thousands of Christians who lived this spirituality and were murdered for it by the state. Liberationists have never been naively optimistic about the prospects of long-term substantive change unaccompanied by protracted struggle and sacrifice, as Gutiérrez's work makes clear. Recently, however, liberation spirituality has begun to turn to certain persons popularly acclaimed as martyrs, such as Archbishop Romero of El Salvador, to sustain a sense of hope, rendering concrete the paradoxical Christ-centred spirituality of cross/resurrection that has been a pillar of this spirituality from the outset.

See also **Dark Night; Franciscan Spirituality; Ignatian Spirituality; Latin American Spirituality; Martyrdom.**

Francisco Boff, *Cry of the Earth, Cry of the Poor*, Maryknoll, NY: Orbis Books, 1997; Pedro Casadáliga and José Maria Vigil, *Political Holiness: A Spirituality of Liberation*, Maryknoll, NY: Orbis Books, 1994; Ignacio Ellacuría and Jon Sobrino (eds), *Mysterium Liberationis: Fundamental Concepts of Liberation Theology*, Maryknoll, NY: Orbis Books, 1993; Ivone Gebara, *Longing for Running Water: Ecofeminism and Liberation*, Minneapolis: Fortress Press, 1999; Gustavo Gutiérrez, *We Drink from Our Own Wells: The Spiritual Journey of a People*, Maryknoll, NY: Orbis Books, 2003; Jon Sobrino, *Spirituality of Liberation: Toward Political Holiness*, Maryknoll, NY: Orbis Books, 1988.

MATTHEW ASHLEY

Lifestyle

see Practice, Spiritual

Light

The metaphors of light and its opposite, darkness, are among the richest and most pervasive in the history of Christian theology and spirituality. The origins of the metaphor of light lie in the Hebrew and Christian Scriptures. In the creation narrative of Gen. 1, light stands for God's presence and action in making order out of chaos. Light in the form of fire sometimes manifests God's presence or guidance, for example when Moses encounters the blazing bush (Ex. 3.2–6) and when God leads the people of Israel as a pillar of fire (Ex. 13.21–22). Light also guides the human quest for God. So, it is in God's light that we see light (Ps. 36); God is a light to the nations (Isa. 51); John's Gospel begins with light entering the world (John 1) and Jesus declares himself to be a light (e.g. John 8.12); in the Gospel of Matthew the ministry of Jesus is introduced by the theme of a dawning light (Matt. 4.12–16); in all the synoptic Gospels Jesus' true nature is revealed in the dazzling light of transfiguration (Matt. 17.1–8; Mark 9.2–8; Luke 9.28–36). In this context, the power of divine light and illumination is contrasted sharply with the darkness of human ignorance or sin – although, as we shall see, in the later Christian mystical tradition the interplay of light and darkness is more subtle.

Liturgically, the theme of the enduring and all-pervading light of Christ illuminating darkness has a daily place in the language of the early morning and evening Offices or prayer of the Church. A thanksgiving for light, the *Lucenarium*, accompanied by the hymn 'Hail gladdening light' (*Phos hilaron*) and dating back to the fourth century, has been restored to occasional use in Western Catholic liturgical use, sometimes as the opening of Saturday vespers, the eve of Sunday, the 'Resurrection Day'. The ceremony has been consistently maintained in Eastern liturgy. The use of light also has a particular association with baptismal regeneration linked to Christ's resurrection. In a number of Western traditions candles are given to candidates during the baptismal ceremony, and the Easter Vigil (a traditional occasion of baptism and renewal of baptismal promises) begins with the kindling of fire, the lighting of the great Easter candle and the passing of its flame to members of the congregation followed by the singing of the Exultet, or hymn to Christ the light, gathered round the Easter candle.

The Christian theological-spiritual tradition expresses a subtle dialectic of knowing and unknowing in relation to God. Without suggesting an excessive contrast or differentiation, the theologians of the early Church can be distinguished as theologians of light or theologians of darkness. The Alexandrian theologian Origen (*c*. 185–255) may be taken as an example of the first. He described the contemplative life in Neoplatonic terms as three ascending stages in a movement upwards towards greater *light*. This 'light-mysticism' expresses an optimistic understanding of the powers of the human mind, illuminated by Christ, to know God in some sense. In the following century, the Cappadocian theologian Gregory of Nyssa (*c*. 335–95), especially in his *Life of Moses*, also represented the contemplative journey in terms of ascent but in this case towards darkness rather than light. He used as his framework of reference the story of Moses' experiences in the book of Exodus. Here the metaphor is the ascent of Mount Sinai as Moses enters into ever deeper clouds of darkness in his encounter with God. Gregory's 'darkness-mysticism' expresses the ultimate incomprehensibility of God who is always more than, always beyond what we can conceive.

In many respects, *The Mystical Theology* of the pseudonymous Denis or Dionysius the Areopagite (probably an unknown sixth-century Syrian monk writing in Greek) proved to have the greatest impact of any patristic theologian on the development of Western mysticism. His theology can be said to balance light and darkness, the way of knowing or imaging and the reciprocal way of unknowing or denial of images. Certainly, an important element of Dionysian theology is the concept of light. God can be spoken of especially as light.

> Light comes from the Good, and light is an image of this archetypal Good. Thus the Good is also praised by the name 'Light', just as an archetype is revealed in its image. The goodness of the transcendent God reaches from the highest and most perfect forms of being to the very lowest. And yet it remains above and beyond them all, superior to the highest and yet stretching out to the lowliest. It gives light to everything capable of receiving it, it creates them, keeps them alive, preserves and perfects them. (*The Divine Names* 4.4 in Luibheid (ed.), 1987, p. 74)

Everything created stems from that initial uncreated light. Each created reality receives the light that is appropriate to its place – a place according to the ordered hierarchy of beings established by God. The cosmos was a kind of explosion of light and the divine light united everything, linking all things by love and with Love. There was, therefore, an overarching coherence. A gradual ascent or movement back towards the source of all things and all light complemented this outward movement of the divine into the cosmos. Everything returned by means of the visible, from the created to the uncreated. The principal theme was the oneness of the universe. Having said this, we need to be careful. An overemphasis on this theology of light, it seems to me, is to misunderstand Dionysius. We may describe God as Light, yet, according to Dionysius' own principles (especially as taught in the *Mystical Theology*), we must also deny the God *is* anything. God is *not* this, not that – not even Supreme Light. Light is the sign that may especially draw us to higher realities. But that reality is ultimately beyond all conception.

> Trinity! Higher than any being,
> Any divinity, any goodness!
> Guide of Christians
> In the wisdom of heaven!
> Lead us up beyond unknowing and light,
> Up to the farthest, highest peak
> Of mystic scripture,
> Where the mysteries of God's Word
> Lie simple, absolute and unchangeable
> In the brilliant darkness of a hidden silence.
> Amid the deepest shadow
> They pour overwhelming light
> On what is most manifest.
> Amid the wholly unsensed and unseen
> They completely fill our sightless minds
> With treasures beyond all beauty.
>   (*Mystical Theology* 1.1 in
>   Luibheid (ed.), 1987, p. 135)

It is the negative, or 'dark', side of Dionysian theology that had such a strong impact on so-called apophatic mystical writings such as the anonymous fourteenth-century English *The Cloud of Unknowing* or aspects of the sixteenth-century Spanish Carmelite, John of the Cross.

On the other hand, the spirituality embodied in religious architecture appears at first sight to express a more colourful and light-filled vision. While there was a diversity of aesthetics – and therefore of theological symbolism – during the Middle Ages (Eco, 1986), there can be no doubt that what can be called 'the spirituality of Gothic' was influenced by the Dionysian emphasis on light. Gothic architectural 'space' has been characterized as, among other things, dematerialized and spiritualized. It thereby expressed the limitless quality of an infinite God through the soaring verticality of arches and vaults. These constituted a deliberate antithesis to human scale. Gothic buildings are notable for another typical characteristic. As Gothic architecture developed, the stone walls of churches were increasingly reduced to a minimum and replaced by vast expanses of glass. The biblical stories portrayed in the stained glass of the windows could teach the worshipper much about the doctrine of God and of salvation. However, there was also a sense in which coloured glass, and its patterned effect on the stonework of the interior of the building, expressed what may be called a 'metaphysics of light'. God was proclaimed as the one who dwelt in inaccessible light yet whose salvific light illuminated the world (see Eco, 1986, ch. IV).

In the end, there are two critical dimensions to the use of the words 'light' and 'darkness' in terms of human encounters with God. First, they are theological metaphors that tentatively point to the nature of the spiritual journey towards God rather than statements about inner psychological states or experiences. Second, as both Denys Turner and Bernard McGinn make clear in their different ways, the metaphors of light and darkness are mutually reciprocal and must be employed dialectically or self-subvertingly in Christian attempts to express the mystery of God as both revealed and hidden (McGinn, 1995, pp. 102–3; Turner, 1995, esp. ch. 11).

See also **Darkness; Dark Night; Illuminative Way; Image and Spirituality.**

Umberto Eco, *Art and Beauty in the Middle Ages*, New Haven: Yale University Press, 1986; Andrew Louth, *The Origins of the Christian Mystical Tradition*, Oxford: Clarendon Press, 1992; Colm Luibheid (ed.), *Pseudo-Dionysius: The Complete Works*, London: SPCK, 1987; Bernard McGinn, *The Growth of Mysticism: From Gregory the Great to the Twelfth Century*, New York: Crossroad, 1994/London: SCM Press, 1995; Denys Turner, *The Darkness of God: Negativity in Christian Mysticism*, Cambridge: Cambridge University Press, 1995.

PHILIP SHELDRAKE

Literature and Spirituality

In a general sense all literature speaks of the human condition and therefore touches on a spiritual dimension but in a more specific way there are works which deliberately embrace an understanding of spirituality and use it as a creative principle. The relationship between literature in Western culture and spirituality takes many different forms. On the one hand accounts of the origin of life, early creation stories and myths from many different sources and cultures have been formative in shaping subsequent literary genres. On the other hand the canon of Scripture has provided a form and a pattern for many different types of storytelling which are still used in contemporary writing. The narrative shape in the Bible with the creation at the beginning and the culmination of the crucifixion and resurrection followed by the final climax in a new heaven and a new earth is one which is often repeated in different ways. It has been dubbed as 'the big picture' and has been deconstructed through the work of postmodern critics in the twentieth century. Nevertheless it is a pattern that is still used and references to biblical forms and images continue to sustain the connection between literature and spirituality. As literary forms change and develop, the link between different kinds of literature and spirituality become more complex. In some periods of history the relationship is sharper than at others.

The idea of a narrative which gives a particular view of life is an often used source for explaining human experience in relation to spiritual values. Most early texts were written in poetic or in ballad form, for example *The Seafarer*, which is an Old English poem of 120 lines. The first part of the poem discusses the perils of life at sea and then moves on to reflect on the shortness of life and the need for faith. The poem reaches its climax with a prayer which provides the context for the poem. *The Wanderer* is another early Old English poem describing the experiences of a wanderer as that of a universal experience and explains through the narrative a message of Christian hope. Another poem of the same period, 'The Husband's Message', describes in an allegorical way the relationship between Christ and the Church. These three poems come from *The Exeter Book* and form part of a larger collection of poems that were copied in 940 and given to Exeter Cathedral by Bishop Leofric. Each of them in their own way illustrates the way in which narrative can be based on an insight into Christian spirituality.

Piers Plowman (1367–70) is the most significant alliterative poem in Middle English; it was thought to be written by William Langland but his authorship is often disputed between the three versions of different lengths. The poem relies on a sophisticated narrative and intricate references to Christian spirituality. The poet describes how he has a vision in a dream of a high tower (Truth), a deep dungeon (Wrong) and a 'fair field full of folk' (the Earth). Then Conscience preaches to the people and Repentance moves them but the way of truth is difficult to find. At this point Piers Plowman comes to offer guidance to the pilgrims if they will help him

plough his half acre of land. Some of them help but others avoid the work and there is a discourse about the different approaches. In the narrative which follows the life of Christ and that of Piers Plowman blend into one. This combination is one that illustrates the power of a narrative that weaves into its structure the same essentials of the Christian spiritual experience. *Sir Gawain and the Green Knight* (1375) is another alliterative poem of the fourteenth century which takes as its theme chivalry, bravery, moral virtue and self-sacrifice. The poem is thought to have been the inspiration behind the Order of the Garter and it reworks the Grail legend. Undoubtedly the most well-read poem of this period is Geoffrey Chaucer's *Canterbury Tales* in which twenty-three pilgrims tell stories which are intended to have a cautionary or a moral purpose. The stories are told in order to shorten the journey to Canterbury, the place of pilgrimage, and the teller of the best story will have a free supper on the return journey.

From the thirteenth century to the sixteenth century biblical dramas known as Mystery Plays were performed in towns all over England; they were previously called the Miracle Plays which were strictly miracles enacted by saints. The different cycles of plays made the biblical stories familiar to those who could not read, using a rare blend of solemn judgement mixed with ribald humour. The productions took place on Corpus Christi day, Christmas, Whitsuntide and Easter, and they reached their fullest development in the fifteenth century and the sixteenth century. The four great cycles of Mystery Plays that have survived are named after the places where they were performed: York, Chester, Coventry and Wakefield. The plays offered a striking visual picture of Bible stories and events before a translation of the Bible was more available. The publication in 1535 of a version of the Bible in English by Miles Coverdale was the first complete text; it was heavily dependent on William Tyndale's translation. Coverdale's Bible was the version that Shakespeare used and it was the text that inspired English Renaissance literature.

It is in the late sixteenth century and early seventeenth century that the relationship between literature and spirituality is at its most interesting. This is seen in particular through the work of the Metaphysical Poets. John Donne's (1572–1631) poems and his sermons interweave spiritual and intellectual imagery. His 'Holy Sonnets' (1610–11) deftly explore some intricate theological themes while his early collection that includes 'Air and Angels' uses unusual images to suggest spiritual insights. Andrew Marvell (1621–78) is probably most famous for his poem

'To his Coy Mistress', but he also wrote poems on spiritual themes. One of his most accomplished is 'The Coronet' in which he reflects on the sort of crown he might offer Christ in place of a crown of thorns, but he realizes that he can offer no crown that is appropriate except one to lay at Christ's feet as a sign of humility.

Of all the Metaphysical Poets, George Herbert (1593–1633) stands out as one whose simplicity of style and exact use of words best expresses Christian spirituality. His poem 'Love' speaks about the nature and intimacy of the believer's relationship with Christ as the key to understanding the importance of communion. Henry Vaughan (1621–95) wrote a number of poems on the same themes and sometimes using the same titles as George Herbert. In the preface to his collection of poems *Silex Scintillans*, he wrote: 'Mr George Herbert, whose holy life and verse gained many pious converts, (of whom I am the least) and gave the first check to a most flourishing and admired wit of his time.'

John Milton's *Paradise Lost* is the outstanding epic poem of the seventeenth century based on the Bible. The poem describes how paradise was lost through Adam and Eve yielding to Satan's temptation and their expulsion from Eden. The poem is made up of twelve books explaining the consequence of the fall of humanity and God's plan for redemption. It is written in a classical style, sometimes dubbed as Milton's 'Grand Style'. The poem has inspired much critical commentary, not least over the question as to whether Satan is the hero of the poem. Milton's achievement is to present a particular interpretation of the fall and its consequences as an epic narrative.

It was in the eighteenth century that the English novel developed and became more established as a distinctive literary genre, with the works of Daniel Defoe (1660?–1731), Samuel Richardson (1689–1761) and Henry Fielding (1707–54). Defoe published *Robinson Crusoe* in 1719; it tells the story of the shipwreck of a man, his survival in difficult circumstances and his eventual rescue. One of the underlying themes is the providence of God in all circumstances. This novel became an inspiration and a pattern for subsequent novels and the themes are frequently reworked in modern literature.

The English novel flourished most noticeably in the nineteenth century beginning with the novels of Jane Austen. The works of the Brontës, Elizabeth Gaskell, Dickens and George Eliot reflect a close knowledge of the Authorized Version of the Bible and of *The Book of Common Prayer*. John Bunyan's *Pilgrim's Progress* (1678) was used by novelists and referred to as a reinforcement of the idea of a novel which illustrated a personal journey and had a clear moral purpose that resulted in the all-important happy ending.

The poetry of Tennyson, Browning and Arnold may be seen as reflecting some of the more complex issues of faith and doubt in the Victorian Age. Matthew Arnold expresses a fear about the loss of faith in God in his poem 'Dover Beach' where he talks about the sea of faith once being full. He reflects:

> But now I only hear
> Its melancholy, long withdrawing roar,
> Retreating, to the breath
> Of the night-wind, down the vast edges drear
> And the naked shingles of the world.

The poem is seen as both encapsulating questions of faith and doubt and also signalling a religionless Christianity: the secular spirituality of the twentieth and twenty-first centuries.

At the end of the nineteenth century Joseph Conrad's novel *Heart of Darkness*, written in 1899 and published in 1902, describes the change from the optimistic imperialism of the nineteenth century to the moral anxiety about the exploitation of Africa by Europeans. The death of Kurtz in the novel symbolizes loss but also an ironic moment of spiritual awareness. He cries out twice: 'The horror! The horror!' T. S. Eliot found Conrad a source of elucidation and inspiration when he was writing *The Waste Land*. He wanted to use the moment of Kurtz's death as an epigraph to his poem but Ezra Pound who edited the poem did not think that Conrad was 'weighty enough' and so the quotation was dropped in favour of a reference to the 'Sybil at Cumae'. Eliot referred to 'The heart of light' in the first section of *The Waste Land* and he picked up on the theme in 'Burnt Norton': 'The surface glittered out of heart of light'. *Four Quartets* is often described as a spiritual classic in the twentieth century because of the intricate and varied ways in which different pathways of faith are explained; in the final section of 'Dry Salvages' Eliot speaks of the importance of the incarnation:

> The hint half guessed, the gift half understood, is incarnation.
> Here the impossible
> Of spheres of existence is actual,

He goes on to explain the reconciliation that is implied in the incarnation. The poem ends with a vision of heaven that reflects the conclusion of Dante's *Divine Comedy*.

There are a number of twentieth-century poets who have written exclusively on spirituality and spiritual insights but those who stand out are: Edwin Muir, R. S. Thomas, Kathleen Raine and Elizabeth Jennings. In fiction the scope is wider since many authors use spiritual allusions and write about spiritual experiences in novels which are not generally understood to come from a context of spirituality. C. S. Lewis's novels and children's books have made a powerful contribution to understanding Christian spirituality. The works of J. R. R. Tolkien have also pointed up the struggle of right against wrong in a spiritual battle. Evelyn Waugh uses the importance of maintaining belief and keeping faith as thematic in a number of his novels. Graham Greene also explores different ways that faith can be interpreted in his writing. More recently, the writers who have been acclaimed in the late twentieth and twenty-first centuries – A. S. Byatt, Peter Carey, Matthew Keane and Yann Martell – have used spiritual themes to mould the worlds that they write about.

The label 'postmodern' has been given to authors whose work is fragmentary, self-reflexive and where the characters seemingly disappear and then reappear. This description could also be applied to the final narrative of John's Gospel where events are disjointed, the author is part of the narrative and Christ after the resurrection appears and disappears eluding recognition. Postmodern writers such as John Fowles, Julian Barnes, Salman Rushdie, Ian McEwan and Angela Carter employ a number of these different techniques. However, they also rely heavily on significant points of historical narrative as a means of exploring human endeavour. In Julian Barnes's *A History of the World in 10½ Chapters*, woodworm eat their way through the furniture of the centuries, providing a deconstructed continuity. The novel concludes with a dream of heaven which is presented in terms of consumerist self-selection. The narrator asks, 'What has happened to the Old heaven?' and is met with the reply: 'Oh it survived for a while, after the new heavens were built. But there was increasingly little call for it. People seemed keener on the new heavens. It wasn't that surprising. We take the long view here.' The culmination of the 'Big Picture' is heaven. Nevertheless the deconstructed version of heaven described by Julian Barnes is entirely dependent on the 'Old Heaven' and looks back at a spirituality that is past in order to explain the present.

See also **Poetry and Poetics.**

Robert Alter, *The Art of Biblical Narrative*, London: HarperCollins, 1981; William Countryman, *The Poetic Imagination*, London: Darton, Longman & Todd, 1999; Paul Fiddes, *Freedom and Limit*, London: St Martin's Press, 1991; Paul Fiddes, *The Promised End*, Oxford: Blackwell, 2000; Gordon Mursell, *English Spirituality*, 2 vols, London: SPCK, 2001; Geoffrey Rowell, Kenneth Stevenson and Rowan Williams (eds), *Love's Redeeming Work*, Oxford: Oxford University Press, 2001; Michael Wheeler, *Heaven, Hell and the Victorians*, Cambridge: Cambridge University Press, 1994; T. R. Wright, *Theology and Literature*, Oxford: Oxford University Press, 1988.

JANE GLEDHILL

Lord's Prayer

Simple yet profound, ancient yet always fresh, deeply Jewish yet available to all, the Lord's Prayer offers the central message of Jesus in the form best suited to its appropriation. Jesus did not come, after all, merely to teach true doctrine and ethics, but to bring about God's kingdom; within that sovereign and saving rule, human beings are caught up with the challenge and invitation to corporate and personal renewal, as deep as the human heart, as wide as the world. To pray this prayer with full attention and intention is to partake in this renewal.

The prayer occurs in Matt. 6.9–13, within the Sermon on the Mount; in Luke 11.2–4, answering the disciples' request for a prayer; and in *Didache* 8.2, which instructs that the prayer be used three times daily. Luke's text is shorter, with some changes in the Greek; Matthew's is the one that has become widespread in the Church, with some traditions also adding *Didache* 10.5 ('remember, Lord, your church . . .'). The doxology ('yours is the kingdom, the power and the glory, for ever') is probably not original, but became part of the prayer very early on in the life of the Church. The prayer clearly stems from an Aramaic original, and it is virtually certain that it represents what Jesus taught.

The prayer is rooted, in shape and content, in older Jewish traditions. But the particular combination of elements marks it out as belonging within Jesus' aim of inaugurating God's kingdom, and his invitation to live by this kingdom in advance of its full appearing. It divides into two parts, the first (in the longer form) containing three petitions about God's purposes and glory, and the second three petitions for human need.

The address, 'Our Father', expresses the intimate trust which characterizes Christian prayer. It evokes the Jewish belief that Israel, God's people, was his firstborn son (Ex. 4.22; Isa. 63.16; 64.8). The Aramaic word *Abba*, 'Father', expresses Jesus' own intimate sense of sonship (e.g. Mark 14.36) and the early Church's sense of sharing that sonship through the Spirit (Rom. 8.16; Gal. 4.6, where the Lord's Prayer may well be in mind).

The first three petitions pray that God's glory and purpose may come to birth throughout creation. God's name is sanctified, held in honour, when his world is ruled by his wisdom and power, and his image-bearing human creatures worship him and reflect his glory in the world. His kingdom comes through Jesus' death and resurrection and his final victory over death itself (1 Cor. 15.24–28), and through every intermediate victory of his love over the powers of the world. The prayer for God's will to be done on earth as in heaven indicates, despite centuries of misunderstanding, that Christianity is not about escaping earth and going to heaven instead, but rather that God wills to renew both heaven and earth and bring them into ultimate unity (Rev. 21).

Emboldened by this trust in God and his kingdom, the last three petitions express the basic needs of those who live between Jesus' initial victory and his final triumph. Bread for today (Matthew) and every day (Luke) symbolizes our constant dependence on the creator. Forgiveness, both of sin and of material debt, is the central blessing of the new covenant (Jer. 31.34; Matt. 26.28), obtained through Jesus' death. The Church here commits itself in turn to forgive (emphasized in Matt. 6.15; 18.21–35). Those who claim the new covenant blessing must live as new covenant people; the heart renewed by God's forgiveness cannot but offer forgiveness to others. The final petition for rescue from danger and evil has two branches. First, we pray to be spared the ultimate test, whether that of fierce temptation or, more specifically, the 'tribulation', the 'time of trial', which in early Judaism was believed to be coming upon the world (compare Matt. 26.41, where it seems that Jesus will face this 'tribulation' alone). Then we pray to be delivered both from evil in general and from 'the evil one'; the original wording could be taken either way, and both may be in view.

From very early, the Lord's Prayer has been at the centre of Christian devotion and liturgy, not least at the Eucharist. Most of the great spiritual writers have expounded it and drawn on it. Alongside its regular use as a straightforward prayer, some have employed it as a framework, allowing other concerns to cluster around its various petitions. Others have used it, like the 'Jesus prayer', as a steady, rhythmic subterranean flow, beneath the bustle of ordinary life. It is, above all, a prayer which unites Christians of every background and tradition. It could energize and sustain fresh growth in shared ecumenical witness and life.

See also **Jesus and Spirituality; Prayer; Synoptic Gospels.**

Leonardo Boff, *The Lord's Prayer: The Prayer of Integral Liberation,* Maryknoll, NY: Orbis Books, 1983; Scott Hahn, *Understanding 'Our Father': Biblical Reflections on the Lord's Prayer,* Steubenville, OH: Emmaus Road Publishing, 2002; Joachim Jeremias, *The Prayers of Jesus,* London: SCM Press, 1967; James Mulholland, *Praying Like Jesus: The Lord's Prayer in a Culture of Prosperity,* New York: HarperCollins, 2002; Alexander Schmemann, *Our Father,* New York: St Vladimir's Seminary Press, 2002; Kenneth W. Stevenson, *The Lord's Prayer: A Text in Tradition,* London: SCM Press/Minneapolis: Fortress Press, 2004; Tom Wright, *The Lord and his Prayer,* London: SPCK/Grand Rapids, MI: Eerdmans, 1996.

N. T. (TOM) WRIGHT

Love

The aim of the Christian life is to love God, God's creation, our fellow humans and our own emerging selves in the most adequate way. Hence, love is the central reference point of Christian spirituality. While all Christians agree on this centrality of love and on the God-given nature of all genuine love, the Christian tradition knows many and at times different approaches to love. Love has never been an unambiguous concept in Christian spirituality. The shifting references to love in ordinary language further complicate the theological efforts to clarify the nature, potential, development and ambiguities of love.

The phenomenon of love appears to be universal in our multicultural and globalizing world. In ordinary language we refer to the possibilities of loving other persons, objects or states of being: we say, for instance, that we love our parents, our homes, our youth. Hence, love is transitive: it relates to some kind of other. We may feel attracted by the otherness of the other. We may experience friendship, attachment, sympathy, loyalty and desire with regard to this other. All forms of love require otherness. The English language speaks also of 'making love', though this expression refers to sexual intercourse rather than to the possibility of producing love in a technical sense. Christian spirituality has been concerned predominantly with the potential of loving God and our fellow human beings, thus with the love of subjects.

Love is not unique to Christian faith and spirituality. Rather the early Church adopted the

Jewish understanding of love and developed it in particular ways. The synoptic Gospels all quote Deut. 6.5–6 and Lev. 19.18 while affirming the dual commandment to love God and the neighbour as the greatest commandment (Mark 12.29–31, Matt. 22.37–40, Luke 10.25–28). Thus both Jews and Christians have emphasized the distinction between love of God and love of neighbour, but also underlined their essential connectedness. In Luke's story of the Good Samaritan the commandment to love is extended to include all human beings without regard for their ethnic, religious or family background (Luke 10.29–37). Everybody is my neighbour. Rather than developing a theoretical discourse on love, the synoptic Gospels show that for Jesus love as the central focus of the human–divine and human–human relationship needs to be practised. His encounters with all kinds of people, for example friends, children, women, beggars, sick and suffering people, sinners, foreigners and enemies, reflect God's universal love. God wishes to gather all around his creative and reconciling presence.

Seen against this widening of the horizon of love, the Johannine texts in the New Testament appear to move into the opposite direction: They limit the focus of Christian love to the inner concerns of this particular community. Here, without paying much attention to the outside world, the primary perspectives are the mutual bond of love for the sake of unity in the community and the example of Jesus' own loving sacrifice (John 15.9–10). However, John's Gospel and letters reflect more deeply on God's being as love and on the connection between knowledge of God and the dynamics of love. 'Whoever does not love does not know God, because God is love' (1 John 4.8).

For Paul, love is the gift of the Holy Spirit and as such it ought to shape the entire life of the individual believer and of the Christian community (Rom. 5.5). Addressing the disunited community in Corinth, Paul presents love as an excellent way of handling conflict, dispute and otherness. He praises faith, hope and love (later on named the three theological virtues), yet singles out love as 'the greatest' and explores it in depth (1 Cor. 13).

The Christian praxis of love, though always conscious of love's divine origin, has been shifting in focus, horizon and praxis since its very beginning. All biblical texts see God's love at work in Jesus Christ and show how God has accepted Jesus' love and confirmed it in the resurrection of Jesus. Different efforts are made to conceive and structure all possible human relationships and actions now in terms of this love.

However, the New Testament texts lack the passion, the desire and the erotic quality of love found in Old Testament passages, such as the Song of Songs, Psalm 42 and Psalm 62.

The passionate desire for union with God returns in the thought of Augustine of Hippo (354–430) who has influenced the spirituality of love more than any other thinker in Western Christianity. Inspired by Neoplatonist philosophy he interpreted the complex biblical heritage on love with clear leanings in the direction of Johannine thinking. For Augustine there exists only one true and lasting form of love, namely the love of God. Hence, whenever we humans truly love, we love God in all our acts of love. The meeting with another human person does not have any co-constitutive character for me as an emerging spiritual subject. Rather if I love that person, I love God in her, and, if she loves me, she loves God in me. Thus, ultimately, only God can be loved; loving the neighbour thus becomes a function of our love for God. God is the highest good, which we all desire. Proper love is always love of God (*amor dei*), never self-love (*amor sui*). For Augustine, love is the way out of our sinful human predicament. Original sin is the framework in which he considers love. His famous dictum 'Love, and do what you will' is misunderstood when read to suggest some general sentiment of the sort 'Love is all you need'. Rather Augustine refers here to the rootedness of all good intentions in love. Since God is love, and love is our origin, 'the actions of men are discerned only according to their root in charity' (*Homilies on 1 John* 7.8).

Since the twelfth century, both Christian mystics and academic theologians have continued to explore love as the centre of Christian spirituality. The mystics emphasized the ecstatic nature of pure love insisting, like Augustine, that all true love is love of God. Human beings become more themselves the more they become like God. Pure love is a mystical experience, pure excess. Ultimately, this love offers intimate knowledge of God. This knowledge can only be attained, if the soul is willing to be transformed by love according to the image of God who is love.

Thomas Aquinas (1225–74) considered love to be one of the three theological virtues besides faith and hope. Love means real friendship between the human being and God and is made possible because of God's goodness and its communication to us humans. The 'light in which we must love our neighbour is God, for what we ought to love in him is that he be in God. Hence it is clear that it is specifically the same act which loves God and loves neighbour' (*ST* 2a2ae.25.1). All of Christian praxis, spirituality and morality

are oriented towards this progressive development in love. Love is the mother of all virtues.
Faith must be shaped by love.

Reformation theologians stressed the priority
of the gift of faith in order to avoid the misunderstanding that human love and desire be
raised to the status of a human condition for
divine salvation. However, they did follow
Augustine when they developed their understanding of love on the basis of the conviction
that human nature was totally spoiled by sin.
Martin Luther distinguished sharply between
God's creative and freely given love, on the one
hand, and human love, on the other hand, that
on its own account never could transcend its
self-centred desires.

Søren Kierkegaard (1813–55) insisted on the
praxis character of Christian love. He distinguished Christian love from worldly love that
always is selective, concerned to be loved in
return and therefore ultimately self-centred.
God's gift of spiritual love comes to us as a command to love our neighbours for their own sake.
Anders Nygren (1890–1978) sharply separated
divine love (*agape*) from human love (*eros*),
while C. S. Lewis (1898–1963), distinguishing
between divine gift-love and human need-love,
overcame this dichotomy somewhat by pointing
to the action of God who kindles a supernatural
appreciative love in the human heart towards
God. Paul Tillich (1886–1965), conscious of the
ambiguities of Christian love, calls for a retrieval
of the erotic quality of desire and for a closer
consideration of the interrelationship between
love and justice.

The history of Christian love thus reveals a
close connection between the respective theological framework and the different approaches
to love. Christian spirituality has always affirmed
the divine origin of love and the connection
between love of God and love of neighbour, yet
the nature and role of the human self as loving
agent in the network of interconnected love relations has remained unclear. Only recently has
the self in the Christian discourse on love been
approached in terms of an embodied self – somewhat surprising in view of the Christian belief in
God's incarnation. Moreover, the ongoing
exploration of the role of gender in the constitution of the human subject will need to be considered more fully in the Christian spirituality of
love. Feminist theologians have drawn attention
to the fact that the stress in Christian spirituality
on overcoming or sacrificing one's self has contributed to the oppression of women in Church
and society. Not only self-centredness and ego-
ism are obstacles to the praxis of Christian love,
but also the lack of a self. Hence, a Christian

spirituality of love must come to terms not only
with the ambiguity of the self, but also with the
potential of human selfhood for love.

Loving attention to the other requires more
than individual acts of charity. It calls for a
radically transformed view of the dignity and
vocation of the human person as God's friend
and of the Christian Church as God's eschatological community called to help renew the
earth. Hence, a Christian spirituality of love
needs to include political, emancipatory, economic, environmental and ecological dimensions. In this way, the praxis of love will reveal
new and surprising ways of being in the world.

A Christian spirituality of love lives from
the energy emerging from the radical difference
between God and human beings, a difference
that creates the desire for closeness, a longing to
enter into the transforming mystery of the
creative and redemptive love of the triune God
for all of his creation.

See also **Agape; Charity; Compassion;
Eroticism; Knowledge.**

Augustine, *Homilies on First John* (415); Werner
G. Jeanrond, *Call and Response: The Challenge of
Christian Life*, Dublin: Gill & Macmillan, 1995;
Helmut Kuhn, *'Liebe': Geschichte eines Begriffs*,
Munich: Kösel, 1975; Bernard McGinn, *The
Presence of God: A History of Western Christian
Mysticism*, 5 vols, London: SCM Press, 1992ff.;
Thomas Aquinas, *Summa Theologiae* 34,
Cambridge: Blackfriars, 1975; Paul Tillich, *Love,
Power, and Justice*, Oxford: Oxford University
Press, 1954.

WERNER JEANROND

Lutheran Spirituality

Lutheran spirituality is a family of spirituality
whose various members resemble one another
through commitment to the thought and
practice of Martin Luther and the Lutheran
Confessions. For Luther (1483–1546), Augustinian monk for years and professor of Bible at
Wittenberg University, theology and spiritual
practice were closely connected. The weight of
scholarly opinion today holds that Luther posted
his Ninety-Five Theses on 31 October 1517
objecting to indulgences and other penitential
practices about a year before he arrived at his
theology of justification of grace through faith
alone. While the grace of forgiveness was
affirmed, justification (being right with God)
was generally understood in both Western and
Eastern Christian theology as predominately a
work of transforming grace, although humans
must do their subordinate part. Luther objected
that this theology fostered an anxious quest to

please God through observance of religious and moral practices. He believed Scripture, particularly Paul, taught differently. Since the work of transformation is always incomplete on earth, Luther said the bedrock of the believer's relation with God is forgiveness. Yet forgiving grace is always accompanied by transforming grace. Indeed, faith as trust in and obedience to God is itself the basic gift of divine transformation. Luther's new theological perspective, including the priority of biblical authority over Church tradition, soon led him to call for reform in many spiritual practices besides penance; the number of sacraments, the Mass, prayers to saints, veneration of relics, monastic vows, to name a few.

Whereas some radical Reformers claimed direct revelations, Luther believed God's grace comes through means that witness to Christ, the Word and sacraments, and he advocated a number of spiritual practices focused on them. To enhance encounter with God's Word Luther emphasized preaching on Scripture, put the liturgy in the vernacular, revived the ancient practice of congregational hymn-singing, and personally translated the entire Bible into German. Luther recognized only two sacraments, baptism and the Lord's Supper, although he wavered for a time on penance and taught that private confession should continue. He insisted on the priority of God's grace in the sacraments and defended infant baptism. He stressed that baptism is of lifelong significance, for daily the Christian is to die to sin and rise to new life in Christ. Weekly Lord's Supper was the norm in Wittenberg, and he strongly encouraged people to receive. Luther rejected transubstantiation, but held that Christ's body and blood are present in, with and under the bread and wine. In keeping with this strongly held view, Luther opposed the destruction of religious pictures and statues. Unlike some other Protestant Reformers, Luther believed that all the arts, but especially music, should be used to praise their creator.

Luther had two other teachings that are of vast importance for the spiritual life. One of these is the priesthood of all believers. While many mistake this to mean that they are authorized to go to God without mediation of a priest, Luther said that the function of priests is to pray for others and teach them about God. So every believer has these priestly responsibilities. However, regularly ordained pastors should preside over the Church's public worship. The second important teaching was vocation. Whereas vocation had come to mean the call to a holier life as a priest or member of a religious order, Luther said God calls people to serve others in and through their station in life or what we might call today their constructive social roles as family members, workers and citizens or civil leaders. Furthermore, the service a simple farmhand renders is just as holy as that of a priest. This elevated the significance of daily life and undercut some of the traditional rationale for a special religious life.

Perhaps Luther's most significant impact on Christian spirituality has been to offer a major alternative to the ascent model of the Christian life. Moses' ascent up Mount Sinai to meet God face to face has long been an inspiration to advocates of Christian mysticism. Stages in this ascent have been variously conceived, but Pseudo-Dionysius' scheme of purgation, illumination and union with God has been prominent. The monastic way of life has been commonly viewed as especially suited to spiritual advancement on this path. The understanding of grace as primarily transformative, the subordinate yet necessary role of humans to prepare themselves for grace, and the higher status given the call to religious life have often supported this ascent model. Luther's views of grace as primarily forgiveness, utter dependence of humans on God for salvation, and the equal holiness of secular service all lead to a different model of the Christian life that is most basically shaped by Paul's imagery of daily dying and rising with Christ. Using Bernard McGinn's distinction between 'mystical elements', such as appear in Paul and John, 'and mysticism proper' that arises with Origen and monasticism, we can recognize mystical elements in Luther's understanding of faith that clings to Christ, but he had serious reservations about monasticism and the ascent model that often underlies it.

Although Martin Luther is clearly the dominant figure in the Lutheran tradition, Lutheran churches and clergy are formally committed to certain confessional writings. In addition to recognizing the primary authority of Scripture, most Lutheran churches subscribe to *The Book of Concord* (1580) that contains three ancient creeds and seven sixteenth-century documents, three by Luther. Most important of the sixteenth-century documents have been The Augsburg Confession (1530), which was written by Philip Melanchthon, Luther's close associate at Wittenberg University, and Luther's *Small Catechism* (1529), which has shaped the understanding of Christian faith for many generations. Commitment to these confessional writings with their teachings on doctrine and practice promotes coherence among the various forms of Lutheran spirituality that have arisen since the foundational period.

Disputes over doctrine arose among Lutherans especially after Luther died in 1546, and were mostly settled with the Formula of Concord (1577). This marked the beginning of Lutheran Orthodoxy, which asserted right doctrine, aggressively combated contrary views, and stressed polemics in pastoral education. In the seventeenth century, spiritual life generally suffered from an overemphasis on doctrine, the devastation of the Thirty Years' War (1618–48), and territorial princes who managed Church affairs for their own ends. Yet there were also signs of vitality. Many fine hymns were written, abundant great religious art music was created by D. Buxtehude, J. S. Bach and others, and some widely used devotional works were written, including *Sacred Meditations* (1606) by Johann Gerhard the greatest Orthodox theologian and *True Christianity* (1606, 1610) by Johann Arndt.

Arndt sounded some of the themes picked up later by Pietism: accent on repentance and a holy life, meditation on Scripture, and less polemic. Pietism began as a religious movement in 1675 with the publication of *Pia Desideria* by Philip Spener, who encouraged small gatherings for meditation on Scripture and support for holy living. Arndt and Spener insisted they were faithful to the Lutheran Confessions, and they shared Luther's accent on the power of faith to bind one to Christ. While Lutheran Orthodoxy had declined in influence by the end of the seventeenth century and Pietism had passed its zenith by 1750, both spread beyond the Lutheran heartlands of Germany and Scandinavia through emigration and foreign missions. Both have contemporary heirs – Orthodoxy in those Lutherans who require full doctrinal agreement for fellowship, and Pietism in evangelical and pentecostal Lutherans who prize religious experiences of new birth.

Luther's legacy includes a paradoxical relation between Christian faith and culture in which faith is open to current modes of thought and practice, yet for the sake of the gospel of Jesus Christ is in some measure critical of them. Lutherans have often failed to practise this, at considerable expense to spiritual vitality. Particularly damaging has been acquiescence to control of the Church by political authority, whether eighteenth-century princes and kings, Hitler's regime, or the democratic states of Germany and Scandinavia. The relation with modern culture has been mixed. While some Lutherans, such as seventeenth-century Christian Wolff, accommodated Christian faith with rationalism and others opposed it with insistence on biblical inerrancy, still others led efforts to reconcile Christian faith with modern natural and historical science. This

tradition initially led by university professors Luther and Melanchthon has included many leading theologians such as Tillich, Bultmann, Nygren and Pannenberg.

Yet great challenges confront this spiritual tradition today. In Scandinavia and Germany secularism and Church weakness have conspired to marginalize the Church. Here where the Church is declining in numbers, Lutherans face the challenge of living and witnessing in a highly secular, religiously pluralistic context. In the religiously diverse culture of North America Lutherans, who claim to be evangelical and catholic, debate whether they should conform more to Evangelicalism or Catholicism. Meanwhile, in developing nations where Lutheran churches are growing, substantial openness to local culture in music, worship patterns and interpreting Scripture have injected new life into the understanding of Scripture and sacramental practice. How can the spirituality centred in the message of justification by grace through faith mediated through Word and sacrament find embodiment in these various cultural contexts today?

See also **Grace; Reformation and Spirituality.**

An excellent discussion of Luther's spirituality with bibliography is Marc Lienhard, 'Luther and beginnings of the Reformation' in *Christian Spirituality: High Middle Ages and Reformation*, ed. Jill Raitt, New York: Crossroad, 1987, pp. 268–99. Another solid discussion of mostly Luther's spirituality with special attention to worship is given by Frank C. Senn, 'Lutheran spirituality' in *Protestant Spiritual Traditions*, ed. Frank C. Senn, New York: Paulist Press, 1986, pp. 9–54. See also Juhani Forsberg, 'Luther on prayer' in *See How They Love One Another*, ed. Paivi Jussila, Geneva: The Lutheran World Federation, 2002, pp. 97–110. Two works that also treat later developments are Eric Lund, 'The problem of religious complacency in seventeenth century Lutheran spirituality' in *Modern Christian Spirituality: Methodological and Historical Essays*, ed. Bradley C. Hanson, Atlanta: Scholars Press, 1990, pp. 139–59; and Bengt Hoffman, 'Lutheran spirituality' in *Spiritual Traditions for the Contemporary Church*, ed. Robin Maas and Gabriel O'Donnell, Nashville, TN: Abingdon Press, 1990, pp. 145–61. The only book-length treatments so far are Bradley Hanson, *A Graceful Life: Lutheran Spirituality for Today*, Minneapolis: Augsburg, 2000; and Bradley Hanson, *Freedom through Grace: Lutheran Spirituality*, London: Darton, Longman & Todd/Maryknoll, NY: Orbis Books, 2004.

BRADLEY HANSON

Macarian Spirituality

Macarius the Great was the near-legendary founder of the monastic colonies of Scete, in the Egyptian wilderness south of Alexandria. This area was also the site of other monastic colonies, such as Nitria and Kellia (the centre of activity for Ammonius and Evagrius), which together constituted a veritable centre of the monastic tradition of the Egyptian wilderness. From this heartland there evolved the collections of stories celebrating the sayings and exploits of the 'Desert' Fathers and Mothers. Macarius himself lived from c. 300–390, and was a dedicated supporter of Athanasius the Great. The monastic historians Palladius (*Lausiac History* 17) and Rufinus (*History of the Monks* 28) speak a little about him, and he features as a sage and ascetic in the collection known as the *Apophthegmata Patrum*; but basically next to nothing was recorded of his life. This was a quality of transparency that made him an ideal candidate for the retrospective attribution of important monastic texts that were not really his. As a figure of high monastic authority and unimpeachable orthodoxy, he was the ideal 'coat-hook' on which to hang a tradition that had come into some degree of conflict in the fifth century and, having been condemned by some episcopal synods, was then looking for a way to preserve its insights and cover up some unfortunate aspects of its past. It is in relation to this latter tradition that the phrase 'Macarian spirituality' is now almost entirely used, though one still finds a degree of confusion in earlier text books, not so aware of the pseudepigraphy involved, that conflate the historical Macarius and the 'Pseudo-Macarius' of the later tradition. If Macarius himself was a straightforward representative of the desert tradition at its height, the latter spirituality was something quite different.

Pseudo-Macarius seems to have lived as a younger contemporary of the Egyptian Macarius, chiefly active in the late fourth century, but was himself a Syrian theologian, writing in Greek. He probably operated originally in eastern Asia Minor and the region of Cappadocia, where he had some contact with St Gregory of Nyssa. He was an important monastic leader of a circle that had earlier been criticized for certain 'excesses' in its spiritual theology. Some modern scholars have identified him as Symeon of Mesopotamia (a theologian-monk named as that group's leader by the historian Theodoret), and accordingly he is now often referred to as either Macarius-Symeon, or Pseudo-Macarius. The criticism of his monastic heritage began to be discernible from the 370s onwards. Some have pointed the finger at Eustathius of Sebaste as being the original founder of the monastic school (he had been an early mentor of St Basil the Great) but the connection is not certain. Greek sources called the movement *Messalians* (a corruption of the Syriac word for 'people of prayer' – *MshLni*). In some Greek texts they were known as the Euchites, but later heresiologists added yet more to the confusion by eventually thinking they were founded by a certain Messalius (who never existed).

What exactly was the objectionable element of the doctrine of this circle is something that those who criticize it themselves do not seem to fully understand. The indefatigable heresy-hunter Epiphanius, who attacked the Messalians in his *Refutation of All Heresies*, in 377, can only find their 'lack of discipline' as grounds for censure; which is a sign that he knew these monks had dared to criticize local bishops, but had little other grounds for explaining their synodical condemnation. Other ancient critics claimed they held that baptism was not sufficient for a Christian life, but that the sacrament's grace had to be constantly supplemented and sustained by prayer; a doctrine that could be heretical, or not, depending on how it was received, by enemy or friend. The movement was condemned at a session of the Council of Ephesus in 431, which cites passages from a key work entitled *Asceticon*. It became clear to later scholars that elements of this text had been taken from the collection of homilies that had been passed down under the name of Macarius. This is how the necessary distinction of Macarius and Pseudo-Macarius was first observed. That distinction then led to the important clarification of the two distinct areas from which the traditions arose, and it was thus noticed, for the first time, that the writings of Pseudo-Macarius represented the early Syrian spiritual tradition (with its typical emphasis on the affectivity of the heart) but at precisely that moment when Syrian ideas on prayer had come to be woven into the larger Christian tradition, in the guise of works of the great Egyptian Macarius. The pseudepigraphal act of salvage, in effect, had not only worked brilliantly, it ensured that distinctive elements of Syrian theology, now successfully attributed to an unimpeachable Desert Father, would be taken up and internationalized as central themes of Byzantine ascetical spirituality. Pseudo-Macarius has been the subject of much close scrutiny in recent decades precisely because this important synthesis now made it necessary to rewrite histories of spirituality.

There are certain themes which, whether 'Messalian' or not (and the relationship of Pseudo-Macarius to any precise Messalian movement is still a controverted matter) do seem to be constitutive for the circle of Syrian ascetics for whom this spiritual master was writing. These are the idea that sin dwells in a human heart like a serpent, and that the human being has a tendency to spiritual dissolution that needs to be offset by 'ceaseless prayer' and inner attentiveness (*prosoche*) that would flower into a genuine sensibility (*aisthesis*) of the presence of the Holy Spirit in the heart of the believer. This monastic family held as axiomatic that a person who was not deeply conscious of the Spirit's presence was clearly unregenerate. Not to feel the presence of the Spirit in one's heart meant that the Spirit was evidently absent from the soul. Those possessed of the Spirit, on the other hand, were said to feel that presence as a vision of light or a deep-seated warmth in the heart. The discovery of the writings of Macarius by the young Wesley led to the inclusion of many of these foundational attitudes in the rise of Methodism. The Macarian school also advocated the abandonment of traditional monastic ideas of hard labour as a form of ascesis, advocating instead a wandering lifestyle, which focused more on spiritual withdrawal and recollection (and which is probably why sedentary local bishops disliked them). As groups of monks wandered, they formed deep and strong bonds with their 'spiritual father' to whom they returned for regular advanced teaching and confession of the heart's secrets. The spiritual father advanced the aims and tenets of the whole group. Clearly Pseudo-Macarius himself was one of the greatest of these 'spiritual fathers' and in his writings set a tone for a quality of close discipleship which would be very significant for much of later Eastern Christian spirituality, which always put a premium on this aspect of close personal guidance by an elder.

Pseudo-Macarius himself presents all these characteristic elements we have mentioned above; indeed the spirituality of the attentive heart, and the constant invocation of *penthos* ('joy-making mourning') are major distinctive contributions which he makes to the development of international Christian spirituality. There is little indication that he himself takes any of these ideas to an objectionable extreme. His works, that is, chiefly the *Great Letter* and the *Fifty Spiritual Homilies*, influenced Gregory of Nyssa's ascetical theology, and went on in later Byzantium to be a major source of the Hesychastic renewal from the eleventh century onwards, when the correlation of ascetic practices, the focus on the deep affectivity of the heart that passionately turns to God, and the · aspiring to luminous visionary experience,

become distinctive characters of Hesychastic spirituality. Many of his ideas were influential for the great Byzantine mystic, Symeon the New Theologian.

See also **Asceticism; Attentiveness; Byzantine Spirituality; Cappadocian Fathers; Early Christian Spirituality; Hesychasm; Tears, Gift of (*Penthos*); Spirit, Holy; Syriac Spirituality.**

J. Gribomont, 'Monasticism and asceticism' in B. McGinn and J. Meyendorff (eds), *Christian Spirituality: Origins to the Twelfth Century*, New York: Crossroad, 1993, pp. 89–112; W. Jaeger, *Two Rediscovered Works of Ancient Christian Literature*, Leiden: E. J. Brill, 1965; G. Maloney (trans.), *Pseudo-Macarius: The 50 Spiritual Homilies & The Great Letter*, CWS, New York: Paulist Press, 1992; J. Meyendorff, 'Messalianism or Anti-Messalianism: a fresh look at the "Macarian" problem' in *Kyriakon: Festschrift: J Quasten 2*, Munster, 1971, p. 585; S. Tugwell, *Ways of Imperfection*, London: Darton, Longman & Todd, 1984, pp. 47–58; S. Tugwell, 'Evagrius and Macarius' in C. Jones, G. Wainwright and E. Yarnold (eds), *The Study of Spirituality*, London: SPCK, 1986, pp. 168–75.

JOHN A. MCGUCKIN

Marriage, Family and Spirituality

The early Christian community posited that discipleship subverts an individual's usual loyalty to the extended patriarchal family upon which Graeco-Roman and Jewish society were based and invites believers into a new family under God's reign. This recreation of family loyalty is found in the Gospels (Mark 3.28–30; 10.28–30; Luke 11.27–28; 14.25–26; 18.28–30; Matt. 19.27–29) and the Pauline letters with their pervasive kinship symbolism of 'brothers and sisters in Christ'. Further, in anticipation of the world passing away, Paul advised against marriage (1 Cor. 7), although he did not see marriage and sexuality as intrinsically sinful.

As the Christian community grew, martyrdom became the archetypal expression of the spiritual life – that life lived under the influence of the Holy Spirit. The popular second-century passion narrative of the martyrdoms of Perpetua and Felicitas – a young North African matron with a nursing child and a pregnant slave girl – show the extent to which the promise of the dawning era allowed some Christians to willingly give up their children or bring dishonour on their families by being baptized.

With the rise of the ascetic movement the idea that sexual activity was obstructive of the higher aspirations of the soul became pervasive.

Virginity was prized and celibacy was expected of bishops, presbyters and deacons. Among those seeking the white martyrdom of the ascetic life, family and marriage were seen as hindrances. For example, the group of wealthy fourth-century Roman matrons who gathered around Jerome equated Christian discipleship with ascetic renunciation. Once widowed, they left children behind in pursuit of holiness in the monasteries of the Palestinian deserts.

As the tradition of special witnesses or saints developed, it was those who had chosen the 'perfect life' of renunciation who were proclaimed holy by popular acclamation. Athanasius' fourth-century *Life and Affairs of Our Holy Father Antony* (of Egypt) who left all he had, including a dependant sister, and fled to the desert was, among other things, a paradigm for the Christian spiritual life. At the same time, early spiritual leaders did address families as to their spiritual responsibilities. John Chrysostom (*c.* 349–407) suggested that Christian families can be praiseworthy if they encourage self-denial, service of the poor, sharing of goods and simplicity of life. Families, in his profoundly social view, should also resist customs of economic and class distinction. However, among the early Church the traditional assumption that family was rightly ordered by patriarchy and had childbearing as its purpose was not challenged.

The dominance of the celibate, monastic spiritual ideal in both Eastern and Western Christianity until the Middle Ages was unchallenged. Similarly, the concept that marriage had procreation as its sole purpose was not questioned. The 'evangelical counsels' that defined the life of perfect discipleship were poverty, chastity and obedience. These vows presumed the renunciation of marriage and family. The spiritual life – life under the influence of the Spirit – was conceived as a counter-cultural life and an anticipation of the eschatological hope in which the things of this world, including all that is tied to death and change, such as sexual congress and childbearing, would pass away.

In the Western Church, the monastic spiritual ideal began to be challenged in the thirteenth century. New forms of discipleship with an apostolic thrust emerged. The mendicant movements, while still requiring celibacy for the members of their primary communities, developed associate (tertiary) orders for lay persons who could follow a modified rule of spiritual formation while married and tending to family responsibilities. Other lay spiritual movements, such as the Beguines, also emerged. These movements did hold up the evangelical counsels as exemplary but they reflected a growing flexibility in the way in which the spiritual life was perceived. Married persons began to appear on official calendars of saints, although it was not for their Christian witness as spouses or parents that they were honoured. Exemplary married queens like Elizabeth of Hungary (renowned for her charity) and Birgitta of Sweden (famous for her prophetic visions) were honoured. Marriage had ceased necessarily to be a hindrance to the pursuit of the spiritual life but it was not the preferred path. Spiritual parenthood was a significant category in medieval literature. Those who nurtured the faithful in their Christian maturation, the spiritual fathers and mothers, were held up as exemplars. But biological parenting was not a focus of interest in that literature. Similarly, the language of spousal intimacy became a staple of celibate mystical discourse yet the physical and emotional intimacy of actual spouses did not preoccupy the thoughts of spiritual writers. At the same time, in the thirteenth century, in the development of sacramental theology in the Western Church, marriage came to be seen as a sacrament, a visible sign of an invisible reality that was a reflection of the faithful union of Christ and his Church.

With the advent of the Christian humanist movement and the changes of late medieval and early modern society, the celibate ideal was more directly challenged. Desiderius Erasmus (*c.* 1466–1536) defied traditional conceptions of the spiritual life by suggesting that marriage might be more desirable than virginity and by praising the spiritual benefits of companionship in marriage. More dramatically, the Protestant Reformation subverted the entire previous spiritual project of Christendom by asserting that marriage and family was the God-ordained vocation of all Christians. Martin Luther (1483–1546) rejected monasticism and celibacy as examples of works-righteousness. Luther considered the family as the place where parents and children could cultivate the Christian ideals of love, sacrifice and trust in God. He saw the family as supporting the existing civil society and focused on intra-familial relationships dedicated to Christ.

The Puritans, heirs of John Calvin's (1509–64) reform, shared Luther's notion of marriage as a holy estate to which most are called. These Reformers carried forward Calvin's view that the relation of spouses is in itself spiritually edifying, although procreation is seen as the primary purpose of conjugal love. Reformed theology focused on the covenantal relationship both of spouses and of God and God's chosen people. The responsibility of the Church, and the family as a cell of the Church, is to bring all of human life to obedience to God in Christ. Thus the social mission of the family is emphasized. Puritans made the family the centre of religious and spiritual formation. The father was the spiritual head of the family and the family in turn was the vehicle of salvation for parents and children. Various spiritual practices, such as journal-keeping, morning and evening family prayer, study of the Bible and domestic catechisms, encouraged spiritual nurture.

The heirs of the Radical Reformation – such as the Anabaptists and Quakers – held different views of discipleship from their mainline cousins. Although they accepted the principle that marriage and family were the God-ordained vocation of most Christians, their sense of the Spirit's working was linked to a radical call. The Christian spiritual life for them implied a radical witness to the values of the Sermon on the Mount. For many this meant that martyrdom or a call to preach or prophesy might take precedence over the duties of family life. For example, if either a man or woman in the early American Quaker community received a call to itinerant ministry, the rest of the community would discern the validity of the call then assume responsibility for his or her children during the period of itinerancy. None of the Reformation churches, mainline or radical, viewed marriage as a formal sacrament of the Church.

Reformers on the Catholic side of the confessional barrier reaffirmed the traditional teaching on the higher call of celibacy in the pursuit of the spiritual life. Yet marriage and family were affirmed as venues where spiritual maturity might be also be cultivated. Popular writer Francis de Sales (1567–1622), in his manual for laity, the *Introduction to the Devout Life*, affirmed that devotion is the call for all persons in all walks of life, married or celibate. He outlined a thoroughgoing programme of spiritual practice – including meditations, prayers and ethical guidelines – that could be adapted to all life circumstances and affirmed that the demands of one's 'state in life' were themselves an expression of the will of God. Francis de Sales, while acknowledging that marriage is significant for the propagation and training of a Christian society, felt that the marriage relationship was even more a friendship directed toward the mutual sanctification of the couple. In the Roman Catholic Church, marriage continued to be considered a formal sacrament.

In the contemporary world, interest in the spiritual dimension of marriage and family has increased across Christian denominations. In part, the ecumenical spiritual renewal occasioned by Vatican II with its 'universal call to holiness' is the starting point for this interest. Larger cultural factors are also at work. Most denominations continue to build upon the spiritual insights of their founders. Evangelical Christian traditions have continued to emphasize the patriarchal model of family and to see the cultivation of family religiosity as a significant feature of discipleship. Mainline Protestant interest in family has manifested itself in family church camps, social services for families and educational programmes for youth. In addition, the impact of Christian feminist theology across the denominations has given rise to new ways of thinking about gender relations and non-patriarchal family structures. The spiritual tasks of extended, blended, divorced, remarried, single, childless and adoptive families have come to the fore.

In Roman Catholicism, the social dimension of the family vocation has been emphasized. Pope John Paul II's three major addresses on the family (1981: *On the Family*; 1983: *Charter on the Rights of the Family*; 1994: *Letter to Families*) stem from the pontiff's personalist philosophy and his idea of the family as the prototype of the 'civilization of love'. John Paul's vision of marriage stresses the equal dignity of husband and wife whose roles are seen as complementary; the intimate heart of marriage is their reciprocal self-giving. But the Christian family is not a self-enclosed community. Rather, his views of marriage, indeed the views of his recent predecessors, are influenced by Catholic social teaching tradition. The Christian family then must participate in and contribute to the common good and have a special concern for the most vulnerable in society. Among some thinkers, the ancient concept of the family as 'domestic church' has been revived and an attempt to articulate its particular spiritual path.

See also **Body and Spirituality; Children and Spirituality; Celibacy; Discipleship; Lay People and Spirituality; Roman Catholic Spirituality; Sexuality; Vocation.**

Don S. Browning and Ian S. Evinson (eds), *The Family, Religion and Culture* Series, Louisville, KY: Westminster John Knox Press, 1996–; Lisa Sowell Cahill, *Family: A Christian Social Perspective*, Minneapolis: Fortress Press, 2000; John Paul II, *On the Family* (Apostolic Exhortation, *Familiaris consortio*), 1981; Michael G. Lawler, *Marriage and Sacrament: A Theology of Christian Marriage*, Collegeville, MN: The Liturgical Press, 1993; John Meyendorff, *Marriage: An Orthodox Perspective*, New York: St Vladimir's Seminary Press, 1973.

WENDY M. WRIGHT

Marriage, Spiritual

see Bridal Mysticism

Martyrdom

The word 'martyr' comes from the Greek word for witness. It was applied as an honorific title to those early Christians who bore witness to their faith in Christ by laying down their lives under persecution. Christ had predicted such a fate for his followers, a prediction soon fulfilled with the death of the first martyr, St Stephen. His death by stoning, as depicted in Acts, recalled the pattern of Christ's death, and in so doing set a pattern for many subsequent narratives.

Stephen's witness, according to tradition, was joined by many of the original apostles, including St Peter, St James and St Paul, as well as the considerable number of Christians who were martyred during the years of sporadic Roman persecution. In this period, when Christianity was an outlawed sect, the willingness to lay down one's life for the gospel was the consummate mark of faithful discipleship – the defining mark of sanctity. Indeed, veneration of the martyrs was the original basis for the cult of saints. The early Christians remembered the anniversary of their deaths – their *dies natalis*, or birthday to eternal life; they gathered at their burial sites and faithfully circulated the accounts of their passion.

Particularly important early texts include the letters of St Ignatius (d. 107), the Bishop of Antioch, who composed his letters to the churches as he was being transported to Rome for execution. Ignatius regarded his impending death as proof of his faith – and a witness to the truth of Christ's promise of eternal reward: 'Then I shall be a real disciple of Jesus Christ when the world sees my body no more.' Among his correspondents was St Polycarp, later Bishop of Smyrna (d. 155), who would eventually meet a similar fate. The account of Polycarp's death, filled with miraculous wonders, set a standard for such narratives. Like the death of St Stephen, it was a death 'conformable to the gospel', a kind of liturgical, or quasi-eucharistic, offering (his burning flesh was like 'bread baking'), by which the Church would be fed and nourished. As Tertullian wrote, 'The blood of the martyrs is the seed of the Church.'

Constantine's conversion ended the era of Roman persecution. And yet the challenge of the martyrs continued to set a standard for faithful discipleship. Beginning in the fourth century the Desert Fathers and Mothers who went into the wilderness were motivated in part by a desire to lay down their lives in a new arena – this time of self-imposed asceticism and sacrifice. In their austerity they offered a 'white martyrdom', in contrast to the 'red martyrdom' of violent death.

And yet the era of martyrdom never truly receded; it simply adapted to new historical circumstances. Some, like St Boniface (d. 754), were struck down in the course of the Church's missionary expansion. Others, most famously St Thomas Becket, Archbishop of Canterbury (d. 1170), died defending the authority of the Church against the encroaching power of the state. The Era of Discovery, which launched a vast new missionary expansion, added many new martyrs – particularly in the 'New World', and in Asia. In Japan a particularly savage period of persecution resulted in the martyrdom of scores of missionaries as well as thousands of lay Christians.

The Protestant Reformation and the subsequent wars of religion introduced a new chapter in the history of martyrdom, as both Protestants and Catholics persecuted one another with zeal. While Catholics honoured the witness of St Thomas More and English Jesuits like Edmund Campion, Protestants revered their own holy martyrs. The suffering of faithful Protestants under the Catholic reign of Queen Mary supplied the material for *Foxe's Book of Martyrs*.

The twentieth century was marked by an enormous rise in martyrdom – possibly more than the total of all previous centuries combined. Persecution by governments and ideologies hostile to Christianity was similar in spirit to the earliest era of Roman persecution – except that the scale was much greater. This included vast numbers of Christians killed by the Nazis, by Communist regimes in the Soviet Union and China, and by anti-clerical forces in countries like Mexico and Spain.

At the same time, however, the twentieth century also brought a widening of the understanding of martyrdom. When Pope John Paul II canonized St Maximilian Kolbe, a Polish priest who died in Auschwitz, he called him a 'martyr for charity'. Kolbe died after volunteering to take the place of another prisoner slated for execution. Thus, a martyr could be someone who died not simply for claiming allegiance to Christ but for bearing witness to one of the evangelical virtues. Unlike martyrs of earlier ages who died for their beliefs or their mode of worship, the martyrs of today might be persons who died for the practice of their faith – a commitment to peace, social justice, human rights or solidarity with the oppressed. Examples might include Dr Martin Luther King Jr, assassinated for his leadership in the Civil Rights Movement, a commitment deeply rooted in his Christian faith; or the

Austrian peasant Franz Jägerstatter, executed for his refusal to serve in the Nazi army; or the Polish priest Father Jerzy Popieluszko, chaplain to the dissident Solidarity movement.

This new understanding of martyrdom received further meaning in Latin America in the 1970s and 1980s, when the Church's emerging 'option for the poor' ran counter to the violent policies of right-wing military dictatorships. Thousands of Christians were tortured and killed – largely lay people, but also priests, nuns and even bishops. What was new in this case was that their persecutors, far from proclaiming hatred for the faith, claimed to be pious Catholics. Among these martyrs was Archbishop Oscar Romero of San Salvador, who was killed in 1980 while saying Mass. Unlike Thomas Becket he was not killed for defending the prerogatives of the Church but for defending justice and the lives of the poor. In that sense, as the Jesuit Jon Sobrino observed, his death was closer to the example of Jesus.

In the light of all this violence, Pope John Paul II was moved to note: 'At the end of the second millennium, the church has once again become a church of martyrs.' One of the striking developments has been a new appreciation for the ecumenical dimensions of martyrdom. The sacrifice of the martyrs – whether Protestant, Catholic or Orthodox – has prompted in some quarters a greater sensitivity to the bonds of ecumenical solidarity. In this spirit the Church of England erected a set of ten statues for Westminster Abbey commemorating a striking array of modern martyrs – Catholic, Protestant and Orthodox. In a similar spirit, in May 2000 the Pope honoured 10,000 'Witnesses of the Faith', martyred during the twentieth century, a prayer in which he acknowledged Christians of all denominations.

The Church has long regarded martyrdom as a special vocation, to which some are called but which none should seek. While the threat of violent death is not an imminent reality for most Christians, the Church still, as it did in the first century, draws food and nourishment from this cloud of witnesses. This is not because only those who die for their faith are true disciples. Daily life supplies its own smaller arenas: the challenge to stand up for a stranger, to defend an unpopular principle, to challenge friends or family when they are wrong. Even when our lives are not at stake the witness of the martyrs – those prepared to go the ultimate distance for their beliefs – reminds us of the gospel challenge to heroism.

The martyrs of every age, including our own, continue to bear witness to Christ and his promise of the resurrection. They remind us that ulti-mately the gospel presents demands that may put us in conflict with our culture, our society, or the state – challenging us, in each situation, to know where our heart's loyalty ultimately lies. A Church that failed to remember its martyrs would be a Church seriously disengaged from the memory of Christ and his witness.

See also **Discipleship; Hagiography; Holiness; Monasticism; Saints, Communion of.**

Bruno Cheno et al. (eds), *The Book of Christian Martyrs*, New York: Crossroad, 1990; Robert Royal, *Catholic Martyrs of the Twentieth Century*, New York: Crossroad, 2000; Jon Sobrino, *Witnesses of the Kingdom: The Martyrs of El Salvador and the Crucified Peoples*, Maryknoll, NY: Orbis Books, 2003.

ROBERT ELLSBERG

Marxism and Spirituality

At first sight, Marxism does not seem to have much space for matters spiritual. Marx himself insisted that 'Christianity has no history whatsoever' and continued 'all the different forms of various times were not "self-determinations" and "further developments" of the religious spirit, but were brought about by wholly empirical causes in no way dependent on any influence of the religious spirit' (Marx, 2000, p. 180). And Engels, who came from a strongly pietistic background, wrote much more on Christianity than Marx – all equally negative. Nevertheless, Marx does refer to humanity's 'spiritual forces' as apparently permanent features of human nature. Many of his comments on religion are insightful and suggestive; and all of his followers – from Austro-Marxists who saw no problem in combining their Marxism with religious belief to those whose version of materialism ruled out any religious statements as a priori false – could find some support in Marx himself.

With the victory of the Bolsheviks in 1917, the dialectical materialism of Soviet orthodoxy pursued a crudely reductionist view of religion, with an opportunistic relaxation as a prop to nationalist sentiment during the Second World War. Outside the Soviet orbit, however, twentieth-century Marxists have spent more time revising the minimal role given to religious and spiritual factors in the tradition they inherited. Two contributions stand out. First, the work of Antonio Gramsci, particularly in his *Prison Notebooks*, provides the subtlest treatment by any Marxist of the role of religion in the historical process. Gramsci was more interested in the type of activity encouraged by Christianity at different times and in difference places than in an examination of its formal content. From his Italian standpoint, Gramsci saw Christianity as a much more differentiated phenomenon than many of his Marxist predecessors. In particular, he did not see Protestantism as more progressive than Catholicism. True, it was the lack of a Protestant Reformation that meant that the Italian people as a whole had not been introduced to the culture and politics of a nation. Nevertheless, Protestantism, by basing itself exclusively on the sacred text of the Bible, had tended to become an intellectual religion divorced from the masses. By contrast, Catholicism had managed, through its liturgy, colour, music and devotion to the saints, to maintain a popular spirituality alongside a doctrinal and intellectual rigidity. Gramsci's remarks on Christian history, although of necessity (he was writing in prison) frequently fragmentary and allusive, are remarkable for their sympathy, insight and suggestiveness. Second, the contribution of what has come to be known as the Frankfurt School is striking. For these writers, the legacy of religion was the idea of perfect justice which, while it might be impossible of realization in this world, yet served as a constant basis of opposition to the powers that were. Although in Adorno, the foremost representative of the Frankfurt School, there is only a limited sympathy with theological motifs, in the work of his younger friend Walter Benjamin, these motifs are more marked: Benjamin derived his theological attitudes from his aesthetics and developed a 'negative' theological position in which mysticism and materialism converged. A more specific example of the suggestiveness of Western Marxism in its treatment of spirituality in the discussion of Jansenism by Lucien Goldmann, a pupil of Lukacs. In his book The Hidden God he brilliantly traces the origins of Pascal's tragic vision to the development of royal power in seventeenth-century France.

Finally, mention should be made of liberation theology and the way in which, particularly in the 1960s and 1970s in Latin America, Christianity was reformulated by theologians (and others) who either declared themselves to be Marxists or who were strongly influenced by the Marxist tradition. In this critical enterprise, liberation theologians have attempted a reinterpretation of traditional Christian ideas through a rigorous application of the Marxist materialist conception of history. For them, the gospel of love may be the general framework of aspiration underlying all human activity: but what the gospel will require in practice – for example, class strife and violence – will be decided by theoretical analysis of a Marxist type. Thus there is no specifically Christian politics or social

theory. Many Christians – including the Vatican – have thought much of liberation theology too Marxist to be Christian. Nevertheless, it is obvious that Marxism contains certain views that some versions of (thereby impoverished) Christianity have failed to propagate: of human beings as essentially social, of solidarity with the poor and outcast, of taking history seriously, and looking towards the future as a critique of the present.

See also Liberation Spirituality; Social Justice; Public Life and Spirituality.

A. Fierro, The Militant Gospel, Maryknoll, NY: Orbis Books, 1977; M. Machovec, A Marxist Look at Jesus, London: Darton, Longman & Todd, 1976; D. McLellan, Marxism and Religion, Basingstoke: Macmillan, 1987; K. Marx, Selected Writings, ed. D. McLellan, Oxford: Oxford University Press, 2000.

DAVID MCLELLAN

Mary and Spirituality

Although central to the teachings and liturgies of Catholic Christianity, Marian spirituality has always overflowed the boundaries of orthodoxy, to give expression to the human longing for God in a multitude of languages, images and practices. Even if one narrows the scope of spirituality to that which is explicitly associated with Christian worship, it would be impossible to summarize the range of beliefs and devotions associated with Mary. Today, New Age, feminist and goddess spiritualities sometimes appeal to the symbolism of the Virgin Mary, while rejecting any association with Christianity. Notwithstanding the plurality of her cult, however, Marian spirituality can only be understood as authentically Christian when it is an integral part of the life of faith. It invites the believer to deepen his or her relationship to Christ, to become incorporated into the community of the Church, and to seek a harmonious balance between the active and contemplative dimensions of a faith expressed in prayer and social action. The Catholic tradition has always differentiated between the adoration that Christians owe to God and the honour accorded to Mary. These points need to be borne in mind when considering Marian spirituality and its potential for Christians today.

Mary was a key figure in the theological controversies of the early Church. It was through affirming Mary as Theotokos – Godbearer – at the Council of Ephesus in 431 that the Church defended its belief in the human and divine natures of Christ. From this theological perspective, Mary's virginal motherhood draws the believer into a space of mystery, where Word meets flesh, time meets eternity, and God becomes human in a Virgin's womb. The Bible says of Mary that she 'treasured up all these things and pondered them in her heart' (Luke 2.19), and it is this silent pondering on the ways of God that has led Marian spirituality to be associated with contemplative prayer.

But devotion to Mary is almost as old as Christianity itself, and the Marian tradition has always been inspired at least as much by popular devotion as by theology and doctrine. The influential if controversial second-century apocryphal gospel, the *Protoevangelium of James*, gives an account of Mary's early life, and many medieval devotions associated with Mary and her mother, St Anne, have their origins in this text and its later interpretations. Further evidence of early devotion to Mary can be found in a work attributed to Gregory of Nyssa, which describes a vision of Mary appearing to Gregory the Wonderworker in the third century. A fragment of an intercessory prayer to Mary, known as the *Sub tuum praesidium*, is believed to date from the third or fourth century. Although the Catholic dogmas of the Immaculate Conception and the Assumption were promulgated in 1854 and 1950 respectively, the celebration of these feasts can be traced back to the sixth and seventh centuries.

The Bible says relatively little about Mary, although it is the source of some of the greatest Marian prayers. The Magnificat comes from Luke's Gospel, as does the first part of the Hail Mary, which is taken from the angel's words at the annunciation and from Elizabeth's greeting at the visitation. The second part of the Hail Mary developed later and in its current form the prayer dates from the sixteenth century. The Hail Mary forms the basis of the rosary, which remains one of the most popular forms of Marian prayer. In John's Gospel, the account of Mary at the foot of the cross has inspired meditations on her maternal suffering, as for example in the *Stabat Mater*, attributed to Jacopone da Todi (1240–1306). Mary has also traditionally been identified with the woman clothed with the sun in the book of Revelation. From the second century, writers such as Justin Martyr and Irenaeus referred to her as the New Eve, based on the Pauline reference to Christ as the Second Adam, and on the Genesis story of creation. Many of the popular Marian titles found in litanies such as the twelfth-century Litany of Loreto have allusions to the Old Testament, and Mary has also been associated with the figure of Wisdom in Prov. 8, particularly with regard to the Feast of the Immaculate Conception.

The Council of Ephesus marked the beginning of a flourishing cult of the Virgin that persisted until the Reformation. With the conversion of Rome, Marian devotion absorbed some of the images associated with the goddess figures of the ancient world, although it would be misleading to describe Mary herself as a goddess. Marian spirituality has also developed along different lines in the Eastern and Western Churches. While the Orthodox Church still draws on the early tradition to represent Mary as an iconic maternal figure who communicates awe and compassion, humility and glory, Western spirituality has reflected changing cultural and historical influences, so that devotion to Mary bears the marks of evolving and sometimes contested beliefs and practices.

The late Middle Ages saw the flowering of Marian devotion in the West, and many of today's prayers date back to that time. Mary was no longer seen as the majestic maternal presence of the early medieval Church, but as a tender and compassionate mother. In the era following the Black Death, images such as the *mater dolorosa* and the *pieta* suggest an association between the suffering of the people and the suffering of the mother of the crucified Christ. The mystery plays, feast days and pilgrimages associated with Mary expressed a spirituality of everyday life, rooted in the seasons and rhythms of nature. But Marian spirituality was also shaped around the desires and ambitions of kings and queens, troubadours and their courtly ladies, mystics and scholarly clerics who looked to the language of the Song of Songs to express a spirituality suffused with eroticism. With the conquest of Latin America, Mary became identified with the indigenous people of Mexico when she reportedly appeared to an Indian convert, Juan Diego, in 1531. Our Lady of Guadalupe has since become a focus for a spirituality rooted in the peoples and cultures of Latin America and, in recent years, identified with their struggle for liberation.

The Reformation saw the rejection of Marian devotion by the Protestant churches, although seventeenth-century Anglican theologians – known as the Caroline Divines – produced a rich seam of Marian literature in the Church of England. With the Council of Trent, the Roman Catholic Church curbed many popular devotions that were deemed to be unbiblical or inappropriate. A robust maternal cult gave way to a more romanticized form of spirituality informed by changing perceptions of motherhood and femininity, with writers such as Mary d'Agreda (d. 1665), Louis-Marie Grignion de Montfort (d. 1716) and Alphonsus Liguori (1696–1787) enjoying widespread popularity.

The mid nineteenth century marked the beginning of an era sometimes referred to as the Marian Century, with a proliferation of often highly sentimental forms of piety proliferating as a reaction against the increasingly rationalist and scientific ethos of the time. As well as the promulgation of the doctrine of the Immaculate Conception (1854), there were numerous reports of apparitions including those at Lourdes (1858) and Fatima (1917). Many religious orders founded in the nineteenth century are modelled on different forms of Marian spirituality.

There was a waning of devotion to Mary in the period surrounding the Second Vatican Council. After heated debate at the Council, it was decided that, rather than issuing a separate document on Mary, she would be included in the document on the Church, *Lumen Gentium*, a move intended to integrate Marian spirituality into the life of the Church as a whole. The Apostolic Letter, *Marialis Cultus*, issued by Pope Paul V in 1974, and Pope John Paul II's 1987 encyclical, *Redemptoris Mater*, sought to articulate a Marian spirituality for the post-conciliar Church, and under the papacy of John Paul II there has been a Marian revival that once again spans a wide spectrum. The growth of ecumenism has seen Catholics and Protestants searching for a shared understanding of Mary's place in the story of salvation. Marian shrines attract many thousands of pilgrims every year, with Marian apparitions being reported in places as far afield as Rwanda (1981) and Medjugorje (1981). In the Roman Catholic Church, there are those who seek a revitalized sacramental life revolving around the institutional structures of the masculine, Petrine Church, and the spiritual life of faith epitomized by the feminine, Marian Church. From a different perspective, liberation theologians look to Mary as the model of a spirituality that expresses itself in solidarity with the oppressed in their quest for justice. While feminists have been critical of what is seen as the impossible ideal of virginal motherhood associated with Mary, there is today a growing movement towards the development of a women's spirituality inspired by feminist reinterpretations of Mary.

There is much in the Marian tradition that can be criticized for its excess or its sentimentality, but there is also much that speaks to the contemporary quest for a spirituality that offers a holistic and integrated understanding of the bodily person in relation to God and to nature. As the human mother of God incarnate, Mary affirms the significance of the body for the Christian faith. As the one whose motherhood of Christ has traditionally been associated with a sense of cosmic redemption, Marian spirituality has the potential to express the joy of a renewed and redeemed creation. And as the one chosen to speak on behalf of all humankind in freely saying 'yes' to the incarnation, she affirms the authority, dignity and holiness of woman before God in the Christian story.

See also Devotions, Popular; Incarnation; Saints, Communion of.

A. M. Allchin, *The Joy of all Creation: An Anglican Meditation on the Place of Mary*, London: New City, 1993; Hans Urs von Balthasar, *Mary for Today*, San Francisco: Ignatius Press, 1988; Tina Beattie, *God's Mother, Eve's Advocate: A Marian Narrative of Women's Salvation*, London and New York: Continuum, 2002; Sarah Jane Boss, *Empress and Handmaid: On Nature and Gender in the Cult of the Virgin Mary*, London and New York: Cassell, 2000; Raymond E. Brown, Karl P. Donfried, Joseph A. Fitzmyer and John Reumann (eds), *Mary in the New Testament*, Philadelphia: Fortress Press/ New York: Paulist Press, 1978; Bertrand Buby, *Mary of Galilee*, vol. 3: *The Marian Heritage of the Early Church*, New York: Alba House, 1996; Ivone Gebara and Maria Clara Bingemer, *Mary: Mother of God, Mother of the Poor*, trans. Phillip Berryman, Tunbridge Wells: Burns & Oates, 1989; Hilda Graef, *Mary: A History of Doctrine and Devotion*, combined edn, London: Sheed & Ward, 1994; William McLoughlin and Jill Pinnock (eds), *Mary for Earth and Heaven: Essays on Mary and Ecumenism*, Leominster: Gracewing, 2002; Michael O'Carroll, *Theotokos: A Theological Encyclopedia of the Blessed Virgin Mary*, Collegeville, MN: The Liturgical Press, 1982; Jaroslav Pelikan, *Mary through the Centuries: Her Place in the History of Culture*, New Haven and London: Yale University Press, 1996; Edward Schillebeeckx and Catharina Halkes, *Mary: Yesterday, Today, Tomorrow*, trans. John Bowden, London: SCM Press, 1993; George H. Tavard, *The Thousand Faces of the Virgin Mary*, Collegeville, MN: The Liturgical Press, 1996; Marina Warner, *Alone of All Her Sex: The Myth and the Cult of the Virgin Mary*, London and New York: Vintage Books, 2000.

TINA BEATTIE

Masculine Spirituality

Masculine spirituality is rooted, consciously or otherwise, in men's sense of self *as men*; that is, in men's social, cultural, physical, sexual and psychological experience, as distinct from that of women.

Once feminist theology opened up the critique of patriarchy within Christian theology and culture, and, together with theologies of Black and of gay and lesbian liberation, challenged the notion of a hegemonic and universal norm in human experience and Christian understanding, it was recognized that spirituality was *gendered* – that is, defined by sexual difference, shaped by the embodied, socio-psychological, historically evolving experience of what it is to be a woman or a man. Masculine experience in itself was no longer regarded as uniform, but formed by class, race and differing cultures, fostering a diverse range of distinctive and sometimes competing masculinities. From this perspective there can be no single or normative spirituality among men, but a plethora of spiritualities, even when, in any particular time or culture, some masculinities may predominate. Social changes in the relationships between women and men, particularly in the post-war, increasingly urban, technological and de-industrial Western communities of the global North, have challenged men's sense of self. Artificial contraception, economic independence and ideological confidence among women have shifted many men's assumptions about themselves and their relationships with women, children and one another. In some men these changes have inspired new spiritualities which are expressions of pro-feminist, pro-gay masculinities, while in others there has been a response that is reactionary and conservative.

Much of the progressive developments in masculine spirituality have been outside mainstream Christianity, predominantly characterized by a broadly pro-feminist, pro-gay consciousness and informed by a variety of contemporary ecological, multi-faith and psychoanalytical concerns. Taking a Jungian approach to gender relations in the West, the poet and psychotherapist Robert Bly articulates in his book *Iron John* a culture of profound loss among men which is in striking contrast to the confidence and eloquence of women at the present time. Men and boys are disconnected from their intrinsic, essential masculine qualities by a culture which has suppressed masculine spiritual and emotional self-realization in pursuit of consumerist goals where men are corporate wage-slaves, distanced from the earth, alienated from their fathers, partners, children and from creative relationships with one another through a regime of environmental exploitation, obsessive work and an absence of constructive male role-models. In this analysis, the Jesus of conventional Christianity – in contrast to vibrant Hindu deities or mythical figures of masculine strength such as the hairy man Iron John – is a neutered Christ-figure who symbolizes men's de-sexualization and disembodiment. Contemporary Western culture func-

tions more as a puerarchy than a patriarchy, dominated by immature and directionless males, a 'sibling society' in which parents can take no genuine responsibility for the proper human development of children because they are so needy themselves.

In response to this profound crisis in masculinity Bly commends a cultural programme of individual and corporate rediscovery for men: a connecting with 'the deep masculine' through careful attentiveness to male experience, embracing both masculine 'wildness' and environmental wilderness in individual and group therapy, looking towards indigenous tribal peoples for models of initiation for boys and the promotion of 'mature' masculinity through fatherhood and other forms of positive mentoring. Bly's approach, and that of others such as Sam Keen, has been to respond to changes in gender relations by arguing for a conscious and interactive shift in masculine identity through an eclectic approach which includes spirituality as one element in an all-embracing, non-credal emphasis on personal development.

Out of these kinds of analyses a men's movement has developed in the West, eclectic and diverse in both theory and practice, generating a range of literature, therapies, retreats and networks for men who are seeking meaning and direction for themselves and their relationships in a time of immense change and uncertainty. Some Christians, most notably Richard Rohr, have developed masculine spirituality along these lines but more emphatically from within the context of orthodox Christianity. Retreats and programmes of spiritual guidance for men use Jungian archetypes as they explore the character of prayer and spirituality specific to men and male experience, such as that developed by Patrick Arnold. From a predominantly conservative evangelical perspective, largely in the United States, the explicitly Christian men's movement 'Promise Keepers' has developed a code of moral values, grounded in a conservative reading of Scripture, which seeks to endorse a divinely ordered model of masculinity and of power-relations within the man–woman dynamic of family, Church and society. The social theology of the Roman Catholic Church has stressed both the complementarity of women and men and also their radical difference within the divinely ordered make-up of creation: men essentially as initiators, leaders and guardians; women as receivers, nurturers and teachers.

Other Christian approaches have embraced the theory that gender identity is socially constructed: culturally formed, always shifting through historical change, and therefore open to renegotiation and radical transformation. Generally these constructionist approaches to masculine spiritualities acknowledge their debt to the women's movement and pay great attention to the diversity of men's experience; they are seeking to co-operate with changes in social structures and transition in gender relations. For example, Roy McCloughry has argued that taking Jesus as the model of mature masculinity, men are called to follow him in furthering God's kingdom by dismantling patriarchal attitudes and practices in their relations with women and one another: overcoming fear, and moving from power to love. James Nelson, in his seminal book *The Intimate Connection*, building on his long-term membership of a men's group, explores his physical, emotional, sexual and spiritual history as a man, and develops a spirituality for men which is grounded in personal, sexual, embodied experience. He argues that the patriarchal model of masculinity which has shaped Western culture for so long, with its linear patterns of thought and its dichotomous, dualistic rationality, has systematized hierarchy and dominance in ways which have done great harm to the planet, the human community, and even to the dominators themselves. A masculine spirituality for the present time is one which enables men to connect with the spiritual as it is embodied within themselves as sexual beings in relation to a diversity of others, all part of a vulnerable ecology.

See also **Body and Spirituality; Feminist Spirituality; Friendship; Homosexuality; Sexuality; Women and Spirituality.**

Robert Bly, *Iron John: A Book About Men*, New York: Addison-Wesley, 1990; R. W. Connell, *Masculinities*, Cambridge: Polity Press, 1995; Elaine Graham, *Making the Difference: Gender, Personhood and Theology*, London: Mowbray, 1995; Roy McCloughry, *Men and Masculinity: From Power to Love*, London: Hodder & Stoughton, 1992; James Nelson, *The Intimate Connection: Male Sexuality, Masculine Spirituality*, Louisville, KY: Westminster John Knox Press, 1988/London: SPCK, 1992; Mark Pryce, *Finding a Voice: Men, Women and the Community of the Church*, London: SCM Press, 1996.

MARK PRYCE

Media and Communications

Spiritual traditions have always been passed on and accessed through whatever media are available. The Christian spiritual tradition has used preaching, memorized sayings, one-to-one conversation, liturgy, personal correspondence, diary and journal to distil and hand on its wisdom. Since the explosion of modern media it has become obvious how message is affected, and even shaped, by the medium in which it is expressed. An example would be the enigmatic wisdom of the Desert Fathers which is handed down in collections of virtually anonymous brief sayings and stories. On the other hand the autobiographical journal form provides an ideal vehicle for the intense and intimate spiritual reflections of St Thérèse of Lisieux. The media which have historically predominated have both created and reinforced the expectation that the scope of 'spirituality' is primarily personal, with social, ethical and ecclesial consequences.

The proliferation of modern media poses important questions for the Christian spiritual tradition. Radio, television, e-mail and the Internet alter the relationship between the private and the public and therefore have an impact on spirituality. What is private and intimate for significant persons is commonly disclosed on public media. The public nature of broadcast and electronic media mean that shared assumptions about faith and practice can no longer be taken for granted. This can most obviously be seen in the history of British broadcasting. Religious programmes have had their place from the beginning, but with a markedly ecumenical emphasis and with an awareness that faith could not be assumed in listeners or viewers. In the USA where the separation of state and Church led to different expectations, and the commercial basis of media operations has allowed for greater consumer choice, it has been easier for radio and television to attract support for particular denominational approaches. Mother Angelica's Eternal Word TV network would be an example, where a highly conservative Catholic ecclesiology and spirituality is promoted as an alternative to secularism.

Modern communications media encourage the proliferation of diverse spiritualities and ensure that, however competitive and critical of one another their advocates might be, they cannot exist in isolation. The Internet can make space for the profound, the foolish and the downright dangerous but it cannot yet provide tools by which the individual might evaluate what he or she finds there.

The immediacy of television and radio is also contributing to the emergence of a new form of public spirituality, which appears to have no particular ecclesial base or authority structure. It comes to light at times of national emergency or disaster, or in response to significant accidents or crimes of violence. Instant images available and repeated on television evoke a response of sympathy. People flock to the site of the tragedy leaving flowers, messages and prayers. The images of the shrines thus created are replayed through television and those create a spiritual feedback loop which often finds further expression in the life and prayer of local churches.

Alongside this new public manifestation of corporate spirituality is an emphasis on the uniqueness of the individual's spiritual experience. If earlier forms of spirituality were seen primarily as a personal matter; it was generally assumed that the interpretation of that experience belonged corporately to the Church. To be outside that body of ecclesial wisdom was to court the charge of heresy. Today the reverse seems true. The Churches emphasize the corporate nature of spirituality at a time when individuals seek to stress the uniqueness of their spiritual experience, looking more for mirroring and affirmation from sympathetic others rather than for judgement about whether their experiences are in line with orthodox teaching. This is perhaps what should be expected from a media-saturated society with its emphasis on personal choice, fulfilment and self-development.

It is phenomena such as these which have led Wesley Carr, a recent commentator on contemporary communications, to conclude that the media are providing for contemporary society the integrative function which once belonged to religion in the medieval age.

See also Cyberspace; Image and Spirituality; Technology and Spirituality.

Wesley Carr, *Ministry and the Media*, London: SPCK, 1990.

ANGELA TILBY

Medieval Spirituality in the West

The centuries between 600 and 1450 CE are extraordinarily significant for the formation and development of Christian spirituality. Spanning almost a thousand years, this vibrant period is witness to the gradual conversion of European tribal peoples and the expansion of Christendom in the Western hemisphere, decisive advances in science and technology, the rise of urban centres and a money economy, and increased knowledge of non-Western cultures. The legacy of medieval spirituality, here defined as a culturally and historically specific guide to and description of the experiential knowledge of the Divine and its presence in nature and in human life, can be reconstructed from numerous sources. They include liturgical rites, sacred architecture, art and music, and the different genres of religious writings such as letters, penitentials, sermons,

saints' lives, and the theological and pedagogical texts composed by mystics and spiritual counsellors. Although much has been lost, the legacy of medieval spirituality is still a vital part of a contemporary search for the sacred: orders founded in the medieval period still exist around the world, European sites and relics of saints and miracle-workers attract pilgrims in search of healing, chants and other liturgical music are being performed for appreciative audiences, monastic buildings still host retreats, and mystical writings continue to be published in numerous world languages. Cognizant of the fragmentary nature of our knowledge, it is still possible to identify three overlapping periods. In each period, climatic, political and economic changes influenced the development of spirituality, as did encounters with other cultures and religions.

Early medieval spirituality may be characterized by a gradual process of cultural conversion and local, that is, site- and clan-specific practices (the sixth to the eleventh centuries). Central medieval spirituality became defined by the proliferation of communal lifestyles, by the development of a body of spiritual literature with a transregional appeal, and by intensified pastoral care for a growing population in cities and rural areas (twelfth and thirteenth centuries). The late medieval period, subject to dramatic climatic and epidemic changes, witnessed a growing mistrust of mystical phenomena, and the simultaneous increase in both more individualized spiritual discipline and the ecclesiastical repression of nonconformist religious views (fourteenth and fifteenth centuries). The thirteenth through the fifteenth centuries mark also what some scholars define as the formation of a persecuting society, with an intensification of anti-Semitism and rejection of marginalized social groups.

Early medieval spirituality. Christian missionaries gained a foothold in European tribal societies through collaboration with noble clans, often through special alliances with aristocratic women. Numerous noteworthy missionaries eventually gained the status of miracle-workers and saints, fiercely protecting their domain even after their deaths. As their status grew, their biographies and cults became embellished with a growing body of stories of dramatic encounters with ill-intentioned 'pagans'. One such famous missionary is St Boniface (d. 753), who was killed by 'pagans' while on a missionary trip to Frisia. St Boniface, born in Wessex, is credited with the conversion of large areas in Germany, including Thuringia and parts of Bavaria. Part of his legend is his miraculous destruction of a sacred oak dedicated to an indigenous divinity.

Despite sometimes dramatic accounts of mass conversions, enforced through the threat of violence and the aggressive destruction of pagan sacred sites, Christianity absorbed well-established magical practices and local clan structures. Hermits and saints took over some of the tasks of pagan holy people, whether as healers or counsellors. Early generations of medieval saints tended to be members of the nobility; their burial sites ensured a growing cult that could anchor Christianity in a particular region. One typical example is St Rupert (d. 718), Bishop of Worms and a member of the Merovingian royal house, who founded several monasteries in remote areas, including a female monastery which he gifted to his niece Ehrentrud. He became the patron saint of Salzburg and surrounding areas after he founded St Peter's monastery in Salzburg.

Following pagan practices, Christian holy days were established in accordance with astronomical cycles (e.g. the Twelve Days of Christmas), or to enhance the fabric of social life, whether to honour ancestors (All Saints' and All Souls' Days) or to minimize social tensions (feast days of status inversions and carnivals). Charms and magical formulas were widely used to help in agricultural work, childbirth, illness and matters of love and lust. If we can trust penitential handbooks, written for confessors, a Christianized use of such practices coexisted with the survival of pagan sacred beings in legends and places of worship. One such powerful miracle-worker is St Radegund (c. 525–87), the Thuringian-Frankish 'queen saint' who founded a royal monastery at Poitiers. The monastery became richly endowed and respected for its support of the arts and education. Learned and strong willed, St Radegund has also been celebrated as a severe ascetic and healer, and is still revered as the patron saint of Poitiers.

Although hermits and loosely organized monastic communities can be found as early as the third century, monasticism became a distinctly medieval phenomenon in aligning economic, governmental and spiritual needs on a large scale. The founding father of medieval monasticism was St Benedict of Nursia (c. 480–547), a brilliant administrator and spiritual director. His Rule is both a seemingly timeless humanistic guide to communal life and an inspirational model for spiritual growth. In the Rule's twelve steps to humility, a practitioner of Benedictine spirituality learns to combine a life of virtue with compassion and love for God to find inner peace and freedom from fear and anxiety.

Central Middle Ages. Although its origins are to be found in Egypt, the institution of Western monasticism as a site for the growth of medieval spirituality came fully into its own after centuries of civil war and invasions in the early medieval period, and accelerated economic growth beginning in the tenth century. Monastic spirituality was fuelled by an intensive search for reform and a return to the apostolic life. Its key proponents were the Cistercian Order, shaped by the forceful and tireless guidance of St Bernard of Clairvaux (1090/91–1153), a mystic and spiritual author of immense influence. It was St Bernard who popularized courtly love mysticism, especially so in his series of sermons on the Song of Songs.

Whereas Cistercians were committed to a cloistered lifestyle, two other key orders became known as mendicant institutions that stressed an itinerant way of life for their male branches. These are the Franciscan Order, founded by St Francis of Assisi (1181/82–1226) and St Clare of Assisi (c. 1193–1253), who fought for the establishment of the female branch; and the Dominican Order, founded by St Dominic de Guzman (d. 1221). Dominican and Cistercian female houses were established across Europe without a founding mother such as St Clare. At one time or another, the female or second orders vastly outnumbered male houses. Monastic orders also branched out into loosely organized lay associations, and produced extraordinary spiritual teachers who taught through personal example, oral and written instructions. An extraordinary representative of these lay organizations is St Catherine of Siena (1347–80), a Dominican tertiary, one of the few female doctors of the Church, and the patron saint of Italy. St Catherine, who attracted a loyal following of a group of women and some men, was a mystic as much as an ardent Church politician, who tried to end the Avignon exile of the papacy through tireless diplomacy and promoted a crusade against Islamic rule. Her writings, all dictated to scribes, include a voluminous collection of letters and a book, simply entitled *The Book*, or *Dialogue*, written between 1377 and 1378.

Side by side with these Church-approved communal efforts which benefited from a pan-European ecclesiastical network, spirituality flourished in countless smaller movements organized around one or more charismatic teachers and miracle-workers. Even in light of the scarcity of remaining records, the variety of belief systems and number of sects and teachers is astounding, and constitutes a veritable 'New Age' movement in medieval garb. Several Church councils, beginning with the Fourth Lateran Council in 1215, and the training and dispatch of a host of papal inquisitors across Europe were intended to curb the proliferation of autonomous spiritual movements. Reforms of the clergy, improved education and a stronger emphasis on Church rites, especially the Eucharist, were also implemented in the effort to create a more homogenous Christian spirituality. An increasing number of spiritual authors, female as well as male, developed a rich psychological vocabulary to describe and teach the human dimension of encounters with Christ, the Virgin Mary, devils and angels. Images of spiritual growth such as ladders, steps and roads became popular. Bold metaphors derived from the Song of Songs and courtly love were employed to denote stages of spiritual development from metaphorical courtship to wedding to setting up a household with Christ as bridegroom and the human soul as bride. Especially in the area of biblical interpretations of the meaning of human life and in the mystical exploration of courtly love, cross-cultural influences from the monotheistic systems of Judaism and Islam came to bear upon Christian spirituality. Christian anxieties about conversions increased as knowledge about the depth of Jewish and Muslim spiritualities became more widespread. Such fear as much as political and economic factors resulted in a rise of anti-Islamic and anti-Judaic polemic and persecution.

In response to a growing urban class of the destitute and chronically ill, women's groups such as the Beguines took on the burdens of care for the sick, and both lay men and women organized spiritual networks to care for leper colonies; special refuges for prostitutes were founded, and saints such as Elizabeth of Thuringia (1207–31) became renowned for their generosity and compassion for the growing class of outcasts.

Late Middle Ages. Affected by devastating outbreaks of the plague, climate changes, the so-called Hundred Years' War, and a deep institutional crisis of the papacy, late medieval spirituality became shaped by penitential and apocalyptic themes, at its most extreme represented in the flagellant movement and excessive individual asceticism. Following the shift of cultural creativity from monasteries to universities and a growing repression of autonomous spiritual beliefs, spiritual writings of this era reflect the intellectual efforts to systematize the poetic and psychological models of previous generations of mystics. Lay spiritual groups emphasized values of the emerging urban burgher class, best perhaps represented in the important *Devotio Moderna* movement. The spirituality of

the *Devotio Moderna*, well informed, suspicious of mystical intensity, and theologically articulate, was developed by lay people and clergy, and found its perhaps strongest voice in the works and ministry of Gerard Groote (1340–84). Before the plague cut short his life, Groote served large congregations through sermons and pastoral care, and wrote numerous treatises outlining his sober programme of Church reforms and disciplined piety. More so than any other spiritual movement, the *Devotio Moderna* produced an abundance of literary works in many genres, including letters, sacred biographies, chronicles, devotional treatises and instructional texts, and a genre unique to the movement, the so-called rapiaries, spiritual notebooks that included quotations and excerpts from other spiritual books, personal thoughts and reflections, and biblical verses. Rapiaries could either be organized chronologically or thematically and were highly individualized expressions of piety. Both men and women collated rapiaries.

At the other end of the spectrum, we find the visionary Jeanne d'Arc (*c.* 1412–31), burned at the stake as a heretic, an illiterate woman of peasant background, and guided solely by a spirituality grounded in mystical experiences and folk stories without the support of theological training or ecclesiastical structures.

It is impossible to point to one single event or change that signalled the end of the medieval era. Nonetheless, scholars would argue that a combination of factors led a change in world view and mentality, including the long-term impact of the Black Death, the rise of an urban culture that eclipsed older models of communication and an existential sense of self and cosmos, now loosely defined as the era of the Renaissance, and the emancipation of the laity from the grip of ecclesiastical, intellectual and religious hegemony.

See also **Beguine Spirituality; Bridal Mysticism; Canonical Communities; Christian Humanism; English Mystical Tradition; Mendicant Spirituality; Nominalism; Rhineland Mystics; Thomist Spirituality; Women Medieval Mystics – and entries for individual monastic orders.**

Caroline Walker Bynum, *Holy Feast and Holy Fast: The Religious Significance of Food to Medieval Women*, Berkeley, Los Angeles and London: University of California Press, 1987; Norman F. Cantor, *In the Wake of the Plague: The Black Death and the World It Made*, New York: HarperCollins, 2001; Aaron Gurevich, *Medieval Popular Culture: Problems of Belief and Perception*, Cambridge and New York:

Cambridge University Press, 1988; Bernard McGinn, John Meyendorff and Jean Leclerq (eds), *Christian Spirituality: Origins to the Twelfth Century*, vol. 16 of WS; R. I. Moore, *The Formation of a Persecuting Society*, Oxford: Blackwell, 1987; Jill Raitt, in collaboration with Bernard McGinn and John Meyendorff (ed.), *Christian Spirituality: High Middle Ages and Reformation*, vol. 17 of WS; Paul Szarmach (ed.), *An Introduction to the Medieval Mystics of Europe*, Albany: State University of New York, 1984; Ian Wood, *The Missionary Life: Saints and the Evangelisation of Europe, 400–1050*, Essex: Pearson Education, 2001.

ULRIKE WIETHAUS

Meditation

There are different kinds of meditation and the definition of the term has changed historically according to which form has enjoyed most contemporary influence. A clear sense today requires understanding the nature and purpose of prayer itself because meditation, in whatever form, is an entry into prayer.

Three periods can be noted. In the early Church *meditatio* was a form of reading and interiorized the meaning of Scripture by means of a particular form of *lectio divina*. Emphasis fell upon prayerful repetition of the chosen text, orally at first and, later in the process, in the heart. This method of meditation was central to the theological creativity of the early centuries. Until St Bernard of Clairvaux meditation was seen, as he said, as a process of 'inverbation' by which the Word became flesh again in the person of the reader. The second phase is characterized by an increasingly scholastic mentality and a diminution of the sapiential influence of monastic prayer. By the seventeenth century, under the influence of the post-Reformation fear of contemplation and of a certain form of Ignatian spirituality, meditation became identified almost exclusively with mental prayer. In increasingly schematic forms it was imposed in the training of clergy and religious but largely failed to lead them to the goal of all Christian prayer which is contemplation. For the third and present phase of meditation we can see more of its significance by returning to the witness of the desert monastic tradition in which the link between meditation and contemplation in the spectrum of prayer was first clearly and experientially perceived.

In his tenth Conference John Cassian describes a method of meditation that he claimed was already an ancient tradition by the fourth century and was adaptable to every kind of person by virtue of a radical simplicity that led ('very easily', he claimed) to poverty of spirit. This poverty was seen as the fruit of a complete renunciation of the 'wealth and abundance of all thoughts'. The practice consists in the continuous repetition of a recommended Scripture verse (*formula*). 'Content with simplicity alone', the meditator is not thinking of the meaning of the verse but using it to move beyond discursive thought altogether into 'pure prayer'. This state of prayer was described by the archetypal founder of the desert tradition, St Antony, as one in which 'the monk does not know that he is praying'. Cassian emphasizes that this method of praying with a single verse is a 'spiritual discipline' that 'embraces the dispositions of every prayer' as its unifying influence compresses all that can be thought and felt into a single act of faith and love.

Cassian recommends this discipline of meditation strongly because it confronts head-on the problem of the distracted mind, experienced even in *lectio divina* when the mind 'is constantly whirling from psalm to psalm . . . fickle and aimless through the whole body of scripture . . . as if it were drunk'. It was also a direct remedy for the dangers of torpor (the 'lethal sleep') and mere reverie (the 'pernicious peace'), which are the most prevalent forms of pseudo-contemplation and occupational hazards for any practitioner of deep prayer. However, the practice of this form of meditation does not replace *lectio divina* (or other forms such as sacramental prayer). On the contrary, according to Cassian it leads to a finer *lectio* in which experience and grace combine to deliver deeper insight and perception. Even more importantly, it leads to that pure prayer which transcends thought and imagination altogether in ecstasy and 'gladness of spirit'.

Cassian's method of meditation thus beautifully illustrates the link between *lectio* and *contemplatio*. Beginning in the form of *lectio* but by reducing the *lectio* to a single continuously repeated verse (*formula*), it goes beyond this aspect of prayer and directly prepares the mind by discipline for the grace that leads into contemplation.

It is this understanding of meditation in succession from Cassian that has gained widespread contemporary acceptance through the influence of the teaching of John Main. He arrived at the right moment to be a major teacher in the late twentieth-century recovery of this tradition. During the prolonged impoverishment of Christian spirituality in the period of theological intellectualization and exclusively 'mental prayer', devotional prayer provided relief from the aridity but rarely any deep engagement in training for truly contemplative experience. For many, contemplation was seen as dangerous or it was presumptuous to aspire to it. With the Second Vatican Council's refreshing of the roots of the tradition contemplation began to regain its centrality. Main saw in the contemporary crisis the need for a practical method of meditation for those seeking contemplative depth. He appreciated the practical relevance of the wisdom of the early Christians for the spirituality of Christians today. In that early tradition the way one prayed was the way one lived. He was able to connect his contemporary rendition of the tradition with earlier manifestations of the same form of meditation in the Christian tradition, such as the Jesus prayer of the Orthodox Church or individual masters like *The Cloud of Unknowing*.

Contemporary spiritual movements such as the World Community for Christian Meditation and Contemplative Outreach show the readiness of lay people today to embrace this ancient, once largely monastic discipline. Even in relation to such a simple method variations arise. The method of 'centring prayer', as taught by Thomas Keating, places more emphasis on the *lectio* aspect of the 'prayer word' and less on the tradition of continuous repetition. The practitioner is advised to repeat the word until distractions have subsided and then to rest in the peaceful state achieved. Sometimes an image is recommended instead of a sacred word. The approach of the World Community for Christian Meditation distinctively emphasizes the poverty of 'pure prayer' and fidelity to the 'mantra' during the period of the meditation. The practitioner is advised to keep saying the word 'in prosperity and in adversity' (Cassian) and the absence of distraction is understood as a state in which self-reflective consciousness has been passed over. Both schools work in spiritual friendship in the vineyard of the contemporary contemplative renewal of the Church. Each has contributed greatly to the recovery of meditation as a practice of contemplative prayer on a wide scale by recommending a simple daily discipline of morning and evening meditation for twenty to thirty minutes and by providing the support of small weekly groups.

Today the ancient practice of meditation has passed beyond the cloister and opened the way to a contemplative Christian life for all, including married people. Yet the ground for this renewal and expansion of the Christian contemplative tradition through meditation was especially prepared by the work of monastic men and women – such as the popularizing scholarship and

prophetic vision of Thomas Merton and the pioneering work of inter-religious dialogue of Bede Griffiths.

The Churches' new openness to inter-faith friendship also illustrates an essential aspect of meditation that is of great value for the Christianity of the twenty-first century. Meditation is a universal tradition found in every major religion. Its difficulties, challenges and fruits at the personal level are almost identical whatever the faith tradition in which it is practised. Each major religion acknowledges the transcendent nature of the experience of ultimate reality and this common recognition of the limitations of intellectual understanding, together with the ascetical realities of the meditation process of purification, creates a common ground that is of supreme significance for human beings in the modern world. With accelerating globalization of the planet, the levels of cultural fragmentation, religious polarization and violence also intensify. A new way of approaching the multiple, common problems of humanity waits to be developed, one which itself demands a new consciousness. Religions that have so often been perverted to justify violence in God's name are now challenged to place greater emphasis on their contemplative dimension and to find the common ground on which a collaborative work for peace and justice can be supported. Meditation is the most practical way this can be realized.

The essential elements of meditation consist of silence, stillness and simplicity. Silence is more than the absence of words; it is the slowing and eventual transcending of thought. When Jesus teaches the avoidance of many words in prayer he points to this aspect of contemplation. Stillness is the freedom from desire that follows the silence of mental thoughts and images. Simplicity is the condition of being in the present moment. These and the other elements of contemplation form the heart of Jesus' teaching on prayer. The Sermon on the Mount shows that contemplation and non-violence are the twin pillars of his teaching and that one cannot be embraced without the other.

The essential teaching on meditation as it is practised by people in all walks of life today offers a simple daily discipline that opens a new understanding of the contemplative life of the Christian. A meditation session of between twenty and thirty minutes is recommended for each morning and evening. These are integrated into other daily duties and forms of prayer. The meditator sits down in stillness of body with the back straight. Then, closing one's eyes lightly one begins to repeat the prayer word or mantra continually with loving attention. John Main, for example, recommended the word 'maranatha'. He advised the meditator to stay with the same words so as to allow the word to sink into the heart as in the Hesychast tradition. No attempt is made to fight distractions by force but simply to let them go and to keep returning to the word. The fruits of meditation are the 'fruits of the spirit' which are manifested in daily life and relationships.

The practice of meditation is the work of contemplation which itself is always gift. Practice shows that meditation goes far further into the mystery of God than mental prayer and, in fact, is the most incarnate way of prayer possible. It is a particularly appropriate practice for members of the religion of the incarnation. A simple practical method of meditation such as that derived from Cassian and described above throws experiential light on the work of the great masters of the Christian mystical tradition whose written works are rich in description or speculation but often lack a specific recommended method. As both the desert tradition and the contemporary contemplative communities show, the teaching of meditation, as of the gospel itself, of which it is a practical spiritual expression, thrives in the personal and oral transmission. No longer regarded as a dangerous or exclusive form of prayer, meditation has recovered its true place at the heart of the Christian life and as the foundation of all Christian spirituality.

See also **Contemplation**; *Lectio Divina*; **Prayer; Senses, Spiritual**.

Anon., *The Cloud of Unknowing*, ed. W. Johnston, New York: Doubleday, 1973; John Cassian, *Conferences*, trans. B. Ramsey, New York: Paulist Press, 1997; L. Freeman, *Light Within*, New York: Paulist Press, 1990; L. Freeman, *Web of Silence*, New York: Continuum, 1993; I. Hausherr, *The Name of Jesus*, Kalamazoo: Cistercian Publications, 1978; Thomas Keating, *Open Mind, Open Heart: The Contemplative Dimension of the Gospel*, New York: Continuum, 1998; J. Main, *Word into Silence*, London: Darton, Longman & Todd, 1980; J. Main, *Essential Writings*, New York: Orbis Books, 2002.

LAURENCE FREEMAN

Memory

Memory lies at the heart of both the Old Testament and the New. In the Old Testament the memory is of YHWH's saving act in the Passover and Exodus, and his continuing love for and redemption of errant Israel. YHWH is represented as remembering his covenant (Gen. 9.15;

Lev. 26.42, 45), and repeatedly urging Israel to do so too (e.g. Chron. 16.12; Ps. 105.5). This memory is expected to recall Israel to her side of the covenant (Ex. 13.3; Num. 15. 40; Deut. 8.2). This becomes one of the major themes of the prophets who constantly recall Israel to the memory of their calling as the people of God, with the cultic and ethical demands that go with that calling (e.g. Jer. 14.10). As the prophets are ignored, YHWH remembers his covenant – but he also remembers Israel's disobedience: a memory balanced by his memory of his own mercy (Hos. 7.2; 8.3; Hab. 3.2).

In the New Testament, that set of memories is not laid aside: rather it is heightened by the memory of what God has now done in the life, death and resurrection of Jesus Christ. For the Christian Church, it is the memory of Jesus that undergirds the life of the Christian community, both its ethical and liturgical life and its hope for the future. This is given special prominence in the Eucharist, where, supremely in the anamnesis, Christ's death and resurrection are both remembered and re-presented to the people of God (Luke 22.19; 1 Cor. 11.24, 25).

Acting as a link between the Old Testament and the New is the memory of God's creation of humankind in his image. '*This* means', as Christian Campe has put it in a lecture on Sloterdijk's most recent work, *Spheres*, 'that when God breathed the spirit into Adam an intimate union was created that from the beginning was absolute resonance. God and man formed a dyadic sphere where each one complemented the other. There is no first and second – only blissful absorption.' One interpretation of the history of Christian (and Jewish) spirituality is to see it as an attempt to re-present the memory of this union, a union which Christians see as mystically recreated in the relationship between Christ and the Church.

Naturally the implications of all these memories always have been and still are much contested. Are they 'dangerous' memories, as Metz and many liberation theologians claim? Or are they, as many types of evangelical and cautious catholic theologians assert, essentially conservative, providing an unalienable core of revelation which is the rock on which the Church can be built?

Modern secular research on memory raises much more disturbing – and exciting – questions. Broadly, most researchers now agree that memory (like indeed the brain that holds the memory) is much more plastic than has traditionally been allowed. It is not that memories are simply true or false: rather it is the case that memories, like identities, are constantly being reframed, refashioned, reinterpreted, according to the context in which they are recalled; the purposes for which they are relevant; the ideological commitments of those who recall them.

Some people find this modern emphasis disturbing for their faith in the religious truth contained in the Scriptures. Like form criticism or reader-response theory, it seems like one more attempt to relativize and therefore trivialize the ground of faith. That is to misinterpret much modern research on memory. Plasticity does not imply irresponsibility or fecklessness with 'the truth'. It is to recognize that in situations in which we take memory very seriously – like a medical history or testimony in court – we are inevitably selective in what and how we remember. But that does not mean that what we remember can or should be dismissed as unreliable: a doctor or jury has to decide, on the basis of all they hear, in what they can put their faith. Most doctors and most juries turn out to be good at doing just that. So it is in the household of faith.

See also **Spirituality and History** (*essay*); **Time; Tradition.**

Gillian Cohen (ed.), *Memory in the Real World*, Abingdon: Psychology Press, 1988; Paul Connerton, *How Societies Remember*, Cambridge: Cambridge University Press, 1989; Charles Elliott, *Memory and Salvation*, London: Darton, Longman & Todd, 1995; James Fentress and Chris Wickham, *Social Memory: New Perspectives on the Past*, Oxford: Blackwell, 1992; J.-B. Metz, *Faith in History and Society*, London and New York: Continuum, 1999.

CHARLES ELLIOTT

Mendicant Spirituality

Innovative religious movements of the thirteenth century embraced a form of life that emphasized poverty and included begging alms (*mendicare* in Latin), giving them the name of 'mendicant' communities. Their members were known as 'friars' (brothers), often identified by the colour of their habit. By 1210 these included the Friars Minor or Franciscans (Grey Friars) and the Friars Preacher or Dominicans (Black Friars). By the middle of the century the Carmelites (White Friars) and Augustinian Hermits (Austin Friars) were included in the category of the mendicants, and in the fourteenth century the Servants of Mary (Servite Friars) were added to their ranks.

The life of Jesus as model. The origins of these new communities may be traced to a renewed interest in the 'life of the apostles' (*vita apostolica*) in the 1100s, noticeable in reformed communities of clergy (clerics regular) and in communities of men and women, with lay and ordained members, such as that of Stephen of Muret (d. 1124), at Grandmont in France; the Poor of Lyons, under Peter Waldo (Valdès) (fl. 1180); and, in northern Italy, the Humiliati. In varying degrees each group included an emphasis on active preaching of penance or conversion, with little or no geographical stability, and reliance on the begging of alms for their support.

In the early 1200s new groups emerged: the Friars Minor founded in Italy, under Francis of Assisi (d. 1226) in 1208/9; and the Friars Preacher, beginning in France in 1215, under the Spaniard Dominic Guzman (d. 1221). With the rise of the Franciscan and Dominican communities, a new emphasis was added: a life modelled explicitly on the Gospel accounts of the life of Jesus with the disciples, including a rhythm of prayer and solitude alternating with demanding ministry among the crowds.

These communities of 'evangelical life' (*vita evangelica*) gave special emphasis to poverty and itinerancy, with the resulting need to depend on begging alms to provide for their needs. Both Francis and Dominic would characterize the mission of their brethren as 'following in the footsteps' of Christ, that is, living in conditions like those of the early disciples, travelling two by two, taking nothing with them for the journey, calling their listeners to 'repent and believe the gospel'.

The Carmelites, originally a mostly lay hermit community in the Holy Land, on their arrival in Western Europe in the 1230s, were organized along the model of the Friars Preacher by the time their rule was approved in 1247, with a more communitarian way of life and engagement in pastoral and priestly ministry, which existed in tension with the memory of their eremitical origins. In a similar way, the Hermits of St Augustine, under the guiding influence of the papacy, moved from their original eremitical life to one more similar to the model of other mendicants, without losing a contemplative dimension to their life. Like the Franciscans and Dominicans, the Carmelites and Augustinians combined the contemplative-eremitical emphasis with the active preaching mission that brought them into contact with the growing populations of the new urban centres of Europe.

Men and women, religious and lay. The men's mendicant communities flourished alongside other religious and lay communities of men and women who shared similar ideals. Women's communities associated with them usually dedicated themselves to an enclosed, contemplative life. In the case of the Franciscans, this 'Second Order' was that of the Poor Ladies (Poor Clares) under the leadership of Clare of Assisi (d. 1253). Among the Dominicans there were early communities of women under Dominican influence at Prouille in France, the reformed community of San Sisto in Rome, and the community of Diana d'Andalo (d. 1236) in Bologna. A 'Third Order' (penitents, tertiaries, *mantellate*) allowed single and married laity, men and women, to live according to the spirituality of the mendicants, among Franciscans, Dominicans, Carmelites and Servites.

Brothers on a journey. The term 'friars' (*fratres*) meaning 'brothers', was used generally to describe the mendicants. These brethren, including lay and ordained friars, lived and prayed together. Their preaching and service to the poor also showed this fraternal dimension, as they journeyed, two by two, from town to town. This brotherly spirit was evidenced in their relations with the faithful, particularly in urban areas, among whom they lived and ministered with an accessibility that heightened their popularity.

A gospel-based model of itinerant preaching informed the spirituality of the mendicant orders. As their numbers grew and their sphere of activity broadened, the mendicants put themselves under immediate papal jurisdiction rather than confining themselves to the jurisdiction of a local diocesan bishop. They moved not only across diocesan boundaries but operated on an international level by the authority granted by the papacy to their superiors. Their ecclesial vision, international in scope, frequently came into conflict with the prevailing parochial and diocesan model of church organization, leading to the famous controversy between mendicants and seculars in the mid 1220s at Paris, in which the new evangelical-itinerant model of spirituality was championed by the Dominican Thomas Aquinas (d. 1274) and the Franciscan Bonaventure of Bagnoregio (d. 1274).

Contemplatives in action. The mendicants reveal a tension between the desire for contemplation in solitude and the demands of public ministry, especially preaching. For the Dominicans the balance was to be achieved through a contemplative atmosphere in the priory, in solemn liturgical celebration, study and silence, in which the Friar Preacher was prepared for the demands of the life of the travelling preacher. Friars Minor were alternately itinerant preachers and contemplatives, moving back and forth between urban conventual houses and more isolated hermitages. Among the Carmelites the strong memory of their eremitical origins in the Holy Land emphasized the contemplative dimension of their life even after their arrival in Europe and their assimilation to the mendicant model. Originally hermits, like the Carmelites, the Augustinians were drawn into the demands of pastoral ministry in urban areas, following a model already found among the Dominicans.

These communities of 'mixed life', both active and contemplative, brought the fruits of their contemplative experience into dialogue with the experience of their lay contemporaries in the emerging towns of medieval European Christianity.

Popular and affective spirituality. The friars were the popular preachers, teachers and spiritual guides of the new urban populations of Europe in the Middle Ages. Their churches, open to the public regardless of parish affiliation, were often constructed with large crowds in mind, with pulpits prominently placed near the centre of a nave designed to serve as a large preaching hall. Their style of preaching, most often in the new vernacular languages, used vivid examples to communicate with an increasingly literate laity. The friars skilfully employed popular music, art, architecture, liturgical and devotional practices to form a new, devout, urban Christian public.

Following the trend begun in Cistercian spirituality, the mendicants emphasized a tender, affective devotion to Christ in events of his life recorded in the Gospels. This spirituality saw the growing use of the Christmas crèche (nativity scene); devotion to the passion of Christ in the 'way of the cross'; to the holy name of Jesus; to the sorrows of Mary during the passion, and the popularization of such practices as the rosary and the recitation of the angelus. The image of Mary as Mother, transformed by a new interest in the events of Christ's life, formed an important element in the spirituality of each of the mendicant orders.

Spirituality for the marketplace. The mendicant orders recruited most of their members from the ranks of the emerging merchant class. And it was to this group in particular that their spirituality was best adapted, proposing a life of Christian discipleship combining prayer with action in society. Frequently such actions focused on restoration of just economic arrangements in towns, relief for the urban poor, the establishment of hospices for the sick, travellers and pilgrims.

The mendicant model of spirituality found in the newly formed universities of the thirteenth century a fertile seedbed for its propagation.

International in character, and with students and masters accustomed to travel from country to country, the university provided the new orders with a rich pool of potential members and a means of propagating the mendicant model of Christian life far and wide.

Through their popular preaching in the vernacular, using lively examples from everyday life, the friars offered a spirituality accessible to the laity in their daily lives. For the increasing numbers of literate lay Christians, the Gospels themselves became texts for spiritual reading and concrete models for behaviour. The friars of the mendicant orders became the leading proponents of a spirituality for the laity in the Middle Ages, making mendicant spirituality virtually identical with the popular religiosity of European Christians until the time of the Protestant and Catholic Reformations and beyond.

See also **Asceticism; Augustinian Spirituality; Carmelite Spirituality; Dominican Spirituality; Franciscan Spirituality; Grandmontine Spirituality; Poverty; Servite Spirituality; Simplicity.**

Herbert Grundmann, *Religious Movements in the Middle Ages: The Historical Links between Heresy, the Mendicant Orders, and the Women's Religious Movement in the Twelfth and Thirteenth Centuries, with the Historical Foundations of German Mysticism*, trans. Steven Rowan, intro. Robert E. Lerner, Notre Dame, IN: University of Notre Dame Press, 1995; C. H. Lawrence, *The Friars: The Impact of the Early Mendicant Movement on Western Society*, New York: Longman, 1994; Lester K. Little, *Religious Poverty and the Profit Economy in Medieval Europe*, Ithaca, NY, Cornell University Press, 1978; Jill Raitt (ed.), 'The Mendicants' in *Christian Spirituality: High Middle Ages and Reformation*, vol. 17 of WS, pp. 15–74.

WILLIAM SHORT

Mercy

Called and commanded to be merciful, Christians remember that mercy is first of all a quality of God. Be merciful as the Holy One is merciful, says Jesus at the end of a teaching on loving one's enemies (Luke 6.36).

The gospel commandment to live mercifully is also a critique of religious practice. Jesus stands in the line of the prophetic tradition of Israel when he chides, 'I desire mercy, not sacrifice' (Matt. 9.13; 12.7. See also Hos. 6.6.). Micah, the eighth-century prophet from the Southern kingdom of Judah, like Amos, his fellow prophet from the North, calls to task those who perpetrate socioeconomic injustice and links this behaviour with failure to dwell in right relation

with God. 'What does the Lord require of you', Micah says, 'but to do justice, and to love kindness, and to walk humbly with your God?' (Micah 6.8). Like Micah, Jesus teaches against religion in the strict sense: it is to God the people must cling, not to worship of God.

The Hebrew rendered as 'kindness' above is *hesed*, more frequently translated as 'mercy' or 'steadfast love'. This is covenant love, embodied in acts of compassion. Often *hesed* is yoked with one of the words translated as 'justice' or 'righteousness'. Justice and mercy are not opposed to one another; they are aspects of the same reality. Their opposite, sacrifice, is a form of bargaining which bypasses the offering of self and does not attend to the poor. In keeping with his Jewish heritage, Jesus brings together righteousness and mercy (*eleos* in Greek) in the Beatitudes: 'Blessed are those who hunger and thirst for righteousness, for they will be filled. Blessed are the merciful, for they will receive mercy' (Matt. 5.6–7). Followers of Christ enter into a dynamic of imitation – to be merciful as God is – but the mercy they offer others also returns to them as blessing.

Christians often trace 'acts of mercy' or 'works of mercy' to Jesus' teaching in Matt. 25.34–40 (see also Isa. 58.6–9 and Luke 4.16–21). The Catholic Christian tradition speaks of seven Corporal Works of Mercy – feeding the hungry; giving drink to the thirsty; welcoming the stranger or sheltering the homeless; clothing the naked; caring for the sick; visiting the imprisoned; and burying the dead; and seven Spiritual Works of Mercy – admonishing the sinner; instructing the ignorant; counselling the doubtful; comforting the sorrowful; bearing wrongs patiently; forgiving all injuries; and praying for the living and the dead.

The intimate relationship between mercy and justice becomes explicit in some contemporary understandings of the works of mercy; their definition continues to include direct service to persons but expands to include social analysis and action. 'Feeding the hungry' comes to mean both giving food and addressing the structural causes of hunger and poverty though policy and public witness. The Catholic Worker Movement in the US, founded by Dorothy Day and Peter Maurin during the Great Depression, engages in both service and social analysis.

Both Dorothy Day and Mother Teresa, twentieth-century community founders, were profoundly committed to the works of mercy in all their unglamorous challenge. Both rooted their work in long hours of prayer. Their analyses of society were different. Maurin and Day – always a critic of what she called 'this filthy, rotten system' – made explicit the relation between poverty and military spending. These differing emphases are also embodied in the forms of community the two women founded in two different socio-cultural contexts: in the case of Mother Teresa, a religious order, the Missionaries of Charity; in that of Dorothy Day, a lay community of personalist, pacifist Christian anarchists. Both founders, however, saw in the face of the poor the face of Christ.

A full century earlier, the Sisters of Mercy, founded by Catherine McAuley in Dublin in 1831, dedicated their community to the service of the 'poor, sick and ignorant', today rephrased as 'uneducated' by the Sisters of Mercy of the Americas. This community's spirituality and mission have broadened to include men and women who are Mercy Associates and young adult members of the Mercy Volunteer Corps who engage one or more years of full-time service with economically poor or marginalized people in the US and Latin America.

The quality of mercy continues to inspire Christians in various forms, including the recently established devotion to the merciful Christ in his passion and death, based in the writings of the Polish Sister of Our Lady of Mercy Faustina Kowalska. In Christian iconography, Mary is represented in several ways as Our Lady of Mercy: with arms extended in prayer, holding chains, lifting up the child Jesus, or sheltering a crowd of people under her protective mantle, safe from evil and harm.

Before God's abundant mercy, Christians plead in prayer, mindful their need for healing and forgiveness. *Kyrie Eleison*, 'Lord, have mercy' is one of the most ancient Christian liturgical formulas, used in both East and West. It has roots in the Psalms (Ps. 51.1–2, 123.2–3) and synoptic Gospels (Matt. 9.27, 15.22, 17.15, 18.33, 20.30, 31; Mark 10.47, 48; Luke 17.13, 18.38, 39). From the same origins comes the 'Prayer of Jesus' or 'Prayer of the Heart' of the Orthodox tradition, repeated constantly until it becomes as intimate as the breath: 'Lord Jesus Christ, have mercy on me' (*Pilgrim*, 1965, pp. 8ff.).

The notion of God's mercy not only originates but endures in Jewish tradition. The Japanese theologian Kosuke Koyama also notes the primacy of mercy as a quality of Allah in the Muslim faith and suggests mercy as a place of convergence for multiple religious traditions. *Hesed*, says Koyama, is 'the measure of community life for humanity' (Koyama, 1997, p. 74).

See also Beatitudes; Charity; Compassion; Discipleship; Ethics and Spirituality; Forgiveness; God, Images of; Psalms; Social Justice.

—————

Dorothy Day, *Loaves and Fishes*, Maryknoll, NY: Orbis Books, 1997 (original edition, New York: Harper & Row, 1963); Kosuke Koyama, 'I desire mercy and not sacrifice: an ecumenical interpretation', The Paul Wattson Lecture, 4 Nov. 1996, *Ecumenical Trends* 26 (May 1997), 73–9; Mary C. Sullivan, *Catherine McAuley and the Tradition of Mercy*, Notre Dame, IN: University of Notre Dame Press, 1995/Dublin, Ireland: Four Courts Press, 2000; *The Way of a Pilgrim* and *The Pilgrim Continues his Way*, trans. R. M. French, New York: Seabury Press, 1965.

JANE CAROL REDMONT

Methodist Spirituality

'The people called Methodist' owe their being and their culturally diverse expressions of spirituality to the ministry and mission of the Revd John Wesley, Methodist by calling, Anglican by birth, Dissenter in background and the widely read 'man of one book'. His preaching and teaching were reinforced by the hymns of his younger brother Charles, hymns still to be found in almost every English-language hymnal.

John (1703–91) and Charles (1707–88) were among the ten surviving children of the Revd Samuel Wesley and his wife Susanna (née Annesley). Both grandfathers had been Dissenting ministers, but each parent had taken the decision to join the Church of England. The Wesley home observed 'a regular method of living', with the children being taught to pray and to read portions of Scripture from an early age. Susanna Wesley devoted time each week to personal conversation with each child, nurturing the spiritual life of each individual.

While undergraduates at Oxford, John and Charles Wesley were founder members of the 'Holy Club', derisively nicknamed 'Methodists' on account of their disciplined regime of prayer and Bible study coupled with work among the poor and in the prisons. This combination of love of God and love of neighbour, of devotional and practical, has become a hallmark of Methodist spirituality. Some years later, in response to a letter from John Wesley which quoted Ps. 37.7 and enclosed some banknotes, Samuel Bradbourne was to write, 'I have often been struck with the beauty of the passage of Scripture you quoted in your letter, but I must confess that I never saw such useful explanatory notes upon it before!'

Attending (reluctantly) the meeting of a 'religious society' in Aldersgate Street, London, on 24 May 1738, John Wesley felt his heart 'strangely warmed' and, as he later wrote, 'an assurance was given me that [Christ] had taken away *my* sin, even *mine*, and saved *me* from the law of sin and death'. Faith became a 'felt' reality, experienced in the heart, a reality the Wesleys were impelled to share. Thus began a mission 'to spread scriptural holiness through the land'. The experience was deeply personal and yet was of universal application. Charles Wesley encapsulates it thus:

> 'Tis Love! 'Tis Love! Thou diedst for *me*!
> I hear thy whisper *in my heart*;
> The morning breaks, the shadows flee,
> Pure, *universal* love thou art;
> To *me*, to *all*, thy mercies move:
> Thy nature and thy name is Love.

The emphasis is on the universal need for salvation and the universal nature of salvation, often expressed in 'the four alls' of Methodism: all need to be saved; all may be saved; all may know themselves to be saved; all may be saved to the utmost. The fundamental conviction that the gospel message is inclusive led the Wesleys and their followers to preach and minister to all – the upper classes and the lower, the churched and the un-churched – and even to those whose religious beliefs differed from theirs. In *A Letter to a Roman Catholic*, John Wesley reflects, 'I think you deserve the tenderest regard I can show, were it only because the same God hath raised you and me from the dust of the earth, and has made us both capable of loving and enjoying him to eternity; were it only because the Son of God has bought you and me with his own blood.' At their best, Methodists believe themselves to be 'friends of all and enemies of none', recognizing with John Wesley that the world is their parish. The spirit of Methodism is catholic and inclusive: '. . . although a difference in opinions or modes of worship may prevent an entire external union, yet need it prevent our union in affection? Though we can't think alike, may we not love alike? May we not be of one heart, though we care not of one opinion? . . . Herein all the children of God may unite . . . they may forward one another in love and in good works.' This wideness of embrace has led to considerable Methodist involvement in the ecumenical movement, both with other Christian churches and in the wider ecumenism of dialogue with those of other religious faiths.

The Nature, Design and General Rules of the United Societies (1743) declares that there is only one condition required of those wishing to be part of a Methodist society – 'a desire to flee from the wrath to come, to be saved from their sins'. This should be made evident, 'first, by doing no harm, by avoiding evil of every kind; . . . secondly, by doing good, by being in every kind, merciful . . . thirdly, by attending upon all the ordinances of God. Such are the public worship of God; the ministry of the word, either read or expounded; the supper of the Lord; family and private prayer; searching the scriptures; and fasting, or abstinence.' Of such significance was this disciplined and ordered life of faith and practice that John Wesley expanded on the theme in the *Minutes of 1744* and in a sermon entitled *The Means of Grace* (1746). Here are identified both 'instituted' means of grace – prayer, public, family and private; searching the Scripture through reading, meditating and hearing; attendance at the Lord's Supper 'at every opportunity'; fasting; Christian conference or conversation – and 'prudential' means of grace, structures within the societies which enabled fellowship and mutual correction. Early Methodist societies were divided into 'classes' and 'bands', in which the members encouraged each other, confessed their shortcomings, heard what others thought of their spiritual progress and prayed together. The value of such small group meetings is now being reclaimed among Methodists in many places.

Methodism has benefited from the extraordinary breadth of interest of its founder, whose personal reading included the early church Fathers, Thomas à Kempis, the Anglican divines, particularly Jeremy Taylor and William Law, continental mystics and pietists. Encouraging his preachers to read similarly widely, he established *The Christian Library*, a collection of fifty volumes of 'practical divinity', which included patristic authors of both East and West, Anglicans, Puritans and more recent Protestants and Roman Catholics.

Methodism has inherited and made peculiarly its own a richness of worship from other traditions. Impressed by the faith of his Moravian friends, John Wesley adopted the practice of the Love Feast, a non-eucharistic sharing of food, prayer, religious conversation and singing, observing that 'we seldom return . . . without being fed, not only with the meat that perisheth, but with that which endureth to everlasting life'. As a service which may be led by a lay person and partaken of by all present, regardless of Church tradition, the Love Feast is being observed again as a fellowship meal.

From the Puritan tradition, and specifically from the brothers Joseph and Richard Alleine, Wesley adapted the Covenant Service as 'a means of increasing serious religion, which has been frequently practiced by our forefathers, – the joining in a covenant to serve God with all our heart, and with all our soul'. This service remains one of the gifts of the Methodist Church to the wider Church.

Another service of fellowship and dedication was the Watchnight Service, now usually, though not exclusively, observed at the turn of the year. On one occasion, hearing that some were spending 'the greater part of the night in prayer, praise and thanksgiving' and 'comparing it to the practice of the ancient Christians', Wesley resolved to join them, taking the practical step of ensuring that the meeting concerned should happen at a time of full moon so that the worshippers might have light for their journeys.

The hymns of Charles Wesley enabled – and continue to enable – the people called Methodist to sing their theology and spirituality. They served as catechetical, devotional and liturgical aids for a people who, for the most part, lacked formal education. Strongly trinitarian, evangelical and eucharistic, they focus on the need for the changed heart and the transformed life and express the universal love of God for all. Through them, the truths of the faith became part of the thinking and living of those who sang them. John Wesley referred to the 1780 collection of hymns, the *Large Book*, as 'a little body of experimental and practical divinity'.

In common with all 'denominational' expressions of spirituality, Methodist spirituality is multi-coloured by the contexts and cultures in which it is espoused. However, the connectional sense fostered by John Wesley between himself and his preachers and societies continues to hold together the world Methodist community and to give a common inheritance of personal discipline and devotion, worship life and social action.

See also **Anglican Spirituality; Evangelical Spirituality; Hymns and Spirituality; Moravian Spirituality; Music and Spirituality; Pietism.**

S. T. Kimborough (ed.), *Orthodox and Western Spirituality*, Crestwood, NY: St Vladimir's Seminary Press, 2002; Gordon S. Wakefield, *Methodist Spirituality*, Exploring Methodism, Peterborough: Epworth Press, 1999; *The Works of John Wesley: Bicentennial Edition*, Oxford: Oxford University Press/Nashville, TN: Abingdon Press, 1975 (in process); Frank Whaling (ed.), *John and Charles Wesley: Selected Writings and Hymns*, CWS, New York: Paulist Press, 1981.

GILLIAN KINGSTON

Military Orders

The 'military orders' are a form of monastic life originating during the Crusades but surviving in modified forms to the present day. Their ethos seems at odds with contemporary understandings of 'spirituality' and these orders are regularly overlooked in histories of spirituality.

The orders consisted of knights dedicated to fighting Muslims in the Holy Land and Spain or pagans in the Baltic. In the mind of the medieval Penitentials, the profession of arms might be unavoidable in a fallen world but was spiritually dangerous. Yet, during the eleventh century, a new ideal of Christian knighthood emerged in the service of the Church. This partly arose from the 'Peace of God' promoted by Church leaders as a way of limiting the destructiveness of warfare. The knightly class were to respect non-combatants and to defend Church property. With the preaching of the First Crusade in 1095, a concept of 'holy war' emerged where fighting might be meritorious. In effect, the new *Christian* knighthood served to divert the aggressive instincts of the nobility into idealistic channels.

The foundation of military orders enabled the knightly class to fulfil a religious vocation without abandoning military roles. A key figure in the early development was St Bernard of Clairvaux who envisaged the life as a spiritual path for lay men with no aptitude for traditional monasticism. Thus in his *In Praise of the New Knighthood* he referred to knights fighting not only flesh and blood but also the spirits of wickedness.

There were three main orders: the Knights of the Temple (Templars), the Knights Hospitaller of St John of Jerusalem and the Knights of the Teutonic Order modelled on the Templars. There were also a number of smaller orders such as Calatrava and Alcántara in Spain and Portugal, founded in the twelfth century during the reconquest of the Iberian peninsula, or the Order of St Lazarus who began running a leper hospital outside Jerusalem in the 1130s and moved from a nursing role to a military role only after *c.* 1244. Two other communities founded for the ransom of Christian captives and with links to the military orders survive to the present day. However, the Mercedarians and Trinitarians are really closer to the mendicant orders.

The Templars originated to protect pilgrims in the Latin Kingdom of Jerusalem and its associated principalities. This became a religious society in 1119 with its headquarters next to the remains of the Jerusalem Temple. The members professed vows of chastity and obedience and lived a community life, attending the Offices sung by the canons serving the Church of the Holy Sepulchre. The Rule, composed by St Bernard, was based on the Rule of St Benedict and Cistercian practices. Like other military orders, there was no provision for traditional monastic study or meditation (some could not read). These practices were replaced by military training or administration. The monastic regime of vigils, fasts and a non-meat diet was moderated at times of military activity. By 1139, the Templars had become an exempt order under a Grand Master, elected by General Chapter, divided into provinces and individual houses called preceptories, many of which managed the European estates that financed military activities in the Middle East. With the collapse of the Latin Kingdom in 1291, the Templars lost their main *raison d'être* and became increasingly unpopular because of wealth and corporate arrogance. Eventually they were accused of heresy and systemic sexual deviance (now accepted as false charges) and dissolved in 1312.

The Knights Hospitaller began by running a hospice for poor and sick pilgrims in Jerusalem under Muslim rule. After the capture of Jerusalem in 1099, the Master, Gerard, persuaded the Latin kings to endow the hospital generously. It founded daughter hospices in the ports of Italy and southern France where pilgrims embarked. By 1113, the Hospitallers were recognized as an exempt order. The twelfth-century Rule was inspired by the Rule of St Augustine and the observances were those of Canons Regular. The Order undertook a military role only after 1118. It was divided into provinces (Priories) with local houses known as commanderies. After the collapse of the Latin Kingdom, the Order gained a new lease of life by capturing the island of Rhodes from the Greeks in 1308. This fell to the Turks in 1522 and the Order resettled in Malta in 1530. This period lasted until Napoleon expelled the Knights in 1798 when they moved their present headquarters to Rome. The Order never abandoned its charitable and nursing work and this gave it a lasting spiritual role as the Knights of Malta under a Grand Master maintaining hospitals in several countries. The Hospitallers also embraced communities of sisters. Some contemporary communities of Canonesses Regular trace their lineage partly to the Hospitaller nuns.

The third large group, the Knights of the Teutonic Order, was created in the Holy Land c. 1189/90. It returned to Europe to convert the Prussians from its mother house at Marienburg near Danzig. The military defeat at Tannenburg (1410) led to decline later accelerated by the defection of their Grand Master to Lutheranism. They still survive as a small Order of clerics and sisters in hospitals, schools and other charitable work with their mother house in Vienna.

See also **Canonical Communities; Religious Life; Rules, Religious.**

Malcolm Barber, *The New Knighthood: A History of the Order of the Temple*, Cambridge: Cambridge University Press, 1994; Alan Forey, *The Military Orders: From the 12th to the Early 14th Centuries*, London: Macmillan, 1992; C. H. Lawrence, *Medieval Monasticism*, London and New York: Longman, 1992 edn, ch. 10; Helen Nicholson (ed.), *The Military Orders: Welfare and Warfare*, Aldershot: Ashgate, 1998; Dominic Selwood, *Knights of the Cloister*, Woodbridge: Boydell & Brewer, 1999.

PHILIP SHELDRAKE

Ministry and Spirituality

It is hard to connect terms as slippery as ministry and spirituality with any degree of precision. Ministry can mean anything from specific sacramental acts performed by ordained or authorized representatives of a church to ordinary and anonymous acts of mercy performed by folk of goodwill. The spiritualities that might underlie or resource even the same conception of ministry are equally varied. Rather than attempting to bolt together two liquid notions too closely, therefore, it is better to admit that in history and practice ministering in a certain spirit has meant faith communities and their members entering into a spiral of interpretation and action, by which they have been led to a greater sense of integrity and purpose.

This spiral, which involves both action and withdrawal, can be further divided into four movements. The first and most active aspect of ministry is a stepping into the world in mission. All established Churches in the West have had to realize that they must engage with the common concerns and needs of people or die, and that ministry cannot simply mean 'keeping the show on the road'. Stepping into the world does not mean being prepared to be absorbed into secular culture but being willing to serve Christ in the people of that culture. This accords with the New Testament, where ministry (*diakonia*) is not used to mean simply caring but embodying and transmitting gospel values. Franciscan spirituality would be a good example of this form of ministerial spirituality, with its keynotes of simplicity, risk and joy.

Liberation theologies have highlighted the imperative to go beyond personal encounter to bring the greatest possible consolation to others. In the second movement of the spiral, ministers are drawn to wrestle with the situations in which people find themselves trapped or marginalized. This entails entering more deeply into the dynamic of situations, looking beyond individual need to name the power structures which cause many to suffer. Without a spirituality which can help ministers identify forms of good and evil at work in the world ministry can easily become confined to meeting existential and private concerns, especially when it is too strongly informed by psychological and therapeutic understandings of the human condition.

This is not to say that insights from the social sciences should be treated with scepticism. Rather, they provide a series of lenses which can help ministers engaged in particular contexts to read the signs of the times within their communities. It is not simply in Latin America where this sort of approach is valid but wherever people are alienated, excluded and oppressed. Enabling this communal discernment is in itself an act of ministry, and involves the courage to face forces far greater than can be salved by individual action. Ignatian spirituality exemplifies one way by which communities have been challenged to overcome resistance to all that is hostile to human nature.

The scale of what stands against human flourishing can be overwhelming, but 'paralysis of analysis' is avoided by bringing provisional and partial understandings of the dynamics of a situation into dialogue with belief. The third movement of the spiral, then, involves a turn to the wisdom of the community. Though spirituality is often evoked to set aside religious truth claims, this has been unhelpfully restrictive, as the Church has always drawn on its traditions to guide its followers through the perplexities of life. Certainly the tradition itself has been used to oppress and alienate and some of its aspects are difficult and even best forgotten, but a Christian spirituality for ministry must involve a creative retrieval of tradition, so that those who seek life can find direction. Dominican spirituality is one example of how priority given to theological study can feed the mind and souls of the people.

The conversation between the social analysis of situations and theological learning will bear fruit, but especially when more than the ideas, concepts and intuitions are involved. A change of mind and heart is also needed, the process lying at the core of all ascetical spirituality and the fourth movement of the spiral. Ministry is not so much about the application of ideas to situations as responding in particular and flexible ways to whatever human needs arise in these situations. So the process of combining ministry and spirituality must leave space for silence and contemplation, where the agents of ministry lay themselves open to being searched and known by God and in light of this having their partial understandings and desires more rightly ordered towards God's greater glory.

The movement into conversion through contemplation is the most personal of all four aspects of this interpretative spiral, but it is in no sense a retreat from ministry in the community. The lives of the Fathers and Mothers of the desert testify to how the movement into the mystery of God and the mystery of the neighbour are indivisible, and to how prayer creates solidarity with all creatures, not simply human. Conversion empowers members of the Church to do the work of ministry in the world by their being sacrificially but distinctly involved in it. This has been demonstrated throughout history by figures as diverse as Teresa of Avila and Thomas Merton who have lived out the monastic ideal for universal benefit.

The four overlapping elements of mission, identification, interpretation and contemplation each contribute to a rounded view of ministry and each suggest a particular emphasis in spirituality. Two final points need to be made, however. First, the spiritualities mentioned above also overlap: Francis was identified with the suffering Christ in prayer; Ignatius took to theology to support his apostolic activity; Dominic and his followers commended the truth by example as well as word. Second, ministry and spirituality are not joined together by ideas or even by a process, but embodied in the very life of the Christian community. Everything that is done, thought and said in ministry finds its source and summit in worship, where the community seeks to discern God's Word and find strength for service. Both ministry and spirituality are ways of talking about the flow of life within and from the whole people of God.

See also **Baptism;** *Diakonia* **and Diaconate; Discipleship; Lay People and Spirituality; Mission and Spirituality; Pastoral Care and Spirituality; Priesthood and Spirituality.**

W. C. Spohn, *Go and Do Likewise: Jesus and Ethics*, New York: Continuum, 2000; M. Volf and D. C. Bass (eds), *Practicing Theology: Beliefs and Practices in Christian Life*, Grand Rapids, MI: Eerdmans, 2002; K. Walters, *Practicing Presence: The Spirituality of Caring in Everyday Life*, Franklin, WI: Sheed & Ward, 2001; R. J. Wicks (ed.), *Handbook of Spirituality for Ministers: Perspectives for the 21st Century* 2, Mahwah, NJ: Paulist Press, 2000.

ROLAND RIEM

Mission and Spirituality

'Mission' is a rich, polyvalent term which many people nevertheless find ambiguous and confusing. To consider only its Christian usage: mission has been employed in both historical and theological contexts and sometimes applied to quite diverse subjects or agendas; it is currently used in reference to the (historical) enterprise of the Church and the very (theological) activity of God; and the adjective missionary is commonly attached to certain kinds of people or attitudes, and not always with approval.

David Bosch developed the venerable but contentious notion that mission is the mother (or heart) of theology, while acknowledging that in the New Testament almost a hundred Greek terms are used for aspects of mission. But since 1952 attention has been redirected to what had been almost forgotten: the subject of mission is God. A famous conference in Willingen, Germany, distinguished a Church-centred mission from a mission-centred Church, noting that the former fails to locate God's salvific work as prior to the Church. *Missio Dei* (the mission of God; God's mission) identifies the Divine activity of self-disclosure as the fount from which everything springs: creation and salvation history, and then the incarnation (God's mission literally brought down to earth) and the extension of this mission through the Church's faithful following of the way of Jesus. In 1965, Vatican II (*Ad Gentes*) echoed these sentiments, recognizing God as both the One who sends and (in Jesus) the Sent One. There is thus a broad consensus that mission and missionary are not synonymous with evangelical pursuits, much less with any form of proselytizing: in fact their *primary* referent is not people at all but God.

If 'mission' is complex, 'spirituality' is surely no less so. But since its history and extension are dealt with elsewhere in this volume, we may turn to consider spirituality and mission together. Within the academic field of spirituality it is not evident that mission occupies a central place, nor that it would make much sense to claim that it should. Spirituality may appear not to need mission – as adjective, complement or corrective. Yet Walbert Buhlmann asserted that 'missionary spirituality' is not one among many spiritualities but an essential feature of every genuine spirituality. Pondering the implications of a missionary God (and of our own call to live in a Godly fashion) may help us to re-evaluate the phrase 'spirituality and mission' and even to identify the contours of a missionary spirituality. Classically, mission is God's sending forth: the Father sending the Son, both sending the Spirit, and the Trinity sending the Church into the world. As an attribute of God, mission's embrace is obviously much wider than the Church's: God's embrace somehow enfolds the whole world. But if mission refers to God, how can we bring spirituality and mission together, and then speak of them in the context of our own lives?

Understood informally, Christian spirituality is a way of being in the world with God. We could explore the enormous variety of possible ways of being, and of actual worlds. We could also consider, not multiple Gods but certainly a multiplicity of understandings (facets or images) of God coexisting in time or in different individuals, or found throughout history. If God's mission is God's perpetual reaching out and gathering in, encountering and embracing, and if the Church's mission (and Christians') derives from God's, some kind of missionary spirituality is indeed constitutive of authentic Christianity.

'Missionary' as an adjective connotes a centrifugal movement. *Missio Dei* characterizes God who is missionary in this sense. St Bonaventure spoke of God as *bonum diffusivum sui*: dynamic or active Goodness, Goodness-in-motion. 'Missionary' is also applied to Christians, followers of Jesus who brought mission down to earth; but we are only missionary if we are true disciples of the Master, pupils of the Teacher, agents of the Saviour. Our first responsibility is to be converted to Christ, to be conformed to him: to 'come' before we 'go'. Conversion, however, demands not merely a 'me-and-God' relationship but a mature turning *of* one's self, *to* God, *for* and *with* others. Such a process requires a *missionary* context: our lives must be turned outward until they resonate with and respond to the lives and needs of the wider human family. Outreach and embrace, reconciliation and healing are the blossoming and fruiting of such conversion: they exemplify the missionary dimension of spirituality. Unless our private or personal relationship with God is transformed into a public or social 'me-and-God-for-and-with-others' relationship, we do not yet have a missionary spirituality; therefore we do not yet have an authentic Christian spirituality. Disciples of Jesus are to respond to the injunction: 'as I have done, so you must do' (cf. John 13.14–15, 34; 14.12). As Jesus' life was missionary, so must ours become.

Through baptism every Christian is commissioned ('co-missioned') to be a disciple, called to be missionary in the Spirit of Jesus. But such a missionary existence must be shaped and sustained by faithfulness to the Christian tradition and to Christ. It must show resilience, because we live in a world of change and because each of us is continuously changing. Every authentic Christian missionary existence is maintained in and through a *missionary spirituality*, or *a spirituality for mission* (and missionaries). The distinction here is well worth pondering.

Spirituality is shaped by and responds to the actual world(s) in which we live and the actual people (images of God) we encounter. It must enable us to discover the significance of our changing selves and of the experiences that a missionary dynamic exposes us to – poverty, victimization, displacement, war: injustice of every kind. Unless a self-proclaimed Christian changes and grows from such experiences, he or she is selfish and shallow, perhaps blatantly unjust, but certainly not yet an authentic Christian disciple.

Jesus was the Incarnate One of God: God-with-us, but also God as-one-of-us. In Jesus people encounter one who was really human, really embodied, neither an imaginary being nor some disembodied or hypothetically spiritual essence. Spirituality can only be lived in an embodied fashion. There are no generic or disembodied people: everyone is particular, and our embodiment is the necessary medium for expressing our spirituality.

As the religion of incarnation par excellence, Christianity should be exemplary in showing how people can embody and live the missionary dimension of faith, as Jesus did. To live deeply in our bodies, ourselves, would then be an authentic expression of spirituality: a way of being holy; a way of conforming our lives to that of Jesus. Yet Christianity has been notoriously ill at ease with incarnation. Christian missionaries have sometimes treated (embodied) people with scant respect and in most un-Godly ways. But since the only way of being human is in and through our bodies, our spirituality must be integrated with our humanness. And since each of us is a person of culture who occupies space, our spirituality requires appropriate and diverse cultural expression. Disembodied spirituality is an oxymoron, an attempt to repudiate our humanity, and implicitly therefore to deny that we are made in God's image: in maleness and femaleness, and notwithstanding our limitations.

The missionary dimension of our faith calls us to reach out, whether just beyond our comfort zone or across the invisible boundaries of race, creed or privilege. Therefore we must be disposed to encounter otherness, alterity. In so doing we discover the alterity of the God who is diffracted through these myriad human lenses, these many ways of being human, these multiple images of God's self. Even without undertaking more formal (missionary) journeys, we discover a multiplicity of ways of being, in our changing selves and those who populate our own familiar worlds. Authentic Christian (missionary) spirituality must attend to and learn from diverse ways of being, and help us live in relationship with different people, changing people, and a changing world. Such spirituality is never a programme and cannot be predetermined, static or fixed; it can only be a process, itself subject to change, transformation, conversion.

Christian spirituality, uneasy in its relationship with the body, has produced people unsure about loving and about how to love. It has tended to dichotomize and oppose body and spirit (as the term 'spirituality' demonstrates). But to love we must first encounter, and we can only encounter real people in real circumstances: in their otherness, their particularity, and their embodied selves. The collocation of 'mission' and 'spirituality' should serve as a challenge and a directive. It should be understood to refer to joyously and honestly incarnate ways of striving for godliness, and of intentionally seeking out new encounters that would challenge our notions of self and God, and focus us on building more inclusive, more mutually respectful and more Godly communities. Spirituality, after all, is empowerment by God's Spirit, whom we invoke to 'come . . . and renew the face of the earth'; it is our way of responding to inspiration, our way of being 'inSpirited' by God's own Spirit, the Spirit of mission.

See also Spirituality and Culture; Spirituality and Social Sciences (essays); Affectivity; Body and Spirituality; Celibacy; Conversion; Inculturation; Ministry and Spirituality.

Stephen B. Bevans, 'Wisdom from the margins: systematic theology and the missiological imagination', Proceedings of the Catholic Theological Society of America, ed. Richard C. Sparks, Berkeley, CA, 56 (2001), pp. 21–42; David J. Bosch, Transforming Mission: Paradigm Shifts in Theology of Mission, Maryknoll, NY: Orbis Books, 1991; Walbert Buhlmann, With Eyes to See: Church and World in the Third Millennium, Maryknoll, NY: Orbis Books, 1990; Anthony J. Gittins, Bread for the Journey: The Mission of Transformation and the Transformation of Mission, Maryknoll, NY: Orbis Books, 1993; Anthony J. Gittins, Reading the Clouds: Mission Spirituality for New Times, Liguori, MO: Liguori Publications, 1999; Beverly Wildung Harrison, 'The power of anger in the work of love', Union Seminary Quarterly Review 36 (Supplementary, 1981), 41–57; Michael Collins Reilly, Spirituality for Mission, Maryknoll, NY: Orbis Books, 1978.

ANTHONY GITTINS

Modernity

see Postmodernity

Monasticism

Christianity holds no monopoly on monasticism, any more than it does on marriage, friendship, or any other fundamental expression of the human spirit. Hence the 'archetypical' power of the monk in Eastern religions, as well as in much of Christianity. Hence too the monastic dimension in every human being, that deepest level at which one seeks 'blessed simplicity', the 'one thing necessary'. And hence the insistence that at the heart of the charism of every religious order – whether Franciscan or Dominican or Jesuit or any other – is the monastic.

The term 'monk' (which can be considered as gender inclusive) is traced etymologically to *monos*, alone, and has been explained in terms of the monk's single-minded focus on God and the consequent marginality required in relation to 'the world', as well as the state of celibacy which is linked to the monastic way, at least in its Christian form.

If monasticism is in a real sense universal, specifically Christian monasticism is profoundly rooted in the Scriptures. Thus from its earliest expression, Christian monastics have interpreted their vocation in the light of the great prophetic and desert figures such as Elijah, Elisha and John the Baptist, as well as the Wisdom tradition. Christ himself, in his withdrawal into the desert at the beginning of his ministry, in his celibacy and in the radical claims of his gospel to leave all things to follow him, in his privileging of 'the poor of Yahweh', and especially his own paschal suffering, death and resurrection, is seen as the primary model of the Christian monastic way. Then Mary as virgin, and the *koinonia* of the apostolic community, including the sharing of goods, and its eschatological character, are also decisive references. The widows and their dedication to prayer and good works are already acknowledged within the New Testament and supported by the Church (cf. 1 Tim. 5.3–16; James 1.27; Acts 6.1), and are invoked by the monastic writers as well as the consecrated virgins.

The Qumran community also bears interesting resemblance to some characteristics of Christian monasticism, as well as Stoic and Platonist groupings, but these did not shape the substance of Christian monasticism.

It was in the early fourth century that monastic life became explicitly and clearly established, in the desert of Egypt, in Palestine and Syria, and in the households of bishops such as Augustine and Cappadocians. Antony of Egypt, if not exactly the founder of Christian monasticism, is certainly reverenced as its principal father, not least because of the very influential *Life of Antony* written by Athanasius (*c.* 357). This key work of interpretive hagiography stresses Antony's evangelical inspiration and austerity, but also his balance of life, gift of discernment, his zeal for orthodoxy, and his victory over the demons through the power of Christ.

Besides the solitary life and communities of hermits (lavras), coenobitic monasticism soon emerged also, particularly through Pachomius, a younger contemporary of Antony. He organized monastic communities with clear structures, and inspired by the apostolic community, and his abbatial successors continued his work. The Pachomian lives and rules proposed the living of a 'holy koinonia' that came to have a major influence in the West, through a Latin translation of St Jerome (d. 420). Jerome's own monastic life in Syria and Bethlehem and his *Life of Paul* further disseminated the monastic way. His deep love of Scripture and work at its translation further linked Scripture and monastic life.

The more eremitical form of monasticism continued to flourish, and the wisdom of the desert abbas and ammas was recorded in various collections of the *Apothegmata* or *Sayings of the Desert Fathers*, often brief and focused responses to the spiritual questions of disciples.

A particularly erudite current of solitary monasticism found its voice in Evagrius Ponticus (d. 399), who was able to combine the deep wisdom of Origen with the lived experience of the men and women of the desert. John Cassian, deeply influenced by Evagrius and other desert abbas, brought this rich experience into the West and made it available through his key writings the *Institutes* and *Conferences*.

St Basil, on the other hand, was very perplexed by the eremitical form, and promoted rather a balanced, gospel-centred communal monasticism. But despite his huge influence on the Eastern Churches, the eremitical life continued to be reverenced also in the East.

In the West the early Christian history is significantly monastic, with St Ninian, who brought a missionary form of monasticism to England before the end of the fourth century, St Germanus, who visited England in the fifth century, St Patrick and his monastic mission to Ireland in the fifth century, St Columba in the seventh century and his foundation of Iona. Celtic Christianity, which was very emphatically monastic, spread from Iona throughout much of England.

St Benedict (d. *c.* 550) wrote his Rule, which drew in a particularly wise way from Basil, Cassian, Augustine and many other earlier monastic sources, especially the *Rule of the Master*. Foundational elements of Benedict's Rule include the balanced daily rhythm of Divine Office, *lectio divina* and work, the warm sense of community in Christ, moderation in directives regarding food, sleep, clothing, etc. The Rule was praised for its balance and lucidity also by Pope Gregory the Great (d. 604), who promoted its spirituality also by writing a delightful *Life of St Benedict*. Pope Gregory transformed his own Roman home into a monastery, and sent from that monastic community St Augustine and his group of monastic missionaries, who founded monasteries and schools, established provinces, dioceses and parishes, laying the foundation for the Ecclesia Anglicana of the Middle Ages and beyond. Indeed not only St Augustine but also the four subsequent Archbishops of Canterbury, the first Archbishop of York, the first Bishop of London, the first Bishop of Rochester and the first Abbot of Canterbury Abbey were all monks from the two groups sent by St Gregory.

By the tenth century the Rule of St Benedict became the standard monastic rule in the West, and in the subsequent 'Benedictine centuries' half the cathedrals of England were staffed by Benedictine monks; hence the Benedictine shape and ethos of British and Anglican spirituality, as noted by authors such as Esther de Waal.

Among the subsequent monastic giants of the Western Church were St Cuthbert (d. 687), and St Hilda (d. 680), both of whom bridged the transition from specifically Celtic Christianity to the Gregorian usages; the Venerable Bede (d. 735), biblical scholar and 'the father of English history', who called St Gregory 'the apostle of the English'; St Anselm (d. 1109), sapiential theologian and spiritual writer, born in distant Aosta, successor of the scholarly Lanfranc as prior of Bec and then Archbishop of Canterbury; and Hildegard of Bingen (d. 1179), immensely gifted poet, theologian and musician.

Western monasticism experienced declines and then reforms throughout the Middle Ages, including the Cluniac reform in the tenth century, the Cistercian renewal sustained energetically by St Bernard (d. 1153), and recoveries of the lavra form, with its communities of hermits gathered around a common church, as with St Romuald (d. 1027) and the Camaldolese, and St Bruno (d. 1101), who laid the non-Benedictine foundations for the Carthusian Order.

With the sixteenth-century Reform in the West, Luther attacked monasticism as tied into 'works righteousness' and spiritual elitism, and in England Henry VIII pursued the dissolution of the monasteries. But monastic life continued in the Roman Catholic Church, though buffeted by state suppressions in several European countries and elsewhere. The renewals were varied in form, stressing the scholarly (as with the Maurists), the ascetical (as with de Rancé and the Trappists), the Gregorian chant (as with Guéranger and Solesmes), the missionary (as with the Ottilien Congregation), or the diversity of forms, from rural eremitical to urban coenobitical (as with the Camaldolese).

And in the East monasticism has had its similar fluctuations, but continues to flourish to the present time in such influential and ancient centres as Mount Sinai and Mount Athos, as well as renewed and new foundations in Eastern and Western Europe, in the USA and elsewhere.

Within Anglicanism a series of monastic and quasi-monastic foundations sprang up within the context of the Oxford Movement, from the nineteenth century on. Eminent monastic scholars and spiritual writers such as Dom Gregory Dix have enjoyed an influence far beyond Anglicanism. Most recently the ecumenical monastery of Taizé has exercised a major influence on young people throughout the world. And currently there are Lutheran and other Protestant monastic communities. In the Roman Catholic Church Thomas Merton, with his dozens of books and hundreds of articles, as well as John Main, Thomas Keating, Basil Pennington and Joan Chittister have been major voices not just of monastic but of wider contemporary Christian spirituality. And monks such as the Benedictine Camaldolese Bede Griffiths have explored the inter-religious dialogue in particularly deep and fruitful ways, given the essential monastic component of Hinduism, Buddhism and Taoism.

The oblate movement, associated with abbeys, monasteries and convents around the world, has helped thousands of lay people to discover their own monastic spirit, while remaining active and ministering beyond the cloister, sometimes, like Dorothy Day, on the front lines of care-giving and prophetic witness. Non-Roman Catholic lay writers, such as Kathleen Norris and Esther de Waal, have explored in fascinating ways the resources of monastic spirituality for all Christians.

Perennial monastic elements, such as worship, contemplation, *lectio*, silence, hospitality, community, solitude and peace can significantly nourish our own postmodern age.

See also **Asceticism; Benedictine Spirituality; Bridgettine Spirituality; Camaldolese Spirituality; Carthusian Spirituality; Cistercian Spirituality; Desert; Eremitical Spirituality; Grandmontine Spirituality; Orthodox Spirituality; Religious Life; Rules, Religious; Taizé, Spirituality of.**

Athanasius, *The Life of Antony and The Letter to Marcellinus*, New York: Paulist Press, 1980; Timothy Fry et al. (eds), *RB 1980: The Rule of St.*

Benedict, Collegeville, MN: The Liturgical Press, 1981; John Cassian, *The Conferences*, annotated by Boniface Ramsey, OP, New York: Paulist Press, 1997; *Encyclopedia of Monasticism*, Chicago: Fitzroy and Dearborn, 2000; Peter King, *Western Monasticism: A History of the Monastic Movement in the Latin Church*, Michigan: Cistercian Publications, 1999; Thomas Merton, *The Silent Life*, New York: Farrar, Straus & Giroux, 1957; D. Rees et al. (eds), *Consider Your Call: A Theology of Monastic Life Today*, London: SPCK, 1978.

ROBERT HALE

Moravian Spirituality

The Moravian Brethren (commonly known as the Moravian Church) descend from the Bohemian Brethren (*Unitas Fratrum*) who followed the evangelical teachings of Peter Chelcicky (d. 1460) and his criticism of the Church for its loss of spiritual simplicity. The Brethren separated from the Catholic Church in Bohemia in 1467. During and after the Reformation period the Brethren, while retaining certain Catholic features in their life and piety, attempted to ally themselves at times with Lutherans and Reformed – although their emphasis on simple dependency on the love of Christ rather than on a struggle for assurance contrasted with later Calvinism. Their most notable leader during the seventeenth century was the humanist and educationalist Bishop John Comenius (considered by some to be the founder of modern educational theory). In 1721, the exiled remnant of the movement amalgamated with the Herrnhut community in Saxony at the invitation of Count von Zinzendorf. John Wesley visited Herrnhut and, while critical of elements of the life and practice, in general terms the pietism of the Moravian Brethren had a significant influence on early Methodism. The Moravian tradition played a prominent role in eighteenth-century Protestant Pietism.

The movement, while organized as a Church with a threefold ministry and liturgical tradition, has always valued common worship, community, service of others, missionary witness, 'quietness' and simplicity of life over credal statements. The Moravian tradition has sometimes manifested quasi-monastic elements (e.g. at Herrnhut or Bethlehem in Pennsylvania) with celibate communities leading a withdrawn life of quiet with property in common. In general, *koinonia* (expressed in spiritual practices such as agapes and foot-washing) has been a strong emphasis in Moravian community and spiritual-ity. The spiritual values of the Moravian tradition, especially discipline, pacifism, material renunciation, simplicity and a religion of the heart, are closely allied to the ideals of the Sermon on the Mount. The tradition has always had an intense devotional element – especially to the humanity of Christ and his sufferings – often expressed in their hymns. The physicality of Moravian devotion to Christ's wounds has sometimes been criticized as exaggerated but the positive result has been tenderness rather than puritanical moralism and a spirituality of compassion rather than law and judgement. Count Zinzendorf may have drawn on the mystical teachings of Jakob Boehme. Certainly, like other Protestant Pietists, the eighteenth-century Moravians appear to have been influenced somewhat by aspects of medieval mysticism and by the teachings of the Spanish Roman Catholic priest and spiritual guide Miguel de Molinos, one of the exponents of a passive, excessively quietist approach to stillness.

The Moravian Church is made up of self-governing provinces, linked by an international synod, and has remained relatively small in number (about 600,000 worldwide). However, the influence of the tradition has been out of proportion to its numbers. Among the more important contributions of the Moravians to the history of Christianity was their influence on the spiritual origins of English Evangelicalism and their work for inter-Protestant ecumenism. Unfortunately, there is a notable lack of current writing on the Moravians available in English.

See also **Education and Spirituality; Evangelical Spirituality; Methodist Spirituality; Pietism.**

L. Bouyer, *A History of Christian Spirituality* 3, London: Burns & Oates, 1969, Part 2, ch. 3; John Comenius, *The Labyrinth of the World and the Paradise of the Heart*, ed. Howard Louthan and Andrea Sterk, New York: Paulist Press, 1998; Peter C. Erb (ed.), *Pietists: Selected Writings*, CWS, New York: Paulist Press, 1983; Peter C. Erb, 'Pietist spirituality: some aspects of present research' and 'The medieval sources of Pietism: a case study' in E. Rozanne Elder (ed.), *The Roots of the Modern Christian Tradition: The Spirituality of Western Christendom* 2, Kalamazoo: Cistercian Publications, 1984; John Walsh, 'The Cambridge Methodists' in Peter Brooks (ed.), *Christian Spirituality: Essays in Honour of Gordon Rupp*, London: SCM Press, 1975.

PHILIP SHELDRAKE

Mortification

see **Practice, Spiritual**

Motherhood of God

The idea of the motherhood of God has become politicized in the contemporary Church, owing to disagreements between feminists and conservatives over the use of inclusive language. Yet the belief that God is maternal as well as paternal has a long history in Christianity, and many would argue that modern Christian spirituality has been diminished by focusing on the fatherhood of God and failing to reflect upon the significance of God's motherhood. It might be helpful to begin by summarizing various explanations that have been offered as to why the Christian understanding of God is almost exclusively shaped around masculine and paternal imagery.

Some scholars argue that the story of creation and the fall in the book of Genesis represents the triumph of Jewish monotheism over the maternal fertility cults of the Canaanite religions. From this point of view, Eve symbolizes the disempowerment of the Great Mother and her replacement by the patriarchal Yahweh God of Israel. Others, however, point to the infrequent use of the word 'father' in relation to God in the Old Testament, arguing that Jewish monotheism represents an ethical rejection of the oedipal father gods of the cults. Whatever explanation one accepts, Christianity inherited from the Hebrew tradition a theological vision that had set its face against the maternal divinities of the ancient world. In addition, early Christians were appalled by the orgiastic decadence of the Greek and Roman fertility cults, and they avoided any association between Christianity and the mother goddesses worshipped in the cults. Feminist theologians argue that the main reason for the exclusion of divine motherhood from Christian theology is the influence of patriarchy, which Christianity inherited from the ancient world and perpetuated in its own institutions and beliefs. Thus Christianity revolves around the Father Son relationship of God and Jesus Christ, reflected in a social and religious order governed by descending hierarchies of paternal authority – kings, priests, lords and fathers – legitimated by the fatherhood of God.

Yet modern psychology and feminist theology call into question the spiritual and ethical desirability of promoting such a one-sided theological vision, arguing that it leads to an authoritarian understanding of God that does not address our human need for symbols of maternal tenderness, nurture and compassion. Object-relations theorists and psychoanalysts such as D. W. Winnicott and Jacques Lacan argue that spirituality and mysticism are closely associated with the early maternal relationship, which constitutes that dimension of the subconscious where creativity, imagination and devotion find release from the constraints and rules of the social order. Elizabeth Johnson suggests that the perennial need for divine maternal qualities has been met by the Marian tradition in Catholic Christianity, but she argues that this has perpetuated a patriarchal theology in which motherhood has been diminished through being divorced from its association with God. She sees the Marian tradition as a source of maternal imagery that needs to be reclaimed as part of the divine mystery. With these ideas in mind, it is necessary to ask what other resources Christianity offers for the retrieval of a sense of God's motherhood that remains faithful to tradition and theologically coherent.

The Old Testament uses a wide variety of images and metaphors for God, the most common of which refer to God as the husband of Israel. However, the imagery of pregnancy, childbirth and motherhood is also used to describe God's love for Israel, as in Isa. 49: 'Can a mother forget the baby at her breast and have no compassion on the child she has borne? Though she may forget, I will not forget you!' (Isa. 49.15). Sometimes, there are alternating maternal and paternal images, which echo the Genesis account of the creation of humankind as male and female in the image of God (Gen. 1.27). In Deuteronomy, God says to Israel, 'You deserted the Rock, who fathered you; you forgot the God who gave you birth' (Deut. 32.18). God's challenge to Job is one of the most richly metaphorical chapters of the Bible, and it invokes a plurality of images to describe the creative activity of God, including both motherly and fatherly images: 'Does the rain have a father? Who fathers the drops of dew? From whose womb comes the ice? Who gives birth to the frost from the heavens when the waters become hard as stone, when the surface of the deep is frozen?' (Job 38.28–30). The Wisdom of God – *Hokmah* in Hebrew, *Sophia* in Greek – is feminine in the Old Testament, as is the *Shekinah*, the presence of God that dwells among the people of Israel. It has been suggested that these feminine images are due to the subliminal influence of the fertility cults with their divine consorts and female deities on the Hebrew religion.

The language of divine fatherhood comes to the fore in the New Testament to describe the relationship of Jesus to God, but Jesus, lamenting over Jerusalem, also likens himself to a mother hen protecting her young: 'O Jerusalem, Jerusalem, you who kill the prophets and stone those sent to you, how often I have longed to gather your children together, as a hen gathers her chicks under her wings, but you were not willing!' (Luke 13.34). St Anselm, writing in the twelfth century, was inspired by this text to reflect on the motherhood of Christ: 'And you, my soul, dead in yourself, run under the wings of Jesus your mother and lament your griefs under his feathers . . . Christ, my mother, you gather your chickens under your wings; this dead chicken of yours puts himself under those wings.'

Some Christians sometimes argue that, although the Bible uses maternal language in relation to God, it never actually calls God 'mother'. The fatherhood of God is therefore an aspect of Christian revelation that cannot be changed to suit cultural or feminist sensibilities. But Christians have always called God mother as well as father. In pre-modern theology, motherhood and fatherhood were understood as gendered social roles of care and responsibility. For early Christians such as Clement of Alexandria (third century) and Gregory of Nyssa (fourth century), God is both a powerful father and a tender and nurturing mother. The fifteenth-century English mystic Julian of Norwich suggests that the idea of motherhood can only be fully understood in the context of God's creative love: 'This fair, lovely word "mother" is so sweet and so natural in itself that it cannot truly be said of anyone but Him, or to anyone but Him, Who is the true Mother of life and of everything. To motherhood as properties belong natural love, wisdom and knowledge – and this is God.' The idea of a maternal God has resulted in some startling devotional imagery. For example, in *The Odes of Solomon*, which dates from the second or third century, we read: 'The Holy Spirit opened His bosom and mingled the milk from the two breasts of the Father and gave the mixture to the world without their knowing.' The seventh-century Council of Toledo declares: 'The Son is begotten or born (*genitus vel natus*) not from nothing, nor from any substance, but from the maternal womb of the Father (*de utero Patris*), that is, from his being.'

Many motherly images arise from the identification between the eucharistic body of Christ and the maternal body of the Church. In the fourth century, St Ambrose wrote of Christ, 'he is a virgin who bore us in his womb; he is a virgin who brought us forth; he is a virgin who nursed us with his own milk'. Mystics such as Catherine of Siena and Teresa of Avila use similar maternal imagery to describe their relationship to God and Christ in highly sensual terms. Catherine refers to Jesus as the soul's 'wet nurse' and to the Holy Spirit as a mother 'who nurses her [the soul] at the breast of divine charity'. Teresa interprets the phrase from Song of Songs, 'Thy breasts are better than wine', in terms of the soul feeding at 'those Divine breasts'.

The disappearance of this kind of language from Christian devotion and worship can be attributed to a number of factors, but the main reasons may be the literal and rationalist (some would say masculine) approach to language which has replaced the richly analogical and symbolic language of the early and medieval Church, and the elimination of feminine imagery associated with Mary, the saints and the maternal Church by Protestantism after the Reformation. However, theology today is informed by a wide variety of voices, including women and those from non-Western traditions who have once again raised the question of the motherhood of God. Beyond the controversies that this has provoked, it seems likely that the advent of postmodernism, with its rejection of rationalist and scientific approaches to religion and its openness to more narrative and symbolic ways of understanding, might allow for the renewal of Christian spirituality through the retrieval of this neglected dimension of the Christian understanding of God. In the words of Pope John Paul I, 'God is our father; even more God is our mother.'

See also **Feminist Spirituality; God, Images of; Women Medieval Mystics.**

———

Barbara Hilkert Andolsenn, 'Feminine names for God and public theology' at http://www.college. holycross.edu/organizations/ctsa/Andolsen.pdf (accessed 23/07/03); Carolyn Walker Bynum, *Jesus as Mother: Studies in the Spirituality of the High Middle Ages*, Berkeley: University of California Press, 1982; Mayer I. Gruber, *The Motherhood of God and Other Studies*, Atlanta, GA: Scholars Press, 1992; Elizabeth A. Johnson, 'Mary and the female face of God' in *Theological Studies* 50 (1989), 500–26; Elizabeth A. Johnson, *She Who Is: The Mystery of God in Feminist Theological Discourse*, New York: Crossroad, 1992; Julian of Norwich, *The Revelation of Divine Love*, trans. M. L. del Maestro, Tunbridge Wells: Burns & Oates, 1994; Avlin F. Kimel Jr (ed.), *Speaking the Christian God: The Holy Trinity and the Challenge of Feminism*, Grand Rapids: Eerdmans, 1992; Sallie McFague, *Models of God: Theology for an Ecological, Nuclear Age*, Philadelphia: Fortress Press, 1987; Rosemary Radford Ruether, *Sexism and God-Talk: Toward a Feminist Theology*, London: SCM Press, 1992; Paul R. Smith, *Is It Okay to Call God 'Mother': Considering the Feminine Face of God*, Peabody, MA: Hendrickson Publishers, 1993.

TINA BEATTIE

Movements, New Religious

New Religious Movements (NRMs) or 'cults', as they are popularly known, emerged as a new phenomenon in the late 1960s and early 1970s. They are mainly associated with Western societies, emanating from the counter-culture and human potential movement of the 1960s. The term 'NRMs' includes a wide range of groups and movements, such as the Unification Church (its members are known as the 'Moonies' in reference to the founder, Reverend Sun Myung Moon), ISKCON (International Society for Krishna Consciousness) or Hare Krishna movement, the Rajneesh Foundation (now Osho movement), the Church of Scientology, The Family (formerly the Children of God), and Transcendental Meditation (TM). Western countries, notably the USA, proved fertile ground for NRMs, but new religions appeared in other parts of the world – in Japan, Latin America, the Caribbean, Africa. Those which began in the USA gradually spread to the UK and from there to Continental Europe.

There is no general agreement among academics about exactly which religious groups and movements should be regarded as NRMs, with standpoint and methodological approach of observers influencing definitions. However, NRMs can be defined by using a chronological criterion, taking the period of their emergence as the main feature. Thus those religious groups and movements are NRMs which have developed mainly since the Second World War and have come to prominence in Western societies in the late 1960s and early 1970s. The years before can be described as formative or dormant periods, years in which the founders or leaders underwent formal education or a kind of spiritual apprenticeship or gathered followers.

Most NRMs started as community-based organizations which drew clear boundaries between themselves and wider society, developed hierarchical structures (even if they denounced these), and had a distinct set of beliefs and teachings formulated by the leadership, often available in some written form, even when communicated orally. These teachings are generally of a syncretic and eclectic nature, drawing from various traditions and belief systems. Teachings and practices have changed or become refined over time or, in some cases, even been thrown over completely. Eclecticism and syncretism are important aspects which distinguish NRMs from previous 'new' religious movements; these had often arisen from dissenting or schismatic processes within established religions or denominations. Another important aspect of NRMs is their international organization and network –

in some ways they resemble multinational corporations. Some NRMs, for example the Unification Church and Scientology, have created numerous offshoots or 'front' organizations. However, internationality does not mean uniformity across the globe: there are variations according to geographical location regarding mode of operation and social insertion. Since their emergence, NRMs have undergone processes of change and maturation, on account of external factors, such as social responses to them, and internal developments, such as the death of leaders and the appearance of a second generation.

There are no reliable statistics about the number of NRMs or their membership in a particular country or globally. Available figures are rough estimates by observers or internally produced membership records. NRMs and their membership are, like their teachings and practices, in continual flux – the very notion of membership needs careful examination – which makes it difficult to capture the numerical importance of NRMs. It is, however, undeniable that their social importance has been disproportionate in relation to actual membership. This is due to the controversies with which NRMs have become associated. Although initially not perceived as problematic, from the mid 1970s onwards, controversies arose from a range of allegations, including 'brainwashing' and 'mind control' to recruit and retain members, exploiting members, 'breaking up families', promoting totalitarian and exclusive world views and autocratic leadership, deceiving the public ('heavenly deception'), and seeking to undermine wider society. While not all NRMs have become controversial or controversial to the same degree, aspects related to particular NRMs have tended to be generalized and applied to NRMs across the board. These tendencies have been fostered by media coverage of NRMs, which has shaped public opinion. A series of dramatic and tragic developments, the mass suicide of the People's Temple in Jonestown, Guyana, in 1978, the 'satanism scare' in the late 1980s, the destruction of the Branch Davidians' compound in Waco, Texas, in 1993, the deaths of Solar Temple members in Switzerland and Canada in 1994 (followed by further deaths in 1995 and 1997), Aum Shinrikyo's sarin gas attack on the Tokyo underground in 1995, and the death of Heaven's Gate members in 1997, trained the media spotlight on the destructive and violent aspects of NRMs and thus reinforced the public's overall negative perceptions.

Given the wide range of NRMs and the lack of clarity regarding the category of NRM, it is difficult to classify them or identify ideal types. One attempt to do this is to divide them into 'families', such those inspired by Eastern traditions (ISKCON, Sathya Sai Baba, Sahaja Yoga, TM), those arising from a broadly Christian context (Children of God, Jesus Army, Worldwide Church of God, Unification Church), those originating in a particular country (Japanese new religions, such as Soka Gakkai, Aum Shinrikyo, the Institute for Research into Human Happiness), those derived from esoteric teachings (Eckankar, Beshara, Gurdjieff and Ouspensky groups), so-called 'self-religions' (est/Centres Network, Life Training, Silva Mind Control), those focusing on extra-terrestrial entities and 'ufology' (the Raël movement, Heaven's Gate), and those with links to the New Age movement (Church Universal and Triumphant). The highly syncretic aspect of NRMs vitiates satisfactory classification, as do diachronic developments which may change the emphasis of teachings or practices over time.

There are various aspects which mark NRMs as new. One is the way in which they have engaged with 'modern' society where they originated. In some ways, NRMs can be seen as a reaction to modernity, a protest against materialism and capitalism, a sign of the self-limiting process of secularization. In this sense, NRMs appear anti-modern: while elevating individual and personal spiritual growth, they advocate a simple, community-oriented lifestyle, without drugs or alcohol, which provides an alternative to life in mainstream society. In other ways, NRMs can be seen to have embraced modernity, by the way they make use of modern means of communication and technology for disseminating ideas and organizing international networks. From a third perspective, NRMs can be seen as products of modernity: their members have been (at least initially) young people (late teens/early twenties) with a 'modern' background, from relatively affluent homes, well educated, with the opportunity to travel. Also, while NRMs rejected mainstream institutions, they created their own institutions, authorities, and authority structures. At the same time, they relied on wider society to support these structures in providing markets for their products and services.

Other aspects which have marked NRMs as distinctly 'new' include the kinds of people which were attracted to them, their visibility, the kind of opposition which they have encountered (a separate movement, the 'anti-cult' movement or 'cult-watching' organizations, formed to combat them), the attention which they have received from the academic community (a substantial body of academic literature now exists on the topic), and the way NRMs have responded to views about themselves.

The overlap between some NRMs and New Age spiritualities suggests inclusion of the New Age 'movement' and neo-paganism in the NRM spectrum. Although they share common roots and draw from similar cultural milieux, they are distinct. The New Age gained momentum slightly later than the NRMs, in the 1980s. Also, its mode of organization is quite different. New Age communities, such as Esalen and Findhorn, are the exception rather than the norm. Generally, New Age consists of a network of groups and individuals without central authorities or leadership or even generally shared teachings. The widespread 'spiritual consumerism' or 'pick-and-choose mentality' points to affinities with postmodernity rather than modernity, but again, opinions differ on this point.

See also **Spirituality and Culture (*essay*); New Age; Postmodernity; Secularization.**

E. Arweck and P. B. Clarke, *New Religious Movements: An Annotated Bibliography*, Westport, CT: Greenwood Press, 1997; E. Barker, *New Religious Movements: A Practical Introduction*, London: HMSO, 1995, 2nd edn; J. A. Beckford, *Cult Controversies*, London: Tavistock, 1985; David G. Bromley and J. G. Melton (eds), *Cults, Religion and Violence*, Cambridge: Cambridge University Press, 2002; P. C. Lucas and T. Robbins (eds), *New Religious Movements in the 21st Century: Legal, Political, and Social Challenges in Global Perspective*, London and New York: Routledge, 2004; C. Wessinger (ed.), *Millennialism, Persecution and Violence: Historical Cases*, New York: Syracuse University Press, 2000; B. R. Wilson and J. Cresswell (eds), *New Religious Movements: Challenge and Response*, London and New York: Routledge, 1999.

ELISABETH ARWECK

Mujerista Spirituality

The word *mujer* means 'woman' in Spanish and *mujerista* refers to the spiritual traditions and scholarly work of Latina and Hispanic women. Led by Ada María Isasi-Díaz, the term *mujerista* was coined by Latina scholars in the United States during the 1980s, with the intent to create an alternative category of theology and spirituality. Latina women scholars desired a unique name that distinguished their work from what is perceived by many as the white, middle-class scholarship that typically falls under the heading 'feminist'. Thus, the creation of *mujerista* spirituality and theology as its own area of study reflects the refusal of diverse groups to universalize the concept of 'woman' beneath a single label, as well as the intent to open dialogue specific to the religious and spiritual concerns of Latina women.

Methodologically and similar to feminist and womanist (African-American women's) spirituality, *mujerista* spirituality begins from women's experience, particularly that of the community of Latina women in North America. In a way similar to the Latin-American liberation spiritualities of scholars such as Gustavo Gutiérrez and Jon Sobrino, *mujerista* spirituality concerns itself with justice for the poor and disenfranchized. Thus, its approach to spirituality is grounded in an ethics that values the body and believes, for example, that the practical, basic bodily needs of food, clothing and shelter must be met before spiritual empowerment and growth is possible. For the *mujerista*, as with liberation theologians in general, the body and soul cannot be separated: for the soul to flourish the body must flourish, and vice versa.

Yet, *mujerista* spirituality distinguishes itself from general liberation spiritualities by recognizing that Latina women are a group whose disenfranchisement is the result of a set of circumstances unique to Hispanic women. The recognition of these particularities, which often includes sexism, prejudice and classism, not only within the larger society but more specifically within a *machista* culture, are therefore central issues of consideration. *Mujerista* work begins with the goal of engendering an experience of self-directed love as central to a Latina's sense of self as well as empowering her to voice her life and experiences. This work is grounded in the Christian faith, a faith that begins from Scripture and the humanity of Christ, a God that lived and died in this world who cared about liberation not only in heaven but within each human life on this earth. Yet *mujerista* scholarship does not stop with concern for the individual, but strives instead toward the overall liberation of Hispanic communities.

The most well-known figure in *mujerista* scholarship is Ada María Isasi-Díaz, whose work spans several decades and comprises a number of books, including *En La Lucha: Elaborating a Mujerista Theology*. Both *En La Lucha* alongside *Hispanic Women: Prophetic Voice in the Church*, co-authored by Isasi-Díaz and Yolanda Tarango, are considered the pioneer texts in the field. Isasi-Díaz has made it her life's work to outline and develop *mujerista* theology and spirituality as a discipline as well as support the scholarship of fellow Latinas in this area. In addition, Isasi-Díaz founded and co-directs the Hispanic Institute of Theology with Latin-American Liberation Theologian Otto Maduro at Drew University where she is a professor.

Though Isasi-Díaz is undoubtedly the most prolific *mujerista* voice to date, *mujerista* theology and spirituality is a growing movement, particularly among Latina scholars within the United States. Several women, including María Pilar Aquino, Daisy L. Machado and Jeanette Rodríguez, editors of the recent anthology, *A Reader in Latina Feminist Theology: Religion and Justice*, have emerged alongside Isasi-Díaz as significant Latina voices. Additionally, while the origins of Latin-American liberation and *mujerista* spiritualities are both predominantly rooted in the Catholic tradition, Aquino, Machado and Rodríguez widen the conversation by including Protestant voices and spiritual perspectives as well.

See also **Feminist Spirituality; Hispanic Spirituality; Liberation Spirituality; Womanist Spirituality.**

María Pilar Aquino, 'Perspectives on a Latina's feminist liberation theology' in Alan Figueroa Deck (ed.), *Frontiers of Hispanic Theology in the United States*, Maryknoll, NY: Orbis Books, 1992; María Pilar Aquino, Daisy L. Machado and Jeanette Rodríguez (eds), *A Reader in Latina Feminist Theology: Religion and Justice*, Austin: University of Texas Press, 2002; Ada María Isasi-Díaz and Yolanda Tarango, *Hispanic Women: Prophetic Voice in the Church*, San Francisco: Harper and Row, 1988; Ada María Isasi-Díaz, *En La Lucha/In the Struggle: A Hispanic Women's Liberation Theology*, tenth anniversary edn, Minneapolis: Fortress Press, 2003; Ada María Isasi-Díaz, *Mujerista Theology: A Theology for the Twenty-First Century*, Maryknoll, NY: Orbis Books, 1996; Jeanette Rodríguez, *Our Lady of Guadalupe: Faith and Empowerment among Mexican-American Women*, Austin: University of Texas Press, 1994.

DONNA FREITAS

Music and Spirituality

The history of spirituality as the lived experience of religion is deeply intertwined with the history of music. Within every major religious tradition music has played both a formative and an expressive role in worship and devotion. At the heart of Jewish and Christian faith experience we find biblical song. From generation to generation music has been employed to offer praise and thanksgiving to God as well as to cry for mercy. Central teachings of each tradition have been expressed musically in temple, synagogue, local church and cathedral. Within Christian history we can trace the role of 'psalms, hymns and spiritual songs' (Col. 3.16) in shaping the character and sensibility of the community's life of faith.

In the Christian tradition, this history is well stated in the 1963 document of the Second Vatican Council, *Sacrosanctum Concilium*: 'The musical tradition of the universal Church is a treasure of inestimable value, greater even than that of any other art . . . sacred music increases in holiness to the degree that it is intimately linked with liturgical action, winningly expresses prayerfulness, promotes solidarity, and enriches sacred rites with heightened solemnity' (Abbot, 1966, p. 171). Singing together in public worship appears as a central practice in nearly all forms of life that exhibit spiritual qualities. All religious traditions manifest a wide range of instrumental, vocal and dance forms in communal rituals.

Understanding the relations between music and spirituality require attention to four things: the body, the emotions, ritual practices and a sense of mystery.

A well-known definition of music speaks of the language of the soul made audible. If we are to understand music as shaping and expressing spirituality, we must begin with the body, for the power of music to 'move the soul' resides in the complex relationship between sound and the body. Because primary rhythms of life are found in the beating heart, the pace of breathing, and in the movements and gestures of the body, ordered sound from 'outside' meets and reflects the 'interior' of human life. Human physicality is at the basis of why music is a primary medium for spirituality. Such communication and formation occur within the practices of specific historic religious traditions as well as in less explicitly religious ways. The body and soul are ready *together* to be touched by music. With appropriate training, we become aware through ordered sound of a sense of what is most real and most valuable to us. How human beings live through time already displays elements of pulse, pitch, pace and rhythm. Music has the power to open those elements to what lies beyond the 'literal' sense of things – joy, sorrow, wonder, gratitude and a sense of the holy.

What makes a particular form of spirituality determinate is, of course, the way in which music (instrumental and vocal) evokes and sustains a particular pattern of emotions and awareness of the life-world. The sound of bells, the rhythm of drumming, the singing of psalms and hymns, and the whole range of ritual song, from 'Kyrie', to 'Gloria' to 'Alleluias' – all these orient us to ways of perceiving our relationships to the world

and to the deity. The fact that chant and other communal song forms articulate sacred texts is crucial to the formation and expression of a particular set of beliefs and emotions. Particular traditions of spirituality are grounded in such practices, enshrined in what are taken to be 'sacred texts' (narratives, teachings, poetry). How God is imaged in sung prayer and praise, as well as in lament, determines the lived experience of God. Yet wordless music also plays a significant role in many religious traditions, especially those that focus on ecstatic states of consciousness.

Within Christianity, Pentecostal traditions employ music toward ecstatic ends. Particularly though not exclusively, African Pentecostal music induces bodily movement and vocalization that express the reception of Holy Spirit. Different levels of intensity mark different musical forms. Most non-Pentecostal Christian musical traditions focus on proclaiming the Word, expressing praise and lament to God, and music in ritual actions such as singing the ordinaries of the eucharistic liturgy, or singing the psalms and prayer responses.

Religious traditions outside Christianity and Judaism involve instrumental and vocal music to induce particular trance states. One can find in Hinduism ecstatic singing and dancing that lead to the love of Krishna and other gods. In some forms of Islam singing and sacred trance are common, and the sound of the call to prayer is itself part of the ritual behaviour of the body at prayer. African drumming awakens the body to praise as well as to communal states of joy or sorrow. Indigenous people's religions, such as among Native Americans, employ dance and chant to embody connections with ancestors and the Creator Spirit. Among the most fascinating topics in the study of spirituality are thus the cross-influences among such traditions, and emerging forms of ritual music.

In addition to music entering the body and evoking and sustaining emotions over time, deeper ranges of spiritual life depend upon the sense of awe and mystery. Both in sung prayer and ritual participation, as well as in the extended musical settings of Christian and Jewish liturgy, there is the possibility of experiencing what Rudolph Otto called the *numinous*. Here some of the highest reaches of the spiritual life, both mystical and moral/ethical, are located.

Music, when brought to the service of ultimate matters can be revelatory. This is why music is considered by Abraham Heschel as well as by Martin Luther as a gift from God to human existence. From time to time human beings have reported that music leads them on a double journey: into the depths of our common humanity, and into the mystery of God.

See also **Spirituality, Liturgy and Worship** (*essay*)**; Art; Aesthetics; Hymns and Spirituality; Spirituals.**

Walter M. Abbott (ed.), 'Constitution on the Sacred Liturgy', *The Documents of Vatican II*, New York: Herder & Herder, 1966, p. 171; Karl Barth, *Wolfgang Amadeus Mozart*, trans. Clarence K. Pott, Grand Rapids, MI: Eerdmans, 1986; Jeremy S. Begbie, *Theology, Music and Time*, Cambridge: Cambridge University Press, 2000; Albert L. Blackwell, *The Sacred in Music*, Louisville, KY: Westminster John Knox Press, 1999; Ivor H. Jones, *Music: A Joy for Ever*, London: Epworth Press, 1989; Don E. Saliers and Emily Saliers, *A Song to Sing, A Life to Live*, San Francisco: Jossey-Bass, 2004; Paul Westermeyer, *Te Deum: The Church and Music*, Minneapolis: Augsburg/Fortress Press, 1998.

DON E. SALIERS

Mystery

Mystery generally signifies a secret or that which is unknowable. It is from the Greek, *musterion*, meaning secret, a secret rite, or a secret teaching. The Latin *mysterium*, in addition to sustaining the Greek meaning, extends the meaning to include anything that transcends human understanding. Theologically, mystery refers to any revealed truth that surpasses human understanding. Scripture frequently describes God as one who knows all things, even that which the human mind could never know or finds incomprehensible.

In the Hebrew Bible, mystery is painted in broad strokes of covenant relationship and the historical unfolding of God's gracious plan of salvation and human liberation. In the New Testament, the mystery of God's purpose of saving love comes to fulfilment in Jesus Christ, whose incarnation and paschal mystery of death and resurrection represent the fullest expression of God's plan of redemption. While the Gospels reveal the 'mystery of the kingdom of God' (Mark 4.11; Luke 8.10), Paul gives the divine mystery of the revelation of God in Christ greater clarity by equating the mystery with Christ's redemptive death on the cross, with inclusion of the Gentiles, and with the final reconciliation of all things to God.

Both the Greek and Latin Fathers saw the mystery of God's saving work in the death and resurrection of Christ operative through initiation into and participation in the sacraments of baptism and Eucharist. Divine realities revealed in the passing on of the doctrinal traditions, especially redemption and resurrection and later incarnation, the Trinity and grace were also defined as mysteries. Wisdom is the result of the experiential processes by which we come to understand the implications of mystery for the Christian life. In his *De Trinitate* (12–14) Augustine suggests that revelation and doctrine work together to reshape our minds, affections and identity. In this sense, the mysteries of God's divine plan that God chooses to convey to us are agents of spiritual cleansing that allow us to arrive at our true destiny: enjoyment of God and ourselves. Augustine makes an important distinction, however, between *scientia* and *sapientia*. *Scientia* is factual knowledge upon which we are able to make judgements on the historical deeds of God in Scripture. But for Augustine, the goal of *scientia* is to move the seeker to *sapientia*, wisdom. *Sapere* in Latin originally meant 'to taste or smell something', and Augustine urged Christians not just to celebrate the mysteries of what God had done for them, but also to taste, enjoy and participate in the mysteries of God's essence. Since the 'essence' of God is justice, wisdom, love and goodness, participation in these qualities *is* the mystery of eternal life with God.

Patristic and medieval writers applied the term mystery not only to sacramental and doctrinal aspects of the Church, but also to the interpretation of Scripture. The mystery of Christ was thought, by diverse writers, to be hidden in both the literal and the spiritual senses of Scripture. The mystery of Christ in the Eucharist was the source of divinization, while the mystery of Christ hidden in the various senses of Scripture was the source of wisdom necessary for our spiritual journey. In medieval, Renaissance and post-Renaissance spirituality, meditations on the mysteries of the life, sufferings and resurrection of Christ became the primary means of contact with the salvific acts of God, of intense identity with Christ, and of the potential for divinization of humanity.

In spite of some considerable Enlightenment rationalism dismissive of mystery, the term and concept has had a potent retrieval in contemporary theology and spirituality. Karl Rahner, for instance, argued that the mystery of the Trinity is equivalent to the mystery of salvation. His claim reverses Augustine's doctrine of God. Rather than seeing the being of God as the locus of spirituality and salvation, Rahner recognizes that 'the economy of salvation *is* the immanent trinity' (cf. 'Mystery' in *Sacramentum Mundi*).

In balancing the experiential and the cognitive, Rahner and others have reoriented mystery in contemporary spiritual theology. Much of this contemporary spiritual theology takes a linguistic and epistemic approach that focuses on mystery as divine incomprehensibility or unknowability. But the focus is not new. Gregory Nazianzus, for instance, writes that 'the divine nature cannot be apprehended by human reason, and . . . we cannot even represent to ourselves all its greatness' (*Oration* 28.11). Pseudo-Dionysius greatly pre-dates contemporary linguistic and epistemic concerns as well. He says, for instance, of the mystery of God, that 'there is no speaking of it [the divine reality] . . . we make assertions and denials of what is next to it, but never of it' (*Mystical Theology* 5). Later, in the seventeenth century Jakob Boehme balanced reason and the divine will, asserting that 'no person's reason or inquisition can suffice to search God's judgments' (*The Way to Christ* 7.1).

As Rudolf Otto famously noted, encounter with the divine is encounter with wonder, awe, even fear. It is an encounter, as Otto called it, with the *mysterium tremendum*. But it is not exclusively so. Mystery, in the context of spiritual growth, also elicits enchantment, beauty and joy. The joy of mystery is expressed well by Angela of Foligno when she writes, 'the joy of the saints [which] is the joy of incomprehension; they understand that they cannot understand' (*Instructions* 2). It is, as Marguerite Porete puts it, joy in a God 'incomprehensible except by Himself . . . it is far better that the soul be in the sweet country of understanding nothing' (*Mirror of Simple Souls* 6.65). Mystery is that 'sweet country of understanding' nothing.

See also **Apophatic Way; Darkness; Eucharistic Spirituality; Holiness; Knowledge; Mystical Theology; Sacramentality and Spirituality; Trinity and Spirituality; Wisdom.**

Angela of Foligno, *The Book of Blessed Angela of Foligno, Instructions* in Paul Lachance (ed.), *Angela of Foligno: Complete Works*, CWS, New York: Paulist Press, 1993; Augustine, *On the Trinity* in Whitney J. Oates (ed.), *Basic Writings of St Augustine* 2, New York: Random House Publishers, 1948; Thomas Keating, *Open Mind, Open Heart: The Contemplative Dimension of the Bible*, New York: Continuum, 2000; *Marguerite Porete: The Mirror of Simple Souls*, trans. Ellen Babinski, CWS, New York: Paulist Press, 1993; *Pseudo-Dionysius: The Complete Works*, trans. Colm Luibheid and Paul Rorem, CWS, New York: Paulist Press, 1987; Karl Rahner, 'Mystery' in Karl Rahner et al. (eds), *Sacramentum Mundi*, New York: Herder & Herder, 1969.

STEVEN CHASE

Mystical Body

see Ecclesiology and Spirituality

Mystical Theology

The Greek verb *muein*, meaning to close, lies at the root of the term 'mystical', referring to that which is hidden or unseen. Early Christian usage of the term suggests a background in both Jewish apocalyptic literature (with its emphasis on the unveiled mysteries of the divine plan) and in a common Hellenistic use of the term to mean whatever is to be held secret. The first Christian uses of the term, beyond the Jewish apocalyptic sense in Pauline literature, refer generally to the hidden depths of divine meaning in the Scriptures. The term came to be applied by analogy to the spiritual significance underlying the practices of Christian worship. Only as an extension of these two uses did the mystical come to apply to the deep intuitive apprehension of the divine mysteries afforded to Christians by means of meditation on Scripture and participation in liturgy. It is worth highlighting this point simply as it differs so considerably from later Western Christian views of 'mystical theology' as the study of various highly extraordinary experiential states of individuals. Patristic and early medieval approaches to mystical theology inevitably contain some account of the preparation for mystical forms of knowing and of the conditions in which such knowledge comes about. Yet they assume such unveilings are an ordinary part of a divinely given cosmos in which the whole creation echoes with a divine self-expression that is radiant beyond the capacity of creatures to declare – except by pointing beyond themselves to a hidden presence. Thus the scriptural and liturgical life of the community serve the divine plan by teaching believers the language of mystical presence and equipping them to pass over into the radiance of divine truth. Origen of Alexandria (*c.* 185–254) in his important *Homily 27 on Numbers* (6–12) interprets the journey of Israel through the wilderness as a foreshadowing of believers' sharing in the death and resurrection of Christ; and for Origin it is through the community's continual participation in that paschal journey that God first trains believers in virtues (a dying to self) and then gradually illumines believers (a resurrection), bringing them to 'a fuller and higher knowledge of the reasons for the Incarnation of the Word of God' (12). Writing several centuries later, the Syrian monk Dionysius the Pseudo-Areopagite (*c.* 500) emphasized even more than Origen the boundlessness of the divine life and hence the bright darkness or cloud of unknowing in which mystical knowledge takes place. In his brief treatise of unparalleled influence, *The Mystical Theology*, Dionysius first recalls the mystical work of the Church in interpreting the hidden meanings of Scripture. Then, using the figure of Moses ascending Mount Sinai (as Gregory of Nyssa (*c.* 332–95) had done in his *Life of Moses*), Dionysius turns to the mystical transformation and encounter with God enacted in the Church's worship. Whereas in the mystical interpretation of the Church's symbolic life (of Scripture and worship) God taught believers via the mediation of visible forms and concepts, now in the direct encounter with hidden divine presence the community's ability to know by means of these figures must be transcended; it is not that the symbolic dimension of mystical theology is ever left behind for it is the ever-present milieu in which direct encounter occurs – apart from the formative environing matrix of Scripture and liturgy the community would have no sensitivity to the divine presence at all. Yet the community's own language and understanding inevitably falters, for 'our words are confined to the ideas we are capable of forming', and in the presence of God who is beyond any conceptual grasp, the mind 'will turn silent completely, since it will finally be at one with him who is indescribable' (*Mystical Theology* 3). The theme of union or participation is thus the capstone of most approaches to mystical theology, for it underlines the uniqueness of the ultimate stages of mystical knowledge as a sharing in the divine self-knowing and ecstatic joy. In *The Journey of the Mind into God* of the great Franciscan theologian Bonaventure (1217–74), for example, the ultimate stages of mystical theology are portrayed as a coming to share, through participation in the death and resurrection of Christ, in the inner-trinitarian knowing and loving of the divine Persons. The historical mission of the Word has clearly figured largely in the shaping of mystical theology, especially as the grounding of all the visible forms and conceptualities that environ the process of mystical knowing. Other writers such as William of St Thierry (*c.* 1085–1158) have emphasized more prominently the equally significant role of the Holy Spirit, energizing contemplation by an infusion of the divine loving and so uniting believers to a divine reality far beyond their rational comprehension. While modern accounts have tended more toward a theology of mysticism (with extensive attention given to various degrees and causes of individual psychological states), this should be distinguished from mystical theology itself. The individualizing turn to the subject of later medieval and early modern thought should not obscure the fundamental trajectory of mystical theology as a form of divine teaching intimately unveiling itself within the community's life of spiritual transformation.

See also **Mysticism** (*essay*); **Ascetical Theology; Mystery.**

Key work with excellent bibliographies: Bernard McGinn, *The Presence of God: A History of Western Christian Mysticism*, multiple vols, New York: Crossroad/Herder, 1991–.

Primary sources: *Origen: An Exhortation to Martyrdom . . . Homily XXVII on Numbers*, trans. Rowan Greer, CWS, New York: Paulist Press, 1979; *Pseudo-Dionysius: The Complete Works*, trans. Colm Luibheid and Paul Rorem, CWS, New York: Paulist Press, 1987; William of St Thierry, *The Golden Epistle*, trans. Theodore Berkeley, Kalamazoo, MI: Cistercian Publications, 1980.

Secondary sources: Andrew Louth, *The Origins of the Christian Mystical Tradition*, Oxford: Oxford University Press, 1981; Mark A. McIntosh, *Mystical Theology: The Integrity of Spirituality and Theology*, Oxford: Blackwell, 1998; Anselm Stolz, *The Doctrine of Spiritual Perfection*, trans. Aidan Williams (originally published 1936 as *Theologie der Mystik*), New York: Crossroad/Herder, 2001.

MARK A. MCINTOSH

Name, Prayer of the

see Jesus Prayer

Native North American Spirituality

It must be noted from the outset that it has only been in the last thirty-five years that Native North American peoples (commonly known as 'Native Americans' in the United States and as the 'First Nations' in Canada) have not had official federal government policies designed to assimilate their cultures and spiritualities. For over one hundred and fifty years previous to that, the intent of government policies related to Native North Americans was to integrate Native peoples into the so-called mainstream of North American society. At the same time, the mission theologies of the various Christian Churches seldom placed any value either on Native cultures or their contexts in the process of Christianizing the original inhabitants of the continent. In examining this history, careful attention must be made not to fall into the error of a kind of presentism which sees and judges the motivations and intentions of either governments or Churches of that time through the prism of what is known today. Nevertheless, to speak of living

Native North American cultures and spiritualities at all is a tribute to the resiliency of these peoples who endured direct assaults on their cultural and spiritual existence over a period of several generations.

Many Native North American peoples resisted assimilation by covert means of practising their cultural and spiritual ways. They often disguised their communal celebrations by having them coincide with national holidays and significant Christian feast days. Many spiritual practices were often conducted 'underground', away from the sight of either government officials or Christian missionaries. Such practices were necessary since many communal ceremonies throughout North America were made illegal by the mid nineteenth century and continued to be so until the early part of the twentieth century. Since the late 1960s and early 1970s, however, Native North American spiritualities have experienced a powerful renaissance. There is no doubt that the liberation and power movements of various minorities in North America at that time, as well as the efforts toward decolonization around the globe, acted as catalysts for this renaissance.

Rather than discuss one, monolithic Native North American spirituality, as if there were such a phenomenon, an authentic approach is to speak of the diversity of North American spiritualities. This diversity certainly existed before contact with the European Newcomers to North America in the late fifteenth and early sixteenth centuries. The continued existence of this diversity indicates a number of elements essential to the nature of Native spiritual traditions. First, this diversity requires viable forms and methods of inter-cultural and inter-religious communication including the means to listen respectfully to the religiously other. A second requirement is the ability to participate in the religious experience of others through rituals and ceremonies. Above all, it requires an understanding of the complexity of cosmic reality such that no one cultural or spiritual vision can encompass all the elements contained within that mystery and that a more profound understanding can be achieved through interaction with others. This diversity means that there really has never been a pure or pristine Native spirituality. Every clan or tribe of Native people accepted and integrated aspects of different spiritual visions of reality that helped them to survive and to achieve a rich and balanced life. This, after all, has been the ultimate motivation of Native spiritual traditions.

Despite the enormous diversity of Native North American cultures and spiritual ways, there are a number of common elements or 'family resemblances' that characterize nearly every Native North American spirituality.

Essential to any understanding of Native North American spirituality is the connection to the land. Over vast expanses of time, Native peoples developed an intimate knowledge of their land and all that it contained for the sake of their survival. This knowledge included the precise activities of various species of animals, the growth patterns of plants for food and medicines and the climatic patterns of their particular region. Further, Native peoples intuited spiritual powers particular to their own homeland. Today, Native peoples continue to reverence their sacred sites from where spiritual knowledge continues to be revealed through ceremonies and rituals. The close observation of the visible and powerfully invisible world around them has meant that Native peoples have never understood themselves to be the pinnacle of the created order nor even its most important part. Most Native peoples continue to understand that even though their place in creation is unique because of their kind of thinking, they are not radically different from the non-human persons within their land. Native North Americans believe that 'we and the land are one'.

A second common element is the emphasis on the communal dimension of life. Survival for Native peoples was not dependent solely on traditional environmental knowledge. It also required the co-operation of the entire tribal community. The importance of creating and maintaining good relations within the extended family or clan and the tribal community ensured the well-being of all. Long before the arrival of the European Newcomers, Native peoples had developed methods for creating treaties and alliances in order to establish spiritual kinships and peaceful relations beyond one's own tribe or nation. Furthermore, the creation of good relationships was not limited to human communities. It included ceremonies to establish and ensure constructive relations with all the elements of creation: plants, animals and spirits. This emphasis on the communal has meant that the fullness of Native North American spiritual life has always been experienced communally rather than apart from family, clan and tribal connections. This has not meant that there is no room for a kind of individualism. Rather, the notion that 'I am because I belong' has been an important characteristic of Native North American spiritualities.

A third element common to all Native spiritualities is the importance of promoting balance and harmony. Native peoples have always recognized that life is a precarious endeavour and not attending to the interdependent nature of creation meant the potential for serious consequences. On a personal level, this translates into the process of integrating all the components of one's life: the physical, intellectual, emotional and spiritual. On a communal level, it translates into a healthy tolerance of diversity and inclusion. There are healing ceremonies to restore the loss of balance that have resulted in personal illnesses and diseases and rituals to engender communal harmony through the use of talking/sharing circles. Today, this important principle of balance is visually represented in the 'medicine wheel', a circle divided into four quadrants with each quadrant being of a particular colour, most often yellow, red, black and white. While the medicine wheel originated among the Native peoples of the Plains, it has become a 'pan-Indian' symbol, representing a holistic view of reality. It has become an important educational tool used by elders and spiritual leaders and introduced in educational curricula for teaching the principles of balance, harmony and integration.

A fourth common element shared by Native North American spiritualities is the importance of visions and dreams. Traditionally, nearly every Native people had a ceremony celebrating the rite of passage into adulthood. Most often within the context of a fast, the ceremony marked the spiritual granting of a unique vision that would orient one's adult life. Today, vision quests or crying-for-a-dream ceremonies are the spiritual means for receiving visions or profound insights that makes one alert, attentive and profoundly conscious of the direction of one's life and all that surrounds it. Visions are not always granted solely through a ceremony. Many Native peoples believe that they are given visions or dreams at critical moments in their lives as gifts from the spirit world. At the root of the spiritual granting of visions and dreams is the belief that spirits can and do communicate directly to the individual with the consequence that, ultimately, visions benefit the entire community.

A fifth common element is the notion of the cyclical nature of life. Rather than a linear process of time, close observation of the natural reveals that phenomena happen in cycles: day follows night, warmth and growth return after a long and harsh winter. The cycle of life continues to be manifest in birth, maturation, gradual degeneration and eventual death, only to be followed again by rebirth. Consequently, many Native peoples continue to affirm a belief in the process of reincarnation. Others have posited a belief in continued life in an afterworld that was not fundamentally different from what is experienced here. Still others believe simply that we return to the soil and become the nutrients necessary for the continuance of the land and all it contains. What the cycle of life has meant fundamentally is that what is important is the here and now. While life is an arduous task to be achieved, it is nonetheless more than survival; life is to be lived in a rich and fulfilling way in accordance with the dynamic processes of creation where salvation is understood as the continuance of the life of the entire community, including both human and non-human members. This belief in salvation as the continuance of the ongoing life of the tribal community has no doubt given Native North Americans the wherewithal to resist the forced annihilation of their spiritual and cultural worlds.

As a result of the cultural and spiritual renewal of Native peoples since the late 1960s, coupled with a more open acceptance of Christian Churches to indigenous cultures and spiritualities, Native Christians have been in the process of integrating Native spiritual ways and the Christian gospel. There remains much discussion about the methods of such an integration and how far such an integration can be achieved without detriment to either Native spirituality or the Christian message. In many ways, Native North Americans are experiencing a new encounter with Christianity. Unlike the historical encounters of the seventeenth and eighteenth centuries, this time Native North Americans are taking ownership of the process.

V. Deloria Jr, *God is Red: A Native View of Religion*, 2nd edn, Golden, CO: North American Press, 1992; V. Deloria Jr, *For this Land: Writings on Religion in America*, ed. J. Treat, New York and London: Routledge, 1999; C. S. Kidwell, H. Noley and G. Tinker, *A Native American Theology*, Maryknoll, NY: Orbis Books, 2001; A. Peelman, *Christ is a Native American*, Maryknoll, NY: Orbis Books, 1995; J. Treat (ed.), *Native and Christian: Indigenous Voices on Religious Identity in the United States and Canada*, New York and London: Routledge, 1996; J. Weaver (ed.), *Native American Religious Identity: Unforgotten Gods*, Maryknoll, NY: Orbis Books, 1998.

DARYOLD CORBIERE WINKLER

Nature Mysticism

The term 'nature mysticism' is commonly understood to denote a spiritual encounter whose defining characteristic is a deep, meaningful and often life-changing communion or unitive experience with the external (natural) world. While individual texts differ to a degree, many additional characteristics can be found in reports of natural mystical experiences: transcendence of space and time, a sense of personal immortality, expansive joy and bliss, moral elevation, intuitive insight into the workings of the universe, luminosity, wonder and beauty.

The clearest expressions of nature mystical experiences can be found in pages penned by philosophers, poets and psychologists. The most characteristic element, communion or union with nature, is evident in the writings of the early twentieth-century philosopher Karl Joel who, while lying on the seashore and feeling the shining water and soft breeze envelop his soul, exultingly remarked that 'Yes, without and within are one'. Similarly, one finds it in the Journals of the French novelist, musicologist and social critic Romain Rolland. Rolland, a deracinated Catholic who engaged in a debate with Sigmund Freud over his unchurched 'oceanic feelings' of eternity, recalled an experience he had as a youth while climbing in the Alps. He relates how he was 'possessed by nature like a violated virgin' and how 'for a moment my soul left me to melt into the luminous mass of the Breithorn . . . Yes, as extravagant as it may sound, for some moments I *was* the Breithorn.' This sentiment is expanded on by Rolland's confidant, the German idealist Malwida von Meysenburg, who wrote how she knelt down in prayer before that 'symbol of the Infinite', the Ocean, and returned 'from the "solitude of individuation"' to the 'consciousness of unity with all that is . . . Earth, heaven and sea resounded as in one vast world-encircling harmony'. The Irish novelist Forrest Reid also writes about a unitive encounter in a passage in his *Following Darkness*. He writes how 'it was as if everything that had seemed to be external and around me were suddenly within me . . . It was within me that the trees waved their green branches . . . that the skylark was singing . . . that the hot sun shone.'

Other elements of the natural mystical experience are emphasized in reports like that of the psychologist R. M. Bucke who, in describing his own experience of what he termed 'cosmic consciousness', speaks of an 'intellectual illumination' through which he came to see that the Cosmos was a 'living presence', that all men were immortal and that the happiness of all was certain. The Indian poet Rabindranath Tagore speaks of an experience in which the world was bathed in a holy radiance, 'with waves of beauty and joy and swelling on every side'. Aldous Huxley speaks of a drug-induced reverie in which his communion with the external world was so intense that time stood still: a 'perpetual present'. While hardly exhaustive, this sampling of texts reflects themes and characteristics of

nature mysticism as found in the writings of a host of other well-known personalities, including Ralph Waldo Emerson, William James, William Blake, Annie Dillard, William Wordsworth and Walt Whitman.

Scholarly debates over the characteristics of and explanations for nature mysticism and its precise relation to other 'types' of mysticism have added nuance and complexity to the seeming unambiguous, straightforward depiction of nature mysticism presented to this point. Indeed the delineation and parameters of the term, which is of relatively recent historical vintage, is in large part due to academic infighting. In this regard no person has come to influence the course of the debate more than the Oxford don R. C. Zaehner and his classic work *Mysticism Sacred and Profane*. Zaehner was in part reacting to historical migrations of the term 'mysticism'. To set the stage: the origin of the term 'mysticism' can be traced back to the Greek Mystery Religions. As Louis Bouyer notes, the Greek use of the term *mustikos* (derived from the verb *muo* (to close) and meaning 'hidden' or 'secret') lacked any direct reference to the transcendent, denoting instead hidden details of ritualistic activities. Bouyer catalogues how the term migrated under the direction of the early Christian Fathers, who emphasized the possibility of accessing the transcendent Divine. However, their use of the terms 'mystical theology' and 'mystical contemplation' implied that mystical encounters with the Divine were accessed only through the auspices of Church and tradition, the Bible and liturgy. In effect, mysticism was always 'churched' mysticism. Another migration occurred during the sixteenth and seventeenth centuries. As Michel de Certeau has observed, one finds for the first time the emergence of mysticism as a noun (*la mystique*) which was correlated with a new religious social type (the 'mystics') and the introduction of the term 'the Absolute', understood as a generic conception of the Divine which existed as a universal, innate, even subconscious dimension of humankind. In sum, the possibility arose that 'mysticism' could be churched or unchurched. If defined as the latter, mysticism came to signify contact with a reality hidden beneath a diversity of institutions, religions and doctrines; a psychological 'subjective experience' divorced from Church and tradition. The latter trend reached paradigmatic expression in the writings of William James, an important figure in the emerging academic study of mysticism who, in his famous *The Varieties of Religious Experience*, framed mysticism in a way diametrically opposed to that Bouyer found in his survey of the early church Fathers. Thus contrary to the latter, James defined religious experience, of which mysticism was the deepest form, as the feelings, acts and experiences of solitary individuals in relation to whatever they might conceive to be the Divine. Tradition and its accoutrements, by which James meant liturgy, ritual, theology and various aspects of Church organization, all essential and crucial for access to the Presence of God for the church Fathers, were now understood by James as secondary phenomena, derived from the primary experiential matrix as located in the individual, and thus essentially unessential for access to the Divine. It is a short step from this to a form of unchurched, non-confessional mysticism, not uncommon today, which valorizes the individual, self-actualization and a technology of altered states.

Zaehner's analysis of nature mysticism presupposed this historical state of affairs. His ire was directed at Aldous Huxley who, in his *Doors of Perception*, espoused a generic form of 'mystical' experience that could be had through the use of psychedelic drugs ('entheogens'). Huxley posited a perennialism in which his own drug-induced visions were equated with the Christian Beatific Vision. His was an unchurched, non-confessional mysticism which focused on the individual and peak experiences, bypassed the need for mediating concepts like confession and grace, and neglected the development of virtues (particularly love and social responsibility). Zaehner's counter, which recalls the early Christian understanding of mysticism surveyed above, proceeded by establishing textual evidence for three universal, cross-culturally valid types of mysticism (nature, monistic and theistic) which he placed in a hierarchical order (theism being the highest). For Zaehner nature mysticism was always directed towards the external world, was devoid of religious (read 'theistic') elements, was equally evident in neurotics (like Huxley), depressives (like John Custance) and healthy minded types (like James and Marcel Proust), and could be explained with respect to Jungian psychology (the expansiveness associated with the numinous Self archetype). In contrast Christian theistic mysticism highlighted personal communion with a loving Deity, turned one inwards to the exclusion of nature, presupposed the Jungian individuated personality, was accessed only through God's grace, and emphasized the primacy of Church, tradition and the virtues. The types of mysticism were, to use Catholic nomenclature, different not simply in degree but in kind.

While Zaehner's analysis has proven to be influential, other theorists have entered the fray, making matters even more complex. Contro-

versies have developed over several aspects of nature mysticism. For example, the question of nomenclature. Otto's notion of 'unifying vision', Underhill's 'illuminated vision of the world', Stace and Marshall's slightly different use of the term 'extrovertive mysticism' all approximate the parameters of nature mysticism yet differ from Zaehner on the question of whether nature contains or reveals a Divine presence. Linked to this are the many forms of churched mysticism, including texts from Upanishadic, Buddhist, Muslim, Native American and Christian mysticism, which contain nature mystical ideation. Similarly, the characteristics of nature mysticism have been debated with some insisting, contra Zaehner, that elements of love, social awareness, a heightened moral sense, creativity and even diverse forms of unity are evident in nature mysticism. Finally, while Zaehner championed a Jungian interpretation of nature mysticism, other explanations have been offered, including Freud's developmental notion of the regression to primary narcissism, the Self psychologist Heinz Kohut's concept of a developmentally mature cosmic narcissism, neuropsychological concepts involving temporal lobe and parietal lobe functions, and various metaphysical and transpersonal theories.

See also **Mysticism; Spirituality, Psychology and Psychotherapy** (*essays*)**; Drugs; Experience, Religious; Literature and Spirituality.**

L. Bouyer, 'Mysticism: an essay on the history of the word' in R. Woods (ed.), *Understanding Mysticism*, Garden City, NY: Image, 1980, pp. 42–56; M. de Certeau, 'Mysticism', *Diacritics* 22.2 (1992), 11–25; William James, *The Varieties of Religious Experience*, Cambridge, MA: Harvard University Press, 1985; Paul Marshall, *The World Transfigured: Mystical Experiences of the Natural World*, Oxford: Oxford University Press, 2005; William B. Parsons, *The Enigma of the Oceanic Feeling*, New York: Oxford University Press, 1999; R. C. Zaehner, *Mysticism Sacred and Profane*, New York: Oxford University Press, 1961.

WILLIAM B. PARSONS

New Age

New Age spirituality is the term that is applied to an amorphous set of metaphysical beliefs, esoteric movements and eclectic practices influencing contemporary Western thinking and religious practices. 'New Age' is as new as it is old. Apocalyptic and eschatological literature found in the ancient Near East, Montanism of the second century, millenarianism, esoteric movements, like Gnosticism, are a few of its historical manifestations. New Age thinking becomes more apparent when a culture is undergoing a change in its historical or religious understanding. The 'New Age' movement of whatever historic period believes itself to be the messianic harbinger of the future, bearing the alternative values, the changed consciousness and the mediating practices required for the personal and planetary transformation that is underway. As psychologist Carl Jung predicted, the 1960s' musical show *Hair* celebrated, and humanistic psychologist Marilyn Ferguson in 1980 reminded us that the Age of Pisces has ended and we are at the dawning of the Age of Aquarius, the age of harmony, peace and understanding.

Sources and influences. There is no one holy text of the contemporary New Age movement, but sources abound. The Hindu Vedas (1800–1200 BCE), the Hermetic tradition, Gnosticism, Greek mystery religions, alchemy, Jewish Kabbalah, Arthurian legends, Celtic Druidism, Renaissance philosophy, Enlightenment humanism, theosophy, shamanism, spiritualism, astrology, Freemasonry and Rosicrusianism contribute to the ideas which inform the loose network of believers and practioners. Past thinkers who have influenced New Age spirituality include: Jakob Boehme (1574–1624), Emanuel Swedenborg (1688–1772), William Blake (1757–1827), Madame Blavatsky (1831–91), William James (1842–1910), Rudolf Steiner (1861–1925), George Gurdjieff (1866–1949) and Peter Ouspenky (1878–1947), Carl Jung (1875–1961), Jiddu Krishnamurti (1895–1986), Arthur Koestler (1905–83), Abraham Maslow (1908–70) and Carl Rogers (1902–87). Contemporary literature is plentiful. An eclectic sample of some writers placed under the heading of New Age in bookstores and Internet sites are: Deepak Chopra, Ram Dass, Marilyn Ferguson, James Lovelock, Carolyn Myss, Marianne Williamson, Gary Zukar, James Redfield, Don Miguel Ruiz, Matthew Fox and John O'Donohue, but hundreds more could be listed. The New Age movement has become a very profitable enterprise offering books, sacred objects, its own music and book publishers.

Beliefs. New Age spirituality has no set dogma or creed. Beliefs are wide ranging. Seven most common beliefs which appear among many of the sources are:

1. *Monism:* all is one and everything that is exists from a single source of energy.
2. *Pantheism:* everything that exists is God or a panentheism.
3. *Humans are divine beings* and the purpose of

the human journey is to discover/recover one's divinity.
4. The discovery/recovery process happens by effecting a change in consciousness or *personal transformation.*
5. *Reincarnation:* the cycle of birth, death and rebirth is necessary to work through any bad karma in order to achieve the awareness of our divinity.
6. *Ecological responsibility:* Mother Earth, 'Gaia', is a living entity and humans must unite to preserve her.
7. *Universal religion:* all religions are simply different paths to the ultimate reality. Universal religion is the mountain with many sadhanas (spiritual paths) going to the summit.

Practices. New Age practices are a blend of ancient disciplines such as meditation, yoga, tai chi, spiritual reading, journalling, pilgrimages, ritual practices and eclectic techniques like the use of crystals, divination tools like runes or tarot cards, astrology, channelling, herbal medicines, organic gardening, hypnosis, homeopathy, massage, acupuncture, therapeutic touch, vegetarianism and chakra balancing. Seminars, conventions, bookstores, informal groupings, books, audio tapes, video films and Internet sites disseminate the thinking.

Sacred sites and centres. There is no central organization or membership list, no formal clergy and no one geographic centre, but rather numerous centres around the globe. Thus, New Age spirituality performs much like an amoeba as far as being unable to pin it down to any defined structure or particular beliefs. However, the dispersed centres do exist that promulgate aspects of its teachings. In Great Britain in 1962, Peter and Eileen Caddy and Dorothy Maclean started the Findhorn Community in a caravan park near Inverness, Scotland. The three communed with nature spirits called 'Devas'. The 'Devas' assisted them in growing enormous vegetables in the notoriously poor soil. Their fame spread and the community grew. Findhorn has become an international centre for spiritual and planetary transformation offering internships and programmes. In 1971, Sir George Trevelyan started the Wrekin Trust. The Trust seeks to explore leading-edge topics in a nonsectarian way. The charity concerns itself with furthering the spiritual nature of humanity and the universe. Glastonbury is another New Age centre with much less defined community structures like Findhorn. Celtic folklore, Arthurian legends and Christian myth surround the mystic of the town. Glastonbury with its Tor, abbey ruins and Chalice Well draws an array of healers, magicians, holistic medicine practioners and goddess worshippers. Ancient stone circles along ley lines in England, Ireland and Brittany have also become sacred destinations for the New Age pilgrim. Many other pilgrimage sites are scattered around the planet, for example Uluru in Australia and Sedona, Arizona in America. New Age tourism has become an effective catechesis programme for New Age spirituality.

In America, the dawning of the New Age erupted at a time of great social stress in the nation. The Civil Rights struggles, the assassinations of public leaders, the Vietnam war created a counter-cultural movement. Many young Americans dropped out, created communes, experimented with drugs and travelled east to learn to meditate. In 1962, Esalen in California was founded as an educational centre for the human potential movement and became a disseminator of New Age thinking. In 1971 the Association for Research and Enlightenment held a discussion group entitled 'New Age Seminar'. In 1977 the Omega Institute in New York opened and is the largest holistic learning centre in America today. Omega Institute states as its mission 'to look everywhere for the most effective strategies and inspiring traditions that might help people bring more meaning and vitality into their lives'.

Possible criticisms. Alongside the innovative and creative elements of New Age spirituality, some commentators, from different perspectives, have raised a number of possible criticisms. These include: superficiality, magical thinking, narcissism, naive optimism, grandiosity, romanticizing of indigenous cultures, non-contextual appropriation of spiritual practices, perpetual process of self-improvement, propensity toward Gnosticism, instant transformation, individualism, consumerism and reductionism.

New Age influence. As a contemporary spirituality movement, without any intentional organizational structures or strategies, smatterings of New Age spirituality can be found in established religious associations as well as in the new centres of education and healing. It is not surprising that as a consequence of transmitting borrowed perennial spiritual realities from various traditions, New Age spirituality surfaces in the established denominations as these religious communities seek to accomplish the task of speaking gospel values in the idiom of contemporary culture, for instance the use of the enneagram for spiritual direction, the adoption of Eastern meditation techniques such as yoga in teaching about prayer, and the use of massage in retreat settings.

See also **Contemporary Spirituality** (*essay*); **Movements, New Religious; Secularization.**

Marilyn Ferguson, *The Aquarian Conspiracy: Personal and Social Transformation in the 1980s*, Los Angeles: J. P. Tarcher, 1980; Robert C. Fuller, *Spiritual But Not Religious: Understanding Unchurched America*, Oxford: Oxford University Press, 2001; Wouter Hanegraaff, *New Age Religions and Western Culture: Esotericism in the Mirror of Secular Thought*, Albany, NY: SUNY Press, 1997; Timothy Miller, *America's Alternative Religions*, Albany, NY: SUNY Press, 1995; Robert Wuthnow, *After Heaven: Spirituality in America since the 1950s*, Berkeley: University of California Press, 1998.

VALERIE LESNIAK

Nominalism

Although what we today call 'Nominalism' never represented a coherent movement and embraced an array of intellectual issues, the concept still offers a meaningful entry into some of the most radical and intellectually innovative changes in medieval Christian thinking about human cognition and religious knowledge.

Nominalism, for lack of a better term, began as a matter of speculative philology and ended as a matter of heresy. In its most profound sense, it represents the liberation of medieval intellectual culture (almost always male) from a reliance on its antecessors in Greek philosophy, science and theory. Nominalism permitted medieval thinkers to create their own distinct epistemologies, and some of their scientific advances, especially so at the University of Oxford. Nominalism also shook the foundations of a holistic world view in which Divine and human reality mirrored each other seamlessly in the human ability to think and conceive of reality. By proposing a deep division between revealed truth that cannot be grasped by the human intellect and rational thought as an entirely separate domain, it thus drove a wedge between magical-intuitive and analytical thinking. In effect, it legitimized a fully secular mode of being human and the notion of autonomous knowledge, whether scientific, political or psychological. It should be noted that we find an equally radical critique of the limits of language in grasping Divine truth in the *via negativa* of mystical theology, which has roots in the Neoplatonic works of Pseudo-Dionysius (active end of fifth, beginning of sixth century). However, the *via negativa* proved to be less divisive in the history of Christian spirituality than Nominalism, not the least because its institutional location was the monastery rather than the university.

Nominalist ideas cannot be separated from the social status and individuality of their proponents, first, because a disproportionate number of nominalist academics were subjected to heresy charges and persecution by the Church, and, second, because medieval academic thought was developed more by individual teachers than by institutions. Nominalism no doubt aided the growing independence of universities from Church influence. In the long run, and certainly unintended by the first generation of nominalist thinkers, it was used to marginalize and delegitimize mystical perception of ultimate reality.

These dramatic socio-cultural and intellectual changes began innocently enough with the development of speculative, or theoretical, grammar. To fully appreciate this fact, we have to remember that in the medieval curriculum, grammar was one of the foundational and most important subjects to be taught. In the realm of speculative linguistics, Nominalism at its extreme proposes that generalized concepts, the so-called universals, do not have truth value and are mere sounds (in Latin, *flatus vocis*). This early form of what is today called discourse analysis was correctly perceived to have radical theological implications, hence the ever-present threat of heresy charges. For example, what would be the consequences for the Church if Father, Son and Holy Spirit would indeed be defined as one being only, and the abstract concept of 'trinity', a keystone of religious orthodoxy, understood to be a mere linguistic abstraction? This view of the Trinity seems to have been the position of an early proponent of Nominalism, Jean Roscelin (d. *c.* 1123/25). Unfortunately, almost all that we know of Roscelin's thought today has been preserved in the writings of his opponent, Anselm of Canterbury (d. 1109), a so-called 'realist'. 'Realism' defended the notion that our language accurately describes a dimension of reality beyond the world of individual-, time- and space-bound phenomena. Anselm gracefully resolved the epistemological question whether abstract concepts could reflect ultimate reality or only the workings of our mind by formulating his famous paradox, 'I believe in order that I may understand' (*credo ut intelligam*). Roscelin's nominalist propositions, not in the least because of Anselm's vigorous attacks and personal influence, were condemned in 1092.

Roscelin's follower, the influential philosopher Peter Abelard (d. 1142), himself subject to several heresy trials, but also the main force behind the spectacular rise of the University of Paris, could best be described as anti-realist or non-realist. Rather than focusing on the Trinity as three distinct persons, he developed a trinitarian model based on three attributes (power, wisdom and love). Abelard contended that what is assumed to be true as generality or as an abstraction denoting a plurality of things or beings does not exist, but that conceptual categories nonetheless constitute a useful fiction in the service of philosophical analysis. In his view, a concept is real in so far as it is a part of speech or discourse (*sermo*). Another brilliant representative of nominalist thought at the University of Paris was Nicolas d'Autrecourt (d. after 1350), who was summoned to a heresy trial in 1340. Nicolas developed a theoretical stance based on the claim of the primacy of individual identity and sense experience in the construction of knowledge.

In the fourteenth and fifteenth centuries, shifting now from Paris to Oxford, Nominalism evolved into a school of thought also known as *via moderna*. The key players were the Franciscan intellectuals Duns Scotus (d. 1308) and William of Ockham (d. 1350). In all of his works, Duns Scotus elaborated on the differences between theological and philosophical epistemologies, and stressed the epistemological importance of individual phenomena. William of Ockham defended the view that we can only truly know existent individual things accessible to the senses. God, however, can only be known intuitively or spiritually. William of Ockham was deeply sympathetic to the radical wing of the Franciscan Order, whose proponents attacked the primacy and privileges of the papacy. Eventually censured by Pope John XXII, William was forced to seek refuge with the anti-papal German King Louis of Bavaria. The persecution of spiritual Franciscans began in earnest with the papal condemnation of their radical stance of apostolic poverty in 1322 and led to a decline of the Franciscan Order, including Franciscan influence in Oxford. Ockham's teachings were disseminated by the German philosopher Gabriel Biel (d. 1495) in Erfurt and Wittenberg.

Nominalism today is valued as the precursor of logical positivism and existentialism and an important tool in critiquing ideologies and their use of 'false universals', but a history of its impact on the course of Christian spirituality still has to be written. The hidden costs of nominalist theories of language and cognition were a gradually growing distrust of spiritual intuition and divine revelation as non-rational and mere fantasy.

See also **Aristotelianism; Medieval Spirituality in the West; Scholasticism.**

M. T. Clanchy, *Abelard: A Medieval Life*, Oxford: Blackwell, 1997; William Courtenay, *Schools and*

Scholars in Fourteenth Century England, Princeton: Princeton University Press, 1987; Sharon M. Kaye and Robert M. Martin, On Ockham, Belmont, CA: Wadsworth, 2001; Gordon Leff, The Dissolution of the Medieval Outlook, New York: New York University Press, 1976; R. I. Moore, The First European Revolution, ca. 970–1215, Oxford: Blackwell, 2000; Heiko Oberman, The Harvest of Medieval Theology: Gabriel Biel and Late Medieval Nominalism, Grand Rapids, MI: Eerdmans, 1962; Robert Pasnau, Theories of Cognition in the Later Middle Ages, Cambridge and New York: Cambridge University Press, 1997.

ULRIKE WIETHAUS

Non-violence

If violence entails doing physical and emotional harm to persons, non-violence is a strategy of confronting violent parties and situations with an activist, non-harmful presence, aiming at ending injury and countering social oppression. Non-violent behaviour may be effected by words, gestures or deeds. It intends to constrain violent action and question social oppression for the sake of opening a horizon toward a situation where violent action loses its lethal character.

Non-violence is not equivalent to pacifism which ordinarily entails withdrawing from scenarios where violence is being enacted. Non-violence is an exercise of power, but not power in a physically coercive sense. It rather attempts to engage the moral, persuasive power of the good to expose and counteract evil. Some of the forms that non-violent action takes are peaceful protest (either silent or with speech) through demonstration or by simple presence; non-co-operation (as in boycotts and strikes); or other forms of communication (letter and e-mail campaigns). Non-violent action may involve individuals or groups or entire social movements.

Non-violent protest as a strategy was reflected upon and refined in the twentieth century especially by Mohandas Gandhi (1869–1948) and Martin Luther King Jr (1929–68). Gandhi strove to create a sociopolitical movement that would end British colonial presence in India. Martin Luther King struggled against racial injustice in the United States, and was the principal architect of the Civil Rights Movement in that country. Both rejected the use of physical aggression to counter the social oppression (and often, outright physical assault) of the opposing powers. The movements both of these figures set in motion were successful in overthrowing peacefully the oppressive forces they encountered. Both, however, met death at the hands of assassins. The examples of these two leaders in non-violent action have inspired a host of other movements in the latter part of the twentieth century. Most notable have been non-violent protest against authoritarian regimes (e.g. the Madres of the Plaza del Mayo in Argentina; protests that brought down Communist governments in Poland, East Germany and Czechoslovakia; protests against military and nuclear installations in Europe and North America; ecological social movements against governmental policies and corporations worldwide).

It is recognized that sustained non-violent action requires a world view or spirituality to undergird continued effort. Several strands are discernible in such spiritualities. One is what might be called an ontology of peace, that is, a belief that relations among persons, societies and the earth itself were intended to be peaceful and non-coercive. Competition, violence and war are aberrations, not a primordial state of nature. A Christian correlate to this is the basic anthropological insight that all human beings are made in the image and likeness of God (cf. Gen. 1.26f.) and that humans and nature are to live in harmony (Gen. 2.24b-25). A Buddhist strand, detectable in the thought of Gandhi, prescribes that human beings should do no harm to any sentient being. For this latter reason, vegetarianism is sometimes associated with non-violent lifestyles.

For Christians, the teachings and action of Jesus constitute a major framework and guide for a non-violent spirituality. The Beatitudes, especially the blessing of peacemakers (Matt. 5.9), inspired both Gandhi and Martin Luther King. The injunctions to love one's enemies and turn the other cheek when one is struck likewise embody Jesus' own action. His preaching of the reign of God as a place where oppression and exclusion would be overcome offers a vision of what a peaceful, non-violent world should be. His own non-resistance to arrest, torture and death provides an example of non-violent behaviour and a giving oneself over to a greater good.

Those promoting non-violent action note that a spirituality of non-violence has to be more than a set of ideas to which one assents. It must grow out of patterns of non-violent discipline and living. Opponents of non-violence point out the situations in which non-violent resistance has appeared to fail. Proponents, on the other hand, note that violent action most often leads to more violence rather than its cessation.

See also Peace; Reconciliation.

Mohandas K. Gandhi, My Experiments with Truth, reprint, Boston: Beacon Press, 1993;

Martin Luther King Jr, *A Testament of Hope*, San Francisco: HarperCollins, 2003; Ron Sider, *Non-violence: The Invisible Weapon?*, Dallas, TX: Word, 1988; Walter Wink, *Jesus and Non-violence: A Third Way*, Minneapolis: Fortress Press, 2003; John Howard Yoder, *The Politics of Jesus*, Grand Rapids, MI: Eerdmans, 1994.

ROBERT SCHREITER

Norbertine Spirituality

The Norbertines is the name commonly used for the Canons Regular of Prémontré (O Praem.) or Premonstratensians founded at Prémontré, France. Norbert of Gennep was born between 1080 and 1085 of a family connected to the court of the Holy Roman Emperor. At an early age he received a benefice as a canon of St Victor's in Xanten and also as a cleric in minor orders was attached to the corps of chaplains around Archbishop Frederick of Cologne. This put him into the circle of the imperial court and it is possible that he accompanied Henry V on his journey to Rome in 1111. That experience, in which Norbert witnessed the humiliation of the Pope by the Emperor, is thought to have triggered Norbert's conversion around the year 1115 and his full engagement in the Gregorian Reform. He was ordained a priest and received papal recognition as a wandering preacher who called both clergy and laity to live the apostolic life modelled on the Acts of the Apostles. Norbert fervently urged his hearers to become 'naked followers of the naked Christ'. His constant efforts to reconcile leaders engaged in armed conflict caused him to be seen and named an apostle of peace, an element of his spirituality strongly emphasized today by his spiritual sons and daughters. In 1120 at the behest of Pope Callixtus II, Bishop Bartholemy of Laon helped Norbert find a location for a reformed monastery for his growing number of disciples. Norbert founded his community as one of canons regular in full harmony with the Gregorian Reform and in strict adherence to the Rule of Augustine. Within a few years Norbert had founded at least seven other such reform monasteries. All were double monasteries in which a core group of clerics was the centre of a much larger local community of lay brothers and sisters who together cared for travellers, the poor and the sick who took refuge in their abbeys. In 1125 Norbert went to Antwerp to help restore regular church life in the face of the disruption fomented there by the followers of the heresiarch Tanchelm who had denied the validity of sacraments, especially the Eucharist, celebrated by unworthy priests.

In 1126 Norbert was named Archbishop of Magdeburg, at that time an outpost for missionary efforts into Eastern Europe. This position drew him back into the circle of court life where he influenced the emperor's support for Pope Innocent II against the anti-pope Anacletus II. Norbert died on 6 June 1134. He was a man of action who left nothing in writing. What we know of his life is based on two medieval *vitae* and contemporary accounts of his ministry. When Norbert was canonized in 1582 the Counter-Reformation interpretation of his Antwerp preaching and of his pattern of bringing warring parties together around the celebration of Mass caused him to be seen as an early apostle of the blessed sacrament.

The organization of Premonstratensian life after Norbert's move to Magdeburg was taken up by Hugh of Fosses, first Abbot of Prémontré, who borrowed from the Cistercians a system of governance designed to establish and maintain a reformed religious life. The chief spiritual authors of this founding era were Adam Scot, Abbot of Dryburgh in Scotland (he later became a Carthusian), Anselm, Bishop of Havelberg, and Philip of Harvengt, Abbot of Bonne-Esperance.

Norbertine foundations broke new ground. They combined the contemplative lifestyle of monks with the pastoral care of canons and thus came to be viewed suspiciously by both those groups. In a significant way Norbert's vision of canonical life prepared the way for the thirteenth-century mendicants who went a step further in the development of the vowed life by eschewing the vow of stability as an essential element of religious life and thus freed themselves for forms of ministry more adapted to the rise of cities and to an economy based more on commerce than agriculture.

Norbertine spirituality, like that of all canons regular, is grounded in Augustine's vision of the apostolic Jerusalem community as the model form for the vowed life. This coming together in unity of mind and heart intent on God is expressed in and shaped by an intense liturgical prayer life, by a strongly ritualized conventual life and by forms of pastoral care in harmony with these forms of spiritual discipline. From the beginnings of the Order until its latest *Constitutions* (1994) the solemn profession formula has provided a synthesis of the Order's spirituality. Here the identifying elements and configuration of the tradition are set out and carried forward. They are:

1. Self-donation to a local church (*Ego N. offerens trado meipsum ecclesiae N.*). This commitment to a church is at the heart of canonical vis-à-vis monastic profession where the self-donation is to the monastic community.

2. Ongoing conversion (*conversio morum meorum*). The specificity of conversion in this tradition is discovered in the challenge of an ongoing life of growth and change in the context of a lifelong commitment to one community committed to the pastoral care of a clearly defined local church.

3. Life in community (*vita communionis*) to be achieved through the living out of vows of poverty, consecrated celibacy and obedience. This is the 'how' of conversion for Norbertine and women. It is rooted in the life of the Trinity and received as gift. In the original medieval formula, poverty and celibacy were not explicitly articulated but were assumed to be integral to the promise of common life and obedience;

4. According to the gospel of Christ and the apostolic life as mediated by the Rule of St Augustine and the order's Constitutions. The present Constitutions identify this apostolic life with: unity of mind and heart, common life, adherence to the teaching of the apostles, perseverance in community prayer with Mary the Mother of Jesus, the centrality of the Eucharist, and testimony to the resurrection of Christ through preaching rooted in contemplation of God's word (*lectio divina*) and other forms of the apostolate.

The concrete shape of this canonical form has varied over the centuries. The uniformity that marked the Cistercians was never as strong among the Premonstratensians although their borrowing of Cistercian forms of governance as a means of establishing and maintaining commitment to reform was an element that made the community attractive to already existing canonical communities adhering to the Gregorian programme. Thus the rapid growth of the Order in its first decades was due as much to existing houses of canons affiliating with Prémontré as it was to new foundations. Already existing chapters could not be expected to accept immediately or completely the liturgical usages of the mother house nor could they abandon the ministries to which they were already committed. From the beginning the houses founded from Prémontré tended to be more monastic while those founded from Magdeburg were often in their origin a strategy towards the evangelization and pastoral care of new towns and parishes. This Prémontré–Magdeburg tension has been a constant throughout the Order's history but it might better be understood as inherent in the perennial attempt to balance a ritualized liturgical and contemplative life with the pastoral demands of a local church. In fact, even in the more monastically

contemplative houses of Western Europe there was always a strong element of pastoral engagement in the care of the poor, the sick and in the hospitality offered to travellers. In time many of these same houses assumed the responsibility for parishes but it was unusual for the assigned pastor to live attached to the parish church without other confrères, especially lay brothers. Since Vatican II an argument for the Magdeburg tradition as more authentically canonical vis-à-vis a seemingly less authentic monastic model at Prémontré has sometimes been marshalled. This may demonstrate a lack of understanding regarding medieval evangelization in and through monastic and canonical implantation. In the West today it may also be a witness to a painful tension between the demands of a liturgically rooted and ritualized contemplative conventual life and the pastoral demands of a highly technologized, mobile and affluent society that highly values individual freedom. Some contemporary Norbertines maintain that the Order's future viability depends upon its success in negotiating this contemporary crisis of identity. A strong case can be made for the viability of Norbertine canonical communities in a Church beset by the scandal of clergy abuse and in need of ministers whose very lifestyle prepares them for a more collaborative apostolate. Evidence for this is clear in a number of Norbertine priories established by groups of diocesan clergy seeking a common life as the base for their ministry and in the phenomenal growth of forms of lay association throughout the Order.

See also **Augustinian Spirituality; Canonical Communities; Conventual Spirituality.**

The Day of Pentecost: Constitutions and Appendices of the Order of Canons Regular of Prémontré, third English edn, DePere, WI: St Norbert Abbey, 1997; Bernard Ardura, *The Order of Prémontré: History and Spirituality*, trans. Edward Hagman, ed. Roman Vanasse, DePere, WI: Paisa Publishing Co., n.d. (French original 1995); Dominique-Marie Dauzet, *Petite Vie de Saint Norber*, Paris: Desclée de Brouwer, 1995; A.W. van den Hurk, *Norbert of Gennep and His Order*, trans. W. J. Smeets and R. Pasensie, Averbode: Altiora, 1984.

ANDREW CIFERNI

North American Spirituality

North America includes the countries of Canada, Greenland, Mexico, the United States of America, all the countries of Central America and the islands which dot the Caribbean. It is meaningless to employ the term North

American spirituality to take in such a large collection of national identities, ethnic groupings and histories. In common parlance, North America refers to the United States and Canada as a natural adjunct. If one dares at all to speak then of North American spirituality, one must do so in very general terms. For as soon as one consigns a certain characteristic to its spirituality several variants coexist along side of it. Perhaps this is part of the spiritual genius that emerged from this vast territory. Thus, in the discussion that follows, the United States will be in the forefront of the discussion.

Historical sketch. North America shares a pre-European and pre-colonial period when a large number of aboriginal peoples thrived and lived from the land. The Iroquois and Inuit of Canada, the Mayan and Aztec of Mesoamerican civilizations, and the Shawnees and Ojibwa of Turtle Island are among some of the First Nations peoples who lived in North America.

Their land-based spiritualities were marked by a radically different approach to the earth, community, space, the individual and the sacred to that of old Europe. Reciprocity, harmony and immanence infused the cultural and social structures of these civilizations. Their respect for the land was judged by 'enlightened' Europeans to be 'uncivilized' and vacuous of 'religion'. Thus, Native Peoples' historical significance in laying the foundations for authentic North American spiritualities has been generally ignored until recently. Today a greater appreciation of indigenous cultures is growing as alternatives are sought to modern culture's propensity to exploit the natural world. Native peoples' understanding of the interrelationship of all beings and their seasonal rhythmic ceremonial practices offer much wisdom as many seek an ecologically sustainable and balanced existence.

In 1492, when Christopher Columbus literally bumped into North America while on his way to India, he ushered in a slow steady stream of explorers and missionaries by 'old Europe's' Catholic sovereigns who were motivated to extend their power, to lay claim to the new resources of the new world and to the 'souls' that inhabited it. Papal politics determined the territories of the new world Spain, Portugal and France would claim. Each of these Catholic countries dealt with indigenous cultures in distinctive ways, some more respectful than others. But Catholicism's hold on the new world would recede within a generation as 'Old Europe' reformed and brought to this land 'dissenters and protesters', the Puritans, Quakers, Mennonites, Lutherans and Jews. The Catholicism of Rome was replaced with the reformed Christianity of Luther, Henry VIII and Calvin. Protestant groups felt a divine commission to experiment in this abundant land. Slowly Enlightenment ideals of life, liberty and the pursuit of happiness and the Greek political principles of republicanism and democracy became prominent. Establishing freedom of religion and the separation of Church and state in the eighteenth century, North America embraced pluralism as fundamental to its ethos. A rich variety of religious awakenings, revivals and reforms would further characterize the history of religious identity of North America. Jonathan Edwards in the eighteenth century would write of 'religious affections'. John Woolman, a Quaker, would combine inner experience with social action leading the campaign to eradicate slavery from American shores. Transcendentalists like Henry David Thoreau fostered nature mysticism while Charles Finney sparked revivalism based upon the 'mighty baptism of the Holy Ghost'. Black slaves, while adopting the faith of their oppressors, significantly reinterpreted Christian notions of deliverance and suffering by meshing their African roots with their new religion, thus contributing a deeply embodied form of spirituality to the American scene.

The hegemony of Protestantism endured through the Civil War era, the rise of industrial America and through the two world wars. Although in the nineteenth century, large numbers of Catholic immigrants from Ireland, Italy, Germany and Poland arrived in America making Catholicism one of the largest denominations in the United States. Traditional Protestant Christian communities also changed over the course of time as new ethnic groups were assimilated and contributed to the religious identity of these congregations. In the latter half of the twentieth century, Presbyterians made room for Korean congregations; Methodists for Swahili-speaking members and the Roman Catholic Church embraced over 12 million Spanish-speaking Catholics. In the last three decades of the twentieth century America has seen the influx of new immigrants from India, Asia, Africa, Caribbean islands and the Middle East bringing Hinduism, Buddhism, Islam, Santeria, Voodoo and other spiritualities to its shores. America is becoming the most religiously diverse nation in the world. The pluralism of Judaism and Christianity which marked America's first two hundred years is now replaced by the pluralism of the world's spiritualities as it enters into the new millennium. Undoubtedly, these global forces will influence the future spiritualities of North America in the years to come.

Some trajectories of North American spirituality. A few trajectories of North American spirituality, which have marked its history and will continue to shape its future, are pragmatism, pluralism, stress on personal experience, and the sense of vitality/innovation.

Pluralism. Owing to the free exercise of religion inscribed in its laws, America has fostered a tolerance for a rich diversity of traditional and non-traditional spiritualities. While many are anchored in familiar denominations (Episcopalians, Baptist, Lutherans, Presbyterians, Catholic, Reformed Judaism), others are attracted to communities more charismatic, evangelical and popular in nature (Shakers, Disciples of Christ, Mormons, Unitarians, Pentecostals, Church for the Fellowship of All Peoples, etc.). But pluralism does not only apply to institutional affiliations. Pluralism in the form of eclecticism marks many individual contemporary North American spiritualities. Individuals may belong to multiple communities for spiritual support concomitantly, or adopt and blend diverse spiritual practices from other religious traditions and cultures and include ancient spiritual texts from other faiths as offering contemporary spiritual insight and inspiration. Pluralism is also reflected in the evolutionary accounts of many spiritual journeys of today. It has become commonplace to hear that an individual baptized Catholic joins the Episcopal Church and then switches membership to the Unitarians or the Interfaith Church. The voluntary character of religious identity in America promotes such spiritual flexibility and ecumenism. And in the coming millennium pluralism will be further challenged as practices from Buddhism, Hinduism, Islam and indigenous cultures are incorporated into America's practice of spirituality, transforming both the traditional spirituality and America's religious sensibilities. Take for example the Western influence on the practice of Buddhism creating a hybrid of 'socially engaged Buddhist practice' or the spirituality of Thomas Merton.

Pragmatism. From its birth at the time of the Enlightenment, American spiritualities have been influenced by the ideals of practical reason, the cultivation of one's natural, human endowments and enlightened self-interest. If something works, one stays with it. If it does not work, one discards and attempts something else. There are positive and negative sides to this approach for one's spirituality. On the one hand, it ties spirituality to actions and consequences, and does not deny materiality, the body and the commonplace of existence. On the other hand, it fails to appreciate the nuance of time necessary for contemplation and the prodigal reality of grace in spiritual development. Moreover pragmatism can easily become a slave to the cultural and economic pressures of commercialism and consumption which in the end exploits the true value of matter. Yet another face of pragmatism in American spirituality is the plethora of self-help books, merchandise, workshops, television programmes which promote tools for living one's best life and encourages a confident self-reliance which leads to the notion that a spiritual identity is achieved through personal effort alone.

Stress on personal experience. No other characteristic perhaps describes spirituality in North America as the stress upon personal experience as witnessed in awakenings, conversions, revivals and charismatic healings. American spirituality has always been highly personal, emphasizing an immediate experience of the sacred. Whether solitary individuals like Ralph Waldo Emerson and Henry David Thoreau or communitarian figures like Martin Luther King and Dorothy Day, rational seekers like Thomas Jefferson or deeply affective mystics like Fanny Crosby, personal experience is normative in determining the authenticity of spiritualities in North America. The stress on personal experience has made North American spiritualities much more receptive to and influenced by psychology. Ever since William James, the practice of spirituality has taken into account the psychological dimensions of faith and at times it has been to the detriment of the communitarian aspects of spirituality.

Sense of vitality/innovation. Possessing a rather short history, unprecedented economic prosperity and the constant challenge of new ideas brought by the continual stream of immigrants to its shores, North American spiritualities enjoy an innovative and optimistic temperament. From the time of America's inception as a land of opportunity and as the location for a 'radical new experiment', American religious sensibility displayed a high regard for the cultivation of the imagination and the ingenuity required to communicate it. The emergence of the 'spirituals' and gospel music as musical forms, the variety of prayer-meeting revivals that met spiritual longings, the design and success of the Twelve-Step programme of Alcoholics Anonymous, the formation of the Catholic Worker movement to meet growing poverty in the country, and the use of technology for evangelism are a few examples of the American religious ingenuity at work. An underlying sense of divine destiny/providence supports the openness to constant change and novelty as well as the willingness to experiment spiritually.

See also **African-American Spirituality; Black Spirituality; Catholic Worker Movement; Hispanic Spirituality; Mujerista Spirituality; Native North American Spirituality; Puritan Spirituality; Quaker Spirituality; Shaker Spirituality; Spirituals; Womanist Spirituality.**

Sydney E. Ahlstrom, *A Religious History of the American People*, New Haven: Yale University Press, 1973; Vine Delorie Jr, *For this Land: Writings on Religion in America*, ed. James Treat, New York: Routledge, 1999; Diana L. Eck, *A New Religious America*, San Francisco: HarperCollins, 2001; Martin E. Marty, *Pilgrims in Their Own Land: 500 Years of Religion in America*, Boston: Little Brown & Co., 1984; Wade Clark Roof, *Spiritual Marketplace: Baby Boomers and the Remaking of American Religion*, Princeton, NJ: Princeton University Press, 1999.

VALERIE LESNIAK

Nothingness

Nothingness as a basic philosophical tenet is commonly associated with Buddhism and atheism more than Christianity, because the ultimate reality in Christianity, God, is held to be something rather than nothing. Yet from three distinct perspectives the concept of nothingness also lies close to the heart of Christianity.

First, the doctrine of creation *ex nihilo* ('out of nothing') was developed largely in reaction to the Platonic view, from Plato's *Timaeus*, that creation is continuous with the divine substance. God as creator is absolutely transcendent and ontologically distinct from creation, so that in relation to the 'something' of creation, the divine cause is a pure 'nothing'. This is the nothingness of *apophasis* ('unsaying'): anything we affirm of God, which necessarily requires creaturely terms, must be more strongly denied as inapplicable to God, because God transcends all language. Though we affirm that God is the cause of creation, we must call this cause a nothing.

Second, central to Christian teaching about Jesus is the kenotic hymn of Phil. 2.6–11, which asserts that Jesus as the Christ 'did not count equality with God a thing to be grasped, but emptied himself (*ekenosen*)' – an emptying which is also translated as 'becoming nothing'. Jesus became nothing in two senses: morally, by taking our sin on himself and dying the death of a criminal on the cross, making him 'to be sin who knew no sin' (2 Cor. 5.21); and ontologically, by taking human nature when he was divine, as the divine Word. In Jesus, God becomes nothing in comparison with what God is, as divine and as morally perfect. The nothingness of Jesus shows the infinite length to which God goes to redeem the world.

Third, repentance and the return to God through self-denial, traditionally understood as the path of *ascesis*, is the realization of our own nothingness before God both morally and ontologically – the same nothingness which Jesus takes on himself. This is the area of the majority of Christian reflection on the meaning of nothingness.

The nothingness of ascesis took on a powerful set of meanings in relation to the monastic tradition of poverty. Poverty as an outward sign was understood as the giving up of everything that made one 'something' in the eyes of the world (1 Cor. 8.2; Gal. 6.3) – possessions, status and family kinship. As an inward sign, it was the giving up of attitudes and idols contrary to simple dependence on God, in poverty of spirit and purity of heart (Matt. 5.3, 8). In the mendicant (lit. 'poor') movements of the twelfth and thirteenth centuries, this long-standing monastic tradition of poverty became intensified, being increasingly applied not just to the moral imitation of Christ's poverty but to participation in Christ's ontological nothingness in his kenotic journey. In the Beguine writers of the late thirteenth century such as Hadewijch of Antwerp (fl. *c.* 1250) and Marguerite Porete (d. 1310), poverty is an ecstatic loss of everything that we are as created, in an 'annihilation' which joins us to Christ's nothingness and brings us into the divine nature. The 'abyss' of our own nothingness is found to be the 'abyss' of God's internal life in the Trinity. Here monastic poverty becomes the point of ontological union with Christ in kenosis, as the soul by becoming nothing becomes one with the Son in the Trinity. This is the focal point for Meister Eckhart (*c.* 1260–*c.* 1328): 'When the soul comes into the One and there enters into a pure rejection of itself, it finds God as in a nothing ... In this nothingness (*niht*) God [is] born' (*German Sermon* 71, *DW* (*German Works*) 3.224.5–7). Nothingness is the key moment of transformation, where God comes to birth in the soul.

This nothingness of ontological union with Christ is regarded with suspicion by the Protestant Reformers, for whom – to generalize – Christ remains exterior to the human soul. When they speak of the human person as nothing, they refer to moral imperfection: sin is the occasion for realizing our moral nothingness before God. We are nothing in comparison with God's grace, contributing nothing and receiving everything (2 Cor. 6.10). By contrast, among the Roman Catholics, moral nothingness not only throws us onto divine grace, but unites us ontologically with Christ, through Christ's passion. Our suffering, our nothingness, may be transformed into Christ's own suffering, making us co-redeemers with Christ – again the link is made through Christ's kenosis. This is the sense in which the late nineteenth-century Carmelite Thérèse of Lisieux referred to herself as a 'poor little nothing (*néant*)'. In her suffering, she said, she was chosen by Love as a 'holocaust', a place of Christ's self-offering in the world. Her nothingness was part of Christ's gift of his own nothingness for the salvation of the world.

As *apophasis*, the language of nothingness is a dialectical language (*see* 'Apophatic Spirituality'). God is only 'nothing' by contrast with our own 'something', and we are only 'nothing' by contrast with God's 'something'. In the end, God is neither something nor nothing, but beyond language. This means that the Christian language of nothingness is not nihilism. God is the ultimate reality, but God's transcendence of all human categories means that 'nothingness', applied both to God and to ourselves, is a valuable dialectical term in our understanding of God and in spiritual progress.

See also **Apophatic Spirituality; Asceticism; God, Images of; Poverty.**

'Néant' in *DS* 11, pp. 64–80.

EDWARD HOWELLS

Obedience

The term is prominent in New Testament Christology, where Jesus is said to have become 'obedient to death, even death on a cross' (Phil. 2.8). This may have a background in the Servant of the Lord (Isa. 52—53), who exemplifies the obedience of Israel to its covenant obligations, even to death. In regard to Jesus, obedience refers to his total submission to his heavenly Father: 'I come not to do my own will, but the will of him who sent me' (John 6.38). Therefore, obedience can be seen as covering Jesus' whole life of loving service, and not just in relation to his sacrificial death on the cross.

Since Christian life is patterned on that of Jesus, it is not surprising that it should involve obedience to the Father. To obey God, however, one must discern God's will, which is communicated to us by various ways and means. God can speak to us directly in prayer. The problem is that our ability to listen has been distorted by sin, and especially by the original disobedience of our first parents (Gen. 3). A time-honoured way of overcoming self-will and delusion is to seek the will of God through the discernment of another person.

The use of spiritual direction was especially prominent among the Desert Fathers of fourth-to fifth-century Egypt and Syria. Typically a disciple joined a master of reputed holiness to learn God's will. Whatever obedience was proffered was strictly a personal matter, with few social ramifications. One was free to choose a master and free to leave. Yet it was recognized that moving from director to director could be a lethal form of spiritual disobedience.

Once Christian ascetics gathered in community, obedience took on other dimensions besides individual spiritual direction. In a large, complex monastic system such as that of Pachomius (south Egypt, fourth to fifth century) obedience was necessary for the good order of the community, which meant the fostering of charity as well as the expediting of economic ends. Recent scholarship shows that Pachomius' reputation for militaristic obedience is quite unfounded.

John Cassian was one of the principal transmitters of Eastern monastic ideas to the West, but he did so according to his own lights. When talking about obedience in *Institute* 4, he promotes it to the primary coenobitic value and puts great emphasis on conformity with the monastic rule and with the superior of the community. For Cassian, one must transcend self-will before attaining the other virtues. But he never explains why self-will is so dangerous or why one should expect to find God's will in the will of the superior. The principal heirs of Cassian in the Latin West were the Rule of the Master and the Rule of Benedict. In both documents, obedience to the abbot and Rule are heavily emphasized and placed in tandem with the passive virtues of silence and humility (RM 7–10; RB 5–7). Obedience is now made the object of an explicit vow.

For the Master, the ordinary monk risks spiritual ruin unless he is guided in all things by the abbot, who is presumed to be a person of deep wisdom and holiness. Again, the greatest danger is to follow self-will, but the Master often equates it with *any* exercise of personal choice. St Benedict backs off from that extreme position, but still stresses the individual, ascetical aspect of obedience.

Benedict is much more sensitive to the horizontal and interpersonal aspects of obedience, or what he calls 'mutual obedience' (RB 71 title). He knows that people cannot live together in Christian love unless they are obedient to one another as well as to the superior. In fact, this kind of obedience is usually more demanding than hierarchical obedience, since it means that we must accommodate ourselves to a variety of characters. Sometimes God speaks to us through rather unattractive people.

Through the subsequent history of religious life, and indeed of all Christian spiritual life, the same dynamics of spiritual obedience have been at work. As religious orders became more active and apostolic, obedience often took on a more objective, institutionalized form. It was no longer only a matter of personal growth but of large public works involving the salvation of numerous other persons. When the subjective and objective aspects of obedience are confused, there is always danger of conflict and unhappiness in the Christian community.

At the turn of the twenty-first century, obedience presents a particularly problematic face, at least in Western, post-industrial society. People today are wary of the claims of blind obedience, given the tragic history of two world wars, mostly caused by the excesses of communism and fascism, and 'savage capitalism'. Today, people are much less ready to offer automatic allegiance to any leader or ideology, including those of religion.

This should be seen as a positive development, although it does not assure that these mistakes will not be repeated. There is a scientifically verified tendency in the human psyche to seek reassurance in a system or person that offers absolute security. Despite the veneer of critical sophistication provided by modern education, many people are still susceptible to the bogus claims of absolute, closed authority.

The problem for religious orders is obvious. The prospect of submission to a religious superior for the good of one's soul is not attractive to many young people today. On the other hand, the intermediate form of obedience found in spiritual direction has become increasingly popular after many centuries of disuse.

See also Asceticism; Benedictine Spirituality; Community; Direction, Spiritual; Discernment; Discipleship; Kenosis; Monasticism; Religious Life; Rules, Religious; Vows.

J. Gribomont et al., 'Obbedienza' in Dizionario degli Istituti di Perfezione 6, Rome: San Paulo Edizioni, 1980, pp. 494–547; T. Kardong, 'Self-will in Benedict's Rule', Studia Monastica 42.2 (Barcelona, 2000), 319–47; A. de Vogüé, Community and Abbot in the Rule of St Benedict, Kalamazoo, MI: Cistercian Publications, 1979, 1.179–253.

TERRENCE KARDONG

Office, Divine

(Also known as Daily Office, Daily Prayer, Liturgy of the Hours, Breviary etc.) The practice of communities and individuals offering prayer at regular points through the day and night goes back to Christianity's early beginnings, and before that probably to Jewish prayer practices.

The book of Acts implies the presence of such a tradition (e.g. Acts 2.15; 10.9; 3.1). Before the fourth century information is slight, but includes references in Hippolytus' Apostolic Tradition to morning, third, sixth and ninth hours, evening, bedtime, and the middle of the night. Plentiful evidence emerges in the fourth century that pious individuals were encouraged to pray especially at these times. In addition, daily public services at morning and evening attracted large crowds; services were ordered liturgically according to the various roles of those present. For many of the common people to pray meant to participate in the liturgy, often with much simultaneous self-expression (a common task of the deacon was to call regularly for silence). This reveals two poles of liturgical prayer: First the daily offering of a sacrifice of praise, seeking quiet, reflective growth in the spiritual life; and, second, a popular public service of praise and prayer which for many was concerned more with obtaining help in coping with the demands of daily life. All of these practices were strongly marked by a sense of being the body of Christ, united by common prayer at set times.

In the same period the monastic tradition came into its own, itself also demonstrating two types of practice: first, groups of devout laity within local congregations who in common performed the 'lesser' hours in addition to public morning and evening prayer, ultimately coming together in resident communities; and, second, those who fled to the desert for a more ascetical life which, while having elements of community, was centred on individual recitation of the entire psalter in numerical order. The one group remained engaged in the midst of society, the other sought sanctity through deliberate marginalization. In all of these practices reference was constantly made to the gospel command to 'pray without ceasing' (1 Thess. 5.17).

The four strands came to overlap. Urban monastic communities adopted recitation of the whole psalter, and this came also to affect the secular liturgy. The distinctive lines soon blurred, and by the time of Benedict the West had two basic forms of daily prayer, monastic and secular, which in fact were now not very different from each other. Each included a daily round in which morning and evening prayer retain their ecclesial character (especially visible in their 'solemn' celebration), while the third, sixth and ninth hours and compline are more characteristically monastic, as is the vigils office with its long readings in the night or early morning, and the first hour or 'Prime' which came to be added. A penumbra of pious practices for the laity arose, which were related to the Divine Office.

In the West the monastic elements came to predominate: from the ninth century in the West there was increasing pressure on clergy to perform the whole round of seven or more offices daily. By the end of the Middle Ages we find offices still performed liturgically in parish churches, and smaller numbers of lay people attending, but now without any active participation. It was increasingly common, however, for individual priests to recite the texts privately, a development encouraged by the appearance of the Breviary, in which the riches of the office were slimmed down, shorn of most of their ceremonial, and condensed into one book. The daily hours of prayer thus came increasingly to be seen as a clerical and monastic preserve in which laity had no part, no responsibility. Popular devotions such as the rosary developed as a compensation to fill this gap. From the fourteenth century came an astonishing flowering of little offices for the laity, ranging from brief memorizable forms, sometimes in rhyme, to miniature versions of the breviary known as Books of Hours. This significant development has remained in vigour till today, both in Roman Catholicism and in some Churches of the Reformation.

In the centuries between the Reformation and the mid twentieth century, however, the daily offices were lost from sight for most ordinary lay people in most places, with significant exceptions, not least the Church of England, where they remained part of the parish round.

The Liturgical Movement, the reforms of the Second Vatican Council, and parallel liturgical renewal in other Western Churches, have brought a renewed awareness of the importance of this form of prayer for all Christians, issuing in recovery of old practices, but also in many forms of imaginative development of the tradition for today's circumstances. This varies from country to country. In France there are significant developments in monasticism and some parishes, in which the ecumenical Community of Taizé has been very influential. In Britain there is a particularly lively ferment of renewal in the Anglican Church. In the USA a great amount of creative academic thinking fails to filter down to parishes and local churches. Renewed, participatory celebration of the Divine Office in local Christian communities seems to be difficult unless lay people are allowed initiative and responsibility, and the right measure of creative freedom is recovered.

The office is often called the prayer of the Church, the voice of the bride addressing the bridegroom (St Ambrose). While late medieval legalism saw it as an obligation on the clergy, it is the vocation of the entire Church. Positive results are emerging from renewing the link of private prayer with the liturgy, for instance in providing forms for individuals or groups to say at an agreed time wherever they are, in association with the public celebrations.

This form of prayer has always included psalms, and there is a substantial literature on the Christian prayer of the psalms. While monasticism has used the whole psalter, the clear tendency in public, ecclesial celebrations of the Office has been selective use of it, according to accessibility and appropriateness.

While in the East the Offices have always been celebrated liturgically, the West's tendency to reduce liturgy to text and inwardness, demoting outward expression to a secondary role, has meant loss of part of Daily Prayer's essence: posture, gesture, ceremonial, setting, music, and the notion of gathering the People of God mean that it is *liturgy*. Ancient practices experiencing a current revival are the Lighting of the Lamps, the Offering of Incense, Commemoration of Baptism at the Font, of the Resurrrection, etc.

An important part of the daily liturgy as the priestly people's offering is intercession. The fundamental textual content of the offices is psalmody followed by intercession. The reading of substantial portions of Scripture only gradually found a place, normally in the night office. Cranmer transferred these to morning and evening prayer in the Anglican reform, where they have gained an established place, while the more recent reforms of Vatican II have created an 'Office of Readings' in the Roman Breviary. Fruitful connections are beginning to be made today with the practice of Bible study.

At the public level the Divine Office is the daily converse of the body of Christ with God in Christ, by the power of the Holy Spirit, sustaining by regular impulses that 'prayer without ceasing' to which the body is called. Individually, each member is both formed and carried, while at the same time assuming the shared responsibility of carrying one another. In it we are steeped in the Scriptures, and thereby in the mystery of salvation history in which we encounter the living Christ. We are strengthened by that in it which encourages us, and toughened by those elements which make not always congenial demands of us, and in ways such as these this practice which stands at the heart of the Christian understanding of prayer builds up both the individual and the body in ways that can defy explanation.

See also **Spirituality, Liturgy and Worship** (*essay*); **Community; Prayer; Psalms.**

George Guiver, *Company of Voices: Daily Prayer and the People of God*, 2nd edn, Norwich: Canterbury Press, 2001; Robert F. Taft, *The Liturgy of the Hours in East and West*, Collegeville, MN: The Liturgical Press, 1993.

GEORGE GUIVER

Oratorian Spirituality

The origins of Oratorian spirituality can be situated within the stream of new movements and communities arising from the Catholic Reformation. The movement developed from the personality and spiritual ministry of the attractive and eccentric St Philip Neri (1515–95). Philip was born in Florence into an ancient family. At eighteen he experienced a conversion and went to Rome where he took up the life of a poor hermit. At the same time he gathered around him a group of young men to whom he gave spiritual guidance. This eventually led to the formation of a Confraternity which met regularly for spiritual exercises and spiritual conversation in which each took an equal role. After Philip's ordination, he led spiritual exercises called an 'oratory' or prayerful devotional meeting. The members discussed devotional books and followed this with a walk, Vespers in a local church, another 'oratory' often dedicated to music, and perhaps a visit to the sick. The Congregation of the Oratory came into informal existence when some of Philip's followers were ordained and a small community began at San Girolamo in 1564.

From then on, lay men took a more passive role as only the clerics preached or conducted discussions. Lay participation in the 'oratory' was reduced to listening and singing. The 'oratory' exercises often lasted several hours and ended with sung canticles from which the musical form known as an 'oratorio' took its name. The Congregation was founded formally in 1575 when it was given the Church of Santa Maria in Vallicella and Philip was elected Provost of the community. The constitutions were begun in 1583 but a final version was not ready for papal approval until 1612. There were serious disagreements about the direction the community should take. Philip continued to believe in the value of informality over rules and was opposed both to any expansion outside Rome or to centralization. In contrast, Antonio Talpa, who took charge of a foundation in Naples, reluctantly sanctioned by Philip, has been characterized not only as rigid but as having a violent temper. He wanted the Congregation to

become a religious order like the Theatines or Jesuits. However, his views did not prevail. The original lay group was nevertheless transformed into a group of priests living in community without vows (there have been a few brother members). The original Congregation continues to exist in Italy, Spain, England, Germany, Latin America and the United States.

In France another form of the Oratory, inspired by Philip Neri's ideals but not an exact copy, was founded by Cardinal de Bérulle in 1611. This Congregation placed a strong emphasis on prayer and on promoting a reformed Catholic priesthood. It played a leading role in the spread of the Catholic Reformation in France and in the development of what became known as the French school of spirituality. Like the Italian Oratory, the French Oratory was a group of priests without formal vows but, unlike the Italian Oratory, was centralized under a Superior-General and General Assembly. As time passed, it specialized in intellectual work, running seminaries and schools.

The keynote of Oratorian spirituality in the Italian tradition is its intimate character based on small numbers of priests in independent houses, each known as an Oratory. Despite Philip Neri's early flirtation with quasi-Franciscan poverty and mendicancy, the Oratorian ethos has generally been warm rather than austere. The members of the more widespread Italian tradition have no formal vows but live a stable life in independent communities with a few simple rules. The members live out of their own income but contribute to the common purse according to their means. There is a common table and common prayers – though not Office in choir. The rich musical liturgies and other services, characteristic of Oratorian churches, are for the benefit of lay people rather than a form of monastic observance. The main work has traditionally been preaching, administering the sacraments and running oratory meetings for lay people. Philip Neri was noted as a confessor and spiritual director and his approach to the practice emphasized individual responsibility and liberty. He believed in the guidance of the Holy Spirit in the life of each person and the importance of penitents discovering for themselves the spiritual path that best suited them.

There has been no female version of the Oratory and the main work of Oratorians has largely been directed at seminarians, clergy or lay men. Despite the victory of Philip Neri's more humane and flexible vision, the core tradition became increasingly clerical. Arguably this has proved a weakness in more recent times as lay people and women in particular have come to play a more active role in spirituality in the Roman Catholic Church. As a generalization, since the Second Vatican Council the houses of the Oratory have become increasingly associated with a more conservative liturgical style and traditional devotional practices.

See also **French School of Spirituality.**

R. Addington, *The Idea of the Oratory*, London: Burns & Oates, 1966; Pierre Janelle, *The Catholic Reformation*, Milwaukee: The Bruce Publishing Co., 1975, chs 6 and 12; V. J. Matthew, *St Philip Neri*, Rockford, IL: Tan Books, 1984; William Thompson (ed.), *Bérulle and the French School: Selected Writings*, CWS, New York: Paulist Press, 1989.

PHILIP SHELDRAKE

Orthodox Spirituality

1. *A spirituality of the Bible and the Church.* It is important to open this article with a disclaimer. In the opinion of the author, there is no different 'Orthodox' spirituality – that is to say, no peculiarly or exclusively 'Orthodox' way of looking at the mystery of God, the human person and the world. Any Orthodox spiritual world view is called to examine the biblical roots (the inspired texts) of the Christian Church and to explore the communion of saints (the inspired lives) of those who have lived out this way. Yet, while there is a remarkable and fundamental unity in the Christian way, both Eastern and Western, there are nevertheless certain distinctive principles that receive greater and more consistent attention in the Orthodox Church. In the article that follows, some of the more basic principles will be briefly proposed and propounded.

2. *Eschatology and spirituality.* 'Eschatology' (or, the study of the last things) is a term with a breadth and spaciousness far greater than any dictionary definition can permit. Most people assume that the last times and the last things imply some apocalyptic or escapist attitude toward the world. It took a long time for theologians to realize that eschatology is not the last, perhaps unnecessary chapter in some course or manual of dogmatics. Eschatology is not the teaching about what follows everything else in this world and in these times. It is the teaching about our relationship to those last things and last times. In essence, it is about the last-ness and the lasting-ness of all things. The Omega gives meaning to the Alpha; this world is interpreted in light of the age to come.

An eschatological vision of spirituality offers a way out of the impasse of provincialism and the evil of confessionalism in our life and in our world. It is the ultimate hope against all hopelessness. It is the conviction that our efforts on this planet are not ours alone, but that the Source and End of all is working in us, through us and above us for the well-being of all creation.

3. *The way of the heart.* The Alpha and Omega of the spiritual life is found not in some other world but in the very heart of the human person. The heart (or, *kardia*) contains the inner treasury and mystery of Orthodox spirituality. More than the seat of emotion and experience, the heart signifies the spiritual centre of the entire human person, body and soul. The heart is also the faculty of reason and a determinant of action, susceptible of both good and evil. To discover one's heart is an act of reintegration, a recovery of a symbolical point of convergence, integrating the entire human person within the cosmos at large. The heart is a symbol of inner harmony and outward communion. Moreover, the heart is the battlefield of the soul, the place of struggle and suffering. As such, it becomes the dwelling place of God and reveals the mystery of divine knowledge and union.

The spiritual aspirant is called to guard the heart, to gather one's intellect within the heart in an act of concentration (or contemplation) and conversation (or prayer). There is no separation between intellectual knowledge, sensual experience and physical action. The culmination of such an attitude is centring the intellect in the heart (or, the *nous* in the *kardia*), which is the ultimate spiritual aim, according to *The Philokalia*. Then, the heart becomes the centre of divine illumination and vision, the meeting-point between God, humanity and the world.

4. *The deification of humanity.* Created in the image and likeness of God (Gen. 1.26), humanity is called to nothing less than *theosis* (or deification, divinization), invited to become no less than divine. Such a conviction is also the result of God's own participation in human life. Athanasius of Alexandria (296–373) claimed that 'God became human in order that we might become deified'. *Theosis* has been a central concept of spiritual life since the second century (with Irenaeus of Lyons), becoming the ruling principle by the fourteenth century (with Gregory Palamas (1296–1359). It is the affirmation of the possibility of a direct and full union between humanity and God, through an authentic synergy and loving sharing but without any fusion or confusion between the two. The weak human nature responds to and is upheld by the initiative of divine grace. Orthodox teaching

insists that this is no union on the level of either essence or person; instead, it is a union on the level of energy. The spiritual person or saint participates in the life, power and glory in a face-to-face encounter and a mutual communion with God.

5. *Apophaticism, theology and asceticism.* Nevertheless, while God's otherness and transcendence are bridged, they are not abolished. God always remains incomprehensible and inaccessible in essence. The apophatic dimension of the Orthodox Church is a critical aspect of theology as well as of spirituality. Not only is God beyond all darkness (signifying our inability or vulnerability as human beings), but God is also beyond all light (symbolizing God's mysterious depth that surpasses everything that we can understand or even experience as human beings, whether intellectually or even spiritually). Apophatic theology received its definitive articulation in Dionysius the Areopagite in the fifth century.

In this respect, theology is a gift of divine grace, a result of pure prayer – as Evagrius of Pontus (346–99) would say. It constitutes the struggle to discover concepts and words that are adequate but do not exhaust the divine mystery. Therefore, theological expression and spiritual experience are not unrelated; mysticism and asceticism are not disconnected. In this respect, there are three deeply interdependent and interpenetrating stages in the spiritual way. Purification involves the cleansing of vices and practice of virtues; illumination comprises the contemplation of human and created nature as God intended it; and union (perfection or deification) implies the visitation of divine grace and vision of divine glory. In the first stage, the human person struggles for liberation from passions that render us corrupt and captive to passionate impulses. In the second stage, the human person receives a perception of the divine presence in the whole of creation. The third stage leads to direct vision and full union with God, who is above and beyond everyone and everything.

6. *Liturgy and mystery: communion and creation.* Above all, theology and spirituality are celebrated as glorification and thanksgiving in liturgy. The spiritual life presupposes participation in the sacraments of the Church. The way of the sacraments and the way of inner contemplation are not alternatives but complementary and united. None can be truly spiritual without sharing in the sacraments; none can be truly Christian without sharing in the communion of saints. As such, the sacraments are neither the end nor the essence of the spiritual life. Yet, they are indispensable means of sharing in divine grace and of receiving the divine 'mysteries' (which is the Greek term for sacraments).

Worship, then, is at the centre of spirituality. What the Orthodox icon does in space and matter, the Orthodox liturgy effects in praise and time. It performs the same ministry of reconciliation, the anticipation – even participation – of heaven on earth. The Orthodox Church retains a liturgical view of the world, proclaiming a world imbued by God and a God involved in this world. Indeed, as Maximus the Confessor (580–662) claimed, the entire world is a 'cosmic liturgy'. In the breadth of the liturgy, we recognize that the world is larger than our individual concerns and the world ceases to be something from which we are estranged but rather becomes something for which we care. The liturgy becomes a celebration of heaven on earth. Thus, our relationship with this world determines our relationship with heaven; the way we treat the earth is reflected in the way that we pray to God.

This introduces and intimates the deeply ecological dimension of Orthodox spirituality. Whenever we narrow the spiritual life to ourselves and our own concerns, we neglect our vocation to transform the entire creation of God. The spiritual aspirant implores God and struggles for the renewal of the whole polluted cosmos. Heaven and earth are full of God's glory; the universe is a burning bush of God's presence. The spiritual person is called to be a prophet in the world. It is not simply the soul that is called to salvation, but the entire human person and the entire created world. Orthodox spirituality upholds an unprecedented affirmation of every particle of creation – to the last speck of dust.

7. *Spiritual direction.* Spiritual direction is the way proposed by the Orthodox Church to guide one along the spiritual journey. It is a test of one's sincerity and struggle. Beyond the narrowly defined aspect of sacramental confession, the spiritual elder – whether male (*geron* or abba) or female (*gerontissa* or amma) – provides a criterion of personal authenticity judged against the depth of tradition and the intimacy of communion. The Orthodox tradition is convinced that we cannot address our passions, we cannot know our heart, without the presence of at least one other person. We require a counsellor, an advisor, a guide. We need someone to consult, someone with whom to share. Indeed, there is something refreshing and even redeeming in simply sharing verbally. There is a healing aspect to the simple act of expressing our thoughts and feelings. We are remarkably related to and

dependent upon one another. Doing by sharing is always better than going alone. Spiritual sharing, then, is a way of spiritual learning. Spiritual consultation is a critical step toward communion. Through this, we learn to be forgiven and to forgive, to be loved and to love. Spiritual direction is the safeguard and measure of all that occurs in the spiritual life.

See also **Apophatic Spirituality; Asceticism; Byzantine Spirituality; Deification; Early Christian Spirituality; Iconography.**

John Chryssavgis, *Beyond the Shattered Image*, Minneapolis: Light and Life Publications, 1999; Tito Colliander, *The Way of the Ascetics*, New York: St Vladimir's Seminary Press, 1985; Thomas Hopko, *The Orthodox Faith, Volume IV: Spirituality*, rev. edn, New York: Orthodox Church of America, 1976; Vladimir Lossky, *The Mystical Theology of the Eastern Church*, New York: St Vladimir's Seminary Press, 1976 (repr. of London: J. Clarke, 1957); Georgios Mantzarides, *Orthodox Spiritual Life*, Brookline, MA: Holy Cross Orthodox Press, 1994; Monk of the Eastern Church, *Orthodox Spirituality: An Outline of the Orthodox Ascetical and Mystical Tradition*, 2nd edn, New York: St Vladimir's Seminary Press, 1996; Kallistos Ware, *The Orthodox Way*, rev. edn, New York: St Vladimir's Seminary Press, 1995.

JOHN CHRYSSAVGIS

Oxford Movement

The Oxford Movement was a movement of theological revival and reform within the Church of England in the nineteenth century. The term is applied principally to the movement led by four members of the University of Oxford between the years 1833 and 1845, namely John Keble (1792–1866), John Henry Newman (1801–90), Edward Bouverie Pusey (1800–82) and Richard Hurrell Froude (1803–36). This chronology was popularized by Newman, writing as a Roman Catholic, in his *Apologia pro Vita Sua* (1864), a retrospective view of his Anglican years. The term is also used more widely to refer to the Anglican 'Catholic' or 'High Church' revival of the nineteenth century.

Newman, Keble, Pusey and Hurrell Froude were all Fellows of Oriel College, Oxford in the 1820s. Though Newman claimed Keble's 'Assize Sermon', preached on 14 March 1833, as the start of the Oxford Movement, its origins lie in dissatisfaction at Catholic emancipation in 1829 (Nockles, 1997, pp. 195–267). The ensuing political crisis over parliamentary reform, which ended with the passage of the Reform Act of 1832 and the new Liberal government's 1833 proposals to reduce and rationalize the Anglican bishoprics in Ireland, reinforced the fear that the establishment of the Church of England was under threat. Keble's sermon was a call to defence of the Church.

Newman, in his *Apologia*, also traced the origins of the movement to the influence of Romanticism, and to reaction against rationalist criticism of religion. In his *Christian Year* (1827), Keble gave poetic expression to the association of sacramentalism and the Romantic cult of nature.

What began as a form of political reaction, prompted by a constitutional crisis, developed into a movement of theological reform. *The Tracts for the Times*, published between 1833 and 1841, sought to remind the Church of England of its doctrinal heritage. The 'Tractarians' claimed continuity with the Caroline Divines of the seventeenth century, though they owed much also to the Nonjurors and to the surviving tradition of High Churchmanship in the Church of England (a tradition they also sometimes disparaged as 'High and Dry').

The Oxford Movement developed new theological perspectives within High Churchmanship. Its leaders strongly emphasized the authority of the ordained ministry, which, in Newman's *Tract 1, On the Ministerial Commission* (1833), was held to derive from apostolic institution and the unbroken chain of episcopal succession. The moderate Tractarian William Palmer, in his *Treatise on the Church of Christ* (1838), developed this into a 'branch theory' of the Church, linking through episcopacy Anglican, Orthodox and Roman Catholic Churches, and unchurching others. This was reinforced by appeal to the Vincentian canon in matters of faith, that is, 'what has been believed everywhere, always and by all', referenced in particular to the Church of the first six centuries, and described as 'the rule of antiquity'.

The movement also sought the renewal of sacramental theology, and particularly eucharistic sacrifice and the real presence of Christ in the consecrated elements. Though Tractarians in general disliked the theology of transubstantiation, their eucharistic doctrine eventually was to lead to the revival of ritual practices similar to those of Roman Catholicism, such as Requiem Masses, reservation of the sacrament, and benediction. Tractarians also encouraged a wider use of sacramental language within the Church of England.

The Tractarians also pioneered a distinctive fusion of the Evangelical cultivation of holiness through conversion with a decisive shift away from Protestant theories of justification. In Newman's *Lectures on Justification* (1838), sanctification was an essential concomitant of justification, implying the indwelling presence of the Holy Spirit, and the need for sustained attention to spiritual discipline, especially through the Eucharist and the practice of confession and penitence.

By the late 1830s, the Tractarians' hostility to the Protestant Reformation was becoming apparent, sealed particularly through publication of the literary *Remains* of Froude in 1838–39. Suspicion mounted that Tractarianism was but a short step to Roman Catholicism, and Newman's conversion in 1845 all but confirmed that fear. His *Tract 90*, published in 1841, had argued that the Anglican Thirty-Nine Articles of Religion could be held consistently with Roman Catholic doctrine, and had provoked an unprecedented storm of protest.

Newman's loss was seen as a catastrophe, removing the movement's most able theologian and influential voice, but this was not the end of it. Under the less charismatic leadership of Keble and Pusey, Tractarianism – or Anglo-Catholicism as it came to be called – continued to grow within the Anglican Church, fanning out from Oxford and the major cities to embrace parishes up and down the country. The Oxford Movement eventually had a worldwide impact on Anglicanism, creating a distinctive theological and liturgical style within it. Though this impact peaked in the mid twentieth century, the Oxford Movement has remained influential within contemporary Anglicanism, and has encouraged ecumenical relationships with other episcopally ordered churches in particular.

See also **Anglican Spirituality; Anglo-Catholic Spirituality; Caroline Divines; Sanctification.**

Primary sources: R. W. Church, *The Oxford Movement: Twelve Years, 1833–1845*, London: Macmillan, 1890; J. H. Newman, *Apologia pro Vita Sua*, London: Longman, 1864.

Secondary sources: S. W. Gilley, *Newman and His Age*, London: Darton, Longman & Todd, 1990; G. W. Herring, *What Was the Oxford Movement?*, London: Continuum, 2002; P. B. Nockles, *The Oxford Movement in Context: Anglican High Churchmanship 1760–1857*, Cambridge: Cambridge University Press, 1994; P. B. Nockles, 'Lost causes and . . . impossible loyalties: the Oxford Movement and the university' in M. G. Brock and M. C. Curthoys (eds), *The History of the University of Oxford, vol. 6: Nineteenth-Century Oxford, Part 1*, Oxford: Clarendon Press, 1997.

JEREMY MORRIS

Pastoral Care and Spirituality

Pastoral care encompasses the wide range of activities designed to embody the loving care of God for people in need. The word 'pastoral' stems from the biblical understanding of God as a shepherd whose care is faithful and reliable (Ezek. 34.1–31; Ps. 23.1–4). Christ is the good shepherd who was sent to the lost sheep of Israel (Matt. 10.6; 15.24; see Luke 15.3–7) and the one who lays down his life for the sheep (John 10.11–16; see Heb. 13.20; 1 Peter 2.25). Others, ordained and non-ordained, are called to provide care for the people of God, but the people remain God's sheep (John 21.15–17; 1 Peter 5.14). Through baptism, Christians are called to carry on the mission of Christ – by healing, guiding, sustaining and reconciling, as well as by feeding the hungry, sheltering the homeless, and working for peace and justice. Concretely, these modes of caring are seen in the Church's catechetical, liturgical, sacramental and social ministries. All these forms of pastoral care seek to promote full human and spiritual development and extend the compassionate reach of the good shepherd to both individuals and groups.

The essence of pastoral care is to continue the compassionate ministry of Jesus today. It consists in being a 'collaborator with Christ' (1 Cor. 3.9) in caring for the needs of people. By consenting to the call to be covenant partners with God who is labouring in all of creation for the good of humankind (Ignatius, *Spiritual Exercises* 236), Christians become the body of Christ and give visible form to the real, though imperceptible, presence of the risen Christ. As such, pastoral care is representational, a standing in place of Christ, wherever there is a cry for support, reassurance and guidance.

Embedded in the story of Jesus' dialogue with the Samaritan woman at the well (John 4.1–42) is the biblical insight that all ministry is a gift from God. The overall structure of the dialogue highlights that it is the Lord who supplies the labour, while others receive a gratuitous share in reaping the rewards. The story opens with Jesus and his disciples arriving at the well of Jacob near Sychar. Jesus sits down beside the well because he is weary (*kekopiakos*) from the journey (4.6). The Greek word for weary contains a root, *kop*, which has two different meanings. Besides meaning 'tired', it also denotes 'labour'. The *kop* root, with its second meaning, reappears in verse 38 to form a Semitic inclusion, a literary device serving like bookends that provides thematic unity to a passage. Here Jesus tells the apostles how blessed they are because 'I sent you to reap that for which you did not labour; others have laboured (*kekopiakasin*), and you have entered into their labour (*kopon*)'. Because they will harvest what they themselves did not sow, the disciples' involvement in apostolic work is a gift that Jesus bestows on them. Jesus is the one who is tired (*kekopiakos*) because he is the one who does all the work. Although they arrived with Jesus, the disciples immediately left the scene to go shopping and are noticeably absent for the whole time that Jesus struggled with the woman, finally bringing her to faith through painstaking and patient efforts. Only when all the work is done, do the disciples reappear.

To embody the presence of Jesus as pastoral ministers is to emulate his sensitivity and compassion for those in need. As with the Samaritan woman, Jesus perceived people and events in a way that issued forth in compassion. The plight of others always stirred Jesus' heart and moved him to reach out in healing and forgiving ways. Once a leper approached Jesus, begging to be cured (Mark 1.40–45). Jesus takes in the reality of this afflicted supplicant, paying close attention to his words and actions. Then, moved with compassion, he reaches out to touch the diseased person. Jesus' therapeutic touch issued forth from a compassionate heart. This episode exemplifies a threefold dynamic that characterizes many of Jesus' ministerial encounters: (1) Jesus is keenly aware of his interpersonal environment, sensitive to the needs of the people around him (contemplative perception); (2) he lets what he perceives stir him to compassion (empathic identification); (3) and moved by compassion, he reaches out to help (caring response). His caring outreach to this leper, ostracized from society on account of his ailment, was typical of Jesus. Other outcasts of his day – women, foreigners, tax collectors and prostitutes – also received compassion from Jesus, even as their religious leaders denied them access to the official channels of healing and reconciliation.

Besides the care of individuals and families, contemporary pastoral care responds to the needs of groups, such as youth, singles, the ageing, the poor and the oppressed. In its two accounts of the miracles of the multiplication of the loaves and fishes, Mark's Gospel illustrates Jesus' sensitive perception and compassionate response to group needs. In the second account (Mark 8.1–10), Jesus is moved to action by his perception of the crowd's hunger. Realizing that the great crowd that had gathered to hear his words was without food, Jesus expressed his concern: 'I feel sorry for all these people; they have been with me for three days now and have nothing to eat. If I send them off home hungry they will collapse on the way; some have come a great distance' (8.2–4).

In contrast, the first account (Mark 6.30–44) indicates that Jesus perceived a different need which, nonetheless, elicited the same compassionate response to the crowd. Here, Jesus is said to have acted because he perceived, not the physical hunger of the crowd for food, but the crowd's hunger for guidance and meaning. Jesus 'took pity on them because they were like sheep without a shepherd, and he set himself to teach them at some length' (Mark 6.34–35). While the two Marcan accounts attribute a different reason for Jesus' compassionate response to the crowd, they point unambiguously to the same sensitive quality of Jesus' perception of others and events. In both accounts, Jesus' ministerial outreach begins with a perception of others that is sufficiently sensitive to arouse feelings of compassionate concern. His penetrating perception of the crowd alerted him to people's physical need for nourishment, as well as to their spiritual need for knowledge and guidance.

The perception of Jesus is characterized by an empathic orientation to others and a broad understanding of their needs as human beings. The miracles of the multiplication of the loaves and fishes dramatize the reality of the incarnation. Christ's divinity is alluded to by his miraculous powers and his humanity is attested to by his grasp of human needs. The mystery of the incarnation celebrates the fact that God was not content to love humankind from a distance, but drew near to love humanity close-by. This divine love flows from an empathic understanding of people because the incarnation allowed God to perceive people and human events not only from a distant divine vantage point, but from the internal frame of reference of a fellow human being. His sensitive and compassionate solidarity with all humankind shaped his pastoral care of people. A spirituality of pastoral care invites people to minister as Jesus did.

In the context of this biblical understanding of the general nature of pastoral care, two specific forms stand out so prominently in modern times that they are often mistakenly identified as coextensive with all of pastoral care: pastoral counselling and pastoral care in hospitals. Both of these ministries have been significantly shaped and influenced by the social sciences, particularly psychology. While acknowledging the important contributions of psychology to pastoral care, some pastoral theologians are concerned that these two forms of pastoral care have so adopted psychological models that the spiritual dimension of pastoral care has been greatly eclipsed (Pattison, 1988; Borchert and Lester (eds), 1985). The modern pastoral care movement has also been criticized for its overemphasis on 'ratio-

technological methods and preoccupations' and its over-optimistic and over-serious desire to change the world and people for the better. People and the situations in which they find themselves, according to this critique, are not always appropriately seen as problems, but 'must ultimately be regarded as mysteries to be loved' (Pattison, 1988; Butler, 1999). In response to these concerns, there has been a call for 'a contemplative approach to pastoral care' (Butler, 1999) and 'revisioning the future of Spirit-centered pastoral care' (H. Clinebell in Borchert and Lester (eds), 1985).

Contemporary pastoral care theorists also emphasize the importance of distinguishing among spiritual direction, pastoral counselling and psychotherapy (Leech, 1989). As a form of pastoral care dating back to the monastic movement of the fourth century and traditionally called *cura animarum*, spiritual direction assists people with deepening their life of faith and union with God and helping them forge a stronger link between gospel values and daily life. Pastoral counselling, on the other hand, resembles psychotherapy in that it is a helping relationship concerned with assisting troubled individuals, couples and families resolve specific problems. What distinguishes pastoral counselling from secular therapy is the involvement of a minister or representative of the Church as the helping professional and the use of a religious framework for diagnosis and response. Besides identifying the psychological dynamics underlying conflicts and difficulties, pastoral counselling encourages people to understand and respond to their plight in terms of such religious categories as forgiveness, reconciliation, repentance, grace, conversion and trustful surrender to God.

See also **Spirituality, Psychology and Psychotherapy** (*essay*); **Compassion; Healing and Health; Ministry and Spirituality; Spiritual Direction.**

G. Borchert and A. Lester (eds), *Spiritual Dimensions of Pastoral Care*, Philadelphia, PA: The Westminster Press, 1985; S. Butler, *Caring Ministry: A Contemplative Approach to Pastoral Care*, New York: Continuum, 1999; C. Gerkin, *An Introduction to Pastoral Care*, Nashville, TN: Abingdon Press, 1997; K. Leech, *Spirituality and Pastoral Care*, Cambridge, MA: Cowley Publications, 1989; S. Pattison, *A Critique of Pastoral Care*, London: SCM Press, 1988.

WILKIE AU

Patience

see **Perseverance**

Patristic Spirituality

see **Early Christian Spirituality**

Pauline Spirituality

Central to Paul's spirituality was his conviction that God has raised Jesus from the dead as the new creation in person and the first fruits of a humanity transformed in his image (cf. 1 Cor. 15.20, 48f.; 2 Cor. 5.17; Rom. 8.29). 'For it is the God who said, "Let light shine out of darkness", who has shone in our hearts to give the light of the knowledge of the glory of God in the face of Jesus Christ' (2 Cor. 4.6). If, as most interpreters hold, this text is coloured by Paul's 'conversion' experience, we may say that this experience was the matrix of Paul's theology and spirituality.

Paul's conviction that the raising of Jesus was the eschatological act of the creator God instilled in him a profound sense that salvation was God's work through and through, a matter of sheer grace. The task of those called to salvation was freely to embrace God's gift.

To speak of salvation as the effect of grace is already to speak of the work of the Holy Spirit. Paul makes no distinction between his experience of Christ crucified and risen and his experience of the Spirit. It is the risen Christ who has become 'life-giving Spirit' (1 Cor. 15.45); and it is the Spirit of Christ that liberates believers from the old aeon of sin and death, reproduces in them the pattern of the crucified and risen one, and makes them, in him, children of God (Rom. 8.2, 12–17; 2 Cor. 3.18; Phil. 3.20f.).

This highlights two important aspects of Paul's spirituality: first, that it is the *risen* Christ who dominates Paul's religious psyche (not, for example, Christ's pre-existence and incarnation, as in the Fourth Gospel); and second, that the risen Christ is precisely the *crucified* one.

The antinomy between a 'theology of the cross' and a 'theology of glory', much exploited in Reformation polemics, is foreign to Paul; indeed, it does away with the central paradox of his spirituality. The cross is indeed central to Paul's thought, but to the extent that the resurrection also is, and vice versa. It was out of darkness that the creator God commanded light to shine, and out of weakness and shame that the redeemer God brought forth Easter. The paradox of power in weakness governs not only Paul's perception of God and of Christ, but also his attitude to life and his interpretation of particular life events (cf., e.g., 2 Cor. 1.8–10; 4.16–18; 11.9–10).

As Abraham's faith expressed itself in 'hope against hope' (Rom. 4.18), so, for Paul, Christian faith is always faith in the God who 'calls into being the things which are not', whether in creating the world, in raising Jesus from the dead or in 'justifying the ungodly' (cf. Rom. 4.5, 17, 24f.).

Already implicit in Paul's initial encounter with Christ is the intuition that the risen Christ is eschatological humankind ('adam') in person (2 Cor. 4.4, 6). He is the 'first fruits', the 'first-born among many brothers and sisters' (1 Cor. 15.20; Rom. 8.29). Humankind's destiny is co-involved with Christ's. This entails their being conformed to the pattern of his existence: suffering and dying with him, in order to enter into glory with him (Rom. 8.17). Paul chides the Corinthians for wanting to bypass the pain of it all (1 Cor. 4.8–13), and opposes their enthusiasm for 'the Spirit' in isolation from Christology and from the context of a community characterized by selfless love in imitation of the crucified (1 Cor. 12—14).

Paul pays little attention to the words, deeds and lifestyle of the historical Jesus or to the 'imitation of Christ' in anything like the sense of a Thomas à Kempis or even of the Gospels. When he speaks of imitating Christ, he means conforming one's actions to the self-giving of Christ in his death.

This was a matter not merely of moral conformity but of real participation. Paul expresses this in various ways: Christians have been 'baptized into' Christ's death, and 'buried with him' ('co buried', as Paul puts it); their adamitic nature has been 'co-crucified' with him; they will be 'united with the image' of his resurrection as they have been 'united with the image' of his death (Rom. 6.3–6). Paul's enigmatic phrase 'in Christ' probably refers to Christ as the field of divine power which permeates and governs the lives of those who submit to him (cf. Ziesler, 1990).

Christians are 'in Christ' in virtue of their solidarity as members of the Church. The Church (which for Paul was primarily the local community of Christians) was the 'body of Christ', the locus of mutual service in the Spirit and therefore the manifestation of Christ's presence in the world. Paul's spirituality had its context in the community of believers and was never individualistic.

At the heart of Paul's spirituality is love. However, Paul hardly ever speaks of Christians loving God or Christ. He speaks rather of God and Christ loving Christians and of Christians loving others (especially fellow Christians: cf. Gal. 6.10). The love that is active in the community is, as it were, the reverberation of God's love for us in Christ, 'poured out in our hearts by the Holy Spirit' (Rom. 5.5). The Christian's love for others is the love with which God loves (cf.

Nygren, 1982). Of course, genuine neighbour love bears all the characteristics of Christ crucified, for it derives from and mirrors God's love (1 Cor. 13; Rom. 5.5–8).

In contrast to the 'gnosticizing' Corinthians of 1 Corinthians, and to all dualistically minded Christians ever since, Paul thought holistically. He did not think that salvation embraced only some 'higher' dimension of the human being. The human being was by definition embodied, and salvation entailed the resurrection of the body (1 Cor. 15). The body was the locus of salvation just as palpably as it was the medium of sexual intercourse (1 Cor. 6.12–17).

It goes without saying that the body that Paul thought constituted the locus of salvation was the body liberated from sin, and transformed (Rom. 8.23; Phil. 3.21; 1 Cor. 15.47–55). However, Paul was no less insistent that it remained the *body*, which in this life, in its very physicality, is the instrument of a person's disobedience or obedience (Rom. 6.16–19). Paul exhorts Christians to offer their bodies (themselves) as a 'sacrifice that is living, consecrated, and pleasing to God'. This is their *logike latreia*, their 'existential cult' (Rom. 12.1–2; 1 Cor. 6.20). Thus Paul 'desacralizes' cult by making the arduous business of ordinariness the 'sacred space' of Christian worship.

It is to be noted, however, that Paul, along with other New Testament writers, had no notion that the Christian's 'mundane worship' included commitment to changing unjust social and political structures: this, no doubt, on the principle that when the ship is sinking no one sets about restructuring the ballroom. For 'the shape of this world is on its way out' (1 Cor. 7.31).

At another extreme, Paul had no notion that holiness had to do with methodologies of prayer or 'spiritual exercises' beloved of later spiritual masters. Of course, individual and communal prayer (of thanksgiving and praise, petition and intercession) was a prominent aspect of Christian living for Paul, but he never regarded it as the object of expertise or as a path to holiness. Holiness, for Paul, meant exhibiting in the context of one's social circumstances the 'fruit of the Spirit', of which the primary manifestation was a cruciform love.

Paul's spirituality is also, and fundamentally, a missionary spirituality. He did 'everything because of the gospel (his missionary task)' (1 Cor. 9.23). His missionary work involved immense hardships, which he rarely mentions, and then only allusively or with embarrassment. He 'died daily' through such hardships (1 Cor. 15.31; cf. 2 Cor. 11.26f.).

Paul's 'dying daily' in pursuit of his mission was his 'asceticism'. He does not appear to have had any appetite for ascetical practices (even if later ascetics were much taken by his 'athletic metaphors and especially by his 'pommelling his body' (1 Cor. 9.2), as they understood that phrase); and he worried about Christians who sought to impose or encourage a particular lifestyle for ascetical reasons (1 Cor. 7). Whatever features early Christianity had in common with the Qumran sectarians, an ascetical regime was not one of them.

Characteristic of Paul's spirituality is his yearning for the future consummation, when 'we shall be with the Lord for ever' (1 Thess. 4.17; cf. Phil. 1.21ff.), when Christ 'will change our lowly body to be like his glorious body' (Phil. 3.21), and when, finally, 'God will be all in all' (1 Cor. 15.28). This yearning flowed from his conviction that the risen Christ is the first-fruits of the imminent eschatological realization of God's plan for creation. Hence the prominence his epistles give to the theme of 'hope' (classic texts are Rom. 5.1–11 and 8.18–39), by which he means looking forward with complete assurance to the inevitable and now imminent completion of God's plan of salvation. Hope, for Paul, is the certitude of faith turned to the future. As such, it is a hope that is exultant even in the midst of ongoing tribulations (Rom. 5.3ff.; 8.24–39).

For Paul, eschatological fulfilment is 'already and not yet'. Whereas this paradox reflects a tension which is entirely positive in Paul, for his perspective was theocentric and cosmic, his interpreters in the West reapplied it to the condition of the individual Christian, which interested them more (cf. Stendahl's 'introspective conscience of the West'). Luther's formulation *simul justus et peccator* (the Christian is 'at one and the same time righteous and sinful', by which Luther meant wholly righteous and radically sinful), characterized the ethos and spirituality of the Lutheran tradition. Catholics have understood the element of truth in Luther's formulation rather more prosaically.

One's view of these matters will depend to a large extent on one's interpretation of Rom. 7.14–25 (the passage that prompted Luther's formulation). Is Paul here really describing *Christian* experience, as Luther supposed? Or is he saying (perhaps unrealistically) that Christians have been delivered from the plight described in Rom. 7.14–25, and now belong squarely in Rom. 8.1–11? And is it perhaps true that (as one Lutheran interpreter has suggested) whereas Luther was wrong to read Rom. 7.14–25 as referring to Christian experience, his own understanding of Christian experience was more realistic than Paul's? One's answers to these questions will doubtless affect how one hears the timbre of Paul's spirituality.

James D. G. Dunn, *The Theology of Paul the Apostle*, Edinburgh: T & T Clark, 1998; Gordon D. Fee, *Paul, the Spirit and the People of God*, Peabody, MA: Hendrickson Publishers, 1996; Michael J. Gorman, *Cruciformity: Paul's Narrative Spirituality of the Cross*, Grand Rapids, MI: Eerdmans, 2001; Richard N. Longenecker (ed.), *The Road From Damascus: The Impact of Paul's Conversion on his Life, Thought and Ministry*, Grand Rapids, MI: Eerdmans, 1997; Anders Nygren, *Agape and Eros* [1930–36], trans. Philip S. Watson, London: SPCK, 1982; Krister Stendahl, *Paul among Jews and Gentiles and Other Essays*, Philadelphia: Fortress Press, 1976; John Ziesler, *Pauline Christianity*, Oxford: Oxford University Press, rev. edn. 1990.

TOM DEIDUN

Peace

It is common to divide the concept of peace into two if not three types of peace. The first type is *pax*, the absence of violence or conflict. Sometimes described as 'negative peace', it is the absence of war. When used of individuals it means an absence of dissention or disturbance. However, when related to the concept of the *Pax Romana*, the peace brought about by the Roman Empire, it takes on more positive connotations, because in that context the absence of conflict was the basis of prosperity, the expression of the rule of law and the flourishing of Roman society throughout the Empire.

Whether understood negatively or positively, the concept of *pax* is not a popular one in Christian thought, though in practice in Christian history it was a much desired state of affairs, enabling the spread of the Christian Church. On the other hand, it will be realized quickly that this form of peace is compatible with dictatorship, oppression and exploitation of human beings, all of which do little for the flourishing of the human spirit, which is essential for any true spirituality.

The second type of peace is *shalom*. This is the dominant concept of peace in Christian thought and spirituality. It is a Hebrew word, expressing a deeper, richer and altogether more positive concept of peace. The root meaning of the word *shalom* means 'whole', and 'it indicates well being in its fullness, spiritual harmony and physical health; material prosperity untouched by violence or misfortune'.

Unlike *pax*, it is not simply a social concept, nor is it simply a personal state. It denotes an integration of all dimensions of personal and social activity, and indicates a harmony both within the individual and in that person's relationship with society. In the Old Testament it is a way of greeting and offering acceptance to the other: 'Peace be to you; do not fear, you shall not die' (Judg. 6.23); 'Peace be to you, and peace be to your house, and peace be to all that you have' (1 Sam. 25.6). In similar vein 'Go in peace' is a valediction rich in meaning.

This deeper meaning of peace was adopted into early Christian thought. Jesus' birth is a proclamation of peace among those with whom God is well pleased (Luke 2.14). In his teaching, 'peacemakers', that is, those who create the conditions of peace, are described as 'blessed' (Matt. 5.9), and after his resurrection he greets his disciples with the words 'Peace be with you' (Luke 24.36; John 20.19). St Paul describes his message as the gospel of peace (Eph. 6.15).

Some writers identify a third form of peace in Christian thought, that of 'inner peace' – the sense of inner calm, well-being and serenity derived from accepting and internalizing the peace of God, which is the foundation of a true spirituality. Others see it as simply the personal dimension of the wider concept of *shalom* already mentioned.

While *shalom* is a deeply religious concept, it is important not to set it in opposition to the concept of *pax*. Implicit in much of St Paul's and other early Christian theologians' attitude to the state is the desirability of the *pax* that only the civil authorities could establish as a prerequisite for the flourishing of *shalom*.

Shalom expresses a quality of relationship with God, with one's self and with others. It leads inextricably to justice, which is a way of being in right relationship with others. It is this integration of the inner life with our social existence that makes *shalom* such a powerful basis for Christian spirituality. Seeking the integration of one's inner life into the mind of God is the basis of penance – the sacrament of reconciliation – reconciliation with God, with one's self and with one's neighbour. From this secure basis the Christian can begin to live truly 'in peace' and enjoy the blessings of God's peace, 'which passes all understanding'.

See also **Ecumenical Spirituality; Nonviolence; Reconciliation.**

Michel Desjardins, *Peace, Violence and the New Testament*, Sheffield: Sheffield Academic Press, 1997; Ulrich Duchrow and Gerhard Liedke, *Shalom: Biblical Perspectives on Creation, Justice and Peace*, Geneva: World Council of Churches, 1989.

KENNETH KEARON

Pelagianism

Traditionally, an early fifth-century heresy that humans can save themselves without 'grace' and did not inherit 'original sin'; therefore, infant baptism is unnecessary, and salvation comes from works. In this caricature it became *the* Western heresy, which, through forcing writers on the Christian life to use a set of binary oppositions (work/grace, sin/redemption, freedom/determinism), has had a distorting influence upon Western spirituality. We can view it historically as one attempt, among others at the time, at Christian self-understanding, where it represents the tendency which stresses human responsibility to take the demands of discipleship seriously and build upon them a lifestyle.

The original aims of the Pelagian group were to promote asceticism and to defend the choice of those who adopted monastic life. In this they opposed the fatalism of late antiquity, as well as other Christians who held that monastic life was no better spiritually than other forms of life: grace was given equally and not enlarged by good works nor diminished by sin. Pelagius preached taking the gospel's demands seriously in lifestyle, and that that adherence mattered for eternity. He preached this not in terms of positive merit, but of culpability: you knew the law, you could have done so but did not, hence you can expect the rich man's reward (Luke 16.19–31). (Recent interest in Pelagianism as a 'lost wisdom' contrasting a human optimism against Augustine's 'pessimism' is historically poorly founded.) Therefore, a sinless life is possible, and it is abhorrent to imagine God imposing impossible demands. In developing this theme it became necessary to hold that humans are innately free to choose their path; the divine side of the relationship being revealing the law and exemplifying it in Jesus. So notions that specific divine gifts were needed to empower a Christian's choice equalled denying freedom, while making nonsense of God as law-giver and judge: could a just God punish for what is impossible without his grace? What God gives (e.g. the example of Christ's life) are external helps to a person choosing to inherit eternal life (cf. Luke 18.18–25).

Other Pelagians looked at the notion of sinfulness inherited from Adam as interpreted from Rom. 5: Adam's disobedience had rendered all 'his seed' flawed, along with his crime's penalty – death (the theory of 'traducianism': Adam's sin is *transmitted* in the act of human generation). Pelagians rejected traducianism as unworthy: it would make God the author of crimes and the persecutor of the newborn. Replying to this, Augustine formulated his understanding of 'original sin' and asked whether or not an infant could gain any benefit from baptism? Baptism made no difference to their salvation or ability to follow the commandments; for infants it merely recognized their entry into the kingdom. Baptism for adults did, however, remove the guilt of their culpable crimes, but Adam's sin was personal to him: God could not act justly yet punish others for his crime. Death is simply a consequence of nature. This was then taken to an extreme where redemption is not a new life, but a life of good choices, while prayer for others is futile: they themselves must choose the good.

The 'orthodox' party was similarly extreme tending to see original sin not as explaining the need for a saviour and the existential condition where simply choosing the good is never that simple (see Rom. 7.19), but as the human morass devoid of ability to do the good without grace. This led many afterwards to recoil from both extremes formulating a theology combining human responsibility with human need. However, such attempts to link extremes, though continually required, were flawed and unsatisfactory. The long-term legacy in Latin spirituality was an inability to create an adequate theology of work; a suspicion of praising human abilities and creativity; a fear of human nature where it touched sexuality (where the transmission of Adam's guilt occurred); and a corresponding need to exempt aspects of the Christian world from that depravity while avoiding the sound of Pelagianism (e.g. the cult of Mary's 'graces' and the later notion of her 'immaculate conception'). The nature of the human–divine relationship was central to the fifth-century disputes: one tendency was to emphasize God equally loving all; another the place of effort; another the need for divine aid to act rightly; with each confident that the relationship could be described. So long as the topic was hedged around with the ancient anathemas, a more rounded approach to the topic could not emerge, hence theology oscillated between the apparent polarities of 'grace'/'work', while the dispute's chronic recurrence is a warning that descriptions of that relationship, in effect spiritualities, should be no less complex than those involved in the relationship.

See also Asceticism; Augustinian Spirituality; Baptism; Calvinist Spirituality; Early Christian Spirituality; Freedom; Grace; Lutheran Spirituality; Monasticism; Work.

Gerald Bonner, 'Pelagianism' in Trevor A. Hart (ed.), *The Dictionary of Historical Theology*, Carlisle: Paternoster Press, 2000, pp. 422–4; Robert F. Evans, *Pelagius: Inquiries and Reappraisals*, London: Adam & Charles Black, 1968; V. Grossi, 'Pelagius – Pelagians – Pelagianism' in Angelo Di Berardino (ed.), *Encyclopedia of the Early Church*, Cambridge: James Clarke & Co., 1992, vol. 2, pp. 665–6; Theodore de Bruyn (trans.), *Pelagius's Commentary on St Paul's Letter to the Romans*, Oxford: Oxford University Press, 1993; Robert F. Evans (trans.), *Four Letters of Pelagius*, London: Adam & Charles Black, 1968; B. R. Rees, *Pelagius: A Reluctant Heretic*, Woodbridge: The Boydell Press, 1988; Eugene TeSelle, 'Pelagius, Pelagianism' in Allan D. Fitzgerald (ed.), *Augustine through the Ages: An Encyclopedia*, Grand Rapids, MI: Eerdmans, 1999, pp. 633–40.

THOMAS O'LOUGHLIN

Penitence

Penitence (Lat. *paenitentia*) is a dimension of conversion corresponding to the Greek idea of *metanoia*, indicating a change of mind or heart. From the same Latin word is derived the word penance which corresponds to the actions which bring about the conversion of heart or flow from the interior conversion. An alternate spelling in Latin is *poenitentia*, which St Isidore of Seville in his *Etymologies* took to mean the punishment (*poena*) attached to the sins that we commit. Other terms associated with penitence and which establish the interior dimension of this term are as follows: contrition, compunction, repentance, remorse; regret, self-reproach, self-reproof, self-accusation, self-condemnation, self-humiliation; stings of conscience, pangs of conscience, qualms of conscience, prickings of conscience, twinge of conscience, twitch of conscience, touch of conscience, and voice of conscience. All these terms underscore the interior quality of penitence whereas penance indicates the exteriorization of the interior attitude of penitence and is associated with the sacrament of confession or penance. Confession links penitence with the acknowledgement of sins while penance is the making of satisfaction for sins committed.

Spiritual direction has often emphasized penitence as sorrow or contrition for one's sins, which leads to the effort to atone for sin, associated with expiation, satisfaction or reparation. In an attempt to judge the quality of interior sorrow, a distinction is made between contrition (true sorrow because sin offends God) – otherwise known as perfect contrition – and attrition (sorrow as a result of fear of punishment) – otherwise known as imperfect contrition. In either case, it is the attitude of the heart and not merely the exterior actions that constitute penitence.

Spirituality links penitence with the virtues of justice and charity. Penitence motivated by justice regards what is due to God and God's punishment, whereas motivated by charity it looks to the human dimension toward self and others. Penitence and penance should not be opposed. The attitude leads to works and the works prepare one for the interior disposition. Works of penitence ideally should lead to self-purification and not self-punishment to satisfy God's justice. Central to the theme of penitence is the call to conversion, a theme found prominently in the sacred Scriptures. Essential to Jesus' message is the call to repentance and reform (Matt. 4.17; Mark 1.15; Luke 5.32; 13.5). John the Baptist had already signalled the clarion call to conversion, which Jesus adopted as vitally important to his message. The apostles in turn carried on the mission of reconciliation, which they inherited from Christ (Acts 2.38).

Spiritual growth therefore requires a sensibility regarding sin, not so much as misdeeds but as the rupture or straining of our relationship with God, neighbour and self. Looking at the other side of the coin, one becomes aware of the love of God and relationship with others. Penitence as a virtue leads to the healing of relationships, and not to shame, meaningless fear or scrupulosity. Penitence understood in its most positive sense is not so much a making of amends or a form of self-punishment, but an acceptance of the responsibilities of being Christian and the call to holiness. It should not lead to works righteousness, an idea fought vehemently by the Reformers, but to a heart open to God. For this reason, a key aspect of penitence is compunction of the heart.

Compunction (Lat. *compunctio*, from *cumpungere*, 'to puncture with') is found in the works of the Fathers of the Church in a number of different patterns, for example compunction of fear, compunction of desire and compunction of the heart. In its original profane use, the word is a medical term, indicating attacks of physical pain. The first ecclesiastical usage toward the end of the second century CE transposes the meaning to signify pain of the spirit, a suffering due to the actual existence of sin and human concupiscence, and as a result of our desire for God. The theological connotation is closely parallel to the biblical idea of *metanoia*, rendered in English as penitence.

In the Scriptures the idea of compunction corresponds to the biblical notion of *katánuxeis*, from the two Hebrew words *tar'élâ* (Ps. 60.5) and *tardémâ* (Isa. 29.10), indicating a lethargic inebriation resulting in spiritual blindness. In the New Testament, the Pentecost speech of Peter (Acts 2.37) employs the notion meaning the supernatural shock which leads to conversion, translated in the Vulgate as *compuncti sunt corde*. To this extent, the most common use associates the idea of compunction with a change of heart.

St Anselm of Canterbury in his *Prayers* proceeded to the awesome fact that God, who knows human beings as they really are, is ever faithful. The love of God pierces the heart (compunction) leading Anselm to consider the cross and passion of Christ as the cost of the faithfulness and love of God for humanity. Assimilated to the cross, the one who prays is involved with the reconciliation of God in Christ. The 'Prayer to Christ' is a clear example of this: 'Why, O my soul, were you not there to be pierced by a sword of bitter sorrow when you could not bear the piercing of the side of your Saviour with a lance? Why could you not bear to see the nails violate the hands and feet of your Creator? Why did you not see with horror the blood that poured out of the side of your Redeemer? Why were you not drunk with bitter tears when they gave him bitter gall to drink?'

See also **Practice, Spiritual; Reconciliation.**

The Prayers and Meditations of St Anselm, trans. Benedicta Ward, Harmondsworth: Penguin Books, 1973, p. 95 (set as verse); David Coffey, *The Sacrament of Reconciliation*, Collegeville, MN: The Liturgical Press, 2001; James Dallen, *The Reconciling Community: The Rite of Penance*, Collegeville, MN: Pueblo, 1986; Michael Driscoll, *Alcuin et la pénitence à l'époque carolingienne*, Liturgiewissenschaftliche Quellen und Forschungen 81, Münster: Aschendorff Verlag, 1999; John Paul II, *Apostolic Exhortation, Penance and Reconciliation in the Mission of the Church*, Synod of Bishops, Rome, 1983, Washington, DC: National Conference of Catholic Bishops, 1984; Robert Kennedy, *Reconciliation: The Continuing Agenda*, Collegeville, MN: The Liturgical Press, 1987.

MICHAEL S. DRISCOLL

Pentecostal Spirituality

Pentecostal spirituality emphasizes a deep, sustainable piety that focuses on divine immanence, a reality that can be the experience of every individual, as was witnessed on the first day of Pentecost in the Acts of the Apostles. This spirituality exercises the totality of human existence and affects one's beliefs, convictions, emotions, thought life and behaviour with regards to God. In Classical Pentecostalism, the emphasis of this spirituality is affirmed through the 'giftings of the Spirit' and the subjective religious experience of 'baptism in the Spirit', all experiences which are understood as normative in the life and work of Pentecostal churches. Classical Pentecostalism owes a lot of its theology and practice to Wesleyan Methodism and the later Holiness Movement which passed on its emotional fervour, Armenian theology, biblical fundamentalism and belief in the 'Second Blessing' of 'entire sanctification' to the Pentecostal movement. In the United States and the United Kingdom as well as the Caribbean, most of the beliefs and spirituality of their Pentecostalism has been as a result of the founder of modern-day Pentecostals, William J. Seymour. Walter Hollenweger (Jones, 1986, pp. 551–2) lists five characteristic features of Pentecostal spirituality: an emphasis on the oral aspect of liturgy, theology and witness cast in narrative form; maximum participation at the levels of reflection, prayer and decision-making; and therefore a form of community which is reconciling; inclusion of dream and vision into personal and public forms of spirituality, so that the dreams function as kinds of icons of the individual and collective, and finally, an understanding of the body/mind relationship which is informed by experiences of correspondence between body and mind.

The emphasis of 'giftings of the Spirit' is very much about charismatic activity. Gifts continue, as they have historically, to distinguish Pentecostal ritual from other Christian liturgies and to serve as a benchmark of its overall spirituality. The manifestation of these gifts plays a central role in the rituals and congregational lives of Pentecostal churches. Gifts symbolize various categories of meaning, namely, Spirit baptism, empowerment and edification.

Although the central Christian message is Jesus Christ, what is critical for the Pentecostal is the personal and direct awareness of and experiencing of the Holy Spirit. The concern is not the exposure as such, but the Holy Spirit who is said to be experienced personally and directly. The Christian life is a matter of the experienced presence and power of the Holy Spirit.

Spirit baptism. Pentecostal spirituality focuses on the coming of the Holy Spirit as a continuing event, because the event recorded at Pentecost in Acts 1 and 2 was not a 'once-for-all event' but it is to be experienced today. This continuing event is the 'baptism in the Holy Spirit'. Other terms include ideas of the Spirit falling upon or coming upon a person who is then 'filled with' or 'receives' the Holy Spirit. Baptism of the Spirit, however, is the term most often used because it expresses for the Pentecostal two things. First is the *totality* of the event; viewing baptism as immersion suggests that the entire person is totally submerged in, and activated by the Holy Spirit. Second is the *uniqueness* of the event: like baptism in water it represents a decisive, therefore unrepeatable experience in the Christian life.

Spirit baptism confirms the presence of the Spirit in the believer's life and an empowerment or gifting. According to this view, speaking in tongues is the initial evidence of the baptism of the Spirit. After this initial event, Spirit baptism continues as the process popularly called the 'spirit-filled life'. The process includes an openness to the Spirit's gifts and a willingness by the believer to operate with these gifts for the edification of the body of Christ. Ideologically, Classical Pentecostalism maintains that Spirit baptism is a doorway into the diverse area of the experience and practice of charismata.

Empowerment. Spirit baptism is more than speaking in tongues and 'experiencing the presence of the Spirit'. This baptism symbolizes an infusion of the divine, a union, with a resulting gifting with power. Pentecostals expect to be 'filled' like the earlier apostles to do the work of God, and like the earlier apostles before Pentecost, they acknowledge the need for empowerment. Spirit baptism, then, symbolizes an ongoing experience of the Spirit, that is, an empowering experience that facilitates and supports the believer in his or her personal life and in serving God and humanity. Although many Pentecostals may expect the sign of tongues to accompany this experience, they do not reduce Spirit baptism to glossalalia. Therefore, while tongues may be understood as symbolizing prayer to and presence of the divine, Spirit baptism as a gift represents the power and empowerment of the Spirit in the Pentecostal's spirituality.

Edification. The practice of gifts reveals that the gifts function as symbols not only of empowerment but of edification. This practice is often referred to as 'ministry,' which implies a focusing outwards to members of the faith community, an intention to fortify and renew, to edify the saints. It follows that Pentecostals believe that God grants gifts to individual believers for the benefit of the whole, that the Church would be strengthened and built up.

Finally, a word on worship, whose practice is at the heart of Pentecostal spirituality. Worship is understood as a way of life, so it is not confined to church services; as the entire service at the church meeting and as a special part of the service within the church meeting. Worship is an encounter with God, in which there is genuine communication between the human and the divine. Therefore a sense of expectancy shapes worship that is both corporate and individualistic. In worship God is seen as involved and as an observer. God is the observer and the congregation performs their praises to God who is immanent.

See also **Baptism; Charismatic Spirituality; Spirit, Holy.**

P. Hills Collins, *Black Feminist Thought, Knowledge, Consciousness, and the Politics of Empowerment*, London: Routledge, 1990; W. Hollenweger, *The Pentecostals*, London: SCM Press, 1972; C. Jones, G. Wainwright and E. Yarnold (eds), *The Study of Spirituality*, London: SPCK, 1986; Steven Land, *A Passion for the Kingdom*, Sheffield: Sheffield Academic Press, 1993; I. MacRobert, *The Black Roots and White Racism of Early Pentecostalism in the USA*, London: Macmillan Press, 1988.

GARNET PARRIS

Perfection

see Journey, Spiritual

Perseverance

Christian moral treatises invariably define perseverance or 'patient endurance' as a particular form of the classical virtue of fortitude. However, the biblical and early Christian use of this term is more carefully nuanced than this definition suggests. In the Scriptures the term 'perseverance' (*hypomone*) has two ranges of meaning. In the Old Testament it is linked to hope and trust in God. In the Septuagint (Greek translation of the Old Testament) *hypomone* is patient waiting, hopeful reliance on the God who alone can act to save his people. It thus contrasts sharply with the Greek understanding of *hypomone* as a courageous virtue summoned from within the self, manifested in courageous resistance. In the Stoic philosophical tradition perseverance comes wholly from within; the emphasis is on the inner strength of the virtuous soul. In the Old Testament perseverance is directed wholly outside the self towards the strength of God. In the New Testament perseverance occasionally describes patient waiting on God (2 Thess. 3.5; Rev. 1.9); but it is more commonly used in the sense of standing fast, patiently 'holding out' in the face of opposition or persecution. This power of resistance does not come from within; rather it is a gift from God (Col. 1.11; Rom. 15.5).

In Christian spiritual writings the term 'perseverance' comes to include elements from both the classical and biblical traditions. It particularly highlights the continuous, unrelenting nature of the struggle against sin in the face of opposition: 'He who perseveres (*hypomeinas*) to the end shall be saved' (Matt. 10.22). In the gospel Christ particularly encourages perseverance in spite of persecution (Matt. 5.10–12), in prayer (Luke 18.1–8), and in the service of God (Luke 12.37–38). Christ's passion and death afford a model of what would later be called 'final perseverance', that persistence in faith and grace until the moment of death that Thomas Aquinas defines as 'abiding in good until the end of life' (*ST* 1a2ae.109.10). The last acts of Christ on the cross, forgiveness and prayer for enemies, provide an example of perseverance that was taken up by the early Christian martyrs; whose judicial death attested to their own profession of faith and who often, in imitation of Christ, prayed for their persecutors as they died.

Perseverance would thus appear to have much in common with the concept of 'spiritual warfare', which also emphasizes that the battle against temptation is ongoing throughout life. However, unlike the aggressive military metaphor of combat, perseverance exemplifies the teaching and example of Christ himself, who (with the exception of the ambiguous incident of the cleansing of the Temple) never employed violence against his human enemies, and forbade his disciples to fight on his behalf. Indeed, one of the most beautiful visual depictions of perseverance is found in late medieval illuminations of the arrest in the garden, where Christ stands serene amid swirling violence; arrested, betrayed, he nevertheless extends his hand to heal the servant attacked by Peter. This visual depiction of enduring compassion also expresses the insight that perseverance is not merely a passive virtue, the simple 'maintenance' of faith or charity despite exhaustion or opposition. Rather, Christian perseverance means persevering in 'doing good', in proclaiming and acting in accordance with the gospel, even in the face of threat or fatigue. And in this sense it can also be distinguished from 'spiritual warfare': the goal is not only to overcome temptation and confute the tempter; perseverance implies continuing to pray and to act in accordance with the gospel in the very presence of the enemy.

G. Kittel (ed.), *Theological Dictionary of the New Testament*, 'hypomenō', vol. 4, pp. 581–8, Grand Rapids, MI: Eerdmans, 1967; J. Pieper, *The Four Cardinal Virtues: Prudence, Justice, Fortitude, Temperance*, New York: Harcourt, Brace & World 1965; Thomas Aquinas, *Summa Theologiae*, 2a2ae.126.

LUKE DYSINGER

Person

Christian spirituality is concerned with a God who changes human beings. Central, therefore, though the category of 'human person' must be to Christian spirituality, its definitions are necessarily fluid. Christianity is defined by its understandings of God and Christ. What it is to be a Christian person is an adventure, a matter of gradual discovery as we engage the Christian tradition. 'We are God's children now'; we know we are being transformed into the likeness of Christ, but what this amounts to 'has not yet been revealed' (1 John 3.2).

Christian teaching about the human person is therefore a matter of keeping questions open rather than a set of answers, which by their nature will be premature. Christianity began with an experience of Christ's resurrection, a sense that the whole human condition had begun to be transformed. The sheer wonder of the experience generates speculation: if Christianity transforms us in *this* kind of way, then our new awareness drives us to reimagine our whole self-understanding, past, present and future. If Christ's resurrection transforms the whole human race, then we are driven to speculate about what must have happened for such transformation to be necessary, or even possible. It is from that train of thought, rather than from any special revelation about palaeontology, that a doctrine of original sin arises – and the question is complicated, rather than removed, by modern scientific discoveries regarding evolution. Moreover, if things went so disastrously wrong, how does that calamity relate to the divine purpose for humanity in creation (humanity as the image of God, whatever that means)? If the new life in Christ is definitive, what will it mean for us to survive death, and just how will this occur? How does our experience of freedom relate to the divine sovereignty?

Such questions lead Christian thinkers down a variety of paths, not necessarily theoretically compatible with each other. Resolutions of the issues about grace and freedom vary between strong doctrines of the bondage of the will and more or less coherent attempts to articulate a real sense in which we remain free under grace. For its part, the question about salvation and creation provokes a spectrum of responses varying from a heavy stress on God's action in Christ somehow supplanting the initial creation to optimistic assertions of an original blessing given within the creation from the beginning. Wisdom depends on understanding such doctrines in connection with the fundamental New Testament experience that led to them – just as the metaphors used by the participants in any deep relationship can be thoroughly misleading if not understood as expressive of *this* particular relationship. Moreover, it is the questions which the experience generates that are the primary bearers of truth and insight, rather than any particular answers we might be inclined to give. Beliefs in, say, the soul continuing to exist after death in separation from the body, are held aright only in tension with an awareness that they emerge from a question that might be answered otherwise. Moreover, the changes characteristic in spiritual growth may often be linked with an exploration of theological options previously overlooked. Thérèse of Lisieux, for example, strikingly echoes Lutheran concerns; and even Melanchthon, let alone later Protestant figures, modified Luther's positions on faith and works.

Christianity does not, of course, exist in isolation. Its contributions enrich and complicate wider discussions and uncertainties about what it is to be human. The main issues in a Christian account of the human person in large part reflect discussions conducted within Western culture more generally. Christianity's belief in some kind of life after death, as well as other doctrines mentioning 'the soul', feed into long-standing, inconclusive philosophical discussions regarding the nature of human consciousness and its possible independence of our bodies, discussions which have recently taken a new turn with the development of neuroscience and of artificial intelligence. Equally contested is the relationship between the individual and society. Much classical Christian theology couches its discussion in terms of the individual and his or her salvation. But a good case can be made for saying that to be personal is necessarily to be interpersonal. If this is so, salvation must be a corporate affair. There are more recent questions, too, about the role of gender, and of ideological distortion. Arguably, the mainstream theological tradition has been shaped by the privileged and powerful, and does not incorporate the wisdom that can be learnt only from the experience of the marginalized. Perhaps our theological categories require thoroughgoing reform.

Neither Western culture in general, nor the Christian Churches in particular, have come to any stable consensus on such issues as these. Nor is there any particular resolution given in Christian revelation. Regarding human nature, the student of Christian spirituality needs to be aware of the tradition's fundamental pluralism and open-endedness. More so than in other branches of theology, it is always a mistake to think that there is only one possible Christian theology of the human. *Imago dei* is an evocative formula that gives Christian theologians wide room to play. It provides venerable biblical association for indefinitely many attempts to conceive the resemblance, and for the whole spectrum of positions balancing resemblance and difference.

The term 'person' is also used to denote the threeness in Christianity's conception of God. Contemporary theologians are divided regarding the advisability of postulating some commonality between the ordinary sense of the word, which probably developed fully only in modernity, and this ancient, technical usage. For both Barth and Rahner, the formula 'three persons in one God' may be too venerable to be abandoned, but it gives the misleading impression that Christianity believes in three Gods. Other modern theologians like to speculate on the divine Persons' communion as a model for human and ecclesial relationships.

See also Spirituality and Theology (essay); Body and Spirituality; Sexuality; Trinity and Spirituality.

David Cairns, The Image of God in Man, London: Fontana, 1973 [1953]; Sarah Coakley, Powers and Submissions: Spirituality, Philosophy and Gender, Oxford: Blackwell, 2002; Roger D. Haight, The Experience and Language of Grace, New York: Paulist Press, 1979; Daphne Hampson, Christian Contradictions: The Structures of Lutheran and Catholic Thought, Cambridge: Cambridge University Press, 2001; Hans Küng, Justification: The Doctrine of Karl Barth and a Catholic Reflection, London: Burns & Oates, 1981 [1958]; Wolfhart Pannenberg, Anthropology in Theological Perspective, Edinburgh: T & T Clark, 1983; Karl Rahner, 'Nature and grace', and 'The hermeneutics of eschatological assertions' in Theological Investigations, 4, London: Darton, Longman & Todd, 1966 [1960], pp. 165–88, 323–46; Josef Ratzinger, Eschatology: Death and Eternal Life, Washington, DC: CUA Press, 1988 [1976].

PHILIP ENDEAN

Petition

see Intercession

Philokalia

1. Philokalic literature. The term 'Philokalia' (a Greek word, signifying 'the love of things (good or beautiful)' is normally used to describe a collection of texts on prayer written between the fourth and the fifteenth centuries by authors of spiritual classics in the Eastern Church. From as early as the fourth century, it came to be adopted as a technical term referring to an anthology of spiritual writings. Thus, Basil the Great and Gregory the Theologian were the first to employ this name for their selections in theology, spirituality and prayer from the works by Origen of Alexandria, which they compiled around the year 360.

Under the same title of Philokalia, two Greek monks and theologians in the eighteenth century, Nikodimos of Mount Athos (1749–1809) and Makarios (Notaras) of Corinth (1731–1805), compiled a similar selection of monastic and ascetic texts. It is the beauty of and love for truth that inspired the editors of this anthology as they chose certain specific texts, which would direct readers through the spiritual stages of purification, illumination and perfection. The authors of this particular collection included such spiritual masters as Antony the Great, Evagrius of Pontus, Maximus the Theologian, John of Damascus, Symeon the New Theologian and Gregory Palamas. All of the texts in the original Philokalia were in Greek. The only Western writer included was John Cassian, whose works had already been translated into Greek during the Byzantine period.

The texts of The Philokalia provide guidelines to and principles of the way of contemplation – 'a mystical school of inward prayer', as Nikodimos himself describes its purpose. It charts a spiritual pathway that leads – through a labyrinth of worldly temptations – to the centre of the heart through the practice of hesychia, namely inward silence and stillness.

2. The editors of the text. The humble editors of The Philokalia were an important and influential part of a spiritual renewal that took place within the Orthodox Church in Greece during the eighteenth century. Makarios was a traditionalist bishop, faithful to the canonical rules and liturgical rituals of the Eastern Church. Nikodimos was well educated and highly intelligent, endowed with a photographic memory. At an early age, Nikodimos encountered three monks from Mount Athos, who introduced him to the traditions and practices of the Holy Mountain as well as to Makarios of Corinth. A prolific author of over one hundred titles, Nikodimos settled on Mount Athos in 1775, spending most of his time in hermitages scattered throughout the renowned and historical monastic peninsula in northern Greece. The two editors themselves met on Mount Athos in 1777.

It was on Mount Athos that the renewal movement, with which both Nikodimos and Makarios were deeply involved and in which both played a formative role, began. Its members – committed and conservative, 'though neither legalistic nor fundamentalist' – were collectively known as

'Kollyvades' (their name reflecting their strict observance of 'the boiled wheat' that was consumed during memorial services). They honoured the traditional doctrines of the church Fathers and were critical of the increasing and negative influence arising from Western teachings introduced into Greece by liberal humanists and intellectuals of the time. The Kollyvades insisted that proper regeneration could only come through an authentic spiritual and theological revival based on a radical rediscovery of the saints and sources of the Church together with their classical Byzantine writings on prayer and contemplation. Nevertheless, curiously, *The Philokalia* – as a text of its time and of its kind – is entirely and characteristically free from any bias against the West.

The Kollyvades were also responsible for an emphasis on the sacramental life as a prerequisite for spiritual renewal. They stressed frequent – indeed, if possible, even daily – Holy Communion, a practice that was fiercely criticized both on Mount Athos (as the monastic haven of the period) and in Constantinople (as the ecclesiastical centre of the period). Under the leadership of Makarios and Nikodimos, the Kollyvades distributed numerous writings of the Fathers, lives of the saints and services of the Church, reminding their contemporaries of forgotten, yet fundamental principles of Orthodox spiritual life.

The same editors of *The Philokalia* further published a companion volume, entitled *Evergetinos*, in 1783, exactly one year after the publication of *The Philokalia*. This book was another collection of texts on prayer, originally compiled by Paulos Evergetinos, the founder of a significant and popular monastery in Constantinople during the eleventh century. The *Evergetinos* was probably intended as a complementary volume, stressing outward action where *The Philokalia* emphasized inward contemplation.

While the editorial responsibility for *The Philokalia* clearly belonged to the more studious Nikodimos, the initiative itself for the work as well as the choice of the material for inclusion – possibly even guided by other similar traditional collections – belonged to the more creative Makarios, who discovered the manuscripts in various libraries of Mount Athos.

3. *The themes of* The Philokalia. The foundational and recurring themes found in *The Philokalia* define the 'inner work' (as Abba Agathon would describe it in the Sayings of the Desert Fathers) of the 'inner person' (as St Paul would define the spiritual centre of the human being in Rom. 7.22, 2 Cor. 4.16 and Eph. 3.16) in order to attain to the 'inner kingdom' (as Christ himself would refer to the inner attitude of the spiritual person in Luke 17.21). The key concepts throughout this spiritual process and along this inner pathway are *hesychia* (or silence, stillness and contemplation) and *nepsis* (or sobriety, vigilance and watchfulness). Indeed, the full and precise title of this anthology is *Philokalia ton Ieron Neptikon* (or, 'Philokalia of the Sacred Neptic Fathers').

The basic purpose and ultimate goal of the spiritual life is theosis (or, deification, divinization), while the primary means or principal way of achieving this goal is prayer, and in particular the Jesus prayer as the powerful invocation and continual repetition of the name of Jesus. The practice of unceasing prayer clearly has its roots in the New Testament (1 Thess. 5.17), but was developed through the ascetic and mystical literature from the fourth to the tenth centuries, finally culminating in a monastic and spiritual movement of the fourteenth century, commonly known as Hesychasm and championed by St Gregory Palamas (1296–1359). It was also sometimes accompanied by the use of a physical technique, which assisted in control of thoughts in the intellect and ceaseless prayer in the heart. However, while the Jesus prayer is a unique tool of contemplation, it is by no means the only means of acquiring theosis, which also presupposes fulfilment and practice of the commandments as well as celebration and communion in the sacraments.

4. *An anthology for all.* In this respect, *The Philokalia* is a book addressed to and beneficial for all readers, as indeed the editors themselves observe in the preface to their anthology. It is not for monastics alone, but is clearly intended to be of interest to all lay readers; similarly, it is not only for Eastern practitioners, but concerns every persevering traveller along the spiritual journey toward the inner kingdom. Even if many of the concepts are difficult to comprehend, sometimes requiring appropriate spiritual direction (at least according to Paisii Velichkovsky), nonetheless the fullness of the spiritual life remains the vocation of every person, irrespective of background or stature, of generation or culture. 'It is surely astonishing that a collection of spiritual texts, originally intended for Greeks living under Ottoman rule should have achieved its main impact two centuries later in the secularized and post-Christian West, among the children of that very "Enlightenment" which St. Makarios and St. Nikodimos viewed with such misgiving' (Kallistos Ware).

Finally, *The Philokalia* is especially refreshing and remarkable as an anthology of spiritual texts inasmuch as it appeals to and includes the intellectual dimension of the human person in the journey toward theosis. It does not promote or proclaim an unlettered or anti-educational form of spirituality. Moreover, *The Philokalia* embraces and encourages a profoundly sacramental approach to the spiritual life, inviting its aspirants to a life of liturgical practice and participation within a community that supports spiritual struggle and growth, rather than a way that admits unbridled individualism or else fosters ascetic isolation.

5. *Editions and translations.* First published in Venice (1782) and later reprinted in Athens (1893), *The Philokalia* was very widely copied, translated and distributed within the Eastern Orthodox Church, being discovered also by J.-P. Migne in the West when the latter was preparing the second section of his *Patrologia Graeca*.

Paisii Velichkovsky (1722–94) produced the Slavonic edition in St Petersburg (1793; reprinted in 1822). This was in fact the translation carried by the pilgrim in the well-known story entitled *The Way of a Pilgrim*. Paisii was a Russian monk who had visited Mount Athos and later settled in Moldavia. Ignatii Brianchaninov (1807–67) produced another translation of *The Philokalia* in 1857, while a third version by Theophan the Recluse (1815–94) appeared in several editions (1883f.), enjoyed wide popularity and had great impact on Russian spirituality and culture during the nineteenth century, even influencing the writings of Fyodor Dostoevsky.

The modern Greek reproduction appeared in Athens (5 volumes, edited anonymously by Epiphanios Theodoropoulos, Astir Publications, 1957–63). In addition, the English translation was prepared by Gerald Palmer, Philip Sherrard and Kallistos Ware (Faber and Faber, 1979–), although the initial translation was a collaborative project. In recent years, a Romanian, French and Italian edition have also appeared, based on the Greek original.

See also **Deification; Hesychasm; Orthodox Spirituality.**

––––––

Constantine Cavarnos, *St Macarios of Corinth*, Belmont, MA: Institute for Byzantine and Modern Greek Studies, 1972; Constantine Cavarnos, *St Nikodemos the Hagiorite*, Belmont, MA: Institute for Byzantine and Modern Greek Studies, 1974; R. M. French (trans.), *The Way of a Pilgrim*, New York: Seabury Press, 1965; E. Kadloubovsky and G. Palmer (eds), *Writings from the Philokalia on Prayer of the Heart*, London: Faber and Faber, 1951; E. Kadloubovsky and G. Palmer (eds), *Early Fathers from the Philokalia*, London: Faber and Faber, 1954;

Kallistos (Ware) of Diokleia, 'The spirituality of the Philokalia', *Sobornost,* incorporating *Eastern Churches Review* 12.2 (London, 1990), 6–24. This is a lucid description of *The Philokalia*, originally prepared with detailed bibliographical notes for *DS* 12, cols 1336–52; *Nicodemus of the Holy Mountain, A Handbook of Spiritual Counsel*, CWS, New York: Paulist Press, 1989; G. Palmer, P. Sherrard and K. Ware (eds), *The Philokalia: The Complete Text*, London and Boston: Faber and Faber, 1979–2003 (see esp. the introduction of vol. 1.11–18).

JOHN CHRYSSAVGIS

Pietism

Pietism is the seventeenth- and eighteenth-century religious movement that gave birth to at least five related forms of spirituality that in various circumstances and ways emphasized spiritual regeneration of the individual and renewal of the Church. Scholars have debated the definition of Pietism. Currently most understand Pietism to embrace several diverse groups, but an earlier generation limited it to the best-known and most widespread, the Lutheran Pietism sparked by Philipp Spener (1635–1705).

Although similar concerns were voiced earlier by Johann Arndt (1555–1621) and reform orthodoxy, Lutheran Pietism began as a movement in 1675 with Spener's *Pia Desideria*, published originally as a preface to Arndt's sermons. Arndt and Spener believed that the Reformation grounded in Luther's understanding of the gospel had gotten off track with Lutheran Orthodoxy's preoccupation with forensic justification and harsh polemics against other views. While in his time Luther had placed the primary accent on God's grace of forgiveness, Arndt and Spener felt their situations called for an emphasis on holiness. Spener's six recommendations for Church renewal in *Pia Desideria* express characteristic themes of Lutheran Pietism: more devotional attention to Scripture including the use of conventicles called *collegia pietatis* (for which others called them Pietists), stress on the priesthood of all believers, focus on love more than knowledge, kinder treatment of those with different beliefs, and more emphasis on holiness and sermons that feed the inner person in the education of ministerial students. August Hermann Francke (1663–1727) followed Spener as leader, and made Halle the centre for reform not only of Church but society through new initiatives in education, inner mission and foreign missions. While Pietism won support from some nobility, it faced opposition from other nobles, Orthodox clergy and repressive laws. Nevertheless, it spread quickly to Scandinavia. Pietist immigrants, pastors and missionaries carried it to every continent in the eighteenth and nineteenth centuries.

Reformed Pietism includes diverse efforts to highlight holiness more than knowledge of doctrine so valued by Reformed Orthodox theology. English Puritanism influenced two forerunners of Pietism in the Dutch Reformed Church through one-time English resident Willem Tellinck (1579–1629), who proposed detailed directions for holy living, and English exile William Ames (1576–1633), who taught theology as knowledge for following God's will. Gisbertus Voetius (1589–1676) and Jodocus van Lodensteyn (1620–77) continued to emphasize conversion and full conformity to God's law, which was called 'precisionism'. The main spokesman of German Reformed Pietism was Friedrich Lampe (1683–1729).

Count Ludwig von Zinzendorf (1700–60) was a godson of Spener and a Halle student active in conventicles. He later purchased an estate that he called Herrnhut, where he received Moravian refugees and others. Zinzendorf organized the community into ten choirs, not for singing, but for mutual prayer, discernment and discipline. For more individual care, these were subdivided into very small groups sometimes called bands. This community eventually became the Renewed Moravian Church. Strongly ecumenical, Zinzendorf saw its members as sent to renew all denominations.

In the German area of Württemberg, Pietism was more loosely related to the Lutheran Church, although its prominent biblical scholar J. A. Bengel (1687–1752) was solidly Lutheran. Here F. C. Oetinger blended pietism with Kabbala and Jakob Boehme in his 'theosophy', and fellowships of peasants and artisans also drew upon the speculative mysticism of Boehme and Swedenborg.

Radical Pietism included a number of persons and groups that were highly critical of the established Protestant churches and often withdrew from them. Their roots were more in spiritualists of the Radical Reformation than in Luther or Calvin. An important German forerunner was Jakob Boehme (1575–1624), a contemporary of Arndt who strongly critiqued the state-supported Lutheran Church and produced several works of speculative mysticism. The best-known individual influenced by Boehme was Gottfried Arnold (1666–1714), who then vigorously attacked the Lutheran Church before eventually moderating somewhat. Jean de Labadie (1610–74) in later life and hymn-writer Gerhard Tersteegen (1697–1769) represented radical Pietism in the Reformed Church.

Although there is considerable diversity among these various forms of Pietism, there are also some significant family resemblances: (1) primary emphasis on regeneration or new birth as a personal experience; (2) holiness of life has priority over knowledge of doctrine; (3) renewal of the Church through conventicles; (4) study and devotional use of the Bible and edificatory literature was much encouraged; (5) ecumenicity that lowered denominational boundaries and encouraged borrowing from other spiritual sources; and (6) a raising of the status of laity and decrease of the distance between clergy and laity. While the heyday of Pietism was in the seventeenth and eighteenth centuries, its influence persisted as a powerful force in Christianity through periodic revivals such as those of lay preacher Hans Nilssen Hauge (1771–1824) in Norway and transplantation to other lands through foreign missionaries. Evangelicalism continues to bear the mark of Pietism.

See also **Evangelical Spirituality; Lutheran Spirituality; Moravian Spirituality; Reformed Spirituality.**

Johann Arndt, *True Christianity*, trans. Peter Erb, CWS, New York: Paulist Press, 1979; Peter Erb (ed.), *The Pietists: Selected Writings*, CWS, New York: Paulist Press, 1983; Philipp Jakob Spener, *Pia Desideria*, trans. and ed. Theodore G. Tappert, Philadelphia: Fortress Press, 1964; F. Ernest Stoeffler, *The Rise of Evangelical Pietism*, Leiden: E. J. Brill, 1965; F. Ernest Stoeffler, *Pietism during the Eighteenth Century*, Leiden: E. J. Brill, 1973; F. Ernest Stoeffler (ed.), *Continental Pietism and Early American Christianity*, Grand Rapids, MI: Eerdmans, 1976.

BRADLEY HANSON

Piety

The term 'Piety' comes from the Latin *pietas* which implies responsibility, duty and devotion to God, a person or country. *Pietas* was also used to denote a type of tenderness, fidelity, reverence, obedience, commitment and affection for one's family, religion and state. In the medieval period, *pietas* also came to mean the offerings one made either financially or in action to religion, family or state. Plato in his work *Euthyphro* provided examples of what he considered true piety, including the definition that piety is the knowledge of how to sacrifice and pray (13d–14a).

We first see piety in the Old Testament included among the seven gifts of the Spirit of the Lord granted to the anointed one in Isa. 11.2. Piety was here defined as 'fear of the Lord', a reverence and devotion above that of mere affectionate regard. The first letter to Timothy discusses at length how the faithful Christian should grow in piety and the manner in which one should live one's life with the mind and heart turned toward God. The letter also points out that God has given us the example of perfect piety in Jesus.

Piety has taken different forms at different points in the history of Christianity. During the early Christian period, *pietas* was most often seen as the reverence one displayed concerning worship of God and belief in the divinity of Christ, along with the proper manner in which one conducted oneself publicly as a Christian. Piety was made evident by the acts one did to show reverence for God and gain purity of heart. These actions included fasting and abstinence from food, drink, sexual relations and other bodily pleasures. They also included almsgiving, the recitation of prayers, and attendance at the liturgy.

As the practice of devotions began to flourish in early medieval Europe, piety was often displayed by the fervour which one showed to various devotions such as eucharistic adoration, devotions to the Virgin Mary, the cult of the saints, the Liturgy of the Hours, the Sacred Heart of Jesus, the rosary, etc. With the rise of Humanism and the Reformation, piety increasingly took on a more personal, interior aspect. Interior warmth and personal love for Jesus became the mark and fruit of true piety. The Pietist movement during the seventeenth and eighteenth centuries emphasized heartfelt religious devotion, ethical purity, charitable activity and pastoral theology, rather than philosophical or systematic doctrinal precision. In his 1675 work *Pia Desideria*, Philipp Jakob Spener spoke of a 'heart religion' to take the place of the dominant, and in his opinion failed, 'head religion'. John Wesley and his Methodist movement were heavily influenced by Pietism. In the twentieth century William James defined piety as a pure and reverent disposition or frame of mind, but James himself had little regard for religious doctrine.

Piety took on a negative connotation in the past decades, often bringing up images of sanctimoniousness, superstition and emotional display. Excessive piety is often viewed as indicative of mental illness or disorder. These negative aspects aside, however, piety remains the virtue and gift which allows one a filial devotion and regard for the things of God, so that they can, in the words of Titus 2.11–13, look forward with happy expectation to the return of Christ Jesus in the glory of God. Piety in its positive aspects allows one the desire and the affection necessary to develop and devote oneself to nurturing an authentic spiritual life. A true spiritual life without authentic piety could not exist within the Christian tradition.

See also **Devotions; Devotions, Popular; Pietism.**

Kathleen Kamerick, *Popular Piety and Art in the Late Middle Ages*, New York: Palgrave, 2002; Dirk Obbink (ed.), *Philodemus: On Piety*, Oxford: Oxford University Press, 1996; Timothy F. Sedgwick, *The Christian Moral Life: Practices of Piety*, Grand Rapids, MI: Eerdmans, 1999; Brad Walton, *Jonathan Edwards, Religious Affections, and the Puritan Analysis of True Piety, Spiritual Sensations, and Heart Religion*, Lewiston, NY: E. Mellen Press, 2002.

HARRIET A. LUCKMAN

Pilgrimage

Pilgrimage is journey to sacred places. Every place has a story, and sacred places are those places whose story is associated with God's self-revelation and with the lives of the holy. It is such places where divine–human encounter has taken place which attract pilgrimage. As a result of the incarnation such encounter is understood by Christians to have taken place most especially, though not exclusively, in the Holy Land. It is there that the phenomenon of Christian pilgrimage began. Though there is some evidence of Christians visiting the holy sites associated with the life and death of Christ in Jerusalem before the conversion of the Emperor Constantine, Christian pilgrimage began in earnest in the fourth century with the visit to the Holy Land of Helena, his mother, in 326. Countless pilgrims followed her, the flow being encouraged by Cyril, Bishop of Jerusalem in the fourth century, who established pilgrimage to the Holy Land in general and Jerusalem in particular as being central to Christian piety. It was he who instituted the *Via crucis*, the route Jesus took from Pilate's house to Golgotha, as a pilgrimage route in Jerusalem. That route is still walked by thousands of Christians. The holy sites were seen as witnessing to the truth of biblical history, but the journeys made to them by Christians have always been undertaken not just for such verification but to recall events that took place there and pray. As they do so, pilgrims seek to become caught up in the passion of their Lord so as to be strengthened in their own witness.

Pilgrimage to Rome, to the tomb of the apostles Peter and Paul, also began to flourish in the fourth century. There gradually emerged a large number of important sites associated with the saints all over Europe, the best known being Santiago de Compostela. Their multiplication was given huge impetus both by the introduction of their use as a public penance in the eighth century and by the loss of the Holy Land in the eleventh and twelfth centuries in the Crusades, so that in later medieval times there emerged a sacred geography of holy sites or shrines, places associated with the lives and deaths of holy men and women, which criss-crossed the continent and which had an enormous effect on the character of Christian faith and practice at that time. Instead of going to the Holy Land, pilgrims would go to the shrine of a saint to be inspired by the Christian witness of that saint and to ask for his or her prayers. Miracles were associated with such prayers and still are, in such places as Lourdes. There arose, too, a system of indulgences, whereby a pious act such as pilgrimage received a reward in the form of a remission of time in purgatory. That, together with straightforward abuse which the incentive for financial gain produced, helped spark the Reformation.

The numbers of people going on pilgrimage declined greatly as a result of the Reformation and though such sanctification of places is not surprising in a religion founded in history and geography, some in the Reformed tradition have continued to question whether pilgrimage is an authentically Christian phenomenon at all. It has certainly been a part of Christian piety from very early times. There developed on the sites of Christian martyrdom from very early times *martyria*, a word which suggests that the place itself bears witness, at which Christians gathered for prayers. Longer journeys to the sites of the martyrdom of the saints for prayer were popular as soon as they were legal. The church Fathers were generally encouraging of pilgrimage (though critical of abuse) and popular piety has ensured its continuance within the Catholic tradition, it now being as popular as ever. In the Reformed tradition there has been a rekindling of interest in pilgrimage of late through spiritual writing which encourages Christians to see their lives as a journey towards God, so that pilgrimage becomes symbolic of life's journey. This notion of pilgrimage as an allegory of Christian life is not new, of course: it has been well characterized from Bonaventure's *Itinerarium Mentis in Deum* to Bunyan's *Pilgrim's Progress.*

Pilgrimage is by no means an exclusively Christian phenomenon: Jews and Muslims as well as Christians journey to Jerusalem, Hindus visit the Ganges, Buddhists go to Sarnath and for Muslims pilgrimage to Mecca is of primary importance. Pilgrimage strikes a chord deep in the human psyche. Anthropologists suggest that both the journey and the destination have great significance, providing a limen, a threshold, that can enable pilgrims to see their lives in a divine perspective. There is also human benefit to be gained from the journey, in that it provides a break from routine, an opportunity to expand horizons, and a chance to reassess priorities. Though it would seem that pilgrimage is universal in its appeal to humanity, Christian pilgrimage is always distinct as a result of its christocentric character. Christians are enjoined by their Lord to take up their cross and follow him who is the beginning and the end of their journey, and pilgrimage can be an important symbol of obedience to that call. This christocentric emphasis is present even when the destination is the tomb of a saint, since the saints provide Christians with inspiration and example in following their Lord.

Christians have found that pilgrimage to the dwelling places of the saints can root them in their Christian past, by reminding them of the Christian history of salvation and inspiring them by the lives of those who have responded wholeheartedly to God's call. Such journeys are pregnant with biblical resonances, beginning with Abraham leaving his homeland to travel in faith to the promised land and ending with Christians bound for their heavenly homeland, the New Jerusalem, as described in Revelation. Pilgrimage thus combines the biblical themes of place and placelessness. It reminds Christians, on the one hand that, as the author of the letter to the Hebrews has it, here they have no abiding city, but are rather continually called to journey forth. On the other hand, it speaks of the promise of Christ that he is going ahead of them to prepare for those who follow him a place to be with him for ever. Medieval pilgrimage shrines were deliberately constructed to combine these two themes, by reminding pilgrims in architecture, glass and stone of their Christian roots and being at the same time a 'slice of heaven', a foretaste of what is to come, pointing Christians towards heaven which is their destination. In this way pilgrimage has a backward and a forward momentum, taking pilgrims in heart and mind back to their Christian heritage and forward to the consummation of all things in Christ. Pilgrimage is thus a very powerful model which links people, places and God together in a way which has great potential because it is at once dynamic and rooted. In an age when people are desperately seeking stability and, at the same time, the ability to deal with rapid change, pilgrimage has much to offer.

See also **Journey, Spiritual; Place; Shrines.**

J. Eade and M. Sallnow (eds), *Contesting the Sacred: The Anthropology of Christian Pilgrimage*, London: Routledge, 1991; V. Elizondo and S. Frayne (eds), *Pilgrimage*, London: SCM Press, 1996; M.-L. Nolan and S. Nolan, *Christian Pilgrimage in Modern Western Europe*, Chapel Hill: University of North Carolina Press, 1989; J. Stopford (ed.), *Pilgrimage Explored*, Woodbridge, Suffolk: York Medieval Press, 1999; V. Turner and E. Turner, *Image and Pilgrimage in Christian Culture; Anthropological Perspectives*, New York: Columbia University Press, 1978; D. Webb, *Pilgrims and Pilgrimage in the Medieval West*, London: I. B. Tauris, 1999.

JOHN INGE

Place

A sense of 'place' is one of the categories of human experience with the strongest impact on how humans see the world and situate themselves in it. There is a vital connection between place, memory and identity. 'Place' involves a dialectical relationship between geographical location and human narrative. Place has become a significant theme in a wide range of writing, including philosophy, cultural history, anthropology, human geography, architectural theory and contemporary literature. Attempts by spirituality to reflect on 'place' must therefore be interdisciplinary, while making connections with theological themes.

Place as a cultural category. We not only live in the world; we have an *image* of the world. The 'world' that surrounds people is not simply raw data but something that carries meaning. This system of meaning is what anthropologists and philosophers understand by 'culture'. But the world is no longer a mosaic of separate cultures and 'place' is not simply local. Technology and rapid travel have increased global connections. Equally, cultures previously viewed as homogeneous are revealed as plural and associated with power issues.

Place and space. Older scientific views of reality suggested that 'space' was absolute, infinite, empty and a priori. 'Place' was a mere division of 'natural' space; a secondary social construction. This view is now problematic. The notion of space as three-dimensional, evenly extended and divisible into commensurate sections is complicated by the theory of relativity and developments in particle physics and even in the psychology of perception. Space does not exist as a simple given; it is subjectively perceived and experienced differently depending on perspec-

tive. 'Space' is now seen as an abstract concept whereas 'place' is physical, specific and relational. Philosophers such as Martin Heidegger, Gaston Bachelard and Edward Casey therefore re-embrace a conviction that place is prior to space (Heidegger, 1975; Bachelard, 1994; Casey, 1996). We 'come to know' in terms of our knowledge of specific places before we know space as in the abstract.

Place and social crisis. The contemporary preoccupation with 'place' reflects a cultural crisis in Western society – a sense of rootlessness and displacement. Human geographers suggest that while it is essential to have 'place identity', we have since World War 2 de-emphasized 'place' for the sake of mobility, centralization or economic rationalization. The French anthropologist Marc Augé distinguishes between place, filled with historical monuments and creative of social life, and what he calls *non-place*, where no organic social life is possible (Augé, 1997). By non-place he means the contexts where we spend increasingly more time – supermarkets, airports, hotels, motorways, in front of the television, sitting at a computer – bringing about a fragmentation of awareness in relation to 'the world'. Unlike non-place, 'place' has three essential characteristics: it engages with our identity, with our relationships and with our history.

Place and belonging. It is this sense of placelessness that underpins the contemporary Western quest for roots. Our longing for place is more than biological or aesthetic. Simone Weil suggests that the hunger for roots is fundamental to our deepest identity, 'To be rooted is perhaps the most important and least recognized need of the human soul' (Weil, 1997, p. 41). Some recent writing on the psychology of place also speaks of *participation* as a key element in being placed. A 'place', as opposed to a 'location' (a mere object 'over there') invites participation in an environment. 'Environment', in the fullest sense, implies different sets of relationships between the natural habitat and human beings.

Place and landscapes. Place obviously involves specific landscapes even if a sense of place is also inherently associated with human events. Landscape is the first partner in the dialectical nature of 'place'. Although place is a human construct, we must not lose sight of the fact that the physical landscape is an active rather than passive partner in the conversation that creates the nature of a place. While a writer like Simon Schama emphasizes the human construction of 'landscape', he does not suggest that there is no *real* nature, merely that there is no *pure* nature (Schama, 1995, pp. 6–7, 61, 81). What we have is an interplay between physical geographies and geographies of the mind and spirit.

Place and memory. If place is firstly landscape, it is also memory. Memory embedded in place, however, involves more than any single personal story; there are deeper narrative currents that gather together all those who have lived there. It is therefore appropriate to think of places as texts, layered with meaning. A hermeneutics of place progressively reveals new meanings in a conversation between topography, memory and the presence of particular people at each moment. 'All human experience is narrative in the way we imaginatively reconstruct it . . . and every encounter of the sacred is rooted in a place, a socio-spatial context that is rich in myth and symbol' (Lane, 1994, p. 19). Thus, there can be no sense of place without narrative.

Place and conflict. Precisely because 'place' involves human narrative, it is not surprising that 'place' is always a contested rather than a simple reality. We only have to think of Jerusalem, sacred to three faiths, or reflect on the disturbing conflict between radically different meanings given to Auschwitz-Birkenau by Polish Christians and Jews (Sheldrake, 1998, pp. 171–5). In deconstructing modernity's belief in objective, 'absolute' place, postmodern critiques assert that *definition* is power. The French Marxist philosopher Henri Lefebvre's analysis of place also reminds us that systems of spatialization are historically conditioned (Lefebvre, 1991). Spatializations are not merely physical arrangements of things; they are also patterns of social action and routine, as well as historical conceptions of the world. The meta-narratives of the people who hold power take over public places; and thus history becomes a story of dominance and repression. The notion that place relates to issues of empowerment and disempowerment forces us to think of multi-localities (locations are different 'places' simultaneously) and multi-vocalities (different voices are heard in each place).

Place and Christian theology. Given the importance of 'place' in culture, as well as the centrality of 'land' and 'temple' in the theologies of the Hebrew Scriptures, it is strange at first sight that the Christian tradition as a whole makes little direct reference to 'place'. Christianity came of age in the Jewish urban diaspora of the Graeco-Roman world. The particularity of place could not be bypassed entirely given the doctrine of the incarnation. However, it is also clear from the Christian Scriptures that the dominant concern for Christian disciples in the apostolic era was to move out from the local into the entire inhabited world, the *oikumene*, in advance of the rapidly approaching last days. Acts 1.8 suggests that Jesus explicitly exhorted his disciples to move beyond Jerusalem to the ends of the earth in pursuit of their mission to preach the kingdom of God. For Christians, God was increasingly to be worshipped in whatever place they found themselves. The experience of 'being in transit', of journey, became a central Christian metaphor.

Western theology has had a great deal more to say about time than about place. Roman Catholic and Anglican considerations have generally limited themselves to space in reference to liturgy. Classical Protestantism has been less happy with the sacredness of place. It affirmed the unbridgeable gulf between the holiness of God and sinful creatures. With Luther it concentrated on the community of disciples, constituted by the Word being proclaimed and the sacraments celebrated. This view tends to encourage a strong ethical emphasis in any theological reflection on place and a suspicion of the sacredness of 'place' as a kind of given.

However, if we take seriously the implications of classical trinitarian and incarnational theology, an ethical approach to 'place' cannot stand alone. The doctrines of Trinity and incarnation imply a divine indwelling in all material reality and a revelation of God through the created order. Truth is not an abstract to be found in some dimension that is 'no place' in particular. Truth must be sought paradoxically in the particularities of place as well as time that have the capacity to speak to us sacramentally of God's presence and promise.

Yet, a theology of place must maintain a balance between God's revelation in the particular and a sense that God ultimately escapes the boundaries of the local. There is a persistent tension in Christianity between what is sometimes referred to as 'place' and 'placelessness'. All 'place' is both here and now, and at the same time a pointer to 'elsewhere'. God's presence cannot be imprisoned in the limitations of place. The divine is to be sought throughout the *oikumene*, the entire inhabited world. The 'catholicity' of place is, for Christians, symbolized most powerfully in the *koinonia* of believers filled with the Spirit and shaped by the Eucharist. This expresses the tension between local and universal with particular strength. On the one hand, every Eucharist exists in a particular time and place. On the other hand, each Eucharist is a *transitus*, a transit point, a passageway between worlds. Eucharistic space enables the particularity of local 'place' to intersect in the risen and ascended Jesus with all times and all places.

See also **Creation Spirituality; Ecological Spirituality; Sacramentality and Spirituality; World.**

Marc Augé, *Non-places: Introduction to an Anthropology of Supermodernity*, London and New York: Verso, 1997; Gaston Bachelard, *The Poetics of Space*, Boston: Beacon Press, 1994; Edward S. Casey, 'How to get from space to place in a fairly short stretch of time: phenomenological prolegomena' in Steven Feld and Keith H. Basso (eds), *Senses of Place*, Santa Fe: School of American Research Press, 1996; Martin Heidegger, *Poetry, Language, Thought*, New York: Harper & Row, 1975; John Inge, *A Christian Theology of Place*, Aldershot: Ashgate, 2003; Belden Lane, *Landscapes of the Sacred: Geography and Narrative in American Spirituality*, Baltimore: Johns Hopkins University Press, 2002; Belden Lane, 'Galesville and Sinai: the researcher as participant in the study of spirituality and sacred space', *Christian Spirituality Bulletin* 2.1 (Spring 1994); Henri Lefebvre, *The Production of Space*, Oxford: Blackwell, 1991; Geoffrey Lilburne, *A Sense of Place: A Christian Theology of the Land*, Nashville: Abingdon Press, 1989; Simon Schama, *Landscape and Memory*, London: HarperCollins, 1995; Philip Sheldrake, *Spirituality and Theology: Christian Living and the Doctrine of God*, London: Darton, Longman & Todd/Maryknoll, NY: Orbis Books, 1998; Philip Sheldrake, *Spaces for the Sacred: Place, Memory and Identity*, London: SCM Press/Baltimore: Johns Hopkins University Press, 2001; Simone Weil, *The Need for Roots*, London/New York: Routledge, 1997.

PHILIP SHELDRAKE

Poetry and Poetics

Poetry is among the earliest forms of human expression, existing in oral traditions before its eventual emergence as a genre of literature. Gaston Bachelard has even called it 'one of the destinies of speech'. Before modernity, poems were characterized by formal criteria of rhythm and meter, and existed in diverse traditions and forms. Before the advent of writing, many cultures produced songs to the gods and those that celebrated deeds of valour, commemorated epic battles, recounted heroic journeys, and so forth. With the advent of printing in the later Middle Ages, poets increasingly saw their work as a production of texts. In modernity, they began experimenting with a wide variety of forms, including blank verse, free verse and prose poems. Poets whose works constituted a distinct literature wrote for a reading public, and readers' tastes as much as their own genius dictated developing styles and sensibilities. It is appropriate to say that it is no longer the *literary form* but the *expressive style* that constitutes a poem in Western culture.

The word poetry derives from the Greek verb *poiein*, a word that means 'to make'. Poetics deriving from this root is a word first found in Aristotle's *Peri poietikes*, a fragmentary treatise 'on the poetic [art]'. He defines it as that branch of knowledge having to do with 'poetry itself and its forms and the specific power of each, the way in which the plot is to be constructed if the poem is to be considered beautiful, of how many and of what parts it is composed, and anything else that falls within the same inquiry'. It is, in other words, a theory of poetry together with the examination of its various formal expressions. Since the nineteenth century, poetics has been categorized in academic terms as a dimension of philosophical aesthetics – that is, not only as a manner of *speaking* and *writing* but as a way of *seeing* and *knowing*. In its popular usage, it suggests the ideal toward which a poet aspires, the horizon of meaning constructed by a given poem. In this sense, poetics describes the dynamic nature of language itself, as well as its function as a communicative art.

Poetry flourished in preliterate cultures, particularly in the context of religious expressions in hymns, prayers and cultic acts. As such we find that poetry occupies a central place within the earliest scriptural traditions of Judaism, as with other religions built upon textual foundations. The psalms come immediately to mind, together with the Song of Songs and Proverbs. Indeed, more than one-quarter of the Old Testament originated in verse form. In the New Testament, form criticism has located fragments of poetry in the Gospels as in the epistles, in the case of the latter in hymnic forms that were probably first used in worship. (See, for example, Phil. 2.5–11, the kenotic hymn; see also, Luke 1.46–55; 2.29–32; Rev. 5.9–10 and 15.3–4, instances that suggest not only an oral source but an oral use, probably in the earliest forms of Christian prayer and liturgy.) Poetry has remained a constant dimension of Christian liturgy, particularly in its chanted forms and in the use of psalms, hymns and other forms of song.

Examples of poems and poetic forms abound in the writings of the early Fathers. This is true not only in hymns and prayers, where one might expect such an occurrence, but also in didactic treatises suggesting an oral use that might have been part of catechetical training. In the Syriac tradition, this is particularly true. These include the *Odes of Solomon*, hymns written by Bardaisan of Edessa (d. 222), and the metrical sermons and hymns of Ephraem the Syrian (d. 373). In the Greek tradition, the literature includes hymns of Clement of Alexandria (d. before 215), Methodius (late third century), Apollinaris of Laodicea (d. 392) and, of course, Gregory Nazianzen (d. *c.* 390). In the Latin tradition, alongside many anonymous examples of early verse, Commodian wrote a lengthy didactic treatise intended perhaps for catechesis, the *Instructions* (fifth century?); other examples include verse attributed to Lactantius, Marius Victorinus, tomb inscriptions by Pope Damasus I, Ausonius and, of course, the writings of Ambrose of Milan (d. 397), widely considered the most important contributor to Latin hymnody in Late Antiquity. Boethius' *The Consolation of Philosophy*, destined to become a standard text for medieval commentary, takes the form of poems interspersed with prose sections of philosophical argument.

The poetic tradition continued in the hymnody of the medieval Church, both Western and Orthodox, as well as in the varied denominations and ecclesial traditions of modernity. Before the rise of the universities in the central Middle Ages, the formal work of theology largely took place within monastic communities and cathedral schools – and, thus, in the context of prayer and liturgy. Poetic form shaped this work within the framework of worship such that faith found expression not only in argument but also in song. The fact that hymns usually find expression in the poetic genre suggests a formal relationship to spirituality as the lived experience and expression of the Christian faith. This provides another example of the suggestion tendered by liturgical scholars that the practice of prayer establishes the shape of belief (*lex orandi, lex credendi*).

Poetry is not simply a possibility for the Church's self-expression and identity as a worshipping community; it establishes what might be called the constitutive grammar of spirituality and of theology itself. The question of the spiritual shape of theology requires that we consider the nature of language and its uses – which is to say, poetics. Knowledge of the divine lies within but always beyond our ability to speak (or write) what we know; the capacities of language always are inadequate to the tasks of human perception. The monastic theologian Bernard of Clairvaux (d. 1153) captures this elegantly when he describes Christ in poetic terms as the *verbum*

abbreviatum, 'the abridged word'. The self-disclosure of God as 'word' occurs *in* but always also *beyond* language. As he observes: 'I have ascended to the highest part of me, and found that the word towers beyond this; I descended to explore the depths, and found that this word is deeper still. When I gaze around, I see the word stretching beyond everything that is outside me; when I gaze within, the word is more inward than this' (*Sermons on the Song of Songs* 74.2.6).

A further insight into this connection between poetics and theology is found in Dante's epic poem, *The Divine Comedy*. Near the end of the final canto of his journey, having reached the mysterious heights of paradise, the narrator concedes: 'How incomplete is speech, how weak, when set/ against my thought!' (canto 33.121–2; translated by Allen Mandelbaum). This is a familiar trope among contemporary poets. Thus, T. S. Eliot observes that 'Words, after speech, reach/ Into the silence' ('Burnt Norton' 5.139–40), and Ellen Hinsey describes 'the Word' as 'Center of utterance, but unreachable/ With voice – compass and goal – Shore towards which all/ Telling rows . . .' ('On the Unlanguageable Name of God' in *The White Fire of Time*, Middletown, CT: Wesleyan University Press, 2002, p. 57). The very nature of language is one of limits; it cannot contain the fullness of human thought, in terms of immanent or transcendent referents. Words lead us toward a dynamic but limited form of cognition at the boundaries where speech and silence meet. As a sacramental dimension of poetry, one might well speak of this as expressing a spirituality shaped at the margins. These establish the proper fabric of prayer and remind us of the transcendent and expansive horizon of worship.

The task of theology is thus shaped by the recognition of the ineffability of human language for the divine, a reality at once immanent in speech and transcending what language can adequately convey. For this reason, poetics captures an essential spiritual dimension of the theological task. Czesław Miłosz speaks of this as an 'eternal insatiability' because the poet 'wants his words to penetrate the very core of reality' and thus 'hopes constantly and is constantly rejected' (*The Witness of Poetry*, Cambridge, MA: Harvard University Press, 1983, p. 74). Such an insight into language-making (i.e., *poiesis*) reminds us that theological language always directs the word toward image and metaphor in a manner exceeding what we can speak. This apophatic dimension of language expresses a poetic spirituality that guides us toward the heights and depths of human experience by the melody of desire. As the poet William Stafford invites us to consider,

'Maybe there's a land where you have to sing/ to explain anything . . .' ('A Course in Creative Writing' in *The Way It Is*, Saint Paul, MN: Graywolf Press, 1998, p. 195). The spiritual insight of such an aesthetic constitutes the original impulse of religion, and remains fundamental to the tasks of theology, liturgy and hymnody in our own day.

See also Mysticism; Spirituality and Scripture (*essays*); Aesthetics; Art and Spirituality; Beauty; Desire; Apophatic Spirituality; Hymns and Spirituality; Knowledge; Literature and Spirituality.

T. S. Eliot, *On Poetry and Poets*, London and Boston: Faber and Faber, 1957; Dana Gioia, *Can Poetry Matter? Essays on Poetry and American Culture*, Saint Paul, MN: Graywolf Press, 2002; Jane Hirshfield, *Nine Gates: Entering the Mind of Poetry*, New York: HarperCollins, 1997; John Hollander, *The Work of Poetry*, New York: Columbia University Press, 1997; Mary Kinzie, *A Poet's Guide to Poetry*, Chicago: University of Chicago Press, 1999; Mary Oliver, *A Poetry Handbook*, San Diego, New York and London: Harcourt Brace, 1994; Theodore Roethke, *On Poetry and Craft*, Port Townsend, WA: Copper Canyon Press, 2001; Muriel Rukeyser, *The Life of Poetry*, Ashfield, MA: Paris Press, 1996; Frank J. Warnke and O. B. Hardison Jr (eds), *Princeton Encyclopedia of Poetry and Poetics*, Princeton, NJ; Princeton University Press, 1965.

MARK S. BURROWS

Postmodernity

'Postmodernity' is a term applied to aspects of contemporary Western cultural experience. Because of the intimate connection between spirituality and culture (de Certeau, 1966), this concept has significant applications to how we interpret the configuration of spirituality in our present era.

The use of the term 'postmodernity', its presumed relationship with the term 'modernity' and the various theories about both (postmodernism) are complex, confusing, realities. In summary, all versions or theories of postmodernism are comments upon whatever is implied by 'the modern' (e.g. Lakeland, 1997, pp. ix–xiv and ch. 1).

It seems reasonable to suggest that in the context of Christian theology and spirituality, 'postmodernity' and 'postmodernism(s)' stand for a critical assessment of 'the Enlightenment project' – particularly a simplistic or naive confidence in the power of human reason, an ordered view of the world and a belief in the inevitability of progress. This simplistic world view must be distinguished from what is genuinely improving about the modern era, especially scientific and industrial-economic developments that continue to benefit humanity. The present cultural period of 'postmodernity' arises essentially from the failure of over-optimistic world views and of scientistic dogmatism.

Paradoxically, while traditional Western religious practice declines there appears to be an ever-increasing hunger for spirituality. Coherent systems of belief about God are no longer presumed necessary for a fruitful spiritual journey. Alongside the breakdown of religious certainties lies a more general fragmentation of collective social consciousness. This inhibits the maintenance of public moral consensus.

Some postmodern theorists argue that it is now impossible to defend any overarching framework of meaning or values. What tends to follow is not merely the detachment of spirituality from belief systems but a privatization of spirituality and its separation from social or public ethics. This 'postmodern' fragmentation is not purely abstract. It lies in the experience of loss and grief that, according to the postmodern theorist Jean-François Lyotard, characterizes our age. What has been lost is the spirit of optimism about the human capacity to solve all problems present at the start of the twentieth century. Nowadays traditional patterns of thought, behaviour and institutions, including religious ones, struggle to deal with a surrounding culture that is impervious to the answers of the past and which presents an overwhelming number of new questions.

First, our understanding of the universe has changed as the result of developments in cosmology and quantum physics. The human race is no longer the 'meaning' of the universe. Second, evolutionary theory is largely unquestioned. The evolution of humankind can no longer be separated from the remainder of life's processes. Third, psychology has become a respected science. This reveals a complex inner world that calls in question the objectivity of human perceptions. Fourth, developments in economics, political theory and the social sciences challenge fixed notions of society. Finally, political events in the twentieth century – two world wars, totalitarianisms, the Holocaust, Hiroshima – decisively undermined over-optimistic visions of human society.

Although 'postmodernity' and 'postmodernism' are notoriously slippery terms, theorists espouse broadly two forms. The first is deconstructive and is especially prevalent among French intellectuals such as Jacques Derrida or Michel Foucault. It involves a radical hermeneutics of suspicion in the face of attempts to create normative interpretations of culture. The second, represented by Hans-Georg Gadamer and Paul Ricoeur, recognizes cultural fragmentation but seeks to reconstruct strategies that enable modest interpretative frameworks without re-establishing a priori norms. Their new process of interpretation seeks to encompass the fact that human experience is diverse and that reality is complex.

Both versions of postmodernism reject the epistemological optimism of modernism. Postmodernism recognizes that all interpretations of 'truth' are culturally conditioned, contingent, morally flawed and intellectually partial. In other words, the postmodern Western world is suspicious of total systems, including theological ones.

Some writers who specifically discuss postmodern spirituality are deeply suspicious of traditional religious language. They reject the necessity of transcendent realities like 'God'. However, others note that postmodernism is not necessarily inimical to Christian spirituality. Indeed, they suggest, postmodern intellectualism is often fascinated with 'the sacred' and is not exclusively committed to some kind of nihilism.

Either way, Western Christian spirituality exists within this ambiguous and unstable culture. So spirituality can no longer be seen simply as the logical consequence of a priori deductive theology. In fact, this kind of theology, separated from 'experience' and praxis, reflected in part the internalization by Christians of a post-Enlightenment opposition between the 'secular' and 'sacred' spheres of human life. Christianity retreated from the vagaries of the social-public realm into an intellectually rigorous but protected world of its own. In contrast, contemporary postmodern spirituality involves an emphasis on experience, engagement and praxis as the immediate contexts for God's self-disclosure and human response. Interestingly a volume on Christian postmodern spirituality suggests that Auschwitz has become *the* symbol of the death of modernism. If so, it should be the 'saints' of the era of the two world wars of the twentieth century who are looked to as prophets of this new spirituality. Some, such as Dietrich Bonhoeffer, adopted a radical stance against politically passive versions of Christianity. Others, such as the Jewish writers Simone Weil or Etty Hillesum, existed ambiguously on the margins of institutional religion.

The most crucial element of a postmodern Christian spirituality is the rejection of modernism's division between the spiritual and secular spheres. If we adopt H. Richard Niebuhr's typology of Christian world views (*Christ and Culture*), the two extremes of 'the Christ of culture' (assimilationist) and 'Christ against culture' (e.g. fundamentalist) are inadequate. Postmodern spirituality must take the secular sphere seriously as an essential ingredient of Christian life. Equally, postmodernism encourages the analysis of the unacknowledged social and cultural agendas that underlie all approaches to spirituality and religion.

Postmodern spirituality crosses boundaries and rejects impermeable divisions. It tends therefore to be ecumenical in spirit, open to other faiths and capable of finding common cause with all people of good will. Conversely, it is less easy to speak of 'Christian spirituality' in the singular and more accurate to think of a plurality of 'spiritualities of Christians'. Exclusive systems increasingly give way to eclecticism. Care is obviously needed when postmodern 'borrowing' crosses into other world faiths. Spiritual neo-colonialism needs to be avoided and the complexities of inter-faith conversation must be acknowledged.

Equally, Christian spirituality is never simply the product or possession of individuals isolated from faith communities or from tradition. Paradoxically, such a view actually intersects with postmodern understandings of the self. The 'modern' idea of the self emphasized its essentially autonomous qualities. In contrast, the postmodern self is not isolated from others or disengaged from the social world but is actually constituted by relationships. Because the self exists in a complex network of relationships there is never such a thing as a completed self.

Furthermore in the Christian tradition there is a paradox of knowing and not knowing in relation to God. The 'apophatic' element, that is, the realization that 'God' is ultimately beyond definition, has received new emphasis in postmodern approaches to theology and spirituality. This is not to say that the riches of trinitarian and incarnational theology are thereby undermined. Recent studies of Christian spirituality in postmodern context speak of a number of needs. Spirituality must take the secular order seriously; be strongly incarnational and engaged with materiality; emphasize the existential quality of God's relating to us and encourage a radical belief in the unconditional love of God (both strong trinitarian themes); speak of the cross as the suffering of God within human suffering; reflect upon the *deus absconditus* in context of an experiential 'absence of God' in contemporary culture.

It is not surprising, therefore, that postmodern thinkers engage strongly with the mystical tradition with its emphasis on the hidden face of

God. The great French intellectual Michel de Certeau drew explicit parallels between post-modern culture and Christian mysticism. The mystic and the postmodern person live in a movement of perpetual departure, wanderers lost in 'the totality of the immense'.

The appropriateness or otherwise of describing some postmodern writing (for example Jacques Derrida) as apophatic/negative theology has been eloquently discussed by the British theologian Rowan Williams. The American theologian David Tracy has suggested that Christian spirituality can be broadly divided into the 'prophetic' and the 'mystical'. Christian theology at best contains both strains. In our postmodern era Tracy suggests that mysticism with its apophatic language is where theologians must turn.

Finally, it is worth noting that the restoration of dialogue between spirituality and theology actually owes something to the theories of postmodernism. First, a 'modern' rationalist approach to knowledge, linked to an emphasis on inwardly consistent but mutually exclusive disciplines has given way to interdisciplinary conversation. The conversation between spirituality and theology, as well as between both and other disciplines such as the social sciences is one of the fruits of this change of perspective. Second, the rise of postmodernism tends to undermine grand theological systems along with other systems of meaning. The study of spirituality, too, now espouses a similar modesty. The interdisciplinary and context-laden nature of the field resists simple systematization by single scholars. It is the age of collected papers, dictionary entries like this – all with limited focuses. The essay replaces the comprehensive narrative history of Christian spirituality. An essay, after all, is not merely a more modest, informal, limited and open-ended piece of writing. It is appropriately, in its fundamental sense, an experiment, a trial, a first tentative attempt at learning.

See also **Spirituality and Culture** (*essay*); **New Age; Secularization.**

Ann W. Astell (ed.), *Divine Representations: Postmodernism and Spirituality*, New York: Paulist Press, 1994; Philippa Berry and Andrew Wernick (eds), *Shadow of Spirit: Postmodernism and Religion*, London and New York: Routledge, 1992; F. B. Burnham (ed.), *Postmodern Theology: Christian Faith in a Pluralist World*, San Francisco: HarperCollins, 1989, esp. Introduction and essays by Geraldine Finn and Rowan Williams; Michel de Certeau, 'Culture and spiritual experience', *Concilium* 19 (1966); Michel de Certeau, *The Mystic Fable*, vol. 1,

Chicago: University of Chicago Press, 1992; David Ray Griffin (ed.), *Spirituality and Society: Postmodern Visions*, New York: SUNY Press, 1988; Paul Lakeland, *Postmodernity: Christian Identity in a Fragmented Age*, Minneapolis: Fortress Press, 1997; Jean-François Lyotard, *The Postmodern Condition: A Report on Knowledge*, Minneapolis: University of Minnesota Press, 1984; David Tracy, *The Analogical Imagination: Christian Theology and the Culture of Pluralism*, New York: Crossroad, 1991.

PHILIP SHELDRAKE

Poverty

This brief entry will examine poverty in the Jewish and Christian Scriptures, in the Christian tradition, and concludes with a brief synthesis.

1. *Poverty in the Jewish and Christian Scriptures.* The various literary traditions of the Jewish Scriptures understand poverty in the material, social context of the community of Israel. Genesis described creation as good and as belonging to Yahweh who intended that it sustain the human community. Physical deprivation in terms of hunger and thirst, the lack of a sufficient dwelling, exploitation by the rich, marginalization, and lack of sufficient land for survival, all posed a threat to the communal well-being of Israel. The selfish appropriation of things by an individual violates the rights of others and results in poverty, an offence against God. That God takes the side of the poor is the refrain of the prophetic literature and the psalms which announce that the Messiah will redress wrongs and inaugurate an eschatological community in which there will be no want. The wisdom literature also sees poverty as God's punishment for sin while material abundance is seen as God's blessing for personal uprightness, judgements which find their meaning in the context of the covenant between Yahweh and Israel.

The Gospels present Jesus who from the outset of his ministry inaugurated the reign of God through preaching and actions as good news to the poor (Luke 4.16–21). The Beatitudes signal that the kingdom of God belongs to the poor (Matt. 5.3; Luke 6.20). Poverty thus appears as an evil that the reign of God must bring to an end. While the Christian Scriptures do not preach in favour of material poverty nor that riches are evil in themselves, they do point to the incompatibility of riches and salvation (Luke 16.13). The parable of the rich man (Matt. 19.16–30) calls for detachment from the idolatry of riches as an integral part of the Christian vocation, an attitude echoed by Paul in the eschatological context of the coming kingdom (1 Cor.

7.29–31), which brings the reward of eternal life and in this life the 'hundredfold' (Mark 10.28–31). Poverty as detachment finds its fulfilment in communion, the sharing of material goods, and in being of one heart and one mind as described in Acts 4.34, realizing the promise of Deut. 15.4 which foretold a time when there would be no one in need in the land.

2. *Poverty in the Christian tradition.* The theme of communion was central to the reflection and life of the early Church. Those who enjoyed the good things of the earth were obliged to use them to alleviate the suffering of the poor as was called for by the *Didache*, by Clement of Alexandria (d. 215) and John Chrysostom (d. 407). Gregory of Nyssa (d. 394) saw the dignity of the poor as the image of Christ, while Gregory of Nazianzus (d. 390) taught charity as the real sign of love for the poor. In the West, Augustine's Rule attempted to take the model of the Jerusalem community described in Acts as the norm of his community, holding all things in common.

The theme of detachment as characteristic of the following of Christ motivated flight into the desert (*anachoresis*). Antony, the first monk, left all things after hearing Matt. 19.21 read in church and engaged in a radical asceticism taking Christ as his example. The lives of the Desert Fathers and Mothers were characterized by renunciation of worldly goods, austerity of life, clothing and food, and supporting themselves through manual labour which was also to benefit the poor. This tradition was transmitted to the West by John Cassian (d. 432) who saw renunciation as the synthesis of the monastic ideal. The Rule of Benedict in the sixth century saw the monastery as the fulfilment of Acts 4.32.

With the advent of the mendicant orders the focus passed to sharing the life of the poor as the realization of the gospel ideal in imitation of Christ. Francis of Assisi (d. 1226) and his friars practised itinerant poverty supported by manual labour, with recourse to begging only when work did not provide for necessities. Francis experienced God as the source of all good, celebrating creation as the reflection of God, thus countering the example of the Cathars who practised a radical asceticism as the rejection of the material world as evil. Dominic (d. 1221) and his brothers practised poverty and humility as the necessary foundation for effective preaching. Through the preaching of the mendicants, the ideal of poverty was embraced by the laity in third orders and confraternities. A mysticism of poverty developed in the fourteenth century with figures such as Meister Eckhart (d. 1328), Angela of Foligno (d. 1309) and others.

In the following centuries these themes of poverty as communion and poverty as detachment gave rise to new movements. Especially since the nineteenth century, the renewal of Church and society was effected by the choice of voluntary poverty. Richard Benson (d. 1915) founded the Society of Saint John the Evangelist to give witness to a disinterested poverty and occasioned the renewal of religious life in the Anglican Communion. Other figures witnessed to poverty through their lives such as Charles de Foucauld (d. 1916) living the mystery of Nazareth in imitation of the poor Christ, and Thérèse of Lisieux (d. 1897) with her little way. The element that emerged in the contemporary period is the link between poverty and justice, especially through the development of base-communities in Latin America and liberation theology. The base-communities realize a Church of the poor on the model of the Jerusalem community described in Acts 4.32. Official teaching of the Christian Churches has challenged Christians to be attentive to the poor and to live lives of detachment.

Synthesis. What emerges from both Scripture and the tradition of the Christian Church has implications for Christian spirituality today. (1) The Christian ideal of communion can only be realized through the concrete sharing of hearts and hands, which implies a detachment of poverty that liberates one from slavery to material things and fosters generosity toward others. (2) The Christian vocation involves a real response to Jesus who invites one to leave all things and follow him, entailing a way of being in the world which recognizes the good things of earth as destined for the use of all. (3) There is an intrinsic relation between poverty and justice in that it is not enough to be detached from material things if one is not engaged for the welfare of others. (4) Given the reality of globalization today, the gospel calls Christians to realize that the Christian ideal of poverty and communion call forth a spirituality of engagement and involvement, in the various forms this may take, with the powers of the world today.

See also **Asceticism; Communion/***Koinonia***; Desert; Detachment; Franciscan Spirituality; Imitation of Christ; Labour, Manual; Liberation Spirituality; Monasticism; Mendicant Spirituality; Religious Life; Simplicity; Social Justice; Vows.**

———

Gustavo Gutiérrez, *The Power of the Poor in History*, Maryknoll, NY: Orbis Books, 1983; Simon Légasse, Aimé Solignac, Michel Mollat, Jean-Marie-R. Tillard and Michel Dupuy, 'Pauvreté Chrétienne', in *DS*, vol. 12, cols 613–97;

Michel Mollat, *The Poor in the Middle Ages: An Essay in Social History*, New Haven, CT: Yale University Press, 1986; John O'Brien, 'Poverty' in Judith A. Dwyer (ed.), *The New Dictionary of Catholic Social Thought*, Collegeville, MN: The Liturgical Press, 1994, pp. 770–6; J. David Pleins and Thomas D. Hanks, 'Poor, Poverty' in David N. Freedman (ed.), *The Anchor Bible Dictionary* 5, New York: Doubleday Press, 1992, pp. 402–24.

MICHAEL W. BLASTIC

Practice, Spiritual

In broad terms, 'spiritual practice' refers to ways in which a particular spiritual vision is both expressed and facilitated in patterns of behaviour, rituals, prayer or other religious disciplines and so on. In much contemporary discourse about 'spirituality', there can on the one hand be a tendency to overemphasize the centrality of spiritual experiences at the expense of the notion of practice, discipline or lifestyle. Yet, on the other hand, there can at times be an equal tendency to create a framework of spiritual practice in isolation from religious belief. The Christian spiritual tradition taken as a whole emphasizes that spiritual vision and spiritual practice go hand in hand. That is, that our religious vision (conceptions of God, world and human life) and our spiritual practices necessarily mutually inform each other. Christian spirituality, in short, is a way of life, a way of addressing the whole of life, a way of being in the world, not merely prayer or beliefs in isolation. A balance of prayer, ascetic discipline and work with and for other people – albeit a balance expressed in a multitude of forms – would be a conventional Christian pattern of spiritual practice. The balance should be at the heart of any contemporary approach to a 'rule of life' where this tradition forms part of spiritual practice and of spiritual direction (for example, in the Anglican tradition and in the commitments made by tertiaries or oblates of religious orders).

Two forms of imbalance have at times characterized Christian approaches to spiritual practice. First, there has sometimes been an excessive emphasis on detached interiority, where inner experiences are given priority or, more broadly, a reduction of spiritual practice to 'a life of prayer', deemed superior to, and detached from, immersion in and engagement with the everyday world. Such an imbalance is critiqued by important elements of the Western Christian mystical tradition (for example, the teachings of John Ruysbroeck on the wickedness of practising inwardness and ignoring ethics) and by various spiritualities of 'the practice everyday life' (for

example, the Ignatian Exercises). Second, while conversion from the values of 'this world' to kingdom values is a fundamental characteristic of Christian discipleship, certain penitential movements throughout the history of Christian spirituality have adopted an excessively negative view of human embodiment or of the material order more generally and thus adopted spiritual practices that speak of a spirit–body dichotomy. An example would be the movements of flagellants who appeared in Western Europe during the thirteenth and fourteenth centuries in response to social, political and religious insecurities and to a sense of God's anger with humankind manifested by these insecurities and by succeeding waves of plague.

The classic way of describing specifically Christian spirituality is in terms of *discipleship*. This emphasizes that to seek to know Jesus Christ is always to follow him and, in some sense, to seek to imitate his way. The notion of 'imitation of Christ', while prevalent during the Middle Ages (e.g. in Franciscan spirituality and in the *Devotio Moderna* movement) raises difficult issues if it is treated in too literal a way (for example, Martin Luther's fear of sliding into salvation by works). That said, the notion of Jesus Christ as teaching the pattern for every Christian life, and of Christian discipleship as a process of seeking to bring one's life into conformity with the call of Christ, would be accepted as normative. As long as one is attentive to the practical absurdities of literalism and to the theological ambiguities, the notion of 'imitation of Christ' still has strong and effective resonances (see, for example, Bonhoeffer's emphasis on disciples bearing the image of Christ as Christ bore the image of God: Bonhoeffer, 1984, ch. 32).

The Christian emphasis on *discipleship*, an active response to and following of the way of Jesus Christ, and on *discipline* (to be understood broadly as training for discipleship) underlines the centrality of praxis (action and doing rather than merely experience) in spirituality. The latter is an embodied contemplative activity of living out Christian faith, individually and collectively, in the transforming context of a response to God in everyday life. A renewed emphasis on 'spirituality-as-practice' demands a re-engagement between spirituality and ethics – two concepts that have frequently been held at a distance from each other. Although a focus on 'praxis' can be defined simply as 'practice', the contemporary usage does not merely mean any and every Christian action or spiritual practice but specifically a practice of the gospel which enhances freedom in the world in all its forms as a fundamental human and Christian value.

Thus, the interplay between spirituality and praxis brings with it a consciousness of social engagement and social transformation as a form of spiritual practice and of Christian discipleship as embodying both a mystical and a prophetic-political faith. The traditional Christian spiritual practice of almsgiving (see, for example, the Rules for Almsgiving in the Ignatian Spiritual Exercises) may be reinterpreted in this way. The various forms of liberationist and Christian feminist spiritualities are two contemporary critical articulations of this view of discipleship and spirituality.

See also **Asceticism; Discipleship; Discipline; Ecological Spirituality; Ethics and Spirituality; Feminist Spirituality; Imitation of Christ; Liberation Spirituality; Social Justice.**

Dietrich Bonhoeffer, *The Cost of Discipleship*, London: SCM Press, 1984; Janet Ruffing (ed.), *Mysticism and Social Transformation*, Syracuse: Syracuse University Press, 2001; Philip Sheldrake, *Images of Holiness: Explorations in Contemporary Spirituality*, London: Darton Longman & Todd, 1987/Notre Dame, IN: Ave Maria Press, 1988; Philip Sheldrake, 'Christian spirituality as a way of living publicly: a dialectic of the mystical and prophetic', *Spiritus: A journal of Christian spirituality* 3.1 (Spring 2003), 19–37; William C. Spohn, *Go and Do Likewise: Jesus and Ethics*, New York: Continuum, 1999.

PHILIP SHELDRAKE

Praise

Praise lies on a continuum that includes all forms of prayerful conversation with God. Whether given in the context of a worshipping community, in informal gatherings, or in solitude behind closed doors, the prayer of praise implies a simultaneous prayer of confession of who we are before God and of God's faithfulness in history. At the same time praise implies a prayer of adoration to the majesty of God and thanksgiving for abundance. Given this continuum, it is not surprising that attempts made to distinguish praise from thanksgiving are particularly difficult. Four basic strategies within the Christian prayer tradition wrestle with the distinctions between praise and thanksgiving in particular, and between praise and other forms of prayer in general. The strategies serve to highlight both the unique nature of praise and the place of praise in the comprehensive arc of verbal prayer.

Friedrich Heiler represents an advocate of a first strategy noting that, especially in the liturgical context, the early Church names praise and thanksgiving as the first two topics of Christian prayer. Both forms of prayer acknowledge God's divine acts in history. They are distinguished, according to Heiler, in that thanksgiving is linked to God's salvation bestowed *upon us* while praise is linked to the greatness and power of God as witnessed *in and through creation*. Prayers of thanksgiving are thus given for God's deeds in the history of redemption while prayers of praise are grounded in God's work in the history of creation (cf. Heiler, 1997, p. xi).

A second strategy makes a distinction based upon the relation between God's being and God's action. Praise and thanksgiving in this formula are like two hands offering a cup of adoration. One hand represents praise as we adore God for who God is in Godself (God's being). A second hand represents thanksgiving as we adore God for what God has done for us (God's action) (cf. Foster, 1992, p. 8). Here again the distinction is valid but it is valid only in the sense that the distinctions lie on a continuum. It is actually very hard to separate who God is from what God has done. In this strategy thanksgiving and praise are tightly interwoven, just as gratitude for what God has done is virtually inseparable from the joy that we find in the fact that God is who God is.

A third formulation groups and distinguishes praise and thanksgiving from petition and intercession. From this standpoint, prayer is placed in the context of human response to a God who first addresses us. In this scheme, praise and thanksgiving represent our response in view of what God has already done for us, while petition and intercession represent our response in view of what we want God to do for us in the future. The distinction is based on abundance and need, but again the distinction serves to highlight the continuum. Praise as a response to abundance simultaneously recognizes our ongoing needs (petition and intercession), our relation to and dependence upon God (confession), and opens our eyes to God's goodness, mystery and holiness (adoration).

A final strategy, grounded in the third-century Greek theologian Origen, highlights the crucial relation between theology and prayer in order to make a distinction between praise and thanksgiving. Thanksgiving for Origen flows from abundance. This abundance in turn brings 'forward for thanksgiving the benefits given many people and those [the pray-er] receives from God'. But for Origen, in the best tradition of patristic spirituality, praise is at once both prayer and a prayerful understanding of doctrine; it is prayer that flows into and out of the *experience* of theology. The power of praise, Origen says, is that which is offered to 'God through Christ, who is praised in Him, and by the Holy Spirit, who is hymned with him' (*On Prayer* 3.33.2). Here the person, being and work of Christ as creator and redeemer is praise. Likewise, the Holy Spirit is a hymn of praise. Praise in this sense is a primal and integral connective reality of the inter-trinitarian relationship itself; it is a mode of our participation in and with the Father, Son and Holy Spirit.

In each of the four strategies, one can detect an instinct to regard praise as first among equals in verbal prayer. A contemporary writer notes that, 'When I give thanks, my thoughts still circle about myself to some extent. But in praise my soul ascends to self-forgetting adoration, seeing and praising only the majesty and power of God, God's grace and redemption' (Hallesby and Carlsen, 1994). Origen is explicit about the elevation of praise above other forms of prayer. In a commentary on 1 Tim. 2.1 which reads, 'First of all, then, I urge supplications, prayers, intercessions, and thanksgivings', Origen says of *all* prayer that 'in the beginning and preface something having the force of praise should be said' (*On Prayer* 3.33.1).

Praise pervades all of Scripture. Indeed, praise seems to be the eschatological fulfilment of a God-appointed vocation. Scripture encourages praise of God's just laws, praise for God's incomprehensible mystery, and praise for the goodness and power God displays through creation. We are called to praise God's name. The Psalms build to a crescendo of praise (Ps. 145–150) in which all creatures, stars, planets, heavens, saints and angels are called to praise God. In quiet times or with shouts, with musical instruments, dancing, song, waving palms or jubilation, expressions of praise connect us to God's eternal shalom.

See also **Adoration; Celebration; Joy; Hymns and Spirituality; Nature Mysticism; Prayer; Psalms; Thanksgiving.**

Richard Foster, *Prayer: Finding the Heart's True Home*, San Francisco, CA: HarperSanFrancisco, 1992; Margaret Guenther, *The Practice of Prayer*, Boston, MA: Cowley Publications, 1998; O. Hallesby and C. J. Carlsen, *Prayer*, Minneapolis, MN: Augsburg Fortress, 1994; Friedrich Heiler, *Prayer: A Study in the History and Psychology of Religion*, Oxford: OneWorld Press, 1997; Origen, *On Prayer* in *Origen: An Exhortation to Martyrdom, Prayer, and Other Works*, trans. Rowan A. Greer, New York: Paulist Press, 1979; John H. Wright, 'Prayer' in *The New Dictionary of Christian Spirituality*, ed. Michael Downey, Collegeville, MN: The Liturgical Press, 1993, pp. 764–75.

STEVEN CHASE

Praxis

see **Practice, Spiritual**

Prayer

Poetic expression most aptly captures the mystery of prayer. Basil Hume describes prayer at its best as 'like being in a dark room with someone you love'. William Blake's 'we are put on earth for a little space that we may learn to bear the beams of love' also goes to the heart of prayer. Both expressions underline the nature of prayer as response to God's gestures toward humanity. Christian writers have discussed the types, methods and stages of prayer for millennia, but even exhaustive treatments of prayer remain partial and inadequate, because of the profoundly personal (not private) nature of prayer. Metaphors that capture the spirit of prayer include the following. Prayer is a gift of God; a soulful conversation; silent contemplation; an expression of wonder; acknowledgement of finitude; the articulation of desire; sharing in God's trinitarian life; an art; raising one's mind and heart to God. There is also paradox in prayer – it is both a privilege and a duty; we do not know how to pray as we ought (Rom. 8.26) and yet are commanded to pray without ceasing (1 Thess. 5.17); we are advised to practise prayer regularly and yet to seek 'mastery' is to miss the point entirely.

1. *Biblical prayer.* Important biblical wellsprings of prayer include Israel's prayer book, the Psalms, and the prayer of Jesus. The psalms arise out of profound awareness of the unconditional love and power of Yahweh, acknowledging human need and dependence on the divine covenant partner. The psalms express virtually every movement of the human heart – praise, anger, trust, lament, compassion, joy, jealousy, intercession, forgiveness, thanksgiving. When we cannot find words to pray, the psalms are at hand to assist us.

The prayer of Jesus is the model par excellence for Christians. In the Gospels, we learn of Jesus' prayer, his trust in God's intimate love and mercy and the ways in which the Spirit worked in and through him (Matt. 11.25–27; Mark 1.9–11; 9.2–8; 14.36; Luke 10.21–22; John 17.1–26). Paul counsels believers that they too are invited to participate in the prayer of Jesus (Rom. 8.15; Gal. 4.6); to make melody to the Lord with full hearts (Eph. 5.20); to pray for each other in the Spirit (Eph. 6.18); to pray without ceasing (1 Thess. 5.17) or anxiety (Phil. 3.17). Matthew (6.9–13) and Luke (11.2–4) record Jesus' teaching of the Lord's Prayer – a way to pray simply and without fanfare, a prayer that is recited daily across the world in both personal and liturgical settings. The Lord's Prayer is a guide to the meaning of prayer. In it one offers praise to God, asks for daily sustenance, forgiveness and protection from temptation.

2. *Characteristics of prayer*. The primary place of prayer is community – the world, the body of Christ, the community of family and friends. Individual prayer is indispensable, but it emerges from, dwells in, and flows back to community. Some prayer can be described as extraordinary – moments in which we are swept off our feet into a world of unifying love. But most of our prayer takes place amid the daily round of living and is therefore best kept simple, brief, ordinary, frequent and human. Creation and incarnation ground Christian prayer in the complexity of daily existence, demanding that it be down-to-earth and portable. We pray not only at designated times, but at any moment of the day, so that God's presence – or at times God's absence – weaves in and out of everything we say, think or do.

Rather than worry about how to pray, one can attend to the prayer that is given in the moment – joy at a spring flower; remorse for our selfishness; pain at loss and disappointment; praise for the wonder of God; frustration at one's inability to pray; active compassion for a street person; healing for illness; forgiveness for offences; gratitude for a new child; lament for those who suffer from hunger, loneliness and war. Prayer that suffuses one's life is holistic, engaging our minds, spirits and bodies; nature and culture; Church and society. There need be no walls around prayer – it can happen at home, in a magnificent cathedral or a humble shopfront, at the office, in the car, or while walking, dancing, climbing, resting, singing or weeping. The eucharistic celebration gathers the prayers of the whole community, as it remembers Jesus' redemptive activities.

Wonder is another foundational element of prayer. Wonder produces gratitude and praise, acknowledging the God who creates, loves and holds the world in existence. A life characterized by wonder is a life open to surprise that refuses to put God in a box, demanding that God be present in predictable ways. Wonder also presumes trust. Prayer acknowledges reliance on God on whose mercy and love we depend. The Gospels challenge us to become childlike by relying on God with confidence and simplicity (Matt. 6.28; 11.25–27; Luke 10.21–22). Julian of Norwich's 'all will be well' captures the disposition of leaning quietly and confidently on God.

Finally, prayer is humble and generous. The tradition contains the record of many holy ones who lived simply before God in the truth of who they were. Their prayer was not puffed up or self-congratulatory. They prayed with clarity about the truth of their creatureliness, their sinfulness and their capacity to become a dwelling place for divinity. Made in the image and likeness of God and baptized into the life, death and resurrection of Christ, the saints model lives of humble and generous prayer. Proximity to the God whose greatest joy is to offer life and love reveals the truth of human nothingness and challenges us to imitate God's love by developing a generous heart.

3. *Obstacles to prayer*. Asceticism is that part of prayer that notices and abandons things that prevent authentic prayer. Preoccupation with self instead of focus on God produces arrogance, smugness, anxiety and hypocrisy. Prayer practice is never immune from engendering false confidence, self-congratulation and anxiety about how one is doing. To approach prayer to 'gain mastery' is to miss the point that prayer is, above all, gift. Fighting distractions can also inhibit prayer. It is often wiser simply to place thoughts and concerns in God's hands.

Frequent prayer can become mechanistic, requiring that we devise ways to renew the freshness of prayer. Preoccupation with performance and 'results' can also lead to an instrumental understanding of prayer. In its deepest sense, what one seeks in prayer is prayer (seeking God's presence) – not a good grade, or the right job, not even health or long life. It is like play in that it does not demand or coerce results. Ultimately one prays not to 'get something', but simply to praise and thank the gracious God of the universe.

Long periods of dryness in prayer can be wearing and frustrating, tempting the one who prays to abandon prayer. When God seems distant or even absent, and prayer seems to produce no fruit, vigilance demands perseverance, courage and trust that somehow in the darkness, the seeds of light are planted and will blossom. A life of prayer requires courage and the will to 'show up' each day – a gesture that in itself is prayer (Luke 11.5–9; 18.2–5). Gregory of Nyssa reminded us that the *desire* to pray is in itself prayer.

Prayer that is motivated primarily by a sense of guilt is unlikely to be genuine prayer. Prayer undertaken because someone will disapprove of me if I don't; because I will fall down in my own image of myself; or because I am afraid of punishment – is bound to be pseudo-prayer, lacking the freedom of raising one's heart to God. The command to pray without ceasing is a valid reason to pray, but at some point the command becomes the true desire of one's heart.

4. *Fruits of prayer.* True prayer bears the fruit of the Spirit – love, joy, peace, patience, kindness, goodness, faithfulness, gentleness and self-control (Gal. 5.22–23). True prayer becomes visible in a life of virtue and leads to conversion, to hearts of flesh, not stone, to embracing change that may be welcome, painful or even terrifying. (Ezek. 11.19). Through trust in a loving God, we open ourselves to the Spirit's power that challenges us to constant change, discovering a new self that allows us to leave the false self behind over and over again. Through prayer, we realize our identity as children and friends of God, liberated from sin and death and alive to the fullness of life. By turning us toward God, all expressions of prayer – monastic, lay, private, public, individual or communal – turn us toward the world. Through prayer, we stand united with all people and especially in solidarity with those who are poor, forgotten and marginalized. Prayer is a way to express hunger for peace and friendship with God for oneself and for the world.

See also **Affirmative Way; Apophatic Spirituality; Attentiveness; Body and Spirituality; Contemplation; Devotions; Discernment; Dreams and Dreaming; Experience, Religious; Imagination; Intercession; Interiority; Jesus Prayer;** *Lectio Divina;* **Lord's Prayer; Meditation; Office, Divine; Prayer, Psychology of; Silence.**

H. Urs von Balthasar, *Prayer*, New York: Sheed & Ward, 1961 [1957]; W. Callahan, *Noisy Contemplation*, Hyattsville, MD: Quixote Center, 1994 [1982]; T. Dunne, *We Cannot Find Words: The Foundations of Prayer*, Denville, NJ: Dimension Books, 1981; R. Goodwin, *Give Us This Day: The Story of Prayer*, Hudson, NY: Lindisfarne Books, 1999; T. Green, *When the Well Runs Dry: Prayer Beyond the Beginnings*, Notre Dame, IN: Ave Maria Press, 1998; T. Merton, *Contemplative Prayer*, New York: Doubleday, 1969; K. Rahner, *Prayers for a Lifetime*, New York: Crossroad, 1995; K. Rahner, *The Need and the Blessing of Prayer*, Collegeville, MN: The Liturgical Press, 1997; S. Tugwell, *Prayer in Practice*, Dublin: Veritas/Springfield, IL: Templegate, 1974.

ELIZABETH A. DREYER

Prayer of the Heart

see Hesychasm

Prayer, Psychology of

The psychology of prayer is a relatively new idea, having grown up with the advent of depth psychology in the twentieth century, beginning with Freud who wanted to replace religion with his psychoanalysis, and Jung who saw his analytical psychology as a way to reconnect with religion. From these two seminal thinkers, a whole new discipline has grown, called depth psychology, that gives an additional way to interpret all forms of human culture, including religious doctrines and rituals. Depth psychology developed many schools of thought in addition to Freud and Jung, such as object relations, self psychology, existential psychology, relational psychology, each of which developed treatment methods to alleviate the mental and emotional anguish of people afflicted with neurosis or psychosis.

The distinguishing contribution of depth psychology to praying is recognition of the human psyche, and especially its unconscious processes, as inextricably present in prayer. Acknowledgement of psychic reality, that we are conscious and unconscious beings, enlarges our understanding of praying. Augustine says God hears our words of prayer (what we consciously intend) and listens to the secret heart of our prayer (what goes on in us unconsciously). Many saints say our very desire to pray is God's spirit already praying in us.

The psyche is also the flesh in which God incarnates, so the psyche's speech is primary, giving voice to the primordial discourse of the images, impulses, hopes, evasions, fears, dreams, desires, fantasies, sexual urges, angers, assertions, needs, that constantly go on in us. Hence everybody prays, whether or not they call it prayer. Every time we ask for help, understanding, strength, in or out of religion, we speak out of us, whether we know it or not. Every time we seek relief for others' pain, or give thanks for the community out of which we emerge, or weep because we feel outside others, we speak our basic human condition.

Prayer is primary because this speech of confession comes first in any act of praying. In prayer we speak out of our flesh, the ground of all our experience, collecting into awareness what our self is saying, both what we know and what we do not know. God hears all our voices and speaks to us in the flesh of our human self and the world. This theological fact changes the way we pray.

Instead of seeing images that come into our mind as we try to pray, or worries about our job or our children, our political or sexual life, as distractions from prayer that we must get rid of or master, we see God meeting us there too, in the flesh of our experience, all of it, all of our self and our world, our conscious and unconscious lives. The Spirit dwells in all these spontaneous manifestations of our life embodied in the world, the world God entered to be among us and with us. Our sense of community thus extends to seeing that despite our differences of culture, country, race, creed or even religion, we all share the same kind of mental life and are inhabited by the same kind of crying out to some kind of transcendent source.

As we collect bits of ourselves into the speech of prayer, confessing them, knowingly now speaking with all the voices in us, these voices focus our attention on the one to whom we are speaking. God becomes the primary focus of our primary, prayerful speech.

Critics of prayer can use psychological categories to reduce prayer to a psychological defence, a protective measure to avoid growing up by using God as a substitute for wrestling with our own choices. We appeal to 'God's will', for example, to evade working out our own responsibility. Or we may use prayer as a narcissistic withdrawal from harsh conflicts in the world, trying to sustain a singular relationship to God and ignore our neighbour.

Once we try to pray, we see its words and feelings and gropings are imbued with an intentionality which the philosopher Husserl calls directional, a subject speaking towards an object, with an awareness of an object, however dim or fuzzy the awareness may be. That object, God, makes us in prayer become aware of the subject we are. Prayer to the source of our being gives us more being, more self. But that is not the primary point of prayer; it is a by-product. The primary point is the other, the one we are seeking in our speech. This is the primary consciousness in which the object, God, appears to us as the subject reaching to us as subjects.

Praying brings into our consciousness personal and group images we have for God (e.g. a mother, score-keeper, guide, or as liberation, sisterhood). These subjective pictures make the vast transcendent near and real to us. Praying also makes us aware of official God-images drawn from Scripture, doctrine and the worshipping community (e.g. rock, refuge, dinner-party host, judge). These objective God-images bind us into the body of faith, the community in the present and in the past and future yet to come. Prayer in addition makes us conscious of what operates in us unconsciously as if it were a god around which our whole life revolves, like a drinking problem or inferiority complex, or like our love for a child.

All these images come forth in praying as the speech of the psyche embodied in our life in the world. Yet prayer bears in on us the knowledge that none of our images can capture the living God. Praying moves us to offer all God-images back into the living God.

See also **Spirituality, Psychology and Psychotherapy** (*essay*); **Prayer.**

Augustine, *Confessions*, Baltimore, MD: Penguin Classics, 1968; A. M. Rizzuto, *The Birth of the Living God*, Chicago: Chicago University Press, 1979; A. and B. Ulanov, *Primary Speech: A Psychology of Prayer*, Louisville, KY: Westminster John Knox Press, 1982.

ANN BELFORD ULANOV

Preaching and Spirituality

The phrase 'Christian spirituality' can be somewhat elusive. Let it be understood here as that which nourishes the life of the Spirit, fosters growth in the Christ-life or forms people in faith and holiness. Similarly 'preaching' admits of various definitions. Whatever form preaching may take (e.g. keregmatic, doctrinal, liturgical, paraenetic etc.) and whatever the context, the act of preaching is communicating the word of God. Preaching, that is, proclaiming the good news of salvation, is rooted in a biblical understanding of God's word as living, active, salvific and effective.

The first account of creation evinces the power of God's own speech ('God said . . . and so it happened'), a theme repeated, for example, in many psalms: 'The voice of the Lord shakes the wilderness of Kadesh' (Ps. 29.8); 'By the word of the Lord, the heavens were made' (Ps. 33.6). The rich biblical term *dabar* YHWH refers not only to the 'word' of God, but also the *magnalia Dei*, God's mighty acts, which continue even today through the unfolding of salvation history.

The biblical prophets preached, and not only a clarion call to repentance but also a word of consolation and promise. Their own preaching was a response to their hearing of the word of God and their acting upon that received word. That God's received word is efficacious – God's word of judgement, at once a word of salvation – is proclaimed in Isaiah: 'So shall my word be that goes out from my mouth; it shall not return to me empty, but it shall accomplish that which I purpose, and succeed in the thing for which I sent it' (Isa. 55.11).

This biblical trajectory of preaching reaches a certain climax in the incarnation of Christ, the very enfleshment of the *dabar* YHWH (cf. John 1.1–4), who preached the 'reign of God' in the midst of God's people. Not only did this Jesus preach through words (cf. Luke 4.18–19), but also through his parabolic deeds: sharing meals with outcasts, forgiving sin, healing the ill, encountering women, etc. This ministry of Jesus continued through his followers, who, after his crucifixion and burial, boldly proclaimed his resurrection through the power of God.

The scriptural witness makes it clear that preaching, especially in parables, was a central part of Jesus' ministry; however, even the so-called 'teaching' of Jesus had a rhetorical quality to it, rendering it close to what modern people might term homiletic. The primary oral culture of the period made the spoken word crucial and preaching was indeed part of the mission of Jesus: 'to gather into one the dispersed children of God' (John 11.52).

This tradition of preaching continues today in church and synagogue (as well as mosque), even in cultures which are in a stage of secondary orality. The first letter of John is instructive for today's preachers:

> We declare to you what was from the beginning, what we have heard, what we have seen with our eyes, what we have looked at and touched with our hands, concerning the word of life – this life was revealed, and we have seen it and testify to it, and declare to you the eternal life that was with the Father and was revealed to us – we declare to you what we have seen and heard so that you may have fellowship with us; and truly our fellowship is with the Father and with his Son Jesus Christ. (1 John 1.1–3)

The goal of the 'preaching event' is to insure this 'fellowship' with the trinitarian God.

One of the earliest accounts of Christian eucharistic celebration by Justin Martyr (*c.* 165) refers to the reading of 'the memoirs of the Apostles [the Gospels] or the writings of the Prophets', followed by the preaching of the leader, who 'verbally admonishes and invites all to imitate such things' (*Apologia* 67). Justin's description is telling; it is on the basis of God's word proclaimed that the assembled Christians are to shape their lives. Thus, the living word takes root in the hearts of believers and bears fruit in their lives. In a similar way, Hippolytus' *Apostolic Tradition* (*c.* 215?) speaks of the cate-chumens' hearing the word for three years with instruction (the variant texts speak in terms of 'catechizing', 'admonishing' and 'preaching'; what is clear is that the 'instruction' was no mere lecture); prior to baptism their lives will be examined: 'Have they lived good lives when they were catechumens? Have they honoured the widows? Have they visited the sick? Have they done every kind of good work?' (*Apostolic Tradition* 20). For Hippolytus the hearing of the word – and its unfolding in the so-termed 'instruction' – should bear fruit in a life of virtu-ous charity. Thus, the 'spiritual instruction' is aimed at a goal, namely continual conversion of life in the Spirit. This connection between preaching and growth in the Christ-life can also be amply illustrated by the so-termed mystagog-ical catecheses of the fourth century. The word of God pre-eminently revealed in Christ was linked with both the scriptural word and the ritual en-gagements of baptism, chrismation and euchar-ist. What can be gleaned from these documents is that the word of God was interpreted in such a way that it related to the lives of the hearers, so as to foster the development of a life of faith and good works.

While the contemporary context for preach-ing is vastly different from ages past, there still remains a strong link between preaching and the nurturing of the life of the Spirit. Whatever else it is, the act of preaching is an act of human com-munication. Recent studies in communication theory point out that speech is not so much about 'speaking', but more about getting a mes-sage 'heard'. Additionally, studies indicate that what is heard is not only the words, but also messages sent non-verbally, as well as para-tactically (through intonation, speed etc.). Human communication is definitely a complex phenomenon.

Further, preaching is more complex than usual ordinary daily communication. It is funda-mentally a self-revelatory act. Underneath the specific words of the sermon/homily lie the embedded values of the preacher: how the preacher views the mystery of God, Christ and the Spirit, and also God's action in the world today; humanity and its status; the Church and its role in the world; Church polity; Church doc-trine; what the views are of theological terms such as salvation, justification, righteousness; how the preacher views the connection between God's word and issues of justice, poverty, peace and so on. Preachers cannot escape that fact that their words convey more than what is said, and the assembled hearers will detect the underlying 'spirituality' of the preacher.

Similarly the assembly comes to hear the word proclaimed and preached, with their own spir-itualities – their views of God, world, people, Church – and how those beliefs and values shape their living response to the indwelling Spirit, and sometimes in circumstances far different from those of the preacher.

Incumbent upon the preacher charged with

nurturing the faith life of the assembly is a purification of motives. What must be proclaimed at all costs is God's word, not merely the preacher's. What is incumbent upon the congregation is that same purification, namely to hear God's word in an unguarded and vulnerable manner.

To be avoided on the part of the preacher is what the United States Roman Catholic Bishops' document *Fulfilled in Your Hearing* mentions: 'speak[ing] ten feet above contradiction' (p. 15). What is a reasonable and attainable goal for the preacher is to be a 'person speaking to people about faith and life' (p. 15). The office of preaching can be realized effectively only when both preacher and hearer have the same goal: an attentive listening to God's word in such a way that it produces a mutually effective and fruitful life of charity.

See also **Spirituality, Liturgy and Worship** (*essay*); **Evangelization; Rhetoric.**

A. Duane Litfin and Haddon W. Robinson (eds), *Recent Homiletical Thought: An Annotated Bibliography* 2, Grand Rapids, MI: Baker Book House, 1983. While not up to date this nonetheless has an excellent divided annotated bibliography. *Homiletic* UMR, 2004 Lone Star Drive, Dallas, TX, USA (214-631-6610). This is a first-rate journal, especially helpful to preachers. It usually has one essay; the rest of the journal is devoted to book reviews divided into various categories.

Walter Brueggemann, *The Prophetic Imagination,* Philadelphia: Fortress Press, 1978; Walter Brueggemann, *Finally Comes the Poet,* Minneapolis, MN: Augsburg/Fortress Press, 1989; Walter Burghardt, *Preaching: The Art and the Craft,* New York: Paulist Press, 1987; Craig A. Satterlee, *Ambrose of Milan's Method of Mystagogical Preaching,* Collegeville, MN: The Liturgical Press, 2002; Gerard Sloyan, *Worshipful Preaching,* Philadelphia: Fortress Press, 1984; Barbara Brown Taylor, *The Preaching Life,* Boston, MA: Cowley Publications, 1993.

JOHN MELLOH

Presence of God

In understanding the meaning of 'the presence of God', the mystical tradition from Scripture onwards contributes most because in this area the intelligence of the mind needs to be enhanced and completed by the intelligence of contemplation.

'To be' means to be present. The presence of God *is* the divine being but it is known to the degree of consciousness awakened in those creatures whom God has called into being to be present to and with God. Presence is inconceivable without relationship. The essence of the divine presence is God's self-presence in the self-transcending relationships of the Trinity. Whatever is not God by nature is called into the trinitarian presence that is God by the grace of its very existence. So, all things share in the divine self-presence. *Theosis*, as the mystical tradition calls it, is the human corollary of the divine presence (2 Peter 1.4). In some further sense, too, all that exists 'in heaven and earth' is being called into this transformed way of being (Eph. 1.10). Human consciousness can only conceptualize and describe experience of God by analogy. Yet it can experientially know the divine presence through the process of its own transformation and the purified levels of its participation in the divine being. 'By thought we can never know him. We know him only by love' (*The Cloud of Unknowing*). The presence of God is known by faith but also by experience. The disciplines of contemplation develop and unite both ways of knowing.

'The unloving know nothing of God for God is love' (1 John 4.7). The mystery of the Trinity reveals Being as communion in love. We become present to God, therefore, to the degree that we are in love, which means to be fully present to what is not ourselves but with whatever we can, on the divine model, be in union with.

The self-saying of God (Logos) results in the existence of all that can say 'I am'. Presence also implies self-knowledge and self-expression. The self-knowledge of the human 'I am' is an echo or reflective icon (*imago dei*) of the God who *is* Being, not *a* Being among others. But 'we can never know God as an object but only by sharing in God's own self-knowledge' (Irenaeus). Human existence itself, when seen as growth in being present to self, to others and to Being (the being-present-to-the presence called spiritual growth) is the best proof of God.

If the 'glory of God is the human being fully alive', to glorify God is not the human idolization of its image of God, but the realization of human potential to be present to the divine presence. The best sign of this will be 'living in love' (John 15.12). Being fully alive is the 'vision of God' and 'we shall become like him when we see him as he is' (1 John 3.2). So by becoming undividedly present, humanity best incarnates the presence of God as relationship in love. Being present, in the non-judgemental sense that Jesus describes the divine presence to 'good and bad alike' (Matt. 5.45), is the ascetical work of contemplation (what Aquinas calls the 'simple enjoyment of what is').

All visible manifestation is the sacrament of God's ineffable presence: in Auschwitz or Assisi. God is not more present in some relationships and less in others because the presence constitutes their very existence. Human reciprocal presence is the variable factor. The diverse beauty of creation reflects, without exhausting, the unbounded creativity of divine presence. Creation is an unfolding of presence rather than the act of a particular being. In seeing this, as the mystics help us to, a merely moralistic picture of a rewarding and punishing divinity dissolves. Yet presence must be interpersonal and so, although 'God does not have favourites', the universal presence of God is immeasurably friendly to all – a reality known at the level of one's own capacity to be present.

The contemplatives assert that we share in the presence of God by cultivating the faculty of attention. Attention is the capacity to love, the nature of prayer and the meaning of worship – the opposite of 'being in two minds' (James 1.8). Correcting the sinful, endemic human state of distraction is the 'practice of the presence of God'. As the mystics teach, to pray is to be present to God with increasing purity and duration. Religious forms of prayer are designed to develop the ability to 'stay awake and pray' continuously. Increasingly the presence of God becomes luminous in everything, sacred or secular, and the very distinction between these states fades. Simultaneously illusion, the root of all evil and the denial of the presence of God, diminishes. We awaken to God's attention to us rushing across the abyss of otherness with the self-abandoned love of the Parent towards the prodigal child.

The distracted, egotistical mind undermines the capacity to be present because presence chooses for the necessary existence of an *other*. But the presence of God is felt as redemptive mercy whenever a genuine effort is made to be present (whether to pray, to pay attention, to love or to be truthful). Thus presence is equally perceptible in suffering and joy.

In Christian faith, Jesus is the fully embodied presence of God in the material, mental and spiritual realms. He brings all into the presence of the Father through the enlightening power of the Spirit. In his teaching and risen life, the presence of God is communicated in ways that awaken the human capacity to self-transcendence, to be present to oneself, to others and to God. Where he is, we are (John 17.21).

See also Mysticism (*essay*); Attentiveness; Contemplation; Experience, Religious; God, Images of; Meditation.

O. Clement, *The Roots of Christian Mysticism*, New York: New City, 1993; L. Freeman, *Jesus the Teacher Within*, London and New York: Continuum, 2001; V. Lossky, *In the Image and Likeness of God*, New York: St Vladimir's Seminary Press, 1985; B. McGinn, *The Growth of Mysticism*, London: SCM Press, 1994; R. Williams, *The Wound of Knowledge*, London: Darton, Longman & Todd, rev. edn, 1990; S. Weil, *Waiting for God*, New York: Harper & Row, 1973.

LAURENCE FREEMAN

Priesthood and Spirituality

A spirituality of priesthood is inseparable from the theology of priesthood that underlies it. But the issue is complicated by the fact that the development of the Church's presbyteral office is itself complex. The New Testament uses a variety of terms for those who exercised roles of pastoral leadership and service in the earliest Christian communities. By the end of the New Testament period, those roles were increasingly being carried out by those called 'elders' (*presbyteroi*) or 'overseers' (*episkopoi*), two titles not always clearly distinguished. Writing in Peter's name as a 'fellow-presbyter' (1 Peter 5.1), the author of 1 Peter exhorts the presbyters in Asia Minor: 'Tend the flock of God in your midst, [overseeing] not by constraint but willingly, as God would have it, not for shameful profit, but eagerly. Do not lord it over those assigned to you, but be examples to the flock. And when the chief Shepherd is revealed, you will receive the unfading crown of glory' (1 Peter 5.2–4). Thus the presbyters are called to humble service, to a pastoral care free of any desire for financial gain or superior status. They share in the ministry of Christ himself, the 'chief shepherd' (5.4), whose suffering (5.1) offers a model of humble service.

As early as Ignatius of Antioch (*c.* 110), the bishop presided over the local community and regulated its liturgy. This was a basic principle in the pre-Nicene Church: the one who presided over the life of the Church presided at its Eucharist. But the same period also saw the gradual evolution of this ministry of pastoral leadership into a cultic, sacerdotal office. As early as 96, the author of 1 Clement compared the order of the Jewish cult, with its high priests, priests and levites, to the order of the Christian community with its apostles, bishops and deacons (40–2). The *Didache* (*c.* 100) recognizes the wandering prophets as eucharistic leaders (10) and calls them 'high priests' (13). The prayer of consecration for the ordination of a bishop attributed to Hippolytus of Rome (*c.* 215) refers to the bishop as 'high priest' (*Apostolic Tradition* 3.4).

Tertullian (d. 225) and Cyprian (d. 258) also speak of the bishop as *sacerdos*. Cyprian extended the term to presbyters, but only in conjunction with the bishop, a usage that has been traditional in the Church. It is also in Cyprian that we find the first reference to presbyters presiding at the Eucharist without the bishop (*Letter* 5).

The charism of presbyteral ministry was a gift for building up the Church. The idea of a vocation is a relatively modern one. In the ancient Church, those with talents for ecclesial leadership were sometimes ordained unwillingly into the office of bishop or presbyter. In the early Middle Ages rural priests, frequently freed serfs or the sons of priests, were more often appointed to their congregations by the feudal lord than by the bishop. Their role was almost exclusively cultic, to offer the Mass and administer the sacraments. And there were other factors contributing to a sacralization of the presbyteral office. Canonists distinguished between the power of ordination and the power of jurisdiction. Theologians defined the sacrament of Holy Orders, not in terms of the bishop's pastoral office but in reference to the priest's role in the offering of the Eucharist. The result of these developments was that priesthood was increasingly understood as a cultic office rather than a ministerial one. The Council of Trent, reacting to the Protestant Reformers, emphasized a visible priesthood with 'the power of consecrating, offering and administering' the body and blood of Christ and forgiving sins (*DS* 1764), but its Decree on Holy Orders neglected to say anything about preaching and leading the Christian community.

The cultic focus of the late Middle Ages was to influence priestly spirituality in the centuries that followed. But it was the so-called 'French School' in the post-Reformation period that was to have the greatest influence on the spirituality of the priesthood in modern times. Its founder, Cardinal Pierre de Bérulle (1575–1629), and those he influenced, Jean-Jacques Olier (1608–57), Vincent de Paul (1581–1660) and Jean Eudes (1601–80), were to shape the culture and spirituality of the priesthood through their enormous influence on priestly formation. Bérulle developed an exalted notion of the priest in his efforts to foster the sanctity of the diocesan clergy. He founded the French Congregation of the Oratory in 1611. His disciples founded congregations that staffed seminaries, de Paul the Congregation of the Missions or Vincentians in 1625, Eudes the Congregation of Jesus and Mary in 1643, later known as the Eudists, and Olier the Society of St Suplice in 1645, the Sulpicians.

At its best, the French School was concretely trinitarian, christological and ecclesial. It saw the humanity of Jesus as the unsurpassable revelation of the Father and Christian life as incorporating the believer into the Son's service and adoration of the Father, and thus into the interpersonal life of the Trinity. For Bérulle, priests bear the character of the Son of God imprinted upon their souls through baptism and the sacrament of orders. He saw the priest's role as most fully realized when celebrating the Eucharist, participating in this way in Christ's great sacrificial offering to the Father. Olier's priestly spirituality was rooted in a sacramental vision of the entire Church, a universal call to holiness, and a mysticism flowing from baptism. A modern study (Chaillot et al., 1984) finds his theology close to that of Vatican II. But Olier's vision was blurred by a work long attributed to him, the *Traité des Saints Ordres*, now recognized as the work of the third superior general of the Sulpicians, Louis Tronson (1622–1700), who reworked some of Olier's writings.

Tronson's theology of orders was an improvement on the earlier Scholastic approach in that it was centred on the ministry of Christ. But the priestly spirituality that flowed from it was far more clerical; it saw the priest as having a unique and superior holiness based on his cultic role. Rejecting the good things of this world in favour of the next, it encouraged asceticism, to discipline the flesh. The priest became increasingly a man apart. It was this otherworldly spirituality, really a truncated version of the spirituality of the French School, that was to shape the culture of those trained in seminaries – nearly all priests after 1850 – down to the Second Vatican Council.

The cultic model of priesthood, based on the sacred functions of worship and sacrifice, largely collapsed in the period after Vatican II. Without rejecting the older tradition, the Council broadened the concept of priesthood by stressing that ordination confers the threefold *munera* of teaching, sanctifying and governing (*Lumen Gentium* 28), thus adding the prophetic and pastoral roles to the cultic, roles that require different skills. It also put the ministerial or hierarchical priesthood in the broader context of the priesthood of Christ and that of the baptized (*Lumen Gentium* 10). But the Council's enlarging of the concept of priesthood and the rediscovery of a more inclusive concept of *diakonia* in its aftermath has led to a crisis of identity for many priests.

The different interpretations of Vatican II's theology of priesthood, placing emphasis on the priest's kerygmatic (Karl Rahner, Joseph Ratzinger), cultic/sacramental (Otto Semmelroth, John Paul II), or community leadership role (Thomas O'Meara, Robert Schwartz) suggest different priestly spiritualities. Pope John Paul II, echoing Bérulle, stresses that the priests are bound in a special way to strive for perfection 'since they are consecrated to God in a new way by their ordination', becoming living instruments of Christ the eternal priest (*Pastores Dabo Vobis* 20). The ministry of a diocesan priest is essentially communitarian, proclaiming the word, celebrating the sacraments, guiding and nurturing a local Christian community. Diocesan priestly spirituality must unite the demands of such an active ministry with a radical experience of being alone with God. A contemporary spirituality for priests needs also to address the integration of sexuality and celibacy. Some have objected that the tendency to define all priests on the model of diocesan priesthood, evident even in Vatican II's *Presbyterorum Ordinis*, slights the special character of religious clergy. Their spirituality more properly is rooted in the concrete circumstances of their ministry and the charism or spirit of their institute, for example Franciscan, Dominican or Jesuit.

The French School may have focused too narrowly on the priest's role at the Eucharist, turning him into a special cultic figure. Yet it remains true that holiness of life should be a central concern for a priest and that priestly ministry is most fully realized in the sacramental celebration of the triune God's transforming presence in the Christian community (cf. 1 Cor. 4.1). Therefore the priest's spirituality must be experienced as a participation in the mystery of God moving into the world in Christ and drawing it back to a communion in the divine life in the Spirit. In this way, the priest serves the priesthood of all the baptized.

See also Discipleship; French School of Spirituality; Leadership; Ministry and Spirituality; Oratorian Spirituality; Pastoral Care and Spirituality; Sulpician Spirituality; Vincentian Spirituality.

George A. Aschenbrenner, *Quickening the Fire in our Midst: The Challenge of Diocesan Priestly Spirituality*, Chicago: Loyola Press, 2002; William M. Thompson (ed.), *Bérulle and the French School: Selected Writings*, trans. Lowell M. Glendon, New York: Paulist Press, 1989; Gilles Chaillot, Paul Cochois and Irénée Noye (eds), *Traité des Saints Ordres (1676) comparé aux Écrits Authentiques de Jean-Jacques Olier (1657)*, Paris: Procure de la Compagnie de Saint-Sulpice, 1984; John W. O'Malley, 'One Priesthood: Two Traditions', in Paul K. Hennessy (ed.), *A Concert of Charisms: Ordained Ministry in Religious Life*, New York: Paulist Press, 1997, pp. 9–24; Pope John Paul II, *I Will Give You Shepherds (Pastores Dabo Vobis)*, Washington, DC: United States Catholic Conference, 1992; Robert M. Schwartz, *Servant Leaders of the People of God: An Ecclesial Spirituality for American Priests*, New York: Paulist Press, 1989.

THOMAS P. RAUSCH

Providence

Providence describes God's action in the world. Traditionally, belief in providence has affirmed the existence of a divine plan and purpose for creation that reflects God's loving care. For human persons, discerning and following God's plan leads to final fulfilment in God, which extends beyond history. In the tradition, providence has been particularly evident in the activities of governance, care and foresight.

Belief in providence sprang first from the Scriptures. God's ordering of all things is a persistent theme in the book of Wisdom. Perhaps the best-known and most dramatic Old Testament affirmation of providence is found in the story of Job. Job is assured that even in the midst of the unthinkable, God cares for him. In the New Testament, the most striking image of providence is Jesus himself, the incarnation of the provident God. The redemptive act of Jesus is seen as the centrepiece of God's providential plan in which people are called to a life of care for one another and to a personal relationship with God.

An early philosophical expression of belief in providence can be found in the writings of the Stoics, who held that providence or *pronoia* is the rule of the divine reason or *logos* over all events. Augustine and Thomas Aquinas, influenced by Stoic philosophy, adopted this notion of providence in a spirituality that underscored the power of God over all creation and emphasized divine transcendence. Providence spirituality involved discovering the plan of God, a plan that was largely hidden. The Church, being the closest to the transcendent God in the order of things, was the custodian of the will of God. Often this spirituality of providence was called on to justify an unhealthy use of power as domination. It fell short in helping people to deal with human suffering and the existence of evil in the world and led to a confused understanding of human freedom.

While contemporary thought continues to view governance, care and foresight as expressions of providence, our knowledge of the world and of God's action in the world has expanded significantly. This has brought about a similar expansion in our understanding of providence. Contemporary physics and mathematics have shown us that the universe is a blend both of order and chaos. It is possible, then, to experience God's providence in the midst of darkness and chaos as well as in moments of peace and order. It is providence that allows us to find meaning in the face of both order and chaos.

Insights from the social sciences suggest that divine–human interaction is most authentic when human persons resist impulses toward selfish desires and choose instead self-transcendence. It is providence that impels us to move from narcissism to self-transcendence and in doing so to expand our capacity for freedom. Contemporary religious thought envisions the divine–human encounter as a dialogue in which God offers human persons unlimited possibilities while always beckoning them to the best of these possibilities.

Modern technology enables the peoples of the world to become more connected and more interdependent. A contemporary spirituality of providence offers the possibility to assist in bringing about the systemic change needed for governance that is directed toward the common good. The aims of providence can be achieved by developing a global ethic, an ethic of care. Providence spirituality supports choices directed toward saving planet Earth and creating living economies. Providence calls us to the kind of discernment that leads to human choices that give witness to God's loving care. Providence spirituality aims at moving the human community from violence to peace, from a culture of rage to a culture of solidarity, from isolation to partnership.

Contemporary providence spirituality reconnects the human community to the wisdom tradition, a tradition that values foresight. It is through strategies of foresight that the transformation of the world is made possible. These strategies bring together heart and head in a spirituality that is both mystical and prophetic. Providence spirituality has been enriched by the insights of feminist theology concerning this connection of head and heart. This theology sees the redemptive act of Jesus as empowerment in the midst of heartbreak and as a call to the discipleship of equals that Jesus preached.

A spirituality of providence offers the human community a glimpse of the new creation. It beckons us to live responsibly and to trust deeply God who is with us and invites us to partnership.

See also **Abandonment; Conversion; Creation Spirituality; Ecological Spirituality; Feminist Spirituality; Grace; Freedom; Journey, Spiritual.**

J. Coultas and B. Doherty, *On Keeping Providence*, Terre Haute, IN: MLX Graphics, 1991; J. Crossan, *Jesus: A Revolutionary Biography*, San Francisco: Harper, 1994; C. LaCugna, *Freeing Theology*, San Francisco: Harper, 1993; S. McFague, *Life Abundant*, Minneapolis: Fortress Press, 2001; J. Polkinghorne, *Science and Providence: God's Interaction with the World*, Boston: Shambhala Publications, 1989; *Providence and Responsibility*, St Louis: Catholic Theological Society of America, 1989.

JOAN SLOBIG

Psalms

I have been accustomed to call this book (Psalms), I think not inappropriately, 'An Anatomy of all Parts of the Soul'; for there is not an emotion of which anyone can be conscious that is not here represented in a mirror. Or rather the Holy Spirit has here drawn to the life all the griefs, sorrows, fears, doubts, hopes, cares, perplexities, in short, all the distracting emotions, with which the minds of people are wont to be agitated. (John Calvin, *Introduction to the Psalms*, 1557)

The psalms excite – the psalms inspire. From the depths of despair to the heights of praise the psalms have excited and inspired both the Jewish and Christian people alike through all generations and for more than three thousand years. Their heritage and influence within the Judaeo-Christian tradition are, beyond a shadow of a doubt, more profound than any other corpus of prayers that are in existence. The psalms, originally an oral tradition, are scriptural, liturgical and sacred. They combine cultic song with artful poetry. The Psalter is a major focus of study and practice and is, in Dietrich Bonhoeffer's words, the 'Prayer Book of the Bible'. The psalms are sung and prayed, preached and meditated upon; they both appeal and intrigue. Furthermore and importantly the psalms resound with all our senses and emotions. Within the rich text of the psalms, colour, imagery and metaphor are all found in abundance. All conditions of humankind are addressed – everything can be spoken to God, nothing need ever be excluded.

The psalms in context. For the purposes of this entry I shall be using the NRSV translation of the Psalms and their numeration. I would also like to make clear that the brevity of this entry only allows for a résumé or taster of this extensive subject. However an extensive list of references is included at the end of the article to aid further study.

The Psalms (the Psalter) comprise 150 songs or poems divided into five 'books' (Ps. 1–41; 42–72; 73–89; 90–106; 107–150). The poetry of the psalms employs the symmetry of parallelism (e.g. one line responds to another, reinforcing the first either positively or negatively). Their title derives from the Greek *psalmoi*, 'songs of praise'. In Hebrew rabbinic literature, the book is called *Sefir Tehillim*, the 'book of praises'. The Psalter is the oldest liturgical book, probably composed between the tenth and third centuries BCE, originally written in Hebrew and later on translated into Latin from the Greek version of the Septuagint. The numbering in the Masoretic Text (Hebrew) differs from that in the Septuagint Text (Greek). The Roman Catholic tradition tends to follow the Greek Text and the Protestant tradition follows the Hebrew Text.

The psalms remain an enigma – a mystery. Scholars have sought to discover and unravel clues as to their deeply complex structure, origin and form. Questions about their exact dating and authorship have been hotly debated and strongly contested and rely largely on historical fact and style. Of the 150 psalms, Ps. 119 is the longest with 176 verses and Ps. 117 is the shortest with 2 verses; 116 psalms have superscriptions; some are attributed to David while others give a specific liturgical or musical instruction. Yet others refer to genre types such as prayer, praise and song and others are simply unfathomable. These superscriptions may well stand as a heading for either a tribute or endorsement of the psalm. The placement of the psalms within the Psalter is also problematical. The psalms appear at times to be thematic, standing in groups or sub-collections, but each psalm can stand independently. They are neither methodological nor systematic. Even the Psalter, as we have it, has no certain or specific order apart from the fact that Ps. 1 and Ps. 150 seem to be perfectly placed. Ps. 1 serves as a preface to the whole Psalter by describing the life of the virtuous person who has sought to fulfil the 'Law' (*torah*) and Ps. 150, as the finale to the whole, expresses unadulterated praise and thanksgiving to God.

The psalms within the Christian tradition. The heritage of the psalms with their ancient Jewish origin has imbued and deeply influenced all praying Christians. Jesus, as a Jew, transmitted and handed on the tradition of the psalms throughout the gospel narratives. Jesus is frequently pictured turning to the Psalter, and citing verses of the psalms – to give further credence to his arguments, to give instruction, or in times of dire need. Such examples can be found for example at an incisive moment (Matt. 22.42–44; Ps. 110.1); or where trust and confidence needed to be instilled in God's loving protection (Luke 12.24; Ps. 147.9); or in

moments of temptation (Matt. 4.5–7; Ps. 91.9–13); or seeking for peace in the final moments of dying (Luke 23.46; Ps. 31.5).

The influence of the psalms as a 'school of prayer' permeated the early Christian Church, for example Athanasius' *Letter to Marcellinus* on how psalms fit the spiritual needs of Christians, or the liturgical sermons of Augustine and the spiritual commentaries of Origen.

The psalms are the backbone and primal language of the monastic tradition. Devotional formation infuses the life of the monk and is twofold. First, it depends upon the communal recitation and liturgical practice of the Psalter sung in chant. Second, the fourfold aspect of *lectio divina* (*lectio, oratio, meditatio* and *contemplatio*) provides the spiritual nurture and contemplative attitude which is the joint necessary requirement for the monastic life. The Psalter is recited in full, usually on a weekly basis. This tradition of recitation has shaped the spiritual and liturgical practice of the Anglican Communion in *The Book of Common Prayer*, the Eastern Orthodox Church and other religious and secular communities.

Music, anthem and song are all inspired by the beauty and unfettered language of the psalms – from Handel's *Messiah* to Elgar's *Dream of Gerontius*; from Gregorian chant to the modern chants of Taizé; from the hymns of Luther to the melodies of Wesley; from the anthem settings of Howells, Stanford and Rutter to the Spirituals of African Americans. Our personal spirituality and prayer is enhanced through listening to, or participating in, the glory of the wondrous sounds of music and voice that are based on psalm settings. In the same way the classical religious poetry of people like Donne, Herbert, Manley Hopkins and many others have been based upon, influenced by and shaped through familiarity with and appreciation of the poetry of the psalms.

The psalms and human emotion. As Christians we pray, and through our prayer we form a relationship with God. The expression of our prayer and the way in which we pray is paramount to our spiritual progress. Prayer without honesty is but a shell. The more self aware we are of our feelings the more likely we are to be transformed into the image of God for whom we are created. To be honest, to find true integrity, we need to explore our feelings and to articulate them in a way where we feel truly heard, truly understood and truly loved. There is no better education in prayer or place where intensification of human experience is better understood than in the Psalter.

During the twentieth century scholars such as Herman Gunkel (in particular) and Claus Westermann, Walter Brueggemann and Bernard Anderson have identified and classified various 'types' of psalms or genres (e.g. praise or hymns, Ps. 8, 19, 33, 100, 145–150; thanksgiving or trust, e.g. Ps. 11, 16, 23, 30, 62, 116, 131; lament or petition, e.g. Ps. 3, 6, 31, 42–43, 51, 102, 130 (individual); Ps. 58, 60, 80, 90 (community)), which can aid us to manoeuvre through the complexity of the texts. The psalms of lament, which verbalize negative concerns and raw perceptions, are the most frequently found 'type' of psalm (approx. forty) and far outweigh psalms of a more positively expressed nature.

For many Christians, complaint and the anger that follows are felt to be inappropriate expressions of prayer. Often these repressed emotions remain unresolved and hidden. This is a serious limitation of emotional authenticity and suggests that the negative is somehow unacceptable. Yet anger plays a dominant part in our lives individually and personally, corporately and globally. In fact the imprecatory or curse psalms (e.g. Ps. 35, 58, 59, 69, 70 (individual) Ps. 12, 83 (community)) are either removed entirely or sectioned off within liturgical settings and prayer books. It is understandable that these psalms, which represent violence, cursing and crying out to God for vengeance on the 'enemy', may pose difficulties for some Christians who find them incompatible with gospel teaching. Nevertheless these cursing psalms authenticate the experience and depth of anger within the human condition.

But just as the psalms cry out in our need so, in the many changing moods and seasons of life, we are able to declare, in the prayer of the Psalmist, our utter dependence and trust in God. Within the textured language of the psalms there is a richness of symbol, imagery and metaphor, which brings prayer into the realms of the poetic imagination. In the same way the intimate language, between the Psalmist and God often sensual and passionate in its declaration, is never shied away from and assumes a closeness and familiarity of relationship. Translations of the psalms are many and it is important for the purposes of prayer to discover for oneself the translation that is most to our taste.

The psalms act in myriad ways. They integrate diversity by focusing intensely on God and providing a space for the whole range and gamut of human emotions and experience to be admitted, accepted and resolved. The psalms allow our desire for God to be fired through ancient poetry and song that remain vibrant and apposite. And, finally, they remind us of our heritage born from the Jewish cult of the Temple and transmitted and handed down through three millennia to Christianity in the twenty-first century.

See also Anglican Spirituality; Benedictine Spirituality; *Lectio Divina*; Monasticism; Music and Spirituality; Office, Divine; Spirituals.

Reginald Box, *Make Music to Our God: How We Sing the Psalms*, London: SPCK, 1996; Walter Brueggemann, *The Message of the Psalms: A Theological Commentary*, Minneapolis: Augsburg Press, 1984; Stephen Breck Reid (ed.), *Psalms and Practice: Worship, Virtue, and Authority*, Collegeville, MN: The Liturgical Press, 2001; Toni Craven, *The Book of Psalms*, Collegeville, MN: The Liturgical Press, 1992; Hermann Gunkel, *An Introduction to the Psalms*, Macon: Mercer University Press, 1998; William L. Holladay, *The Psalms through Three Thousand Years: Prayerbook of a Cloud of Witnesses*, Minneapolis: Fortress Press, 1996; James L. Mays, *The Lord Reigns: A Theological Handbook to the Psalms*, Louisville, KY: Westminster John Knox Press, 1994, Konrad Schaefer, *Berit Olam: Studies in Hebrew Narrative and Poetry*, Collegeville, MN: The Liturgical Press, 2001.

SUSIE HAYWARD

Public Life and Spirituality

Christian faith is communal; to believe means to be part of a community of disciples that is the Church. Discipleship also involves engaging one's wider community, the diverse sphere of common life, the public realm. Christian spirituality is intensely personal, yet at the same time must be public. In fact, persons are shaped in engagement with public life. Unfortunately, overly individualistic and therapeutic notions of spirituality have undermined the public dimension of faithful living. While movements such as liberation theology in Latin America and political theology in Europe countered this trend, still scholarship in spirituality and public life needs far more attention.

Public life includes but extends beyond politics. Public life is the sphere of common life in a society, a space of encounter, dialogue, debate and shared activity. Spirituality takes shape at least in part in this common sphere, where persons are at least partially formed and educated, where they explore their identity and seek material goods for survival, and where they express their values and visions. Thus, spirituality cannot help but be public. What is needed is greater reflectiveness about the formative power of the public sphere and a more conscious openness to express and embody Christian faith in this dimension of human living. At the same time,

Christian spirituality has been uncritically united to varied social and political campaigns, risking the transcendence and credibility of faith. A critical look at the relationship between spirituality and any particular situation is imperative.

Christian spirituality can take diverse forms in the public sphere, depending on the demands of the social context, theological viewpoint and individuals' particular gifts. Christians can stand over against the dominant social and political structures, calling for change in a prophetic stance. Anglican Archbishop Desmond Tutu (1931–), for example, took this position in the struggle against apartheid in South Africa. So too did Dorothy Day (1897–1980) in her long protest against capitalistic excess and war in the United States. The prophetic mission has gone hand in hand with a holistic understanding of spirituality – and a sharp critique of 'other-worldly' and 'privatistic' notions of faith. In proclaiming prophecy, however, religious groups do risk becoming identified with a single issue, leaving a vacuum in identity and leadership once that problem has been conquered, or undermining Church credibility if the position is misguided.

Some assert that the Church, by its very nature, must be counter-cultural. Contemporary theologian Stanley Hauerwas, for example, warns that Christians must not be assimilated into society. Rather the Church is a distinct community with particular practices and norms; it actually is an alternative *polis* in its own right.

Other Christians choose to work directly within political systems as elected officials, a position that requires a delicate balance between seeking to enact one's beliefs and responding to the diverse interests of a pluralistic populace. So too do Christian organizations exercise political roles as public policy lobbyists or, in the case of the Conference of Religious in Ireland, social partners in the government. These are complex vocations, involving compromise and an ability to translate one's beliefs into public language. Moreover, different political structures pose particular issues for spirituality. In the United States, a democratic political structure and strict separation of Church and state affirm the value of the individual and the freedom of religious institutions from state control, yet also may unnecessarily eclipse religious beliefs from public spaces. In a situation of religious establishment such as in the United Kingdom, Christianity plays a prominent official public role yet finds itself weak amid a highly secular population.

Politics is one form of public engagement. Yet work more broadly must be considered as a highly formative public practice. People of faith serve, for example, as educators, librarians, lawyers, social service providers and medical professionals in secular institutions. They may not discuss their faith explicitly, but their work still can be a public spiritual practice that aims to foster human development. This is the kind of implicit presence, captured by the image of lay people as invisible leaven in the loaf, promoted by the Second Vatican Council (1962–65).

Of course, two of the oldest forms of public Christian spirituality are worship and evangelism. To worship is a public act, bringing together the corporate body in a common space to proclaim the good news and to remember Christ at the Eucharist. The call to make disciples even more assertively demands engagement with the wider public. While implicit presence can be a form of evangelism, Christians also embody their spirituality by explicitly witnessing to their faith in the hope of gaining followers of Christ. Public prayer, care and testimony are vital parts of Christian spirituality.

Spirituality is wrongly understood as first and foremost a matter of individual, interior religious experience. Rather, Christian spirituality is both personal and public, thriving in the interplay between moments of contemplative solitude and active engagement. Teachers such as Thomas Merton (1915–68) recognized this dynamic, and they sought to show how one can integrate contemplation in a life of action. Scholars of mysticism too have begun to point out how even great figures in the history of Christian mysticism (e.g. Meister Eckhart, Teresa of Avila, Ignatius of Loyola and Quaker leaders) worked for social transformation. This remains the task: to seek God deeply in the midst of public living.

See also **Spirituality and Culture (*essay*); Global Spirituality; Interiority; Liberation Spirituality; Peace; Secularization; Social Justice; Vatican II and Spirituality; Work.**

José Casanova, *Public Religions in the Modern World*, Chicago: University of Chicago Press, 1994; Stanley Hauerwas, *In Good Company: The Church as Polis*, Notre Dame: University of Notre Dame Press, 1995; Thomas Merton, *Contemplation in a World of Action*, Garden City, NY: Doubleday & Co., 1971; Janet K. Ruffing (ed.), *Mysticism and Social Transformation*, Syracuse, NY: Syracuse University Press, 2001; Desmond Tutu, *No Future without Forgiveness*, New York: Doubleday, 1999; Claire Wolfteich, *American Catholics through the Twentieth Century: Spirituality, Lay Experience, and Public Life*, New York: Crossroad, 2001.

CLAIRE E. WOLFTEICH

Purgative Way

The Purgative Way is the first of the three ways of the Christian life often referred to as the 'classical spiritual itinerary': the Purgative Way, the Illuminative Way and the Unitive Way. Each of these 'ways' together, though described separately with their own salient characteristics and method of prayer, form a single journey that leads the Christian ever more deeply in the life and love of God in this world, the one world, that God and humans share alike. Although often presented in a linear fashion the 'three ways' are not separate and independent aspects of religious development but rather are attempts to describe the various movements of grace in our life that are cyclical in nature. Even those 'advanced' in their spiritual pilgrimages recognize that something of each of the three ways continues to deepen and grow as they strive to mature in faith over the course of an entire lifetime. Even the most secular of psychologists will recognize that we never arrive 'once and for all' but are continually involved in the ongoing task of conversion and human growth. The foundations for the three ways of the Christian life are already visible in the writings of Christian antiquity. In Heb. 5.11–14 and 6.9–12, along with many other New Testament texts such as Eph. 4.12–16, we have indications that development in the spiritual life is viewed as progressive in nature; it can be practised, that is, learned. For example, the texts from Hebrews indicate in a general way that there are persons who are beginners in their Christian journey and those who are masters. The writer of Hebrews describes those 'living on milk' because they are still 'babies'; he talks about those that are 'mature' and those who are 'teachers'. The author speaks of 'training' and thus, along with those who are 'beginners' and 'masters', we will have those who are further advanced, that is, those who are neither beginners nor yet masters. Likewise, the text speaks of those who have learned and practised the Christian life but have fallen away from it and need to practise some more!

In the second century, with the growing emphasis on personal perfection and bodily asceticism, there were a significant number of people who moved to the deserts of the Middle East in order to achieve the goal of personal perfection in the Christian life as monks and religious. They described their journey of faith in various ways. Origen (d. 254) wrote of 'purification, learning and love'. Basil the Great (d. 379) adopted the already existent description of 'beginners', 'proficients' and 'perfects' after he became a monk and dedicated himself

to the ascetic lifestyle. Bernard of Clairvaux (d. 1153) wrote of the threefold progression of 'fear, hope and love' in the life of the Christian with reference to the biblical Song of Songs. Thomas Aquinas (d. 1274) spoke of the progression of 'virtue and charity', and the 'three degrees of charity', thus once again accepting the widespread belief that the Christian life was developmental in nature.

However, it is in the writings of a contemporary of Aquinas that the Purgative, Illuminative and Unitive Ways are explicitly mentioned with respect to the life of the ordinary Christian and not necessarily to those who had dedicated themselves to the ascetic lifestyle as a monk or religious. It was Bonaventure (d. 1274), in his *De Triplici Via*, based on the Dionysian terms and writings from the sixth century which were then widely diffused in Latin in Europe, who explicitly describes what would become for future Christian generations the 'classical spiritual itinerary' of purgation, illumination and union. Although many Christian writers used this terminology after Bonaventure to characterize and describe the Christian journey, it would only be later, in the sixteenth century, that a thorough and systematic analysis of the three ways was achieved by John of the Cross at the height of mysticism in Europe at the time and, paradoxically, at the height of the dreaded Spanish Inquisition.

John of the Cross (d. 1591) carefully analyses the threefold way in his commentaries *The Dark Night (DN), The Ascent of Mount Carmel (A), The Spiritual Canticle (SC)* and *The Living Flame of Love (F)*. Since John of the Cross is recognized as the Western mystic that described, systematized and analysed most thoroughly the Purgative, Illuminative and Unitive Ways, his work will be used in a summary way as the basis for the presentation below.

The Purgative Way is commonly associated with the state known as the Beginners (*see A* 2.17 ff.). The need to set out on the Purgative Way comes as a result of the recognition that, as we have grown into maturity and adulthood, there is a further need for growth and maturation: an individual has come to understand that she or he has a desire for *something more* that can only be achieved by moving beyond his or her current debilitating boundaries and dispositions. This awareness is not meant to negate everything about our life, but it is meant to help us 'correct' what *is* debilitating and life-draining. Thus, the Purgative Way describes the journey of somebody setting out to re-form primary attitudes that, to date, may have well guided the individual but, due to their own limitations, are now preventing the individual from further personal and spiritual maturation.

Entry into the Purgative Way is characterized by the recognition that 'I need to do something about my life!' The individual has become aware of the need to change and desires to do something about it. In Christian terms one might describe this initial phase as entering into an acute awareness of the 'sinfulness' of one's life, that is, an awareness of one's failures toward others, self, God and creation that has expressed itself hereto in greed, sloth, pride, false opinions, bad habits and so on. During the First Week of the Spiritual Exercises of Ignatius of Loyola (d. 1556) the retreatant is exhorted to examine in great detail his or her life in order to become deeply aware of his or her personal need for growth and conversion in light of past failures such as these.

Thus, entry into the Purgative Way is not merely the onset of the felt need to confess one's sins, but rather, it is a state of consciousness that propels the individual into an integral reformation of the foundations of his or her life. Often the individual will set out to perform works of charity, become more intentional and habitual about prayer, and seek to refocus inordinate passions that distract from his or her primary commitments in life. In short, an individual launched along the Purgative Way seeks to become more disciplined about many aspects of his or her life in order to move from 'self centred-ness' to 'other-centred-ness'. The goal is to live with a greater freedom in relationship to others, the world, to God and to oneself. The Purgative Way questions 'business as usual'. For example, one may decide to schedule a regular daily time for personal prayer and meditation. Frequently 'the beginner' will use Scripture passages, religious statuary or icons to assist in focusing attention on what is known as discursive prayer (the conscious and deliberate 'saying' of prayers that assists in conceptualizing and evaluating one's own life in view of the gospel of Jesus Christ). What the Purgative Way begins to correct is our false sense of reality and our relationship to it. Our current categories of knowledge are questioned and reshaped in order to enter ever more deeply into the life and grace of God that first called us forth along the Purgative Way. Most significantly, the Purgative Way seeks to purify our image of God, thus reorientating us toward the truth of God in our life and in the life of the world.

Thus, negatively, the Purgative Way is a movement away from bad habits, sinful behaviour and unhealthy attachment to material things. Positively, however, the Purgative Way is a movement toward more truthful relationships, more authentic self-giving to others and a more conscious decision to perform acts of charity, prayer and almsgiving.

The dialectic of asceticism characterizes the Purgative Way: we intentionally open ourselves up to God's grace in our life in order to move more positively in this world; but as we choose to change old habits in order to adopt new ones God's transforming grace becomes ever more apparent and takes deeper root. Thus, the goal of the Purgative Way is not to gain a disciplined mastery over our life but rather (and paradoxically) to 'lose control' of our life and hand our life over to God's loving grace such that we can live ever more fully and lovingly in this one and only world which God and humanity share.

See also **Conversion; Illuminative Way; Journey, Spiritual; Triple Way; Unitive Way.**

E. W. Trueman Dicken, *The Crucible of Love: A Study of the Mysticism of St Teresa of Jesus and St John of the Cross*, New York: Sheed & Ward, 1963; K. Kavanaugh and O. Rodriguez, *The Collected Works of St John of the Cross*, Washington: Institute of Carmelite Studies, 1991; Steven Payne, *John of the Cross and the Cognitive Value of Mysticism*, Norwell: Kluwer Academic Publications, 1990; David B. Perrin, *For Love of the World: The Old and the New Self of John of the Cross*, Bethesda: International Scholars Press, 1997.

DAVID PERRIN

Purification

see **Purgative Way**

Puritan Spirituality

Puritanism thrived in seventeenth-century Britain and America as a movement of spiritual renewal, largely Calvinist in sympathy. The term 'Puritan' was first used in the 1560s for those in the Church of England who resisted the Elizabethan Settlement, scorning its failure to realize a thoroughgoing scriptural reform of church life and piety. Puritans insisted that the whole of one's experience be brought under the lordship of Christ, and were thus criticized for their emphasis on 'precision' in the spiritual life. Prior to the work of Perry Miller and others in modern Puritan scholarship, these were a people often misunderstood and abused. H. L. Mencken reflected a popular stereotype in defining Puritanism as 'the haunting fear that someone, somewhere might be happy'. While it varied immensely in its particular expressions of piety, the Puritan spirit was generally marked by a greater joy and engagement in life than often has been realized. By the early eighteenth century, the movement gave way to the evangelical piety of Isaac Watts in England and Jonathan Edwards in America.

The diversity of those called 'Puritans' included irenic Presbyterians like Richard Baxter, Independents (or Congregationalists) like John Owen, Separatists like John Smyth (to whom Baptists trace their roots) and radical believers (from George Fox's Quakers with their stress on the Inner Light to Fifth Monarchy Men anticipating a new millennial kingdom). In America, the term embraced the separating Puritans who settled at Plymouth under William Bradford in 1620, as well as non-separatists who came to Massachusetts Bay under John Winthrop in 1630. Jerald Brauer distinguishes four different types of Puritan piety – nomist, evangelical, rational and mystical – seen respectively in the obedience to Scripture urged by Thomas Cartwright, the fellowship with Christ emphasized by Richard Sibbes, the dependability of reason taught by John Milton, and the mystical union extolled by Francis Rous (Brauer, 1987). In short, the heterogeneity of Puritanism was as remarkable as its unanimity in understanding the Church as a community of 'visible saints'.

Undergirding the whole of Puritan spirituality was an Augustinian vision of God's alluring beauty and astounding majesty. The Puritan writers of the Westminster Confession (1646) particularly emphasized the latter, urging that 'according to the secret counsel and good pleasure of his will' and 'out of his free grace and love alone', God 'hath appointed the elect unto glory' (Westminster Confession of Faith, 3.5–6). This conception of God's sovereign power, joined with the reality of human sin, naturally prompted Puritans to ask how repentant believers could be assured of God's promise of faithful relationship. They found their answer in the covenant. Through the covenantal bond, an untamed God of holy majesty willingly 'tamed' Godself, entering into loving, intimate relationship with those who had been estranged from God by sin.

In expounding the character of this covenantal relationship, some Puritans focused on the intimacy that God establishes with believers who are engrafted into the covenant community. Others put greater stress on God's infinite power and wisdom, developing a 'federal theology' (from *foedus*, the Latin word for 'covenant') that emphasized the divine decrees of election and reprobation. Hence, Puritan spirituality could express itself in the deeply personal and 'affective

theology' of Richard Sibbes (with its celebration of holy desire), as well as in the austere logic of William Perkins' *Golden Chain* (with its detailed explication of double predestination).

Union with Christ became the most important theme in Puritan spirituality, as it had been for Calvin himself. Thomas Watson spoke in characteristically Puritan fashion when he described God as 'a *delicious* good', insisting that such a truth should 'ravish the soul with pleasure', giving it 'rapturous delight and quintessence of joy' (Watson, 1898, p. 17). Puritan sermons were full of passionate reminders that Christ is a bridegroom who longs to be joined with his bride the Church. Sermons and commentaries on the Song of Songs flourished in Puritan circles on both sides of the Atlantic. Francis Rous, in his *Mystical Marriage* (1656), could urge the Christian's 'hottest affection' toward Christ as the Spouse of the soul. 'Look on him so that thou maist lust after him; for here it is a sin, not to look that thou maist lust, and not to lust having looked' (Rous, 1656, p. 687). John Cotton in New England could speak of the Puritan preacher as the 'breasts of Christ' from whom the faithful members of the congregation can suck the milk of the Word (Cotton, 1655, p. 198). An unembarrassed intimacy thus marked the Puritan understanding of union with Christ, made possible by a covenant of marriage binding God to God's people.

At the same time, however, the Puritan preoccupation with soteriology led other theologians of the movement to an intricate analysis of the *ordo salutis* of birth and growth in the spiritual life. Using the language and rational systematizing of Peter Ramus, a Calvinist critic of Aristotilian Scholasticism, they developed a detailed calculus of sanctification. Popular Puritan writers like William Perkins of Cambridge and William Ames (author of *The Marrow of Theology*), outlined step by step the various dimensions of God's preparatory grace in the process of salvation, including God's foreknowledge, the divine decree, predestination and effectual calling. Subsequently, the pattern went on to plot the individual's exercise of faith/repentance, God's work of justification and adoption, and the movement toward progressive sanctification through the use of the means of grace. Along the way, attention would be paid to the nature of conversion and how a believer could be assured of salvation.

Devotional practices that emerged out of this Puritan covenant theology included an emphasis upon baptism and the Lord's Supper as seals of the covenant, incorporating believers into the close-knit community of the faithful. Preaching became virtually a 'third sacrament', with highly expository sermons and the singing of psalms forming the liturgical heart of Puritan worship. But most distinctive to the piety of the Puritan saints were spiritual practices which began at home, reaching out from there to sanctify the whole of one's life in the world.

Puritan believers practised a daily routine of private and family prayer that suggested a parallel to the monastic canonical hours. These included morning prayer on rising, table grace at meals, nightly reading and catechizing of the family, and evening prayer before bed. Sabbath observance involved family catechesis before the morning service, a careful review of the sermon over the family lunch, and further reading and prayer through the rest of the day. A regular examination of conscience was also encouraged through the use of personal diaries. Moreover, the Puritans were inveterate readers – not only of the Bible, but also of devotional manuals like Richard Rogers' *Garden of Spiritual Flowers*, martyrologies like John Foxe's *Book of Martyrs*, and emblem books like Francis Quarles's *Emblems, Divine and Moral*. Metaphors of the spiritual life as 'journey' and 'combat' predominated in Puritan spiritual writing, as exemplified by John Bunyan's *Pilgrim's Progress* and John Downame's *The Christian Warfare*. Spiritual handbooks relating the experience of faith to the worldly vocations of the faithful were also popular, as in John Flavell's *Husbandry Spiritualized* and Cotton Mather's *The Religious Marriner*, written respectively for farmers and sailors.

By means of these various devotional aids, Puritan believers worked through the storms and joys of their spiritual lives. In times of persecution or when they were tempted to despair, they fell back on the comfort of unconditional election, identifying the attacks of the spiritual enemy in trying to discourage the soul, and seeking assurance through the inner witness of the Spirit and the signs of grace in their lives. At all times they attended to the exercise of Divine Providence in the world around them, interpreting personal, local and national affairs as signs of God's presence. English Puritans after the failure of the Commonwealth could see their afflictions as a sharing in the sufferings of Christ. American Puritans could read their New World experience through the lens of ancient Israel's sojourn into the wilderness. For the Puritan mind, a sovereign and loving God was indelibly present in all the turnings of history.

Puritanism as a movement was as medieval as it was modern. It could echo the bridal mysticism of Bernard of Clairvaux in the warmth of its 'monastic' piety while fostering the development of the individual through its intense self-scrutiny and criticism of hierarchical forms. Like the French spirituality to which it was contemporary, Puritan spirituality offered a juxtaposition of opposites – merging the deepest conception of union with Christ to the loftiest vision of God's inaccessible grandeur.

See also **Calvinist Spirituality; Election (Predestination); Reformed Spirituality.**

———

Jerald C. Brauer, 'Types of Puritan Piety', *Church History* 56.1 (March 1987), 39–58; Patrick Collinson, *The Elizabethan Puritan Movement*, London: Methuen, 1967; John Cotton, *A Brief Exposition . . . upon the whole Book of Canticles*, London: T. R. & E. M., 1655, p. 198; Janice Knight, *Orthodoxies in Massachusetts: Rereading American Puritanism*, Cambridge, MA: Harvard University Press, 1994; Richard C. Lovelace, 'The Anatomy of Puritan Piety: English Puritan Devotional Literature' and Charles Hambrick Stowe, 'Puritan Spirituality in America' in L. Dupré and D. Saliers (eds), *Christian Spirituality: Post-Reformation and Modern*, New York: Crossroad, 1989, pp. 294–323 and 338–53; G. F. Nuttall, *The Puritan Spirit*, London: Epworth Press, 1967; Charles Hambrick-Stowe, *The Practice of Piety: Puritan Devotional Disciplines in Seventeenth-Century New England*, Chapel Hill, NC: University of North Carolina Press, 1982; Francis Rous, *The Mystical Marriage*, London: R. W., 1656; Gordon Wakefield, *Puritan Devotion*, London: Epworth Press, 1987; Thomas Watson, *A Body of Divinity*, London: Passmore & Alabaster, 1898.

BELDEN C. LANE

Purity of Heart

The biblical concept of 'purity of heart' juxtaposes two different but related ideas: first, the notion of ritual and moral purity; second, the concept of the heart as the centre of human personality and identity. In ancient Israel the necessity for purity was a consequence of God's infinite holiness. Impurity could be contracted through direct violation of the Law or through contact with an impure person, place or thing. Ritual cultic purification restored the person who had contracted 'uncleanness' and often required animal sacrifice or symbolic lustrations with water. The prophets denounced purification that was merely exterior and cultic: they emphasized instead the need for inward, moral purity; and they stressed that the innermost self must constantly turn back to God and remain focused on him. In ancient Israel the deepest level of human personality and the source of the noblest human emotions was believed to be the heart. To attain purity of heart required turning away from sin and keeping one's inward gaze on God and his Law. New Testament teaching on purity of heart borrows strongly from the Old Testament prophetic tradition. Purity is not primarily a question of external observance (Matt. 23.25–26; Luke 11.39–41), but of inward forgiveness from sin and renewed grace. It is through faith in Christ that God purifies the heart (Acts 15.9).

Although Christian spirituality was at first almost indistinguishable from Jewish piety, it took written form in the Greek *koine*. In Greek philosophy and physiology it is not the heart but rather the *nous* that is the centre of human personality, the core 'self'. There is no exact English equivalent for *nous*. It is sometimes translated as 'intellect' or 'mind'; but in addition to being the centre of thought, it was also considered the organ of contemplation, the centre of our longing and capacity to behold the divine. In Christian spiritual writings what is said of the 'heart' in the Scriptures thus came to be understood of the *nous*, which was often identified with the image of God. The road to purity of heart thus entails moral and doctrinal preparation for Christian contemplation, the vision of God. Repentance, turning away from sin, and the inward purification they facilitate, is only a starting point. Purity of heart is the gateway to Christian contemplation.

From the early fourth century the 'pure of heart' whom Jesus promised 'shall see God' (Matt. 5.8) have been identified in Christian spiritual writings with those who receive from God the gift of *apatheia*, 'dispassion' or 'freedom from compulsion'. Although this term, borrowed from Stoic philosophy, had been used by earlier writers such as Clement of Alexandria, its most eloquent defender was the fourth century hermit, Evagrius Ponticus (d. 399). His disciple John Cassian (d. 435) translated *apatheia* as *puritas cordis*, 'purity of heart', and described this virtue as the immediate goal (*skopos*) of the Christian ascetic. Purity of heart leads in its turn to the final end (*telos*), which is the kingdom of heaven (*Conference* 1). Cassian's overwhelming popularity ensured that in the Christian West the biblical term 'purity of heart' would serve as the means by which the monastic doctrine of *apatheia* would be universally transmitted and known. In the Christian East, however, the term *apatheia* has been used in its own right down to the present time, even by such vitriolic critics of Evagrius as John Climacus (d. 649).

The freedom bestowed by *apatheia* is not freedom from temptation, since certain temptations continue until death (Evagrius, *Praktikos* 36). Rather, *apatheia* refers to freedom from the inner storm of 'passions', irrational drives which in their extreme forms would today be called obsessions, compulsions or addictions. The attainment and maintenance of this state, at least in varying degrees, has always been one of the principal goals of Christian asceticism.

It should be noted that neither the biblical phrase 'purity of heart' nor the more technical *apatheia* describe a static or purely passive state. Once attained, purity of heart can be lost. Freedom from the storm of one kind of passion does not guarantee freedom in all other dimensions of the inner life. Continuous reliance on the grace of God and daily striving are essential components of this gift. Finally, purity of heart is not only a state of being; it implies outward movement. Purification prepares the way for love and deeds of charity (1 Peter 1.22, Heb. 9.14).

See also Apatheia; Asceticism; Freedom; Interiority; Person; Purgative Way.

G. Bunge, *Earthen Vessels: The Practice of Personal Prayer According to the Patristic Tradition*, San Francisco: Ignatius Press, 1996; *John Climacus, The Ladder of Divine Ascent*, trans. C. Luibheld, CWS, New York: Paulist Press, 1982; *John Cassian, The Conferences*, trans. B. Ramsey, CWS, New York: Paulist Press, 1997, Conference 1; 'On the Eight Thoughts', 'The Monk', 'Chapters on Prayer', in *Evagrius of Pontus, the Greek Ascetic Corpus*, trans. R. E. Sinkewicz, Oxford: Oxford University Press, 2004.

LUKE DYSINGER

Quaker Spirituality

The Society of Friends arose amid the religious, social and political experimentation of the Puritan Revolution in England in the mid seventeenth century, one of many radical religious groups to flourish during Oliver Cromwell's rule. George Fox emerged as a prominent figure of the movement. His intense religious search, first among Puritan pastors and then among separatist groups, led him to despair that any human teacher could 'speak to his condition'. He experienced 'that there was an ocean of darkness and death, but an infinite ocean of light and love, which flowed over the ocean of darkness'. This light was the Light of Christ, who alone could 'teach his people himself'. He wrote further of a revelation that 'the nature of those things that were hurtful without, were within', that is, though he had not committed great evils, the capacity for them lay within him, as did the power of the Light to overcome them. This led to a sense of connection with other tempted human beings and the ability to minister to them.

Other seekers who came to Friends likewise experienced the Light as that which at first exposed their capacity for evil but then led to the victory of good over evil within them. A sense of inward peace followed, often after a lengthy internal conflict, and a deep sense of community with other Friends who had been through the same harrowing experience. This sense of victory energized them to labour to transform the social order into a godly society characterized by justice and righteousness. Drawing on the imagery of the book of Revelation, some Friends described this process as 'the Lamb's War'.

Other Friends preferred love language to martial imagery. Although 'Truth's testimony' may be 'against you', Sarah Blackborrow urged her reader to love truth. In an otherwise prophetic proclamation, she drew upon Proverbs and the Song of Songs in language reminiscent of medieval mystics for its ecstatic quality, inviting readers to the feast in Wisdom's house:

A Love there is which doth not cease, to the seed of God in you all; and therefore doth invite you every one . . . to return into it, that into Wisdom's house you may come, where there is a feast provided . . . the well-beloved of the Father is here, and this is he who is the fairest of ten thousand . . . long did my soul thirst after him . . . Now all you who thirst after your beloved, come into Wisdom's house . . . Oh! love truth and its Testimony . . . that into my Mother's house you all may come, and into the Chamber of her that conceived me, where you may embrace, and be embraced of my dearly beloved one.

Quaker spirituality has always integrated its inward and outward dimensions. The experience of earliest Friends was intensely interior. The light of Christ is available to all, without the mediation of liturgy or clergy. The same Spirit that gave forth the Scriptures could lead the faithful into new truth. Quakers met for worship in silence, open to the possibility that anyone might minister in words to the worshipping community.

Quaker meeting for worship is a group contemplative practice. Both apophatic and kataphatic methods are used to 'centre down', to quiet oneself to be open both to divine presence and to other worshippers. This focus on ministering to the gathered meeting and on being open to divine leadings distinguishes Quaker worship from private contemplation, which Quakers also practised. Early Quaker Robert Barclay described meeting for worship:

When assembled, the great work of one and all ought to be to wait upon God . . . to feel the Lord's presence, and know a gathering into his name indeed . . . there the secret power and virtue of life is known to refresh the soul, and the pure motions and breathings of God's Spirit are felt to arise . . . every one puts forth that which the Lord puts into their hearts . . . though there be not a word spoken, yet is the true spiritual worship performed, and the body of Christ edified.

Individual spiritual leadings developed into corporate testimonies, the ethical stands of the Society of Friends that are a central expression of their spirituality. These are often described as the testimonies of peace, simplicity, equality and integrity. In 1650 George Fox was offered release from Derby prison if he would accept a captaincy in Cromwell's army, but he declined, explaining that he 'lived in the virtue of that life and power that took away the occasion of all wars', and that he 'was come into the covenant of peace, which was before wars and strifes were'. Friends' practice of integrity looked back to the injunction of Jesus to 'let your yea be yea and your nay nay'. Like other radicals, Quakers refused to take oaths since oath-taking implied that one need not be honest otherwise. Fidelity to this testimony proved costly in the courts, for refusal to take the oath of allegiance resulted in long imprisonments and forfeiture of property. Integrity also led Friends to refuse to bargain or haggle when selling in the marketplace, which seriously challenged merchants' customs but later ironically enriched some Quakers. The Quaker testimony of equality began with the conviction that anyone, female or male, young or old, might be called to minister in words to the worshipping community. An early opening of George Fox was that theological training alone, 'being bred at Oxford or Cambridge was not enough to fit and qualify man to be ministers of Christ'. Women's speaking in public worship was scandalous to many outsiders, and it opened the way to a broader testimony on human equality, which came to embrace the anti-slavery and women's rights movements in the nineteenth century, and movements for civil and human rights in the twentieth.

The death of Cromwell meant the end of the Puritan revolution. The English monarchy was restored in 1660, and a vengeful Parliament enacted laws intended to stamp out nonconformity to the established Church. Until the Act of Toleration in 1689, Friends and other dissenters suffered waves of persecution. By then the fiery urgency of the youthful movement had waned.

The exuberant beginnings gave way to classical formulations, to a life characterized by quiet discipline, and to the articulation of a Quaker culture among 'God's peculiar people'. A 'hedge' separated Friends from non-Friends: exogamy led to excommunication or 'disownment'. Simplicity became a uniform 'plain dress'. Although the hedge lent a monastic air to Quaker devotion at this time, it was not the full social withdrawal of ancient anchorites or Anabaptist communitarians: William Penn initiated a Holy Experiment in colonial Pennsylvania that fostered religious toleration, treated Native Americans with honesty and dignity, and enlisted no militia. Inwardly, the confidence of earlier Friends gave way to suspicions of one's own motives. Self-watchfulness became central as Friends aimed for purity of heart.

Quakerism in the eighteenth century was more respectable, if still regarded as odd in the eyes of the wider world, though the radical ethics of the earliest generation continued and developed in new directions. The colonial New Jersey tailor John Woolman, a gentle mystic and unrelenting abolitionist, represents the genius of Quakerism in this era. His spiritual life integrated the inward and the outward: the intense feeling of community experienced in group worship was extended to an intimate closeness or 'a near sympathy' with oppressed slaves, Native Americans and the poor. His writings also explore the relationships among the traditional testimonies: a life of material simplicity fosters peace and human equality, just as unbridled greed led the way to slavery, oppression and war.

In the nineteenth century Friends gradually lowered the hedge between themselves and the wider world. Liberal and evangelical influences competed, leading to schisms in the USA, though Friends in Ireland and Britain avoided such major divisions. Evangelical Friend Elizabeth Fry's work for prison reform in England and progressive Lucretia Mott's leadership in anti-slavery and women's rights movements illustrate Quaker work for social justice in that era. Evangelical Friends in the twentieth century, often identifying themselves more with fellow evangelicals than with Quaker distinctives, carried on a vigorous mission work, numerically most successful in Kenya and Bolivia. Liberal friends, through the influence of Caroline Stephen and Rufus Jones, came to see themselves as part of the wider phenomenon of Christian mysticism. Thomas Kelly continued their democratization of the mystical life, holding it up as available to all. The 1900s also saw efforts at the reunification among divided Friends, and perhaps the most creative developments in the peace testimony.

The Friends Service Committees in Britain and the USA shared the Nobel Peace Prize in 1947 for relief efforts after the end of the war in Europe. Others continue to look to Quakers for their ethical testimonies, voteless decision-making, integrity of the inward and outward life, and their commitment to education. It may well be Friends whose first language is not English who may shape new directions for the twenty-first century.

See also **Contemplation; Shaker Spirituality; Silence; Social Justice.**

Hugh Barbour and J. William Frost, *The Quakers*, Richmond, IN: Friends United Press, 1994; Michael L. Birkel, *Silence and Witness: Quaker Spirituality*, London: Darton, Longman & Todd/Maryknoll, NY: Orbis Books, 2004; Howard H. Brinton, *Quaker Journals: Varieties of Religious Experience among Friends*, Wallingford, PA: Pendle Hill Publications, 1972; Mary Garman et al., *Hidden in Plain Sight: Quaker Women's Writings 1650–1700*, Wallingford, PA: Pendle Hill Publications, 1996; Douglas V. Steere, *Quaker Spirituality: Selected Writings*, Mahwah, NJ: Paulist Press, 1984.

MICHAEL L. BIRKEL

Quietism

Quietism strictly refers to the propositions condemned by the Holy Office, Pope or other ecclesiastical tribunals in the seventeenth century, allegedly taught or implied in some of the writings of, principally, the Spaniard Miguel de Molinos (1628–96) and the French writers Jeanne-Marie Bouvier de la Motte (Mme Guyon: 1648–1717) and the Archbishop of Cambrai, François de Salignac de la Mothe Fénelon (1651–1715). In view was an extreme form of spiritual passivity, endangering the role of the human faculties and other creaturely means of salvation in the Christian life. As such, quietism is a form of a wider tendency among religions to exaggerate the otherwise legitimate impulse to surrender to the initiative of the divine partner. The term 'quietism' itself may be derived from Teresa of Avila's 'prayer of quiet', while the term 'quietists' appears to have been used both by Molinos's enemies as early as the 1680s and more positively by adherents in Naples.

Recent scholarship is characterized by two tendencies. First, a revisionist study of the sources, with particular attention to sociopolitical influences, generally inclines toward a more positive reading of the principles: condemned positions are at most 'implied', perhaps resulting from a too unsystematic approach to the issues involved by the writers themselves, who were more interested in spiritual practice than in theological theory. A general atmosphere of anti-mysticism on the part of the opposing parties also seems to have played a significant role in the accusations levelled. Second, this distance between practice and theological theory illustrates a dissatisfaction with the prevailing theory on the part of our principles, and an accompanying attempt to seek alternatives in the soil of spiritual practice. For example, if works righteousness were in the theoretical ascendancy, on both the ecclesial and personal levels, one might understand the felt need to seek correctives to this in a form of passive surrender to the promptings of grace on the level of practice. Epistemologically this might manifest itself in the tension between analytic reason and affective intuition, or, equivalently, the tension between propositional doctrinalization and mystical experience. With hindsight today one is inclined to realign both the theory and the practice, rather than simply oppose one to the other.

After working in Spain as a priest in Valencia, Molinos's ministry in Rome extended from 1663 to his death in the prison of the Holy Office, where he resided for nine years as a result of his condemnation. A noted confessor, spiritual guide and author, his spiritual directorship of a Valencian confraternity in Rome gained him influential friends in the Curia. But the growing opposition to celebrated Italian quietists eventually brought a similar opposition to his own views. On 20 November 1687, Pope Innocent XI ratified the decree of the Holy Office condemning sixty-eight propositions of Molinos in the papal bull *Coelestis Pastor*. The official files of the trial have vanished, however.

Molinos's *The Spiritual Guide* sets forth the journey from imperfect to perfect contemplation; the later *Defence* offers an apparently unsuccessful apology of the former in synthesized form. An early treatise recommending frequent Communion suggests the ecclesial and sacramental dimension of his spirituality, although this dimension was inadequately attended to in the *Guide*. The *Guide* presupposes a distinction between discursive meditation and undifferentiated contemplation. All contemplation is a form of non-differentiating quiet, whether in its active, imperfect and acquired form, to which all are called, or in its perfect and passively infused form. Molinos considers the latter that to which all the others are ordered. The *Guide* explores the dispositions of acquired contemplation and its struggles (book one), the need for a spiritual director (book two), and the summit of perfect contemplation (book three).

Molinos cites Teresa of Avila and alludes to John of the Cross's teaching, but lacks their theological and pastoral amplitude of thought.

Representative issues left unresolved by Molinos would be: (1) Why is contemplation necessarily higher in value than meditation? (2) What is the role of grace, even in acquired contemplation, and the role of human action in passive contemplation? (3) How does one make the transition from acquired to passive contemplation? Is this purely the work of grace, or is some human effort involved? Molinos seems to presuppose both, paradoxically. But if it be purely the work of grace, why all the attention to acquired contemplation, not to mention the earlier background of meditation by spiritual beginners? And what happens to the role of the Church and its sacraments, qua created instruments of salvation, if all be grace? On the other hand, if perfect contemplation is the result of human effort in any way, how can it be purely passive contemplation? The relation between grace and human effort, or between perfect contemplation and imperfect contemplation/ meditation, finds an implied resolution in the union between divinity and humanity in the incarnation. Molinos does not explore this, although he does not seem to deny the salvific role of the incarnate Word throughout the entire Christian life in the *Guide*.

Molinos's shadow reaches France in the works of Mme Guyon. Strengthened by her friendship with the Barnabite priest François Lacombe after her husband's death, for approximately five years she exercised her gift of 'spiritual maternity', a grace she believed she received in 1682, by propagating her views on prayer.

Molinos's condemnation strengthened the anti-mystical forces in France, however, and both Lacombe and Mme Guyon found themselves eventually imprisoned. She was freed through the influence of Mme de Maintenon, who invited her to continue her apostolate at her girls' school of St Cyr, which was then influenced by the thought of Fénelon, whom Mme Guyon had amicably met somewhat earlier. Her influence over the students and others aroused renewed suspicion, and so she requested a theological commission to examine her work. Unfortunately the celebrated Issy Conference (1695), during which she was defended by Fénelon, condemned her *A Short and Easy Method of Prayer* and her *Commentary on the Canticle*, Bossuet exercising the preponderant influence. After various imprisonments, she was released in 1703 upon signing a submission.

Viewing prayer in affective terms, the *Short Method* studies the stages of love's purification, stressing that the divine being can only be found in a darkness of faith which transcends formulas. The soul is presented as not inactive (against the charge of quietism), for despite the negations, the asceticism demanded is very real and demanding. Mme Guyon's *Spiritual Torrents* later elaborated the stages of the soul's 'annihilation': agony, death, burial, corruption, reduction to ashes, resurrection. The *Commentary on the Canticle* describes the 'pure love' to which the soul finally comes, in which God is loved purely for himself alone, and combines nuptial and 'burial' mystical symbolism, for the marriage with God occurs as the soul expires in the arms of God, fully 'annihilated'. Even sympathetic readers will encounter some questionable expressions of extreme passivity, along with ambiguity over whether the loss of a 'distinct' view of Christ at the spiritual summit means the loss of all saving connection to him.

Fénelon's defence of Mme Guyon already dogged his reputation, and his *Explication of the Maxims of the Saints on the Interior Life* (1697), in which he sought to defend disinterested, pure love as the authentic form of mysticism, finally brought the full weight of Bossuet's power against him. Although he had been named the Archbishop of Cambrai only in 1695, he now found himself banished from the court of Louis XIV, who in turn pressured the unwilling Pope Innocent XII to condemn twenty-three propositions from the *Explication* on 12 March 1699. Fénelon submitted, but remained a sought-after spiritual guide until his death.

Pure love, while a strain in Mme Guyon's thought, seems more central for Fénelon. Somewhat paradoxically, 'pure love talk' enables one to appropriate the new humanism of the times, but in a manner consistent with the asceticism of the tradition. Heightened attunement to humanist love intensifies the need to purify it through heightened 'disinterestedness'. Even were one to end up in hell, hypothetically entertained, the true mystic would have that disinterested calmness that rests in God's presence. This can be read as imprudently fanatic passivity (Bossuet's view). Fénelon sees it as the kind of pure love which is at the same time a pure, disinterested hope in God's goodness.

Fénelon exemplifies an attempt to relink fruitfully mystical experience, Scholastic theology, sacramental life and ecclesiastical doctrine, although one senses that he did not quite articulate these amply enough. A further working through of the issues of grace and human response already in tension at the Reformation, extreme passivity and extreme activity were symptoms of a struggle taking place on a larger ecclesial and social canvas. The condemnations arguably retarded a workable resolution for a long time to come.

See also **Annihilation, Spiritual; Contemplation; French School of Spirituality; Hesychasm; Indifference; Love; Meditation.**

Louis Cognet, *Post-Reformation Spirituality*, trans. by P. Hepburne Scott, Twentieth Century Encyclopedia of Catholicism 41, New York: Hawthorn Books, 1959; Louis Cognet, 'Guyon (Jeanne-Marie Bouvier de la Motte)' in *DS* 6, cols 1306–36; Leszek Kolakowski, 'Quietism' in *The Encyclopedia of Religion* 12, New York: Macmillan, 1987, pp. 153–5; Alistair Mason, 'Quietism' in *The Oxford Companion to Christian Theology*, ed. A. Hastings et al., Oxford: Oxford University Press, 2000, pp. 589–90; Eulogio Pacho, 'Molinos (Michel de)' in *DS* 10, cols 1486–514; Friedrich von Hügel, *The Mystical Element of Religion as Studied in Saint Catherine of Genoa and Her Friends* 2, London: James Clarke & Co., 1961, pp. 129–81.

WILLIAM THOMPSON-UBERUAGA

Radical Spirituality

see **Social justice**

Rapture

see **Ecstasy**

Reading, Spiritual

see *Lectio Divina*

Recollection

The most common way to define prayer as recollection is to make a distinction between *active recollection* (also known as acquired recollection) and *infused recollection* (also known as passive or mystical recollection). Active or acquired recollection involves one's own efforts aided by natural grace to acquire habitual recollection of God's presence. Infused recollection is dependent on supernatural grace whereby God alone summons the soul into a collected state and gathers the faculties of the soul around the unifying centre of God's presence. A second variation is that between *actual recollection* (an act of prayer based on a sudden thought of God) and *habitual recollection* (continuous awareness of God's presence in and through all things). Since these categories are integrated rather than oppositional, recollection is often referred to as a virtue that contains a contemplative element. In this sense recollection serves as an important point of connection between the so-called active and contemplative life. One of the most sustained discussions of the distinctions between active and infused recollection can be found in the writings of Teresa of Avila in chapters 15 and 16 in *The Life*, in chapters 28 and 29 in *The Way of Perfection*, and in *The Interior Castle* where she discusses acquired recollection in the first three 'mansions' and infused recollection in the fourth.

As an integral part of contemplation and prayer, recollection is typically taught and practised according to three interrelated forms. A first form seeks to 'centre' and 'collect' the soul. A second focuses on recollection as a form of constant prayer lived in habitual consciousness of the presence of God. A third relies on the symbolic imagination, perception and senses to 'relive' gospel stories, experiences of sacred place and personal history.

In the first form of recollection, 'collectedness' is the opposite of 'wandering' or *perigrinatio*. Recollection in this sense finds a unifying centre, a home within the self. This form of recollected prayer is known by a variety of names including centring prayer, the prayer of presence and the Quaker practice of 'centring down'. Historically, various Church spiritual writers have explored this centring aspect of recollection. Recollection for John Climacus involved the will to 'fight always with your thoughts in order to call them back when they wander (*peregrinatio*)' (*Ladder of Divine Ascent* 4). Augustine practises recollection as he acknowledges the God who 'brings together what is scattered' within himself (*Confessions* 10.40).

The second principle of recollection seeks to fulfil Paul's injunction to constant prayer through habitual recollection of God's presence. In this form, even the smallest details or chores become means for recalling to memory the active presence of God. Two of the most distinctive statements of this form of ongoing prayer are found in Jean-Pierre de Caussade's *Sacrament of the Present Moment* and Brother Lawrence of the Resurrection's collection of writings and letters known collectively as *The Practice of the Presence of God*. For Brother Lawrence, for instance, recollection is the holiest and most necessary practice in the spiritual life. It 'consists in taking delight in and becoming accustomed to God's divine company . . . at every moment, without measure' (*Spiritual Maxims* 6).

The third principle, *symbolic recollection*, covers a range of literature, prayer and spiritual practice. Here, the symbolic imagination, the senses, the body, mind, heart, perceptions and intuition are all used to 'remember', enter into and relive a gospel story, a sacred place or personal history. The mechanics of symbolic recollection go back at least to Plato's myth in the *Phaedrus* of the soul as charioteer drawn by two horses, one representing honourable desires and the second dishonourable desires. Guided by reason represented by the charioteer, the horses can fly through an opening in the dome of heaven that leads to supersensible reality. But the two contrary desires make controlling the flight difficult and more often than not the soul falls back to earth, incarnate. The soul can, however, return to its proper home through memory (*anamnesis*) which contains the Forms glimpsed in the heavens. Though Plato's 'doctrine of recollection' is rejected by Augustine and other theologians (except Origen) on the basis of its implication of the pre-existence and the reincarnation of the soul, these same theologians do take elements of Plato's myth, teaching that God can illumine the mind, senses and imagination so that the soul is able to achieve some insight into eternal truths.

Richard of St Victor, using symbolic recollection, echoes Plato's myth, though he substitutes the Forms of heaven with the Truth of Scripture: '[Scripture] describes invisible things through the forms of visible things and impresses the memory of them upon our minds through beauty' (*Twelve Patriarchs* 15). Julian of Norwich embodies memory as she prays, 'as a gift and a grace from our Lord, may my body be filled full of recollection and feeling of his blessed passion' (*Showings* 3). The classic disciplines of examen of conscience (recollection used to uncover areas in our life in need of cleansing and purification) and examen of consciousness (recollection of God's presence throughout the day and our response to God's presence) are also examples of this form of recollection. Both are important, for example, in Ignatian spiritual formation and are present concretely in the Anglican William Law's integration of devotion and virtue in his *Serious Call to a Devout and Holy Life* (16).

Recollection is a varied and flexible form of prayer and devotion. Its intent is not to suppress turmoil or pain of this world, but rather to let it go; in its active and passive forms it is a self-abandonment to divine providence and unifying grace. In both its active and contemplative forms it is a way of life attentive to God's presence in the world.

See also **Attentiveness; Contemplation; Examination of Conscience/Consciousness; Meditation; Memory; Prayer; Reflection.**

William A. Barry, *Paying Attention to God: Discernment in Prayer*, Notre Dame, IN: Ave Maria Press, 1990; Brother Lawrence of the

Resurrection, *The Practice of the Presence of God*, trans. Salvatore Sciurba, Washington, DC: ICS Publications, 1994; Henri Nouwen, *The Way of the Heart*, New York: Seabury Press, 1981; Dominic Scott, *Recollection and Experience: Plato's Theory of Learning and Its Successors*, Cambridge: Cambridge University Press, 1995; *Teresa of Avila, The Interior Castle*, trans. Kieran Kavanaugh and Otilio Rodriquez, CWS, New York: Paulist Press, 1979.

STEVEN CHASE

Reconciliation

The theme of reconciliation is central to an understanding of salvation in Christian faith, and therefore also to spirituality. Theologically, there are two dimensions to reconciliation. In the vertical dimension, reconciliation is about God's bringing about the forgiveness of sin, effecting a new communion with the sinner. It is in this form that the Pauline writings address reconciliation (e.g. Rom. 5.1–11; 2 Cor. 5.17–20; Col. 1.20). The sacramental understanding of reconciliation in the liturgical traditions of Christianity focuses especially on this vertical dimension, emphasizing its being effected through the saving mystery of Christ.

The horizontal dimension of reconciliation stresses overcoming alienation between human beings. Reconciliation in this sense is based upon a wider social sense of reconciliation, whereby enmity between parties is set aside, and a new relationship is set up. The interest in this horizontal dimension of reconciliation has been heightened in recent times by the need to overcome the effects of civil conflict within countries, the reassertion of the rights of native peoples colonized by outsiders, the effects of domestic physical and sexual abuse, and other rifts in human relationships.

Reflection on the specifically Christian understanding of reconciliation in recent years has led to a clearer understanding of what Christian spirituality contributes to healing broken situations. Whereas processes of reconciliation in the wider society usually begin their efforts by trying to change the mind and heart of the wrongdoer, Christian understandings of reconciliation begin with God's healing the wounds of the victim. This stance has grown out of two insights. First of all, Christians understand God as one who gives special preference to the poor, the excluded and the disadvantaged. Viewed from this perspective, God cares in a special way in the first instance for the victim. Second, the victim sometimes forgives the wrongdoer, even when the wrongdoer has not repented and

sought forgiveness. Christians believe that God provides a special gift to the victim in order to do this. Added to this is the fact that often a wrongdoer never repents. When such is the case, does this mean that the victim is excluded from healing and held for ever hostage to the intransigence of the wrongdoer? Reconciliation thus understood, therefore, is the moment wherein God restores the humanity of the victim, a humanity that has been wrested from the victim in the act of wrongdoing.

But this restoration is not a return to the status quo. Such a forgetting of the wrongdoing would once again injure the victim. It would be saying, in effect, that what happened was not as serious as the victim perceived, or that the victim is not important enough to be so injured. Rather, the restoration that takes place in reconciliation brings the victim to a new place, making of the victim a 'new creation' (2 Cor. 5.17). That 'new place' often entails a call of the victim to further the work of reconciliation that has been begun in the victim by reaching out to other victims as well.

This furthering of the work of reconciliation begun by God constitutes a ministry of reconciliation. Such a ministry begins by creating 'safe spaces' wherein victims may examine their wounds and start to experience the healing that God offers them. The concept of safety is important because the risk of exposing and examining wounds must not lead to harming the victim once again. Within those zones of safety, ministers of reconciliation strive to create an experience of hospitality for the victim. The human hospitality the victim experiences can serve as a prelude to the experience of God's grace, the ultimate hospitable gift that restores the victim's humanity.

These dynamics play themselves out in social reconciliation as well, that is, in the healing of entire societies. The emphasis in this case, however, is healing the memories of the past and developing structures so that heinous events can never happen again. To achieve this, emphasis is placed on (1) truth-telling about what had happened, (2) the pursuit of justice for victims, and (3) the creation of social structures that will prevent past events from being repeated.

See also **Forgiveness; Healing; Memory; Nonviolence; Redemption.**

John Paul Lederach, *The Journey Toward Reconciliation*, Scottdale: Herald Press, 1999; John Milbank, *Being Reconciled*, Oxford: Blackwell, 2003; Robert Schreiter, *Reconciliation: Mission and Ministry in a Changing Social Order*, Maryknoll, NY: Orbis Books, 1992; Robert

Schreiter, *The Ministry of Reconciliation: Spirituality and Strategies*, Maryknoll, NY: Orbis Books, 1998; Miroslav Volf, *Exclusion and Embrace: A Theological Exploration of Identity, Otherness and Reconciliation*, Nashville: Abingdon Press, 1996.

ROBERT SCHREITER

Redemption

Redemption – 'setting free' – is the most important of the terms used by Jews and Christians to specify the meaning of salvation. Exegetically and theologically, the questions to be asked are: who redeems human beings; from what are human beings redeemed; how are human beings redeemed; and for what are they redeemed? The varying answers to these questions, as well as giving substance to Christian doctrine, also generate quite different understandings of the shape of the spiritual life.

The concept of redemption finds its origins in the law codes of ancient Israel as well as in the paradigmatic events of the Exodus and the Return from Exile. So a person or an animal could be redeemed from punishment or simply obligation and ownership, including slavery, through a process of redemption, *pdh*, which would be accomplished by the redeemer, *g'l* (the words are not to be strictly differentiated), and this might involve the payment of a ransom, *kpr* (see Ex. 21.29–30; Lev. 25.47–55; 1 Sam. 14.27; 2 Sam. 14.11). However, it is not clear that redemption always came with a price. In particular God may simply act as the deliverer, without having to give anything in redemption (Isa. 52.3). So God redeems his people from Egypt by his power, releases them from slavery and brings them to the promised land where they are to be his faithful people (Ex. 6.6). This language of deliver/redeemer was also to be applied to the Exile (Jer. 16.14–15) and indeed developed into faith in God as a deliverer from sin (Isa. 44.22) and death (Job 33.28).

The New Testament, while using redemption language a little more sparingly, nonetheless gives it great prominence, drawing both on the vocabulary of deliverance in the Septuagint and also on the world of the slave market, sacral manumission and ransoming. So the Christian has been bought, *agorazo* (1 Cor. 6.20). The Christian is set free from the power of the world, the flesh, Law, sin, death and Satan (John 1.13; Gal. 3.13; Rom. 8.21; Titus 2.14; Col. 1.13). In parts of the New Testament the means of redemption is also specified – the blood of Christ (Rom. 3.24–25). Christ is the ransom, *lutron* (Mark 10.45). However, the means of redemp-

tion is not always specified and this has led to considerable later theological debate, which will be considered below. Finally, the purpose of redemption is both true freedom now (Gal. 5.1) and also eternal life (John 3.16). We must further note the distinctive synoptic language of the kingdom, which is marked out by tangible redemption now as well as in the world to come (Luke 4.18–20).

The lack of complete precision in the means of redemption has spawned a variety of theologies of the atonement: in brief, is a redemption payment made, and to whom, or is the effect in the heart of the believer (objective or subjective)? The mainstream characterization of patristic atonement theology is of the *Christus Victor* type, where Christ by rising again from death defeats the power of Satan, including death, and because he has united humanity with himself thereby redeems humankind. It is a deliverer model of redemption; Christ as humanity's representative. However, for some Patristic theologians, the redemption price was the death of Christ, which was the ransom paid to Satan to require him to free captive humanity (Origen). By the Middle Ages this theology was thought to give Satan too much power and, in a feudal context, Anselm advanced the satisfaction theory. Christ, as the God-man able to make the perfect sacrifice, 'satisfies' God's offended justice and dignity. This 'Latin' theory of the atonement – wherein redemption is redemption mostly from divine punishment – was to be further refined during the Reformation (Calvin more than Luther) into 'penal substitutionary atonement'. Christ takes on himself the punishment rightly due to humankind from a holy wrathful God, thereby winning salvation for the predestined or, in later versions, those who choose to believe. In modern Evangelicalism the severity and apparently unjust tone of this view – 'Father kills Son to meet demand of abstract inflexible justice' – has been softened into 'self-substitution' (John Stott). The third classic version (Peter Abelard) is sometimes confusingly called 'exemplarist'. Strictly speaking the point of the 'example' of Christ's death was to move human hearts to repentance. In more modern theologies his death becomes a way of identifying God with the suffering of the world and the power of Christ's sacrifice is in the thoroughness of this identification (Jürgen Moltmann).

If redemption is conceived primarily as forgiveness of sins and a release from the punishment due for sin (more sharply as escape from the wrath of God), then the corresponding spirituality may focus on the individual's acceptance of their sinful state, of Christ's substitutionary death for them and then of an assurance that this is the case. Such a spirituality may be combined with public and personal proclamation of this faith, so that others too may be similarly rescued. This is an account of classic Protestantism (though without the elements of predestination so prevalent in the sixteenth century, which tended to produce a model of the Christian life less focused on the 'personal decision for Christ' and more on discerning the signs of election). The attractive power of this spirituality can be found in the conviction of liberation experienced by the believer, who believes their sins to have been wiped away and that this is done not on the basis of any merit of their own, but simply by faith in the action of God in Christ.

A spirituality focused on redemption of the human life from the power and consequences of sin can also be expressed in a classically Catholic mode. Here the sacraments – baptism as the washing away of the effects of original sin and the Mass as the moment of reappropriation of the sacrificial merit of Christ's death – provide the shape for a more prolonged vision of the Christian life, where the journey from enslavement to sin is only slowly achieved in sanctification.

A spirituality more focused on redemption as liberation from human mortality (which is in itself a product of human sinfulness) can be said to be associated with Eastern Orthodoxy. Here the emphasis is on Christ's gift of divine life to humankind by virtue of his union with humanity in the incarnation and the spirituality more focused on participation in the Godhead in worship and contemplation.

Finally, a modern interpretation of redemption would emphasize less humanity's slavery to sin and vulnerability to God's judgement, and more the tangible slaveries – poverty, race, gender – which human beings still experience, and the crucial role of God, Christians and other people of good conscience, in bringing real liberation now, rather than leaving the oppressed with the distracting hope of a spiritual or future redemption.

Reflecting on the biblical account of redemption may enable some creative fusion. So, redemption is normally a costly process. 'Sacrifice' is a constant presence. In the New Testament it is clear that it is God in Christ who bears the cost. In both the Jewish and Christian Scriptures, God is believed to provide forgiveness of sin to individuals and communities and also real liberation from current experiences of oppression, whether they are political, legal, military, connected with health or culture or indeed experiences of spiritual oppression,

because these two sets of realities cannot be divorced. But it is also clear that such experiences of redemption are never complete and it is part of the Judaeo-Christian hope that there will be a final redemption when the suffering and injustice of the whole created order will be put right in the new creation (Isa. 11.6–9; Rom. 8.23). As Michael Ramsey argued: 'The Church will see every part of its mission in the total perspective of the reconciliation of mankind [*sic*] to God and of heaven as the goal for every man and woman made in the divine image.'

See also **Deification; Grace; Incarnation; Jesus and Spirituality; Person; Reconciliation.**

————

S. T. Davis, D. Kendall, G. O'Collins (eds), *The Redemption: An Interdisciplinary Symposium on Christ as Redeemer*, Oxford: Oxford University Press, 2004; Doctrine Commission of the Church of England: *The Mystery of Salvation*, London: Church House Publishing, 1995; J. Moltmann, *The Crucified God*, London: SCM Press, 2001; G. O'Collins, *Christology*, Oxford: Oxford University Press, 1995; C. Rowland, *The Cambridge Companion to Liberation Theology*, Cambridge: Cambridge University Press, 1999; J. Stott, *The Cross of Christ*, Leicester: InterVarsity Press, 1986; S. Sykes: *The Story of Atonement*, London: Darton, Longman & Todd, 1997.

ALAN BARTLETT

Reflection

1. *Definition and a philosophical approach.* Reflection may be defined as an activity through which the mind grasps the nature of truth and its own nature and activity. According to Johann Baptist Lotz, in implicit reflection, consciousness is always consciousness of self or turns back on itself as it grasps its object.

Lotz identifies several types of explicit reflection. In *psychological* reflection, humans consider inward experience, examining the spiritual and sensible acts of knowledge, purpose and feeling. Through this process, they become aware of the body–soul distinction. *Logical* reflection concerns itself with the abstract nature of human knowledge and relies on mental realities such as concepts, judgements and deductions. It determines if the connections made in thought are correct. *Ontological* reflection considers the ultimate nature of mental acts. There are two types. First, reflection on the theory of knowledge concerns itself with the nature of truth. Second, reflection on the metaphysics of knowledge traces the possibility of truth by examining a priori conditions for it within the subject. Through *metaphysical* reflection, humans become aware of being. Finally, in *transcendental* reflection, human consciousness becomes aware of being as the supreme condition of possibility of human acts. A second type of transcendental reflection concerns itself with the interpretation of being, asking how it may be justified as the ultimate condition of the possibility of consciousness.

Lotz traces the rich history of the philosophical concept of reflection from its origins in the writings of Neoplatonists to its further development in the works of Augustine, Bonaventure, Aquinas, Descartes, Kant and Hegel. The fullest development of the notion of reflection in twentieth-century philosophy may be found in the work of Gabriel Marcel who distinguishes between primary and secondary reflection. According to Marcel, the aim of primary reflection is problem-solving. It is abstract thinking in which there is a distinction between subject and object. In secondary reflection, the distinction between subject and object breaks down – it involves the contemplation of mysteries that, in turn, comprehend us.

2. *Reflection in theology*. Both systematic and practical theologians have considered the nature of reflection. Paul Tillich, Bernard Lonergan, Schubert Ogden and David Tracy have each addressed the character and fruits of reflection. In Volume 1 of his *Systematic Theology*, Tillich uses the term 'ultimate concern' to express the existential nature of reflection in theology. Only those propositions that concern us ultimately may properly be considered the object of theological reflection. Further, only those concerns that have the power of threatening and saving our being may be considered ultimate.

Bernard Lonergan concerns himself with the dynamic nature of human consciousness through which humans come to know and to act upon what is known. He develops a four-phase process of knowing that incorporates reflection. According to Lonergan, we come to know through experiencing, reflecting and understanding, judging and deciding, which leads inevitably to action. The human quest for understanding, goodness and love drives this search for knowledge. Lonergan has summarized his approach in terms of the transcendental imperatives: 'Be attentive, be intelligent, be reasonable, be responsible, be loving and, if necessary, change' (Tracy, 1991, p. 152). Thus he posits that conversion may be one fruit of the reflective process, and he understands it as a radical transformation requiring the development of a new foundation for all of one's thoughts and actions.

Like Lonergan, Ogden views reflection as fundamental in living. It aims to promote the art of life. Reflection enables engagement in a complex praxis of life lived in relationship to others and to the entire cosmos. The capacity for reflection enables us to not merely lead our lives but to live them, since reflective understanding allows us to consent to life and to live with vitality. According to Ogden, we ground our lives in faith that normative principles governing our existence have unconditional validity and that life lived in accordance with them is worth living. These normative principles include truth, beauty and goodness.

David Tracy draws on the work of critical theorists, feminists and liberation theologians to remind us of the fragility of reflection. It results from the tension the postmodern self experiences between conscious awareness and the awareness of otherness. This tension is experienced within, in the unconscious, and without in the plurality of ideologies. He emphasizes that all experience and understanding, all reflection, is hermeneutical. Further, in interpretation, we must rely on hermeneutics of suspicion and retrieval because of the existence of systemic distortions in our individual and communal lives.

Finally, practical theologians, such as Robert Kinast, use the term 'theological reflection' to describe a type of theological method. In it, reflection upon experience within particular contexts is correlated with the tradition for the sake of improved praxis.

3. *Implications for spirituality*. Sandra Schneiders' approach to human spirituality emphasizes its nature as experientially grounded, integrative, consciously pursued and involving self-transcendence toward an ultimate value. Given this commonly accepted definition, the role of reflection would appear crucial in the development of a personal spirituality and in the appropriation of lived tradition(s) in its formation. Through reflection upon experience one discerns the ultimate concern, tests the validity of it in relation to culture and tradition, and shapes one's life praxis in relation to it. The postmodern approach to reflection reminds us of the partiality of this enterprise. It also highlights the humility required in the face of what Tracy describes as interruptive historical realities, such as the Holocaust. These call forth strategies of resistance, attention and hope to counter the evil they exemplify and remind us ultimately of the finite nature of all reflection.

See also **Attentiveness; Discernment; Ministry and Spirituality; Pastoral Care and Spirituality; Recollection.**

Robert L. Kinast, *Let Ministry Teach: A Guide to Theological Reflection*, Collegeville, MN: The Liturgical Press, 1996; Beth Kostelac and James L. Connor, 'Theological reflection: Woodstock's way of working', *Woodstock Report* 31 (December 1992), pp. 3–7; Johannes Baptist Lotz, 'Reflection' in K. Rahner (ed.), *Sacramentum Mundi: An Encyclopedia of Theology* 5, New York: Herder & Herder, 1970, pp. 189–90; Schubert Ogden, 'On teaching theology', *Criterion* 25 (Winter 1986), 12–14; Sandra Schneiders, 'Religion vs. spirituality: a contemporary conundrum', *Spiritus* 3 (Fall 2003), 163–85; Paul Tillich, *Systematic Theology* 1, Chicago: University of Chicago Press, 1951; David Tracy, 'Recent Catholic spirituality: unity amid diversity' in Louis Dupré and Don Saliers (eds), *Christian Spirituality: Post Reformation and Modern*, vol. 18 of WS, pp. 143–73; Louis Dupré, *Plurality and Ambiguity: Hermeneutics, Religion, Hope*, Chicago: University of Chicago Press, 1987.

JANE F. MAYNARD

Reformation and Spirituality

The closest the Reformation era came to what we today understand by the term 'spirituality' is comprehended in the medieval term 'piety' (*pietas*). *Pietas* was manifested in devotion toward God and duty toward others. In the late Middle Ages this often involved the performance of ritual acts, for example attendance at Mass, pilgrimages, charity toward the poor, providing votive Masses for the dead. The Protestant Reformation tried to effect a significant change in acts of piety, but devotional readings designed to inculcate 'true religion' were remarkably similar between Protestants and Catholics.

Public worship. Many of the acts of piety practised by late medieval Christians were regarded by Protestant Reformers as fostering works-righteousness, that is, an attempt to get a blessing out of God apart from faith (trust) in God's promises. Martin Luther did not reject the performance of good works, but he consistently held that good works should be expressions of gratitude to God and love for the neighbour that are a response to a relationship with God based on justification by faith for Christ's sake. A true reform of piety required a consistent preaching of God's forgiveness and use of the means of grace, the word of God and the sacraments of Christ. The Christian was not just to attend Mass but hear sermons and receive Holy Communion. Pilgrimages, indulgences, votive Masses and other acts of piety were to be converted into deeds of loving service to the neighbour.

Luther effected a thorough restructuring of public worship that was more or less followed by other Reformers. The daily Masses were suppressed unless there were communicants; votive Masses were entirely abolished. In their place were daily prayer services with sermons. In Lutheran Church orders these daily services retained the character of the Divine Office and were called Matins (morning prayer) and Vespers (evening prayer). Especially in churches with schools the prayer offices continued to be sung by choirs, often in a mixture of Latin and German or another vernacular language. Expository sermons were preached as entire books of the Old and New Testaments were read chapter by chapter. On some days the sermons were based on catechetical texts such as the Ten Commandments, Apostles' Creed, and Lord's Prayer. Luther's *Large Catechism* is actually an editing of sermons preached by Luther on the parts of the Catechism.

On Sundays and festivals of the Church year in Lutheran Churches a full Service of the Word and the Lord's Supper was celebrated which followed the historical Order of Mass in Latin or German or a mixture thereof. The readings were the historic epistle and Gospel pericopes. In Reformed Churches the continuous reading of Scripture chapter by chapter was practised. It took time to prepare preachers who could deliver the kind of sermons the Reformers wanted and even more time to prepare congregations who could understand such sermons. Therefore the Reformers produced postils or books of homilies with sermons that could be read publicly to the congregation or read privately in the home.

Many of the Reformed Churches followed the example of Ulrich Zwingli in having Communion four times a year, which was a significant increase over the Middle Ages in which the faithful often received Communion once a year at Easter. In Reformed practice the entire congregation was prepared to receive Communion by lengthy penitential services. In Lutheran practice individual confession and absolution continued to be practised, at Luther's urging, and communicants were also examined for their knowledge of the Catechism when they announced their intention to receive Communion, particularly its teaching on the Lord's Supper. In time Saturday Vespers became a time of preparation for Holy Communion with the laying-on of hands in absolution for those who had made a general or particular confession of sins. A form of non-compulsory private confession was retained in the Anglican Prayer Books; a form of confession and absolution was devised from the Sarum Rite and the Cologne Church Order. A general penitential order was provided in the Communion Service and preceded Morning and Evening Prayer in the 1552 Prayer Book.

A revolutionary change occurred in the ambience of public worship from the visual emphasis of Catholicism to the auditory emphasis on Protestantism. Worshippers were not to look at pictures but listen to the word. In Reformed practice images were removed from church buildings in acts of iconoclasm and communicants sat while bread and cups of wine were passed to them by ministers. Buildings were whitewashed so as to remove any vestige of idolatry and to keep the mind from being distracted so that worshippers could concentrate on the word of God. By and large iconoclasm did not occur in Lutheran church buildings; pictures were valued for having a teaching purpose.

Nevertheless, the Reformers agreed with St Paul that 'faith comes from what is heard'. A significant development for piety in both Lutheran and Reformed practice was congregational singing. The singing of vernacular hymns by the congregation was practised in Germany during the Middle Ages, especially in juxtaposition with the Graduals and Sequences of the Mass. Luther made the congregational hymn central to public worship, especially in the German Mass (1526). Lutheran hymns were initially based on liturgical and catechetical texts. Later hymns were lyrical meditations on a text of Scripture (e.g. Luther's 'A mighty fortress is our God', Philipp Nicolai's 'Wake, awake, for night is flying'). Ulrich Zwingli in Zurich eschewed hymn-singing in public worship but John Calvin in Geneva, after experiencing congregational hymn-singing in Strasbourg, encouraged the development of metrical psalmody. These hymns (Lutheran chorales, Reformed metrical psalms) could be sung at home in family devotions as well as in public worship.

Private devotions. The emphasis on the word in both Reformation and Counter-Reformation ritual resulted in a practice of private devotions based on meditative reading and prayer. Early Reformation prayer books continued the tradition of the Books of the Hours (*Horae*) or Prymers (as they were called in English) that filled private devotional needs in the late Middle Ages. Some included traditional material but eliminated legendary material, indulgences, pruned the list of saints and removed some of the Marian prayers while subtly pressing the doctrinal distinctions of the Reformation. Luther's *Little Prayer Book* (1522) contained prayers related to the parts of the Catechism as well as prayers to be used for the days and seasons of the Church year and the needs and occasions in life, but singled out the Pater Noster as the exemplary Christian prayer. Luther's *Little Catechism* (1529) was not only a book that the head of the household could use to teach his household; it also included meal graces, prayers upon arising in the morning and retiring at night, and tables of household duties drawn from biblical citations.

Luther's devotional books and others like them proliferated to such an extent that King Henry VIII in England worried about 'the dyversitie of praier bookes that are nowe abroade', authorized an official English 'Primer, set foorth by the kynges majestie and his Clergie, to be taught, lerned, and read: and none other to be used throughout all his dominions' (1545). This Primer was traditional in many ways: it included a compete set of the eight canonical Hours, the Litany and Dirge, and Psalms of the Passion, but it eliminated promises of indulgences and trimmed prayers to the saints and to Mary. The 1549 *Book of Common Prayer* not only regularized public worship but included a collection of prayers that could be used at home. The primers published during the reign of Mary I, in both Latin and English, returned to the format and content of the earlier, Catholic French-printed primers. Elizabeth I's English Primer (1559) reinstated her father's Primer of 1559, including the eight canonical hours, the Dirge and Commendations, although she permitted editions of the Edwardian Primer also to be published during her reign. In spite of the efforts of Tudor monarchs to authorize an official primer, private printings of diverse prayer books also continued.

Toward the end of the sixteenth century prayer books became more elaborately structured around themes, such as the passion, death and resurrection of Christ. Such prayer books differed in style but not in focus from the mysteries of the rosary. In fact, prayer books often attained an ecumenical readership that defies confessional divisions. One of the most popular prayer books in the sixteenth century was written by the Spanish Dominican Luis de Granada, whose fivefold stages in prayer – preparation of the soul, reading, meditation, thanksgiving and petition – was replicated in other prayer books. We see in this development a movement away from relating private prayer to public prayer and toward a cultivation of the spiritual life initiated by examination of conscience and humiliation. Not surprisingly, by the end of the sixteenth century there was a resurgence of interest in the writings of medieval mystics such as Bernard of Clairvaux, Thomas à Kempis, and Johann Tauler, even among Protestants.

See also **Spirituality, Liturgy and Worship**
(*essay*); **Anabaptist Spirituality; Anglican Spirituality; Baptist Spirituality; Calvinist Spirituality;** *Devotio Moderna*; **Devotions, Popular; English Spirituality; Lutheran Spirituality; Medieval Spirituality in the West; Moravian Spirituality; Office, Divine; Preaching and Spirituality; Puritan Spirituality; Reformed Spirituality; Scandivanian Spirituality.**

Louis Bouyer, *A History of Spirituality* 3, New York: Seabury Press, 1982; Bengt R. Hoffman, *Luther and the Mystics*, Minneapolis: Augsburg, 1976; Steven E. Ozment, *The Reformation in the Cities*, New Haven and London: Yale University Press, 1975; Frank C. Senn (ed.), *Protestant Spiritual Traditions*, Mahwah, NJ: Paulist Press, 1986; Helen C. White, *The Tudor Books of Private Devotion*, Madison: University of Wisconsin Press, 1951.

FRANK C. SENN

Reformed Spirituality

The Reformed tradition came into being in the city states of Switzerland during the complex spread of the Reformations of the 1520s and 1530s. It was a subtly varied tradition from the beginning, flavoured by the different emphases of each city's Reformers. For example, the covenant theology which developed in Zurich initially under Zwingli, but principally thanks to Bullinger was distinctively different from the Calvinist orthodoxy which dominated Geneva by the 1550s. If the former found its spiritual centre in God's relationship with the whole of creation, the latter all too easily slipped from Calvin's reticence before the scriptural fact of election into the precise mathematics of predestination. Christians who look back to those years and those thinkers as determinative are part of the Reformed tradition, although ecclesiologically they may be part of different communions. Most, however, will belong to churches that adopt either a Presbyterian or Congregational ordering, as was recognized by the merging of the International Congregational Council and the World Alliance of Reformed Churches in 1970.

Reformed thought changed out of all recognition between the final edition of Calvin's *Institutes* (1559) and the publishing of the *Westminster Confession* (1647). The courageous encounter with Scripture which had crafted the first generations of the Reformation gave way to the Scholasticism of federal theology (Lat. *foedus* = covenant) which made covenant the determining principle of its schema and turned the relationship between God and humanity into an inherently legal one. Grace was almost subordinated to law. However, although federal theology remained in the ascendant until the mid nineteenth century, Reformed thought remained diverse. The Arminian controversy, which came to a head at the Synod of Dort in 1618, was an intra-Reformed debate. Similarly, Friedrich Schleiermacher (1768–1834), the first systematician to see a way through the Enlightenment impasse, and Jonathon Edwards (1703–58), America's greatest theologian who redrew classical Augustinian and Calvinist thought for a post-Newtonian universe, were both members of the Reformed family.

That breadth and variety has remained a characteristic of the Reformed family in the nineteenth and twentieth centuries. It embraced the extremes of the Mercersberg High Church movement of John Williamson Nevin (1803–66) and Philip Schaff (1819–93) as well as the proto-fundamentalism of Princeton's Charles Hodge (1797–1878) and his son Archibald, and Benjamin Warfield (1851–1921). In the twentieth century, the great neo-orthodox theologians Karl Barth (1886–1968) and Emil Brunner (1886–1966) were Reformed pastors, but so too were those redoubtable inheritors of Schleiermacher's mantle, John Oman (1860–1939) and John Hick.

Theologically and spiritually the Reformed tradition was grounded in a recovery of the transcendent otherness of God. That was radical and shocking in the early years of the sixteenth century, for Europe had been formed by a religious culture which had for a thousand years been defined by the close immanence of God in the sacraments, the physicality of the saints and their relics, holy places and (most significantly of all) the eucharistic host. Finite things, the Reformed argued, could not contain the infinite. Only God could bridge the gap between God and humanity, and God had done so in Christ, as the Scriptures and dominical sacraments bore witness. God came as the Word made flesh, a Word witnessed to by the words of Scripture, made real by the Spirit through the words of a preacher. A spirituality of the ear thus replaced a spirituality of the eye. The architectural and artistic setting for worship had to accommodate itself to this paradigm shift in perception. Whitewashed walls and a plain Communion table replaced instructive murals and distracting images. What mattered were words.

Reformed spirituality is scriptural. Along with other traditions of the Reformations, the Reformed restored the balance between word and sacraments in worship. Preaching became a sacramental activity. Refusing to listen to godly preachers, said Calvin, was 'like blotting out the face of God which shines upon us' (*Institutes* 4.1.5). Scripture is important because God is encountered through it. Theologically the Reformed have therefore emphasized the primacy of Scripture over reason and tradition; spiritually they have encouraged daily private worship centred on Scripture reading. Matthew Henry's (1662–1714) *Exposition of the Old and New Testaments* (1708–10) and Philip Doddridge's (1702–51) *The Family Expositor* (1738–56) are but two of the finest examples of the ways in which the Reformed sought to make Scripture devotionally and theologically accessible for private devotion. Each family was intended to be a micro-church, gathered daily around the Word.

Reformed spirituality allows God to be God in all God's otherness and strangeness. The sovereignty of God is absolute. God is not, for the Reformed, egalitarian, but given to particularity and choice – a people, a land, individuals like Abram and Sarai, Joseph and Mary. The basic reality of human living for the Reformed is that men and women have to do with the living God. The 'chief end' of human beings, according to the opening question of the *Westminster Shorter Catechism* (1647), is 'to glorify God and enjoy him forever'. That is a classical statement of Reformed piety. That is what life is for. All living is in that sense vocational, a response to God's calling. The doctrine of election was intended both to defend the particularity of God's activity and to emphasize that those choices had nothing to do with human merit. Nineteenth- and twentieth-century Reformed theology has called into question the classical statements of the doctrine of double-predestination (as stated in the *Westminster Confession of Faith*, ch. 3, for example). Barth considered them lacking in scriptural warrant, and he and others have re-stated the doctrine Christologically. The spiritual consequences of election have been both liberating and enslaving. The misinterpretation of the doctrine in Reformed history has resulted in the justification of exploitation, oppression and apartheid. However, when understood correctly as election to service, following Christ to the cross and beyond, it has been intensely liberating, both individually and corporately (as seen, for example, in the Barmen Declaration of the Confessing Church in 1934).

If life is vocational for the Reformed, that vocation is lived out in a world which Calvin termed 'the theatre of God's glory'. The Reformed, like most Protestants, do not recognize a difference between the sacred and the secular. God is Lord of all, and vocation therefore belongs as much to the banker and the politician as the priest. Discipleship is about engagement, not withdrawal. Together they are part of the priesthood of all believers who are required to raise their particular space and time to God in prayer, and to allow God into their space and time through their service.

At the heart of Calvin's spirituality was the mystical union between Christ and the believer. For Calvin this was an intensely corporate experience, expressed in baptism. It was through the life of the Church, the ministry of the Word, the administration of the sacraments and the liturgy that believers received everything that Christ was and is. He had a remarkably high doctrine of the Church: 'there is no other way to enter into life unless this mother conceive us in her womb, nourish us at her breast, and lastly, unless she keep us under her care and guidance until, putting off mortal flesh, we become like the angels' (*Institutes* 4.1.4). Reformed spirituality takes the visible Church seriously. Membership and commitment are important – hence the Communion tokens and cards which were used at varying points in history to ensure that members had received the benefits of Communion.

The marks of the Church were, for Calvin, the true preaching of the Word and the proper administration of the sacraments. He was more concerned with the centre than the circumference. The classical Reformers never considered themselves to be doing anything other than reforming the Church. Their quest was not for schism, but unity. As Calvin wrote in his *Commentary on the Epistle to the Ephesians*, 'God cannot be torn into different parts. It cannot but be our duty to cherish holy unity . . . Faith and baptism, and God the Father and Christ, ought to unite us, so as almost to become one human being.' The concern for the unity of the Church which has been a mark of the international Reformed community in the last century is a natural expression of the Reformed heritage. It is no accident that in the twentieth century two of the most creative experiments in Christian community, the Iona Community and Taizé (borrowing generously and deliberately from Catholic patterns of Christian living), were the creation of Reformed pastors, George MacLeod and Roger Schutz.

See also **Calvinist Spirituality; Puritan Spirituality; Reformation and Spirituality; Taizé, Spirituality of.**

Alister McGrath, *Roots that Refresh: A Celebration of Reformation Spirituality*, London, Hodder & Stoughton, 1991; Elsie Anne McKee (ed.), *John Calvin: Writings on Pastoral Piety*, Mahwah, NJ: Paulist Press, 2001; Howard L.

Rice, *Reformed Spirituality: An Introduction for Believers*, Louisville, KY: John Knox Press, 1991.

DAVID CORNICK

Reign of God

The significance of the reign of God (called in earlier translations of the Scriptures the 'kingdom of God') for Christian spirituality stems from its importance in Jesus' own spirituality as it is described in the New Testament. Its central place in the memory of Jesus' relationship with God is demonstrated by the petition found in the Lord's Prayer, 'Your kingdom come, your will be done on earth as in heaven'. Most of the Christian scriptural writings agree that it provided a crucial framework for how his first-century followers interpreted Jesus' life and mission.

The reign of God announced by Jesus draws on the expectations of the Jewish people for the ultimate and sure fulfilment of God's purpose for the creation – both earth and heaven. It provides a key to Jesus' relation to Jewish Scripture and tradition, especially the prophetic and apocalyptic literature. It anticipates the transformation and renewal of the earth, abundance and celebration, social and economic justice, an end to oppression, the overcoming of suffering and death, intimacy with God and harmony within the whole created order – all implied by the Hebrew word *shalom*. Jesus' own teaching, his 'mighty acts' and his resurrection are all interpreted in the New Testament as 'signs' of the appearance of God's reign. Early Jewish Christian identification of Jesus as the anticipated Messiah is directly related to the belief that in him, God's reign had begun and would soon be established in its fullness.

With the passage of time, the eschatological dimension of early Christian faith became less important and Christians lost their hope in the transformation of this world. The reign of God came to be identified on the one hand with the ultimate fulfilment of God's purposes beyond history – in heaven – and on the other with the Church as the means by which salvation is achieved. Yet the rich imagery of the reign of God continued to attract Christians, especially those whose dire human condition made the hope of a 'new heaven and new earth' most compelling.

In the period following the Second World War, the reign of God re-emerged as a focus of Christian theology and spirituality. European theologians such as Jürgen Moltmann, Wolfhart Pannenberg and Dorothee Soelle rediscovered the importance of 'the future' as a category for Christian faith and insisted that the God who embraced the creation in Christ has hopes for this world. In the United States, James Cone and other African-American theologians examined the roots of Black Christian spirituality in its rich musical tradition. They discovered in the lyrics of the spirituals a profound hope for escape from slavery and misery into a land of promise identified with God's reign.

The renewal unleashed by Vatican II (1962–65) proved to be a watershed in reclaiming the reign of God as a primary category for Christian spirituality. While its primary effects were felt among Roman Catholics, its influence touched every major Christian tradition. The Council urged the Church to use the Bible as its primary resource for interpreting the multiple contexts in which Christians live. In Latin America, Africa and Asia, this initiative gave birth to thousands of 'base communities', small groups of poor Christians on the lowest rungs of society who learned to pray and read the Bible in the light of their own experience of suffering and oppression. They identified the promise of the reign of God which they found in the story of the Hebrew people with their own longing and zeal for liberation from every kind of misery. Biblical stories like the Exodus and the Return from Exile inspired hope for a future radically different from the past or the present, while the struggles of the Hebrew people to achieve God's promises motivated action on behalf of the changes awakened by that hope.

The dream of creating societies which would reflect the justice, peace and abundance of God's reign led many to radical political action, in which they were joined by clergy and religious and to which the repressive regimes against which they were fighting responded with brutal violence. The Jesuit Jon Sobrino, who has worked for many years among the poor of El Salvador, argues that *only* a spirituality based on the reign of God could adequately reflect the faith and hope of the people with whom he works. More recently, the reign of God has provided an important perspective for spiritualities that respond to ecological concerns and encourage an attentive reverence for the earth as God's creation.

Spiritualities that take the reign of God as their starting point affirm a God of both compassion and justice, who can be trusted to take the side of the victims of this world. They consider the Bible as the primary locus for identifying God's nature and purpose. They give priority to the values of God's reign as the Scriptures identify them, especially justice and mercy. They assume that a relationship with God through Christ in the power of the Spirit is inevitably expressed in solidarity and community with those who suffer and in engagement in the struggle to overcome their pain. While trusting that God's purposes will ultimately prevail, faith in the future is balanced by willingness to create 'signs of God's reign' in the present through acts of mercy, political action and, when necessary, acts of resistance against those forces that oppose the values of the reign of God. Traditional Christian acts associated with spirituality, such as prayer and fasting, are reinterpreted as actions in solidarity with the suffering and as creating signs of the presence of the reign of God in the here and now.

See also **Eschatology; Jesus and Spirituality; Lord's Prayer; Social Justice; World.**

Leonardo Boff, *Cry of the Earth, Cry of the Poor*, Maryknoll, NY: Orbis Books, 1997; James H. Cone, *The Spirituals and the Blues: An Interpretation*, Maryknoll, NY: Orbis Books, 1992; Marie Dennis et al., *Oscar Romero: Reflections on His Life and Writings*, Maryknoll, NY: Orbis Books, 2000; Gustavo Gutiérrez, *We Drink from Our Own Wells: The Spiritual Journey of a People*, Maryknoll, NY: Orbis Books, 2003; Choan-Seng Song, *Jesus and the Reign of God*, Minneapolis: Fortress Press, 1993; Elsa Támez, *The Amnesty of Grace: Justification by Faith from a Latin American Perspective*, Eugene, OR: Wipf and Stock 2002.

JOHN T. KATER JR

Relationships

In the Judaeo-Christian tradition spirituality is conceived of as an expression of relationship with God, neighbour and self. Human relationship with God is to be characterized by complete love, obedience and faithfulness (Deut. 6.4). Human beings are commanded by God to respect one another and to live together in justice and holiness as a matter of personal and communal integrity (Lev. 19.17). The Gospels draw these relationships together as the core of what it is to be holy: 'The first commandment is this: "Hear O Israel, the Lord our God is one; and you shall love the Lord your God with all your heart, and all your soul, and all your mind, and all your strength." The second is: "You shall love your neighbour as yourself"' (Mark 12.28–31; see also Matt. 22.34–40; Luke 10.25–28). In the epistles love of neighbour is the 'royal law' (James 2.8), fulfilling God's call to holiness of living (Rom. 13.8; Gal. 5.14).

Relationship with God, one another, fellow creatures and with the earth is inherently part of what it is to be human (Gen. 1 and 2). Material life in all its forms finds its origin and ongoing meaning as God's creation, which is in itself (in Christian interpretation) the out-working of the co-operative relationship between the persons of the Holy Trinity: Creator, co-creating Word, and life-giving Holy Spirit. Just as this divine life of the Trinity shares a dynamic spiritual economy of love, so creation is formed as an ecology, an ordered and relational network of material interdependence and connectivity. Human beings in particular are made in the image of God (Gen. 1.26ff.), to live as persons in community (marriage, kin, tribe, nation, neighbour, city, religious fellowship), having an intrinsic relationality which sustains a tendency towards procreation, communion, communication and constructive co-operation. In the primal state, and in its heavenly restoration, all creatures find their vocation to worship the Creator and to abide with one another in harmony (cf. Ps. 148 and 150; Isa. 11.1–9; Rev. 7.9ff.).

In fallen creation these relationships are distorted or even broken; this state of sin is characterized by exploitation and alienation on every level, so that human beings are distanced from God, one another, the creation and from aspects of themselves. The salvation of God in Christ restores these relationships, and makes available reconciliation with God, with neighbour (including creation and community as well as between individuals) and within the self. Spirituality is concerned with the ordering of personal relationships and with the proper participation of individuals in the Church and society – the discipline of appropriate prayer, penance and service to God and neighbour. Yet spirituality has also been concerned with the new corporate patterns of relationship which emerge as the social reality of what it is to be 'in Christ', characterized by values of mutuality and inclusivity which allow former distinctions (Jew/Greek, male/female, slave/free) no spiritual or moral relevance (e.g. Eph. 4 and 5; Col. 3; Gal. 3.25ff.). This vision has found a variety of practical implications for discipleship in different historical and social contexts, such as the campaign for the abolition of slavery, or for the ordination of women, as well as the expression of Christian concern for the quality of social relationships through healthcare and education, workers' rights, the peace movement, development work, the campaign for fairer terms of international trade, or in environmental politics.

For individuals, spiritual companionship/direction, pastoral care and counselling, and psychotherapy, all offer ways to find personal integration and spiritual maturity within the self and in the intimate realm of personal relationships.

See also Charity; Community; Communion/ *Koinonia*; Creation Spirituality; Ecological Spirituality; Healing and Health; Person.

MARK PRYCE

Religious Life

Rooted in the human longing for the Absolute, Christian religious life is a distinctive lifestyle which is both simple and complex. In its simplest description, it is a call and a commitment to live for God through following Jesus. It is complex and multifaceted in that it is deeply personal and influenced by both the time and the place in which it exists. Religious life takes its inspiration from the gospel and traces its beginnings to early Christianity.

Two contemporary forms of that life are the 'contemplative' or monastic life and what is referred to in *Perfectae Caritatis*, the document from Vatican II on religious life, as institutes where 'the very nature of religious life requires apostolic action and services' (8). At times a religious congregation takes its inspiration from a particular school of spirituality, for example Benedictine, Dominican, Carmelite or French School. In other cases a group identifies more closely with a founder or foundress unrelated or loosely related to these schools of spirituality.

Development of religious life as work of the Spirit. Religious life is a prophetic phenomenon in the Church. Its origins, its development and its renewal are marked by the newness which characterizes all works of the Holy Spirit. Most histories of religious life trace its growth and development in a linear fashion. They tend to underline the early movement from the cities to the desert, the development of monasticism, the mendicant movement and finally the apostolic movement. The growth of this charismatic way of life, however, was not so neatly developmental as such an outline might indicate. As a work of the Holy Spirit, religious life is most often expressed in the creativity and surprise of the Spirit. One of these moments of newness for religious in the Catholic tradition was Vatican II which called for the co-operation of all religious in the process of renewal. This renewal, both personal and communal, was to involve 'two simultaneous processes: (1) a continuous return to the sources of all Christian life and to the original inspiration behind a given community and (2) an adjustment of the community to the changed conditions of the times' (*Perfectae Caritatis* 2).

Perfectae Caritatis spoke of a 'wonderful variety' of religious communities, of 'varied gifts' and the 'diversity of their spiritual endowments'. The ongoing efforts of canon law to find cate-gories which define religious congregations give evidence of the newness of the Spirit who is constantly creating without the limitation of categories. Only with the hindsight which is a gift of the Spirit can common threads be recognized.

The active or ministerial form of religious life is more widespread among women than among men today. Its history embodies the impulse of the creative Spirit. What is distinctive about this form of life is its focus on ministry and its mobility. It grew out of the needs of society and flourished especially after the French Revolution which left so many people marginalized and bereft of assistance. In these ministerial congregations, the cloister legislated for women was necessarily mitigated and certain practices of religious life such as the Divine Office recited in choir were replaced. It was only with the promulgation of *Conditae a Christo* in 1900 that women in these ministerial congregations, that is, with simple vows, not living in cloister and dedicated to apostolic works, were recognized officially as religious.

An ecclesial and prophetic life. Religious life is an ecclesial life. Its position within the ecclesial community is essential, though at times ambiguous and difficult. Authorized, guided and supported within the Church, religious are by their prophetic vocation called to be faithful, loving and critical. Religious profess publicly their intent to imitate the form of life of Jesus, to walk in his footsteps, to be as he was – totally reliant on God through poverty, always seeking the will of the One he called and experienced as Father, choosing celibacy as the expression of a deep personal loving relationship with God and others. It is the conscious and free choice of celibacy for the sake of God's reign that unifies the total gift of oneself to God. As evangelical counsels, these three realities of poverty, obedience and consecrated celibacy are deeply rooted in the gospel.

Community and ministry are likewise intrinsic to religious life. Solidarity with the marginalized and the outcasts of society has prompted religious to respond to those in need through education, healthcare and other human and social services. They do this in memory of Jesus who went about doing good: healing the sick, forgiving the sinner, restoring dignity to those deprived of it in the eyes of others. Ministry and community overlap in the life of Jesus as he draws outcasts, women and children in from the margins, enabling them to take their rightful place in the community of disciples. How the elements of community and ministry are lived within an individual congregation today depends on that group's understanding of itself, its history, tradition and its particular law. At their best, religious witness to the Absolute of God and to God's loving concern for all. Contemplation of the face of Christ, especially as it is revealed in the faces of the poor, nourishes the gift of their life to others.

Religious life and culture. The forms of religious life are deeply affected not only by the charism, the history and the tradition of each religious institute but also by the culture in which the life is lived. There is no one time or place which is privileged in this regard. Like the gospel itself, religious life is a seed sown in the world. It falls on the ground and potentially bears fruit in any age, on any continent. In the nineteenth and twentieth centuries, the relationship of religious to the world was at times described as 'separation' from the world. The understanding behind this expression, especially detrimental to women, often led to a distancing from the realities of everyday human life and from the laity whose primary task was seen as being in the world. Separation from the world today is often understood as taking a counter-cultural stance whenever gospel values are threatened.

Not identical with any one culture, religious life is profoundly shaped by the surrounding culture. The perennial 'essentials' look quite different in diverse geographical areas and/or in various historical settings. Poverty, for example, is lived on the African continent in a way that is quite different from the way it might be lived in Asia or the Americas. So also the vow of obedience is understood and expressed quite differently in a democratic society than in an autocratic one. In both, it requires ongoing discernment of God's will through the mediation of the religious community, its constitutions and those to whom authority is confided. How this search is structured and facilitated will differ according to the culture.

If cultures affect the expressions of religious life, so do the values of that life influence the cultures in which they exist. These cultures must be renewed by encountering the gospel. Humanity is to be transformed from within by persons who themselves are renewed. Just as all the faithful are called to evangelize human culture and cultures in a profound way, so are religious called to recognize and transform the values of the culture, both local and global, in which they live.

Newness and the future. The challenges to religious life of a postmodern, globalized and violent world are enormous. Religious require faith and fidelity to the Spirit who continues to inspire creativity and hope in the human heart. Religious life calls for continued openness to the other and to otherness. It requires as well the realization that inspired expressions of religious life will continue to arise out of contemplative discernment and love for God and humanity.

See also **Apostolic Spirituality; Benedictine Spirituality; Canonical Communities; Carmelite Spirituality; Celibacy; Cistercian Spirituality; Conventual Life; Community; Dominican Spirituality; Franciscan Spirituality; French School of Spirituality; Ignatian Spirituality; Jesus, Society of; Mendicant Spirituality; Monasticism; Obedience; Poverty; Rules, Religious; Servite Spirituality; Vows.**

Joan Chittester, *The Fire in These Ashes: A Spirituality of Contemporary Religious Life*, Kansas City: Sheed & Ward, 1995; Catherine M. Harmer, *Religious Life in the 21st Century: A Contemporary Journey into Canaan*, Mystic, CT: Twenty-Third Publications, 1995; Sandra M. Schneiders, *Finding the Treasure: Locating Religious Life in a New Ecclesial and Cultural Context*, Religious Life in a New Millennium, vol. 1, New York/Mahwah, NJ: Paulist Press, 2000; Sandra M. Schneiders, *Selling All: Commitment, Consecrated Celibacy, and Community in Catholic Religious Life*, Religious Life in a New Millennium, vol. 2, New York/Mahwah, NJ: Paulist Press, 2001; Vatican Congregation for Institutes of Consecrated Life and Societies of Apostolic Life, 'Starting afresh from Christ: a renewed commitment to consecrated life in the third millennium', *Origins* 32 (2002), 130–48.

MARY MILLIGAN

Renaissance

see **Christian Humanism**

Resurrection

The resurrection of Jesus of Nazareth occupies such a central place in early Christian faith and life that it touches and affects almost everything else, spirituality included. Mainstream Christian theology has always affirmed the resurrection both of Jesus and also, still in the future, of all who belong to him. But resurrection as a theme has had a surprisingly varied subsequent career, not always being fully integrated into Christian reflection either about the future life or its present anticipations.

The earliest Christians lived in the world of first-century Judaism, where resurrection (which always means embodied future life; never, until second-century Gnosticism, a non-bodily immortality) was widely accepted, on the basis of texts like Dan. 12 and 2 Macc. 7. These and other texts (some of which referred also, metaphorically, to the restoration of Israel) reflect the Jewish belief in God as creator and judge, committed thereby to putting the created order to rights, including restoring to life those who had died for their loyalty to God and Torah. This Jewish belief, developed especially by the Rabbis, always referred to the future raising of all God's people at the day of judgement. By contrast, the early Christians believed that Jesus' resurrection had anticipated this, launching the project of God's future world within the present one and thus generating a new category of time in which the present age of corruption and decay was already overlaid with the new age of forgiveness and life. In addition, the Christians made resurrection central to their life and thought in a way Judaism had never done, and emphasized its character as neither the resuscitation of the body which had died, nor its abandonment, but its transformation into a new kind of physicality no longer subject to decay or death. While at one level this provokes a powerful set of historical questions (why did this mutation in traditional belief occur?) to which the best answer is the high probability of the actual bodily resurrection of Jesus, it also again gives characteristic shape and content to the spirituality which based itself on Jesus and particularly on his death and resurrection.

This shows itself in the New Testament in a wide variety of ways. In John, Jesus himself is 'the resurrection and the life' (11.25), so that to follow and believe in him is to embrace life itself. John 20 then tells the story of Easter in such a way as to emphasize that this is the start of the new creation ('the first day of the week'), inviting Jesus' followers to discover their new identity and vocation as sharing in both the benefits and the tasks of the new world.

In Paul, Rom. 8 envisages God eventually doing for the whole creation, not just for believers, what he did for Jesus at Easter, so that the present condition of Christians is both an anticipation of that future (seen particularly in holiness of life) and a patient endurance in the suffering, and the groaning in inarticulate prayer in the power of the Spirit, which indicate the tension between what is already true and what is not yet true. Rom. 4 analyses Abraham's faith – as the model for Christian faith – in terms of his belief that God could give life where there was only death. Rom. 6 discusses baptism in terms of dying with Christ and being raised with him, so that one can now 'walk in newness of life', a theme paralleled in Gal. 2.19–21. Likewise, Eph. 1 and Col. 3 understand the Christian to be so solidly 'in Christ' that he or she is already 'raised with him', so that the power of God which

effected Jesus' resurrection is already at work in their lives. The massive treatment of resurrection in 1 Cor. 15 unveils the underlying argument of much of the letter, not least the bracing ethical commands (God will raise your body, therefore it matters what you do with it now) in chapter 6 and the assurance in chapter 13 that faith, hope and love will last into God's future world. In particular, Phil. 2.5–11 (though not mentioning the resurrection specifically, it is clearly implied) and 3.20f. speak of the risen Jesus in terms which indicate that he is the true Lord of the world, while Caesar, who claims to be king, lord and saviour, is not. This is stated in summary form in Rom. 1.4: the resurrection is the means by which God declares Jesus to be 'son of God in power'. Thus, though resurrection remains anchored both in the fact of what happened to Jesus and in the reality awaited by believers on the last day, it comes forward from the first and backwards from the second to transform, and give characteristic shape and content to, several interlocking aspects of Christian experience, from prayer to politics, from devotion to doctrine.

Resurrection informs the spirituality of the early Fathers in a variety of ways. Aside from the defence of the doctrine against obvious pagan sneers, we find it as part of the challenge to martyrdom, as the ultimate destiny for which the 'medicine of immortality', that is, the Eucharist, will prepare Christ's people (Ignatius), and, developing Paul's insight, as the central meaning of baptism (especially e.g. in the Easter rites developed by Cyril of Jerusalem). The sheer physicality of resurrection was celebrated by second- and third-century Fathers over against the dualism of the Gnostics, undergirding the call not to a passive or detached spirituality but to a robust ethic and a refusal to compromise with the idolatrous demands of paganism, especially the Caesar-cult. As with Jewish belief, resurrection correlates closely with believing in God as creator and judge. To soften either part is to take a step away from resurrection; conversely, to emphasize resurrection is always to embrace a theology and spirituality in which the created order, itself basically good, is to be put to rights, starting with Jesus and hence to be anticipated in the present life rather than postponed to an ultimate future.

In the Middle Ages and the Reformation, however, resurrection seems to have taken something of a back seat in spirituality and theology. Unlike the Eastern Church, which retained a strong sense of the resurrection in connection with both sacraments and spirituality, the Western Church barely mentions it in the medieval canon of the Mass – an omission followed by Cranmer and only rectified, though without as yet much integration into eucharistic theology itself, in contemporary rites. Bernard and Aquinas both insist on the importance of the bodily resurrection. But the medieval stress (not least in writings like those of Dante and, later, Bunyan, and in paintings like Michaelangelo's Sistine Chapel) on souls being taken to either heaven or hell, coupled with a residual Platonism that devalued the material world in favour of the 'spiritual', meant that just as Christology had concentrated on the incarnation, so eschatology concentrated on 'going to heaven'. The huge concentration of devotional art and music on the details of the passion and death of Jesus contrasts with the paucity of equivalent meditation on the resurrection. For centuries, many Christians simply failed to notice that the key New Testament texts spoke of the renewal of earth itself, with God's kingdom eventually combining heaven and earth in one (Rev. 21—22). The liberal scepticism of the Enlightenment reinforced this omission, which is only now being made good with the stress in the last fifty years on a more historical approach to Easter, a less Platonic view of the cosmos and the future, and a more robust liturgical celebration of Easter. A glance at typical Western Easter hymns reveals an interesting dichotomy between those which introduce the theme of the renewal of creation and those which assume that the main point is 'life after death', as opposed to the second-stage life after 'life after death' of the New Testament. Thus Easter sometimes collapses into sentimental piety, failing to sustain the clear-cut ethic and sacramental theology of the early Church.

Resurrection has, however, made an interesting return in various theologies of liberation. Some have mistakenly supposed that a liberationist meaning could only be achieved by downplaying the bodily resurrection itself, but in fact it is bodily resurrection which confronts tyranny with the news that death, its ultimate weapon, has been defeated. The promise of the creation's renewal, and the news of this being anticipated at Easter, undergirds all Christian ecological work. Coventry Cathedral, rebuilt after its wartime bombing but with the shell of the old building visible from inside the new one, speaks powerfully of resurrection and hence of hope and peace. And it is resurrection, by invoking God's future, renewed world and suggesting that this renewal can be anticipated in the present, which enables us to understand how there can be a Christian theology of 'place' which is not a lapse into either sentiment or magic.

At the heart of a resurrection-based spirituality there will always remain the personal encounter with the risen Jesus, and here the Gospels remain peerless sources for prayer, meditation and sacramental life. The two disciples on the road to Emmaus, whose hearts burn within them as the risen (but unrecognized) Jesus opens the Scriptures to them and who then recognize him in the breaking of the bread, are described in such a way as to set a pattern for all Christian discipleship (Luke 24.11–35). Jesus' meeting with the weeping Mary – including the haunting 'Do not hold on to me' – provides the basis for genuine comfort (John 20.11–18). His confrontation with Thomas, and his refutation of his doubts, challenge Christian spirituality at the point of epistemology (Thomas wants to 'know' by touching, and Jesus invites him to do so; nevertheless, seeing is enough to convince him; but Jesus speaks of a faith that does not even need sight) (John 20.24–29). His commissioning of the disciples (20.19–23) is the foundation of all Christian mission; his breakfast with them by the shore is replete with sacramental overtones and signs of new creation; and his final conversation with Peter, simultaneously forgiving and challenging, conveys the very heart of Christian devotion, vocation and mission. To know the risen Jesus is to hear one's own name spoken with the question and command: 'What is that to you? Follow me!' (John 21.22).

See also Cross and Spirituality; Jesus and Spirituality; Johannine Spirituality; Pauline Spirituality; Synoptic Gospels.

S. Davis, D. Kendall and G. O'Collins (eds), The Resurrection: An Interdisciplinary Symposium on the Resurrection of Jesus, Oxford: Oxford University Press, 1997; R. N. Longenecker (ed.), Life in the Face of Death: The Resurrection Message of the New Testament, Grand Rapids: Eerdmans, 1998; G. O'Collins, Easter Faith: Believing in the Risen Jesus, London: Darton, Longman & Todd, 2003; Oliver O'Donovan, Resurrection and Moral Order: An Outline for Evangelical Ethics, 2nd edn, Leicester: Apollos/ Grand Rapids, MI: Eerdmans, 1994; T. F. Torrance, Space, Time and Resurrection, Edinburgh: The Handsel Press, 1976; Rowan Williams, Resurrection: Interpreting the Easter Gospel, London: Darton, Longman & Todd, 1982; N. T. Wright, The Resurrection of the Son of God, London: SPCK/Minneapolis: Fortress Press, 2003.

N. T. (TOM) WRIGHT

Retreats

The concept of a 'retreat' has a long and varied history. In the Christian context the invitation of Jesus to 'come away and rest awhile' (Mark 6.31) is often thought of as the first invitation to 'make retreat'. Although a complete history of formal retreats through the centuries is impossible to construct, there are bits and pieces of information to be gleaned through various writings, seen in the lives of 'saints' such as Thérèse Couderc, founder of the Cenacle Sisters, Madeline Sophie Barat, Society of the Sacred Heart, Vincent Pallotti who began the Society of the Catholic Apostolate and in the archives of many women's and men's religious communities, both Anglican and Catholic.

The original inspiration for 'retreat' can be traced to the notion of a 'retreat of the whole Church' in the forty-day season of Lent as codified after the Council of Nicaea (325) and to the development of monasticism as a form of collective retreat. There is little evidence for any kind of organized retreat during the Middle Ages apart from the practice of pilgrimage. As a formal process, retreats were introduced during the Catholic Reformation of the sixteenth century. St Ignatius Loyola and the Society of Jesus (Jesuits), founded in 1540, contributed enormously to the growth of the retreat movement across the globe, having conducted lay retreats as early as 1538 in Siena in Italy, spreading to other areas and continuing worldwide to the present day. This was followed in the early seventeenth century by St Francis de Sales, St Vincent de Paul and their followers. The first retreat houses appeared in France during the seventeenth century. Other religious communities have also made a particularly large contribution to the development of retreats. Among them are the Franciscans, Passionists, Dominicans, Benedictines, Redemptorists, Oblates of Mary Immaculate, Adorers of the Precious Blood to name only a few Roman Catholic communities.

In the Anglican tradition, the practice of retreats was adopted in the Church of England as a result of the Oxford Movement and the first recorded formal retreat took place in Oxford in 1856. A number of Anglican religious communities such as the Society of St John the Evangelist (Cowley Fathers), the Community of the Resurrection (Mirfield, England) and the Sisters of Bethany had a particularly strong association with retreat work and spiritual guidance from the start. A major expansion of retreats took place during the twentieth century under the inspiration of such figures as Evelyn Underhill and Reginald Somerset Ward.

The modern experience of retreats may be traced to the late nineteenth and early twentieth centuries. In the United States the impetus for the revitalization of retreats came from a layperson by the name of Sidney Finlay of New York. It is safe to say that initially the modern retreat movement was by and large a development within the Roman Catholic and Anglican traditions. Yet throughout its history, retreatants have included persons from many religious denominations. What has changed significantly in the last few decades is the opening of retreat centres under the sponsorship of other Western Christian traditions – Lutheran, Baptist, Methodist and Presbyterian among them. Beyond the Christian tradition, there are also a number of Buddhists centres.

Professionalization. A more contemporary development within the retreat movement is the recognition of the need for ongoing formation for persons leading retreats and renewal programmes, better preparation for persons managing centres and the need of retreat personnel to be in communication with one another, networking and co-operating for the good of the entire retreat movement. In the UK, the National Retreat Association has been formed and consists of the Association for Promoting Retreats (mainly Anglican), Baptist Union Retreat Group, Methodist Retreat Group, National Retreat Movement (mainly Roman Catholic), Quaker Retreat Group, United Reformed Church Silence and Retreat Network. These associations have members in England, Ireland, Scotland, France, the Czech Republic and Channel Islands. In the United States and Canada, Retreats International (Roman Catholic in origin) serves some 350 member retreat/renewal centres while the North American Association of Retreat Directors (NARDA), of Protestant origin, attempts to bring together those who direct such centres. Recently the Graduate Theological Foundation, in co-operation with Retreats International, has instituted an MBA in Retreat Center Management in recognition of the need to better prepare persons for the unique combination of 'business and spirituality' necessary in managing retreat and renewal centres.

Purpose of retreat. The term 'retreat' can be misleading in that it could easily conjure up the idea of 'escape' from the world. The experience of 'retreat' does include a 'stepping aside' from ordinary routine for a time to reflect and to pray, to slow down, to be still and to listen. This 'coming apart' is meant to aid retreatants in integrating their relationship with the Divine, their spirituality, as that is experienced in the marketplace and home – in the world. Ideally, the experience of 'retreat' motivates the individual to recognize the significance of prayer, quiet, solitude in the everyday in order to be a more 'balanced' participant in every aspect of life. Spirituality concerns the whole of life and how all of life is lived in the presence of God. Retreat times, ideally, help us to wake up to the fact of the ever-present Reality in which 'we live and move and have our being'. Service, in the world, ought to be one of the fruits of such spiritual awakening.

Types of retreats. In the early days of the retreat movement, the 'closed retreat' would be a common phenomenon. Retreats for men only, women only, girls only or boys only were held, consisting of conferences by a 'retreat master', time for the retreatant to reflect on input, celebration of Mass, often Benediction of the Blessed Sacrament with exposition. During some of these 'closed retreats' there might be an opportunity for retreatants to speak privately with the 'retreat master' but otherwise the general order of the day was silence.

Through the years a great variety of retreat styles has emerged. It is still common to find many retreat centres offering some form of the Spiritual Exercises of St Ignatius in the 'directed retreat experience', lasting from a short retreat of several days to the traditional four-week format. The Nineteenth Annotation retreat is also becoming more and more popular. This is a method of experiencing the Ignatian Exercises in the midst of daily life where retreatants commit themselves to a certain time of prayer each day with specific Scripture passages and then meet with a spiritual director at regular intervals, often weekly, to reflect upon what has happened in their prayer or meditation as that impacts on daily life.

Topical or thematic retreats have also become commonplace. A group of persons gather at a retreat centre and spend time reflecting and praying around a specific theme such as 'forgiveness', 'compassion', 'the life of Jesus'. Usually there is a retreat leader who offers some thoughts and reflections, passages from Scripture or other anecdotal material touching upon the chosen theme. Retreatants are then given time and space to pray with the material they have heard. Sometimes there are opportunities for conversation among the retreatants concerning what is happening for them in this process. At other times silence is maintained throughout. This type of approach is often referred to as a 'guided retreat' and usually does include some type of communal worship service depending upon the setting and the group.

Many persons opt for a 'private retreat' experience where an individual retreatant takes some time for prayer, reflection, silence and solitude at a chosen place. Many retreat centres have 'hermitages' where private retreatants may stay if they choose.

Various movements, all across the globe, have emerged through the years providing highly structured retreat experiences. The Cursillo (sometimes described as a 'short course on Christianity') is one such example and originated on the Spanish island of Mallorca under the direction of Bishop Juan Hervas. The Cursillo is a community experience that includes a series of talks presented by persons who themselves have gone through the Cursillo experience. Follow-up groups and meetings are established to build upon what has taken place in the initial retreat.

'Christ Renews His Parish', or CHIRP as it is called, is a similar kind of process geared toward the renewal of parish life via the spiritual renewal of parishioners. Similarly structured retreat experiences focused on young people have been popular in the last several decades. 'Teens Encounter Christ' (TEC) is one such example. 'Marriage Encounter' is a worldwide structured retreat experience which, while past its zenith in popularity, still continues. There is a similarly structured weekend retreat experience for couples preparing for marriage called 'Encounter'.

Summary. During the last few decades, at the time of and following Vatican II, there has been a great effort to heal the splits between body, mind and spirit caused by a dualistic attitude. The results of this growth are very visible in the retreat movement and programmes for renewal, prayer and retreat. In most, if not all, English-speaking countries this shift is reflected in offerings that speak to mind/body/spirit integration. It is not uncommon to find retreat centres and retreat facilitators offering opportunities for various kinds of 'healing touch' within the overall retreat experience. Such efforts seek to reclaim and celebrate the reality that our bodies truly are temples of the Holy Spirit deserving of reverence and respect.

The hunger for a spirituality that both nourishes and challenges is being expressed everywhere by persons from a wide range of backgrounds, cultures and religious affiliations. It is to retreat centres and houses of prayer and renewal that many of these persons go seeking a place of hospitality, safety, peace – a place where conversations that matter may take place, where real questions may be voiced and where some guidance is available.

See also **Direction, Spiritual; Ignatian Spirituality.**

ANNE LUTHER

Rhetoric

The art of persuasion is one of the principal living legacies of pre-Christian Graeco-Roman culture. The Greek philosopher Aristotle (384–322 BCE) and the Roman politician Cicero (106–43 BCE) remain its most influential exponents. Rhetoric originated in the instruction of public speakers, but thanks to their systematizing efforts became a practical philosophy, pedagogical theory, literary aesthetic and civic ethic.

Rhetoricians follow the guiding principle of decorum, ever adapting to the specific requirements or varying arguments made for particular historical audiences. Rhetoric thus encourages a thoroughly contextual and practical approach. Its proponents recognize three types of persuasive situations. Forensic rhetoric, usually in a court of law, establishes guilt or innocence. Deliberative rhetoric, typically in a legislative assembly, argues in favour of future courses of action. Epideictic rhetoric characterizes many occasions for public speaking, pleasing audiences by assigning praise or blame to individuals. Rhetoricians pursue three ways to convince audiences. Logos focuses on rational and evidentiary argumentation. Pathos appeals to the emotions of hearers. Ethos relies on the good character of the speaker or writer to bolster her or his case. Beyond these general principles, rhetoricians often provide detailed practical guidance, especially concerning the stages of composition. The most influential are invention, or how to come up with good arguments; disposition, deciding the order of one's speech; and adornment, or how to use specific words, phrases and images for maximum effect. Rhetoricians teach their students to adopt the style most apt to the rhetorical situation and the specific audience.

Rhetoric has always attracted charges of sophism, tempting many Christian writers to reject it altogether. In the West the influential work of Augustine of Hippo (354–430) assured the survival of the art of persuasion. His On Christian Doctrine is a complete rhetorical manual. He teaches pupils how to interpret symbols as God's persuasive action; how to understand the varied rhetorical nature of Holy Scripture; and how to use oratorical tools to preach deeply moving sermons. For reasons related both to the complex history of documentary distribution and the feudal political situation, rhetoric was incorporated in medieval pedagogy in a central but truncated form. Nevertheless, monastic writers developed the art of letter-writing to an unprecedented degree. And they preserved the documents that from the fourteenth century onward would spur the full recovery of the rhetorical civic spirit

which became characteristic of the city states of the Renaissance. Humanists such as Desiderius Erasmus (1466–1536) and Reformers (both Protestant and Catholic) such as John Calvin (1509–64) were thoroughly schooled in rhetorical principles that affected their combative careers and the substance of their theologies. Calvin, for instance, says he wrote his *Institutes of the Christian Religion* in the judicial mode to defend persecuted French Protestants. Therein he referred to scriptural revelation as God's 'baby talk' to woo human children. In the mid seventeenth century, weariness after a century of religious warfare and the rise of new scientific methods led to a growing mistrust of the persuasive art. Nonetheless a robust tradition of public speaking survived, leaving its mark on many sermons and political utterances. In our day postmodern critiques have encouraged a broadbased revival of rhetoric that has spurred, for instance, self-conscious rhetorical Christian theology.

In the study of spirituality rhetorical lenses incline researchers to appreciate the specific situation and audience addressed in a primary text, and how this accommodation influences the substance of the argument. Familiarity with stylistic conventions significantly assists the interpretive effort. Finally, one may appreciate how rhetorical training influences the mystic's conception of divine communication.

See also **Interpretation** (*essay*); **Aristotelianism**; *Devotio Moderna*; **Christian Humanism**; **Preaching and Spirituality**.

Augustine, *On Christian Doctrine*, New York: Macmillan, 1958; John Calvin, *Institutes of the Christian Religion*, Philadelphia: Westminster Press, 1960; Don H. Compier, *What is Rhetorical Theology? Textual Practice and Public Discourse*, Harrisburg, PA: Trinity Press, 1999; Kathy Eden, *Hermeneutics and the Rhetorical Tradition: Chapters in the Ancient Legacy and Its Humanist Reception*, New Haven, CT: Yale University Press, 1997; George A. Kennedy, *Classical Rhetoric and Its Christian and Secular Tradition from Ancient to Modern Times*, Chapel Hill: University of North Carolina Press, 1980; James J. Murphy, *Rhetoric in the Middle Ages: A History of Rhetorical Theory from St Augustine to the Renaissance*, Berkeley: University of California Press, 1974.

DON H. COMPIER

Rhineland Mystics

Narrowly considered, the Rhineland mystics include a number of men and women, mostly Dominican friars and nuns, as well as an informal network of Beguines and lay persons known as 'the Friends of God' influenced by the teaching of Meister Eckhart, Heinrich Süs (Henry Suso) and Johann Tauler, who flourished in Germany and northern Switzerland during the early fourteenth century. More accurately, this 'Eckhartian' circle represents the flowering of a spiritual movement embracing a much longer period of time, a wider range and a more disparate membership who share a number of characteristics:

- a profound yearning for and awareness of the immediate presence of God within human consciousness and 'in all things';
- an emphasis on simplicity of life, material and spiritual poverty, gospel preaching and active love for others, especially the poor, sick and suffering;
- a popular, urban-centred spirituality;
- vernacular expression in preaching and writing;
- at least a tendency toward an inclusive and egalitarian model of human and ecclesial relations;
- typical adherence to the Neoplatonic, 'Dionysian' spiritual doctrine reintroduced into Europe early in the thirteenth century.

Rhineland mysticism shares many of these features with the mystical spirit finding expression at the same time in England, France and Italy. But it is distinguished by its geographical locale, popularity, intensity and influence.

Traversing the heart of north-western Europe for over eight hundred miles from the Rheinwaldhorn Glacier to the North Sea, the Rhine was the major line of commerce and communication from Switzerland through modern Liechtenstein, Austria and Germany, to the Netherlands. Along its banks and tributaries were found the most densely populated areas of medieval Europe, including the cities of Basle, Strasburg and Cologne. Even Augsburg, Magdeburg, Bingen, Trier and Erfurt, as well as parts of Flanders and Holland, fell within its ambit spiritually as well as culturally and commercially. To such places were drawn the new mendicant Orders, especially the Franciscans and Dominicans. But the roots of Rhenish mysticism extend back into the eleventh and twelfth centuries, when new currents of religious renewal reached central and western Germany.

Benedictine, Augustinian and Cistercian monasteries of men and women had punctuated the Rhineland for hundreds of years. The influence of the twelfth-century Benedictine abbess Hildegard of Bingen remained powerful for many years. The enthusiasm of the spiritual renaissance known as the *vita apostolica* had also borne fruit in associations of devout lay men and women in towns and cities, cultivated by the preaching missions of saints such as Bruno von Hartenfaust and Norbert of Xanten, whose later monastic orders, the Carthusians and Praemonstratensians, continued to provide inspiration and direction.

During the thirteenth century, mystical tendencies were fostered by the saintly Cistercian nuns of Helfta – the abbess Gertrude of Hackeborn, her sister Mechthild, and St Gertrude the Great (1256–1302). Into their midst came the fiery Beguine, Mechthild of Magdeburg (*c.* 1210–82), old, nearly blind and carrying her single astonishing work, *The Flowing Light of the Godhead*, which was soon translated into Middle High German and circulated widely.

The coming of the mendicant friars in the thirteenth century contributed the spark that set the Rhine Valley aflame spiritually. Franciscans were in Cologne by 1221. David of Augsburg (1200–72) and Lamprecht of Ratisbon (*c.* 1215–60), who preached and wrote mystical verse in German, must be counted among the earlier Rhineland mystics. The success of the Dominicans, who arrived in the same year, was even more impressive. The growth of houses of friars and especially nuns during the second half of the thirteenth century was prodigious. Many were permeated with the mystical yearnings of the previous era, augmented by the emphasis on study and preaching characteristic of the Order.

At the same time, houses of Beguines such as Beatrijs of Nazareth (1200–68) and Hadewijch of Antwerp (fl. 1220–40) were multiplying in the Lowlands and other parts of Western Europe. Often the spiritual direction of these devout, apostolic and mystically oriented women was placed in the care of the mendicants. Solitary figures such as Mechthild of Magdeburg also relied on the friars. Her director and eventual editor was the Dominican Heinrich of Halle, where her younger brother Baldwin was prior. Peter of Dacia similarly directed and promoted the teachings of the remarkable mystic Christine of Stommeln (1242–1312).

The fountainhead of the 'golden age' of Rhineland mysticism was St Albert of Lauingen, 'Albert the Great' (*c.* 1200–80), the teacher of Thomas Aquinas and a host of German friars, perhaps including Eckhart. Albert arrived from Paris with young Thomas in tow in 1248, when he founded the great *studium generale* in Cologne. Drawing Dominican students from Germany and beyond, the School of Cologne grew famous because of Albert's ambitious plan to forge a philosophical-theological synthesis of ancient Greek, Christian, Jewish and Islamic thought. Central to his vision was the integrating role of Christian Neoplatonism found in Augustine but especially in the newly rediscovered Dionysian corpus including the *Mystical Theology* that had such a profound impact on the era with its emphasis on apophatic spirituality ('unknowing').

Albert's more famous students were more or less drawn to Neoplatonic mysticism – Thomas Aquinas and the brothers John and Gerard Korngin less so, while Ulrich Englebert of Strassburg, Dietrich of Freiburg, Berthold of Moosburg and Eckhart adopted the main features, tempered by the Aristotelianism of Aquinas. As notable preachers, teachers and writers, their influence on generations of Dominican nuns and friars was enormous and spread far beyond the confines of the Order.

The outstanding contributors to the tradition of Rhineland mysticism were Eckhart (*c.* 1260–1328) and his disciples Heinrich Süs (1295–1366) and Johann Tauler (*c.* 1300–61). Their ministry and personal friendships among the nuns, Beguines and laity encountered in their work established the nucleus of the movement later called 'the Friends of God'. Sermons and letters were exchanged and circulated among convents and houses throughout the Rhineland and beyond. The diocesan priest Heinrich von Nördlingen (*c.* 1310–*c.* 1379) similarly guided many of the nuns, supplying the translation of Mechthild's *Flowing Light of the Godhead* to the monastery at Engelthal as well as a copy of Aquinas's *Summa Theologiae*.

Although less scholastic in their formation than the friars, the Dominican nuns of the Rhineland were imbued with both a love of learning and a mystical yearning for immediate encounter with God. Many had been Beguines who were drawn to the Dominican cloister by the combination of study and apostolic spirituality that were its chief characteristics. Others were of aristocratic, even royal, parentage. Sometimes whole monasteries of Augustinian, Benedictine and Cistercian nuns changed affiliation to the Dominicans during the second half of the thirteenth century – if only temporarily.

Among the nuns who figure prominently among the Rhineland mystics are Margaret Bender (1291–1351), prioress of Engel Hal; Elspeth Stag (*c.* 1310–*c.* 1360), prioress of Toss in Switzerland, the devoted friend and amanuensis of Heinrich Süs; Adelphi Longman; and Christine Bender. Their own writings, usually in the form of revelations and commentary, have recently attracted scholarly and popular attention. The convent chronicles of the Dominican nuns, the *Schwesternbücher*, were circulated among the monasteries, and have become important sources of linguistic study as well as evidential material regarding the spirituality of the period.

Beyond the Dominican pale, several works are associated with Rhineland mysticism. The writings of Rulman Merswin (1307–82), self-styled lay leader of the movement after Tauler's death, are of lesser importance theologically and spiritually. But two anonymous works of the latter period are of special importance: *The Book of Spiritual Poverty*, which was for a long time attributed to Tauler, and the *Theologia Germanica (Deutsch)*, written by a Teutonic Knight. Finally, the great Jan van Ruusbroec (1293–1381), while distancing himself from the excesses of later Rhineland mysticism, incorporated essential teachings of the 'golden age' in his own writings. Elsewhere, elements of Rhineland mysticism can be found in the English classic, *The Cloud of Unknowing*, written sometime in the latter part of the fourteenth century. The writings of Nicholas of Cusa (1400–64) still reflect its influence, which can also be found in St John of the Cross (1542–91).

After the repression of the Beguines and Beghards at the Council of Vienne in 1311/12 and the papal condemnation of seventeen of Eckhart's propositions in 1329, Rhineland mysticism tended to diverge into opposed tendencies. Orthodox followers of Eckhart, especially Süs and Tauler, and the later Ruusbroec and his disciple Gerard Groote, tempered the more extreme expressions of mystical union favoured by their Meister and abandoned the philosophical dimension of the Cologne Dominicans almost entirely.

But by the end of the century, radicals among the Friends of God movement veered into perceived heresy. The last leader associated with the Friends of God, Nicholas of Basle, was condemned and burned at the stake at Vienna in 1409. The influence of Eckhart and the Friends of God survived among the mystical Anabaptists, however, and found a home among their descendants, the English Baptists, the Mennonites, the Amish and Hutterites. Beginning the mid nineteenth century, the recovery of authentic sermons and other documents of Eckhart, Süs and Tauler, as well as texts pertaining to the Beguines and the Dominican nuns of the Southern Rhineland, followed by the publication of critical editions and studies of these, led to a renewed interest in all aspects of the renaissance of the thirteenth and fourteenth century Rhenish mysticism.

See also **Mysticism (*essay*); Anabaptist Spirituality; Apophatic Spirituality; Beguine**

Spirituality; Bridal Mysticism; *Devotio Moderna*; Dominican Spirituality; English Mystical Tradition; Neoplatonism.

J. M. Clark, *The Great German Mystics*, Oxford: Oxford University Press, 1949; Oliver Davies, *God Within: The Mystical Tradition of Northern Europe*, London: Darton, Longman & Todd, 1988; Leonard Hindsley, *The Mystics of Engelthal: Writings from a Medieval Monastery*, New York: St Martin's Press, 1998; Rufus Jones, *The Flowering of Mysticism in the Fourteenth Century*, New York: Hafner Publishing Co., 1971 (facsimile of 1939 edn); Alain de Libera, *Introduction à la mystique rhenane d'Albert le Grand à Maître Eckhart*, Paris: OEIL, 1984; *La Mystique Rhénane* (Colloque de Strasbourg, May 1961), Paris: Presses Universitaires de France, 1963.

RICHARD WOODS

Ritual

Ritual can be described as patterned symbolic activity. There are many definitions and interpretations of ritual because it carries within it the ambiguity of the multivalent symbol. Ritual in the twentieth century became an object of study in the fields of anthropology, psychology, sociology, semiotics and the arts. The field of liturgical studies, which has always had an interest in ritual, has been increasingly dependent on the work of social scientists who investigate ritual beyond the liturgical arena.

Especially after the liturgical reforms of Vatican II liturgiologists have employed the findings of such anthropologists as Arnold van Gennep and Victor Turner. The latter in particular developed the notion that ritual is a social, symbolic process. It is both expressive and creative of culture that develops through a process called social drama. Both men were interested in the rites of initiation. They understood ritual in terms of the three-stage process of the rites of passage: separation, marginality and reintegration. Liminality that refers to threshold or anti-status experiences characterizes the experience of marginality. Their studies bequeathed to liturgists language and concepts to probe more deeply into various liturgical celebrations.

The twentieth century also saw a renewed interest in symbolic realism. This rediscovery of the power of symbols is noted in particular in the works of Freud and Durkheim. For psychology, symbols arise out of the unconscious dimension of the person. Prominent in ritual studies in psychology has been Erik Erikson who believed that ritual was an important element in one's person-

al development. Another important psychologist in the study of symbolism was Carl Jung who understood symbol in terms of the individualization process. Symbol represents the small visible part of a large unconscious reality. In general in psychology, ritual is an important component in psychosocial personality development. Ritual can assist a person to achieve a more balanced world view because it embraces both the rational and pre-rational aspects of the human being. Because ritual is the medium point between purely programmed activity and pure spontaneity it can provide a structure or channel through which feelings can be appropriately expressed. It provides a safety valve for emotional reactions that could become chaotic for lack of boundaries. A more human life requires some structure.

Sociology has focused the study of ritual in the areas of language, the structuring of human behaviour and the disclosure of meaning through social interaction. A study of ritual language reveals that language is more than the mere communication of information. It transcends its own structure and moves into the most profound areas of human existence. The language of liturgy and spirituality is the language of metaphor and poetry. It is provocative, prophetic and performative in the sense that it demands commitment from those who use that language. Ritual language expresses the beliefs, the stories and the identities of persons in community. In this sense it can be said that ritual creates community.

Ritual can structure human behaviour because it is a form of embodied knowing. It is an emotional, imaginative and kinesthetic form of understanding. Ritual is the way humans construct and organize their world because through its enactment the ritual creates a pattern of meaning in the human body. For instance, Ronald Grimes explores ritual from the point of view of speech acts in that saying something is also doing something. It is through participation in specific rituals that participants reorder their lives as in the case of the Christian sacraments.

For sociologists the meaning of a society's culture resides in the symbols it employs. Because ritualization takes place in community it is a major form of communication of traditions and customs out of which culture is composed. Ritual builds community by helping people acquire a sense of identity and by promoting their participation in a community of shared meaning. Here in particular it is important to note that the study of ritual texts alone cannot yield the meaning of a ritual. A text must be performed to surrender its meaning.

Many of the approaches described above understand ritual as a kind of performance. The ritual scholar Catherine Bell is critical of such approaches. She sees them as creating a dichotomy between practice and theory, that is, ritual is an action but it is filled with a belief or some conceptual conviction. For her, ritual is situational so that its meaning can only be discerned in its context. The Christian Eucharist receives its full meaning in the Christian community of believers but would have a different or deficient meaning outside that context.

An important characteristic of ritual according to Bell is that it is a strategic practice. For instance in liturgy baptism is a strategic practice to bring people into the Christian community and reconciliation is a strategic practice to restore one to community.

It is Bell's concern for the place of power in ritual which is of particular significance for scholars of liturgy and spirituality. Rituals that seemingly play a positive place in human life can be misunderstood because they unknowingly promote unjust structures or are ways in which groups are disempowered. Her analysis is helpful for understanding how feminist liturgies and Hispanic popular religion can undermine unjust structures and provide alterative forms of ritualization to official public rituals whose control tradition has invested in a relatively small exclusionary group.

See also **Spirituality, Liturgy and Worship** (*essay*); **Sacramentality and Spirituality; Symbol.**

Catherine Bell, *Ritual: Perspective and Dimensions,* New York: Oxford University Press, 1997; Catherine Bell, *Ritual Theory, Ritual Practice,* New York: Oxford University Press, 1992; Erik Erikson, *Toys and Reasons: Stages in the Ritualization of Experience,* New York: W. W. Norton, 1977; Ronald L. Grimes, *Beginnings in Ritual Studies,* Lanham, MD: University Press of America, 1982; Victor Turner, *Dramas, Fields, and Metaphors: Symbolic Action in Human Society,* Ithaca, NY: Cornell University Press, 1974; Victor Turner, *The Ritual Process: Structure and Anti-Structure,* Ithaca, NY: Cornell University Press, 1977.

JAMES L. EMPEREUR

Roman Catholic Spirituality

In general, Roman Catholic spirituality does not differ, essentially, from Catholic spirituality more generally understood with its emphasis on liturgical worship, a strong sense of tradition and a sacramental orientation. In that broad sense, Roman Catholic spirituality has more funda-

mentally in common with Orthodox or Anglican spirituality than it would with, say, Congregational or Quaker spirituality. However, Roman Catholic spirituality does exhibit its own 'tone' and has orientations that are peculiar to its own history and tradition.

In the modern Catholic tradition from the time of the Catholic Reformation of the late sixteenth century and, especially, in the period of the Baroque, Catholic spirituality took on a particular series of emphases that lasted until the shifts engendered by events leading up to, and the celebration of, Vatican II. Those emphases were partially a reaction to certain critiques of the Protestant Reformation and partly derive from the energies of the reformation within the Roman Catholic tradition itself. Such trends are so various that only the broadest taxonomies may be noted.

The Tridentine emphasis on the real presence of Christ in the Eucharist with the attendant doctrine of transubstantiation led to a whole panoply of paraliturgical practices of eucharistic devotions ranging from encouragement of prayer before the reserved sacrament to exposition and blessing with the Eucharist in a short service called 'Benediction' or exposition over a stipulated period of time with attendant adoration such as the so-called 'Forty Hours Devotion' (obligatory in churches according to the old code of canon law (1918); recommended in the new code (1983)). Religious orders of both men and women were founded in the modern period to increase devotion to the blessed sacrament. In the modern period as much attention was paid to the presence of Christ in the Eucharist as was to the reception of Christ in Communion. Only in the early twentieth century did a pope (Pius X) encourage frequent reception of the sacrament.

Marian devotion, always a part of the larger Catholic tradition, received new emphasis in the modern Roman Catholic Church both by the definition of new Marian dogmas like the Immaculate Conception (1854) and the Assumption (1950) and the emphasis on devotion to Mary in the Baroque period. The fifteenth-century devotional practice of the rosary was so encouraged in the modern Church that it became almost a hallmark of Roman Catholic piety with communal recitation in churches; months (October) devoted in a special way to the rosary; rosary devotions at funeral wakes; pious associations related to rosary devotionals; religious communities devoted to its practice; and so on.

Devotions to the saints, harshly criticized in Reformation circles, continued to play a part in the popular religious life of Roman Catholics. The names of saints were commonly given to children; saints largely popular in given ethnic areas were honoured in public ways on their feast days. Pious practices, carried over from medieval usages, still found their place in churches (e.g. the blessings of throats on Saint Blaise's day in February); medallions of particular saints were frequently worn or used in other fashions. Visits to shrines or chapels annexed to churches dedicated to Mary or one of the saints were ubiquitous in Roman Catholic communities.

One instrument of the reform movement within Roman Catholicism from the sixteenth century on was the founding of new religious orders of men and women to invigorate the life of piety and religious observance. Sixteenth-century communities like those of the Jesuits and the reformed Carmelites fostered an interest in practices of meditative prayer. The Jesuit practice of the Spiritual Exercises led to the retreat movement while the Carmelite reform spread to France, which, in turn, spawned a whole range of pious practices now collectively known as the French School of spirituality.

The slow rise of communities of religious women like the Sisters of Charity and religious brothers (e.g. the Christian Brothers) who engaged in the good works of education, nursing care, asylum labours and care for the elderly was one of the most important developments of modern Roman Catholic life. When one distinguishes the traditional cloistered monastic orders and the mendicants like the Franciscans, it is important to note that most active orders of religious brothers and religious sisters are a post-Enlightenment phenomenon. Their spiritual life reflected most of the emphases found in modern Catholic spirituality: mental prayer; pious exercises like the rosary; visits to the blessed sacrament and the stations of the cross (a devotional practice systematized only in the eighteenth century); abbreviated forms of the liturgical hours (frequently in the form of the Little Office of the Blessed Virgin Mary); frequent sacramental confession and daily attendance at Mass.

The reforms attendant on the efforts of Vatican II did not suppress most devotional practices but did provide new opportunities as a result of a recovery of older spiritual practices. Reforms in the liturgy encouraged greater participation in the eucharistic liturgy made easier by the possibilities allowed by the shift to the vernacular. The flourishing of biblical studies oriented prayer towards biblical emphases with an increased reliance on prayers inspired by the Bible and especially the psalms. The ancient practice of the contemplative reading of Scriptures (lectio divina) became widespread. Research into the sources of specific schools of spirituality (ressourcement) reinvigorated such traditional practices as Ignatian prayer, monastic usages for laity, and interest in the contemplative practices associated with the Carmelite tradition. The openness of the Council to the great non-Christian religious traditions made it possible for many to make use of such Eastern disciplines as the use of the mantra in prayer because of analogues in the Christian tradition (e.g. in centring prayer) or Zen sitting. New reform movements, often lay-initiated movements, like the Cursillo, Neo-Catechumenate, Contemplative Outreach, Focolare, flourish in the contemporary Church as do newer, often conservative, religious orders like the Legionnaires of Christ or Opus Dei.

A couple of extremely important new intuitions developed in the contemporary period. One firm point is the recovery of the idea that union with God in contemplative prayer is not some extraordinary grace available to the chosen few but the fulfilment of the life of grace open to all as a result of their baptism in Christ. The other advance is the firm linkage made between the life of prayer and the need for social justice. Contemporary Roman Catholic spirituality is unanimous in its resistance to the view that the development of the spiritual life is merely for the perfection of the individual independent of, or indifferent to, the suffering of the world. Authentic Roman Catholic spirituality seeks to cultivate participation in the trinitarian life of God as the model and energy source for all who see themselves, like the Trinity of Persons, bound to all who bear within themselves the image and likeness of God. This more communal view of spirituality has had its strongest proponents among those who write from a liberationist point of view.

The present situation in Roman Catholic spirituality reflects both the inherited devotional practices whose roots go back to the Middle Ages, refracted through the reform efforts following on the Council of Trent and its aftermath, as well as new energies unleashed by the reforms after Vatican II. Like the good householder of the gospel, this spirituality attempts to bring forth old things and new.

See also Spirituality, Liturgy and Worship (essay); Catholicity and Spirituality; Ecclesiology and Spirituality; Sacramentality and Spirituality; Tradition; Vatican II and Spirituality.

James Bacik, Spirituality in Transition, Kansas City: Sheed & Ward, 1996; Gustavo Gutiérrez, We Drink from Our Own Wells, Maryknoll, NY: Orbis Books, 1983; William Resier, To Hear

God's Word Listen to the World: The Liberation of Spirituality, New York: Paulist Press, 1997; James F. White, *Roman Catholic Worship: Trent to Today*, New York: Paulist Press, 1995.

LAWRENCE S. CUNNINGHAM

Rules, Religious

'Religious rules' are normative texts which set out the spiritual principles guiding members of religious communities. Rules tend to be composed either by founders of communities as a spiritual testament or by their successors as a means of giving lasting definition to a spiritual tradition.

'Rules' are not a simple genre of spiritual writing. However, certain common features can be summarized. Rules set out the particular ethos and purpose of religious communities and their way of life. A rule may also contain norms to guide individual members or communities as a whole. Rules have generally been distinguished from 'constitutions'. The latter are administrative documents that address practical matters, are often applications of a foundational rule to the needs of specific times and places and are revised according to changing circumstances. In contrast, a rule is not essentially a *legislative* document but a *wisdom* document or medium for the communication of a particular spiritual ethos. Rules should be thought of as introductions to a tradition rather than reductions of the tradition to a static 'essence'. That is to say, rules lay open a tradition but are not a complete description. For example, the final chapter of the Rule of St Benedict (ch. 73) points beyond itself to 'teachings of the holy Fathers' and to other rules of life.

The earliest 'wisdom documents' of Christian monasticism were lives of the great founders (e.g. the *Life of St Antony* by Athanasius) or collections of sayings (e.g. the *Apophthegmata Patrum*). These writings belong to a period of informality. Once institutionalization took place, for example with the foundation of large coenobitic communities in Egypt in the fourth century, normative texts began to appear. Traditionally Pachomius (*c.* 290–346) has been thought of as the founder of coenobitic life with the beginnings of the monastery at Tabennisi *c.* 320. His Rule is credited with being the first, with a significant influence on the later Rules of St Basil in the East and St Benedict in the West. This move codified the monastic way of life and the hierarchy to which the individual should give obedience. It provided a vehicle of continuity but, equally, it moved away from the spontaneity of obedience to a spiritual father or mother. Obedience was now to a rule of which the superior was the spiritual interpreter and legal monitor.

Christian monasticism has been dominated by three Rules, St Basil in the Eastern Church and St Benedict and St Augustine in the West. The Rule of St Basil relates to Basil the Great (*c.* 330–79), one of the three theologians referred to as the Cappadocian Fathers. He bequeathed to Eastern monasticism the ethos on which it is still based. The title 'Rule' (the *Asceticon*) is perhaps a misnomer as the material is fundamentally an anthology of advice. Even during Basil's lifetime a number of versions of the *Asceticon* were in circulation and questions of authenticity are complex (see Holmes, 2000). Two versions should be mentioned. The Small *Asceticon* is the earliest collection and is probably the version that influenced the Rule of St Benedict. The most widespread form, the Great *Asceticon* in its Vulgate version, has influenced most modern translations. The tone of Basil's 'Rules' is strict yet relatively moderate compared to the extremes of early desert asceticism. The emphasis is on community life and a balance of liturgy, manual work and other tasks. Provision is made for the education of children and for the care of the poor.

There is also a dispute about the 'textual labyrinth' of the so-called Rule of St Augustine and about whether it was written by Augustine. Whatever the case, this is likely to have been the oldest Western rule which in turn influenced the Rule of St Benedict and inspired hundreds of religious communities of varying forms (e.g. canonical, military and mendicant), including, since the nineteenth century, several Anglican ones. The 'Rule' actually refers to two texts, the *Ordo Monasterii* and the *Praeceptum* supplemented by a letter of Augustine (Letter 211) that seems to be a version of the *Praeceptum* addressed to women. Although the influence of the Rule was overtaken by that of St Benedict, it had a major resurgence in the late eleventh century when it was adopted by the new communities of clerics known as Canons Regular and parallel communities of women. The resurgence was further expanded by the adoption of the Rule by several of the new mendicant orders. This resurgence is explained by its flexibility, emphasis on fraternal community and relative openness to outside work. These features spoke to the ethos of new spiritual movements of the time and to the spiritual needs of the inhabitants of the new cities.

The Rule of St Benedict, written in sixth-century Italy, is the most important rule in the history of the Western Church in terms of widespread influence. In the period from the sixth to the tenth centuries it gradually replaced other Rules such as those of Martin of Tours and of Columbanus. While the Rule draws on the Rule of St Basil, the Rule of St Augustine and others, the predominant background influence seems to be the Rule of the Master (although there are still some authorities who maintain a reverse influence or that both Rules rely on a common source now lost). While the Rule is characterized by its moderation, urbanity and balance, it nevertheless presupposes a life of withdrawal from the outside world. The outward-looking ethos of the Augustinian tradition is largely absent although hospitality to strangers (who are to be received as Christ) is a major injunction. The central task of the monk is the *opus Dei* or common prayer supplemented by personal meditation, spiritual reading (*lectio*) and work. The success of the Rule is probably explained mainly by its healthy balance of work, prayer and rest and its balance between the values of the individual spiritual journey and of common life under the authority of an abbot chosen by the monks.

The Second Lateran Council (1139) formally recognized three rules, St Benedict and St Augustine in the West and St Basil in the East. The Fourth Lateran Council (1215) went further and prescribed that no new rules should be recognized. All communities founded after that date had to choose one of the ancient rules. Several thirteenth century mendicant orders (Dominican, Servite and Augustinian) adopted the Rule of St Augustine. The early Bridgettines were forced to give precedence to the Rule of St Augustine and to use their new Rule of St Bridget only as a subsidiary document. It has often been said that there was only one exception to this prohibition of rules outside the ancient three, the Rule of St Francis approved in 1223. However this is too simple. At least two orders predating 1215, the Grandmontines and the Carthusians, had their own Rules or Customary (albeit influenced by the Rule of St Benedict). The Carmelites could also trace their origins back to hermits living in the Holy Land under the Rule of St Albert. The Rule was modified as the Carmelites became coenobitic and mendicant in the thirteenth century but was never replaced. The new forms of religious life that proliferated after the Reformation either adopted one of the ancient Rules in order to be a canonical religious order (e.g. the Ursulines took the Rule of St Augustine), or bypassed that status and contented themselves with modest constitutions. One exception was the Society of Jesus which was recognized as a religious order with solemn vows and whose Constitutions of St Ignatius are de facto treated as a Rule.

Religious rules are, as already noted, wisdom documents. We need an adequate theory of interpretation beyond textual fundamentalism if we are to do justice to their spiritual wisdom. Rules are 'spiritual classics' in the sense made familiar by the theologian David Tracy. While rules are historically conditioned, they cross the boundaries of time or place and retain their importance in new contexts. While rules, like all spiritual classics, begin in particular historical contexts, they have a capacity to disclose a world of meaning in a potentially infinite succession of interpreters in quite different contexts. Equally, rules are only really interpreted through *performance*. They are texts to be lived. Good musicians interpret a piece of music creatively rather than slavishly while remaining within conventions set by the composer's score and by the subsequent tradition of interpretation. So, for example, those who over many centuries have sought to live according to the Rule of St Benedict have 'performed' the text in strikingly different ways. There is no single, 'closed' interpretation of a rule as new aspects are revealed whenever it confronts new horizons. Rules set boundaries but the boundaries make space for a diversity of lived interpretation. At the same time they enable communities to recognize the broad stream of tradition within which they seek to live. Finally, rules offer signposts that enable us to recognize family resemblances in a diversity of lived interpretations past and present.

See also **Monasticism; Religious Life.**

Luke Eberle (trans.), *The Rule of the Master*, Kalamazoo: Cistercian Publications, 1977; Timothy Fry (ed.), *The Rule of St Benedict*, Collegeville: The Liturgical Press, 1980; George Ganss (trans.), *The Constitutions of the Society of Jesus*, St Louis: Institute of Jesuit Sources, 1970; Augustine Holmes, *A Life Pleasing to God: The Spirituality of the Rules of St Basil*, London: Darton, Longman & Todd, 2000; George Lawless, *Augustine of Hippo and His Monastic Rule*, Oxford: Clarendon Press, 1987.

PHILIP SHELDRAKE

Rule of Life

see **Practice, Spiritual**

Russian Spirituality

The conversion of the Russian people to Orthodox Christianity was under way from about 988. Patterns of devotion and models of sanctity were derived from the Byzantine world. But their assimilation gained momentum since the new religion used a language (Church Slavonic) which was reasonably familiar to the people. Earlier Moravian and Bulgarian missions had generated the requisite translations from the Greek. There was therefore no delay in introducing services and Scriptures in translated form.

The fruits and guarantors of Orthodox tradition were the saints. The Russians were soon to generate their own. Over the succeeding centuries, the humblest of them seemed to gain special favour. Some of their authentic features survived the efforts of hagiographers and icon painters to universalize their image and their message. The life of Theodosius of Kiev (d. 1074) reveals the subtle features of an irenic, self-effacing monk. The reading of a document like this must have persuaded many a novice to follow in his way. Equally engaging were the biographies of later saints like Sergius of Radonezh (c. 1314–92) or Seraphim of Sarov (1759–1833). The relics of such saints encouraged pilgrimage and veneration.

It was Seraphim who pointed out that religious routines were no more than a prelude to the all-important 'acquisition of the Holy Spirit': 'however good in themselves, prayer, vigils, fasting and other Christian practices serve only as a means for this to be achieved'.

This was one way of defining the monastic life. Elsewhere, it was matched by an insistence on the very rigours which Seraphim had critically assessed. Among the earliest of Russian monks were stern ascetics, and their ways found favour even with the non-monastics in the centuries to come. A common practice was to fortify the life of prayer by fasting or restrictions in the diet. It was a practice rooted in the Middle Ages, but accepted widely to this day. Hence four Lenten periods in the year, not to mention days of abstinence each week (Wednesday and Friday). At such times no food derived from animals was served. In this way, as in others, self-discipline was anticipated and commended.

'Everything has to be done decorously and in order', insisted Joseph of Volok (1439–1515) in his monastic Rule. Indeed, order could be venerated in itself. This might involve unquestioning observance of the rubrics. By contrast, a critical approach to rubrics, let alone consideration of their possible reform, could spell disaster. For orthopraxis and orthodoxy were supposed to be at one. In the mid seventeenth century, supporters of tradition (Old Ritualists was to be their designation) preferred secession from the established Church and an early death in preference to changes in the spelling of their saviour's name. Only an iota was at stake.

Concern for order could affect the Russian world at large. All the greater was the need for a corrective. It was provided in the form of individuals who challenged desiccation in the system by the chaos of their lives. They cast themselves as fools for Christ. In their lives they demonstrated the supremacy of faith to logic, and of nonsense to all 'proper' ways of life. It was believed that their outrageous words and interventions could affect the highest in the land. Basil the Blessed (d. 1550) and Nicholas of Pskov (d. 1576) were fools in Christ who gained a hearing from no less a tyrant than Ivan IV. But there were fools in modern times as well.

Monastic discipline could itself provide the setting and the shelter for the life of prayer of individuals over and above the services prescribed for all. At some stage in the fourteenth century the Russians were to gain a new dimension for their spiritual life through continued contacts with Byzantine churchmen. Sergius of Radonezh was early to engage in Hesychastic prayer. By the time of Nil of Sora (1433–1508) there are writings which reveal directly what it meant. Here was an unremitting search for inner stillness, involving ceaseless prayer (1 Thess. 5.17). Central to this prayer was the invocation of the name of Jesus. A fruit of such prayer could be the experience of eternal light.

The influence of Hesychasm was to be promoted by the publication of The Philokalia (1782), followed by translations into Church Slavonic (1793) and, in due course, Russian (1876–90). The work assembled writings of the Fathers, which are influential to this day.

Those who practised Hesychastic prayer (by no means only the monastics) were advised to use experienced elders to monitor their progress and to guard them from delusions. Here was a specific function for spiritual fathers, who also played a wider role in parishes throughout the land. Since early times, Communion could be taken only after the confession of one's sins. It was a requirement which was judged to be the more appropriate since Communion was rare. Not until the nineteenth century were countermeasures taken, and even then it was considered 'daring' to receive the sacrament more frequently than in the penitential seasons. Nevertheless, here was a form of pastoral care for all and sundry, which could encourage understanding of the Church's teaching. By contrast, the average parish priest was not expected to offer guidance through his sermons.

In general, services retained and still retain their medieval form. Over the centuries, a process of accretion has modified the detail, but there is little prospect of liturgical reform. Central to the life of each community is the eucharistic celebration, which is experienced with appropriate dignity and awe. All sacraments and sacramentals emphasize that matter may be sanctified since it was party to the incarnation. Matter is thus richly used in worship, which has its tactile, visual and olfactory aspects. Non-instrumental music also plays its part. In the early centuries this was monophonic, as were its Byzantine models. Since the seventeenth century, harmonization has become the norm, influenced by the Christian West. The role of beauty in the worship of the Church is never questioned. An early medieval legend suggests that it was the very beauty of the service which most impressed those envoys of the Russian ruler who visited Byzantium in search of a religion for his people.

The services invariably involve the body of the Church as a coherent whole. As essential to her structure as to her inner being are such factors as collegiality, conciliarity, a life in common. Much of this was summarized in the Russian term *sobornost*. It was itself derived from the teachings of the theologian A. S. Khomiakov (1804–60).

Collegiality involves a social aspect also. It encourages the recognition of a Christ who is incarnate in one's fellow human being. Hence the clouds of incense which are offered to the persons present at a service. Thus acknowledged is that which is divine in each. Such recognition can impel the Christian also to engage in charitable works. Role models for engagement of this kind are Joseph of Volok (1439–1515), Juliania Lazarevskaia (d. 1604) and Maria Skobtsova (1891–1945).

The institutional forms of the Russian Orthodox Church were changed as part of the Westernizing policies of Peter the Great (1722). But the liturgical and spiritual strata of its life in the succeeding centuries remained remarkably consistent with its past.

From 1917 the Soviet state sought to eliminate religion from the public and private life of its citizens. All beliefs and practices were to be severely tested in the process, and much was wilfully destroyed. Earlier, good order had been cherished: Church life was now without its comeliness or form. Martyrdom became a common prospect. This brought astounding dedication to the fore.

Liberation from the yoke of atheist Communism in the 1990s resulted in reversion to older patterns of behaviour. Pious traditions were revived with fervour, often with a folkloristic zeal. In the process it could seem as if the harrowing experiences of Soviet times no longer leavened the believer's life. There were believers, rather, who were ready to consider 'Holy Russia' (a seventeenth-century designation) as datum

rather than as aim, and segregated from the outside world at that.

See also **Byzantine Spirituality; Deification; Fools, Holy; Hesychasm; Iconography; Jesus Prayer; Orthodox Spirituality;** *Philokalia;* **Staretz.**

Primary source: George Fedotov, *The Treasury of Russian Spirituality*, New York: Sheed & Ward, 1948/ London: 1950.

Secondary sources: George Fedotov, *The Russian Religious Mind* 1 and 2, Cambridge, MA: Harvard University Press, 1966; N. Gorodetzky, *The Humiliated Christ in Modern Russian Thought*, London: SPCK, 1938; George Maloney, *Russian Hesychasm. The Spirituality of Nil Sorskii*, The Hague/Paris: Mouton, 1973.

SERGEI HACKEL

Sabbath

The origins of the Sabbath are lost in history. The Hebrew Bible's opening description of God's creation of the universe culminates in the reference to God resting on the seventh day (Gen. 2.2), as a result of which that day came to be known as the Sabbath (from the Hebrew *shabbat*, which means simply 'rest'). From the start, then, God was defined by more than work, and so were human beings who were made in the divine image and likeness (Gen. 1.27). From the start too, a key dimension of Sabbath observance is thus not just to rest, but to participate in God's rest, an idea crystallized in Ps. 95 (or *Venite*), and which patristic writers were to develop extensively: for theologians like Augustine of Hippo or Bede the Venerable, our willingness to keep Sabbath time inserts us into a different, future-oriented dynamic, for it allows us a glimpse of the life of heaven (e.g. Augustine, *Confessions* 13.35–6).

In the Ten Commandments, the injunction to keep the Sabbath occupies a pivotal place as the fourth commandment, linking together true worship (the subject of the first three) with moral righteousness and justice (the subject of the remaining six) (Ex. 20.1–17). In the great charter of holiness found in Lev. 19, the keeping of the Sabbath is the only command to appear twice (Lev. 19.3, 30); and in later chapters of the same book this observance is extended to sabbatical feasts (Lev. 23.15–21), months (Lev. 23.23) and years (Lev. 25.4), the process culminating in the celebration of the jubilee year (Lev. 25.10). In these extensions of the Sabbath, its fundamental principles – rest and restoration – are applied not just to the people of Israel as a whole, but to slaves, the land and all living things as well.

There is much uncertainty about how far these principles were ever practised; but it is likely that the keeping of the Sabbath really took effect during the Exile of the Israelites in Babylon. In such a context, Sabbath-keeping became a defiant act, subverting the lifestyle of the oppressor, and enabling those who had been forced to leave behind their holy places to find hope and meaning instead in holy time. It is worth noting that in the description of the Ten Commandments in Deuteronomy, the Sabbath is explicitly linked with the importance of remembering God's liberating act in the Exodus (Deut. 5.15); and for centuries thereafter, Jewish people in exile or captivity have found in the observance of the Sabbath a way of refusing to conform to the values of their oppressors.

The attitude of Jesus to the Sabbath has been much discussed; but it appears likely that his encouragement to his followers to find their rest in him (see Matt. 11.28) is a way of extending the principles of the Sabbath to the whole of the Christian's relationship with God in Christ. The writer of the letter to the Hebrews argues that those described in Ps. 95 as not entering God's rest are the disobedient and those who lack faith (Heb. 3.18–19), but that 'a sabbath rest still remains for the people of God; for those who enter God's rest also cease from their labours as God did from his' (Heb. 4.9–10). The resurrection of Jesus took place on the first day of the week, not the seventh; but, just as Jews in exile observed the Sabbath as a way of marking their distinctiveness, so Christians came to mark Sundays as a way of doing the same. By the second century CE the Christian Sunday was referred to as 'the eighth day'; and Christians were encouraged to keep it by coming to public worship, engaging in acts of mercy, resting from their normal work, and seeking to avoid what Tertullian called 'every posture of anxious care'.

Later Christians varied in their attitude to the Christian Sabbath. Luther, reacting against what he took to be the legalistic sabbatarianism of the Catholic Church, downgraded the Sabbath altogether as a Mosaic and thus redundant institution, arguing that 'Scripture has abrogated the Sabbath-day'. By contrast, Calvin and those who followed him defended Sunday as a legitimate Christian replacement for the Sabbath, preferring to christianize the Old Testament Law where Luther had sought to distinguish sharply between Law and Gospel. In the pluralistic, postmodern world of contemporary Christianity, there has been an increasing recognition that the divinely given rhythm of work and rest adumbrated in Genesis has much to offer societies where unemployment, overwork and the peri-lous substitution of consumerist 'leisure' for true Christian play threaten to make life either stressful or meaningless.

See also **Leisure**.

___

Tilden Edwards, *Sabbath Time: Understanding and Practice for Contemporary Christians*; Minneapolis: Seabury Press, 1982; Tamara C. Eskenazi et al. (eds), *The Sabbath in Jewish and Christian Traditions*, New York: Crossroad, 1991; Robert K. Johnston, *The Christian at Play*, Grand Rapids, MI: Eerdmans, 1983.

GORDON MURSELL

Sacramentality and Spirituality

A fundamental presupposition in reflecting on the relationship between 'sacramentality' and 'spirituality' in a specifically Christian mode is that there is a God who searches for human beings and makes it possible for them to search for God in their turn. So 'sacramentality' has to do with how human beings are open to the promise of divine grace and the transformative Spirit of God in human affairs; and 'spirituality' has to do with how human beings become most fully themselves in relation to God.

The context of the interaction of human beings with God, with one another and with the non-human beings with whom we are inter-adapted and co-evolved is deemed to be 'creation'. The whole cosmos teems with expressions of divine generosity and life-giving resource, and is a limitless source of wonder and gratitude, as its immensity and microscopic energies and detail are explored. In principle no knowledge or insight from any source need be excluded in advance in human engagement with this divinely constituted context which may manifest divine transformative presence. At all times it is crucial, however, to recall that such engagement with a divine presence may not lead to the confusion of a divine creator with creation. Attempts to discern and to respond to God's freely bestowed grace have a certain is/is not character, so a certain wariness and discretion may be a mark of spirituality, as well as a willingness in the present era to live somewhat adventurously. That means learning not only from inherited resources both non-verbal and verbal across the whole spectrum of Christian believing, but from at least some non-Christian religious traditions. Christian believers now have the opportunity to learn from one another and from other devout believers and indeed non-believers beyond the scope of any discernibly ecclesiastical organization in an unprecedented way.

Further, since human beings now engage with

their world in ways not merely unknown but unforeseen in the past, sacramentality and spirituality both need re-exploring in respect of genuinely novel domains of the human creativity which may provide clues to divine engagement with human beings. New dimensions of imagination and willingness to take risks, live with unpredictability and recover from mistaken judgements as to where the divine is to be discerned are all required. For instance, we can not ignore the creativity evident in the running of airlines and high levels of technological enterprise any more than that of the world of entertainment. And for many human beings, involvement with the young, whether or not as 'genetic' parents, and the realms of work, paid or unpaid, public or private, including time spent in voluntary organizations and associations, and manifold forms of social and political life are important. Sacramentality and spirituality are not therefore to be construed in terms of what we may too narrowly construe as 'religion' if we take seriously the conviction that our context is that of 'creation'. In any case, the 'public service' or 'liturgy' of Christian worship has to do with *koinonia hagion* (commonly taken to mean 'holy communion'), that is, with the making common of the holy and the sanctification of the common or the ordinary, to which worshippers are dismissed at the end of specifically Christian ceremony. Many forms of human activity provide inescapable reminders of our interdependence on one another, of the extent to which human beings become themselves in interaction with one another, and thus yield clues to what it is to be open to the possibility of transformative divine presence. The 'Sanctus' of Isa. 6.3, central to some liturgy, is but one reminder of the way in which divine splendour and authority may be disclosed in unexpected ways, and, as in its original religious and political context, continues to have significant implications for life together.

The specifically Christian shaping of life (of which the Apostles and Nicene Creeds give the essential frame of reference) requires in addition acknowledgement that God has acted and continues to act in a personal way in incarnation. In other words, while we learn to think through the consequences of engagement with our world in freshly illuminating ways, we also focus particularly on God's flesh-taking in a particular person. The focus on Christ as sacrament makes possible coherence, selectivity and discrimination in understanding sacramentality. For God in incarnation is discerned to be not only creator and enlivening Spirit, but redeemer – the most signal exercise of creative initiative.

The point here is that sacramentality and spirituality require clarity about the fact that interdependence also means acute vulnerability, and the capacity to inflict damage. The human species in particular is capable of depths of malice beyond that of other beings. Creativity is especially exhibited in God's continuing to companion us, rather than leaving us to our own efforts to extricate ourselves from the harms we inflict on one another and our environment, required though we are to do what we must and can. So to the 'Sanctus' must be added the 'Kyrie eleison, Christe eleison', a continuous plea for mercy, closely allied to the practice of intercessory prayer especially for those who bring harm to others. Lament over evil also keeps human beings open to the discernment of the justice as well as the mercy which manifests divine presence, notwithstanding many difficulties concerned with establishing where justice may lie and what it may require of us to effect it. In addition, the creative discontinuity of forgiveness may also enable the discovery of unexpected opportunity for those who may find themselves graced to open up the future for themselves and others by not being bound by the harms of the past.

The key doctrines for focusing attention on God's commitment to redemption with many implications for a specifically Christian understanding of sacramentality and spirituality are those of the ascension of Christ, and the renewed outpouring of the Spirit. The ascension represents both Christ's transformed humanity and the exuberance for him and those redeemed by God through him of a repossessed paradise, as well as the continuous availability of grace, love and communion with God for all who respond to God's initiatives. Christ mediates human salvation, whether understood as God's viewing human beings in Christ (justification) or through Christ's effecting human fulfilment (sanctification). The outpouring of the Spirit on Christ himself and on others in and through him secures the continuity of divine grace manifest in creation while enabling those committed to him to track and signpost redemption by specific sacraments. The creeds and the 'Gloria' of Christian liturgy set out the framework of confidence within which commitment by believers in the redemption brought about through him is to be sustained. Fundamental is the priority of loyalty to God sustained in worship, and the alliance of human beings with God's defeat of evil.

The appropriate human response to God's redemptive activity is that of discipleship (John 15.12–17). This text identifies Christ and his mission, his gift of life and understanding of

God to others, his choice of some human persons to be especially close to him, and the request that they show to others the love which he has shown them, to become 'sacramental' themselves. Such discipleship requires the patience and courage to endure and to embrace change in self-perception, and perception of others and of God. The changes may sometimes be difficult, not least because they may require resistance to some elements in oneself and one's culture, restraint in one's way of living, and putting up with considerable misunderstanding.

The changes may for some be marked by stages, though these may not be tidily distinguishable. Such stages have been known, for instance, as purgation, illumination and union, or as justification, sanctification and glorification, and there are no doubt others. Variation is necessary, given the extraordinary differences between human beings in their particular situations. Discipleship in most Christian communities is marked by a rite of transition (baptism, chrismation and some ceremony of commitment) into the realm where human beings find new identities, and new stabilities through change may be sought and established. Whether specific ceremonies are identified as 'sacrament' and whether these are two or more in number, or whether sacramentality is very broadly construed, they will necessarily be multiple in meaning in sustaining human beings throughout their lives. They will, however, both evoke God-Christ-Spirit, and invite the participation of believers both in engagement with the fullness of their present reality while seeking to draw them ultimately beyond it.

See also **Baptism; Body and Spirituality; Creation Spirituality; Eucharistic Spirituality.**

Bishop Hilarion Alfeyev, Jessica Rose (ed.), 'Sacraments' (including 'Monasticism') in *The Mystery of Faith: An Introduction to the Teaching and Spirituality of the Orthodox Church*, London: Darton, Longman & Todd, 2002, pp. 130–66; Sarah Anderson (ed.), *Of Women and Angels: The Virago Book of Spirituality*, London: Virago, 1998; Richard H. Bell with Barbara L. Battin (eds), *Seeds of the Spirit: Wisdom of the Twentieth Century*, Louisville, KY: Westminster John Knox Press, 1995; David Brown, *God and Enchantment of Place*, Oxford: Oxford University Press, 2004; David Brown and David Fuller, *Signs of Grace: Sacraments in Poetry and Prose*, London and New York: Continuum, 2003; articles on 'Lay Spirituality', 'Priestly Spirituality', and 'Spirituality, Liturgical', written by members of an ecumenical team, in Peter E. Fink (ed.), *The New Dictionary of Sacramental Worship*, Dublin: Gill & Macmillan, 1990; David Impastato (ed.), *Upholding Mystery: An Anthology of Contemporary Christian Poetry*, New York: Oxford University Press, 1997; Gordon Jackson, *The Lincoln Psalter: Versions of the Psalms*, Manchester: Carcanet Press, 1997; articles on 'Baptism', 'Blood', 'Body', 'Eucharist', 'Forgiveness', 'Penance', 'Prayer', 'Preaching', 'Sacrament', 'Spirituality', 'Symbolism', written by members of an ecumenical team, in Adrian Hastings, Alistair Mason and Hugh Pyper (eds), *The Oxford Companion to Christian Thought*, Oxford: Oxford University Press, 2000; Kathleen Norris, *Amazing Grace: A Vocabulary of Faith*, New York: Riverhead/Oxford: Lion, 1998; Helen Oppenheimer (ed.), *Profitable Wonders*, London: SCM Press, 2003; Geoffrey Rowell and Christine Hall (eds), *The Gestures of God: Explorations in Sacramental Theology*, essays from an ecumenical colloquium held in 2003, London and New York: Continuum, 2004; R. Wuthnow, *Creative Spirituality: The Way of the Artist*, Berkeley and Los Angeles/London: University of California Press, 2001.

ANN LOADES

Sacred

According to the classic understanding of the religious anthropologist Mircea Eliade, 'the sacred' is the opposite of 'the profane' (from the Latin, *pro fanum* 'outside' or 'in front of' the temple). In other words, 'sacred' stands for the transcendent order or what is ultimate rather than finite. 'The sacred' concerns what matters most deeply to people – typically centred on human meaning and destiny. Although the notion of 'the sacred' is sometimes used broadly, it most appropriately refers to a religious world view. By extension, it may be applied to places, persons, events, times or actions that relate people to the source of ultimate meaning.

In biblical terms, 'the sacred' or 'holy' is identified first and foremost with God. In a specifically Christian understanding, God is revealed *in* and not simply by the person of Jesus of Nazareth at a particular time and place. Consequently, the foundations of a Christian understanding of the sacred are that God is manifested 'in the flesh' and in history. This implies a radical sense that the sacred, while transcendent, is also immanent. Potentially, therefore, no aspect of time and place is inherently more sacred than another and conversely no aspect is inherently profane. In Johannine and Pauline literature, 'the world' can designate what is opposed to God revealed in Jesus Christ but this does not imply a rejection of the created order. On the contrary, the Christian Scriptures offer a positive theology of creation and of history, strongly reinforced by the doctrine of the incarnation. Indeed, in John's Gospel (ch. 3) God sends the Son in order to save the world because God loves it. Theologically, two extremes are to be avoided: on the one hand equating 'the sacred' only with what is other than the ordinary and material or, on the other hand, submersion in the ordinary to such a degree that the transcendent dimension of the Christian vision of God is undermined.

Religious faiths, including Christianity, often associate an intensified sense of 'the sacred' with particular sites, situations, actions and people. However, the Christian Scriptures also suggest that Jesus and the early Christian community were ambivalent towards sacred places such as the Jerusalem Temple. For example, Jesus warns his disciples not to be wedded to the Temple for it will be destroyed (Matt. 24.2). Jerusalem (and indeed any holy place) is relativized in Jesus' conversation with the Samaritan woman (John 4). The first martyr Stephen denounces the Temple (Acts 7) and in the book of Acts in general Jerusalem is left behind in favour of witnessing throughout the whole world. So it appears that Christianity, while continuing to revere the sacred places of Judaism, especially those associated with the life of Jesus, abandons the intense link between 'the sacred' and a particular land, a particular city and Temple, an ethnically defined 'holy people' and laws that separate sacred from profane things and actions. So, the holiness of the new people of God – those who follow Jesus – is no longer marked by boundaries of ritual purity (e.g. circumcision, dietary laws). The story of Jesus prolonged in the life of the Christian Church, and the theology of God incarnate, map out a new geography of 'the sacred'. 'The sacred' is now manifested particularly in Jesus' mystical body – the community of followers dispersed throughout the world seeking to live the story of Jesus in every place.

Despite these foundations, it has to be admitted that, historically, Christian spirituality has often adopted a less inclusive attitude to the world and to everyday existence. At times it supported a hierarchy of holiness with certain classes of people deemed to be in closer contact with 'the sacred'. This hierarchy became associated with some version of separation from everyday life available notably in the lifestyles of members of monastic communities or celibate clergy. What is problematic, theologically and spiritually, is not the validity of such lifestyles but the notion of hierarchical holiness. Against this, the Christian Scriptures, notably the Pauline literature, refers to Christians in general as 'holy' or 'the holy ones' or called to be holy (e.g. Rom. 1.7; 1 Cor. 1.2; 2 Cor. 1.1; Eph. 1.1; Phil. 1.1; Col. 1.2). Thus, it is all those with faith in Jesus Christ who are set apart for God. This more general sense of the call to all Christians to reveal the sacred is reaffirmed by the documents of Vatican II, most notably the Dogmatic Constitution on the Church (Lumen Gentium), ch. 5 entitled 'The Call of the Whole Church to Holiness'.

In principle, in the light of Scripture reaffirmed in contemporary thinking, Christian spirituality as a way of responding to 'the sacred' finds its sources of inspiration, as well as its contexts of practice, in each and every place and in the multiplicity of activities that constitute 'everyday life'.

See also Holiness; Place; Time; World.

Peter Brown, *Authority and the Sacred: Aspects of the Christianisation of the Roman World*, Cambridge: Cambridge University Press, 1995; Mircea Eliade, *The Sacred and the Profane: The Nature of Religion*, New York: Harcourt Brace, 1959; Philip Sheldrake, *Spaces for the Sacred: Place, Memory and Identity*, London: SCM Press/ Baltimore: Johns Hopkins University Press, 2001.

PHILIP SHELDRAKE

Sacred Heart

The Sacred Heart is a devotional image that was one of the defining symbols of Roman Catholicism from the late seventeenth to the mid twentieth centuries. The modern form of the devotion is closely associated with the visions of Margaret Mary Alacoque (1647–90) a French Visitation nun from Paray-le-Monial. From 1673 to 1675 she received a series of 'great revelations' in which she reported Jesus' appearance to her, his designation of her as the 'Apostle of his Sacred Heart', the mystical exchange of his heart and hers and his request to establish a series of devotional practices in honour of his heart. These practices include Thursday night adorations of the blessed sacrament, Communion on the first Friday of each month and a yearly liturgical feast on the Friday following the feast of the Body and Blood of Christ. Margaret Mary's visions were promoted by Claude de Colombière SJ (1641–82) and, after her death, by a series of Jesuit fathers and by members of the Visitation Order.

The symbol did not originate with the Visitandine but had evolved in varied theological, visual and literary forms over the previous centuries. Its roots go back to the patristic era as the Church Fathers, among them Augustine,

Ambrose, Cyprian and Jerome, reflected allegorically on Scripture. They saw the Church as originating in the heart of God, as born from the pierced side of Christ as Eve had been born from Adam. Similarly, they saw the blood and water that flowed from his side as representing the sacraments of Eucharist and baptism. Origen saw John, the beloved disciple, as the contemplative who rests on the breast of the beloved, near to the heart. The medieval period elaborated these insights and saw the rise of various forms of popular devotion including visual imagery of the heart of Christ, first as part of the popular devotion to the sacred wounds, then as a separate visual devotional image. Private medieval devotion to the heart of Christ was widespread and fostered by the Benedictine, Carthusian, Franciscan, Dominican and Cistercian Orders. Prayers with the heart of Christ as their focus flourished. Conflation of key texts from the Song of Songs encouraged a mysticism of the heart. The side wound was the cleft in the rock, the opened portal through which the beloved entered the bridal chamber of divine love, the heart, the nest of the dove. A number of medieval visionaries, chief among them Mechtild of Hackeborn (d. 1299), Gertrude the Great (1256–c. 1302) and Catherine of Siena (c. 1347–80) reported experiences in which Christ revealed to them his heart or exchanged his heart for theirs. Associations with the heart and eucharistic piety increased. In the early modern period the devotion was integrated in new ways into the Jesuit, Salesian and Eudist spiritual traditions. Francis de Sales' (1567–1622) spiritual theology imagined a world of interconnected hearts: the heart of God and human hearts conjoined by the crucified heart of Christ. Jean Eudes (1601–80) developed the devotion's first systematic theological and liturgical foundations. The devotion in the form that Margaret Mary envisioned, with its emphasis on adoration and reparation for the outrages committed against divine love, especially the sacrament of the Eucharist, achieved widespread importance during the French Revolution where it became the standard of counter-revolutionary forces. The Sacred Heart devotion was established as a universal practice within the Roman Catholic communion in 1856 by Pope Pius IX and spread to all corners of the Catholic world. Consecrations by families, parishes and other groups occurred frequently. In 1899 Leo XIII consecrated the entire human race to the Sacred Heart. In the first half of the twentieth century theologians, notably Karl Rahner sj, attempted to ground the popular devotion in a sound theology. Since the reforms of Vatican II the Sacred Heart, along with other traditional devotional practices, has not figured prominently in theological or liturgical thought.

See also **Devotions, Popular; Jesus and Spirituality.**

Annice Callahan, *Karl Rahner's Spirituality of the Pierced Heart: A Reinterpretation of the Devotion to the Sacred Heart*, Lanham, MD: University Press of America, 1985; Leo Scheffczyk (ed.), *Faith in Christ and the Worship of Christ: New Approaches to Devotion to Christ*, trans. Graham Harrison, San Francisco: Ignatius Press, 1986; Joseph Stierli (ed.), *Heart of the Saviour: A Symposium on Sacred Heart Devotion*, trans. Paul Andrews, New York: Herder & Herder, 1958.

WENDY M. WRIGHT

Saints, Communion of

This theme occurs in the third section, on the Holy Spirit, of the three traditional sections of the Apostles' Creed, indicating that both sanctity and communion are gifts of the Spirit, and indeed that the Spirit is the intrinsic link between both. The Spirit makes holy, and this holiness is formative of community. Inasmuch as spirituality is derived from the Spirit, then such spirituality will bear the marks of a community-forming holiness. This Creed also invites us to link these considerations with the trinitarian nature of God, which governs each of its three sections (Father, Son, Spirit). The communion of saints reflects the trinitarian communion of Father, Son and Spirit, with which it is linked through the Spirit. One senses the biblical roots of this credal teaching, namely, the Spirit as the sanctifier and source of fellowship (1 Cor. 1; 2; 12, etc.).

The Creed also suggests subsidiary insights. For example, if each of the Creed's three traditional sections parallel each other, then each becomes mutually illuminating, as in psalmodic parallelism. As the Father (first division) creates heaven and earth, so the work of the Spirit (third division) spans both realms: 'I believe in the Holy Spirit . . . and life everlasting'. This suggests that the communion of saints is both earthly and heavenly, foreshadowing the traditional tripartite view of the Church as militant (on earth), suffering (in purgatory) and triumphant (in heaven). As the Son (second division) ascended into heaven and intercedes for us at the Father's right hand, so the Spirit (third division) enables us to share in that intercessory work of the Son. The suggestion is that such intercession forms us into a community. The communion of saints is largely a community built up through intercession on behalf of one another, possessing a Christological character. Such intercession would seem to be one of the primitive roots of the place of the saints in Christian thought and worship, reflected in the New Testament counsel of mutual intercession by all sanctified believers (Eph. 1.1, 18–19), and then in the later patristic cult of the martyrs and confessors.

The Creed's 'bulge' in its central, Christological portion intensifies the centrality of Christ and the implied Christological shaping of the communion of saints (along with all the other articles confessed). Thus, our birth as a Church and communion reflectively parallels Jesus' birth; our co-operative intercessory work parallels Mary's co-operative motherhood of Jesus; our need to have our sins forgiven parallels Jesus' suffering and death (for our sins); our own resurrection into the heavenly communion parallels Jesus' own resurrection. The teaching on the body's resurrection intriguingly suggests both a communitarian and a personalistic dimension to the communion of saints. Our bodies link us one with another, rendering us mutually vulnerable, and yet their unique specificity suggests our individuality.

Writers commonly point to the biblical narrative structure which the Apostles' Creed reflects. Situating the theme of the communion of saints within this narrative structure suggests and exhibits the biblical roots of the theme. The synoptic theme of the 'reign or kingdom of God' intimates the corporate and very visible, perhaps even structural, nature of the communion of saints. The Johannine and Pauline writings, while not ignoring the theme of the kingdom, use equivalent symbols to stress perhaps more the qualitative, love dimension (the 'mystical' dimension of John?) and the fellowship of mutually reinforcing charisms (Paul). 'Kingdom' language is almost of necessity more hierarchical, while the Pauline shared charisms suggests a greater mutuality of ministries and so a more shared form of spirituality.

Inasmuch as the Creed is an outgrowth of the early baptismal formulas, the communion of saints can also be said to be a further thinking through of the meaning of baptism itself. The early connection of baptism with Eucharist perhaps enabled Hilary to suggest the eucharistic Communion as a model of the communion of saints (*Commentary on the Psalms* 64.14). Keeping the biblical and baptismal/eucharistic origins of the theme in mind somewhat softens the unresolved historical questions regarding the more precise and immediate factors leading to the phrase's addition to the Creed. For example, was its addition a critique of Vigilantius' supposed condemnation of the cult of martyrs? Or was it aimed against Donatism's elitist view of

sanctity? This illuminates the pairing of 'the holy, catholic church' with 'the communion of saints'. This would suggest that it is not the separatist Donatists who alone constitute the true communion of saints; the simple and even sinful baptized of the Catholic Church is that communion, at least in part.

The complex albeit compact richness of the theme, suggested by the above, already suggests something of the chequered history the teaching exhibits, as well as the route to a balanced presentation. Different periods will typically stress or overstress one dimension, thus fostering a return to the teaching's sources and a regaining of forgotten aspects. At the same time, as insight into the teaching develops, we must allow for the possibility that what one party might consider a deviation, another might perhaps rightly consider a legitimate development. Some examples follow.

The teaching challenges the tendency to slide into forms of individualism, isolationism and analogous one-sidedness. The corporate quality of Christian life needs attending to, if this teaching is to be taken seriously. The retrieval of the centrality of the kingdom of God in Jesus' teaching among today's biblical critics can be taken as corroborative of this teaching's deepest tendencies. The further retrieval of the sociopolitical dimension of the kingdom, among biblical critics employing social scientific methods of analysis, and among political, liberation and feminist theologians, also has played a helpful role in this endeavour.

This is connected with the teaching's implied critique of elitism. For example, the tendency to so stress singular individuals that their corporate solidarity with others is obscured. Something of this was behind the Reformation's critique of the cult of saints of Roman Catholicism, particularly the cult of Mary. This overlooks the Pauline teaching of the Spirit's sanctification of all Christians, and the mutual yet distinct charisms with which all are gifted and for which each is made accountable. In this sense, the communion of saints and the priesthood of all believers are mutually reinforcing teachings.

The teaching also challenges, sometimes in subtle ways, the natural tendency of institutions to slide into juridicism and an ecclesial 'structuralism'. The Spirit is the giver of holiness and the one who forms community. The Spirit's work cannot be reduced to structures or laws. A legitimate distinction needs to be made between community on the one hand and on the other institutional structures which are meant to foster such community. Community is deeper than structure, although there need be no intrinsic incompatibility between them. The God who creates the body and other material realities is also the Spirit who sanctifies. The heritage of the Western, Roman Church strongly builds on its structural, institutional genius. The Roman, juridical process of canonization of saints attests thereto. At the same time, this needs balancing by the other, 'mystical' or pneumatological dimension, rather more emphatically stressed by the Eastern Orthodox and some Reformation traditions. The 'saints' is a category extending beyond the officially canonized, and must be such, if the Spirit is to be the final giver of holiness. Just as the Spirit has a way of keeping the canon of Scripture open to new interpretations, so we might suggest that the Spirit has a way of keeping our canonical list of saints open and even relativized.

The communion of saints also challenges excessively narrow views of the true fellowship of the sanctified. As the Spirit spans heaven and earth, so the fellowship embraces not only the living, but also the dead and the yet to be born. We are linked in a vast network of all humans, past, present and to come. This suggests that a true spirituality will foster accountability not only to our current concerns, but to our ancestors and our progeny. How we treat history's dead (its victims especially) and its yet to be born is a measure of our spirituality.

Along these lines, one might even see an ecological dimension in the teaching, indicating that the fellowship of the saints extends to the cosmos at large. It is well known that both a personalistic and a more neuter reading of *communio sanctorum* have existed side by side in the tradition (Alexander of Hales, Thomas Aquinas, etc.). By and large our interpretation above has followed the personalistic view. However, the neuter interpretation of the Latin *sanctorum* would tend to stress the fellowship as one of sharing in the 'holy things' (namely, the sacraments, especially the Eucharist). Of course, thinking through the meaning of the sacraments would naturally lead to the view that no contrariety need exist between the two views. In any case, an ecological reading might be considered a contemporary extension of the 'neuter' stream of interpretation.

See also **Communion/*Koinonia*; Ecclesiology and Spirituality; Ecological Spirituality; Eschatology; Intercession; Martyrdom; Pauline Spirituality; Spirit, Holy; Trinity and Spirituality.**

Nicholas Ayo, *The Creed as Symbol*, Notre Dame: University of Notre Dame Press, 1989; Stephen Benko, *The Meaning of Sanctorum Communio*, trans. David L. Scheidt, Studies in Historical Theology 3, Naperville, IL: A. R. Allenson, 1964; Yves M. J. Congar, *I Believe in the Holy Spirit* 2, '*He Is Lord and Giver of Life*', trans. David Smith, London: Geoffrey Chapman, 1983, pp. 15–23, 52–64; Elizabeth Johnson, *Friends of God and Prophets: A Feminist Theological Reading of the Communion of Saints*, New York: Continuum, 1998; J. N. D. Kelly, *Early Christian Creeds*, 3rd edn, London: Longmans, 1972; William M. Thompson, *Fire and Light: The Saints and Theology*, New York: Paulist Press, 1987.

WILLIAM THOMPSON-UBERUAGA

Salesian Spirituality

Salesian spirituality is a Roman Catholic spiritual tradition that takes as its point of reference the religious vision of Francis de Sales (1567–1622) and Jane Frances Frémyot de Chantal (1572–1641). Francis, a Savoyard, was the reforming Bishop of Geneva, a charismatic preacher and popular spiritual writer. Jane, the widowed French baroness de Chantal was, with her mentor and friend Francis, the foundress of the Order of the Visitation of Holy Mary. The distinctive spiritual vision that they promulgated grew out of the fertile seedbed of early modern Catholicism with its roots in Christian humanist thought and the ferment of Catholic ecclesial and spiritual reform. Salesian spirituality is often seen as the first flower of the seventeenth-century French spiritual renaissance.

Central to Salesian spirituality is its vision of a world of conjoined divine and human hearts. Human beings are created by and for the God of love and endowed with a desire to return in love to God. This God-directedness is discovered especially in the heart – the dynamic, holistic core of the person. Human hearts are created to beat in rhythm with the heart of God, whose inner trinitarian life is one of reciprocal love between the divine persons. Yet while they desire this, human hearts, wounded in the fall, do not reflect the divine heartbeat. The crucified heart of Jesus is thus the necessary mediator between human and divine hearts. Jesus' invitation to 'come and learn from me . . . for I am gentle and humble of heart' (Matt. 11.28–29) is key in this mediation. Authentic human life consists in 'living Jesus', allowing the gentle, humble heart to dwell in each human heart. From the transformed heart all action will then flow.

The spiritual life, which is a process of gradually exchanging heart for heart, is seen as open to all men and women of every station and walk of life. Francis and Jane felt that in their time God was raising up 'devout souls' in every corner of the Church to leaven the loaf of a renewed Christian society. In this process, hearts ablaze with the love of God are essential. Every form of communication – preaching, teaching, writing, spiritual guidance, daily exchanges – is potentially a medium through which heart might speak to heart and the love of God be kindled. Further, relationships of love – familial, spousal and communal – encourage the realization of a conjoined world of hearts. Salesian spirituality contains one of the most highly articulated theories of spiritual friendship in the Christian world.

The Salesian vision was spread not only by the personal witness of Francis and Jane but through his popular writings and through the order of the Visitation. The founders' reputation for sanctity, cast in the heroic mould of post-Tridentine Catholicism, gained them visibility. He was canonized in 1665, she in 1767; he was made a Doctor of the Church in 1877.

The *Treatise on the Love of God* is Francis' most ambitious work that describes 'the birth, growth, decline, activities, benefits and perfections of God's love' and provides the theory behind his vision. The *Introduction to the Devout Life*, written for lay persons and encouraging a spiritual maturity adapted to the demands of work and family, is his most influential work. It is the *Introduction* that is credited with introducing the universal call to holiness into Roman Catholic tradition. The *Introduction* became one of the most published and translated of spiritual classics – by the end of the nineteenth century over four hundred editions had appeared.

The Salesian spirit was also disseminated through the Order of the Visitation, founded in 1610. This innovative women's community was originally designed as a simple congregation for women not eligible for other forms of vowed religious life – widows, the physically handicapped, those with frail health, the young and those of mature age. Visitandines were to be daughters of prayer who lived like Jesus by engaging in the practice of the 'little virtues' (gentleness, humility, patience, simplicity, cordiality) within a community and, to a limited extent, with neighbours. In less than a decade, due to ecclesial pressure applied in the process of expansion, the congregation was altered to become a formal, enclosed, contemplative order. By Jane de Chantal's death there were over eighty houses in Europe. In the United States and in France after the Revolution the Visitation monasteries sponsored schools. Although the Order was severely diminished during the French Revolution, in the twenty-first century the Visitation has foundations in the British Isles, Western, Eastern and Southern Europe, North and Latin America.

Besides Jane de Chantal, the most celebrated Visitandine is Margaret Mary Alacoque (1647–90). Her visions of the Sacred Heart of Jesus became the basis of the worldwide devotional cult that flourished through the nineteenth and early twentieth centuries. The Visitation actively promoted the devotion in its early days, sponsored lay sodalities for that purpose and especially in eighteenth-century France were associated with the Catholic anti-revolutionary and anti-republican cause that took the Sacred Heart as its standard.

In the middle of the nineteenth century, during what has been called the 'Salesian Pentecost', Salesian spirituality received renewed impetus. Bishop Rey of Annecy with Fr Pierre Mermier (1790–1862) sponsored the Missionary Oblates of Saint Francis de Sales of Annecy and (with Mother Echernier) the Sisters of the Cross of Cavanod to conduct internal missions in a de-christianized land. The Missionary Oblates later sent personnel to India, where the group flourished. In the Piedmont, Don Bosco (1815–88) established an active apostolic family under the Salesian aegis. The family included the Salesians of Don Bosco, the Daughters of Mary Help of Christians (with Mother Mazzarello) and a society of lay co-operators. By the twenty-first century the Salesians of Don Bosco had become the third largest men's religious order in the world. They are known for their ministry with disadvantaged youth. The gentle pedagogy that is the backbone of their ministry is derived from the teachings of Francis de Sales. In Paris, Archbishop de Ségur (1820–81), an avid devotee of Francis, facilitated networks in the capital and provinces designed to promulgate Salesian spirituality. He encouraged Fr Henri Chaumont (1838–96) to start a spiritual association for diocesan priests and, along with Mme Carré de Malberg, created the Daughters of Francis de Sales for lay women. From these foundations came the Indian Missionaries of Mary Immaculate and a lay man's association, the Sons of Francis de Sales.

With the sponsorship of Ségur and Mermillod and Mother Mary de Sales Chappuis (1793–1875) of the Troyes Visitation, other religious associations guided by the Salesian spiritual vision were formed. Fr Louis Brisson (1817–1908) with Léonie Aviat established the Oblate Sisters of Francis de Sales to minister to young female urban workers. With Chappuis, Brisson founded the Oblate Fathers of Francis de Sales as a teaching congregation with the express purpose of promoting Salesian spirituality. Today these later communities have a global reach and, along with the Visitation Order and the ever-popular *Introduction to the Devout Life*, continue to disseminate the Salesian spiritual vision.

See also **Devotions; Devotions, Popular; French School of Spirituality; Friendship; Christian Humanism; Monasticism; Roman Catholic Spirituality; Sacred Heart.**

Primary sources: Francis de Sales, *Introduction to the Devout Life*, trans. John K. Ryan, New York: Doubleday, 1982; Francis de Sales, *Treatise on the Love of God*, trans. John K. Ryan, Rockford, IL: TAN Books, 1974; *Francis de Sales and Jane de Chantal: Letters of Spiritual Direction*, trans. Péronne-Marie Thibert, CWS, Mahwah, NJ: Paulist Press, 1988.

Secondary sources: E. J. Lajeunie, *Saint Francis de Sales: The Man, the Thinker, His Influence*, trans. Rory O'Sullivan, Bangalore, India: SFS Publications, 1986; Elisabeth Stopp, *Madame de Chantal: Portrait of a Saint*, 1st edn, London: Faber and Faber, 1962; 2nd edn, Stella Niagara, NY: DeSales Resource Center, 2002; Wendy M. Wright, *Bond of Perfection: Jeanne de Chantal and François de Sales*, 1st edn, Mahwah, NJ : Paulist Press, 1985; 2nd edn, Stella Niagara, NY : De Sales Resource Center, 2001.

WENDY M. WRIGHT

Salvation

see Redemption

Sanctification

Historically, Christianity has concerned itself with three main issues concerning sanctification: (1) the relation of the grace of God and faith; (2) the question of sanctification and justification; and (3) the degree to which one could obtain sanctification in this life.

The writings of the early Christian period contain little concerning the actual doctrine of sanctification as we have it in the churches today. Rather, the early Christians were more concerned with a type of moral understanding of holiness where one depended on faith and works to identify with the risen Christ. It was by living and acting as another Christ that one obtained salvation. By living a holy and just life following baptism, one became in varying degrees a vessel of the Holy Spirit. The more the Spirit lived in the person, the more God the Father would see the Son mirrored in that soul, and the more worthy one would be to lead the Christian community. *The Shepherd of Hermas* and the *Didache* both speak of living a just and upright life of single-mindedness as a sign one was a follower of Christ and so saved. The Holy Spirit strengthened the devoted Christian in the paths of holiness, and by growing in this image of the Son, one grew in holiness and grace. Following this

notion of holiness and the identification of sanctification with justification, the ascetical movement gained momentum and gradually came to be seen as the best and safest route to holiness and sanctification, and, in the Eastern tradition, to deification.

The first Christian writer to develop doctrinal ideas and language for sanctification was Augustine of Hippo, whose ideas profoundly influenced Western European theology both Catholic and Protestant. Augustine did not distinguish between sanctification and justification, but he did understand justification as intimately included in sanctification. Never able to completely separate himself from his early Manichaean tendencies, Augustine viewed human nature as completely corrupted in the fall. Because of this profound corruption, the human person was naturally incapable of extricating him- or herself from the bondage of sin without a supernatural intervention of divine life. According to Augustine, this divine intervention happened through the sacraments, which by the sixteenth century developed into the seven sacraments of the Catholic tradition.

Augustine's teachings greatly influenced medieval theology and found its most developed form in the thought of Thomas Aquinas. For Aquinas, justification and sanctification were not clearly distinguished, but justification included the infusion of divine grace (sanctifying grace) as something substantial into the human soul. This grace is a divine gift and enables the soul to be lifted to a higher level of being and allows it the knowledge, possession and enjoyment of God. This grace comes from the inexhaustible merits of Christ and is imparted to believers through the sacraments.

The Reformers preferred to speak of sanctification by emphasizing the incompatibility of sin and redemption rather than the Roman Catholic understanding of nature and supernature. The Reformers made a clear distinction between justification and sanctification, considering justification as a legal act of divine grace and sanctification as a moral recreation of human nature. The Reformers believed one was justified by faith alone, yet this justification was followed by sanctification since God would send the Spirit of Christ into the hearts of the justified. For the Reformers, the Holy Spirit is the Spirit of sanctification.

In Pietism and Methodism, great emphasis was placed on a constant interior, emotional fellowship with Christ as the means of sanctification. Wesley not only distinguished between justification and sanctification, but separated the two and spoke of sanctification as the second gift of grace following the first which was justification by faith.

With the rise of rationalism and Kant's moralism, sanctification was understood not as a supernatural work of the Holy Spirit, but as merely moral improvement by the will and natural powers of the human person. Schleiermacher considered sanctification the progressive domination of the God consciousness with the human person over and against the morally defective world consciousness.

Recently, certain trends in theology and spirituality have begun discussing sanctification solely in terms of moral character and moral improvement, to the neglect of the supernatural character of grace so prevalent in earlier theologies both Roman Catholic and Protestant.

See also **Baptism; Deification; Election (Predestination); Grace; Holiness; Methodist Spirituality; Pietism; Redemption; Sacramentality and Spirituality.**

Donald Alexander (ed.), *Christian Spirituality: Five Views of Sanctification*, InterVarsity Press, 1988; Donald Alexander, *The Pursuit of Godliness: Sanctification in Christological Perspective*, Washington: University Press of America, 1999; Oswald Bayer, *Living by Faith: Justification and Sanctification*, Grand Rapids, MI: Eerdmans, 2003; Kenneth J. Collins, *John Wesley: A Theological Journey*, Nashville, IN: Abingdon Press, 2003; David Peterson, *Possessed by God: A New Testament Theology of Sanctification and Holiness*, Grand Rapids, MI: Eerdmans, 1995.

HARRIET A. LUCKMAN

Scandinavian Spirituality

Despite national differences related to social, historical and cultural conditions, the Scandinavian countries (here: Norway, Sweden and Denmark) do have several important religious traits in common. It can therefore be regarded as justifiable to speak of a 'Scandinavian spirituality', although important national differences must not be overlooked.

In prehistoric time all three countries seem to have had fairly common religious practices related to ancient tribal religion. Due to communications and contacts established through trade and settlements, large parts of the Scandinavian area from the mid eighth to late eleventh century went through a shift from ancient tribal religion to Christianity. In this process, Christianity rapidly became part of the ideological foundation of the gradually developing Scandinavian kingdoms. The kings presented themselves as both protectors of Christianity and patrons of the Church.

This symbiosis between religion and power found a strong symbolic expression through royal saints like Knud of Denmark, Eric of Sweden and above all Olav of Norway (see below).

When describing the historical development and the content of a Christian spirituality within the realms of medieval Scandinavia, one might distinguish between three different, but related and interactive dimensions. First, the development can be studied as an integrated part of the history of how all the main European religious traditions also reached Scandinavia, and how the various monastic and mendicant orders contributed to this cultural and spiritual development. A remarkable aspect of this process is seen in the way impulses from abroad compounded with innate manners of expression both in Skaldic literature, hagiographic sagas and in visual art (rune stones, woodcarvings and stave churches). Second, a broader picture of the content of the developing Scandinavian spirituality is afforded through pastoral sources such as letters and wills, statements from provincial synods, Mass commentaries, homilies and manuals for clergy. Here Christianity was literally translated into Old Norse language and mentality, and especially the homilies to the people (*ad populum*) tell us much about how religion was meant to permeate ordinary life. Third, medieval Scandinavian spirituality also included and integrated important elements from popular religion, viewed as a broad spectre of religious rites, folklore and customs, related to, but still in tension with, the more formal levels of religion. Historically, this was a result of a gradual religious acculturation, conditioned by both the general openness of pre-Christian religious practices to influences from abroad, and Christianity's ability to assimilate old religious customs.

When looking at the history of the medieval Scandinavian spirituality, there are several reasons to highlight the extraordinary contributions of two individual persons. First, the importance of St Olav of Norway could hardly be overestimated. This is shown in the role of his shrine in Trondheim (the Cathedral of Nidaros), a foundation for the Norwegian Church province, and during many centuries a goal for pilgrims from all over Scandinavia and many parts of Europe. Of great importance was also St Olav's role as church patron in several European countries, as well as the late twelfth-century hagiographic and liturgical texts which tried to apply evangelical and monastic values to St Olav as an ideal of a Christian ruler. Second, from the fourteenth century Bridget (Birgitta) of Sweden also stands forth with special importance. She was the founder of the monastic order which carries her name, and deserves a place not only in the history of Scandinavian spirituality, but also in the history of European spirituality. In her revelations central spiritual traditions converged: the basic liturgical life, the thirteenth-century mendicant spirituality and the bridal mysticism of the twelfth-century Cistercian tradition.

The secular rulers played a crucial part when the Protestant Reformation during the sixteenth and seventeenth centuries was introduced in the Scandinavian realms. This resulted in the establishment of state churches based on the Lutheran confessions in all three countries. Vernacular Bible and liturgy, Lutheran devotional literature, evangelical hymns and catechetical manuals together laid the foundation for an evangelical Lutheran spirituality. During the seventeenth and eighteenth centuries corresponding developments are detectable within the Scandinavian churches due to changing traditions within both theology and pastoral life. Seventeenth-century Lutheran Orthodoxy inspired a considerable wave of religious poetry, which through official and unofficial hymn books contributed substantially to the parishioners' devotional life. Lutheran Orthodoxy also represented a characteristic 'religion of the heart', a kind of Protestant mysticism and an impulse which developed into eighteenth-century Pietism. It represented a renewed focus on religious experience and a marked zeal for Church reform, promoting a genuine individual Christian faith and a lifelong commitment to personal perfection and holiness as followers of Jesus. During the 1730s the Danish theologian Erik Pontoppidan (d. 1764) – who served both as a university professor in Denmark (Copenhagen) and later as bishop in Norway (Bergen) – published *Sandhed til gudfrygtighed* (*Truth Unto Godliness*, 1737), an explanation of Martin Luther's *Small Catechism*, with a marked pietistic emphasis. This book, perhaps like no other single publication, extensively informed large parts of (especially) Norwegian spirituality for almost two hundred years. Other excellent sources to a Lutheran 'theology of the heart' in Scandinavia are to be found in the hymn-writing of the era, notably the Danish clergymen Thomas Kingo (d. 1703) and Hans A. Brorson (d. 1764). The orthodox Kingo, whose hymn book of 1699 became the official hymn book of the Danish and Norwegian Churches for nearly two hundred years, reflects an interiorization of church liturgy and lectionary through meditation and compunction, while the Pietistic Brorson in his hymns shows a strong influence from the tradition of bridal mysticism, combined with a markedly pietistic psychology of conversion.

The altering of political and social class structures at the beginning of the nineteenth century coincided with and was in some ways empowered by the growing influence of a lay revival spirituality which strongly opposed both rationalistic theology and many aspects of the inherited religious power structures and traditions. Of great importance in this context is the remarkable lay peasant leader Hans Nielsen Hauge (d. 1824) from Norway. He developed and propagated a spirituality which in a characteristic way combined a mystically oriented personal piety (influenced by Johann Arndt and Johannes Tauler), which focused on daily repentance and a holy life, with a strong emphasis on the believer's active responsibilities in society, and especially their contribution to the development of industrial life. Through his own example and those of thousands of his followers, H. N. Hauge deeply influenced industrial, political and spiritual development in Norway during the nineteenth century.

Another important contribution to late nineteenth-century Scandinavian spirituality, especially as it developed within the Low Church's lay missionary organizations in Sweden and Norway, came through the Swedish lay preacher C. O. Rosenius (d. 1868). Through his numerous publications, and together with the outstanding female hymn-writer of his movement, Lina Sandell (d. 1903), Rosenius represented an evangelical spirituality which focused upon Christ's atonement and the free gift of salvation through faith and divine grace alone. This became in many ways an important counterpoint to an older pietistic *Ordo Salutis* which stressed the importance of experienced penitence and remorse as a necessary prelude to faith.

In Denmark, two outstanding writers contributed lastingly to modern Christian spirituality during the nineteenth century. First, the famous philosopher Søren Kierkegaard (d. 1855) developed a radical interpretation of individual human existence and Christian discipleship. Through his prolific writings he strongly influenced not only twentieth-century existential philosophy, but also important parts of theology and spirituality within the Scandinavian context. Second, the clergyman and hymn-writer Nikolai F. S. Grundtvig (d. 1872) developed a bold sacramental reinterpretation of Lutheranism which opposed both seventeenth-century orthodoxy and eighteenth-century Pietism and Enlightenment. Grundtvig's view of Christianity was strongly influenced by the theology of the Church Fathers (notably Irenaeus), and by early medieval sources of the exchange between the gospel, old Nordic mythology and a Germanic mentality, especially as witnessed in Anglo-Saxon poetry. Grundtvig's influence is still considerable in Denmark and even in Norway, both through his theology and his numerous hymns. He has inspired a characteristic 'free-minded' Christianity based on the apostolic creed, baptism, Eucharist and the oral proclamation of the biblical message, interpreted in accordance with this cultic context.

The nineteenth century also marked a gradually broader denominational variation, as the restrictions of an older confessional state constitution were loosened and a new legislation of religious freedom was inaugurated (first in Norway in 1845). A large-scale emigration to the United States during the second half of the nineteenth century also eventually resulted in new impulses of congregational and devotional life that were brought from America back to the 'old world'. During the nineteenth century and at the beginning of the twentieth century, this led to a more open and ecumenical climate, and gradually one finds the establishment of smaller, for example, Methodist, Baptist and Pentecostal congregational life alongside the dominant Lutheran state churches.

With this historical sketch as background, one could point to the following observations as characteristic contours in a tentative map of present-day Scandinavian spirituality. First of all one should point to the fact that on a broader cultural level, the nineteenth and twentieth century processes of secularization and pluralization have led to a considerable loss of relevance of formal religion, and also to a more intense debate on the relation between state and Church. On a formal, juridical level this process led to the separation of the traditional bonds between state and Church in Sweden in the year 2000. Apparently, the process is moving in the same direction within the Church of Norway. On a religious level one can observe that although the vast majority of the population in the three countries is still baptized members of the dominant Lutheran folk churches, just a minor part (approx. 3 per cent) regularly attend the main Sunday services. This loss of existential relevance of the Christian faith and the diminishing participation in the liturgical life of the Church is of course a challenge to the development of a meaningful Christian spirituality. On a parish level and related to the praxis of congregational life, one tries to meet this challenge in various ways. All the Scandinavian churches have gone through significant liturgical reforms, which have confirmed their adherence to the Western liturgical pattern. At the same time, the values of a lay evangelical spirituality centred on preaching and prayer are still strong, and at its best contributing to a fruitful tension between sacrament and 'heart' in devotional life. At the start of the twenty-first century the variety of spiritual traditions has increased among other things due to the general ecumenical climate. This has opened the doors for co-operation and influences in many directions. In this context the Porvoo Agreement (1996) between the Nordic and Baltic churches and the Anglican churches in Britain and Ireland, marks an important event. The Agreement opens up significant possibilities for new developments within Church life, not least those related to liturgical spirituality. The future will show if those possibilities will be realized in ways that contribute to a broader and more varied spiritual life. Within several Free Churches and also in lay Christian organizations within the established Lutheran churches, one finds considerable influences from evangelical and charismatic types of spirituality. Especially in Norway over the last few years there has been a renewed concern for evangelization in the form of strategic programmes for so-called 'church growth', mainly inspired from the USA. In Sweden and Norway the ecumenical climate, together with traditions related to a 'spirituality of the heart', has also led to the development of retreat movements. Most often these movements find their main inspirations in a modified Ignatian type of spirituality, drawing on traditions of mysticism, liturgical life and biblical meditation. In this context and in relation to the developing ecumenical climate, it is also of importance to recognize the fairly rapid growth of various minor contemplative and monastic communities within the Roman Catholic Church. The importance of this is not only related to the Roman Catholic tradition. Through open ways of communication – in prolific, popular writings, in the conduct of open retreats and in the offering of systematic 'spiritual guidance' to a large number of clergy and lay persons from other Christian traditions – the contemplative communities contribute in significant ways to the development of a Christian spirituality within the larger context of Scandinavian Christianity.

It might be fair to say that the rapid globalization through mass media and Internet has to a large extent undone the feeling of living culturally on the edges, and to some extent torn down the fences between different spiritual traditions. This opens the religious landscapes in new, fascinating ways. The new religious movements and the development of highly privatized and syncretistic so-called 'New Age' spiritualities also is part of the picture in the Scandinavian countries. But at the same time important traits are also related to elements of a vague 'folk' religious tradition that is still there, at the turn of the millennium perhaps even stronger than before. This is apparent in many ways, but perhaps most strongly evidenced in the roles formal religion and Church liturgy continue to have in public life on both festive and tragic occasions. While it is still too early to draw firm conclusions, one possible interpretation of this situation could be that life for many in a postmodern society seems to have increased the importance of some kind of belonging to a religious tradition and/or the formal Church. But the premises for this belonging often differ rather strongly from the frameworks of traditional theology and spirituality as understood by the Church leadership. In this and other ways the existential challenges related to the fragmented conditions of postmodern life have been put on the agenda. This creates uncertainty and ambivalence. In a cultural context dominated by secularization and materialism, one can observe signs of constructive responses to this situation both in a new diversity of Christian spiritual practices, and in a new openness for Christianity in all its liturgical, ethical and intellectual aspects as a meaningful way to the interpretation of life experiences in their historical and cultural contexts.

See also **Bridal Mysticism; Bridgettine Spirituality; Lutheran Spirituality; Pietism.**

A. M. Allchin, *N. F. S. Grundtvig: An Introduction to his Life and Work*, Aarhus: Aarhus University Press, 1997; T. A. Dubois, *Nordic Religions in the Viking Age*, Philadelphia: University of Pennsylvania Press, 1999; L. S. Hunter (ed.), *Scandinavian Churches: A Picture of the Development of the Life of the Churches of Denmark, Finland, Iceland, Norway and Sweden*, London: Faber and Faber, 1965; J. Kristjánsson, *Eddas and Sagas*, Reykjavik: Íslenska bókmenntafélag, 1997; E. Molland, *Church Life in Norway 1800–1950*, Minneapolis: Augsburg Publishing House, 1957.

LEIF GUNNAR ENGEDAL AND
JAN SCHUMACHER

Scholasticism

Scholasticism refers to a cultural movement in Western intellectual history distinguished from the earlier culture of monasticism by new knowledge, new institutions of learning and new methods of study. It is difficult to be precise about where and when Scholasticism emerges as a distinctive cultural force but it is already well under way at the beginning of the twelfth century and is generally regarded as having reached its highest manifestation by the middle of the thirteenth century.

The process of receiving new knowledge, in particular from the Muslim world, is an important strand in the emergence of Scholasticism. Knowledge of mathematics, astronomy, physics, medicine and other scientific subjects increased dramatically in Western Europe after the eleventh century. Boethius had already translated some of Aristotle's logical works and more became known in the twelfth century. By the thirteenth century Aristotle's ethical, psychological, metaphysical and physical works were translated. The scholastic period was firstly then about learning, receiving this vast quantity of new knowledge, and thinking through its implications for what had been understood up to then.

The monasteries which had preserved the learning of the ancient world through Europe's 'Dark Ages' were gradually overtaken, first by the schools attached to them, then by the cathedral schools, and finally by the universities founded at the beginning of the thirteenth century. The *scholasticus* was the teacher in the monastic or episcopal school. The term was inherited from the ancient world where *scholastikos* referred to those sufficiently free from the cares of material life and public affairs to devote themselves to the culture of the mind whether as students, scholars or teachers.

The key intellectual tension in Scholasticism concerned the place to be allowed to dialectic or logic in the interpretation of received truth. Some regard Boethius as the first Scholastic for already having explicitly raised the question of relating faith and reason. It was an issue in the ninth-century controversies about the Eucharist and the twelfth century saw sustained and bitter struggles about it between Bernard of Clairvaux and the School of St Victor on one side, and Peter Abelard and Gilbert de la Porrée on the other. In the thirteenth century it became a controversy about the use of Aristotle's philosophy and it came to a head in the 1277 Parisian condemnation of radical Aristotelians. The new knowledge challenged received opinions in many areas.

The new institutions of learning were settings in which meditation and exposition were supplemented by the more vigorous and dialectical disputed question, a method of teaching that persisted in the universities of Europe down to modern times. Abelard is credited with having given birth to this new method in his work *Sic et Non*, a collection of incompatible and even contradictory statements from traditional authorities: how were these to be interpreted and on what basis might they be reconciled. Alexander of Hales formalized the method of the disputed question and paved the way for the transition from collections of sentences that merely gathered traditional teachings, to the great *summae*, works of creative interpretation and synthetic reconstruction.

Anselm of Canterbury (1033–1109) is the most important figure of the early Scholastic period. He thinks and writes in the style of Augustine, who was for the Middle Ages the paradigmatic Christian thinker. At the same time Anselm is keen to do justice to the demands reason rightly makes on the believing mind. His arguments for the existence of God are still valued as worthy of philosophical attention in spite of being found in a confession of faith in which Anselm, like his much-admired master, searches with his reason for the God he already knows by faith.

The Scholastic period is also characterized by the emergence of new forms of religious life, another indication of intellectual and religious change. The Cistercians of the twelfth century were founded partly to counteract the anti-intellectualism of the great Cluny tradition, and the speedy involvement of Cistercians in intellectual and political life indicates that a new kind of monk had indeed emerged. Other Scholastics of the twelfth century were Canons Regular, particularly Hugh and Richard of the cathedral school of St Victor. Whether the cathedral town of Chartres can claim a school of its own has been disputed but a series of remarkable scholars had a more or less strong association with the town. The thirteenth century saw another new form of religious life, that of the friars, who earned their living neither from monastic labour nor from pastoral benefices but by asking alms in return for their work of preaching and teaching.

For twelfth-century Scholastics, Plato's *Timaeus* and the book of Genesis together supported a characteristic appreciation of the world as intriguing and worthy of study in itself, while being sacramental and theophanic, revealing to eyes properly equipped the glory of God hidden within it. There was a simple confidence in the wise ordering of the world and in the capacity of human reason to seek and find the truth about it. William of Conches brought to bear on this revered synthesis new scientific knowledge learned from the Muslim world, while Robert Grosseteste carried this further in the thirteenth century equipped now with knowledge of Aristotle's physical and metaphysical works. We see in William and Robert the beginnings of 'science' as it came to be understood in the modern period: observation, method, experiment, hypothesis of cause and effect, and so on.

If the twelfth century is still about Christian theology and Platonism, the thirteenth century is about Christian theology and Aristotle. The use of his ideas in Christian thought is the great intellectual controversy of high Scholasticism. Although united in defending their new form of life, the Franciscans and Dominicans tended to disagree about how philosophy was to be understood in its relationship with theology. The Franciscans, in particular St Bonaventure, were more reserved about the aspirations of purely philosophical reasoning while the Dominicans, notably Albert the Great and Thomas Aquinas, seem more confident that truth attained by reason will not contradict truth accepted in faith. Thomas explicitly addresses his contemporaries' concerns about the effects of philosophical thinking on theological work. Far from diluting the wine of faith with the water of philosophy, he says, the person who puts philosophy at the service of faith is turning water into wine (*Commentary on Boethius de Trinitate*, q.2, a.3, ad 5).

For Scholastic thinkers, light is at the centre of their appreciation of God's presence in things, a light that shines within creation but also within the human mind equipped to know and appreciate the truth of creation. Light might well be taken as the fundamental divine attribute for a culture centred on the pursuit and enjoyment of the truth through learning and teaching. The most accessible evidence of this Scholastic metaphysics or spirituality of light is found not in texts but in the cathedrals and their stained-glass windows. These buildings articulated physically what Scholastic culture believed about the hidden presence of the divine light and the transcendent sweep of the created order, lifting the mind towards God seen within and through that order. Abbot Suger at St Denis, in what he built and in what he wrote, explains how philosophical, theological, spiritual and architectural ideas coalesced in the celebration of God as light.

A key figure in this is Pseudo-Dionysius the Areopagite, a sixth-century Syrian monk, whose works retained quasi-scriptural authority for the Latin Scholastics. Joseph Pieper emphasizes how the Pseudo-Dionysian tradition acted as a corrective, its conviction that all reality is unfathomable holding in check the scholastic tendency towards rationalism. God is beyond all symbolic representation, positive affirmation and intelligible negation, Pseudo-Dionysius says, and is attained finally in a mystical theology beyond being and knowing. This apophatic and theocentric mysticism, so important for later mystical currents in England, the Low Countries and elsewhere, may seem in contrast with the kataphatic and Christological mysticism associated with Bernard and some of the women writers of the Middle Ages.

But the thinkers of this period were capable of keeping both in mind. Thomas Aquinas for example says that theology, the intellectual pursuit of the truth of God, is both *scientia*, a knowing, and *sapientia*, wisdom. If God is light then it is a light so bright that it will be experienced as darkness by human minds. To know that we do not know is then the highest wisdom. If we do attain to some knowledge and experience of God as the gospel teaches (John 17.3) it can only be along ways intelligible to us: in symbol, language, sacramental celebration, a historical community and study of the sacred text.

Above all it is Christ who is our way to God. If Scholasticism is rationalist on one side it is warmly devotional on another. The humanity and suffering of Christ move to centre stage in the art, liturgy and devotion of this period. The close collaboration between many friars and the communities of women attached to their orders produced what seems like a marriage of scholastic theology and mystical spirituality. The men, for example Eckhart and Ruysbroeck are also mystics, while the women, for example Hildegard and Catherine of Siena, are also theologians.

In fact this kind of marriage is found again in the writings of John of the Cross. He lived during the period of a new Scholasticism, the sixteenth and seventeenth centuries, when theologians such as Cajetan, Suárez, Banez and Molina worked on a fresh synthesis of faith and reason in a radically different cultural and intellectual context. Neo-Scholasticism belongs to another radically different moment in the history of Christian thought, the nineteenth and twentieth centuries, when significant efforts were made throughout the Catholic world to show how Christian theology and faith may be supported by philosophy and reason.

The dangers in Scholasticism are more obvious perhaps than those that beset other spiritual and intellectual traditions. Its strength lies in its respect for the human mind and for traditions of learning, in its conviction that hard thinking is an essential component of religious faith, and above all in its understanding of God as truth and light. Only the contemplation of truth stills the questioning mind. Only what is intellectually satisfying quenches the thirst for understanding. Only the Divine Wisdom captivates the mind so as to cause it to burst into love.

See also **Aristotelianism; Cistercian Spirituality; Dominican Spirituality; Franciscan Spirituality; Intellectual Life and Spirituality; Light; Medieval Spirituality in the West; Monasticism; Neoplatonism; Nominalism; Norbertine Spirituality; Rhineland Mysticism; Thomist Spirituality; Victorine Spirituality; Women Medieval Mystics.**

G. R. Evans (ed.), *The Medieval Theologians: An Introduction to Theology in the Medieval Period*, Oxford: Blackwell, 2001; Mary T. Malone, *Women and Christianity, Volume 2: The Medieval Period AD 1000–1500*, Dublin: Columba Press, 2001; Erwin Panofsky, *Gothic Architecture and Scholasticism: An Inquiry into the Analogy of the Arts, Philosophy, and Religion in the Middle Ages*, Penguin USA, 1981; Joseph Pieper, *Scholasticism*, South Bend, IN: St Augustine's Press, 2001; R. W. Southern, *Scholastic Humanism and the Unification of Europe I: Foundations*, Blackwell: Oxford, 1995; R. W. Southern, *Scholastic Humanism and the Unification of Europe II: The Heroic Age*, Blackwell: Oxford, 2000; Maurice de Wulf, *An Introduction to Scholastic Philosophy: Medieval and Modern, Scholasticism Old and New*, trans. P. Coffey, Eugene, OR: Wipf and Stock, 2003.

VIVIAN BOLAND

Scottish Spirituality

Spirituality is not a word that trips easily off the Scottish Presbyterian tongue. However, if it is defined in terms of encounter with God, a lived experience of faith and a disciplined life of prayer and action, then there is a long and distinctive tradition of Scottish spirituality which can be found as much in the Church of Scotland and other Presbyterian denominations as in the Scottish Episcopal and Roman Catholic Churches.

It is probably fair to say that non-Scots have often found more of a spiritual 'buzz' in Scotland than have the native inhabitants. Dr Johnson's well-known reaction to Iona epitomizes an English attitude to the particular spirituality of the Highlands and Islands which has also manifested itself in the creation of the myth of 'the spiritual Gael' and the construction of romanticized notions of Celtic Christianity. A sense of the holiness of place is also a feature of the indigenous Scottish spiritual tradition, however, as is an emphasis on the physical and a generally more rugged, strenuous and intellectual approach than characterizes the gentler and smoother spirituality of the English. Strongly biblical in origin and ethos, and specifically influenced by the Psalms, Scottish spirituality has had a particular attachment to the Word – and the word – and has found its main expression in the literary forms of poems, hymns, sermons and prayers rather than through music or visual art.

Any review of Scottish spirituality must surely

start with the devotional literature that came out of the monastery on Iona in the centuries following its foundation by Columba around 563. Of the many poems attributed to Columba himself the most likely to come from his hand is the rather forbidding *Altus Prosator*. Its emphasis on the sovereignty of God, the terrible reality and consequences of the fall and the power of Christ's redemption introduce themes which crop up again and again in later Scottish devotional literature.

Surviving manuscripts indicate a rich devotional life in the monasteries of medieval Scotland, as demonstrated in the 'Lauds for the Feast of Columba' in the *Inchcolm Antiphonar*, the office for visiting the sick in The Book of Deer, and the fine collection of Gaelic poems and hymns in the *Book of the Dean of Lismore*. The end of the Middle Ages witnessed a flowering of Scottish spirituality in the work of three poets, William Dunbar, Gavin Douglas and Robert Henryson. Much of their verse was of a devotional character and the best of Dunbar, notably his ode on Christ's birth, *Rorate, celi desuper!*, stands comparison with Milton.

The Scottish Reformation produced a new emphasis on popular participation in both public worship and private devotion. The earthy, incarnational, Lutheran-influenced *Good and Godly Ballads* written by the Wedderburn brothers of Dundee enjoyed only a short reign before being supplanted by the Calvinist metrical psalms which were to play a dominant role in Scottish Reformed worship for the next three centuries. Most of those that found their way into the 1564 Scottish Psalter were of English provenance but the Scots could at least lay claim to 'All people that on earth do dwell', the work of the Borderer William Kethe. They also appropriated the Shorter Catechism drawn up by the Westminster Assembly of divines in 1647 much more enthusiastically than their co-religionists south of the Border.

Generations of Scots were brought up on the metrical psalms and the Shorter Catechism with its opening message that the 'chief end of man' is 'to know God and enjoy him for ever'. Knowledge rather than enjoyment of God predominated in much Reformed Scottish spirituality. The Kirk's approach to worship has often struck its critics as being dour and gloomy but it has never been accused of dumbing down or trivializing. In the Scottish spiritual tradition following Christ has always been understood as an affair of the mind as well as of the heart and the emotions. Awe in the face of the majesty of the Almighty has been accompanied by a lively interest in arguing and disputing about his attributes and

wrestling with difficult theological issues. In English and especially in Anglican spirituality there has been a clearer divorce between the devotional and the intellectual aspects of Christianity whereas in Scotland they have gone together. Scots think on their knees and pray standing up.

One aspect of this intellectual approach to spirituality has been the number of Scottish devotional classics written by academics. A prime example are the *Spiritual Exercises* noted down between 1624 and 1647 by John Forbes of Corse, first Professor of Divinity at King's College, Aberdeen. The letters written between 1636 and 1638 by Samuel Rutherford, Professor of Divinity and Principal of St Mary's College, St Andrews, combine evangelical passion and assurance with a rich and daring use of human metaphors to describe the all-sufficient grace and loveliness of Christ. Perhaps the most influential piece of Scottish devotional writing in the seventeenth century was *The Life of God in the Soul of Man* (1677), written by Henry Scougal, Professor of Divinity at King's College, Aberdeen, which defines true religion as 'a union of the soul with God, a real participation in the divine nature, the very image of God drawn upon the soul'. It had a profound impact on both John Wesley and George Whitefield.

The ultra-Calvinist and antinomian emphasis on election, characterized in James Hogg's *Private Memoirs and Confessions of a Justified Sinner* (1824), undoubtedly made for an unappealing, self-righteous element in the Scottish spiritual psyche in the eighteenth and nineteenth centuries. However, evangelical Presbyterianism was also responsible for introducing more nourishing and affirming spiritual fare into the Kirk in the form of the Biblical Paraphrases which were widely sung from the late eighteenth century.

A striking feature of Scottish religious life throughout the nineteenth century were the great spiritual revivals or awakenings which often took place in the context of the twice-yearly communion seasons. They were particularly marked in the Gaelic-speaking Highlands and Islands. Gaelic spirituality was also distinguished by fervent preaching and the singing of spiritual songs and hymns. The work of the three great Gaelic evangelical bards of the eighteenth and nineteenth centuries, Dugald Buchanan of Perthshire, John MacDonald of Ferintosh and Peter Grant of Grantown, has the same quality as Columba's – the sovereignty of God is described through his mighty works of creation and illustrated through the vivid physical imagery of the psalms, there is a strong emphasis on the fall, redemption through Christ and the covenant of grace and there is also an intense sense of spiritual pilgrimage.

Hymnody provided the richest and most characteristic expression of Scottish spirituality in the nineteenth century. Among the finest examples are Horatius Bonar's 'I heard the voice of Jesus say' and 'Light of the world! For ever, ever shining', John Drummond Burns' 'Hushed was the Evening Hymn', Walter Chalmers Smith's 'Immortal, Invisible, God only Wise', Norman Macleod's 'Courage, brother, do not stumble' and George Matheson's profoundly theological as well as devotional 'Make me a captive, Lord, and then I shall be free' and 'O love that wilt not let me go'. The greatest Scottish spiritual writer of the age was the Congregationalist minister (and émigré to England), George MacDonald, whose fairy tales coloured by Christian and mystical symbolism and shaped by powerful allegories of good and evil, so influenced C. S. Lewis.

The twentieth century saw native Scots beginning to appreciate their Celtic inheritance and also view it through the rose-tinted glasses that English visitors had worn. This trend was begun by Alexander Carmichael, the ecumenically minded excise officer who collected the Gaelic prayers, blessings and charms from the Highlands and Islands and translated them into English as the *Carmina Gadelica*. He drew especially on the rich spiritual tradition of the Roman Catholic communities in the southern Hebridean islands which had been largely unaffected by the Reformation. Kenneth Macleod's *Songs of the Hebrides* (1909–21), Alistair Maclean's *Hebridean Altars* (1937), and G. R. D. McLean's *Poems of the West Highlanders* (1961) provided a rich storehouse of devotional material which has been much plundered by modern editors for anthologies of Celtic Christian prayer. The academic contribution to Scottish spirituality was maintained by John Baillie, Professor of Divinity of Edinburgh, whose *Diary of Private Prayer* (1936) remained in print for more than fifty years.

The giant of twentieth-century spirituality, George MacLeod, resembled Columba in many ways. Of aristocratic birth, he was a natural leader of people and carried out his visionary project of rebuilding the ruined abbey buildings on Iona and establishing them as the home of a community dedicated to peace, justice and finding new ways 'to touch the hearts of all'. His carefully crafted prayers are shot through with powerful physical imagery and had a mystical, cosmic feel as well as being wholly earthed in the real world.

Recent decades have seen a significant revival of spirituality in Scotland thanks in part to the growth and influence of the ecumenical movement and increasing contact between Presbyterians, Episcopalians and Roman Catholics in places like Scottish Churches House in Dunblane. The ecumenical Iona Community has made spirituality one of its priorities and its Wild Goose Worship and Resource Group has hugely enriched the liturgical life of churches of all hues with prayers and songs which are both highly poetic and grittily incarnational. The work of its leader, John Bell, widely recognized as one of the most creative figures in contemporary worship and hymnody, is deeply rooted in the Scottish tradition of rigorous engagement with Scripture, theological ambiguity and acknowledgement of suffering. He has also consciously gone back to and sought to promote the psalms, the source of so much Scottish spirituality.

See also **Celtic Spirituality; Calvinist Spirituality.**

———

Meg Bateman, Robert Crawford, James McGonigal (eds), *Scottish Religious Poetry: An Anthology*, Edinburgh: Saint Andrew Press, 2000; Thomas Owen Clancy and Gilbert Markus (eds), *Iona: The Earliest Poetry of a Celtic Monastery*, Edinburgh: Edinburgh University Press, 1995; Adam Philip, *The Devotional Literature of Scotland*, London: James Clarke, 1923; Martin Reith, *Beyond the Mountains: Some Scottish Studies in Prayer and the Church*, London: SPCK, 1979; David Wright (ed.), *The Bible in Scottish Life and Literature*, Edinburgh: Saint Andrew Press, 1988.

IAN BRADLEY

Secularization

Secularization is a deeply debated and highly contested concept. In general, the word is used to describe the relatively recent decline of religion in the Western world. However, even with this very basic understanding, there are some immediate problems. First, religious affiliation in the USA – in theory a liberal, modern state – remains vibrant. Second, Europe seems to be the exception rather than the rule when it comes to a general decline in religious interests. Third, it is far from clear that religious interests necessarily decline in direct proportion to the rise of industrialization, modernity, globalization and the like. At the height of the Industrial Revolution in Victorian Britain, church attendance stood at record levels. In post-war Britain, new denominations and new religious movements have flourished.

Defining the term. Although the term 'secularization' has lapsed into popular usage, the proper definition lies in a cluster of prior sociological understandings. Technically speaking, Bryan Wilson argues that secularization relates to the diminution in the social significance of religion. In other words, its application covers such things as: the sequestration by political powers of the property and facilities of religious agencies; the shift from religious to secular control of various of the erstwhile activities and functions of religion; and the general decline in the proportion of their time, energy and resources that people devote to religious concerns; the decay of religious institutions; the supplanting, in matters of behaviour, of religious precepts by demands that accord with strictly technical criteria, and so forth (Wilson, *Religion in Sociological Perspective*, 1982).

Similarly, Larry Shiner argues that there are six characteristics that identify the process of secularization. First, the *decline of religion*: 'previously accepted symbols, doctrines and institutions lose their prestige and influence. The culmination of secularization would be a religionless society'. Second, *conformity with 'this world'*: 'the religious group or the religiously informed society turns its attention from the supernatural . . . the culmination of secularisation would be a society totally absorbed with the pragmatic tasks of the present and a religious group indistinguishable from the rest of society'. Third, the *disengagement of society from religion*: 'society separates itself from the religious understanding which has previously informed it in order to constitute itself as an autonomous reality and consequently to limit religion to the sphere of private life'. Fourth, the *transposition of religious beliefs and institutions*: 'knowledge, patterns of behaviour and institutional arrangements which were once understood as grounded in divine power are transformed into phenomena of purely human creation and responsibility'. Fifth, the *desacralization of the world*: 'the world is gradually deprived of its sacred character as man and nature becomes the object of rational-causal explanation and manipulation. The culmination of secularisation would be a completely "rational" world society in which the phenomenon of the supernatural or even of "mystery" would play no part'. Sixth, and finally, a *movement from a 'sacred' to a 'secular' society*: 'this is a general concept of social change, emphasizing multiple variables through several stages . . . the culmination of secularisation would be a society in which all decisions are based on rational and utilitarian considerations and there is complete acceptance of change' (Shiner, 1967, pp. 207–20).

Comment. Several objections can be raised against the secularization thesis. First, apparent religious decline (in terms of formal attendance at a place of worship or belonging to a religious organization) must be measured against other voluntary organizations or associations. Granted, fewer people belong, formally, to a Christian denomination when compared to the inter-war or Victorian periods, but almost all forms of association have declined steeply since those days. There are fewer Scouts and Guides, trade union membership has waned, and there are now fewer members of the Conservative Party than there are Methodists. Recreationally, there are fewer people in our cinemas and football grounds than seventy years ago – yet no one can say these activities are in decline. Indeed, it is a sobering thought that in an apparently secular Britain, there are still more people in church each weekend than watching a game of football.

Second, there is reason to doubt the idea that fewer and fewer people are turning to official or mainstream religion. For example, the Victorian period saw a revival of religion and religious attendance that lasted for about forty years. Yet the beginning of the eighteenth and nineteenth centuries were the very opposite of this: church attendance was, on the whole, derisory. The evidence for church attendance during medieval times is contestable; with some scholars asserting that religious observance was strong and others arguing that it was at best patchy.

Third, this haphazard, semi-secular, quiet (but occasionally rowdy and irreverent) English Christianity continues well into successive centuries. James Woodforde's *Diary of a Country Parson* provides an invaluable window into the life of the clergy and the state of English Christianity in the eighteenth century. Again, a close reading of the text suggests that whatever secularization is, it is not obviously a product of the Industrial Revolution. Woodforde clearly thinks it is reasonably good to have 'two rails' (or 30 communicants) at Christmas or Easter, from 360 parishioners. Such figures would be low by today's standards in some rural communities. Woodforde tells us that the only time his church is ever full is when a member of the royal family is ill, or when there is a war on. Generally, the context of his ministry is one where he baptizes, marries and buries the people of his parish, but the week-by-week Sunday attendance is not something that would get many ministers of his age into a frenzy of excitement.

Fourth, statistical surveys continually support the thesis that Europe is a place where the vast majority of the population continues to affirm their belief in God, but then proceeds to do little about it. So church attendance figures tend to remain stubbornly low. Yet this is not a modern malaise, but is rather a typical feature of Western societies down the ages. Granted, there have been periods of revival when church attendance has peaked. But the basic and innate disposition is one of believing without belonging; of relating to the Church, and valuing its presence and beliefs – yet without necessarily sharing them. Or, as the classic aphorism puts it, 'I cannot consider myself to be a pillar of the church, for I never go. But I am a buttress – insofar as I support it from the outside.'

Contemporary perspectives. Scholars are divided on how to interpret contemporary society and its apparent secularity. Sociologists such as Peter Berger have effectively repented from their predictions of the 1960s, and now argue that Western society, with all its capitalism and consumerism, remains religious. Historians can now show that increased church attendance may be a response to social unease and dislocation. The Industrial Revolution and the resettlement of post-war Britain both saw a rise in church attendance that may be viewed as a reaction to social upheaval.

Other scholars such as Callum Brown have argued that secularization is neither a product of the Industrial Revolution nor of Enlightenment thinking, but is in actual fact a rather more recent phenomenon. In *The Death of Christian Britain* (2000), Brown argues that the cultural revolution of the 1960s has broken the cycle of intergenerational renewal that was so essential to Christianity's survival. The rise of popular culture has done more than any other thing to marginalize Christianity (and religious observance in general), and provide people with other arenas for absorption and entertainment.

Similarly, Robert Putnam's *Bowling Alone* (2000) shows that the rise of popular culture in the USA has had a deleterious effect upon many different types of association and voluntary societies. Putnam's thesis demonstrates that 'negative social capital' has built up to such an extent that religious affiliation may ultimately be affected. In a country where churchgoing is a normal activity – as many as 50 per cent of the population attend on a regular basis – Putnam's thesis may point to some interesting future trends.

That said, Danielle Hervieu-Leger's (2000) work suggests that religious memory still persists in societies that are apparently acquiring religious amnesia. Although the cycle of intergenerational renewal may be distorted by the invasiveness of popular culture, her work suggests that religion only mutates under such conditions. It may be pushed from the public sphere to the private realm, but it still appears to be able to shape society at critical points. Far from turning its back on religion, modern societies seem to be perpetually absorbed by it – something argued more than a quarter of a century ago by David Martin (1978).

But lest this sound too complacent, it is important to remember that there is *something* in secularization. True, whatever that process is supposed to describe, it can probably never do justice to the intrinsically inchoate nature of religious belief that characterized the Western European landscape and its peoples long before the Enlightenment, let alone the Industrial Revolution of the nineteenth century and the cultural revolutions of the twentieth century. 'Standard' secularization theories are weak and unconvincing because they tend to depend on exaggerating the extent and depth of Christendom. They assume a previous world of monochrome religious allegiance, which is now (of course) in tatters. But in truth, the religious world was much more plural and contested before the twentieth century ever dawned.

So what, exactly, has changed? Despite an understandable reticence to accede too much ground to proponents of secularization theses, it can still be readily acknowledged that the twentieth century was the most seminal and challenging period for the churches in all of time. Leaving aside its own struggles with pluralism, postcolonialism, modernity, postmodernity and wave after wave of cultural change and challenge, the biggest issue the churches have had to face up to is, ironically, a simple one: choice. Increased mobility, globalization and consumerism have infected and affected the churches, just as they have touched every other aspect of social life. Duty is dead: the customer is king. It is no surprise, therefore, to discover churches adopting a consumerist mentality, and competing with one another for souls, members, or entering the marketplace itself and trying to convert tired consumers into revitalized Christians.

Thus, fewer regular or frequent churchgoers now attend church twice on a Sunday, which was once normal practice. For most, once is enough. Many who do attend on a regular basis now attend less frequently. Even allowing for holidays and other absences (say through illness), even the most dedicated churchgoer may only be present in church for 70 per cent of the Sundays in any given year. Many clergy now remark on the decline in attendance at Days of Obligation (i.e., major saints days, or feast days such as the Ascension). The committed, it seems, are also the busy. The response to this from among the more liturgical churches has been to subtly and quietly adapt their practice, whilst preserving the core tradition. For example, the celebration of Epiphany may now take place on the Sunday nearest to 6 January, and not on the day itself. Most Roman Catholic churches now offer Sunday Mass on Saturday evenings, in order for Sunday to be left as a family day, or for whatever other commitments or consumerist choices that might now fall on the once hallowed day of rest.

Added to this, we also note the rising number of 'new' spiritualities, their range and volume having increased exponentially in the post-war era. Again, choice (rather than upbringing, location, etc.) is now a major factor in determining the spiritual allegiances that individuals may develop. Moreover, it is not easy to discern where the boundaries now lie between leisure, exercise and spirituality. As the consumerist-individual asserts their autonomy and right-to-choose, clear divisions between religion and spirituality, sacred and secular, and Church and society are more problematic to define. Thus, consumerism and choice simultaneously threatens but also nourishes religion and spirituality. Spiritual self-help books and other products, various kinds of yoga and meditative therapies, plus an ample range of courses and vacations, all suggest that religious affections and allegiances are being transformed in contemporary society rather than being eroded. 'Secular' society seems to be powerless in the face of a curiously stubborn (and growing) social appetite for inchoate religion and nascent spirituality, in all its various forms.

Conclusion. While it is true that many in Western Europe are turning from being religious assumers to religious consumers, and are moving from a culture of religious assumption to religious consumption, in which choice and competition in the spiritual marketplace thrive, there may be little cause for alarm. Three reasons come to mind.

First, even in the most modern societies, there is still demand for religion that is public, performative and pastoral. Furthermore, there are thousands and thousands of private spiritualities and beliefs that flourish in modernity, demonstrating that faith does not wither and die in our culture. Many churches have seen a rise in numbers since the terrorist attacks of September 11th 2001. Religion mutates, and continues to live on.

Second, religion is remarkably resilient in the modern age. Much of our 'vernacular religion' – such as the celebration of Christmas – reveals a nation that still enjoys its carols, nativity plays

and other Christian artefacts that long ago moved beyond the control of the Church to become part of the cultural furniture. Religion is still in demand and, where it is absent, it is more often than not created, or the gap filled with new forms of spirituality. In the absence of religion, people tend to believe anything rather than nothing, and the task of the Church must be to continue to engage empathetically with culture and society, offering shape, colour and articulation to the voices of innate and implicit religion.

Third, the churches can respond to the challenge of an apparently faithless age with a confidence founded on society (yes, society), which refuses to leave religion alone. Often, the best that churches can do is to recover their poise within their social and cultural situations, and continue to offer a ministry and a faith to a public that wish to relate to religion, without necessarily belonging to it. With rare exceptions in history, this is what all clergy have had to work with most of the time: it is both an opportunity and a challenge.

In short, the statistics for church attendance, if read crudely, retell one of the great lies of the modern age, namely that secularization is 'real'. It is, rather, a sociological and interpretative construct that is placed upon select data. Secularization theories tend not to take 'implicit' or 'folk' religion that seriously; and neither do the theorists pay much attention to the rising interest in spirituality. Equally, the appeal of fundamentalism and new religious movements in the West, to say nothing of the explosive growth in Christianity and Islam in the developing world, are also dismissed.

Ultimately, crude readings of church attendance or membership figures say very little about the faith of a nation; believing and belonging should not be confused. In contemporary Western society, very few people choose not to relate at all to the Church, or to mainstream religion. In any secular age, there is space and demand for religion, faith and spirituality. This is important, for it reminds us that religion provides enchantment within modernity, and that churches are often the only bodies that provide public and open places within a community for tears, grief, remembrance, laughter and celebration.

See also **Spirituality and Culture (*essay*); New Age; Postmodernity; Public Life and Spirituality.**

Callum Brown, *The Death of Christian Britain*, London: Routledge, 2000; Grace Davie, *Religion in Britain Since 1945*, Oxford: Blackwell, 1994; Danielle Hervieu-Leger, *Religion as a Chain of Memory*, Cambridge: Polity Press, 2000; David Martin, *A General Theory of Secularisation*,

Oxford: Blackwell, 1978; Martyn Percy, *Salt of the Earth: Religious Resilience in a Secular Age*, London: Continuum, 2002; Robert Putnam, *Bowling Alone*, New York: Simon & Schuster, 2000; Larry Shiner, 'The concept of secularization in empirical research', *Journal for the Scientific Study of Religion* 6 (1967), 207–20; Bryan Wilson, *Religion in Sociological Perspective*, Oxford: Oxford University Press, 1982.

MARTYN PERCY

Self

see **Person**

Senses, Spiritual

The notion of 'spiritual senses' seems to have arisen with the Alexandrian theologian Origen (*c.* 185–255), especially in his interpretation of the Song of Songs as the summit of the mystical life (see Lawson, 1957). Origen's understanding is based on a Platonic distinction between the inner, spiritual person formed in the image of God, and the outer material person formed from the mud of earth. One can also define two loves, *eros* and *agape*. While true love is one, according to Origen *eros* can be misunderstood in a carnal way. In the highest human state, contemplation of God, there is a pure, spiritual passion for what is invisible. As the outer person has five material senses, so the inner person has five spiritual senses. Gregory of Nyssa (*c.* 335–95) was undoubtedly influenced by Origen but explored more deeply the nature of the soul's experience of divine darkness. In the darkness of union the soul cannot *see* but somehow *feels* the presence of the divine – especially through smell, taste and touch. The idea of the five spiritual senses had a significant influence on later Western mysticism, for example on Bernard, Bonaventure and, more surprisingly, on Ignatius of Loyola.

In contemporary terms, the concept of 'spiritual senses' seems problematic because it suggests a division between the bodily and the spiritual dimensions of human existence. Even if we look beyond outdated anthropologies, the question remains as to whether or not a reformulation has any practical value.

One answer might be that 'spiritual senses' speak of an *integration* of the sensory with the spiritual dimension of human experience. In that way, the notion can be reinterpreted as *retaining* the connection between contemplation and embodiment. Second, 'spiritual senses' counteract any tendency towards a purely intellectualist understanding of consciousness of or 'union' with God. Third, the notion emphasizes that however close to God we grow, the encounter involves the whole self, including the senses.

Although frequently overlooked, references to the 'spiritual senses' are present in a spiritual tradition that is still influential today – the Ignatian Spiritual Exercises. For example, in the Introductory Annotations (Spiritual Exercises 2), Ignatius speaks of the person making the Spiritual Exercises being filled and satisfied not by much information but by an 'interior savour'. However, the most explicit reference is in the 'prayer of the senses', or 'application of the senses' (e.g. Spiritual Exercises 121–6), offered as the fifth and final prayer of the day from the Second Week onwards. New meditative material is not used but 'the five senses of the imagination' are passed over the material of previous prayer. Such an exercise can be reduced to a technique where one tries to imagine particular sensual details of a gospel scene ('feel the wind in the hair') in order to deepen contemplative awareness. However, from the evidence of some early 'directories' (additional material on guiding the Exercises), it seems clear that the 'prayer of the senses' follows in the long tradition of 'spiritual senses', especially as taught by Bonaventure in his *Journey of the Soul into God*. However, at a time when contemplative-mystical interiority was viewed with suspicion, this approach was entirely ignored in the final text of the Official Directory of 1599 in favour of a less subtle exercise of active imagination (de Guibert, 1972, pp. 246–7; Palmer, 1996, pp. 132–3 and pp. 321–3). The Ignatian 'application of the senses' stands for a level of intensification, simplification and contemplative depth that Ignatius Loyola seeks but that cannot be a question of method alone.

In this matter, Karl Rahner's comments are helpful (Rahner, 1979). Not everyone can be said to have all or even any of the 'spiritual senses'. Two things are needed to restore them: God's grace and practice. Rahner suggests that the usefulness of the concept is in terms of expanding our experience of contemplation of God. First, 'spiritual senses' enable us to discern well. They represent a kind of delicate spiritual sensitivity where we develop a 'feel' for God's will, and insight into God's desire. Second, 'spiritual senses' are a way of representing the richness of the soul's experience of God in contemplation. They suggest a depth that is not captured solely by 'vision' or 'knowledge'.

A recent writer on the 'spiritual senses', Enzo Bianchi (Bianchi, 2003), suggests that they have a wide application for all Christians in that the celebration of the Eucharist ideally involves the 'spiritual senses'. The Eucharist incorporates believers into 'the mystery' of God and yet also involves all the senses: hearing (the word), seeing (the ritual), tasting (the eucharistic elements), smelling (incense, for example), touching (our fellow believers, for example in the kiss of peace). Here the human senses are ideally refined and transfigured so that what is perceived and received is not merely something external but a deeper reality (so the Word in and through the words). This is not something accessible only to an elite but is the true purpose of eucharistic participation.

See also **Mysticism (*essay*); Contemplation; Ignatian Spirituality; Meditation.**

Enzo Bianchi, *Words of Spirituality: Towards a Lexicon of the Inner Life*, London: SPCK, 2002, ch. 4, 'Senses and spirit'; Joseph de Guibert, *The Jesuits: Their Spiritual Doctrine and Practice*, St Louis: The Institute of Jesuit Sources, 1972; George Ganss (ed.), *Ignatius Loyola: Spiritual Exercises and Selected Works*, New York: Paulist Press, 1991; Andrew Louth, *The Origins of the Christian Mystical Tradition: From Plato to Denys*, Oxford, Clarendon Press, 1981; R. P. Lawson (trans.), *Origen: The Song of Songs – Commentary and Homilies*, Ancient Christian Authors 26, London, 1957; Martin E. Palmer (ed.), *On Giving the Spiritual Exercises: The Early Jesuit Manuscript Directories and the Official Directory of 1599*, St Louis: The Institute of Jesuit Sources, 1996; Karl Rahner, 'The beginnings of a doctrine of the five spiritual senses in Origen', *Theological investigations* 16, London: Burns & Oates, 1979, pp. 81–103.

PHILIP SHELDRAKE

Servite Spirituality

The Order of Servants of Mary (Servites) was founded about 1245 when a group of Florentine merchants withdrew from a penitential lay confraternity to Monte Senario, some twelve miles distant. This first foundation was characterized by the desire of these men (canonized in 1888 as the Seven Holy Founders) to live a life of prayer and penance, under the protection of Our Lady. In this they showed themselves part of two popular medieval movements, one steeped in penitential observances, the other in service to Mary.

Beginning in 1250 other foundations were made, first in central Italy and then farther north, even in Germany. The original characteristics continued and, following a collective vow of poverty made the following year, the Order began to adopt typical 'mendicant' structures and apostolates. The contemplative and eremitical characteristics weakened and the Marian element became more pronounced.

Faced with the raging conflict of the secular clergy with the mendicants that culminated in the suppression of many of the smaller mendicant orders by the Second Council of Lyons in 1274, the Servants of Mary abandoned completely the ban on ownership of property, while retaining in most places a life of true material poverty and the right to collect alms from the faithful, as was the custom of other mendicant orders. At the same time the Marian aspect of Servite life was increasingly emphasized so that by 1317, when the *Legenda de Origine Ordinis*, the first narrative history of the foundation period, was written, St Philip Benizi (d. 1285), prior general during the difficult years after the Second Council of Lyons, was presented as the example of the authentic Servant of Mary, and the concept of Marian service was developed in great detail.

By the time the Order was definitively approved by Benedict XI in 1304 the major characteristics of Servite spirituality were well established: Marian devotion, apostolic service to others, fraternity or community life (especially important because the Order's very foundation was the work of a group of men together), and poverty or austerity of life. Certainly other aspects of Christian spirituality were also present but these seem most characteristic and indeed they continued through the centuries, being modified or re-emphasized according to the needs of the times.

Devotion to Mary in the early years of the Order was seen as the total dedication of the person to God and to Mary as a means to fulfil one's dedication to God. This total dedication was expressed in certain devotional practices of the time, for example the recitation of certain prayers such as the Angelic Salutation and the Salve Regina, liturgical celebrations such as the Vigil of our Lady and the celebration of the Mass of the Blessed Virgin on Wednesdays and Saturdays in addition to the Marian feasts of the period, and the dedication of Servite churches to Mary. It was also manifested in the seal of the prior general, the artwork in their churches and choir books and their vow formula.

By the Renaissance their Marian devotion began to be increasingly focused on the sorrows of Mary, so that in the period following the Council of Trent devotion to the Seven Sorrows of Mary became the characteristic Servite Marian devotion. This was modified slightly after Vatican II by incorporating into such devotion a consideration of the continued suffering of Christ in his body the Church today as the present constitution states: 'Since the Son of Man is still being crucified in his brothers and sisters, we, Servants of his mother, wish to be with her at the foot of those countless crosses in order to bring comfort and redemptive cooperation.'

The poverty and austerity witnessed in the lives of the first friars on Monte Senario became a recurring beacon calling the Order back to its original fervour. In the early 1400s the rebuilding of Monte Senario materially and spiritually was an expression of the need for reform in the Order. From Monte Senario friars went to northern Italy to found the Congregation of the Observance which lasted until shortly after the Council of Trent. The reforms in the Order after Trent certainly were institutional and structural, but the guiding light of the reform was the *Lettera Spirituale* of Angelo Maria Montorsoli, prior general 1597–1600. His basic principle was that reform of religious life must begin with the observance of the vow of poverty, understood primarily in the material sense. This too was the emphasis in the life and constitutions of the Hermits of Mount Senario (1593–1780). The concept of evangelical poverty was again stressed in the present constitutions of the Order, but with a different meaning: 'Work, the sharing of goods and a moderate style of life constitute the witness to poverty voluntarily undertaken by Servite communities.'

Service of others was an integral part of Servite spirituality from the beginning. At first this was exercised simply within the conventual Church with liturgical services offered in the presence of lay people, hearing their confessions and burying their dead. This expanded in later centuries to include scholarly pursuits such as teaching in universities and publishing books, whose themes frequently dealt with Our Lady. Servites maintained churches and shrines dedicated to Mary. In the nineteenth century parochial work provided an outlet for ordained friars which assured the continuance of the Order in places where religious foundations were suppressed and it also provided an economic base when other financial sources had been confiscated by governments. In the twentieth century this spread to include organized missionary work on all continents.

Many religious congregations of women and lay groups, inspired by the same ideal, grew up around Servite communities. Others already in existence, attracted by the same ideal, associated themselves with the Order. Each group is a unique expression of lay or consecrated life, and all participate in a common vocation, while maintaining relationships of spiritual and apostolic co-operation.

Finally the value of community life has been present since the foundation of the Order and the example of the founding friars, of St Philip Benizi, St Peregrine Laziosi, St Anthony Pucci, St Juliana Falconieri and other beatified brothers and sisters, have been an abiding inspiration as Servites work together in groups and also co-operate with other groups to build the kingdom of God.

See also **Eremitical Spirituality; Mendicant Spirituality; Poverty; Rules, Religious.**

V. Benassi, O. J. Dias and F. M. Faustini, *A Short History of the Servite Order*, Rome: General Secretariat for the Servite Missions, 1987; G. M. Besutti osm, E. M. Casalini osm and C. M. Borntrager osm, 'Servites (Ordre des Servites de Marie)' in *DS* 15, cols 695–730; F. A. Dal Pino, *I frati Servi di santa Maria dalle origini all' approvazione (1233 ca.-1304)*, 2 vols, Louvain: Université de Louvain, 1972; F. A. Dal Pino, *Brothers and Servants. The Seven Holy Founders of the Servite Order*, 2nd edn, Chicago: Friar Servants of Mary, 2004; C. M. Ross osm, *The Charism of the Servants of Mary*, Chicago: Friar Servants of Mary, 1983; *Sources for the History and Spirituality of the Servants of St Mary*, vol. 1, *From 1245 to 1348*, Sotto il Monte (Bergamo): Servitium editrice, 2000; vol. 2. *Dal 1349 al 1495*, Gorle (Bergamo): Servitium editrice, 2002 (only in Italian).

PEREGRINE M. GRAFFIUS.

Sexuality

Contemporary writing about sexuality and spirituality, whether from the perspective of theology, psychology or religious practice, is about integration: how two things quite different or seemingly different can be brought together. The relevance of sexual theology for spirituality consists in the concern of both for human bodily behaviour.

Sources for a theology of the connection between spirituality and sexuality are the same as those for any systematic effort: Judaeo-Christian tradition and other spiritual traditions, the cultures in which we live, the reported experience of people. Like most other aspects of human behaviour, sexual experience is understood as in a rear-view mirror. Only after the cycle of feelings, activities, storytelling and gratitude or regret have been completed does one make sense of her new sexual reality in the light of her full human experience. People know from their experience whether sexual arousal is about more than lust, and that sexual delight is not always selfish. For many couples the sexual relationship they share makes life richer and more spiritually significant.

The present state of thinking about sexuality in the context of spirituality cannot be evaluated without recalling something of its historical antecedents and their more immediate contributions to contemporary theory and practice. It is also necessary to understand in some degree the sources of the widespread contemporary challenge to rules of gender and traditional sexual ethics. In our time the traditional functional relationships between men and women are all but dead.

This article will necessarily limit its consideration to Western traditions of spirituality. It will begin with a brief historical overview, consider next those factors which have rendered traditional concepts problematic, and finally focus on central issues that now engage reflection on the spiritual-sexual lives of human persons.

Overview. The polytheistic religions of ancient Greece and Rome saw sexual love as connected to particular gods and goddesses and sexual practices could be considered sacred ritual actions in the appropriate religious contexts. Sex was treated as 'sacramental' in the sense that it was a way of communing with the divine through its human counterpart. The sacredness of sexuality was, however, separate from its function in regard to reproduction. A severely dualistic mindset separated the sacred (beautiful) and the worldly (practical), and transmitted such a view through influential philosophies, art and literature.

The Jewish tradition by and large saw the sexual life as a secular affair, to be regulated by other than religious means. There was no divine consort involved in creation, and no divine model for living sexually. The Hebrews, in contrast to their pagan neighbours, demythologized human sexuality. In the Song of Songs and in the book of the prophet Osee, the joyous mysteries of human desire and union are used as a metaphor to bring people to understand something of the covenant with God. They are not used to suggest that directives came from the transcendent Being to regulate and give meaning to such desire and union. Marriage and reproduction were considered a religious duty, but were not seen as a source of connection to the divine.

With Christian traditions a diversity of theologies of sexuality emerges. Jesus gave no particular teaching on sexuality other than on the value of monogamous marriage. Much of this is paralleled in the teaching of the rabbis. His novelty seems to have been the freshness of his approach, sweeping aside quibbles about the Law, and his open relationship with all manner of people. His attitudes are to be seen as much in his actions as in his recorded teachings. It would be unusual for a Jew of Jesus' time to be celibate, yet there is no evidence for his marriage or other sexual involvement. Jesus attracted male and female disciples, and on the day of Pentecost the Holy Spirit seems to have descended on the twelve disciples and their female companions, 'the women, and Mary the mother of Jesus' (Acts 1.14).

Paul was a Jew, but also a Roman citizen, wrote all his letters in Greek, came from Tarsus in Asia Minor, and introduced some new ideas into the Hebrew background. One could say that Paul re-sacralized marriage with his use, in Eph. 5.25, of the pagan symbolism of the union of holy one with his people ('even as Christ loved the church, and gave himself for it'). The image of the sacred marriage is taken by Paul as a symbol of divine redemption and a pattern for earthly union. Yet he was an 'ad hoc' teacher, not a systematic one, and he also wrote, 'The flesh lusts against the spirit, and the spirit against the flesh, and these are contrary the one to the other' (Gal. 5.17). Many interpretations have attempted to show a broader than physical meaning to the concept of 'flesh' but such obvious dualism was later used to justify asceticism and to deprecate sex.

Many forms of Gnosticism affected the early Christian Church, developing on trends from pagan religions and philosophies that regarded matter as inherently evil. In the second century, Marcion condemned marriage and procreation as the works of Satan. By the end of the third century the extreme dualism of Manichaeism profoundly influenced Augustine of Hippo. Manichaeans held that matter was concupiscence, a 'disorderly motion in everything that exists'. Matter or concupiscence was female, the 'mother of all the demons', and the soul was imprisoned in it. The object of religion was to release the soul and severe asceticism was practised to this end. The Manichaean religion spread rapidly, was known in Rome by the fourth century and was influential in North Africa. Historians have not been able to trace the exact connection of its ideas with later sects, such as the Cathari of the twelfth century and the Jansenists of the seventeenth, but the resemblance can be seen with many who stress the contrast of soul and body and regarded sex as unclean. The sexual ethics of St Augustine and its legacy, that is, only when sexual intercourse had the purpose of procreation was sexual desire ordered according to reason, and therefore not sinful, became the norm for future teaching and legal pronouncements. In addition to a general prohibition of anything that produces sexual pleasure for its own sake (not justified by the purpose of procreation), Thomas Aquinas opposed contraception because it intended nonprocreation and because it constituted an injury against an unborn child and/or the human species.

Affirmation of the potential of sexual intercourse for expressing and effecting interpersonal love. The rise of the courtly love tradition and new forms of mystical theology in the twelfth century introduced the assertion that sexuality can be a mediation of interpersonal love. Some voices, including Abelard and John Damascene continued to argue that concupiscence does not make sexual pleasure evil in itself. Thomas Aquinas worked out a theory of love that could have asserted that sexual intercourse could be an aid to interpersonal love (*ST* 2a2ae.26.11) and he intimated that marriage could make possible a high form of friendship between male and female (*Summa Contra Gentiles* 3.123). Some say he broke with Augustine's theory of procreative sex and fully justified marital intercourse as an expression of the good of fidelity.

In the fifteenth century writers such as Denis the Carthusian began to speak of the possible integration of spiritual love and sexual pleasure. Martin Le Maistre, teaching at the University of Paris, argued that when sexual pleasure is enjoyed for its own sake it contributes to the general well-being of the persons involved. Nonetheless, surprisingly little change occurred before the twentieth century.

Modern Roman Catholic teaching reaffirmed the procreative ethic in reaction against the Protestant decision to accept birth control. Little by little theologians such as Bernard Haring and Josef Fuchs began to move in the direction of allowing that sexual intercourse in marriage without a procreative intent and for the purpose of fostering marital union should not be considered sinful. Vatican II taught explicitly that the love essential to marriage is uniquely expressed and perfected in the act of sexual intercourse. It made no distinction between the primary and secondary ends of marriage, thus accepting non-procreative marital intercourse. Sexuality was, however, still seen by most established religions as primarily an occasion of moral danger rather than spiritual growth.

New knowledge about sexuality through the science of sexology has contradicted previously held beliefs about the meaning and potentiality of human sexuality. Arguments for the male being the only active principle or for the unnaturalness of certain sexual activities was undercut by growing evidence from the animal as well as the human world. Cultural views of sexuality were discovered to be different in different societies. Sexual need and desire began to be articulated not as the result of sin but a natural drive, integral to the human personality, not fixed but formed by complex factors from earliest childhood.

Through feminist research women became aware of the irrationality of sexual taboos, and struggled to find new freedom from past prohibitions. Equality and mutuality changed from being unthinkable to being a measuring stick of the appropriateness of sexual relations between persons. The contemporary hope has been to free once more the power and beauty of sexuality for the whole of human life.

Contemporary approaches. (1) The integration of sexuality and spirituality still requires the disassociation of sex from symbols of defilement, sin and guilt, especially by religious bodies. This critical, historical work is ongoing.

(2) Some theorists have introduced the principles of justice – affirming the dignity of persons and groups of persons – as a norm that would replace the reproductive norm as the public meaning of sexuality. Similarly, new understandings of the nature and role of women give rise to norms of equality and mutuality in sexual relations between women and men. Sexual union, for all its physical pleasures, also symbolizes a spiritual union of two people. It may well be that sexual energy opens a current of spiritual energy that forms a transcendent bond between people who are deeply in love. If human nature is understood to be essentially open to sexual expression in any intense relationship – and more or less virtuous as they are more or less mutual, active and integrated into the whole of human personhood – it is quite natural for attitudes regarding marriage and divorce, contraception, masturbation and homosexuality to change. All of us – single or married, gay or straight, celibate or sexually active – show each other the many ways to love.

But this remains open to debate. Which sexual activities contribute to and which prevent the integration of sexuality into the whole of human life is not in every case evident. Moreover, there is little dialogue between thinkers who construct ethical systems and those who are concerned with personal spirituality.

(3) Sexuality is seen by some as a language for the sacred, spiritual-carnal realm of the interpersonal. The metaphor of language is constructive, offering its own ethics and recognition of limits. Besides creating life, sex is an avenue of self-expression, a means of making a statement about our connection to our own bodies and our relation to the world around us. Sexuality is used as a form of exchange and, in certain circumstances, a type of currency. Many people use sex as a means to an end, which may produce a 'fair exchange' or result in exploitation.

(4) Some have begun to approach the question

from the side of spirituality and to propose that there is reciprocal growth (or stuntedness) between one's sexual health and spiritual health. Becoming aware of sexual power and capable of managing it is also the key to spiritual adulthood. Our sexuality provides the rites of passage that also contain spiritual tasks and achievements.

- When we become *aware of being sexual beings*. This awareness is sometimes gradual and sometimes explosive and sudden, but with it comes our sense of adult identity, of being a centre of power, a subject who can connect with others, a person. Sex education is meant to give a context of responsibility and goodness to this dawning awareness. However, all too often it is characterized in individuals by a sense of shame and fear. The awareness meant here is not that there is sex *our there* (in the movies, adults, novels, etc.) but *in here*. Most often this awareness dawns in middle school and is characterized by increased curiosity, experimentation and concern with body image. When a child is abused and catapulted prematurely into sexual awareness, much remedial work must be done. This stage corresponds with the tasks of spirituality – coming to self-knowledge and self acceptance. Practically it means identifying more with peers than parents, overcoming shame and false guilt, acknowledging orientation, beginning to be aware of one's love map (patterns of attraction and arousal). The rites here are rock concerts, mall crawls, group dates, and food, dress and hair arrangements.
- When we *perceive our capacity and need for intimacy*. Most often this begins in parental closeness and same-sex sharing of secrets and private fears and desires. It is the power of being connected on emotional and intellectual as well as physical levels and is an essential component of adult sexual maturity. Ritual moments are best friends' symbols, sleepovers, special moments, anniversary places. Practically, it means allowing oneself to be vulnerable and open to another. The differences in male and female child-raising sometimes mean that women find intimacy easier than men and attain its skills more easily.
- When we experience *ecstasy or self-transcendence*. In sexual terms this may be referred to as 'orgasm' but no sexologist presumes to define precisely what is meant by that term. James Prescott identifies four levels of orgasm, and suggests that most people don't experience more than the second level. An ecstatic state is neither exotic nor as rare as often imagined. It can be produced by religion, art, sex and even simple movement. Ritual moments are as commonplace as roller-coaster rides, running, dancing, horseback-riding or swinging on a swing, but may be as socially charged as first intercourse. No human being develops fully without both intimacy and ecstasy and no lifestyle is capable of sustaining a person's growth which does not include some experience of ecstasy. It is often said that men seek and accept ecstatic behaviours more easily and earlier than women. The way this produces passage or transformation of the self is that an ecstatic state temporarily dissolves the boundaries of the self, so that one experiences part of a larger whole, then the boundaries are reconstituted in a new, hopefully enlarged sense of self.
- *When we choose commitment or love*. Love is often revealed through a breakthrough experience, associated with the birth of a child, or the almost-loss of someone. With commitment the moments of passage may be single or multiple. The rituals that accompany the commitment are very well known: giving and accepting a ring, clothing, and other symbols of self (cheque books!). While society puts a premium on weddings as rituals of commitment, earlier and other societies celebrated different stages of commitment with different religious ceremonies to mark first menstruation, 'going steady', engagement, marriage, parenthood. Anniversaries are ritual times showing sexual relationship (commitment) as a completed rite of passage. Divorce and remarriage, gay and lesbian partnership, while controversial, also beg for ritual public celebration. The ritual connects a particular couple's sexual union to those before, after and around it, and assures the couple of society's support and its acknowledgement of divine blessing on their union.

These moments in which sexual development signals personal passage and transformation are truly passages in the ancient sense of initiatory mystery because they cause, not just signal, the shift from child to adult, alone to connected, consumer of the emotional resources of humanity to generator of life and love.

(5) The enhancement of sexuality can be mandated as part of a theory of virtue. Contrary to the platonic notion that repression of sex produces intellectual and spiritual power, sex itself may enable a concentration of powers so that the deepest and most creative springs of action are tapped close to the centre of personal life. One must not overstate the claim, however. We know that sexual desire left to itself is not even able to

sustain its own ardour. There is growing general evidence (the rise in impotence and sexual boredom) that sex is not the indomitable drive it was thought to be when it *was* culturally repressed. More and more theorists are coming to the conclusion that sexual desire without interpersonal love leads to disappointment and a growing meaninglessness. The other side of that conclusion is that sexuality is an expression of something beyond itself. Its power is a power for union and its desire a desire for transcendence.

For the lesbian or gay or bisexual spiritual person, as for the heterosexual, the challenge of intimacy begins in the call to come to know ourselves and then to love and trust who we are. Our identity – and this includes our sexual identity – grounds our ability to be faithful to other people and to values. The spirituality of the homosexual, transsexual or bisexual person, like everyone else, goes through the stages of self-discovery, self-acceptance and self-transcendence. Coming out to one's parents and associates can be experienced 'as coming in' to one's own centre. It appears to be a condition for the intimacy and ecstasy that makes life fulfilling. When we 'come in', we know the exhilaration that is felt as sexuality begins to be incorporated into our lives; the joy of being fully ourselves before those we love and before God.

Kundalini yoga teaches a way of managing sexual energies of the psyche and body and bringing about a kundalini experience, an ecstatic state of spiritual ecstasy reached through disciplining one's sexual energy. Rather than allowing the normal release of sexual energy through a physical orgasm, kundalini spiritual practice directs the sexual energy to rise up the spine and culminate in a spiritual union with the divine. Mystics have been said to experience altered states of consciousness during deep moments of meditation that included orgasmic release.

Any spirituality of sexuality has to include a way of articulating how celibacy plays in the spiritual life of a human being and the community. No longer thought to be delivered from the dangers of friendship, affection and love, celibates, especially males, are now feared to be open to the temptations and distortions that come with loneliness. As in all charismatic gifts, religious celibacy is a personal capacity of an individual, intensified by the power of the Holy Spirit for the good of the community. Various spiritualities of celibacy have been proposed.

• It is chosen for the sake of the kingdom of God, a choice that cannot be made so wholeheartedly by the husband and householder. It is suitable for leadership because it embodies a higher moral standard.

• It is chosen as a sign of the eschatological kingdom, the reign of God to come at the end of time. In this view it challenges our present domestic concerns and witnesses to future value by living virtually within that future environment.

• It is a vocation to work in places and apostolates that are potentially dangerous and do not leave the time or energy for a committed partner. What is chosen is to work with the poor or ill or politically oppressed, and celibacy is enjoined because, in justice, the demands and dangers associated with that particular work should not be inflicted on a spouse.

• In the Roman Catholic Church, celibacy is linked historically with priesthood. In this practice it is a religious discipline required by the Church of all ordained priests.

• To live as celibate can be recognized as a personal call, a mysterious aspect of one's own journey of faith, one's sacred contract, whether alone or with a community. This lifestyle allows a particular individual in particular circumstances to love better and more generously.

See also **Agape; Body and Spirituality; Celibacy; Desire; Eroticism; Homosexuality; Love; Masculine Spirituality; Relationships; Women and Spirituality.**

Helen Fisher, *The Anatomy of Love: A Natural History of Mating, Marriage and Why We Stray,* Ballantine Books, 1994; Caroline Myss, *Anatomy of the Spirit: The Seven Stages of Power and Healing,* New York: Three Rivers Press, 1996; David Schnarch, *Passionate Marriage: Love, Sex and Intimacy in Emotionally Committed Relationships,* New York: W. W. Norton & Co., 1997; Joan Timmerman, *Sexuality and Spiritual Growth,* New York: Crossroad, 1992; Evelyne Eaton Whitehead and James Whitehead, *The Wisdom of the Body: Making Sense of Our Sexuality,* New York: Crossroad, 2001.

JOAN H. TIMMERMAN

Shaker Spirituality

Shaker spirituality reflects a core set of religious values which the Believers accommodated to changing community circumstances over the course of more than two centuries of continuous history. These spiritual values found expression in two different spheres, the setting of public worship and the world of everyday activities. Neither sphere alone is a sufficient depiction or measure of the spiritual traditions of the Shakers.

The origins of the United Society of Believers in Christ's Second Appearing lie in eighteenth-century England among the dissenting portions of the religious population. Known initially as Shaking-Quakers, the earliest Believers engaged in spirit-directed ecstatic worship outside the established religious communities, setting themselves in opposition to the Church of England and to other dissenting religious communities. In this small sectarian circle Ann Lee (1736?–1784), an illiterate factory worker, emerged as a leader. Lee, a charismatic visionary, experienced opposition from both ecclesiastical and civil authorities because of her willingness to express religious dissent prophetically by disrupting worship services. For their actions, she and other Believers spent time in prison. In 1774, in part as the result of a vision, Ann Lee led a handful of followers to America.

In America, after an initial period when the group disappeared from the historical record, a small but growing community of Shakers emerged under Lee's leadership. Located in an area adjacent to Albany, New York, the members experienced hostility and periods of incarceration during the American war for independence because of their commitment to pacifism. Beginning in 1781 Lee led a successful missionary journey in eastern New York and parts of New England that lasted for more than two years. Converts attracted to the Believers' gospel formed the nuclei of several new Shaker communities scattered across these regions. During these years Shaker spirituality expressed in the worship setting remained largely spontaneous and spirit-driven, creating a strong bond among the Believers. It also proved a source of curiosity for persons outside the community. Observers told of strange practices during worship; some apostates even charged the community with promiscuity and drunkenness during the meetings.

Following the death of Lee in 1784, her English and American disciples shaped a communal organization that structured life for the members in every aspect of their existence. James Meacham, one of the first American leaders, organized the community's public worship; his decisions had the practical effect of reducing the spontaneity of the spiritual exercises and of regulating the physical expressions in worship. Dances and marches with songs and hymns became standard activities in Shaker meeting houses. These rituals integrated converts into the community and created the powerful sense of a spiritual family. The most creative period in the history of Shaker worship was known as 'Mother Ann's Work' or the Era of Manifestations.

Beginning in 1837 in New York and then spreading throughout Shaker villages from the east coast to the Ohio Valley, this period witnessed a new burst of ecstatic and spirit-directed worship. For more than two decades in the mid nineteenth century, chosen Believers or 'instruments' received spirit messages and songs as well as new rituals of all kinds. Shaker religious exercises involving bodily expression – whirling, dancing, jumping, falling – again filled the meeting houses. These creative manifestations attracted so much attention that for a time the leadership closed the meetings to non-Shakers. Elaborate outdoor rituals were also carried out by the Believers at special sacred sites at each village. In the second half of the nineteenth century when numerical decline set in, the Shaker communities did not enjoy the same amount of success in attracting new converts. About the same time the Society experienced a new openness to the 'world' which formerly it had condemned. There were also outside influences on Shaker worship. On some occasions, for example, Protestant ministers were invited into Shaker meeting houses to preach an evangelical message. The Shakers joined with spiritualists, participating in seances and trance activities. They adopted the use of musical instruments and sang hymns that were not a product of their own tradition. They also abandoned the dances and marches which formerly had been unique to Shaker worship.

The twentieth century witnessed continuing numerical decline, geographical retreat to the east coast, and the near complete feminization of the society. By 1960 only three villages remained, staffed by a handful of Believers who were not in close unity with one another. New members were rare, but one convert, Brother Theodore Johnson who joined the Sabbathday Lake, Maine, community, exercised a powerful influence on the spirituality of the Believers. Johnson joined with other Believers at that site in a revival of traditional Shaker spirituality. He also brought into the community a positive view of other Christians and an interest in ecumenical worship. Although his status as a Believer was an issue of controversy, his presence was a major factor in stabilizing the situation at Sabbathday Lake and in fostering the renaissance of Shaker studies in the closing decades of the twentieth century.

But the formal worship setting is only one of the two contexts where Shaker spirituality has been evident throughout the history of the society. The daily experiences of the Believers provide another forum for discovering the spiritual dimensions of Shaker life. From the time of origins to the present, the Believers have viewed everyday activities as powerful expressions of their spirituality. During the formative years of the tradition under Ann Lee, the first Believers faced animosity from their neighbours and physical harassment from religious opponents. The willingness of Lee and her associates to witness boldly to their beliefs and to persevere in the face of suffering and opposition was evidence of the strength of their spiritual commitment to the Shaker cause. The emergence of a nascent communal society in these early years created the sense of extended family. The Believers came to regard Lee as their mother; thus the name 'Mother Ann' became her honorific title. Lee's immediate successor, her English colleague James Whittaker, instituted strict regulations requiring the abandonment of conventional families. Husbands and wives separated, and children were no longer cared for only by their biological parents. The new families were spiritual families, and they required sacrifice and renunciation on the part of the Believers.

During the years of geographical expansion at the start of the nineteenth century when the Society moved into the Ohio Valley and other western transappalachian areas, Believers found themselves burdened with the task of building community structures and facing new uncertainties. Lucy Wright, the leader in the Society's ministry in New Lebanon, New York, called for sacrifice and investment of a sort that the Believers had not previously experienced. Millennial Laws newly promulgated controlled all aspects of community life. Missionaries ventured into distant and sometimes threatening locales as they spread the Shaker gospel. The remarkable economic success enjoyed by the Shaker communities, both east and west, came at the expense of long hours of toil by both brothers and sisters who laboured willingly for the community rather than for their own financial advancement. These Believers also abandoned conventional family life – sexual relations, special love, relationships with their biological children – for life in the Shaker family presided over by elders and eldresses. Celibacy and obedience were virtues that separated Believers from the ways of the 'world'. The decades of numerical decline presented the Believers with new challenges. No longer was the Society able to boast of its economic success, or to attract admiring glances from outsiders. Now the community was forced to weather difficult times. As the villages closed down, the surviving members sought solace and strength in the spiritual traditions of the past. Individual Believers rose to the occasion and asserted religious commitment and resolution. Even when they disagreed about the proper

strategy for the future, faithful Believers, such as Sisters Bertha Lindsey at Canterbury, New Hampshire, and Mildred Barker at Sabbathday Lake, found strength in the spiritual traditions of the Society.

Ultimately, the conflict between these last two villages was resolved by natural processes. Now the future of the Society remains in the hands of the remaining Believers at Sabbathday Lake. Their spiritual strength is evident in the persons of Sister Francis Carr and Brothers Arnold Hadd and Wayne Schmidt. The daily labour they invest in community life in the kitchen, library and fields as well as the leadership they express in the meeting house combine to reflect the dual sense of 'labour' that is explicit in the Shaker saying, 'Hands to work and hearts to God'. Although few in number, the contemporary Believers are surrounded by hundreds of enthusiastic supporters and friends who look positively upon the spiritual values expressed in Shaker life and worship.

See also **Celibacy; Community; North American Spirituality; Quaker Spirituality.**

Edward Deming Andrews, *The Gift to be Simple: Songs, Dances and Rituals of the American Shakers*, New York: Dover Publications Inc., 1962; Edward Deming Andrews, *The People Called Shakers: A Search for the Perfect Society*, New York: Dover Publications Inc., 1963; Priscilla J. Brewer, *Shaker Communities, Shaker Lives*, Hanover, NH: University Press of New England, 1986; John T. Kirk, *The Shaker World: Art, Life, Belief*, New York: Harry N. Abrams Inc., 1997; Daniel W. Patterson, *The Shaker Spiritual*, Princeton, NJ: Princeton University Press, 1979; Stephen J. Stein, *The Shaker Experience in America: A History of the United Society of Believers*, New Haven, CT: Yale University Press, 1992; Robley E. Whitson (ed.), *The Shakers: Two Centuries of Spiritual Reflection*, CWS, New York: Paulist Press, 1983.

STEPHEN J. STEIN

Shrines

The original meaning of the word shrine is a box or case containing sacred relics of a saint, it being derived from the Latin *scrinium*, a case or chest for books or papers. It was later used to describe the area of a church in which such relics are to be found. In the Catholic tradition such shrines have always been the end point of pilgrimages and miracles often associated with the relics placed there. The miraculous power of the material is attested to in the Acts of the Apostles where we learn that when handkerchiefs and scarves which had been in contact with St Paul's skin were carried to the sick, they were rid of their diseases and the evil spirits came out of them. Later, the notion that God could work miracles through saints' bones or *brandea* (cloths which had been in touch with them) grew with alacrity. The author of *The Martydom of Polycarp* wrote in AD 156 that the martyr's bones were more valuable than refined gold. Pope Gregory the Great, in the sixth century, sent filings of what were believed to be the chains of St Peter, and which he considered to be the most precious of all relics, enclosed in crosses to his friends. The cult of the saints was of huge importance in medieval Christianity: almost all cathedrals had at their heart a shrine containing the relics of a saint, and those which were not affected by the Reformation still do. So, for example, the shrine of St James remains the visible goal of pilgrims on the Santiago pilgrimage route. Not all shrines contain relics: Marian shrines have arisen where the Blessed Virgin has appeared and many of these, such as those at Lourdes in France and Walsingham in England, remain very popular destinations for pilgrims. The common thread between all shrines is the link with a place of a holy person or persons.

Modern Catholic teaching includes within the definition of a shrine any places towards which an itinerary of faith converges, places whose purpose is to celebrate God's involvement with creation through the lives of his people down the Christian centuries. Shrines are to be found in sacred places where divine–human encounter has taken place, where saints have lived and died and where holiness has been manifested. Looked at in this way, a shrine is a reminder of the salvific work of the Lord. Thus in the same way as the shrines of the people of Israel (Shechem, Bethel, Beersheba, Silo) were all linked to stories of the Patriarchs and were memorials of their encounter with the living God, so the shrines of the Christian Church are memorials to encounter with that same living God who remains faithful. Shrines are an effective physical reminder of the fact that the creation is not a system closed onto itself, but one created by a God who is still intimately involved in it through the life of those he has called to himself in Christ. Pilgrims make their way to such shrines in order to be reminded of God's commitment to the world and to ask for the intercession of saints, whether or not they hope for a miraculous intervention by God as a result of such prayer. Pope John Paul II referred to shrines as 'permanent antennae of the good news'. Thought of in this way, their function is not only be a reminder of past salvific acts on God's part but a call to holiness in the present

and a pointer to God's future. The medieval cathedrals built around the shrines of saints were constructed to be symbolic of heaven and so have a forward-looking momentum. They were intended to point pilgrims towards their heavenly homeland and as a result encourage them on their journey towards it. There are thousands of these shrines throughout the world. Indeed, if their purpose is to celebrate God's involvement with the world in this manner, very many Christian churches could fit into the category of shrine. Understanding them as such could enhance the power of their witness to the Christian faith.

See also Devotions; Devotions, Popular; Holiness; Intercession; Pilgrimage; Place; Sacred.

P. Brown, *The Cult of the Saints. Its Rise and Function in Latin Christianity*, Chicago: Chicago University Press, 1981; *The Shrine. Memorial, Presence and Prophecy of the Living God*, Vatican City: Pontifical Council for the Pastoral Care of Migrants and Itinerant People, The Vatican 8 May 1999; *The Shrine a Privileged Place for a Meeting between God and His People, a Pilgrim in Time*, Vatican City: Proceedings of the XIV Plenary Meeting of the Pontifical Council for the Pastoral Care of Migrants and Itinerant People, The Vatican, 23–25 June 1999; D. Webb, *Pilgrims and Pilgrimage in the Medieval West*, London: I. B. Tauris, 1999.

JOHN INGE

Silence

Most monastic traditions impose limitations on conversation and many spiritual masters point to the necessity of vigilance in this matter even for those living in a non-monastic ambience. Today in a world in which entertainment, noise and communication predominate, it is important to appreciate that spirituality demands a different emphasis. Regular periods of silence and retreat seem essential for spiritual growth.

For St Benedict and the Western monastic tradition, silence joins with humility and obedience as the prime determinants of a spiritual attitude to life. 'Because of the seriousness of silence, permission to speak should be rarely granted to perfect disciples even when it concerns conversation about good, holy and edifying matters' (RB 6.3). This instruction was taken literally during the Middle Ages and a sign language was developed to avoid the necessity of speech. This practice continued with the Cistercians of the Strict Observance (Trappists) until Vatican II.

The spiritual discipline of silence or restraint of speech operates at many levels. Different factors contribute to that state of tranquillity which makes possible greater attention to the non-sensate realities of the spiritual world. At different times, according to circumstances, more effort in one particular area will have a positive impact on one's spiritual life.

1. *Reduction of physical noise*. The stimulus of sound is difficult to ignore. Noise makes concentration difficult and attention to inward realities almost impossible. This means that any attempt at meditation or prayer needs to begin with an effort to remove ourselves from the alienating effects of noise, and to allow the organism to quieten down after it has been battered by living in a noise-filled environment.

2. *Avoidance of the sins of the tongue*. Although, in itself, speech is morally neutral, the epistle of James (3.1–12) and many writers of the monastic tradition see in silence the only effective means of neutralizing our tendency towards sins of the tongue. This means learning to control the flow of speech so that it does not become the vehicle for unconscious malice in the form of contention, detraction, domination, contempt of others and pride.

3. *Conservation of energy*. Silence is at the service of intense living. Time spent in idle conversation is time not spent in more useful activities; attention given to trivialities lessens our capacity for serious endeavour. Although many people find relaxation in talking, it can sometimes serve as a means of escaping from or postponing the imperatives of their personal situation. In addition, those of an introverted nature experience excessive talking as de-energizing.

4. *Listening*. It is not possible to speak and to listen at the same time. Without the discipline of silence it becomes impossible to engage in meaningful dialogue, since this involves leaving aside one's personal thoughts and endeavouring to hear what the other is saying. Our own urgency to speak prevents our absorbing what the other is expressing and often causes us to rush to fill the pauses that are a necessary part of what is being communicated.

5. *Concentration*. The inner noise due to the multiplicity of thoughts is the ultimate source and power of emotional disturbance, temptation to the vices and distraction in prayer. Vigilance over the thoughts and over inner and outer dialogue is essential for leading a peaceful life, in relative freedom from doubt and inconsistency, with an unhindered capacity to be refreshed in prayer, Excessive talking is both the cause and the expression of mental dispersion.

6. *Listening to the heart*. A certain element of withdrawal is necessary if one is to give priority to spiritual realities. Such solitude and silence allows concerns to be seen in perspective and in proportion and facilitates attention to the more profound murmurings of the Spirit dwelling in the heart and of one's own conscience.

7. *Apophasis*. At a certain point both in prayer and in life, God's presence is experienced as a profound dissatisfaction with all attempts to express the divine reality in language. This results in an attraction towards a reverent silence, a preference for unknowing, and a sense of the appropriateness of negative images like desert and darkness.

See also Asceticism; Apophatic Spirituality; Cistercian Spirituality; Discipline; Eremitical Spirituality; Hesychasm; Monasticism.

———

Primary sources: *RB* 6, 'On Restraint of Speech'; *RM* 8, 'What should be the Mode and the Measure of the Disciples' Silence'.

Secondary sources: Hans Urs von Balthasar, 'The Word and silence,' in *Explorations in Theology I: The Word Made Flesh*, San Francisco: Ignatius Press, 1989, pp. 127–46; Michael Casey, 'Inner noise' in *The Art of Sacred Reading*, Melbourne: HarperCollins, 1995, pp. 91–7; Oliver Davies and Denys Turner, *Silence and the Word: Negative Theology and Incarnation*, Cambridge: Cambridge University Press, 2002; David Tomlins, 'The meaning and value of silence in Christian living', *Cistercian Studies* 17.2 (1982), pp. 172–80; Ambrose Wathen, *Silence: The Meaning of Silence in the Rule of St Benedict*, Cistercian Studies Series 22, Washington: Cistercian Publications, 1973.

MICHAEL CASEY

Simplicity

Though most spiritual traditions endorse 'simplicity' as an important value, specifying its precise significance within those traditions is no simple matter. Christian authors, for example, use the term to characterize, among other things, the nature of God, moral probity, childlikeness, and even particular styles of personal prayer, liturgical celebration and daily living.

In the Hebrew Scriptures, 'simplicity' is typically associated with perfection, integrity and sincerity of heart. Those who find favour with God, such as Noah, Abraham, Jacob and Job (Gen. 6.8–9; 17.1; 25.27; Job 1.1) are said to be *tam* (perfect), among those who walk in *tamîm* (integrity), terminology that may originate in a cultic context requiring whole and unblemished sacrificial victims. In ancient Greek biblical translations these words are often rendered as *haplous* (simple) or *haplotes* (simplicity), which in turn are often rendered as *simplex* and *simplicitas* in the Latin Vulgate. The psalmist's confidence that 'the decree of the Lord is trust-worthy, giving wisdom to the simple' (Ps. 19.8; cf. Ps. 119.130; Prov. 1.4; 9.4), finds an echo in Jesus' cry of praise to the Father that 'what you have hidden from the learned and the clever you have revealed to *nepiois*' (Matt. 11.25; Luke 10.21), a Greek expression which can mean 'children' or 'the simple'. In such passages later authors would find the grounds for linking Christian simplicity with evangelical 'childlike-ness' or 'spiritual childhood', though in Paul *nepios* and its cognates usually carry a negative connotation of moral or spiritual immaturity, while *haplous* is used for wholehearted gener-osity (compare 1 Cor. 13.11 with 2 Cor. 8.2; 9.10–13). Elsewhere in the Gospels Jesus declares 'if your eye is *haplous*, your whole body will be filled with light' (Matt. 6.22; Luke 11.34), in contexts which seem to relate the 'single' eye to singleness of heart, in contrast to all 'double mindedness'. Similarly, early Christian texts of the sub-apostolic era frequently present disciple-ship as involving a fundamental choice between the 'two ways' of darkness and light, the former associated with *dipsychia* (duplicity, hesitation) and the latter with 'simplicity' (*Letter of Barnabas*, cf. *Didache, Shepherd of Hermas*).

The terms *simplex* and *simplicitas* likewise occur often in Latin patristic literature. Though sometimes used in the pejorative sense to indi-cate naivety or ignorance, in Augustine and others one can still find the biblical contrast between the 'simple heart' and the 'double heart'. Monastic traditions of both the East and West present 'simplicity' as a key monastic virtue, in contrast to the complexity of worldly life or scholastic thinking, and recognize a process of gradual 'simplification' in prayer.

The classic medieval defence of God's absolute simplicity is found in the *Summa Theologiae* of Thomas Aquinas (1a q. 3; on human *simplicitas* see 2a2ae.109.2; 111.3). Meister Eckhart delves further into the mystical implications of this metaphysical doctrine, declaring that 'God is infinite in his simplicity and simple by reason of his infinity,' so that if the soul 'is to be united with God, she must be simple as God is simple', returning to the ultimate simplicity of being itself, beyond all distinctions. Jan van Ruusbroec brings out more clearly the volitional compon-ent in discussing 'simplicity of intention', a theme also found in a famous passage from the *Imitation of Christ* affirming that the human person 'is borne up from earthly things on two wings: simplicity and purity', and that 'simplicity is in the intention' while 'purity is in the affec-tion' (2.4). John of the Cross advocates letting go of a multiplicity of attachments and devotions to

rest in 'the simplicity of faith' (*Ascent of Mount Carmel*, 3.43.1), and describes the process of becoming so transformed in 'the simplicity and purity of God' that the soul is left 'clean, pure, empty of all forms and figures, purged, and radi-ant in simple contemplation' (*Spiritual Canticle* 26.16).

Discussions of simplicity among later authors often focus on its moral and psychological aspects. Vincent de Paul and Francis de Sales, for example, typically relate simplicity to humility, purity, straightforwardness and lack of pretence. Other authors influenced by the seventeenth-century French School of spirituality use the term in specifying a particular stage of prayer, variously called 'prayer of simplicity', 'prayer of simple regard' or 'prayer of simple presence', which they tend to identify with the 'active recol-lection' described by St Teresa of Avila. In our own time, simplicity is often treated popularly in terms of lifestyle issues or aesthetic principles (e.g., in Twelve-Step programmes and the envi-ronmental and liturgical movements, or in con-temporary presentations of the religious vow of poverty as a commitment to 'simplicity of life').

In short, the term 'simplicity' seems to refer to no single quality but rather to a complex set of interrelated themes, whose common thread for Christians may perhaps be found in the 'greatest commandment' (Matt. 22.34–40; Mark 12.28–34; Luke 10.25–28). Christian simplicity must be ultimately rooted in a total and undivided love of a supremely simple and loving God, yet simul-taneously expressed in loving concern, not only for one's diverse neighbours, but for a cosmos of seemingly infinite complexity, created and sustained by the same divine love.

See also Mysticism (*essay*); Contemplation; Darkness; French School of Spirituality; Light; Prayer; Poverty.

Y. de Andia, V. Desprez and M. Dupuy, 'Simplicité' in *DS* 14, cols 892–921; J. Bauer, 'Simplicity' in J. Bauer (ed.), *Sacramentum Verbi*, New York: Herder, 1970, vol. 3, pp. 847–8; S. Payne, 'Simplicity' in Michael Downey (ed.), *The New Dictionary of Catholic Spirituality*, Collegeville, MN: The Liturgical Press, 1993, pp. 885–9.

STEVEN PAYNE

Singleness

The spiritual notion of singleness is most often associated with the human heart and will, and is first seen in the Old Testament teaching on the necessity of loving God with one's whole heart. This single-heartedness (*yahed lebabi*) of

Ps. 86.11, speaks of walking in the ways of the Lord with one object and one goal. The single heart was a pure heart, and was a sign of wisdom (Wisd. 1.1).

Jesus would advocate this singleness or purity of heart in the Sermon on the Mount, and the notion of a single-minded devotion of the mind and heart to God was a recurring theme in early Christian writings. It was the single-hearted who would see God, and it was singleness of life that would win one God's favour. Duplicity was condemned as the antithesis of this purity of intention and 'double-mindedness' was considered contrary to Christian teachings and lifestyle.

Singleness of mind and intention would also be a recurring theme in medieval spirituality, particularly in the mystical theology of the Rhineland mystics and medieval woman mystics. In the *Brautmystik* of this time period, the union between Christ and his beloved were often seen as the union of mind, soul and body, to create a singleness of complete union between the lover and the beloved. Kierkegaard would discuss singleness of heart in his own work, defining it as the willing of one thing: God.

The notion of singleness, however, also included a physical lifestyle as early as the Syrian ascetics of the second and third centuries. The Syrian term *ihidaya*, much as the Greek *monachos*, indicated a person who had chosen to live a life of aloneness, or singleness, in imitation of the single, alone, Christ. Together with this physical 'aloneness' or 'singleness' one would also attain a singleness or purity of heart. The notion behind this understanding was that in order to live a life most in conformity with the life of Jesus, one had to attain purity or singleness of heart which was most easily, and in some circles only, attained through a life of physical solitude and aloneness, or singleness. These early groups of *ihidaya* or *monachoi* would become the precursors of later monasticism both in Orthodoxy and Roman Catholicism. The early Syrian and Greek Christian monks would use the word 'singleness' as contemporary spirituality uses the words 'celibacy' and 'virginity', as well as 'purity of heart'.

In contemporary understanding, 'singleness' most often refers to the physical state of being single, unmarried, and not in a committed physical and emotional relationship of any type. While contemporary 'singleness' may not take on the spiritual sense of the first centuries of the Christian era, the contemporary option of living a single unmarried life as a deliberate choice without religious vows or specific religious community or affiliation, brings new questions and challenges to the notion of vocation and human

spiritual fulfilment. States in life recognized by the Christian churches as callings or vocations, such as marriage, religious vows and ordination, see the primary source of grace being found in a committed relationship with a community often of choice such as spouse and children, religious community or the clerical community. Each of these lifestyle choices has a unique relationship to the larger community and world, and one's vocation or calling in life is to live out the grace of that committed relationship. The state of singleness – living as a single, unattached person – as practised in today's world, however, has yet to find recognition and articulation of its particular role among the people of God. While the single life is most often regarded by society as a temporary transitional lifestyle while waiting or preparing for marriage, religious vows or ordination, there is a growing sense that there exists a definite vocation and call by God to the life of a single person as a state in life all its own without vows to any other person or institution. While the theology and spirituality of the vocation to singleness is still awaiting a clear articulation, the elements of emotional, psychological, intellectual and physical freedom the single life affords arise as appealing elements, particularly in countries where the modern trend toward individualism and autonomy have gained popular and philosophical ground. Less comfortable elements of aloneness and loneliness, separateness and insecurity, while not unique to the single life, do stand out as its more common and unpleasant elements in ways that are unique to its own lifestyle. Where traditional religious hermits or even isolated vowed religious or diocesan priests may have needed to address these same issues, the respect and financial support afforded them by the Church or their communities set them apart from today's single person who must provide for themselves financially and live in the world of employment and economics, as well as negotiate contemporary societal norms which still view people in committed relationships of one type or another as the norm for healthy adults.

Despite the present ambiguity concerning the vocation to the single life without religious vows or commitments to an exclusive person or institution, as a viable vocation and lifelong way of life, the growing practice and questions offer fruitful and engaging notions of the human person's relationship with God. The contemporary choice for a lifelong single lifestyle also raises the question of the human need or lack thereof for a concrete community, and the questions of maturity, discernment, strength of character and sense of identity, and responsibility required of someone contemplating a life lived without a spouse or religious community.

See also **Celibacy; Monasticism; Purity of Heart; Syriac Spirituality; Virginity.**

Sebastian Brock, *Spirituality in the Syriac Tradition*, Kerala, India: SEERI, 1989; Ruth Goring, *Singleness: A Life Grounded in Love: 10 Studies for Individuals or Groups*, Downer's Grove, IL; InterVarsity Press, 2002; Diane Leclerc, *Singleness of Heart: Gender, Sin, and Holiness in Historical Perspective*, Lanham, MA: Scarecrow Press, 2001; Harriet Luckman and Linda Kulzer (eds), *Purity of Heart in Early Ascetic and Monastic Literature*, Collegeville, MN: The Liturgical Press, 1999; Mary O'Brien and Clare Christie (eds), *Single Women: Affirming Our Spiritual Journeys*, Westport, CT: Bergin & Garvey, 1993.

HARRIET A. LUCKMAN

Social Justice

While notions related to justice were at the heart of Aristotle's *Nichomachean Ethics* and Thomas Aquinas' *Summae*, 'social justice' is a relatively new notion. General justice, for both, subordinated all human behaviour to the common good; particular justice was expressed in commutative justice, restorative justice and distributive justice.

Commutative justice defined relationships among a group's members. It sought equality based on fair standards for reciprocity (the give and take of human relationships); it also rejected unnecessary encroachment on others' rights. Restorative justice sought to reconcile conflicted parties in a way that enabled them to find common ground for beginning anew on a more equal footing in a broken relationships. Distributive justice ordered the goods of the community in a way that enabled the most seriously injured to have access to their basic needs.

Social justice builds on all three kinds of justice noted above. Indeed, social justice can be considered as a kind of umbrella holding not only these three forms, but all other forms of justice.

While seminally contained in Catholic Social Teaching since *Rerum Novarum* ('Of New Things'), the 1891 encyclical of Pope Leo XIII, the notion achieved a new acceptability in *Quadragesimo Anno* ('After Forty Years'), written by Pope Pius XI in 1931. In this letter, Pope Pius XI showed that social justice encompasses the common good of all, including respect for human rights (commutative justice) and a rightly ordered distribution of benefits and burdens (distributive justice).

Building on the corpus of papal writings that constitute the core of Catholic Social Teaching, the US Catholic bishops stated in 1978: 'In Catholic thought, social justice is not merely a secular or humanitarian matter. Social justice is a reflection of God's essential respect and concern for each person and an effort to protect the essential human freedom necessary for each person to achieve his or her destiny as a child of God' (*To Do Justice* 8, Washington DC: US Conference of Catholic Bishops, 1978).

In the Old Testament, Justice was a name of God, a key identifier (Jer. 23.6). It defined God's nature (Isa. 30.18) as well as God's activity (Gen. 18.25; Ps. 9.5). God's purpose vis-à-vis all in creation involves the establishment of justice. The two main Hebrew words for justice were *misphat* and *tsedâqâh*, *tsedeq* or *tsadâq*. To know Yahweh is to do justice (Jer. 22.13–16). To be in right relationship with God demanded of God's people that they promote just relations with each other and, especially, those marginalized (the widow, the orphan and alien) and those denied the community's resources (via almsgiving and fasting). In the Septuagint, *tsedâqâh*, *tsedeq* or *tsadâq* got translated as *dikaiosune*. If human beings were to be just in a way that reflected God's justice they needed to observe God's will by caring for others who were marginalized and without resources.

In the four Gospels of the New Testament, it appears nine times, seven being found in Matthew (Matt. 3.14; 5.6, 10, 20; 6.1, 33; 21.32; Luke 1.75; John 16.18). Because it is found seven times in Matthew, with five of these in the Sermon on the Mount and two of these dividing the eight beatitudes, Matthew's Gospel has often been called 'The Gospel of Justice'. Indeed the opening words of Jesus find him saying that he must undergo John's baptism to 'fulfil' all *dikaiosune* (3.15). Furthermore, those who will follow him must image a *dikaiosune* that is greater than that of the scribes and Pharisees (5.20).

Since all human relationships must image those of God and, since God's nature is expressed in trinitarian dynamics, all human relationships must witness to the Economic Trinity wherein the three Persons relate to each other in such a way that their very identity ('I AM') is realized only in so far as all three Persons share fully in the resources of the Commonwealth (Reign/Reality/ Life) of God. From this understanding of God's communitarian nature and functioning, theological anthropology posits three key concepts that undergird social justice: (1) the dignity of every person that is realized in the greatest freedom possible; (2) relationships of solidarity that are realized in the greatest forms of participation possible; and (3) equity in sharing of resources that ensure the maximal degree of meeting human needs.

Building on this theological anthropology, social justice demands that: (1) the basic right of freedom for the many (persons) cannot be undermined in ways that ensure the control of the few; (2) the need for social security and solidarity take precedence over the desire for control by the few; and (3) the needs of the many take precedence over the wants of the few.

The document in Catholic Social Teaching that most succinctly summarizes the biblical basis for justice as well as the human cry for justice is the 1971 statement from the Synod of Bishops. At this meeting, which, for the first time, had a very significant number of Church leaders from less-developed nations (who, therefore, were experiencing the lack of social justice within their nations and among the nations of the world), they declared that their 'analysis of the situation of the world' revealed a 'network' of domination that denied people their basic need for freedom as well as dynamics that kept the 'greater part of humanity' from sharing in the earth's basic resources. This led them to call for a renewed effort for 'action on the part of justice'. They further declared that this situation manifested a 'grave sin' of social injustice that demanded conversion to God's word. In one of the few places where any leaders in the Roman Church admitted their own need for conversion, they also declared: 'While the Church is bound to give witness to justice, she recognizes that anyone who ventures to speak to people about justice must first be just in their eyes. Hence we must undertake an examination of the modes of acting and of the possessions and the lifestyle found within the Church itself.'

If Jesus came proclaiming the gospel of the 'reign of God' and if the 'reign of God' is grounded in trinitarian relationships, community at every level of the world must reflect its maker. This demands that social justice ground every relationship throughout society.

See also **Feminist Spirituality; Liberation Spirituality; Public Life and Spirituality; Reign of God.**

Synod of Bishops, 'Justice in the World' in Joseph Gremillion (ed.), *The Gospel of Peace and Justice: Catholic Social Teaching since Pope John*, Maryknoll, NY: Orbis Books, 1976; Michael H. Crosby, *House of Disciples: Church, Economics and Justice in Matthew*, Portland, OR: Wipf & Stock, 2004; John Donahue, 'Biblical perspectives on justice' in John Haughey (ed.), *The Faith that Does Justice: Examining the Christian Sources for Social Change*, New York: Paulist Press, 1977.

MICHAEL H. CROSBY

Society and Spirituality

Religion and society should not really be divided as subjects or objects. Their relationship is fundamental to religion, and has been conceived by some as inherent to the nature of society. Societies invariably have hereditary values that lead to individual and collective views on behaviour, beliefs and attitudes. It is generally a mistake to try and define religion outside such social patterning. Religion and spirituality provide a variety of templates for the ordering of individual and collective courses of action, and for culture more generally. Often, religion gives expression to the most cherished or critical moments of social life. Moreover, most major religions have social vision: they wish to see some degree of congruence between social organization and the faith that they espouse.

Typically, the presence of religion within society is characterized by both sacred and social cultivation. Even in faiths where a high doctrine of revelation is claimed, the expression of the spirituality will be social and disseminated. However, it is in national, local or state religions that one can most easily see the complex connectedness between religion and society. For example, occasions such as Remembrance Sunday, Mothering Sunday, Harvest Festival and the celebrations of Christmas and Easter within the Western Christian tradition can be highly flavoured with cultural artefacts that have not originated from within the heart of the religious tradition. Medieval mystery plays, equally, can be nascent spiritual vehicles for pursuing a particular social agenda that is relevant to its cultural context. The popularity of singing carols at Christmas is an example of commonplace spiritual and cultural material being widely used outside the control of mainstream religion.

The etymology of the word 'religion' comes from two Latin words meaning 'to persistently bind together'. Religion, by its very nature, is socially experienced and expressed, and is concerned with having an impact on social realms that are beyond the sacred. Correspondingly, divisions between 'religion' and 'society', although commonplace, are invariably false. This is because religion exists not only in its own right, but is also public, and finds that its materials, sacred truths, stories, images and ideas are part of the wider cultural furniture. Even an apparently innocent phrase such as 'Happy Christmas' bears testimony to this.

In early Christian tradition there was an expectation that religion and society were essentially indivisible. Even in the earliest Christian communities, the expectation that Christ would return soon did not mean the followers of Jesus could become separatist. They were to continue working, paying taxes and ordering their lives as peaceable law-abiding citizens. Moreover, they could also draw on their considerable Jewish heritage, which included an emphasis on prophetic resistance to social injustice. Stephen, the first Christian martyr, had responsibility for presiding over the giving of alms.

Augustine (354–430) wrote about the interdependency between the temporal order and the eternal order in the *City of God*. Several centuries later, Thomas Aquinas (1225–74) also meditated upon the compatibility between heavenly and earthly realms, and between ecclesiastical and civil orders. During the Reformation, John Calvin (1509–64) attempted to order the city of Geneva as a kind of theocracy. In modern times, liberation theologians have attempted to resist social injustice through hermeneutics and praxis, and in so doing have sought to show how the values of the kingdom of God may be brought to bear upon social ordering, economics and human rights. In their way, each of these explorations saw the relationship between religion and society as consisting of the interdependencies between the ideal and the concrete, and sought to find ways to reduce the distance between the two such states.

Theories of religion and society. The discipline of the sociology of religion is, in part, an attempt at categorization – 'establishing normative epochs' for meaning. It concerns itself with describing phenomena in ways that can almost be characterized as commonsensical, creating categories of meaning and knowledge in order to give a 'social' account of what it sees. From the very genesis of sociology, 'religion' has tended to be treated like a 'thing' – an 'object' of scientific analysis – and deconstructed accordingly. Correspondingly, religion is broken down into its (alleged) constituent parts (e.g. sacred–profane), or referred to in functional terms (e.g. 'social legitimization', 'projection'). Like many modernist human sciences, however, it often fails to see *itself* as a construction of reality, social or otherwise. As Catherine Bell points out: 'That we construct "religion" and "science" is not the main problem: that we forget we have constructed them in our own image – that is a problem' (Bell, 1996).

In saying this, Bell reminds us that a 'pure' description of phenomena is not possible. Both the human sciences and theology (or the language of faith) are engaged in an interpretative task, and describe what they see according to the prescribed rules of their grammar of assent. In the case of the sociology of religion, this often tended to assume a humanist-orientated perspective, which has sometimes imagined itself to be 'neutral'. Thus, sociologists described what they saw, while theologians and religious people were said to 'ascribe' meaning to the same phenomena. On the other hand, those who have had spiritual experiences feel that what they experience is 'real', and the sociological account is therefore deemed to be at best complimentary and at worst unrepresentative. Invariably, both approaches forget that 'religion' is something of a complex word with no agreed or specific definition.

The genesis of the problem lies in nineteenth-century approaches to religion. Marx and Feuerbach, among others, distinguished between 'essence' and 'manifestation' in religion. Social, moral and scientific critiques of religion tended to see religion as a 'thing' that could be explained (away) in terms of the applied point of reference. For Durkheim, religion was 'a unified set of beliefs relative to sacred things' (1912). For Marx, it was 'the opium of the people' (1844) – the self-conscious, self-feeling of alienated humanity. For Freud, it was dreams and primal rites that became religious rituals (1939).

Properly speaking, it was Durkheim who first described religion as 'something eminently social' in his *Elementary Forms of the Religious Life* (1912) – regarded as a landmark in both sociological theory and the academic study of religion. Durkheim's main concern was the relationship of the individual to society. He was not concerned merely with isolated intellect, but believed that the order, arrangement and coherence of society derived from minds that were constantly interacting. For him, collective ideals were always socially derived and maintained. Religion thus became associated with collective social orientation.

Similarly, Max Weber was also concerned to discover how cultures are formed. He observed that religious ideas have independent causal significance in systems of social action or processes of social change. He used as his primary example the interdependence between Protestant theology as a motive for action, and the capitalist economic system as the resultant action. In general, argued Weber, religion is an ideology which supplies motivation within society. The economic or social situation of a particular place can be linked historically to the religious ideas that have influenced the people within that place, and may continue to provide legitimization to social arrangements.

Although the contributions of Durkheim and Weber are fundamental in how we have now come to see the relationship between religion and society, other contributors have also added significantly to the debate. In 1912, Ernst Troeltsch (1865–1923), drawing from Weberian theory, differentiated between what he regarded as the two dominant forms of the social organization of religion – church and sect – in his *The Social Teaching of the Christian Churches*. He argued that these distinct forms vary because of their attitude towards society, with churches accepting the social order and lending it credibility, and sects distancing themselves from the socially constructed ways of living.

One of the more important contemporary theorists has been Talcott Parsons (1902–79). In his *The Structure of Social Action* (1937), he details the way in which society exists as a set of institutions beyond the control of each individual, but yet within the grasp of collective human action. Similarly, Thomas Luckmann and Peter L. Berger emphasize 'the social construction of reality', and argue that religion is a collation of human ideals which become infused into a 'sacred canopy' of meaning that provides explanations about existence and the relationship humans have with the world, and with the universe as a whole. Religion, for Berger and Luckmann, does not just exist in the established religious institutions such as churches. Rather, 'invisible religion' (or nascent spirituality?) resides in the symbolic universes of meaning which simultaneously justify social institutions and the ways in which we live our everyday lives, by attributing to them the status of ultimate reality.

Religion and society today. Religion is thoroughly a part of society and cannot be separated out entirely from its context as though there was somehow a pure essence that could be studied. Equally, society takes such a hand in creating and ordering religion that society itself cannot be properly understood without some reflection upon religious ideals and practices. In the wake of the terrorist attacks on September 11th 2001, many cultural commentators have reflected upon the extent to which the destruction of the World Trade Center in New York was an attack on American imperialism or secularism, or, alternatively, a trenchant statement about the defence of militant Islam.

However, what may also be noteworthy are the evocative spiritual responses to such disasters (e.g. Hillsborough, Zeebrugge and other national calamities come to mind). In response to '9/11', many places of worship were filled to overflowing. Countless candles, flowers and tributes were left by 'Ground Zero', often accompanied by heart-rending messages that expressed 'implicit' religious and spiritual sentiments. Even the formal religious acts that were subsequently to memorialize the many dead tended to be more open in their appreciation of 'operant' spirituality than 'official' religious sentiments.

But for those who study secularization, implicit religion, new religious movements and fundamentalism, the reassertion of explicit religion within 'secular' Western society will hardly come as a surprise (implicit or 'invisible' religion having been rejected). While many religious groups are content to accommodate culture within their expression of faith, there are many traditions that resist such moves. In the latter case, the tension between religion and society can become extreme, and occasionally lead to violence. But the majority tradition is one of adaptation. Individuals, communities and societies constantly seek the spiritual in the midst of the apparently secular.

In conclusion, we note three particular issues that focus the study of religion and society and its impact of spirituality for the immediate future. First, globalization appears to lead to an increase in spiritual pluralism. Under such conditions, societies that have been ordered through one particular religion now find themselves having to adjust, and needing to accommodate a range of faiths within the public sphere. This can create some ambiguities, and occasionally can lead to tensions between competing convictions. At this point, society can appear to be less coherent, and may struggle to reconcile some of its religiously funded but implicit values with other more explicit faith claims.

Second, there seems to be little evidence that spirituality is becoming less of a feature within contemporary society. The interest in spirituality – religious and sacred sentiment outside the immediate control of formal religion – has been burgeoning for many years in the Western world. It would seem that in the midst of consumerism and secularization, people are turning more than ever to texts and techniques that inspire and enchant. This appears to result in the continual (if somewhat diffuse) infusion of spirituality at every level of society, suggesting that society, no matter how atomized and incoherent, persists in its quest for sacral meaning amid the everyday reality of mundane modernity.

Third, religion and spirituality continue to thrive in the gaps between the ideal and the real, and between formal and operant religion. At its most visible, religion offers a means for expressing and ordering public grief, celebration and memorialization, at local, national and international levels. It is precisely at the breaking points of human existence that religion lends the strength and vision to society to reconfigure itself, and imagine new beginnings. Religion, in other words, still has the marked capacity to enable society to exceed itself, and in so doing, improve upon the present and build for the future. Religion is that which 'binds' things together; spirituality is its expression. Individuals, ideas, communities and nations, set alongside their pain, grief, hopes, healing and celebration, are brought together in ways that continue to sustain and nourish societies, enabling them to see beyond the immediate and transitory, and catch a glimpse of something timeless and ultimate. Societies, it would appear, have always needed this. But religion not only provides it – it gives birth to the very societies that continue to seek the something that is more than human.

See also **Spirituality and Culture; Spirituality and Social Sciences** (*essays*); **Public Life and Spirituality; Social Justice.**

C. Bell, 'Modernism and postmodernism', *Religious Studies Review* 3 (July 1996), 190–7; R. N. Bellah and P. E. Hammond, *Varieties of Civil Religion*, New York: Seabury Press, 1980; P. Berger, *The Sacred Canopy*, New York: Doubleday, 1967; E. Durkheim, *Elementary Forms of the Religious Life*, London: Allen & Unwin, 1912; Talcott Parsons, *The Structure of Social Action*, McGraw-Hill, 1937; E. Troeltsch, *The Social Teaching of the Christian Churches*, New York: Macmillan, 1912; M. Weber, *The Theory of Social and Economic Organization*, New York: Free Press, 1957.

MARTYN PERCY

Sodalities

see Community; Devotions

Solitude, Solitary Life

see Eremitical Spirituality

Song of Songs

'All the world is not worth the day that the Song of Songs was given to Israel; all the writings (*Kethubim*) are holy but the Song of Songs is the holy of holies' (Mishna Yadaim, 3.5).

This quote reflects the reverence with which the Song of Songs was regarded by the early rabbis. The book itself has generated considerable controversy regarding its literary integrity, its genre and its interpretation. Some scholars contend that it is really an anthology of discrete poems. Today, most maintain that the eight chapters should be interpreted as a unit composed of several different poems.

There are basically four ways that the Song has been interpreted: allegorically; as a cultic re-enactment; as a dramatic performance; and literally. The marriage metaphor characterizing the love relationship between God and Israel (Isa. 54.5; Hos. 2.14–20) or between Christ and the Church (2 Cor. 11.2; Rev. 19.6b–8) provided a precedent for an allegorical interpretation. The vocabulary and suggestion of fertility rituals persuaded others that the Song was influenced by the marriages rites of the gods Damuzi and Inanna (Hebrew Tammuz and Ishtar). Other commentators perceived the basic features of a drama with refrains and choruses. Finally, similarity between these poems and some Egyptian love poems led many to conclude that the Song of Songs is simply erotic lyric poetry.

While the first and preferred method of interpretation of the Bible traditionally has been the literal approach, the opposite has been true with this book. Perhaps the sexual imagery has been too suggestive and has offended the sensitivities of many. This and the fact that God is never mentioned have led some to conclude that the poems were originally secular. Until recently, most commentators presumed that they were not to be understood literally but must possess some concealed religious meaning. One Jewish approach was a kind of historical allegory that recounted Israel's story from the experience of the Exodus to the advent of the Messiah. The Christian allegory was either ecclesiological, describing the relationship between Christ and the Church, tropological with moral implications, or Mariological, seeing the Virgin Mary as the pre-eminent type of the Church.

The history of interpretation shows that the allegorical and/or mystical interpretive approaches lent themselves to a spiritual understanding of the Song of Songs. This is probably because the passionate love between the couple in the Song could be seen as a metaphor of the even more passionate love between God and the individual soul invited to mystical union. In such an interpretation, the amorous imagery, which otherwise might have been too explicit for some, was often muted by being spiritualized. This allowed one to revel in the sensuality of the Song without being overwhelmed by its eroticism.

As early as Origen (*c.* 240 CE), Christians began to read the book with devotional eyes that viewed the relationship described there as a spiritual marriage. This interpretation was endorsed by such influential authors as Gregory of Nyssa, Jerome, Ambrose, Theodoret and Cyril of Alexandria. It took on added significance in the mysticism of the Middle Ages with the writings of Gregory the Great, William of St Thierry, Venerable Bede, Bernard of Clairvaux, as well as the sixteenth-century writers Teresa of Avila and John of the Cross. A comparable spiritual allegorical approach is also found in Jewish writers such as Philo of Alexandria and Maimonides.

When allegory is employed in spiritual interpretations, the nature imagery and exchange between the lovers are read as double entendre, saying one thing but meaning another. In a typological approach, the book is read literally as an account of human love, but a love that is merely a type of the all-encompassing love that God has for humankind. With the advent of critical scholarship, allegorical or typological interpretations have generally given way to literal readings, though these earlier approaches are still widespread among many Protestant Evangelicals and are found within some traditions of spiritual theology. Critical biblical scholarship regards the book as a collection of erotic love poetry that celebrates the passion between a woman and a man. The very eroticism, that prompted interpreters to adopt an allegorical approach, today contributes to a contemporary understanding of the significant role that sensuality plays in a healthy spirituality.

The woman in the Song of Songs is identified as the Shulammite, perhaps the feminine form of the name Solomon (7.1(6.13)). Some commentators refer to her as a girl or a maiden, thus featuring her presumed unmarried state. However, the connotation of youthfulness also suggests immaturity, a trait that conflicts with the book's depiction of the woman. Refuting her brothers' impression of her (8.8), this woman describes herself as full-figured (8.10). Furthermore, she is quite independent of societal restraints, in contrast to women in a traditional patriarchal society. While she may be rather young, this is a mature woman, not a naive girl.

Although the Song is a tribute to mutual love, its focus is the amorous disposition of the woman. Her words open and close the Song and her voice is dominant throughout. Most of the poems of yearning are uttered by her (1.2–4; 2.6; 8.1–3). She is the one who is love sick (2.5; 5.8), longing to follow her beloved (1.4), and she is the one who celebrates their mutual belonging (2.16–17; 6.3). She takes the initiative, seeking him in the privacy of her room (3.1; 5.6b) and in public streets (3.2; 5.7). She seeks to protect their love from public scrutiny, and possible criticism (1.7; 8.1) does not prevent her from venturing out, alone at night, in search of him, even jeopardizing her own safety. She is neither slow to speak erotically (1.2, 4, 13; 3.4) nor embarrassed by the titillating language that the man uses to describe her body (4.5–6; 7.2–10a (1–9a)). It is clear that this woman is driven by love, not inhibited by social opinion nor by some narrow sense of sexual propriety.

The Shulammite's description of the charms of her lover and the pleasures of their lovemaking, though often symbolic, is quite provocative. Her beloved is comely and agile like a young stag, renowned for its sexual prowess (2.8–9, 17; 8.14). She extols the beauty of his body part by part, moving from his head to his thighs (5.10–15). She rhapsodizes about the impassioned delights they experience that intoxicate like wine (1.2; 2.4; 7.10), and about those that can be savoured like luscious fruits (2.3; 4.16; 7.14). She tells how various luxurious aromas enhance the ardour of their passion (1.3, 12–14; 6.2). Sensuous metaphors such as these not only evoke vivid images but can arouse desire as well. This woman is not intimidated by eroticism.

The words of the young man are either in answer to the woman's questions or in dialogue with her. They provide the reader with his perception of her. She is beautiful (1.15; also 2.10b, 13; 4.1, 7; 6.4, 10; 7.7), the fairest among women (1.8; also 5.9; 6.1). No woman can compare with her (2.2; 6.8–10); her beauty is unblemished (4.7). The jewellery that adorns her makes her resplendence rival the most ornate of Pharaoh's chariots (1.9–11). Her eyes have enraptured him (4.9; 6.5), even though they are as gentle and innocent as doves (1.15; 4.1). Every part of her body is enchanting (4.1–5; 6.5b-7; 7.2–6, 8–10a), and her voice is sweet to the ear (2.14). He compares her to a garden that is fruitful yet inaccessible to all but him (4.12–15; 5.1). This man has been smitten by love. His interest in the woman is certainly erotic, but there is no indication that he desires her merely for his own pleasure. This desire is mutual, seeking mutual fulfilment. The woman is not being used; she is being loved.

The Song moves from the experience of intense longing to that of blissful enjoyment, and then to longing once more. The woman seeks her absent lover and finds him, only to seek him again. The lovers are separated from each other, joined in an ecstatic embrace, and then apart once again. This alternation between presence and absence, possession and loss, exhilaration and dejection accurately characterizes the ebb and flow of human love with its various combinations of desire, anticipation and consummation. Everything about this love is mutual. Both the woman and the man move from one emotion to the other. At times she is the initiator, at other times she is reserved. He is variously the object of her search and a forceful suitor. Neither of the lovers has to be cajoled. The tryst is an encounter sought and enjoyed by both lovers.

While the book certainly applauds the glories of lovemaking, more importantly it celebrates the depth of the commitment shared by the woman and man; 8.6–7 has been described as the highpoint of the entire Song. The seals mentioned may refer to amulets with apotropaic powers that were often worn around the neck or on the arm. The Shulammite asks that her lover allow her to be for him just such an amulet, a sign of the love that they share. She maintains that their love possesses a force that can easily rival the power of death and Sheol, the place of death. It can even withstand the chaotic primal and flood waters. Neither death nor chaos is a match for the love that joins these two together. No power from the netherworld and no treasure from this world can compare with the strength and the value of human love.

See also **Spirituality and Scripture** (*essay*); **Carmelite Spirituality; Cistercian Spirituality.**

Dianne Bergant, *Song of Songs: The Love Poetry of Scripture*, Hyde Park, NY: New City Press, 1998; Dianne Bergant, *Song of Songs*, Berit Olam Series, Collegeville, MN: The Liturgical Press, 2001; Marcia Falk, *The Song of Songs*, San Francisco: Harper, 1990; Michael V. Fox, *The Song of Songs and the Ancient Egyptian Love Songs*, Madison, WI: University of Wisconsin Press, 1985; Roland E. Murphy, *The Song of Songs*, Minneapolis, MN: Fortress Press, 1990; Renita Weems, 'Song of Songs' in *The Women's Bible Commentary*, ed. Carol A. Newsom and Sharon H. Ringe, London: SPCK, 1992, pp. 156–60.

DIANNE BERGANT

Soul

The human individual's inherent capacity for selfhood, self-awareness and subjectivity, the principle of human knowing and responsible freedom, has in Christian tradition and much of philosophical history been called 'soul'. Post-Enlightenment authors have used such terms as 'infinite striving' (Lessing), 'self-explication of the Idea' (Hegel), 'the difference between ego and superego' (Freud), 'existentiality' (Jaspers), 'thereness' (Heidegger), 'primordial realization of the future' and 'kernel of existence' (Bloch). Jürgen Moltmann speaks of 'the soul of our life'. 'Our "soul,"' he says, 'is to be found wherever we are utterly given to life, passionately interested and involved' (Moltmann, 1998, p. 12f.). Thinkers have related 'psyche' to 'soul' in vari-

ous ways, including within 'psyche' such powers as emotion and imagination.

However 'soul' may be defined, what is agreed within the Christian tradition is that human beings are spirit as well as flesh. Yet we have no experience at all of this spiritual aspect of ourselves except as rooted in our physicality, in our bodies. The theory of how soul and body, the spiritual and the physical, are joined in the human person has fascinated philosophers and religious thinkers for at least as long as history and literature have been recorded. The practical implications of the question are pivotal to an integrated Christian spirituality.

Christian theology prior to the modern era sought understanding of the question predominantly in Greek philosophy. The explanation for this fact lies to a great extent in the spread of Greek power and culture in the Mediterranean region just prior to the beginning of the Christian era. Greek dominance led to the translation of the Hebrew Scriptures into Greek (the Septuagint), the adoption of current Greek philosophical terminology into that translation and into the Jewish and Christian Scriptures that would follow, and the strong influence of Platonic and Aristotelian reasoning on the interpretation of the Scriptures and on related theological questions for centuries to come.

Plato, building on the work of his master Socrates, argued that the soul (*psyche*) as the principle of life is both pre-existent and immortal. He described the soul as simple, spiritual and divine, though imprisoned for a time in a material body. This soul knows spiritual things (the forms) only through memory from its spiritual pre-existence. It is destined to be released from the material through death and subsequent rebirths and deaths, eventually to become one again with God, with the eternal and unchanging good, true and beautiful.

In Aristotle's thought, the human person is by definition *both* soul and body, not merely, as for Plato, soul imprisoned in and using body. The soul is the form, the 'livingness' of the body. On this concept Thomas Aquinas in the thirteenth century built his presentation of soul as the body's form (*ST* 1.76).

On the question of human immortality, Aquinas departed from Aristotle. In the Aristotelian scheme only the supra-individual world-soul, not the individual soul, is immortal. But because Aquinas defined the soul as an individual spiritual substance, he saw it as capable of living on independently after the body's death. His interpretation has largely shaped Christian theology up to the present in regard to this issue, though the various Christian traditions and individual thinkers within those traditions have in more recent centuries varied in their views regarding the mode of that immortality, especially for the interlude between death and 'the last day'.

Karl Rahner pointed out that treatment of the soul as form ('livingness') of the body is a philosophical approach whose implications would preclude ever dealing with either soul or body independently of the other, in life or in death. If these implications had been fully appreciated by Aquinas himself and by his disciples, he contended, Christian thinking might have been led away from Platonic dualism. But the dualistic emphasis, the dichotomy and even opposition between soul and body characteristic of Platonism and Neoplatonism, in fact prevailed in Christian theology and spirituality until the biblical renewal of the twentieth century converged with post-Cartesian anthropology to bring new insights and raise new questions still unanswered, the latter particularly in regard to individual eschatology.

Biblical understandings. The human person as presented by the Hebrew Scriptures is an undivided unity of flesh and spirit. Two terms are used in Hebrew to refer to the human spirit: *nephesh* and *ruach*.

Nephesh, often inaccurately translated 'soul', is the inner being of the human creature, intimately linked with breath and blood, and seen as the seat of the emotions and passions. Though it springs from the life-breath or spirit (*ruach*) of God, in our flesh (*basar*) it is inherently subject to death. In primitive Semitic thought and in some Hebrew references, *nephesh* is imaged as a kind of diminutive version of the body that escapes in death through the mouth or nostrils or other opening, such as a wound. When God breathes into Adam's nostrils, Adam becomes a 'living *nephesh*' (Gen. 2.7). In death this *nephesh* dies (as in Num. 23.10: 'May my *nephesh* die the death of the just'), and it continues in existence as a 'dead *nephesh*' (as in Num. 6.6, where the Nazirite is not to enter a place where there is a 'dead *nephesh*'). The term can also denote the human individual (as in Gen. 46.18) or the locus of emotion (as in Ps. 42.1).

The reality expressed by the term *ruach* is often very close to that expressed by *nephesh*. However, *ruach* does not have the same physical overtones, though its most literal sense is that of wind or breath. It usually implies intense activity and energy: the life-breath or spirit of God, or the inner strength and vitality of a human being.

These two Hebrew terms passed into the Septuagint and then into the Christian Scriptures as the Greek *psyche* and *pneuma* respectively. But in the Christian Scriptures the centrality of the Pentecostal experience brings about a new coalescence between them. Both are now gathered into a concentration on life in the Spirit of Christ as the only true life.

Psyche in the Christian Scriptures does not carry the physical connotations inherent in the Hebrew *nephesh*. Thus one is cautioned by ancient superstition to guard one's *nephesh* from escape by not sleeping with one's mouth open and to avoid sorceresses who snare *nephashot* in their magic wristbands (Ezek. 13.18). But Jesus proposes that to safeguard one's *psyche*, one must surrender it to God's care (Matt. 6.25) and even be ready to lose it (Matt. 16.25; Mark 8.35; Luke 9.24; John 12.25). Yet it *is* to be safeguarded in this paradoxical way, for it is more precious than the whole world or anything else that might be offered in exchange for it (Matt. 16.26; Mark 8.36f.). *Psyche* is thus intimately associated with the concepts of selfhood and of life that has eternal value.

As with the Hebrew *ruach*, *pneuma* in the Christian Scriptures refers to the human spirit and principle of action as well as to the divine. However, a new complexity is introduced. Though the reference to *basar* ('flesh') in the Hebrew Scriptures implies weakness and mortality in contrast to God's might and eternity, it involves no moral judgement. In the Christian Scriptures, especially in the Pauline and Johannine texts, 'spirit' (*pneuma*) and 'flesh' (*sarx*) come to be morally opposed, and 'flesh' becomes a symbol not simply of weakness and mortality but of legalistic and even sinful obstruction of the Spirit of God. As the Spirit of God (*ruach*) had rushed upon David and entered into the prophets, so the Spirit (*pneuma*) comes upon Jesus at his baptism, is given to the disciples when Jesus breathes on them after the resurrection, and fills them at Pentecost according to Jesus' promise. Thereafter the Christian is to live no longer as *sarx* (nor even merely as *psyche*) but as *pneuma*, in the very specific sense of living according to the holy Spirit of God in Jesus. It is to be stressed that 'flesh' and 'spirit' are not opposed here in a dualistic sense of body and soul; their opposition in early Christian thought as expressions of human non-response or response to God's Spirit continues to assume the Hebrew view of the human being as indivisibly body and spirit.

The human person: physical and spiritual. Neither the Hebrew nor the Christian Scriptures attempt a philosophical analysis of human nature, and such an analysis should not be read out of either the Hebrew/Aramaic or Greek terminologies as used there. The Bible does witness to a view of the human person as a being at once bodily and spiritual, and different generations of biblical writers wrestled in their own contexts with the meaning of that reality. There is, however, no biblical base for the dichotomy between soul and body that very early began to characterize Christian thinking under the influence of Platonism. In this respect, modern anthropology is nearer to biblical thought than the intervening nineteen centuries of Christian tradition.

Human experience of the spiritual is derived only through bodily behaviour. We cannot even think about the spiritual without language, which in turn is utterly dependent upon physical experience. An entirely independent reality known as 'soul' can no more exist than a purely mechanical, unconsciously acting body can. Whatever may be the form of human immortality, it must somehow ultimately encompass both the spiritual and the physical aspects of one's individual being; it cannot be simply a matter of 'saving one's soul'. And while one lives in time, an integrated spirituality cannot address the soul without addressing bodiliness as essential to humanness and holiness. Pauline and Johannine themes of opposition between 'spirit' and 'flesh' need to be reclaimed in their original intent, rescued from a flawed tradition that identified 'flesh' with everything physical rather than with all that is not filled with, and driven by, the Spirit of God. After all, the same letter to the Romans that develops the spirit–flesh opposition sings of the redemption of all creation in freedom.

See also **Afterlife; Body and Spirituality; Dualism; Interiority; Johannine Spirituality; Neoplatonism; Pauline Spirituality; Person.**

Daniel A. Helminiak, *Religion and the Human Sciences: An Approach via Spirituality*, Albany, NY: State University of New York Press, 1998; Jürgen Moltmann, *Is There Life after Death?* Milwaukee, WI: Marquette University Press, 1998; W. Pannenberg, *Anthropology in Theological Perspective*, Philadelphia, PA: Westminster Press, 1985; Anton Pegis, *Saint Thomas and the Problem of the Soul in the Thirteenth Century*, Toronto: Pontifical Institute of Medieval Studies, 1983.

SUZANNE NOFFKE

Space

see **Place**

Spirit, Holy

The Holy Spirit is fundamental to a Christian understanding of spirituality. Indeed, formally and properly, spirituality does not in the first place concern the experiences of the human spirit itself, or even the expression of religious belief in piety and practice, but rather the effect of the divine Spirit on individual and corporate life. When St Paul referred to the *pneumatikos*, the 'spiritual', his mind was on the activity and presence of the Holy Spirit in and among God's people. His attention was not on the fulfilment of the human spirit through religious practice but on the impact of God's life on human life. Paul and other New Testament writers were drawing on a rich Jewish inheritance in which the Spirit of God was seen as *God in action* in the world and *God present* with his people: creating and sustaining all things, choosing and shaping a covenant people, inspiring and equipping agents and leaders for his purposes and, through them, promising a future in which God's power would be unmistakably present, and his activity fully manifested in a redeemed creation. The life and death of Jesus Christ, followed by his resurrection and by the outpouring of the Spirit, convinced a small but remarkably significant proportion of first-century Jews that the reign of God, promised through the Spirit, had begun in an anticipatory way among them. The evidence was before their eyes in the presence and activity of God *through the Spirit* in Christian communities and people. The day of the Lord had arrived: God was dwelling with his people.

Hence, although it was some three hundred years before the Holy Spirit was credally defined at the Council of Constantinople as 'the Lord, the giver of life', the logic of the classical Christian confession of the divinity of the Spirit was implicit in early Christian conviction. The Spirit is not merely a means by which God affects the created world but is the very life-giving presence of God in and to the world. The same creed went on to set the Spirit's identity within a fully trinitarian understanding of God's being, stating that the Holy Spirit 'proceeds from the Father' and 'with the Father and the Son, is worshipped and glorified'. Later the Western Church added 'Filioque' to the creed, claiming that the Spirit proceeds from the Father 'and the Son'. Although the Eastern Church continues to disagree on the propriety of the insertion, Western and Eastern Christians agree that the Spirit is both *deserving* of worship and *dedicated* to the mission of the Father to redeem the world through the coming of the Son. The Spirit, therefore, though fully divine in status, is often described as 'self-effacing', because the ministry of the Spirit is to make known the face of the Father revealed in the face of Christ, and to fulfil the ministry of the Son by drawing humanity into a reconciled relationship with God within a renewed created order.

Paradoxically, therefore, while the Spirit is fundamental to spirituality, the Spirit is not the focus of spirituality. This makes the work of the Spirit difficult to describe. Attempts to do so often make use of the images, such as fire, water, wind and dove, that the Bible uses to allude to the presence of the Spirit. An alternative method, and one more likely to preserve the personal identity of the Spirit, is to explore some of the titles that Scripture gives to the Spirit. For example, the Holy Spirit is called the *Spirit of life* (Rom. 8.1). The creative work of the Spirit in bringing life into being and maintaining its existence is the basis of all spirituality. Life itself is a gift of God's Spirit and all forms of life have a spiritual quality because they are dependent on God's decision to create through the Spirit's power.

The Spirit is also the *promised Holy Spirit* (Eph. 1.13), the one to be given fully and extensively in the future which the triune God is preparing for the world. The eschatological Spirit, the Spirit of God's future, is intimately involved in the perfecting of creation and in the bringing forward of the character and conditions of the future into the present. Every example of good being chosen, evil thwarted and of justice, peace and mercy being yearned for, is evidence of the Spirit's work in human life and, therefore, of genuine spirituality.

However, Christian sense can only be made of the life-giving and world-perfecting work of the Spirit by an understanding of the Spirit as the *Spirit of Christ* (Phil. 1.19). As Irenaeus put it, God creates by the two hands of the Word and the Spirit. The Word becomes incarnate through the overshadowing of the Spirit, proclaims the good news of the kingdom through the anointing of the Spirit, offers himself up in death through the Spirit and is raised to life by the power of the Spirit. Sent by the ascended Christ, the Spirit continues the messianic ministry of Jesus in the Church and, with the whole of the created order, strains for the consummation of salvation in the recreation of earth and heaven and in the manifestation of the children of God as joint-heirs with Christ. In other words, the promised Holy Spirit has been poured out through the eschatological event of Jesus Christ, manifesting, in the present, the life of the age to come. Where the character of Christ is seen, the values of Christ affirmed and the actions of Christ performed, there the Spirit is to be found, shaping spirituality. But the Spirit's work is supremely evident in lives which have become identified with Christ through faith and baptism,

solidarity with his people and commitment to his mission.

As the Spirit of Christ, the Holy Spirit is also the *Spirit of truth* (John 16.13). Each individual search for truth and every truth-seeking community is marked by the Spirit of the one who came to bring us the truth that will set us free. Education is liberation and the Spirit is the divine educator who leads us into all truth by searching out all things, even the depths of God, and revealing them to us (1 Cor. 2.1–13). The fullest truth about God, according to the gospel, is the passionate grace of the cross of Christ in which humanity has been remade and evil overcome. The Spirit's work is to unfold the meaning of Christ's cross – and everything that surrounded it – and to impress upon the world its implications for human life.

The Spirit is also the *Spirit of fellowship* (2 Cor. 13.13), the one who brings us into relation with others and into relation with God. Human friendships and families, communities and societies, networks and nations which display love for the other, demonstrate the activity of the Spirit binding people together in covenantal ties. The spirituality of covenantal love is perfectly expressed in the Triune life of fellowship, a pattern of participative existence which the Spirit seeks to embed in human life by drawing us to the life that Christ lives before the Father. Hence, the fellowship that the Spirit brings does not annihilate difference but, rather, intensifies distinctiveness. The Spirit leads us to the freedom to be the particular people God wants us to be. However, the Spirit reveals this personal identity by bringing us into interdependent relationships with others in which we recognize that the different gifts we have been given by the Spirit are given for the common good (1 Cor. 12.7). This is why the community of the Church is described as 'God's temple', where the Holy Spirit dwells (1 Cor. 3.16). Here, the followers of Christ are to experience the life-giving presence of the Spirit in lives lived together (bound by a common baptism) and which receive the empowerment of the Spirit through each other (in the fellowship and ministry of the eucharistic community).

The most common name for the Spirit in the New Testament is the *Holy Spirit* – the sanctifying Spirit by whom we are made holy. The deep instinct in many forms of spirituality for moral transformation is the result of the Holy Spirit's action on the human spirit awakening an awareness of the divine goodness and of human failing. The abiding attractiveness of Jesus to those both in and beyond the Church has much to do with the self-evident holiness of his life. The ministry of the Holy Spirit, from whom Christ was born, in whom Christ lived and died, and by whom Christ was raised from the dead, includes transforming people and communities in Christlike ways so that with him, 'pure in heart', they may see God (Matt. 5.8; Heb. 12.14).

The effect of the divine Spirit on the human spirit is most profoundly seen in the area of prayer and worship. Rather than devotions which we do as ways of relating to God, they are our response to the prior activity and presence of God in the world and, accordingly, they are both initiated by the Spirit of God, and performed through the Spirit of God in us, as we allow ourselves to be drawn into the divine life of love and to share in the triune conversation of joy.

See also **Charismatic Spirituality; Communion/** *Koinonia*; **Holiness; Pentecostal Spirituality; Presence of God; Quaker Spirituality; Sanctification; Shaker Spirituality; Trinity and Spirituality.**

Gary D. Badcock, *Light of Truth and Fire of Love: A Theology of the Holy Spirit*, Grand Rapids, MI: Eerdmans, 1997; Yves Congar, *I Believe in the Holy Spirit* 1, London: Geoffrey Chapman, 1983; Gordon Fee, *God's Empowering Presence: The Holy Spirit in the Letters of Paul*, Peabody, MA: Hendrickson, 1994; John McIntyre, *The Shape of Pneumatology: Studies in the Doctrine of the Holy Spirit*, Edinburgh: T & T Clark, 1997; Thomas A Smail, *The Giving Gift: The Holy Spirit in Person*, London: Hodder & Stoughton, 1988; John V. Taylor, *The Go-Between God: The Holy Spirit and Christian Mission*, London: SCM Press, 1972.

CHRISTOPHER COCKSWORTH

Spiritual Conversation

This mutual self-revelation focuses on the reverent disclosure of the deeper realities of two or more people's lives. Like all authentic dialogue, spiritual conversation presupposes trust, acceptance and a desire to learn from one another. When this kind of dialogue takes place within a context of faith, the participants also encounter something of God's existential word. Therefore, the subject matter of spiritual conversation is rich and includes, for example, reflections about how one finds God in the everyday realities of life, of one's personal search for meaning and authenticity, of one's struggles and graces, of one's sinfulness and forgiveness, of the enduring significance of the life and death of Christ, of the challenges of living an authentic spiritual life in an age of cynicism and doubt.

Such conversation can characterize the rela-

tionship between two old friends or a long-standing faith-sharing group. But it can also emerge more spontaneously, as a grace of the moment, a gift of needed disclosure and acceptance. What is crucial is that such exchanges be honoured with a confidentiality and reserve. What people disclose in spiritual conversation ought to remain in the context of the trusted couple or group. No one should be compelled to share his or her life. True spiritual conversation must be free and, ultimately, liberating.

The deeply religious opportunity within such spiritual conversation is suggested in the encounter between Moses and the Lord, speaking 'face to face, as one speaks to a friend' (Ex. 33.11), and in the final discourse of Jesus in John 17. To engage in true spiritual conversation is to imitate something that is divine and holy. For this reason there is a long tradition that describes prayer as conversation between the man and woman who seeks the very face of God and the God who responds. Such prayerful conversations are moments both of revelation as God opens himself to the person in prayer and of surrender as the man or woman in prayer allows, as it were, the divine to be at home in one's heart. This intimate prayer or colloquy is the touchstone of Ignatian prayer.

Within the Christian community spiritual conversation can contribute to the context for spiritual direction, fraternal government in religious communities, and deepening friendship among apostolic workers. Clearly the adaptation of spiritual conversation to these areas of church life needs to be done prudently and authentically. For example, while some spiritual direction can be mutual, the finality in spiritual direction is not mutual sharing but discerning guidance in prayer, life and service. Generally in a spiritual direction environment one of the participants is the pastoral and spiritual leader, while the other seeks help. It is not strictly based on mutual self-revelation. Similarly in fraternal governance the service of the superior or community leader is to lead and, therefore, there is again no expectation of mutual revelation. While it would be helpful for apostolic colleagues to share deeply their spiritual and religious ideals, and there may be occasions when such exchanges offer rich opportunities for growth, there must be a prudent and respectful willingness to allow all the participants to share only as they wish and when they wish. Finally, in this age of heightened diversity but also of a genuine searching for ways to bridge religious, philosophical and even spiritual divisions, disciplined but authentic spiritual conversation can also be a powerful opportunity for ecumenical growth and co-operation.

See also **Attentiveness; Direction, Spiritual; Friendship; Hospitality; Ignatian Spirituality.**

Thomas H. Clancy, *The Conversational Word of God*, St Louis, MO: Institute of Jesuit Sources, 1978; J. Peter Schineller, 'Conversation in Christian life and ministry' in *Ministerial Spirituality and Religious Life*, ed. John M. Lozano, Chicago, IL: 1986, pp. 91–116; Sandra M. Schneiders, *The Revelatory Text: Interpreting the New Testament as Sacred Scripture*, 2nd edn, Collegeville, MN: The Liturgical Press, 1999; David Tracy, *Dialogue with the Other: The Inter-Religious Dialogue*, Louvain: Peeters Press/Grand Rapids, MI: Eerdmans, 1990.

HOWARD GRAY

Spirituals

An extensive body of song transmitted in oral folk traditions arising principally in American revivals in the eighteenth and nineteenth centuries. There are two streams of spirituals, referred to simply as 'white' and 'black'. White spirituals originated as folk hymns and ballads appearing first in the religious revivals of the early eighteenth century (the 'Great Awakening' of the 1740s) and then in the ensuing 'camp-meeting spirituals' of the frontier. Black, or negro spirituals as they became known, had origins in the experience of slavery among peoples of African descent. While there are distinct differences in texts, melodic lines and performance styles, there is clear evidence of mutual influence between these two categories of the spiritual.

Texts of the early white spirituals were intensely personal religious expressions, with strong imagery drawn from Scripture and individual experience. In contrast to the hymns of Watts and the metrical psalm tradition, the texts of these spiritual songs were free from doctrinal constraints, and served as testimony and witness to conversion. For example, James Davenport, an early Separatist evangelist, published this text in 1742: 'Come and taste along with me/ Consolation running free/From my Father's wealthy throne/Sweeter than the honeycomb.' Some of the early tunes to which these texts were sung bear strong resemblances to secular folk tunes from the British Isles, while others are by known early American composers such as Jeremiah Ingalls, whose *The Christian Harmony* (1805) is the first source of such tunes.

The camp-meetings – outdoor protracted religious gatherings – produced spiritual songs that expressed evangelical fervour in very simple and often repetitive lines. Most of these employed refrains and tag lines such as 'Glory hallelujah!' inserted between lines of known hymns by Watts and Wesley. Baptists and Methodists of the early nineteenth century were known for enthusiastic singing of such styles, as in 'Where, O where are the Hebrew Children? (sung three times)/Safe in the promised land'. The spirituality of these songs was often orientated toward heaven, or toward the time of individual conversion, salvation and judgement. Many of the white spirituals were published in collections, mostly in a series of tune books used in 'singing schools'. Among the most famous are the *Kentucky Harmony* (1816), *The Southern Harmony* (1835) and the shape-note 'bible' of B. F. White and E. J. King called *The Sacred Harp* (1847).

African-American spirituals carry the profound emotional import of human suffering, ecstatic hope and deep yearning for freedom. This internationally prized stream of spirituals constitutes the largest body of distinctively American folksong, numbering well into the thousands. The classical black spiritual was forged in the convergence of African heritages of song and ritual and the encounter with Christianity under the conditions of slavery. Some of these are directly traceable to plantation work songs among slaves, while others spring from improvizational forms in worship gatherings. Some of the tunes may have been composed by particular folk musicians, but nearly all of them remain unknown. The rhythmic complexity and characteristic vocalization patterns of these spirituals reflect both lamentation and praise, the latter traceable to dancing ritual contexts of the 'ring shout', found in slave gatherings for worship. While the exchange between black and white traditions is well known, the indelible crucible of captivity yearning for freedom marks the distinctive depth of spirituality in black spirituals.

The explicit Christian images of the passion of Christ are reflected in well-known examples of the laments: 'Were you there when they crucified my Lord?' and 'Nobody knows the trouble I've seen'. Images of death and exile are present in such spirituals as 'Sometimes I feel like a motherless child'. While lament and sorrow are present, these songs often carried double meanings, encoding under religious imagery specific messages not recognizable to the slave owners. So 'Steal away to Jesus' spoke also of getting to freedom in the North. The biblical images of 'Beulah land' or of 'Canaan' became bearers of more than hope for heaven – code phrases for escape. One can hear this in 'Swing low, sweet chariot, comin' for to carry me home'. Other biblical images are used as protest, as in 'Go down,

Moses'. When the line 'tell ole Pharoah to let my people go' is sung, more than the children of Israel is being signified. These elements of protest and codes of hope make the African-American spiritual especially durable and accessible to other peoples in oppression and captivity. Out of these texts and many of the tunes came the powerful 'freedom song' traditions which animated the Civil Rights Movement of the twentieth century.

Black spirituals have supplied composers and arrangers with a rich set of resources for choral work. Beginning with the Fisk Jubilee Singers in the late nineteenth and early twentieth centuries, an international repertoire of these beloved songs has encircled the globe. Spirituals will continue to express a depth of spiritual yearning, biblical lament and praise, and joyous affirmation of freedom as new generations discover these treasures of text and music, and new composers continually return to the deep wells of inspiration they contain.

See also **African-American Spirituality; Hymns and Spirituality; Music and Spirituality.**

Buell E. Cobb, *The Sacred Harp: A Tradition and Its Music*, Athens: University of Georgia Press, 1989; James H. Cone, *The Spirituals and the Blues: An Interpretation*, Maryknoll, NY: Orbis Books, 1991; George Pullen Jackson, *White and Negro Spirituals*, New York: Augustin, 1943; John Lovell Jr, *Black Song: The Forge and the Flame*, New York: Macmillan, 1972; Eileen Southern, *The Music of Black Americans*, 2nd edn, New York: Norton, 1983.

DON E. SALIERS

Sport and Spirituality

Sport involves the participation of an individual or team in what is usually a competitive game, but also extends beyond competition to include participation in recreational athletics. What distinguishes games that fall under the category of sport, from a game like chess, is that while chess requires investment of the mind in terms of strategy, participation in sport rests on the physical performance of the human body. Participation in the Summer/Winter Olympic Games and/or football's World Cup are often acknowledged as the highest examples of sporting achievement for athletes and spectators alike across the world.

The relationship between sport and spirituality can be illuminated on a number of levels, but is also a relatively new topic for the field. In his 1976 *The Joy of Sports*, Michael Novak explores sports as a religion in its own right. The intense

passion, love and excitement he experienced while watching a game or in following a particular team compelled him to probe a number of issues in this anthology, including: why and how sports capture him so completely, in body, mind and spirit; what significance these feelings hold in terms of religion and spirituality; and a defence of play as a legitimate topic of intellectual enquiry. Novak describes the sports fan as a kind of religious believer, whose faith, love and ritual participation in relation to a team operates at the same level as any organized tradition, only without official recognition on a religious level. He urges readers not to overlook the role of 'the spirit' as we play and watch sports.

Whether spectator or participant, the same intense emotion and total physical and mental engagement described by Novak that is often associated with athletics has led others to suggest that sports and mystical experience are connected. In *Flow: The Psychology of Optimal Experience*, Csikszentmihalyi describes 'flow' as an 'optimal', epiphany-like experience where a person becomes 'lost' or totally immersed in a particular task or situation, in a manner similar to a mystic who becomes momentarily immersed or unified with the divine. Csikszentmihalyi suggests the physical challenges that athletics present to the human body create the necessary conditions that spark a flow experience. Michael Murphy and Rhea White's *In the Zone: Transcendent Experience in Sports* expresses similar sentiments about the relationship between mysticism and athletics. Like William James's *The Varieties of Religious Experience*, through discussions with athletes from a range of sports, Murphy and White relay the various qualities of detachment, ecstasy, surrender, mystery and awe described in interviews as evidence of the 'mystical sensations' prominent across athletic experience.

In addition to sports and mysticism, interest in the relationship between sports and the experience of ritual, symbol, religious metaphor and culture, as well as faith, are popular topics in contemporary dialogue. A recent issue of *The Living Light* was devoted entirely to 'Sports as Religious Education', exploring participation in athletics (as player and/or spectator) as integral to the moral development and faith lives of both youths and adults. Several articles suggest that through athletics humans experience rhythms similar to the liturgical cycle, sporting events as similar to the ritual of Mass, as well as extraordinary examples of faith and the human spirit, providing religious metaphors and resources worthy of great attention by religious educators.

With regard to women in particular, the passage of Title IX in 1972 in the United States, a policy that established the right to equal participation among women and men in sports teams at schools and institutions of higher education, has opened new doors to younger generations of women and their potential for spiritual experience and growth through athletics in the ways mentioned above. As the first generation of women to benefit from Title IX reaches adulthood, today young girls share with boys the opportunity to experience the body in the unique forum that athletics provides, as well as aspire to various female sporting icons like soccer star Mia Hamm, a privilege formerly reserved almost exclusively for boys and men. The famous sporting company Nike, named after the Greek goddess Nike, the goddess of (athletic) victory, has engaged in extensive outreach regarding the relationship between girls and women, their bodies, identity and sports, even launching a website: www.nikegoddess.com

While investigating the importance of sport in relation to spirituality in general may be a relatively young area, the topic of women, sport and spirituality in particular has tremendous potential, since the women who have benefited from the opportunity to participate in sports are just now coming of age. Spirituality, a field that privileges experience as foundational for understanding the divine, will benefit greatly as research into the experience of sport is developed, particularly as younger generations seek alternative forums in which to understand the spiritual life, and a generation of women for the first time experience athletics as an integral part of growing up.

See also **Body and Spirituality; Leisure.**

Mihaly Csikszentmihalyi, *Flow: The Psychology of Optimal Experience*, New York: Harper-Perennial, 1990; Robert J. Higgs, *God in the Stadium: Sports and Religion in America*, Lexington, KY: University Press of Kentucky, 1995; Tara Magdalinski and Timothy John Lindsay Chandler, *With God on Their Side: Sport in the Service of Religion*, New York: Routledge, 2002; Bernard L. Marthaler (ed.), 'Special feature: sports as religious education', *The Living Light* 9.2 (Winter 2002); Michael Murphy and Rhea A. White, *In the Zone: Transcendent Experience in Sports*, New York: Penguin/Arkana, 1995; Michael Novak, *The Joy of Sports: End Zones, Bases, Baskets, Balls, and the Consecration of the American Spirit*, New York: Basic Books, 1976; Susan Saint Sing, *Spirituality of Sport: Balancing Body and Soul*, Cincinnati, OH: St Anthony Messenger Press, 2004.

DONNA FREITAS

Stability

In the context of Christian spirituality, 'stability' refers primarily to the monastic, and especially the Benedictine, practice of perseverance in a particular community and in one's commitment to seeking God through that community's monastic practices. In its larger usage it can refer to any analogous perseverance to a particular Christian vocation and practice.

Stability has its roots in the Jewish and Christian Scriptures, although key biblical themes would seem to militate against it. Christ's own earthly ministry was one of journeying from place to place, and his mandate to the apostles to go and preach to all nations would seem to imply a very itinerant model for gospel living; hence the missionary model of the monks of Ireland and Syria, and the later apostolic congregations of the Roman Catholic and Anglican Churches.

But very early on, the domestic churches offered the example of a more stable living of the gospel. And at the deeper level, stability finds its ground in the central gospel affirmation of God's persevering covenant fidelity and love. God is faithful to us, and calls us to abide always in that love: 'Abide in me as I abide in you. Just as the branch cannot bear fruit by itself unless it abides in the vine, neither can you unless you abide in me . . . abide in my love' (John 15.4, 9). Thus Christians are to remain 'steadfast in the faith, without shifting from the hope promised by the gospel' (Col. 1.23); they are to be 'rooted and grounded in love' (Eph. 3.17). Following this theme, Cyprian and other Fathers stressed the need to remain stable in the faith until death.

One emphasis of the desert tradition had to do with stability: 'Sit in your cell and your cell will teach you everything.' A particularly radical form of this stability was lived by the stylites. Basil decreed that the monk who had committed himself to a monastery should not leave, except in the case of service to the Church or because the monastic community had lost its spirit. The Councils of Chalcedon (451) and Nicea II (787) echoed this decree. The first translation into Latin of the *Life of Antony* rendered the Greek term for firmness or tranquility of spirit (*katastasis*) as 'stability' (*stabilitas*). Perseverance in the cell, and more generally in the place one has settled, is recommended in Cassian's *Conferences*, which conclude with this point (*Conferences* 24.3–7). In the Rule of the Master, stability is mentioned in the introductory materials to the rite of profession, and in the conclusion (RM 89).

Stability finds a special place and emphasis in the Rule of St Benedict, as the first of the three 'promises' which the professing monk is to make: 'When he is to be received, he comes before the whole community in the oratory and promises stability, fidelity to monastic life (*conversatio morum*), and obedience' (RB 58). St Benedict draws from the Rule of the Master and from Basil and the currents of the Egyptian tradition noted above in requiring his monks to stay in the monastery except for necessary journeys (RB 50–1; 67). St Benedict was particularly appalled by gyrovague monks 'who spend their entire lives drifting from region to region, staying as guests for three or four days in different monasteries. Always on the move, they never settle down, and are slaves to their own wills and gross appetites' (RB 1). The Rule does not condemn all journeying monks (and thus the *monachi peregrini* – RB 61), nor does it exclude monks being sent out for a particular task (RB 51; 67); and it directs that 'all absent brothers should always be remembered at the closing prayer of the Work of God' (RB 67). But St Benedict certainly calls his own monks basically to persevere 'in the monastery until death' (RB Prologue), in fidelity to God's call and in faithfulness to the monastic family. Thus the conclusion of the chapter on the 'Tools of Good Works': 'The workshop where we are to toil faithfully at all these tasks is the enclosure of the monastery and stability in the community' (RB 4). But Benedict is implicitly open to passage of a monk to another monastery and explicitly allows transfer to the eremitical life (RB 1). Thus, Benedict legislates for 'stability of place', but not in an absolute way, and the essential is always 'stability of heart' to the larger monastic family and to the regular monastic observance. The stable bond of union of the brethren is Christ himself, and their ongoing hope is that he will bring them 'all together to everlasting life' (RB 72).

A splendid witness to Benedictine stability is the Venerable Bede, foremost scholar in Scripture and history of Anglo-Saxon England, who entered monastic life as an oblate at the age of seven, at Wearmouth, and shortly after was transferred to the foundation of Jarrow in 682, where he persevered over fifty years until his death in 735. He loved the monastic rhythm and studies, and that stability sustained his 'special delight: always to learn, to teach, and to write'.

St Romuald (d. 1027), father of the Camaldolese Benedictines, who practised 'stability of heart' if not 'stability of place', as he journeyed throughout Italy to found and renew monasteries and hermitages, teaches in the desert tradition the substance of the spirituality of stability as he urges in his Short Rule: 'Sit in your cell as in paradise . . . Above all realize that you are in

God's presence; hold your heart there in wonder as if before your sovereign.' Since God is present in one's dwelling and one's community, one need not search for God elsewhere.

St Peter Damian (d. 1072), disciple of the Romualdian reform, enriched the theology of Christian stability, teaching that where even one Christian is, there the whole Church resides. Thus stability, even in a hermit cell, cuts the monk off from none of the Christian community.

Another model of stability is Julian of Norwich (*c*. 1342–after 1416), who lived for years the enclosed life of an anchoress, in a cell adjoining a parish church in Norwich. In a tumultuous time of plague, war and social unrest, from her stable solitude she was able to assure us that 'all will be well and all will be well and all manner of thing will be well' (*Showings* 27, long text). The anchorite form of monastic living, rooted in early Christianity, was more formalized in the Middle Ages, with the bishop himself permanently enclosing the anchorite within the cell. The Ancren(e) Rule is an early thirteenth-century expression of this particularly intense form of stability.

A later great witness to stability is Brother Lawrence of the Resurrection, whose 'practice of the presence of God' has inspired Catholics and Protestants alike to discover God in the immediate here and now and to remain in that presence. Brother Lawrence's own life expressed his fidelity to this practice, and he lived over fifty years in the Paris Carmelite monastery he first entered, until his serene death in 1691.

The more recent institutes founded after Trent with simple vows often included the vow of stability, not to a particular place or community but to the congregation.

T. S. Eliot writes of 'the still point of the turning world' (*Four Quartets*). Christian stability wants to be there. It can be argued that Christian stability is particularly needed, and urgently so, in our own restless, rootless age, where commitments are very fragile and conditional, and the first response to difficulty can be to 'up sticks' and move on elsewhere. Whatever be the Christian vocation, we are all certainly called to 'stability of heart', to abide faithfully in God's persevering love.

See also **Benedictine Spirituality; Camaldolese Spirituality; Cistercian Spirituality; Desert; Monasticism.**

M. Lohrer, 'Towards a meaning of monastic stability', *Benedictine Confluence* 3 (1970), pp. 4–8; J. McMurry, 'Monastic stability', *Cistercian Studies* 1 (1966), pp. 209–24; A. Roberts, 'The meaning of the vow of stability', *Collectanea*

Cisterciensia 33 (1971), pp. 257–69; G. Rocca, J. Rezac and A. de Vogue, 'Stabilita', *Dizionario degli Istituti de Perfezione* 9, Roma: Edizioni Pauline, 1997, pp. 106–16; A. Wathan, '"Conversatio" and stability in the Rule of Benedict', *Monastic Studies* 2 (1957), pp. 1–44.

ROBERT HALE

Staretz

Staretz or starets is the Russian equivalent of the Greek term *geron*, elder. Such elders – spiritual guides – were to be found in the early monastic world. But they were not necessarily ordained or even tonsured in order to perform their role. It was a role which came to obviate or supplement the predetermined structures of their church. In the absence of a generally accepted method by which elders were selected, it was the individual who gravitated to the elder of his choice. The elder offered spiritual insight, counsel and support.

Support might well depend on more than words with all their limitations. When Antony the Great (*c.* 251–*c.* 356) asked a monk why he never posed a single question on his annual visits, he received the answer, 'It is enough for me to see you, father'. The very presence of the elder could offer inspiration. All the more might Antony attract adherents such as this, since he had earlier lived in prayerful isolation. His followers could hope to gain from this experience when he made himself available once more. It was a pattern of return which was to be repeated by elders of the centuries to come. Spiritual guidance by the elder of one's choice was to be most favoured in the Orthodox milieu.

The spoken or the written word, often aphoristic, was also influential in conveying insights to the seeker. Not that such teaching was invariably intended for the world at large. 'My advice to you is fashioned according to your inner and outer circumstances,' wrote Makarii of Optino (1788–1860). 'Hence they can be right only for you.' Such fine-tuning of the Christian message was valued by his correspondents.

The role of an elder did not coincide with that of a confessor. Formal confessions would be encouraged. But an elder might prefer a follower to venture on a comprehensive revelation of his thoughts in order to achieve a better understanding of his person. Such a revelation had to be a willing contribution. According to a Russian elder of the early Soviet period, Aleksei Mechev (1859–1923), it was itself a mark of maturation, and could bear much fruit. Mechev was familiar with elders of the Russian monastery at Optino, where daily revelations were encouraged as part

and parcel of monastic life. Here was a practice which had ancient roots. It was familiar to sixth-century masters.

While an elder might guide dependants in a variety of ways, it was Hesychastic prayer which demanded his involvement most of all. The postures and exertions which involved practioners in the pursuit of inner prayer needed to be supervised for fear of damaging their equilibrium. Such was the insistence of Theophan the Recluse (1815–94), and of elders like him.

The eighteenth-century revival of Hesychastic prayer, marked by the publication of *The Philokalia* (1782), made new demands on elders. Paisii Velichkovskii (1722–94) translated *The Philokalia* into Slavonic: he encouraged followers of his to have recourse to elders. Such was his reputation that many were to heed him. Paisii was to work from Niamets in Moldavia.

Optino was among the monasteries most obviously affected by him. In due course, its community determined that it would appoint a single elder at a given time. Unusual decision that it was, it needed to be validated by the local bishop. The monastery was to house a remarkable sequence of elders until its closure by the Soviet authorities in 1923. This included Makarii Ivanov (1788–1860) and Amvrosii Grenkov (1812–91). Amvrosii was unwontedly to draw additional attention to the elders since he served as a model for Dostoevsky's romanticized starets Zosima in *The Brothers Karamazov* (1879–80). Hence the popular belief that elderdom was most of all at home on Russian soil.

The Optino elders served as consultants to all who came their way. The same is true of Seraphim of Sarov (1759–1833). After years of seclusion (1810–25), this humble monk opened his doors to anyone who wished to see him (1825–33).Though an individual's contact with the elder might be limited to seconds, it was believed that these could link him with the very source of grace. If people were unable to make the arduous pilgrimage to an Amvrosii or a Seraphim, the literate among them could be served by correspondence. Seraphim wrote little, but Amvrosii's correspondence was voluminous, as was that of his predecessor, Makarii. Another elder, Theophan the Recluse was inaccessible to visitors by choice. But his correspondence was wide-ranging, penetrating and perceptive. He continued a tradition of the distant past. The letters of two reclusive monks of the early sixth century, John and Varsanuphius, were addressed to monastics and laity alike.

In modern times, persecution of religion under Soviet rule would often separate an elder from his flock – hence another need for correspondence. Should he be imprisoned, this necessarily aligned him with those who were in urgent need of succour and support. It was a ministry for which the elder Tavrion Batozskii (1898–1978) remained profoundly grateful. Tavrion survived decades of penal exile and of prison camps. Later he was visited by thousands. It was a different kind of 'return'.

See also **Hesychasm; Jesus Prayer; Orthodox Spirituality;** *Philokalia;* **Russian Spirituality.**

Primary sources: Barsanuphe et Jean de Gaza, *Correspondence,* trans. Lucien Regnault et al., Solesmes, 1972; Chariton of Valamo, *The Art of Prayer: An Orthodox Anthology,* trans. E. Kadloubovsky and E. M. Palmer, ed. Timothy Ware, London: Faber and Faber, 1966; Macarius starets of Optino, *Russian Letters of Direction 1834–1860,* ed. and trans. Iulia de Beausobre, London: 1944.

Secondary sources: J. Dunlop, *Staretz Amvrosy: Model for Dostoevsky's Staretz Zossima,* Belmont: Nordland, 1972; Valentine Zander, *St Seraphim of Sarov,* Guestwood, NY: St Vladimir's Seminary Press, 1975.

SERGEI HACKEL

Struggle

see **Combat, Spiritual**

Suffering

The response of Christians to the experience of suffering, especially the suffering of the innocent and the good, has inevitably been influenced by their world view. Thus most early Christians, knowing less about the causes of natural phenomena, tended to see God's hand in everything that happened to them, and hence frequently sought to understand suffering as some form either of punishment or of warning. Later, with a more developed scientific world view, Christians began to wonder whether God really did cause everything to happen as it did, and eventually to question the very existence of a loving (let alone an omnipotent) God: the catastrophic earthquake that struck Lisbon on All Saints' Day 1755, killing thousands of people, many of whom were at Mass at the time, became a watershed in this regard; and the unspeakable horror of the Shoah, or Holocaust, in which six million Jews perished at the hands of the Nazis, made an authentic spiritual response to the reality of suffering even more difficult.

Central to the Christian's spiritual response to suffering is the crucifixion of Jesus. It is a paradox that those generations closest to the historical Jesus in time and geography tended to emphasize the exalted Christ, whose victory over death on the cross brought hope of eternity to those who were suffering then. Later generations – for example, late medieval European Christians afflicted by the Black Death, or Latin American Christians in the twentieth century oppressed by unjust and brutal regimes – drew strength instead from the image of the suffering, human Jesus. Thus, Julian of Norwich's *Showings* (or *Revelations) of the Divine Love* (*c.* 1373–93) and the Peruvian Gustavo Gutiérrez's *On Job: God-Talk and the Suffering of the Innocent* (1986) alike explore how the suffering God both shares and transforms the suffering of human beings.

The spiritual response of Christians to suffering has not been restricted to words or books. Early Christian iconography often celebrates the triumph of the martyrs (including biblical figures such as Daniel in the lions' den) in the face of terrible persecution. In the Catholic tradition, the possession of relics of the saints provided a focus for the impassioned prayers of local people, who believed that the saint's intercession might assist them in time of need (the medieval *clamor,* or shouts of entreaty and anger before the relic of a saint who appeared indifferent to human suffering, seems to have been common in different parts of Europe). Crucifixes and altarpieces depicting the tortured Christ (such as the Isenheim altarpiece of *c.* 1516 by Matthias Grünewald, now in the museum at Colmar); pilgrimages to holy places (such as the shrine of our Lady at Lourdes in southern France, the result of the experiences of St Bernadette Soubirous, a poor young local woman, in 1858); the singing of 'spirituals' and gospel music by poor black Christians in the southern United States of America – all these represent different patterns of spiritual response to the experience of suffering.

Yet perhaps the supreme manifestation of the Christian response to suffering is to be found in texts that in origin were not Christian at all: the Psalms of the Hebrew Bible, or Old Testament. In making their own these ancient yet timeless prayers, many of which give rise, in word and song, to the full range of different human responses to the reality of suffering (including anger, denial, resignation, despair and hard-won hope), Christians have prayed them in the light of Christ's passion and crucifixion, allowing themselves to hurl questions at God ('My God, my God, why have you forsaken me?') in the conviction that only a God who enters into the depths of their suffering can help them to find meaning within it. In so doing, they have discovered that the courage to ask questions of God can empower them also to go on asking questions of those evil forces which cause so much human suffering to occur. And in the process, prayer and theology come together; for the honesty and directness of this kind of prayer has led sufferers like the biblical Job not only to subvert easy and complacent pieties but even to discover, in and through their suffering, a living God who shares it with them.

See also **Cross and Spirituality; Martyrdom; Psalms.**

Walter Brueggemann, *The Psalms and the Life of Faith*, Minneapolis, MN: Augsburg Fortress Press, 1995; Gustavo Gutiérrez, *On Job: God-Talk and the Suffering of the Innocent*, trans. Matthew J. O'Connell, Maryknoll, NY: Orbis Books, 1987; Ruth Harris, *Lourdes: Body and Spirit in the Secular Age*, London: Penguin, 1999; *Julian of Norwich, Showings*, trans. Edmund Colledge and James Walsh, CWS, New York: Paulist Press, 1978; Gordon Mursell, *Out of the Deep: Prayer as Protest*, London: Darton, Longman & Todd, 1989; Dorothee Soelle, *Suffering*, trans. Everett R. Kalin, Philadelphia, PA: Fortress Press, 1975.

GORDON MURSELL

Sufism and Christianity

The term 'Sufism' is derived from the Arabic *'taṣawwuf'*. Etymologically, many roots are given for the derivation of the term: *ṣafa'* (purity); *ṣaff* (rank), an allusion to the supposedly higher calling of Sufis; *ṣuffah* (bench), referring to the bench at Medina where the first companions of the Prophet sat and finally, *ṣūf* (wool) from the garb traditionally associated with the first Sufis. In broad terms the name refers to that mystical or esoteric strand of Islam that has been inherent in the faith since its beginnings. As Chittick points out, already in the tenth century CE Būshanjī (d. 959) could complain that 'Today Sufism is a name without a reality, but it used to be a reality without a name' and, as Chittick adds, 'Nowadays the name has become relatively well known, but the reality has become far more obscure than it ever was in the past.' It should also be noted, as pointed out by Carl Ernst, that the term 'Sufism' was largely invented by Western Orientalists wanting a term to refer to the various aspects of Islam that they found attractive and acceptable. The difficulty in defining the term reflects the intrinsic complexity and variety found within Islam itself, not only temporally and spatially but culturally and linguistically.

From the time of the Prophet, Islam has traditionally delineated three areas of teaching – that pertaining to practice, knowledge and interiority – or, simply put, to body, mind and heart. The teachings attributed to the 'Sufis' have then tended to concentrate on the latter realm – that of the heart, often referred to in Islamic texts as *ma'rifah* (knowledge or recognition) and requires knowing one's inmost self and ultimately God. The Sufi, then, remembers or recalls this hidden knowledge and helps others to come to it. Consequently, much Sufi teaching emphasizes the nearness, presence and immanence of God rather than God's distance and transcendence. The key Quranic verses quoted in this respect are 'We are nearer to him than the jugular vein' (50.16) and 'He is with you wherever you are.' (57.4).

Accordingly, the Sufis often confound reason and the rational mind to allow the heart to open to God. Thus Jalāl al-Din Rūmī (d. 1273) writes in the *Mathnawī* 'The philosopher kills himself with thinking, his back is turned to the treasure. Most of those destined for Paradise are simpletons, so that they escape from the mischief of philosophy.' Like Eckhart and others in the Christian tradition they have a great love of paradox and use surprise and shock to teach their pupils, not hesitating to use stories of sexual transgression, alcohol and the eating of forbidden foods to convey their message. The state of *hairat* (blessed perplexity) is essential to the journey to union with the divine and importance has often been attached to the states of annihilation (*fanā*) and subsistence (*baqā*).

Following the pioneering work of Miguel Asin Palacios at the beginning of the twentieth century, scholars have renewed interest in the possible interrelatedness between the Christian and Sufi mystical traditions. Asin Palacios suggested that certain texts of, for example, the Andalusian Sufi tradition may well have influenced the Spanish Christian writers Ss Teresa of Avila and John of the Cross. In particular he referred to the writings of Ibn Abbād of Ronda (d. 1390) and his teaching on the importance of dryness and contraction in prayer as prefiguring the teachings of, among others, St John of the Cross. Subsequent scholarship has built on the pioneering work of Asin Palacios so, for example, contemporary scholars such as Catherine Swietlicki (see in particular *Spanish Christian Cabala: The Works of Luis de Leon, Santa Teresa de Jesus and San Juan de la Cruz*) and Luce López Baralt (see *San Juan de la Cruz y el Islam*) suggest that the Iberian Jewish population may well have acted as the intermediaries for the transmission of this tradition to Christianity. As López-Baralt points out, the ninth-century work *Maqāmāt al-qulūb* (*The Stations of the Heart*) by Nūrī of Baghdad already contains many of the symbols found in both the *Zohar* and the Spanish Christian mystical tradition. However, it is difficult to make a direct causal link between the three traditions and we may never be able to prove the influence categorically one way or the other.

In more recent times a direct influence is discernible between Sufi writings and those of Thomas Merton (1915–68). The American Cistercian drew heavily on Sufi teachings in his later talks and writings. From 1966 until his death in 1968 he gave a series of talks to the novices of Gethsemani Abbey, Kentucky, directly about Sufism (see Baker and Henry, 1999). Sufi terms such as annihilation and blessed perplexity occur frequently in these last lectures and writings.

On the other side, some commentators have suggested that the Sufi tradition itself was influenced by the Christian presence in Islamic lands. Thus, Louis Massignon in his biography of the ninth-century Sufi martyr Ḥusayn ibn Manṣūr al-Ḥallāj (857–922) suggests that he resembled Jesus in several respects, not least because, like Jesus, he prayed for his executioners but also that he was executed for identifying so closely with the Godhead in his famous saying: 'Anā al-Haqq' ('I am the Truth'). Other scholars have suggested Christian influences in the writings of, among others, Rūmī and Farīd ud-Dīn Attār (d. 1220).

With the recent publication of many good critical editions of classic Sufi texts and the growth of Sufi groups in the West the complex and interactive relationship between Sufism and Christianity looks set to continue and develop.

See also **Islam and Christianity.**

———

M. Asín Palacios, 'Un precursor hispano-musulman de San Juan de la Cruz' in *Al-Andalus* 1, 1933; R. Baker and G. Henry, *Merton and Sufism: The Untold Story*, Fons Vitae, 1999; W. Chittick, *The Sufi Path of Love*, Albany, 1983; C. Ernst, *Words of Ecstasy in Sufism*, Albany, 1984; L. López-Baralt, *San Juan de La Cruz y el Islam*, Hiperión, 1985; L. Massignon, *La Passion d'al-Hosayn-ibn-Mansour al-Hallāj*, Paris 1922; T. Merton, *Raids on the Unspeakable*, London: Burns & Oates, 1977; R. Nicholson, *The Mathnawī of Jalālu'ddin Rūmī*, London, 1925–71; A. Schimmel, *Mystical Dimensions of Islam*, University of North Carolina Press, 1975; C. Swietlicki, *Spanish Christian Cabala: The Works of Luis de Leon, Santa Teresa de Jesus and San Juan de la Cruz*, Columbia: University of Missouri Press, 1986.

PETER TYLER

Sulpician Spirituality

'Sulpician spirituality' broadly denotes the spiritual formation fostered by the priests of the Society of St-Sulpice, who are diocesan priests specializing in seminary and priestly formation. In a more limited but probably more common sense, it denotes the style of spirituality taking its central guidance from the work and writings of Father Jean-Jacques Olier (1608–57), the pastor of St-Sulpice in Paris (whence the name 'Sulpician'), who belonged to the founding constellation of the French School of spirituality, and who founded the Society in 1641. These meanings overlap.

Bérulle's themes permeate Olier's writings, but Olier typically replaces the Pseudo-Dionysian 'exitus-reditus' pattern with a Pauline and Johannine paschal rhythm. Bérulle's more 'objective' approach (rarely does he reveal, except indirectly, his personal experience) is complemented by Olier's greater attentiveness to our and his personal ('subjective' in this sense) experience of the mysteries of Jesus and Jesus' companions. Hence he stresses the role of the Spirit, who brings us into this participation.

This pneumatological experientialism helps to protect Olier's attention to the personal pole from derailing into psychologism or emotionalism. It also helps avoid ecclesial triumphalism. He offers sober analyses of the subtle ways in which we can be disordered by sin, reflecting the Augustinian revival of the French School. Yet the Spirit who exposes our disordered interiority also brings us into all the mysteries of Jesus' life, and so there is a stronger note of hope and resurrection triumph in Olier. We have received in Christ more than we have lost through sin, he writes in his *Catechism* (1.19). This seems to be a (still somewhat contested) theological dividing line between Olier's 'toughness' and the Jansenists' 'rigourism', which he opposed.

Olier seeks a renewal of both presbyterate and laity, and while this involves institutional and pastoral strategies, the stress falls upon interior transformation. In this regard, Olier's teaching on prayer is central. In the history of Christian spirituality it is perhaps what typically is meant by 'Sulpician spirituality'. Prayer in the Sulpician mode is nothing other than our participation in the mysteries of Jesus (usually connected with the liturgical calendar and rites). Olier's sensitivity to our inability to corral the Spirit made him hesitate to offer 'methods' of prayer; the key was to be attuned to how the Spirit may be guiding us. Absent clear direction from the Spirit (*Introduction to the Christian Life and Virtues*, ch. 4), he recommended what has become the celebrated 'affective' style of Sulpician prayer, as over against more discursive styles, sometimes characterized as the 'Jesuit' ('Ignatian') mode, although this contrast hardly applies to Ignatius Loyola and his Spiritual Exercises. Later generations of Sulpicians encumbered the more balanced affective approach of Olier with discursive distinctions. Perhaps Jesuits did the same with Ignatius' Exercises.

Olier's 'easy method' can be shortened to 'Jesus before our eyes, in our heart and in our hands' (cf. Deut. 6.6, 8), or 'adoration, communion and co-operation' (of which Evelyn Underhill was quite fond). He prefers the term 'co-operation' to resolution, reflecting a Tridentine Augustinianism, joining the human will to the Spirit's grace (*Catechism* 2.8). The 'method' corresponds to a holistic anthropology (mind, the interior depths of the psyche, and action), expressing how the Spirit can christify the whole person. This is likely the method's attractiveness. The reverent imagination, savouring, and discernment found in Loyola's Spiritual Exercises reflect an equivalent anthropology, not surprisingly, since Bérulle was initially formed by them.

The Society of St-Sulpice has a long history now, surviving suppression under the French Revolution (1790) and again by Napoleon (1811), and now entering into a rich globalization through its missions, first in Canada and the United States, and now in Vietnam, Japan, South America and Africa. Reflecting trends in the larger Church, it has known various phases (from developing the initial thought of Olier on through to nearly forgetting it, and now recovering it through the return to the founder's charism fostered by Vatican II). Relatively early (by the end of the seventeenth century), Olier's more mystical experientialism was being turned into a form of moralism and asceticism on the one hand, and a more didactic, discursive mode of prayer on the other. The famous *Particular Examens* in its redaction under Louis Tronson (1690), disseminated in the Sulpician seminaries, already displayed these features: the priest is modest, disciplined, austere in piety. J.-A. Emery's *The Spirit of Saint Thérèse* (1775) signals a return to a more mystical-biblical orientation, receiving more prominence through the renewal of interest in the French School, coupled with the contemporary biblical and theological renaissance after Vatican II, to which the Sulpicians have made notable contributions.

See also **Augustinian Spirituality; French School of Spirituality; Ignatian Spirituality; Priesthood and Spirituality.**

Bérulle and the French School: Selected Writings, ed. William M. Thompson, trans. Lowell M. Glendon, CWS, New York: Paulist Press, 1989; Raymond Deville, *The French School of Spirituality: An Introduction and Reader*, trans. Agnes Cunningham, Pittsburgh: Duquesne University Press, 1994; Irénée Noye, 'Saint-Sulpice (Compagnie des Prêtres de)' in *DS* 14, cols 170–81; J. J. Olier, *Catechism of an Interior Life*, trans. M. Edward Knight, Baltimore: John Murphy & Co., 1855; Pierre Pourrat, *Father Olier, Founder of St Sulpice*, trans. W. S. Reilly, Baltimore: Voice Publishing Co., 1932; Aelred Squire, *Asking the Fathers: The Art of Meditation and Prayer*, Wilton, CT: Morehouse-Barlow/New York: Paulist Press, 1973, pp. 147–58.

WILLIAM THOMPSON-UBERUAGA

Swedenborgian Spirituality

An historical and contemporary movement of churches and seekers taking its name and inspiration from Emanuel Swedenborg (1688–1772), an eighteenth-century Enlightenment Swedish nobleman who underwent a dramatic mid-life spiritual crisis that resulted in a vocational change from physical scientist to Christian prophet.

Swedenborgian spirituality is small but worldwide, manifesting in several denominations that span the liberal–conservative spectrum. In thirty works written during Swedenborg's remaining years, he claimed to produce a 'revealed' inner sense to the Jewish and Christian Scriptures, a disclosure he asserted constituted the second coming of Christ. Though confining himself to a ministry of publication, enthusiastic readers of mostly Anglicans, Methodists and Baptists formed in England after his death, which led to a separatist controversy and the founding of The General Conference of the New Jerusalem in 1787. Other Swedenborgian organizations formed during the subsequent century in North America, Switzerland and Australia, and in the second half of the twentieth century Swedenborgianism took root with some vigour in black African populations (Ghana, South Africa and Mauritius), Japan and South Korea, all as mission fields of the older organizations. Today five Swedenborgian denominations worldwide total 60,000 members, with the substantial majority in Africa.

Steeped in the mathematical and philosophical frameworks of Descartes, Newton, Leibniz and Wolff, Swedenborg was influenced by the rationalist philosophy of science in the Enlightenment and also by Pietist spirituality (his father, Bishop Jesper Svedberg, was a prominent Pietist Lutheran reformer). Versed as well in ancient

Greek philosophy, Swedenborg is often labelled Neoplatonist; reminiscent of Proclus and Plotinus he portrayed an elaborate hierarchy of spiritual realms reaching into union with the 'divine *esse*', which is anterior to creation. Primary stress was laid on understanding divine causality and order in the cosmos and in history as necessary for effective spiritual development. Targeting logical fallacies of both Roman Catholicism and Reformation theology, Swedenborg heralded a 'New Church' founded upon a rational understanding of the cosmos and of Christianity. William Blake, alternately a Swedenborg enthusiast and critic, claimed Swedenborg believed in 'salvation by understanding'. Such a characterization, however, is only half the picture. Swedenborg's Pietistic leanings insisted on ethical progress as a certain result of true faith. Also in keeping with Pietism, Swedenborg minimized the role of ecclesiastical structures and taught that the individual always had immediate access to Christ through prayer and right study of the Scriptures. He taught a positive view of anthropology: those sincerely seeking Christ received 'divine influx' which guided a psychospiritual process called regeneration, a term Swedenborg borrowed from Pietist writers. Regeneration involved faithful effort to co-operate with Christ in the redemption, whereby the Holy Spirit gradually reformed the will and the understanding through application of spiritual effort in a life of usefulness. Heavenly life was said to begin in this world, as spiritually causal structures connected the seeker's diligence with angelic and divine activity working on their behalf. Extensive attention to influences from spiritual realms and to life after death have often led to a comparison with spiritualism, but Swedenborg and Swedenborgians have always denounced occult activity.

Historically, spiritual practice in the churches has centred on liturgical worship as the primary activity. Music, prayers and liturgical responses support the central event: an interpretive sermon rationally approaching the divine through an explication of various inner levels of meaning in biblical texts. Though Swedenborg never referenced the ancient and medieval allegorical tradition, Swedenborgian hermeneutics is strikingly similar to the spiritual exegesis of Origen, Pope Gregory I, John Cassian and Bernard of Clairvaux, with the main difference being a claim to precision of meaning exacted through Swedenborg's 'science of correspondences'. Recently, the majority of English and North American groups have become increasingly 'Low Church' and contemporary in worship style, while Asian and African congregations incorporate local cultural features in style of worship.

Swedenborg's most significant impact occurred in nineteenth-century America as Swedenborg's metaphysics was appropriated broadly by healing theologies, utopian communitarian groups, Transcendentalists, Spiritualists and Romance poets and artists. Despite teaching a High Christology, Swedenborg's rational approach to metaphysics laid the groundwork for pluralism, and drawing upon these aspects the most liberal branch initiated the 1893 World Parliament of Religions under the leadership of Charles Carroll Bonney. That denomination, the General Convention of Swedenborgian Churches of North America, continues to promote interfaith dialogue.

Though Swedenborg holds the status of a prophet among most Swedenborgians, the limit of his authority is hotly contested. In liberal circles other authors and movements have been appropriated for over a century, while the largest branch, the General Church of the New Jerusalem, believes his works have such final authority as to exclude interest in other spiritualities. American psychologist Wilson Van Dusen in the latter decades of the twentieth century developed Swedenborgian spiritual practices oriented towards Swedenborg's own spiritual practice and moved significant numbers of Swedenborgians toward the practice of meditation, dream interpretation and reliance upon personal experience.

See also **Allegory; Dreams and Dreaming; Enlightenment Thought; Exegesis, Spiritual; Pietism; Neoplatonism.**

Ernst Benz, *Emanuel Swedenborg: Visionary Savant in the Age of Reason*, trans. Nicholas Goodrick-Clarke, West Chester, PA: Swedenborg Foundation, 2002, originally published as *Emanuel Swedenborg: Naturforscher und Seher*, Munich, 1948; Inge Jonsson, *Visionary Scientist: The Effects of Science and Philosophy on Swedenborg's Cosmology*, West Chester, PA: Swedenborg Foundation, 1999, originally published as *Emanuel Swedenborg*, Boston: Twayne Publishers, 1971; Robert Kirven, *A Concise Overview of Swedenborg's Theology*, Newtonville, MA: J. Appleseed & Co., 2003; Emanuel Swedenborg, *Heaven and Its Wonders and Hell: Drawn from Things Seen and Heard*, trans. George F. Dole, West Chester, PA: Swedenborg Foundation, 2000, originally published as *De Coelo et Ejus Mirabilibus et de Inferno, ex Auditis et Visis*, London, 1758; Wilson Van Dusen, *The Presence of Other Worlds: The Psycho-Spiritual Findings of Emanuel Swedenborg*, San Francisco: Harper & Row, 1975; William Woofenden, *Swedenborg Explorers Guidebook: A Research*

Manual, West Chester, PA: Swedenborg Foundation, 2002.

JAMES LAWRENCE

Symbol and Spirituality

The topic of symbolism is part of semiotics, the study of signs. Sometimes the word 'symbol' is used interchangeably with 'sign', as when we speak of mathematical symbols, international symbols for road signs, words as symbols, and so forth. In religion it is useful to restrict 'symbol' to large-scale thematic signs that are defined in networks of other symbols and that usually find expression in several media such as language, visual and plastic arts, music, drama and perhaps architecture. In Christianity, for instance, the events of Jesus' life as recounted in the New Testament have taken on large-scale symbolic meaning, as well as more general concepts such as creation, fall, atonement, resurrection, sanctification, Church as Body of Christ, Bride of Christ, Ark of Salvation, or Jesus as cosmic Christ, Second Person of the Trinity, the saving Way, Truth and Life, and as Friend.

Spiritually relevant religious symbols need not be conceptually consistent but often are confluences of several thematic traditions. For instance, the New Testament represents Jesus as a sacrifice both in the sense of the Passover sacrifice in Egypt by which the firstborn of the Israelites were saved and as the scapegoat sacrifice of the atonement ritual in Leviticus that takes away the sins of the world. Families of conceptually inconsistent symbols resonate together under master symbols, such as 'Jesus as Sacrifice', to provide pivotal points for liturgy, meditation, theological reflection and other devotional practices.

The function of religious symbols in spiritual life is rarely to provide only a description of some religiously important reality. In fact, religious symbols in spiritual contexts are often fantastical, exaggerated or bizarre. The Hindu and Buddhist symbols of the dancing divine figures brandishing swords and wearing belts of skulls do not mean to assert that any gods look, dress or behave like that; rather their spiritual function is to scare the devotee out of a complacent view of ultimacy. The Spiritual Exercises of St Ignatius of Loyola involve visualizations of scenes, say, from the life of Jesus Christ, that by no means have to be accurate portrayals of persons, their dress or architectural surroundings; their function rather is to transform the soul of the devotee into more Christlike habits. The function of engaging religious realities by means of symbols is to transform the soul so that it is better in tune with those realities. Religious practice involves living with those symbols, perhaps for a very long time, so as to become enabled to engage the religious elements in a true way.

Nineteenth- and twentieth-century philosophy has helped to understand this pragmatic, non-descriptive function of religious symbols, or at least some of them. Charles Peirce, the founder of pragmatism, distinguished between iconic and indexical dimensions of reference in symbols. Iconic reference says that the object-reality is 'like', perhaps isomorphic with, the symbol. For instance, a cross on a Christian altar refers iconically to the cross on which Jesus died (Peirce's example). Indexical reference establishes a causal connection between the reality and the interpreter, as pointing to an object causes the interpreter to turn his or her head to look. Religious symbols usually have both iconic and indexical dimensions of reference. Used in processes of devotion, however, the indexical, causal, transformative, dimensions can be very strong, whereas the iconic dimensions are often false if taken literally. The philosopher Alfred North Whitehead offered a similar theory of symbolic reference that combines a causal dimension of perception with imaginative constructions. Susanne K. Langer has elaborated this theory for religious symbols.

Some religious symbols important for spiritual life point to what is ultimate and infinite, to what cannot literally be expressed in finite terms, for instance symbols of God and creation. These symbols fix on elements that, on the one hand, are finite and determinate, such as the existence of the world, or of goodness, or of meaning, and, on the other hand, are that without which the world we take for granted would be different or lacking. They are symbols of finite things that are world-founding. These symbols can be called 'finite–infinite contrasts' because the finite elements point beyond to what, without the creation of those finite elements, would be non-finite or infinite. Symbols such as these are broken symbols: they can be used for spiritual purposes only with the understanding that they are inadequate and point beyond themselves. Like theology, spirituality is apophatic with its fundamental broken symbols.

See also **Apophatic Spirituality; Kataphatic Spirituality.**

Edwyn Bevan, *Symbolism and Belief*, London: George Allen & Unwin, 1938; reprint edn Boston: Beacon Press, 1957; *Ignatius of Loyola: The Spiritual Exercises and Selected Works*, ed. George E. Ganss, CWS, New York: Paulist Press, 1991; Susanne K. Langer, *Philosophy in a New*

Key: A Study of the Symbolism of Reason, Rite, and Art, 3rd edn, Cambridge, MA: Harvard University Press, 1956; Robert Cummings Neville, *The Truth of Broken Symbols*, Albany, NY: State University of New York Press, 1996; Robert Cummings Neville, *Symbols of Jesus: A Christology of Symbolic Engagement*, Cambridge: Cambridge University Press, 2001; Alfred North Whitehead, *Symbolism: Its Meaning and Effect*, New York: Macmillan, 1927; reprint edn, New York: Fordham University Press, 1985.

ROBERT CUMMINGS NEVILLE

Synoptic Gospels, Spirituality of

Since redaction criticism has helped us to see more clearly that the Gospels were written from faith for faith, it is legitimate to enquire into what they show and tell about the sense of the presence of God and how to live in response. That divine presence, so the Gospel writers want their hearers and readers to know, is revealed most fully in Jesus Christ in whose transforming power participation is made possible, by faith, through the Holy Spirit. The opening sentences of 1 John are apt evocations of what we find in the Gospels and how we should come to them: 'That which was from the beginning, which we have heard, which we have seen with our eyes, which we have looked upon and touched with our hands, concerning the word of life . . . that which we have seen and heard we proclaim also to you . . .' (1 John 1.1–3). The Gospels, in other words, are testimonies of faith in Christ from start to finish – written remembrances and imaginative expressions of profound encounters with the divine Son of God, intended to mediate him to others as the basis for faith, repentance and new life.

What, then, are the main ingredients of this spirituality? The most important ingredient is testimony to a decisive revelation of the divine in time, space and person. The person is Jesus of Nazareth in whom God's eschatological Spirit is seen to be present in a unique way. The time is that of the culmination of salvation history in the drawing near of God's rule of justice and peace ('the kingdom of God') with the coming of God's Messiah. The space or place is God's people Israel and their Temple in Jerusalem, now decisively reinterpreted in the light of the Messiah's death and resurrection, the coming of the Spirit and the mission to all nations.

This testimony is mediated in significant ways. It is mediated through the Scriptures now read prophetically and charismatically as pointing to the fulfilment of God's saving purposes for Israel and the nations in the coming of the Spirit-endowed Son of God. Typical of this is the fact that, for Mark, the 'beginning of the gospel of Jesus Christ' is a complex of scriptural quotations (Mark 1.2–3) of eschatological import; and that, for Matthew, the events of Jesus' life are interpreted repeatedly as taking place 'to fulfil what the Lord had spoken by' one or other of the biblical prophets (e.g. Matt. 1.22–23; 2.5–6, 15, 17–18, 23).

But the testimony is not just mediated scripturally. It is mediated also through the experience of the first followers of Jesus, experience displayed in the form of compelling narrative testimony to the sense of God's presence and power in Jesus of Nazareth crucified and risen. Typical here is Mark's emphasis on the epiphanic quality of God's presence in Jesus signalled by the recurring motif of awe and wonder at what Jesus says and does (e.g. Mark 1.27–28; 2.12; 4.41). Typical in Luke is the exultation which is evoked in people of all kinds by the breaking in of the new age with the coming of the Spirit-filled Messiah (e.g. Luke 1.44, 47; 2.10; 24.41, 52–53).

In general, therefore, the spirituality of the three synoptic Gospels has much in common, especially in their grounding in a theology, Christology and eschatology which are both fundamentally scriptural and shaped also by ideas and practices (e.g. messianism and scripture interpretation) current in the Judaism of their day. At the same time, redaction and composition criticism have shown decisively that each Gospel has its own distinctive theology and spirituality. The New Testament canon, with its remarkable multiplicity of Gospels, offers a wonderful polyphony of voices testifying in their various and unique ways to the manifestation of the divine presence in Jesus of Nazareth.

1. *Matthean spirituality*. For Matthew, as for all the evangelists, Christian spirituality is both theocentric and christocentric. It is based on the sure experience of the fatherly grace of God by which it is possible to say in response, 'Our Father, who art in heaven' (Matt 6:9). This experience of grace is grounded in a profound sense of the presence of God – above all, in Jesus, who is 'God with us' (Matt. 1.23; 28.20). In Jesus the Son of God, heaven and earth have touched for salvation and judgement, and God's new people is brought into being to live as 'the light of the world' (Matt. 5.14). This revelation of grace is at one and the same time a summons to repentance and a life of 'righteousness' (*dikaiosune*), which is Matthew's favourite term for the active obedience to the demanding will of God taught and practised by Jesus himself (cf. Matt. 3.15; 5.6, 10, 20). Put simply, grace and obedience, divine

initiative and human response, are two sides of the same coin in the economy of the kingdom of heaven made present in Jesus.

In fact, much of the Gospel of Matthew is given over to an attempt to display what kind of obedience is the appropriate response to the divine presence in Jesus. For a start, there is the demand for single-minded commitment. The choice which Jesus places before his disciples is a choice between incompatible ways which allows no compromise. It is a matter of either/or: God or mammon (6.24); the narrow gate and the hard way or the wide gate and the easy way (7.13–14); being found on the Last Day among the sheep or among the goats (25.31–46).

A corollary of the demand for total commitment is the summons to obedient and humble practice of the will of God as taught by Jesus in the five great extended discourses (Matt. 5—7; 10; 13; 18; 23—25). Spirituality is about learning to be a follower in the school of Jesus (cf. Matt. 11.28–30; 13.51–52), by receiving Jesus' teaching and putting it into practice. Central to this practice is the double command of love of God and love of neighbour (cf. Matt. 5.38–42, 43–48; 19.19; 22.34–40), alongside which must be placed the profound concern with forgiveness and reconciliation (Matt. 5.21–26; 18.21–35) as well as the exercise of 'the weightier matters of the law, justice and mercy and faith' (Matt. 23.23). This is what constitutes true 'righteousness' as the only adequate response to the presence of the heavenly Father in Jesus the Son. The nature of this righteousness is epitomized memorably in the parable of the sheep and the goats with which the teaching of Jesus comes to a climactic end (Matt. 25.31–46). There, true righteousness is shown to be a matter of discerning the presence of Jesus the heavenly Son of Man in his persecuted, destitute brothers and sisters on earth and responding in acts of love and self-dispossession on their behalf.

2. *Marcan spirituality.* Whereas in Matthew spirituality is a response to the sense of the fatherly presence of God and the abiding presence of Jesus God's Son (cf. Matt. 28.20), what is striking in Mark is the hiddenness of God, the secrecy surrounding Jesus' identity as the Son of Man and, at the end, Jesus' mysterious absence (cf. Mark 16.1–8). Both Gospels have a spirituality grounded in the revelation of God, Christ and the Spirit, yet the nature of their spiritualities is significantly different (though not necessarily incompatible). In particular, whereas Matthew focuses on that aspect of spirituality which concerns the moral life, in Mark the emphasis is on spirituality as the outworking of a certain kind of

epistemology. At the heart of this epistemology is the subversive and world-transforming idea that the nature of reality is revealed, not in God's presence but in his absence, not in God's power but in his weakness – better still, that God's presence is to be sought and found precisely in his absence, and that God's power is revealed precisely in his weakness.

This helps to explain Mark's overwhelming Christological focus on Jesus as the Son of Man who '*must* suffer' if God's will is to be done, Satan conquered and the 'many' from all nations ransomed for God (cf. Mark 8.31; 9.31; 10.32–45). It also helps to explain the understanding of discipleship of Jesus as cruciform, in imitation of Christ: 'If anyone would come after me, let him deny himself and take up his cross and follow me' (Mark 8.34–35). In ways which resonate with the theology of the cross in the letters of Paul, Mark's vision of God is the paradoxical vision of the revelation of God in the crucifixion of the Son of God. With its roots in Jewish apocalyptic (e.g. the book of Daniel), Marcan spirituality represents the astonishing insight that suffering is not defeat but redemption, and that the way to find life is to surrender it, since God is the sovereign God who brings life out of death.

Mark's cruciform spirituality has many corollaries. One is the need for faith expressed in prayer, since only by faith and prayer can the truth about the hidden God, the suffering Son of Man and the call to take up one's cross be received (cf. Mark 9.14–29). A second corollary is the need for a basic change of outlook and expectations summed up in Jesus' call to 'repent and believe in the gospel' (Mark 1.15). The portrayal of the disciples as persistently obtuse is Mark's way, by means of irony, of showing how radical is the change of outlook required and how many are the obstacles (e.g. Mark 9.33–37; 10.32–45; cf. 4.1–20). What is required, third, is a spirituality of discernment and vigilance (cf. Mark 13.32–37). Only thus will times of testing be endured and the way of the cross embraced, in hope of the kingdom of God and eternal life. In all this, it is Jesus himself who shows the way (e.g. Mark 14.32–42).

3. *Lucan spirituality.* If Matthean spirituality is about the practice of righteousness in response to the gracious presence of God in Jesus and Marcan spirituality is about faith, cross-bearing and prayerful attentiveness to God's hidden presence in imitation of the suffering Son of Man, Lucan spirituality is about the joyful acknowledgement of the universal salvation made possible by the dawning of the age of the

eschatological Spirit with the coming of the Messiah. Whereas a disciple in Matthew is a learner in the school of Jesus, and in Mark one who follows Jesus 'on the way' in fear and trembling, in Luke a disciple is a joyous, Spirit-inspired, recipient of salvation.

As an expression of gratitude to God, joy (*chara* and cognates) is probably the most distinctive aspect of Lucan spirituality. Uniquely among the Gospels, joy in God is an aspect of the life of Jesus himself (cf. Luke 10.21). It is also a recurring motif in the teaching of Jesus – especially in the parables of losing and finding in Luke 15 (at vv. 5–7, 9–10, 22–24, 32) – and in the stories of conversion arising out of encounter with Jesus (e.g. 19.1–10, at v. 6). Joy is a response to grace and salvation. It expresses the gospel's fundamental claim that the coming of Jesus is 'good news to the poor' (cf. Luke 4.18), the culmination of the mighty acts of God for the salvation of the world.

Related to joy are repentance and conversion (cf. Luke 7.36–50; 15.11–32; 19.1–10; 23.39–43). For Luke, repentance is the only appropriate response to the in-breaking of the new age and is a prerequisite of forgiveness and salvation. It involves a change of heart and life orientated on Jesus and the kingdom of God. Furthermore, those most likely to repent are 'the poor', those whose physical, social and spiritual circumstances render them open and receptive to divine grace (cf. Luke 6.20–23). The transformation which results is often portrayed in acts of hospitality and the festive sharing of food. Table-fellowship, with its overtones of the messianic banquet of the end-time, is for Luke a primary embodiment and enactment of the salvation Jesus offers (cf. Luke 14—15; 22.7–30).

However, Luke is interested, not only in how the life of faith begins, but also how it is sustained. This has a 'vertical', God-ward dimension. Characteristic here are the exercise of a faith that perdures (cf. Luke 8.12, 50; 24.25) and the practice of prayer after the example of Jesus himself (e.g. Luke 6.12; 9.18, 28–29; 11.1; 18.1–8; 22.40–46; 23.34, 46). On the 'horizontal' plane, spirituality is a matter of public witness by word and deed to the 'good news' of the Gospel. Pre-eminent here are acts of testimony to the salvation that has come in Jesus (e.g. Luke 8.47). Equally important are acts of self-dispossession for the sake of the poor and destitute, of which the story of the Good Samaritan is the classic representation (Luke 10.25–37). For Luke, as for the biblical tradition as a whole, love of God and love of neighbour are inseparable aspects of whole-hearted response to the one true God.

See also **Spirituality and scripture** (*essay*).

S. C. Barton, *The Spirituality of the Gospels*, London: SPCK, 1992; B. E. Beck, *Christian Character in the Gospel of Luke*, London: Epworth Press, 1989; S. R. Garrett, *The Temptations of Jesus in Mark's Gospel*, Grand Rapids, MI: Eerdmans, 1998; C. D. Marshall, *Faith as a Theme in Mark's Narrative*, Cambridge: Cambridge University Press, 1989; B. Przybylski, *Righteousness in Matthew and His World of Thought*, Cambridge: Cambridge University Press, 1980; G. N. Stanton, *The Gospels and Jesus*, 2nd edn, Oxford: Oxford University Press, 2002.

STEPHEN C. BARTON

Syriac Spirituality

Alongside the Christianity of Graeco-Roman antiquity, whose adherents spoke primarily Latin in the West and Greek in the East, other centres of Christian theology and spirituality existed. Foremost among these was the Syriac-speaking church, centred upon Antioch and Edessa, encompassing a large area of what today are eastern Turkey, Syria and much of northern Iraq and Iran. The Syriac-speaking areas were divided between the Roman and the Persian Empires, and all too often were the scene of bitter warfare between them. This situation did not, however, prevent theological and spiritual interchange between the divided parts of Syrian culture. Indeed, the two greatest early spiritual writers of the Syriac spiritual tradition were Aphrahat the Persian sage, and St Ephrem, who lived first in Nisibis, then later in Edessa, in the Roman Empire. In the centuries that followed, great theological leaders arose in both parts of Syrian culture and produced works of spiritual depth, even after the area of Syrian cultural predominance was overwhelmed by the Islamic conquests of the seventh century.

The beginnings of Syriac spirituality are unclear, as is the actual process of introduction of Christianity to Syrian culture. Syria was probably evangelized by Judaeo-Christians from Palestine, who brought with them the influences of the Essene communities, as well as an extreme asceticism and tendency to devalue both marriage and sexuality, found both in Qumran and among Jewish Christian splinter groups such as the Encratites and Elkaisites. The scant literature extant from earliest Syriac Christianity, especially the *Acts of Judas Thomas* and the *Odes of Solomon*, seems to bear this out. Important too for the Syriac spirituality of the fourth century is the marked absence of Hellenistic models of theology and scriptural interpretation. Syriac Christianity remains faithful to the techniques of rabbinical midrashic interpretation, and is strongly influenced by Jewish targumic models.

It is in the *Acts of Judas Thomas*, a work that displays clear Gnostic overtones, that we first meet that emphasis on virginity (*btuluta*) and abstinence within marriage (*qaddishuta*) that remain a central part of early Syrian spirituality. Even in the *Book of Steps*, however, a work of the fourth century considered 'orthodox', there is a clear distinction made between those believers who are 'just' and those who are 'perfect'. The just lead lives in community, have occupations, get married and have families. They can be saved if they live upright lives, but they receive only the 'pledge' of the Holy Spirit, a sort of first install-ment. The perfect strive for lives of complete renunciation, and consecrate themselves wholly to the service of God and the Church. They receive the fullness of the Holy Spirit as their reward. The lifestyle of the perfect, although sharing many of the values of monasticism, is at most proto-monastic, as they live their lives within the larger community, not in complete solitude.

In the *Demonstrations* of Aphrahat we find a number of treatises that deal with the spiritual life, more especially with purity of heart. This purity is achieved through abstinence, prayer and the sacraments of baptism and the Eucharist. Prayer is seen as a sacrifice in and of the heart, a sacrifice that God accepts by consuming it with the fire of the Holy Spirit. Aphrahat's treatises emphasize the central role of the Holy Spirit, and contribute to the development of the 'Spirit-mysticism' so characteristic of Syrian thought.

Aphrahat's attitude toward marriage and marital sexuality, as instituted by God, is posi-tive, in contrast to earlier Syrian writers. This attitude and the emphasis on prayer and the sacraments as avenues open to all Christians, as occasions for reception of the Holy Spirit, evi-dence a positive re-evaluation of 'non-perfect' Christians. At the same time the privileging of virginity and celibacy continues. In his *Demon-stration VI* Aphrahat speaks of the 'Sons and Daughters of the Covenant' (*bnai/bnay qyama*). These Christians live celibate lives, assist in the celebration of the communal liturgies and aid the deacons and priests. They are part of the community, but occupy a privileged position within it. Through their voluntary renunciation of earthly attachments they are able to make greater spiritual progress than others.

Aphrahat also refers to these 'Covenanters' as *ihidaye*. This term is central to Syrian spirituality and possesses an extraordinary richness of theo-logical and spiritual meanings: the single ones; the celibate; those possessing singleness of heart

and mind. *Ihidaya* can also refer to Adam in his pre-fallen state, as well as to Christ the *Only-Begotten*. Through prayer, ascetic practice and baptism the *ihidaye* seek to rejoin Adam in Paradise by being joined to Christ, the Second Adam. The *ihidaye*, through prayer and contem-plation also imitate the 'watchfulness' of the angels (called 'Watchers' in Syriac), who con-template the divine mysteries. There is a strong eschatological element to this spirituality, in striving to re-enter Paradise during this life by baptism, and in living the life of the heavenly angels through contemplation and celibacy.

Saint Ephrem of Nisibis (*c.* 306–73) shares many of Aphrahat's spiritual ideas, but is a more gifted theologian, whose insights concerning God, human beings and creation are expressed poetically in hymns full of metaphor and para-dox. This use of paradox is Ephrem's response to the simultaneous transcendence of God and God's immanence in creation. God is unap-proachable and unknowable, yet also appre-hended in the types and symbols that God has given in nature, particularly in the life of Christ, the Word made flesh. It is in prayer and contem-plation of these types and symbols that the human eye becomes 'luminous' or 'limpid', like a polished mirror, capable of reflecting the light of the Trinity.

The sacraments of baptism and the Eucharist are, for Ephrem, essential elements of the ongo-ing manifestation of God's presence and power in the world. Fire, as a symbol of divine power, flares up in the Jordan at Christ's baptism. Fire is present in the eucharistic wine, and fills those who partake of it with the power of the Holy Spirit.

Mysticism of the Spirit is also central to Ephrem's understanding of Christian growth, divinization and salvation. Ephrem posits a tri-partite division of human nature into body-soul-spirit. Spiritual progress leads the believer away from the physical toward the psychic, and finally to the spiritual. Ephrem also adds a fourth ele-ment: progression toward, and absorption into, the Holy Spirit. This final absorption occurs only after the resurrection. This gradual divinization is achieved through sexual abstinence, medita-tion, prayer and fasting, but most especially through the Eucharist.

By the end of the fourth century Hellenistic culture and theology exerted an increasing impact upon Syrian spirituality. The writings of Egyptian monasticism, and most importantly the works of Evagrius of Pontus, become known in Syria. Evagrius, a monk and disciple of Origen, exposes the Syrian tradition to a Christian spirituality deeply influenced by Pythagorean mysticism and Neoplatonic philosophy. To the theology of Ephrem, which attempts to decipher something of the nature of God from the types and symbols that God has given in creation, Evagrius adds a theology that is apophatic, describing God primarily in the terms of the *via negativa*. Evagrius adopts the tripartite Origenian model of spiritual progress that begins with the stage of practical asceticism, in which one strives to overcome physical and emotional passions. The second stage is *gnosis* or *theoria*, where the believer contemplates both material and rational, incorporeal creation. The final stage of development is *theologia*, the mystical contemplation of the Trinity itself. Under the influence of Evagrius, the Syriac writers strive to achieve an integration of the heart-centred traditional Syrian spirituality with a Hellenistic theology that is more purely intellectual and philosophical.

We can observe the beginnings of this integration in the writings of Philoxenus of Mabboug (d. 523) who, while yet giving a central place to a spirituality of the heart, considers the achievement of spiritual knowledge to be the path to mystical union with God. Asceticism brings enlightenment as well as fullness of Spirit. Philoxenus presents his spiritual theology most characteristically in his *Letter to Patricius*. Philoxenus' exact contemporary, Jacob of Serugh (d. 521), shows himself less influenced by Hellenistic spirituality. Jacob's verse homilies continue the spiritual tradition of Ephrem, in poetry of warmth and gentleness that avoids the theological polemic so prevalent in his time.

As a result of the breakdown of Christological consensus after the Councils of Ephesus and Chalcedon, the Syriac churches in the Persian and the Roman Empires broke both with each other and with the imperial church of Constantinople and Rome. Largely rejecting the compromise solution achieved at Chalcedon, the Syrian Church of the East in Persia adhered to the Antiochian Christology of Theodore of Mopsuestia, while much of the Church of Western Syria embraced an uncompromising form of the Christology of St Cyril of Alexandria. Curiously, despite the theological tensions between Eastern and Western Syria, the spiritual works of writers from both areas show a marked commonality of emphasis in the value placed upon the prayer of the luminous heart, upon the working of the Holy Spirit, and upon the intellectual ascent to God. Although generally little known in the Western tradition, the writings of such writers as John of Dalyatha, Martyrius, Dadisho Qatraya, Joseph Hazzaya and especially Isaac of Nineveh, would richly repay modern study. The spirituality of the Syrian tradition is marked by an incarnational theology, possessing a positive valuation of the created order. As such, it offers a valuable corrective to a Christian spiritual tradition that all too often has privileged an exclusively intellectual search for God

See also **Asceticism; Apophatic Spirituality; Monasticism; Neoplatonism.**

Primary sources: Aphrahat, 'Selected Demonstrations' in *Nicene and Post-Nicene Fathers* series 2, vol. 13, Edinburgh: T & T Clark/Grand Rapids, MI: Eerdmans, 1997; S. Brock (ed.), *The Syriac Fathers on Prayer and the Spiritual Life*, Cistercian Studies Series 101, Kalamazoo, MI: Cistercian Publications, 1987; *Ephrem the Syrian. Hymns*, ed. K. McVey, CWS, Mahwah, NJ: Paulist Press, 1989; A. Mingana (ed.), *Early Christian Mystics*, Woodbrooke Studies 7, Cambridge, UK: W. Heffer & Sons Ltd, 1934.

Secondary sources: S. Beggiani, *Introduction to Eastern Christian Spirituality. The Syriac Tradition*, Cranbury, NJ: Associated University Presses, 1991; S. Brock, *The Luminous Eye. The Spiritual World Vision of Saint Ephrem the Syrian*, Cistercian Studies Series 124, Kalamazoo, MI: Cistercian Publications, 1992; R. Murray, *Symbols of Church and Kingdom: A Study in Early Syriac Tradition*, Cambridge: Cambridge University Press, 1975.

ALAN G. PADDLE

Taizé, Spirituality of

The Taizé Community grew from the passionate commitment of Roger Schutz (Brother Roger) for communal living as a parable of reconciliation in the strife-torn Europe of the 1940s. The son of a French Reformed pastor who was himself unafraid to pray in a Catholic church, Roger read theology at Lausanne and Strasbourg. After the fall of France in 1940 he felt called to help refugees, and bought a house in the isolated village of Taizé which was a couple of miles south of the Vichy demarcation line. Here he practised by himself the rhythm of prayer, which he had previously experimented with at university, while keeping open house for refugees and the displaced. Someone denounced him to the Gestapo while he was paying a visit to Geneva in 1942. He was unable to return to the house until 1944, but began the communal life of what was to become the Taizé community in a flat near Geneva cathedral, joined by three friends, including Max Thurian.

Immediately the war ended, Roger returned to Taizé, founding a community devoted to reconciliation. At first it was harsh and difficult. There were attacks on the German prisoners of war to whom the Community ministered. The brothers also took in orphaned boys, who were cared for by Roger's sister Geneviève. It was indicative of the Community's long-term commitment to the poor and oppressed. The Community grew slowly – the first seven brothers took their vows in 1949. Roger's monastic ideals can be traced from an eighteen-page pamphlet he wrote in 1941, which developed into the *Introduction to Community Life* (1944) and *The Rule of Taizé* (1952/3). The essence of the gospel was to be found in three words which exemplified the spirit of the Beatitudes – joy, simplicity and mercy. They were to be the characteristics of the community's life. The *Introduction to Community Life* stated, 'Through our day let work and rest be quickened by the Word of God. Keep inner silence in all things and you will dwell in Christ. Be filled with the spirit of the beatitudes, joy, simplicity and peace.'

The Community was to be 'a parable of reconciliation'. They have firmly resisted both pressure to become a church and the thought that they are a monastic order within Protestantism. The first Catholic brother took his vows in 1969, and the Community embraces brothers of many different ecclesial backgrounds. They are a community, not an order. However, together, gathered in prayer and in community, they are an image of the future reconciled Church, a small reflection of what will one day be.

Their ministry was from the first marked by a passion for reconciliation, and living as far as possible in anticipation of unity. Brother Roger's instinctive (and very Reformed) understanding of provisionality provided the dynamic for this. Friendships were established, most notably with John XXIII, Paul VI, Patriarch Athenagoras of Constantinople, and Eugene Carson Blake of the World Council of Churches. All found in Taizé, in John XXIII's words, 'a springtime of the Church'.

In 1951 the brothers formed their first fraternity, living among the poor in the mining community of Montceau-les-Mines. Since then small fraternities have been planted across the world, sharing the life of the poorest. Struggle and contemplation are held in tension. After living for a while in Calcutta in 1976, Brother Roger and Mother Teresa explained that the division between Christians became unbearable when their daily living confronted all that wounds humanity.

Taizé became a place of pilgrimage for the young. That was neither planned nor expected, but it became a major part of the Community's ministry. They come for many reasons, but at the heart of any visit is the thrice-daily rhythm of prayer, and a liturgy which combines Scripture, silence, intercession and simple music that provides a doorway to contemplation. Here young people are listened to, and allowed to explore who they are and what they are called to become. It was out of this experience that Brother Roger called a 'Council of Youth' in 1974, making clear the connections between contemplation, prayer, social commitment and politics. It was a remarkable ecumenical occasion, attended by forty thousand young people, and that in its turn led to the 'Pilgrimage of Trust on Earth', a multi-level attempt to nurture Christ's peace and reconciliation across the world.

Brother Roger has said that the community do not want there to be 'a spirituality of Taizé'. They have no particular 'method', and have found no solutions to either ecumenical divisions or the pastoral care of the young. They are rather 'a parable', and just as a parable invites us into its world, the community invite visitors into theirs, to discover something of what will one day be.

See also **Community; Ecumenical Spirituality; Monasticism; Reconciliation.**

J. L. Balado, *The Story of Taizé*, London: Mowbray, 1980; Rex Brico, *Taizé: Brother Roger and His Community*, London: Collins, 1978; Kathryn Spink, *A Universal Heart: The Life and Vision of Brother Roger of Taizé*, London: SPCK, 1986.

DAVID CORNICK

Taoism

see Daoism and Christianity

Tears, Gift of (*Penthos*)

The tears that accompany repentance, conversion and inward renewal are linked both in the Scriptures and in the later Christian spiritual tradition with the concept of *penthos*, 'mourning' that purifies the soul. In the Old Testament *penthos* is especially mourning for the dead expressed in tears and lamentation; but it is also the sorrow and grief that accompanies prophesied disaster. Similarly, *penthos* in the New Testament is also mourning with tears; but it is a grief that leads to a determination to act or change (2 Cor. 12.21; Rev. 18).

The Christian doctrine of tears/*penthos* flowers in the fourth-century deserts of Egypt. To weep for one's sins was for many Desert Fathers the central and all-encompassing act of monastic piety (*Sayings*, Latin *Systematic Collection*, bk 3). The hermit Evagrius Ponticus (d. 399) recommends that one begin with tearful prayer in order to 'calm the wildness within the soul' and obtain forgiveness of sins (*On Prayer* 5–6). Prayer with tears is a gift one should request from God, but tears and *penthos* are not ends in themselves: they afford humility and lead to pure prayer, eventually to that simplest and purest of all prayer that is contemplation. If, however, one becomes overly preoccupied with tears, their presence can become a cause of pride and thus of sin: 'you have turned the antidote of passion into a passion' (*On Prayer* 7–8).

John Climacus (d. 649), whose *Ladder of Divine Ascent* is read each Lent by every Orthodox monk and nun, compares tears shed in prayer with the sacrament of baptism. Such tears, he claims, are in one sense greater than baptism itself: namely, that they wash away postbaptismal sin. Such tears are also a sign that we have received the gift of love, and that our prayers have been accepted by God (*Ladder* 7). Symeon the New Theologian (d. 1032) extols and describes two kinds of tears: bitter tears of repentance and fear, and sweet tears of joy. He does not stress this distinction, however; and he describes both mingled sorrow for sin and delight at forgiveness, as well as a progression from sorrow to joy. He likens prayer with tears to a second baptism, and regards tears as a preparation for contemplation and the indwelling of the Holy Spirit. But tears are not only a means of preparation, they are for Symeon the sign of the Spirit's indwelling 'in light and fire': 'When a person has the light of the Holy Spirit inside himself . . . he pours forth a ceaseless flood of tears that both refreshes him and arouses the flame of his longing. These tears of his become even more copious; and having been purified by their flood, he shines forth even more brilliantly' (*Theological Chapters* 3.21).

In the Christian West, too, compunction and prayer with tears are highly regarded. John Cassian, like his master Evagrius, encourages tears during prayer which he regards as one – but only one – of the signs of genuine compunction. Compunction, literally the sense of being 'inwardly pierced', may be manifested in a variety of ways: shouts of joy; profound silence; inarticulate groans; 'floods of tears' (*Conferences* 9.27). Cassian describes the many different states tears can express: repentance from sin; longing for heaven; meditation on the last judgement; compassion for the terrible state of hardened sinners. Like Evagrius, Cassian warns against too much reliance on tears, and stresses that they should never be forced (*Conferences* 9.29–30). Other Western spiritual writers who recommend tearful prayer include: Benedict of Nursia (Rule 4.57; 52.4); Peter Damian (d. 1072);

Bernard of Clairvaux (d. 1153); Ruysbroeck (d. 1381); and Ignatius of Loyola (d. 1556).

Finally, it should be borne in mind that the frequency with which tears accompany prayer or any other spiritual practice may be heavily influenced by social and psychological factors. In the modern era in non-Mediterranean Europe and North America the public, external expression of most deep emotions is strongly discouraged; and for this reason the gift of tears may be uncommon. In the relative absence of this traditional sign of compunction, sincerity and divine grace, it may be well to recall Evagrius' reminder that tears are not a goal but rather a means towards the goal of humble, honest conversation with God.

See also **Asceticism; Byzantine Spirituality; Early Christian Spirituality; Humility; Monasticism.**

Evagrius of Pontus, the Greek Ascetic Corpus, trans. R. E. Sinkewicz, Oxford: Oxford University Press 2004, 'Chapters on Prayer'; I. Hausherr, *Penthos: The Doctrine of Compunction in the Christian East*, Kalamazoo, MI: Cistercian Publications, 1982; *John Cassian: The Conferences*, trans. B. Ramsey, CWS, New York: Paulist Press 1997, 'Conference 9'; *John Climacus: The Ladder of Divine Ascent*, trans. C. Luibheid, CWS, New York: Paulist Press, 1982; *Symeon the New Theologian: The Practical and Theological Chapters, and the Three Theological Discourses*, trans. J. P. McGuckin, Kalamazoo, MI: Cistercian Publications, 1982.

LUKE DYSINGER

Technology and Spirituality

Being human involves the use of tools. And it is the use of tools, recorded as far back as 2.6 million years ago in the genus *Homo*, that has brought spirituality and technology into a relationship that has persisted, and will persist, as long as *Homo sapiens* inhabits the earth. The reason for this is that technology, like spirituality, is part of a process through which human beings invest life with order and meaning. Technology, from the Greek *techne*, means 'know-how', The term 'technology', generally speaking, pertains to the realm of made things; it is part and parcel of the material world. Spirituality, on the other hand, concerns itself with incorporeal matters. Both technology and spirituality improve the quality of human experience; technology through the invention of machines and artefacts designed to make life easier and more materially satisfying; spirituality by insisting material life can be made meaningful in ways that transcend the physical.

Spirituality and technology, if viewed as 'systems' of thought with specific ends in mind, have dramatically different goals. Technology is based upon the scientific method, and the application of that method to the invention and production of commodities for the marketplace. Technology is both ends and means, and continually so, because new discoveries rely on the existence of earlier methods and mechanisms. Spirituality is itself goal-oriented, but its goals are hardly those of technology. The goals of spirituality are profound, and enduring, while those of technology, no matter how remarkable or esoteric, remain essentially mundane. These distinctions must be kept in mind when considering areas in which technology and spirituality appear to overlap. There is a built-in limit to such intersections, since the nature of spiritual enquiry is neither scientific nor technological. 'Know-how' is not the ultimate value. Why we exist, why we are here, and to what purpose, are questions beyond the scope of every machine ever designed. Nor is it in the nature of technology to illuminate such concerns. This is not to say, however, that technology can be of no use at all in fostering spirituality.

The basic function of technology is to multiply the powers of human senses and organs. In doing so, technology makes it possible for humans to overcome their physical limitations. The microscope and the telescope make vision more acute, the telephone and the radio enable us to hear voices at great distances, a plane substitutes wings for the legs we are born with. Tools and machines give us strength our bodies do not naturally possess, and vastly increase our productive capacities. Yet the sensibility that produces such life-enhancing inventions is not merely utilitarian; it is fuelled by a desire for a higher level of satisfaction. At heart, *Homo faber* is a person who seeks to understand how things work. And while it is true that sometimes this seeking leads to undesirable and unintended results, such results are most often due to human fallibility. There are also instances when the curiosity that drives *techne* has an almost spiritual overtone, as when microscopes, telescopes, deep-sea probes and satellites are used to reveal extraordinary aspects of the world and the cosmos that would have remained unknown without the use of such inventions. If looking into nature reveals the presence of God, then technology, no matter how unintentionally, has certainly aided in this search.

Historically, linkages between spirituality and technology have occurred primarily in the fields of communication and transportation. One of the earliest examples of such a conjunction

between spirituality and technology is the carving of pictorial glyphs, used to track commodities, on temple records six thousand years ago in Sumeria. Three millennia later, these same Sumerians were writing on clay tablets with reed styluses. Progress and invention, of course, were slow, but in the fifteenth century BCE, a Semitic people living in the South Sinai invented the alphabet, an invention that converted simple record-keeping into a powerful tool that eventually made it possible for different cultures, with different spiritual outlooks, to communicate. Another, more recent, example of an overlap between spirituality and technology is the construction of roads, most notably in Rome. The Romans, of course, were famous for road-building. And at the height of the Roman Empire, more than fifty thousand miles of roads knitted together Roman territories stretching from Mesopotamia to what is now Great Britain. It is difficult to imagine the map of modern Christianity looking as it does without the existence of these roads, and their effect on the mobility of the early disciples.

An even more significant convergence of spirituality and technology took place in the fifteenth century, with Gutenberg's invention of movable type. A papal indulgence, printed at Mainz in 1454, is the first dated use of this technology in Europe. And no later than 1455, the Gutenberg Bible, also printed in Mainz, became the first complete book printed with the new technology. The spread of printing technology expanded the flow of information, both sacred and secular, throughout Europe, and ultimately played as significant a role in the launch of Protestantism as did theological disputes. The social-political effect of this new technology was to weaken the hold of the Catholic Church in Western Europe, and to advance the cause of literacy. The subsequent rise of literacy further undermined the Catholic Church as a spiritual authority by allowing people to choose between Scripture and their own personal revelations as sources of spirituality. In the modern world, improvements in transportation and communication technologies continue to encourage the spread of spirituality, so much so, in fact, that it might be argued (after Hegel) that quantitative change really does lead to qualitative change. Today, geography no longer impedes the spread of spirituality. The words of a televised evangelist reach anywhere, as long as there is a satellite to transmit and direct the signal. People living on opposite sides of the world can be in almost immediate contact at the click of a mouse, or the touch of a button on a computer keyboard. Communications technology continues to accelerate the process begun in Sumeria, a process that has now taken us from our small and circumscribed neighborhoods into cyberspace.

Technology, old and new, is not without its critics. When Noah's descendants tried building a tower at Babel, God confused their speech, forcing them to abandon the project. In the Greek myths, Prometheus is punished for teaching lowly humans how to use fire, a figurative usage that entails the creation of technology. The historical connection between *techne* and the development of weapons (military technology) has long been studied by scholars, among them Lewis Mumford. Mumford also bemoans the dehumanizing effects of large-scale systems. Max Weber, following upon insights supplied by Karl Marx, observes that the rationalized modern workplace is peopled mainly by 'disenchanted' workers. And more recently, Jacques Ellul, elaborating on this theme of alienation, worries that an ever more ubiquitous technology will serve to disconnect us completely from what it means to be human. There is little question that mass society, with its mass production and delivery systems, is a difficult place for people to feel connected to other human beings in ways that matter. And in Ellul's pessimistic view of 'technique', an almost deterministic over-reliance on endless technological change without regard to purpose has led us to the brink of spiritual tragedy. Ellul may overstate the case, but there is cause for concern.

Technology presents many challenges to spirituality. Even those who are sanguine about the future of convergence between technology and spirituality admit that research in areas like cloning, robotics, artificial intelligence and military technology gives them pause. In these endeavours spiritual-ethical concerns seem to have been pushed aside by the relentless march of invention. Other technological pursuits, like cyberspace, appear to offer hope for increasing spirituality. Proponents believe an inexpensive global network, linking friends and strangers over the Internet, possesses significant potential for transmitting the word of God, and for helping to increase spirituality worldwide. Such expectations appear to be overly optimistic, although they are grounded in an appreciation of what communications technology has already accomplished in the way of abetting spirituality. But for every champion of cyber-spirituality, there is a sceptic who sees lonely people staring at a monitor. And there is no denying that the telephone, the automobile, radio, television and the computer, which have helped convert the world into a global village, have also pushed people away from associational life. Technology is Janus-faced. And technological possibilities, no matter how much we might wish otherwise, are not necessarily spiritual opportunities.

See also **Contemporary Spirituality; Spirituality and Science (*essays*); Cyberspace; Ecological Spirituality; Enlightenment Thought; Media and Communications; New Age; Postmodernity.**

Lewis Mumford, *Technics and Civilization*, New York: Harcourt-Brace, 1934; Jacques Ellul, *The Technological Society*, New York: Knopf, 1964 (*La Technique ou l'enjeu du siècle*, Paris: Librairie Armand Colin, 1954); Erik Davis, *Techgnosis*, New York: Harmony Books, 1998; Ignacio L. Gotz, *Technology and the Spirit*, Westport, CT: Praeger, 2001.

GEORGE O'HAR

Thanksgiving

In Christian prayer, thanksgiving, adoration, praise and blessing are intimately related. The Hebrew Bible promotes this family of prayer by implication: it contains no independent vocabulary of thanksgiving distinct from praise. Though *yadah* from the Hebrew is generally translated as 'thank', *hillel* as 'praise', and *toda* as 'gratitude', they are often synonymous and the distinctions hard to identify. Still, thanksgiving does have independent characteristics that are gleaned from the Hebrew, clarified in the New Testament, identified in early Church doctrine and practice, and made to come to life in the Eucharist.

Though appearing early in the Hebrew Bible, a vocabulary of thanksgiving as gratitude is often indistinct – the thank-offering itself was an offering of peace or fellowship in the sacrificial system of the Mosaic covenant. Thanksgiving in the sense of gratitude is more common in the Psalms, where 'give thanks to the Lord, for the Lord is good' is a common phrase. Many psalms of lament conclude with thanksgiving. Such conclusions indicate that the honesty of lament is yet embraced in the 'but yet' of the believer's confidence in God's steadfast love and tender mercies which then lead to thanksgiving.

With the New Testament thanksgiving becomes more sharply defined. This definition reaches its culmination in the bread and wine of the Lord's Supper. The word Eucharist itself (from the verb *eucharisteo* and its cognate noun *eucharistia*), meaning thanksgiving, is used in the early Church to describe the sacramental quality of the supper. Thanksgiving, exemplified most concretely in the Lord's Supper, becomes in the New Testament a motive for life and conduct, a general attitude toward life's blessings and trials, and an essential component of prayer.

Paul turns thanksgiving into a way of life: it should, he says, be given at all times and for all things (1 Thess. 5.16; 2 Thess. 2.13; Phil. 4.6). Thanksgiving seems, more than any other form of prayer, to be Paul's answer to the question of how to pray without ceasing. In all things, Paul urges his listeners to 'give thanks praying'. In the Gospels, as modelled by the life and words of Christ, thanksgiving and praise to God become key elements of Christian life and faith. In John, identity and union of the believer with Christ through the Holy Spirit both enkindles thanksgiving and transforms the life of those thus united to Christ into an offering of thanksgiving. In this sense thanksgiving is the attitude of prayer equivalent to the life of faith.

Thanksgiving, as eucharistic, as union with Christ, as a way of life, and as a form of constant prayer is also a prayer of confession. To give thanks to God is to imply a confession of God's sovereignty, redemptive power, eternal wisdom and holy mystery. Equally, to give thanks to God is to imply a confession of our own servanthood, sinfulness, powerlessness, wandering and mortality. That confession is at the heart of prayers of thanksgiving is reflected also in Scripture. The Hebrew word *yadah* for 'thank' is often used in situations where 'confess' might be a better translation (cf. Ps. 35.18).

Similarly, Jesus prays, 'I thank you, Father, Lord of heaven and earth, because you have hidden these things from the wise and intelligent and have revealed them to infants' (Matt. 11.25; Luke 10.21). In this prayer, the word translated as 'thank' is the verb meaning rather to 'confess', used for confessing sins as well as blessings. As with adoration, praise, and blessing, the circular network of prayer that passes through thanksgiving runs as well directly through confession.

While gratitude is an ever-present response of appreciation for the bounty of God's love for us, prayers of thanksgiving are generally made for specific gifts and blessings. As Paul says, a reasonable person contemplating the beauty and goodness of creation can know something of God: 'for since the creation of the world, God's invisible qualities – God's eternal power and divine nature – have been clearly seen, being understood from what has been made.' But only the faithful give thanks for the *gift* of creation: 'for they [those without faith] knew not God, *they did not honor God as God or give God thanks*' (Rom. 1.20–21). For Paul, ingratitude and unbelief are virtually synonymous.

Gratitude and thanksgiving are thus based on the belief that all creation is from God. Yet while it is true that all prayer, in some sense, consists in thanking God for everything, it is also true that thanking God for everything means maintaining precision, attention and clarity in prayer. For as George Buttrick reminds us, 'the prayer of thanksgiving should be quite specific: I thank thee for *this* friendship, *this* threat overpassed, *this* signal grace. "For all thy mercies" is a proper phrase for a general collect, but not a private gratitude. If we are "thankful for everything", we may end by being thankful for nothing' ('Prayer').

According to Origen, thanksgiving 'is a statement of gratitude made with prayers for receiving good things from God'. These 'good things' can be material gifts, spiritual gifts or simply thanksgiving as an acknowledged benefit of a gift. In any of these cases, for Origen thanksgiving opens a window on to both the goodness of creation and the holiness of God (*On Prayer* 1.14). Whether we follow Brother Lawrence, who found reason for prayer in the small and ordinary, or Gregory of Nyssa, who found prayer in a dark cloud beyond mind, 'the last thing that is necessary for prayer is that we give it in thanksgiving' (Spener, 'God-pleasing prayer' 3.10).

See also **Adoration; Celebration; Desire; Eucharistic Spirituality; Joy; Praise; Prayer; Suffering.**

George A. Buttrick, 'Prayer' in Richard Foster and James Bryan Smith (eds), *Devotional Classics: Selected Readings for Individuals and Groups*, San Francisco, CA: HarperSanFrancisco, 1993, pp. 100–5; Pat Collins, *Prayer in Practice: A Biblical Approach*, Maryknoll, NY: Orbis Press, 2001; Philipp Jakob Spener, 'God-pleasing prayer', in Peter C. Erb (ed.), *Pietists: Selected Writings*, CWS, New York: Paulist Press, 1983, pp. 88–93.

STEVEN CHASE

Theoria

The word *theoria* had a long and respectable empirical and philosophical career before it ever gained a technical sense among the Christian spiritual writers. The new Christian uses were related to the older semantic, but *theoria*, as it was increasingly used to describe a spiritual faculty, represented a much more acutely sharpened sense of the word, and one can certainly conclude that this intensity made of it almost a neologism of the Byzantine Christians. Generally *theoria* meant awareness or perception. The fifth-century Syrian theologian Theodoret used it to describe Adam and Eve's sudden realization of their nakedness in his *Commentary on Genesis*.

Several contemporaneous biblical commentators used it also, in a relatively new and special sense, to signify what they meant about the 'spiritual sense' of Scripture, as distinct from the historical or material meaning of the text. A 'theoretic interpretation' thus meant a higher allegorical reading, rather than a speculation, in ancient exegesis. Most Greek Christian writers used *theoria* in its more common sense, however, of seeing or perceiving. But since *theoria* was a particularly apt word for noetic vision, or the function of the human psyche when engaged in the highest level of discernment and scrutiny (such as philosophy or scientific speculation) it was obviously destined in the hands of Christian writers to become a highly favoured term for spiritual awareness, and this was how it was predominantly used by monastic and spiritual authors. Gregory of Nyssa in his sixth *Homily on Canticles* shows that by the end of the fourth century the word had acquired a high technical sense of the purest and most refined form of human contemplation of the divine activity and presence in the psyche or the world. But it is perhaps Evagrius of Pontus (late fourth century) who most developed the word in its specific application to the spiritual life. Evagrius (Letter 12) described *theoria* as the 'final goal of wisdom' and used it as a synonym for the kingdom of God. It was, for him, that state of consummation which the ascent of soul to divine communion can bring about through prayer. Contemplation (*theoria*) of the iconic patterns of the forms of the world (what we might today call the higher levels of philosophical attentiveness and reflective meditation) open up for the monk, in Evagrius' understanding, an acuity of intellectual vision that itself serves as the midwife of 'spiritual knowledge' (*gnosis*). Evagrius' spiritual vocabulary survived the condemnation of its originator to become foundational for Christian spirituality. In wider patristic thought, the intellective awareness signified by *theoria* was always closely related to, but not to be confused with, spiritual knowledge. In later writings of the West, and in some modern studies, this distinction has not been so carefully observed, since Western contemplative traditions often used the notion of 'contemplative vision' as the highest marker of a human consciousness of God, whereas the earlier patristic tradition was always most cautious about using 'vision' as a final term of reference for 'communion' with the divine. The word *theoria* also implied a state of spiritual achievement demonstrably more advanced than that described as *praktikos* (practical or ascetical exercises) which first demanded the attentions of the novice. Practical exercises in terms of the

length of prayers, or fasting, and (of course) moral repentance, prepared the soul by purifying it, in the monastic understanding, for a higher-level engagement in the life of *theoria*. This in turn was expected to lead to the mystical communion with God. The close and systemic relation of most of these technical words to describe the new Christian theology of prayer can be seen in the following short passage from Evagrios: 'When the spiritual intellect (*nous*) practises the ascetical life (*praktikos*), with God's help, and draws near to mystical knowledge (*gnosis*), then it ceases to have much awareness at all (*prosoche*) of the sub-rational affairs of the soul (*psyche*); for contemplative knowledge (*theoria*) carries it on high and detaches it from the senses (*aistheta*)' (Evagrius, *Praktikos* 38).

See also **Byzantine Spirituality; Contemplation.**

V. Lossky, *The Mystical Theology of the Eastern Church*, Cambridge: James Clarke [1957], 1973, pp. 196–216; J. A. McGuckin, *Standing in God's Holy Fire: The Tradition of Byzantium*, London: Darton, Longman & Todd/New York: Orbis Books, 2001; T. Spidlik, *The Spirituality of the Christian East*, Kalamazoo, MI: Cistercian Publications, 1986.

JOHN ANTHONY MCGUCKIN

Thomist Spirituality

The term refers to the spiritual life and teaching of St Thomas Aquinas (1225/26–74) and of those who belong to his school. As a child, so it is said, Thomas was already asking the question 'what is God?' and this remained the central preoccupation of his life. He opted for the Dominicans rather than the Benedictines for reasons that remain unknown, but the intellectual concerns of the new Order may have appealed to him as well as its commitment to countering the neo-Manichaean ideas of the Cathars. In practice this meant developing a theological approach in which an appreciation of the goodness of creation was central.

Thomas had already been introduced to the philosophy of Aristotle at Naples and his studies under Albert the Great in Paris strengthened his interest in the newly translated works of Aristotle. On the face of it Aristotle seemed less promising an ally for Christian theology than the more religiously minded Plato. In fact there was little of Plato's work available in the thirteenth century although he had already had a significant impact on the development of theology in the patristic period. In any case Thomas found in Aristotle the ally he needed for supporting the theological affirmation of created reality. Issues that are central to Christian life and thinking such as creation itself, human individuality and integrity, grace and freedom, incarnation and sacrament – all receive fresh and exciting treatment in the light of Aristotle's scientific, ethical and metaphysical teachings.

Thomas's holistic anthropology – his understanding of the essential unity of body and soul in the human individual – is a distinctive and original contribution to human thought. Much moral and spiritual wisdom follows from his conviction that the human is essentially a physical being, that the soul needs the body just as the body needs the soul, and that there is no human knowing, even the highest forms of spiritual understanding, that does not depend on what has been experienced physically. It has been claimed that Thomas is the first Christian philosopher to take the corporeal character of human existence calmly. For Thomas the human body is even essential to what he calls 'the well-being of our eternal happiness': no one had given such honour to the human body before.

With characteristic provocativeness, G. K. Chesterton says that Thomas, with Francis of Assisi, saved the West from spirituality. By this he means that the affirmation of the goodness of creation by Francis and Thomas strengthened a characteristically Christian understanding of the Word becoming flesh and of God seeing all that he had made and finding it very good. The world itself is already a gift from God by virtue of the mystery of being or existence that is found at the heart of the smallest thing there is. On this view all one needs is an ant or a leaf to initiate a meditation on existence that will lead ultimately to God. In the thought of Thomas Aquinas we find a mysticism of being in which the divine presence is recognized primarily in God's creative and continuing emanation – Thomas does not fear the term – that is the being of things. Because it is created in the image of God the human creature has the capacity to receive the gift of being with awareness and gratitude.

His most famous work, the *Summa Theologiae*, was intended as a moral theology, concerned with the living out of the Christian life understood as the human creature's pilgrimage of return to God. A key structuring theme of this work is *beatitudo*, blessedness or bliss. Thomas uses this term to characterize the trinitarian life of God in which creation and salvation originate. He uses it also to refer to the final end or fundamental desire that moves human beings to moral and spiritual searching. *Beatitudo* is what Jesus Christ brings because it is he who in fact opens the way for human entry into the blessed life of God. Thomas did not live to write the parts of the *Summa* devoted to eschatology but it is clear from what he did write that the blessedness to which we may now look forward is beyond anything human hearts can conceive.

Thomas speaks of the human appropriation of *beatitudo* in terms of grace and deification. His understanding of grace is essentially trinitarian. The Son and the Spirit have been sent by the Father to bring the world within God's embrace so that it might share in God's own life of knowing and loving. Grace refers to the strengthening and elevation of nature that attends the indwelling of the divine persons. Grace operates within the human capacities for knowing and loving and conforms human beings to 'the Word that breathes Love'. Graced humanity is Word-bearing and loving, made to be like God.

In practice this happens through the virtues or gifts of faith, hope and charity with the many actions, expressions, initiatives and practices to which they give rise and which constitute the pastoral and spiritual life of Christian individuals and communities. The life of the believer, stimulated and sustained by Christ in his Church, is nevertheless a life lived in mystery, since in this life, Thomas says, we can only be united with God as with an unknown. Faith is profoundly paradoxical for him. It is a firm assent unsupported by evidence sufficient to satisfy the intellect. It is a speaking or articulation whose hold on truth reaches beyond what the words used contain. It touches a reality signified by those words, which yet remains unknown. 'It is in the dark night of ignorance', he writes, 'that we come closest to God in this life' (in *1 Sentences* 8.1.1).

For Thomas, wisdom means knowing that we do not know God. We are *viatores* or travellers who live in a tension towards that which is and is not yet ours. We live then by hope, a virtue whose characteristic act is prayer, which Thomas describes as 'the interpreter of desire'. Prayer is the struggle of mind and mouth to find words for what the heart wants.

Thomas understands charity to mean friendship with God. No longer simply creatures or servants, we are established in friendship with God by Jesus Christ (John 15.15) so that we become God's partners and co-workers in caring for the world and guiding its progress. It is in this friendship of charity that we begin already to experience *beatitudo* as we are brought to participate in the nature of God who is love.

Christ won this gift for us through his passion and the sacraments are the fruits of his passion. They adapt the gift of divine life or grace to the kind of creature we are: linguistic, sign-making, social, political, physical, ritual-celebrating and historical. We know from the witnesses who testified to his way of living that Thomas's personal spiritual life was centred on the celebration of the Eucharist. His devotion to the Eucharist is still to be seen in the poetry he composed to accompany the liturgies of Corpus Christi. Having been to confession and celebrated the Eucharist, he then spent his day studying the Word of God, trying to penetrate and expound wisdom's truth in a sustained and creative theological life.

In his life of Jesus, Thomas describes him as a wandering teacher whose mission was to serve truth in a life of poverty, prayer and preaching. Thomas sought to imitate this way of living, devoting himself without reserve and without ambition to the ministry of study and teaching. Some sections of the secular clergy reacted strongly to the emergence of the mendicant orders and sought to have their way of life disallowed. Thomas wrote a number of works in defence of the new form of religious life. At the heart of the friar's life, he said, is obedience, the highest exercise of human freedom as a person entrusts himself completely to God and to God's unfolding plan for the world. He argued that this was a valid way of following Christ whose love and obedience are the world's salvation.

Thomist spirituality, at least as we see it in Thomas himself, combines intellectual dedication and discipline with a comparatively simple life of prayer and liturgical practice. On 6 December 1273, the feast of St Nicholas, Thomas had an experience during the Eucharist that led him to give up writing. He had often cited a saying of Pseudo-Dionysius to the effect that the search for God involves not just learning about divine things but experiencing them, literally 'suffering' them (*non solum discens sed et patiens divina*). This saying became reality for him on that day. He had given his life to contemplation, meaning the study of the Word of God. Now, it seems, he was brought to that place of silence of which the Christian mystical tradition had always spoken, into those mists within which – as Thomas well knew – God is said to dwell.

See also **Analogy; Aristotelianism; Body and Spirituality; Creation Spirituality; Deification; Dominican Spirituality; Intellectual Life and Spirituality; Medieval Spirituality in the West; Mendicant Spirituality; Obedience; Person; Scholasticism.**

Thomas F. O'Meara, *Thomas Aquinas Theologian*, Notre Dame, IN: University of Notre Dame Press, 1997; Walter H. Principe, *Thomas Aquinas' Spirituality*, Toronto: Pontifical Institute of Medieval Studies, 1984; J.-P.Torrell, *Saint Thomas Aquinas: Spiritual Master*, trans. Robert Royal, Washington, DC: Catholic University of America Press, 2003; Simon Tugwell, *Albert and Thomas*, CWS, New York: Paulist Press, 1988; James A. Weisheipl, *Friar Thomas d'Aquino: His Life, Thought, and Works*, Oxford: Blackwell, 1974, 2nd edn, Washington, DC, 1983; A. N. Williams, *The Ground of Union: Deification in Aquinas and Palamas*, Oxford: Oxford University Press, 1999.

VIVIAN BOLAND

Time

Interestingly, 'time' is not a prominent theme in books on Christian spirituality even though time and the sanctification of time are central to a religion whose foundational doctrine is God's 'incarnation' at a particular historical moment. Christian spirituality exists *in time* – in other words, it is always historical and contextual and, in the words of Rowan Williams, has 'closed off the path to "timeless truth"'. Christian spirituality points to 'the affirmation of history, and thus of human change and growth, as significant' (Williams, 1990, pp. 1–2).

We apprehend our world in terms of space and time and these provide the framework of our experience. In that sense, 'time' like 'place' is a critical cultural category through which human beings organize their understanding of human existence and the world around them. How we perceive time determines our rhythms of life, how we behave and how we value the different elements of our lives.

The human concept of time has changed and consequently the way history is written has also changed. The concept of time has gone through three historical phases: cyclical, linear and 'chaotic' (see Fernández-Armesto, pp. 246–9). Although cyclical and linear conceptions of time have coexisted throughout much of history, linear time gradually asserted its superiority. In this context, the Old Testament writings are very important, especially the Genesis creation story. In contrast to the beauty of a cycle with no beginning and no end, the book of Genesis posits a unique act of creation that inaugurated change and the flow of time. Judaism retained cyclical themes of recurrence but preferred a predominantly linear model of time. Particular events might be repeated or be echoed (e.g. the annual commemoration of the Passover) but history taken as a whole was unique. This view passed over into both Christianity and Islam. In Christianity, the linear model of time was reinforced by the unique event of the incarnation and the emphasis on the permanent sufficiency of Christ's sacrifice on the cross made 'once for all'. In turn, this belief pointed forward to the final victory of God in Christ – a teleological-providential view of history led by God ever onward towards a redemptive climax.

Such a view of time is now confronted by the arrival, in Western cultures at least, of a concept of time that is no more than chaotic flux. This is partly a philosophical question of denying the 'objective' nature of cultural categories such as 'time' and its consequent relegation to a subjective, mental construction which is necessarily plural and contested. This new conception of time was reinforced by the work of Albert Einstein and subsequent scientific studies on 'time'. Time is not absolute but depends on the observer's standpoint (literally and metaphorically). Equally, some cosmologists speculate that time might itself be reversible and actually be reversed if, in some unimaginable future, the universe begins to contract.

Since Augustine's *Confessions*, Christianity has engaged with philosophical questions about time. Time is the condition of human existence, and of human becoming, and time is inextricably linked to the contingent-created order (time and the world are created together). Time is, if you like, the measure of the absolute difference between God and human existence. Unlike humankind, God is conceived as having neither memory nor expectation of future possibility but as existing in a complete and joy-filled 'present'. How, then, can time-bound humanity and the eternal God engage with each other? In a sense, such philosophical issues are not the paramount ones for spirituality. Yet, from another angle they stand forcefully for the sheer 'otherness' of God, the mysterious nature of divine–human encounters and for the priority of an apophatic-mystical stance not only to religious language but also to the nature of spiritual experience.

Christian life and practice have been dominated by concepts of time. The Church's life is marked by a series of temporal cycles – although one has to admit that their power is considerably diminished in contemporary Western culture where time has become increasingly fluid rather than rhythmic. Each day celebrates liturgically the division between day and night (and symbolically between light and dark) and in some Christian communities, for example monastic ones, the whole day is punctuated by times of prayer. These operate on a number of levels: as thresholds between different activities, as a framework for a rhythmic rather than random pattern of life, and as regular moments for recollecting the continuous presence of God. A

weekly cycle not only provides a regular holy day set aside for worship but a boundary between labour and rest. The cycle of the year is to be lived out in redemptive terms in relation to Christ's life from conception to ascension, marked by alternating fasting and feasting, rather than simply in terms of the natural seasons (although there are clearly many ways in which these two views of the year's passing overlap).

It has been suggested that Christianity lives with at least four concepts of 'time' (see Rayment-Pickard, 2004). In reality, these are not alternatives but are to be held in creative tension. 'Catastrophic time' highlights the inexorable process of time moving towards death and the fact that 'destiny is dust', as it were. The contemplation of such contingency and of time's ruin has played a significant part in the development of Christian spiritual discipline or asceticism. 'Apocalyptic time' expresses a spirituality of waiting and anticipation – that ultimate meaning will 'come to us' rather than be artificially constructed by our limited imaginations. 'Kairic time' (from the Greek *kairos*, implying 'time-as-opportunity') focuses attention on the vital importance of the present moment and of finding meaning in the ordinary, in what is *given now*. In many respects *kairos* time is in the foreground of the New Testament. God's saving action in the life-death-resurrection of Jesus is said to be 'in the fullness of time' (Gal. 4.4). This overflows into the sense that for all whom Jesus addresses, 'this is the favourable time', now 'the time is fulfilled (Mark 1.15; Matt. 4.17). The call to welcome the kingdom of God, to turn to God, is an urgent *now*. Finally, 'prophetic time' does not accept things as they are but both envisions and then actively promotes an ideal 'end' for time (both in the sense of completion and purpose). Such a view of time fuels different forms of political or liberation spiritualities.

In the broadest possible terms, Christianity treats time as a tightly bound, threefold pattern of memory, engagement with the present and anticipation of the future. On the one hand, past and future are not escape routes from dissatisfaction with the present. On the other, a sense of being involved in a stream of time breeds a sense of responsibility for a time beyond ourselves and relativizes an obsession with the unique importance of our 'present moment'. For the Christian community, 'time' conceived as a whole is portrayed in eschatological terms as emanating from and returning to divine eternity. Both the Christ-centred and eschatological dimensions of time are most powerfully realized in the regular celebration of the Eucharist. Here, Christ's redemptive life, death and resurrection are re-presented as real and effective for each succeeding generation. At the same time, in every contingent eucharistic 'moment', past, present and future are mystically gathered in an intersection of time and eternity.

A number of features of contemporary Western culture underline the shifting patterns of 'time' and provide a challenging context for Christian approaches to time to be reconceived. In summary, these features involve the crumbling away of the time boundaries that defined people's lives for centuries. For example, the impact of micro-technology, among other factors, means that we live increasingly in a 24-hour world where distinctions between night and day are blurred. Equally the traditional boundaries between a working week and Sabbath rest are rapidly being eradicated. The resulting 'crisis' of time presents itself as a fragmentation of time and the problem of a lack or loss of time. This heightens our awareness of 'running out of time', the imperative of 'saving time', the pressure to avoid anything that is 'a waste of time' and so on. The cultural pressures are towards immediacy, speed, obvious productivity and completion *now*. In this context, Christian spiritual values such as attentiveness and waiting, recognizing our unfinished nature and living in hope and expectation, take on a new urgency and prophetic potency. Faithfulness and perseverance become critical challenges for everyone. It is worth recalling that one of the most powerful symbols of time in both the Hebrew Scriptures and the Gospels is the desert. The desert is both a space and a time. Desert 'time', whether for the people of Israel in Exodus or for Jesus in the synoptic Gospels, is a period both of waiting and of testing (see e.g. Deut. 8.2). Symbolically, the 'time of the desert' stands for an apparent non-time, a between-time, a 'useless' time, yet the kind of time that, if allowed for, teaches humanity the crucial lessons of patience and perseverance.

See also **Spirituality and History** (*essay*); **Afterlife; Eschatology; Hope; Journey, Spiritual; Perseverance; Sacred; World.**

___

Enzo Bianchi, *Words of Spirituality: Towards a Lexicon of the Inner Life*, London: SPCK, 2002, esp. ch. 11; Richard K. Fenn, *The End of Time: Religion, Ritual and the Forging of the Soul*, Cleveland: The Pilgrim Press/London: SPCK, 1997; Felipe Fernández-Armesto, 'Time and history' in Kristen Lippincott, with Umberto Eco, E. H. Gombrich et al., *The Story of Time*, London: Merrill Holberton, 1999; A. J. Gurevich, *Categories of Medieval Culture*, London and Boston: Routledge, 1985, ch. 4; Hugh Rayment-Pickard, *The Myths of Time:* *From St Augustine to 'American Beauty'*, London: Darton, Longman & Todd, 2004; Rowan Williams, *The Wound of Knowledge: Christian Spirituality from the New Testament to St John of the Cross*, London: Darton, Longman & Todd/ Cambridge, MA: Cowley Publications, 1990.

PHILIP SHELDRAKE

Tradition

Tradition, from the Latin root *tradere*, means in essence 'to hand on'. Customarily tradition refers to an approved teaching, and carries greater weight than teaching that is not time-honoured or handed on from generation to generation. Tradition allows for transmission of the identity, continuity, and the productive unfolding of the message of revelation in the community of faith. It connotes what is indispensable and essential to the self-understanding of a community. Its role in Christian spirituality is central.

While the meaning of Christian spirituality is not self-evident, it does however concern itself with the lived experience of Christians, with the reaction of individuals to Christian faith, and with the religious consciousness and practice that spring from that faith. It is concerned less with doctrine and more with the ways in which Christianity shapes individuals who are part of the Christian community and the collective and social dimensions that have been so important to the lived experience of Christian faith.

The Bible tells us that a whole 'cloud of witnesses' (Heb. 12.1 NRSV) testifies to the tradition that shapes Christian life. To understand Christian spirituality is to have some sense of what has gone before, how that 'before' forms the contours of the community, and how it applies to Christian life today in positive and negative ways. In other words having a clear account of the background and development of the story of Christian spirituality is critical to the quest for knowledge about its tradition.

Implicit in the employment of the adjective 'Christian', of course, is that such spirituality must have something to do with Jesus Christ. In fact, even though people have known Jesus in countless and varied ways, it nonetheless is clear that to speak of Christian spirituality is to speak of the lived encounter with Jesus Christ in the Holy Spirit. The recorded evidence of that encounter comprises the Christian spiritual tradition.

A distinction must be made between authentic and inauthentic traditions. Inauthentic tradition is an accretion that somehow distorts an authentic tradition, whereas authentic tradition places the receiver of that tradition in contact with the original source of a teaching, in this case Jesus Christ. This contact guarantees that all present and future development of a person, group or movement is legitimate, for to be out of contact with the authentic tradition is to be in danger of deviating from the original source. Contact with Jesus Christ is understood as life-giving; great care therefore is given to defining and handing on authentic tradition. No Christian spirituality of any value can stand apart from authentic tradition.

Authentic Christian tradition exists in diverse manifestations, each forging a legitimate elaboration of the encounter with Jesus Christ, thus allowing for use of the plural 'traditions' when describing varying expressions that do not conflict, but instead complement one another. Christianity, for example, has within the New Testament several different approaches to the experience of Christ referred to as Johannine, Pauline, Lucan, Matthean and Marcan.

Early Christianity saw the emergence of two major traditions established along geographic and linguistic lines: that of the East and that of the West. These traditions are marked by variations in theology, liturgy, culture and temperament. Within these great traditions live others, constituting traditions within traditions. In the West different spiritualities arose in different places like France, Spain and the Rhineland, each having a history, emphasizing a method, and placing stress on particular key concepts, though each has as its goal knowing and loving God in Jesus.

Contemporary theologian Gustavo Gutiérrez suggests three stages in the formation of a Christian spiritual tradition. First, persons from the past have powerful religious experiences as they live their Christian faith that give them new insight into the life of the Spirit or a new way of understanding God's word or a different approach to their discipleship to Jesus. Next, they or people close to them reflect upon the experience and attempt to express it in any of several ways: through their writing; through artistic expressions; in the formation of followers; by composing prayers; by preaching and teaching; or by founding some new kind of Christian community. Some are such lasting insights that new 'schools' of spirituality are founded like those of the Augustinians, Cistercians, Victorines, Dominicans and Jesuits. Tradition also manifests spiritualities that derive from quite specific 'types' within Christianity. Examples include mission spiritualities, liberation spiritualities, feminist spiritualities and lay spiritualities. Third, these experiences and the traditions founded from them enter into the broader stream of the Christian tradition. Gutiérrez indicates that 'they are not the end of the line . . . they are offered to the ecclesial community as a new way of being Christian' (Gutiérrez, pp. 52–3). Subsequent generations of Christians build upon, draw from and modify these traditions. They become part of the public and social nature of the Christian spiritual tradition.

Any spirituality of value must be located within the authentic tradition, both of Christianity in general and of a grouping within its authentic tradition. Suggesting otherwise is to imply that spirituality has need of neither the truth of the broad tradition nor the specificity of the more particular tradition. Tradition is so comprehensive a concept as somehow to touch upon all human activity. Yet for every human activity there is a precedent that exerts influence; nothing stands completely by itself or has a completely private life. Christian spirituality is never simply in the Christian tradition but is qualified in some way by still another and more specific tradition. Central to Christian tradition is the notion that to be Christian is to be united with God in Jesus Christ through a Spirit-led communion with others; thus the public and social nature of Christian spirituality. Tradition in Christian spirituality involves attending not only to Christian experience, but also to how that experience becomes articulated and communicated for the sake of the individual spiritual journey and for the sake of the common task that is inherent in Christian discipleship.

Most of what is written about Christian spiritual tradition is written essentially as a guide to the faithful for devotional purposes. Saints and mystics of the Church are often portrayed as lonely and isolated persons who wrestle with their vision of God in their attempt to understand God's ways. In a sense, there is no such mystic or saint, for mystical experience as it is described closely interrelates with the religious and cultural tradition from which it comes. These persons may also be seen as speaking for a community whose thought patterns and language they reflect. The community in turn interprets, and seeks to understand and apply the spiritual knowledge they have gained. Their experiences have to be understood and interpreted within the context of the corporate belief of the Church and of the society of which that Church is a part.

Contemporary interest in the Christian spiritual tradition is increasing, not only for its own sake, but also because Christian identity can be discovered precisely in the religious sense and spiritual experience of humankind. Christian tradition recognizes that growing together in prayer and love is an integral part of God's purpose of 'gathering all things into one in Christ' (Eph. 1.10). Ordinary men and women of prayer and love increasingly recognize this truth in these days of wide ecumenism.

The temptation to be swept along unreflectively by some contemporary fashion is real. This is why knowledge of the spiritual classics and their tested wisdom is necessary. Tradition enables women and men of the present era to enquire with discerning hearts and minds into the stories of significant spiritual figures and movements of the past to acquire understanding. It is from the friends of God, these guides who have wide and perceptive knowledge of the Christian tradition and its spiritual paths, that the truth of Christianity is received. Guides who spring forth from the tradition help others to find their way and to distinguish between the heart of their teaching and the superficial conditioning of their own era. No authentic Christian spirituality can remain indifferent to the insights of the tradition in which it stands. Standing within a tradition teaches Christians from the experience of the past. Simultaneously, Christians add to that tradition.

See also **Christian Spirituality: Definition, Methods and Types; Spirituality and Culture; Spirituality and History (essays).**

Yves Congar, *Tradition and Traditions: An Historical and a Theological Essay*, trans. M. Naseby and T. Rainborough, London: Burns & Oates, 1966; Ewert Cousins (gen. ed.), World Spirituality: An Encyclopedic History of the Religious Quest (WS), New York: Crossroad, 1985–; Josef Rupert Geiselmann, *The Meaning of Tradition*, New York: Herder & Herder, 1966; G. Gutiérrez, *We Drink from Our Own Wells*, Maryknoll, NY: Orbis Books, 1983, pp. 52–3; C. Jones, G. Wainwright and E. Yarnold (eds), *The Study of Spirituality*, London: SPCK/New York: Oxford University Press, 1986.

MARYGRACE PETERS

Transformation

see Journey, Spiritual

Trappist Spirituality

see Cistercian Spirituality

Trinity and Spirituality

From a contemporary Christian perspective, the term 'spirituality' does not refer to just one dimension of the Christian life, such as prayer or the pursuit of virtue, recollection or ascetic practice. Rather, 'spirituality' or 'the spiritual life' pertain to the whole of the Christian life, living in and through the Spirit of God, the Spirit of Christ. It entails being conformed to the person of Christ, brought into communion with God and others through the presence and power of the Holy Spirit. This is to say that all Christian spirituality is *ipso facto* trinitarian spirituality. Be that as it may, it must be recognized that in the history of Christian spirituality, approaches to Christian living may be more or less attentive to the trinitarian moorings of life in Christ by the Spirit to the glory of the Father. The focus here is on an explicitly trinitarian spirituality, informed by Scripture, the traditions of Christian spirituality, and the renaissance of interest in the doctrine of the Trinity and its implications for Christian spiritual life in the contemporary Church and world.

Trinity. The doctrine of the Trinity is often thought to be dense and abstract, with little practical import for the Christian life. However, the Trinity is the central mystery of Christian faith and life. It is the source of all the other mysteries of Christian faith, the light that enlightens them (*Catechism of the Catholic Church* 234). If the Trinity is thought to be obscure and ethereal, cloudy rather than clear, the possibilities for understanding the other mysteries of the Christian faith are not promising.

In the last decade and more, there has been a renaissance of interest in the doctrine of the Trinity and its far-reaching implications for every dimension of the Christian life, inclusive of the spiritual life. Many contemporary studies, converging as they do on the relational character of the divine mystery, have helped bring three insights of enduring value to the fore: (1) whatever is said of the mystery of God must begin by attending to the incarnate Word, Jesus Christ, and to the presence and action of the Spirit of God in human life, history, the world and the Church; (2) the mystery of God is profoundly relational, and this relational mystery is expressed in the language of Father, Son, Spirit; (3) the doctrine of the Trinity is an eminently practical teaching, expressing not only who and how we understand God to be, but what we think human persons are called to be and become: created to glorify God by living in communion with God and one another through Christ in the Spirit.

Most contemporary feminist perspectives have been attentive to the difficulties with understanding God in purely, or even primarily, masculine imagery. But 'Father' is not God's proper name. Neither is 'God' God's proper name. Nor does the name 'Son' exhaust the depth and complexity of God's Word disclosed in Jesus of Nazareth. 'Father', 'Son', 'Spirit' are names that designate relationships rather than who God is in God's fullness. God is inexhaustible mystery. But through the process of naming, beginning in the Old Testament and continuing through early Christian history and beyond, the three names 'Father', 'Son' and 'Spirit' emerge in relation to one another and to a people. They bespeak the profoundly relational character of the divine mystery, the One whose name is beyond all naming: 'God is love' (1 John 4.8).

Interpersonal communion. Efforts to spell out the practical implications of the Trinity for the spiritual life move in two general directions. The first stresses the Trinity as model of interpersonal communion. Beginning with the distinctiveness of the works of Father, Son and Spirit in the economy of salvation, and retrieving an understanding of person as being toward and for the other, rather than as a self-contained individual, this approach looks to the category of *perichoresis* in trinitarian theology as a way of speaking of the relationship of Father, Son and Spirit as equal, mutual and interdependent. Human relationships in all spheres of life are to be brought into conformity with the equality, mutuality and interdependence that characterize the divine life. Such an approach to the spiritual life emphasizes distinctiveness of persons who are what they are, and become who they are, only in deepening of relationships, in a personal communion of equality, mutuality and interdependence, which is a share in the divine life.

From the perspective of Trinity as interpersonal communion, human life in Christ by the Spirit is a call to loving communion with God, others and every living creature. The trinitarian doctrine is expressive of what it means to participate in the life of God through Jesus Christ in the Spirit. A fresh understanding of God as Father, Son and Spirit, and the understanding of person as a distinct one toward-and-for-the-other in relationship which is at the heart of trinitarian doctrine can greatly enrich our understanding of Christian life in the Spirit.

Participation in mission. A second approach to Trinitarian spirituality is focused on participation in mission, sharing in the mission of Word and Spirit. By the mystery of the incarnation, God's love is manifest, present to the human reality. The incarnate Word is light amidst darkness, the divine life amidst human life. Jesus is God's Word in flesh. The Father speaks a Word, and his name is Jesus Christ, the Son. Here 'Word' is understood not just as an instrument of verbal communication. Word is God's expressivity, God's language, God's speech. But speaking is not possible without breath. Indeed speaking and breathing are ineluctably related. In Word and Spirit, God is speaking and breathing the divine life in the world.

From this perspective trinitarian spirituality is nothing more, or less, than a baptismal spirituality. In baptism we are conformed to Christ, anointed with the Spirit, gifted by the Father to live as sons and daughters of God, brothers and sisters in Christ. This is to participate in the mission of Word and Spirit, manifest in the fullness of the incarnational *kenosis* of Christ, but in a particular way in the baptism of Jesus in the Jordan by John.

As soon as Jesus was baptized he came up from the water, and suddenly the heavens opened and he saw the Spirit of God descending like a dove and coming down on him. And a voice spoke from heaven, 'This is my Son, the Beloved, my favor rests on him.'
Then Jesus was led by the Spirit out into the wilderness to be tempted by the devil. (Matt. 3.16–17—4.1).

Word is Love heard and seen. *Spirit* is the principle of Love's creativity and bonding. In the Son and the Holy Spirit, God is speaking and breathing. Word is what is said; Spirit is the saying. What is said in the saying is Love. But Love expressed and bonding takes many different forms. To participate in the mission of Word and Spirit is to see and to share in the manifold manifestations of human expressivity and creativity as they disclose the divine reality. The Christian call is to live with and in the missions of Word as expressivity and Spirit as creativity, communicating and bringing forth in all that is said and done the one Love. In human expressivity and in various configurations of human creativity and bonding, something of the magnitude of the God who is three in one Love is made manifest. The gift and task of Christian life in the Spirit is to cultivate, nurture and sustain the great variety of the manifestations of the magnitude of God's love in all forms of expressivity and creativity.

In such an understanding of trinitarian spirituality, human life and destiny are realized not in the pursuit of personal sanctification, or the soul's perfection, nor is it found in the exercise of individual rights and liberties, but in all those creative expressions of Love that lead to a fuller communion in the one Love.

Whether informed by the doctrine of the

Trinity understood in terms of interpersonal communion, or as a participation in mission, a Christian spirituality which is trinitarian through and through is shaped by a strong sense of the gift of God's Love. For the doctrine of the Trinity is the way by which Christians try to speak of the ineffable mystery of God's constant, eternal giving as gift. By accepting this gift, the one who lives in Christ through the Spirit participates in the divine life. Every response to this gift is a deepening in the dynamic of deification – being conformed to the person of Christ, brought into communion with God and others through the presence and power of the Holy Spirit.

Caution must be taken in the face of tendencies to understand the Trinity as a model of how to live the Christian life. Theologies of the Trinity as a model of interpersonal communication and communion often give rise to subtle and not so subtle anthropomorphic approaches to Christian life and spirituality. It is rather more helpful to understand both the Trinity and spirituality in terms of an economy of gift, so that Christian life in the Spirit, that is, trinitarian spirituality, is a whole way of living freely and responsibly with, in and from the gift given through the Word and in the Spirit.

See also **God, Images of; Jesus and Spirituality; Mission and Spirituality; Spirit, Holy.**

David Coffey, *Deus Trinitas: The Doctrine of the Triune God*, Oxford and New York: Oxford University Press, 1999; Michael Downey, *Altogether Gift: A Trinitarian Spirituality*, Maryknoll, NY: Orbis Books, 2000; Catherine Mowry LaCugna, *God for Us: The Trinity and Christian Life*, San Francisco: Harper, 1991.

MICHAEL DOWNEY

Triple Way

The *triple way* or *threefold path* is a traditional Christian way of referring to the stages of spiritual development or transformation. Although not as widely used today, this threefold concept has had considerable influence on the development of the Christian spiritual tradition. The term is most often used to refer to the stages of *purification* or *purgation*, *illumination* and *union*.

Clement of Alexandria (*c.* 150–214) and Origen (185–254) drew on Christian Scripture (e.g. Eph. 4.11–24; Luke 20.36) and Greek, Neoplatonic traditions to produce the first formulations of the idea. Thus, in *Stromateis 5* Clement sees the goal of the Christian life as the *theoria* or 'vision of God', referring to Plato and combining *theoria* with the older Platonic term

of *epopteia* (see McGinn, p. 372). This *theoria* is obtained from the dual processes of attaining knowledge (*gnosis*) and the practice of love (*agape*) in ethical activity (*ethike*). Central to this process is the ordering of the passions (*pathe*), akin to the Stoic attainment of *apatheia* as exemplified in the life of Marcus Aurelius (121–180). The idea of 'mystical stages of development' (*tas prokopas tas mystikas*) leading to both *apatheia* and 'divinization' (*theopoiesis*) clearly owes much to Plato, expecially the narrative of 'the Cave' in the *Republic* (see Turner in this respect) as well as Old Testament sources such as Moses' command to follow God in Deut. 13.4. This idea of the preparation for life in the Trinity through purification and illumination would remain central in all subsequent formulations of the Triple Way throughout the tradition.

Origen draws on Clement's ideas, elaborating and developing them. In the *Commentary on the Song of Songs*, he sees the three books of Wisdom (Proverbs, Ecclesiastes and the Song of Songs) as corresponding to the three stages of spiritual development: Proverbs to the *ethike* (*philosophia moralis* – 'a seemly manner of life'), Ecclesiastes to *physike* (*philosophia naturalis* – 'right attitude to the natural order') and the Song of Songs to *enoptike* (*philosophia inspectiva* – 'contemplation of things divine and heavenly'). The soul, then, is first purified through the practice of ethics and virtues; it then learns to contemplate the world as God made it, and finally comes to vision of God and union with the divine.

By the time Evagrius of Pontus (344–99) was writing, the threefold tradition had clearly been well established. Being a follower of Origen's theology he continued where Origen had finished in developing the exposition of the threefold path. His clearest exposition of the path is in his *Treatise on Prayer* where his theology is combined with the pithy wisdom of the Desert Fathers and Mothers, especially their teaching on purification and the overcoming of temptation and demons. He takes the three paths as established but modifies the description of the stages to *praktike*, *physike* and *theologia*. *Praktike* is still the development of virtues – the word is somewhat unusual and corresponds to what we would now call 'the active life' as opposed to the 'contemplative life' (cf. Gregory Nazianzen); for Evagrius, however, it presupposed the *hesychia* of the monk, that is, the life of struggle with the demons to overcome temptation and subdue the passions in silence and solitude. *Physike* remains the same as in Origen – the stage of natural contemplation, seeing God in created reality. *Theologia* is knowledge (*gnosis*) of the Holy Trinity leading to contemplation of God as God is. The most important development associated with Evagrius is the division of the Christian life into that of active spiritual struggle and passive contemplation (prayer that is received) – the *physike* seems to correspond to the overlapping period in between these two stages. For Evagrius, in prayer the mind returns to its primordial state in *nous* beyond all mental knowing.

The early Church's exposition of the Three Ways reaches its final and fullest development in the writings of the anonymous scholar Denys (or pseudo-Denys) the Areopagite, believed to have been writing in Syria some time in the fifth century. Denys introduces for the first time in *The Celestial Hierarchy* the threefold path as it would come to be understood in all consequent tradition, that is, as the path of purification, illumination and union: 'the hierarchical order imposes on some the reception of purification, on others to purify; on some to receive illumination, and on others to enlighten; on some, again, to receive perfecting, and on others to perfect' (*CH* 3.2). From Denys onwards the tradition becomes firmly established in Christianity's understanding of spiritual development.

By the High Middle Ages scholars debated whether the triad marked a temporal succession or whether the various stages could be simultaneously experienced. Thus the Franciscan school associated with St Bonaventure (1218–74, see in particular *De Triplici Via*) suggested that whereas beginners could experience a taste of union, 'perfects' still had imposed on them the need for purification. On the other hand, the Carthusian school associated with Hugh of Balma (second half of the thirteenth century, see in particular his *De Mystica Theologia*) suggested that only after the beginner's stage of purification has been accomplished can the proficient move to illumination before attaining the perfection of the final stage of union (see also the writings of Vincent of Aggsbach during the fifteenth century Tegernsee Debate).

The tradition can be seen throughout the mystical writings of the High Middle Ages and into the modern period. Writers such as Ignatius of Loyola (1491–1556), Teresa of Avila (1515–82) and John of the Cross (1542–91) all make use of the threefold path in their writings. Ignatius relates the First Week of his *Spiritual Exercises* to the way of purification, while Weeks Two and Three correspond to that of illumination. Likewise, in Teresa's *Interior Castle* the first mansions refer to the state of purification, those in the middle to that of illumination and the final mansions to that of union. John's masterful expositions of the purgative way in his *Dark Night of the Soul* and *Ascent of Mount Carmel* are justly cele-

brated, while his *Spiritual Canticle* and *Living Flame of Love* relate more to the other two stages.

Despite an interest in the subject continuing well into the twentieth century (see, for example, Reginald Garrigou-Lagrange (1877–1964), Joseph de Guibert (1877–1942) and Adolphe Tanquerey (1854–1932)) the hold of the concept on Christian imaginations has lessened in recent years. Karl Rahner, in a famous critique of the concept in his *The Theological Investigations* 3 challenged the convention of thinking of the spiritual life in terms of distinct stages.

Recent work has tended to relate the threefold path to more contemporary psychological understandings of human faith development, most notably in the work of James Fowler, who builds on the work of psychologists such as Carl Jung and Erik Erikson to present a sevenfold division of faith development integrated into human psychological development.

Present work in the Orthodox tradition (see, for example, Dumitru Staniloae's *Orthodox Spirituality*) retains the classic threefold path using terminology virtually unchanged from that of Evagrius and the early patristic writers.

For contemporary Christians it still has use for describing the stages of spiritual development and remains relevant in the field of spiritual direction and accompaniment.

See also **Conversion; Illuminative Way; Journey, Spiritual; Purgative Way; Unitive Way.**

J. Fowler, *Faithful Change*, Nashville, TN: Abingdon Press, 1996; R. Garrigou-Lagrange, *The Three Ways of the Spiritual Life*, London: Burns & Oates, 1938; A. Louth, *The Origins of the Christian Mystical Tradition*, Oxford: Clarendon Press, 1981; B. McGinn, *The Foundations of Mysticism: Origins of the Fifth Century*, London: SCM Press, 1991; K. Rahner, 'Reflections on the problem of the gradual ascent to Christian perfection' in *The Theological Investigations, 3*, trans. Karl-H. and Bonigace Kruger, London: Darton, Longman & Todd/Baltimore, MD: Helicon Press, 1967; D. Turner, *The Darkness of God: Negativity in Christian Mysticism*, Cambridge: Cambridge Univeristy Press, 1998.

PETER TYLER

Union with God

see Mysticism; Unitive Way

Unitarian Spirituality

The Unitarian movement, especially in the United Kingdom, has undoubtedly been influenced to a considerable extent by the ethos of Rational Dissent, a tradition which believed that the Spoken Word was the supreme sacrament, and that Scripture readings and an intellectual sermon characterized by argument and apologetic were the most important constituents of public worship. Many of its supporters, the English Presbyterians in particular, anxious to avoid anything likely to encourage unseemly 'enthusiasm', preferred a set liturgy to extemporary prayer. It was probably these aspects of the tradition which gave rise to the view that Unitarians are suspicious of spirituality, and that they prefer the company of those who consider intellectual understanding, social protest and good works to be of greater value than spiritual devotion. S. T. Coleridge, an enthusiastic convert to Unitarianism in his youth, soon deserted the movement because of what he saw as its deplorable lack of spirituality.

But the Rational Dissenters themselves were by no means unaware of the importance of emotion, and arguments among them about the relative merits of reason and feeling were not unknown. When the eminent Anglican clergyman Gilbert Wakefield resigned his living in 1770 and joined the Rational Dissenters, he wrote a pamphlet denying the value of public worship. The poet Anna L. Barbauld, daughter of Dr Aikin, Principal of Warrington Academy, wrote a reply, in which she admitted with sorrow that 'the spirit of devotion is at low ebb amongst us'. This she blamed on too philosophical a view of religion, and she pleaded for a greater trust in emotion. Joseph Priestley, Presbyterian minister and mechanistic determinist, protested that this was to encourage superstition. Priestley himself, however, in a sermon on *Habitual Devotion* preached in 1791, was quite prepared to declare that 'he who practises such devotion sees God in everything, and everything in God. He dwells in love and walks with God all day long'. Priestley's disciple Thomas Belsham, who died in 1829 and who has sometimes been called the last of the Rational Dissenters, was chiefly known in his own day as an erudite biblical scholar, a powerful intellectual debater, and a critic of the superstitious excesses of Arian theology. But one of his biographers says that his private personal diary, with its 'prayers, sighs, doubts and hopes, frank addresses to God in sunshine and in gloom', reveals 'a sensitive soul, living constantly in the presence of God'.

One suspects that this was also true of the other leading Unitarians in the nineteenth century. The situation was in any case considerably transformed by the major changes in Unitarianism which occurred in the latter half of the century, largely under the influence of James Martineau, who had himself been influenced by American Transcendentalism. Martineau, a man in whom great intellect was matched with deep personal spirituality, reinvigorated the prayer-book tradition, endowing it with new poetic power, and this continued to dominate Unitarianism until well into the twentieth century.

The second half of the century, however, saw further dramatic changes. Liturgy and set prayers were for the most part discarded, and there were constant attempts to give free worship greater spiritual depth. New rituals were introduced, old ceremonies abandoned or reinterpreted. The use of candles (once beyond the pale for those of Puritan descent) was welcomed, and the ceremonial lighting of a flaming chalice (the new icon of worldwide Unitarianism, borrowed from the Radical Reformation) became a standard feature of Unitarian worship. What is more, thanks to the movement's long-established concept of open revelation, inspiration was found not only in the Judaeo-Christian tradition, but also in all the great world faiths. The use of theistic language was discouraged and there were imports from Celtic spirituality, New Age thinking, agnostic humanism, feminist theology, and neopaganism.

These changes were not achieved without controversy. Some Unitarians, aware of the dangers inherent in what has been appropriately called 'supermarket religion', made vigorous efforts to safeguard the Christian tradition within the movement. Even those more inclined towards comprehension and a multi-faith approach often lamented the movement's neglect of private personal spirituality and its apparent inability to give its adherents a true awareness of the *mysterium tremendum*. Practical attempts to remedy the situation have usually evoked little positive response, and it is probably still the case that most Unitarians, like the Quakers, continue to believe that true personal spirituality is best demonstrated by good works and a keen social conscience.

See also **Spirituality and the Dialogue of Religions (***essay***); Anabaptist Spirituality; Postmodernity; Puritan Spirituality; Quaker Spirituality.**

G. Chryssides (ed.), *Unitarian Perspectives on Contemporary Religious Thought*, London: The Lindsey Press, 1999; A. J. Long, *Current Trends in British Unitarianism*, Belfast: The Ulster Unitarian Christian Association 1997; D. McGuffie, *The Hymn Sandwich: A Brief History of Unitarian Worship*, London: Worship Committee of the Unitarian General Assembly, 1982; A. E. Peaston, *The Prayer Book Tradition in the Free Churches*, new edition, Cambridge: James

Clarke, 2003 [1964]; M. Smith (ed.), *Prospects for the Unitarian Movement*, London: The Lindsey Press, 2002; T. Wintle (ed.), 'Essays on spirituality', *The Unitarian Universalist Christian* (the quarterly journal of the American Unitarian Universalist Christian Association), 43.1 (Spring 1988).

ARTHUR LONG

Unitive Way

The Unitive Way refers to the third of a threefold spiritual itinerary that includes the following: Purgative Way, Illuminative Way and Unitive Way. These three 'ways' comprise the 'classical spiritual itinerary', which has been fairly well defined as such from the thirteenth century on. See the entry 'Purgative Way' for a brief history of the concept of the 'classical spiritual itinerary'. John of the Cross (d. 1591) carefully analyses the threefold way in his commentaries *The Dark Night of the Soul* (*DN*), *The Ascent of Mount Carmel* (*A*), *The Spiritual Canticle* (*SC*), and *The Living Flame of Love* (*F*). Since John of the Cross is recognized as the Western mystic who described, systematized and analysed most thoroughly the Purgative, Illuminative, and Unitive Ways, his work will be used in a summary way as the basis for the presentation below as well as the other entries concerning the classical spiritual itinerary.

Following the 'dark night of the soul' which characterizes the later part of the Illuminative Way the spiritual pilgrim enters the Unitive Way. Those who enter this way are known as the 'perfects'. In contrast to the marked shift in one's prayer life that characterizes the transition from the Purgative Way to the Illuminative Way no such dramatic change takes place in the transition from the Illuminative Way to the Unitive Way. Perhaps one could speak of a change in degree of intensity of contemplative prayer as opposed to the radical shift from discursive prayer to contemplative prayer that marks the change between the other two ways. In the Illuminative Way the pilgrim would have experienced certain 'touches of union', that is, transitory experiences of the closeness of God. However, what is different about the Unitive Way, in contrast to the Illuminative Way, is the experience of the habitual presence of God in one's life: there is a quality of 'immediacy' experienced in one's relationship to God. John of the Cross describes this presence as the experience of being 'one with God'. With the entry into the Unitive Way there is the establishment of a 'substantial' union with God (*SC* St. 20 and 21, 12–13). Whereas before there were periods when the pilgrim felt the absence of God, there exists

now the experience of the habitual presence of God deep within (*SC* St. 2.5).

John of the Cross speaks of the Unitive Way as the 'highest state attainable in this life', also known as the state of the 'spiritual marriage':

This spiritual marriage is incomparably greater than the spiritual betrothal, for it is a total transformation in the Beloved, in which each surrenders the entire possession of self to the other with a certain consummation of the union of love. The soul thereby becomes divine, God through participation, insofar as is possible in this life . . . It is accordingly the highest state attainable in this life. (*SC* St. 22.3)

The Unitive Way represents the completion of the transformative process of conformity of the person's life to that of God's. The pilgrim has been drawn fully into participation of the divine nature. All of one's life is directed toward the love of God in this world. Inordinate affections, desires, or impulses all but cease to exist and thus cease to drive the person toward unwanted actions or harmful decisions. In psychological terms the individual has achieved an extremely high level of personal integration and maturity. The individual 'ordinarily inclines and moves toward God in the first movements of its intellect, memory, will, and appetites, because of the great help and stability it has in God and its perfect conversion toward him' (*SC* St. 27.7). In the Unitive Way the pilgrim enjoys an incredible 'habitual sweetness and tranquillity that is never lost or lacking' (*SC* St. 24.5).

John cautions us, however, that an individual who has entered the Unitive Way is still capable of falling into sin, even though she or he is highly unlikely to do so. The attraction to evil, in contrast to the intense attraction to the love of God and the absolute Good, has no compelling hold over the pilgrim in this journey of life. As John says 'old lovers hardly ever fail God, for they now stand above all that would make them fail him' (*SC* St. 25.11).

John of the Cross makes an interesting observation that concerns the way we come to know things of the created order in the Unitive Way: instead of knowing God through the symbolic expressions of God manifest in the created order, the individual 'knows creatures through God' (*F* St. 4.5). The individual has come to know the created world through the loving perspective of God. Thus, in a very strong way the pilgrim in this state experiences both his or her 'humanity' and 'divinity' through the order of creation. All of reality is experienced as being taken up into God's sublime love: the fullness of redemption has won its way in the life of the individual; the power of the cross shines forth in divine and human glory.

With the Unitive Way one has reached the highest level of development possible in this life but John still acknowledges that 'love can grow deeper in quality . . . and become more ardent' (F Prologue 3). Mortal, bodily existence prevents a more complete union with God and thus the intense desire for an even fuller union with God remains (F St. 1.27–8). Even though profound, one's 'knowledge of God' is still obscure due to its incompleteness. God, on this side of eternity, is unfathomable. In the Unitive Way life will continue, with its disappointments and losses, joys and celebrations, until mortal death ushers the pilgrim into the eternal embrace of the Beloved Other. At that time, in the fullness of the state of glory, one will be 'face to face' with God.

See also **Carmelite Spirituality; Dark Night; Illuminative Way; Journey, Spiritual; Purgative Way; Triple Way.**

K. Kavanaugh and O. Rodriguez, *The Collected Works of St John of the Cross*, Washington: Institute of Carmelite Studies, 1991; Steven Payne, *John of the Cross and the Cognitive Value of Mysticism*, Norwell, MA: Kluwer Academic Publications, 1990; David B. Perrin, *For Love of the World: The Old and the New Self of John of the Cross*, Bethesda, MD: International Scholars Press, 1997; E. W. Trueman Dicken, *The Crucible of Love: A Study of the Mysticism of St Teresa of Jesus and St John of the Cross*, New York: Sheed & Ward, 1963.

DAVID PERRIN

Vatican II and Spirituality

In the sixth paragraph of the Decree on the Renewal of Religious Life (*Perfectae Caritatis*) there is a demand that vowed religious undertake an earnest study of the 'accepted classics of traditional Christian spirituality' (*e germanis spiritualitatis Christianae fontibus*). That exhortation is the only time in the published documents of Vatican II where the word 'spirituality' occurs. Despite the infrequent use of that word in the documents of Vatican II there is no doubt that the Council was deeply concerned with the Christian spiritual life in general but, more specifically, caused a fundamental shift in how the Christian life is to be lived. Indeed, it could be argued that Vatican II was more centrally concerned, because of its fundamentally pastoral orientation, with the ordinary spiritual development of ordinary Christians than any council in history.

To understand that shift in Christian spirituality we might begin with the nodal fifth chapter in the Dogmatic Constitution on the Church (*Lumen Gentium*) entitled the 'Universal call to holiness in the Church'. That chapter rightly noted that while among all the faithful there are 'different kinds of life and its different duties, there is one holiness cultivated by all who are led by the Spirit of God' (5. 41). In a sense that assertion is a Christian commonplace but it was also, given certain developments in Christian history, an antidote to the penchant to overvalue 'states of perfection' in which the clerical and vowed religious constitute a body devoted to Christian perfection while the larger body of Christians were less concerned with such issues and the passive recipients of the 'fruits' of such labours. By a common baptism and a common allegiance in the Spirit to Jesus Christ, all are called to holiness.

So central is the emphasis on the common call to holiness that the other emphases of Vatican II can be seen as highlighting those instrumentalities by which such holiness can be nurtured. Thus, to cite an obvious example, the Constitution on the Sacred Liturgy (*Sacrosanctum Concilium*), which made sweeping changes in the entire sacramental life of the Church, did so in order to allow all Christians to participate fully in the public worship of the Church. The conciliar consensus could not be more explicit: 'The Church wants all believers to be led to take a full, conscious and active part in liturgical celebration. This is demanded by the very nature of the liturgy itself . . .' (2.14). That participation was not merely seen as advancing a fuller sense of solidarity but as bringing forth the presence of Jesus Christ as 'fully present in His church', especially in the liturgy in his sacrifice re-presented in the Eucharist, in his sacraments, through his Word proclaimed, and in our prayers and hymns (1.7). Further, in stipulating that the whole range of sacramental actions be reformed, that effort was orientated for 'the nourishment of the Christian life' (3.59).

The shift to an emphasis on proper participation in the liturgical life of the Church should be seen in tandem with a renewed focus on the charisms granted by the indwelling Spirit of God which enrich the Church. These gifts exist among 'the faithful of every rank' which render them 'fit and ready to undertake the various tasks and offices which help the renewal and the building up of the church' (*Lumen Gentium* 2.12). The highlighting of charisms provide a foundation for understanding the theological significance of prophetic critique, spiritual guidance, teaching, various non-ordained ministries, and the other impulses which are so much a part of the contemporary Church. Such charisms flow out of baptismal life and form the background for the development of solid theological investigation that must accompany all spiritual writing and praxis in the Church.

Three other documents coming from Vatican II also deeply reorientated the shape of contemporary spirituality within the Roman Catholic Church. The Decree on Ecumenism (*Unitatis Redintegratio*) not only affirmed the common spiritual inheritance of all Christians (the Word of God; the theological virtues of faith, hope and charity; the gifts of the Spirit, and so on) which form a basis for dialogue but, more crucially, affirm the workings of grace outside the 'visible bonds' of the Catholic Church. Catholic spirituality can be nourished by an encounter with various expressions of spiritual practice of other Christians but can also co-operate with them, for instance, in common prayer and other forms of Christian activity both spiritual and social.

Second, by acknowledging the promptings of divine grace outside the Christian religion in its decree on the Church's Relation to Non-Christian Religions (*Nostra Aetate*), encouragement is given to those who seek out the wisdom of those faith traditions beginning with the Jewish tradition to which we are inexorably bound. Post-Vatican II spirituality has been immeasurably enriched by the spiritual exchanges that take place, at times at a very deep contemplative level, with those traditions. The Catholic Church, this decree asserts, 'rejects nothing of those things which are true and holy in these religions' since they 'frequently reflect a ray of truth which enlightens everyone' (2).

The many fruitful dialogical exchanges with various bodies of religious believers are a direct result of the assertions of *Nostra Aetate* that the presence of God's grace is operative among all religious believers. That such exchanges are present only at the margins of Catholic consciousness is belied by the many efforts of Pope John Paul II to foster such exchanges, most famously by his presence, in 1986, with representatives of all the majors religious of the world at Assisi to pray for peace in the world, an exchange repeated in the same place in 2002.

Finally, the unprecedented Pastoral Constitution on the Church in the World of Today (*Gaudium et Spes*) addressed itself to people everywhere to share, as its title suggests, both the hopes and joys of common humanity. The very orientation of that document indicates that however one is going to live a Christian life it has to be lived with a sense of being part of a common humanity. That orientation gives power to forms of spirituality (e.g. various liberationist spiritualities) that combine spiritual practice in the light of the 'signs of the time'.

When reflecting on the explosive interest in Christian spirituality in the nearly two generations since Vatican II finished its deliberations (1965) it is obvious that much of its health depends on the orientation given by the Council. The re-examination of the vast tradition of Christian spiritual writing, the willingness to learn from other traditions, the central focus on the Word of God, the many diverse 'forms' of Christian prayer found in almost any parish, the newer movements of Christian nurture, the proliferations of ministries, a heightened awareness of the needs of the poor and disadvantaged, the renewal of liturgical celebration – all flourish because of encouragement from Vatican II.

For all of those accomplishments it should also be said that Vatican II was not a final word but a starting place. More than one critic has noted the Council's rather thin pneumatology, its somewhat heady optimism about human possibility, its embryonic words about ecumenism and inter-faith relations, and so on. Nonetheless, what the Council did do was encourage the Catholic Church to look back to its roots (*ressourcement*) while looking forward to the future. That dialectic, of course, reminds us of another element highlighted by the Council: we are a pilgrim church, which means, we are not there yet.

See also **Contemporary Spirituality** (*essay*); **Roman Catholic Spirituality.**

Norman P. Tanner (ed.), *Decrees of the Ecumenical Councils*, 2 vols, Washington, DC: Georgetown University Press, 1990; Herbert Vorgrimler (ed.), *Commentary on the Documents of Vatican II*, 5 vols, New York: Herder & Herder/London: Burns & Oates, 1967.

LAWRENCE S. CUNNINGHAM

Victorine Spirituality

The Victorine spiritual tradition, originating at the Abbey of St Victor in Paris, was a primary source of the great spiritual awakening of the twelfth century. The Victorines represent a transitional phase that brought the monastic mystical tradition into contact with practices of intellectual reflection emerging in the schools of Paris. The high point of the community and its spirituality was mainly during the Middle Ages although the Abbey itself survived until its suppression during the French Revolution. The Victorine synthesis of scholarship, mysticism, liturgy, exegesis, aesthetics, ethics, contemplation and compassion serves as a model for contemporary spiritual life.

The Victorines, 'Regular' or 'Augustinian' Canons, lived as a clerical community dedicated to a common life of poverty, celibacy and obedience under the Rule of St Augustine. Though the authorship the Rule has been called into question, there is a real sense of spiritual continuity between Augustine's influence and the twelfth-century communities of canons that included the Victorines at Paris. The Rule is grounded in evangelical values and impulses, and forms the basis of the Victorine ideal: spiritual and contemplative exploration of the inner person accomplished under the guidance, supervision and love of the community intent on union with God through imitation of Christ as an example for others.

William of Champeaux founded the Abbey at St Victor in 1108. Based on William's fame as teacher, the community grew, adding contemplative elements, a new sense of liturgical formation, and an emphasis on learning and scholarship foreign to most other communities of Augustinian Canons.

Hugh of St Victor (d. 1141) was the first great master of St Victor. The most prolific of all Victorine writers, Hugh, with the possible exception of his student Richard of St Victor, was the most influential teacher to emerge from the Abbey. Hugh is often called 'alter Augustinus' because of his deep reliance on and astute interpretations of St Augustine. He blended Augustine's practical teachings on contemplative life with the theoretical writings of Dionysius the Areopagite. His works cover the range of the arts and sacred science taught in his day. A great mystical writer, Hugh was also a philosopher and a Scholastic theologian of the first order. In the areas of doctrine, preaching and contemplation, St Bonaventure considered Hugh to be the 'master' of all previous spiritual luminaries of the Church. Hugh's major works include On the Sacraments of the Christian Faith, considered by many to be the first Scholastic summa. His Didascalicon serves as an outline for training Christian scholars in philosophy, spirituality and theology, while serving as a methodological guide for reading Scripture. His thinking on the anagogic theme of rising from visible symbols to the invisible things of God is most clearly expressed in his Commentary on the Celestial Hierarchy of Dionysius the Areopagite. Hugh's scriptural commentaries include literal, allegorical and tropological (moral) interpretations of the Pentateuch, the books of Kings, Ecclesiastes, Jeremiah, Joel and the Song of Songs. His important mystical works include On the Moral Ark of Noah, On the Mystical Ark of Noah, On the Nature of Love, On the Power of Praying, and In Praise of Charity.

Richard of St Victor (d. 1173) the premier Victorine mystic, contemplative, and creative theologian, has had immense impact on Christian spirituality. Dante said of Richard that he was, 'in contemplation more than human' (Paradiso 11.132). Many of Richard of St Victor's works combine biblical exegesis with apophatic theology, the life of virtue, and contemplative teaching. Works of Richard's that have made important contributions to the history of spirituality include the Twelve Patriarchs (or Benjamin Minor), which describes the preliminary stages of the life of virtue leading to contemplative awareness, the Mystical Ark (or Benjamin Major), which systematizes Richard's insights concerning levels of contemplative consciousness, On Elimination of Evil and Promotion of Good, which focuses on the life of virtue, meditation and contemplation, and On the Four Degrees of Passionate Charity, which sketches the itinerary of the 'path of love' leading to more perfect service of neighbour and, ultimately, union with God. In his great doctrinal treatise, On the Trinity, Richard finds in the human experience of love a basis for contemplating the mystery of the Trinity.

Particularly adept at uniting heart and mind in contemplative speculation, Thomas Gallus (d. 1246) was known and revered from the thirteenth through the sixteenth centuries, primarily as a commentator on the Dionysian writings and as an exegete of the Song of Songs. Recently rediscovered, his writings include three commentaries on the Song of Songs, a Commentary on Isaiah 6, two mystical treatises, On the Seven Grades of Contemplation and The Mirror of Contemplation, and two major works on the Dionysian corpus.

Achard of St Victor (d. 1171) makes no sharp distinction between theology, preaching and meditation. As with other Victorines, he combines figurative use of theological imagination with technical logic. Achard's surviving works consist of fifteen sermons and two metaphysical treatises, On the Distinction of the Soul, Spirit, and Mind and On the Unity of God and the Plurality of Creatures. The last of the sermons, Sermon 15, is in actuality a mystical tract on the contemplative life and is often referred to as The Treatise on the Seven Deserts. In this work, the human soul, having deserted God becomes like a desert, a 'region of unlikeness' to God. But through the action of Christ, symbolized by his forty-day stay in the desert, the soul begins a journey of ever deepening intimacy and likeness to God. However, in the final desert, Achard moves naturally from this process of deification to identification with Christ through compassionate service to neighbour.

Taken as a whole the Victorines offer a range of resources for our contemporary quest for meaning, connection and relationship. These include their focus on the life of Christ as a model of charity and compassion, their insistence on awakening to the mystery and wonder of God, their ability to join corporate life in a network of mutual respect and guardianship, and finally, their keen sensitivity to the rhythms of God's felt presence, absence, and return.

See also **Mysticism (*essay*); Apophatic Spirituality; Augustinian Spirituality; Canonical Communities; Contemplation; Exegesis, Spiritual; Medieval Spirituality in the West; Mystical Theology.**

Achard of St Victor: Works, trans. and introd. Hugh Feiss, Kalamazoo, MI: Cistercian Publications, 2001; Steven Chase, *Contemplation and Compassion: The Victorine Spiritual Tradition*, London: Darton, Longman & Todd/ Maryknoll, New York: Orbis Press, 2003; *The Didascalicon of Hugh of St Victor: A Medieval Guide to the Arts*, trans. and introd. Jerome Taylor, New York: Columbia University Press, 1961; *Richard of St Victor: The Twelve Patriarchs, The Mystical Ark, Book Three of the Trinity*, trans. and introd. Grover Zinn, CWS, New York: Paulist Press, 1979; *Richard of St Victor: Selected Writings on Contemplation*, ed. Clare Kirchberger, London: Faber and Faber, 1957.

STEVEN CHASE

Vincentian Spirituality

Origins and history. Vincentian spirituality is to an unusual extent the inherited ethos of a set of communities, rather than a set of tenets. Aside from two substantial biographies of Vincent de Paul (more correctly Depaul), one written soon after his death in 1660 and the other more than a century later, his followers did little to publicize him or his spirituality, until the 1920s. Then a third biography appeared, by Pierre Coste, who had already published fourteen volumes of Vincent's works. These works consist almost entirely of letters and addresses to the members of the two communities he founded. Henri Bremond wrote of the letters, 'I did not find a line in them that is banal.'

Vincent Depaul was born in 1581, the third son of a farming family. He was gifted, and his parents decided he should follow an uncle's example and become a priest. After two years of schooling with the Franciscans at Dax in southwest France, he went to study theology at the University of Toulouse. There he maintained himself partly by conducting a highly regarded school and partly by securing ordination to the priesthood at the un-canonical age of nineteen. He continued his studies for a basic theology degree for four more years, which were followed by a long search for a satisfactory church position.

Nothing came his way until he was made a chaplain/almoner at the court of ex-Queen Marguerite (Reine Margot) in Paris in 1610. Instead of being drawn into the life of high society by this appointment, however, he consciously sought out the circles in Paris which were devoted to the improvement of Catholic life, in the spirit of the Council of Trent. In their different ways, Pierre de Bérulle, André Duval and Francis de Sales became his mentors, most significantly the last mentioned.

In 1612 Vincent secured his first appointment to a parish – Clichy, near Paris – where he rebuilt the church, promoted frequent confession and Communion and started a school for youngsters interested in the priesthood. His mentors moved him from there to the post of tutor with the highly influential De Gondi family, which had the right of nomination of the bishops of Paris. It was not work he found entirely congenial, but he made his position a platform for pastoral work, re-evangelization in fact, among the neglected country people of his employers' vast estates. He extended his concern to the galley-slaves who manned the fleets under De Gondi's command, and secured a notable improvement in their conditions. These initiatives led to the establishment of one of his four major organizations, the Congregation of the Mission. Initially it was a community of priests financed by the De Gondis to preach missions on their lands, but in due course it extended its scope throughout France and to parts of Italy and Poland, where it became established during Vincent's lifetime, and sent missions to Ireland, Scotland, North Africa and Madagascar. Even before founding his congregation in 1625, Vincent had begun to establish societies or 'conferences' of lay people in various localities, to organize the relief of the poor there. These were known as 'Confraternities of Charity', and are the antecedents of present-day Vincentian movements such as the Society of St Vincent de Paul. Vincent's best-known foundation, the Daughters of Charity, came about as a way of sustaining and developing the work of the lay confraternities of charity. From 1632 they were virtually a religious community working outside their convents in the cities and villages of

France, an almost unheard-of novelty. Their foundation was largely due to the giftedness of Louise de Marillac, the natural daughter of a very prominent family, who under Vincent's guidance became a powerful force for promoting the development of women and eliminating poverty in France. Vincent's final foundation was known as 'the Tuesday Conferences', weekly meetings of clergy in Paris and other cities who wanted to progress spiritually and as priests in the way Vincent had many years before.

Key texts. Hardly any of this work found expression in writing for publication. Nonetheless, Vincent and Louise and their followers lived and worked according to a set of clear and profound Christian principles. These are set out most systematically in the Rules they drew up for their congregations, the *Common Rules* of the Congregation of the Mission, also known as Lazarists or Vincentians (*RCW*, pp. 83–118), and the Common Rules of the Daughters of Charity, finally published only after the death of the two founders in 1660 (*RCW*, pp. 167–93). The word 'common', while it chiefly distinguishes the rules from those for particular office-holders, also has the overtone of 'ordinary' or 'unexceptional': while the members made sanctity their goal, they chose the normal practices of good Tridentine Catholics as the means to attain it, inspired chiefly by Francis de Sales' *Introduction to the Devout Life*. In addition to these texts (published in the volume of Classics of Western Spirituality mentioned in the bibliography below), some of Vincent's letters, addresses to his followers, and some of Louise's spiritual reflections, are of great significance. For example, Vincent's address on prayer and other matters to Antoine Durand (*C*, pp. 80–8), his address to his priests and brothers on charity (*CCD*, 12, pp. 260ff., French edn), and his address on the objectives of the Congregation of the Mission (*RCW*, pp. 135–50). Among Louise's writings which deserve special mention are her report to Vincent on some lay charitable conferences she had visited (*RCW*, pp. 252ff.), the account of her conversion experience at Pentecost 1623 (*RCW*, p. 226) and her reflections on the Immaculate Conception of the Virgin Mary (*RCW*, pp. 228ff.). An important text from after Vincent's time is the instruction on the method to be used in preaching produced by his successor in the Congregation of the Mission, René Alméras (*Circulaires des Supérieurs Généraux de la CM*, Paris 1877, vol.1, pp. 75ff., French edn). These, like practically everything written by Vincentians or Daughters of Charity until comparatively recently, are directed to an internal readership. The writer in

the Vincentian tradition who has the greatest claim to fame is Frédéric Ozanam, one of the founders of the Society of St Vincent de Paul, who was at the forefront of the restoration of the Catholic Church in post-Revolutionary France.

Key people. The outstanding figures in almost four hundred years of Vincentian institutional history are mainly those who became saints. Apart from Vincent and Louise themselves, they belong to the late eighteenth and nineteenth centuries: a group of six sisters and three priests who were martyred for their fidelity to the papacy during the French Revolution; an Italian missionary bishop, Justin de Jacobis, who was a key figure in the establishment of Catholicism in Ethiopia and a forerunner of missionary inculturation, along with his Ethiopian fellow-worker, the martyr Ghebre-Michael; Rosalie Rendu, who initiated Frédéric Ozanam and his companions into the service of 'les misérables de Paris'; Catherine Labouré, a visionary who communicated the Medal of the Immaculate Conception ('the Miraculous Medal') to the Church, but who spent her entire life as a Daughter of Charity working unknown at a home for elderly workmen near Paris; Francis Clet and John Gabriel Perboyre, who were martyred as missionaries in China, the latter of whom especially has left some valuable prayers and spiritual writings; Frédéric Ozanam himself, and Marco Antonio Durando, a Vincentian priest, the founder of a religious congregation of women, and important in the spiritual life of nineteenth-century Turin. While not a few others in the Vincentian movement have been prominent, such as Jean-Baptiste Etienne who restored the communities after the French Revolution, Fernand Portal, the ecumenist, and Annibale Bugnini, a leading figure in the Vatican II liturgical renewal, it is central to the Vincentian spirit to prize holiness above everything else. In Perboyre's words, 'The one thing necessary is the imitation of Christ.'

Key values. As set out by Vincent, the basic values in the movement he founded are: simplicity, that is, plain speaking, plain writing, and undeviating pursuit of gospel values, especially lovingkindness; humility, after the example of Christ; gentleness, great sensitivity to people's feelings; mortification, acceptance of the cross; and above all, zeal for God's glory and the temporal and eternal welfare of the human race. Vincent had a keen sense of Christ's presence among the poorest people of his time. This perception explains his profound respect for, and his extraordinary creativity in the service of, people whom others regarded as outcasts. Hence, perhaps, the comparative obscurity in which the Vincentian movement has unfolded. What explains its vitality are the trinitarian depth to which both Vincent and Louise invite their listeners and readers, and an axiom that comes closer to a metaphysical principle than almost anything else in the body of Vincentian writing: '*totum opus nostrum in operatione consistit*' – 'our only task is to accomplish our proper work' (*C*, p. 104; *CCD* 11, p.41, French edn).

See also **Charity; French School of Spirituality; Ministry and Spirituality; Oratorian Spirituality; Pastoral Care and Spirituality; Priesthood and Spirituality; Roman Catholic Spirituality; Salesian Spirituality.**

P. Coste, *Correspondence, Conferences, Documents*, 14 vols: 1–8 and 13, New York: New City Press, 1985 (CCD); *Life and Labours*, 3 vols, London: Burns, Oates & Washbourne, 1934; J. Dirvin, *St Louise de Marillac* , New York: Farrar, Straus & Giroux, 1970; A. Dodin, *Vincent de Paul and Charity*, New York: New City Press, 1993 (C); J. M. Roman, *St Vincent de Paul, A Biography*, London: Melisende, 1999; Frances Ryan and John Rybolt (eds), *Vincent de Paul and Louise de Marillac, Rules, Conferences and Writing*, CWS, New York: Paulist Press, 1995 (RCW); L. Sullivan (ed.), *The Spiritual Writings of Louise de Marillac*, New York: New City Press, 1991.

MYLES REARDEN

Virginity

In Christian spiritual writings the term 'virginity' has three different ranges of meaning. Prior to the fourth century, treatises on virginity by such authors as Cyprian (d. 258) and Tertullian (d. *c.* 225) were primarily exhortations to faithfulness and chastity intended for unmarried women. From the mid fourth century such treatises were generally encomia of the monastic life intended for communities of nuns. A third range of meaning, common throughout Christian history, interprets virginity allegorically as the state of the Christian soul espoused to Christ, awaiting the wedding feast of heaven.

In the early Church virginity embraced 'for the sake of the kingdom of heaven' (Matt. 19.10–12), or out of a sense of eschatological urgency (1 Cor. 7.25–31), or to serve the Church more freely (1 Cor. 7.32–35) quickly provided a visible witness to the moral imperatives of the Christian gospel. In *The Body and Society* Peter Brown has shown that the longing for an unambiguous, visible sign of Christian identity caused celibate life to be particularly emphasized, precisely because it was equally incomprehensible and scandalous to both contemporary pagans and Jews. The

possibility that Christians, particularly young Christian women, could attain a sense of personal identity and freedom apart from tightly enmeshed networks of family obligations and social status was shocking to non-Christians. The example of virgin-martyrs who interpreted their lives not as wasted but as fulfilled beyond the power of pagan imagination was a powerful witness both to those outside the Church and to those within it. To deliberately embrace the unmarried state became a vivid sign of contradiction that unambiguously emphasized the spiritual and eschatological nature of the Christian covenant.

Communities of Christian celibates, particularly celibate women, may have enjoyed quasi-official status in the Church from apostolic times. Hints, but no explicit description of their organization and goals, are scattered throughout the early patristic literature. Their existence as long-standing institutions is taken for granted by the Council of Elvira (*c.* 306). With the rise of Christian monasticism in the late third and early fourth centuries, the term 'virgins' came to refer primarily, if not exclusively, to communities of monastic women, who celebrated official liturgies of consecration from at least the early fourth century.

With the Church's radical reversal of fortune in the fourth century, the older eschatological and spiritual significance of virginity gradually came to be expressed in the new social and hierarchical context. Consecrated virginity, in the sense of monastic life, now enjoyed official recognition within the state Church. It was only natural that the question of the relative merits and status of virginity vis-à-vis the married state should arise. In the Syrian Church an over-exaltation of celibate life as the proper fulfilment of baptism was eventually condemned as the 'Encratite heresy'. Yet when Jovinian (d. *c.* 405) attempted to define marriage as the superior and more natural state, he was vigorously opposed by Jerome (d. 420) and eventually condemned. Consecrated virginity came to be regarded as the 'higher' Christian vocation and the surer road to heaven, despite the fact that marriage in the West was later defined as a sacrament, while the consecration of virgins and profession of monastic vows was not (Thomas Aquinas, *ST* 2a2ae.186–9, Suppl. 41–2).

The allegorical interpretation of virginity in Christian tradition has always been tied to the allegorical interpretation of the Song of Songs. This exegetical approach is part of Christianity's inheritance from Judaism, for the rabbis had long regarded Solomon's epithalamion as a symbol of God's love for his people. In the Christian mystical tradition Solomon's canticle was interpreted both in an ecclesiological sense as the love of Christ for the Church, and in a personal-mystical sense as Christ's love song to the betrothed (baptized) soul. This imagery recurs not only throughout mystical-exegetical treatises intended for the spiritual elite, such as writings on the Song of Songs by Origen (d. 254), Gregory the Great (d. 604) and Bernard of Clairvaux (d. 1153), but it is also central to the baptismal catecheses of Ambrose of Milan (d. 397), which were preached to ordinary Christian catecheumens. Thus virginity has been extolled throughout the history of Christianity both as a universal symbol and a particular vocation.

In the utilitarian modern world, perhaps even more than in antiquity, the need exists for a means of expressing the value of human life in terms of its potential for intimate union with Christ, rather than by its biological or social 'productivity'. Thus it is vital to reinterpret the traditional tension between the respective meanings of Christian marriage and consecrated virginity as lifegiving and mutually illuminating. Christian marriage and consecrated virginity each require the witness of the other to fully attest to the eschatological dimensions of the Christian gospel, the goodness and beauty of creation, and the passionate, intimate love of the Christian God.

See also Asceticism; Celibacy; Chastity; Monasticism.

Peter Brown, *The Body and Society: Men Women, and Sexual Renunciation in Early Christianity*, New York: Columbia University Press, 1988; Evagrius of Pontus, 'Exhortation to A Virgin' in *Evagrius of Pontus, the Greek Ascetic Corpus*, trans. R. E. Sinkewicz, Oxford: Oxford University Press, 2004; Constance Mews (ed.), *Listen Daughter, The Speculum Virginum and the Formation of Religious Women in the Middle Ages*, London: Palgrave Publishers, 2001; Origen, 'Prologue to the Commentary on the Song of Songs', in *Origen: An Exhortation to Martyrdom, Prayer and Selected Works*, trans. R. A. Greer, CWS, New York: Paulist Press, 1979.

LUKE DYSINGER

Virtue

Virtue in the Christian tradition denotes both the orientation of a person's character towards the good and the application of knowledge of this good to concrete circumstances. While there are many theories of virtue, they all share this dual focus on both the moral character and on the concrete circumstances of moral living.

Moreover this concern with the character and its formation has operated, historically, as an important corrective to the occasional legalistic and act-centred tendencies that also form part of the moral tradition. From the beginning Christians associated the acquisition of virtue with the Holy Spirit. However the enduring theological significance of virtue also owes a great deal to the centrality of the concept in the philosophy of Aristotle. For Aristotle virtue is intimately connected with the person's apprehension of what it means to live the good life, to have *eudaemonia* or well-being. This pursuit of the good life, however, is something that must be cultivated and reinforced through good choices and good actions. Virtue is thereby neither pre-existing nor guaranteed. Rather it is nurtured through the repetition of good behaviours, and thus becomes a *habitus*. However, it is not only the execution of good decisions that helps cultivate a virtuous disposition: the manner in which such actions are performed is also significant. Thomas Aquinas took up this Aristotelian sense of virtue as a condition of the person's character, but read it through an Augustinian lens so that in the *Summa Theologiae* we are presented with a distinctively Christian account of virtue and the virtues.

The virtuous person, then, is one who lives life in accordance with the good and who cultivates the practice of the virtues through his or her decisions and actions. Traditionally the virtues were characterized as being either cardinal or theological, the cardinal being particularly associated with the moral realm. The ability to recognize the good and to apply it in each particular context is itself the highest of the cardinal virtues, that is, prudence. Prudence, almost indistinguishable from Aristotle's practical wisdom or *phronesis*, thereby guides the operations of our conscience. Fortitude strengthens our will and regulates our fears. Temperance manages our passions, moderating in particular our sensual desires. The fourth of the cardinal virtues, justice, works towards the construction and maintenance of fair and honourable relationships in society. Justice thus attends to the social and relational context in which the person strives to live a virtuous life. These four cardinal virtues are central to the moral life and form the basis of ethical decision-making. However for the Christian, the theological virtues of faith, hope and charity (love) are equally, if not more, significant. While the cardinal virtues are adequate to enable the person to apprehend and live a humanly good life, the theological virtues are necessary in order to bring the person into union with God. They are called theological because they are regarded as being infused by God in the person and they enable each individual to enter into a relationship with God. They thereby create the spiritual grounding for the moral character and orientate it towards God.

While virtue has long had an illustrious career in the fields of ethics and spirituality, its re-emergence in the late twentieth century has been significant. A return to a person-centred, biblically based ethics in Catholicism (mandated by Vatican II), together with a greater focus on philosophical ethics among Protestant ethicists, has resulted in the relocation of virtue in ethics, so that it is again centre stage. Moreover this in turn has created a context in which the intrinsic relationship between spirituality and ethics can again come to the fore within the Christian tradition. The theorists of virtue ethics have generated a focus on narrative and community in the formation of the moral character (Hauerwas and MacIntyre). They have also highlighted the significant role that liturgy and prayer have in the life of moral communities. Recognizing the importance of imagination and aesthetics (Keane and von Balthasar) in the moral life of the person and the community is also a hallmark. Virtue ethics is attentive to the capacity of spirituality to nourish the moral life of the person and regards ethics and spirituality to be necessarily intertwined. In fact the traditional language of holiness in spirituality is closely aligned with that of the cultivation of virtue. Thus the person-centred, developmental approach to the moral life that is characteristic of virtue ethics accentuates the strong connections that exist between the spiritual and moral aspects of the person's life.

See also **Aesthetics; Communion/*Koinonia*; Ethics and Spirituality; Imagination; Holiness; Person.**

S. Hauerwas, *A Community of Character: Toward a Constructive Christian Social Ethic*, Notre Dame, IN: University of Notre Dame Press, 1981; A. MacIntyre, *After Virtue: A Study in Moral Theory*, Notre Dame, IN: University of Notre Dame Press, 1981; G. Meilender, *The Theory and Practice of Virtue*, Notre Dame, IN: University of Notre Dame Press, 1988; J. Porter, *The Recovery of Virtue: The Relevance of Aquinas for Christian Ethics*, Louisville, KY: Westminster/ John Knox Press, 1990; M. Slote, *From Morality to Virtue*, New York: Oxford University Press, 1992.

LINDA HOGAN

Vision of God

see **Presence of God**

Visionary Literature

Visionary literature refers to a body of writings in which persons, usually characterized as mystics, describe their faith experiences through 'direct' sensory vision (sight and sound, or even smell and touch) or by intuitive inner vision. The individuals writing about their visions describe themselves as actually 'seeing' the subject or the object of the vision in question. The visions are accompanied by a deep-felt conviction of the truthfulness, for themselves and for others, of what has been 'seen'. Thus the visions are written down in order to pass on received messages, admonitions, or other revelations given to the Christian community from God through the individual in question.

There is some biblical evidence for this phenomenon, as demonstrated in New Testament texts such as Mark 16 or Matthew 28 who proclaim 'We have seen the Lord!' However, the flowering of 'visionary literature' took place in the twelfth to fourteenth centuries during which time a number of mystics, largely women mystics, underwent extraordinary visionary experiences. These visions are characterized by emotional intensity, seemed 'fantastic' in nature, and were often 'irrational'. They were sometimes accompanied by weeping, tears, screaming, stigmata, extreme loss of appetite and illnesses of all kinds.

The subjects of the visions included, among many other things, vivid images of God's majesty on a throne, Jesus on the cross, images of heaven and hell, and angels. The visions were accompanied by profound insights into the nature of love and of evil, the need for personal and ecclesial conversion, the nature of the relationship between God and the world, or the meaning of creation and redemption. Thus, visionary literature can usually be divided into three general categories: visions of devotion (where love is aroused and deepened); visions of doctrine (a teaching or interpretation of a current doctrine of the faith); and visions of prophecy (revelation of God's love or hope for the world).

One must ask the question: how is it determined which visionary experiences are authentic and which are not? Beyond the question of authenticity comes a further question: what was 'seen' may have had meaning for the visionary, but who is to say that it should have meaning for us as well? Some general criteria that have withstood the test of time have been discerned by the Christian community through the ages in order to authenticate visionary experiences as a reliable source of inspiration for the individual and the larger Christian community. For example, the visionary must first herself or himself be living an authentic, holy, and liberating Christian life, a life that is affirmed by the Christian community as truly such. The visions are sometimes accompanied by a cure from some illness that authenticates the vision and testifies to the liberating power of Christ in this way. Furthermore, the teachings of the visionary must not contradict the Scriptures, or authentic teachings based on the Scriptures. If it is a true vision the visionary does what they are 'told' despite Church restrictions or other cultural restrictions that may dictate otherwise.

On this latter point we have as an example the visions of Catherine of Sienna (1347–80) which called her to speak out against the abuses of power plaguing the Church at the time. Clergy, bishops, and popes alike strove for office and position instead of humble service to God's people. Furthermore, in 1376 Catherine met with Pope Gregory XI, in order to persuade him to move back to Rome after a period of some seventy years during which time the popes had taken up residency in Avignon, France, due to political turmoil in Italy. This was a bold suggestion on the part of Catherine, especially given the meagre influence of women in Church and state affairs at the time. However, her vocal criticisms of the abuse of power in the Church, and the return of the Pope to Rome, testify to the strength of the inspiration she received in her visions. Catherine wrote many letters as well as her well-known book *The Dialogue*.

Other women contributing to the explosion of visionary literature during the twelfth to fourteenth centuries include the following: Hildegard of Bingen (1098–1179) as recorded in her *Life, Know the Way* (known as *Scivias*), and *The Book of Divine Works*; Mechthild of Magdeburg (1210–83) as recorded in *The Flowing Light of Godhead*; Julian of Norwich (1342–c. 1416) as recorded in *Showings of God's Love*; and Margery Kempe (1373–1440) as recorded in *The Book of Margery Kempe*. A male counterpart visionary during this time was Henry Suso (1295–1366); see his *Life, Little Book of Truth*, and *Little Book of Eternal Wisdom*. A contemporary contributor to the body of literature known as 'visionary literature', is Caryll Houselander (1901–49); see her *The Passion of the Infant Christ*.

See also **Mysticism (*essay*); English Mystical Tradition; Women Medieval Mystics.**

Monica Furlong, *Visions and Longings: Medieval Women Mystics*, Boston, MA: Shambhala, 1996; Shawn Madigan, *Mystics, Visionaries, and Prophets: A Historical Anthology of Women's Spiritual Writings*, Minneapolis, MN: Fortress Press, 1998; Elizabeth Petroff (ed.), *Medieval Women's Visionary Literature*, New York: Oxford University Press, 1986.

DAVID B. PERRIN

Vocation

The Latin word *vocare* means 'to call, summon or invite', or 'to call by name'. Thus a 'vocation' always comes to us from outside ourselves, often from someone in authority. Once called, we are expected to respond by drawing near to the caller, or by performing the action to which we are bidden, or by accepting the identity bestowed upon us in the name we have been given. When God is the one who calls, our response to vocation is of ultimate significance – even a matter of life and death.

In the Old Testament, there is a common human vocation implicit in the very act of creation with its attendant command to have dominion over the earth (Gen. 1.27–28). Subsequently, God calls both the people of Israel (Isa. 43.1) and individuals such as Abraham (Gen. 12.1), Moses (Ex. 19.3), and the prophets Samuel (1 Sam. 3.4) and Isaiah (Isa. 49.1). In each case, the invitation is not only to intimate communion with God, but also to mission on behalf of the community – or in the case of Israel, for the sake of the nations (Isa. 42.6). A similar pattern is found in the Gospels when Jesus, after calling his disciples to follow him (Matt. 4.19), then commands them to minister to those in need (Matt. 10.1) and appoints them as his apostolic representatives (Luke 6.13). The concept of 'calling' features prominently in the Pauline writings, where Christians are 'called to be saints' (Rom. 1.7) and exhorted to live a life worthy of their calling (Eph. 4.1).

Before Christianity became the established religion of the Roman Empire, Christians understood their vocation from God as a call to radical conversion from death into life. To accept baptism was to renounce evil and become a new creature in Christ. For many, this conversion required giving up an occupation involving violence or immorality; in certain communities, even celibacy was considered obligatory. By the Middle Ages, when infant baptism had become the usual practice, the Church came to accept that most people would fulfil their Christian responsibility through faithful service within the normal bounds of family and community life. Even the term 'vocation' came to be restricted to those persons who followed a 'special' calling as a monk, nun, priest, prince or king.

Reacting against this restricted notion of vocation were sixteenth-century Reformers like Martin Luther and John Calvin, who insisted that every duty undertaken out of love for God and neighbour was a true Christian vocation. Thus the mother rocking the cradle and the shoemaker at his last were fulfilling callings every bit as sacred as that of the preacher in the pulpit. As these examples imply, the Reformers tended to assume traditional roles assigned in accordance with gender and class. They urged Protestant Christians to accept the conventional demands of their social stations as God-given vocations. Nevertheless, the Reformers were successful in inspiring people to consider the whole of human life as the appropriate arena for Christian discipleship.

In the Roman Catholic Church, Vatican II returned to the biblical and patristic sources to recover a more inclusive understanding of vocation in which 'all Christians in any state or walk of life are called to the fullness of Christian life and to the perfection of love' (*Lumen Gentium* 13). Contemporary Christians of diverse traditions now acknowledge both the universality of God's call and the need for discernment in order to determine how that call is particularized for each individual. In contrast to the popular culture which so readily equates a sense of vocation with the desire for self-fulfilment, Christians today affirm the truth of Frederick Buechner's dictum: 'The place God calls you to is the place where your deep gladness and the world's deep hunger meet' (*Wishful Thinking*, New York: Harper & Row, 1973, p. 118).

See also **Baptism; Conversion; Discernment; Discipleship; Election (Predestination); Election, Ignatian; Lay People and Spirituality; Religious Life; Vows.**

John C. Haughey (ed.), *Revisiting the Idea of Vocation: Theological Explorations*, Washington, DC: Catholic University of America Press, 2004; Renée LaReau, *Getting a Life: How to Find Your True Vocation*, Maryknoll, NY: Orbis Books, 2003; Parker J. Palmer, *Let Your Life Speak: Listening for the Voice of Vocation*, San Francisco: Jossey-Bass, 2000; M. Basil Pennington ocso, *Called: New Thinking on Christian Vocation*, New York: Seabury Press, 1983; Douglas James Schuurman, *Vocation: Discerning Our Callings in Life*, Grand Rapids, MI: Eerdmans, 2004; Gordon T. Smith, *Courage and Calling: Embracing Your God-Given Potential*, Downers Grove, IL: InterVarsity Press, 1999.

ARTHUR G. HOLDER

Vows

The making of vows or promises to God is part of the relationship between God and the chosen people expressed throughout the Old Testament in the notion of covenant (Ex. 34.10). The essential covenant promise is of mutual love and fidelity between God and the community of the faithful. The initiative in this call to reciprocal love comes from God (Ex. 6.7; Deut. 4.20), whose call to respond is in itself a grace. Within that general promise, some received a specific call to dedicate their lives entirely to God in a way that bore public witness to the call to holiness that belongs to all (1 Sam. 1.22; Isa. 6.1–9). The evangelical counsels of poverty, chastity and obedience derive from the life of Christ who renounced the acquisition of personal property (Luke 9.58) and the exclusive commitment to one other expressed in marriage and family life (Matt. 12.46–50; Matt. 19.10–12), and who was obedient to his Father's will to the point of death (Luke 22.39–42; Heb. 5.7–10). Christ's call to discipleship proposes the life of the evangelical counsels to all Christians within the multiplicity of their chosen ways of life. The religious vows are a particular development of the baptismal call to discipleship (*Lumen Gentium* 44). The drive to money, sex and power lies at the heart of the human psyche and is, in itself, neutral. The process of conversion to the values of the kingdom involves the transformation of this drive so that its fulfilment is not an end in itself but a means of growing into the fullness of human personhood expressed in the freedom of love and service of God and others.

From the earliest beginnings of the Church some felt called to a radical following of Christ through the implicit and later explicit practice of the evangelical counsels (*Perfectae Caritatis* 1). While this did not always involve the profession of these counsels through vows, there derived from the life of the desert hermits a way of life characterized by liturgical prayer, the public profession of the counsels and a life led in common that came to be expressed and supported by canonical vows. The monastic vows of stability, conversion of life and obedience derive from the same Biblical call to self-dedication, but are lived in the specific framework and tradition of the early period of consecrated life within the Church (Rees et al., 1978, p. 128).

Later developments of more mobile forms of religious life led to the standardizing of religious vows as poverty, chastity and obedience, although some orders take other additional vows (such as hospitality, among the Brothers of St John of God, or especial obedience to the Pope, among the Jesuits).

Since the reform of religious life resulting from Vatican II, the name of these vows has been called into question. Married Christians are also called to love chastely, in a single-hearted commitment to the other that is a reflection of God's liberating love, which neither exploits nor dominates, and accepts one's own and others' bodies as temples of the Holy Spirit (1 Cor. 6.19). The renunciation of the genital expression of sexuality is not a value in itself unless aimed at the transformation of the human capacity to love in freedom. The notion of obedience bears connotations of feudalism and servitude that no longer hold in cultures that take the autonomy and accountability of individuals in society for granted. In the light of endemic world poverty and the disparities of income even in the developed world, the security enjoyed by most religious can seem far removed from any realistic notion of destitution, which many religious orders are dedicated to overcoming rather than imitating.

Despite the crisis of confidence in promises both in public and private life in the Western world (Radcliffe, 1999, p. 31), the spiritual reality behind vowed living retains a compelling sign value. Celibate chastity challenges a world of sexual exploitation and the disintegration of committed relationships, bearing witness to the grace of fidelity given by God whose love is everlasting (Jer. 31.3). Obedience, whose Latin root *ob+audire* means to listen intently, refers not to loss of autonomy but to the finding of the true self through the discernment of God's will in a contemplative openness and availability that characterized the prophets and disciples (1 Sam. 3.10) and Mary the mother of God (Luke 1.38). The sharing of the common life and renunciation of private goods and property are not only a form of personal renunciation (Matt. 19.27–30) for the sake of the kingdom, but a sign of solidarity with Christ in the poor that proclaims a value for human life beyond purely economic judgements. This radical imitation of Christ poor, chaste and obedient comes in response to the transforming power of Christ who is our holiness and our freedom.

See also **Chastity; Obedience; Poverty; Vocation.**

———

A. DiIanni, *Religious Life as Adventure: Renewal, Refounding or Reform?*, New York: Alba, 1994; *Lumen Gentium* in *The Documents of Vatican II*, ed. W. Abbott, London: Geoffrey Chapman, 1967; J. Merkle, *Committed by Choice*, Collegeville, MN: The Liturgical Press, 1992; J. B. Metz, *Followers of Christ: The Religious Life and the Church*, London: Burns & Oates, 1978; F. Moloney, *Disciples and Prophets: A Biblical Model for the Religious Life*, London: Darton, Longman & Todd, 1980; D. O'Murchu, *Poverty, Celibacy and Obedience: A Radical Option for Life*, New York: Crossroad, 1999; *Perfectae Caritatis* in W. Abbott (ed.), *The Documents of Vatican II*, London: Geoffrey Chapman, 1967; T. Radcliffe, *Sing a New Song*, Dublin: Dominican Publications 1999; D. Rees et al., *Consider Your Call: A Theology of Monastic Life Today*, London: SPCK, 1978; S. Schneiders, *Finding the Treasure*, New York: Paulist Press, 2000; S. Schneiders, *Selling All*, New York: Paulist Press, 2001; A. Van Kaam, *The Vowed Life*, Denville, NJ: Dimension Books, 1968; C. Yuhaus et al., *Religious Life: The Challenge for Tomorrow*, New York: Paulist Press, 1994.

GEMMA SIMMONDS

Warfare

see **Combat, Spiritual**

Wealth

see **Consumerism**

Welsh Spirituality

Great was Christ in all eternity,
Great in taking the nature of man,
Great in dying on Calvary hill,
Great in breaking the power of death,
Truly great is he now,
Ruler over heaven and earth.

(*Caneuon Ffydd*, p 232)

This is the first verse of a well-known hymn from the early nineteenth century. Its writer, Titus Lewis (1773–1811) is a typical example of the great company of Nonconformist preachers and hymn-writers who carried forward the work of the Methodist revival which had begun in Wales, as it did in England in the 1730s (Meic Stephens, 1998). It was a revival which in its Welsh form, Calvinist in doctrine, Welsh in language, had a decisive influence on the whole development of Welsh society for the best part of two centuries. Indeed, under its influence a distinct Welsh Nonconformist culture came into being which gave a particular colour to the life of Wales, social, cultural and intellectual, well into the twentieth century.

When we look at this verse of Titus Lewis's hymn we see at once that it presents us with a spirituality which is firmly rooted in Christian doctrine. The whole theme of these lines is Christological, centring on the person of Jesus Christ, as made known in the Scriptures of the Old and New Testaments and in the faith and worship of the early Christian centuries. It celebrates the pre-existent Christ, the incarnate Christ, Christ who dies on the cross, and who in dying overcomes the power of death. It celebrates the ascended Christ now at the right hand of the Father, in whom all things in heaven and on earth are gathered together into one. It comes from an evangelical tradition of Christian faith and worship which has been extremely reluctant to make use of visual imagery in either its teaching or its life. But through its use of poetic imagery it presents us with a striking verbal equivalent of the Byzantine icon of Christ Pantocrator as we find it in the dome of the churches of Eastern Christendom, an icon which of course Titus Lewis could never have seen.

That the heart of a tradition of evangelical hymnody should be wholly centred on the person of Christ is perhaps not surprising. Perhaps less expected is the centrality of the doctrine of the Trinity in this same body of hymns. Here the Calvinist emphasis on the saving counsel of God from all eternity takes a particular form. God is seen from before creation, already holding the salvation of fallen humanity in God's heart and mind.

In this picture of the eternal counsel of the Three in One, 'the design of great love', as the hymn writers term it, we have again a verbal equivalent of one of the most famous of Orthodox icons, the icon depicting the hospitality of Abraham, often known as the Old Testament Trinity. It is commonly said that this icon is painted in such a way as to draw the viewer into the circle of the three divine persons. This thought of our entering into the very life of the Three in One is perhaps less common in the Welsh hymnody of these times, but it finds a clear expression in some of the greatest verses in one of the greatest of all Welsh hymn-writers, Ann Griffiths (1776–1805). She speaks of heaven as 'Abundant freedom of entrance ever to continue/Into the dwelling places of the Three-in-One/Water to swim in not to be passed through/ Man as God and God as man' (Allchin, 1987, p. 16). Here we see how Ann Griffiths' hymns unite a passionate intensity of longing with a remarkable intellectual clarity, 'Not heat without light, nor light without heat', as her earliest biographer put it.

We have been looking at a late manifestation of Welsh spirituality. We have seen a tradition which reveals itself above all in a tradition of sacred poetry, a poetry of praise and thanksgiving. We can trace the development of this tradition, not only in recent centuries, but throughout the whole history of Wales, from the fifth and sixth centuries till today. It was as the Roman armies left Britain in 410, and as the Anglo-Saxon invaders from Northern Europe took over more and more of the eastern side of southern Britain, that the British inhabitants of the island, retreating into the west, began to become aware of themselves not only as Britons but also as *Cymry*, those who live together, fellow countrymen, comrades. With this growth in national consciousness, there came a more rapid but no less decisive awareness of themselves as Christians, whose heritage reached back into the period of the Roman occupation of the island but whose sense of identity was greatly strengthened by the vigour of the monastic movement which in these early centuries swiftly reached the westernmost parts of the old Christian world, having travelled from Egypt and Palestine. A brief period of two or three centuries, 'The Age of the Saints', created a group of churches in the Celtic lands, Wales, Ireland, Western Scotland, Isle of Man, Cornwall, Brittany; a group of churches sometimes mistakenly referred to as 'The Celtic Church'. This western Christian world in the first Christian millennium forms the historical foundation of the 'Celtic Christianity' which has so much fascinated and sometimes perplexed readers and students during the last generation (Davies, 1996).

This early Celtic Christian world had its two main centres, one in Ireland, the other in Wales. In Wales it is marked from the beginning, as it was in the eighteenth and nineteenth centuries, by a combination of fervour and clarity, of doctrine and devotion. It is also marked by an extraordinary tenacity and resilience. Throughout the centuries the Celtic peoples of the west have known repeated periods of outward defeat and devastation. Inwardly, however, they have maintained a continuity of vision and understanding which has almost unconsciously conveyed to the people of our own time something of the fullness of that first-millennium Christianity.

A particular kind of sacred poetry has, for more than twelve centuries, flourished in Wales in a great variety of ways. It has always contained at its heart the conviction that the work of the poet must be primarily the praise of God in himself, and in and through his work in creation and redemption. This work of praise is a sacred, priestly calling, the gift of the Holy Spirit enabling God's people to articulate God's praise.

One of the few pieces of sacred poetry in Welsh, which we can definitely date in the first millennium, is a poem written in the margin of an eighth-century Latin manuscript found in the university library at Cambridge. It is a poem of nine three-line verses, a poem at once trinitarian and incarnational, celebrating the work of God both in creation and in redemption. Of the nine verses six (3–5 and 6–8) are explicitly trinitarian though in interestingly different ways. Verses 6 to 8, for instance, speak of the call to worship the eternal Trinity, a call given first to angels and saints in heaven, then to the whole people of God in this world, and then to the poet himself in his own particularity. Thus in this poem the poet insists that this work of praise is something altogether universal and at the same time altogether personal. It is both these things at once. Again and again the poets exclaim 'I too offer my praise' (Allchin, 1997, pp. 1–10).

Much of this earliest poetry in the period before the twelfth century is anonymous and difficult to date, but when examined theologically much of it seems to reflect the proportions and understanding of first-millennium Christianity with remarkable skill. This is a form of Christianity which in its main outlines was common to East and West. Not only to the Latin and Greek worlds inside the old Roman empire, but also to Coptic and Armenian to the East and to Celtic in the West, fusing together into one Old Testament and pre-Christian traditions of praise poetry (Allchin, 2003, pp. 317–33).

The history of Welsh spirituality in the six centuries from 1130 to 1730 cannot be confined to the history of Welsh poetry, though it finds its heart and centre there. The poetic tradition shows remarkable continuity and constant powers of renewal. At its heart there is this theme of the praise of God, a theological poetry, much of which has as yet been very little studied. Here the work of the Centre for Higher Welsh and Celtic Studies in the University of Aberystwyth is of great significance. Of the poets of the period 1350–1500, usually considered from the literary point of view as the Golden Age of Welsh poetry, much is now in print, though much remains unpublished. Some is of real theological value. This is a field where much is being done and much remains to be done.

What is the present situation of Welsh spirituality? The question is difficult to answer, especially for someone who is not Welsh. The institutional decline common to all churches of Western Europe is certainly evident in Wales and it is a decline which, for social and cultural reasons, began to manifest itself already in the years following World War 1. The future of the Welsh language, which as we have seen has always been central to the spiritual tradition, is very uncertain in the twenty-first century, as is the case with all minority languages (Densil Morgan 1999, *passim*). The present situation is one that joins anxiety with hope.

One thing however is clear and that is that in the middle of the twentieth century (1935–80), four Welsh poets emerged in whom, in a variety of ways, this ancient tradition of sacred verse, the poetry of praise, received a new and unforeseeable expression. John Saunders Lewis, David Gwenallt Jones, Waldo Williams, and Euros Bowen were all writers whose roots were in the world of Welsh Nonconformity, Calvinistic Methodist, Baptist and Congregational. All of them, for a variety of reasons, felt themselves called to transcend the denominations in which they grew up. All of them, in very different literary idioms, found themselves called to make their own this fifteen-hundred-year tradition of sacred poetry of which we have spoken in this article and in a remarkable way they succeeded in doing so.

Here at least English-language material, both translation and commentary, is accessible. Thus these four 'doctors of the Church', who so unexpectedly emerged in the middle of the twentieth century, are part of an unfolding story which still goes on and which demands fuller attention on the part of those who are prepared to recognize, in this western part of southern Britain, the presence of a tradition of spirituality which can sometimes bring first-millennium Christianity alive for us in our own day in surprising ways.

See also **Celtic Spirituality.**

A. M. Allchin, *Ann Griffiths: The Furnace and the Fountain*, Cardiff: University of Wales Press, 1987; A. M. Allchin, *Praise Above All: Discovering the Welsh Tradition*, Cardiff: University of Wales Press, 1991; A. M. Allchin, *God's Presence Makes the World: The Celtic Vision through the Centuries in Wales*, London: Darton, Longman & Todd, 1997; A. M. Allchin, 'The heir of resurrection: creation, cross and resurrection in early Welsh poetry', in John Behr, Andrew Louth and Dimitri Conomos (eds), *Abba: The Tradition of Orthodoxy in the West, Festschrift for Bp. Kallistos Ware*, New York: St Vladimir's Seminary Press, 2003; Mark Atherton (ed.), *Celts and Christians: New Approaches to the Religious Traditions of Britain and Ireland*, Cardiff: University of Wales Press, 2002; Euros Bowen, *Priest and Poet*, trans. Cynthia and Saunders Davies, Cardiff: Church in Wales Publishing, 1993; *Caneuon Ffydd*, Cardiff: Pwyllgor Llyfr Emynan Cydenwadol, 2001; Joseph Clancy. *Mediaeval Welsh Poems*, Dublin: Four Courts, 2003; N. G. Costigan, *Defining the Divinity: Mediaeval Perceptions in Welsh Court Poetry*, Aberystwyth; University of Wales Press, 2002; Oliver Davies, *Celtic Christianity in Early Mediaeval Wales*, Cardiff: University of Wales Press 1996; Oliver Davies (ed.), *Celtic Spirituality*, CWS, New York: Paulist Press, 1999; D. Densil Morgan, *The Span of the Cross: Christian Religion and Society in Wales 1914–2000*, Cardiff: University of Wales Press,

1999; D. Gwenallt Jones, *Sensuous Glory: The Poetic Vision of Gwenallt Jones*, ed. A. M. Allchin, Densil Morgan and Patrick Thomas, Norwich: Canterbury Press, 2000; Jenny Rowland (ed.), *Early Welsh Saga Poetry: A Study and Edition of the Englynion*, Bury St Edmunds: Boydell & Brewer, 1990; J. Saunders Lewis, *Selected Poems*, trans. Joseph Clancy, Cardiff: University of Wales Press, 1993; Meic Stephens (ed.), *Companion to the Literature of Wales*, Cardiff: University of Wales Press, 1998; Waldo Williams, *The Peacemakers*, trans. Tony Conran, Llandysul: Gomer Press, 1997.

A. M. ALLCHIN

Wesleyan Spirituality

see Methodist Spirituality

Wisdom

Augustine spoke for Christians throughout the ages when he acknowledged God as 'the Wisdom in whom and from whom and through whom all things are wise which anywhere are wise' (*Soliloquies* 1.3) But what does it mean to be wise? When Clement of Alexandria (following Stoic tradition) said that wisdom is 'the knowledge of things divine and human, and their causes' (*Stromateis* 1.5), he surely meant to imply far more than the accumulation of information, or even the attainment of insight. In Christian understanding, to be wise is to discern the divinely ordained pattern within nature and experience, and then to follow the prescribed way of living well so as to be in right relationship with God.

The classic expressions of Hebrew wisdom are found in the Old Testament books of Proverbs, Job and Ecclesiastes, all of which offer profound reflections on the meaning of life, true happiness, virtue and vice, and the challenges of coping with suffering, loss, finitude and death. Key to their perspective is an insight that is repeated several times: 'The fear of the Lord is the beginning of wisdom' (Prov. 9.10). Passages in many other Old Testament books reflect similar concerns and make use of the same literary forms (e.g. proverbs, aphorisms, instructional discourse, debate and hymnic poetry).

Among the so-called apocryphal or deutero-canonical books of the intertestamental period, the Wisdom of Solomon and Ecclesiasticus (also known as the Wisdom of Jesus Ben Sirach) are clearly in the wisdom genre, but with more explicit reference to the events and heroic figures of salvation history. In these later books, as in Proverbs 1—9, there appears the personified figure of Lady Wisdom (Heb. *hokmah*, a feminine noun), which has been variously interpreted as a hypostasis of the attributes of Yahweh, an appropriation of Near Eastern goddesses, or the embodiment of social roles enacted by women in Israelite society.

The synoptic Gospels present Jesus as a teacher of subversive wisdom who habitually employed proverbs and parables. Moreover, Luke sees Jesus as the child and prophet of Wisdom (Gk. *sophia*), while in Matthew he is presented as Wisdom incarnate (11.19). The prologue to John's Gospel identifies Jesus as the Word (Gk. *logos*) and follows the Jewish author Philo in assimilating that Word to the same Wisdom who was present with God in creation. Paul also declares that Christ is 'the power of God and the wisdom of God' (1 Cor. 1.24), but he insists that the wisdom of this world is not the same as God's wisdom, which is revealed only in the suffering of the Saviour on the cross (1 Cor. 2.1–5). The Epistle of James (3.17) similarly contrasts earthly wisdom with 'the wisdom from above', which is 'first pure, then peaceable, gentle, willing to yield, full of mercy and good fruits, without a trace of partiality or hypocrisy'.

The early Church Fathers readily identified Wisdom with the second Person of the Trinity. Both sides in the Arian controversy appealed to Wisdom's words in Prov. 8.22 ('The Lord created me at the beginning of his work') with reference to the status of the Logos, although they predictably interpreted this verse in very different ways: for Arians, it indicated that the Son was a creature; for the proponents of Nicene orthodoxy, it suggested that the Son was with the Father from the very beginning, even before the creation of the world. Justinian's famous church of Hagia Sophia in Constantinople was dedicated to Christ as Holy Wisdom, as were many other churches in both East and West. However, some authors such as Theophilus of Antioch and Irenaeus identified not Christ but the Holy Spirit as God's Wisdom.

Many early Christian texts might be classified as forms of 'wisdom literature'. The *Odes of Solomon* is a Syriac collection of hymns in praise of God as creator and redeemer, often reminiscent of the great lyric passages in Job or Ecclesiasticus. The *Sayings of the Desert Fathers* presents the desert monastics as venerable (although not necessarily well-educated) sages who teach through aphorism, story and enacted parable. The opening words of the Rule of Benedict ('Listen, O son, to the precepts of the master, and incline the ear of your heart') clearly echo Prov. 4.20, and the entire rule is filled with practical advice about daily life interspersed with exhortations to virtue, obedience and fear of the Lord.

Medieval theologians frequently spoke of Christ as Divine Wisdom, sometimes ascribing to him the feminine characteristics of the Old Testament figure. Thus Bede's commentary on Proverbs is thoroughly Christological in its interpretation; for example, 'Wisdom (Lat. *sapientia*) has built herself a house' (Prov. 9.1) is taken as an allegorical figure of the incarnation. Biblical texts describing personified Wisdom were frequently applied to Christ in the liturgy, and Alcuin even composed an entire Mass of Holy Wisdom in this vein. But as early as the seventh century, the same texts were being read on feasts of the Virgin Mary as well; in medieval art and sculpture, she is often depicted as the 'Seat of Wisdom' enthroned on a chair, with the Christ child as Incarnate Wisdom on her lap. In addition, Lady Wisdom was often conflated with representations of Lady Philosophy such as that of Boethius in his *Consolation of Philosophy*.

In the late nineteenth and early twentieth centuries, Russian Orthodox theologians Vladimir Solovyev and Sergei Bulgakov developed speculative forms of 'sophiology' in which the feminine Sophia is seen as the divine splendour manifest in the beauty of creation, and even as the *ousia* (essence) by virtue of which the three *hypostases* of the Trinity are held in unity. Influenced by the Platonic notion of the world-soul, the idealist philosophy of Schelling, and the mystical writings of Jakob Boehme, sophiology is well known among the Orthodox, but it has not found widespread acceptance there.

In contemporary spirituality, there is considerable debate over the value and appropriateness of sapiential theology and language, especially in relation to issues of gender. Feminist participants in the controversial Reimagining Conference held in Minneapolis in 1993 were invited to offer prayers to 'our maker, Sophia' as a way of overcoming the patriarchal connotations of traditional trinitarian language. Many church people saw this as syncretism or 'goddess worship', while others believed that it was a timely recovery of a neglected strand within the Orthodox Christian tradition.

More recently, some feminist scholars have argued that sapiential theology has always been inextricably linked to the interests of the social and political elite, from the sages of the Solomonic court to the male proponents of Wisdom Christologies in the New Testament. Other scholars, however, respond that wisdom traditions in Scripture have been effectively integrated with prophetic and apocalyptic traditions, so that Wisdom Christologies carry a deep commitment to social justice, as well as an appreciation of the kind of folk wisdom accessible to women as well as to men in that cultural context. Whatever the future of sapiential theologies may be, it is clear that the search for wisdom will always belong at the heart of Christian spirituality.

See also **Spirituality and Scripture** (*essay*): **Feminist Spirituality; Knowledge.**

María Pilar Aquino and Elisabeth Schüssler Fiorenza, *In the Power of Wisdom: Feminist Spiritualities of Struggle*, London: SCM Press, 2000; Stephen C. Barton (ed.), *Where Shall Wisdom Be Found?: Wisdom in the Bible, the Church and the Contemporary World*, Edinburgh: T & T Clark, 1999; Katharine Dell, *'Get Wisdom, Get Insight': An Introduction to Israel's Wisdom Literature*, London: Darton, Longman & Todd, 2000; John Eaton, *The Contemplative Face of Old Testament Wisdom in the Context of World Religions*, London: SCM Press/Philadelphia: Trinity Press International, 1989; Barbara Newman, *God and the Goddesses: Vision, Poetry, and Belief in the Middle Ages*, Philadelphia: University of Pennsylvania Press, 2003, esp. ch. 5, 'Sapientia: the goddess incarnate'; Elisabeth Schüssler Fiorenza, *Jesus: Miriam's Child, Sophia's Prophet: Critical Issues in Feminist Christology*, New York: Continuum, 1994.

ARTHUR G. HOLDER

Womanist Spirituality

Womanist spirituality is a vital, expressive, revolutionary, embodied, personal and communal resistance-based way of life and theoretical discourse, based upon the rich lived, yet oppressive, experiences of women descended from the African diaspora, who as social beings in relationship with the divine, celebrate life and expose injustice and malaise. The womanist locus is not a narrow single-mindedness focusing exclusively on issues of sexism, racism or classism, but is, instead, a wide sweeping panorama confronting all three of these negative 'isms', and many more. Injustice stems from all oppressions, for example racism, classism and sexism, homophobia, ecological pollution, ageism, ableism and the misuse of power. Womanist, derived by Alice Walker from the term 'womanish', refers to women of African descent who are audacious, outrageous, in charge, responsible, serious, courageous and wilful. A womanist is a black feminist or feminist of colour. Womanism celebrates women's lives and cultures; embraces love for women, sexually and/or nonsexually; and is inclusive as it cares for the ultimate health, wholeness and survival of all people. The tremendous capacity for love involves the spectrum of culture, creation, Spirit, people and self. Womanist emancipatory spirituality embraces hope and transformation towards engendering mutuality and community, and honors the *imago dei* in all persons; it builds on the essential goodness of humanity and focuses on liberation amid personal and societal fragmentation in general, and faith-based discourse in particular. Honouring the *imago dei* in all persons presses womanist spirituality to explore questions of engagement and identity, sacrality, power, sacred texts and narratives which shape questions of authority, rituals and history; ethics regarding matters of values, behaviour, visibility and integrity; and location and stories, which concern matters of autobiography, culture, aesthetics, ecology and community. Many, though not all dogmas are open, adaptable to, and embracing of womanist spirituality. While many first-generation womanist scholars are Christian, women and men of the African diaspora of many faiths live, teach, preach and create embodying womanist spirituality.

Womanist spirituality is a dance, that process of empowerment where one connects with the divine, and the divine within self, nature and world to enhance every fibre of human life. This process, which may occur in formal, informal, conscious and unconscious ways, is the experience of living out the sacred, which includes, but is not exclusive to religion, worship or denominational commitments. Such power denotes an influence, permission, and an ability to choose, make decisions and affect change responsibly. This holy vitality sustains womanists when it seems all hope is lost and any efforts to make a difference futile. Rosita deAnn Mathews notes that womanist spirituality is also a paradoxical energy: one which leads and serves, resists evil and oppression by using power from the periphery. This womanist way of being requires that all actions be thought through with a keen prophetic awareness which names the action for what it is and analyses its existence in love. Womanist spirituality as power from the periphery gains strength from other places to exist, and may interrupt an oppressive system. Such engagement helps create a new spirit, protects one's soul from invasion, retains creativity and renews faith. Using power from the periphery, womanist spirituality works within its ethical framework to nurture personal and communal spirituality and responsibility, practises integrity, competence, dignity and truth. This power allows one to maintain commitment and not compromise authority. Womanist spirituality

honours respect for compassion, courage, life and inclusiveness. One example of womanist spirituality as power from the periphery is bell hooks' thesis *Killing Rage*.

Killing Rage disrupts those cultural productions and pedagogical strategies that celebrate white privilege, male supremacy: all hegemonic, oppressive discourse, which diminishes, denigrates and destroys ideas, possibilities, spirits, communities, individuals and bodies. *Killing rage*, the fury and anger that brews amid violence, is painful. Without an outlet, such rage can become intense grief and garbage. This rage holds a spirituality that is a place of aliveness, of immediate presence, a gift of subjectivity. *Killing rage* helps us name, unmask and engage the self and others in profound politicization and self-recovery, towards courageous action and resistance that helps one grow and change. *Killing rage*, as womanist, empowered spirituality from the periphery is an electrifying tool for change in public and private.

Emilie Townes explains that womanist spirituality involves a 'blaze of glory', bespeaking its eschatological and apocalyptic dimensions grounded in redemption and salvation. Such a vitality calls one to engage social witness, social analysis, biblical and theological reflection, ethical examination and mother wit or communal wisdom in naming and defying all of the 'isms' used to oppress. Womanist spirituality is embodied in the lived experience of justice and love, according everyone respect and dignity as children of God. This spirituality is prophetic, sees trouble upon the horizon, wants to confront wrong, and organizes for righteousness. Karen Baker-Fletcher sees such embodied spirituality when God is the strength and source of all creation. As human beings connect with the source of life within, they covenantally connect with God's speech, voice and word, in Anna Julia Cooper's language, as 'A Singing Something'. Embodied womanist spirituality moves one toward communal wholeness, liberation and flourishing, connecting with the dynamic energy-matter in creation, grounded in that force which holds, encompasses and interconnects us towards healing and provides wisdom, insight, endurance, new meaning, acting in harmony with God; promoting respect and dignity for all life; it is ecological. Womanist spirituality embraces a sense of the divine who gives empowerment for survival, healing, resistance and liberation. Baker-Fletcher comments that this life-affirming, embodied spirituality supports deliverance and salvation towards balance as justice. Womanist spirituality provides one with a powerful wholeness and healing with seven gifts: voice, vision, naming, tar/glue qualities of community building, regeneration, re-memory, and the interconnectedness of survival, resistance and liberation. These gifts signal humanity's interconnection with God/Spirit; prophetic speech, and the transformation of oppression; the capacity for equality; a cohesiveness of community; the transference of knowledge, wisdom and cultural heritage; the ability to make historical meaning; and the willingness to thrive, resist oppression, and reclaim freedom from the colonization of soul and mind.

Emilie Townes observes that womanist spirituality knows the stories of the community, past and present. The boundaries of community extend to the larger world with concern for everyone's health and well-being; that is, one cares about the well-being of all persons, whether they are oppressed or opressor. Extending community means not being crippled to do good even while under the oppressive aegis of dominant societal culture. Such spirituality emerges out of hope, love and intergenerational, communal wisdom. As lived, vital experience, womanist spirituality also yearns and works for wholeness and wellness of individuals, which involves an attitude of self-awareness where one knows how to be assertive, inquisitive, determined, astute and oppose the hegemonic status quo. Such a spirituality involves integrity and responsibility for gathering knowledge about self and the community. Kelly Brown Douglas notes that, with the individual as sacred, womanist spirituality involves an intimate connection with God/Spirit, thus one's sexuality. Sexuality, the elemental dimension of human beings that dictates sensual, intimate, affective, emotional and sexual relationships, is central to womanist spirituality because it involves an individual's relationship with God. Spirituality involves everything about human life, the power to be relational, self-transcending and fully engaged in freedom.

Womanist spirituality is also a process of being in the presence of Mystery of/and the Beautiful, where human beings have ultimate intimacy with a power that is both within and greater than themselves. As co-creators sustained through hope and love, this sexual power exudes a holiness that gives one strength to endure and overcome. Such a spirituality allows for the manifestation of the beautiful in culture and embraces justice that teaches one to celebrate differences and see new possibilities of engagement. With embodied spirituality comes a cultural resiliency and its flexibility, where formerly oppressed communities can orchestrate their own cultural expressions and values toward the pursuit of identity and community building. Womanist spirituality involves a gifted grace, a theology of relationality. This embodied relationality of thought, being and existence presses one to question origins, structures and being. This spirituality of relationality involves a process of working for justice, of human beings creating systems that are catalysts for change, rooted in ultimate source of all reality. Interconnections with the divine and all creation is a vitality of ecological empowerment and embodied spirituality.

Womanist spirituality as social witness personifies an attitude and commitment for justice. This hope-filled vision blends the divine and the human as empowered grace, rooted in God/Spirit's love, a love via compassion and justice, worship and dedication as social witness. Rosetta Ross posits that activity as witness connects faith with protest, and affirms divine presence within people. That is, God within shapes how people see, understand and connect with the world, and allows one to meet external challenges with authority, trusting God will provide. Such a witness is spirituality as a living response that affirms one's embodiment of grace, of lived divine norms, in opposition to injustice and hegemony. Womanist spirituality embraces the butterfly's regal graced transformation, the fertile creativity of the kokopelli (the mythical Hopi symbol of the hump-backed flute-player and trickster), the deep roots of the oak tree, with a passion of life that signals unspeakable joy.

See also **Feminist Spirituality; Liberation Spirituality; Mujerista Spirituality.**

Karen Baker-Fletcher and Garth Kasimu Baker-Fletcher, *My Sister, My Brother: Womanist and Xodus God-talk*, Maryknoll, NY: Orbis Books, 1997; Kelly Brown Douglas, *Sexuality and the Black Church: A Womanist Perspective*, Maryknoll, NY: Orbis Books, 1999; bell hooks, *Killing Rage: Ending Racism*, New York: Henry Holt, 1995; Rosita deAnn Mathews, 'Using power from the periphery: an alternative theological model for survival in systems' in Emilie Townes (ed.), *A Troubling in My Soul: Womanist Perspectives on Evil and Suffering*, Maryknoll, NY: Orbis Books, 1993; Rosetta E. Ross,. *Witnessing and Testifying: Black Women, Religion, and Civil Rights*, Minneapolis, MN: Augsburg/Fortress, 2003; Emilie Townes, *In a Blaze of Glory: Womanist Spirituality as Social Witness*, Nashville, TN: Abingdon Press, 1995; Alice Walker, *In Search of Our Mother's Gardens: Womanist Prose*, New York: Harcourt Brace Jovanovich, 1983, p. xi.

CHERYL A. KIRK-DUGGAN

Women and Spirituality

Why single out women? Because, although there is a general meaning of the term spirituality, there is no such thing as generic spirituality. In general, spirituality refers to the experience of life energized by desire for self-transcendence in love, in free commitment to goodness and truth (i.e., a philosophical and psychological definition), or religious spirituality means this desire activated by the Holy Mystery as each religion (in this case, Christian) understands this. Because spirituality refers to *experience*, it cannot simply be generically Christian spirituality. Rather, it must be human experience as embodied in this or that Christian in a particular culture, sex, race and class. It is shaped by the richness and complexity of this person's family history, psychology, education and whatever else influences one's reaching out in love and freedom.

Consequently, one's spirituality is deeply influenced by gender, to take just the topic of this article. Here gender refers not to biological sex (female) but to the meaning one's culture gives to that sex. Gender means the pervasive, socially constructed meaning of sex given to women at any historical period. Until recently, female was usually equated with 'feminine', meaning such things as intuitive, emotional, receptive, motherly, more closely related to nature and matter than to culture and spirit, guardian of virtue in the midst of an aggressive masculine world, complement to the leadership natural to men. Today, when these meanings are no longer universally accepted, female gender identity is ambiguous for many and even problematic when some women create new meanings and strive to communicate with women and men who regard more traditional meanings as the only ones characteristic of truly spiritual or Christian life. Once we accept the inseparability of Christian spiritual growth and concrete human reality, this combination of freedom and problems alerts us to important issues for women.

Why women's spirituality is problematic. Three realities cut across class and racial lines making Christian spirituality problematic for women. First, women's humanity is restricted. Most patterns of family and education around the world reinforce two roles for women: the object of attraction for males and the one who lives for others. The feminist movement addresses these issues by helping women develop the critical consciousness and equitable social structures that honour autonomy yet integrate autonomy into relationships of authentic mutuality and collaboration. Christian women deserve networks of assistance in relating feminist goals and

spiritual development. For example, spiritual direction can support the self-knowledge that all great spiritual teachers regard as the root of discernment of spirits. Second, Christian tradition has legitimated women's restriction. It has functioned, and sometimes continues to serve as one of the most effective means of reinforcing detrimental images (e.g. woman as characteristically prone to vanity and seduction, or naturally most suited for nurture and self-sacrifice, thus poorly equipped for leadership). The language of 'difference' between women and men is too often manipulated to evade real equality in church and society. Third, absorption of prevailing God-images hinders women's spiritual development (and men's). Most Bible translations use only masculine pronouns for God; lectionaries exclude most of the texts that image God as female; official preaching and teaching reinforce the assumption that maleness is closer to divinity. This prevents women from affirming themselves as images of God and restricts women from using their own experience as a revelation of God's attributes and action. It prevents a woman from presuming 'the holy' is like her.

Supporting women's spirituality. Given this situation, what supports women's spiritual growth? First, self-knowledge promotes mature spiritual discernment. Second, finding and creating a theology that affirms women's experience becomes necessary. Third, creating structures of Church and society that confirm, contradict and continue with women according to their spiritual needs is an ongoing challenge.

1. Self-knowledge. What makes self-knowledge Christian is either conscious commitment to identity as a disciple of Jesus in the community of believers given over to the liberating work of Jesus, or self-knowledge cultivated as the root of spiritual discernment. Teresa of Avila, in *The Interior Castle* (1.2) teaches that no matter how mature one may become one never finds self-knowledge is superfluous because it is the foundation for spiritual discernment. She warns against introspection that becomes self-preoccupation, or worse, becomes a subtle kind of control forcing one toward spiritual 'progress' according to one's own design. True self-knowledge comes through interpersonal relationships with God and with those we choose and those we chance upon through life's events; it comes through prayer, work and facing adversity. It teaches us that life comes especially through a kind of death to old ways of thinking and feeling about God, self and others, in order to move into new more inclusive ways that we would and could not create ourselves. As contemporary psychologists such as Kathleen Fischer have demonstrated (*Women at the Well*, 1988), this traditional way of integrating independence and relationship is compatible with insights from feminist psychology.

2. Creating new theology. A second way of fostering women's spiritual development is finding and creating a theology that functions therapeutically for women. That is, it includes women's experience, affirms women's intrinsic value, and legitimates women's full ministry in the Church and society, in contrast with the long tradition that has assumed women's subordination or ignored their contributions. Creating this theology is a long-range project with three central tasks:

a. Recover and evaluate. First, feminist scholars (i.e., women and men aware of women's history of subordination and committed to equality for women) *recover* women lost in Christian tradition. For example, Margaret Carney (1989) has uncovered Clare of Assisi, formerly seen only in the shadow of St Francis, revealing her as the first woman to author a rule of life for nuns and the co-founder of Franciscan spirituality, preserver of Franciscan values while friars were losing sight of the original charism. *Evaluation* is also crucial at this phase. For example, Elizabeth Liebert (2001), along with two colleagues, has examined the *Spiritual Exercises* of Ignatius of Loyola in light of women's experience of giving and receiving these famous guidelines for prayer and commitment to Christ. Through critique and creative re-examination, she has uncovered their liberating possibilities and reclaimed the *Exercises* for women's spirituality.

b. Reinterpret the foundation. Feminist scholars' second task is creative, original interpretation of theology's very foundation so that it loses its power to intimidate or restrict women. Here biblical and doctrinal scholarship is crucial. For example, Sandra M. Schneiders (1999) has demonstrated how and why the Bible can be both divine revelation and an expression of sinful sexism. In *Freeing Theology* (1993), Catherine LaCugna edits the work of ten scholars presenting a comprehensive introduction to each foundational theme (e.g., revelation, Christ, Trinity) not as a review of what is problematic in male-centred theology, but positively from a perspective that honours women's experience, creating a stream of theology that cannot be used to subordinate women.

c. Construct an expanded foundation. A third task of renewed theology requires moving into uncharted waters: construction of a theology of holy Mystery using women's experience as the primary and focal reference. Elizabeth Johnson's *She Who Is* (1992) gives women and men an inspiring and challenging theology of the Trinity with its implications for spiritual growth. Constance FitzGerald's essay, 'Impasse and Dark Night' demonstrates how women's social and ecclesial impasse reveals classic signs of the way Holy Wisdom transforms humans. Ivone Gebara's *Longing for Running Water* (1999) takes the experience of poor Brazilian women with whom Gebara lives as a foundation for an eco-feminist theology of cosmic communion. Delores Williams' *Sisters in the Wilderness* (1993) roots theology of redemption in the experience of African American women. Because all theology and spirituality arise out of a particular social location, attention to the inseparable links between women and spirituality can alert us to the way our entire spiritual tradition has been shaped.

3. Constructing social and ecclesial structures. Women's spiritual growth calls for social and ecclesial structures that can confirm, contradict and continue with women according to their spiritual needs. In order to know how to accomplish these three tasks there must be sensitivity to women's developmental needs. For example, for women embedded in restrictive or male-centred notions of self and God, helpful structures would *confirm* caring relationships, while *contradicting* denial of self-care and avoidance of the conflict resulting from self-affirmation or emerging feminist consciousness. *Continuing* support would be crucial while women deal with the anger that is the sign of mature differentiation from unhealthy dependency. At another stage of spiritual development, for women embedded in adult autonomy and desire for control, helpful structures would *confirm* this mature independence while *contradicting* avoidance of the vulnerability and spiritual darkness inevitable in spiritual maturity. A *continuing* community of ministerial collaboration, compassion and gospel challenge would be central while women experience the temptation to cynicism or withdrawal that comes with awareness of the inadequacy of all social structures short of final cosmic transformation.

See also **Contemporary Spirituality; Feminist Spirituality; Growth, Spiritual; Masculine Spirituality.**

————

Margaret Carney, 'Francis and Clare: a critical examination of the sources', *Laurentianum* 30 (1989), 25–60; Katherine Dyckman, Mary Garvin and Elizabeth Liebert, *The Spiritual Exercises Reclaimed: Uncovering Liberating Possibilities for Women*, New York: Paulist Press, 2001; Constance FitzGerald, 'Impasse and Dark Night', in J. W. Conn (ed.), *Women's Spirituality: Resources for Christian Development*, 2nd rev.

edn, New York: Paulist Press, 1996, pp. 410–35; *The Collected Works of St Teresa of Avila*, Vol. 2, trans. Kieran Kavanaugh and Otilio Rodriguez, Washington, DC: Institute of Carmelite Studies, 1980; Sandra M. Schneiders, *The Revelatory Text*, 2nd edn, Collegeville, MN: The Liturgical Press, 1999; Mary Jo Weaver, *Springs of Water in a Dry Land: Spiritual Survival for Catholic Women Today*, Boston: Beacon Press, 1993.

JOANN WOLSKI CONN

Women Medieval Mystics

The study of mysticism is inevitably textually mediated, a fact particularly important to remember in the case of women mystics. There were doubtless women who had mystical experiences whose voices will remain forever silent, but prior to 1200 there are no significant records of them. Women like Hildegard of Bingen (1090–1179) and Elisabeth of Schönau (1129–65) wrote of their visionary experiences, but the content of their works is not concerned with mysticism as such. However, after 1200 there is a plethora of written evidence for women's mystical experience.

This flowering of women's mysticism was nurtured by changes in the religious atmosphere of the thirteenth century: the development of vernacular languages and the growing literacy among the laity; the movement of religious life out of the monastery into the marketplace, with its fresh emphasis upon penance, poverty and preaching; and the mood of pastoral reform inspired by the Fourth Lateran Council (1215) which fostered a deepening sacramental and devotional practice among the laity. These movements combined to open to a wider variety of Christians the opportunity for experiencing and giving expression to mystical union with God. Women were significant contributors to the new forms of mysticism which emerged as a result.

Literary genres appropriate to this new mysticism differ from the scriptural commentary or mystical treatise proper to earlier monastic settings. Hagiography became more common and innovative. The use of poetry to express mystical experience grew significantly. An important poetic innovation was the combination of religious themes with the language and forms of secular courtly love poetry. Above all, the visionary account typifies the mystical expression of medieval women. The visions described in these accounts are best interpreted not literally but as imaginative visualizations of the mystical encounter between God and the self and the Christian story of salvation this encounter represents. In a church where women had no officially recognized authority to speak, visions gave women's experiences and messages divine validation.

Our knowledge of the women mystics of the High Middle Ages comes from two types of sources: *vitae* written by admirers who were often male clerics, and personal accounts of mystical experience produced by the women themselves, usually with the help of others, again frequently male clerics. The question of the authenticity of the records of these women is thus an inevitable aspect of their study. What follows focuses primarily on texts authored by women.

The immense influence of Francis of Assisi (1181–1226) stimulated new expressions of mysticism among his female followers. Of first importance is Clare (1196–1253), rightly recognized as the co-founder of the Franciscan movement and the first woman in history to write her own rule and have it approved by ecclesiastical authority. The mystical element in Clare's writings looks back to the twelfth-century bridal mysticism of Bernard of Clairvaux, but also exhibits a distinctive Franciscan flavour in its stress on the virtues one acquires through mystical identification with Christ: radical poverty, humility and charity. The most important Franciscan woman mystic is the tertiary Angela of Foligno (*c.* 1248–1309), whose *Book* describes the spiritual life as a journey of some thirty steps, beginning with standard devotion to and imitation of the passion of Christ, but ending with one of the richest accounts of mystical union to be found in Christian history. Franciscan elements in Angela's mysticism include the fact that Francis plays a strong mediatorial role, and even the highest stages of mystical union represent a deepening participation in the passion of Christ. Three aspects of Angela's mysticism, however, make her different from most Franciscans and more like the Beguine mystics: her description of the role of the Trinity in mystical union, her focus on apophatic theology, and her description of God and the soul as mutual abysses.

Mary of Oignies (1176–1213), known through the *vita* written by the Augustinian champion of the Beguines, James of Vitry (1160/70–1240), is the archetype of Beguine mystical piety. She combined extravagant ascetical practice and apostolic activity with prolonged experiences of ecstatic rapture, often precipitated by eucharistic devotion. Three other Beguine mystics, Hadewijch of Brabant (first half of thirteenth century), Mechthild of Magdeburg (1208–1282), and Marguerite Porete (d. 1310), produced some of the greatest mystical works of the thirteenth century. We know virtually nothing about the lives of these women, apart from what little we can glean from their writings.

Hadewijch, author of 31 letters, 45 poems in

stanzas, 16 poems in couplets, and a book of visions, is the clearest example in the Western tradition of 'love mysticism', which expresses the experience of union with God in a highly erotic vocabulary influenced by both the Song of Songs and secular courtly love literature. Hadewijch's writings do not present any systematic doctrine of the mystical life, but three basic themes can be isolated: the nature and activity of Love which is both God (*Minne*) and the felt effects of that Love in the human self (*minne*); the description of the relationship between God and the soul as entering into a mutual abyss; and participation in the sufferings of Christ as a perpetual aspect of mystical union.

Mechthild wrote *The Flowing Light of the Godhead*, a curious compilation of seven books of varying length and genre. She saw herself as a sort of evangelist, inspired by God to produce a work resembling the Book of Revelation. Her book has a confessional character, akin to Augustine's *Confessions*, wherein the meaning of Mechthild's life and religious experience is seen as paradigmatic for her readers. Its prose is intermittently broken up with bursts of lyric poetry of such fine quality that Mechthild is considered one of the major religious poets of the thirteenth century. Her major image is that of a flowing movement which suggests the perpetual activity of the Trinity particularly vis-à-vis creation. Like Hadewijch, Mechthild is a representative of love mysticism, and her work is full of erotic descriptions of her union with God.

Marguerite Porete was executed as a relapsed heretic in Paris on 1 June 1310 over her refusal to recant the ideas presented in her book *The Mirror of Simple Souls*. Ironically, the book was one of the most widely disseminated mystical works in the Middle Ages, translated into four languages, and circulated anonymously. Marguerite was condemned for advocating a form of antinomian freedom from ecclesiastical jurisdiction in connection with the abuses of the so-called Free Spirit heresy. Her book is dialogic throughout, with three main speakers: the Soul (not always to be identified with Marguerite), Lady Love and Reason, with the occasional addition of other participants. Marguerite's mystical teaching sees the spiritual life as an itinerary of seven stages, including three kinds of 'death' necessary for the desired goal of annihilating union with God.

The mystical practices of early thirteenth-century Cistercian women have much in common with Beguine mysticism. Beatrice of Nazareth (1200–68) is arguably the first woman writer of the new mysticism. Her *Seven Manners of Loving* is also the first book of spiritual guidance written by a woman. Like the Beguines, Beatrice combines the mysticism of commentaries on the Song of Songs with the themes of courtly love literature. The sevenfold itinerary of the soul toward union with God is described in terms of alternate longings and satisfactions, torment and peace. Toward the end of the thirteenth century, the Cistercian monastery of Helfta produced two mystical writings of significance: *The Herald of Divine Love* by Gertrude the Great (1256–1301) and *The Book of Special Grace* by Mechthild of Hackeborn (1240–98). The impetus to create these may have been inspired by the presence in the community of Mechthild of Magdeburg, who retired there towards the end of her life. However, these writings have more in common with earlier monastic traditions of theology and liturgy than they do with Mechthild's writings and are generally more serene in tone.

The tremendous outpouring of literature by and about women mystics began to peter out in the fourteenth century, possibly due to a heightening of ecclesiastical disapproval of any form of unregulated religious life or unauthorized teaching by women. However, several important voices from that century deserve mention.

Women followers of Dominic (1170–1221) came into their own as mystical writers in the fourteenth century. Through the nine known 'Sister Books' written between 1310 and 1350, we learn about the mystical practices of the German Dominican cloisters. These books, written by women, about women, for women, formed an original genre: part history, part hagiography, part mystical narrative, a kind of 'community hagiography' designed to proclaim God's approval of their monasteries. Several Dominican nuns also authored books of revelations: Margaret Ebner (1291–1351), Christine Ebner (1277–1356), and Adelheid Langmann (1312–75). The most important Dominican woman mystic is Catherine of Siena (1347–80), the tertiary and great Doctor of the Church, who authored nearly four hundred letters which provide a wonderful window into her personality, some two dozen prayers, and her *Dialogue*, through which she communicated the teachings she learned through her conversation and union with God. Catherine is the quintessential example of contemplation thoroughly integrated with action; what she experienced in contemplation compelled her into action that involved service to the sick poor, political involvement in both civic and ecclesial affairs, and the foundation of a monastery. Since God for her was both 'gentle first Truth' and 'Charity itself', her way to God can be described as a lived dynamic or perichoresis of truth and love.

Two other significant women mystics of the fourteenth century were Bridget of Sweden (1303–73), a contemplative in action like Catherine, author of eight books of revelations and founder of the Bridgettine Order, and Julian of Norwich (1342–c. 1416), the anchoress who authored two versions of her *Showings*.

See also Mysticism (*essay*); Beguines; Bridal Mysticism; Bridgettine Spirituality; Cistercian Spirituality; Dominican Spirituality; English Mystical Tradition; Flemish Mysticism; Franciscan Spirituality; Medieval Spirituality in the West; Mendicant Spirituality; Rhineland Mysticism.

Primary sources: See translations of primary sources in the CWS series, all published by Paulist Press, New York: Francis and Clare (1988), Angela of Foligno (1993), Hadewijch (1980), Mechthild of Magdeburg (1998), Marguerite Porete (1993), Gertrude of Helfta (1993), Margaret Ebner (1993), Catherine of Siena (1980), Birgitta of Sweden (1990), Julian of Norwich (1978).

Secondary sources: Leonard P. Hindsley, *The Mystics of Engelthal: Writings from a Medieval Monastery*, New York: St Martin's Press, 1998; Amy Hollywood, *The Soul as Virgin Wife: Mechthild of Magdeburg, Marguerite Porete and Meister Eckhart*, Notre Dame, IN: University of Notre Dame Press, 1995; Bernard McGinn, *The Flowering of Mysticism: Men and Women in the New Mysticism – 1200–1350*, vol. 3 of *The Presence of God: A History of Western Christian Mysticism*, New York: Crossroad, 1998; Mary T. Malone, *Women and Christianity*, vol. 2: *From 1000 to the Reformation*, Maryknoll, NY: Orbis Books, 2002; Elizabeth Alvilda Petroff (ed.), *Medieval Women's Visionary Literature*, Oxford: Oxford University Press, 1986.

JOAN M. NUTH

Work

Work is a spiritual issue – one that presses questions about dignity, justice, creativity, holiness and the meaning of human activities. In contemporary developed societies, where one's job often becomes a key to human identity, work also is central to individual and cultural self-understandings. Thus, work carries a complex spiritual dimension and can even be considered a spiritual practice. While work as spiritual practice has been somewhat neglected in classical Christian literature, nevertheless several critical texts point us to a fuller understanding of this dimension of Christian spirituality.

One of the reasons for the neglect of work as a distinct subject is the overall neglect of lay spirituality in classical Christian writings on spirituality – particularly in Roman Catholic teaching. Because the celibate life was seen as more perfect than lay life 'in the world', many Christian writings express ambivalence about the holiness of secular activities, including work. Moreover, as contemplative mysticism and accompanying extraordinary experiences grew dominant as the mark of sanctity by the late Middle Ages, ordinary, ascetical practices such as work took second place as an inferior kind of spiritual path (Vauchez, 1993).

However, resources can be recovered from within the Christian tradition to explore and validate the spirituality of work. Monastic founder St Benedict of Nursia (c. 480–c. 547), for example, points to the virtue of labour. In his influential Rule, he advocates a moderate daily balance among prayer, *lectio divina* ('holy reading'), manual work and rest – hence the contemporary Benedictine motto '*Ora et Labora*' ('Pray and Work'). The Benedictine incorporation of work has precedents in the early desert monastics, who did not shun humble labor.

St Francis de Sales (1567–1622), Bishop of Geneva and spiritual guide, encouraged lay people that they too could aspire to perfection. In his *Introduction to the Devout Life* and his numerous letters of spiritual direction, de Sales wrote that true devotion could be lived amidst life in the world and the hectic responsibilities of daily work. Reflecting his aristocratic social milieu, de Sales wrote that gentlemen, soldiers, kings and mothers could live devoutly. So often, he pointed out, we associate perfection with a particular path different from our own, rather than embracing the challenges of the paths on which we actually walk. Simply love God fully and fervently in the midst of your daily work – this is true devotion, he wrote.

De Sales was responding in part to the association of perfection with virginity, affirmed at the Council of Trent, and the related neglect of the lay spirituality. This was a major concern too of the Protestant Reformers. Martin Luther (1483–1546), for example, criticized the idleness and corruption of the clergy as he reasserted the dignity and holiness of ordinary work. He asserted the priesthood of all believers and argued for the vocation of the secular person in his or her occupation and household duties. John Calvin (1509–64) too strongly emphasized the worldly calling and the importance of ascetic discipline. The twentieth-century sociologist Max Weber theorized, in fact, that Calvinistic notions of vocation and worldly asceticism may have unintentionally propelled the development of modern capitalism (*The Protestant Ethic and the Spirit* of Capitalism). Fearing for their salvation, the Puritans looked to economic success as marks of election. Their industry and frugal discipline produced capital, spurring on economic development and the classic 'Protestant work ethic'.

While this validation of work carries many positive consequences, the work ethic also has led to a distorted view of human work. Work has become mechanized, over-glamorized, and even an obsession for many contemporary consumerist societies. Lost is the Benedictine balance, in which work formed one part of a rhythmic life with God. To counter an unfree attachment to work, writers such as the Jewish theologian Abraham Joshua Heschel have pointed back to the importance of Sabbath (see his classic book *The Sabbath*). The command to observe Sabbath (Deut. 5.12–16; Ex. 20.8–11) guides human beings back to their true nature – creaturely, limited, yet liberated. In resting from work one day per week, human beings claim their dignity, honour the Creator, and affirm too the holiness of their work.

John Paul II also took seriously the demeaning, dehumanizing potential of work in his 1981 encyclical *On Human Work* (*Laborem Exercens*). He advocated justice for labourers, including a fair wage, adequate to support a family, and decent working conditions. Work, wrote the Pope, is a vocation and a distinguishing mark of humanity. People are called to work in imitation of God the Creator and of Christ who laboured. Work builds up the common good. John Paul II thus proposes a spirituality of work that rests on the personhood of the worker, the importance of community, and a bold call for human beings to serve as co-creators with God.

Vatican II (1962–65) has been a critical support to a Christian spirituality of work. The Council affirmed the importance of the lay vocation 'in the world' – in their work, family and political activities. Indeed, the laity were called to be church in the world, to infuse the secular sphere with the spirit of God, like leaven dispersed invisibly in bread yet causing it to rise. Work was part of the lay mission in the world and could be a means of sanctification (see the Dogmatic Constitution on the Church (*Lumen Gentium*) 40; the Decree on the Apostolate of Lay People (*Apostolicam Actuositatem*) 2). Thus, the Council did much to bridge the sacred and the secular, a dichotomy that for too long obfuscated the powerful spiritual dimensions of human work.

Spirituality scholars have begun to examine the relationship between work and spirituality, a topic that has ignited interest across religious faiths, and among seekers outside of religious traditions. A strong business-and-spirituality movement today seeks to incorporate integrity, values and wholeness in work that can seem impersonal and deadening to the spirit. At the same time, women's sharply changing work roles must prompt new reflection on notions of women's holiness and vocation. It is vital that Christian spiritual leaders and scholars attend to the question of work, bringing both the wisdom of the tradition as well as pertinent critiques of its oversights.

See also Asceticism; Benedictine Spirituality; Business and Spirituality; Calvinist Spirituality; Consumerism; Lay People and Spirituality; Lutheran Spirituality; Marxism and Spirituality; Public Life; Salesian Spirituality; Vatican II and Spirituality; Vocation.

John Haughey, *Converting 9 to 5: A Spirituality of Daily Work*, New York: Crossroad, 1989; Abraham Joshua Heschel, *The Sabbath*, New York: Farrar, Straus & Young, 1951; John Paul II, *On Human Work: Laborem Exercens*, Boston, MA: Daughters of St Paul, 1997; Gregory F. Pierce (ed.), *Of Human Hands: A Reader in the Spirituality of Work*, Minneapolis, MN: Augsburg Fortress, 1991; Dorothee Soelle with Shirley A. Cloyes, *To Work and To Love: A Theology of Creation*, Minneapolis, MN: Fortress Press, 1984; Claire Wolfteich, *Navigating New Terrain: Work and Women's Spiritual Lives*, New York, Paulist Press, 2002.

CLAIRE E. WOLFTEICH

World

The theme of 'the world' in relation to Christian spirituality is complex. It may be thought of in two ways. First, in terms of the physical universe, ever-developing scientific understanding has an impact on how we think about existence and thus on our spiritualities. Second, 'the world' is a symbolic reality capable of different spiritual evaluations. It is the second sense of the word that is the subject of this entry.

In the New Testament, 'the world' is defined ambiguously. It is what God created and is thus good (Rom. 1.20). It is loved by God and is saved by the incarnation (John 3). In general, 'the world' carries most ethical and theological weight in the Johannine and Pauline writings. The former are particularly exercised by the theme. In the Johannine corpus is to be found apparently the most negative evaluations. So, for example, the disciples do not belong to the world (John 15.19) and are in the world but not of it (John 17.11). Christ is said to have overcome the world (John 16.33) and God's kingdom is not of this world (John 18.36). There is, therefore, a superficial contradiction in John between God's love of the world and other passages that enjoin a rejection of it. A Christian interpretation of 'the world' needs to steer a careful course between rejecting creation or history and being in thrall to what is transient. An eschatological perspective strongly present in the New Testament portrays the present order and age as 'passing away' and highlights the promise of an 'age to come'. However, Christian apocalyptic is ambiguous. The absolute separation of this age from the age to come is shaded. The new creation is said to be already here (2 Cor. 5.17) and salvation is available here and now through the ministry of Jesus and not merely in the future (e.g. Luke 19.9).

The tension between a positive and a negative evaluation of 'the world' remains strong in the literature of the early Christian centuries. In particular, many early theologians combated the influence of gnosticism which denigrated the material world and promoted a non-material, otherworldly perfection. Thus, central aspects of the 'materiality' of Christian theology and spirituality, the humanity of Christ, the Eucharist and external works of charity, were apparently denied as obstacles to true enlightenment (gnosis). As early as Ignatius of Antioch (early second century), the *Letter to the Smyrneans* warned against such tendencies. Later, Irenaeus (c. 130– c. 200) conducted a vigorous anti-gnostic campaign, defending the reality and importance of the material as well as spiritual nature of human life (his *Against Heresies*). Although the major Eastern theologians such as Origen and the Cappadocians repudiated Gnosticism, the intellectualist slant in Origen (influenced by Platonic philosophy) was preoccupied with heavenly knowledge where the soul 'ascended' from the bodily and material realm towards union with the divine. In his division of the world into two societies (*City of God*), Augustine (354–430) appears to undermine a proper valuation of the material world. However, the two societies (City of God and human city) co-exist and are better thought of as two dynamisms in human life (desire for God, versus desire for what is immediate and transient) that exist *within* history.

The subsequent history of Christian spirituality expresses the tension implied by being 'in the world but not of it'. Different traditions and practices express this differently. On the one hand, the monastic concept of *fuga mundi* or 'flight from the world' suggests not a rejection of creation but an alternative, counter-cultural critique of 'worldliness'. On the other hand, the tradition of Christian humanism arising from the Renaissance appreciated the integrity of 'the world' both in its natural and its social senses. Both spiritual traditions express something important. However, if unbalanced, the ascetic tendency undermines the spiritual value of everyday life and embodiment, while the humanist tendency is in danger of abandoning any critique of making 'the world' an end in itself.

It is worth noting two attempts to create a typology of Christian spiritualities in relation to 'the world' and 'human history'. Edward Kinerk identifies four types of spirituality in terms of how they interpret the world as a potential place for expressions of the authentic (Kinerk, 1981). He assumes that all Christian spiritualities facilitate a transformation from the inauthentic to the authentic. Importantly Kinerk views all four types as equally valid expressions of Christian spirituality. In contrast, Geoffrey Wainwright (drawing upon Niebuhr's *Christ and Culture*) adopts a more complex fivefold typology based on how spiritualities balance the kingdom of God with 'the world' (Wainwright, 1986). First, in 'Christ against culture', the world and the kingdom are in conflict and the kingdom *replaces* the world. Second, 'Christ of culture' over-identifies kingdom and world. Both of these types are interpreted as deficient. In the third, 'Christ above culture', Christ raises creation in his redemptive action. The fourth type, 'Christ and culture in paradox', emphasizes conflict and God's prophetic judgement on the world. Finally, 'Christ the transformer of culture' is supported by Wainwright as the most balanced type. This emphasizes both a positive view of 'the world' and its transformation.

See also **Spirituality and Science; Spirituality and History** (*essays*); **Christian Humanism; Environment; Ecological Spirituality; Eschatology; Monasticism; Sacred.**

Edward Kinerk, 'Towards a method for the study of spirituality', *Review for Religious* 40.1 (1981), pp. 3–19; H. Richard Niebuhr, *Christ and Culture*, New York: Harper & Row, 1951; Philip Sheldrake, *Spaces for the Sacred: Place, Memory, Identity*, London: SCM Press/Baltimore: Johns Hopkins University Press, 2001; Geoffrey Wainwright, 'Types of spirituality' in C. Jones et al. (eds), *The Study of Spirituality*, London: SPCK, 1986, pp. 592–605.

PHILIP SHELDRAKE

Yoga

Yoga is an infuriatingly diffuse term which defies precise definition. Etymologically it derives from a Sanskrit root meaning 'to join' and is cognate with the Latin *iugum* which gives us the English 'yoke'. The yogic tradition of ascetical practice grew up in an uneasy symbiosis with the all-dominating sacrificial ritual of the Vedic religion. Very generally, it can be applied to all sorts of spiritual striving by analogy with the physical action of joining or harnessing oxen to a cart. Yoga can, therefore, be translated as 'spiritual exercise' and be made to apply very loosely to any way or practice which leads to *moksha* or 'release'. More specifically it refers to a whole series of spiritual practices, both those of heterodox *sadhus* or *sannyasis*, wandering holy men who continue to proliferate in modern India, and the more orthodox sages to whom are ascribed the philosophical texts of the Upanishads. For the latter group Yoga amounts to a personal appropriation of the Vedic tradition, an interiorization of the external ritual achieved through a series of physical and mental techniques.

The classical Yoga system, expounded by the sage Patañjali in the *Yoga Sutra*, gathers together eight traditional practices – *yama* or restraint, *niyama* or discipline, *asana* or bodily posture, *pranayama* or breath-control, *pratyahara* or withdrawal from sensory objects, *dharana* or concentration, *dhyana* or meditation and finally *samadhi* – a term which Mircea Eliade translates as 'enstasy', in deliberate distinction from ecstasy, a certain sense of inward isolation or interior stillness (Sanskrit *kaivalyam*). Underlying all the practices is the general technique of 'one-pointedness' (Sanskrit *ekagrata*) of concentration, anchoring the naturally wandering mind on a single focus. Hence the stated aim of the classical Yoga: *cittavrttinirodha*, the 'suppression of the modifications of the mind'. Forms of yoga practice are to be found in all Indian ascetical traditions, ranging from the theistic spirituality of the Bhagavad Gita – where the person of Krishna becomes the focus of attention – to the strictly non-theistic forms of Buddhism and Jainism. In principle the general technique or method, concentrating the attention on one point, can be separated from the specific religious aim or metaphysic. Hence the variant forms which have led not just to a rich culture of Yoga-practice within the Indian religious tradition but to various adaptations to Christian prayer as well.

How far can Christians make use of this culture of inner concentration? As a way of *preparation* for prayer or meditation the incorporation of certain yoga techniques into Christian prayer seems unproblematic. The first two groups of practices of the classical Yoga are necessary preliminaries to any form of asceticism. Some degree of formal yet relaxed posture is also nec-

essary and is recommended by various Christian mystics and writers. Even regulation of the breathing is not totally foreign to the Christian tradition; the 'third way of praying' in Ignatius' *Spiritual Exercises*, for instance, in which familiar prayers are set in rhythm with the breathing, is a fascinating parallel. Nevertheless, the distinction between technique and aim is never entirely clear-cut and does not allow for a simple grafting of Christian belief on to some supposedly neutral yogic 'prayer-method'. Much depends on the focus of 'one-pointedness' and the extent to which Christians can make Christ the centre of their prayer while using particular yogic methods.

In responding to this issue, two contrasting ways in which technique and aim work together need to be distinguished. According to the classical yoga pattern, by concentrating on a regular rhythm the meditator develops a mood of deep inner relaxation. This is the sort of experience described in the 'great sayings' of the Upanishads. The *Atman*, the essence of individuality is identified with the ground of Being or *Brahman*; the one becomes deeply grounded in the other. In other words, the resulting form of concentration reflects the nature of the initial focus. At this point, an important sub-distinction has to be made. If the focus of attention is completely lacking in cognitive or affective connotations – for instance, in the practice of controlling the breathing – then the primary experience, isolation from all external stimuli, may become very much a *self*-consciousness. Everything, including the meditator's individuality, is absorbed into the single focus of attention; my sense of self becomes very much bound up with the rhythm of the breathing. If, however, the focus is a word, symbol or icon which evokes an affective relation, it may well deepen an already existing relationship with that to which the given focus points. This latter direction is clearly less problematic than the former. The danger, however, is that in both – though clearly in different degrees – the element of faith can be ignored or, at any rate, downplayed. Technique can become all-important, reducing the relationship *established by God's Spirit* to an almost automatic process which the meditator can control at will, a sort of meditative Pelagianism.

This danger is largely obviated by another way of integrating technique and aim, that associated with the Buddhist appropriation of the yoga tradition. The Buddhist form of yoga is deeply suspicious of the discourse of 'self' – let alone of any practice which would seek to isolate and privilege one particular experience. On the other hand, Buddhism does recommend the basic technique of focused concentration – even if it takes it in a different direction. The meditator is guided by the quality of *sati* (Pali) or *smrti* (Sanskrit), usually translated as mindfulness, a careful attention to *the entire contents of consciousness*. Although beginning with an initial concentration on one point, the aim is precisely to *avoid* absorption into the focus; it is important to refrain from identifying with the object. More positively, the technique is to observe the object, whether it lacks any specific cognitive or affective 'content' or is familiar and meaningful and evokes a particular response. In practice, the meditator does not seek one focus to the exclusion of others but by simply observing and being sensitized to one focus manages to become sensitized to the presence and influence of others. Often the immediate focus of attention has a much more dynamic quality, something which moves or changes as it is observed; for example, the breathing, a sound, a feeling, or a relationship with another person. In other words, the meditator attends to the present moment and allows what is experienced to take its own form. Unlike the yogic method of 'breath-control', therefore, the Buddhist simply watches and notes what happens. The primary experience is detachment, a willingness to watch – and, for the Christian meditator, to wait upon God and the promptings of the Spirit.

See also **Body and Spirituality; Buddhism and Christianity; Hesychasm; Hinduism and Christianity; Meditation; Practice, Spiritual.**

J.-M. Déchanet, *Christian Yoga*, London: Search, 1960; Mircea Eliade, *Yoga, Immortality and Freedom*, Princeton, NJ: Princeton University Press, 1969; Georg Feuerstein, *Textbook of Yoga*, London: Rider, 1975; Thomas Matus, *Yoga and the Jesus Prayer Tradition*, Ramsay, NJ: Paulist Press, 1984.

MICHAEL BARNES

Zen and Christianity

The dialogue between Zen Buddhism and Christianity has proved to be one of the most creative interreligious engagements of the last half century. Many Christians have taken up forms of Zen practice, and some have even been commissioned as authentic Zen teachers by Japanese *roshis*. Very roughly, two approaches to this dialogue of religious practice can be distinguished. The first would discern behind the engagement some sort of *philosophia perennis* which overcomes all dualisms; the focus here is on experiencing the one ultimate reality which exists somehow above or beyond the particularities of religious languages. The second speaks more

about the complementarity of equally valid traditions; the object is to enter into another spiritual universe and to explore the shared space in which the two traditions enhance and support each other. If the former is based on an intuition of sameness, the latter is more content to take as its starting point the reality of difference. Neither position is unproblematic philosophically or theologically, but what holds them together is a conviction that the meeting point of religious traditions lies in prayer and contemplation.

This is the main reason Zen has proved such an attractive – and productive – basis for dialogue. However, particular motivations vary. For Thomas Merton the engagement was, for the most part, intellectual and only at the very end of his life, before his tragic death in Bangkok in 1968, did he encounter Buddhism first-hand. One can only speculate what theological commentary Merton might have produced on a dialogue of practice which was still at the level of polite conversation. Pioneering work had been done in the years after World War 2 by a handful of Jesuits in Japan. For Hugo Enomiya Lassalle, the practice of Zen was a logical extension of his missionary commitment – a form of inculturation into the spiritual world of Japan to which he had committed his life. For his contemporary, Heinrich Dumoulin, the interest was more strictly academic. His highly influential *A History of Zen Buddhism* chronicles an engagement which reaches back to the days of St Francis Xavier. Apart from some fascinating details which show that the dialogue was by no means a one-way process, Dumoulin explicitly raises the theological issue about the relationship between two very different approaches to mysticism. Their successors, such as William Johnston and Kadichi Kadowaki, follow in the same tradition, claiming to practise not pure Zen under a Buddhist master but a Zen-influenced Christian contemplation. For Kadowaki, Zen and Christianity differ as to their ultimate aims, but in terms of practice and structure show many similarities. Johnston is responsible for a whole series of popular but often deeply insightful books on Christian mysticism which have taken their inspiration from the broader dialogue of religions.

For many practitioners, especially in Europe and the United States, the dialogue has a more personal aspect. In the heady but disorientating days of the post-Vatican II 1960s, Zen enabled many Christians to find a new depth to spiritual lives long deadened by decades of neo-Scholasticism. Willigis Jäger, a German Benedictine who runs a Zen-Christian centre in Würzburg, is perhaps the most radical. He argues that the Zen experience of *satori* or awakening is identical to what is taught about mystical experience by Eckhart, John of the Cross and the author of *The Cloud*. The myths, rituals and symbols of religious traditions are transcended in inner personal conviction; all religions, including Christianity and Buddhism, have to be understood as culturally conditioned attempts to speak of what can only be properly recognized in the silence of an intuitive mystical knowing. Others prefer to avoid speculative questions and to stick with practice. Robert Kennedy, a Jesuit from New York, is one of the most eloquent exponents of a Catholic Christianity rooted deep in his own lived experience of faith. His wonderfully poetic style of writing speaks of Zen as a way to overcome the human tendency to theorize by total immersion in a stillness where an intuition of God's immanence can be realized. Elaine McInnes, a Catholic sister who learned her Zen practice in Japan and subsequently set up a centre in the Philippines, speaks in similar vein of Zen prayer leading to a sense of being deeply infused with the divine. For both these practitioners Zen and Christian prayer are different but parallel paths. Christian categories are not to be replaced by Buddhist, as if they are mere variants on a common theme; rather Zen strengthens the Christian commitment to enter into the utter mystery of God after the manner of the self-emptying of Christ.

The theme of *kenosis* has proved one of the most fruitful, and controversial, areas for theological dialogue between the two traditions. Masao Abe, a leading philosopher of the Kyoto school and probably the best-known Zen Buddhist commentator on the dialogue with Christianity, reads Jesus' example back into the very nature of God: the self-emptying of the Son has its origins and true nature in the self-emptying of the Father, the *kenosis* of God. For Christians, of course, the Christological hymn of Phil. 2 does not easily bear such a 'metaphysical' reading of the inner nature of God. What drives Abe, however, is less an exact exegesis than an antipathy towards dualism in any shape or form. Buddhism, he insists, overcomes dualistic thinking since its point of departure lies not with some ultimate 'essence' of things with which human beings seek to enter into relationship but with the guiding concept of *śunyata* or emptiness, which Abe calls the 'interpenetration and mutual reversibility of all things'. Christian theologians, such as Hans Küng, David Tracy and Donald Mitchell, argue that the distinction between God and creatures cannot be so easily relativized or subsumed into the supposed 'higher' truth of Zen. At stake for these theologians is the integrity of Christian faith which is formed not by personal asceticism nor by the most sophisticated of philosophical dialectics but by the self-revealing act of God himself whose Word speaks out of God's own silence.

Not all Christian practitioners of Zen would see the need to engage in such a consciously theological dialogue. Indeed most would see in the sharing of silent meditation the only resolution possible. But questions for the Christian understanding of God and what makes for human flourishing cannot be avoided. Is it possible to bring together the 'cosmic' language of Buddhism and the more obviously anthropological discourse of Christianity? Or are the two strictly incommensurable? Is there any role for the Christian Scriptures and theological doctrine beyond what Buddhists would refer to as 'skilful means', a practice useful for a particular moment on the spiritual path but ultimately to be discarded as one approaches the 'higher' reaches of contemplation and union with God? Is the personal dimension of Christian faith to be ultimately transcended? If so, what happens to the Christian sense of the person as the one called into being by God? More importantly, what happens to Christ?

Any good dialogue will sensitize participants to hidden assumptions about the other and to the danger of practising a certain type of spiritual colonialism. If the dialogue is to avoid the worst excesses of the single-minded pursuit of personal enlightenment, then it will be important to remember the broader ritual and even devotional context of Zen practice without which the language of *śunyata* and *satori* cannot be understood fully. The ceremonial side of the tradition with its strongly monastic culture and doctrinal study is easily ignored. In other words, Zen remains a Buddhist tradition and cannot be turned into some cross-religious meta-tradition without doing it violence. Zen does, of course, cultivate what often appears as a thoroughly iconoclastic attitude towards religious structures. But a typically Buddhist pragmatism, the capacity of the tradition to adapt to particular needs and circumstances, should not obscure the role which is played by language and symbol in giving it a particular shape. If Buddhism can only be properly understood against the background of its Indian matrix in the middle of the first millennium BCE, then attention also needs to be paid to the Chinese and Japanese culture which has shaped Zen in a particular way. Each tradition has its own integrity which must be respected.

It does not follow, of course, that there is nothing to be learned from the engagement beyond an esoteric lesson in oriental history. The experience of so many Christian practitioners is that Zen clears the mind and enables that right channelling of human desire which is the goal of all good spirituality. The question, however, is whether or not such a participation in another tradition is likely to enhance that life-giving pattern of human transformation which is given in Christ. Does the dialogue with Zen provoke anything more significant than guarded discussions about the dangers of syncretism and neo-pelagianism? Does it enable the love of God which flows from the *imitatio Christi* to flourish within the individual and the community of faith? Perhaps the only judicious response which is possible is to note another dimension of the 'Zen experience' – that parallels and similarities only ever emerge against a backdrop of greater difference and otherness. In other words, distinctions are not levelled out in favour of some easily assimilated commonality but invite an attitude of patient waiting on what always remains a greater and unpredictable mystery, however that mystery is named or not named. Strangely, the most positive aspect of the dialogue is the emergence of a space where – to put it in Christian terms – the meditator is free to let God be God. The space allows resonances and echoes to be heard. Just as key terms, such as *kenosis* and *śunyata*, for all their manifold differences, can provoke important theological reflection on the human quest for God, so Zen practices like sitting meditation and even the paradoxical *koan*, probing riddles designed to frustrate the conceptualizing capacity of the mind, may produce an imaginative response from within the Christian vision of the world.

Johnston's insight, that the cross of Christ is *the* Christian *koan* is persuasive; Christ challenges the desire to possess the perfect pattern. If he is right, then Christology may well turn out to be not peripheral but central to the dialogue.

That inter-faith dialogue should raise such questions does not mean that the practice of Christian faith cannot be deepened or indeed transformed by immersion in another conceptual world. Indeed there is something of an irony in the fact that a tradition which refuses all talk about the ultimate should enable Christians to experience the reality of God more profoundly. It is perhaps for this reason that the real value of this 'dialogue of religious experience' lies less in the identification of some 'middle ground' beyond the particularities of religious language than in the questions it raises both for the more conceptual or theological dialogue and for spirituality.

See also **Spirituality and the dialogue of religions** (*essay*); **Buddhism and Christianity; Kenosis; Meditation; Nothingness; Yoga.**

Heinrich Dumoulin, *A History of Zen Buddhism*, London: Faber, 1963; J. K. Kadowaki, *Zen and the Bible*, New York: Orbis Books, 2002; Robert Kennedy, *Zen Gifts for Christians*, New York: Continuum, 2000; Robert Kennedy, *Zen Spirit, Christian Spirit*, New York: Continuum, 2001; Hugo Enomiya Lassalle, *Zen Meditation for Christians*, La Salle, IL: Open Court, 1974; William Johnston, *Christian Zen*, Dublin: Gill & Macmillan, 1979.

MICHAEL BARNES

INDEX OF NAMES AND TITLES

This index includes names and titles given in the bibliographies to each entry only if these are also mentioned somewhere in the text. With the exception of Mary, it does not include characters from the Bible. The letters a and b after a page number indicate that discussion of the person (or work) is confined to the page's left or right hand column respectively. Within certain lengthy entries, numbers in **bold** indicate the major discussions.